KT-403-536

ervices

WITHDRAWN

RISK
MANAGEMENT

RISK MANAGEMENT

EMMETT J. VAUGHAN
University of Iowa

John Wiley & Sons, Inc.
New York • Chichester • Brisbane • Toronto • Singapore

S 658, 155 VAU

Cover Photo: J. A. Kraulis/Masterfile

Acquisitions Editor	Whitney Blake
Marketing Manager	Leslie Hines
Production Editor	Melanie Henick
Text Designer	Initial Graphics Systems, Inc.
Cover Designer	Madelyn Lesure
Manufacturing Manager	Mark Cirillo
Illustration Coordinator	Eugene Aiello

This book was set in 10/12 New Baskerville by V&M Graphics and printed and bound by Donnelley/ Crawfordsville. The cover was printed by Phoenix Color.

Recognizing the importance of preserving what has been written, it is a policy of John Wiley & Sons, Inc. to have books of enduring value published in the United States printed on acid-free paper, and we exert our best efforts to that end.

Copyright © 1997, by John Wiley & Sons, Inc.

All rights reserved. Published simultaneously in Canada.

Reproduction or translation of any part of
this work beyond that permitted by Sections
107 and 108 of the 1976 United States Copyright
Act without the permission of the copyright
owner is unlawful. Requests for permission
or further information should be addressed to
the Permissions Department, John Wiley & Sons, Inc.

ISBN: 0-471-10759-X

Printed in the United States of America

10 9 8 7 6 5 4 3 2

To Erin, Jessica, Katie, Kelli, Matthew, Meagan, Michael, Moria, Patrick Emmett, Ryan, and Tyler

Preface

The subject matter of this book is a branch of applied economics, called *risk management*, which has as its objective the reduction and elimination of certain types of risks facing businesses and other organizations. It is a scientific approach to the problem of dealing with these risks that seeks to achieve identifiable objectives by avoiding, reducing, and transferring risk. Risk management evolved from the field of corporate insurance buying, and because of its ancestral roots is generally included as a part of the course sequence for students who are majoring in risk and insurance.

This book has been in the process of preparation for nearly four decades. Since 1958, when I was an undergraduate student majoring in economics and insurance at Creighton University—barely two years after the term *risk management* first appeared in the literature—the subject of risk management has held my fascination. Over the next five years, the term risk management and articles on the subject began to appear with increasing regularity. In 1963, I entered the ranks of insurance faculty, the same year in which Professors Robert I. Mehr and Bob A. Hedges published the first textbook on risk management, their classic *Risk Management in the Business Enterprise*. In a sense, risk management and I entered the academic world together.

Over the years, I have used several risk management textbooks, all of which have served me and my students well. At the same time, these texts treated some areas in ways differently from what I would have preferred. Eventually, like many other faculty, I developed my own course structure that emphasized the features of the discipline that I considered important, at the expense of other topics. This book reflects this evolution of my view of risk management.

The title of the book reflects my view that *risk management* is both an art and a science. Risk management as a science involves the application of the scientific method to the process of managing risks and the use of the decision theory in solving risk management problems. Fundamentally, risk management is a problem in decision making. More specifically, it is a problem of decision making under conditions of uncertainty. Once a problem is identified, related information is analyzed and evaluated. Alternative solutions are identified, and the one with the greatest potential for success is selected. Were it not for the advances in scientific decision making, it seems doubtful that risk management would have evolved as a discipline.

As important as the contributions of the scientific approach have been, it seems indisputable that risk management is also an art. In a sense, risk management as an art begins where risk management as a science stops. After all of the data has been gathered, evaluated and analyzed, a decision must be made. Sometimes the analysis will point to the decision, but this is not always the case. Then the risk manager must make a decision based on the *feel* of the situation, or based on experience with other similar situations. The art of risk management is based on the willingness to make decisions and take action even when all of the desirable information is not available.

DESIGN OF THE BOOK

The text is designed for use in a college introduction to the field of risk management. Because the risk management course occurs at different levels in the curriculum of different schools, *Risk Management: the Art and the Science* is designed to serve as a text in two types of courses, reflecting the place in the curriculum at which the course in *Risk Management* is located. At some schools, risk management is the first course in the sequence for students majoring in risk management and insurance. At other schools, it is a capstone course that is taken after the student has taken a range of other courses related to the field of risk and insurance. I have tried to write a book that can be used at either level. Depending on the level at which the course is offered, the emphasis can be altered to accommodate the preference of the instructor and the curriculum.

Although I believe that the book can be used as the text for either a first course or a capstone-type risk management course, a word of explanation is in order for students who will use it in the advanced course. It is conceivable that the book may be used in a program in which *Fundamentals of Risk and Insurance* or *Essentials of Insurance* (of which the author is a co-author) have been used at the lower level. Students who have used the *Fundamentals* or *Essentials* book will find that there is some repetition in the material from those texts in the current book. More specifically, Chapters 10, 11, 12, 13 and 14, which deal with the insurance as a device for dealing with risk, draw heavily on chapters in the *Fundamentals* and *Essentials* books. The inclusion of this material in this book was necessary to round out the treatment of risk management for those students for whom this book is an introduction not only to risk management, but to insurance as well.

In addition to serving as a text for students majoring in risk management and insurance—either as a first course in the sequence or as an advanced course—the text can also serve as a self-contained treatment of the subject for students who will take only a single course in risk management. These will include MBA students who want (and need) an orientation to this important managerial function.

WHY STUDY RISK MANAGEMENT?

The reasons for studying risk management are varied. For some, the study is undertaken in preparation for a career in the field. A course in risk management such as those for which this text is designed is normally a part of a sequence that constitutes a major in the field of risk and insurance or risk management and insurance.

In addition to those who study risk management in preparation for a career, others will study it as a part of a general business curriculum, or as an elective in another major.

Still others study insurance as a part of the discipline of risk management, the managerial function that aims at preserving the operating effectiveness of the organization. Personally, I believe that the study of risk management should be considered *essential* for all business students, since I believe that it is a part of the common core of knowledge with which all business students should be familiar. Although some have argued that the study of insurance *per se* is a narrow specialty, the broader discipline of risk management—of which insurance buying is only a part—is clearly a function that all future managers should understand. A proper understanding of the methods of dealing with exposures to loss is essential to organizational leaders. Although insurance is only one of the techniques that can be used to deal with pure risks, risk management decisions presuppose an understanding of the nature and functions of insurance.

Because the study of risk management and insurance draws on different disciplines, it is sometimes considered a subset of one of them. Thus, in many colleges and unversities, insurance and risk management are a part of the finance curriculum, reflecting the financial nature of the risk management function. In other schools, it is considered a part of economics, while in still other schools it is located in another department. This organizational ambiguity reflects the confusion concerning what the study of risk management and insurance entails.

In fact, risk management is a separate and distinct discipline, which draws on and integrates the knowledge from a variety of other business fields. In a micro sense, it is a discipline in which a variety of methodologies are brought to bear on a significant problem.

ACKNOWLEDGMENT

I have been supported and encouraged in writing this book by many people. First and foremost are the members of my family, all of whom sacrificed much to assist me. I thank them all for their help, but more importantly for their understanding.

First, I owe much to *my teachers*, whose influence left an indelible mark on me and on this book. I include within the broad rubric of *my teachers* the authors of the books and articles on the subject of risk management that have shaped my view of risk management. Among the many in this category, I include my colleague of many years, Professor Michael Murray, who has shared his insights with me over the years and whose influence on my ideas has been significant.

I am grateful to all my friends and seminar students over the past thirty years who, in the course of discussions had given me ideas and helped me to understand points that had baffled or irritated me. They could not have known this at the time, and it would be exceedingly difficult for me to accurately list all of those who helped in this way.

In addition, I owe a debt of gratitude to the reviewers, who offered valuable suggestions that helped to shape the final work. They were Ann Butler, Patricia A. Cheshier, Kenneth J. Crespas, Richard Corbett, Stephen M. Avila, George B. Flanigan, Ken Huntley, and Lazarus Angbazo.

I owe special thanks to Dr. Therese M. Vaughan, who abandoned our plans for co-authoring the book when she became commissioner of Insurance for the State of Iowa. I also owe a special debt of gratitude to Professor Timothy S. Vaughan of the University of Northern Illinois. When asked to review Chapter 9 on measuring risk, he rejected virtually everything I had written, and replaced it with the far more understandable discussion that is included in the text. His enormous assistance on this (and other) chapters contributed significantly to the final work and helped me to avoid errors that would otherwise have marred the book. I am also grateful to Mary Susan Vaughan, a doctoral student at the University of Iowa, who reviewed the book as it progressed. Her insights and suggestions were extremely helpful to me in many sections of the book.

Finally, I thank Jan Koopman, who assisted in the preparation of the manuscript.

From the teachers who will use this book as a text, I will be grateful to receive advice concerning any errors that should be corrected and any material that should be added or omitted when it is revised. To the students who will be compelled to read it, I extend the hope that the material presented will seem as exciting and interesting as it has seemed to me.

Emmett J. Vaughan
Iowa City, Iowa

Contents

Contents

CHAPTER 1

The Risk Management Problem

CHAPTER OBJECTIVES

When you have finished this chapter, you should be able to

Identify the techniques developed by our primitive ancestors to deal with risk.

■

Identify and describe the human innovations associated with business and commerce that were invented to deal with risk.

■

Explain why the dollar amount of losses caused by natural perils tends to increase over time.

■

Define and explain the meaning of the term *risk*.

■

Distinguish among the terms *risk*, *peril*, and *hazard*.

■

Identify and explain the classes of hazards.

■

Differentiate between pure risk and speculative risk.

■

Differentiate between fundamental and particular risk.

■

Describe the categories into which pure risk may be subdivided.

■

Identify and explain the principal methods of handling risk.

⁙ The Human Race and Risk   ■ ■ ■ ■ ■ ■ ■ ■ ■ ■ ■ ■ ■ ■ ■ ■ ■

The entire history of the human species is a chronology of exposure to misfortune and adversity and of efforts to deal with these risks. Although it is perhaps an exaggeration to claim that the earliest profession was risk management, it can be argued that from the dawn of their existence, humans have faced the problem of survival, not only as individuals but as a species. The initial human concern was a quest for security and avoidance of the risks that threatened extinction. Our continued existence is testimony to the success of our ancestors in managing risk.

It is not difficult to imagine the perils that threatened primitive man, or the apprehension that the hazardous environment fostered. Shivering in the cold, suffering pangs of hunger, and hunted by savage beasts that were stronger and faster and bit harder, humans faced an environment that was a combination of incredible perils and hazards. Overall, the environment was one of chronic risks of deprivation and hunger. Although we can only speculate about how primitive people dealt with these risks, we can imagine the difficulties early humans faced in the slow and steady progress toward security.

Many of our primitive ancestors' responses to risk were identical to those of other animals. Without a great deal of thought, people who were threatened by dangerous beasts fled—if not the first time the beast was encountered, at least thereafter. In addition to their instinctive reactions to risk, they learned to avoid dangerous areas and situations. But their instinctive reactions to risk and their learned behavior do not adequately explain our ancestors success in managing the risks they faced. Other humanlike creatures, such as *Homo erectus* and *Homo Sapiens neanderthalensis* reacted to threats in these ways but, despite the fact that they were larger and stronger, failed in their efforts to manage the threats to their existence. They failed to achieve the ultimate goal of risk management, which is survival. In contrast, anatomically modern humans (*Homo Sapiens Sapiens*) not only survived but flourished.[1] The difference was the unique human gift of reason. Men and women think, and it is in their ability to think that they deal with risks in ways that are different from those of other creatures. Although men and women share with lesser animals the instinctive reactions to some risks, their most significant achievements in managing risk are those that stem from their thinking nature. Indeed, it can be argued that one of humanity's defining characteristics is the way in which the race deals with risk. The human species distinguished itself from lesser species not only by its inclination to address existing adversity, but also by its ability to anticipate adversity and to prepare for it. Having experienced misfortune or having observed the misfortune of others, men and women developed measures that would reduce the likelihood of such misfortune. Humans learned to improve on the achievements of others. In the words of Blaise Pascal, the race progressed, as each generation remembered at least a part of what earlier generations had learned. Although progress was agonizingly slow, humans learned to manage the risks they faced in

---

[1]Anthropologists now distinguish between the archaic *Homo Sapiens* (*man the wise*) and *Homo Sapiens Sapiens* (Man the Double Wise), the ancestors of the modern human race.

new ways and developed new approaches to managing risks. Many of the measures that were originally devised to reduce risk eventually became cornerstones of human development and rank among humanity's greatest achievements.

Man's initial achievement in dealing with risk was to create tools, which increased his chances of survival in two ways. First, they served as weapons of protection from larger beasts. In addition, they simplified the process of obtaining food. The first tools were likely weapons—rocks, clubs, and sharpened sticks that served as primitive spears. Whether the first tools were devised to help people address the uncertainty of tomorrow's food supply, or to keep from being today's food for those animals higher in the food chain, they served both functions. Above all, tools reduced risk and helped the species to survive.

Like certain other species, humans banded together, for both defensive purposes and social interaction. In this way, they gained protection through strength in numbers and were able to share resources. This, in turn, resulted in sharing prosperity and adversity and, ultimately, risk.

Humans also learned to prepare for adversity by *saving* for the future, both collectively and individually. A significant innovation occurred with the domestication of animals, which was an early form of saving. By capturing rather than killing an animal, humans created a reserve for future consumption. The innovation of saving was also the beginning of the concept of private property. The hunter who refrained from killing an animal today so that the animal would be available to provide meat tomorrow created a vested interest in the animal that was a property right. Although most early property rights were tribal (rather than individual), these tribal rights eventually became individual rights. When humans began to cultivate some wild grasses, grains, roots, and fruits that had formerly been collected, tribes began to claim areas as their own. Originally, the area was held in common and the tribe protected it from interloper. When the tribal spirit began to disintegrate, the notion of ownership passed from the tribe to the family and the individual.

By the dawn of history some 50 centuries ago (which we date from the time men began to write), humans in many different parts of the world had learned to manage the risks that threatened their ancestors. They had learned to defend themselves and to provide for their material wants on something other than a day-to-day basis. They had learned to accumulate for the future and to live together in communities. As wealth grew in modest increments, they invented laws to govern their relationships. They were, in a word, becoming civilized.

This is not to suggest that civilization and urban life eliminated misfortune and risk. The fortifications and walled cities unearthed by archaeologists are mute testimony to the fact that with increases in wealth came increased risk. Although many of the risks that had threatened primitive men and women disappeared, new risks arose. There was frequent warring among rival states, and entire cities were sometimes razed to the ground. Famine and pestilence were periodic reminders of the vulnerability of the race, and the perils of nature sometimes destroyed what men and women had built. But the worst was past. Men and women had learned to manage risks, and the race had survived. In the process of surviving, men and women had created technological, social, and legal advances that led humanity out of the darkness of primitive existence.

EVOLUTION OF BUSINESS RISKS

We do not know when trading and commerce began, but clearly it originated early in the existence of the human race and it allowed men and women to take advantage of specialization, thereby increasing the general availability of goods and the accumulation of reserve stocks. This, in turn, provided a cushion against misfortune. It is not a stretch to suggest that business itself was one of humanity's early efforts to deal with risk. Equally important, from the inception of commerce, those engaged in business and commerce have faced risks and have developed techniques for dealing with risk. Two innovations in particular are noteworthy. As early as 3000 B.C., the Babylonian civilization exhibited a highly developed commercial sector with money and a legal system.

Money

Although there is some debate concerning exactly when money was first used, without doubt its effect was dramatic. The inevitable consequence of private property had been the evolution of a market economy, but until the invention of money, commerce was on a barter basis. The invention of money revolutionized commerce, private property, and the accumulation of wealth. By providing a new way of keeping score, it had important implications for managing risks. In primitive societies, risk management efforts focused on the preservation and protection of self and property from the perils that could cause loss. With the introduction of money as a medium of exchange and store of wealth, wealth could be held in the form of tangible property or as financial assets that could be exchanged for tangible property. Tangible assets that were lost or damaged could be replaced, provided the owner had financial assets when a loss occurred. The invention of credit meant that assets could be acquired even by those who did not have financial assets, provided someone was willing to lend them money. This, in turn, created risks for the lender, which they addressed by imposing interest charges for loans.

The Legal System

The second innovation was the development of a legal system. Although laws originally developed as tribal conventions, they eventually became more formalized. Hammurabi (1792 to 1750 B.C.) created his famous Code of Hammurabi by collecting earlier Sumerian and Akkadian regulations in a single place. Again, we can argue that the invention of laws was a distinctly human effort to deal with risk. By defining individual rights and responsibilities, the legal system created a framework whose basic function was to protect those rights.

Other Commercial Innovations

Although commerce brought rewards, it also involved risks because the goods that were to be traded were exposed to loss. Early traders voluntarily assumed these risks primarily because the potential for gain was greater than the risk of loss.

Because reducing the chance of loss increased the likelihood of gain, those engaged in commerce devised inventive approaches to dealing with risk.

For example, as early as 3000 B.C., Chinese merchants used the technique of *sharing* risk. These merchants shipped their goods by boat down river, and because of treacherous rapids, not all the boats made it safely. To reduce the impact of losses on any one individual, the merchants devised the plan of distributing their goods on each other's boats. Thus, when a boat was dashed to pieces on the rocks, the loss was shared by all rather than falling upon a single individual.

About 1200 years later the Great Code of Hammurabi provided for the *transfer* of the risk of loss from merchants to moneylenders. Under the provisions of the code, a trader whose goods were lost to bandits was relieved of the debt to the money-lender who had loaned the money to buy the goods. Babylonian moneylenders undoubtedly padded their interest charges to compensate for this transfer of risk. The Phoenicians and later the Greeks adapted this innovation to the risks of sea trade. Loans were made to shipowners and merchants engaged in trade, with the ship or cargo pledged as collateral. The borrower was offered an option whereby, for a somewhat higher interest charge, the lender agreed to cancel the loan if the ship or cargo were lost at sea.[2] In this way, the risk of loss was transferred from the owner of the boat or cargo to the lender. These contracts were referred to as *bottomry contracts* when the ship was pledged and *respondentia contracts* when the cargo was the security.

In about 900 B.C. on the island of Rhodes, another ingenious device for sharing risk was conceived. Rhodian sea merchants occasionally had to lighten their load in the midst of heavy storms. Because the ships often contained cargoes owned by different parties, one can imagine the debate over whose goods got tossed. The solution was an agreement that all owners in the venture were to "come into contribution together with the value of the ship and the goods that are saved." This principle has come down to us as the maritime principle of *general average*.

GROWTH OF BUSINESS RISKS

We can leave humankind at the beginnings of civilization and fast forward through the rise and fall of the Egyptian, Greek, and Roman civilizations, past feudalism, past the rise of the merchant class and mercantilism, to the Industrial Revolution and the beginnings of our modern capitalistic market economy. Modern capitalism emerged after a series of events over several centuries that produced the conditions necessary for a capitalistic market society. These included private ownership of the means of production, the spirit of acquisitiveness, the profit motive, competition, and the operation of a market economy.[3]

---

[2]The additional interest on such loans was called a *premium*, a term that has become a part of insurance terminology, indicating the payment made by the insured.

[3]Most economic historians now agree that there is no single starting point for the capitalist system. Rather, the growth of capitalism has been evolutionary, consisting of a series of increments in capitalist practice.

With the growth of enterprise and the need to raise large amounts of capital, another innovation aimed at limiting risk emerged, the corporation. The earliest versions of the shareholder form of business organization, from which the modern corporation evolved, appeared in Europe near the end of the seventeenth century and were known as joint stock companies. A corporation addresses risk in two ways. The first is by allowing multiple investors to share the risk of enterprise by pooling invested funds. This feature also exists in the case of partnerships and other joint ventures and is independent of the second way that the corporation addresses risk, which is by limiting the liability of investors to the amount of their investment. Legally, a corporation is an artificial person, with rights and responsibilities separate from those of its owners and, with limited exceptions discussed later in the text, limits the liability of owners to the amount of their investment.

The Industrial Revolution witnessed the application of steam to the production process, and with steam came new risks. The early steam engines were hazardous mechanisms, and explosions were common. Proposals to locate a steam boiler in or near a community in the early 1800s evoked protest marches and resistance that augured the nuclear plant protests of the twentieth century. Not only was the risk of explosion great, but steam power created other risks. Steam-powered machines were far less prone to stoppage by obstructions than human-powered devices; they continued to grind away, oblivious to the hands and arms that got entangled in gears. It soon became evident, at least to the workers, that industrialization was a mixed blessing. The high toll in terms of injuries to workers eventually led to legislation that made the employer liable for damages to the injured worker. Electric power followed steam and was in turn followed by nuclear power. With each new era, new risks arose. Because many of the old risks remain, the inventory of risks that must be addressed increases geometrically. As a consequence, the modern business corporation and its not-for-profit cousins face a profusion of risks, both known and unknown.

RISKS OF THE MODERN BUSINESS ENVIRONMENT

Although the risks that threatened our earliest ancestors have disappeared, they have been replaced by new risks that accompanied advancing technology. Many of the risks facing business today were unknown a generation ago. Some of them have arisen from changes in the legal environment and include potential liability for a profusion of new transgressions—environmental damage, discrimination in employment, sexual harassment, and violence in the workplace. Yet other risks have accompanied the emergence of the age of information technology—interruptions of business resulting from computer failures, privacy issues, and computer fraud. The bandits and pirates that threatened early traders have been replaced by hackers who engage in vandalism and commit electronic larceny. Daily newspapers indicate the simultaneous threat of the new-age hazards and the age-old perils of nature. The hazards posed by the nuclear age were demonstrated by the incident at the Three Mile Island nuclear facility in Pennsylvania in 1979 and the accident at the Soviet Union's Chernobyl plant in April 1987. The potential ravages of nature are evidenced by the over $22 billion in damages caused by Hurricane Andrew, by the floods of near-biblical proportions in the midwestern United States in 1993, and by the earthquakes in California and Kobi, Japan, in 1993 and 1994. And the bombing of the World Trade Center in 1993 and the Oklahoma Federal Building in 1995 serve as reminders that it is not just nature that can cause death and destruction but people as well. Although losses that affect a single individual or a single firm are less spectacular, for the party who suffers the loss, they are no less devastating.

As might be expected, with the increasing array of risks, the dollar amount of losses arising from accidents has also increased. Interestingly, however, the increasing dollar amount of losses is not solely a function of the increasing number of risks. Even those losses that arise from the perils of nature—windstorms, earthquakes, and floods—have exhibited an increasing severity. Nor is the increasing severity merely a reflection of inflation; the dollar total associated with these losses continues to increase even when adjusted for inflation. Although the number of earthquakes, floods, and windstorms occur at essentially the same rate as in the past, each new catastrophe seems to exceed previous losses. The reason, of course, is simple: today more wealth, more investment, and more assets are exposed to loss. As business has become more capital intensive, and as the technology of production equipment becomes more costly, capital investment increases. With the growth in capital investment, the risk of financial loss also increases.

⠶ The Concept of Risk ■

In its broadest sense, the sense in which we have used it thus far in our discussion, the term *risk* means exposure to adversity. Although our usage of the term in this loose sense has been adequate for our discussion up to this point, it is now time to define the term more precisely.

Every field of knowledge has its own specialized terminology, and terms that have very simple meanings in everyday usage often take on different and complicated connotations when applied in a specialized field. One such term is risk. Economists, statisticians, decision theorists, and insurance theorists have long discussed the concepts of "risk" and "uncertainty" in an attempt to construct a definition of risk that is useful for analysis in each field of investigation. Up to the present time, they have not been able to agree on a single definition that can be used in each field. A definition of risk that is suitable for the economist or statistician may be worthless as an analytic tool for the insurance theorist. The fact that each group treats a different body of subject matter requires the use of different concepts. Although the statistician, the decision theorist, and the insurance theorist all use the term *risk*, each may mean something entirely different.

The definition of risk differs from one discipline to another, and even within the same field there are sometimes contradictory definitions. Insurance and risk management are a case in point. In part because the field is relatively new and in part because risk management writers and insurance theorists have attempted to borrow the definitions of risk used in other fields, there are contradictory definitions of *risk* even in this field where risk is the central object of study.

To compound the problem, people in the insurance business use the term *risk* to mean either a peril insured against (e.g., fire is a risk to which most property is exposed), or a person or property protected by insurance (e.g., many insurance companies feel that young drivers are not good risks). We will avoid using the term in these ways and instead will use it in the abstract to indicate a situation in which an exposure to loss exists.

CURRENT DEFINITIONS OF RISK

If we were to survey the best-known insurance textbooks used in colleges and universities today, we would find a general lack of agreement concerning the definition of risk.[4] Although the insurance theorists have not agreed on a universal definition, all the definitions share two common elements: indeterminacy and loss.

- The notion of an indeterminate outcome is implicit in all definitions of risk: the outcome must be in question. When risk is said to exist, there must always be at least two possible outcomes. If we know for certain that a loss will occur, there is no risk. Investment in a capital asset, for example, usually involves a realization that the asset is subject to physical depreciation and that its value will decline. Here the outcome is certain and so there is no risk.

- At least one of the possible outcomes is undesirable. This may be a loss in the generally accepted sense in which something the individual possesses is lost, or it may be a gain smaller than the gain that was possible. For example, the investor who fails to take advantage of an opportunity "loses" the gain that might have been made. The investor faced with the choice between two stocks may be said to "lose" if he or she chooses the one that increases in value less than the alternative.

OUR DEFINITION OF RISK

We define risk as a condition of the real world in which there is an exposure to adversity. More specifically, "Risk is a condition in which there is a possibility of an adverse deviation from a desired outcome that is expected or hoped for."

Note first that in this definition risk is a condition of the real world; it is a combination of circumstances in the external environment. Note also that in this combination of circumstances, there is a *possibility* of loss. When we say that an event is possible, we mean that it has a probability between zero and one; it is neither impossible nor definite. Note also that there is no requirement that the possibility be measurable, only that it must exist. We may or may not be able to measure the degree of risk, but the probability of the adverse outcome must be between 0 and 1.

---

[4]The term *risk* is variously defined as (1) the chance of loss; (2) the possibility of loss; (3) uncertainty; (4) the dispersion of actual from expected results; or (5) the probability of any outcome different from the one expected.

The undesirable event is described as "an adverse deviation from a desired outcome that is *expected* or *hoped for*." The reference to a desired outcome that is either expected or hoped for contemplates both individual and aggregate loss exposures. The individual hopes that adversity will not occur, and it is the possibility that this hope will not be fulfilled that constitutes risk.[5] If you own a house, you hope that it will not catch fire. When you make a wager, you hope that the outcome will be favorable. The fact that the outcome in either event may be something other than what you hope constitutes the possibility of loss or risk.

In the case of an insurer, actuaries predict some specified number and amount of losses and charge a premium based on this expectation. The amount of predicted losses is the desired outcome that the insurer expects. For the insurer, risk is the possibility that losses will deviate adversely from what is expected. Because uncertainty is the actuarial measure of risk for an insurer, some writers define risk as uncertainty. Although this is a meaningful definition from the insurer's perspective, it is less than satisfactory from the individual's point of view.

UNCERTAINTY AND ITS RELATIONSHIP TO RISK

Because the term *uncertainty* is often used in connection with the term *risk* (sometimes even interchangeably), it seems appropriate to explain our view of the relationship between the two concepts.

The most widely held meaning of *uncertainty* refers to a state of mind characterized by doubt, based on a lack of knowledge about what will or will not happen in the future. It is the opposite of certainty, which is a conviction or certitude about a particular situation. A student says, "I am certain I will get an A in this course," which means the same as "I am positive I will get an A in this course." Both statements reflect a conviction about the outcome. Uncertainty, on the other hand, is the opposite mental state. If one says, "I am uncertain what grade I am going to get in this course," the statement reflects a lack of knowledge about the outcome. Uncertainty, then, is simply a psychological reaction to the absence of knowledge about the future.[6] The existence of risk—a condition or combination of circumstances in which there is a possibility of loss—creates uncertainty on the part of individuals when that risk is recognized.

The individual's conviction or lack thereof (certainty or uncertainty) about a specific situation may or may not coincide with the conditions of the real world. The student who says, "I am certain I will get an A in this course" may actually get a B, a C, a D, or even an F. Uncertainty varies with the person's knowledge and atti-

---

[5]There is not general agreement on the point that risk involves exposure to adversity. Some writers maintain that risk does not necessarily imply that outcomes are adverse. See Neil A. Doherty, *Corporate Risk Management* (New York: McGraw-Hill Book Co., 1985), p. 1.

[6]In addition to its meaning as a psychological phenomenon, a second possible meaning of the term *uncertainty* relates to probability and is contrasted with a second meaning of certainty; a situation in which the probability of an event is 100 percent. An event may be said to be impossible (probability $= 0$), certain (probability $= 1$) or uncertain. Used in reference to the likelihood of an event, uncertain simply means that the probability is judged to be between 0 and 1.

tudes. Different attitudes are possible for different individuals under identical conditions of the real world. It is possible, for example, for a person to experience uncertainty in a situation in which he or she imagines that there is a chance of loss, but where no chance of loss exists. Similarly, it is possible for an individual to feel no uncertainty regarding a particular risk when the exposure to loss is not recognized. Whether or not a risk is recognized, however, does not alter its existence. When there is a possibility of loss, risk exists even whether or not the person exposed to loss is aware of the risk.[7]

THE DEGREE OF RISK

It is intuitively obvious that risk is greater in some situations than in others. Just as we should agree on what we mean when we use the term *risk*, we should agree on the way(s) in which risk can be measured. Precisely what is meant when we say that one alternative involves "more risk" or "less risk" than another?

It would seem that the most commonly accepted meaning of "degree of risk" is related to the likelihood of occurrence. We intuitively consider those events with a high probability of loss to be "riskier" than those with a low probability. This intuitive notion of the degree of risk is consistent with our definition of risk. When risk is defined as the possibility of an adverse deviation from a desired outcome that is expected or hoped for, the degree of risk is measured by the probability of the adverse deviation. In the case of the individual, the hope is that no loss will occur, so that the probability of a deviation from what is hoped for (which is the measure of risk) varies directly with the probability that a loss will occur. In the case of the individual, we measure risk in terms of the probability of an adverse deviation from what is hoped for. Actuarial tables tell us, for example, that the probability of death at age 52 is approximately 1 percent and that at age 79 it is about 10 percent. At age 97, the probability of death increases to nearly 50 percent. Using the probability of an adverse deviation from the outcome that is hoped for, we view the risk of death at age 79 as greater than that at age 52, but less than that at age 97. The higher the probability that an event will occur, the greater is the likelihood of a deviation from the outcome that is hoped for and the greater the risk, as long as the probability of loss is less than 1.

In the game of Russian roulette, more risk exists when there are two bullets in a revolver's six chambers than just one. Adding a third bullet increases the risk, as does adding the fourth and fifth. Adding the fourth and fifth bullets increases the probability of a deviation from the hoped-for outcome. And if a sixth bullet is added, the player can no longer expect or even hope that the outcome will be

---

[7]Some authors equate our notion of uncertainty with *subjective risk*, which is a person's perception of risk. An individual may perceive risk where it does not exist. (Navigators in Columbus's day perceived a risk of falling off the edge of the world.) They may also fail to perceive risk when it does exist. The distinction between objective risk and subjective risk (i.e., between risk and uncertainty) is important because subjective risk affects the decisions people make. Ideally, they should make decisions based on actual risk (i.e., objective risk). Better information reduces uncertainty (improves subjective risk estimates) and leads to better decisions.

favorable. The sixth bullet makes the outcome certain, and risk no longer exists. If the probability of loss is 1.0, there is no chance of an outcome other than that which is expected and, therefore, no hope of a favorable result. Similarly, when the probability of loss is 0, there is no possibility of loss and therefore no risk.

In the case of a large number of exposure units, estimates can be made about the likelihood that a given number of losses will occur, and predictions can be made on the basis of these estimates. Here the expectation is that the predicted number of losses will occur. In the case of aggregate exposures, the degree of risk is not the probability of a single occurrence or loss; it is the probability of some outcome different from that predicted or expected. Insurance companies make predictions about losses that are expected to occur and charge a premium based on this prediction. For the insurance company, then, the risk is that its prediction will not be accurate. Suppose that based on past experience, an insurer estimates that 1 out of 1000 houses will burn. If the company insures 100,000 houses, it might predict that 100 houses will burn out of the 100,000 insured. But it is highly unlikely that 100, and only 100, houses will burn. The actual experience will undoubtedly deviate from the expectation, and insofar as this deviation is unfavorable, the insurance company faces risk. Therefore, the insurance company makes a prediction not only with respect to the number of houses that will burn, but also estimates the range of error. The prediction might be that 100 losses will occur and that the range of possible deviation will be plus or minus 10. Some number of houses between 90 and 110 are expected to burn, and the possibility that the number will be more than 100 is the insurer's risk. Students who have studied statistics will note that when one of the standard measures of dispersion (such as the standard deviation) is used, risk is measurable, and we can say that more risk or less risk exists in a given situation, depending on the standard deviation.

At times we use the terms *more risk* and *less risk* to indicate a measure of the possible size of the loss. Many people would say that more risk is involved in a possible loss of $1000 than in that of $1, even though the probability of loss is the same in both cases. The probability that a loss may occur and the potential severity of the loss if it does occur contribute to the intensity of one's reaction to risk. It seems, therefore, that a measurement of risk should recognize the magnitude of the potential loss. Given two situations, one involving a $1000 exposure and the other a $1 exposure, and assuming the same probability in each case, it seems appropriate to state that there is a greater risk in the case of the possible loss of $1000. This is consistent with our definition of risk, since the loss of $1000 is a greater deviation from what is hoped for (that is, no loss) than is the loss of $1. On the other hand, given two situations where the amount exposed is the same (e.g., $1000), there is more risk in the situation with the greater probability of loss.

Although it may be difficult to relate the size of the potential loss and the probability of that loss in the measurement of risk, the concept of expected value may be used to relate these two facets of a given risk situation. The expected value of a loss in a given situation is the probability of that loss multiplied by the amount of the potential loss. If the amount at risk is $10 and the probability of loss is 0.10, the expected value of the loss is $1. If the amount at risk is $100 and the probability is 0.01, the expected value is also $1. This is a very useful concept, as we will see later.

RISK DISTINGUISHED FROM PERIL AND HAZARD

The terms *peril* and *hazard* are often used interchangeably with each other and with *risk*. However, to be precise, it is important to distinguish these terms. A peril is a cause of a loss. We speak of the peril of "fire" or "windstorm," or "hail" or "theft." Each of these is the cause of the loss that occurs. A hazard, on the other hand, is a condition that may create or increase the chance of a loss arising from a given peril. It is possible for something to be both a peril and a hazard. For instance, sickness is a peril causing economic loss, but it is also a hazard that increases the chance of loss from the peril of premature death. Hazards may be classified into four broad categories:

- *Physical hazard* consists of those physical properties that increase the chance of loss from the various perils. Examples of physical hazards that increase the possibility of loss from the peril of fire are the type of construction, the location of the property, and the occupancy of the building.

- *Moral hazard* refers to the increase in the probability of loss which results from evil tendencies in the character of an insured person. More simply, an insured person's dishonest tendencies may induce that person to attempt to defraud the insurance company. A dishonest person, in the hope of collecting from the insurance company, may intentionally cause a loss or may exaggerate the amount of a loss in an attempt to collect more than the amount to which he or she is entitled.

- *Morale hazard*, not to be confused with moral hazard, results from the insured persons' careless attitude toward the occurrence of losses. The purchase of insurance may create a morale hazard, since the realization that the insurance company will bear the loss may lead the insured to exercise less care than if forced to bear the loss alone.

- *Legal hazard* refers to the increase in the frequency and severity of loss that arises from legal doctrines enacted by legislatures and created by the courts. Jurisdictions in which legal doctrines favor a plaintiff represent a hazard to persons or organizations who are sued at tort. Although legal hazard is greatest in the field of legal liability, it also exists in the case of property exposures. In a jurisdiction where the law imposes obligations on property owners to clean up debris from property losses or demolish damaged buildings, the exposure to loss is increased.

Clearly, "moral" and "morale" hazards are important only from the insurer's perspective; they cause insured losses to be inflated. From the perspective of the risk manager, they are not particularly important. Two additional hazards, however, are of importance to the risk manager: legal hazards and criminal hazards. Legal hazards arise out of statutes and the decisions of the courts. The hazard may vary from one jurisdiction to another. Statutory liability increases the likelihood of loss, and liberal court awards increase the potential severity. Criminal hazards, like moral hazard, arise out of the dishonest tendencies of human nature. Criminal hazard may exist in employees and nonemployees, and increase the likelihood of loss from theft and embezzlement.

CLASSIFICATIONS OF RISK

Business generally involves the investment of assets. The hope is that this investment will generate a profit. If things do not go as planned, the investor can suffer a loss, and this possibility of loss represents the risk of entrepreneurship. Businesses may fail or suffer loss as a result of a variety of causes. The differences in these causes and their effects constitute the basis for different classifications of risk. The sources of risk may be classified as dynamic or static, pure or speculative, and fundamental and particular.

Financial and Nonfinancial Risks

In its broadest context, the term *risk* includes all situations in which an exposure to adversity exists. This adversity sometimes involves financial loss and sometimes not. Some element of risk is involved in every aspect of human endeavor, and many of these risks have no (or only incidental) financial consequences. In this text, we are concerned with those risks that involve a financial loss.

Financial risk involves the relationship between an individual (or an organization) and an asset or expectation of income that may be lost or damaged. Thus financial risk involves three elements: (1) the individual or organization who is exposed to loss, (2) the asset or income whose destruction or dispossession will cause financial loss, and (3) a peril that can cause the loss.

The first element in financial risk is that *someone* will be affected by the occurrence of an event. During the devastating midwestern floods of 1993, millions of acres of farmland as well as thousands of buildings were severely damaged by floodwaters, causing billions of dollars in financial loss to owners. In addition, according to the game commissions in the affected states, the effect of the flood on wildlife in the area was severe. Although the loss of thousands of deer, pheasants, and trees perhaps diminished the quality of life for residents of the area, there was no financial loss resulting from the destruction of the wildlife and fauna.

The second and third elements in financial risk are the thing of value and the peril that can cause the loss of the thing of value. The individual who owns nothing of value faces no financial risk. Furthermore, if nothing could happen to the individual's assets or expected income, there would be no risk.

Static and Dynamic Risks

A second important distinction is between static and dynamic risks.[8] *Dynamic risks* are those resulting from changes in the economy; they arise from two sets of factors. The first set are factors in the external environment; the economy, the industry, competitors, and consumers. Changes in these factors are uncontrollable, but all have the potential to produce financial loss to the firm. The other factors that can produce the losses that constitute the basis of speculative risk are manage-

---

[8]The dynamic–static distinction was made by Alan H. Willett, *The Economic Theory of Risk and Insurance* (Philadelphia: University of Pennsylvania Press, 1951), pp. 14–19.

ment's decisions within the firm. The management of every organization makes decisions on what to produce, how to produce it, how to finance the production, and how to market what is produced. If these decisions result in the provision of goods and services that the market accepts at an adequate price, the firm will profit. If not, it may suffer loss.

Dynamic risks normally benefit society over the long run, since they are the result of adjustments to misallocation of resources. Although these dynamic risks may affect a large number of individuals, they are generally considered less predictable than static risks, inasmuch as they do not occur with any degree of regularity.

Static risks involve those losses that would result even if no changes in the economy occurred. If we could hold consumer tastes, output and income, and the level of technology constant, some individuals would still suffer financial loss. These losses arise from causes other than the changes in the economy, such as the perils of nature and the dishonesty of other individuals. Unlike dynamic risks, static risks are not a source of gain to society. Static losses involve either the destruction of the asset or a change in its possession as a result of dishonesty or human failure. Static losses tend to occur with a degree of regularity over time and, as a result, are generally predictable. Because they are predictable, static risks are more suited to treatment by insurance than are dynamic risks.

Pure and Speculative Risks

One of the most useful distinctions is that between pure risk and speculative risk.[9] *Speculative risk* describes a situation that holds a possibility of either loss or gain. Gambling is a good example of a speculative risk. In a gambling situation, risk is deliberately created in the hope of gain. The student wagering $10 on the outcome of Saturday's game faces the possibility of loss, accompanied by the possibility of gain. The entrepreneur or capitalist faces speculative risk in the quest for profit. The investment made may be lost if the market does not accept the product at a price sufficient to cover costs, but this risk is borne in return for the possibility of profit. The term *pure risk*, in contrast, is used to designate those situations that involve only the chance of loss or no loss. One of the best examples of pure risk is the possibility of loss surrounding the ownership of property. The person who buys an automobile, for example, immediately faces the possibility that something may happen to damage or destroy the automobile. The possible outcomes are loss or no loss.

The distinction between pure and speculative risks is an important one because normally only pure risks are insurable. Insurance is not concerned with the protection of individuals against those losses arising out of speculative risks. Speculative risk is voluntarily accepted because of its two-dimensional nature, which includes the possibility of gain. Not all pure risks are insurable, and a further distinction between insurable and uninsurable pure risks may also be made.

---

[9]Although the distinction between pure and speculative risk had been introduced earlier, Albert H. Mowbray formalized the distinction. See Albert H. Mowbray and Ralph H. Blanchard, *Insurance, Its Theory and Practice in the United States*, 5th ed. (New York: McGraw-Hill. 1961), pp. 6, 7.

Fundamental and Particular Risks

The distinction between fundamental and particular risks is based on the difference in the origin and consequences of the losses.[10] *Fundamental risks* involve losses that are impersonal in origin and consequence. They are group risks, caused for the most part by economic, social, and political phenomena, although they may also result from physical occurrences. They affect large segments or even all of the population. *Particular risks* involve losses that arise out of individual events and are felt by individuals rather than by the entire group. They may be static or dynamic. Unemployment, war, inflation, earthquakes, and floods are all fundamental risks; the burning of a house and the robbery of a bank are particular risks.

Throughout history, risks have increased, both in variety and in complexity. With every new risk, humans have attempted to devise responses. Over time, a variety of social contracts have emerged regarding how risk will be addressed and who will bear the losses associated with risk. In some eras the emphasis has been on collective measures, whereas in others it has been on individual measures. Because fundamental risks are caused by conditions more or less beyond the control of the individuals who suffer the losses and because they are not the fault of anyone in particular, it is held that society rather than the individual has a responsibility to deal with them. Collective measures to address risk are found throughout history. They include, first, government itself. A fundamental purpose of government is to guarantee the security of the people. National governments maintain armies and provide protection against the risk of invasion or conquest by other nations. Police forces are established to protect citizens from a variety of threats, and national laws are enacted to define personal rights that are to be protected. In addition to the collective measures adopted to protect citizens from physical harm, governments may also be responsible for economic and social programs whose goals and objectives are to protect individuals from harm. Although some fundamental risks are dealt with through private insurance,[11] it is an inappropriate tool for dealing with most fundamental risks. Usually, some form of social insurance or other government transfer program is used to deal with fundamental risks. Unemployment and occupational disabilities are fundamental risks treated through social insurance. Districts suffering flood damage or earthquakes are areas eligible for federal funds.

Particular risks are considered to be the individual's own responsibility, and are inappropriate subjects for action by society as a whole. The individual deals with them through the use of insurance, loss prevention, or some other technique.

The exact place at which the line should be drawn between collective measures to protect against risk and individual measures is a value judgment that embodies the collective preference of a society. With the development of a free-market capitalistic society, there is a tacit agreement regarding responsibility for particular

[10]The distinction between fundamental and particular risks is based on C. A. Kulp's discussion of risk (which he referred to as "hazard"). See C. A. Kulp, *Casualty Insurance*, 3rd ed. (New York: Ronald Press, 1956), pp. 3, 4.

[11]For example, earthquake insurance is available from private insurers in most parts of the country, and flood insurance is frequently included in contracts covering movable personal property. Flood insurance on real property is available through private insurers only on a limited basis.

risks. In a free-market capitalistic society, the economic risks associated with production and commerce are generally borne by those whose funds are invested. These are the parties that realize the gains from success in the market, and they are also the interests that suffer the losses.

CLASSIFICATIONS OF PURE RISK

It would be impossible in this book to list all the risks confronting an individual or business, but we can briefly outline the nature of the various pure risks that we face. For the most part, these are also static risks. Pure risks that exist for individuals and business firms can be classified as (1) personal risks, (2) property risks, (3) liability risks, and (4) risks arising from the failure of others.

Personal Risks

These consist of the possibility of loss of income or assets as a result of the loss of the ability to earn income. In general, earning power is subject to four perils: (a) premature death, (b) dependent old age, (c) sickness or disability, and (d) unemployment.

Property Risks

Anyone who owns property faces property risks simply because such possessions can be destroyed or stolen. Property risks embrace two distinct types of loss: direct loss and indirect or "consequential" loss. Direct loss is the simplest to understand: if a building is destroyed by fire, the owner loses the value of the building. This is a direct loss. However, in addition to losing the value of the building itself, the owner also loses the use of the building during the period required for reconstruction. The owner of a house loses a place to live, and the business firm loses the income that would have been earned through use of the building. Property risks, then, can involve two types of losses: (1) loss of the property and (2) loss of use of the property resulting in lost income or additional expenses.

Liability Risks

The basic peril in the liability risk is the unintentional injury of other persons or damage to their property through negligence or carelessness; however, liability may also result from intentional injuries or damage. Under our legal system, the laws provide that one who has injured another, or damaged another's property through negligence or otherwise, can be held responsible for the harm caused. Furthermore, our legal system also decrees that an employer or other principal is responsible for the acts or omissions of agents or employees and can be held liable for their negligence. Liability risks, therefore, involve the possibility of loss of present assets or future income as a result of damages assessed or legal liability arising out of either intentional or unintentional torts, or invasion of the rights of others.

Risks Arising from Failure of Others

When another person agrees to perform a service for you, he or she undertakes an obligation that you hope will be met. When the person's failure to meet this obligation would result in your financial loss, risk exists. Examples of risks in this category would include a contractor's failure to complete a construction project as scheduled, or a debtor's failure to make payments as expected.

❖ The Burden of Risk ■

Regardless how risk is defined, the greatest burden in connection with risk is that some losses will actually occur. When a building is destroyed by fire, or money is stolen, or a wage earner dies, there is a financial loss. When someone is negligent and that negligence results in injury to a person or damage to property, there is a financial loss. These losses are the primary burden of risk and the primary reason why individuals attempt to avoid risk or alleviate its impact.

In addition to the losses themselves, risk has other detrimental aspects. The uncertainty as to whether the loss will occur requires the prudent individual to prepare for its possible occurrence. In the absence of insurance, one way this can be done is to accumulate a reserve fund to meet the losses if they do occur.[12] Accumulation of such a reserve fund carries an opportunity cost, for funds must be available at the time of the loss and must therefore be held in a highly liquid state. The return on such funds will presumably be less than if they were put to alternate uses. If each property owner accumulates his or her own fund, the amount of funds held in such reserves will be greater than if the funds are amassed collectively.

The existence of risk may also have a deterrent effect on economic growth and capital accumulation. Progress in the economy is determined to a large extent by the rate of capital accumulation, but the investment of capital involves risk that is distasteful. Investors as a class will incur the risks of a new undertaking only if the return on the investment is sufficiently high to compensate for both the dynamic and static risks. The cost of capital is higher in those situations where the risk is greater, and the consumer must pay the resulting higher cost of the goods and services or they will not be forthcoming.

Finally, the uncertainty connected with risk usually produces a feeling of frustration and mental unrest. This is particularly true in the case of pure risk. Speculative risk is attractive to many individuals. The gambler obviously enjoys the uncertainty connected with wagering more than the certainty of not gambling; otherwise he or she would not gamble. But here it is the possibility of gain or profit, which exists only in the speculative risk category, that is attractive. In the case of pure risk, where there is no compensating chance of gain, risk is distasteful. Most

---

[12]One great danger of this approach is the possibility that a loss may occur before a sufficient fund has been accumulated.

people hope that misfortunes will not befall them and that their present state of well-being will continue. Although they hope that no misfortune will occur, people are nevertheless likely to worry about possible mishaps. This worry, which reduces a feeling of well-being, is an additional burden of risk.

Techniques for Dealing with Risk ■ ■ ■ ■ ■ ■ ■ ■ ■ ■ ■ ■ ■

Because risk is distasteful, we attempt to deal with it through avoidance, reduction, retention, and transfer. In some cases, two of these approaches—transfer and retention—are combined to create a fifth technique, risk sharing.

RISK AVOIDANCE

Risk is avoided when the individual or organization refuses to accept it even for an instant. The exposure is not permitted to come into existence. This is accomplished by merely not engaging in the action that gives rise to risk. If you do not want to risk losing your savings in a hazardous venture, then pick one where there is less risk. If you want to avoid the risks associated with the ownership of property, do not purchase the property but lease or rent it instead. If the use of a particular product promises to be hazardous, don't manufacture or sell it.

The avoidance of risk is one method of dealing with risk, but it is a negative rather than a positive technique. For this reason it is sometimes an unsatisfactory approach to dealing with many risks. If risk avoidance were used extensively, the business would be deprived of many opportunities for profit and would probably not be able to achieve its objectives.

RISK REDUCTION

Risk may be reduced in two ways. The first is through loss prevention and control. Safety programs and loss-prevention measures such as medical care, fire departments, night security guards, sprinkler systems, and burglar alarms are all examples of attempts to deal with risk by preventing the loss or reducing the chance that it will occur. Some techniques are designed to prevent the occurrence of the loss, whereas others, such as sprinkler systems, are intended to control the severity of the loss if it does happen. From one point of view, loss prevention is the most desirable means of dealing with risk. If the possibility of loss could be completely eliminated, then risk would also be eliminated. And yet, loss prevention can also be viewed as an inadequate approach to dealing with risk. No matter how hard we may try, it is impossible to prevent all losses. In addition, in some cases the loss prevention may cost more than the losses themselves.

Risk may also be reduced in the aggregate by use of the law of large numbers. By combining a large number of exposure units, reasonably accurate estimates can be made of the future losses for a group. On the basis of these estimates, an organization such as an insurance company can assume the possibility of loss of each exposure, and yet not face the same possibility of loss itself. We discuss this concept in greater detail in Chapter 10.

RISK RETENTION

Risk retention is perhaps the most common method of dealing with risk.[13] Organizations, like individuals, face an almost unlimited number of risks; in most cases nothing is done about them. When some positive action is not taken to avoid, reduce, or transfer the risk, the possibility of loss involved in that risk is retained.

Risk retention may be conscious or unconscious. Conscious risk retention takes place when the risk is perceived and not transferred or reduced. When the risk is not recognized, it is unconsciously retained. In these cases, the person so exposed retains the financial consequences of the possible loss without realizing that he or she does so.

Risk retention may also be voluntary or involuntary. Voluntary risk retention is characterized by the recognition that the risk exists, and a tacit agreement to assume the losses involved. The decision to retain a risk voluntarily is made because there are no alternatives more attractive. Involuntary risk retention takes place when risks are unconsciously retained and also when the risk cannot be avoided, transferred, or reduced.

Risk retention is a legitimate method of dealing with risk; in many cases, it is the best way. Every organization must decide which risks to retain and which to avoid or transfer on the basis of its margin for contingencies or ability to bear the loss. A loss that might be a financial disaster for one organization might easily be borne by another. As a general rule, risks that should be retained are those that lead to relatively small certain losses.

RISK TRANSFER

Risk may be transferred from one individual to another who is more willing to bear the risk. Transfer may be used to deal with both speculative and pure risk. An excellent example of the use of the transfer technique for dealing with speculative risks is the process of hedging. Hedging is a method of risk transfer accomplished by buying and selling for future delivery, whereby dealers and processors protect themselves against a decline or increase in market price between the time they buy a product and the time they sell it. It consists of simultaneous purchase or sale for immediate delivery and purchase or sale for future delivery, such as the

---

[13]Some writers use the term *risk assumption* rather than *risk retention*. Because "to assume" implies that the object is somehow "taken on," retention, which implies that something is "kept," is more appropriate. The distinction is a semantic one, but risks are retained, and the losses that occur are assumed.

sale of futures in the wheat market at the same time that a purchase is made in the spot market.[14]

Pure risks are often transferred or shifted through contracts. A hold–harmless agreement, in which one individual assumes another's possibility of loss, is an example of such a transfer. For example, a tenant may agree under the terms of a lease to pay any judgments against the landlord which arise out of the use of the premises. Contractual transfers of risk are quite common in the construction industry, but are also used between manufacturers and retailers with respect to the product liability exposure.

Insurance is also a means of transferring risk. In consideration of a specific payment (the premium) by one party, the second party contracts to indemnify the first party up to a certain limit for the specified loss that may occur.

RISK SHARING

Risk sharing is a special case of risk transfer; it is also a form of retention. When risks are shared, the possibility of loss is transferred from the individual to the group. However, sharing is also a form of retention in which the risks "transferred" to the group are retained, along with the risks of the other members of the group.

Risk is shared in a number of ways by individuals and organizations. One outstanding example of a device through which risk is shared is the corporation. Under this form of business, the investments of a large number of persons are pooled. A number of investors may pool their capital, each bearing only a portion of the risk that the enterprise may fail. Insurance is another device designed to deal with risk through sharing, as one of the basic characteristics of the insurance device is the sharing of risk by the members of the group.

⠿ Business Risk Management ■ ■ ■ ■ ■ ■ ■ ■ ■ ■ ■ ■ ■ ■ ■ ■ ■

From earliest times, humankind has demonstrated an aversion to risk and an inherent hunger for security. We have seen that much of the growth in human knowledge was prompted by the perils and hazards of the environment. Many of the economic and social institutions that have evolved were created in response to risk. Those engaged in business and commerce, in particular, have been concerned with risk. Because business generally requires the investment of assets, risk is an inherent part of a business operation. As we have seen, a business faces pure risks and speculative risks. The remainder of this book is a summary of the

---

[14]Hedging operations are made possible by speculators who buy and sell futures contracts in the hope of making a profit as a result of a change in price. The speculator attempts to predict the prices months in advance of delivery and buys and sells on the basis of these estimates. It is the speculator's willingness to buy and sell futures that makes possible the hedging process, and it is to the speculator that the risk is transferred.

ways in which businesses deal with pure risk. More specifically, this book is a treatment of a branch of applied economics, which has been designated *risk management*. Risk management is a scientific approach to the problem of pure risk, and its objective is the reduction and elimination of pure risks facing the business firm. Risk management evolved from the field of corporate insurance buying and is now recognized as a distinct and important function for all businesses and organizations.

Before turning to our discussion of risk management as a function of business, it seems appropriate that we briefly consider the suggestion that is sometimes made that risk management is superfluous and even counterproductive to the interest of corporate owners. Although the argument focuses on insurance since insurance is an alternative to other risk management methods, the argument that businesses ought not to insure is, in effect, an argument that risk management is unnecessary.

DIVERSIFICATION AS A SOLUTION FOR PURE RISKS

Modern financial theory in the form of the *capital asset pricing model* (CAPM) suggests that the value of a firm is equal to the discounted (present value) projected flow of income it will generate for its owners. According to the CAPM model, sophisticated investors will require a higher rate of return (i.e., will use a higher discount rate in projecting the cash flows) for stocks that carry a higher degree of risk. Furthermore, it is argued, sophisticated investors do not consider diversifiable risk, and such risks therefore do not affect a stock's rate of return. Because investors diversify their asset holdings, they require a risk premium only for bearing systematic (nondiversifiable) risk. In other words, systematic or *market risks* are priced, but diversifiable risk is not. Consequently, it is observed, reducing risks at the corporate level which are diversifiable at the portfolio level does not benefit stockholders.

Following from this premise, it has been argued that corporations should never purchase insurance. In theory, stockholders can deal with pure risks much as they deal with speculative risks, through diversification. According to the theory, the purchase of insurance by a corporation reduces the return to stockholders by more than the reduction in risk. Because the long-run cost of insurance is always more than the amount that is paid out in losses, the return on investment to stockholders will be higher in a diversified portfolio of stocks that do not purchase insurance than for the same stocks if insurance is purchased. Some corporations might suffer catastrophic loss and fail, but the overall return to investors will be higher without insurance than with it.

As in the case of many theories, this theory contemplates a narrow set of conditions and ignores certain other important features. First, the diversification strategy is relevant only for those organizations whose ownership is widely disbursed and which can be included in a diversified portfolio. Closely held organizations and other business entities in which the value of the business represents a major part of the owners' wealth are not susceptible to diversification.

A more generalized argument against the diversification strategy for pure risks can be constructed from financial theory itself. Some financial theorists have argued that although total risk may not affect the required rate of return on stocks, large amounts of diversifiable risk, if unmanaged, can significantly reduce the value of the firm. Proponents of this thesis argue that while diversifiable risks may not affect the investor's discount rate (the denominator in the discounted cash-flow model), it can significantly reduce the expected cash flows (the numerator). The impact of risk on the firm's projected cash flows stems from the effect of risk on the variety of constituencies with which the firm must deal.[15]

A high degree of risk will affect customers, suppliers, and the workforce. Customers become increasingly reluctant to deal with a business firm when they perceive that it has excessive risk and might face financial distress in the future. First, there is apprehension that a firm in financial stress will produce lower quality products. There is also a concern that the firm may not be around to provide service on the products that it sells and consumers are likely to turn to less risky firms as a more dependable source of products. The same influence can also affect suppliers. The higher the risks facing the firm, the less likely it is that suppliers will offer preferential terms. Although this is most evident in the case of suppliers of credit, it is a factor for other suppliers as well. Finally, a firm's employees are also affected by excessive risk because of the close connection between the risks of the organization and their personal risks. Riskier firms will have to pay employees more than other firms to induce them to commit their services to the organization. The higher the risks facing the organization, the greater the likelihood that employees will demand higher salaries or leave the firm. The net effect of these influences on a firm with high risk will be to increase its costs of operation, thereby placing it at a competitive disadvantage in the market and increasing the likelihood of ultimately failing.

Because high risk can increase the firm's costs, it will decrease the cash flows and can ultimately increase the likelihood of bankruptcy. This compounding effect, in which pure risks increase market risks, suggests that insurance companies have a comparative advantage in dealing with pure risks. Contrary to the argument that the return will be higher on a diversified portfolio of stocks of noninsuring firms than on a similarly diversified portfolio for insuring firms, precisely the opposite effect may be true. The failure to manage an organization's risks can have an adverse effect on the corporation's earnings and prospects for survival.

RISK MANAGEMENT AND SPECULATIVE RISKS

Although the traditional focus of risk management has always been pure risks, there are some who argue that the distinction between pure and speculative risks is disappearing (if it ever existed) and that the risk manager's responsibility in the future will include both pure and speculative risks.

---

[15]D. Mayers and C. Smith, "The Corporate Insurance Decision," *Chase Financial Quarterly* 1982, pp. 47–65.

Corporate managers are concerned (or should be) about the total risk portfolio of the firm and attempt to manage risks, regardless of the source. They buy insurance to protect against losses that may arise from pure risks, and they use commodity and financial futures to hedge against fluctuations in interest rates and foreign exchange rates. In some cases, they avoid risky activities, even when the potential returns are high. In most cases, the decisions about how the organization will deal with the various risks it faces have been made independently; one person (or department) deals with pure risks, another deals with the risk of interest rates and fluctuations in foreign exchange, and others deal with production and market risks. Critics argue that since the separate decisions collectively affect the total risk of the firm, they should be integrated into a single framework that will determine the totality of risk, including both pure and speculative.

Recently, some risk managers (and risk management scholars) have expressed the view that the traditional focus of risk management on pure risk has been too narrow. As a consequence, they argue, risk managers have missed opportunities to expand their responsibility to newly developing risks, such as interest rate risk, currency conversion risks, credit risks, and derivatives. The responsibility of risk managers, they argue, should be expanded to include other risks, especially those relating to other facets of finance.

The aspirations of those who would like the risk manager to assume responsibility for other forms of financial risk is perhaps understandable. After all, the greater the responsibility, the more important the position within the organization. "Risk is risk," they argue, "and the distinction between pure risk and speculative risk is an artificial one created and perpetuated by academics." In support of this position, they point to the fact that some innovative insurance-like contracts cover risks that were historically considered to be speculative risks.

The disinclination of other risk managers to enter into the field of derivatives, futures, and options is also understandable. Whether the distinction between pure and speculative risk is real or artificial, they say, the techniques used to address some types of risks differ significantly from those used to address others. The disagreement is not about whether financial risks susceptible to treatment by derivatives, futures, and options should be managed, but whether they should be managed by the same person who manages the risks of fires, explosions, embezzlements, and legal liability. Nor do they disagree that someone needs to manage the organization's total risk portfolio. The disagreement is whether this overall management of risk should be done by the risk manager. There are some risk managers who are convinced that the evolution of risk management into a wider field might make it irrelevant. The assertions of expansionists to the contrary, they see clear and unequivocal distinctions among risks and have no problem in delineating pure risks from speculative risks.

The reason that decisions about different risks have been made separately is not that the risks arise from different sources, but because the techniques that are used them are fundamentally different. Some risks managers who have the financial expertise to deal with certain speculative financial risks may get the opportunity to do so, but it is far from inevitable that risk management will expand to include other types of financial risk. Although some risk managers have the expertise to deal in the arena of hedging, futures, options and derivatives, there are others who do not, or who feel sufficiently challenged by their existing responsibilities. For the foreseeable future, these risk managers will comprise the overwhelming majority of the profession. The student may defer judgment on this issue until we have examined the nature of the techniques that are used to deal with pure risks.

IMPORTANT CONCEPTS TO REMEMBER

Code of Hammurabi	morale hazard	risks arising from failure
bottomry contracts	legal hazard	of others
respondentia contracts	financial risk	burden of risk
general average	dynamic risks	risk avoidance
risk	static risks	risk reduction
uncertainty	speculative risk	risk retention
subjective risk	pure risk	risk transfer
degree of risk	fundamental risks	risk sharing
peril	particular risks	risk management
hazard	personal risks	capital asset pricing model
physical hazards	property risks	diversifiable risks
moral hazard	liability risks	

QUESTIONS FOR REVIEW

1. In what ways did prehistoric humans deal with risk?

2. Identify the techniques designed to address the problem of risk that developed with the evolution of business.

3. Define risk and distinguish it from uncertainty.

4. Risk may be subclassified in several ways. List the three principal ways in which risk may be categorized, and explain the distinguishing characteristics of each class.

5. The distinction between pure risk and speculative risk is important because only pure risks have traditionally been considered insurable. Why is the distinction between fundamental and particular risk important?

6. List the four types of pure risk facing the individual or an organization and give an example of each.

7. Distinguish between *perils* and *hazards* and give an example of each.

8. Briefly distinguish among the four categories into which hazards may be divided and give an example of each.

9. List the techniques listed in the chapter that may be used in dealing with risk and give an example of each technique.

10. What are the two principal ways in which the impact of risk may be felt by an individual or an organization?

QUESTIONS FOR DISCUSSION

1. Explain how pure risk has an adverse effect on economic activity generally and on the organization specifically.

2. Is all risk undesirable? Explain and illustrate your answer.

3. To what do you attribute the increasing severity of losses in the economy?

4. Briefly state the argument that is sometimes put forth regarding the absence of a need for insurance by corporations. Do you agree or disagree with the argument?

5. Do you believe that the distinction between pure and speculative risk is useful, or is it an artificial dichotomy. Should the risk manager's responsibility be expapnded to include the management of other financial risks?

SUGGESTIONS FOR ADDITIONAL READING

Greene, Mark R., James S. Trieschmann, and Sandra G. Gustavson. *Risk and Insurance*, 8th ed. Cincinnati: South-Western Publishing, 1992. Chapter 1.

Greene, Mark R. and Oscar N. Serbein. *Risk Management: Text and Cases*, 2nd ed. Reston, Va.: Reston Publishing Company, 1983. Chapters 1, 13.

Hammond, J.D., ed. *Essays in the Theory of Risk and Insurance*. Glenview, IL: Scott, Foresman, 1968.

Hardy, C.O. *Risk and Risk Bearing*. Chicago: University of Chicago Press, 1923.

Head, G.L. "An Alternative to Defining Risk as Uncertainty." *Journal of Risk and Insurance*, XXXIV, No. 2 (June 1967).

Houston, D.B. "Risk, Insurance, and Sampling." *Journal of Risk and Insurance*, XXXI, No. 4 (Dec. 1964).

Knight, F.H. *Risk, Uncertainty and Profit*. Boston: Houghton-Mifflin, 1921.

Kulp, C.A., and John W. Hall. *Casualty Insurance*, 4th ed. New York: Ronald Press, 1968. Chapter 1.

Mayers, D. and C. Smith. "The Corporate Insurance Decision," *Chase Financial Quarterly* 1982, pp. 47–65.

Mehr. R.I., and B.A. Hedges. *Risk Management in the Business Enterprise*. Homewood, IL: Richard D. Irwin, 1963. Chapter 1.

Mowbray, A.H., R.H. Blanchard, and C. Arthur Williams. *Insurance*, 6th ed. New York: McGraw-Hill, 1969. Chapter 1.

Pfeffer, I. *Insurance and Economic Theory*. Homewood, IL: Richard D. Irwin, 1956.

Vaughan, Emmett J. and Therese M. Vaughan. *Fundamentals of Risk and Insurance*, 7th ed. New York: John Wiley and Sons, Inc., 1996.

Willet, A. *The Economic Theory of Risk and Insurance*. Philadelphia: University of Pennsylvania Press, 1951.

Williams, C. Arthur, and Richard M. Heins. *Risk Management and Insurance*, 6th ed. New York: McGraw-Hill, 1989. Chapter 1.

Wood, Oliver G., Jr. "Evolution of the Concept of Risk," *Journal of Risk and Insurance*, XXXI, No. 1 (March 1964).

CHAPTER 2

The Risk Management Solution

CHAPTER OBJECTIVES

When you have finished this chapter, you should be able to

Describe the evolution of modern risk management and identify the strategic development that led to the transition from insurance management to risk management.

•

Define and explain the meaning of the term *risk management*.

•

Distinguish between risk management and insurance management.

•

Identify the steps in the risk management process.

•

Identify the various reporting relationships that the risk management function may assume within an organization.

•

Identify the qualifications that are desirable for an individual assigned to a risk management position.

Introduction

Risk management is a scientific approach to the problem of dealing with the pure risks faced by individuals and businesses. It evolved from corporate insurance management and has as its focal point the possibility of accidental losses to assets and income of the organization. Many business firms have highly trained individuals who specialize in dealing with pure risk. In some cases this is a full-time job for one person, or even for an entire department within the company. Those who are responsible for the entire program of pure risk management (of which insurance buying is only a part) are risk managers. Although the term *risk management* is of recent vintage, the actual practice of risk management is as old as civilization itself. In the broad sense, risk management is the process of protecting one's person and assets. In the narrower sense, it is a managerial function of business, which uses a scientific approach to dealing with risks. As such, it is based on a specific philosophy and follows a well-defined sequence of steps. In this chapter, we examine the distinguishing features of risk management.

The History of Modern Risk Management ■ ■ ■ ■ ■ ■ ■

The general trend in the current usage of the term risk management began in the early 1950s. One of the earliest references to the concept in literature appeared in the *Harvard Business Review* in 1956.[1] In that article, the author proposed what, for the time, seemed a revolutionary idea; that someone within the organization should be responsible for "managing" the organization's pure risks:

> The aim of this article is to outline the most important principles of a workable program for "risk management"—for so it must be conceived, even to the extent of putting it under one executive, who in a large company might be a full-time "risk manager."

At this time, many large corporations already had a staff position referred to as the "insurance manager." This was an apt title, for the position usually entailed procuring, maintaining, and paying for a portfolio of insurance policies obtained for the benefit of the company. The earliest insurance managers were employed by the first of the giant corporations, the railroads and steel companies, which employed insurance managers as early as the turn of the century. As the capital investment in other industries grew, insurance became an increasingly significant item in the budget of firms. Gradually, the insurance-buying function was assigned as a specific responsibility to in-house specialists. In 1929, insurance buyers met informally in Boston to discuss problems of mutual interest. In 1931, the American Management Association established its Insurance Division for the purpose of exchanging information among members and publishing news and information of interest to corporate insurance buyers. In 1932, the Insurance Buyers of New York (which later became the Risk Research Institute) was organized. In 1950, the National Insurance Buyers Association was organized; this later became the American Society of Insurance Management.

Although risk management has its roots in corporate insurance buying, it is a distortion to say that risk management naturally evolved from corporate insurance buying. Actually, the emergence of risk management signaled a dramatic, revolutionary shift in philosophy, occurring when attitudes toward insurance changed. For the

---

[1]See Russell B. Gallagher, "Risk Management: A New Phase of Cost Control," *Harvard Business Review*, (September–October 1956).

insurance manager, insurance had always been the standard approach to dealing with risks. Although insurance management included techniques other than insurance (such as noninsurance or retention and loss prevention and control), these techniques had always been considered primarily as alternatives to insurance. The insurance manager viewed insurance as the accepted norm or standard approach to dealing with risk, and retention was viewed as an exception to this standard.

Many of the earliest insurance buyers were skilled insurance technicians, often hired from an insurance agency or brokerage firm. They understood the principles of insurance and applied their knowledge to obtain the best coverage for the premium dollars spent. Traditional insurance textbooks had always preached against the dollar-trading practices that characterized some lines of insurance, and most insurance buyers knew that economies could be achieved through the judicial use of deductibles. Despite these precursors of the risk management philosophy, the notion persisted that insurance was the preferred approach to dealing with risk. When insurance was generally agreed to be the standard approach to dealing with pure risks, the decision not to insure was courageous indeed. If an uninsured loss occurred, the risk manager would surely have been criticized for the decision not to insure. The problem was that too little consideration was given to the soundness of insurance-buying decisions. The insurance manager's function was to buy insurance, and while this buyer attempted to get the most coverage for the insurance dollar, he could hardly be criticized for buying insurance. After all, that was his job.

The change in attitude toward insurance and the shift to the risk management philosophy had to await management science, with its emphasis on cost-benefit analysis, expected value, and a scientific approach to decision making under uncertainty.

The transition from *insurance management* to *risk management* occurred over a period of time and paralleled the development of the academic discipline of risk management. It is not clear whether the academic discipline led or followed, for developments in the corporate and academic worlds appear to have occurred simultaneously. Without question, however, the work of academics supported developments in the corporate sector. Through a fortuitous accident of timing, the risk management movement in the business community coincided with a reappraisal of the curriculum in business colleges throughout the United States. During the early 1950s, two studies of the curriculum were published in the United States, one by Gordon and Howells, and the other by Pierson.[2] Both studies concluded with stinging criticisms of the business college curriculum, stating that business colleges were not preparing their students for managerial careers, but instead were bogging down in explaining the specific functions and activities of business.

Business schools soon began to change their curricula, adding new courses and changing the focus of established courses. The most significant changes in the curriculum were the introduction of *operations research* and *management science*, marking a shift in focus from descriptive courses to normative decision theory.[3] Whereas

---

[2]Robert A. Gordon and James E. Howell. *Higher Education for Business* (New York: Columbia University Press, 1959) and Frank C. Pierson, et. al., *The Education of American Businessmen* (New York: McGraw-Hill, 1959)

[3]Operations research, also known as operational research, deals with a broad range of mathematical applications that describe complex systems. Operations research is said to have originated during World

previous courses described how and why people chose among options, prescriptive decision theory now focused on how choices should be made.

Not surprisingly, insurance faculty were among the first business academics to embrace decision theory. They were trained in actuarial science, the mathematical underpinning of insurance, and as the earliest quantitative specialists in business schools, they were knowledgeable in the methodologies of decision theory. Equally important, they had an inventory of interesting questions to which these tools could be applied in business situations—questions involving the choices among the techniques that could be used to address risk. Academics not only began to question the central role that had always been assigned to insurance, but now also developed the theoretical justification for the challenge.

Intuitively, some insurance buyers independently reached the same conclusions about the supremacy of insurance as a method for dealing with pure risks as the academics who applied the new decision models. With time, the more sophisticated corporate managers came to realize that there might be more cost-efficient ways of dealing with risk. Perhaps the most effective approach, they thought, would be to prevent losses from happening in the first place, and to minimize the economic consequences of the losses they were unable to prevent. From this simple beginning came the discipline of risk management, which is based on the notion that management, having identified and evaluated the risks to which it is exposed, can plan to avoid the occurrence of certain losses and minimize the impact of others. Risk control—the elimination or reduction of risk—became a major factor in risk management. Increased emphasis on control, which goes beyond altering the probability of loss and seeks also to minimize the severity of losses, led to consideration of risk financing alternatives other than insurance. The ultimate conclusion was that the cost of risk could be *managed* and held to the lowest levels possible.

The risk management philosophy made sense, and it spread from organization to organization. When the insurance buyer's professional association decided to change its name to the Risk and Insurance Management Society (RIMS) in 1975, the change signaled a transition that was well underway. The Risk and Insurance Management Society publishes a magazine called *Risk Management,* and the Insurance Division of the American Management Association publishes a wide range of reports and studies to assist risk managers. In addition, the Insurance Institute of America developed an education program in risk management featuring a series of examinations leading to a diploma in risk management. The curriculum for this program was revised in 1973, and a professional designation, Associate in Risk Management (ARM), was instituted.

Risk management grew out of a merger of engineering applications in the military and aerospace programs, financial theory, and insurance. Many of the concepts that originated in academic halls, however, were taken over and applied in the corporate world.

War II, when Allied scientists were engaged in designing air-defense strategies, solving logistical problems, and assisting in other aspects of military operations. It is now a common management tool and is applied to such areas as production scheduling, inventory policies, transportation systems, and risk management.

❖ Risk Management Defined ■ ■ ■ ■ ■ ■ ■ ■ ■ ■ ■ ■ ■ ■ ■ ■ ■ ■

As a relatively new discipline, risk management has been defined in a variety of ways, but a unified theme appears in virtually all of the definitions that have been proposed: risk management is concerned principally with pure risk and involves managing those risks. Although these two points help us understand what risk management is, they do not adequately describe the essence of the concept. We propose the following definition of risk management.

> Risk management is a scientific approach to dealing with pure risks by anticipating possible accidental losses and designing and implementing procedures that minimize the occurrence of loss or the financial impact of the losses that do occur.

This definition, though not all encompassing, provides a good starting place for our discussion. To provide a better understanding of the boundaries of the risk management function and to differentiate the boundaries from those of other disciplines, we will briefly examine several aspects of the definition.

SCIENTIFIC APPROACH

We have described risk management as a "scientific approach" to the problem of pure risks. Yet risk management is not a science in the same sense as are the physical sciences, any more than management itself is a science.[4] As the term is generally understood, a "science" is a body of knowledge based on laws and principles that can be used to predict outcomes. Scientists seek to discover and test the laws of the science through laboratory experiments aimed at discovering the laws that govern events. Risk managers, unable to use the standard method of physical sciences, the controlled experiment, instead depend on rules (laws) derived from the general knowledge of experience, through deduction, and from precepts drawn from other disciplines, particularly decision theory. The fact that risk management is not a science, however, does not preclude its use of the scientific method.

RISK MANAGEMENT TOOLS

As stated in our definition of risk management, a fundamental part of the risk management function is designing and implementing procedures that minimize the occurrence of loss or the financial impact of the losses that do occur. This indicated the two broad techniques used in risk management for dealing with risks. The techniques we identified in Chapter 1 can be grouped into two broad approaches: risk control and risk financing.

---

[4]Efforts to create a "science" of management started with Frederick W. Taylor, "the father of scientific management." Taylor experimented in the application of the scientific method to management problems, attempting to use controlled experiments in which various elements were held constant. See Frederick W. Taylor, *Scientific Management* (New York: Harper & Row, 1911), p. 31.

Risk Control

Broadly defined, *risk control* techniques are designed to minimize, at the least possible costs, those risks to which the organization is exposed. Risk control methods include risk avoidance and the various approaches to reducing risk through loss prevention and control efforts. In the case of risk avoidance, the individual or organization refuses to accept any exposure to loss arising from a particular activity.

Risk reduction consists of all techniques that are designed to reduce the likelihood of loss, or the potential severity of those losses that do occur. It is common to distinguish between loss prevention—those efforts aimed at preventing losses from occurring—and loss control—those efforts aimed at minimizing the severity of loss if it should occur. Examples of loss-prevention techniques include steps to reduce the number of employee injuries by installing protective devices around machinery. Other risk-reduction techniques aim at reducing the severity of those losses that actually do occur, such as, for example, the installation of sprinkler systems. These are loss control measures. Other methods of controlling severity include segregation or dispersion of assets and salvage efforts. Although dispersion of assets will not reduce the number of fires or explosions that may occur, it can limit the potential severity of the losses that do occur. Salvage operations after a loss has occurred can minimize the resulting costs of the loss.

The sophistication of risk control efforts can vary widely. Whereas the small mercantile establishment may simply use strategically located fire extinguishers and deadbolt double locks as risk-reduction techniques, the giant corporation has an elaborate sprinkler system and security personnel. In both cases, however, these techniques constitute the application of risk control to the exposure involved.

Risk Financing

Risk financing, in contrast to risk control, focuses on guaranteeing the availability of funds to meet those losses that do occur. Fundamentally, risk financing takes the form of retention or transfer. All risks that cannot be avoided or reduced must, by definition, be transferred or retained. Frequently, transfer and retention are used in combination for a particular risk, with a portion of the risk retained and a part transferred.

The form that risk financing techniques may assume can also vary considerably. Retention, for example, may be accompanied by specific budgetary allocations to meet uninsured losses and may involve the accumulation of a fund to meet deviations from expected losses. Retention may also be less formal, without any form of specific funding. A larger firm may use a retrospectively rated program, various forms of self-insured retention plans, or even a captive insurer. The small organization uses deductibles, noninsurance, and various other forms of retention techniques. Nonetheless, the approach of both organizations is the same.

Transfer may take the form of contractual arrangements (such as hold-harmless agreements), the subcontracting of certain activities, or surety bonds. Transfers of this type are essentially a form of risk control. Transfer of risk through the purchase of insurance contracts is, of course, a primary approach to risk financing.

In deciding which of the techniques should be used to deal with a given risk, the risk manager must consider the size of the potential loss, its probability, and the resources available to meet the loss if it should occur. The benefits and costs in each approach must be evaluated, and then, using the best information available, the decision is made.

DISTINGUISHING CHARACTERISTICS OF RISK MANAGEMENT

We can gain a better understanding of the risk management function and its place in the organization by distinguishing risk management from general management and from insurance management.

Risk Management Distinguished from General Management

Risk management differs from general management in its scope. Although both deal with risk, the type of risks they handle differs. General management is responsible for dealing with *all* risks facing the organization, including both speculative risks and pure risks. In contrast, the risk manager's area of responsibility is narrower in scope, being limited primarily to pure risks only. General managers, who have stewardship of the firm's assets and income, delegate to risk managers the duties associated with pure risks, and the risk manager becomes responsible for conserving the assets and the income of the organization from losses associated with pure risks. Thus, the risk manager is responsible for part of general management's responsibility. More specifically, the risk manager is responsible for that segment of general management's mission that relates to pure risks.

Risk Management Distinguished from Insurance Management

The risk manager evolved from the insurance manager, but the two terms are often used interchangeably, without a great deal of attention paid to the actual role of the individual. In order to distinguish between the risk manager and insurance manager, a functional approach should be used.

Risk management, having evolved from insurance management, is concerned primarily with *insurable* risk. The more appropriate realm of risk management, however, is *pure* risk. In other words, the risk manager cannot ignore those pure risks that are not insurable. A good example is shoplifting losses. Although shoplifting losses represent a pure risk exposure, it is not generally insurable on an economical basis. Risk management is, therefore, broader than insurance management in that it deals with both insurable and uninsurable risks, and the choice of the appropriate techniques for dealing with these risks. Insurance management involves the use of techniques other than insurance (e.g., noninsurance or retention as an alternative to insurance), but for the most part it is restricted to the areas of those risks considered to be insurable.

As noted earlier, risk management also differs from insurance management in philosophy. Insurance management involves techniques other than insurance, but in general these other techniques are considered primarily as alternatives to insurance. Whereas the corporate insurance buyer traditionally emphasizes the most insurance for the dollar spent, the risk management concept concentrates on reducing the cost of dealing with risk by whatever techniques are most appropriate. Under this scheme, insurance is viewed as simply one of several approaches for dealing with the firm's pure risks.

Insurance managers view insurance as the accepted norm or standard approach to dealing with risk, and retention as an exception to this standard. As they contemplate their insurance program, they ask, "Are there any risks that I should retain?" "How much will I save in insurance costs if I retain them?" In viewing loss-prevention measures, they ask, "How much will this measure reduce my insurance costs?" "How long will it take for a new sprinkler system to pay for itself in reduced fire insurance premiums?" Risk managers, in contrast, view insurance as simply one of several approaches to dealing with pure risks. Rather than asking "Which risks should I retain?" they ask, "Which risks must I insure?"

The difference is obviously one of emphasis. The insurance management philosophy sees insurance as the accepted norm, and retention or noninsurance must be justified by a premium reduction that is "big enough." Under the risk management philosophy, it is insurance that must be justified. Because the cost of insurance must generally exceed the average losses of those who are insured, the risk manager believes that insurance is a last resort and should be used only when necessary.

Risk management then, is something more than insurance management, in that it deals with both insurable and uninsurable risks, but it is something less than general management, in that it does not deal (except incidentally) with business risk.

HENRI FAYOL AND RISK MANAGEMENT

Although use of the term *risk management* dates from the 1950s, the function itself had been recognized earlier. For example, the famous French management authority, Henri Fayol, writing in 1916, divided all industrial activities into six broad functions, including one—which Fayol called security—that sounds surprisingly like our modern concept of risk management. Fayol's six broad functions are:

1. Technical activities, which include production, manufacture, and adaptation.

2. Commercial activities, which include buying and selling.

3. Financial activities, which involve finding sources of capital and managing capital flows.

4. Security activities, which consist of protecting the property and persons of the enterprise.

5. Accounting activities, which consist of recording and analyzing financial information about the activity.

6. Managerial activities, which consist of organizing, planning, command, coordination, and control.

Fayol's definition of the security function coincides rather closely with our current understanding of risk management and might easily serve as a definition of risk management in a modern textbook:

> The purpose of this function is to safeguard property and persons against theft, fire and flood, to ward off strikes and felonies and broadly all social disturbances or natural disturbances liable to endanger the progress and even the life of the business. It is the master's eye, the watchdog of the one-man business, the police or the army in the case of the state. It is generally speaking all measures conferring security upon the undertaking and requisite peace of mind upon the personnel. The object of this (security activity) is to safeguard property and persons against theft, fire and flood, to ward off strikes and felonies and broadly all social disturbances or natural disturbances liable to endanger the progress and even the life of the business.[5]

The other five functions described by Fayol all developed as well-defined academic disciplines and became divisions in the corporate structure headed by a vice president. "Security," however, got lost in the shuffle, and Fayol's six-function division of business activities was not resurrected until the 1950s.[6]

■ The Risk Management Process ■ ■ ■ ■ ■ ■ ■ ■ ■ ■ ■ ■ ■ ■ ■

The suggestion that risk management represents a scientific approach to dealing with pure risks implies that the process involves a logical sequence of steps. Having defined and traced the development of risk management, we will now examine the steps in the risk management process. While separate discussion of each of these steps is useful for the purpose of analysis, the reader should understand that in actual practice the steps tend to merge with one another.

The six steps are as follows:

1. Determining objectives

2. Identifying risks

3. Evaluating the risks

4. Considering alternatives and selecting the risk treatment device

5. Implementing the decision

6. Evaluating and reviewing

[5]Henri Fayol, *General and Industrial Management* (New York: Pitman Publishing Corp., 1949), p. 4. This is an English translation of the book originally published in French in 1916.

[6]The growth of risk management as a business practice and a profession has led to an increased interest in the subject as an academic discipline. In December 1984, the American Risk and Insurance Association (the professional association of university professors of insurance and risk management) submitted a petition to the Standards Committee of the American Assembly of Collegiate Schools of Business, (AACSB), requesting that Risk Management and Employee Benefit Education become part of the common body of knowledge taught at institutions accredited by the AACSB.

DETERMINING OBJECTIVES

The first step in the risk management process is to decide precisely what the organization would like its risk management program to do. To obtain maximum benefit from the expenditures associated with risk management, a plan is needed. Otherwise, the tendency is to view the risk management process as a series of isolated problems rather than as one single problem, and there are no guidelines to provide for logical consistency in dealing with the organization's risks.

There are a variety of possible objectives for the risk management function. They include maintaining the organization's survival, minimizing the costs associated with pure risk, and protecting employees from accidents that might cause death or serious injury. The first objective of risk management, however, like the first law of nature, is survival; to guarantee the continuing existence of the organization as an operating entity in the economy. Risk management contributes to the attainment of the organization's goals by assuring that it will not be prevented from attaining these goals by losses associated with pure risks.

Unfortunately, the one step in risk management process that is most likely to be overlooked is determining the objectives of the program. As a consequence, in many firms risk management efforts are fragmented and inconsistent. Many of the defects in risk management programs stem from the absence of clearly defined objectives for the program. (We discuss the determination of risk management objectives in Chapter 5.)

Risk management objectives are often formalized in a "Corporate Risk Management Policy," which states the objectives and describes policy measures for their attainment. Ideally, the objectives and the risk management policy should be a product of the company's board of directors, since they are ultimately responsible for preserving the organization's assets. In formulating the objectives and the risk management policy, the board of directors may receive advice from the risk manager acting as a staff adviser.

IDENTIFYING RISKS

Obviously, before anything can be done about the risks an organization faces, someone must be aware of them. We say "someone" because this phase of the risk management process is often delegated to an outside party, such as an insurance agent or a risk management consultant.

It is difficult to generalize about an organization's risks because differences in operations and conditions give rise to differing risks. Some risks are obvious, whereas many can be overlooked. In order to discover the important risks facing the firm, most risk managers use a systematic approach to the problem of risk identification.

Tools of Risk Identification

The more important tools used in risk identification include internal records of the organization, insurance policy checklists, risk analysis questionnaires, flow process charts, analysis of financial statements, inspections of the firm's operations, and interviews. These, combined with a vivid imagination and a thorough understanding of the organization's operations, can help to guarantee that important exposures are not overlooked.

Combination Approach Required

The preferred approach to risk identification consists of a combination approach, in which all risk identification tools are brought to bear on the problem. In a sense, each tool can solve a piece of the puzzle, and combined they can be of considerable assistance to the risk manager. But no individual approach or combination of these tools can replace the diligence and imagination of the risk manager in discovering the firm's risks. Because risks may arise from many sources, the risk manager needs a wide-reaching information system designed to provide a continual flow of information about changes in operations, acquisition of new assets, new construction, and changing relationships with outside entities. (The risk identification process is discussed in greater detail in Chapter 7.)

EVALUATING THE RISKS

Once the risks have been identified, the risk manager must evaluate them. This involves measuring the potential size of the loss and the probability that the loss is likely to occur and then providing some ranking in order of priorities. Certain risks, because of the severity of the possible loss, will demand attention prior to others, and in most instances there will be a number of exposures that are equally demanding.

Any exposure that involves a loss that would represent a financial catastrophe ranks in the same category, and no distinction is made among risks in this class. It makes little difference, for instance, if bankruptcy results from a liability loss, a flood, or an uninsured fire loss. The net effect is the same. Therefore, rather than ranking exposures in some numerical order of importance, it is more appropriate to rank them into general classifications such as critical, important, and unimportant. One set of criteria that may be used to establish a priority ranking focuses on the potential financial impact of the loss. For example:

- *Critical risks:* all exposures to loss in which possible losses are of a magnitude that will result in bankruptcy.
- *Important risks:* those exposures in which possible losses will not result in bankruptcy, but will require the firm to borrow in order to continue operations.
- *Unimportant risks:* those exposures in which possible losses can be met out of the firm's existing assets or current income without imposing undue financial strain.

Assignment of individual exposures to one of these three categories requires determining the amount of financial loss that might result from a given exposure and assessing the firm's ability to absorb such losses, which involves measuring the level of uninsured loss that could be borne without resorting to credit and establishing the firm's maximum credit capacity.

CONSIDERING ALTERNATIVES AND SELECTING THE RISK TREATMENT DEVICE

The next step is to consider the techniques that should be used to deal with each risk. As we have already noted, these techniques include risk avoidance, retention, sharing, transfer and reduction. In practical application, the risk manager focuses on four of these techniques: avoidance, reduction, retention, and transfer. (The principles that dictate the choice of one approach over the others are discussed later in this chapter.)

This phase of the risk management process is primarily a problem in decision making: more precisely, it is deciding which of the techniques available should be used in dealing with each risk. The extent to which the risk manager must make these decisions alone varies from organization to organization. Sometimes the organization's risk management policy establishes the criteria to be applied in the choice of techniques, outlining the rules within which the risk manager may operate. If the risk management policy is rigid and detailed, the risk manager has less latitude in the decision making. He or she therefore becomes an administrator of the program rather than a policymaker. In other instances, where no formal policy exists or where the policy has been loosely drawn to permit the risk manager discretion, the risk manager's responsibility is much greater.

In attempting to determine which technique to use in dealing with a given risk, the risk manager considers the size of the potential loss, its probability, and the resources that would be available to meet the loss if it should occur. The benefits and costs involved in each approach are evaluated and then, on the basis of the best information available and under the guidance of the corporate risk management policy, the decision is made.

IMPLEMENTING THE DECISION

The decision to retain a risk may be accomplished with or without a reserve and with or without a fund. If the decision is made to include the accumulation of a fund, the administrative procedure must be inaugurated to implement the decision. If the decision is made to use loss prevention to deal with a particular risk, the proper loss prevention program must be designed and implemented. The decision to transfer the risk through insurance must be followed by the selection of an insurer and negotiations for placement of the insurance.

EVALUATING AND REVIEWING

Evaluation and review must be included in the program for two reasons. First, the risk management process does not take place in a vacuum. Things change: new risks arise and old risks disappear. Therefore, the techniques that were appropriate last year may not be the most advisable this year, and constant attention is required. Second, mistakes are sometimes made. Evaluation and review of the risk management program permits the risk manager to review decisions and discover mistakes, hopefully before they become costly.

Although evaluation and review should be continuing functions of the risk manager, some firms also hire independent consultants periodically to review their program. These consultants are independent advisers who may be hired to evaluate the entire risk-management program or particular segments of the program. Although, they are typically employed by business firms that are unable or unwilling to create the position of risk manager within the organization, many firms that already have a risk manager may consider an outside review to be desirable.

Misconceptions About Risk Management ■ ■ ■ ■ ■ ■ ■ ■

The misunderstanding about risk management reflects both a misreading of the literature and defects in the literature itself. Much of the material published in the area of risk management originated in the academic world. The other major source has been the practicing risk managers of large national concerns. As a result, two misconceptions have developed concerning risk management. The first is that the risk management concept is applicable principally to large organizations. The second is that the risk management approach to dealing with pure risks seeks to minimize the role of insurance.

UNIVERSAL APPLICABILITY

A reading of much of the literature dealing with the concept of risk management would easily lead us to conclude that risk management has useful application only for the large industrial complex. This misconception stems from the fact that many of the techniques with which writers have been preoccupied (e.g., self-insurance plans, captive insurers) do apply primarily to giant organizations. Because most of the articles on risk management have been written by practicing professional risk managers, it is natural that they would write about the techniques they use in their own companies, and virtually all professional risk managers are employed by large organizations. But it cannot be overemphasized that the risk management philosophy and approach applies to organizations of all sizes, even though some of the more esoteric techniques may have limited application in the case of the average organization.

The risk manager's position within the corporate framework has grown, and risk management has become a recognized term in businesses of all sizes. Although the small firm obviously cannot afford a full-time professional risk manager, the principles of risk management are basically common sense applied to the process of dealing with certain risks. This common-sense approach applies just as properly to the small organization as it does to the giant international firm. The approach may differ in scope and complexity, and the form that the tools assume may vary with the size of the organization, but their essential nature is the same.

ANTI-INSURANCE BIAS?

The second misconception about risk management—that it is anti-insurance and that it seeks to minimize the role of insurance in dealing with risk—also stems from the risk management literature. Writers from the academic world, preoccupied with techniques that apply principally to giant organizations, have concentrated on risk management techniques other than insurance. In fact, many academic writers have assiduously avoided writing about insurance in the risk management process in order to avoid being stigmatized as "insurance" professors. The new professors of risk management have therefore relegated insurance to a subordinate role in the risk management process, and have focused instead on other approaches to dealing with risk, such as risk control, risk retention, risk avoidance, and captive insurance companies.

If asked about the philosophy of risk management, many practitioners in the insurance field would respond that the major thrust of risk management is on the retention of risk and the use of deductibles. Retention is indeed an important technique for dealing with risks, but it is not necessarily the central approach.

Contrary to the popular notion, the essence of risk management is not on the retention of exposures. Rather it is on dealing with risks by whatever mechanism is deemed most appropriate, and in many instances, commercial insurance will be the only acceptable approach. Although the risk management philosophy suggests that some risks should be retained, it also dictates that some risks must be transferred. The primary focus of the risk manager should therefore be on identifying the risks that must be transferred to achieve the primary risk management objective. Only after this determination has been made does the question of which risks should be retained arise. More often than not, deciding which risks should be transferred also determines which risks will be retained: the residual class that does not need to be transferred.

■ The Risk Manager's Job ■ ■ ■ ■ ■ ■ ■ ■ ■ ■ ■ ■ ■ ■ ■ ■ ■ ■ ■

Not every corporate employee who deals with insurance functions is a risk manager. In fact, in some organizations the person responsible for insurance-related activities is far removed from the risk management arena. Insurance-related positions can be found in most organizations but with dramatically different responsibilities.

The term *risk manager* can be used in a functional sense to mean anyone who performs the risk management job, regardless of whether that person is an employee of the organization, an outside consultant, or an agent or broker. As the term is used in this book, however, it refers to an individual employed by the organization who is responsible for the risk management function.

Even when viewed from this perspective, every organization has a risk manager who must make decisions relating to the pure risks facing the organization. In a large corporation the risk manager is a well-paid professional who has a specific title and job description that relates to the management of risks. In the small company this individual may be the president or managing partner. In a moderate-sized company, he or she may be the chief financial officer or someone on an intermediate-staff level.

RESPONSIBILITIES AND DUTIES OF THE RISK MANAGER

One way to obtain a precise understanding of the risk manager is to take a look at what he or she does. Basically, the risk manager:

1. *Assists in developing risk management policy.* Generally, risk management objectives and policy are approved by the organization's highest level policy-making body. However, the risk manager helps management in identifying risk management objectives and prepares a statement of policy for consideration and approval by top management.

2. *Engages in risk identification and measurement.* Risk identification is perhaps the most difficult risk management function. Not only is it a never-ending task, but also the risk manager cannot know whether it has been done properly, or whether some obscure exposure to loss has been overlooked. The risk identification process requires a far-reaching information system that will alert the risk manager to new exposures as they arise. Although the risk manager has ultimate responsibility for identifying and measuring risk, outside consultants, as noted earlier, are often retained to assist in this function.

3. *Selects risk financing alternatives.* While loss-prevention and control measures can reduce the amount of risk, some risk will always remain, and so the organization must choose between retention and transfer for these remaining risks. Based on a knowledge of the organization's financial structure, the risk manager recommends the technique to be used or in some cases makes the choice.

4. *Negotiates insurance coverage.* The risk manager must first determine what insurance is needed and must then go to the insurance market to obtain the best combination of coverage and cost. This function is usually carried out through an agent or broker, although sometimes it may be done directly with the insurers. In the insurance-buying function, the risk manager is involved in selecting the agent or broker and generally participates with the agent or broker in selecting the insurer.

5. *Manages claims.* Negotiating settlements with insurers can be an involved, protracted process, particularly in the case of large property losses or business interruption losses. With regard to claims for liability and workers compensation, the risk manager must see that reporting procedures are adequate, that claims adjusters are the best available, that reserves are fre-

quently checked, and so on. Self-insured claims require even more careful attention. Subrogation (recovery) procedures against third parties must be initiated and followed through, and claim expenses (investigations, expert witnesses, legal, etc.) must be properly controlled.

6. *Supervises internal administration.* This function includes supervising the maintenance of risk-related records, such as loss statistics and the risk management manual, monitoring insurance renewals, and maintaining property schedules and valuation or appraisal records.

7. *Communicates with other managers.* The risk manager communicates with other managers within the organization, as well as with parties outside the organization, through formal documents—such as the *Risk Management Manual*—through regular written communications, and through personal contact. The risk manager must inform other managers about the scope of the organization's insurance program, request information for risk identification, and provide guidance in the area of loss and claim procedures.

8. *Handles accounting.* In many multidivisional organizations, the risk manager must allocate risk and insurance charges equitably among cost centers. Much of this function involves informed judgment.

9. *Administers risk functions.* The risk manager's many administrative duties include supervising contractors' certificates of insurance, monitoring insurance expirations, assisting the legal department in developing standards for purchase orders, leases, and other contracts, and related functions.

10. *Supervises loss prevention.* Although risk managers cannot be experts in all phases of loss prevention, they should have a general knowledge of the area backed by their own loss information. This knowledge should enable every risk manager to determine the best method of obtaining what loss-prevention counsel is needed. The most effective risk manager has direction over the safety function, but even when a separate department handles this function, the risk manager, with available loss data, can provide useful support.

11. *Manages employee benefits.* Roughly one-third of currently practicing risk managers are also responsible for employee benefits. Some consider this part of risk management, but others disagree, arguing that employee benefits are not risks, but costs deliberately assumed for a business purpose. However, most agree that risk management and managing employee benefits are separate professional fields, calling for different kinds of expertise.

The extent to which any particular risk manager has responsibility for all 11 functions varies from organization to organization. Periodic surveys conducted by the Risk and Insurance Management Society reveal that such responsibility varies with the size of the organization. In some instances, risk managers are also responsible for the firm's employee benefit plans, whereas in other cases, their responsibility is limited to those risks that threaten the firm itself.

In spite of the emphasis of the literature on noninsurance techniques, such as retention or self-insurance, the most common responsibility of risk managers is negotiating insurance coverage. Indeed, more than two-thirds of risk managers in businesses of all sizes reported negotiation of insurance coverage as one of their principal responsibilities. In contrast, responsibility for risk financing increases with the size of the firm. For firms with more than $500 million in sales, three-fourths of the risk managers are responsible for risk financing.

About one-fourth of the risk managers reported having some responsibility for loss-prevention activities within their organizations. A higher percentage reported more responsibility for safety and fire engineering, however, than for security, which seems to indicate that in most companies responsibility for loss prevention is fragmented.

TRAINING AND QUALIFICATIONS OF RISK MANAGERS

What training and experience prepare risk managers for their demanding job? Risk managers have taken a variety of paths to their corporate positions. Many employers look for someone with an insurance background, broker, company, or related experience, although today some employers are demanding actual experience in corporate risk management. Other companies give the position to someone with a related professional background—engineer, lawyer, accountant, administrative analyst, and so on. In some corporations, especially those in which the employee benefit program predated the risk management department, the risk manager may be an employee benefit specialist with incidental responsibility for the organization's property and liability exposures. Often, the risk manager is an account executive from a brokerage firm who has been enticed into the risk management position. At the same time, some executives believe that experience with an insurance company or brokerage firm may create an undesirable bias in favor of insurance, and some firms have therefore avoided risk managers from the insurance field.

In discussing the qualifications required of a risk manager, one practicing risk manager offered this tongue-in-cheek summary:

> The skills and qualifications of a well-rounded corporate risk manager are fairly simple and easy to state: Being as proficient at underwriting as any seasoned professional in a solid property and casualty insurance company, expert at handling and adjusting claims in all lines, possessing a solid background in engineering as well as industrial hygiene and having a strong foundation in medicine is virtually essential. It goes almost without saying that the risk manager must be a professional accountant and well versed in the nuances of cash management and financial forecasting. He or she should possess an extensive legal education. To top it all off, the person needs to be an excellent writer and speech-maker, and be recognized as a strong negotiator, salesman and politician.[7]

It would be amazing to find all these qualifications in any one person. Any risk manager will have some of these strengths but will be lacking in other areas. When

---

[7]A.H. Seiple, Jr., "A Practitioner Looks at Risk Management's Corporate Function," *Risk Management* (September 1982), p. 24.

a risk manager personally lacks specific background strengths, he or she either tries to be selective in building a staff to add people who complement personal strengths, or draws on the strengths of the company's other staff departments. The risk manager who lacks legal education, for example, tends to draw more heavily on the company's law department. By the same token, a risk manager with a degree in engineering will rely less on the company's industrial or mechanical engineers than the manager who lacks an engineering background.

Until quite recently, there seemed to be no reason to prefer any particular background. Because risk management encompasses so many fields, it is virtually impossible to find an expert in everything related to risk management. Consequently, risk managers have tended to be specialists in one particular phase of risk management (e.g., insurance or loss prevention) or generalists without expertise in any of the specific subdisciplines of risk management. With the growth of professional studies in risk management, however, this view has changed. Although the study of risk management does not attempt to create professionals who are experts in all risk management fields, it does address the interrelationships of risk management techniques. More importantly, it creates a conceptual framework that assists in choosing among risk management alternatives. In short, the emphasis in the study of risk management is on *management* in the decision-making sense. Persons trained in risk management are uniquely equipped for organizing, planning, leading, and controlling the organization's risk management functions.

POSITION IN THE ORGANIZATION

In general, risk managers are assigned to one of three corporate departments, depending on the firm's history and development of risk management. In some organizations, the risk manager evolved from the insurance manager, who has traditionally worked in the finance division or under the comptroller. In these companies, risk management is viewed as a financial function and so belongs to the *finance division*. In companies where the risk manager evolved from the employee benefits manager, the risk manager may be in the *personnel division*. Finally, in companies where the risk manager developed from the safety function, the risk manager will generally be assigned to the division that traditionally housed the safety director, usually the *production division*.

Most risk managers have a financial orientation, reporting to a vice president of finance, treasurer, or comptroller. There is a growing school of thought, however, that says the risk manager should be in a less specialized department, reporting to an executive vice president or even the president to illustrate the companywide scope of risk management activities.

According to a 1996 survey conducted by RIMS, 39 percent of respondents reported their title was risk manager, 34 percent said their title was director of risk management, and 14 percent reported the title Vice President.[8]

[8]"Climbing Corporate Ladder Pays Off For Risk Managers," *Business Insurance* (April 1, 1996), p. 27.

The Nonprofessional Risk Manager ■ ■ ■ ■ ■ ■ ■ ■ ■ ■ ■

Only a small number of organizations can afford a full-time professional risk manager; therefore, most risk management activities are performed by persons other than professional risk managers. In smaller firms, the risk manager has other duties as well. In the smallest firms, the risk manager may very well manage everything; this person's job imposes an extremely heavy burden, for it requires the utmost precision if loss is to be avoided. Decisions must be made as to what kind of insurance is to be purchased, how much, and from whom. If the insurance coverage is inadequate and a loss occurs, the firm will suffer a financial loss. If the business is overinsured, the loss is just as real in terms of the premiums that should not have been spent.

Certainly, the nonprofessional risk manager needs all the help he or she can get, and so may seek advice from many sources. In the last analysis however, the decision remains his or her burden. Unfortunately, the risk managers who must depend on the services of others cannot always be certain that their advisers are genuinely interested in advising, as distinguished from selling. For this reason, the nonprofessional risk manager should understand the principles of risk management, knowing enough about it to recognize whether his advisers have any real expertise, to determine when help is needed, and then to be able to see whether the kind of help he needs will be forthcoming.

RISK MANAGEMENT AND THE INDIVIDUAL

Risk management evolved formally as a function of business. Insurance managers became risk managers, and with the transition certain principles of scientific insurance buying, which had always been used to some extent, were formalized. These principles are largely common-sense applications of the cost-benefit principle, and they are equally applicable to the insurance-buying decisions of the individual or the family unit. Like the business firm, the individual or family unit has a limited number of dollars that can be allocated toward the protection of assets and income against loss. Personal risk management is concerned with the optimal allocation of these dollars and employs the same techniques as does business risk management. In order to achieve maximum protection against static losses, the individual must select from among the risk management tools of retention, reduction, and transfer. Although the primary emphasis in this book is on commercial risk management and insurance buying, the basic principles discussed apply equally well to the individual and family unit.

Outside Risk Management Services ■ ■ ■ ■ ■ ■ ■ ■ ■ ■ ■

The three major sources of external assistance are risk management consultants, consulting affiliates of national brokers, and insurance companies or their subsidiaries.

RISK MANAGEMENT CONSULTANTS

Among the better known risk management consulting organizations are Tillinghast, Ebasco Risk Management Consultants, Inc., Risk Planning Group, RIMCO, the Wyatt Company, Warren, McVeigh & Griffin, Inc., Betterly Risk Consultants, Risk and Benefit Systems, Insurance Buyers' Council, Inc., and Stone and Webster. These organizations provide a cafeteria of services from which the risk manager can choose. As an example, Tillinghast, the largest of these independent consultants, provides diverse services to its clients in both the public and private sectors: designing insurance programs, auditing existing insurance and self-insurance programs, analyzing risk management department operations, conducting feasibility studies for captives, managing offshore and onshore captive insurers, preparing specifications for all portions of an insurance program and evaluating responses to bid specifications, and designing, implementing, and monitoring loss control procedures.

Several independent specialty organizations have been formed to respond to the specific needs of risk management departments. For example, Corporate Systems offers a risk management accounting system for evaluating self-insurance, which helps a corporation in its financial and risk analysis forecasting. Equifax Risk Management provides support services in loss control and claims administration. GAB Business Services, Inc., has established a safety and loss-prevention program in the workers compensation and general products liability areas.

INSURANCE AGENTS AND BROKERS

Initially the insurance agents' reaction to the risk management movement was divided. In general, their responses fell into one of three classes: fear, indifference, or enthusiasm. When corporate insurance buyers and risk managers formed their professional organizations, some agents feared that these organizations might be an attempt to bypass the traditional distribution system, of which they had always been the central figures. In addition, the literature dealing with risk management on topics such as self-insurance and retention of risks appeared to minimize the role of insurance in the risk management process.

Other agents viewed the development of risk management as a phenomenon far removed from their sphere of operation, feeling that it was of interest primarily to larger organizations, and had little relevance to the smaller and medium-sized accounts that constituted their special domain. For this group, the risk management concept was a distant, nebulous concept that revolved around massive self-insurance programs and captive insurance companies.

Finally, some agents recognized the risk management concept as an opportunity for the professional agent to serve his or her clients. Faced with the decision as to the response that should be taken, these agents embraced risk management theory and attempted to develop services that could be offered to those clients that pursued the risk management philosophy. Many insurers and national brokers, accustomed to servicing large commercial accounts, adjusted their operations and began to offer services oriented toward risk management. This course of action has proven to be the wisest. Although many giant corporations employ skilled technicians in their insurance buying or risk management department, countless business organizations cannot afford an in-house risk management staff. The need for professional advice on insurance and other aspects of risk management has created new opportunities for agents to be of service to insurance buyers. Today, most of the large brokers (e.g., Alexander and Alexander, Frank B. Hall, Fred S. James, Marsh and McLennan, Johnson and Higgins) have established their own subsidiaries that provide consulting services. These organizations offer services for their own in-house clients and also compete with independent consultants for outside business.

Some observers maintain that insurance agents and brokers cannot provide objective risk management counsel because of the conflict of interest inherent in the commission system by which they are compensated. But this conflict is not new; it has existed for many years and the professional agent has long been aware that placing commission income above the client's interest results in only a short-term gain, if any gain at all.

As the once-distinct lines among firms in the financial services market continue to face, it is conceivable that commercial banks will become another source of risk management services. Although federal banking law has required a separation between banking and other forms of commerce,[9] a number of the nation's largest banks have been increasingly active in the insurance field, generally through partnerships with insurance brokerage houses. This phenomenon is perhaps best illustrated by the activities of J. P. Morgan, which entered into a partnership called *Trident* with the international insurance broker, Marsh & McLennan in the early 1990s. Trident has emphasized property/casualty insurance start-up ventures, friendly acquisitions and other strategic opportunities arising from restructurings and realignments already under way in the global insurance industry. The partnership has been instrumental in the creation of a number of specialty insurers and reinsurers, including EXEL, ACE, Centre Re, SCUUL and Mid Ocean Reinsurance.[10] In 1993, when the membership at Lloyd's voted to permit corporate investors, the Marsh & McLennan and J. P. Morgan partnership was among the first entities to take advantage of the opportunity. We will undoubtedly see additional activity by banks in the field of insurance and conceivably in other risk management services, probably through partnerships with insurance brokerage firms.

---

[9]The National Banking Act of 1864 bars national banks from engaging in any activity that is not banking or incidental to the power of banking. Banks are not permitted to underwrite insurance and are allowed to engage in insurance agency activities under a limited exception to the general rule separating banking and commerce. Banks are permitted to sell credit life and health insurance, and banks in communities with populations of less than 5000 are permitted to operate insurance agencies. In 1996, the U.S. Supreme Court ruled that the National Banking Act preempts state laws that prohibit the sale of insurance in communities with populations under 5000. See Steven Brostoff, "Top Court Gives Banks Green Light," *National Underwriter, Property & Casualty/Risk and Benefits Management Edition.* (April 1, 1996).

[10]"New Bermuda Company to Reinsure Lloyd's Syndicates," *Best's Insurance News,* (July 1, 1993).

OUTSOURCING RISK MANAGEMENT FUNCTIONS

Although the trend is new, some firms, including the international giant, IBM, had adapted the concept of *outsourcing* to the risk management function. An increasing number of firms—both large and small—employ an outside organization on a continuing basis to perform risk management-related functions that have traditionally been performed internally. Although there is general agreement that the ultimate risk management decisions and responsibility must remain within the organization, an increasing number of companies are outsourcing many of the routine administrative functions related to risk management.

Actually, for most smaller businesses, outsourcing the functions of risk identification and measurement have always been the norm. Smaller firms find it impractical to manage all phases of their risk management program and depend on insurance agents and brokers to perform the risk identification and measurement function. Often, they have also received assistance in deciding what should be done about individual risks. The outsourcing trend reflects something of a reversal, in which organizations that have acquired the expertise to perform such functions are now hiring others to perform the functions. Larger organizations hire ongoing service for various reasons: to assist the risk manager in areas outside his or her field of specialized knowledge; to provide guidance for a corporate officer who handles risk management as a secondary responsibility; to provide counsel on markets for specialized coverages; to assist when problem lines are renewed; and to provide information on new coverages. Generally, the organizations to which risk management functions have been outsourced are insurance brokerage firms.

IBM is a good example. During the period from 1987 to 1995, IBM reduced its risk management staff from 62 persons operating worldwide to eight. The staff reduction was achieved by shifting most of the risk identification work in foreign operations to insurance brokers. The company actually considered eliminating its risk management department completely, but decided that the company's fiduciary responsibility to shareholders and partners required that final risk management decisions must be made within the organization.[11]

Although the firms that have turned to outsourcing generally appear to be satisfied with the results, the motivation has generally been to a report of a high level of satisfaction with the results. Most firms have turned to outsourcing have done so not by choice, but in response to corporate downsizing. The one point on which there is universal agreement, however, is that the ultimate risk management decisions about how much risk to retain and which risks should be transferred must be made internally.

[11]See Dave Pelland, "Outsourcing: More Efficient Risk Management?" *Risk Management* (May 1995).

IMPORTANT CONCEPTS TO REMEMBER

insurance management
risk management
operations research
management science
risk control
loss prevention
loss control
risk financing
insurable risk

Henri Fayol
security function
risk management process
determination of objectives
identification of the risks
evaluation of the risks
considering alternatives and
    selecting the risk
    treatment device

implementing the decision
evaluation and review
insurance policy checklists
risk analysis questionnaires
flow process charts
critical risks
important risks
unimportant risks
risk management policy

QUESTIONS FOR REVIEW

1. Identify the two broad approaches to dealing with risk that are recognized by modern risk management theory.

2. Identify and briefly describe the four basic techniques available to the risk manager for dealing with the pure risks facing the firm.

3. List and briefly describe the six steps in the risk management process.

4. The text states that the emergence of risk management was a revolution that signaled a dramatic shift in philosophy. What was this change in philosophy?

5. Briefly describe the development of risk management as a function of business in the United States. What, in your opinion, were the primary motivating forces and the strategic factors that led to the development of risk management?

6. Describe the responsibility of the risk manager and the risk manager's position within the organization.

7. What is the relationship between risk management and insurance management? In your answer you should demonstrate an understanding of the difference between the two fields.

8. Describe the relationship between risk management and general management. In what ways does a risk manager become involved in the overall supervision of the firm?

9. Describe the criteria that the text suggests be used in prioritizing risks in terms of their importance.

10. Identify two common misconceptions about risk management, and explain why these misconceptions developed.

QUESTIONS FOR DISCUSSION

1. Which of the six steps in the risk management process do you believe is the most difficult for the risk manager? Which would you suspect is the most frequently overlooked or neglected?

2. In some sense, a risk manager must be a "jack of all trades," because of the breadth of his or her activities. Identify several areas in which a risk manager should be knowledgeable, and explain why this would be useful for the risk manager. What type of educational background should a risk manager have?

3. In a large, multi-division company, risk management may be centralized or decentralized. Which approach, in your opinion, is likely to produce the greatest benefits? Why?

4. The American Risk and Insurance Association has argued that risk management should be added to the required core of knowledge in business administration. To what extent do you agree or disagree that risk management should be a required course in a business curriculum?

5. About one-third of risk managers report that they are responsible for employee benefits. To what do you attribute this low percentage of risk managers with such responsibility? What are the arguments for and against assigning responsibility for employee benefits to the risk management department?

SUGGESTIONS FOR ADDITIONAL READING

Allen, T.C., and R.M. Duvall. "A Theoretical and Practical Approach to Risk Management," *Risk Management*. New York: The American Society of Insurance Management, 1971.

American Management Association. *The Growing Job of Risk Management:* AMA Management Report 70. New York: American Management Association, 1962.

Barlow, Douglas. "The Evolution of Risk Management," *Risk Management* (April 1993), pp. 38–45.

Carter, Robert L. and Neil A. Doherty. *Handbook of Risk Management.* Middlesex, England: Kluwer-Harrap, Rembrandt House, 1976.

Doherty, Neil A. *Corporate Risk Management: A Financial Exposition* (New York: McGraw-Hill Book Company, 1985).

Ealy, Thomas V. "Bringing Risk Management Into the Boardroom," *Risk Management* (April 1993), pp. 30–37.

Fayol, Henri. *General and Industrial Management* (New York: Pitman Publishing Corporation, 1949).

Gallagher, Russell B. "Risk Management: A New Phase of Cost Control," *Harvard Business Review*, September–October 1956.

Hampton, John H. *Essentials of Risk Management and Insurance.* New York: American Management Association, 1993.

Head, George W., Michael J. Elliot, and James D. Blinn. *Essentials of Risk Financing.* vol. I and II. Malvern, Pa.: Insurance Institute of America, 1993.

Head, George L., and Ron C. Horn. *Essentials of Risk Management*, vols. I and II, 2nd edition. Malvern, PA: Insurance Institute of America, 1991.

Kamei, Toshiaki. "The Nature and Classifications of Risk Management," *Kansai University Review of Economics and Business* (March 1991).

Kloman, Felix H. "Risk and Response: Beyond 2000," *Risk Management* (April 1995), pp. 65–72.

MacDonald, Donald L. Corporate Risk Control. New York: The Ronald Press, 1966.

Mehr, R.I., and B.A. Hedges. *Risk Management in the Business Enterprise.* Homewood, Il.: Richard D. Irwin, 1963. Chapter 1.

Pelland, Dave. "Outsourcing: More Efficient Risk Management?," *Risk Management* (May 1995)

Seiple, A.H., Jr. "A Practitioner Looks at Risk Management's Corporate Function," *Risk Management* (September 1982).

Snider, H.W., ed. *Risk Management.* Homewood, Ill.: Richard D. Irwin, 1964.

Taylor, Frederick W. *Scientific Management* (New York: Harper & Row, Publishers, Inc., 1911).

West, Kathryn Z. "Risk Management for the Middle Market," *Risk Management.* (January 1966), pp 33–35.

Williams, C. Arthur, and Richard M. Heins. *Risk Management and Insurance,* 6th ed. New York: McGraw-Hill, 1989. Chapters 1, 2.

Young, Peter C. "The Transformation of Risk Management," *Public Risk* (September/October 1991).

CHAPTER 3

Risk Management Decisions

CHAPTER OBJECTIVES

When you have finished this chapter, you should be able to

Identify the two broad approaches to dealing with risk that are recognized by modern risk management theory.

Identify and illustrate the nonscientific approaches to risk management decisions.

Explain generally the way in which utility theory may be used in risk management decisions.

Identify two decision models from the field of decision theory that may be used in risk management decision making, and explain the circumstances in which each is applicable.

Identify the three rules of risk management and explain how they relate to the management science decision models.

Identify the three broad categories of insurance coverage and describe the distinguishing characteristics of each category.

▓ Introduction ■

In this chapter, we turn to the process by which risk management decisions are made. We examine some of the decision-making processes that have been suggested and define the criteria that should be used in risk management decisions. Risk management decisions are concerned primarily with the third step in the risk management process; selecting the technique that will be used to deal with the

NAPIER UNIVERSITY LIBRARY

risks that have been identified and measured. Before turning to our discussion of these decisions, it will be helpful to consider the alternatives from which the risk manager can choose: the tools of risk management.

The Tools of Risk Management ■■■■■■■■■■■■■■■

In general, the risk manager's risk treatment techniques—the tools of risk management—are the same as those used by others, which were discussed in Chapter 1. In the current terminology of risk management literature, these techniques are classified as risk control and risk financing. Risk control focuses on minimizing the firm's risk of loss and includes the techniques of avoidance and reduction. Risk financing concentrates on arranging the availability of funds to meet losses arising from the risks that remain after risk control techniques are applied, and includes the tools of retention and transfer. Although the various risk management techniques are usually discussed as if they were separate and distinct, more often than not they are used in combination with each other. In fact, it is the process of combining the application of risk control and risk financing techniques that represents the art and science of risk management.

Risk Management Decisions ■■■■■■■■■■■■■■■

Once risks have been identified and measured, a decision must be made regarding what, if anything, should be done about each risk. This is the basic risk management problem. Several approaches to risk management decisions are possible.

INSTINCTIVE AND INSTITUTIONAL REACTIONS TO RISK

Humans react to adversity in a variety of ways. At the personal level, the natural instinct for self-preservation dictates that we take whatever measures are available to avoid injury or loss. Such reactions are not decisions, but rather innate instincts of self-preservation. In addition to these instinctive reactions to danger, personal loss prevention and control measures might be classified as a learned behavior. "Don't play with matches," "Don't tease the dog," "Don't run with scissors," are all risk management axioms that are instilled in the individual from an early age. Individuals acquire a body of principles that dictate patterns of action designed to protect and preserve. They become innate standards for behavior that, while sometimes violated, represent rules for personal loss prevention and control.

Another part of human behavior in responding to risk is institutionalized. People almost automatically purchase automobile insurance and homeowners insurance. Although economists posit a rational purchaser who makes marginal calculations based on utility, many insurance-buying decisions are actually dependent and subordinated decisions. The youthful driver does not really want to buy automobile insurance; he or she simply wants to drive a car. Legal requirements and societal conventions dictate, however, that insurance must be purchased. Similarly, although some consumers probably make a rational choice to purchase or not to purchase homeowners insurance, for the overwhelming majority, there is really little choice. Unless the individual has sufficient resources to purchase a home for cash, there will be a mortgage, and the mortgagor will insist on insurance. In short, convention dictates many risk management and insurance decisions at the personal level.

When we move from consideration of the individual to the organization, the standards and rules become more complex and more formalized. Because hazards increase with the complexity of the activity, the instinctive and institutionalized patterns of behavior that serve as the foundation for personal risk management are inadequate and the choices become more complicated.

"GOOD" AND "BAD" RISK MANAGEMENT DECISIONS

One of the complexities in risk management decisions is in distinguishing good decisions from bad ones. Because risk management involves decision making under conditions of uncertainty, the decisions are sometimes judged as good or bad in ways that are inappropriate. Consider the following examples:

- Joe Smith, the risk manager for ABC, Inc., elects not to purchase the umbrella liability policy suggested by his broker. The umbrella policy would have provided $5 million in coverage, but at a cost of $13,000. The year passes uneventfully without any liability losses. Smith has therefore saved the company $13,000.

- Mary Jones, risk manager for XYZ, Inc., elects to include a $100,000 deductible in the fire insurance policies covering her firm's plant. The premium credit is $18,000. Unfortunately, six weeks after the deductible provision is added to the policy, the building suffers a $200,000 loss, of which XYZ must bear $100,000. Mary's decision was ill-advised and cost the firm $82,000.

- Bill Johnson, against the advice of his agent, elects to carry collision coverage on his firm's five-year-old truck, which is valued at $1000. The premium for the collision coverage is $150. The wisdom of Johnson's decision is confirmed when the truck is destroyed in a collision and the firm collects $1000.

Is it reasonable to conclude that Smith's decision not to purchase the umbrella policy was a good one? Clearly, the decision resulted in a saving in premium dollars. Did Mary make a poor decision? After all, there is little question that her choice cost the firm $82,000. And can anyone argue that Bill's decision was not perceptive?

It should be obvious that there is something terribly wrong with our labeling each of these decisions as "good" or "bad" based on the outcome. Simply put, we cannot evaluate a decision made under conditions of uncertainty in light of what happens after the decision is made. Instead, the evaluation must be made on the basis of the information available at the time the decision is made.

Suppose that you and I wager a dollar on the flip of a coin. As I flip the coin, you say "call it" and I say "heads." Is my choice of *heads* a good decision or a bad decision? Knowing what I knew about the probabilities—that *heads* is as likely as *tails*—the decision is as good a decision as I can make. (*Tails* would, of course, have been an equally good decision.) Now suppose that as a result of the toss, the coin ends up tails and I lose my dollar. Does this change the quality of my decision? Reasonable people should agree that the decision was as good a decision as I could make, even though the outcome was different from the one I predicted.

Now let us change the scenario dramatically. Suppose that I offer to wager $50,000 on the flip of the same coin ($50,000 which, by the way, I don't have). You accept and flip the coin. The outcome in this case is, as I predicted, a head.

One of the decisions in the preceding scenario was a *good* one, while the other decision was *bad*. The decision to bet a dollar that the outcome of the flip was a good one—at least as good a decision as I was able to make. Although the outcome was unfavorable, the decision itself was good. The second decision, in which I wagered $50,000 that the outcome would be a head—money I did not have—was a bad decision, despite the fact that the outcome was favorable.

If decisions made under conditions of uncertainty are to be judged as good or bad, they must be evaluated in light of the information available at the time the decision is made—that is, before the outcome is known. On what basis should the decisions be judged good or bad? Although several criteria may be used, the preceding scenario suggests one: how bad it will hurt if the decision is wrong, that is, the penalty associated with an unfavorable outcome. As we will see shortly, this criterion is used in many risk management decisions.

COST-BENEFIT ANALYSIS

Cost-benefit analysis attempts to measure the contribution that a risk management technique makes to the risk management process by determining whether, and by how much, the technique's benefits exceed its the cost. The greater the benefits for a given cost, or the lower the cost for a given level of benefits, the more cost effective the particular technique is thought to be. Actually, cost-benefit analysis can be used to judge any business decision where benefits and costs can be determined. When benefits are realized over time (or when costs are incurred over time), they are expressed as discounted cash flows.

Although cost-benefit analysis is a good technique for risk management decision making, the nature of risk situations creates impediments to its use. Whereas costs are generally measurable, benefits may not be. This, of course, is not unique to insurance decisions. Many of the problems addressed by decision theory are those for which the answer is not intuitively obvious.

UTILITY THEORY AND RISK MANAGEMENT DECISIONS

One school of thought proposes that utility theory be used as an approach to risk management decisions. Utility theory was originally introduced to explain the nature of the demand function. According to neoclassical economists, the utility or satisfaction derived from economic goods does not increase proportionately with increases in the good. In a somewhat overworked example, economists argue that one derives greater satisfaction from the first cup of coffee than from the second, and greater satisfaction from the second cup than from the third. Because people derive less satisfaction from additional units of a commodity, they are willing to pay less for these additional units, which partially explains the downward-sloping demand curve with which most students are familiar. From this point of departure, economists also hypothesized that, for most persons, money also has diminishing marginal utility. If one's income doubles from say, $40,000 to $80,000, his or her satisfaction level will less than double. Elementary economics textbooks illustrate the diminishing marginal utility of money graphically with charts such as the one presented in Figure 3.1. As shown in the figure, the increase in wealth from $40,000 to $80,000—a 100 percent increase—yields only a 50 percent increase in utility, from 600 utils to 900 utils.[1]

In an often cited article, Professors Friedman and Savage developed a theoretical explanation for the apparent inconsistencies in human behavior with respect to risk.[2] Friedman and Savage were intrigued by the pattern of consumer choices with respect to insurance and other decisions involving uncertainty. They noted that some people will purchase insurance, indicating a distaste for uncertainty, whereas other people gamble, indicating that they prefer risk to certainty.[3] To explain this

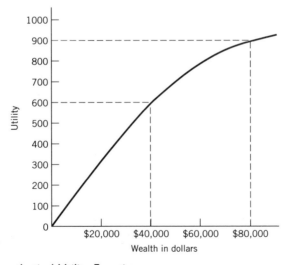

Figure 3.1 Hypothetical Utility Function

[1]The term *util* is simply a term invented by economists as the unit of measure for utility.

[2]Milton Friedman and L.J. Savage, "The Utility Analysis of Choices Involving Risk," *Journal of Political Economy* 56 (August 1948), 279–304.

[3]Diminishing marginal utility theory has been used to argue against gambling on the grounds that, even if the gambler breaks even over the long run, the disutility from losing will be greater than the utility from winning. This argument ignores the utility or satisfaction the gambler derives from gambling (which is separate from the utility of the money won). Diminishing marginal utility has also been used as an argument to support progressive taxation and the equalization of incomes.

anomaly, Friedman and Savage hypothesized that people who buy insurance have a utility curve that appears concave to the base, bending downward, as indicated in Figure 3.1. Gamblers, in contrast, have a an upward-bending utility curve, convex to the base.[4]

Adherents of utility theory as an approach to risk management decision making use the expected value concept to compare different states of uncertainty. This is done by constructing a utility curve for the individual, which then serves as a basis for insurance decisions. The process is described as follows:

> For each sum of money loss to which a person is exposed, a utility value is assigned. These values are multiplied by the probability of loss and a total expected utility of loss is derived. The implications for risk-handling methods are important and may be illustrated by reference to a decision as to whether or not to purchase insurance.[5]

In the proposed methodology, the expected loss of utility resulting from risk management decisions is computed by substituting a *utility index number* for the dollar losses associated with the decision. The initial step in the expected utility model approach is to derive the individual's utility function. Several approaches have been suggested for this task, but in general they involve asking the subject a series of questions concerning the amount he or she would pay to eliminate the possibility of loss of a given magnitude.[6]

Once the individual's utility function has been derived, it is used as a surrogate for the dollar amount of loss in a calculation that multiplies utility units by the probability that each level of loss might occur. This calculation is made for each decision being considered and the decision that produces the lowest expected loss of utility is selected.[7]

To illustrate the concept, suppose, for example, that the individual whose utility curve is indicated in Figure 3.2 has $80,000 in assets, consisting of a $60,000 bank account and a $20,000 automobile. Suppose, too, that there is a 10 percent chance that his auto will be demolished, he will have $60,000 in the bank and his $20,000 car or $80,000 in assets, which the utility curve indicates will give him roughly 900 utils. If he does not buy insurance and the car is demolished, he will be forced to replace the car and will be left with only $40,000 in his bank account which, combined with his (new) $20,000 car, will leave him with $60,000 in assets. At this point, his utility will be 750 utils. Because the probability that the car will be demolished is 10 percent, the consumer's satisfaction without insurance is equal to the probability of a collision (.10) times his utility if a loss occurs plus the probability of no loss (.90)

---

[4]A convex utility curve implies that the individual has an increasing marginal utility for money and is a risk seeker. Insurance buyers, who have a concave utility function, are risk averse.

[5]Mark R. Greene and Oscar N. Serbein, *Risk Management: Text and Cases* (Reston, Va.: Reston Publishing Co., 1983), p. 52.

[6]We will not discuss the process by which the utility function is derived primarily because we believe that it is an essentially useless tool for risk management decisions.

[7]Mark R. Greene and James S. Trieschman, *Risk and Insurance,* 7th ed. (Cincinnati, Oh.: SouthWestern Publishing Co., 1988), pp 590–598.

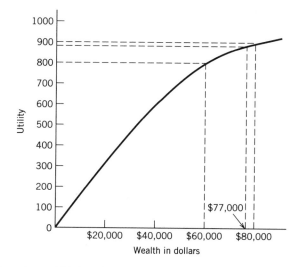

Figure 3.2 Hypothetical Utility Function

times his satisfaction if the loss does not occur. Accordingly, the individual's expected level of satisfaction without insurance is $(.9 \times 900) + (.1 \times 800) = 890$ utils.

Now suppose that the subject determines that the cost of insuring his car will be $3,000. If he purchases the insurance, he is guaranteed a net wealth position of $77,000 ($80,000 minus the $3,000 premium). If he does not purchase insurance, his utility is 890. If his utility of a certain position of $77,000 is greater than his utility for the uncertain position of a 90 percent chance of $80,000 plus a 10 percent chance of $60,000, he will purchase the insurance by the purchase of insurance, and he will not buy it if his utility is diminished.

Although this explanation of the expected utility model is extremely brief anf admittedly superficial, it is sufficient for our purpose, which is to explain why we do not believe it merits more serious consideration.

What Does the Utility Function Express?

To determine the usefulness of a utility function such as that depicted here, we should examine exactly what the utility function expresses. It is a summary of the individual's psychological attitudes at a specific point in time. It encompasses his or her optimism or pessimism, historical experiences, and other unidentifiable factors. The utility function for two individuals will differ significantly, which leads to different decisions for a specific set of circumstances. Smith's utility function may indicate that a risk should be transferred, whereas Brown's utility function may indicate that the risk should be retained. This suggests that there is no "right" or "wrong" decision with respect to risk situations. We argue to the contrary—that for a given risk situation, there is a correct solution and a variety of incorrect solutions. This solution exists independently of the individual's attitudes, which may be flawed by ignorance, experience, or unknown psychological factors.

A first problem with the use of utility theory in risk management decision making is that the utility function is a theoretical concept, and most economists agree that an individual's utility function is constantly changing with the environment. A utility function constructed at some point in time may be accurate only for that particular point in time. More importantly, there is a serious question as to whether a person's utility function can be derived by asking questions about hypothetical situations. In fact, tests generally indicate that the results produced by the hypothetical question approach are invalid and unreliable.[8]

Actually, it can be argued that little is gained by constructing a utility function. We can determine utility preferences more directly by simply observing the individual's decision. If the derived utility function indicates that the individual should not purchase a particular form of insurance and he or she makes the purchase, this simply signifies that the individual's utility preference at the time of purchase differs from that expressed in the constructed utility function. When theory and reality are in conflict, it is the theory that should be rejected, not the reality. The decision to purchase or not to purchase a particular insurance coverage is, in fact, an expression of the individual's utility preference at that particular time. Other decisions, such as those made with respect to hypothetical situations from which the utility function was derived, are irrelevant.

Finally, another problem associated with the use of utility theory in risk management decision making is that of whose utility function to use. In the case of a corporation, it is the stockholders' assets that are exposed to loss, but the decisions relating to the risk of loss of those assets are delegated to the risk manager. Could we construct a "consolidated" utility function for all stockholders? If not, and it seems unlikely, should we substitute the risk manager's utility function for that of the stockholders?

Economists constructed the theory of marginal utility in an attempt to explain *why* people make the consumer choices they do. As such, it is an interesting theoretical explanation of why people make the decisions they make with respect to risk situations. It does not and is not intended to provide guidance on the decisions people *should* make. Utility theory can explain why an alcoholic spends his money as he does—because the purchase of alcoholic beverages maximizes his utility. It does not, however, reveal anything about how he should spend the money.

Attempts to construct the utility function for a risk manager, and then to use this function in risk-making decisions, are clearly misdirected. It can be argued that one objective of risk management is to change the utility function of decision makers. Using a utility function (real or hypothetical) as the basis for risk-related decisions could conceivably lead to more consistent decisions, but there is no reason to believe that those decisions would be good. They might be consistent—but consistently bad decisions. At the risk of repetition, utility theory is useful in explaining why individuals might make decisions in a certain way, but it has little to recommend it as a methodology for making good decisions.

---

[8]Paul Slovic, "Assessment of Risk Taking Behavior," *Psychological Behavior* 61 (1964): 220–233.

DECISION THEORY AND RISK MANAGEMENT DECISIONS

Modern risk management originated with the introduction of decision theory, a branch of management science, to business decisions. *Management science* is a broad discipline that includes all rational approaches to decision making that are based on the application of scientific methodology. It includes the subdisciplines of operations research, decision sciences, information sciences, behavioral sciences, and some aspects of systems analysis. The past two decades have witnessed the growth in the application of quantitative techniques to the decision making process. Although a variety of names have been applied to the methodology involving quantitative approaches to decision making, the most widely known and accepted name is *operations research* (*OR*). Actually, operations research can be defined broadly to include a multidisciplinary approach to decision making. Under this definition, many people use the terms *operations research* and *management sciences* almost interchangeably.

The types of problems addressed by the OR approach are those for which there is no obvious solution. This approach therefore aims at identifying the *best* decision or solution to the problem. Although analysis of a problem situation almost always includes some qualitative considerations, a significant part of most operations research studies is based on quantitative decision making techniques. The most commonly used quantitative techniques in OR decision-making are statistical analysis (which includes probability theory, regression analysis, statistical sampling, and testing hypotheses) and simulation. Both qualitative and quantitative analysis of a problem provides important information for the decision maker. In many cases, the decision maker draws on both sources in making the final decision.

Decision Theory

Decision theory (or decision analysis) can be used to determine optional strategies when a decision maker is faced with several decision alternatives and an uncertain or risk-filled pattern of future events. This is precisely the situation facing the risk manager in the common risk management situation.

The analyst's first step in the decision theory approach to a given problem is to list all decision alternatives available to the decision maker. The second step is to list all future events that might occur. These future events—which are beyond the decision maker's control—are referred to as "states of nature" for the problem. It is assumed that the list of possible states of nature includes everything that can happen and that the states do not overlap. Although the explicit recognition of all possible outcomes is a characteristic of scientific decision making, in many risk management situations this step is often intuitive.

In decision theory terminology, the outcome from a certain decision and the occurrence of a particular state of nature are referred to as the "payoff."

Types of Decision-Making Situations

The literature reports three classes of decision-making situations, based on the decision maker's knowledge about the states of nature.

1. *Decision making under certainty:* One and only one state of nature exists, and the decision maker knows with certainty the future event.

2. *Decision making under risk:* More than one state of nature exists, and probability estimates are available for all states.

3. *Decision making under uncertainty:* More than one state of nature exists, but nothing is known about the probability or chance of occurrence for the various states.

Thus decision making under certainty means that the outcomes of each option are known with certainty. The major problem associated with the process of decision making under certainty is the determination of the tradeoffs among conflicting objectives—for example, quality versus price. Cost-benefit analysis was one of the specialties developed for this problem.

If the probability can be predicted from past experience or observation, the situation is described as decision making under risk. When the probability of different outcomes can be predicted with certainty, expected values can be computed to determine the most favorable outcome.

Finally, decision making under uncertainty means that the probability of occurrence of each outcome is not known. Analysis of decision making under uncertainty describes a decision problem in terms of a payoff matrix, a rectangular array whose rows represent alternative courses of action and whose columns represent so-called states of nature. The term *states of nature* refers to conditions that determine the consequences of a chosen action and that are assumed to be mutually exclusive and exhaustive.

Criteria for Decision Making Under Risk

The basic decision theory approach is to identify all possible outcomes, and then assign a value to these possible outcomes based on their likelihood and the "payoff." The notation

$$V(d3, S1) = \$100,000$$

is interpreted to read, the "payoff" (value) of decision 3, given state 1, equals $100,000. The payoff for each decision under each possible state of nature is identified, and then, depending on the criteria used, the decision is made.

Expected Value

Decision theorists view expected value as a reasonable criterion for decision making under risk—that is, when the probability data are available for the states of nature. Decisions under risk can be made using either an expected value or expected opportunity loss decision criteria. The expected value of a decision alternative is the sum of the weighted payoffs for the alternative. The weight for each payoff is the probability that the payoff occurs multiplied by the value.

In the risk management situation, for example, expected value might be used to compare the purchase of insurance for a particular exposure with retention. For the purpose of simplification, assume a loss exposure of $100,000, for which the probability is estimated to be .01. Assume further that insurance against loss from this exposure will cost $1500 annually. The expected value for the two possible choices (insure and retain), given the two possible states of nature (no loss and loss occurs), would be computed as follows:

	State 1 No Loss	State 2 Loss Occurs	Expected Value
Insure	−$1,500 × .99	−$1,500 × .01	$1500
Retain	$0 × .99	−$100,000 × .01	$1000

Applying the expected value criterion, we find that the decision to retain is the most attractive. Based on adding the expected values for the decision "Insure," the expected value of the decision is −$1500: (−$1500 × .01 + −$1500 × .99). For the decision "Retain," the expected value is −$1000. If the decision is made on the basis of expected value, since −$1000 is less than −$1500, retention will be selected as the appropriate decision. It may be noted parenthetically that, given an accurate estimate of probabilities, the expected value criterion will always suggest retention over transfer through insurance. This is because the premium for insurance includes not only the expected value of the loss, but the cost of operating the insurance mechanism as well. Assuming that the insurer has an accurate estimate of probability, the cost of insurance is *always* greater than the expected value of a loss.

Two problems are associated with the expected value model. The first is that the expected value model requires that the decision maker have dependable information on the probabilities. Although there is considerable literature that suggests otherwise, accurate probability estimates are not available as often as desired. Second, and more important, even when accurate probability estimates are available, actual experience can deviate from the expected value. Although the *long-run* expected value of the retention strategy is $1000, a loss of $100,000 could be sustained. If a $100,000 loss is unacceptable to management, the long-run expected value is irrelevant. Following the bankruptcy that results from the uninsured $100,000 loss, little consolation can be had from the fact that the retention strategy would have been the cost-effective strategy in the long run if the firm had survived.

Decision Making Under Uncertainty

When nothing is known about the probability of the possible outcomes, the expected value model cannot be used and a different approach is required. One such approach is the so-called maximin strategy, in which the decision maker attempts to maximize the minimum possible profits. The minimum payoff for each choice is listed, and the maximum of the minimums is selected as the alternative. For problems such as those in the area of risk management, in which payoffs such as costs are to be minimized, the maximin approach is reversed, in that the decision maker lists the costs associated with each decision. The recommended decision then corresponds to the minimum of the maximum costs, which gives rise to the term *mini-*

max. Minimax cost is a variation of the maximin profit strategy; it is used when the objective is to minimize the maximum cost.

Minimax Regret

A second strategy—minimax regret—measures the payoff under each of the decisions in terms of the "regret" that the decision maker will feel for each decision given each of the possible states of nature. Thus:

	State 1 *No Loss*	State 2 *Loss Occurs*	*Maximum* *Loss*
Insure	−$1,500	−$1,500	−$1500
Retain	$0	−$100,000	−$100,000

Because the choice that will yield the smallest maximum loss is transfer, this choice will minimize the maximum loss.

Minimax regret seeks to avoid "hurt." In this illustration, the implications of the greatest regret (the uninsured $100,000 loss) are so distasteful that the $100 premium is chosen as the choice in which the regret will be minimized. Although decision theorists have couched the argument differently, prudence suggests that a different strategy be adopted in those situations in which one of the possible states of nature associated with a given choice is unacceptable. In risk management, the premise on which the minimax cost or minimax regret strategies are based is the often quoted axiom that the probability that a loss may or may not occur is less important than the possible severity of the loss if it should occur.

Decision theorists propose use of the minimax cost strategy as a conservative approach when the probability is not known. Risk management maintains that even when there is a good estimate of the probability, the risk management objective requires avoiding the possibility of ruin, even when the probability is small.

The minimax cost or minimax regret strategies are appropriate when the maximum cost associated with one of the possible states of nature is unacceptable to management. This would be the case, for example, when the potential loss that might arise is beyond the firm's ability to bear; the situation in which one of the states of nature would result in bankruptcy and would result in failure to achieve the risk management objective.

Although the expected value strategy will always point to retention as the preferred approach, a *minimax* strategy will always suggest transfer. The obvious key, then, is to determine the situations in which each strategy should be applied. Fortunately, this question was addressed in the first textbook on the subject of risk management,[9] and the answer was provided in the form of three simple rules.

[9]Robert I. Mehr and Bob A. Hedges. *Risk Management in the Business Enterprise* (Homewood, Il.: Richard D. Irwin, 1963). Chapter 1.

THE RULES OF RISK MANAGEMENT

With development of risk management as a special functional area of management, increased attention has been devoted to formalizing its principles and techniques, so as to provide guidelines in the risk management decision-making process. One of the earliest contributions to the risk management field was the development of a set of "rules of risk management." These rules are simply common-sense principles applied to risk situations:

1. Don't risk more than you can afford to lose.
2. Consider the odds.
3. Don't risk a lot for a little.

Simple as they appear, these three rules provide a basic framework within which risk management decisions can be made. Unfortunately, they are sometimes misunderstood and are often neglected.

Don't Risk More Than You Can Afford to Lose

The first and most important of the three rules is "Don't risk more than you can afford to lose." Although it does not necessarily tell us *what* should be done about a given risk, it does tell us which risks about which *something* must be done. If we begin with the recognition that when nothing is done about a given risk the firm retains the possibility of loss arising out of that risk, deciding the risks about which something must be done boils down to determining which risks cannot be retained. The answer is explicitly stated in the first rule.

The most important factor in determining which risks require some specific action is the maximum potential loss that might result from the risk. Some losses can be financially devastating, literally wiping out the assets of the firm, whereas others involve only minor financial consequences. If the maximum potential loss from a given exposure is so large that it would result in an unbearable loss, retention is not realistic. The possible severity must be reduced to a manageable level, or the risk must be transferred. If severity cannot be reduced and the risk cannot be transferred, it must be avoided. In decision theory terms, "don't risk more than you can afford to lose" identifies the decisions for which the minimax cost or minimax regret strategy is appropriate.

The question of the size of a risk that can safely be retained is a complicated and technical one. The level of retention for individual risks is directly related to the total loss-bearing capacity, and this in turn depends on the firm's cash flow, liquid reserves, and ability to increase the cash flow in the event of an emergency. For every business firm, some losses can be met out of cash flow, others require dipping into cash reserves, and still others require borrowing. Some losses might be greater than all of these cushions could absorb. The amount that a firm "can afford to lose" will obviously vary from firm to firm. The level will also vary over time, depending on the resources that might be available at the time of a loss.

Consider the Odds

The individual who can determine the probability that a loss may occur is in a better position to deal with the risk than would be the case without such information. However, undue significance can be attached to such probabilities, for the probability that a loss may or may not occur is less important than the possible severity if it does occur. Even when the probability of loss is small, the primary consideration is the potential severity.

This is not to say that the probability associated with a given exposure is not a consideration in determining what to do about that risk. On the contrary, just as the potential severity of loss indicates the risk about which something must be done (that is, the risks that cannot be retained), knowing whether the probability that a loss will occur is slight, moderate, or quite high can help the risk manager decide what to do about a given risk (although not in the way that most people think).

A high probability is an indication that insurance is probably not an economical way of dealing with the risk. This results from the fact that insurance operates on the basis of averages. Based on past experience, the insurer estimates the amount it must collect in premiums to cover the losses that will occur. In addition to covering the losses, it must cover the costs of operating the company. Therefore, paradoxical though it may seem, the best buys in insurance involve those losses that are least likely to happen. The higher probability of loss, the less suitable is insurance as a device for dealing with the exposure.

Consider the relationship between the premium an insurer must charge for insurance and the average expected loss. Because the insurer must pay certain expenses in addition to the amount of losses, the premium is always greater than the average loss of those who are insured. Suppose, for the sake of illustration, that 100 property owners each own a building valued at, say, $10,000. If the probability of loss is 1 percent, 1 out of every 100 buildings will burn, and the loss will be $10,000. When this $10,000 loss is shared by the 100 owners, the cost of losses is $100. The insurer might add 50 percent of the average loss per insured to cover expenses, and charge each buyer $150. Now suppose that we increase the probability of loss to 10 percent. Ten buildings will burn, and the total losses will be $100,000. The average loss per insured is now $1000, and the insurer will charge $1500. If the probability of loss is 25 percent, 25 buildings will burn, the losses will be $250,000, and the insurer will charge $3750. As the probability of loss increases, so does the premium for a given dollar of protection.

In the most extreme case, if the probability of loss is 100 percent, all of the buildings will burn and total losses will be $1 million. The average loss per insured is $10,000, and the insurer would charge $15,000 for insurance on each $10,000 building. Obviously, the purchase of insurance under these conditions would be absurd, for the insurance buyers would be paying more in premiums than the value exposed to loss. Yet for the insurance-buying public as a whole, the cost of insurance is always greater than the average loss per insured. The higher the probability of loss, the higher will be the average loss per insured, and the higher will be the premium. In those instances where the probability of loss is very high, insurance buyers simply engage in trading dollars with insurance companies, paying premiums to collect those losses that are certain to happen.

The best buys in insurance are those in which the probability is low and the possible severity is high. The worst buys are those in which the size of the potential loss is low and the probability of loss is high. The most effective way to deal with those exposures in which the probability of loss is high is through loss-prevention measures aimed at reducing the probability of loss.

The second rule of risk management, "consider the odds," suggests that the likelihood or probability of loss may be an important factor in deciding what to do about a particular risk. But which risks? Logically, the use of probability in risk management decision making is properly limited to those situations in which the decisions to be considered are not in conflict with the first rule of risk management: "Don't risk more than you can afford to lose." For decisions in which one of the possible states of nature is ruin, the minimax cost or minimax regret strategies are appropriate.

Having limited our application of probability to situations in which ruin is not one of the possible outcomes or states of nature, it becomes clear that even in this limited set of decisions, situations in which probability theory is useful abound. Among the more fertile fields for analysis are the selection of deductibles, the choice of retrospective rating plans, and the decision to insure or retain the loss of physical damage to vehicles.

Don't Risk a Lot for a Little

The first rule provides guidance for those risks that should be transferred (those involving catastrophic losses in which the potential severity cannot be reduced), and the second rule provides guidance for those risks that should not be insured (those in which the probability of loss is very high). Still they leave a residual class of risks for which another rule is needed. This residual class is the subject of the third rule.

In essence, the third rule dictates that there should be a reasonable relationship between the cost of transferring risk and the value that accrues to the transferor. It provides the guidance in two directions. First, risks should not be retained when the possible loss is large (a lot) relative to the premiums saved through retention (a little). On the other hand, in some instances the premium that is required to insure a risk is disproportionately high relative to the risk transferred. In these cases, the premiums represent "a lot," while the possible loss is "a little."

Although the rule "don't risk more than you can afford to lose" imposes a maximum level on the risks that should be retained, the rule "don't risk a lot for a little" suggests that some risks below this maximum retention level should also be transferred. The maximum retention level should be the same for all risks, but the actual retention level for some exposures may be less than this maximum. As a matter of fact, since the rating structures vary according to different lines of insurance, it is advisable to set the actual level of retention for each risk individually on the cost-benefit basis implied in the third rule.

Risk Characteristics as Determinants of the Tool

Clearly, some risks should be transferred, and some should be retained. It is also clear that both transfer and retention are satisfactory in other cases, and that avoidance or reduction is necessary. What determines when a given approach should be used?

The characteristic of the risk itself determines which of the four tools of risk management is most appropriate in a given situation. Each of the tools should be used when it is the most appropriate and least expensive means of achieving the financial security that the business owner desires. Under what circumstances is each of the tools appropriate?

Based on the foregoing discussion, we can summarize a few general guidelines with respect to the relationship of the various tools and particular risks. The accompanying matrix categorizes risks into four classes, based on the combination of frequency (probability) and severity of each risk. Although real-world risks are not divided so conveniently, the model still provides a useful technique for analysis, and it is possible to formulate some general conclusions by considering the various combinations of frequency and severity in the chart.

	High Frequency	*Low Frequency*
High Severity		
High Severity		

When the possible severity of loss is high, retention is not realistic and some other technique becomes necessary. However, we have also noted that when the probability of loss is high, insurance becomes too costly. Through a process of elimination, we reach the conclusion that the appropriate tools for dealing with risks characterized by high severity and high frequency are avoidance and reduction. Reduction may be used when it is possible to reduce either the severity or the frequency to a manageable level. Otherwise, the risk should be avoided.

Risks characterized by high frequency and low severity are most appropriately dealt with through retention and reduction—retention because the high frequency implies that transfer will be costly, and reduction to reduce the aggregate amount of losses that must be borne.

Risks characterized by high severity and low frequency are best dealt with through insurance. The high severity implies a catastrophic impact if the loss should occur, and the low probability implies a low expected value and a low cost of transfer.

Finally, those risks characterized by low frequency and low severity are best handled through retention. They seldom occur, and when they do happen, the financial impact is inconsequential.

Although not all risks fit precisely into the categories shown in the chart, many will. When the probability or severity is not clearly "high" or "low," the principles may be modified by judgment.

The Special Case of Risk Reduction

Because insurance has traditionally been considered the major technique for dealing with risks, it tends to receive major attention, and because retention is clearly seen as an alternative to insurance, it also receives considerable notice. Unfortunately, because the direct benefits of loss prevention and control methods are often elusive and difficult to measure, sometimes the tendency is to slight this important technique. In the past, risk managers have sometimes encountered resistance from management with respect to expenditures recommended for loss-prevention measures.

From a theoretical perspective, decisions regarding the application of risk management techniques should be made on the basis of a marginal benefit-marginal cost rule. This means that from the viewpoint of minimizing costs, each of the techniques for dealing with risk should be utilized when that particular technique represents the lowest cost approach to the particular risk in question. In addition, a given technique should be used only up to that point at which the last dollar spent achieves a dollar reduction in the cost of losses or risk, and no further. However, this basic principle must sometimes be modified in the case of loss-prevention and control methods. Humanitarian considerations and legal requirements may dictate that loss-prevention and control measures go beyond the optimal marginal cost-marginal benefit point. For example, federal legislation in the form of the Occupational Safety and Health Act requires employers to incur expenses for job safety loss-prevention and control measures that might not be justified on a pure cost-benefit basis.[10]

RISK MANAGEMENT AND INSURANCE BUYING

Although insurance is only one of the techniques available for dealing with the pure risks that the individual or the firm faces, many of the risk management decisions culminate in a choice between insurance and noninsurance. Although the basic principles of risk management have already been discussed, it may also be useful to examine the application of a few of these principles to the area of insurance buying.

---

[10]Decisions with respect to loss prevention in connection with employee injuries have been greatly affected by OSHA. The Williams-Steiger Act, better known as the Occupational Safety and Health Act (OSHA), of 1970 established a new agency within the U.S. Department of Labor, the Occupational Safety and Health Administration, which is empowered to set and enforce health and safety standards for almost all private employers in the nation. There are mandatory penalties under the law of up to $1000 for each violation and optional penalties of up to $1000 for nonserious violations. Penalties may be assessed for every day that an employer fails to correct a violation during a period set in a citation from OSHA. In addition, an employer who willfully or repeatedly breaks the law is subject to penalties of up to $10,000 for each violation. Any willful violation of standards resulting in an employee's death, upon conviction, is punishable by a fine of up to six months' imprisonment, or $10,000. The maximum penalty under the law is life imprisonment for killing an OSHA inspector.

Common Errors in Buying Insurance

In general, the mistakes that most people make when buying insurance fall into two categories: buying too little and buying too much. The first, which is potentially the more costly, consists of the failure to purchase essential coverage, which can leave the individual exposed to unbearable financial loss. Unless the insurance program is designed to protect against the catastrophes to which the individual is exposed, an entire life's work can be lost in a single uninsured loss. Conversely, it is possible to purchase too much insurance, buying protection against losses that could more economically be retained. The difficulty in buying the right amount of insurance is compounded by the fact that it is possible to make both mistakes at the same time. Although most people spend enough to provide an adequate insurance program, too often critical risks are ignored, leaving gaping holes in the overall pattern of protection, while unimportant risks are insured, using valuable premium dollars that would be more effectively spent elsewhere.

Some insurance buyers turn the entire decision-making process over to an outside party, such as an insurance agent or broker. In a sense, they delegate the responsibility for both policy decisions and administration to this outside party. Although such a course of action may relieve the insurance buyer of the decision burden, it may not result in an optimal program. When the decisions involved in the purchase of insurance are delegated to an outside party, the tendency is to insure exposures that might be retained. An insurance agent does not enjoy being in a defensive position when a loss takes place, and when charged with the overall responsibility for the insurance decisions, he may decide to protect himself as well as his client by opting for more, rather than less, insurance. Although a competent agent or broker is a valuable source of advice, the basic decision rules should be made by the person or persons most directly involved, for these decisions are likely to involve large financial considerations over the long run, either in terms of premiums paid or losses sustained if hazards are not insured.

The Need for a Plan

The basic problem facing any insurance buyer is that of taking the best possible advantage of the available premium dollars. In order to obtain maximum benefit from the money expended, some sort of plan is needed. Otherwise, the tendency is to view the purchase of insurance as a series of individual isolated decisions rather than as a single problem, and there are no guidelines to provide for a logical consistency in dealing with the various risks faced.

A Priority Ranking for Insurance Expenditures   Such a plan can be constructed to set priorities for the allocation of premium dollars on the basis of the previously discussed classification of risks into *critical*, *important*, and *unimportant*, with insurance coverage designed to protect against these risks classified as *essential*, *important*, and *optional*.

1. *Essential:* coverage that protects against loss exposures that could result in bankruptcy. (Insurance coverage required by law is also essential.)

2. *Important:* coverage that protects against loss exposures that would force the insured to borrow or resort to credit.

3. *Optional:* coverage that protects against losses that could be met out of existing assets or current income.

The Large Principle—Essential Coverages First The primary emphasis on essential coverage follows the first rule of risk management and the axiom that the probability that a loss may or may not occur is less important than the possible size of the loss. Because the organization must of necessity assume some risks and transfer others, it seems only rational to begin by transferring those that it could not afford to bear. One frequently hears the complaint, "The trouble with insurance is that those who need it most are those who can least afford it." There is considerable truth in this statement. The need for insurance is dictated by the inability to withstand the loss in question if the insurance is not purchased. Thus, although it is true that those who need insurance are those who can least afford it, it is also true that they are the ones who can least afford to be without it. In determining whether or not to purchase insurance in a particular situation, the important question is not "can I afford it?" but rather "can I afford to be without it?"

When the available dollars cannot provide all of the essential and important coverage the individual or organization wants to carry, the question becomes where to cut. One approach is to assume a part of the loss in connection with coverage. This can be done by adding higher deductibles, thereby freeing dollars for other coverage that is desired. In many lines of insurance, full coverage is uneconomical because of the high cost of covering small losses. If coverage for small losses is eliminated through deductibles, the premium credits granted may permit the purchase of other important coverage.

Insurance as a Last Resort—Optional Coverages As we have seen, insurance always costs more than the expected value of the loss. This is because, in addition to the expected value of the loss (the pure premium), the cost of operating the insurance mechanism must also be borne by the policyholders. For this reason, insurance should be considered a last resort, to be used only when absolutely necessary.

It is in connection with this characteristic of insurance that many people fail to appreciate the appropriate function of insurance. The insurance principle should not be utilized for the purpose of indemnification for small relatively certain losses. These can more desirably be carried as part of a business's cost of production (or as one small cost to an individual of maintaining himself and his family). In many instances, these small, relatively certain losses can be eliminated from the insurance operation by excluding them or by using a deductible. Insurance companies, by providing indemnity for such small losses in their contracts, are as guilty of the misuse of the insurance principle as are the insureds who buy them.

There is nothing intrinsically wrong with optional coverage, but it is not a very good way to spend the limited number of dollars available for the purchase of insurance. If the individual's psychological makeup is such that protection against even the smallest type of loss is desirable, it is probably all right. The real problem with respect to such coverage is that the individual who insures against small losses often does so at the expense of exposures that involve losses that would be financially catastrophic. Although an individual or business firm might be expected to desire some optional coverage, such coverage should not be purchased until all important coverages have been purchased—and, of course, all essential coverage should be purchased before premiums are spent on the less critical coverage. In this way, the premium dollars spent will be spent where they are most effective—protecting first against losses that could result in bankruptcy, next against losses that would require resort to credit, and finally, when all other exposures have been covered, against risks that could be met out of existing assets or current income.

IMPORTANT CONCEPTS TO REMEMBER

tools of risk management
institutional reactions
instinctive reaction
cost-benefit analysis
utility theory
utility function
diminishing marginal utility
management science
decision making under
   certainty
decision making under risk

decision making under
   uncertainty
expected value
minimax regret
rules of risk management
don't risk more than you
   can afford to lose
consider the odds
don't risk a lot for a little
frequency
severity

Occupational Safety and
   Health Act (OSHA)
essential insurance
   coverages
important insurance
   coverages
optional insurance
   coverages
large loss principle
insurance as a last resort

QUESTIONS FOR REVIEW

1. Identify and illustrate the non-scientific approaches to risk management decisions.

2. What characteristics distinguish good decisions from bad decisions in risk management?

3. Describe cost-benefit analysis and explain how it can be useful in risk management decision-making. What are the difficulties in its use in risk management decisions?

4. Explain what is meant by the term management science and identify the major subdisciplines discussed in the text that are used in risk management decisions.

5. Describe the process by which decisions are made using an expected value strategy. To what extent is this strategy useful for risk management decisions?

6. Which of the decision models described in the text seems to you to be the most appropriate strategy for risk management decisions?

7. Three rules of risk management proposed by Mehr and Hedges are discussed in this chapter. List these rules and explain the implications of each in determining what should be done about individual exposures facing a business firm.

8. Why are loss prevention and control measures subject to different considerations than the choice with respect to other techniques for dealing with risk?

9. Explain how knowing the frequency and severity of loss for a given exposure to loss is helpful in determining what should be done about that exposure.

10. Identify the three categories into which insurance coverages may be priority ranked, indicating the nature of the exposure or risks to which each applies.

QUESTIONS FOR DISCUSSION

1. The principles and rules of risk management appear to be just plain common sense. In view of this fact, how do you account for the widespread violation of these rules in insurance buying today?

2. Explain the relationship, if any, among the statements: "Don't risk more than you can afford to lose," "Those people who need insurance most are those who can least afford it," and "Insurance should be considered as a last resort."

3. What are the implications of the observation that "the cause of a loss is less important than its effect?"

4. Do you agree or disagree with the text's position on the use of utility theory in risk management decisions? Explain the basis for your agreement or disagreement.

5. In an effort to reduce insurance costs, the risk manager of a medium sized manufacturing firm cancelled the property insurance on the firm's $8.5 million plant and equipment, for which the annual premium was about $265,000. Two years later when the action was discovered, the risk manager was called on the carpet by a horrified Vice President of Finance. "What were you thinking of?" demanded the VP. "What if we had had a loss?" "But," responded the risk manager, "we didn't have a loss. The fact that I saved the firm over half a million dollars in the past two years is proof that the decision was the right one." If you agree with the risk manager, help him convince the Vice President that he is right. If you disagree, help the VP convince the risk manager that he is wrong.

SUGGESTIONS FOR ADDITIONAL READING

Friedman, Milton and L.J. Savage, "The Utility Analysis of Choices Involving Risk," *Journal of Political Economy*, LVI (August 1948) 279–304.

Green, Mark R., and Oscar N. Serbein. *Risk Management: Text and Cases.* Reston, Va.: Reston Publishing Company, 1983. Chapter 3.

Mehr. R.I., and B.A. Hedges. *Risk Management: Concepts and Applications.* Homewood, Il.: Richard D. Irwin, 1974. Chapter 2.

————. *Risk Management in the Business Enterprise.* Homewood, Il.: Richard D. Irwin, 1963. Chapters 3, 11.

Ralston, August R., ed. *Risk Management Manual,* Santa Monica, Ca.: (loose-leaf service with monthly supplements), vol. 3, sections 1 and 2.

Slovic, Paul. "Assessment of Risk Taking Behavior," *Psychological Behavior,* 61 (1964) pp. 220–233.

Williams, C. Arthur, and Richard M. Heins. *Risk Management and Insurance,* 6th ed. New York: McGraw-Hill, 1989. Chapters 13, 14.

CHAPTER 4

Evaluation and Review of Risk Management Programs

CHAPTER OBJECTIVES

When you have finished this chapter, you should be able to

Describe the importance of the evaluation and review phase
of the risk management process.

■

Explain the two principal reasons for the evaluation and review phase
in the risk management process.

■

Identify and briefly describe the steps in the risk management audit.

■

Describe the general differences between a risk management audit
and an insurance survey.

■

Describe the general format of a risk management audit report.

■ Introduction ■

In theory, evaluation and review represent the final step in the risk management process. In actual practice, however, it is often the first step in managing risks. In fact, about the only time the risk management steps occur in the "textbook" sequence is in the case of a newly established organization that has no risk management program. Seldom does the risk manager begin with a clean slate. More often than not, the risk manager is faced with the responsibility of evaluating and reviewing an existing risk management program. In the real world, past decisions regarding program objectives, existing risks, and the importance of those risks have resulted in a particular type of risk management program. The risk manager comes onto the scene to find an existing program with an underlying set of objectives—formalized or not—and an implicit ranking of the exposures in terms of their importance. It is this existing program with which the risk manager is concerned. Throughout his or her career, the risk manager is generally occupied with the final phase of the process, evaluation and review, continually reevaluating the program's objectives, searching for new exposures or risks that may have been overlooked, and confirming the wisdom of past decisions.

As previously noted, evaluation and review are important to the risk management process for two reasons. The first reason is that things change. Risk management solutions that were appropriate in the past may no longer be appropriate. New risks emerge and old risks disappear. In some cases, a new risk results from developments outside the organization. The growth of litigation over employment discrimination and other employment-related practices during the late 1980s and early 1990s is an example.

A second, equally important reason for continuing evaluation and review of the risk management program is that mistakes are sometimes made. Exposures may be overlooked. The measures that were selected to address the risks may not have been the most appropriate, or they may not have been properly implemented. Persistent review of the program provides an opportunity to discover past errors, hopefully before they become costly.

General Evaluation and Review ■ ■ ■ ■ ■ ■ ■ ■ ■ ■ ■ ■ ■ ■ ■

How does one review a risk management program? Basically, by repeating each of the steps in the risk management process to determine whether past decisions were proper in the light of existing conditions and if they were properly executed. The risk manager reevaluates the program's objectives and repeats the identification process to assure, insofar as possible, that it was performed correctly. Then the manager evaluates the risks that have been identified and verifies that the appropriate decision was made on how to address each risk. Finally, the implementation of the decisions must be verified to make sure they were executed as intended. Thus, although the evaluation and review phase of the risk management process comes last in theory, it is a repetitive and continuing function for most risk managers.

EVALUATION AND REVIEW AS MANAGERIAL CONTROL

Managerial functions have traditionally been defined to include organizing, planning, leading and controlling. The evaluation and review phase of the risk management process is the managerial control phase of the risk management process.

The purpose of controlling is to verify that operations are going according to plans. Control requires (1) setting standards or objectives to be achieved; (2) measuring performance against those standards and objectives; and (3) taking corrective action when results differ from the intended results. Managerial control requires an appraisal of the reasons that operating results are different from those planned, and decisions as to what action is needed. In this context, it should be recognized that a disastrous loss need not occur for performance to deviate from what is intended. Because risk management deals with decisions under conditions of uncertainty, adequate performance is measured not only based on whether the organization has survived, but whether it would have survived under a different set of more adverse circumstances. The existence of an inadequately addressed exposure with catastrophic potential represents a deviation from the intended objective. It is this type of deviation from objectives that the risk management control process is intended to address.

Risk Management Audits ■■■■■■■■■■■■■■■■■■

Although evaluation and review is an ongoing process that is performed without interruption, the risk management program should periodically be subjected to a comprehensive review called a *risk management audit*. Most people are familiar with the term *audit* as it is used in the accounting field, where it refers to a formal examination of financial records by public accountants to verify the accuracy, fairness, and integrity of the accounting records. The term *audit* has a second meaning, which is any thorough examination and evaluation of a problem, that is implied in the term risk management audit. A risk management audit is a detailed and systematic review of a risk management program designed to determine if the objectives of the program are appropriate to the needs of the organization, whether the measures designed to achieve those objectives are suitable, and whether the measures have been properly implemented.

INTERNAL AND EXTERNAL AUDITS

As the term *risk management audit* is used by some writers, it is an analysis of the program conducted by someone from outside the organization. While risk management audits *may* be conducted by an external party, they may also be performed internally. When the risk management department has the required in-house expertise, it may establish a system for internal audits of the risk management function on a regularly scheduled basis. Although internal audits may lack the objectivity of external audits and are not substitutes for external audits, they can provide many of the same benefits. The benefits of internal audits will be maximized to the extent that they are conducted—to the extent possible—in the same way as an external audit. Because internal audits should follow the same procedure as an external audit, we will focus on the external audit.

Reasons for an Independent External Risk Management Audit

An independent (external) risk management audit has much to recommend it. Among the many advantages, the following are among the most important:

- Objectivity. The most important benefit of an external audit is the objectivity of the reviewers. Because external auditors bring a detached perspective to the review, they can be more objective about the decisions that have been made.

- Expertise. External auditors may bring expertise to the analysis that does not exist within the organization. This is particularly true when the firm being audited operates in a specialized field with unique exposures and the auditor has experience auditing organizations in that field.

Many external risk management audits are event-oriented. They are triggered by an acquisition or merger, or when a problem is encountered in a particular area. Losses or premiums in a particular area may appear to be out of control, or there may be difficulty in obtaining a particular line of insurance. Occasionally, a risk management audit is commissioned because management has reservations about the performance of the risk manager or the risk management department. In this case, the audit is a performance review of the risk manager.

Sometimes, an external risk management audit will be commissioned by the risk manager or the risk management department to support a change in the program or an initiative that needs to be sold to top management. A recommendation by an outside party often carries greater weight with the executive office than do the recommendations of the regular staff.

Although the services of an external consultant can be valuable in all of the above circumstances, risk management audits also make sense when there is no crisis. Ideally, a risk management audit should be viewed as a routine, integral part of the risk management process. A logical motivation for an external audit is to obtain a fresh, unbiased perspective. Expert, objective reviewing may uncover critical flaws in the program that have gone undetected by the risk manager because of his or her closeness to the program.

Selecting the External Auditor

External risk management audits are most often performed by individuals or companies engaged exclusively in risk management consulting activities. The management services divisions of some of the major public accounting firms offer risk management consulting services, including risk management audits. In addition some of the larger insurance brokerage firms have affiliated organizations that specialize in insurance audits. The major source of expertise for risk management audits is risk management consultants.

Selecting a consultant to perform the risk management audit requires care. There is little regulation of risk management and insurance consultants. Although about half the states require consultants to be licensed, requirements for entry into the field are modest. Although an examination may be required, it is generally no more difficult than the licensing examination for insurance agents.[1] Other states have no requirements for the licensing of consultants. A few states do not allow an individual to hold both an agent's or broker's license and an adviser's license.

Many auditors are members of the Society of Risk Management Consultants, a national association of independent risk management consultants. Members of this association are distinguished from other risk management consulting organizations in the fact that they may not be affiliated with an insurance company or insurance intermediary (i.e., agency or brokerage firm).

The consultant retained to conduct an external risk management audit should be an individual or organization with experience in the particular industry or segment of the economy to be audited. The experience should be confirmed by obtaining a list of the consultant's previous clients, who should be contacted to determine their satisfaction with the auditor's performance.

STEPS IN THE RISK MANAGEMENT AUDIT

Whether the evaluation and review of the risk management program is conducted internally or by an external auditor, the process will generally include the following steps:

1. Evaluate risk management objectives and risk management policy.
2. Identify and evaluate exposures to loss.
3. Evaluate the decisions for dealing with each exposure.
4. Evaluate implementation of risk treatment techniques selected.
5. Recommend changes for improvement in the program.

Review Risk Management Objectives and Policy

The first step in evaluating a risk management program is to review the risk management policy of the firm and determine the objectives of the program. The evaluation of a risk management program involves measuring that program against some standard, and the objectives of the program represent the logical standard for such an evaluation. Even when the organization does not have a formal written risk management policy, analyzing the existing procedures and pattern of protection can indicate the existence of a *de facto* policy.

Once the objectives of the program have been identified, they are evaluated to determine their suitability for the organization. This evaluation will generally include a review of the organization's finances and its ability to bear losses to which it is exposed. The goal here is to determine whether the objectives of the program are

---

[1]The following twenty-six states provide for licensing of risk management consultants, insurance consultants, insurance counselors, or insurance advisers: Alaska, Arizona, Arkansas, Connecticut, Delaware, Florida, Georgia, Idaho, Indiana, Iowa, Kentucky, Maine, Massachusetts, Michigan, Minnesota, Montana, Nebraska, New Jersey, New York, North Dakota, Oklahoma, Oregon, Texas, Vermont, Virginia, and Wyoming.

consistent with the organization's finances and ability to bear loss. When the risk management objectives are defective, new objectives are formulated and suggested to management for approval. Where practice is inconsistent with policy, the two should be reconciled, either by changing the objectives or changing the way in which the organization deals with its risks. In those instances in which the objectives are hazy, a recommendation should be made that the organization formalize its philosophy with respect to risk management by adopting a formal risk management policy.

Risk Identification

After the objectives have been defined and evaluated, the next step is to identify the organization's existing exposures. The techniques used to identify risks in a risk management audit are essentially the same as those used in the risk-identification phase of the risk management process.[2]

This step consists of an analysis of operations to determine the various exposures to loss. It serves as a check on the identification procedures that have been used in the past. When major exposures have been overlooked, the audit should identify the measures that may be used to address them and recommend the most appropriate of the alternatives. If a previously recognized exposure has been inadequately addressed, corrective measures should be recommended.

Consideration of Alternatives

Once the risks facing the organization have been identified and measured, the auditor considers the various approaches that may be used in dealing with each risk. This step should include a review of the extent to which risk avoidance and risk reduction have been used to deal with the organization's risks. It should also consider whether any of the retained risks ought to be transferred, or whether risks that have been insured might more appropriately be retained.

Evaluate Risk Management Measures that Have Been Implemented

The next step is to evaluate the past decisions on how each exposure is to be addressed and to verify that the decision was properly implemented. This step will include a review of both loss control measures and loss financing.

The review of the organization's risk control program should determine first, whether loss prevention and control measures have been applied to each of the exposures that were identified and, if not, why not. Although the possibility of risk control measures should be considered for all exposures identified, those exposures in which the potential severity is high should be a primary focus, followed by those exposures in which loss frequency is high. In some organizations, there is a tendency to focus on risk control measures in a particular area, while ignoring measures that might be applied in other areas. One way to assure that risk control measures have

---

[2]The tools and techniques used in the risk identification process are discussed in Chapter 6.

been considered for all exposures is to consider the exposures that have been identified one by one, considering the loss control measures that might be used to reduce the frequency of loss or loss severity. As in the case of insurance, loss control checklists can help the auditor to ensure that options for loss control measures have not been overlooked. Audits for risk control measures are discussed in the next section.

The review of risk financing measures should address the choices that have been made regarding transfer and retention. The main concern is that those risks that the organization could not afford to bear and that cannot be reduced to a manageable level have been transferred. The review of risk financing may also include a review of the contracts that have been arranged to effect the transfer of risk. With respect to insurance, the auditor first considers whether the insurance coverages that have been purchased are appropriate to the needs of the organization. When this is confirmed, the auditor analyzes whether the risks that should be transferred have actually been transferred. Additional considerations in auditing the insurance program are discussed in the next section.

SCOPE OF THE RISK MANAGEMENT AUDIT

A complete risk management audit, whether it is an internal or an external audit, should include a review of the entire risk management program. Although the ideal is a comprehensive review of all facets of the total risk management program, practicality often dictates which different phases of the risk management program should be audited separately. In practice, separate audits are often performed to address three separate aspects of the risk management program. The three broad areas that an audit may address are:

1. Risk Management policy and administration.
2. Risk control.
3. Risk financing (insurance).

The scope of the audit will depend in part on the expertise of the auditor and in part on the size and complexity of the organization being audited. In some cases, the risk management audit will address all three areas. In other instances, separate audits will be conducted for one or all of the three areas. The larger and more complex the organization, the more specialized the measures to address risks are likely to be. Because risk management consulting organizations differ in their expertise, it may be necessary to address the auditing of risk financing and risk control measures separately. In our discussion, we will review the comprehensive version of the risk management audit, understanding that the extent to which the risk management audit addresses insurance coverages and loss control measures can vary, depending on the terms of the engagement.

Audit of Risk Management Policy and Administration

An audit of the risk management policy and administration focuses on the broad features of the risk management program: the objectives of the program, the responsibility and authority of the risk manager, and the question of whether the policy and risk management organization are consistent with objectives.

Issues relating to policy are whether the objectives of the program have been clearly defined, whether they are suitable to the organization, and whether they have been formalized in a written risk management policy statement.

With respect to the administration of the program, the audit will consider the manner in which risk management personnel performs the risk management function. This will include a review of the risk management manual and risk management operating procedures. Pertinent questions involve the existence of a disaster plan, the structure and adequacy of risk-management records, and the general procedures used in identifying risks and implementing decisions.

Auditing the Risk Control Function

As in the case of the risk management audit, generally an audit of the risk control function is a comprehensive review of the measures that have been implemented to control risks. As discussed in greater detail in Chapter 9, risk control measures differ according to the types of loss at which they are aimed. The specialized nature of loss prevention and control for diverse types of exposures may dictate that specialized audits will be required for the evaluation and review of these measures. These may include:

- Safety audits.
- Security audits.
- Environmental compliance audits.
- Claim handling audits.
- Computer security audits.
- Property loss control audits.

Often, a single consultant will not have the expertise to address all of these areas, and it may be necessary to retain the services of several specialists. For each of the listed areas, there are professional consultants available to review and evaluate the measures that have been implemented to deal with the organization's risks. As in the case of risk management audits, generally when in-house expertise exists, the external audits should be supplemented by periodic internal audits.

In some areas, risk control services may be available to the organization in connection with insurance. Industrial safety programs offered by workers compensation insurers are typical. One area that is often addressed separately is employee safety. Although the insurance company that provides the organization's workers compensation insurance may provide loss control services, some managers question whether an insurance company has the proper incentives to control losses, especially when the insurance is written under a loss-sensitive rating program, in which the final premium fluctuates directly with the losses suffered. For this and other reasons, independent safety audits are among the most common external risk management audits.

Although risk management consultants will generally have the expertise to audit loss control measures in the areas where the application of such measures has been common (e.g., employee safety programs, property protection, and fleet safety programs), specialty consultants may be required for areas such as environmental compliance, employment-related practices, product liability exposure, and electronic data processing security. Among the other sources of safety audits, some insurance companies provide loss prevention and control services for nonpolicyholders on a fee basis. Some national insurance brokerage companies provide loss prevention and control services on a similar basis. The major providers of safety audit services, however, are independent safety engineering firms.[3] In choosing a consultant for auditing the risk control function, the most important consideration is the experience of the consultant in dealing with the exposures of the particular industry of which the organization is a member.

Audit of the Insurance Function

As suggested earlier, an audit of the insurance function may be conducted at two levels. At one level, the audit addresses insurance broadly, evaluating its role in the overall risk management program. This approach begins with risk management policy and objectives as a given, and focuses on whether the risk manager's decisions concerning what insurance coverages should be purchased is consistent with the objectives set forth in the risk management policy.

The second approach to auditing the insurance function is a more detailed review of the insurance program, which examines the coverages that have been purchased in greater depth, including a detailed analysis of the way in which the coverage is written. The insurance coverage in force is analyzed to determine whether it provides the protection that was intended by the risk manager. The risk manager's intent in purchasing insurance is to implement a decision to transfer part of the organization's risk to the insurer. The problem that may arise is that the transfer is accomplished by contract, and it is the contract that defines what risk is transferred, not the risk manager's intention. Because insurance contracts are complicated instruments with insuring agreements and exclusions designed to limit coverage to specific defined risks, the contracts must be reviewed to determine whether the risks the insurer has agreed to cover include all aspects of the risk the risk manager intended to transfer. In some situations insurance buyers discover that a risk that they thought had been transferred to the insurer is, in fact, excluded from coverage. Determining precisely what the insurance contract covers and what it does not is a demanding process, but it is an indispensable phase of both the risk management audit and the insurance survey.

The audit of insurance programs is more highly developed than are risk control audits or comprehensive audits. In fact, the risk management audit itself is, in some ways, patterned after a technique used by insurance agents long before the evolution of the risk management concept. This technique was known as an

---

[3]The annual directory of safety consultants, published in the October 9, 1995 edition of *Business Insurance*, lists 73 safety consulting organizations. The October 2, 1995 edition of *Business Insurance* lists 109 environmental compliance consultants. Assistance in locating safety auditing firms is available through the American Society of Safety Engineers, 1800 Oakton Street, Des Plaines, Illinois 60018-2187, (708) 692-4121.

insurance survey. Although the term *insurance survey* is used loosely within the insurance industry and so means many different things to different people, it originally had a definite and specific connotation. Namely, it was used as a term of art to describe a particular type of analysis and review of an insurance program. The following description, extracted from the training materials used by a large multiple-line insurer thirty-five years ago, captures the essence of the concept:[4]

WHAT IS AN INSURANCE SURVEY?

A complete Insurance Survey is a twofold project provided as a service by an agent or broker to an insured or a prospective insured. It consists of two divisions, each of which comprises several subdivisions. The producer, first of all, makes a thorough survey of the risk for the purpose of determining all exposures to which it is subject. He also takes note of any conditions in the risk which might be changed and thereby eliminate or reduce the hazards, whether they pertain to property loss or bodily injury. He then makes an exhaustive examination of all existing insurance, to see if it is written correctly and in a manner most favorable from the insured's standpoint. The final step in this part of the Survey is a comparison of the existing insurance with the disclosed exposures to discover whether or not loss from such exposures has been effectively blocked by that insurance.

The second part of the project is a comprehensive analysis, in writing, setting forth the details and conclusions developed by the survey. Although the manner in which this information is presented will vary, all of the phases covered in the first part will be dealt with to some extent in this second part. Each exposure will be pointed out and an estimation of its severity made. If there is no criticism of the existing insurance, this will be mentioned. If, on the other hand, errors are found, any shortcomings which are brought to light will be recounted.

The most important feature of the report will be the presentation of a complete insurance program and the necessary steps to be taken in order to achieve such a program. This, of course, is the goal toward which all the time and effort put into the project have been aimed. This is the "blueprint" from which the producer and the insured may work to build a bulwark against calamitous loss.

The description is surprisingly similar to what we now call a risk management audit. Obviously, however, there are differences, and it may be helpful at this juncture to identify those differences.

The definition of the insurance survey presented in the quotation makes specific reference to the agent's efforts to identify "conditions in the risk which might be changed and thereby eliminate or reduce the hazards." From this it seems clear that the insurance survey, properly executed, was never intended to focus on insurance alone; loss prevention and control recommendations were an essential part of the survey technique.

In what way, then, did the insurance survey differ from a risk management audit? Basically, in the same ways that insurance management differs from risk management. Although the insurance survey considered loss prevention and control mea-

---

[4]*Insurance and Suretyship Course,* Chapter 24, "Survey Selling," Education Department, Royal-Globe Insurance Companies, 1962.

sures as well as insurance, risk control measures are regarded primarily as auxiliary to the major tool of insurance. Also, it is noteworthy that retention and self-insurance are conspicuously absent from the description of the insurance survey. At the risk of overstating the case, it is probably accurate to say that the primary focus of the insurance survey was on the *adequacy* of the insurance coverage, rather than on its *propriety*. Because the insurance survey developed in the era before risk management concepts were widely discussed, the failure of practitioners to focus on retention is perhaps understandable. After all, no agent wants to be in a defensive position when a loss occurs. The major question addressed with respect to insurance in the survey is usually "Is there enough?" The risk management audit asks this question as well, but also asks regarding insurance "Is there too much?"

The insurance survey is still widely used by insurance agents and brokers. It may be called a survey, an insurance audit, or a *stewardship report*. A distinguishing characteristic is usually its detail. It consists of a review of existing insurance contracts to determine whether all needed forms of insurance have been included, whether the existing insurance policies are mechanically correct (that is, the names, addresses, amounts, and so on), whether the premium computations are correct, and whether the proper endorsements have been used. The primary focus of an insurance survey is on the adequacy of insurance coverage. The review seeks to determine if there are any uninsured exposures.

Naturally, a systematic approach to the analysis of insurance contracts is required. The person or persons analyzing the insurance coverage will often use standardized insurance policy checklists that list the possible endorsements and modifications to insurance policies that are possible. Although the details of the analysis differ from one line of insurance to another, the auditor usually follows a standard methodology for analyzing insurance contracts built around the following questions:

- Who is protected?
- What property is protected?
- Where is it protected?
- What perils are insured?
- What losses are covered?
- What locations are covered?
- What conditions suspend or limit coverage?

When analysis of existing coverages indicates inadequacies in the insurance protection in force, specifications will be prepared for substitute or replacement coverage suitable to the needs of the organization.

Comprehensive Audit Versus Functional Audit

Although a risk management audit is the most comprehensive, there is a place for audits that address a particular risk management function, such as safety audits and insurance surveys (insurance audits). In fact, insurance audits and safety audits are usually conducted more frequently than are complete risk management audits. Almost by definition, most insurance audits are external audits, and are usually conducted by insurance practitioners, although sometimes by risk management or insurance consultants.

Complete Audit Versus Special Problem Audit

Besides the possibility of separate audits to address policy and administration, insurance, and risk control, a comprehensive risk management audit should also be distinguished from consulting services that address a specific problem or situation. Occasionally, an organization may retain an outside consultant to review a specific area of the risk management program, such as the administration of the program, the insurance coverage, or the loss prevention and control program. In addition, a consultant may be retained to assist with a major decision for which the risk management department lacks expertise. This might include, for example, the preparation of specifications to solicit bids for the insurance program or the evaluation of the feasibility of self-insurance or a captive insurance company.

THE RISK MANAGEMENT AUDIT REPORT

Besides their common objectives, internal and external audits share another similarity—their formality. Evaluation and review are an ongoing part of the risk management process. The internal audit is distinguished from the continuing review process by its comprehensive nature and the fact that it culminates in a formal report. Unlike the continuing evaluation and review process that seeks to identify flaws whenever possible, the audit follows a standard procedure to produce a formal evaluation. Usually, the risk management audit will be formalized in a written report detailing the findings of the auditor. Where appropriate, the report will include written recommendations for change or modification in the program.

The Audit Report

The preparation of a written report of the risk management audit is only a small part of the audit process. It is also one of the most difficult parts for many persons. Actually, this need not be the case. Once the difficult steps of risk identification, analysis of exposures, and program design have been completed, all that remains to complete the process is to transmit the analysis to paper. With the advent of automated word processing systems, the process has become greatly simplified. Like attorneys and other professionals whose principal product is advice, persons engaged in risk management auditing have found ways to boilerplate their recommendations and to avoid reinventing the wheel in communicating with individual clients.

The risk management audit is complete only when the analysis and recommendations culminate in a written report to management, summarizing the findings of the analysis and making recommendations for improvement in the program.

Arrangement and presentation of the report may take many forms. It may begin with a complete picture of all the exposures, followed by a discussion of the measures that have been implemented to address the exposures. We prefer a somewhat different arrangement, in which each exposure is discussed, together with the measures that have been selected and implemented to address that exposure. Based on this approach, the risk management audit is divided into three basic parts: the executive summary, the body of the report, and a schedule of existing insurance.

Executive Summary   The first section of the report, the Executive Summary, includes an overall evaluation of the program and a summary of the recommendations that have been made throughout the body of the report. Recommendations for changes in the insurance program should include an estimate of the approximate cost and should refer the reader to the place in the body of the report in which the recommendation is discussed in greater detail. For example, a typical recommendation might state: "Purchase $5,000,000 umbrella liability policy. Approximate annual cost, $13,000. See page 22." The purpose of the Executive Summary, as its title implies, is to briefly summarize the recommendations without the explanation and justification, which are contained in the body of the report.

Body of the Report   The second section, the body of the report, consists of a narrative discussion of the various exposures facing the organization, the measures that have been adopted to address these risks, and the recommendations for change. Whatever the sequence used, the discussion of each exposure should treat four areas:

1. *The exposure to loss:* This is a brief explanation of the problem that must be dealt with.

2. *The existing solution:* This is a statement of the steps that have been taken in the past. When insurance has been used, a brief explanation of the existing coverage is included. When the audit addresses both risk control and risk financing, an observation of the application of each should be included for each exposure identified. If either of the techniques have not been applied to a particular exposure, the observation should indicate whether this is acceptable. If it is not, the subject should be addressed in the following section, which deals with remaining problems.

3. *Any remaining problems:* Any part of the exposure that is inadequately protected should be noted. For example, if the limits of coverage are inadequate, or if the scope of the perils insured against is not ideal, it should be noted. If loss prevention and control measures are inadequate, the deficiencies should be noted.

4. *Recommendations for change:* Here the report proposes the solution to the remaining problems that were noted under item 3 above.

Because the evaluation of a risk management program implies some standard against which the program is judged, this should be outlined in the introduction to the report. If the corporation has a formal risk management policy or formal policy with respect to insurance buying, this policy will serve as the standard. In the absence of a corporate policy, the classification of risks described in Chapter 3 might be used. Risks are classed as critical, important, and unimportant, and the insurance coverages designed to address these risks are classed as *Essential, Impor-*

tant, and *Optional.* This classification reinforces the notion that the potential severity of loss is the most important consideration in determining what should be done about a given exposure. It will also result in an allocation of available premium dollars that protects against the most important risks first.

Schedule of Existing Insurance When the audit includes a review of insurance coverages, a schedule of the existing insurance is included in the report. This schedule should list each policy in effect, the name of the company and agency handling the coverage, a brief description of the coverage, the expiration date, and the premium. It is designed to show, in one place, the total insurance program, together with pertinent facts about each of the coverages.

How Often?

A major question concerning risk management audits is the frequency with which they should be prepared. A distinction may be made between internal audits, conducted by the organization's own risk management personnel, and external audits. Because most businesses operate on a fiscal year budget, annual reviews are probably the norm for internal audits. An annual review of the organization's risk management program gives risk management personnel an opportunity to prepare a concise summary of their performance for management, and at the same time raises any critical issues that need to be addressed by the organization's policymakers.

The ideal frequency for external audits is less clear. A comprehensive audit of a major risk management program will involve significant costs. At the same time, there is clearly a benefit in having an outside organization review the risk management program to judge its suitability for the organization. Although there is no hard and fast rule, those engaged in the risk management consulting field generally recommend that an audit be performed about once every five years.

EXPERT SYSTEMS IN RISK MANAGEMENT AUDITS

Given the enormous amount of knowledge required to match complex insurance coverages with the risks of diverse businesses, it was probably inevitable that computer-based expert systems would eventually make their way into the risk management area. The variety of issues that must be considered, as indicated by the preceding discussion, makes risk identification a logical application of the *expert system* concept. As the term is generally used, an expert system is a computer program that acts like an expert consultant in diagnosing problems. Expert systems use a large database of knowledge relevant to the specific subject matter combined with structured rules of inference to draw conclusions.

The first expert system for risk management and insurance-related problem-solving was an integrated, industry-specific risk analysis software that combines risk identification features with insurance programming capability. The product, PS4, was developed for insurance agents and is marketed by Professional Software Systems, Inc. of Coeur D'Alene, Idaho. Running on a personal computer, the program is a tool for analyzing the risk exposures and insurance needs of over 620 specific industries, from accountants to zoos. The program is periodically updated to reflect changes in insurance coverages, new exposures, and additional risk considerations.

Although the key feature of the system, in the view of many users, is in risk identification, the system's capabilities are not limited. In fact, it was designed for insurance agents and has integrated components beginning with the risk identification survey, written proposal to a prospect, and applications to insurers for the various forms of insurance that the analytical phase indicates are needed. In the context of our present discussion, which deals with risk management audits and insurance surveys, the principal benefit of the PS4 system is its integration of functions. From the detailed, industry-specific risk identification questionnaires and checklists which are useful in identifying the organization's risks to the ability to generate written reports and proposals, PS4 parallels the evaluation and review phase of the risk management process.

RISK MANAGEMENT AUDITS AS GUIDES TO ACTION

The end result of the risk management audit should be an objective evaluation of the strengths and weaknesses of the risk management program. The risk management audit that discovers weaknesses in the program creates an opportunity to correct the flaws in the program and create a stronger program. Obviously, it will do the audited organization no good at all if a report is merely placed on the shelf "for future reference." While many of the discussions in an audit will provide a useful reference for years to come, most audit reports contain solid recommendations that are worthy of immediate implementation. Also, they normally contain suggestions for further investigation or consideration. The actions taken by top management after the audit has been completed will determine whether it has been worth its time and cost.

IMPORTANT CONCEPTS TO REMEMBER

risk management audit	de facto policy	expert system
insurance survey	stewardship report	safety audit

QUESTIONS FOR REVIEW

1. In what sense is the evaluation and review phase not the final step in the risk management process?
2. What are the reasons for the evaluation and review phase in risk management?
3. How, generally, does one conduct the evaluation and review phase of the risk management process?
4. Define what is meant by the term *risk management audit*.
5. Describe the steps in a risk management audit.

6. Evaluation implies some standard against which the risk management program is judged. What should be that standard and how should it be defined?

7. Describe the general differences between a risk management audit and an insurance survey.

8. What type of analysis is recommended for reviewing the manner in which insurance coverages have been written?

9. Why is the analysis of insurance coverages an essential part of the evaluation and review of a risk management program?

10. Identify and briefly describe the three broad facets of a risk management program that should be addressed by a risk management audit. Why are all three facets not addressed in some risk management audits?

QUESTIONS FOR DISCUSSION

1. How would you go about the process of selecting an external organization to perform a risk management audit?

2. What are the advantages of internal audits? What are the disadvantages?

3. Insurance audits are performed by internal staff, by external risk management consultants, and by insurance agents and brokers. What, in your opinion, are the advantages and disadvantages of insurance audits performed by each of these parties?

4. Which phase of the risk management program—policy and administration, risk financing, or risk control—requires auditing most frequently? Why?

5. Insurance agents and brokers analyze and review the risks of their clients on a regular basis. Some agents and brokers provide their clients with a written *stewardship report,* outlining the results of such reviews. To what extent do you believe that such reports are beneficial (a) to the client and (b) to the agency or brokerage firm? Why?

SUGGESTIONS FOR ADDITIONAL READING

Gallagher, Russel B. *Auditing the Corporate Insurance Function,* AMA Research Study 68 (New York: American Management Association, 1964).

Head, George L., ed. *Essentials of Risk Control,* 2nd ed., vol. I, Malvern, Pa.: Insurance Institute of America, 1989. Chapter 11.

Insurance and Suretyship Course, Chapter 24, "Survey Selling," Education Department, Royal-Globe Insurance Companies, 1962.

Levick, Dwight E. *Risk Management and Insurance Audit Techniques,* 3rd ed., Boston, Ma.: Standard Publishing Company, 1995.

Ralston, August R., ed. *Risk Management Manual,* Santa Monica, Ca.: (loose-leaf service with monthly supplements), vol. 3, section 14.

CHAPTER 5

Risk Management Objectives

CHAPTER OBJECTIVES

When you have finished this chapter, you should be able to

Explain why defining risk management objectives is a critical step
in the risk management process.

■

Describe the two broad classes into which risk management objectives can be divided,
and identify the objectives that may be established within each class.

■

Identify the primary risk management objective and explain why it is preeminent.

■

Describe the characteristics of an effective risk management policy.

⚎ Introduction ■■■■■■■■■■■■■■■■■■■■■■■■■■■■■

Now that we have examined some of the basic principles of risk management
and insurance buying, we can turn to the important considerations in the
design of a risk management program, the objectives of the program. Planning
is generally recognized as a critical phase in the management process, and
establishing objectives has become a standard managerial practice. Managing an
organization's risks requires establishing objectives for this function. It is therefore fitting that we examine some suggested objectives for the risk management
function.

As we noted, the first step in the risk management audit is to evaluate the
objectives of the program. Unless these objectives are clear, there may be wide
disagreement on the desirable courses of action, and this disagreement can

carry over into the audit itself. In the absence of reliable guidelines to direct them, the personnel charged with purchasing insurance face the heavy burden of deciding alone which risks to insure and which to retain. In this chapter, we examine the broad objectives of risk management and see how these objectives are translated into the organization's risk management policy. In addition, we examine some of the factors that should be considered in the design of the risk management policy.

The Need for Risk Management Objectives ■ ■ ■ ■ ■ ■

Most risk management programs evolve over a considerable period of time. As new exposures develop, measures are taken to deal with them. Sometimes insurance policies are purchased to protect against exposures that arise, and at other times loss-prevention measures may be implemented. When properties are acquired and as new exposures develop, insurance policies are added to protect against the possible losses that these exposures entail, or, in some cases, the decision may be made not to insure the exposure. Even when considerable effort is devoted to coordinating the expansion of a program, defects inevitably develop and the program becomes marked by gaps and inconsistencies. Many programs lack insurance coverage that should be considered essential, while at the same time they include coverage against risks that might more appropriately be assumed. In some cases, insurance is purchased against the entire possibility of loss, with either a small deductible or no deductible at all, whereas in other instances major risks are uninsured. Often, loss-prevention and control measures are totally neglected.

Usually, the gaps and inconsistencies in an organization's risk management program are easily correctable. But while existing defects can be corrected through changes in the program, such changes may result in only temporary improvement. A meaningful change, which will serve not only to correct defects but also to protect against recurrence of such deficiencies, requires other modifications. To correct existing defects and to guard against future inconsistencies, attention should focus on the cause of the defects. In most cases the defects stem from the absence of a clearly defined risk management philosophy.

Objectives for the risk management function are no less important than objectives for other divisions of the organization. Fundamentally, an organization's management is concerned that all personnel assigned decision-making functions perform their duty wisely and in the interests of the organization. Consequently, most organizations provide guidance to their decision makers in the form of objectives. From the organization's perspective, the term *objective* refers to long-range results that are to be achieved. The objectives for the risk management program should set forth the goals to be attained in the management of pure risks. These objectives then provide the framework for risk management decisions relating to specific risks.

Objectives of Risk Management ■ ■ ■ ■ ■ ■ ■ ■ ■ ■ ■ ■ ■

It is inadequate to talk about a single objective of risk management, just as it is inadequate to talk about a single objective of business or any other organization. Most organizations will, of course, have multiple objectives, and most functions within the organization will also have multiple objectives. An organization or a division within an organization may have one dominant mission, but other goals will also demand recognition. The production department, for example, may be responsible for producing goods of the quantity and quality laid down by a master production schedule, but it will be expected to produce those goods at a certain cost. The risk management function is no different. Among its multiple objectives, the following are the most common:

- To guarantee post-loss adequacy of resources.
- To minimize the cost of dealing with pure risk.
- To protect employees from serious injury and death.
- To meet legal and contractual obligations.
- To eliminate worry.

Whenever an organization has multiple objectives, the objectives sometimes conflict one with the other. Under such circumstances, a decision must be made as to which takes precedence. It is not enough, therefore, merely to identify the objectives of risk management; we must also identify the objective that transcends others, the objective that represents the risk manager's "key result area," or the objective that justifies the very existence of the risk management function. To identify the risk key result area, we must ask what precisely it is that the organization hopes to achieve through the risk manager's efforts. Why do organizations engage in risk management activities?

SELECTING THE KEY RESULT OBJECTIVE

Most writers suggest multiple objectives for the risk management function and as the two major objectives, usually include mitigating the effects of risk and minimizing cost. Williams and Heinz define risk management as "the *minimization of the adverse effects* of risk *at minimum cost* through its identification, measurements, and control."[1] A careful examination of this definition suggests that there are two objectives; minimizing the adverse effects of risk and minimizing the cost of doing so. Mehr and Hedges, in their classic *Risk Management: Concepts and Applications,* suggest that risk management has a variety of objectives, which they classify into two categories: pre-loss objectives and post-loss objectives. They propose the following objectives in each category:[2]

[1] C. Arthur Williams and Richard M. Heinz, *Risk Management and Insurance* (New York: McGraw-Hill, 1964), p. 11. Emphasis added.
[2] Robert I. Mehr and Bob A. Hedges, *Risk Management: Concepts and Applications* (Homewood, Ill.: Richard D. Irwin, 1974), p. 4.

Post-Loss Objectives	*Pre-Loss Objectives*
Survival	Economy
Continuity of operations	Reduction in anxiety
Earning stability	Meeting externally imposed obligations
Continued growth	Social responsibility
Social responsibility	

According to Mehr and Hedges:

> In the great majority of cases, the pre-loss objectives relate to economy and to avoidance of anxiety, while post-loss objectives relate to the completeness and speed of recovery. Together, they produce the dominant risk management goal; an economical pre-loss assurance that post-loss recovery will be satisfactory.[3]

This "dominant goal," like the purpose suggested by Williams and Heinz, has two parts. Where Williams and Heinz specify "minimizing adverse effects" and "minimum cost," Mehr and Hedges stipulate "economical pre-loss assurance" and "satisfactory post-loss recovery." Which goal takes precedence when the two are in conflict?

It is clear that whatever the objectives of the organization might be, they can be achieved only if the organization remains in existence. If the organization's existence is destroyed, of course none of the objectives, whatever they may be, is attainable. The first objective of risk management, like the first law of nature, is survival: to guarantee the continuing existence of the organization as an operating entity in the economy. In this sense, the primary function of risk management is to fill a supportive role in the organization's hierarchy of objectives. The primary goal of risk management is not to contribute directly to the other goals of the organization—whatever they may be.[4] Rather, it is to guarantee that the attainment of these other goals will not be prevented by losses that might arise out of pure risks. This means that the most important objective is neither to minimize costs nor to contribute to the profit of the organization. Nor is it to comply with legal requirements nor to meet some nebulous responsibility related to the firm's social responsibility. It can and does do all of these things, but they are not the principal reason for its existence. Rather, the principal objective of risk management is to preserve the operating effectiveness of the organization. For most organizations, this objective can be translated into the simpler goal, "to avoid bankruptcy."

Given the importance of the survival objective in the risk management function, and the uncertainty as to costs, we propose the following primary objective for the risk management function.

---

[3]*Ibid.*, p. 4.

[4]The other objectives of the organization may or may not include the objective of maximizing profit. The common belief that "the objective of a business firm is to maximize profits" is part of American folklore. It probably got started as an assumption to simplify economic theory. Because there is an element of truth in the statement, however, it became an easy way to talk about a complex problem. Maximizing profit may not be the objective of the organization. On the other hand, even when the objective is not to maximize profit, it is clear that a business firm must cover its costs if it is to survive and must also generate a return on the investment of its owners if it is to attract and retain capital.

The primary objective of risk management is to preserve the operating effectiveness of the organization; that is, to guarantee that the organization is not prevented from achieving its other objectives by the losses that might arise out of pure risk.

The risk management objective must reflect the uncertainty inherent in the risk management situation. Because one cannot know what losses will occur and what the amount of such losses will be, the arrangements made to guarantee survival in the event of loss must reflect the worst possible combination of outcomes. If a loss occurs and, as a result, the organization is prevented from pursuing its other objectives, it is clear that the risk management objective has not been achieved. Though not immediately obvious, it is equally true that the risk management objective has not been achieved when there are unprotected loss exposures that could prevent the organization from pursuing its other objectives should the loss occur, even if the loss does not occur. For this reason, the objective refers to losses that *might* arise out of pure risks.

OTHER OBJECTIVES

In addition to survival, to which we assign primacy among the objectives of risk management, there are a number of subsidiary objectives, some of which may conflict with the first objective and with each other.

Economy

The first of the subsidiary objectives of risk management is economy. Here, the goal is to reduce the cost of dealing with pure risks to the lowest level possible, consistent with the first objective of survival. It goes without saying that economy should not be achieved at the cost of adequate provision for potentially catastrophic losses. Although Mehr and Hedges classify economy as a pre-loss objective, there are instances in which economy—the cost of dealing with risk—can be a post-loss objective as well. Many loss reduction measures are implemented after the loss has occurred, and the decisions that are made at this time can have an impact on the ultimate cost of the loss and on the cost of dealing with risk.

Reduction in Anxiety

The objective of reducing anxiety, which Mehr and Hedges refer to as the objective of a *quiet night's sleep,* refers to the peace of mind that comes from the knowledge that appropriate measures have been taken to address adversity. When potentially catastrophic exposures remain unprotected, or when management simply does not know whether such exposures have been addressed, the uncertainty and mental unrest can distract managers from other considerations. In the extreme, worry and discomfort that arises from uncertainty regarding the survival of the organization can have a deleterious effect on the health and well-being of the organization's management. Worry drains energy—energy that would be more productively employed in other channels. The peace of mind that comes from the security of a well designed and executed risk management strategy allows managers to direct their energies toward growth and profitability.

The objective of a quiet night's sleep refers to the peace of mind not only for the risk manager, but for the organization's other executives, for the board of directors, and for stockholders. It can even extend to parties outside the organization, such as creditors, suppliers, and consumers. As noted in Chapter 1, customers, suppliers, and creditors prefer to do business with a firm whose prospects for survival are good, as compared with a firm whose survival is questionable. It naturally follows that these parties will prefer to do business with firms that have arranged to deal with the threats to their survival.

Earning Stability

The goal of stable earnings stems from the effect that wide variations in earnings can have on owners and third parties. Stockholders prefer stable earnings to earnings that fluctuate widely. Because investors will generally prefer a stable flow of income, risk management can also contribute to the firm's overall performance by reducing variations in income that might result from losses associated with pure risks. This is done in several ways, as discussed later in the text. Minimizing fluctuations in income that result from losses associated with pure risk aids planning and is a desirable goal in itself. In addition, reducing the variation in income can also help to maximize the tax deductions for losses and minimize the taxes on profits. Because uninsured losses are deductible only to the extent that they may be offset against earnings, a firm's long-term tax burden will be lower when earnings are relatively stable over time. Although the *Internal Revenue Code* makes provisions for carrying losses back and forward as charges against past and future profits, the provision is subject to limitations that can result in the loss of a large deduction that exceeds the taxable income in the carry-back and carry-forward periods.

Continued Growth

Maximizing profits is not always a dominant goal in an organization. Among the other goals that are often mentioned in corporate objectives is growth. For an organization with a record of strong growth, the ability to continue that growth may be among the organization's most important goals. When growth is an important organization goal, protection against threats to that growth is an important risk management objective. Properly conceived and executed risk management strategies can facilitate continued growth in the event of a loss that might otherwise threaten that growth.

Meeting Externally Imposed Obligations

The objective of meeting externally imposed obligations relates to the organization's relationships with other organizations and with the state. Many of the contracts that are used in business relationships deal with the question of who will be responsible for losses under specified conditions. Creditors, for example, generally require that the borrower secure insurance to protect property that is pledged as collateral. Contracts with provisions of this type create an obligation to an outside party that the risk management process must address. In addition to the obligations that arise under contracts, the organization may also have obligations that are imposed by law. State and federal laws may require that organizations engaged in certain types of activities purchase specified forms of insurance. Common carriers, for example, are required by state and federal laws to purchase automobile liability insurance and also insurance that covers the property being transported. All states impose obligations on employers to compensate workers who are injured in the course of their employment and require that the employers insure this obligation or qualify as a self-insurer. Other statutes require safety measures designed to protect employees or the general public.

Social Responsibility

Mehr and Hedges classify social responsibility as both a pre-loss objective and a post-loss objective. The pre-loss aspect of social responsibility relates the variety of social obligations facing the firm because of its relationship to its employees, to other organizations, and to society in general.

The loss prevention and control measures that are an integral part of the risk management process produce socially desirable benefits. To the extent that these measures prevent the destruction of assets or injury to individuals, society benefits. In addition, when a firm goes bankrupt, employees as well as owners suffer. If appropriate risk management strategies protect the organization against catastrophic losses, bankruptcies are avoided and the disruptions caused by bankruptcies are also avoided.

The objective of social responsibility often conflicts with the objective of economy.

Measuring Attainment of Objectives

One problem in connection with all of the objectives is in determining whether or not they have been achieved. With respect to the first objective—survival—it is possible that a firm will survive merely because the risk management program is never tested. A firm that has neglected important exposures may be fortunate and never suffer a loss in an unprotected area. The measure of the adequacy of a risk management program is not whether the organization survives, but whether it could have survived under a different set of conditions.

QUANTITATIVE OBJECTIVES

Ideally, objectives should be quantifiable whenever possible. Although none of the objectives we have discussed thus far is quantifiable, many risk management departments have established quantifiable objectives. Several objectives might be considered. One is the total amount spent on insurance premiums. The problem here is that the level of insurance expenditures is sometimes influenced by factors over which the risk manager has little or no control—primarily the cyclical nature of the insurance industry and the intensity of the competition in the property and liability insurance field. Insurance premiums may fall, without any effort on the risk manager's part. Similarly, they may increase through no fault of the risk manager.

A better subject for quantitative objectives is the number of accidents or injuries in areas toward which loss-prevention and control measures have been directed. As discussed in Chapter 26, the Occupational Safety and Health Administration publishes annual statistics on injury rates by industry. These and the organization's past losses provide useful benchmarks for establishing quantitative goals in the area of employee injuries.

Another measure of performance that some firms have used as a performance standard, if not an objective, is the cost of risk, which is the total expenditures for risk management, including insurance premiums paid and retained losses, expressed as a percentage of revenues. RIMS publishes annual studies on the cost of risk, which makes it convenient for the risk manager to compare the risk management costs of the organization with other firms in the same industry. Although the cost of risk varies from industry to industry, it generally averages something in the neighborhood of 1 percent of revenues. (For a firm whose net profit represents 10 percent of revenues, the cost of risk represents about 10 percent of profit.) As in the case of insurance premiums, the cost of risk may fluctuate because of factors over which the risk manager has no control. Still, it is a useful standard when properly interpreted. It can also serve as the basis for a risk management objective relating to cost.

VALUE MAXIMIZATION OBJECTIVES

At least one scholar has argued that the ultimate goal of risk management is the same as the ultimate goal of the other functions in a business—to maximize the value of the organization. Neil Doherty suggests that the objective of management generally, and therefore the objective of the managers to whom responsibilities have been delegated (including the risk manager) is value maximization.[5] As we noted in Chapter 1, modern financial theory suggests that this maximized value is reflected in the market value of the organization's common stock. According to this view, risk management decisions should be appraised against the standard of whether or not they contribute to value maximization. It is a view with which it is difficult to disagree. It is also a view that is not inconsistent with the objectives as outlined above. With limited exceptions, all of the objectives discussed above do, in one way or another, contribute to value maximization. The difference is specificity. Value maximization is the ultimate goal of the organization, and is a reasonable standard for appraising corporate decisions in a consistent manner. At the same

[5]Neil A. Doherty, *Corporate Risk Management*, (New York: McGraw-Hill Book Company, 1985), Chapters 1 and 2.

time, the value maximization objective has some limitations. The first is that it is relevant primarily to publicly held firms whose stock is publicly traded.

RISK MANAGEMENT'S CONTRIBUTION TO THE ORGANIZATION

Risk management can contribute to the organization's general goals in several ways. The first and most important way is in guaranteeing, insofar as possible, that the organization will not be prevented from pursuing its other goals as a result of losses associated with pure risks. Because survival is a prerequisite to value maximization (and to virtually everything else), the primary contribution of risk management is in assuring that the organization is not prevented from pursuing value maximization (and other objectives) by the losses that arise from pure risks. If risk management made no contributions other than guaranteeing survival, this alone would seem to justify its existence. But risk management can contribute to corporate and organizational goals in other ways.

Risk management can contribute directly to profit by controlling the cost of risk for the organization; that is, by achieving the goal of economy. Since profits depend on the level of expenses relative to income and to the extent that risk management activities reduce expenses, they directly increase profits. There are several ways in which risk management activities can directly affect the level of costs. One, of course, is in the area of insurance buying. To the extent that the risk manager is able to achieve economies in the purchase of insurance, the reduced cost will increase profits. In choosing between transfer and retention, the risk manager will select the most cost-effective approach. This means that expenses for risk transfer will generally be lower in organizations where the choice between transfer and retention considers the relative cost of each approach.

Risk management can also reduce expenses through risk control measures. To the extent that the cost of loss prevention and control measures is less than the dollar amount of losses that are prevented, the expense of uninsured loss is reduced. In addition, since loss prevention and control measures can also reduce the cost of insurance, risk control has a dual effect on expenses. Risk control measures that reduce the cost of losses include those measures that prevent losses from occurring.

In addition to the reduction in expenses associated with losses, risk management can, in some instances, increase income. The ability to resume operations quickly following damage to the organization's assets, for example, will minimize the loss of income that would otherwise be sustained by the organization.

It can also be argued that when the pure risks facing an organization are minimized, through appropriate control and financing techniques, the firm has greater latitude in the speculative risks it can undertake. Although it is useful to distinguish between pure and speculative risks with respect to the manner in which they are addressed and the responsibility for dealing with them, there are inevitable tradeoffs between pure and speculative risk in the overall risk portfolio of an organization. It has been argued that the total amount of risk that an organization faces is important, since firms with higher total risk are more likely to find themselves in financial distress. When the organization faces significant pure risks that cannot be reduced or transferred (or that simply have not been reduced or transferred), its ability to bear speculative risk is reduced. By managing the amount of pure risk, risk management increases the firm's ability to engage in speculative risks.

Risk management can also permit an organization to engage in activities that involve speculative risk by minimizing the pure risks associated with such ventures. Consider, for example, the organization contemplating an entry into international markets. This decision will create both pure and speculative risks for the organization. If the combination of pure and speculative risks exceeds the risk threshold that management is willing to accept, the international venture may be abandoned. If, on the other hand, the risk manager can reduce the level of pure risk, the aggregate pure and speculative risk may be reduced to a level that management finds acceptable. To illustrate, suppose the corporation's top management is considering setting up a subsidiary in a politically troubled country. The threat of expropriation may appear to be too great and might cause management to reject the opportunity in favor of a safer but less profitable alternative. However, if the risk manager reports that political risk insurance is available and reasonably priced, management may decide in favor of the opportunity and thereby generate an increased revenue and profits. The risk manager, who theoretically is responsible for managing all pure risks and can choose from many alternative risk treatment methods, is also in a position to contribute substantially to the operating results of the corporation.[6]

The Risk Management Policy ■ ■ ■ ■ ■ ■ ■ ■ ■ ■ ■ ■ ■ ■ ■

A policy is a general guide to action. It is a standard organization plan that translates objectives into more specific guidelines. Although a policy does not tell a person exactly what to do, it does point out the direction to go. Some of the more familiar policies common in business are "we sell only for cash," or "we promote from within." In each instance, some important aspect of a recurring problem has been singled out and a guide established for dealing with it. Just as the organization needs a formal policy with respect to its other activities, a risk management policy can help provide guidance for the risk manager and the risk management department.

In practice, policies vary considerably in precision and in the degree of guidance they offer. In some cases, they constitute carefully drawn rules that are to be followed in all cases; in other instances, they are general guides to action which leave the operating manager considerable discretion. The same is true with respect to risk management policies.

THE NEED FOR A RISK MANAGEMENT POLICY

The first step in designing a proper risk management program is for management to formalize its philosophy with respect to the role of insurance in the organiza-

---

[6]See Marshall W. Reavis, "The Corporate Risk Manager's Contribution to Profit," *The Journal of Risk and Insurance*, XXXVI, No. 4 (September 1969), pp. 473–479.

tion's overall risk management program by identifying the objectives of the program. Once the objectives have been identified, they should be operationalized through the adoption of a formal risk management policy. Such a policy should, among other things, outline the exposures to be insured and those to be retained, so that dangerous gaps do not develop in the future.

For rather obvious reasons, the development of a risk management policy cannot be done by someone outside the organization. Major policy decisions related to insurance should be made by the highest policy-making body in the organization—such as the Board of Directors—because these decisions are likely to involve large financial considerations, either in terms of premiums paid over the long term or risks assumed if hazards are not insured. In addition, it is the Board of Directors and the professional managers of the firm, after all, who are responsible for preserving the organization's assets.

A risk management policy statement of the type suggested here is of immeasurable value in future insurance decisions. In the absence of some sort of reliable guidelines, the individuals who are charged with responsibility for purchasing insurance and the insurance agents who act as advisers on insurance matters are faced with multiple choices and decisions. Each of these decisions must be individually considered and settled, and perhaps defended at some time in the future. Since neither the firm's risk manager nor the agents want to be in a defensive position when a disaster strikes, they tend to protect themselves, as well as the firm, by recommending more rather than less insurance, and they wait for explicit instructions before taking any action that will reduce the level of existing protection. By providing guidance for those responsible for programming and buying the firm's insurance, a formal risk management policy statement will provide the basis for achieving a logical and well-balanced program.

DEVELOPING A RISK MANAGEMENT POLICY

As we have noted, determining the risk management policy for a particular organization involves decisions that can be made only by the management of that organization. In designing the risk management policy, several important factors need to be decided.

Basic Objectives of the Risk Management Program

Initially, we can probably agree on the basic purposes of a risk management and insurance program. We have suggested that the first objective should be to preserve the operating effectiveness of the organization: to make sure that the organization is not prevented from achieving its other objectives by the pure risks facing the organization and the losses that may arise from these risks. Implied in this objective is avoidance of financially catastrophic losses that would impede the organization's basic functions.

An equally important objective is the humanitarian goal of protecting the organization's employees from accidents that might result in death or serious injury. Subsidiary goals may focus on costs, the preservation of public relations, and so

99

on. Although broad general goals such as these are valuable as an initial point of departure, to be really useful the risk management policy must be more specific, specifying maximum retention limits per area of exposure, so as to provide guidance to the risk manager with respect to which risks are to be transferred and which are to be retained. The greatest gaps in most insurance programs arise from the failure to recognize that all risks that could result in a given dollar amount of losses are equally important. This shortcoming can be overcome by specifying maximum risk retention limits.

The Maximum Retention Limit

A maximum retention limit should be set for each area of exposure, specifically delineating the exposures to loss that will not be retained. Setting this limit is one of the most difficult decisions in formulating a risk management policy, but it is a decision that must be made if extreme risks are to be avoided.

The question of the size of risk that can be safely assumed is a complicated and technical one. The basic philosophy of risk management dictates that an organization should assume risks as large as it can afford. The amount that a particular organization can afford depends, of course, on its cash flow, liquid reserves, and the availability of funds from outside the organization in the event of an emergency. Determining the maximum amount of loss that can be absorbed safely requires measurement of the cash flows and determining the possibility of increasing those flows.

For a business firm, the cushion available to absorb losses consists of the assets of the firm (existing assets and future income), credit, and claims against others that may arise out of the loss. It is the available funds from whatever source, that can be depended upon in the event of loss. Obviously, the ability of any organization to absorb loss is enhanced by the availability of liquid assets earmarked as a reserve for contingencies. Because the operating budgets of many firms do not provide a wide margin of cash to cover irregular losses, some risk managers deem it advisable to establish an uninsured loss reserve fund. The existence of such a fund helps to guarantee the availability of assets in the event of a catastrophic loss or a series of uninsured losses. At the same time, it gives the firm greater flexibility in its insurance-buying decisions. Uninsured loss reserve funds are discussed in greater detail in Chapter 14. Suffice it to say here that the existence and size of such a fund are important determinants of the maximum retention limit established in the risk management policy.

In the case of public bodies, such as municipalities or other governmental entities, which are not profit-making organizations, when uninsured losses exceed available resources the entity must go to the source of its revenue—principally the taxpayers—for funds to meet the loss. Although it may be possible under some circumstances to defer increasing taxes by substituting an increase in debt, this of course simply postpones the increase. Furthermore, many states place statutory limits on the amount of debt that a public entity may incur, usually expressed as some percentage of the assessed valuation of property within the municipality. This means that in the absence of cash reserves and without insurance, the burden of loss may fall immediately on the taxpayers. Although the ability to levy taxes is a potential source of funds and might conceivably be considered part of the city's loss-bearing capacity in setting a maximum retention level, it would seem that elected and appointed officials should prefer to avoid increasing taxes to meet uninsured losses whenever possible. If the ability to levy additional taxes is considered in establishing the maximum retention level, some reasonable limit should be placed on the extent to which this source of funds will be considered. For example, a maximum permissible tax increase might be set at 5 or 10 percent.

After careful consideration of these various factors, the organization should select an aggregate loss-retention level, indicating the total amount of uninsured losses that it could bear in a given year. Because cash flow will vary over time, this aggregate retention level might also be specified on a variable basis. For example, a given organization might establish a maximum retention level for all retained losses during any fiscal year as the larger of, say, $50,000 or 10 percent of the firm's annual working capital.

Converting the aggregate level to a maximum retention level per area of exposure cannot be scientific under most circumstances, and any level selected will be somewhat arbitrary. However, since there is no limit to the number of occurrences that may take place in a given time period, it does not seem unrealistic to specify a maximum retention limit per area of exposure of one-fifth to one-tenth of the annual aggregate limit.

Once the maximum retention level per area of exposure has been established, the person or persons charged with responsibility for the risk management policy should take whatever steps are necessary to guarantee that the organization is not exposed to losses in excess of the specified amount. This may involve risk control efforts that reduce the potential severity of loss, or it may involve the transfer of exposures that might result in loss in excess of the maximum retention limit.

One additional point should be made in order to avoid confusion. The maximum retention limit stipulates that those risks that might result in loss in excess of a specified amount will be transferred. It does not necessarily imply that all exposures that might result in losses below this amount will be retained. As a matter of fact, many lesser exposures will probably be transferred as well. The essential point here is that all of the catastrophic exposures will be transferred.

Minimum Retention Level

The question of insurance coverage for those loss exposures that may result in loss below the maximum retention level can be determined on a case-by-case basis, but in order to reduce the number of marginal decisions that must be made in programming and purchasing insurance coverages, we believe that it is also advisable to set a minimum level of retention or assumption—a dollar level of loss below which insurance will not be purchased. The minimum level of assumption per area of exposure might be set at $1000, for example, which would mean that insurance would not be purchased to protect against any risk in which the potential exposure is less than $1000 and that insurance coverages would include a deductible of at least $1000, whenever possible. Exception would be made in those instances in which the coverage in question does not lend itself to including the deductible or where the insurance coverage is required by law or by contract. This retention level would be a minimum, and in some instances the level of retention would be higher and could range as high as the level selected as the maximum retention level.

Under this scheme, the level of risk retention for various areas of exposure would not necessarily be the same. In fact, because of differences in the rating structures for different lines of insurance, it is probably advisable to determine the level of retention for each of the lines on the basis of the premium credits available for including a deductible. However, setting maximum and minimum retention levels should help to introduce an element of logical consistency into the insurance program and avoid assumption of catastrophic exposures, while at the same time purchasing insurance against losses that would be inconsequential in their financial impact. In addition, it should provide sufficient flexibility to guarantee the selection of the most appropriate deductibles from a cost perspective.

Funding the Retention Program

When the risk management policy specifies a maximum retention limit, it may also be reasonable to address the question of funding for retained losses. Given the formulation of a rationally conceived maximum retention level per area of exposure, there remains the problem of accounting for the losses that arise from retained risk and guaranteeing the availability of funds to meet the losses that occur. Often this will require that the retention program be supported through some form of tangible reserves. It should be recognized that a certain amount of uninsured loss is likely to occur under any insurance program, and when the program has been designed with the intentional retention of those risks that are likely to produce only moderate losses, the likelihood of uninsured losses occurring is even greater. When an organization elects to retain some of its risks through elimination of previously carried insurance or through increased deductibles, appropriations should be made for the uninsured losses that will probably take place.

Although many organizations make budgetary allocations to cover some uninsured losses, in most instances these allocations are on a year-to-year basis, with no carryover of unexpended funds and without a reserve for unexpectedly large losses. This practice ignores the wide variations in experience that may occur over time.

Prudence sometimes suggests that an organization embarking on a risk-retention program consider establishing a reserve for uninsured losses. This fund can be established through an initial appropriation and can be increased annually until it reaches a level equal to the maximum annual retention limit established under the risk management policy (for example, 1 to 2 percent of the annual budget). If chargeable losses deplete the balance of the fund below the specified target level, additional appropriations should be provided, not to exceed some predetermined amount. The fund may also be augmented through the addition of any allocations for uninsured losses that are not required to cover losses during that fiscal year.

The existence of such a fund should guarantee the availability of assets in the event of a catastrophic loss or a series of uninsured losses, and at the same time give the organization greater flexibility in its insurance-buying decisions.

Employee Injuries

As noted earlier, the risk management policy should specifically address corporate policy regarding possible injuries to employees. It should state without qualification the corporation's policy to provide safe working conditions for its employees and the idea that under no circumstances will the risk of serious injury or death of employees be considered an acceptable risk. Besides reflecting management's attitude, this statement can serve an additional function. The Occupational Safety and Health Administration has the power to levy fines against employers for violation of the Occupational Safety and Health Act standards. Under some circumstances, the amount of the fine may be reduced upon a showing that the employer acted in good faith in attempting to comply with the provisions of the law. Although a statement of corporate policy in the risk management policy will not in itself guarantee a reduction in a fine, it may serve as part of an overall pattern demonstrating good faith.

SAMPLE RISK MANAGEMENT POLICY STATEMENT

As an illustration of the general nature of a risk management policy, a sample risk management policy statement follows this section. The retention limits in this policy statement are arbitrary, but they indicate the basic approach. Individual organizations would, of course, modify the retention levels (and perhaps other aspects of the statement) to suit their own circumstances.

Whatever limits are finally selected, the risk management policy should then become the framework within which insurance decisions and other risk management decisions are made. Once the risk management policy has been adopted, it should be reviewed periodically in light of the loss experience and accumulated loss reserves to assure that changing conditions are taken into consideration.

SAMPLE RISK MANAGEMENT POLICY

1. It shall be the policy of Iowa Pork Packers, Inc. to avoid, reduce, or transfer the risk of loss arising out of property damage, legal liability, and dishonesty in all cases in which the exposure could result in loss that would bankrupt or seriously impair the operating efficiency of the firm.

2. It shall be the policy of Iowa Pork Packers, Inc. to provide safe working conditions for its employees. Under no circumstances will the risk of serious injury or death of employees be considered an acceptable risk.

3. It shall be the policy of Iowa Pork Packers, Inc. to assume the risk of loss arising out of property damage, legal liability, and dishonesty in all cases in which the exposure is so small or dispersed that a loss would not significantly affect the operations or the financial position of the firm.

4. Insurance will be purchased against all major loss exposures which might result in loss in excess of $100,000 or 10 percent of the projected annual working capital through the purchase of appropriate forms of property and liability insurance against the widest range of perils and hazards available.

5. Insurance will not be purchased to cover loss exposures below the amount of $10,000 unless such insurance is required by law or by contract, or in those

instances in which it is desirable to obtain special services such as inspection or claim adjustment in connection with the insurance.

6. The administration of the risk management program will be under the direction of the Risk Manager, such responsibility to include placement of insurance coverages, maintenance of property appraisals and inventory valuations, processing of claims and maintenance of loss records, and supervision of loss prevention activities.

7. Safety and loss prevention recommendations by OSHA officials and insurance company loss prevention personnel will be given serious consideration and implemented whenever feasible. In those instances in which such recommendations are not implemented, a written justification for nonimplementation will be filed with the Board of Directors by the company officer making the decision.

8. Insurance will be placed only in insurance companies rated A+ or A in *Best's Policyholders Ratings*. Insurance placed in any other companies will require a written report of the particulars, such report to be filed with the Board of Directors by the Insurance Administrator.

IMPORTANT CONCEPTS TO REMEMBER

post-loss objectives	social responsibility	risk management policy
pre-loss objectives	economy	maximum retention limit
survival	reduction in anxiety	uninsured loss reserve fund
continuity of operations	meeting externally imposed	aggregate loss retention
earning stability	obligations	level
continued growth	cost of risk	minimum retention level

QUESTIONS FOR REVIEW

1. Explain why defining risk management objectives is a critical step in the risk management process.

2. Why are objectives needed in a risk management program?

3. Describe the two broad classes into which risk management objectives can be divided, and identify the risk management objectives that may be established within each class.

4. Identify the primary risk management objective and explain why it is preeminent.

5. Describe the role of quantitative objectives in risk management.

6. Describe the general nature of a corporate risk management policy.

7. Explain the concept of a maximum retention limit in a corporate risk management policy. On what should the maximum retention limit of a corporate risk management policy be based?

8. Describe the purpose of a minimum retention limit in a corporate risk management policy.

9. Describe the general nature and purpose of a reserve for uninsured losses.

10. Describe Doherty's thesis of the *value maximization objective.*

QUESTIONS FOR DISCUSSION

1. Describe what you believe are the essential characteristics of a good risk management policy statement.

2. Describe risk management's direct contribution to profit.

3. Explain the purpose and intent of each of the provisions in the sample risk management policy included at the end of the chapter.

4. Prepare a risk management policy statement for yourself, and be prepared to explain the rationale for each of the provisions in the statement.

5. Risk management can be justified only insofar as it contributes in some way to attaining the objectives of the organization. In what way(s) does the risk management function make such a contribution?

SUGGESTIONS FOR ADDITIONAL READING

Doherty, Neil A. *Corporate Risk Management: A Financial Exposition* (New York: McGraw-Hill Book Company, 1985).

Greene, Mark R. and Oscar N. Serbein. *Risk Management: Text and Cases,* 2nd ed. Reston, Va.: Reston Publishing Company, 1983, Chapter 1.

Head, George L., ed. *Essentials of Risk Control,* 2nd ed., vol. I, Malvern, Pa.: Insurance Institute of America, 1989. Chapter 1.

Mehr, Robert I., and Bob A. Hedges. *Risk Management: Concepts and Applications.* Homewood, Ill.: Richard D. Irwin, 1974. Chapter 2.

Mehr, R.I., and B.A. Hedges. *Risk Management in the Business Enterprise.* Homewood, Il.: Richard D. Irwin, 1963. Chapter 10.

Reavis, Marshall W. "The Corporate Risk Manager's Contribution to Profit," *The Journal of Risk and Insurance,* XXXVI, No. 4 (September 1969), pp. 473–479.

Rosenbloom, Jerry S. *A Case Study in Risk Management.* Englewood Cliffs, NJ: 1972, Chapter 1.

Smith, Michael L., and C.A. Williams, Jr. "How the Corporate Risk Manager Contributes to Company Value," *Risk Management* (April 1991).

Williams, C.A., and Richard M. Heinz. *Risk Management and Insurance* (New York: McGraw-Hill, 1964).

CHAPTER 6

Risk Identification

CHAPTER OBJECTIVES

When you have finished this chapter, you should be able to

Explain why risk identification is generally considered to be the most difficult step
in the risk management process.

•

Identify the contributions that insurers have made to the practice of risk identification.

•

Identify the circumstances and challenges that gave rise to systems safety.

•

Explain how the system safety approach to risk identification differs from
the approach that had previously been used to identify risks.

•

Identify and briefly describe the major tools that are used in the risk identification process.

•

Identify and briefly describe the techniques that are used in conjunction with
risk identification tools to identify risks.

•

Explain how the analysis of financial statements may be useful in risk identification and
also examine the inadequacies of financial statements for risk identification.

⬛ Introduction ■

Before anything can be done about the risks facing an organization, someone must
identify those risks. Although this is a simple statement, the actual process of risk
identification is an agonizing one. As observed earlier, it is a never-ending task, for
new risks are arising constantly. In addition, one can never be absolutely certain
that the job has been done properly. In this chapter, we examine some of the tech-

niques of risk identification, focusing on the tools that are available to assist the risk manager in this process.[1]

◆ Responsibility For Risk Identification ■ ■ ■ ■ ■ ■ ■ ■ ■ ■

In an organization large enough to have a full-time risk manager, risk identification and measurement are primary functions. For the in-house risk manager, risk identification is continuous and depends on a wide-reaching communication network generating a constant flow of information about the organization's activities.

But what about the smaller company that does not have professional staff? Unless there is someone within the organization with insurance expertise, outside help will be required. Some organizations rely on periodic audits from risk management consultants to see that the job is being performed properly; others use the consultant on a continuing retainer basis. However, generally, most firms without in-house staff rely on the agent or broker. Therefore, all insurance agents and brokers should, of course, be thoroughly conversant with the techniques of risk identification and measurement. Even though their compensation is generally from the sale of insurance, they will often be called upon to act as advisers in the risk management function. The producer who can perform continuing risk analysis for clients and provide periodic detailed information will become valuable to clients.

Outside parties such as agents, brokers, and consultants can provide valuable service in the risk identification phase, but it is difficult for anyone outside the organization to fully understand the operations of the firm. For this reason, completely delegating the risk identification function to an outside party is not a satisfactory solution to the problem. When an outside party is retained to identify risks, the individual within the organization who is responsible for the risk management function should recognize that this outside party is going to need help in the risk identification process, and should be prepared to participate with the outside party in identifying the organization's exposures.

Actually, the process of identifying the risks facing an organization is a two-party job. Internal personnel are familiar with the operations of the organization, whereas the professional insurance agent, broker, or risk management consultant is a specialist in handling risk. Together someone from inside the firm and the external risk specialist make an ideal team for identifying exposures. But the inside party must be willing to furnish the external party with the information needed to accurately assess the loss exposures. Whether or not there is a full-time risk manager, someone in the organization has, or should have, responsibility for risk and insurance. This person, whether it be the president, industrial relations manager, personnel manager, operations manager, treasurer, chief financial officer, secretary, or controller, should marshal all the resources available to see that the risk identification process is completed.

---

[1]Risk identification and measurement are so closely related that some writers combine the two into a single function. Although there is a close relationship and risk identification inevitably involves some intuitive measurement, we prefer to separate the functions simply because it breaks the process into manageable chunks. Risk measurement is discussed in Chapters 7 and 8.

✖ Risk Identification Methodologies   ■ ■ ■ ■ ■ ■ ■ ■ ■ ■ ■ ■ ■

Risk identification techniques have been developed simultaneously by professionals from different disciplines, each focusing on their own specialty. These professionals include insurance practitioners, fire safety personnel, security specialists, industrial loss-prevention engineers, accountants, and physicists and engineers in military and space programs. Because each group has been concerned with a somewhat different problem, the strategies and techniques they have adopted for identifying hazards have also differed. These strategies and techniques testify to the persuasiveness of the risk problem and to the ingenuity with which humankind has addressed this problem.

Generally, risk identification techniques developed as part of loss-prevention and control efforts. It is fundamental that before a risk can be treated, it must be recognized. Consequently, loss-prevention efforts in various disciplines have focused on risk identification as a point of departure. Initially, risk identification was an instinctive process; when an accident or loss occurred, people naturally sought to avoid the circumstances or conditions that caused the loss. One can envision the first time a prehistoric human attempted to pick up a burning coal. It is likely that word spread quickly that this was an inadvisable practice. Similarly, after a few encounters, people learned to avoid carnivorous animals that were larger and faster than they were.

Eventually, risk identification became more sophisticated, especially after humans learned to communicate by writing. Information of losses became more widely disseminated, and the inventory of risks derived from personal experiences was enlarged by information on the experiences of others. Formal risk identification emerged when such inventories of losses were recorded and shared with others.

IDENTIFICATION BASED ON PAST LOSSES

Until recently, the primary methodology of risk identification was the observation of losses that had already occurred. As a rule, risk identification did not occur until a loss had taken place. Once a loss occurred, people sought measures that would prevent the reoccurrence of loss from the same source. People learned that there was a risk of loss by fire because houses burned. They learned that electricity could be a hazard as well as a beneficial tool because people were electrocuted, and that while the horse provided a convenient means of locomotion, they could also kick people.

Insurance companies played a major role in developing risk identification techniques, and most of the methods they developed were based on analysis of past losses. Often, insurance company personnel were interested in identifying not only risks, but also the hazards associated with those risks. Insurance safety engineers working in the field of employee safety gathered a significant body of information as losses occurred, and from this information base created exposure templates or exposure checklists for hazard identification. Insurers also developed insurance policy checklists, which in effect identified the various risks for which they offered coverage.

Although the risk identification checklists they produced naturally focused on the perils and hazards against which they offered protection, these early risk identification tools provided a base on which risk identification could be constructed.

Insurance underwriters also contributed to the body of knowledge relating to risk identification. *Underwriting* is the process of deciding whether to insure a particular exposure and the rate at which it will be insured. As a part of the underwriting process, insurance company personnel often conduct inspections of the applicant's premises to gather information about the hazards. Based on these inspections, the underwriter decides whether it will insure the applicant and sometimes what corrective measures will be required before coverage will be written. Underwriters discovered by experience the types of hazards that were likely to give rise to loss, and this information became part of the science of risk identification.

Insurance rating practices also contributed to the risk identification process. Insurance pricing is based on probability theory. Based on an analysis of past experience, insurance actuaries attempt to predict future losses. Because losses vary with the hazards involved (i.e., conditions that increase the likelihood of loss), the identification of hazards is fundamental to the rate-making process.

In the field of fire insurance, for example, rates differ according to the construction, occupancy, protection, and exposure of the property to be insured. Other things being equal, the rate for masonry buildings is lower than the rate for frame buildings, but higher than the rate for fire-resistive structures.

In the field of industrial injuries, insurance-rating bureaus maintain extensive databases, classifying losses according to occupation. In addition, the historical record of losses is also useful in identifying the causes of past losses, which then serve as a basis for loss-prevention and control measures.

Workers compensation premiums for many employers are computed on an "experience rating" basis, which reflects the employer's past history of losses. The Experience Modifier Worksheet, computed by the workers compensation rating bureau, provides historical data that indicate whether the firm's losses have been average, above average, or below average. Because the cost of workers compensation varies directly with the past loss experience, it provides information that is useful in the risk evaluation process.

SYSTEMS SAFETY TECHNIQUES

In the 1960s, the engineers and scientists engaged in U.S. military and aerospace initiatives developed a new approach to risk identification. As noted above, historically, risks have been identified by experience—that is, after a loss has occurred. Because much of the activity in which the military and space program was involved represented new frontiers, another approach was needed. In addition, the risks with which aerospace engineers were concerned did not lend themselves to transfer, and so the concentration was primarily on loss-prevention efforts.

The military and space program's major contribution to the body of knowledge concerned with loss prevention and control was in the introduction of the *systems* approach to safety. The term *systems safety* is generally used to describe a collection of logic and mathematical techniques that are continually applied to the detection and correction of hazards from the early conceptual stage of a product right on through its detailed design and operation. It includes a study of operating procedures, test procedures, inspections, scheduled top management reviews, and attention to nontechnical areas such as readability of manuals and motivation of workers.

The complexity of the space program and the newness of the equipment with which the scientists were working meant that there was little in the way of historical data on the perils and hazards that might cause loss. Moreover, the systems with which the engineers were occupied were so complex that a new approach to hazard identification was required.[2] To cope with this situation, the scientists developed a variety of techniques that are collectively known as *systems safety* and that are now becoming part of the risk manager's arsenal.

Systems safety is not new with respect to objectives, as some of its proponents seem to imply. Its objectives are the same as those in the conventional safety areas explained up to this point—that is, to identify causes of losses and either eliminate them or minimize their effects. It is new, however, in the sense that it applies the most advanced management skills, including the use of mathematics and computers, in the most comprehensive manner to attain its objectives. Systems safety also differs from conventional safety in that it places great emphasis on the identification of possible causes of losses before the losses happen. In programs such as those for which systems safety was developed, the traditional approach of waiting for an accident to happen and then investigating to determine its cause left much to be desired. Instead, scientists searched for and found models that could be used to anticipate accidents and to devise corrections before they happened. This involved the detailed analysis of each component, each action, and each interrelationship in the system in order to determine, insofar as is possible, what could go wrong. This analysis was accomplished through the use of computers, mathematical modeling, prototypes, simulation, and logic. The objective of the systems safety approach was, in simple terms, to determine in advance the optimal methods of design and manufacture that would provide the greatest possible safety.[3]

Whether systems safety would have developed in the absence of the enormous resources that were devoted to the space program is debatable. What is clear, however, is that the funds that were spent and the successes that were achieved produced a new range of tools that have become useful in the private sector. Increasingly, systems safety has found a niche in colleges of engineering (and in some colleges of business administration) across the country. With a growing cadre of safety engineers trained in these methods, insurance companies have incorporated

[2]See Jerome Lederer (Director, Manned Space Flight Safety, NASA), *Best's Review, Property Liability Edition*, 7, No. I (May 1970): 48. Think of the enormous work and costs involved in applying systems safety in the Apollo program. Lederer says that over 15 million parts are involved in a single launch, with 5.6 million parts in the Apollo vehicle, including 1.5 million operational systems. Hence, he says, a reliability of 99.9 percent would mean 5,600 malfunctions!

[3]J.L. Recht, "Systems Safety Analysis: An Introduction," *National Safety News*, 42, No. 6 (Chicago: National Safety Council, December 1965).

many elements of systems safety into the services they offer their clients. Similarly, safety consulting organizations provide unbundled systems safety services.

Several features distinguish the systems safety approach from the traditional loss-prevention methodology. The principal feature, however, is the emphasis on identifying possible causes of accidents before the accident occurs, rather than attempting to determine causation by analysis of past accidents.[4]

✖ Risk Identification Tools ■

Exposure identification is an essential phase of both risk management and insurance management. Because insurance management is the older field, the technique of identifying insurable exposures was already highly developed when the risk management movement began. Many of the procedures that insurance agents and insurance managers had used to identify insurable exposures were expanded and adapted to aid in identifying other risks for which the risk manager is responsible.

Risks lurk in such obscure places that no single approach to risk identification is adequate. A variety of tools are available to assist in risk identification, including questionnaires, checklists, and procedure guides. As we noted in our earlier discussion of the risk management process, the preferred approach to risk identification is a combination approach, in which all the tools available are brought to bear on the problem. The risk manager must employ many techniques, not only initially, but on a continuing basis to keep abreast of all changes and developments that can create new exposures. But no individual approach or combination of tools can replace the diligence and imagination of the risk manager in discovering the risks to which the organization is exposed.

The term *risk identification tools* encompasses several standard forms and checklists that are designed to facilitate the risk identification process. As such, these tools differ from documents within the organization that may provide a part of the risk picture. The following tools are unrelated to the organization whose risks are to be identified, but provide guidance in organizing and interpreting the information that is gathered by risk identification techniques.

RISK ANALYSIS QUESTIONNAIRES

The key tool in the risk identification process is a risk analysis questionnaire, also sometimes called a fact finder. These questionnaires are designed to lead the risk manager to the discovery of risks through a series of detailed and penetrating questions, and in some instances, this instrument is designed to include both insurable

---

[4]Because it is primarily concerned with loss control, systems safety is discussed in Chapter 9, which deals with loss control measures. Because an essential part of the systems safety approach is the identification of hazards, it is appropriate that it at least be mentioned here.

and uninsurable risks. Unfortunately, because these questionnaires are usually designed to be used by a wide range of businesses, they cannot include unusual exposures or identify loss areas that may be unique to a given firm.

The function of the risk analysis questionnaire is often misunderstood. Sometimes a risk management consultant or an insurance agent will approach a client with the questionnaire, fully expecting to proceed through an agonizing series of questions from start to finish. Other consultants and agents reject the use of lengthy questionnaires because they anticipate an adverse reaction from clients. These practices and attitudes are based on a fundamental misunderstanding of the purpose and function of the questionnaire.

The risk analysis questionnaire is designed to serve as a repository for the information that is gained from documents, interviews, and inspections. The information in the completed questionnaire is gained from an analysis of documents, inspections, records, and interviews. Its purpose is to lead the person attempting to identify exposures through the identification process in a logical and consistent fashion.[5]

EXPOSURE CHECKLISTS

A second important aid in risk identification and one of the most common tools for risk analysis is a risk exposure checklist, which is simply a listing of common exposures. An almost infinite number of checklists is available, ranging from very short to extremely detailed. They are useful in jogging the memory before and after inspections, but generally should not be used during an inspection. Following a "laundry list" narrows the inspector's vision and can result in overlooking unique exposures. Insurance company checklists typically list only those exposures included as insured perils on standard insurance policies. Obviously, a checklist cannot include all possible exposures to which an organization may be subject; the nature and operations of different organizations vary too widely for that. However, it can be used effectively in conjunction with other risk identification tools as a final check to reduce the chance of overlooking a serious exposure.

INSURANCE POLICY CHECKLISTS

Insurance policy checklists are available from insurance companies as well as from publishers specializing in insurance-related publications. Typically, such lists include a catalogue of the various policies or types of insurance that a given business might need. The risk manager simply consults such a list, picking out those policies applicable to the firm. A principal defect of this approach is that it concentrates on insurable risks only, ignoring the uninsurable pure risks.

---

[5]One of the most comprehensive risk analysis questionnaires is published by the Insurance Division of the American Management Association (AMA). However, like other questionnaires, it cannot deal with the unusual facets of a firm's operations, and therefore is not a complete solution to the problem of risk identification. The Risk Identification Appendix contains a risk analysis questionnaire loosely based on the AMA's questionnaire.

Because the insurance needs of various types of business vary, industry-specific checklists are preferred. A number of such checklists are available, one of the most useful of which is the *Coverages Applicable* manual by Roy McCormick, published by the Rough Notes Company of Indianapolis, Indiana. It outlines the various types of insurance that might be needed by approximately 600 different business and professional risks and is revised annually. *Coverages Applicable* also includes a brief discussion of the nature and scope of coverage listed.

Although *Coverages Applicable* is a useful starting point, it merely indicates the inventory of insurance coverages that might be applicable to a particular type of organization. It does not address the myriad of endorsements and modifications that may be required to tailor the coverage to the unique exposures of the organization under consideration. Other more detailed coverage checklists, however, are available from other sources. Some insurers develop application forms for their packages policies that inventory the entire range of operations available in these packages. Although such tools are limited to the products the insurer sells, these forms can still be useful in risk identification.

EXPERT SYSTEMS

In a sense, an expert system used in risk identification incorporates the features of risk analysis questionnaires, exposure checklists, and insurance policy checklists in a single tool. The PS4 product we touched on briefly in Chapter 4 is a good example. Although the report-generating capability previously discussed is a valuable benefit, the system's real niche is in the risk identification phase of risk management.

The detailed, industry-specific risk survey questionnaire and loss control forms incorporate all of the questions that are usually included in a risk analysis questionnaire, but in an industry-specific format. The survey questionnaires are detailed and specific and lead the user through a series of penetrating questions designed to assist in identifying not only common exposures, but also those that may be unique to the specific industry. The industry-specific insurance coverage checklists can be used in tandem with the in-depth analysis of insurance coverages that is also included.

In addition to these features, which are directly related to the risk identification function, the integrated nature of the program allows the user to generate written proposals to clients or prospects. An additional feature consists of ongoing account-handling features, which allows the editing and storage of certificates of insurance, insurance binders, and commercial applications.

■■ Risk Identification Techniques ■ ■ ■ ■ ■ ■ ■ ■ ■ ■ ■ ■ ■ ■ ■

The risk identification tools described earlier provide a framework within which we can interpret information derived from four risk identification techniques: orientation, analysis of documents, interviews, and inspections.

ORIENTATION

The first step in risk identification is to gain as thorough a knowledge as possible of the organization and its operations. The risk manager needs a general knowledge of the goals and functions of the organization. If the organization is small and the risk manager is also president of the company, he or she will need no further indoctrination. A risk manager, on the other hand, may need to acquire information on the operations of the organization. If the individual performing the risk identification function is an external party—an agent or consultant encountering the organization for the first time—he or she will need to become familiar first with the general practices of the particular industry and then with the activities of the specific firm itself.

If the organization is a public corporation, the best place to start is with the latest annual report and financial statement. These documents will provide general information. A great deal more depth can be obtained from the SEC Form 10-K, which all U.S. public corporations use. This document provides detailed summaries of the firm's various activities and may also list all locations. If the organization is a closely held corporation, a partnership, or a sole proprietorship, it will be more difficult to get anything definitive in writing. Here, the financial statements are a good place to start, but the operations themselves will probably have to be described by an individual in the company. If the organization is a public body, it will usually have an annual budget that is somewhat comparable to an annual report, but considerably more detailed in outlining the various departments and the extent of their operations. Although these documents can provide a general orientation, more detailed information will have to come from other sources.

ANALYSIS OF DOCUMENTS

The history of the organization and its current operations are recorded in a variety of records. These records represent a basic source of information required for risk analysis and exposure identification. As a starting point in the risk identification process, the auditor should obtain certain internal and external documents that summarize the activities and history of the organization. These documents include the following:

1. Latest Dun and Bradstreet Report
2. SEC 10-K Report
3. Copy of annual report
4. Latest balance sheet
5. Latest income statement
6. Sample of advertising literature
7. Catalogue, if any
8. Sample of letterhead

9. Sample of packaging
10. Purchase order form
11. Installation and service agreements
12. Sales agreements
13. Copy of lease agreements
14. Copies of any other contracts
15. Latest payroll audit (two years) by insurer
16. Latest inventory valuation report
17. Latest appraisal on buildings and contents
18. Account receivable balance in last 24 months
19. Schedule of vehicles
20. Personnel roster
21. State motor vehicle reports for drivers
22. Fire rate makeup
23. Workers compensation experience modification
24. General liability experience modification
25. Automobile liability experience modification
26. Buy–sell agreement
27. Flowchart of operations
28. Copy of risk management policy
29. Copy of agreement to indemnify officers
30. Copy of safety policy
31. Copy of safety rules
32. Three-year loss record and claim experience

Some of the documents on the list are available internally, whereas others are obtained from external organizations. Although the value of some of the documents should be relatively obvious, the information that can be derived from others is not immediately apparent. However, several of the risk identification tools discussed in the following section are useful in extracting pertinent information.

Analysis of Financial Statements

Properly used, financial statements can be a valuable source of information for the risk identification function. Both the balance sheet and the operating statement (profit and loss statement) are excellent sources of general information about the organization. Although financial statements are only one facet of an organization's record system, they represent an important source of data for the risk identification function. The organization's balance sheet, for example, reveals the existence of various types of assets, which leads the auditor to seek information on the possible losses to which such assets are exposed. The balance sheet may also indicate the existence of negotiable securities, which might be impossible to detect during an inspection. Similarly, it can also indicate how much cash or working capital is available as a measure of loss-retention capability. On the liability side of the ledger, stockholders' equity and reserves are other indicators of the firm's ability to retain risk. Footnotes to the financial statement will show possible or pending liability suits or claims.

The income and expense classification in the income statement may also indicate areas of operation of which the risk manager was unaware. The profit and loss statement provides a measure of indirect loss exposures, such as business interruption, and is needed to estimate the exposure to fidelity losses. The income statement also indicates past income flows, which can be helpful in assessing the organization's ability to absorb losses.[6]

Although financial statements can be useful in risk identification, they often lack the detailed information needed to judge the significance of the exposures they reveal. For example, although a large amount of cash may be shown, this exposure is much different if the bulk of that money is on deposit at banks than if most of it is held in safes at various company locations. Unfortunately, most balance sheets do not distinguish cash on deposit from cash on hand. Similarly, if the firm holds securities as a short- or long-term investment, the risk of criminal loss is greatly increased if the securities are negotiable, but a balance sheet usually does not separate negotiable from nonnegotiable securities.

Another fundamental problem is that the risk manager must concentrate on more than just aggregate values—he or she must watch for disbursements or concentrations of values as well as for changes in assets and operations. The financial statements probably do not tell the risk manager how the firm's assets are distributed among its locations, the values of business personal property at various locations, or the existence of personal property of others that may be in the organization's custody.

Flowcharts

In some cases, analysis of a flowchart of the operations may alert the risk manager to unusual aspects of the firm's operations which give rise to special risks. A flowchart of an organization's internal operations—revealing the type and sequence of its activities—views the firm as a processing unit and seeks to discover all the contingencies that could interrupt its processes: damage to a strategic asset located in a *bottleneck* within the firm's operations; the loss of the services of a key individual or group through disability, death, or resignation; or damage to cargo en route from one firm location to another. Especially when extended to include the flow of goods and services to and from customers and suppliers, the flowchart approach to risk identification can highlight potential accidents that can disrupt the firm's activities and its profits.

---

[6]Some writers view analysis of income statements as a primary means of risk identification. The financial statement method of risk analysis was proposed by the risk manager of a national corporation, and has become a more or less standard approach to the risk identification problem. See A. Hawthorne Criddle, "A Theory of Risk Discovery," *National Insurance Buyer,* 6, No. 1 (January 1959).

The most positive benefit of using flowcharts is probably that it forces the risk manager to become familiar with the technical aspects of the firm's operations, thereby increasing the likelihood of recognizing special exposures. A flowchart is especially useful in a multiplant organization where goods flow from one location to another, but may also be used to advantage with a single plant. A simple flowchart will show goods that come into the building, the source, mode of transportation, where title passes, what is done to the goods inside the building, and how they are shipped out. Although there are undoubtedly some organizations in which the flowchart approach will yield information that is not otherwise discoverable, it has limited applications.[7]

Organization Charts

In the case of a large organization, an organization chart will reveal the various divisions within the organization and reporting relationships. It can reveal the existence of units of which the auditor might otherwise be unaware, and it can also indicate persons who should be interviewed as additional sources of information. It will also provide the risk identifier with an understanding of the nature and scope of the organization's operations.

Existing Policies

Although some will view as heresy the suggestion that a review of the existing policies can be helpful in the risk identification stage, we believe that the existing contracts are an important tool in risk identification. The auditor will need the existing policies to evaluate the adequacy of the coverage anyway, and it therefore makes sense to obtain them when other information is being gathered. If the auditor is the client's insurance agent, he or she may already have copies of the policies that have been written through the agency. However, unless the agent handles the client's entire account, he or she will not have copies of all contracts. If the client is reluctant to permit the policies to leave the organization's files, photocopies should be made.

Loss Reports

Another important source of information that can aid in risk identification is the organization's record of its own past losses. A large organization should have regular reports of all public liability and workers compensation losses and potential claims, regardless of size. Some organizations will also suffer regular property losses. Examination of loss records will indicate the kinds of losses that have occurred, which may be useful in assessing the degree of risk of certain activities or operations.

The value of loss records in risk identification will depend on the completeness of the records and the form in which they are maintained. Ideally, loss records

---

[7]The use of flowcharts in risk analysis was popularized by a practicing risk manager in a giant corporation. See A.J. Ingley, "Problems of Risk Analysis," *The Growing Job of Risk Management*, AMA Management Report No. 70 (New York: American Management Association, 1962), pp. 137–138.

should be maintained for all losses, both those covered and those not covered by insurance. Such information is useful both in completing the risk identification phase and in deciding what approach should be used to deal with the risks.

Contracts and Leases

It is often impractical for the risk manager to review contracts before they are signed. However, the risk manager should reach an agreement with the persons responsible for contracts concerning what terms and conditions in each type of contract are of concern. Agreement should be reached on what issues are important from a risk management viewpoint and which nonstandard documents the risk manager should review. The risk manager should certainly see the documents after they are signed. Contracts contain requirements to carry insurance, to name additional insureds, to give notification in case of cancellation, and to assume liability. Therefore, a method of routing all contracts to the risk manager should be developed.

When an outside party such as a risk management consultant or an insurance agent or broker conducts the risk identification process, copies of all contracts and leases should be obtained for analysis.

Fire Rate MakeUp

Although less accessible today than formerly, the fire-rating organization's engineering report for each building is a valuable source of information for the auditor. In the initial interview with a client, the auditor should obtain an Agent of Record letter, which is an authorization from the client to the insurance-rating organization to provide the engineering reports on which the organization's fire insurance rates are based. The Agent of Record letter will permit the auditor to obtain a copy of the fire rate makeup prior to a physical inspection of the property. The fire rate makeup is used to compute the schedule rate of certain commercial buildings, where the rate is determined by adding debits and subtracting credits from a base rate, which represents a "standard building." The debits and credits represent those features of the building's construction, occupancy, fire protection, and neighborhood that deviate from the standard. Through the application of these debits and credits, the physical characteristics of each schedule-rated building determine that building's fire insurance rate.

Analysis of the fire rate makeup both before and after the inspection is part of the process of developing audit information. By examining the sheet before the physical inspection, the auditor becomes aware of the charges that have been made and can look for the deficiencies to see whether they can be eliminated. In some cases, a meeting with members of the rating bureau may be in order to determine whether improvements warrant re-rating the structure.

Experience Modification Letters

In some lines of insurance, most notably workers compensation, general liability, and automobile liability, the insured's own past loss experience enters into determining the premium to be charged for current protection. Experience rating imposes surcharges or grants credits to the insured, adjusting the premium upward or downward, depending on the extent to which experience has deviated from the average experience of the class to which the insured belongs. Usually, experience rating is used only when the insured generates a premium large enough to be considered statistically credible. The current "experience modifier" for workers compensation, general liability, and automobile liability insurance can provide a vivid indication of the insured's past loss experience and may be helpful in identifying areas that require attention.

Other Documents

The risk manager cannot always depend on others in the organization to report what is happening in the organization, which means that he or she must be constantly alert for new and changing exposures. A good way to do this is to review key documents on a regular basis. Ideally, these documents should be forwarded to the risk manager as a standard practice. The risk management auditor may not have access to all the documents in the following listing. However, where possible, these documents should be reviewed in the search for exposures.

- *Minutes of Board of Directors Meetings.* These minutes outline plans that may call for risk planning in advance.
- *Request for Funds.* Before new buildings or machinery are acquired, the project must be proposed and approved by various departments. The Request for Funds form can easily be routed to the risk manager, who will then have a good source of information with respect to planned changes and developments that may give rise to new exposures.
- *Company Manuals.* Administrative, controller, and other manuals often contain provisions relating to risk, insurance, claims, safety, fire protection standards, and the like.
- *Miscellaneous.* Depending on the company, the risk manager may need to check such documents as bylaws (for officer indemnification clauses), purchase orders, standard construction contracts, descriptive literature, catalogues, advertising, and rental agreements.
- *Annual Reports.* The annual report to stockholders should not reveal any information of which the risk manager is unaware. However, the risk manager should review the annual report precisely to determine whether or not it does. If the annual report reveals exposures of which the risk manager was unaware, it is an indication that something in the risk management information system is defective.

Although this list is not exhaustive of the various documents and information sources the risk manager may consult in risk identification, the documents listed are among those that are most frequently used as sources of information on the risks of the organization.

INTERVIEWS

Another important source of information that can aid in risk identification is the interview with key personnel within the organization. Some information is not recorded in documents or records and exists only in the minds of executives and employees. Interviews with various parties within an organization are sometimes required to dig this information out and to add it to the general information that is used to identify exposures. The number and scope of such interviews will depend largely on how familiar the person performing the identification function is with the organization and its activities. In the case of an external auditor, particularly in an initial risk analysis, interviews should be held with every person who can contribute information. This will generally start with the president or general manager for an overview of operations and goals. Where appropriate, interviews with the following parties should also be included.

- Operations Managers. The managers of each of the various departments within the organization can provide information regarding precisely what is being done in each department. Information of this nature may reveal exposures that are not otherwise evident.

- *Chief Financial Officer.* The vice president of finance or other chief financial officer can provide information on the company's financial condition, what money and security exposures exist for check writing, and what loss of certain facilities would mean from a financial standpoint.

- *Legal Counsel.* The legal department (or the firm's outside attorney) can provide information as to what major contracts exist, which hold-harmless agreements are used, and the liability exposures of which he or she is aware.

- *Plant Engineer.* The plant engineer can indicate the existence of critical machinery, the extent of maintenance programs, and more technical details regarding operations. The chief engineer can answer questions on research, development, and quality control.

- *Purchasing Agent.* The purchasing agent can provide information with respect to purchase order terms used (i.e., FOB point of origin or FOB destination) and the degree to which the firm is protected by hold-harmless agreements from manufacturers or purchasers of goods.

- *Personnel Manager.* The industrial relations manager can provide data on the status of union contracts regarding safety and workers compensation. In addition, when the employee benefit program is included in the audit, the bulk of the information related to these programs is generally available from the personnel department.

- *Plant Nurse.* The plant nurse can provide insights into the type of injuries occurring, into use of loss-prevention techniques such as pre-employment physicals and audiograms, and into the extent of possible outside personal malpractice insurance.

- *Safety Manager.* If the firm has a safety manager, he or she should also be interviewed, not only to determine the nature and extent of the firm's safety procedures, but also to gain a better knowledge of operations in general. The safety manager is usually well acquainted with the plant processes and can provide insights into hazards that few other persons in the organization can match.

- *Employees and Supervisors.* The principal reason for interviewing employees and foremen is to get a feel of the people in the plant. Casual conversations with employees and supervisors may reveal the existence of hazards of which top management is unaware. It can also show whether there is any strain between employees and foremen or management—a sign of poor morale. Plant morale is an important factor in employee accidents and employee dishonesty.

- *External Parties.* External parties often provide insights that cannot be gained elsewhere. The firm's attorney and certified public accountant can be especially helpful in this respect. When the auditor is someone other than the client's insurance agent or broker, the agent or broker can also be an important source of information regarding past risk management decisions.

In addition to these structured interviews, informal conversations with company personnel at all organizational levels can help the risk manager uncover pertinent loss exposure information that could not be readily or accurately relayed in written reports. Conversations with workers may highlight some unsafe equipment or work practices not mentioned in the formal reports. By interviewing senior management, the risk manager can learn the degree of pure risk with which top management is comfortable—the risks the firm wants to absorb, wholly or in part, and those it wishes to transfer. These expressions from top management will help the risk manager identify those exposures that, for the organization as one firm, are particularly important.

Structured Interview Guide

Another tool, similar in many respects to the risk analysis questionnaire, is the structured interview guide, designed for use by insurance agents in eliciting information from clients. A structured interview guide consists of a series of general questions about the organization and its activities. It is much shorter and less detailed than the risk analysis questionnaire, and it serves a different purpose. The structured interview guide elicits general information that supplements information extracted from the documents obtained from the organization, and is inserted, along with other information, in the risk analysis questionnaire.

INSPECTIONS

A physical inspection of property is probably the best way to obtain a good knowledge of operations. Just as one picture is worth a thousand words, one inspection tour may be worth a thousand checklists. An examination of the firm's various operation sites and discussions with managers and workers will often bring attention to risks that might otherwise have been undetected. The inspection will be most useful if it is preceded by a thorough orientation as described above. Many things can be missed if the risk manager does not have some idea of what he or she is looking for. On the other hand, the risk manager should always be alert to discover activities that may not be apparent. The inspection of the premises is one of the most important parts of the process of developing the survey information because

- It helps to familiarize the auditor with the organization.
- It helps to indicate areas of possible rate reduction and improvements from a fire protection standpoint, which will make the risk more attractive from an underwriting standpoint.
- It may reveal areas of possible loss that would not otherwise be discovered and may therefore assist in making recommendations for loss prevention and coverage.

One inspection should be made with the owner or an employee who can answer any questions that may arise. It is helpful to carry a camera on this inspection, and if one is available, a portable tape recorder or transcribing machine helps in taking notes. Following this first inspection with the client or an employee, the auditor may wish to make additional inspections alone. On his second inspection, the auditor may wish to prepare a chart of the premises, noting locations of property, safes, protective devices, and any other features that will be needed in preparation of the report. Ideally, the inspector should have a copy of the *fire rate makeup*, the engineer's report on which the fire insurance rate for the building is predicated. The inspector can make note of the specific hazards for which charges have been made in the fire rate makeup.

If the building is a manufacturing or assembly process, it may be effective to follow the work flow in the inspection. This means beginning where raw materials enter the building, following the materials to their storage area, and then going through the various processes to completion as finished products. This allows the inspector to examine the process and to note features that might represent a bottleneck or critical hazard. However, the work-flow approach should not distract the inspector from seeing every spot of the entire plant.

Risk Management Information Systems ■ ■ ■ ■ ■ ■ ■ ■ ■

Although the risk identification tools and methods discussed in this chapter are necessary for determining the risks facing an organization, they are not sufficient to guarantee the detection of new risks as they emerge. To identify new risks, the risk manager needs a far-reaching information system, which yields current information on new developments that may give rise to risk. In addition, the risk manager needs a system of maintaining the wide range of information that affects the organization's risk.

RISK MANAGEMENT POLICY MANUAL

The *Risk Management Policy Manual* is a central depository for all risk management and insurance-related corporate policies. It should include a complete set of all policies, ranging from the corporate risk management policy itself to individual policies that address such diverse subjects as the use of company automobiles by employees for personal business or whether corporate executives traveling on company business should purchase the collision damage waiver on rented cars. Other policies may address claim-reporting requirements, corporate responsibility for the employee's property on the employer's premises, and any other issues for which corporate policies have been established. Defining such policies in writing eliminates the need to address the issue and make a decision when a loss has already occurred. Most organizations use a numbering sequence that facilitates the addition of new policies as they are adopted.

Copies of the *Risk Management Policy Manual* should be distributed to units within the corporation as a way of communicating what the risk management department expects and what the other departments may expect from the risk management department.

RISK MANAGEMENT RECORD SYSTEMS

Fundamentally, risk management is a problem in decision making. Information about the organization's risks are the raw material for these decisions. Records and statistics on losses and premiums are essential tools of the risk management profession, and without adequate records, it is difficult to analyze the risks facing the organization and to determine the advisability of retaining certain risks. In addition, records relating to property valuations, past losses, and other critical pieces of information should be readily available to the person or persons responsible for administering the program.

Although the specific records that will be retained within the risk management department will vary, the following types of information should be maintained in the office of the risk manager. Some of these items of information may also be maintained elsewhere in the organization, but all of them should be readily available to the risk manager.

1. *Property Valuation Schedule.* This schedule should include the insurable values of all buildings, contents by building, plus a separate schedule of vehicles or mobile equipment. It can be maintained through continual revision as new properties are added and old locations are dropped, with the values periodically updated to reflect increased construction costs.

2. *Vehicle and Mobile Equipment Schedule.* In administering new acquisitions, sales, and exchanges of motor vehicles, the insurance administrator must have access to pertinent vehicle information.

3. *Requests for Insurance Bids and Coverages.* This file should be maintained when requests for bids are made to insurers or when requests for insurance coverages

are made. Copies of the requests for coverage need be kept only until the requested policies have been received. Requests for bids may be retained on a more permanent basis to facilitate preparation of future bid requests.

4. *Insurance Register and Insurance Policies.* The insurance register may be kept with the insurance policies in force, or it may be maintained in a section of the insurance manual, but it should contain a list of all policies currently in force, with the expiration date and the annual premium. The schedule of existing insurance contained in this report may serve as the initial schedule for the insurance register.

5. *Claim Report File.* A claim report file should be established to permit keeping track of and following up on payments due from insurance companies. The claim report file should be structured in a way that allows the risk manager to monitor progress on individual claims as well as aggregate claims. Because the claim file will also provide a database for analysis of losses, the information recorded for each claim should include not only the informa-tion required by the insurer, but also data the risk manager needs for analysis of hazards.

6. *Loss Data.* The loss data file should contain a record of all losses, including both insured and uninsured losses. These data will permit analysis of loss patterns for making decisions regarding the purchase of various forms of insurance and the deductibles to be utilized.

7. *Premium and Loss Comparison.* This special file should contain a record of premiums and losses by type of insurance. This information, with the loss data on uninsured losses, will provide a basis for analysis of the efficiency of the premium dollar spent.

RISK MANAGEMENT INFORMATION SYSTEMS

Much of the information required for this risk management information system already exists within most organizations in an unstructured form. The information becomes more useful when it is combined into a useful database that facilitates analysis; that is, when it is integrated in a *risk management information system* (RMIS). A number of vendors sell prepackaged risk management information system software, but many organizations have developed their own in-house systems.

The purpose of RMIS is to support the risk management decision process. By consolidating quantitative aspects of the risk management function in a relational database, coded by organizational unit, RMIS provides the raw material for risk management decisions.

Information for RMIS comes from several sources. First, information on losses comes from the firm's insurer or, in the case of self-insured losses, from the third-party administrator (TPA) who is responsible for settling losses. For retained losses that are not paid by a TPA, the data must be input by the risk management department. In addition to the information on losses, data on premiums and other risk-related expenditures are available from internal sources, but must be entered into the system by the risk management department.

The consolidation of the various types of risk-related data in a RMIS can provide inputs for the decision process in several ways. First, the information on losses—insured and uninsured—provides useful information for the selection of deductibles and other retention decisions. In addition, when losses are properly coded to indicate causes, RMIS is useful in identifying areas when loss control measures should be directed. The losses should be related to the organizational structure. This means that losses and claims should be traceable to individual operating units within the organization, much like a cost accounting system. This allows allocation of costs to the organizational unit responsible for the losses. It also helps to identify areas in which losses are higher than average. The database will also usually include a unit-by-unit inventory of exposure data, summarizing information that is pertinent to risk measurement. Budgeted costs associated with risk, such as premiums paid, losses, and loss control exposures represent another part of the database. Finally, RMIS usually includes data on the cost of risk management administration. These costs include administrative costs for the risk management division, the cost of consultants and outside services, and other direct costs related to risk management.

INTERNAL COMMUNICATION SYSTEM

In addition to the records component of the risk management information system, the risk manager needs to create information channels that ensure that all information relating to the risk management function is channeled to the risk management department. Among the concerns that the risk manager should be informed about are the following:

1. New construction, remodeling, or renovation of the firm's properties.
2. Introduction of new programs, products, activities, or operations, especially those that require specialized equipment.
3. Acquisition through purchase, lease, or rental of new locations.
4. Litigation involving the organization or any of its employees with respect to their activities as employees of the organization.
5. Progress on claims in the process of settlement or litigation; information channels in this area are required not only from insurance companies, but also from lawyers involved in the litigation.
6. Recovery progress of workers during periods of disability, including the worker's ability to return to work on a light-duty basis. Communication in this area requires information both from the injured worker and from physicians.
7. Information on hiring activities throughout the organization. Because hiring may occur in a variety of places throughout an organization, the risk manager requires information on the extent to which different standards are required or are used in the hiring process.

Although the preceding list is not exhaustive, it indicates the broad range of information sources that need to be established if the risk manager is to be alerted to new exposures as they evolve within the organization.

IMPORTANT CONCEPTS TO REMEMBER

systems approach to safety
identification tools
risk analysis questionnaires
fact finders
exposure checklists
insurance policy checklists
coverages applicable
orientation
analysis of documents

analysis of financial
    statements
financial statement method
flow charts
fire rate makeup
experience modification
    letters
experience modifier
structured interview guide

inspections
risk management
    information systems
risk management policy
    manual
risk management record
    systems

QUESTIONS FOR REVIEW

1. Explain why risk identification is generally considered to be the most difficult step in the risk management process.

2. Identify the contributions that insurers have made to the practice of risk identification.

3. Identify the circumstances and challenges that gave rise to systems safety.

4. Explain how the systems safety approach to risk identification differs from the approach that had previously been used to identify risks.

5. Identify and briefly describe the broad techniques that are used in the risk identification process.

6. Describe the general nature of (a) a risk analysis questionnaire, (b) an exposure checklist, (c) an insurance policy checklist, and (d) a structured interview guide. What are the advantages and disadvantages of each in the risk identification process?

7. In what way(s) may flowcharts be useful in the risk identification process?

8. Identify the insurance-related documents that may be available to the risk manager and explain how each may be useful in the risk identification and measurement process.

9. Explain what is meant by an expert system and how such systems may be used in the risk identification process.

10. Describe the components of a risk management information system and explain the function the RMIS serves.

QUESTIONS FOR DISCUSSION

1. Of the approaches to risk identification discussed in the text, which is the preferred approach?

2. Who, in your opinion, should perform the risk identification function? Should it be performed internally, or should it be delegated to an outside party?

3. Discovery of the risks an individual or organization faces is one of the most difficult tasks in the risk management process. How would you go about determining the risks you face?

4. Explain how the analysis of financial statements may be useful in risk identification and also the inadequacies of financial statements for risk identification.

5. What information that is useful in risk identification and measurement may be gained from the internal documents listed in the Analysis of Documents section of the chapter?

Suggestions for Additional Reading

Criddle, A. Hawthorne. "A Theory of Risk Discovery," *National Insurance Buyer*, VI, No. 1 (January 1959).

Ingley, A.J. "Problems of Risk Analysis," *The Growing Job of Risk Management*, AMA Management Report No. 70 (New York: American Management Association, 1962), pp. 137–138.

Lederer, Jerome. "Manned Space Flight Safety, NASA," *Best's Review, Property Liability Edition*, vol. VII, No. I (May 1970).

Mehr, R.I., and B.A. Hedges. *Risk Management: Concepts and Applications.* Homewood, Il.: Richard D. Irwin, 1974. Chapters 7, 8.

Ralston, August R., ed. *Risk Management Manual.* Santa Monica, Ca.: (loose-leaf service with monthly supplements), vol. 1, section 1.

Recht, J.L. "Systems Safety Analysis: An Introduction," *National Safety News*, vol. XCII, No. 6 (Chicago: National Safety Council, December 1965).

Rao, Geetha. "Anatomy of an Accident: How Forensic Engineers Determine What Went Wrong," *Risk Management* (October 1995).

CHAPTER 7

Risk Evaluation: Measuring Severity

CHAPTER OBJECTIVES

When you have finished this chapter, you should be able to

Identify and explain the Prouty measures of severity.

•

Identify the three broad categories into which risks may be classified according to their potential severity and describe the characteristics of each.

•

Identify the two reasons for measuring the severity of the potential loss that can arise from a particular exposure.

•

Explain the provisions of the Internal Revenue Code relating to the taxation of property insurance recoveries.

•

Identify the factors that determine the magnitude of a business interruption loss.

•

Explain the general method by which the potential severity of employee dishonesty losses can be measured.

Introduction

In this chapter, we begin our examination of the process whereby the risk manager attempts to evaluate the risks facing the organization. "Evaluation" implies some ranking in terms of importance, and ranking suggests measuring some aspect of the factors to be ranked. In the case of loss exposures, two facets must be examined: the possible severity of loss, and the possible frequency or probability of loss. We begin our discussion by examining the process of measuring loss severity, and we treat frequency in the next chapter.

❖ Importance of Loss Severity in Ranking Exposures ■■■■■■■■■■■■■■■■■■

The first rule of risk management—don't risk more than you can afford to lose—suggests that it is the size of a potential loss that dictates what ought to be done about a particular exposure. At least it suggests that the size of a potential loss is the factor that dictates the exposures about which *something* must be done.

Actually, there are two reasons why potential severity must be measured. First, some notion of severity is necessary for classifying risks. Whether a particular exposure is ultimately classed as critical, important, or unimportant depends on the potential severity of loss. In addition, the magnitude of the potential loss must also be measured to determine the amount of insurance that should be purchased when the decision is made to transfer the risk. A lack of precision in determining the amounts of insurance to be purchased can result in unnecessary costs and, in the case of inadequate coverage, sometimes unbearable costs. If the amount of insurance is too low, the firm itself must bear the uninsured loss. If the amount of insurance purchased is higher than required, there is also an unnecessary cost. As we will see, different degrees of precision are required for the purpose of (1) classifying risk and (2) determining the amount of insurance to be purchased. In the first case, the severity is measured against the organization's ability to bear losses. In the second case, the cost of the insurance purchased can vary directly with the precision of the valuation estimate. It is for this reason that different measures of severity may be considered for different purposes.

❖ The Prouty Measures of Severity ■■■■■■■■■■■■

The risk manager of a large national corporation has suggested a classification for measuring loss severity, based on a system used by insurance underwriters. Richard Prouty has proposed that for each potential loss, the risk manager should estimate two measures of loss: the *maximum possible loss* (MPL) and the *probable maximum loss* (PML).[1] The *maximum possible loss* is the worst loss that could occur, given the worst possible combination of circumstances. The probable maximum loss, on the other hand, is the loss that is likely, given the most likely combination of circumstances.

The distinction between the MPL and the PML is derived from the art of the underwriter. In assessing exposures being considered for insurance, property insurance underwriters attempt to estimate the MPL for each property. Although

---

[1]Richard Prouty, *Industrial Insurance: A Formal Approach to Risk Analysis and Evaluation* (Washington, D.C.: Machinery and Allied Products Institute, January 19, 1960).

the underwriter recognizes that it is conceivable that a 10-story building to be insured could burn to the ground, he or she also realizes that this is highly unlikely. Most fires are discovered in their incipient stages. Fire departments respond to alarms quickly, and most losses are controlled. In the case of a building with a sprinkler system, the chances of a total loss are quite remote. Therefore, rather than focusing on the total value of the structure, the underwriter attempts to determine the magnitude of the *most likely* loss. Given the underwriter's spread of risk and the numerous properties in his or her risk portfolio, this is a reasonable strategy.

It may also be a reasonable strategy for the risk manager with a large number of properties. If the risk manager's exposure to loss approximates that of an insurance underwriter—that is, if there are a large number of properties geographically dispersed—perhaps the maximum probable loss is a useful concept. For the risk manager with a single structure, or a limited number of properties, however, the important measure of severity is the *maximum possible loss.*

THE LOSS UNIT CONCEPT

One of the most relevant measures of severity, which unfortunately has not been widely discussed, is the *loss unit.* The loss unit is the total of all financial losses that can result from a single event, taking into consideration the various exposures. One of the best examples of the loss unit computation is the total losses that might have occurred in the bombing of the World Trade Center in 1994. Although the total property damage and business interruption that resulted from the bomb exceeded $600 million, the loss could have been worse. The loss unit in this case could include the total value of the building itself, the loss of rental income during the period of reconstruction, the workers compensation benefits payable to workers who might have been killed or injured, and the potential liability for injury to customers and tenants. Computing the loss unit requires calculation of the maximum possible loss for each of these exposures and then aggregating the totals. The significance of the loss unit lies in the fact that although an organization might be able to retain certain of the exposures individually, there is no guarantee that losses will occur individually. The loss unit is an attempt to alert management to the potential catastrophe that could result under the worst possible conditions.

◼ Measuring Property Loss Exposures ◼ ◼ ◼ ◼ ◼ ◼ ◼ ◼ ◼ ◼ ◼

Damage to property may be a source of two types of loss, direct and indirect. In this section, we focus on measuring the severity of direct loss to property in order to determine the exposure that arises out of the loss of the property itself. Indirect loss, which involves the loss of income that stems from the loss of the property, is discussed separately.

LOSS SEVERITY—REAL PROPERTY

It should be recognized at the outset that the risk manager's measure of loss severity is usually unrelated to the values for the property that may appear on the organization's books of account. Book values—which are based on historical costs and fictitious depreciation rates—have little to do with the actual loss that the organization would suffer if the asset were damaged or destroyed. Book values are based on historical costs and are modified by depreciation conventions that often overstate the value to gain the tax advantages associated with rapid depreciation.

From the risk manager's perspective, two measures of value for real property are possible: the actual cash value and the replacement cost of the property. *Actual cash value* is an insurance term that defines the value as current replacement cost less depreciation. As such, it may be a useful measure of value for the risk manager. But the conditions of the organization must be considered, and the actual loss that would be sustained if the property were destroyed may make replacement cost a more appropriate measure of value.

Most standard forms of property insurance provide coverage on an *actual cash value basis*. Historically, this approach was adopted in order to enforce the principle of indemnity, which holds that the insured should be compensated for the loss that he or she suffers and no more. In many instances, however, the "actual cash value" indemnification does not provide indemnification for the insured's total loss, and special endorsements are available to provide payment on other than an actual cash value basis under specialized circumstances.

The other value that can be used to measure the potential severity of real property losses is *replacement cost,* which is the cost of reconstructing the building with like kind and quality. Like actual cash value, replacement cost is an insurance term; it describes an option under which the insurer will pay loss without a deduction for depreciation, provided the insured has purchased coverage based on the replacement cost value of the property. The difference between replacement cost value and actual cash value, then, is depreciation. Because actual cash value is determined by deducting depreciation from replacement cost, valuation of real property must begin with an estimate of the replacement cost of the structure. Three approaches may be used to estimate building replacement costs; estimates or bids by building contractors and appraisers, construction cost indexes, and average square foot costs.

Contractors and Appraisers

Logically, the most accurate measure of the cost of replacing a structure is the amount that is actually spent for replacement. When the insured hires a builder to reconstruct a damaged building or when a tradesman is hired to make repairs, the amount actually paid is the replacement cost of the damaged or destroyed property.

A professional appraisal firm may be retained to estimate the replacement cost value of a structure. In this case, the appraisal firm serves as a surrogate for the contractor. In preparing an estimate of the replacement cost of a structure, professional appraisal firms perform the same cost calculations as would a contractor developing a bid for construction of the building. Firms such as Lloyd-Thomas Appraisal Company, Marshall-Stevens Appraisal Company, Industrial Appraisal Company, Rau Appraisal Company, or the American Appraisal Company all provide professional advice in this area. The drawback to this approach is that the appraisal costs money, and the small insured may feel that he cannot afford the expense of a professional appraisal.

Some insurance companies and a few insurance agencies provide property valuation services. This is probably the best approach for the small to medium-sized organization. Assistance from insurance companies, though less desirable than a professional appraisal, is certainly cheaper, and, in addition, it is more accurate than the results a risk manager unschooled in property appraisal might obtain working alone.

Internal Appraisals

Although a professional appraisal by a contractor or an appraisal firm is the preferred approach, some organizations perform their own appraisals, especially when the original cost of the structure is known and it is relatively new. In addition, when a professional appraisal has been made in the past, some organizations perform the computations internally to update such appraisals. Also, some risk managers periodically compute property values to determine whether a professional appraisal is required. Finally, some organizations perform their own appraisals for economy. When the appraisal is performed internally, one of two approaches is generally used: a construction cost index or a square foot cost method.

Construction Cost Indexes

A second approach to estimating current replacement cost values is to adjust the original construction cost of a building to current construction costs through the use of a construction cost index. Like a consumer price index, a construction cost index expresses the costs for one time period as a percentage of the cost for some arbitrary earlier point in time. A construction cost index would appear as shown in Table 7.1.

The application of a construction cost index is relatively simple. The original cost of the structure is multiplied by the index value for the current year. A structure built in 1926 at a cost of, say, $1 million, would cost $15,715,000 to construct in 1995 ($1,000,000 × 1571.5). The only problem that arises is that not all buildings were built in 1926, and we need to be able to compute the current replacement cost of buildings that were built in years other than the base year of the index. Fortunately, the base year of a cost index is purely arbitrary, and the base year can be converted to any year simply by dividing the index number for the current year by the index number for the new base year. For example, assume that the building under consideration was constructed in 1985. We are interested in the cost of constructing the 1985 building in current terms. To compute the replacement cost value of a structure built in 1985, we convert the base year of the cost index to 1985.

$$\frac{\text{Index value for indexed year}}{\text{New base-year index value}} = \text{New Index Value}$$

Table 7.1 Construction Cost Index, 1982–1995

	1926 = 100	
1926	=	100.0
****		*****
1982	=	1136.2
1983	=	1176.7
1984	=	1224.4
1985	=	1249.6
1986	=	1266.6
1987	=	1278.3
1988	=	1329.4
1989	=	1362.4
1990	=	1382.6
1991	=	1397.4
1992	=	1420.4
1993	=	1469.9
1994	=	1518.7
1995	=	1571.5

Thus, for example, if we divide the 1980-indexed value for 1992 (232.0) by the 1980-indexed value for 1985 (126.6), we obtain the 1985-indexed value for 1992:

$$\frac{1571.5}{1249.6} = 140.2$$

As shown in the table, construction costs in 1985 were 1249.6 percent of construction costs in 1926; construction costs in 1995 are 1571.5 percent of the 1926 construction costs. Construction costs in 1995 were therefore 140.2 percent of construction costs in 1985. Multiplying the original 1985 cost of $1 million produces a 1995 replacement cost of $1,402,000. The same indexing process would be applied to any additions to the structure, using the year in which the addition was made as the indexing base year.

Construction cost indexes are useful tools for estimating replacement costs. The use of a cost index requires data on the original cost of the structure and the existence of an index that accurately reflects the changes in costs for the particular type of property to be valued. Because construction costs can vary geographically, some construction cost indexes reflect costs only in a particular region. In some cases, a territorial multiplier is used to convert a national index to a specific locality. One of the most widely used sources of building and construction costs, the appraisal firm Marshall and Swift publishes a national construction cost index in its publication, the *Stevens Valuation Quarterly*, which is available at most libraries. Territorial multipliers are included, that reflect differences in construction costs by area.

Although application of a construction cost index is an effective approach to determining current replacement costs, it is not always possible. Often, information on the original cost of the structure is not available. In this case, a different approach must be used, such as the square foot cost method discussed in the following section. When original cost data are available, they can be used to generate a replacement cost value that can be tested against the values generated by the square foot cost method.

Square Foot Construction Costs

The replacement cost of a building can be determined by comparing the subject building to a building whose costs are known. Obviously, this approach is workable only when a credible database of building costs exists that can be applied to the particular structure under consideration. Generally, this means an organized collection of known costs, collated and averaged to make them more useful.

In the United States, there are several dependable sources of average square foot cost information for various types of buildings. Generally, these cost data are accumulated by professional appraisal companies, who offer the services of their engineers and architects to property owners who desire a specific appraisal of their property. The major appraisal firms are Marshall and Swift, Rau Appraisal, Boeck Appraisal, and Lloyd-Thomas Appraisal. Several of these appraisal firms compile valuation databases from their appraisals. The *Stevens Valuation Quarterly*, published by Marshall and Swift, is perhaps the best known of these databases. This publication is a loose-leaf manual with quarterly supplements that lists construction costs for a wide variety of building types and other structures. The construction costs published in the manual are an average of the costs for buildings of various types actually appraised by Marshall and Swift.

Stevens Valuation Quarterly *Spot Cost Method*   The *Stevens Valuation Quarterly* is an appraisal tool widely used by the insurance industry for estimating insurable values. In the *Valuation Quarterly Spot Cost Method* approach, the replacement cost of a building is found by comparing the construction and dimensions of the subject building with the construction and dimensions of similar buildings whose costs are known. The simplest accurate measurement of size relationship is by means of the floor area, so the costs in the *Valuation Quarterly* are normally on a square foot cost basis, with special costs for items that do not fit accurately into this method.

The square foot costs in the *Stevens Valuation Quarterly* vary by occupancy and type of construction. The occupancy classifications reflect the differences in construction among occupancy classes (for example, churches versus hotels, and hotels versus hospitals). For each occupancy, the square foot replacement costs are presented for five major types of construction.[2] The format of the Spot Cost values is indicated in Figure 7.1.

[2]The construction classes are similar to but not identical with the classifications used by insurers in determining fire rates for commercial properties.

INDUSTRIALS

Costs include an amount of office commensurate with the general quality of the structure. Typically, for manufacturing this is between 4% and 12% of the total area. Wiring and piping used in the manufacturing process are not included.

CLASS	COMPONENT PARTS	LOW	AVG.	GOOD	EXCL.
A	Basic Structure	$18.85	$27.28	$39.46	$57.09
	Exterior Wall	6.20	8.48	11.61	15.90
	Heating and cooling	.90	3.44	5.24	8.15
	Elevators	1.01	1.27	1.60	2.01
	Total cost per square foot ...	**$26.96**	**$40.47**	**$57.91**	**$83.15**
B	Basic Structure	$17.31	$25.38	$37.19	$54.52
	Exterior Wall	6.13	8.40	11.50	15.74
	Heating and cooling	.89	3.41	5.18	8.07
	Elevators	1.00	1.26	1.58	1.99
	Total cost per square foot ...	**$25.33**	**$38.45**	**$55.45**	**$80.32**
C	Basic Structure	$11.56	$19.03	$31.33	$51.57
	Exterior Wall	5.75	7.70	10.31	13.80
	Heating and cooling	.88	2.07	3.41	7.98
	Total cost per square foot ...	**$18.19**	**$28.80**	**$45.05**	**$73.35**
D	Basic Structure	$11.28	$18.13	$29.15	$46.87
	Exterior Wall	4.37	6.20	8.78	12.44
	Heating and cooling	.87	2.03	3.35	4.94
	Total cost per square foot ...	**$16.52**	**$26.36**	**$41.28**	**$64.25**
S	Basic Structure	$11.56	$18.56	$29.80	$47.85
	Exterior Wall	3.37	5.23	8.12	12.59
	Heating and cooling	.88	2.05	3.38	4.99
	Total cost per square foot ...	**$15.81**	**$25.84**	**$41.30**	**$65.43**

	SUBSTITUTION REFINEMENTS	LOW	AVG.	GOOD	EXCL.
W	Brick, common	$ 7.61	$ 9.61	$12.14	$15.34
	block backup	6.81	8.43	10.43	12.90
	grouted or cavity	7.49	8.93	10.65	12.70
A	Concrete block	5.42	6.91	8.80	11.22
	Concrete and glass panels	9.15	10.59	12.27	14.21
	Concrete, formed	6.35	7.90	9.82	12.20
L	tilt-up or precast	5.02	6.53	8.48	11.02
	Masonry veneer, Class D	5.74	8.05	11.30	15.86
	Metal and glass panels	10.53	13.72	17.88	23.30
L	Metal, corrugated or ribbed	2.98	3.76	4.75	5.99
	sandwich panels	5.66	7.29	9.40	12.12
	Steel studs, stucco panels	5.38	6.31	7.41	8.69
S	wood or aggregate panels	6.01	7.07	8.30	9.76
	Stucco, Class D	4.39	5.28	6.34	7.63
	Tile, structural clay	5.64	6.91	8.48	10.40
	Transite or galbestos	4.32	5.45	6.89	8.71
	Wood siding	4.43	5.40	6.57	8.01
H	Electric, baseboard or cable	$ 1.36	$ 1.72	$ 2.17	$ 2.74
	wall heaters	.65	.78	.94	1.13
	Forced air	1.41	1.81	2.33	3.00
	Furnace, floor or wall	.74	.89	1.08	1.30
	Hot water, baseboard/radiators	2.50	3.25	4.23	5.51
	Space heaters, gas with fan	.59	.80	1.10	1.49
E	Steam, with boiler	2.34	2.98	3.79	4.82
	without boiler	1.88	2.45	3.19	4.14
A	Central A.C., hot/chilled water	6.42	8.15	10.34	13.12
	warm and cool air	3.72	4.80	6.19	7.98
T	Package A.C., short ducts	2.69	3.55	4.68	6.16
	Heat pump	3.00	4.07	5.53	7.50
	Evaporative cooling	1.33	1.56	1.83	2.14
	Refrigerated cooling only	1.78	2.51	3.53	4.98
	Ventilation, fans & ducts	.44	.55	.68	.85

10/95

VALUATION QUARTERLY
© 1995 by MARSHALL & SWIFT, L.P. All rights reserved.

Figure 7.1 Spot Cost Values

Construction Classifications Insurance companies and their rating organizations have established construction classifications for the purpose of determining the fire insurance rate on different types of buildings. These classifications reflect the degree to which a particular type of construction will resist the effects of fire. Most building construction falls into five broad classes:

1. **Class A Fire-Resistive Buildings:** A "Class A" fire-resistive building is characterized by a steel frame, which may be bolted, welded, or riveted together.

This steel frame is covered by at least 4 inches of concrete or other fire-resistive material. The floors and roof of a Class A structure are usually reinforced concrete on steel decking or formed slabs resting on the frame, or poured so that they become an integral part of the frame. As an alternative, they may consist of prefabricated panels and may be mechanically stressed.

2. **Class B Fire-Resistive Buildings:** A "Class B" fire-resistive building is characterized by a reinforced concrete frame in which the columns and beams are either formed or precast reinforced concrete. Precast beams or columns are usually mechanically stressed. Like the Class A buildings above, a Class B building is fire resistant. The floors and roof of Class B structures are usually reinforced concrete on steel decking or formed slabs resting on the frame, or poured so that they become an integral part of the frame. As an alternative, they may consist of prefabricated panels and may be mechanically stressed.

3. **Class C Masonry Buildings:** Class C buildings are partially fire resistant. They are characterized by masonry or reinforced concrete construction. The walls are usually load bearing. In some cases, the roof or upper floors may be supported by exposed steel, concrete, or wood joists or trusses. Masonry buildings may have combustible or noncombustible floors and roofs.

4. **Class S Buildings:** Class S buildings are characterized by incombustible construction and prefabricated structural members. The exterior walls may be steel studs or an open skeleton frame with exterior coverings consisting of prefabricated panels or sheet siding. Upper floors and roof are supported on steel joists or beams. The "ground" floor may be a concrete slab on grade. Upper floors and roof may consist of metal deck, prefabricated panels, or sheathing.

5. **Frame (Class D) Buildings:** Frame buildings are those with exterior walls, floors, and roof of combustible construction, or buildings with exterior walls of noncombustible or slow-burning construction with combustible floors and roof.

The published square foot costs represent the final cost of construction to the owner, including average architect's and engineer's fees, normal interest on building funds during the process of construction, labor and materials, normal site preparation, including grading and excavation, utilities from the structure to the lot line, and the contractor's overhead and profit.

If a building is to be valued on the basis of the cost per square foot of constructing it, someone must obviously determine the area of the building, expressed in square feet. Unless blueprints or construction plans are available, this may require the appraiser to determine the dimensions of the structure by measuring it. Although "measuring out" a building is usually a relatively simple task, it can become complicated in the case of complex structures. The recommended approach is to follow the same methodology in every case. Start at a selected corner of the structure, and measure to the next "corner." Write the measurements down and prepare a rough structure as you record the dimensions. When the dimensions from one corner to the next are recorded, turn the corner and measure in a new direction until you reach the next corner, recording the measurements until you reach the starting point. At this point, you can "prove" the accuracy of the measurements by adding the dimensions for opposite sides.[3] The area can then be computed using standard geometric formulas.

Size and Shape Modifiers

A square (equilateral rectangle) structure will enclose the maximum area per lineal meter of perimeter. The greater the departure of the building's structure from a perfect square, the greater the deviation in square foot area from the optimum represented by a square. In addition, straight walls are less expensive to construct than are corners and angles. As a result, the square foot construction cost of a structure varies not only with the dimensions of the structure, but also with its shape. Appraisers recognize the influence of size and shape through the use of "modifiers," which reflect the influence of these factors on average square foot cost. The size and shape modifiers used in the *Stevens Valuation Quarterly* are indicated in Figure 7.2.

MEASURING PERSONAL PROPERTY EXPOSURES

Business personal property is a generic term that refers to the contents and other movable property owned by the organization. It generally consists of machinery and equipment and furnishings, as well as raw materials and inventories.

Machinery, Equipment, Furnishings

Machinery, equipment, and furnishings, like buildings, may be insured on an actual cash value or on a replacement cost basis. The actual cash value of machinery, equipment, and furnishings can be estimated in one of two ways. Since, for personal property, actual cash value is approximately equivalent to market value, the market value of the property can be determined from suppliers of the type of property involved. If there is a used market in the type of property under consideration, a reasonably close estimate of the actual cash value of the property can be obtained by determining what it would cost to replace the property in the marketplace.

The second approach to estimating actual cash value follows the procedure discussed earlier in connection with real property. Replacement cost indexes are available which indicate the current replacement cost for property of different ages, given the original cost of the property. (The replacement cost index of the *Stevens Valuation Quarterly* in Figure 7.3 is typical.) If a piece of equipment was acquired in year X for $1500, and the prices for that type of equipment have increased 50 percent, the current replacement cost of the property is $2250. This approach is probably simpler and less time consuming than attempting to determine market values for a large amount of equipment, but it is workable only if the original cost of the equipment is available.

---

[3]Experienced appraisers and adjusters have found that the measurement process is greatly simplified if measurement is conducted on the roof of the structure.

MODIFIERS
HEIGHT MULTIPLIERS

FOR FINISHED AND MULTIPLE-RESIDENTIAL BUILDINGS, (See Page C-1) the base wall height is 10 feet. Add or deduct 3% for each foot deviation.
FOR PLAIN BUILDINGS, the base wall height is 10 feet. Add or deduct 2% for each foot deviation for those occupancies designated as Plain on Page C-1. For unfinished shells use a 1% differential.
FOR BASEMENTS, add or deduct 2% for each foot deviation from the base height of 10 feet.

MULTISTORY BUILDINGS

Add .5% for each story over three, above ground, to all SPOT COST base costs. See Page B-8 for further explanation. Add .3% to ADDITIVE base costs.

SIZE AND SHAPE MULTIPLIERS

The main influence on cost variation due to the size and shape of buildings is the amount of wall area in relation to floor area. The purpose of the following tables is to provide a multiplier to adjust for this variation. Multiply the basic cost in either the Spot Cost or Additive Cost Section by the FINISHED BUILDING or PLAIN BUILDING (See Page C-1) multiplier under the approximate shape of the subject building and opposite the area corre- sponding to the nearest single floor area. In multistory buildings with varying single floor areas, an average floor area should be approximated. Do not use these tables if the exterior wall is priced from the Unit-in-Place Cost Section. For rural structure costs, Page B-94 & B-95, use the PLAIN BUILDING SIZE MODIFIERS deducting 15% from the multipliers.

FOR ALL BUILDINGS EXCEPT SINGLE FAMILY RESIDENCES

Single Floor Area	Approximately Square		Rectangle Or Slightly Irregular		Long Rectangle Or Irregular		Very Irregular	
	FINISHED	PLAIN	FINISHED	PLAIN	FINISHED	PLAIN	FINISHED	PLAIN
600	1.28	1.50	1.34	1.59	....	....	....	....
800	1.23	1.42	1.28	1.51	....	....	....	....
1,000	1.19	1.36	1.26	1.47	1.29	1.52	....	....
1,200	1.16	1.32	1.21	1.39	1.26	1.45	....	....
1,500	1.12	1.25	1.18	1.32	1.22	1.39	....	....
2,000	1.08	1.20	1.12	1.25	1.16	1.31	1.20	1.36
2,500	1.06	1.16	1.08	1.20	1.13	1.25	1.16	1.30
3,000	1.04	1.13	1.06	1.16	1.10	1.21	1.13	1.26
3,500	1.03	1.10	1.05	1.13	1.08	1.17	1.10	1.22
4,000	1.01	1.08	1.03	1.11	1.06	1.14	1.08	1.19
5,000	.99	1.06	1.01	1.09	1.04	1.12	1.06	1.15
6,000	.97	1.04	.99	1.07	1.02	1.10	1.05	1.13
7,000	.96	1.03	.98	1.04	1.00	1.08	1.03	1.11
8,000	.95	1.02	.97	1.03	.98	1.06	1.02	1.09
10,000	.94	1.00	.96	1.02	.97	1.04	1.00	1.07
12,000	.93	.99	.95	1.00	.96	1.02	.98	1.05
14,000	.92	.98	.94	.99	.95	1.00	.96	1.04
16,000	.91	.97	.93	.98	.94	.99	.95	1.02
18,000	.90	.96	.92	.97	.93	.98	.94	1.01
20,000	.89	.95	.91	.96	.92	.97	.93	1.00
25,000	.88	.94	.90	.95	.91	.96	.92	.99
30,000	.87	.93	.89	.94	.90	.95	.91	.98
40,000	.86	.92	.88	.93	.89	.94	.90	.97
50,000	.85	.91	.87	.92	.88	.93	.89	.96
60,000	.84	.90	.86	.91	.87	.92	.88	.95
80,000	.83	.89	.85	.90	.86	.91	.87	.94
100,000	.82	.88	.84	.89	.85	.90	.86	.93
125,000	.81	.87	.83	.88	.84	.89	.85	.92
150,000	.80	.86	.82	.87	.83	.88	.84	.90
200,000	.79	.85	.80	.86	.81	.87	.82	.89
300,000	.78	.84	.79	.85	.80	.86	.81	.88

VALUATION QUARTERLY
© 1990 - MARSHALL & SWIFT - PRINTED IN U.S.A.

1/90

Figure 7.2   Size and Shape Modifiers

When market values for used property are available, they provide a good approximation of actual cash value. On the other hand, when the starting point is the cost of new property—either determined from sellers or through replacement cost indexes—the actual cash value can be obtained by deducting a proper allowance for depreciation. Although this will always involve an element of judgment, the *Stevens Valuation Quarterly* provides a useful table of depreciation rates for various types of contents. (See Figure 7.4). The table in this figure includes a suggested salvage value for various types of equipment and an annual percentage

COMPARATIVE EQUIPMENT COSTS

Basis 1926 = 100%

YEARLY

INDUSTRY	1995	1994	1993	1992	1991	1990	1989	1988
Average of all	1020.4	985.0	958.0	939.8	928.5	910.2	886.5	841.4
Airplane mfg.	1221.8	1174.9	1145.3	1127.6	1119.9	1102.3	1078.8	1027.5
Apartment	763.5	739.5	714.2	696.1	684.4	670.2	651.2	619.0
Bakery	969.1	930.9	903.0	886.3	874.6	855.3	832.5	789.1
Bank	794.9	773.4	749.3	732.5	721.2	711.1	694.7	662.5
Bottling	1033.6	994.3	968.5	952.8	943.4	925.5	903.0	853.2
Brewery and distillery	1254.3	1208.9	1181.0	1162.7	1150.4	1125.0	1094.0	1033.0
Candy and confectionery	1244.2	1194.7	1159.1	1138.2	1122.7	1095.9	1064.5	1006.6
Cannery (fish)	1217.8	1169.9	1133.3	1111.7	1095.7	1070.9	1041.6	985.7
Cannery (fruit)	1225.1	1180.1	1140.3	1114.4	1094.7	1069.9	1040.5	985.2
Cement mfg.	1022.3	987.5	965.9	951.0	943.3	925.0	900.7	857.5
Chemical	1014.0	977.9	958.3	946.1	939.1	919.2	895.9	847.8
Church	870.9	847.9	813.4	787.1	767.9	753.2	732.5	697.8
Clay products	1015.8	981.8	959.3	942.3	932.9	913.9	887.5	843.8
Contractors' equipment	1185.1	1153.4	1125.2	1095.3	1075.3	1050.1	1017.3	970.9
Creamery and dairy	1066.4	1023.6	996.5	980.5	968.5	945.6	919.2	866.9
Dwelling	741.6	717.5	694.2	678.2	667.9	653.8	635.5	604.4
Elec. equip. mfg.	1015.1	968.7	945.8	935.7	934.8	924.2	906.4	857.5
Elec. power equipment	953.6	905.8	887.4	881.5	884.8	879.1	864.4	814.9
Flour, cereal and feed	1003.6	964.9	939.4	924.8	916.3	897.5	874.9	829.2
Garage	1140.5	1102.0	1073.9	1054.2	1040.4	1018.2	991.5	943.9
Glass mfg.	952.2	914.9	894.6	881.6	876.6	861.7	840.8	796.3
Hospital	944.0	908.8	883.1	866.8	855.4	836.6	813.4	770.7
Hotel	899.4	869.8	842.0	822.7	807.9	788.5	764.8	726.4
Laundry and cleaning	873.5	843.0	820.9	805.7	797.4	781.2	760.2	721.7
Library	969.6	937.2	906.6	887.3	876.6	861.9	840.4	798.2
Logging equipment	1067.9	1034.9	1006.4	984.7	969.3	949.9	925.1	884.3
Metalworking	1156.4	1113.4	1085.9	1070.3	1061.0	1038.9	1011.2	963.8
Mining and milling	1051.3	1019.8	992.7	971.8	955.6	934.2	906.0	859.6
Motion picture	1135.1	1097.9	1065.0	1039.6	1025.7	1009.6	984.3	932.3
Office equipment	863.1	838.6	818.1	805.9	798.7	787.1	768.3	732.6
Packing (fruit)	1153.5	1118.6	1079.2	1047.7	1025.8	1003.0	974.2	924.3
Packing (meat)	1064.3	1025.8	996.3	977.6	963.5	939.7	911.9	864.1
Paint mfg.	1034.3	995.7	971.8	955.9	947.8	929.0	905.2	857.0
Paper mfg.	985.5	953.2	925.2	904.4	892.4	875.1	853.1	808.8
Petroleum	1066.5	1028.9	1008.3	998.6	990.9	966.0	942.0	895.9
Printing	931.9	898.6	877.0	863.7	860.7	848.5	835.0	791.8
Refrigeration	1209.6	1165.9	1135.6	1114.2	1101.5	1077.6	1049.3	994.3
Restaurant	840.8	812.8	786.7	769.0	755.2	736.2	713.6	677.0
Rubber	1101.2	1063.7	1039.1	1019.2	1009.1	986.7	959.9	912.7
School	959.8	927.9	899.0	880.1	867.3	848.6	824.3	782.7
Shipbuilding	1162.4	1122.8	1097.2	1078.7	1069.5	1050.1	1023.6	973.3
Steam power	1002.9	964.5	944.5	933.8	929.5	914.3	890.8	841.0
Store	1000.6	970.9	937.5	914.3	899.7	884.1	861.6	819.2
Textile	1081.1	1049.2	1022.7	1003.2	991.1	969.5	945.6	900.4
Theater	847.7	820.3	795.1	779.2	770.1	756.9	737.2	700.7
Warehousing	850.1	826.7	800.2	782.0	771.2	757.7	740.2	708.5
Woodworking	1002.9	975.0	942.9	911.6	894.0	879.3	856.4	811.5

1/96

VALUATION QUARTERLY
© 1996 by Marshall & Swift, L.P. All rights reserved.

Figure 7.3 Equipment Cost Index

for depreciation, by class. More specialized valuation tables may also be available. Libraries, for example, generally use average costs calculated by a national library association. Other associations have similar aids.

Inventory and Raw Materials

The standard insurance valuation of inventory and raw materials is on an actual cash value basis. This generally means replacement cost minus depreciation. In most cases, the only depreciation applicable to inventory or raw materials is obsolescence, as might be the case with outdated stock. In most jurisdictions, the obsolescence factor is considered in computing the depreciation on property, and therefore it enters into the computation.

FIXTURES AND EQUIPMENT

DEPRECIATION PERCENTAGE TABLES

The percentages in the following table are rough "rule of thumb" guides only and are based on equipment in average condition. When the condition of the equipment under study is other than average, use the Condition Modifiers found in Section S. If the estimate is for insurable value only, we recommend using 80% of the indicated percentages and then applying condition modifiers.

Industry	Annual Depreciation	Salvage Value	Industry	Annual Depreciation	Salvage Value
Airplane mfg.	10.2	10%	Laundry-dry cleaning	10.2	10%
Apartment	9.7	10%	Library	10.2	10%
Bakery	8.5	10%	Logging equip.	16.9	10%
Bank	11.4	10%	Metal working	10.2	12%
Bottling	8.5	10%	Mining, milling	10.2	8%
Brewery, distillery	8.5	8%	Motion picture	8.5	12%
Candy, confectionery	7.0	10%	Office equipment	10.2	12%
Cannery-fish	10.3	8%	Oil refining	6.4	7%
Cannery-fruit	8.5	8%	Packing-meat	8.5	7%
Cement mfg.	5.1	8%	Paint mfg.	10.8	7%
Chemicals	10.8	6%	Paper mfg.	7.9	7%
Church	10.2	10%	Printing	9.2	10%
Clay products	6.8	7%	Refrigerating	10.2	8%
Construction equipment	16.9	14%	Restaurant	12.0	14%
Creamery-dairy	8.5	11%	Rubber	7.3	9%
Dwelling	9.7	12%	School	10.2	10%
Elec. equip. mfg.	10.2	10%	Shipbuilding	7.5	9%
Elec. power equip.	3.4	10%	Steam power	3.6	10%
Flour, cereal, feed	6.0	8%	Store	11.4	10%
Garage	10.2	10%	Textile	10.7	8%
Glass mfg.	7.3	8%	Theater	10.2	12%
Hospital	9.8	12%	Warehousing	11.4	10%
Hotel	10.2	10%	Woodworking	10.2	10%

The tables below are furnished primarily for the experienced equipment appraiser who has knowledge of the normal lives of fixtures and equipment, as a check against his other methods of determination of the total depreciation of equipment.

EFFECTIVE AGE IN YEARS	30	25	20	15	12	10	8	5
			TYPICAL LIFE EXPECTANCY IN YEARS					
1	2	2	3	5	6	8	10	15
2	3	5	7	10	13	16	21	31
3	5	7	10	15	20	24	33	48
4	7	10	14	21	27	33	46	66
5	9	13	18	27	34	42	57	77
6	11	16	22	32	42	51	67	82
7	14	19	26	38	50	61	74	
8	16	22	30	45	57	70	78	
9	18	25	35	51	64	76	80	
10	21	29	40	57	71	79		
11	24	32	45	63	76	80		
12	26	36	50	69	78			
13	29	40	55	74	80			
14	32	44	60	77				
15	35	48	65	79				
16	39	52	69	80				
17	42	56	73					
18	46	61	76					
19	49	66	78					
20	53	70	79					
22	60	74						
24	66	77						
26	72	79						
28	77							
30	79							

VALUATION QUARTERLY
© 1996 by MARSHALL & SWIFT, L.P. All rights reserved.

1/96

Figure 7.4   Equipment Depreciation Percentages

The major problem in determining the measure of loss for inventory stems from the inventory valuation conventions used by accountants, which can present a distorted picture of the actual cash value of the property. Many firms use either a "first in–first out" or "last in–first out" convention. Neither is a proper measure of insurable value. Properly measured, the inventory or raw materials should be valued at replacement cost; "next in–already here."

Tenant's Improvements and Betterments

Tenant's Improvements and Betterments are alterations or additions made to real property at the expense of a tenant. The tenant of a structure may spend a substantial sum in modifying and improving a structure owned by someone else. Usually, these improvements become a part of the building, and will belong to the building owner, depending on the terms of the lease.[4]

Assume that Brown owns a newly constructed building, with a replacement cost value of $1 million. Now assume that White, the tenant, installs improvements at a cost of, say, $200,000. The investment by White increases the value of Brown's building, raising the replacement cost value of the structure to $1.2 million. This is the value of Brown's interest in the structure and the amount he would lose in the event the structure is destroyed.

White, on the other hand, has an interest in the intangible "use value" of the improvements. White made the $200,000 investment in the expectation that he would enjoy the use of the improvements for at least the term of the current lease, and perhaps longer. If the building is destroyed, White will suffer the loss of use of the improvements. The exact amount of White's loss will depend on when the improvements are destroyed and the period of use anticipated and guaranteed by the lease at the time of installation. If, for example, the destruction occurs shortly after installation, White will lose the full $200,000 in use value that is lost. If, on the other hand, the improvements are destroyed after five years and White's lease still has five years to run, White will have lost one-half the expected use value.

Valuable Papers and Records

Still another area that requires special attention is the possible loss that can arise from damage to or loss of valuable papers and records. Unfortunately, this is a difficult area to measure, and most organizations have given little thought to what it would cost to replace the organization's records if they were destroyed. About the only approach that seems available with respect to measuring the potential severity of the valuable papers and records exposure is to calculate—at a reasonable internal labor rate—the cost of reconstructing the information in the records. There

---

[4]Insurance with respect to tenant's improvements and betterments creates a disproportionate number of problems in the insurance field, to a large extent because the insurable interest of such improvements is not always clearly understood. It is possible for both the building owner and the tenant to have an insurable interest in improvements to real property made at the expense of a tenant. Furthermore, it is possible that the value of the improvements may be insured by both parties, and that payment may be made to both parties in the event of a loss. This often misunderstood principle is discussed in Chapter 17.

will be instances in which an attempt to measure the value by this method will indicate that it would not be possible to reconstruct the records, thereby raising an entirely different type of question. If the records cannot be reproduced, what is the measure of value that their destruction would represent to the firm?

TAX TREATMENT OF PROPERTY LOSS INSURANCE RECOVERIES

Because a significant difference sometimes exists between the actual value of an asset and the value for which the asset is carried on the firm's books, insurance recoveries will often exceed the book value of the asset that has been destroyed. This, in the view of the Internal Revenue Service, poses a problem.

It should be noted first that a business is allowed a deduction for the book value of property that is destroyed by an accident, such as a fire or windstorm. If the book value of the asset is the same as the insurance recovery, the deduction for the damaged property offsets the insurance proceeds. The problem arises when the insurance proceeds exceed the book value of the asset.

Suppose, for the purpose of illustration, that the XYZ corporation owns a building that it has insured for its replacement cost value of $10 million. The book value of the asset—its original cost less accumulated depreciation—is, say, $5 million. In the event of a loss, XYZ's deduction for the building is limited to its depreciated basis of $5 million. The insurance recovery of $10 million therefore exceeds the deductible basis by $5 million, and XYZ realizes a taxable gain. This type of loss and recovery is termed an *involuntary conversion* and is subject to special tax treatment under *Internal Revenue Code* Section 1033(a). In the event of an involuntary conversion, the taxpayer is given the option of recognizing the gain (and paying taxes on the gain), or deferring taxation of the gain. If XYZ elects to do so, it can recognize the $5 million in taxable gain, pay the appropriate tax, and enter the new building built with the insurance proceeds in its books with a $10 million basis. As an alternative, XYZ may, under Section 1033(a), elect to defer taxation of the gain. In this case, the new $10 million building is entered in the books at the same basis as the building that was destroyed.[5]

⬛ Measuring Indirect Loss Exposures ■ ■ ■ ■ ■ ■ ■ ■ ■ ■ ■ ■

Indirect loss (also called consequential loss) consists of the other financial losses that result from the damage or destruction. For example, if you own a building worth $1,000,000, and that building is destroyed by a fire, you lose the $1,000,000 in value that the building represents. However, you also lose the use of the build-

---

[5]The choice between recognition and deferral of the gain may require complex calculation of the benefits under the options. It may be advantageous to pay the tax and receive a new basis that can then be depreciated.

ing for the period of time that it takes to rebuild it. The loss of use of the building is one form of indirect or consequential loss.

Indirect or consequential losses have traditionally been divided into two categories: "time element" and non-time element. Non-time element consequential loss coverages include various forms of consequential damage, such as the reduction in the value of clothing parts when companion parts are damaged, or losses that result from, but are not a part of the direct damage. The owner of a building that is partially destroyed by fire may suffer an additional loss, for example, if the building code requires that buildings of one type be rebuilt with superior construction. Laws that require demolition of the undamaged portion of a structure are another form of "indirect loss."

Time element exposures, as the designation implies, are those indirect loss exposures in which the amount of loss is usually a function of time. The loss arising from these exposures results from the inability to use an asset and consists of the reduction in income or the additional expenses occasioned by that loss of use. Time element exposures include business interruption, extra expense, contingent business interruption and extra expense, and the leasehold interest exposure.

MEASURING BUSINESS INTERRUPTION EXPOSURES

In the case of business interruption, the measure of loss for most organizations is the expenses that would continue during a period of shutdown, as well as the profits that would be lost during that period. When a firm is forced to suspend operations as a result of damage to its facilities, the income that had previously been earned ceases. In spite of the fact that the income ceases, some expenses will continue during the period of restoration. This might include, for example, depreciation, interest on mortgages and other indebtedness, the salaries of executives, employees under contract, and perhaps other employees, maintenance expenses, advertising, and, in some instances, utilities.

At the same time, some expenses will probably be discontinued during the period of interruption. Expenses such as light, heat, power, water, and telephone, for example, may be totally discontinued. In the case of rented property, the rent may be suspended during the period of restoration. Often, a part of the workforce will be let go during the period of interruption.

Period of Interruption

In general, the loss that will be sustained is measured in terms of the period that will be required for restoration, commencing with the date of the loss and continuing until the damaged property is restored to usable condition. Under some circumstances, an organization may be able to continue its operations at another location, or perhaps on a reduced basis at the location where the damage occurs. Although generally it is not possible to predict in advance how severely the firm's premises will be damaged, and therefore to determine whether or not operations could be continued at the existing location, it may be possible to determine what other facilities might be available in the event of loss.

When a mercantile establishment is interrupted, it loses sales, and the most appropriate measure of loss is the reduction in sales, less the cost of the goods sold and the expenses that do not continue during the period of interruption. When a manufacturer is interrupted, on the other hand, it loses production. The distinction between "sales" and "production" can be illustrated by the case of a manufacturer producing seasonal goods for sale at a future point in time. The manufacturer of Christmas tree ornaments might, for example, continue production throughout the year, but sell the bulk of its production during the months of September, October, and November. An interruption during the months of March, April, and May would not result in a reduction in sales during that period, precisely because no sales were being made. However, the lost production would be translated into reduced sales during the following September, October, and November.

A firm's business income goes to pay the expenses of operations and, to the extent it exceeds those expenses, a profit. It is thus composed of two elements: expenses and profits. For the purpose of understanding the business interruption exposure, it is helpful to subdivide expenses further into those that would continue in the event of a shutdown and those that would not continue. Thus,

Business income = Continuing Expenses + Noncontinuing Expenses + Profit

In the event of an interruption of business operations, some expenses will continue, and some will be abated. Logically, the loss sustained by the firm whose business is interrupted consists of the expenses that continue and the profit that would have been earned during the period of interruption.

Determining the potential severity of a business interruption loss is basically a prediction. More specifically, it is a prediction of the future income and expenses of the firm, and the period that would be required for restoration. The first item of information that is needed is an estimate of the period of interruption, which is a function of the period of time required for restoration. The logical approach is to assume the worst possible contingency—a total loss—and compute the potential loss in terms of the time that would be required to restore the premises in the event of such a loss. The *Stevens Valuation Quarterly* includes estimates of the time required to construct buildings of various types for specified occupancies. See Figure 7.5. Difficult to obtain machinery, which might not be readily available and which might thereby delay resumption of operations, should be considered in determining the period of restoration.

Once the period of interruption has been determined, it is necessary to predict the maximum loss that could be sustained during that period. This will vary with the seasonality of the business and with the trend in earnings. A highly seasonal business could lose a substantial portion of its income during a short period of interruption. In addition, since it is future income and expenses that would be lost, the estimate of the potential loss should consider increases in earnings over time. Finally, because expenses that do not continue are not payable under the business interruption forms, to the extent that such expenses can be identified, they should be deleted.

GENERAL INFORMATION

CONSTRUCTION TIME

The following table of average periods of construction lists points on empirical curves, which have been developed from figures for actual construction jobs. The data was adjusted for time lost due to labor shutdowns and extreme cases were discarded. No adjustments were made for holidays, inspection delays, or other minor shutdowns. Figures are the number of contract days from groundbreaking to completion of project.

DESIGNED OCCUPANCY	PROJECT COST (in thousands of dollars)			
	100	200	500	1,000
Apartments, low-rise	100	145	200	240
Auditoriums/Clubhouses	105	135	185	235
Banks	95	120	165	210
Churches	120	160	235	315
Department Stores/Shopping Malls	-----	-----	-----	280
Dormitories	120	150	205	260
Garages/Parking Structures	105	135	195	250
Governmental Buildings	120	155	220	280
Hotels/Motels	115	145	195	245
Hospitals	-----	-----	270	325
Industrial Buildings	100	125	165	205
Libraries	105	190	300	385
Medical Office Buildings	120	180	260	320
Nursing Homes	160	195	250	305
Office Buildings	110	135	185	225
Residences/Town Houses	95	125	180	240
Restaurants	120	155	220	285
Retail Stores/Markets/Disc. Stores	105	160	235	290
Schools/Colleges	145	180	240	295
Veterinary Hospitals	130	175	255	340
Warehouses	90	110	150	185

DESIGNED OCCUPANCY	PROJECT COST (in thousands of dollars)			
	5,000	10,000	20,000	50,000
Apartments, low-rise	340	385	-----	-----
Apartments, hi-rise	425	500	575	675
Auditoriums/Clubhouses	410	520	665	910
Banks	375	475	-----	-----
Churches	610	815	1090	-----
Department Stores	415	490	575	720
Dormitories	445	565	710	-----
Garages/Parking Structures	460	600	-----	-----
Governmental Buildings	515	665	860	1200
Hotels/Motels	415	520	655	885
Hospitals	510	620	755	975
Industrial Buildings	335	410	510	675
Libraries	580	665	750	-----
Medical Office Buildings	455	515	575	-----
Nursing Homes	480	585	710	-----
Office Buildings	370	460	570	760
Restaurants	515	-----	-----	-----
Retail Stores/Markets/Disc. Stores	415	470	-----	-----
Schools/Colleges	485	600	740	985
Warehouses	315	390	-----	-----

1/95

VALUATION QUARTERLY
© 1995 – MARSHALL & SWIFT. All rights reserved.

Figure 7.5   Time Required for Reconstruction

Employee Expense

One of the major considerations in estimating a potential business interruption loss is the need to continue the employee payroll during a period of interruption. In some instances, all employees are critical to the success of the firm and must be retained for the resumption of operations. In other cases, the workers could be easily replaced and do not therefore represent a "necessary continuing expense."

Loss of Earnings After Restoration

In estimating the possible loss that can result from an interruption of business operations, consideration should also be given to the possibility that earnings may not return to their previous level immediately upon physical restoration of the premises. In some instances, the loss of earnings may continue past this point in time. Consider, for example, the case of a restaurant. In the event of fire forcing a suspension of operation, customers may turn to other restaurants in the area, and the business following the reopening may be far lower than the business immediately preceding the fire or other peril that occasioned the interruption.

EXPENSES OF CONTINUING OPERATIONS

Some types of businesses cannot shut down their operations in the event of a fire, and so may have to continue operations at some other location, usually at an increased cost. Expenses to continue operations following damage to facilities may include those incurred for temporary premises and equipment, moving, extra labor, advertising, printing, travel for employees, and so on. The amount of these extra expenses is estimated from available information and is projected for the anticipated period that will be required to resume normal operations. The expenses in the organization's profit and loss statement provide a point of departure for projecting future expenses, including those that would be required to continue operations. Standard extra expense worksheets, usually included in a risk analysis questionnaire, are used as a guide in the projections.

CONTINGENT BUSINESS INTERRUPTION

Contingent business interruption refers to the loss resulting from interruptions which are caused by a fire or other insured peril at premises that are not owned, controlled, or operated by the firm. Contingent business interruption losses occur

1. When the firm depends on one or a few manufacturers or suppliers for most of the materials or services to conduct business. The firm on which the insured depends is called the *contributing property*.
2. When the firm depends on one or a few businesses to purchase the bulk of its products. The business to which the bulk of the insured's production flows is called the *recipient property*.
3. When the firm depends on a neighboring business to help attract customers to its place of business. The "attracting" business is commonly referred to as a *leader property*.

CONTINGENT EXTRA EXPENSE INSURANCE

The *contingent extra expense* exposure refers to the loss sustained in the form of extra expenses that are incurred as a result of damage to or destruction of property that the firm does not own, control, or operate. It is similar to contingent business interruption in the sense that it is property of some other firm, rather than the firm's own property, whose destruction would cause the loss. A contingent extra expense exposure exists, for example, in instances where a manufacturer has a low-cost source of raw materials. Shutdown of the supplier's plant would force the insured to obtain these materials elsewhere at a higher cost.

THE LEASEHOLD INTEREST EXPOSURE

Leasehold interest refers to the value of the asset that exists when an individual or organization enjoys a favorable lease, which might be terminated if the premises leased were destroyed. A lessee may suffer financial loss as a result of the termination of a lease, particularly when the rent specified in the lease is below the current market, and many leases provide for cancellation in the event of damage to the premises. This, coupled with a rent in the lease that is below the market, creates a potential loss for the lessee.

Suppose, for the same example, that a firm has leased property for $1000 a month under a contract that does not provide for escalation of the rent, but that contains a provision for the cancellation of the lease in the event of fire damage to the premises. Suppose also that the increases in rents since the inception of the lease make it impossible to secure similar quarters at less than $2000 a month and that the current lease has six years to run. This situation creates a leasehold interest of $1000 a month for the 72-month period remaining in the lease.

A leasehold interest arises from the cancellation clause in a lease, and the increase in property values or rents since the inception of the lease. Generally, the measure of loss is the difference between the rent the tenant is paying under the lease and the rent that would have to be paid elsewhere for the balance of the lease.

In simplest terms, the measure of value in the case of a leasehold interest, is the difference between the rent payable under the lease and the rent that would be required in the absence of the lease. The insured's right to continue payment of the amount specified in the lease is a contractual one, and it is this right that constitutes the basis for the insurance. It should be clear that the amount of the tenant's interest varies over time with current rental costs. The leasehold interest value at any point in time depends on the prevailing rental rates for equivalent facilities.

Because the amount of the leasehold interest exposure is a function of time, and because the loss, if one occurs, will be sustained over a period of time, measuring the leasehold interest exposure involves discounting to calculate the present value of the loss. The value of the leasehold interest exposure is a lump sum, equal to the discounted present value of the difference between the bargain rate in the lease and the cost of equivalent facilities in the market. The net leasehold interest will vary over time, decreasing with the number of months left to run in the lease. The magnitude of the exposure diminishes over time.

For the purpose of illustration, let us return to our initial example of the firm with a lease that has six years to run, with a guaranteed rent of $1000 when prevailing rents for similar facilities are $2000. The leasehold interest is $1000 a month.

The *net* leasehold interest is the present value of $1000, discounted at some rate of interest for 72 months. If we use 6 percent, reference to a present value table indicates that the present value of $1 a month for 72 months at 6 percent is indicated to be $60.6425. The present value of $1000 a month for 72 months, and the present value of the insured's leasehold interest is therefore $60,643.

◼ Measuring Criminal Loss Exposures ◼ ◼ ◼ ◼ ◼ ◼ ◼ ◼ ◼ ◼

The major area of criminal loss is employee dishonesty. For many years, there was no satisfactory way to determine how great the exposure was in this area. Although it seemed clear that the amount an embezzler could get away with was somehow a function of the organization's assets and cash flow, there was no precise formula for measuring possible loss severity. Then, many years ago, the Surety Association of America, in conjunction with the American Institute of Certified Public Accountants devised a series of Dishonesty Exposure Indexes that may be used to roughly estimate the fidelity exposure. Separate formulas are available for public bodies, banks, and mercantile or manufacturing firms. Based on certain financial measures, a Dishonesty Exposure Index is computed, and then, through reference to a table based on these indexes, the *minimum* amount of fidelity coverage is derived. The Dishonesty Exposure Indexes were devised to determine the amount of employee dishonesty insurance an organization should purchase. Despite this origin, they are basically a means of measuring the exposure. They are useful in determining whether the risk should be transferred or retained and, if it is to be transferred, the limits of coverage that should be purchased.[6]

◼ Measuring Legal Liability Exposures ◼ ◼ ◼ ◼ ◼ ◼ ◼ ◼ ◼ ◼

Regrettably, there is little we can say about the process of measuring potential severity in the case of legal liability. It is an exposure for which there is virtually no maximum. Reference to the daily newspapers provides a stark reminder of the fact that the size of damage awards has grown significantly.

The record case for a single injury involved the Ford Motor Company and a $128,466,280 judgment for injury to a single person. The gas tank of a Ford Pinto exploded, permanently disabling the claimant. Although the judgment was reduced on appeal, the size of the initial judgment indicates the attitudes of jurors. The Dalkon Shield, an intrauterine birth control device, was taken off the market in 1974, in the face of hundreds of suits against its manufacturer A. H. Robins Company. After a quarter of a billion dollars had been paid in judgments, over 3000 cases remained unsettled.

The world's largest asbestos manufacturer, the Denver-based Manville Corporation, filed for reorganization under the bankruptcy laws on August 26, 1982 to

[6]The Dishonesty Exposure Index is discussed in greater detail in Chapter 20.

hold at bay the thousands of product liability cases planned or pending against its subsidiary, Johns-Manville. The move not only held up an estimated 52,000 potential lawsuits (which could cost $2 billion to litigate) but also put a barrier between the company and its creditors. Prior to filing for reorganization, new lawsuits had been coming in at a rate of 500 per month, with about 16,500 suits already pending. (Mansville is only one of a group of 260 companies facing similar claims.)

An even greater catastrophe illustrating the magnitude of the liability exposure was the December 3, 1984 accident at Union Carbide's plant in Bhopal, India, which killed more than 3800 people. The Union Carbide loss, which shocked the world, occurred when an insecticide plant owned jointly by Union Carbide and the Indian government leaked toxic gas. The gas, of which the main ingredient was the chemical methyl isocyanate, killed more than 3800 local residents and injured tens of thousands. The accident was the worst ever experienced by the chemical industry. In October, 1991, India's Supreme Court upheld a controversial $470 million settlement.

A catastrophic liability loss of more recent vintage involves the suits against three U.S. manufacturers of breast implants, Dow Corning Corporation, Bristol-Meyers Squibb Company, and Baxter International, Inc. In 1994, a federal judge approved a $4.25 billion product liability settlement between breast implant makers and women who say they were injured by the implants. Dow Corning has since filed for bankruptcy.

Although all of these cases have involved large national manufacturers or corporations, they illustrate the magnitude of the damage, injury, and deaths for which businesses can be held liable. It is a mistake to assume that only large national organizations are exposed to catastrophic losses. After all, the determinant of the severity of the liability loss is not the size of the organization that is held responsible, but the number of people injured or the damage caused by the actions of the organization or its employees. Many authorities believe that given the current state of our tort system, we currently have no answer to the question, "How much liability insurance is enough?"

IMPORTANT CONCEPTS

maximum possible loss (MPL)
probable maximum loss (PML)
loss unit
actual cash value
replacement cost
principle of indemnity
construction cost index
square foot cost method
class A fire resistive building
class B fire resistive building
class C masonry building
class S building

class D frame building
size and share modifier
next-in already-here
tenant's improvements and betterments
valuable papers and records
Section 1033(a)
indirect loss
consequential loss
time element loss
non-time element loss
business interruption exposure

period of interruption
continuing expenses
noncontinuing expenses
contingent business interruption exposure
contingent extra expense exposure
extra expense exposure
contributing property
recipient property
leader property
leasehold interest exposure
dishonesty exposure index

QUESTIONS FOR REVIEW

1. Explain the two reasons why it is important that the potential severity of losses associated with an exposure be measured.

2. Why is precision in determining the amount of insurance important for the organization?

3. Identify and describe the two measures of severity suggested by Prouty. Which of these measures is the more important for the risk manager? Why?

4. Describe the loss unit concept. Why is the concept important to the risk manager?

5. Define and distinguish between actual cash value and replacement cost.

6. Identify the three basic approaches that can be used to determine the value of real property.

7. Describe the five general classes into which commercial structures are classified according to type of construction.

8. Describe the provisions of the Internal Revenue Code relating to (a) deductions for uninsured property losses, and (b) taxation of insurance recoveries.

9. What is the conventional measure of an organization's loss in the event of an interruption of business?

10. Describe the nature of the contingent business interruption and contingent extra expense exposure and identify the circumstances under which these exposures can arise.

QUESTIONS FOR DISCUSSION

1. Describe the nature of an involuntary conversion, as defined in the *Internal Revenue Code*. What decisions does this I.R.C. provision require the risk manager to make? What considerations are relevant to such decisions?

2. Why is measuring the severity of a business interruption loss considered more complicated than the problem of measuring a potential loss to real or personal property? In your answer, discuss the issues that must be addressed in measuring severity of a business interruption loss.

3. Brown currently rents a commercial building from an estate at an extremely favorable rate. Whereas equivalent facilities would cost $10,000 a month, she is able to lease the building for $6,000, but the lease is on a month to month basis. Compute Brown's leasehold interest in the property.

4. What characteristics of employee dishonesty losses complicate the process of measuring the potential severity of such losses? How can the potential severity be measured?

5. How can the potential severity of the liability exposure be measured?

SUGGESTIONS FOR ADDITIONAL READING

McDougall, Donald B. "Fixed Asset Appraisals: An Overlooked Opportunity to Save $$," *Public Risk* (March/April 1995).

Prouty, Richard. *Industrial Insurance: A Formal Approach to Risk Analysis and Evaluation* (Washington, D.C.: Machinery and Allied Products Institute, January 19, 1960).

Ralston, August R., ed. *Risk Management Manual*, Santa Monica, Ca.: (loose-leaf service with monthly supplements), vol. 2, section 7. "Valuations."

Marshall & Swift. *Stevens Valuation Quarterly* (Los Angeles, Ca.: (loose-leaf service with quarterly supplements).

CHAPTER 8

Risk Evaluation: Measuring Frequency

CHAPTER OBJECTIVES

When you have finished this chapter, you should be able to

Explain two interpretations of probability and three approaches to estimating probability.

■

Identify and briefly describe the three probability distributions that are likely to be of interest to the risk manager.

■

Explain the concept of a random variable.

■

Explain the concepts of expected value and variance of a random variable.

■

Compute estimates of the mean and variance of a random variable, and describe the implications of sampling error when computing the estimate.

■

Distinguish between a binomial distribution and a Poisson distribution and determine which is more appropriate for different situations.

■

Compute and interpret simple regressions and explain how regression analysis may be useful to the risk manager.

■

Describe simulation models and explain how simulation may be useful to the risk manager.

✖ Introduction ■

In the preceding chapter, we examined some of the measures of loss severity that can be used in assessing the exposures facing the organization. We turn now to the more difficult task of attempting to estimate loss frequency and severity distributions. The first of these gives the distribution of the number of losses per year from a given exposure, whereas the second is the distribution of the dollar amount lost when a loss occurs. Often, the goal of the risk manager here is to combine these two distributions to derive the distribution of total annual losses, which depends upon both the number of losses that occur and the severity of the individual losses. As we will see, knowledge of these three distributions can be useful in making decisions among alternative risk treatment devices, such as retention and insurance. We will also see, however, that identification of loss distributions is not always easy, and many assumptions must be made along the way. Consequently, the results must be interpreted with caution. Statistical theory does indeed have many applications in risk management, but it cannot be applied blindly. Before discussing the derivation of the frequency and severity distributions, therefore, we will briefly review some basic concepts of probability and statistics. In addition, we will consider some limitations on the use of statistics in risk management.

✖ Usefulness of Quantitative Analysis ■ ■ ■ ■ ■ ■ ■ ■ ■ ■ ■

There was a time when kings and emperors had astrologers at court to help them plan for the future. It is easy to understand the cult of the astrologer at court. After all, the astrologer was an astronomer, and if a person has success in predicting eclipses by stargazing, why should he or she not have equal success in predicting the course of more mundane matters by considering the disposition of heavenly bodies? And while we scoff at the naiveté of the astrologer's cult, we can sympathize with the desire to predict the future.

Today, many businesses have statisticians and forecasters for the same purpose. Although the theoretical underpinnings of statistical analysis have more validity than that of the stargazers of long ago, the opportunity for misuse is as present today as it was then. Errors in the use and interpretation of statistical techniques can lead to false conclusions that are hazardous when used in decision making. The problem is that it is very easy to do arithmetic on historical data or subjectively estimated figures. What is difficult is properly interpreting the relevance of these computations as they relate to some current risk management problem. It is an easy and fatal step to think that the accuracy of one's arithmetic is equivalent to the accuracy of information to be applied to the problem at hand. Unfortunately, there is no more common error than to assume that because prolonged and accurate mathematical calculations have been made, the results are automatically applicable to the real world. One of the greatest dangers in the current emphasis in business schools on statistics and other forms of quantitative analysis is the failure to provide adequate training with respect to the question of when these tools are appropriate and when they are not. Unfortunately, there is an almost irresistible temptation to use quantitative tools to solve every problem, simply because the tools "are there," even when the situation does not merit their use and when the results may be counterproductive.

This is not to suggest that probability theory and other quantitative techniques are not useful in risk management decision making. Indeed, in the proper circumstances, quantitative techniques are extremely useful in risk management decisions. This is not at all surprising. One of the earliest applications of quantitative analysis in business was in the insurance field where the pricing process relies heavily on probability theory. Because probability theory serves as the basis for insurers' pricing decisions, it is only logical that risk managers would use the same techniques in evaluating insurance as a risk management alternative. But it is important that probability theory and quantitative analysis be placed in their proper perspective and used when they are appropriate aids in risk management decisions.

There are a number of areas in which statistical inference can be properly used in the risk management process. In this chapter, we examine some of the applications of quantitative measurement in the risk management process. Bear in mind that one goal of the risk manager should be to strike the proper balance when it comes to the use of quantitative tools in evaluating risks and making decisions. While there is certainly no mathematical formula that adequately reflects all considerations relevant to a particular risk management problem, nor is there an individual so skilled at subjective analysis that his or her decision making couldn't be enhanced by some consideration of relevant historical data.

Because students in a course in risk management are likely to have differing backgrounds and expertise in the area of quantitative analysis, we have provided a brief review of some statistical concepts in this chapter. We recognize that the following discussion of probability is likely to be as boring to the learned as it is confusing to the novice. We therefore suggest that the "learned" turn over the pages until they find something more interesting, while we explain this useful concept to the novice.

PROBABILITY THEORY

Some notions are impossible to define adequately. Such ideas are found to be based on the universal experience of nature and are intuitively understood, but often difficult to define. Probability is one such notion. The dictionary tells us that "probable" means "likely." Further reference gives us the not very helpful information that "likely" means "probable." Clearly, we should be able to do better than that. Probability theory is that body of knowledge concerned with measuring the likelihood that something will happen and making predictions on the basis of this likelihood.

Early in the history of modern risk management, the insurance buyer of a major corporation suggested that risk managers might find it productive to use broad generalizations about the likelihood of loss, classifying probability as *almost nil* (meaning that, in the opinion of the risk manager, the event is probably not going to happen), *slight* (meaning that while the event is possible, it has not happened and is unlikely to occur in the future), *moderate* (meaning that the event has occasionally happened and will probably happen again), and *definite* (meaning that the event has happened regularly in the past and is expected to occur regularly in the future).[1] Although probability estimates such as these may be of some help in risk management decisions, one is reminded of the famous quotation from Lord Kelvin:

> When you can measure what you are talking about, and express it in numbers, you know something about it; but when you cannot measure it, when you cannot express it in numbers, your knowledge is of a meager and unsatisfactory kind.

It is always helpful when we can measure things on a ruler instead of simply calling them "large" and "small." Probability is simply a measure of, or a statement of our belief of, the likelihood of an event. We measure probability on an imaginary ruler, marked at one end with a zero and unity at the other. The high end of the scale, marked unity, represents absolute certainty. Any proposition about which there is no doubt whatsoever finds its place at this point on the scale. For example, the probability that the reader will eventually die is equal to unity because it is absolutely certain that we will all die some day. Using the letter P to stand for probability, we would write P (you will die some day) = 1. The bottom end of the scale, marked zero, represents absolute impossibility. The probability that the reader could run a mile in 30 seconds is zero, because failure would be absolutely certain. The statistician here would write P (you could run a mile in 30 seconds) = 0.

Events that are neither certain nor impossible lie between the two ends of our imaginary ruler, and are assigned values proportional to their relative likelihood of occurrence. Thus if we believe that the likelihood of some event A occurring is twice that of event A not occurring, we would write $P(A) = 2/3$ and $P(not\ A) = 1/3$. Note that for any event A, one of the two events A and *not A* must occur, but the two events A and *not A* could never occur simultaneously. (When two events could never occur at the same time, we say the events are *mutually exclusive*. When at least one of two events must occur, we say the two events are *collectively exhaustive*.) Thus, $P(A)$ will always equal $1 - P(not\ A)$, with values between 0 and 1 proportional to the relative likelihood of event A occurring versus not occurring.

Accordingly, any time we have a set of n mutually exclusive and collectively exhaustive possible outcomes, the assertion that each of these outcomes is equally likely dictates that each outcome be assigned probability $P = 1/n$. For example, assuming that the two possible outcomes of a coin toss ("heads" and "tails") are equally likely, we must assign $P(heads) = P(tails) = 1/2$. Similarly, given a well-shuffled deck of 52 playing cards, the probability of drawing any one of the 52 equally likely cards is $1/52$.

So far, we have set up our scale on which the probability of events may be specified. How do we arrive at an actual measure of the probability of real-life events? There are three ways, and we will consider them each in turn. Before doing so, however, it may be useful to distinguish between two interpretations of probability. The first of these interpretations is the *relative likelihood* interpretation used to illustrate the concept of probability thus far, which refers to the relative likelihood of an event occurring versus not occurring on any single trial. The second interpretation is one of relative frequency and relates to the number of times a certain event would

---

[1]See Richard Prouty, *Industrial Insurance: A Formal Approach to Risk Analysis and Evaluation* (Washington, D.C.: Machinery and Allied Products Institute, 1960).

occur over a large number of identical trials. The relative frequency interpretation states that the *proportion* of trials in which some event A occurs will approximately equal the probability of event A as the number of trials becomes large. Thus if the probability of drawing the ace of spades from a well-shuffled deck of 52 cards is $1/52 = 0.01923$, then over a large number of identical trials we would draw an ace of spades approximately 1.923 percent of the time. Both of these interpretations are useful in risk management.

Determining the Probability of an Event

To obtain an estimate of the probability of an event, one of three methods can be employed. The first technique to be discussed involves identifying subsets of a sample space of mutually exclusive, collectively exhaustive, and equally likely outcomes. The probability of an event A can then be defined as:

$$P(A) = \frac{\text{number of outcomes for which event } A \text{ occurs}}{\text{total number of possible outcomes}}$$

Thus, we know the probability of flipping a head is $1/2$ because there are two equally likely possible outcomes, one of which is a *head*. Similarly, given a well-shuffled deck of 52 cards, if the event A is "draw an ace of spades," then $P(A) = 1/52$, as only one of the 52 possible outcomes results in event A. If the event B is "draw an ace", then $P(B) = 4/52$, as four of the 52 equally likely outcomes results in event B. Similarly, if the event C is "draw a black card," then $P(C) = 26/52 = .5$. These probabilities are deducible from the nature of the event. Because they are determined in this manner (i.e., based on causality), they are called *a priori* probabilities.

While this approach to measuring probability is quite useful for demonstrating various probability concepts, the underlying framework of equally likely simple outcomes has little practical application other than analyzing various games of chance. Note, however, that both the relative frequency and relative likelihood interpretations can be applied to these probabilities. In the long run, we would expect to draw an ace $4/52 = 7.69$ percent of the time over a large number of trials, while on any *single* trial the measure of relative likelihood for drawing an ace is $4/52$.

The second approach to measuring probability involves *empirical estimation* and is based on the fact that the relative frequency of an event approaches the underlying probability of that event over a large number of identical trials. Thus after observing the number of times a certain event has occurred over a large number of trials performed under essentially the same conditions, the proportion of trials in which the event has occurred becomes an estimate of the underlying probability of that event. Suppose, for example, that we are interested in mortality rates for 21-year-old males, i.e., the probability that a 21-year-old male will die before reaching the age of 22. Although there are only two possible outcomes, ("dies," "doesn't die"), it would be absurd to assume that the two outcomes are equally likely and assign probability $1/2$ to each. We put the question to an actuary who tells us that the probability that a 21-year-old male will die before reaching age 22 is 0.00183. What does that mean? It means that someone has examined mortality statistics and discovered that, in the past, 183 men out of every 100,000 alive at age 21 have died before reaching age 22. Barring changes in the underlying causes of these deaths, in the future we can expect about the same proportion of 21-year-old males to die before reaching age 22. Moreover, for some randomly drawn male having just turned 21 (in the absence of any additional information relevant to health, lifestyle, or other determinants of mortality), our estimate of the probability that this individual will die before reaching age 22 is $183/100,000 = 0.00183$. These probabilities, computed after a study of past experience, are called *a posteriori* or empirical probabilities.

There are a few points from the above example that merit review: 1) Historical data provides an *estimate* of the "true" underlying probability P, but does not reveal the "true" P itself. Intuition and statistical theory both suggest that the more data available (all else constant), the more precise will be the probability estimate. 2) In the procedure described above, the clause "barring changes in the underlying causes of these deaths," highlights an implicit assumption that the "true" probability P is not (rapidly) changing over time. In general, the degree to which P may be changing over time becomes critical when the desire to use more data to estimate P also means using *older* data. 3) Any probability statement is a reflection of what we know, and what we don't know, at the time of that statement. The mortality rate described above, for example, does not automatically condemn every male on his 21st birthday to a probability of 0.00183 of dying within the next year. Given additional information about any *specific* 21-year-old male, we may revise the initial estimate based on aggregate mortality data (the marginal or prior probability) upward or downward to form a revised estimate (a *conditional* or *posterior* probability).

The third approach to assigning probabilities is *subjective* probability estimation. For example, the coach of a football team may state that his team has a 70 percent chance of winning the conference title this season. Such a statement would not reasonably be based on empirical observation that his team has won seven out of the last 10 conference championships, as the players and skills on his and all the other conference teams change from year to year. Rather, such a statement is based on his knowledge of his players' skills relative to the skills of other players in the conference for his particular season, his own experience regarding the level of performance required to win a conference championship, and so on. Nonetheless, the same two interpretations of the probability statement may be applied. Implicitly, this coach is saying that if this season were to be repeated a large number of times with the exact same players under the exact same conditions, he believes his team would win the championship about 70 percent of the time. As such, he is also saying that the relative likelihood of this team winning *this particular season* is about .70, yet there are a number of undetermined chance events which will influence whether or not they actually do.

RANDOM VARIABLES

Thus far, we have discussed the probability of various events such as flipping a head, drawing an ace of spades, dying within a year after reaching the age of 21, and so on. We now turn to estimating probability distributions for random variables.

Put simply, a random variable is a numeric outcome whose value depends on some chance event or events. A random variable is described by its probability distribution, which indicates the probability for each value that the random variable might possibly assume.[2] Random variables are usually represented by a capital letter. For example, we might define the random variable X to be the value observed on a single roll of a fair die. Since there are six equally likely outcomes, the probability distribution for the random variable X would be presented as:

Table 8.1. Probability Distribution for the Value Observed on a Single Roll of a Fair Die

x	$P(X = x)$
1	1/6
2	1/6
3	1/6
4	1/6
5	1/6
6	1/6

As the set of all possible values for a random variable are mutually exclusive and collectively exhaustive, the sum of the probabilities in any discrete probability distribution must equal one. Of course, the symbolic name assigned to a random variable need not always be the letter X. Given the discussion of the previous chapters, we can define three random variables of particular interest in certain risk management situations:

$N =$ the total number of losses experienced during a giving year.

$L_i =$ the dollar value of the i_{th} loss experienced during the year. (Thus L_1 is the dollar value of the first loss, L_2 is the dollar value of the second loss, L_3 is the dollar value of the third loss, . . . , L_N is the dollar value of the N_{th} loss experienced during the year.)

$T =$ the total dollar value of all losses experienced during the year, i.e. $T = L_1 + L_2 + L_3 + \ldots + L_N$

EXPECTED VALUE AND VARIANCE OF A RANDOM VARIABLE

The probability distribution for a random variable contains a large quantity of information, describing the relative likelihood of each possible value that the random variable might assume. It is often convenient to synthesize this information into two summary pieces of information, i.e., the *expected value* (also called the *mean*) of the random variable and the *variance* of the random variable.

---

[2]This discussion assumes the random variable is discrete. A discrete random variable is one for which all possible values are "countable," and thus occupy distinct points, rather than continuous ranges, on the real number line. The possible values are typically the non-negative integers or some subset of the non-negative integers, which will be our assumption unless otherwise noted. The concepts examined in this section generally apply to continuous random variables as well, but development of the concepts for continuous random variables would require integral calculus.

Expected Value

For any discrete random variable X, we can define the expected value of the random variable as:

$$E[X] = \sum_x x \cdot P(X = x)$$

Put simply, the expected value of a random variable is a weighted average of all possible values for that random variable and is computed by multiplying each possible value by its respective probability and summing the results. For example, if we define X as the value of a single roll of a fair die, then $E[X] = 1(\frac{1}{6}) + 2(\frac{1}{6}) + 3(\frac{1}{6}) + 4(\frac{1}{6}) + 5(\frac{1}{6}) + 6(\frac{1}{6}) = 3.5$. The expected value, or mean of a random variable X, may also be represented by the notation μ_X or simply μ if the identity of the random variable under consideration is understood.

As with probability, there is a long run average interpretation of expected value as well as an interpretation that applies to any single trial. The long run average interpretation of the expected value relates to the long run average value of the random variable over a large number of trials. Thus if a fair die were rolled a large number of times, the random variable X defined above would equal one about $\frac{1}{6}$ of the time, two about $\frac{1}{6}$ of the time, three about $\frac{1}{6}$ of the time, and so on. In the long run, if we added up all the realized values of X and divided by the total number of trials, the average value of X would approach the expected value of 3.5 as the number of trials becomes large. Moreover, the expected value of 3.5 is the "single best guess" of the value that will be realized on any *single trial*, in the sense that guessing this value would minimize the average squared deviation between the value guessed and the actual value realized over a large number of trials.

The preceding example also demonstrates a critically important concept when dealing with expected values (or averages) in risk management. Note that the value realized on a single roll of a die is 1, 2, 3, 4, 5, or 6, and in no case is it ever equal to 3.5. It is important to remember that the expected value of a random variable is not necessarily the value that is going to occur, and should never be treated as the value that *will occur* on any single trial. Although the expected value is always our single best guess of the value that will be realized, we must also remember that this guess will be wrong. Many decision makers facing risk management scenarios fall into the trap of treating the expected value as the value that will occur, rather than simply as a measure of central tendency for the probability distribution at hand. Forgetting the random variation above and below the mean inevitably generates improper risk management decisions.

Under what circumstances, then, is the expected value of loss a useful measure in the risk management process? In general, the usefulness of an expected value lies in the degree to which an organization could absorb potential losses both above and below the expected (average) loss, and thus survive to realize as a long run average the expected loss. Conversely, for those situations in which there is some relevant probability of catastrophic loss which the organization could not survive, basing the decision to retain such a risk solely on the expected loss is flawed. This decision implicitly ignores the fact that the expected loss is simply the average loss that would be realized over a large number of exposures, but is not the loss that is guaranteed (or even likely) to occur on any single exposure.

Measures of Dispersion: Variance, Standard Deviation, and Coefficient of Variation

Having noted that the realized value of a random variable will vary randomly above and below the mean, it is useful to have a measure of the magnitude of this variability. The *variance* of a random variable X is defined as:

$$\text{VAR}[X] = \sum_{x} (x - E[X])^2 \cdot P(X = x)$$

The variance is a weighted average of the *squared difference* between the possible values of the random variable and the expected value of that random variable.

Suppose for example, that there are four convenience stores on the north side of town, and we have determined the following probability distribution for the number of those stores that will be robbed during the coming year. Letting the random variable N represent the number of those stores that will be robbed during the coming year, we have:

Table 8.2   Probability Distribution for the Number of Stores That Will Be Robbed on the North Side

x	$P(N = x)$
0	.05
1	.20
2	.50
3	.20
4	.05
SUM:	1.00

The mean and variance of this random variable would be computed as:

$E[N] = .05(0) + .20(1) + .50(2) + .20(3) + .05(4) = 2$

$\text{VAR}[N] = .05(0-2)^2 + .20(1-2)^2 + .50(2-2)^2 + .20(3-2)^2 + .05(4-2)^2 = 0.8$

Suppose we also have the following probability distribution for four convenience stores on the south side of town:

Table 8.3   Probability Distribution for the Number of Stores That Will Be Robbed on the South Side

x	$P(N = x)$
0	.10
1	.25
2	.30
3	.25
4	.10
SUM:	1.00

The mean and variance for the south side distribution would be computed in a similar manner:

$$E[N] = .05(0) + .20(1) + .50(2) + .20(3) + .05(4) = 2$$
$$VAR[N] = .10(0-2)^2 + .25(1-2)^2 + .30(2-2)^2 + .25(3-2)^2 + .10(4-2)^2 = 1.3$$

Although both probability distributions generate the same mean, the distribution for the south side neighborhood has greater variance. This can be seen more clearly in Figure 8.1, which displays the *probability mass function* for the two random variables. Compared to the north side distribution, the south side distribution has smaller probabilities of realizing values close to the mean and larger probabilities of realizing values far away from the mean. The variance is thus a measure of *dispersion around the mean* that will be realized over a large number of identical trials. The variance of a random variable X is often represented by the notation "σ^2_X", or simply "σ^2" if the identity of the random variable under consideration is understood.

Often it is convenient to know the *standard deviation* of a random variable, which is simply the square root of the variance. The standard deviation is generally represented using the notation σ_X or simply σ. Thus the standard deviation of the north side distribution discussed previously is $\sigma = \sqrt{0.8} = 0.89$, while the standard deviation for the south side distribution is $\sigma = \sqrt{1.3} = 1.14$. The standard deviation is particularly useful if the random variable in question is normally distributed, for in this case the mean μ and the standard deviation σ together define the entire probability distribution.

It is also useful, sometimes, to compute the *coefficient of variation* for a random variable, which is the standard deviation divided by the mean. This division has the effect of scaling the standard deviation and allows comparison of the dispersion of two or more random variables relative to the magnitude of their respective average values.

Estimating the Mean and Variance

Like probabilities, the mean and variance of a random variable can be empirically estimated. Suppose we have collected n observations of some random variable X (call our data $x_1, x_2, x_3, \ldots, x_n$). We can now compute:

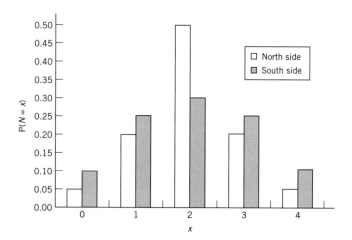

Figure 8.1 Probability Distributions for Number of Stores That Are Robbed

$$\overline{X} = \frac{\sum\limits_{i=1}^{n} x_i}{n}$$

and

$$s^2 = \frac{\sum\limits_{i=1}^{n} (x_i - \overline{X})^2}{n - 1}$$

Here $\overline{X}$ is called *sample mean* and provides an estimate of the true mean μ which in practice is usually unknown. Similarly, s^2 is called the *sample variance*, and provides an estimate of the true variance σ^2.

Suppose that we are interested in estimating the mean and variance of the value observed on the single roll of a fair die. Pretend for now that we know nothing about the six equally likely outcomes and must resort to estimating μ and σ^2 empirically. (If we did know the exact probability distribution displayed in Table 8.4 we could compute the "true" values $\mu = 3.5$ and $\sigma^2 = 2.92$.) If we rolled a single die ten times, we might observe the following data:

6 1 5 3 5 2 4 4 2 4

Based on this sample, our estimates of μ and σ^2 would be computed as follows:

Table 8.4 Computation of $\overline{X}$ and s^2 for Dice Rolling Data

i	x_i	$(x_i - \overline{X})$		
1	6	$(6 - 3.6)^2$	=	5.76
2	1	$(1 - 3.6)^2$	=	6.76
3	5	$(5 - 3.6)^2$	=	1.96
4	3	$(3 - 3.6)^2$	=	0.36
5	5	$(5 - 3.6)^2$	=	1.96
6	2	$(2 - 3.6)^2$	=	2.56
7	4	$(4 - 3.6)^2$	=	0.16
8	4	$(4 - 3.6)^2$	=	0.16
9	2	$(2 - 3.6)^2$	=	2.56
10	4	$(4 - 3.6)^2$	=	0.16
sum:	36	sum:		22.40

$$\overline{X} = \frac{36}{10} = 3.6,$$

$$s^2 = \frac{22.40}{9} = 2.49$$

Thus our estimate of μ is $\overline{X} = 3.6$, and our estimate of σ^2 is $s^2 = 2.49$. Of course, we could just as easily have rolled the following ten values:

1 1 5 3 4 1 5 2 6 3

in which case our sample mean and variance would be $\overline{X} = 31/10 = 3.1$ and $s^2 = 30.90/9 = 3.43$. A third sample of $n = 10$ observations may have resulted in the following data:

$$2\ 4\ 3\ 2\ 5\ 3\ 1\ 6\ 4\ 3$$

and our sample mean and variance would be $\overline{X} = 33/10 = 3.3$ and $s^2 = 20.10/9 = 2.23$. (The enthusiastic reader should perform computations similar to those demonstrated above in order to verify these results.)

Exactly what does all of this mean? It means that when μ or σ^2 (or any other parameter used to describe a random variable as we will see later in the chapter) is estimated using historical data, there is still uncertainty regarding the *true* value we are trying to estimate. When we compute $\overline{X}$ as an estimate of μ, we must remember that $\overline{X}$ is entirely a function of our limited data and is not equal to the mean that would be computed if we had a much larger number of observations.[3]

We must also always remember that historical data used to compute $\overline{X}$ and s^2, strictly speaking, only provide estimates of the μ and σ^2 that existed in the past, back when the data was generated. Before we make a leap of faith and assume that this same data also helps to estimate the μ and σ^2 that will exist in the future, we must address the question of whether the basic nature of the random variable being studied is changing over time. In making predictions based on historical data, the risk manager implicitly says, "If things continue to happen in the future as they have in the past, and if our estimate of what has happened in the past is accurate and precise, this is what we may expect . . .". Although there are statistical techniques such as trend analysis and linear regression which help to anticipate future changes in our data, predicting the future should always involve some degree of subjective evaluation of the manner in which the surrounding environment is changing.

PROBABILITY MODELS FOR RISK MANAGEMENT

Putting aside the simple examples of flipping coins and rolling dice, risk managers are often interested in three random variables which characterize the risk faced by an organization. We will let the random variable N represent the *number of losses* that will occur within a given time period (usually one year). The random variable L will represent the *dollar value* of any single loss that occurs, and the random variable T will represent the total dollar value of all losses incurred during a given time period (again, usually one year). The random variable N thus relates to the frequency of loss, while L relates to the severity of losses. If we let L_1 represent the severity of the first loss incurred during a given year, L_2 the severity of the second loss incurred during the year, and so on, then $T = L_1 + L_2 + L_3 + \ldots + L_N$.

Suppose we have a rental property manager who owns 100 houses, and this manager is interested in characterizing the number of these houses that will catch fire

---

[3]Actually, there is a statistical relationship between the variance of a random variable X, and the variance of the random variable $\overline{X}$ used to estimate μ_X. If the random variable X has variance σ^2, and $\overline{X}$ is computed as the average of n independent pieces of data, then the variance of $\overline{X}$ is equal to σ^2/n. Thus, as the sample size n increases, $\overline{X}$ becomes a more precise estimate of μ_X.

during the upcoming year. In this case, the possible values for the random variable N are $0, 1, 2, \ldots , 100$. Our task in constructing a probability distribution for N is to assign a probability to each of these possible values.

How could we proceed? One approach would be to examine the history of these 100 houses and count the number of years in which zero houses caught fire, the number of years in which one house caught fire, the number of years in which two houses caught fire, and so on. The problems with this approach should be apparent. If these 100 houses are relatively new, we may have only a few years of such data. Moreover, it is very likely that none of these 100 houses have ever burned, making it impossible to evaluate the probability that one or more houses will catch fire within a year's time under this approach. Conversely, if these 100 houses are each 50 years old, the number of houses that burned 30 to 50 years ago (when the houses were relatively new) may be of little use in predicting the number that will burn next year.

This discussion serves to highlight the fact that it is generally difficult to evaluate the probabilities of rare events solely through historical analogy. However, given an understanding of some basic laws of probability, it may be possible to apply a *model* which describes the situation at hand, and use historical data to estimate certain *model parameters* rather than to estimate the required probabilities directly. As will be seen this approach allows us to make more efficient use of available data. Two useful models for characterizing frequency of loss are the binomial model and the Poisson model.

The Binomial Model

The binomial model is appropriate when we have some given number of exposures to loss, which we will represent with the letter n. Each of these exposures will result in either 0 or 1 losses. (No single exposure will ever result in more than one loss during the time interval in question.) Moreover, the model assumes that each exposure has the same probability P of generating a loss, and thus probability $1 - P$ of not generating a loss. Finally, the model assumes that the n exposures to loss are *independent* of one another. Thus, whether or not any one exposure generates a loss has no bearing on whether any of the remaining exposures generates a loss.

Under these assumptions, the probability distribution for the total number of losses sustained is given by the following formula: [4]

$$P(N = x) = \frac{n!}{x!\,(n - x)!}\, p^x (1 - p)^{n-x} \qquad x = 0, 1, 2, \ldots, n.$$

If the probability distribution for N follows the above formula, it can be shown that $E[N] = np$ and $VAR[N] = np(1 - p)$.

Applying the binomial model to the rental manager's one hundred houses, we assume that each house has the same probability p of catching fire once during the upcoming year, and probability $1 - p$ of not catching fire. Suppose we are able to esti-

---

[4]The notation $x!$ (called X factorial) represents the number $x(x - 1)(x - 2) \ldots (3)(2)(1)$, or $x! = x(x-1)!$ where $0! = 1$. Thus, $0! = 1$, $1! = 1$, $2! = 2 \times 1 = 2$, $3! = 3 \times 2 \times 1 = 6$, $4! = 4 \times 3 \times 2 \times 1 = 24$, and so on.

mate that $p = 0.0001$ for each house. Since there are 100 houses, we have $n = 100$ and we may now compute:

$$P(N = 0) = \frac{100!}{0!\,100!}(0.0001)^0(0.9999)^{100} = 0.990049$$

$$P(N = 1) = \frac{100!}{0!\,99!}(0.0001)^1(0.9999)^{99} = 0.009901$$

$$P(N = 2) = \frac{100!}{2!\,98!}(0.0001)^2(0.9999)^{98} = 0.000049$$

and so on. The expected value for the number of houses that will burn is $np = 100(0.0001) = .01$, and the variance under this model is $np(1 - p) = 100(0.0001)(0.9999) = 0.009999$.

How would the parameter p be estimated? Under the binomial model, we need not restrict ourselves to only the history of these 100 houses. Rather, we can look at a large number of houses assumed to have a similar propensity of catching fire and apply what we have learned. Suppose that nationwide, out of 100,000 similar houses, ten burned last year. We could now estimate $p = 10/100,000 = .0001$. Of course, the fact that we can only estimate p implies that the binomial formula only provides estimates of the probabilities in question. Moreover, we must also remember that the relevance of the probabilities computed using the binomial probability formula depends on the degree to which the model assumptions are met. In the case of the binomial model, the critical assumptions are that the probability of loss is the same p for each exposure, and the various exposures to loss are independent of one another.

The Poisson Model

The binomial distribution is generally used to model the number of losses that will occur as a function of some finite number of exposures to loss, and some probability P that any single exposure will generate a loss within the specified time period. The *Poisson model*, in contrast, can be applied when we consider each small instant of time that passes to be an exposure to loss. In this sense, the organization faces a virtually unlimited number of exposures to loss within a given year. If we consider each small instant of time that passes to have the same (very small) probability of generating a loss, independent of every other small instant of time, then the probability distribution for the number of losses that will occur during a given time period is given by the following formula:

$$P(N = x) = e^{-\lambda}\frac{\lambda^x}{x!} \qquad x = 0, 1, 2, \ldots$$

Here λ is the average number of losses sustained during the time period in question and e is the constant 2.71828. Note that the Poisson distribution is defined by a single parameter $\lambda = E[N]$.

Suppose a certain manufacturing facility has sustained the following number of losses per year during the past five years:

Again, in the absence of some probability model, we would be limited to using the relative frequency approach to estimate the probability distribution for the number of losses that will occur during any given year. Following this approach, we would estimate P($N = 0$) = ⅗, P($N = 1$) = ⅖, and P($N = 2$) = ⅕. Note that under this approach, our estimate of the probability P($N > 2$) is equal to zero, as we have not observed more than two losses per year in our historical data. Surely, however, the fact we have not experienced more than two losses per year in the past five years does not mean that we would never experience three or more losses per year. The problem is that, by definition, rare events will show up very infrequently in our data. Using probability models and theoretical probability distributions allows us to "fill out the tails" of the probability distribution, hence to estimate the probability of events that have not yet occurred.

In order to apply the Poisson distribution to construct a probability distribution, we must estimate $\lambda = \text{E}[N]$. The above data generates a sample mean $\overline{X} = (1 + 2 + 0 + 1 + 0)/5 = 0.8$. Using $\lambda = 0.8$ in the Poisson probability equation, we could compute:

$$P(N = 0) = e^{-0.8}\frac{0.8^0}{0!} = 0.4493$$

$$P(N = 1) = e^{-0.8}\frac{0.8^1}{1!} = 0.0359$$

$$P(N = 2) = e^{-0.8}\frac{0.8^2}{2!} = 0.0014$$

and so on.

When is the Poisson distribution an appropriate model? One useful concept in deciding to use the Poisson distribution lies in the fact that when the number of losses per year follows a Poisson distribution, the time between losses is said to have the "memoryless" property. Put simply, this means that the amount of time that will pass before the next loss occurs does not depend on the amount of time that has passed since the last loss that occurred.

This slightly counterintuitive notion can be explained within the industrial accidents example used above. Suppose the plant employs a large number of workers. Each of these employees may have an accident at any time, independent of when any other employee has an accident. (The fact that one employee has an accident neither causes nor prevents other employees from having accidents.) Thus, the time until the next accident does not depend on how much time has passed since the last accident, as a large number of different employees are involved. Since the memoryless property applies, the Poisson distribution is appropriate for modeling the number of accidents that will occur within one year's time. More generally, the Poisson distribution is useful for modeling the number of events that occur along a time continuum, when the events occur randomly, one at a time, during the period in question.

A Note of Caution

In the previous section we examined the use of probability models and theoretical probability distributions. We noted that the use of theoretical probability distributions may help the risk manager in "filling out the tails" of the probability distribution, thus providing estimates of the probabilities of rare events that would be infrequently observed in historical data. This is likely to be useful information when it comes time to select among the alternative risk treatment devices.

Having argued in support of the usefulness of theoretical distributions, a caution is in order. Too often, a particular distribution is chosen for no reason other than the risk manager's familiarity with it. A number of alternative distributions are available, each generating a different pattern of probabilities for the outcomes. It is important, therefore, that the distribution be chosen with appropriate attention to the degree to which it "fits" the current problem.[5]

Severity Distributions

The previous chapter examined some considerations in estimating the maximum possible loss from a single occurrence and considered the importance of this value in decisions to insure or not to insure. Knowledge of the entire severity distribution will further enable the firm to make decisions on the mechanism for financing the risk. For example, when a building catches fire, it may be a total loss. Knowing the maximum possible loss is more than the firm is able to handle, and combining this with a risk management objective of preventing bankruptcy will lead the firm to conclude that the entire risk should not be retained. Alternately, however, the loss may be only partial. A knowledge of the distribution of partial losses is important in deciding how much of the risk to transfer. The attractiveness of alternative retention levels will depend in part upon the firm's exposure to loss under each alternative.

The severity distribution provides the alternative loss amounts from a given occurrence and their associated probabilities. Suppose, for example, that the firm is concerned with loss by fire to a warehouse and has determined that the appropriate way to value the direct loss is on the basis of replacement cost. The replacement cost for the warehouse is estimated to be $500,000. Thus, the maximum possible loss is $500,000. Considering all possible partial losses, the risk manager has derived a severity distribution which appears as follows:[6]

Table 8.5 Loss Severity Distribution

Loss	Probability
$0 to $20,000	.40
$20,000 to $100,000	.30
$100,000 to $200,000	.20
$200,000 to $250,000	.05
$250,000 to $500,000	.05
Total	1.00

[5]To help with this process, statisticians have developed "goodness of fit" tests. These are statistical procedures which basically consider the probability that the observed outcomes could have been generated by the assumed distribution. If that probability is low, the risk manager may conclude the distribution is not valid for describing the loss process under consideration.

[6]In this example, we are considering the direct loss only. In reality, the entire loss, including the loss of revenues or extra expenses during the time it takes to repair the warehouse should be considered.

Of course, this discussion has bypassed the question of how the severity distribution is estimated. Identification of a severity distribution is in some respects more difficult than the identification of the frequency distribution. Part of the reason for this is the large number of possibilities that may occur. Notice that the distribution in the table gives only partial information, breaking loss amounts into six intervals. In fact, any dollar amount may occur in the event of a loss, each with its own probability. Since it is unlikely that we have observed every possible outcome, it is not possible to completely specify the severity distribution solely by examining the distribution of past losses.

As with frequency distributions, one alternative is to fill out the severity distribution using an appropriate theoretical distribution. Not surprisingly, the theoretical distributions likely to be of value in describing the severity of losses are not the same as those of value in describing the frequency of losses. Some distributions which have been suggested for explaining the severity of losses are the lognormal distribution, the exponential distribution, and the Pareto distribution. The same cautions apply in using a theoretical distribution to estimate the severity distribution for losses. A particular distribution should be chosen not because of the risk manager's familiarity with it, but because it is appropriate in that situation.

The Total Annual Loss Distribution

Because the frequency distribution shows the distribution of the number of occurrences per year and the severity distribution shows the distribution of the dollar amount lost per occurrence, they may be combined in a special way to obtain the distribution of the dollar amount lost per year, or the total annual loss distribution. The process by which the frequency and severity distributions are combined, known as convolution, is beyond the scope of this text. Frequently a computer is used to simulate the annual loss distribution given the frequency and severity distributions. In some cases when theoretical frequency and severity distributions are used, a mathematical formula for the total annual loss distribution may be derived. However derived, this third distribution may provide information useful to the risk manager when deciding between alternative insurance programs, loss prevention programs, and retention.

CORRELATION AND LINEAR REGRESSION

Throughout this chapter, we have relied from time to time on the assumption that two or more random variables are independent of one another. This basically means that knowing the value of one random variable provides no additional information about the value that the other random variable may assume.

Correlation

Frequently, we face the situation where two or more random variables are in some way related to one another. When such relationships can be identified and measured, they may be useful to the risk manager, since knowing the value that one random variable has assumed does give us additional information for predicting the value of the related variable. To the extent that changes in one value vary directly with some other value, regression analysis is a useful tool for projecting future events.

When two variables tend to move in the same direction, such that when one random variable assumes a relatively large value and the other also tends to be relatively large, the two values are said to be *positively correlated*. Conversely, when two random variables tend to move in opposite directions, such that when one variable is relatively high, the other tends to be relatively low, we say that the two values are *negatively correlated*.

When such data are analyzed, the initial step is to plot the points on a *scatter diagram* either manually or with one of the many computer spreadsheets with graphic functions. By convention, the *dependent variable* (i.e., variable we would like to be able to predict) is called Y and is plotted on the Y axis, and the variable on which Y depends (the independent variable) is designated X and is plotted on the X axis. Independent variables can be demographic factors or certain management projections, such as next year's payroll, shipments, total miles driven, and so on.[7] If the diagram indicates points extending diagonally across the surface from the lower left-hand corner to the upper right, this is the first suggestion of a positive functional relationship. If the points extend from the upper left-hand corner to the lower right-hand corner, a negative functional relationship is indicated.

Consider, for example, the data displayed in Table 8.6, a somewhat overworked example of the number of work-related injuries incurred by a manufacturing firm, along with the number of hours worked each year during the period 1985 through 1995.

Table 8.6 The Number of Work-related Injuries Incurred by a Manufacturing Firm

Year	Number of Employee Hours Worked	Number of Lost-Time Injuries
1986	1,000,000	11
1987	1,320,000	14
1988	1,275,000	11
1989	1,150,000	12
1990	1,500,000	13
1991	1,100,000	9
1992	1,600,000	15
1993	1,700,000	18
1994	1,650,000	15
1995	1,800,000	17

[7]Sometimes it may be difficult to identify a variable with which the value one is interested in predicting is correlated. One expedient that may be productive—if used with care—is to use time as the predictor variable. Usually, however, the independent variable is a random variable other than time.

Although an exact relationship may not be evident from the tabular presentation of data, intuition suggests a positive correlation between these two variables, and this is confirmed when the relationships are plotted on a graph, as in Figure 8.2. Here, the number of hours worked has been plotted on the horizontal axis as variable X, while the corresponding number of accidents is plotted on the vertical axis as variable Y.

Although the plotted points do not fall precisely in a straight line, we can see that the values tend to scatter randomly above and below an imaginary line drawn through the plotted points. There is an expected element of variability in the data, but it is clear that there is a relationship and that a change in the number of hours worked is likely to be accompanied by a change in the number of loss-time injuries. With this information, the risk manager can make predictions concerning the probable level of work-related injuries in the future, if he or she knows the number of hours that will be worked.[8]

Regression Analysis

It is simple in an example such as this one to see the historical relationship between the two variables. More importantly, our intuition and understanding of the situation would lead us to expect a relationship such as this prior to examining the data.

Once we have an intuitively justifiable model, it is then useful to measure the relationship between or among the variables. This is performed by *regression analysis,* which calculates the parameters for the specified model which results in the best fit for the data. For example, when a scatter plot suggests a linear relationship such as in Figure 8.2, regression can be used to solve for the parameters of the model:

$$e[Y] = a + bX$$

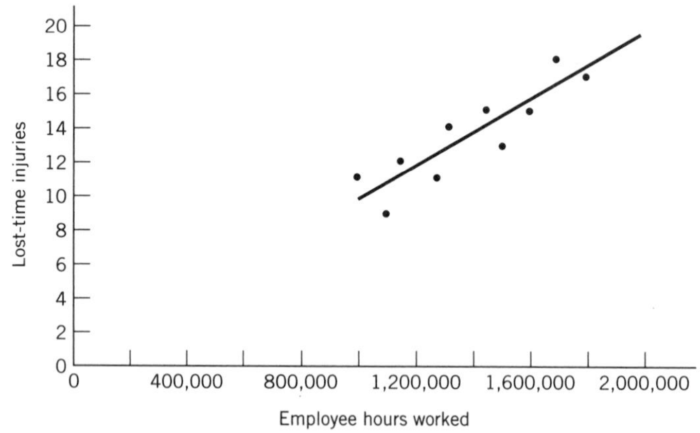

Figure 8.2   Lost-Time Accidents Per Employee Hours Worked

[8]Understand that correlation does not imply causality. Although workers compensation losses may vary directly with the number of hours worked, it does not necessarily follow that increasing the number of hours worked causes an increase in work-related injuries. All that it suggests is that work-related injuries and the number of hours worked increase or decrease in tandem. For the purpose of forecasting, this is all one needs to know.

Here, a is the value of the regression line at its origin (i.e., where $X = 0$) and b describes the change in the expected average value of Y that accompanies a given change in X. Note that the expression $a + bX$ does not produce the exact value of Y, but only the average value of Y when X assumes a given value. In this sense, the regression model explains that variation in Y is related to X, but cannot predict variation in Y due to factors unrelated to X.

To obtain the a value, the following formula is used:

$$a = \frac{\sum X^2 \sum Y - \sum X \cdot \sum XY}{N \cdot \sum X^2 - \left(\sum X\right)^2}$$

and the formula for b, showing the change in expected value for Y for a given change in X is

$$b = \frac{N \cdot \sum XY - \sum X \cdot \sum Y}{N \cdot \sum X^2 - \left(\sum X\right)^2}$$

If a linear model is inadequate, a curve may be used. If, when the points have been plotted on a scatter diagram scaled with the logarithms of X and Y (or with one of these logarithmically scaled), an examination of the scatter of points suggests correlation, and a straight line may be passed through the points, a logarithmic function may be appropriate for the analysis.[9]

SIMULATION MODELS

One of the more useful applications of probability theory in risk management is its use in simulation models. Such models use mathematical equations to represent the various functions within the risk environment and indicate the likely outcomes of the various choices. Simulation models vary from simple to very complex. Regardless of their size or complexity, the models serve the same basic purpose: to permit risk managers to test various scenarios and determine the most likely outcomes for various decisions.

There are two general categories of computer models: deterministic models and probabilistic models.

- Deterministic models are characterized by consistent results. They do not explicitly recognize random variation in the environment being modeled. If a deterministic model is run many times with exactly the same values for all of the input factors, it will produce exactly the same output each time.

- Probabilistic models, also called stochastic models, explicitly recognize randomness or uncertainty. The range of chance variation may be quite large in some models.

[9]There are three types of functions that may be distinguished. *Arithmetic functions* exist when a given absolute change in X produces a certain constant absolute change in Y. *Logarithmic functions* exist when a given percentage change in X brings about a certain constant percentage change in Y. Finally, a *curvilinear function* exists when a change in Y associated with X is not constant in either absolute or relative terms but is variable depending on the value of X.

Since risk management scenarios are subject to chance variation, one might conclude that a probabilistic model would be the better planning instrument for a risk manager. In practice, both types of simulation are useful in risk management decisions.

One type of stochastic model—a *Monte Carlo* stimulation—is used to create a total loss profile for an organization, based on past experience and theoretical probability distributions. The model's association with gambling stems from the fact that the output from such a model is not determined solely by the inputs but is also subject to some element of chance variation. The mathematical distributions that are used to model loss frequency include the normal distribution, the Poisson distribution, and the negative binomial. Severity distributions are generally modeled through the use of the Log-normal and Gamma distributions.

Deterministic models also have many applications in risk management, and are particularly useful in choosing among alternatives. As discussed later in the text, simulation models may be extremely useful in choosing among insurance alternatives where the premium is sensitive to losses during the policy period. In workers compensation and health insurance, for example, insurance coverage is available on a "cost-plus" basis, but subject to a maximum and minimum premium. Simulation models are useful in considering "what if" for various assumed levels of loss.

INSURANCE RATES AND UNDERWRITING AS RISK MEASUREMENTS

Although unquestionably some organizations are large enough and have sufficient loss experience to apply probability theory, they represent a small portion of the business population. Most businesses are small and medium-sized, which means that there are limits to the extent to which they can apply probability theory. This does not mean, however, that these organizations have no notion of their loss frequency; it means simply that their experience is not a sufficient sample on which to make credible predictions.

Although the conventional notion of risk measurement contemplates measuring frequency and severity of the organization's risks by the risk manager, it should be remembered that the pricing practices of insurers are based on probability theory, and the insurance rate for a particular exposure represents a measurement of risk. After analyzing past experience, insurance actuaries attempt to predict future losses. Because losses vary with the hazards (i.e., conditions that increase the likelihood of loss), actuaries attempt to divide the population of risks into groups with different loss-producing characteristics for the purpose of deriving rates that will reflect the probability of loss. The insurance rate is, in a rough sense, a measure of loss frequency and severity.

Underwriting is the process by which an insurer decides whether or not to insure a particular exposure, and if so, the rate at which it will be insured. When an insurance company refuses to accept a particular risk, it is because the underwriter judges that the hazards associated with that risk are too high in relation to the price that the insurer can charge. Because the price and acceptability of the risk to the insurer are based on the hazards associated with the subject of the insurance, both the rate and acceptability of the risk to an insurer are useful indicators of the hazards associated with the exposure.

Even when the firm does not have sufficient data to construct a probability function for its various exposures, a rough approximation of expected losses can be determined based on premiums for insurance coverages. Because the premium charged by an insurer is based on expected losses (the so-called *pure premium*) the expected loss for a particular line of insurance can be estimated from the allowance in the premium intended for the payment of losses. For example, consider the following situation. *XYZ* Corporation has 60 vehicles, consisting principally of private passenger autos. The physical damage premium for collision coverage on the vehicles is $250 each per year, or $15,000 per year. The expected loss ratio for automobile physical damage is about .65. This means that according to the insurer's estimate, the expected loss for *XYZ* is about $10,000. If *XYZ*'s losses are in fact less than $15,000, it will be cheaper for *XYZ* to retain the risk of loss rather than purchase insurance.

This is not surprising. The premium for insurance coverage is based on the expected average loss, but because of the expense loading, will always be greater than the expected average loss. The major reason for the purchase of insurance is that the organization's *actual* losses may exceed *expected* losses. This, you will recall, is the essence of risk; the possibility of a deviation from what is expected. If one could be certain that actual losses would be less than or equal to expected losses, there would be no reason to purchase insurance.

A FINAL CAUTION REGARDING ADEQUACY OF THE FIRM'S DATA

Many of the decisions involving the use of quantitative analysis are in the choice between commercial insurance and retention. In these cases, the risk manager considers the likely cost that will be incurred as a result of the two possible choices, usually insurance or retention. In this context, it is useful at the outset to recognize several axioms that may not be immediately obvious.

The first is that insurers use probability theory in computing the prices they will charge for their insurance. Indeed, insurers "invented" the use of probabilities in decision making. Insurance rates are based on the past losses of the insurer or on the losses of numerous companies collected by advisory organizations. In computing the rates, insurers use sophisticated actuarial techniques and a massive loss database. However, even with a significant history of losses upon which to draw, the actuaries' estimates of future losses are sometimes—even often—off the mark.

When an individual firm uses probability theory to project its own loss experience for comparison with the loss estimates of the insurer, there is an implicit assumption that the experience of the individual firm may be different from the larger population on which the insurer's loss estimate is based. When the predicted losses for an individual firm indicates a substantial difference from the insurer's rate, the difference may be due to one of two factors:

1. The loss experience of the firm may actually be different from that of the larger population on which the insurer's prediction is based.

2. The estimate of losses by the firm or by the insurer may be in error.

Given the difference in the size of the populations on which the predictions are based, most authorities would probably reject the contention that the projections of the individual firm are likely to be more accurate than those of the insurer. As noted earlier in the chapter, one drawback in relying solely on historical loss data of the organization to estimate a frequency distribution is that only losses that have occurred in the past can be observed. The risk manager must recognize that there is some positive, although perhaps small, probability that future experience will be significantly different from that of the past. This "tail" of the distribution, showing the likelihood of rare occurrences, is of particular importance to the risk manager, who is often interested in the worst case scenario. Although the use of industry-wide data and theoretical probability distributions may help the risk manager in filling out the tails of the probability distribution, care is required, since there may be differences between the organization and the general industry population. No two firms are ever identical; differences in employee training, loss prevention efforts, and other factors can affect the suitability of industry data for a particular organization.

Finally, it should be recognized that conditions within a firm rarely remain stable over time, suggesting that past data may be obsolete. A new production process, a new safety program, a change in the number of employees or their levels of training may all affect the frequency of employee injuries. The same holds true in other areas. Changes in economic conditions, the legal environment, social attitudes, and the employer's operation may all affect the frequency distribution of the firm's loss exposures over time. Using the past loss data which does not reflect these changes will adversely affect the accuracy of the estimated frequency distribution. Where the risk manager can identify trends in losses over time, it may be possible to adjust past data to reflect these changes. This process is known as "trending" the data. This is another area in which errors may enter into the estimation process, since inaccurate adjustment of the data may produce inaccurate estimates of the frequency distribution.

IMPORTANT CONCEPTS

probability	variance	correlation analysis
relative likelihood interpretation	standard deviation	negative correlation
relative frequency interpretation	coefficient of variation	positive correlation
	sample mean	dependent variable
	sample variance	independent variable
a priori probability	binomial model	standard error of estimate
a posteriori probability	Poisson model	coefficient of correlation
conditional or posterior probability	severity distribution	simple correlation
	total annual loss distribution	multiple correlation
marginal or prior probability	simulation model	underwriting
random variable	Monte Carlo simulation	pure premium
probability distribution	deterministic simulation	
expected value	regression analysis	

QUESTIONS FOR REVIEW

1. Describe the three ways in which probability may be determined.

2. Distinguish between the two interpretations of probability discussed in the chapter.

3. Define the terms random variable and probability distribution.

4. Describe what is meant by a probability distribution and identify the two summary pieces of information that synthesize the information in such distributions.

5. Of what value is the mean of a probability distribution to the risk manager?

6. Identify and distinguish between the two types of simulation models that are used in risk management.

7. Of what use are theoretical probability models to the risk manager? Of the models discussed in the chapter, which do you believe is probably the most useful?

8. Briefly explain the reasons that the risk manager must use caution when relying on the firm's historical data in risk management decisions.

9. What, in your opinion, is the principal advantage of probability to the risk manager? What is the principal disadvantage?

10. Given the following record of automobile collision losses, estimate the mean of the probability distribution and the standard deviation.

Year	Number of Losses
1991	13
1992	17
1993	15
1994	19
1995	14

QUESTIONS FOR DISCUSSION

1. Identify five types of loss a risk manager might be interested in predicting and an independent variable that might provide a basis for such predictions.

2. The risk manager of a national trucking company has accumulated information on the number of accidents and miles driven by year. Plot the data on a scatter diagram. What conclusions are suggested by the results?

Year	Accidents	Million Miles Driven
1981	6	1.125
1982	14	2.655
1983	18	3.388
1984	22	3.655
1985	24	3.921
1986	31	4.450
1987	41	5.050
1988	59	5.330
1989	67	5.680
1990	81	6.340
1991	88	6.560
1992	110	7.220
1993	135	7.890
1994	145	7.960
1995	186	8.245

3. The ABC Corporation has averaged 30 collisions annually over the past five years. The losses have been remarkably consistent and the risk manager has assumed that losses follow a Poisson distribution. What is the probability that the firm will suffer 40 losses in the coming year?

4. ABC Corporation has extensive data on the firm's history of both automobile losses and workers compensation losses. The risk manager is interested in determining whether there is a correlation between the two. Do you believe that the two types of losses are likely to be correlated? Why or why not?

5. Identify an independent variable with which you suspect each of the following types of losses is likely to be correlated:
   a. shoplifting losses
   b. employee injuries
   c. flood losses
   d. windstorm losses

SUGGESTIONS FOR ADDITIONAL READING

Cummins, J.D. and L.R. Frielander. "Statistical Analysis in Risk Management," *Risk Management* (September 1978–April, 1979).

Doherty, Neil A. *Corporate Risk Management* (New York: McGraw Hill Book Company, 1985), Chapters 2, 4.

Financial Applications for Risk Management. Fireman's Fund Insurance Companies and Risk Sciences Group, Inc., 1983.

Greene, Mark R. *Decision Analysis for Risk Management—A Primer on Quantitative Methods* (New York: The Risk and Insurance Management Society, 1977).

Jablonski, Mark. "Using Probabilistic Risk Analysis," *Risk Management.* (March 1966).

Lauri, J.J. and N.A. Baglini. *Principles of Property and Liability Underwriting* (Malvern, Pa.: Insurance Institute of America, 1977).

CHAPTER 9

🔲🔲🔲🔲🔲

Risk Control:
General Considerations

CHAPTER OBJECTIVES

When you have finished this chapter, you should be able to

Explain how a business might use risk avoidance in dealing with risk and why avoidance is subject to limitations in its application by businesses.

▪

Distinguish between loss-prevention and control measures.

▪

Explain the difference in philosophy between the domino theory and energy release theory of accident causation.

▪

Define systems safety and describe the systems safety techniques described in the chapter.

▪

Describe the nature and purpose of disaster planning.

▪

Identify the four broad areas toward which risk control measures should be directed and describe the general nature of each.

■ Introduction ■

Avoiding losses has always been one of humanity's greatest concerns, and risk control was undoubtedly the first risk management technique. Primitive man lived in caves and sometimes in trees to protect himself from dangerous wild beasts. The first practitioner of loss prevention was probably the human who climbed a tree to escape a saber-toothed tiger. The history of civilization is a record of humanity's attempts to deal with threats to well-being by forces of nature and other perils.

In this chapter, we explore some of the reasons why corporate attitudes toward risk control have changed, and examine the concept of risk control in a generic sense, focusing on the general principles of risk control. We will consider the specific applications of risk control to individual exposures in later chapters.

It should be understood that neither this chapter nor the later chapters on risk control are intended as a crash course in loss prevention and control. The loss-prevention and control measures that are appropriate for the variety of hazards that can produce losses differ from hazard to hazard. They encompass fire prevention engineering and industrial safety, security measures, legal analysis, and a variety of engineering applications. These are highly sophisticated disciplines, for which people prepare through years of education and training. It would be presumptuous to suggest that we can summarize these disciplines in a few pages. Hopefully, however, the discussion will place risk control in perspective in the risk management process, and give an appreciation of the contribution that risk control makes to achieving the risk management objectives.

■: Risk Control Generally   ■ ■ ■ ■ ■ ■ ■ ■ ■ ■ ■ ■ ■ ■ ■ ■ ■ ■ ■

Risk control has been an integral part of the risk management process since the concept of risk management was conceived. In those firms where risk management is recognized as an important organization function, risk control efforts are generally an important part of the corporate program. To begin our discussion, let us briefly review the distinction between the two major techniques of risk control—risk avoidance and risk reduction.

RISK AVOIDANCE

Technically, avoidance takes place when decisions are made that prevent a risk from even coming into existence. Risks are avoided when the organization refuses to accept the risk even for an instant. An example is a firm that considers manufacturing some product but, because of the hazards involved elects not to do so. The high incidence of medical malpractice claims in some fields has resulted in a shortage of practitioners in these areas. This is risk avoidance. Although the line between risk avoidance and risk reduction or risk transfer is sometimes a hazy one, whether a particular action is avoidance, reduction, or perhaps transfer is academic. Once the risk exists, it is more appropriate to classify the measures used to eliminate it or minimize it as loss prevention rather than avoidance. The distinction, however, is merely semantic. In either case, the efforts to minimize risk constitute risk control efforts.

The classic example of risk avoidance by a business firm is a decision not to manufacture a particular product because of the inherent risk. Given the potential for product liability claims that may result if a consumer is injured by a product, prudence dictates that a business consider carefully the potential for liability losses and weigh this potential against the profit that might be made by producing the product. Often, it is judged that the risk is not worth the potential gain.

Although avoidance is the only alternative for dealing with some risks, it is a negative rather than a positive approach. If avoidance is used extensively, the firm may not be able to achieve its primary objectives. A manufacturer cannot avoid the risk of product liability by avoiding the risk and still stay in business. For this reason, avoidance is, in a sense, the last resort in dealing with risk. It is used when there is no other alternative.

Risk avoidance should be used when the exposure has catastrophic potential and the risk cannot be reduced or transferred. Generally, these conditions will exist in the case of risks for which both the frequency and severity are high. The high potential loss severity dictates that the risk not be retained, and the high frequency virtually guarantees that insurance will not be economically feasible.

RISK REDUCTION

The term *risk reduction* is used to define a broader set of efforts aimed to minimize risk. Other terms that were formerly used, and that have been displaced by the more generic term *risk reduction*, include *loss prevention* and *loss control*. The term *risk reduction* is considered to include both loss-prevention and control efforts. Broadly speaking, loss-prevention efforts are aimed at preventing the occurrence of loss. Although it is obviously impossible to prevent all losses, it is also clear that some losses can be prevented. In addition, loss control efforts can be directed toward reducing the severity of those losses that do occur. In other words, some risk control efforts aim at reducing frequency, and others seek to reduce the severity of the losses that do occur. Those risk control measures designed to reduce the frequency of loss focus on preventing losses from occurring. These include not only engineering measures, but education and enforcement as well. Those risk control measures aimed at reducing the severity of the losses that do occur include a variety of approaches. Some, such as sprinkler systems, are designed to mitigate damage by retarding the force causing the damage. Others, such as salvage activities and rehabilitation seek to reduce the financial loss resulting from the event by maximizing the after-loss value of the person or property that was damaged.

◼ Historical Neglect of Risk Control   ◼ ◼ ◼ ◼ ◼ ◼ ◼ ◼ ◼ ◼ ◼ ◼ ◼

Although the situation has changed dramatically with the growth of risk management, there was a time when risk control was a relatively neglected function. This was true for several reasons.

In theory, risk control measures should be used when they are the most effective technique for dealing with a particular risk. Furthermore, loss-prevention and control measures should be used up to the point at which each dollar spent on such measures will produce a dollar in saving through reduction in losses. This is simple marginal benefit–marginal cost analysis. Unfortunately, applying this kind of analysis to the risk control process is complicated by several factors.

First, the timing of the expenditures for loss control and the benefits from reduced losses are different. Loss-prevention costs must be incurred here and now, but the benefits they will generate are all in the future. Furthermore, the benefits are more elusive, requiring measurement of something that does not happen (losses). Although such measurement is possible, experience has shown that few businesses historically were inclined to attempt to do so. Given the uncertain nature of the future benefits from loss reduction and the immediate cost, it is probably not surprising that the expenses often lose in competition with other funding needs. Because the benefits of loss-prevention and control efforts are difficult to measure, expenditures in this area are sometimes difficult to justify on a cost-benefit basis and as a result lose in competition with other funding needs.

Still another factor was that, until recently, state and federal regulations were less stringent. There were fewer regulations to comply with, since less was known about the health hazards associated with various types of occupational positions. Where hazards were recognized, they were often assumed to be inherent in the industry or occupation; hence, minimum attention was given to their control or elimination. In the field of consumer products, it was widely accepted that safety was the user's responsibility, since few governmental regulations or judicial rulings made manufacturers responsible for their products' end use. Consumerism, government regulations, and the tort system have created an entirely new environment, and have gotten the attention of the business world with a vengeance. Government regulations have imposed new responsibilities on business firms with respect to the safety of both their employees and their consumers. In addition, changes in the tort system have created new incentives for effective loss-prevention programs.

Today, the neglect of risk control is more a historical footnote than a fact. Owing partly to the growth of risk management but more to mandated risk control measures that are dictated by state and federal laws, risk control programs are an important facet of every organization's efforts to deal with risk.

GOVERNMENT STANDARDS

The theory behind government regulations related to safety is that businesses will not implement the desired safety measures unless they are compelled to do so. In some instances, it is theorized, businesses underestimate the benefits of safety measures. In other cases, legislators have simply concluded that the public interest—defined in terms of injuries and deaths prevented—outweighs corporate profits in importance. Once adopted, the statutory standard becomes mandatory for all businesses covered by the law.

Occupational Safety and Health Administration (OSHA) regulations are perhaps the best example of statutory loss control standards. OSHA was a legislative recognition of the fact that businesses must sometimes be compelled to make loss-prevention expenditures. The law was passed in 1970 to force employers to incur loss-prevention costs related to employee safety without regard to marginal benefit–marginal cost analysis. If the employers could not find justification for employee safety expenditures on a cost-benefit basis, Congress would give them the incentive to do so by imposing penalties for failure to do so.[1]

State and local building and fire codes represent another example of government mandates for loss-prevention and control measures. These codes are based on models developed by the National Fire Protection Association (NFPA) to define the construction and occupancy.[2] The NFPA standards are published annually in loose-leaf and bound editions and updated continuously through the actions of many technical committees representing broad-based industry and government memberships. The individual standards that comprise the code are directed principally at fire prevention, detection, and suppression.

VOLUNTARY STANDARDS

In addition to the statutory standards enacted by the Congress and state and local legislatures, there are also a number of voluntary or consensual standards that have been adopted by nongovernment groups to provide private advisory guidance. Although these standards are not legally binding, they can have an important influence on the safety efforts of those to whom they are intended to provide guidance.[3] Often, voluntary standards gain significance because they are used as performance measures by insurance companies. The standards promulgated by the Underwriters Laboratories (UL) are a case in point. Although UL certification of a product is voluntary on the part of the manufacturer, most commercial insurance companies will provide product liability insurance only to manufacturers who use UL-approved materials or whose products bear the UL label. The UL tests a wide variety of products for conformance with its own safety standards, most of which have as their primary objective the personal safety of users of the tested products.

The line between statutory standards and voluntary standards is sometimes hazy. When OSHA was enacted, for example, many of the statutory standards that were originally adopted were verbatim extracts from private standards of organizations such as the National Fire Protection Association.

✠ The Risk Manager and Risk Control ■ ■ ■ ■ ■ ■ ■ ■ ■ ■ ■ ■

Risk control has been an integral part of the risk management process since the concept of risk management was conceived. In those firms where risk management is recognized as an important organization function, risk control efforts are generally an

---

[1]As with other federal regulatory agencies, OSHA standards are promulgated through publication in the Federal Register. Following the prescribed period for public comment, if any, they are then codified in the Code of Federal Regulations (CFR). The OSHA Standards are grouped in the Code at 29 CFR 1910 (Title 29 of the Code of Federal Regulations, Part 1910).

[2]*Fire Protection Handbook*, 17th ed., National Fire Protection Association, Quincy, Mass., 1991.

[3]In the United States, when a voluntary standard is judged to be of general importance, the developing organization submits it to the American National Standards Institute (ANSI) for adoption.

important part of the corporate program. Risk control measures support both transfer and retention. Companies that insure all or part of their risk find that loss experience is their most valuable negotiating point with respect to availability, coverage, and premium costs. Poor or escalating loss experience is usually met by restricted availability of coverage and higher premiums. The organization with good loss experience is likely to find that insurance markets for its risks are readily available.

Ideally, a well-designed loss-prevention and control program should encompass four major areas:

- Personnel safety
- Automobile (fleet) safety
- Liability loss control
- Property protection
- Security

Loss-prevention in each of these areas is a technical and highly specialized function, and often requires the expertise of specialists. Most loss-prevention and control strategies were originally conceived as a response to a perceived problem and are specific to that problem. Although the underlying approach may theoretically be the same, different skills are required. Preventing employee injuries obviously calls for a different kind of expertise than reducing the risk of a directors' and officers' liability suit, or preventing embezzlement, but all require a similar mixture of technical skills in order to choose the ideal loss control measures from a variety of alternatives.

The success of a corporate loss control program is dependent on the quality of management it receives. It seems clear from our discussion of the earlier failure of the risk control function in organizations that risk control requires an advocate within the organization: someone who is responsible for the overall coordination of the risk control function, regardless of the particular area of loss involved. Many authorities believe that responsibility and authority for the development of a total loss-prevention and control program should be vested in a single person. The risk manager, by virtue of his or her familiarity with the exposures of the organization and the costs arising from such exposures, is a logical person to whom such responsibility might be assigned. Although the risk manager will rarely possess the wide range of skills required for a comprehensive loss-prevention and control effort, what he or she really needs is the ability to recognize the need for risk control and the managerial skills necessary to accomplish the desired goal through the efforts of those who have the needed skills.

Other arrangements are, of course, possible. In those firms in which a safety director already exists, that individual's position might be enlarged to include responsibility for total loss prevention, not just personnel safety. In other firms, where there is no safety director, responsibility for this function should be assigned as part of the total responsibility to a director of loss prevention and control. Regardless of the title or the proportionate amount of time devoted specifically to the risk control area, the person must have clear designation of both responsibility and authority for the program.

✖ Theories of Accident Causation ■ ■ ■ ■ ■ ■ ■ ■ ■ ■ ■ ■ ■ ■

In later chapters, we will consider specific loss-prevention and control measures for individual exposures. As a foundation for those discussions, it may be helpful to review the general theory of accident causation. Understanding why accidents happen can be useful in designing programs for their prevention. To date, no one has developed a dominant general theory of why accidents occur. Instead, there are two separate theories, each of which has some explanatory and predictive value.

1. The *domino theory,* developed by H. W. Heinrich, a safety engineer and pioneer in the field of industrial accident safety.
2. The *energy release theory,* developed by Dr. William Haddon, Jr., of the Insurance Institute for Highway Safety.

Although these authors were concerned with different types of loss (Heinrich with industrial accidents and employee injuries, and Haddon with highway safety), both are general theories in the sense that they may be applied across the entire range of loss prevention and control. The Heinrich theory, which is the older of the two, is still widely cited and has many adherents. Haddon's theory is more general and being the newer of the two theories, is less well known. Each theory has numerous adherents, and much of the literature reflects one or the other of the two theories (but seldom both). For some reason, writers tend to emphasize one theory and ignore the other (but seldom both).

HEINRICH'S DOMINO THEORY

According to Heinrich, an "accident" is one factor in a sequence that may lead to an injury. As illustrated in Figure 9.1, the factors can be visualized as a series of dominoes standing on edge; when one falls, the linkage required for a chain reaction is completed. Each of the factors is dependent on the preceding factor. In Heinrich's theory

1. A personal injury (the final domino) occurs only as a result of an accident.
2. An accident occurs only as a result of a personal or mechanical hazard.
3. Personal and mechanical hazards exist only because of the fault of persons.
4. Faults of persons are inherited or acquired as a result of their environment.
5. The environment is the conditions into which an individual is born.

The domino theory states that when an injury or property damage takes place, all five factors are involved. If the fifth domino falls, it is because the first domino fell causing the others to fall in turn. If one of the factors in the sequence leading to an accident can be removed, the loss can be prevented. For example, eliminating an unsafe act makes the action of the preceding factors ineffective.

Heinrich held that a person responsible for loss control should be interested in all five factors, but be concerned primarily with accidents and the proximate causes of

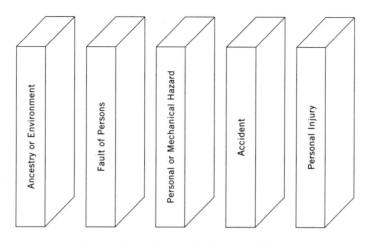

Figure 9.1 Heinrich's Domino Theory

those accidents. The factor preceding the accident (the unsafe act or the mechanical or physical hazard) should receive the most attention. If this third domino can be removed, the sequence will be interrupted, even if the first two dominos fall.

What is the primary cause of accidents? Unsafe acts of persons or unsafe mechanical or physical conditions? The answer is very important because it tells the loss control specialist where to direct the most attention. For Heinrich, the answer was clear. After a study of 75,000 industrial accidents, Heinrich concluded that 98 percent of all accidents are preventable and that it should be possible to reduce industrial accident costs with some form of loss control. Among the 75,000 cases he studied, Heinrich charged 88 percent to the unsafe acts of persons and 10 percent to dangerous physical or mechanical conditions. The remaining 2 percent were termed "Acts of God." Some accidents involve both unsafe acts and conditions. In these cases, Heinrich assigned responsibility to the primary cause. Heinrich also emphasized that accidents, not injuries or property damage, should be the point of attack. According to Heinrich, an accident is any unplanned and uncontrolled event in which the action or reaction of an object, substance, person, or radiation that *could* result in personal injury or property damage. Note that in this context, an "accident" need not actually result in injury or property damage. If a person slips and falls, an injury may or may not result, but according to Heinrich, an accident has taken place. According to Heinrich, "An injury is merely the result of an accident." This observation is the basis for the philosophy of loss-prevention and control that places the emphasis on attempting to control the frequency of accidents. The accident itself is controllable. The severity or cost of an injury that results when an accident occurs is difficult to control. Although Heinrich's work concentrated on employee injuries, his theory seems suited to any situations in which conduct of the victim is important.[4]

[4]Heinrich, H.W. *Industrial Accident Prevention* (4th ed.) (New York: McGraw-Hill Book Co., 1959).

WILLIAM HADDON'S ENERGY RELEASE THEORY

Instead of concentrating on human behavior, Haddon treats accidents as a physical engineering problem. Accidents result when energy that is out of control puts more stress on a structure (property or person) than that structure can tolerate without damage. The model is generic, and situations in which "energy is out of control" could include fire losses, accidents, industrial injuries, and virtually any other situation in which injury or damage can result. Accidents can be prevented by controlling the energy involved or by changing the structures that the energy could damage. More specifically, Haddon suggested ten strategies designed either to suppress conditions that produce accidents or to enhance conditions that retard accidents.

1. *Prevent the creation of the hazard in the first place.* Examples of efforts aimed at the preventing hazards include licensing of drivers, no-smoking rules that eliminate cigarettes from restricted areas, and a ban on manufacture and sale of dangerous toys or other products protects consumers.

2. *Reduce the amount of the hazard brought into being.* Efforts aimed at controlling the amount of hazard include highway speed limits, limiting horsepower in vehicles, and limiting the voltage in electrical appliances.

3. *Prevent the release of the hazard that already exists.* This includes measures to control the release of energy, such as fuses and automatic shut-off controls on machines.

4. *Modify the rate or spatial distribution of release of the hazard from its source.* Examples include brakes on vehicles, electrical transformers, dams and levees for flood control, and pressure relief valves on boilers.

5. *Separate in time or space the hazard and that to be protected.* Examples include all types of separators, such as divided highways, traffic lights, pedestrian malls, one-way streets, the isolation of persons with communicable diseases, and avoiding congested traffic.

6. *Separate the hazard and what is to be protected by interposing a material barrier.* Examples include fences and similar barriers to protect property, fire walls, machine guards, bullet proof vests, automobile seat belts and airbags, child-proof medicine containers, and imprisioning criminals.

7. *Modify relevant basic qualities of the hazard.* Examples include electrical transformers, noncaustic cleaners, lead-free paint, and fat-free foods.

8. *Make what is to be protected more resistant to damage from the hazard.* Examples include fire and earthquake resistant buildings, crash resistant vehicles, alteration-proof checks, and properly designed shipping containers.

9. *Begin to counter the damage already done by the hazard.* Examples include first aid and emergency response medical services, separating damaged from undamaged property and protecting property from further damage.

10. *Stabilize repair and rehabilitate the object of the damage.* Examples include the rehabilitation of injured workers, salvage operations and restoration of damaged property.

Haddon's ten strategies can be grouped according to whether they (a) focus on controlling the amount of energy that exists or the rate at which it is released (strategies 1 through 4); (b) aim at protecting persons or property from the energy that is released (strategies 5 through 7), or (c) attempt to mitigate the effects of the energy on persons or property (strategies 8 through 10). Generally speaking, the larger the amount of energy generated relative to the resistance level of the property or persons exposed to the energy, the lower numbered (the earlier) the strategy must be employed to control it. In the ultimate case—where the amount of energy generated is large and the object exposed to damage is highly vulnerable—the only effective approach may be to prevent the creation of the hazard (Strategy 1).[5] The strategies may, of course, be combined to address a given hazard in different ways.

THE TWO THEORIES COMPARED

The difference between the Heinrich and Haddon theories can be viewed as a difference in emphasis. Both theories explain a sequence that leads to damage or injury. Unlike Heinrich, who places most of the blame for accidents on human behavior that leads to mechanical or physical hazards, Haddon concentrates on the physical engineering aspects of the conditions that give rise to accidents.

Approaches to Loss Prevention and Control ■■■■■■■■■■■■■■■■■■■■■■■■■■■

The differing emphasis in Heinrich's theory and Haddon's theory provide a basis for understanding the different approaches to loss prevention and control. Efforts to prevent losses and to reduce the impact of those losses that do occur take place in virtually every phase of human activity. Some of these are sophisticated, whereas others are simple and reactive. Various ways of classifying loss-prevention efforts have been suggested.

One of the most widely accepted classifications is to divide loss-prevention efforts by the object of the effort. Some such efforts are aimed at mechanical and environmental factors, and seek to eliminate hazards; these are referred to as the *engineering approach.* Other loss-prevention measures focus on the individual and seek to modify human behavior; these use the *human behavior approach.*[6]

---

[5]Haddon, William, Jr., M.D., "On Escape of Tigers: An Ecological Note," in C.W. Wixom (ed.) *Key Issues in Highway Loss Reduction* (Washington, D.C.: Institute for Highway Safety, 1970).

[6]The dichotomy between the engineering approach and the human behavior approach is illustrated by the debate over the choice between seatbelts and airbags in automobiles. The National Safety Council's insistence on the airbag is a manifestation of the low esteem in which the engineering approach holds the human inclination toward safety. Although all American automobiles now come equipped with safety belts, they also have inflatable airbags, mainly because people do not use the seatbelts.

ENGINEERING APPROACH

The engineering approach to loss prevention and control emphasizes the elimination of unsafe physical conditions by such measures as fire-resistive construction, burglary-resistant safes, boiler inspections, and safer cars. The basic premise in the engineering approach is that people have little regard for their own personal safety and that it is inherent in human nature to commit careless acts. Safety engineering must protect people from themselves.

HUMAN BEHAVIOR APPROACH

The human behavior approach stresses safety education and the motivation of persons. Proponents of this approach to loss prevention argue that most accidents are committed by unsafe acts, and that the greatest gains in safety and loss prevention can be achieved through efforts aimed at modifying human behavior. The efforts aimed at modifying human behavior include education and enforcement.

Education   The first ingredient in the human behavior approach to risk control is education. Education serves two important functions. First, it alerts those exposed to loss to the existence of the hazards they face and impresses on them the consequences of the losses to which they are exposed. Hopefully, it creates a heightened sense of concern over the individual's own safety. Second, education can provide guidance on the "safer way" of performing certain functions. Safety education, television safety ads, posters, safety committees, and safety rules are all examples of the *educational* facet of the human behavior approach to loss prevention.

Enforcement   For some inexplicable reason, many people feel immune to injury from the hazards they face. Since the individual's own concern for his or her safety is often insufficient to motivate the desired conduct, rules and regulations must be enacted and enforced. Traffic laws, municipal building codes, plant safety rules, and the plethora of similar regulations and their enforcement are examples of the "enforcement" aspect of the human behavior emphasis in loss control.

RISK CONTROL TECHNIQUES

The desire for survival is a basic human trait, and broadly speaking, loss control techniques include all of the actions of individuals that are prompted by the desire to avoid injury or loss. For this reason, it is impossible to create an inventory of loss-prevention and control efforts of individuals. Even in the more limited case of the control techniques that are planned and implemented as part of the formal risk management process, the inventory of techniques is virtually endless.

It is possible, however, to describe broad control techniques into which the virtually endless array of specific approaches can be classed. Haddon's strategies, for example, represent such a classification and provide a convenient roadmap for planning the attack on losses. They include both efforts to prevent the occurrence of loss (loss prevention) and efforts to minimize the costs of those losses that are not prevented.

Control Measures and Time of Application

Another way by which loss control measures can also be classed is according to the time at which they are applied. One classification of "timing" categorizes the measures according to whether they are applied before the accident, at the time of the accident, or after the accident. Haddon suggests that loss-prevention efforts can be classified as pre-event actions, simultaneous-with-event actions, and post-event actions. Pre-event actions are efforts aimed at preventing the loss event. In the case of auto accidents (Haddon's principal area of concern) pre-event actions include licensing, vehicle inspection, and driver education programs. Simultaneous-with-event actions include all of the efforts that are designed to "package" and protect the driver when an accident does occur. Post-event actions might focus on medical care and treatment to injured drivers.

Control Measures and Mechanism

Another classification focuses on whether the loss control measure is aimed at the person, the mechanical device or mechanism, or the environment within which the accident occurs. Some loss-prevention measures are directed toward each of these instrumentalities. Driver education, for example, focuses on the person; automobile safety standards focus on the machine; and road signs, stop-lights, and intersection control focus on the environment.

When the time of application and the mechanism toward which the loss control measure is directed are combined, we can construct a matrix that summarizes the possible combinations of loss-prevention and control techniques (see Figure 9.2).

Thus the loss-prevention measures may be directed toward nine possible combinations of timing and mechanism. They are aimed at each part of the person–machine environment complex, before, at the time of, and after the accident.

	Prior to Event	At Time of Event	After Event
Individual			
Machinery			
Equipment			

Figure 9.2 Timing and Targets of Control Measures

SPECIALIZED LOSS CONTROL TECHNIQUES

As previously noted, the array of loss-prevention and control techniques is virtually endless. About all one can hope to do is provide a means whereby the techniques can be classified. Although the classifications discussed earlier are the most common, there are several techniques which are sometimes ignored in the discussion of loss prevention and control. These techniques are separation of assets, salvage, rehabilitation, redundancy, and noninsurance transfers.

Separation of Assets

Separation of assets can work to control severity. During World War II, for example, the risk of loss arising out of the manufacture of munitions was conducted at numerous small plants rather than at a few large ones. The purpose of this separation approach was to limit the value of assets exposed to loss in a single occurrence. This approach is applicable to property losses generally and is also aimed at crime exposure to minimize both the likelihood and amount of loss.

Salvage

When efforts aimed at preventing the occurrence of a loss fail and the loss occurs, the amount of the loss can be reduced by immediate action to protect the remaining value that has not been damaged. Such efforts can substantially mitigate the damage that would otherwise be incurred. Salvage efforts include not only those efforts designed to protect property from further damage, but also arranging for the sale or other disposition of undamaged property at the highest price.

Rehabilitation

Rehabilitation is, in a sense, the salvage function applied to human beings. The rehabilitation of workers who have been injured on the job reduces the financial loss from the injury, both for the worker and for the employer who must compensate the injured worker. Significant advances in the science of rehabilitation have decreased the costs of compensating injured workers.

Redundancy

Although not often thought of as a loss control technique, redundancy can help to prevent the adverse effects of accidents. "Standby" generating facilities in the event of power outages, alternate sources of materials and supplies, and duplicate safeguards on dangerous machines are all examples of redundancy in the loss control effort. The classic example of redundancy in safety measures is found in the U.S. space program, where redundant systems have been refined to a high art as loss control measures.

Noninsurance Transfers

Some risk transfers—most notably insurance—are a form of risk financing. Other types of transfers are more appropriately classified as risk control measures. These risk-control transfers include a variety of business activities, such as leasing, subcontracting, and contractual arrangements that alter the incidence of loss. Leasing property, for example, avoids the risks associated with ownership. The use of subcontractors to perform certain functions can result in the transfer of the risk associated with those functions to the subcontractor. Another type of risk transfer that falls within the rubric of risk control consists of contractual transfers of risk that are auxiliary to another contract or agreement. Such agreements are referred to as *exculpatory agreements, holdharmless agreements,* and *indemnity agreements.* Such agreements arise in connection with a variety of contractual relationships, including construction contracts, purchase orders, lease of premises agreements, automobile lease agreements, maintenance and service agreements, and easement agreements.

Under an exculpatory agreement, one party agrees to release the other party from liability for damage arising out of a particular activity. A landlord might, for example, agree by contract to release the tenant from any liability arising out of damage to the leased property, regardless of the tenant's negligence or fault. An indemnity agreement goes further and requires one party to pay for damage or loss for which he would not otherwise be responsible. Finally, a holdharmless agreement obligates one party (the indemnitor) to keep the other party (the indemnitee) from financial loss arising from what falls within the scope of the contractual provisions. The loss may be damage to or destruction of property belonging to the other party or liability to a third party. For example, a contractor might agree to defend and indemnify the owner of a project for liability to injured third parties arising from the owner's and contractor's negligence. If a member of the public is subsequently injured and brings suit against both the contractor and owner, the owner would be protected by the hold harmless agreement. This protection is, of course, defined and limited by the indemnitor's ability to make good on the promise to indemnify.

It should go without saying that the agreement between two parties cannot affect the rights of a third party who is not a party to the contract. A party may shift his liability to another party by contract only so far as the other party is concerned. If *A* agrees to indemnify and hold *B* harmless from any and all liability arising out of the activity, nothing prevents *C* from suing *B*. If *B* is held liable, *A* has simply agreed to pay the judgment. If *A* cannot, for some reason, meet the obligation under the contract, *B* remains legally liable to *C*.

Actually, the classification of these types of transfers as risk control methods can be debated. Generally, risk control reduces risk. When a risk is transferred to another party, it has not been eliminated, but merely shifted to another party. From this perspective, contractual transfers of risk do not reduce risk, at least not in the aggregate. From the perspective of the transferor, however, the risk is reduced, so we will consider these as risk control measures.

Systems Safety ■

Systems safety, an approach to loss prevention and control that has general applicability, first appeared in the United States during the 1950s. It is a branch of and developed from systems engineering, the application of engineering skills to the design and creation of complex systems. It evolved in response to increasingly complex problems that needed to be solved and for which traditional approaches were inadequate.[7] As the title indicates, systems safety views a process, a situation, a problem, a machine, or any other entity as a system—rather than as just a process, situation, problem, or machine. The term *system* means any collection or composite of resources that are to be changed into outputs. These resources include materials, personnel, procedures, technology, facilities, time, and other factors. An accident occurs when a human or a mechanical component of a system fails to function when it should. The objective of systems safety is to identify these failures and either eliminate them or minimize their effects.

The initial stimulus for systems safety was the creation of the intercontinental ballistic missile (ICBM) system, which was to serve as the key element in the nation's cold war strategy of deterrence through the threat of nuclear retaliation. Later, systems safety was applied to the U.S. space program.[8]

Systems safety is not a single methodology but a variety of different techniques designed to analyze systems and identify potential system failures. These different techniques seem to have been invented simultaneously by many individuals at about the same time. The simultaneous development of the systems safety approach by multiple individuals is not surprising; systems safety has a common-sense basis and follows the logical problem-solving approach that engineers had always used in attempting to solve a problem. Because the problems that it addressed were complex, the common-sense logic approach was supported by mathematical tools that are common to engineering projects. The concurrent development of conceptually identical but methodologically different approaches to identifying system failures produced a variety of techniques, many of which differ primarily in detail. The multiple authors also generated a variety of names, some of which describe what are virtually identical techniques.[9] The common theme in these methodologies is the premise that accidents result from system failures and that they can be prevented by identifying those failures before they occur.

---

[7]For an interesting perspective on the development of the systems approach to risk identification (and systems safety), see Vernon L. Grose, *Managing Risk: Systematic Loss Prevention for Executives* (Englewood Cliffs, N.J.: Prentice Hall, 1987). Grose, a pioneer in the application of systems methodology to controlling risk, began his career as an applied physicist at Boeing and later became director of reliability at Litton Industries and director of applied technology at Northrop Ventura. In these positions, he managed risks in NASA's Projects Mercury, Gemini, and Apollo. In 1969, he was appointed to the NASA Safety Advisory Group for Space Flight. He later served as a member of the National Transportation Safety Board and the National Highway Safety Advisory Commission.

[8]Although the term *systems safety* was not formally used until sometime after the end of the Second World War, the basic concepts of systems engineering—and systems safety—predates the use of the term by a significant period. The engineers who supervised the construction of the pyramids were dealing with a system and doubtless needed to consider a variety of complex interrelationships.

[9]Systems safety methodologies include literally dozens of different approaches. The popularity of the systems safety approach is indicated by the existence of the Systems Safety Society, a professional association of systems safety engineers.

DISTINCTIONS BETWEEN SYSTEMS SAFETY AND TRADITIONAL APPROACH TO SAFETY

Although the techniques of systems safety differ in methodology, they share certain similarities. Among these similarities are the ways in which they differ from traditional approaches to safety.

A first distinction between systems safety and the traditional approaches to safety is in the emphasis systems safety places on identifying losses that have not yet occurred. Whereas the conventional approach to loss prevention and control had been to wait until an accident or loss happened, and then find the cause, there was no experience on which the military planners and space scientists could call. Furthermore, the "wait and see" approach was unacceptable for the types of accidents that might occur in managing a nuclear deterrent system or a manned space project. Instead of relying on experience—of which there was none—scientists searched for and found models that could be used to anticipate accidents and devise corrections before they occurred. At the risk of oversimplification, this involved the detailed analysis of each component, each action, and each interrelationship in the system to determine, insofar as possible, what could go wrong. This was accomplished through the use of logic analysis, mathematical modeling, prototypes, and simulation. Systems safety attempts to identify potential failures before they occur so that measures can be taken to prevent their occurrence.[10]

A second difference in systems safety was its abiding faith in the principle of causality. Systems safety rejects the notion that accidents are a matter of chance—something that simply happens. Instead, accidents are seen as created phenomena, facilitated by choices or decisions. Viewed from this perspective, accidents are not an inevitable part of the workplace, not *acts of God*, or simply unlucky breaks. If the causes of accidents can be identified, then they can be prevented. Equally important, the prevention can be achieved by eliminating the efficient cause. By recognizing and identifying multiple causes in a chain of causality, systems safety analysis means that an accident can be prevented by eliminating some, but not necessarily all, of the causes of the accident.

Still another difference between systems safety and traditional approaches to safety was in the total emphasis on preventing accidents. Whereas traditional safety measures were often viewed as an adjunct or supplement to risk transfer, the risks addressed by systems safety were not susceptible to treatment by risk financing. The objective of systems safety was the total elimination of critical failures, which, given the nature of the projects to which it was originally applied, were deemed unacceptable.[11] Hence, the motto *zero defects*.

Neil Armstrong's first step on the lunar surface on July 20, 1969, climaxed the stunning success of the greatest scientific achievement ever accomplished by man to that date. What made the Apollo XI program possible was a combination of loss

[10]J.L. Recht, "Systems Safety Analysis: An Introduction," *National Safety News* 92, No. 6 (Chicago: National Safety Council, December 1965).

[11]See Jerome Lederer (Director, Manned Space Flight Safety, NASA), *Best's Review, Property Liability Edition* 7, No. I (May 1970): 48.

control disciplines and engineering skills that brought about the design and assembly of the most reliable flight products ever produced. Of all contributions to this success, the application of a system approach was probably the overriding key. At all stages of design, manufacture, and operation, the person-machine environment subsystems were considered as interrelated, interdependent components of the overall system.

SYSTEMS SAFETY TECHNIQUES

We will limit our discussion to two of the most popular systems safety techniques in order to *illustrate* the systems safety approach, not to provide instruction in use of the techniques.

Hazard Mode and Effect Analysis

Hazard Mode and Effect Analysis (HMEA) attempts to identify potential system failures through detailed analysis of identified hazards.[12] HMEA triggers many questions that can provide guidance regarding the measures that might reduce or eliminate the likelihood of loss. Basically, the analysis attempts to summarize not only the system component whose failure could trigger a loss, but also the importance of the failure and the measures that can prevent the failure.

The actual HMEA analysis is generally summarized in tabular form, as shown in Table 9.1. The analysis may be prepared at any level of complexity—system, subsystem, component, or detail part. Although it is usually initiated in the early stages of a project and kept up to date through the system's life cycle, it can be applied at any time during that cycle. The specific questions that are addressed in HMEA analysis are indicated in the first column of Table 9.1. The second column provides a brief description of the information that is required in response to the headings in column 1. Finally, the third column illustrates the information that might be entered for a very simple system failure—a flat tire on an automobile. Although this example uses a simple failure for the purpose of illustration, the technique is, of course, applicable to considerably more complex systems. In fact, the success of Project Apollo—the manned exploration of the moon—is partially credited to HMEA because it was the primary type of analysis that was employed to foresee risks and their effects.

Fault-Tree Analysis

Fault-Tree Analysis (FTA) is designed to identify system faults by identifying the causes of events. It is usually performed by a graphic diagram (called a *fault tree*) that traces the relationships between all minor events that could ultimately lead to a major undesired event.

---

[12]Like many other systems safety methods, HMEA goes by many names. It has also been called Reliability Analysis for Preliminary Design (RAPD), Failure Mode and Effect Analysis (FMEA), Failure Mode, Effect, and Criticality Analysis (FMECA), and Fault Hazard Analysis (FHA).

Table 9.1 Column Entries in Hazard Mode and Effect Analysis

Hazard MODE	Hazard MECHANISM	Hazard CAUSE	Hazard EFFECT	Hazard SEVERITY	Hazard DETECTION	Hazard PROBABILITY	Hazard DETERRENTS	Hazard PREVENTIVE ACTION	Hazard CONTROL RESOURCES
The undesirable event that could occur or the desirable event that could fail to occur.	The hardware or software that could cause the failure.	The ultimate physical, chemical or human reasons that the mechanism could occur.	The immediate functional result of a hazard mechanism—a short range view, limited to the system element for which the analyst has personal responsibility.	The ultimate impact of the malfunction (mode) on system objectives—determined by consensus.	The very first indication or observable exhibition of a hazard mechanism.	A rough estimate of the malfunction's likelihood—determined by consensus.	Response to question, "Is it possible to eliminate this hazard mechanism?" If answer is yes, then list why it was not done. If no, state why it is impossible.	Action that would, if implemented, either eliminate or control a hazard mechanism.	Dollar value of all resources required to implement preventive action—determined by consensus.
Flat tire	Worn tires puncture	Failure to replace tires Sharp object in road	Tire goes flat	Could result in loss of control of vehicle	Steering begins to wobble Tire makes thumping noise	10 percent	Partial deterrents: replace tires, avoid driving over sharp objects	Replace tires	New set of tires, $500.

In contrast to the somewhat hazy origins of HMEA, the origin of Fault-Tree Analysis is well known. It was invented in 1959 at Bell Laboratories to address what developers of the USAF Minuteman intercontinental ballistic missile (ICBM) system felt was an excessive risk in the system. After an intensive effort by engineers and designers, the Minuteman was ready to be deployed to silos. Each missile, which carried a nuclear warhead, was preprogrammed to a target in the Soviet Union. To ensure a rapid launch response in the event of a Soviet attack, the system had been designed with the launch and guidance systems operative 24 hours a day. The concern was whether one or more malfunctions could conceivably result in an accidental launch, triggering World War III. Although the system had been subjected to extensive HMEA-type analyses, Department of Defense personnel wanted further assurance that the unthinkable would not occur. Although all components had been tested and verified, the concern was not about the components but about the total system. Was there anything, the experts at Bell Laboratories asked, that could permit the inadvertent launch of a missile. The idea they came up with was a logical analysis of causality in which the necessary elements in a chain of causality that leads to a launch were identified and tested for infallibility. The new type of analysis was called Fault-Tree Analysis.

FTA is usually summarized graphically. A *fault tree* has two major elements: (1) logic diagramming, which connects, by means of *and* and *or* gates the subevents that contribute to the ultimate undesired event at the top of the tree and (2) the subevents themselves. Construction of the tree begins at the top with the ultimate undesired event. The tree is progressively constructed downward by successive repetitions of the question, "What must happen for the event (or subevent) to occur?" The necessity and sufficiency of each subevent in the causality of the following event is indicated by the type of gate, *and* or *or*. If more than one subevent at a given level must occur before the event above them will result, an *and* gate is used. On the other hand, if a single subevent will cause the event at the next higher level to occur, those subevents lead to an *or* gate. Once the chain of causality has been identified and the significance of the subevents determined, the FTA provides a roadmap for prevention measures.

Obviously, the description of causality in the fault tree must be as complete as possible. An incomplete fault tree may ignore a critical link in the chain of causality, thereby precluding addressing the specific condition that could prevent the loss. An FTA chart for an accident using a power saw is illustrated in Figure 9.3. In a more complete version of a fault tree, probabilities are assigned to the subevents at each level. This permits the analyst to calculate the probabilities of events at the higher levels of the tree. For those events controlled by *and* gates, the joint probabilities of the multiple events that must occur to produce the result are computed. Thus, if the occurrence of event A requires that B and C both occur and the probability that B will occur is .10 and the probability that C will occur is .20, the probability that A will occur is .02 (.10 × .20). If the occurrence of B requires that *either* E or F occur and the probability that E and F will occur is .20 and .30, respectively, the probability that either E or F will occur is .44 percent (i.e., the probability of E plus F, minus the probability of both E and F).

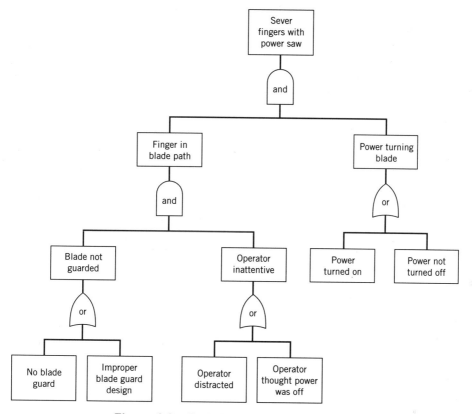

Figure 9.3   Fault-Tree Analysis Logic Chart

◆ Sources of Assistance for Risk Control ■ ■ ■ ■ ■ ■ ■ ■ ■ ■ ■ ■

Numerous organizations in our society are dedicated to promoting safety and loss prevention. Interestingly, many of these organizations have direct ties with the insurance industry. Indeed, many of the major advancements in risk control have come directly from the efforts of insurance companies, both individually and collectively. For example, much of our current knowledge about industrial safety and the protection of employees from the hazards of the workplace originated from the efforts of the insurers writing workers compensation insurance. The first researchers to address the problems associated with injury in the workplace were insurance company employees, and their studies have provided much of the knowledge still used in loss-prevention programs today. The loss-prevention engineering divisions of insurers remain one of the most important sources for information in this area.

Major gains in the area of fire loss prevention have also come from the insurance industry. Some insurers, most notably the Factory Mutuals and the Industrial Risk Insurers, focus as much on loss-prevention services for their insureds as on indemnification for losses and have been a strategic element in promoting fire safety. The National Fire Protection Association, which was formed in 1896, grew out of the loss-prevention efforts of insurers. Insurance companies also created the Underwriters Laboratory which investigates and tests electrical materials and other products to determine that fire prevention and protection standards are met. The organization was formed to test the electrical apparatus developed for the world exposition in Chicago in 1894. It continues to this day as a major factor in industrial and home fire safety.

Among the earliest efforts in preventing losses related to boiler explosions one also finds the insurance company. The Hartford Steam Boiler Inspection and Insurance Company, organized in 1866, offered loss-prevention engineering services and guaranteed the results of these services by promising indemnification in the event of an explosion.

Underwriters Salvage Company assists insurance companies in the adjustment of losses through the reclamation, reconditioning, and disposition of damaged goods. In this way it assists in an important post–loss control measure. Other insurance organizations that engaged in important loss-prevention activities include the Insurance Committee for Arson Control, the Insurance Crime Prevention Institute, the Defense Research Institute, and the Insurance Institute for Highway Safety. The insurance industry also works closely with and supports the efforts of the National Safety Council and similar public safety organizations.

LOSS CONTROL SERVICES AVAILABLE FROM INSURERS

In view of the historical emphasis of insurers on loss-prevention and control efforts, it is not surprising that insurance companies remain one of the most widely used sources of loss-prevention and control assistance. In some lines of insurance, such as boiler and machinery insurance, the loss-prevention and inspection services are perhaps the major reason why coverage is purchased.

Insurers conduct loss control activities both for their own benefit and as a service to their insureds. The major benefit to the insurer is in making accounts more profitable by reducing the amount of losses. Equally important, an insurer's loss control specialists can sometimes devise ways to improve loss experience to an extent that allows the insurer to write an account that would otherwise be unacceptable.

Insurer loss control services provided to insureds help the insured to reduce the cost of losses and of its insurance program. Insurers provide three general levels of loss control services.

The first level—a physical survey—serves primarily for the collection of underwriting information on a customer's loss exposures. The loss control representative seeks to evaluate the physical hazards affecting the customer's exposures and to determine management commitment to loss control and employee attitude toward appropriate safety behavior patterns. In this way, the loss control representative may obtain insights into both moral and morale hazards.

The second level of insurers' service—risk analysis and risk improvement—advances the first level to what might be considered the normal practice for most insurers. In addition to a physical survey and hazard evaluation (level one), the insurer's loss control personnel analyze the customer's claims-loss history and submit formal written recommendations to the business owner or manager concerning ways to reduce hazards. To support the risk analysis and improvement process, the insurer's loss control personnel may provide training, informational, or counseling services.

A safety program is a series of presentations on any of various safety-related subjects, intended to raise workers' awareness of loss exposures and appropriate safety behaviors. The objectives of safety programs are to develop positive safety attitudes among all workers; to improve workers' understanding of safety-related matters; and to help workers accept responsibility for their role in the organization's safety program.

The third level of insurer loss control services—safety management programming—represents a "full-service" approach to safety assistance. The process begins with a total evaluation of the policyholder's operations, as in risk analysis and improvement activities. After reviewing the evaluation with the insured, the insurer's loss control specialists assist the insured in establishing loss control objectives, selecting appropriate loss control measures, organizing the resources necessary to implement the chosen loss control measures, and setting up procedures for monitoring the program. The consultation process usually includes periodic visits to the insured's premises to monitor the program.

Insurers differ in the extent to which they emphasize loss control services. For some insurers, such as the Factory Mutuals, loss-prevention and control services are a critical element in the product mix, and many insureds purchase coverage from these companies to access their loss-prevention services.[13]

OTHER RISK CONTROL RESOURCES

In addition to the traditional sources of assistance, other resources are available to the organization for specialized risk control needs.

The Legal Profession

Lawyers are not normally considered as loss-prevention and control specialists, but it is clear that in the post-loss phase of liability loss control, they are the major players. Once an event has occurred that could give rise to a lawsuit and to legal liability, the engineering and human behavior approaches to loss prevention are replaced by the legal efforts at loss control. Defense attorneys who specialize in

---

[13]Insurance trade associations are also a source of assistance in loss prevention and control. Major insurance trade associations that play an important role in loss prevention include the American Insurance Association, the Alliance of American Insurers, the National Association of Independent Insurers, and the Insurance Information Institute, which conduct research in loss-prevention methods and lobby for loss control laws. Specialized insurance industry organizations involved in safety include the Insurance Institute for Highway Safety, National Automobile Theft Bureau, and the Insurance Crime Prevention Institute. Other organizations include the National Safety Council and the National Fire Protection Association.

defending and negotiating settlements for bodily injury and property damage are loss control specialists in the same sense as a sprinkler system is a mechanism for controlling the damage caused by fire.

Accountants

The accountant is a major loss-prevention and control specialist in the field of employee crime. By designing and implementing internal controls in the organization's financial recordkeeping system, the accountant seeks to minimize the potential for dishonesty among the organization's employees. Auditing is a major loss-prevention tool for employee dishonesty and is effective in controlling both the frequency and severity of loss.

Disaster Planning ■

In the midst of the floods that devastated the midwestern states during the summer of 1993, the author received a frantic call from the president of a midwestern manufacturing plant asking for information on disaster plans. Specifically, the request was whether an "off-the-shelf" plan was available that might provide guidance in the firm's disaster recovery operation. The problem, of course, is that the time to think about a disaster plan is before the disaster occurs, not afterward. As a concluding note in this chapter on risk control, it seems appropriate that we touch briefly on this important pre-event action for post-event loss control.

The need for advance planning to establish procedures in the event of a disaster is obvious. At the time of a disaster, normal operating procedures, the chain of command, and communication links may be interrupted. Confusion and chaotic conditions can prevent normally effective executives from taking the steps that are required to reduce the severity of the losses resulting from the disaster, whatever it may be. The objective of a disaster control plan is to allow those responsible for the enterprise during an emergency to focus on the solution of major problems. To accomplish this objective, the disaster plan establishes an emergency organization, designed to perform specific tasks before, during, and after a disaster. It also establishes priorities for the use of resources available at the time of the disaster and thereafter.

Basically, a disaster plan provides management with a planned course of action to guide it in disaster or emergency situations. Although the disaster plan must be prepared for the specific organization, it usually follows a common pattern. It lists the types of disasters that may occur, explains the duties of the emergency coordinator, and outlines the steps that are to be taken before, during, and after a disaster.

A disaster plan does not contemplate all the specific conditions that could be produced by a flood, an explosion, or a terrorist threat. The range of possible disasters makes detailed planning for every type of disaster virtually impossible. What a disaster plan attempts to do is to provide a general plan of action that is sufficiently broad and flexible to accommodate a variety of emergency situations. Properly prepared and executed, a disaster plan can make the difference between the organization's survival when a disaster occurs and the inability to recover. For most organizations, a primary objective of the plan is to facilitate resumption of normal operations as quickly as possible following a disaster.

ORGANIZATION DISASTER PRIORITIES

An initial step in developing the disaster plan is to establish priorities that will be followed in resolving conflicts in developing the plan. This advance determination of priorities will guarantee that appropriate attention is given to the rankings and that decisions regarding priorities do not have to be made under the confusion and pressures of an actual disaster. Although every organization must set its own priorities, the following presents the types of priorities in their order of importance.

- First, to protect human life.
- Second, to prevent or minimize personal injury.
- Third, to prevent and minimize the potential damage to physical assets.
- To restore normal operations as quickly as possible.

With these priorities established, measures aimed at achieving the priorities can then be identified. Those directed toward protecting human life and preventing injuries will include plans for evacuating personnel and providing the required shelter, protecting persons who must remain in threatened areas, and providing medical assistance for the injured. Measures aimed at minimizing property damage will include plans for removing threatened property when time allows, maintaining critical records at alternate sites, and adapting common-sense measures designed to protect and preserve property at the time of and after the disaster. Measures to restore normal operations quickly will include making advance arrangements to relocate certain functions (such as computer operations), identifying alternative facilities, and providing for the resupply of materials and replacement of equipment.

DEVELOPING THE PLAN

The initial step in developing the disaster plan should be the identification of the persons who will be responsible for creating the plan. Because the disaster plan will require coordination of multiple functions, an *ad hoc* committee is likely to provide the most efficient group. Responsibility for coordinating the planning process should be assigned to a coordinator or chair of the committee. The committee members, who are generally the representatives of the departments and divisions that will have responsibilities in the event of a disaster, should be appointed to assist and advise the coordinator in preparing the plan. Typically, these departments will include personnel, risk management, security, safety, plant engineering, and public relations.

A disaster plan does not require the creation of a new organization structure. The existing structure, temporarily reconfigured for the disaster situation, can perform the functions required at the time of a disaster. A single individual—conceivably the coordinator who supervised the completion of the disaster plan—should be designated as the emergency coordinator, with extraordinary authority at the time of a disaster. This will help to ensure that the normal organization structure will not be an impediment to actions necessary at the time of a disaster. The coordinator will typically be an official with regular responsibility for handling emergencies, such as the director of security or the risk manager.

When completed, the disaster plan should address issues such as management succession, the creation of alternate headquarters and, when needed, appropriate data processing facilities, emergency communications facilities, protection of records, public relations and news control, emergency medical care, warning systems, evacuation procedures, and restoration procedures. Planning for the contingencies in these areas can serve to minimize confusion at the time of a disaster and help to reduce losses.

SUMMARY

As a result of developments over the past two decades, attitudes toward risk control have changed, albeit slowly. Establishing an effective loss control program has been proven beyond any reasonable doubt to be a sound investment. The benefits derived from organized safety programs and other loss control programs have included such factors as preservation of life and limb, increased worker efficiency, reduction in insurance rates, and lower levels of losses in general. Advances in loss control techniques, accompanied by documented records of success, have increased management's awareness of the need for and benefits of risk control efforts. Increased data on the efficiency of loss control measures, combined with statutory requirements, have elevated risk control to an unprecedented level.

IMPORTANT CONCEPTS

government standards	post-event action	physical survey
voluntary standards	separation of assets	risk analysis and risk
consensual standards	salvage	improvement
domino theory	rehabilitation	safety management
energy release theory	redundancy	programming
engineering approach	systems safety	disaster plan
human behavior approach	principle of causality	emergency coordinator
pre-event action	Hazard Mode and Effect	
simultaneous-with-event	Analysis (HMEA)	
action	Fault-Tree Analysis (FTA)	

QUESTIONS FOR REVIEW

1. Describe the conditions in which risk avoidance should be used and explain why it is used in these circumstances.

2. To what can the historical neglect of the risk control function be attributed?

3. Explain what is meant by government standards and explain in what way(s) they affect the risk management function of an organization.

4. Explain what is meant by voluntary or consensual standards and explain the role they play in the risk management process.

5. Identify the five areas toward which risk control measures may be directed.

6. Identify and distinguish between the two general theories of accident causation.

7. Describe the general thesis of Heinrich's Domino Theory.

8. Describe the general thesis of Haddon's Energy Release Theory.

9. Describe the two general approaches to loss prevention and control.

10. Explain the classification of loss prevention and control measures according to their time of application.

QUESTIONS FOR DISCUSSION

1. Identify the classification of loss prevention and control measures based on the object toward which the measure is directed.

2. Explain how each of the following represents an approach to risk control: (a) separation of assets; (b) salvage; (c) rehabilitation; (d) redundancy.

3. Describe the origins of systems safety.

4. Distinguish between Hazard More and Effect Analysis (HMEA) and Fault-Tree Analysis (FTA), indicating the approach of each technique to hazard identification.

5. Identify the priorities for a disaster plan described in the text. Do you agree or disagree with the priorities?

SUGGESTIONS FOR ADDITIONAL READING

Bird, Frank E., and Frank J. Loftus. *Loss Control Management.* Loganville, Ga: International Loss Control Institute, 1976.

Christine, Brian. "Disaster Management, Lessons Learned." *Risk Management* (October 1995), pp. 19–34.

Clemens, P.L. "A Compendium of Hazard Identification and Evaluation Techniques for System Safety Applications," *Hazard Prevention* (March/April 1982).

Cox, Jack E. and Robert L. Barber. "Practical Contingency Planning," *Risk Management* (March 1996), pp. 15–20.

Doherty, Neil A. *Corporate Risk Management* (New York: McGraw Hill Book Company, 1985). Chapter 13.

Fire Protection Handbook, 17th Edition, National Fire Protection Association, Quincy, Ma. 1991.

Grose, Vernon L. *Managing Risk: Systematic Loss Prevention for Executives* (Englewood Cliffs, NJ: Prentice Hall, 1987).

Haddon, William, Jr., M.D., "On Escape of Tigers: An Ecological Note," *Technology Review* (May 1970). .

Haddon, William, Jr., M.D., "What We're Talking About," in C.W. Wixom (ed). *Key Issues in Highway Loss Reduction* (Washington, D.C.: Institute for Highway Safety, 1970).

Hammer, Willie. *Handbook of System and Product Safety.* Englewood Cliffs, NJ: Prentice-Hall, Inc. 1972.

Head, George L., ed. *Essentials of Risk Control,* 2nd ed., vol. I, Malvern, Pa.: Insurance Institute of America, 1989. Chapters 9, 10 and 11.

Heinrich, H.W. *Industrial Accident Prevention* (4th ed.) (New York: McGraw-Hill Book Company, 1959).

Heinrich, H.W., Dan Petersen, and Nester Roos. *Industrial Accident Prevention: Safety Management Approach,* 5th ed. New York: McGraw-Hill Book Company, 1980.

Koska, Detlef K. "Turn Disaster to Your Advantage With an Operations Recovery Strategy," *The John Liner Review* (Fall 1995).

Lederer, Jerome. *Best's Review, Property Liability Edition,* Vol. VII, No. I (May 1970).

Moore, Pat. "The Day After: Disaster Recovery and Service Coordination," *Public Risk* (May/June 1995).

Petersen, Dan. *Techniques of Safety Management* 2nd ed. New York: McGraw Hill Company, 1978.

Ralston, August R., ed. *Risk Management Manual,* Santa Monica, Ca.: (loose-leaf service with monthly supplements), vol. 2, sections 3 and 9.

Recht, J.L. "Systems Safety Analysis: An Introduction," *National Safety News,* Vol. XCII, No. 6 (Chicago: National Safety Council, December 1965).

Walsh, Timothy J. *Protection of Assets* Santa Monica, Ca.: The Merritt Company (loose-leaf service with monthly supplements), Section I, Introduction.

CHAPTER 10

Risk Financing: Insurance Transfers

CHAPTER OBJECTIVES

When you have finished this chapter, you should be able to

Define insurance from the viewpoint of the individual and of society.

Identify and explain the two essential features in the operation of insurance.

Identify and explain the desirable elements of an insurable risk.

Explain what is meant by adverse selection and why it is a problem for insurers.

Describe the three broad fields into which insurance may be classified, citing the distinguishing features of each.

Distinguish between social insurance and private insurance.

Identify the major classes of private insurance.

Distinguish among the various types of insurers, based on their legal form of ownership and distribution systems.

Introduction ■

The risk control techniques discussed in the preceding chapter will not eliminate all risks facing the organization. Although risk may be reduced, some risks will remain. These remaining risks are addressed by the second broad approach to risk management, risk financing. The techniques of risk financing, retention and transfer, are mutually exclusive and collectively exhaustive. Risks that are not transferred are retained.

In this chapter, we begin our discussion of risk financing with an examination of insurance, a contractual arrangement by which risk is transferred to another party. Although there are other types of contracts that also involve the transfer of risk (such as leases, construction contracts, and holdharmless agreements), these arrangements are fundamentally different in nature from insurance, and we treat them as risk control techniques. Insurance is a more formal social technique that uses the law of averages to reduce risk and spread the losses that do occur. We begin with a brief examination of the insurance mechanism, focusing on its nature and the manner in which it addresses risk. We then examine some common types of insurance and the structure of the insurance industry.

The Nature and Functions of Insurance ■ ■ ■ ■ ■ ■ ■ ■

A brief discussion of how insurance works vis-à-vis the risk management process may help us understand why some exposures are more susceptible to treatment by insurance than are others.

RISK SHARING AND RISK TRANSFER

Insurance in its simplest aspect has two fundamental characteristics:

- Transferring or shifting risk from one individual to a group.
- Sharing losses, on some equitable basis, by all members of the group.

Let us assume that there are 1000 buildings in a community and, for simplicity, that the value of each building is $100,000. Each owner faces the risk that his or her building may catch on fire. If a fire does occur, a financial loss of up to $100,000 could result. Some buildings will undoubtedly burn, but the probability that all will burn is remote. Now, let us assume that the owners of these buildings enter into an agreement to share the cost of the losses as they occur, so that no single individual will be forced to bear an entire loss of $100,000. Whenever a building burns, each of the 1000 owners contributes his or her proportionate share of the amount of the loss. If the building is a total loss, each of the 1000 owners will pay $100 and the owner of the destroyed building will be indemnified for the $100,000 loss. Those who suffer losses are idemnified by those who do not. Those who escape loss are willing to pay those who do not because by doing so they help to eliminate the possibility that they themselves might suffer a $100,000 loss. Through the agreement to share the losses, the economic burden of the losses is spread throughout the group. This is essentially the way insurance works, for what we have described is a pure assessment mutual insurance operation.

The operation of such a plan poses some difficulties, the most obvious being the possibility that some members of the group might refuse to pay their assessment at the time of a loss. This problem can be overcome by requiring payment in advance. To require payment in advance, it is necessary to have some idea as to the amount of those losses. They may be calculated on the basis of past experience. Let us now assume that on the basis of past experience, we can predict with reasonable accuracy that two of the 1000 buildings will burn. We could charge each member of the group $200, making a total of $200,000. In addition to the cost of the losses, there would no doubt be some expenses in the operation of the program. There is also a possibility that our predictions might not be entirely accurate. We might, therefore, charge each member of the group $300 instead of $200, thereby providing for the payment of expenses and also providing a cushion against deviations from our expectations. Each of the 1000 building owners will incur a small certain cost of $300 in exchange for a promise of indemnification in the amount of $100,000 if his or her building burns down. This $300 premium is, in effect, the individual's share of the total losses and expenses of the group. If losses and expenses are less than the $300, the excess may be returned to the participants. If losses and expenses exceed the $300, it may be necessary to go back to the participants for additional funds.

As an alternative to the preceding scenario, a properly funded organization could contract directly with each of the building owners to provide the insurance. In this case, the insurer would charge the $300 and pay all losses and expenses. If a surplus were generated, it would be retained by the entrepreneurial organization. If a loss resulted, it would be borne by the organization.

INSURANCE DEFINED FROM THE VIEWPOINT OF THE INDIVIDUAL

Based on the preceding description, we may define insurance from the individual's viewpoint as follows:

> From an individual point of view, insurance is an economic device whereby the individual substitutes a small certain cost (the premium) for a large uncertain financial loss (the contingency insured against) that would exist if it were not for the insurance.

The primary function of insurance is the creation of the counterpart of risk, which is security. Insurance does not decrease the uncertainty for the individual as to whether the event will occur, nor does it alter the probability of occurrence, but it does reduce the probability of financial loss connected with the event. From the individual's point of view, the purchase of an adequate amount of insurance on a building eliminates the uncertainty regarding a financial loss in the event that the building should burn down.

RISK REDUCTION THROUGH POOLING

In addition to eliminating risk at the level of the individual through transfer, the insurance mechanism reduces risk (and the uncertainty related to risk) for society as a whole. The risk the insurance company faces is not merely a summation of the risks transferred to it by individuals; the insurance company is able to do something that the individual cannot, and that is to predict within rather narrow limits the amount of losses that will actually occur. The accuracy of the insurer's predictions is based on the law of large numbers. By combining a sufficiently large number of homogeneous exposure units, the insurer is able to make predictions for the group as a whole. This is accomplished through the theory of probability.

Because the insurance company bases its rates on its expectation of future losses, it must be concerned with the extent to which actual experience is likely to deviate from predicted results. For the insurance company, risk (or the possibility of financial loss) is measured by the potential deviation of actual from predicted results, and the accuracy of prediction is enhanced when the predictions are based on and are applied to a large number of exposure units.

If the insurance company's actuaries or statisticians could predict future losses with absolute precision, the insurer would have no possibility of loss. It would collect each individual's share of the total losses and expenses of operation and use these funds to pay the losses and expenses as they occurred. Premium income would always be sufficient to pay losses and expenses. If the predictions are not accurate, the premiums that the insurer has charged may be inadequate and risk therefore exists for the insurer. To the extent that accuracy in prediction is attained, risk is reduced.

Although probability theory plays an important role in the operation of the insurance mechanism, insurance does not always depend on probabilities and predictions. Insurance arrangements can exist in which the participants agree to share losses and to determine each party's share of the costs on a post-loss basis. It is only when insurance is to be operated on an advance premium basis, with the participants paying their share of losses in advance, that probability theory and predictions are important.

INSURANCE DEFINED FROM THE VIEWPOINT OF SOCIETY

In addition to eliminating risk for the individual through transfer, the insurance device reduces the aggregate amount of risk in the economy by substituting certain costs for uncertain losses. These costs are assessed on the basis of the predictions made through the use of the law of large numbers. We may now formulate a second definition of insurance:

> From the social point of view, insurance is an economic device for reducing and eliminating risk through the process of combining a sufficient number of homogeneous exposures into a group to make the losses predictable for the group as a whole.

Insurance does not prevent losses,[1] nor does it reduce the cost of losses to the economy as a whole. In fact, it may very well have the opposite effect of causing losses and increasing the cost of losses for the economy as a whole. The existence of insurance encourages some losses for the purpose of defrauding the insurer, and, in addi-

---

[1]This statement is not intended to disparage the loss-prevention activities of insurance companies. In many forms of property and casualty insurance, attempts to reduce loss are perhaps the most important feature of all, but these loss-prevention activities are not essentially part of the operation of the insurance principle. Insurance could exist without them, and they could and do exist without insurance. Insurance in and of itself does not favorably alter the probability of loss.

tion, people are less careful and may exert less effort to prevent losses than they might if the insurance did not exist. Also, the economy incurs additional costs in the operation of the insurance mechanism. Not only must the cost of the losses be borne, but also the expense of distributing the losses on some equitable basis adds to this cost.

INSURANCE: TRANSFER OR POOLING?

The two definitions of insurance—from the individual viewpoint and from the societal viewpoint—reflect two different views of insurance, and have divided insurance scholars for at least the past half century. The first viewpoint emphasizes the transfer of risk, and does not attempt to explain how the risk is handled by the transferee. The second viewpoint emphasizes the role of insurance in reducing risk in the aggregate, which it does by pooling. Some writers maintain that the essential requisite in the insurance mechanism is the transfer of risk, whereas others argue that it is the pooling or sharing of risks.

Adherents of the transfer school point out that there are numerous examples of what are clearly insurance transactions, in which risks that are transferred to insurers are not pooled. There seems to be more or less general agreement on the point that insurance involves the transfer of risk. Even in risk-sharing mechanisms, such as post-loss assessment plans, risk is transferred from the individual to the group. Those who emphasize the pooling of risk point out that it is this feature of insurance that distinguishes insurance from other risk transfer techniques. Although they admit that pooling itself involves risk transfer (from the individual to the group), it is the pooling or combination of risks that makes the insurance mechanism.

The definition of insurance from the individual perspective, as a device for the transfer of risk and the substitution of a small uncertain cost for a large uncertain loss, seems to be the better definition. It applies to all mechanisms we would call insurance, and it applies only to them. In contrast, the pooling definition does not apply to all mechanisms that are considered insurance, and so it is somewhat less satisfactory. The *essential* feature of insurance is risk transfer. Pooling is an important technique available to the transferee, but it is not a requisite, and insurance transactions can occur in which the risk that is transferred is unique and in which there is no pooling. Although insurance *generally* involves the reduction of risk in the aggregate, which is achieved by pooling, insurance transactions need not involve pooling.

Both definitions are useful, however. The definition of insurance from the individual's perspective defines the essence of insurance, based on its essential component, transfer. The definition of insurance from society's perspective is a functional definition, and explains how insurance usually achieves the transfer function.

INSURANCE AND GAMBLING

Perhaps we should make one final distinction regarding the nature of insurance. It is often claimed that insurance is a form of gambling. "You bet that you will die, and the insurance company bets that you won't" or "I bet the insurance company $300 against $100,000 that my house will burn." The fallacy of these statements should be obvious. In the case of a wager, there is no chance of loss, and hence no risk, before the wager. In the case of insurance, the chance of loss exists whether or not an insurance contract is in effect. In other words, the basic distinction between insurance and gambling is that gambling creates a risk, whereas insurance provides for the transfer of existing risk.

THE ECONOMIC CONTRIBUTION OF INSURANCE

Property that is destroyed by an insured contingency is not replaced through the existence of an insurance contract. True, the funds from the insurance company may be used to replace the property, but when a house or building burns, society has lost a want-satisfying good. Insurance as an economic device is justified because it creates certainty about the financial burden of losses and because it spreads the losses that do occur. In providing a mechanism through which losses can be shared and uncertainty reduced, insurance brings peace of mind to society's members and makes costs more certain.

Insurance also provides for a more optimal utilization of capital. Without the possibility of insurance, individuals and businesses would have to maintain relatively large reserve funds to meet the risks they must assume. These funds would be in the form of idle cash, or would be invested in safe, liquid, and low-interest-bearing securities. This would be an inefficient use of capital. When the risk is transferred to the professional risk bearer, the deviations from expected results are minimized. As a consequence, insurers need keep much smaller reserves than would be the case if insurance did not exist. The released funds are then available for investment in more productive pursuits, resulting in a much greater productivity of capital.

Elements of an Insurable Risk ■ ■ ■ ■ ■ ■ ■ ■ ■ ■ ■ ■ ■ ■ ■ ■

Theoretically all possibilities of loss can be insured, but some are not insurable at a reasonable price. For practical reasons, insurers are not willing to accept all the risks that others may wish to transfer to them. To be considered a proper subject for insurance, certain characteristics should be present. The four prerequisites listed next represent the "ideal" elements of an insurable risk, which means that certain risks that do not have them can still be insured.

1. *There must be a sufficiently large number of homogeneous exposure units to make the losses reasonably predictable.* Insurance, as we have seen, is based on the operation of the law of large numbers. A large number of exposure units enhances the operation of an insurance plan by making estimates of future losses more accurate.[2]

---

[2]The reader is no doubt aware of the much publicized instances in which Lloyd's writes insurance on the physical attributes of an important star, or insures against loss from some unique event. Although these exposures do not meet the desirable element of an insurable risk—that there be a large

2. *The loss produced by the risk must be definite and measurable.* It must be a type of loss that is relatively difficult to counterfeit, and it must be capable of financial measurement. In other words, we must be able to tell when a loss has taken place, and we must be able to set some value on the extent of it.

3. *The loss must be fortuitous or accidental.* The loss must be the result of a contingency; that is, it must be something that may or may not happen. It must not be something that is certain to happen. If the insurance company knows that an event in the future is inevitable, it also knows that it must collect a premium equal to the certain loss that it must pay, together with an additional amount for the expenses of administering the operation. Depreciation, which is a certainty, cannot be insured; it is provided for through a sinking fund. Furthermore, the loss should be beyond the control of the insured. The law of large numbers is useful in making predictions only if we can reasonably assume that future occurrences will approximate past experience. Because we assume that past experience was a result of chance happening, the predictions concerning the future will be valid only if future happenings are also a result of chance.

4. *The loss must not be catastrophic.* It must be unlikely to produce loss to a very large percentage of the exposure units at the same time. The insurance principle is based on a notion of sharing losses, and inherent in this idea is the assumption that only a small percentage of the group will suffer loss at any one time. Damage that results from enemy attack would be catastrophic in nature. There are additional perils, such as floods, which, though they would not affect everyone in the society, would affect only those who had purchased insurance. The principle of randomness in selection is closely related to the requirement that the loss must not be catastrophic.

RANDOMNESS

The future experience of the group to which we apply our predictions will approximate the experience of the group on which the predictions are based only if both have approximately the same characteristics. There must be a proportion of good and bad risks in the first group equal to the proportion of good and bad risks of the group on which the prediction is made. Yet, human nature acts to interfere with the randomness necessary to permit random composition of the current group. The losses that are predicted are based on the average experience of the older group, but there are always some individuals who are, and who realize that they are, worse than average risks. Because the chance of loss is greater for these risks than for the other members of society, they have a tendency to desire insurance coverage to a greater extent than the remainder of the group. This tendency results in what is known as *adverse selection*—the tendency of the persons whose exposure to loss is

---

number of exposures—the transactions are still insurance. The underwriters at Lloyd's are able to engage in such practices because they substitute mass underwriting (where a single risk is spread among many insurers) for the mass of exposures and because the premiums charged for such coverages are heavily loaded, that is, higher than probability requires.

higher than average to purchase or continue insurance to a greater extent than those whose exposure is less than average. Unless some provision is made to prevent adverse selection, predictions based on past experience would be useless in foretelling future experience. Adverse selection works in the direction of accumulating bad risks. Because the predictions of future losses are based on the average loss of the past (in which both good and poor exposures were involved), if the experience of the future is based on the experience of a larger proportion of bad risks, it will be worse than that of the past, and the predictions will be invalid.

Adverse selection long caused private insurers to avoid the field of flood insurance. The adverse selection inherent in insuring fixed properties against the peril of flood is obvious. Only those individuals who feel that they are exposed to loss by flood are interested in flood insurance, and yet in the event of a flood, there is a likelihood that all these individuals would suffer loss. The element of the sharing of the losses of a few by the many who suffered no loss would not exist. Although some insurers have written coverage against flood on fixed properties, the coverage has not generally been available from private insurers for those who need it most.[3]

ECONOMIC FEASIBILITY

Sometimes, an additional attribute is listed as a requirement of an insurable risk—that the cost of the insurance must not be high in relation to the possible loss or that the insurance must be economically feasible. We can hardly call this a requirement of an insurable risk inasmuch as the principle is widely violated in the insurance industry today. The four elements of an insurable risk are characteristics of certain risks that permit the successful operation of the insurance principle. If a given risk lacks one of these elements, the operation of the insurance mechanism is impeded. The principle of "economically feasible insurability" is not really an impediment to the operation of the insurance principle, but rather a violation of the principles of risk management and common sense.

Self-insurance

The term *self-insurance* has become a well-established part of the terminology of the insurance field, despite disagreement as to whether or not such a mechanism is possible.[4] From a purely semantic point of view, the term *self-insurance* represents a definition impossibility. The insurance mechanism consists of transfer of risk or pooling of exposure units, and since it is impossible to pool with or transfer risk to oneself, it can be argued that self-insurance is impossible. However, the term is widely used, and we ought therefore to establish an acceptable operational definition, semantically incorrect though it may be.

Under some circumstances, a business firm or other organization can engage in the same types of activities as a commercial insurer dealing with its own risks.

---

[3]After decades of agitation for the government to "do something" about flood exposure, a federal flood insurance program was enacted in 1968. This program is discussed in Chapter 17.

[4]For example, see Matthew Lenz, Jr., "Self-insurance, Semantics, and Other Hang-ups," *CPCU Annals*, 28 (June 1975).

When these activities involve the operation of the law of large numbers and predictions regarding future losses, they are commonly referred to as "self-insurance."[5]

Even apart from its semantic shortcomings, self-insurance is an overworked term. Few companies or organizations are large enough to engage in a sound program meeting the requirements outlined here. In the majority of cases, risks are simply retained without attempting to make estimates of future losses. In many cases, no fund is maintained to pay for losses. Furthermore, until the fund reaches the size where it is adequate to pay the largest loss possible, the possibility of loss is not eliminated for the individual exposure units.

The Fields of Insurance ■ ■ ■ ■ ■ ■ ■ ■ ■ ■ ■ ■ ■ ■ ■ ■ ■ ■

Insurance is a broad, generic term embracing the entire array of institutions that deal with risk through the device of sharing and transfer of risks. Insurance may be divided and subdivided into classifications based on the perils insured against or the fundamental nature of the particular program. Basically, the primary distinction is between private insurance and social insurance. In addition to these two classes, we will also examine a third class of quasi-social insurance coverage called *public benefit guarantee programs*.

Private insurance consists largely of voluntary insurance programs available to the individual as a means of protection against the possibility of loss. This voluntary insurance is usually provided by private firms, but in some instances, it is also offered by the government. Private insurance is usually voluntary, and the transfer of risk is normally accomplished by means of a contract. *Social insurance,* on the other hand, is compulsory insurance, usually operated by government, whose benefits are determined by law and whose primary emphasis is on social adequacy. In general, the benefits under social insurance programs attempt to redistribute income based on some notion of "social adequacy," and individual equity is of secondary importance. The largest social insurance program in the United States is the social security system. Other social insurance coverages include workers compensation, unemployment insurance, and the Medicare program.

Unfortunately, there is no single criterion that can be used to distinguish private insurance from social insurance. Further complicating the situation, the designations "private" and "voluntary" are both slightly misleading: some "private insurance" is sold by the government,[6] and not all compulsory insurance is social insurance. With the exception of workers compensation, which is a social insurance sold by private insurers, our discussion will focus on private insurance.

---

[5]Technically, such programs are retention programs that employ insurance techniques. In spite of its semantic shortcomings, the term *self-insurance* is a convenient way of distinguishing the retention programs that utilize insurance techniques from those that do not. Self-insurance is discussed in greater detail in Chapter 14.

[6]Examples of some types of private insurance sold by the government include life insurance, available through the Veterans Administration, federal crop insurance, and crime insurance, which is sold by the U.S. Department of Housing and Urban Development in areas where crime insurance is not available from private insurers at affordable rates.

THE INSURANCE INDUSTRY

It is self-evident that the complicated device known as insurance does not come into existence by itself. Someone must estimate the probability of loss, collect the funds necessary to compensate those who suffer loss, make payments for the losses that occur, and provide for the general administration of the program. This is the function performed by insurers. Let us turn now to a discussion of the private insurance industry.

CLASSIFICATION OF PRIVATE INSURERS

Insurers may be classified according to the type of insurance they sell, their place of incorporation and licensing, their legal form of ownership, and their distribution system.

Insurers Classified by Type of Product

It is possible to distinguish among three types of insurers, based on their products. Life insurers sell life insurance and annuities and, in some cases, accident and health insurance. Property and liability insurers sell all types of insurance designed to indemnify for damage to property and for legal liability. Finally, health insurers sell accident and health insurance.

The reason for this specialization of insurers by product line is partly technical and partly historical. From the beginning of insurance in the U.S. until about the time of the Civil War, there was little regulation of insurance, but most insurers elected to specialize, writing a single line of insurance. As state regulation of insurance evolved, most states enacted laws limiting the type of insurance a company was allowed to write. Under this so-called *monoline system,* three types of insurers emerged: fire insurers, casualty insurers, and life insurers. A fire insurance company could write fire and marine insurance but not casualty or life insurance. Casualty insurers could write only casualty insurance, which consist of workers compensation insurance, various types of liability insurance, boiler and machinery insurance, and crime insurance. Neither fire nor casualty insurers could write life insurance and life insurers could not write fire and casualty insurance. This monoline form of organization was unique to the United States. British and European companies more often than not received charters that gave them authority to sell insurance of all kinds anywhere in the world.

There were three reasons for the compartmentalization that was built into the American system. First, it was supposed that the monoline system would allow insurers to specialize in a particular field of insurance and develop a proficiency that would enable them to cope better with technical problems. Second, it was felt that the segregation of insurance by class would permit a more accurate appraisal of the financial qualification required for each type of insurance and that regulatory requirements could be established to fit each class. Finally, insurance regulators feared that there was a danger in combining fire insurance, which seemed more subject to catastrophes, with life insurance. The various conflagrations, such as the New York fire of 1835, helped to reinforce this opinion.[7]

Shortly after the end of World War II, the monoline form of organization began to disappear. Individual states began to change their laws to allow multiple-line operations, in which fire and casualty insurers were allowed to cross the barriers that had separated them. By the mid-1950s, all but a few states had changed their laws and the monoline form of operation was replaced by multiple line operations. The changes did not completely destroy underwriting compartmentalization. It merely permitted the companies in the field of property and casualty insurance to cross the traditional barriers when an insurer met the capital and surplus requirements of each line. It did not, in most cases, eliminate the barrier between life insurance and property and liability insurance. Consequently, the insurance industry may currently be divided into the three broad fields of life insurance, health insurance, and property and liability insurance.

Life Insurers Life insurers sell life insurance, annuities, and sometimes accident and health insurance. These coverages are sold on both an individual and a group basis. The risk manager's use of life insurers is generally in connection with the organization's employee benefit program and sometimes in protecting the organization against the financial loss associated with the death of key employees.

Health Insurers Health insurers are specialty insurers that sell accident and health insurance (or, more simply, *health insurance*). Health insurance is defined as "insurance against loss by sickness or accidental bodily injury."[8] The "loss" may be the loss of wages caused by the sickness or accident, or it may be expenses for doctor bills, hospital bills, medicine, and similar medical expenses. Health insurers, like life insurers, provide coverage on both an individual and group basis.

Property and Liability Insurers Property and liability insurers sell those forms of insurance designed to protect against losses resulting from damage to or loss of property and losses arising from legal liability. These coverages are those that were sold by separate fire and casualty insurers in the monoline era and which were formerly referred to as *fire* and *casualty* insurance. The older terminology is gradually being displaced, and the dichotomy between *fire* and *casualty* is slowly giving way to the more descriptive division between *property* and *liability* insurance. The term *property insurance* now refers to fire insurance, marine insurance, and those coverages formerly classified as casualty that are concerned with losses to real and personal property. *Liability insurance,* of course, refers to those coverages pertaining to the legal liability exposure. Although property and liability are the preferred terminology, it should be noted that *fire* and *casualty* are still widely used in some circles.

---

[7]During the early years of the property insurance industry in the United States, catastrophe losses wiped out many companies. The most well known of these losses were the great New York City fire of 1835, which wiped out 23 of the 26 New York companies and almost wiped out New York; the 1871 Chicago fire, which made Mrs. O'Leary's cow famous; and the fire that accompanied the 1906 San Francisco earthquake.

[8]The Commission on Insurance Terminology of the American Risk and Insurance Association.

The major lines of insurance sold by property and liability insurers include fire insurance, ocean marine insurance, inland marine insurance, automobile insurance, liability-other-than auto, workers compensation insurance, boiler and machinery insurance, crime insurance, credit insurance, and title insurance. In addition, these insurers also sell another type of financial contract that is often confused with insurance—surety bonds. The following brief description of these coverages will provide background for the discussion that follows.

Fire insurance is a form of property insurance designed to cover damage to buildings, furniture, fixtures and other personal property at fixed locations. The term fire insurance, although widely used, is a misnomer because although fire was the original peril for which protection was provided, coverage may now be provided under the *fire insurance* line against virtually all insurable perils. There are two basic approaches with respect to the perils for which coverage is provided. Under the first approach, called "named-peril" coverage, the specific perils against which protection is provided are listed in the policy, and coverage applies only for damage arising out of the listed perils. Under the second approach, called "open-peril coverage," the policy lists the perils for which coverage is not provided, and loss from any peril not excluded is covered.[9] Coverage may be provided for both direct loss (i.e., the actual loss represented by the destruction of the asset) and indirect loss (i.e., the loss of income and/or the extra expense that is the result of the loss of the use of the asset protected).

Marine insurance, like fire insurance, is designed to protect against financial loss resulting from damage to owned property, except that here the perils are primarily those associated with transportation. Marine insurance is divided into two classes: ocean marine and inland marine.

Ocean marine insurance policies provide coverage on all types of oceangoing vessels and their cargoes. Policies are also written to cover the shipowner's liability. Originally, ocean marine policies covered cargo only after it was loaded onto the ship. Today the policies are usually endorsed to provide coverage from "warehouse to warehouse," thus protecting against overland transportation hazards as well as those on the ocean.

Inland marine insurance is something of a contradiction in terms. The field developed as an outgrowth of ocean marine insurance and "warehouse-to-warehouse" coverage. As population spread across the United States, transportation came to play a crucial role in the development of business. With the growth of transportation facilities, a demand arose for insurance to protect against losses to products being shipped. Originally, inland marine developed to cover goods being transported by carriers such as railroads, motor vehicles, or ships and barges on the inland waterways and in coastal trade. It was expanded to cover instrumentalities of transportation and communication such as bridges, tunnels, pipelines, power transmission lines, and radio and television communication equipment. Eventually, it included coverage on various types of property that is not in the course of transportation, but that is away from the owner's premises.

---

[9]This latter approach was formerly referred to as "all risk" coverage, and you may still hear it referred to as such. There is a concerted effort to avoid the term "all risk," however, because it was frequently misunderstood by insurance buyers. The term "open-peril" coverage is gradually replacing the term "all risk."

Automobile insurance provides protection against several types of losses. First, it protects against loss resulting from legal liability arising out of the ownership or use of an automobile. Coverage is also provided against loss resulting from theft of the automobile or damage to it from many different causes. Finally, it includes a special form of accident insurance that covers injuries suffered in auto accidents.

Liability insurance embraces a wide range of coverages. The form with which most students are familiar is automobile liability insurance, but there are other liability hazards as well. Coverage is available to protect against nonautomobile liability exposures such as ownership of property, manufacturing and construction operations, the sale or distribution of products, and many other exposures.

Workers compensation insurance provides for the payment of the obligation state statutes impose on employers for injuries to employees in the course of employment. Because the benefits are determined by law and the coverage is compulsory, workers compensation insurance is considered to be a social insurance coverage, even though it is sold by both private insurers and by state funds.

Boiler and machinery insurance was one of the earliest casualty coverages. The operation of boilers is an exposure to life and property because of the hazard of explosion from internal pressure. Furthermore, various forms of machinery are subject to accidental breakdown that may necessitate lengthy and expensive delays in production. To prevent losses, boiler and machinery insurers maintain an extensive inspection service, and this service is a primary reason for the purchase of the coverage.

Burglary, robbery, and theft insurance are casualty coverages designed to protect the property of the insured against loss resulting from the criminal acts of others. Because a standard clause in these crime policies excludes acts by employees of the insured, they are referred to as "nonemployee crime coverages." Protection against criminal acts by employees is provided under fidelity bonds, which are discussed shortly.

Credit insurance is a highly specialized form of coverage (available to manufacturers and wholesalers) that indemnifies insureds for losses resulting from their inability to collect from customers. The coverage is written subject to a deductible equal to the normal bad-debt loss and with a provision requiring the insured to share a part of each loss with the insurer.

Title insurance is still another narrowly specialized form of coverage.[10] Basically, it provides protection against financial loss resulting from a defect in an insured title. Under a title insurance policy, the insurer agrees to indemnify the insured to the extent of any financial loss suffered as a result of the transfer of a defective title. In a sense, title insurance is unique in that it insures against the effects of some past event rather than against financial loss resulting from a future occurrence.

Fidelity and Surety Bonds Fidelity and surety bonds represent a special class of risk transfer device, and opinions differ as to whether bonds should be classified as insurance. As a matter of fact, there are certain fundamental differences between a bond and an insurance policy, and, strictly speaking, it can be argued that some bonds are

---

[10]Title insurance is clearly a form of property insurance and whether it should be classified as "casualty" insurance is debatable. Historically, it has been written by specialty insurers, but it is generally classified as a casualty coverage by the state insurance codes.

not contracts of insurance. In general terms, a bond is an agreement by one party, the "surety," to answer to a third person, called the "obligee," for the debt or default of another party, called the "principal." In other words, the surety guarantees a certain type of conduct on the part of the principal, and if the principal fails to behave in the manner guaranteed, the surety will be responsible to the obligee.

Bonding is divided into two classes: *fidelity bonds* and *surety bonds*. Fidelity bonds protect the obligee against dishonesty on the part of his or her employees and are commonly called "employee dishonesty insurance." In most respects, they resemble insurance more closely than do surety bonds, and many authorities consider them to be a form of casualty insurance.

Most surety bonds are issued for persons doing contract construction, those connected with court actions, and those seeking licenses and permits. Basically, the *surety bond* guarantees that the principal is honest and has the necessary ability and financial capacity to carry out the obligation for which he or she is bonded. The surety obligates itself with the principal to the obligee in much the same manner that the cosigner of a note assumes an obligation with a borrower to a lender. The primary obligation to perform rests with the principal, but if the principal is unable to meet the commitment after exhausting all his or her resources, the surety must provide funds to pay for the loss. In this event, the surety may take possession of the principal's assets and convert them into cash to reimburse itself for the loss paid.

Although there is a difference of opinion as to whether bonds are actually insurance, insurance regulators normally include them within the framework of the contracts they regulate. Furthermore, property and liability insurers sell these bonds, and suretyship is normally considered to be part of the property and liability insurance business.

Classification By Place of Incorporation and Licensing

A *domestic* insurer within any given state is an insurer that is incorporated within that state, or, if it is not incorporated, was formed under the laws of that state. A *foreign* insurer is one that is incorporated in another state of the United States or formed under the laws of another state. *Alien* insurers are incorporated or formed in another country.

A licensed (or *admitted*) insurer with regard to any particular state is an insurer that has been granted a license to operate in that state. An unlicensed (or *nonadmitted*) insurer is one that has not been granted a license. Agents and brokers (except surplus lines brokers) are licensed to place business only with admitted companies. Surplus lines brokers are licensed to place business with nonadmitted insurers, but only if licensed insurers will not write it. Licensing status is also important for purposes of reinsurance.

Classification by Legal Form of Ownership

Insurers can be classified as proprietary, cooperative, and government insurers. Proprietary insurers are organized to earn a profit for their owners; proprietary insurers include capital stock insurers, Lloyds, and insurance exchanges. Cooperative insurers are organized to provide insurance for their members, who are also the owners of the insurer. Within this framework, nongovernment insurers may be grouped into the following classes.[11]

1. Capital stock insurance companies
2. Mutual insurance companies
3 Reciprocals or interinsurance exchanges
4. Lloyd's associations
5. Health expense associations

Capital Stock Insurance Companies These companies are organized as profit-making ventures, with the stockholders assuming the risk that is transferred by the individual insureds. If the actuarial predictions prove accurate, the premiums collected are sufficient to pay losses and operating expenses while returning a profit to the stockholders. The capital invested by the stockholders provides funds to run the company until premium income is sufficient to pay losses and operating expense. In addition, it provides a surplus fund that serves as a guarantee to the policyholders that the contracts will be fulfilled. The distinguishing characteristics of a *capital stock insurance company* are as follows: (1) the premium charged by the company is final—there is no form of contingent liability for policyholders; (2) the board of directors is elected by the stockholders, and (3) earnings are distributed to shareholders as dividends on their stock.

Capital stock insurers more or less dominate the field of property and liability insurance, accounting for approximately *two-thirds* of the premium volume, even though they comprise less than *one-third* of the total number of property and liability companies. In the life insurance field, where approximately 90 percent of the companies are capital stock insurers, they write slightly more than 60 percent of total premiums.

Mutual Insurance Companies In contrast to a stock company, a *mutual insurance company* is owned by its policyholders. Mutual insurers are organized for the purpose of providing insurance for their members. Normally, a mutual company is incorporated, and in many states this is a legal requirement. The distinguishing characteristics of a mutual insurer are its lack of capital stock and the distribution of earnings. Any money left after paying all costs of operation is returned to the policyholders in the form of dividends. Included in the concept of "costs" that must be paid is the addition to the surplus of the company. Unlike the capital stock company, the mutual company has no paid-in capital as a guarantee of solvency in the event of adverse experience. For this reason, mutual insurers need to accumulate a surplus to protect against such adverse contingencies as heavy losses or a decline in investment return. Mutual insurers write about one-third of the property and liability premium volume in this country and slightly over one-half of all life insurance premiums.

---

[11]Although not technically a separate form of insurer, the captives and pooling groups discussed in Chapter 15 are sometimes mentioned as another group. Generally, a captive or pooling group will be organized under one of the forms listed above.

A limited number of mutual insurers issue assessable policies in which the insured has a contingent liability and is subject to assessment if losses exceed advance premiums.[12] However, all states permit mutual insurers to issue nonassessable policies when they have attained a specified level of fiscal strength. Normally, when a mutual company has the same financial strength required of a capital stock company writing the same type of business, it may be permitted to issue nonassessable policies. An advance premium mutual company issuing nonassessable policies is usually operated like a capital stock company. The advance premium that is collected is intended to be sufficient to cover all losses and expenses. If it is not, the additional costs are paid out of the accumulated surplus. All the larger mutual carriers in the United States operate on this basis. However, unlike the capital stock companies, the premium is not fixed and definite, and any excess of premium income over costs may be returned to the policyholders as dividends.

In the final analysis, there are few practical differences between a mutual company operating on an advance premium basis with nonassessable policies and a capital stock company. Although the policyholders own the mutual company in theory, there are no vested rights of ownership for these policyholders except in the case of liquidation. Furthermore, the policyholders theoretically control the company, but this is on a basis equivalent to the theoretical control of the stockholders over the management in a large corporation with many individual stockholders.[13]

Reciprocals A reciprocal exchange (also called an interinsurance exchange) is a particularly American innovation, and though accounting for only a small segment of the insurance industry (there are about 50 in existence), it is a significant insurer. Reciprocal exchanges are sometimes confused with mutual insurers, and while the two are similar, they also differ in a fundamental way. A *reciprocal* is an unincorporated group of individuals, called subscribers, who exchange insurance risks. Each member (or subscriber) is both an insured and an insurer: as a member of the group, the individual is insured by each of the other members and, in turn, insures each of them. In a mutual organization, members of the group assume their liability collectively; in a reciprocal exchange, each subscriber assumes his or her liability severally (meaning separately) as an individual, and not as a member of the group. The advantage of this arrangement is that the liability of each subscriber is limited. Although some reciprocals provide for a limited assessment of the members, one member cannot be called upon to assume the liability of a defaulting member. The premium paid by each subscriber is maintained in a separate account, and the subscriber's share of each loss is paid from his or her account.

[12]Some mutual insurers operate on a post-loss assessment basis, in which premiums are payable after a loss occurs. The nuclear energy industry operates a post-loss assessment mutual to provide liability insurance for losses arising out of nuclear incidents. In addition, some mutuals charge an advance premium but reserve the right to levy additional assessments if losses exceed the advance premiums collected. *County mutuals* authorized by the insurance laws of many states usually operate as advance premium assessable mutuals.

[13]Fraternal societies are specialized forms of mutual insurers. Basically, fraternal societies are nonprofit organizations that operate on the basis of "lodges," with a representative form of government. Fraternals have concentrated their activity primarily in the field of life insurance, although they sometimes sell sickness and accident insurance. Because fraternals are considered to be charitable institutions, they do not pay federal income tax or state premium tax.

The chief administrator of the reciprocal program, the *attorney-in-fact*, derives authority through a power of attorney granted by each of the subscribers, which is used to commit the members as insurers of each other's property. The attorney-in-fact receives some percentage of the gross premiums paid by the subscribers (usually about 25 percent) to cover the expenses of operating the program. Reciprocals confine their operations to the property and casualty fields. The portion of the total premiums written through interinsurance exchanges is relatively small. In 1995, only about 6 percent of all property and casualty premiums were written through reciprocals.

Lloyd's Associations   *Lloyd's associations*, strictly speaking, do not themselves underwrite insurance. Lloyds associations include Lloyd's of London and American Lloyds.

Lloyd's of London is the oldest and perhaps the most famous insurance organization in the world. Generally, Lloyd's is a corporation for marketing the services of a group of individuals. The organization itself does not issue insurance policies or provide insurance protection. The actual insurance is underwritten by the 40,000 underwriting members of the association. Technically, each member is a separate "insurance company," issuing policies and underwriting risks separately or collectively with other members. In a sense, Lloyd's is similar to the New York Stock Exchange, in which the actual physical facilities are owned by the stock exchange and are made available to members for the transaction of business. It is governed by a group known as the Committee of Lloyd's, which establishes standards with which members must comply.

Originally, each underwriter at Lloyd's conducted business as an individual proprietor or as a member of one of 400 syndicates. No corporations or other limitations on liability were permitted, and every member of Lloyd's exposed his or her entire personal fortune in addition to business assets.[14] In 1993, Lloyd's adopted a new system of operation permitting corporations with limited liability.

Normally, policies written through Lloyd's are issued by the individual underwriters, and each underwriter assumes a fraction of the risk. The Lloyd's policy contains the statement, "Each for his own part and not for one another," indicating that the underwriters assume liability and that each underwriter is liable only for his or her own commitments. Historically, however, solvent members have assumed the liabilities of defaulting members for public relations reasons.

In addition to the individual liability that results from the severability of the underwriters, another problem arises. In the event of a dispute concerning coverage under the policy, technically each of the individual underwriters must be sued. In practice, however, if suit is brought against one underwriter under a contract and it is successful, the remaining members pay their portion of the loss without the necessity of further litigation.

Although Lloyd's of London is famous throughout the United States, it is licensed in only two states, Illinois and Kentucky. Each Lloyd's policy issued in the United States contains a clause in which the underwriters agree to submit to the

---

[14]Standards for admission of underwriters are both severe and rigid. It was not until 1968 that non-British members were admitted, and women were not admitted to membership until 1969.

jurisdiction of either of these two states or any other court of competent jurisdiction in the nation.[15]

The *American Lloyd's associations* attempt to emulate the success of (and capitalize on the fame of) Lloyd's of London. An American Lloyd's is simply a group of individuals who operate an insurance mechanism using the same principles of individual liability of insurers as Lloyd's of London. Following the practice at Lloyd's of London, each underwriter assumes part of a risk and is liable only for his or her portion of the risk. Individual underwriters have no obligation to cover losses for which a defaulting member is responsible. Although this is essentially the same system used by Lloyd's of London, many American Lloyd's lack the strict regulation that the original Lloyd's imposes on its members. Most states have laws prohibiting the organization or licensing of American Lloyd's. Those American Lloyd's that do exist operate almost exclusively in the property insurance field.

Insurance Exchanges   *Insurance Exchanges* are similar to Lloyd's associations. In 1979, Florida, Illinois, and New York enacted legislation authorizing the formation of "insurance exchanges," patterned after the method of operation used at Lloyd's, in which a number of underwriters participate in providing insurance under a single contract. The exchanges were created to insure large, unusual, or hard-to-insure exposures. The Florida and New York exchanges encountered financial difficulties, and both closed in 1988. The Illinois exchange continues to operate successfully.

Health Expense Associations   *Health Expense Associations* are unique to the field of health insurance. They include Blue Cross and Blue Shield associations and certain health care providers, such as *Health Maintenance Organizations* and *Physician Hospital Organizations.* The Blue Cross and Blue Shield plans are nonprofit associations usually organized under special state enabling legislation to provide for prepayment of hospital and surgical expenses. The Blue Cross plans were originally organized by individual hospitals to permit and encourage prepayment of hospital expenses. Blue Shield plans were organized by physicians for the same reason. Both Blue Cross and Blue Shield market "service" contracts under which service benefits, rather than a dollar indemnity, are provided to insured members. Thus, although a commercial insurer's contract might, for example, provide for payment of a specific dollar amount per day while the insured is confined to a hospital, a Blue Cross contract would provide a semiprivate room in a member hospital.[16]

Health Maintenance Organizations (HMOs) and Physician Hospital Organizations (PHO's)—also sometimes called Organized Delivery Systems (ODSs)—are health care providers that also act as insurers by virtue of the manner in which they charge for their services, which is called *capitation.* Under the capitation approach,

---

[15]Despite the fact that Lloyd's is licensed in only two states, it provides insurance in other states as well, under the provisions of state *excess and surplus line laws* discussed in Chapter 12.

[16]The laws under which Blue Cross and Blue Shield plans were organized originally exempted the plans from the state insurance premium tax and from other provisions of insurance laws. A number of states have eliminated the exemption from the premium tax in recent years. Prior to the Tax Reform Act of 1986 (TRA-86), Blue Cross and Blue Shield plans were exempt from federal taxes, but TRA-86 repealed this exemption for years after 1986.

individual subscribers pay an annual fee and in return receive a wide range of health care services. A Health Maintenance Organization (HMO) provides health care services to enrollees on a fixed prepayment basis. This prearranged health care is provided to an enrolled group within a specified geographic area. An HMO is a complete health care organization that combines both the delivery and the financing of comprehensive health service. Hospital Physician Organizations are a type of joint venture in which hospitals and physicians combine to provide a full range of health care services to subscribers. PHOs are paid a capitated fee (per enrollee fee) for the services they provide.

Government Insurers

In addition to the social insurance coverage discussed in the preceding chapter, both the federal and state governments are also engaged in the field of private or voluntary insurance.[17] The government's private insurance programs have developed for diverse reasons. In some cases, they have been established because the risks involved did not lend themselves to private insurance, because either the hazards were too great or the private insurers were subject to adverse selection. In other instances, they originated because of the private insurers' inability or reluctance to meet society's needs for some form of voluntary insurance. In a few cases, government voluntary insurance programs have been established as tools of social change, designed to provide a subsidy to particular segments of society or to help solve the social ills afflicting individual classes of citizens. Finally, government insurance programs have sometimes been founded on the mistaken notion that such programs could somehow repeal the law of averages and provide insurance at a lower cost than would be charged by private insurers.

Federal Private (Voluntary) Insurance Programs   Over the years, the federal government has engaged in a number of voluntary insurance fields. In many programs, the government cooperates with private insurers, providing reinsurance or other forms of subsidy in meeting risks that the private insurance industry could not meet alone.

Voluntary programs that the federal government has operated in the past but that are no longer active include war risk insurance for the U.S. merchant marine and other property owners, nuclear energy liability insurance, and federal riot reinsurance. Private insurance programs currently operated by the federal government include servicemen's and veterans' life insurance, U.S. Postal Service insurance coverage, Federal Crop Insurance, Mortgage Loan Insurance through the FHA and VA, the National Flood Insurance Program, the Federal Crime Insurance Program, a surety bonding program offered through the Small Business Administration, a fidelity bonding program offered through the U.S. Department

---

[17]A government insurer, as used here, means an insurance enterprise operated by the state or nation, with the government or a government agency collecting premiums (or taxes in the case of some social insurance plans) and assuming liability for the payment of losses. It also includes instances in which the government provides reinsurance for other insurers or participates with them in assuming the risk of loss as a transferee. It does not cover self-insurance funds established for the protection of government property or insurance programs operated by the government exclusively for the benefit of its employees.

of Labor, and credit and political risk insurance through the U.S. Export Import Bank and the Overseas Private Corporation.

State Private (Voluntary) Insurance Programs   Like the federal government, a number of individual states offer private or voluntary insurance, but in a far more limited form. The state programs that do exist more often than not compete with those of the private insurance industry. About half the states sell workers compensation insurance. In addition, the state of Wisconsin operates a state life insurance fund, and Maryland operates a state automobile insurance fund.

Classification According to Distribution System

The agent or broker has always been the central figure in the insurance marketing process, but the relationship between the agents and the companies they represent can be, and is often, quite varied. Over the years, several marketing forms have evolved, each of which has as its goal the attainment of efficiency in distribution and service.

Life Insurance Distribution System   With the exception of a small amount of life insurance that is sold through the mail, most life insurance is sold by agents or brokers. The agent may work through a general agency or a branch office. Most agents are independent contractors, but they may also be employees of the general agency or insurer. Life insurance companies originally insisted that individual agents represent them exclusively, but increasingly the trend has been toward multiple company representation and brokerage of life insurance. Brokers place the insurance they write with a number of insurers, selecting the insurer most appropriate to the situation.

General agents are independent businesspeople empowered by the company they represent to sell life insurance in specified territories and to appoint subagents. The general agency receives an overriding commission on all business written by its subagents out of which it pays agency expenses. The fact that the general agent hires, trains, and compensates subagents makes the general agency a relatively inexpensive and riskless way to start in a new area.

In the *branch office system,* the sales force is supervised by a branch manager who, in contrast to the general agent, is a salaried employee of the insurance company. Branch office expenses are paid by the home office, for the branch office is simply an extension of the home office. The agents assigned to a branch office may be employees of the insurer or independent contractors. At one time, the branch manager received only a salary, but in recent years many branch managers now receive additional compensation on the basis of the productivity of the agents supervised.

Property and Liability Distribution Systems   In the field of property and liability insurance, companies may be classified as (1) those who operate through the American Agency System and (2) the "direct writers." The agents who operate through the American Agency System are known as independent agents, whereas those who represent direct writers are called captive agents.

Independent agents normally represent several companies, dividing the policies they sell among those companies according to their choice. They own their expirations, which means that they may place the renewals of sold policies with some other insurer if they choose to do so. This alternative often gives the independent agent strategic power that it can use to the benefit of clients. However, because even the independent agent is first and foremost a representative of the insurance company, he or she also has an obligation to the company. One implication of the ownership of renewals by the independent agent is that it prevents the insurance company from paying a lower commission on renewal business. If a company represented by an independent agent were to attempt to pay a lower commission on renewal policies than on new ones, the agent could simply place the policy with a different company, making it new business for that company.

Direct writers operate through salaried representatives (as in the case of the Liberty Mutual Insurance Company) or through *exclusive* or *captive agents* (as in the case of Nationwide, State Farm, and Allstate).[18] The compensation of the salesperson may be in the form of a salary, or it may be a commission, based on the premium volume. In the case of the exclusive agent, it is normally commission. The key point is that the agent or the salaried employee does not own the expirations. He or she has no choice as to where the policy is to be renewed. Because the agent cannot transfer the business written to another insurer, the direct-writing company can pay a small renewal commission or none at all.

The *ownership of renewals* is the most important difference between the two types of agents, and from this difference arise still other distinctions in the method of operation. Since the direct-writing agent receives little or no commission on renewals, the premiums on policies written by direct writers are generally lower than those of companies operating through the American agency system. In addition, it means that the production of new business is of crucial importance for the direct writing agent. In a sense, the life insurance agent is in the same position; he or she is a captive agent, representing only one company. Since for the life insurance agent, like the direct-writing agent in property and liability, the renewal commission is quite low, his or her income depends on the generation of new business. The independent agent, on the other hand, places greater emphasis on the retention of accounts presently serviced, since the commission on these accounts is the same as the commission on new business.

Direct Response Distribution of Insurance Life insurance, health insurance, and property and liability insurance are all sold by insurers operating under a "direct response" system. These insurers do not use agents, rather, they promote the sale of insurance by mass media advertising and by direct mail.

Advantages and Disadvantages of Alternative Marketing Systems No one marketing system is best for all insurance consumers. The independent agency system is likely

---

[18]Technically, companies that operate through exclusive agents are not "direct writers" but rather "exclusive-agent companies." However, the term *direct writer* is commonly used in reference to both companies operating through salaried representatives and those operating through exclusive agents.

to be most satisfactory for those buyers of insurance who have very complex insurance needs or who consider service more important than cost. The exclusive agency and direct writer systems have been most successful in dealing with insurance buyers who have relatively simple needs, primarily individuals, families, and small main-street type businesses. However, a number of direct writers specialize in commercial risks, especially workers compensation insurance. These include Employers Mutual of Wausau and Liberty Mutual Insurance Company. Because some direct writers have strengths in particular lines of insurance, there are occasions when no other insurer fits the needs of the organization quite as well as does a particular direct writer. In these cases, the risk manager may place the insurance directly with the direct-writing company's sales representative, or the business may be placed with the direct writer by the organization's agent or broker. Although direct writers do not usually pay a fee to independent agents or brokers, the agent or broker may negotiate a fee for placement. The broker's fee for acting as intermediary with a direct writer is usually based on the net premium (i.e., the direct writer's premium without an added commission). Depending on the line of insurance and the premium for the risk being transferred, the agent's negotiated fee might range from as low as 1 percent to as much as 10 percent.

Mass Marketing and Group Property and Liability   Mass merchandising involves efforts to sell insurance, either personal lines or commercial lines, to individual purchasers whose only relationship is membership in a common organization. In the commercial lines area, mass marketing programs have generally taken one of two forms: *trade association plans* and *safety group plans.*

Under trade association plans, firms that are members of a sponsoring trade association are eligible to participate in the group program, which is usually subject to individual underwriting requirements, but makes coverage available on a discounted basis. The source of the discount is generally a reduced agent's commission and savings in insurer administrative expenses.

Safety group programs are not typically restricted to members of a trade association, but are usually available to any firm in the selected industry, provided the firm agrees to undertake a loss control program specified by the insurer. Coverage is usually subject to individual underwriting. The savings in a safety group program stem from the same sources as association group programs. In addition, savings in loss costs are anticipated from the safety programs that are a basic part of safety group programs.

CORPORATE COMBINATIONS

To further explain the structure of the insurance industry, we should briefly examine some of its unique corporate relationships, which include insurance company groups and cooperating underwriting syndicates.

Insurance Company Groups

Many insurance companies operate in groups, often called *fleets*, which consist of a number of insurance companies under common ownership and often under common management. Insurance company groups developed during the monoline era and were designed to permit the writing of both property and casualty coverage by insurers under a common management. Because a fire company could not write casualty coverage and a casualty company was forbidden to issue fire coverage, the logical solution was to form two companies and operate them in tandem. Although this reason for company fleets no longer exists, the form of operation persists, and the overwhelming preponderance of the property and liability insurance business is written by insurance companies that are members of a company group.[19]

Initially, company fleets limited their operations to the property and liability field, but over time these groups expanded to include life insurers. State Farm Mutual, founded in 1922, added a life subsidiary, State Farm Life Insurance Company, in 1929. One by one, the other major property and liability insurers also acquired or formed life insurance company subsidiaries. Eventually, life insurance companies acquired or formed property and liability insurers. As a result, most insurance company fleets now include both property and liability insurers.

Underwriting Syndicates

In addition to the other forms of cooperation, insurers sometimes join together in *underwriting syndicates* for the purpose of handling risks that would be beyond the capacity of an individual company. In these syndicates, which are found primarily in the property and liability field, insurers make use of the basic insurance principle of spreading risk and sharing losses.

The Associated Factory Mutual Insurance Companies   The *factory mutuals* are a group of four direct-writing mutual insurers specializing in underwriting property insurance on highly protected exposures, usually involving large concentrations of value.[20] Insurance purchased from one of the companies is shared on a percentage basis among all four companies. The basic emphasis of the factory mutuals is on loss prevention, and only high-grade and sprinklered risks are insured. Applicants are rigidly inspected both before and after the issuance of the coverage. The initial premiums are substantially higher than the amount anticipated to be needed for losses and expenses, with the excess premium returned to the policyholder as a dividend at the end of the year. Although the factory mutuals comprise only a small number of companies, the system is a significant factor in the insurance market, particularly for larger insureds.

[19]There are about 290 groups, comprised of slightly more than 1100 insurers operating in the property and liability field, that write about 90 percent of the industry's total premiums.

[20]The factory mutual concept dates from 1835, when Zachariah Allen, the owner of a textile mill, organized the Manufacturers Mutual Fire Insurance Company of Rhode Island. Allen, distressed because existing insurers granted no rate concessions to factories in which proper attention had been devoted to loss prevention and control, decided to organize a company that would recognize superior construction and loss-prevention efforts. The four factory mutuals currently in existence are the Allendale Mutual Insurance Company, Arkwright-Boston Manufacturers Mutual Company, Philadelphia Manufacturers Insurance Company, and Protection Mutual Insurance Company. In addition, these companies own a stock company, the Affiliated Factory Mutual Insurance Company, that insures high-quality risks that do not meet the requirements of the factory mutuals.

Industrial Risk Insurers   Industrial Risk Insurers (IRI) is an underwriting syndicate of about 45 stock insurers that was formed in December 1975 through the merger of two syndicates, the Factory Insurance Association (FIA) and the Oil Insurance Association (OIA). Like the factory mutuals, the IRI emphasizes loss prevention and specializes in large exposures. However, unlike the factory mutuals, in which the originating company issues the policy and then reinsures a portion with other insurers, the IRI itself issues the insurance, and the coverage is shared among the member companies on a predetermined basis.

Improved Risk Mutuals   The Improved Risk Mutuals is an underwriting syndicate composed of 18 mutual insurance companies, which combine to write insurance on larger and higher valued properties than any one of the companies could individually insure. To a somewhat lesser extent than the factory mutuals and the IRI, the improved risk mutuals specialize in writing highly protected risks.

Nuclear Energy Pools   Insurance for liability arising out of nuclear accidents is provided by an insurance industry pool, American Nuclear Insurers, up to $200 million. In addition, a mutual insurance assessment association, consisting of nuclear reactor operators, provides an additional $7.5 billion in coverage on a post-loss assessment basis.[21] Property insurance is provided by the nuclear pools and by two offshore industry mutual insurers, Nuclear Electric Insurance, Ltd. and Nuclear Mutual Ltd. In 1995 the nuclear pools and industry mutuals provided over $1 billion primary and $1 billion excess property insurance.

Other Voluntary Syndicates   In addition to the factory mutuals, the IRI, and the improved risk mutuals, several similar syndicates have been formed to deal with specialized exposures or concentrations of values in particular industries. For example, two syndicates, the Associated Aviation Underwriters and the United States Aircraft Insurance Group, offer insurance for aviation risks. The American Hull Insurance Syndicate represents its members in competition with international marine insurers, specializing in oceangoing ships of American registry. The Railroad Insurance Underwriters provides a market for insuring rolling stock and, in addition, insures fixed-location property owned by the railroads.

REINSURANCE

Reinsurance is a device whereby an insurance company may avoid the catastrophe hazard in the operation of the insurance mechanism. As the term indicates, reinsurance is insurance for insurers. It is based on the same principles of sharing and transfer as insurance itself. In a reinsurance transaction the insurer seeking reinsurance is known as the "direct writer" or the ceding company, while the company

---

[21]Nuclear reactor operators are subject to assessment up to $63 million per reactor, plus an additional 5 percent assessment if needed, making the potential assessment per nuclear reactor $66,150,000. If coverage from the industry pools and assessments are inadequate to cover a catastrophic loss, Congress can appropriate additional funds and then tax the owners of the nuclear reactors to cover the appropriation.

assuming part of the risk is known simply as the "reinsurer." That portion of a risk that the direct writer retains is called the "net line," or the net retention. The act of transferring a part of the risk to the reinsurance company is called "ceding," and that portion of the risk passed on to the reinsurer is called the "cession."

Reinsurance had a very simple beginning. When a risk that was too large for the company to handle safely was presented to an insurer, it began to shop around for another insurance company that was willing to take a portion of the risk in return for a portion of the premium. A few current reinsurance operations are still conducted in this manner, but the ever-present danger that a devastating loss might occur before the reinsurance becomes effective led to the development of modern reinsurance treaties. Reinsurance may provide protection against a comparatively large single loss, or a large number of small losses caused by a single occurrence.

Types of Reinsurance Treaties

There are two types of reinsurance treaties: facultative and automatic. Under a *facultative treaty*, each risk is submitted by the direct writer to the reinsurer for acceptance or rejection. Although the terms under which reinsurance will take place are spelled out, the direct writer is not obliged to submit a risk to the reinsurer and the reinsurer may accept or reject risks that are submitted. Until the risk has been submitted and accepted, the direct writer carries the entire risk. Under the terms of an *automatic treaty*, the reinsurer agrees in advance to accept a portion of the gross line of the direct writing company or a portion of certain risks that meet the reinsurance underwriting rules of the reinsurer. The direct writer is obligated to cede a portion of the risk to which the automatic treaty applies.

Reinsurance in Property and Liability Insurance

There are two essential ways in which risk is shared under reinsurance agreements in the field of property and liability insurance. The reinsurance agreement may require the reinsurer to share in every loss that occurs to a reinsured risk, or it may require the reinsurer to pay only after a loss reaches a certain size. The first arrangement is called *proportional reinsurance* and includes quota share and surplus line reinsurance. The second approach is called *excess loss* reinsurance. In the case of proportional reinsurance, the direct writer pays the reinsurer a proportionate share of the premium (less an allowance for expenses) based on the percentage of the risk the reinsurer assumes. The reinsurer then becomes responsible for the unearned premium reserve and the payment of losses based on the division of the risk between the parties. In excess reinsurance, the direct writer, in effect, purchases insurance with a high deductible. The premium for excess loss reinsurance is a small fraction of the direct writer's premium.

Another method of reinsurance is pooling. The pooling arrangement may be similar to that used in aviation insurance, under the terms of which each member assumes a percentage of every risk written by a member of the pool. This pooling arrangement is a form of proportional reinsurance. On the other hand, the pool may provide a maximum loss limit to any one insurance company from a single loss, as is the case with the Workers Compensation Reinsurance Bureau. After a member of the pool has suffered a loss in excess of a specified amount (i.e., $100,000 as a result of one disaster), the other members of the pool share the remainder of the loss.

Reinsurance in Life Insurance

In the field of life insurance, reinsurance may take one of two forms: the term insurance approach or the coinsurance approach. Under the *term insurance approach*, the direct writer purchases yearly renewable term insurance equal to the difference between the face value of the policy and the reserve, which is the amount at risk for the company. The *coinsurance approach* to reinsurance in life insurance is similar to the quota share approach in property and liability insurance; the ceding company transfers some portion of the face amount of the policy to the reinsurer, and the reinsurer becomes liable for its proportional share of the death claim and for a share of the policy reserve.

Functions of Reinsurance

Reinsurance serves two important purposes. The first, which is fairly obvious, is to reduce the spreading of risk. Insurance companies are able to avoid catastrophic losses by passing on a portion of any risk too large to handle. In addition, through excess loss reinsurance arrangements, a company may protect itself against a single occurrence of catastrophic scope. Smaller companies are permitted to insure exposures they could not otherwise handle within the bounds of safety.

The second function reinsurance performs is not as immediately obvious: it is a financial function. As explained in Chapter 12, state laws allow an insurer to record premiums received as income only as the time for which the protection is provided passes. Further, the insurer must establish a liability for unearned premiums called the *unearned premium reserve*. Because insurers generally incur a high percentage of the non-claim cost associated with a policy when the policy is written, an insurer whose premium volume is expanding will generally have expenses that exceed recordable income. This produces a decrease in the insurer's surplus. Because the amount of premiums an insurer may write depends on the amount of its surplus, this poses a dilemma for the insurer. In the absence of some other alternative, an insurer could expand only to a certain point and would then be required to stop and wait for the premiums to become earned, freeing surplus.

Reinsurance provides a solution to this dilemma. When the originating insurer reinsures a part of its business using proportional reinsurance, it pays a part of the premium to the reinsurer. The reinsurer then establishes the unearned required premium reserve, and the direct writer is relieved of the obligation to maintain such reserves. Since the direct writer has incurred expenses in acquiring the business, the reinsurer pays the direct-writing company a commission for having put the business on the books. The payment of the ceding commission by the reinsurer to the direct writer means that the unearned premium reserve is reduced by more than cash is reduced, resulting in an increase in surplus. In this way, excess capacity of one insurer may be transferred to another insurer through reinsurance.

IMPORTANT CONCEPTS TO REMEMBER

insurance defined from the viewpoint of the individual
insurance defined from the viewpoint of society
randomness
adverse selection
economic feasibility
pooling
elements of an insurable risk
self-insurance
private insurance
social insurance
monoline operation
multiple-line operation
ocean marine insurance
inland marine insurance
fire insurance
named-peril coverage
open-peril coverage
health insurance
casualty insurance
property insurance
liability insurance
surety bonds
surety
principal
obligee
credit insurance
title insurance

life insurance
domestic insurer
foreign insurer
alien insurer
capital stock insurance company
mutual insurance company
assessment mutual
advance premium mutual
assessable policy
fraternal insurer
reciprocals
Lloyd's association
insurance exchange
attorney-in-fact
excess and surplus line law
Blue Cross
Blue Shield
health maintenance organization
service contract
physician hospital organization
capitation
government insurer
National Flood Insurance Program
Federal Crime Insurance Program
SBA Surety Bond Program

Federal Fidelity Bonding Program
Export-Import Bank
Overseas Private Investor Corporation
agent
broker
binding
American Agency System
direct writer
independent agent
captive agent
ownership of renewals
direct response system
general agent
branch office system
personal producing general agent
company groups
fleets
underwriting syndicate
factory mutuals
Industrial Risk Insurers
advisory organization
rating bureaus
CPCU
CLU

QUESTIONS FOR REVIEW

1. List and explain each of the desirable elements of an insurable risk.

2. Identify the two fundamental functions involved in the operation of the insurance mechanism.

3. Give examples of three uninsurable exposures and indicate why each is uninsurable.

4. Identify and distinguish between the two major classes of marine insurance.

5. Briefly explain the fundamental difference between an insurance contract and a surety bond.

6. List the types of insurers as classified by legal form of ownership, and briefly describe the distinguishing characteristics of each type.

7. Describe the general nature of the two major distribution systems used in the property and liability field. Of what significance are the distinctions between the systems of significance to the risk manager?

8. What are captivating health care providers? In what ways are these insurers similar and dissimilar to other health insurers?

9. What are the general methods of operation of Lloyd's of London, and why does it receive such wide publicity?

10. Identify the various costs that are common to all insurers and explain the extent to which these costs may differ from one insurer to another.

QUESTIONS FOR DISCUSSION

1. Suppose that the members of your class enter into an agreement under whose terms all would chip in to pay for the damage to any automobile owned by a class member that was damaged in a collision. Explain if this is insurance and whether you would be willing to participate.

2. A friend tells you about a plan for the formation of an insurance company which will issue insurance policies to protect a person who buys stock against a decline in the value of that stock. Explain why you believe the scheme will or will not work.

3. Adam Smith wrote, "People of the same trade seldom meet together, even for merriment and diversion, but the conversation ends in a conspiracy against the public, or in some contrivance to raise prices." To what extent do you believe that this observation holds true with respect to the various cooperative organizations in the insurance field?

4. "When an insurer is successful in its efforts to select insureds from the better than average classes, the gain in its competitive position is magnified by the impact of this success on its competitors." Explain what is meant by this statement.

5. At one time it was suggested that the problem of providing insurance protection against loss by flood be met by providing coverage against the flood peril as a mandatory part of the Standard Fire Policy. Do you agree with this solution? Why or why not?

SUGGESTIONS FOR ADDITIONAL READING

Athearn, James L., Travis Pritchett, and Joan T. Schmit. *Risk and Insurance*, 6th ed. St. Paul, MN: West Publishing, 1989. Chapter 4.

Denenberg, Herbert S. "The Legal Definition of Insurance." *Journal of Risk and Insurance*, XXX, No. 3 (Sept. 1963).

Doherty, Neil A. *Corporate Risk Management* (New York: McGraw Hill Book Company, 1985), Chapter 10.

Faulkner, E.J., ed. *Man's Quest for Security*. Lincoln, Ne: University of Nebraska Press, 1966.

Gibbs, D.E.W. *Lloyds of London: A Study of Individualism*. New York: St. Martin's Press, 1975.

Greene, Mark R., James S. Trieschmann, and Sandra G. Gustavson. *Risk and Insurance*, 8th ed. Cincinnati: South-Western Publishing, 1992. Chapters 3, 23, 26.

Kulp, C.A., and John W. Hall. *Casualty Insurance*, 4th ed. New York: Ronald Press, 1968. Chapter 1.

Lenz, Matthew, Jr. "Self-Insurance, Semantics, and Other Hang-Ups." *CPCU Annals*, XXVIII (June 1975).

Mowbray, A.H., R.H. Blanchard, and C. Arthur Williams. *Insurance*, 6th ed. New York: McGraw-Hill, 1969. Chapters 5, 6.

Nelli, H.O., and R.A. Marshall. *The Private Insurance Business in the United States*. Research Paper 48. Altanta, GA: Bureau of Business and Economic Research, Georgia State College, June 1969.

Pfeffer, I. "The Early History of Insurance." *CPCU Annals*, XIX, Nos. 11, 19, 23 (Summer 1966).

Reinmuth, D. *The Regulation of Reciprocal Insurance Exchanges*. Homewood, IL: Richard D. Irwin, 1967.

Rejda, George E. *Social Insurance and Economic Security*, 2nd ed. Englewood Cliffs, NJ: Prentice-Hall, 1984.

Smith, Barry D. *How Insurance Works: An Introduction to Property and Liability Insurance*, 2nd edition. Malvern, PA: Insurance Institute of America, 1994.

Webb, Bernard L.; Howard N. Anderson; John A. Cookman; and Peter R. Kensicki, *Principles of Reinsurance*, Vol. I and Vol. II. Malvern PA: Insurance Institute of America, 1990.

Williams, C. Arthur, and Richard M. Heins. *Risk Management and Insurance*, 6th ed. New York: McGraw-Hill, 1989. Chapter 12.

CHAPTER 11

Risk Financing: Practical Considerations in Insurance Buying

CHAPTER OBJECTIVES

When you have finished this chapter, you should be able to

Explain the general concept of insurance rate-making.

∎

Identify the four broad approaches to insurance rates.

∎

Explain the function of insurance advisory organizations in the rate-making process.

∎

Explain the purpose of underwriting and the relationship between underwriting and rates.

∎

Describe the evidence that indicates the extent of competition in the insurance industry.

∎

Explain the purpose of and the manner in which the excess and surplus line market operates.

∎

Describe the important considerations in selecting an insurance agent or broker.

∎

Identify and explain the important considerations in selecting an insurer.

Introduction ∎∎∎∎∎∎∎∎∎∎∎∎∎∎∎∎∎∎∎∎∎∎∎∎∎∎

An applicant for insurance sometimes makes the surprising discovery that the insurance company is not particularly interested in providing the desired coverage. Insurance companies are in business to sell insurance, and it is therefore unexpected when an insurer rejects an applicant or refuses to renew coverage that has been written in the past. It is similarly difficult for consumers to understand the periodic shortages of insurance in the marketplace, during which insurance becomes unavailable for entire classes of insurance buyers. While certainly insurers are in business to sell insurance, they may have good reasons to refuse a particular applicant. In this chapter, we examine some of the practical aspects of insurance buying. Because pricing is a key variable in insurance availability, we begin with a brief discussion of insurance rate-making, followed by the related subject of insurance underwriting. We will then be in a position to explore the competitive nature of the insurance industry and the implications of this competition for insurance buyers.

⚙ Insurer Pricing ■

An insurance rate is the price per unit of insurance. Like any other price, it is a function of the cost of production. However, in insurance, unlike other industries, the cost of production is not known when the contract is sold, and it will not be known until some time in the future, when the policy has expired. One fundamental difference between insurance pricing and the pricing function in other industries is that the price for insurance must be based on a prediction. The process of predicting future losses and future expenses and allocating these costs among the various classes of insureds is called rate-making.

A second important difference between the pricing of insurance and pricing in other industries arises from the fact that insurance rates are subject to government regulation. Virtually all states have laws imposing statutory restraints on insurance rates. These laws require that insurance rates must not be excessive, must be adequate, and may not be unfairly discriminatory. Depending on the manner in which the state laws are administered, they impose differing limits on an insurer's freedom to price its products.

In addition to the statutory requirements that rates must be adequate, not excessive, and not unfairly discriminatory, certain other characteristics are considered desirable. To the extent possible, for example, rates should be relatively stable over time, so that the public is not subjected to wide variations in cost from year to year. At the same time, rates should be sufficiently responsive to changing conditions to avoid inadequacies in the event of deteriorating loss experience. Finally, whenever possible, the rate should provide some incentive for the insured to prevent loss.

SOME BASIC CONCEPTS

A *rate* is the price charged for each unit of protection or exposure and should be distinguished from a *premium*, which is determined by multiplying the rate by the number of units of protection purchased. The unit of protection to which a rate applies differs for the various lines of insurance. In life insurance, for example, rates are computed for each $1000 in protection; in fire insurance, the rate applies to each $100 of coverage. In workers compensation, the rate is applied to each $100 of the insured's payroll.

Regardless of the type of insurance, the premium income of the insurer must be sufficient to cover losses and expenses. To obtain this premium income, the insurer must predict the claims and expenses, and then allocate these anticipated costs among the various classes of policyholders. The final premium that the insured pays is called the *gross premium* and is based on a *gross rate*. The gross rate is composed of two parts, one designed to provide for the payment of losses and a second, called a *loading*, to cover the expenses of operation. That part of the rate that is intended to cover losses is called the *pure premium* when expressed in dollars and cents, and the *expected loss ratio* when expressed as a percentage.

Although some differences exist among different lines of insurance, in general, the pure premium is determined by dividing expected losses by the number of exposure units. For example, if 100,000 automobiles generate $30 million in losses, the pure premium is $300:

$$\frac{\text{Losses}}{\text{Exposure units}} = \frac{\$30{,}000{,}000}{100{,}000} = \$300$$

The process of converting the pure premium into a gross rate requires addition of the loading, which is intended to cover the expenses that will be required in the production and servicing of the insurance. The determination of these expenses is primarily a matter of cost accounting. The various classes of expenses for which provision must be made normally include commissions and other acquisition costs, general administrative expense, premium taxes, and an allowance for profit and contingencies. In converting the pure premium into a gross rate, these expenses are usually treated as a percentage of the final rate, on the assumption that they will increase proportionately with premiums. Because most of the expenses do actually vary with premiums, the assumption is reasonably realistic.

The final gross rate is derived by dividing the pure premium by a *permissible loss ratio*. The permissible loss ratio is the percentage of the premium (and so the rate) that will be available to pay losses after provision for expenses. The conversion is made by the formula

$$\text{Gross rate} = \frac{\text{Pure premium}}{1 - \text{Expense ratio}}$$

Using the $300 pure premium computed in our previous example, and assuming an expense ratio of 0.40, we see that

$$\text{Gross rate} = \frac{\$300}{1 - 0.40} = \frac{\$300}{0.60} = \$500$$

Although the pure premium varies with the loss experience for the particular line of insurance, the expense ratio also varies from one line to another, depending on the commissions and the other expenses involved.

Advisory Organizations

As we have seen, the accuracy of an insurer's predictions increases with the number of exposures on which they are based. In the property and liability field, insurers pool loss statistics to increase the accuracy of the rate-making process. By pooling their loss statistics, insurers support *advisory organizations* (also called *rating bureaus*) that use these statistics as the raw material for computing trended loss costs (i.e., pure premiums). Some larger insurers maintain their own loss statistics and compute their own loss costs.[1] In either case, the insurer then adds a loading, which reflects its unique expenses, to the loss costs to derive a final rate. Some of the more important advisory organizations are the following:

1. *The Insurance Services Office (ISO)*: The Insurance Services Office provides a wide range of advisory, rating, and actuarial services relating to property and casualty insurance, including the development of policy forms, loss information, and related services for multiple-line coverage. It computes and publishes trended loss data for most property and liability insurance lines other than workers compensation. The ISO was originally owned and controlled by insurance companies. In 1994, ISO members approved a new structure in which the organization's board consists of seven noninsurers and four industry representatives.

2. *The American Association of Insurance Services (AAIS)*: The American Association of Insurance Services performs approximately the same functions for its subscribers as does the ISO.

3. *The National Council on Compensation Insurance*: The National Council on Compensation Insurance develops and administers rating plans and systems for workers compensation insurance.

At one time, rating bureaus used the loss statistics reported by their members to compute advisory rates, which the bureaus then filed with state insurance departments on behalf of their members. Nonbureau companies either maintained their own loss statistics and filed their rates independently, or used the bureau rate as a point of departure, modifying it to reflect their own experience and expenses. Because insurers that used rates filed by bureaus charged the same rates for coverage, during the 1980s industry critics argued that the activities of rating bureaus constituted a form of price-fixing and that these activities permitted the industry to operate as a cartel. Although it may be argued that the system of advisory rates did not prevent the industry from operating in a highly competitive manner, major rating bureaus responded to the criticism in 1989 when they decided to discontinue filing advisory rates on behalf of their members.[2] In 1989, the ISO announced its decision to stop providing advisory rates to its members. Instead, it now provides insurers with trended loss costs only. Insurers develop and add their own factors for expenses, profits, and contingencies. In 1990, the National Council of Compensation Insurance and the Surety Association of America announced that they would follow the same practice.[3]

---

[1] The rate-making function in a life insurance company is performed by the actuarial department or, in smaller companies, by an actuarial consulting firm.

[2] The accusation that advisory rates constituted a system of price-fixing ignores the fact that insurers were free to participate in bureaus or file their rates independently, thereby precluding the price-fixing and market-sharing activities of a cartel. In fact, a significant portion of the market is controlled by nonbureau companies, which develop their own rates and price their products individually.

[3] There are no rating bureaus in the life insurance field. However, the Society of Actuaries, a voluntary association of actuaries, holds periodic meetings for the exchange of information with the goal of improving premium determination.

Adjusting the Level of Rates

When rates are initially established for any form of insurance, the rate is by definition an arbitrary estimate of what losses are likely to be. Once policies have been written and the loss experience on the policies emerges, the statistical data generated become a basis for adjusting the level of rates. Past losses are used as a basis for projecting future losses, and the anticipated losses are combined with estimated expenses to arrive at the final premium.

Any change in rate levels indicated by raw data is usually tempered by a credibility factor, which reflects the degree of confidence the ratemakers believe they should attach to past losses as predictors of future losses. The credibility assigned to a particular body of loss experience is determined primarily by the number of occurrences, following the statistical principle that the greater the sample size, the more closely will observed results approximate the underlying probability. To obtain a sufficiently large number of observed losses for achieving an acceptable level of credibility, the ratemaker must sometimes include loss experience over a period of several years. The less frequent the losses in a particular line of insurance, the longer the period needed to accumulate loss statistics necessary to achieve a given level of credibility.

One of the principal drawbacks of a long experience period is that when the interval is too long, the underlying conditions that influence frequency and severity are likely to have changed, and adjustments reflecting such changes must be included in the rate-making process. One approach is to weight the experience of the most recent years more heavily than that of the earlier years. Another technique is the use of trend factors. A *trend factor* is a multiplier calculated from the trend in average claim payments, the trend of a price index, or some similar series of data. The trend indicated by past experience is usually extended into the future to the midpoint of the period for which the rates will be used.

TYPES OF RATES

The approach to setting rates is quite similar in most instances, but two different types of rates can be distinguished: class and individual.

Class Rates

The term *class rating* refers to the practice of computing a price per unit of insurance that applies to all applicants possessing a given set of characteristics. For example, a class rate might apply to all types of dwelling of a given kind of construction in a specific city. Rates that apply to all individuals of a given age and sex are also examples of class rates.

The class-rating system permits the insurer to apply a single rate to a large number of insureds, simplifying the process of determining their premiums. In establishing the classes to which class rates apply, the ratemaker must compromise between a large class, which will include a greater number of exposures and thereby increase the credibility of predictions, and one sufficiently narrow to permit homogeneity. For example, a rate class could be established for all drivers, with one rate applicable regardless of the age, sex, or marital status of the driver or the use of the automobile. However, such a class would include exposures with widely varying loss potential. For this reason, numerous classes are established, with different rates for drivers based on factors such as those listed. Class rating is the most common approach in use by the industry today and is used in life insurance and most property and liability fields.

Individual Rates

In some instances, the characteristics of the units to be insured vary so widely that it is deemed desirable to depart from the class approach and calculate rates on a basis that attempts to measure more precisely the loss-producing characteristics of the individual. The four basic individual rating approaches are judgment, schedule, experience, and retrospective ratings.

Judgment Rating   In some lines of insurance, the rate is determined for each individual risk on a judgment basis. Here the processes of underwriting and rate-making merge, and the underwriter decides whether or not the exposure is to be accepted and at what rate. *Judgment rating* is used when credible statistics are lacking or when the exposure units are so varied that it is impossible to construct a class. This technique is most frequently applied in the ocean marine field, although it is also used in other lines of insurance.

Schedule Rating   *Schedule rating*, as its name implies, makes rates by applying a schedule of charges and credits to some base rate to determine the appropriate rate for an individual exposure unit. In commercial fire insurance, for example, the rates for many buildings are determined by adding debits and subtracting credits from a base rate, which represents a standard building. The debits and credits represent those features of the particular building's construction, occupancy, fire protection, and neighborhood that deviate from this standard. Through the application of these debits and credits, the physical characteristics of each schedule-rated building determine that building's rate.[4]

Experience Rating   In *experience rating*, the insured's own past loss experience enters into the determination of the final premium. Experience rating is superimposed on a class-rating system and adjusts the insured's premium upward or downward, depending on the extent to which his or her experience has deviated from the average experience of the class. It is most frequently used in the fields of workers compensation, general liability, and group life and health insurance. Generally, experience rating is used only when the insured generates a premium large enough to be considered statistically credible.

Although the exact method of adjusting the premium to reflect experience varies with the type of insurance, the general approach is usually the same. The insured's

---

[4]Schedule rating is used less frequently today than in the past. In 1976, the Insurance Services Office introduced a new class-rating program for many types of commercial buildings that had previously been schedule-rated, leaving only the larger and more complex buildings to be schedule-rated.

losses during the experience period are compared with the expected losses for the class, and the indicated percentage difference, modified by a credibility factor, becomes a debit or credit to the class-rated premium. The experience period is usually three years, and the insured's loss ratio is computed on the basis of a three-year average. The credibility factor, which reflects the degree of confidence the ratemaker assigns to the insured's past experience as an indicator of future experience, varies with the number of losses observed during the experience period.

The experience-rating formula used in general liability insurance illustrates the principal. The formula is:

$$\text{Modification} = \frac{\text{Actual Loss Ratio} - \text{Expected Loss Ratio}}{\text{Expected Loss Ratio}} \times \text{Credibility}$$

Assuming, for the purpose of illustration, that the expected loss ratio is 60 percent and that the insured has achieved a 20 percent loss ratio, and further that the credibility factor is 0.20, the computation would be:

$$\frac{0.30 - 0.60}{0.60} = 0.50 \times 0.20 = 10\%$$

The comparison of the actual loss ratio and the expected loss ratio indicates a 50 percent reduction in premium. However, the indicated reduction is tempered by the credibility factor, resulting in a 10 percent credit.

In most instances, the use of experience rating is mandatory for those insureds whose premiums exceed a specified amount.

Retrospective Rating   A *retrospective-rating* plan is a self-rated program under which the actual losses during the policy period determine the final premium for the coverage, subject to a maximum and a minimum. A deposit premium is charged at the inception of the policy and then adjusted after the policy period has expired, to reflect actual losses incurred.[5] In a sense, a "retro" plan is like a cost-plus contract, the major difference being that it is subject to a maximum and a minimum. The formula under which the final premium is computed includes a fixed charge for the insurance element in the plan (the fact that the premium is subject to a maximum), the actual losses incurred, a charge for loss adjustment, and a loading for the state premium tax. Retrospective rating is used in the field of workers compensation, general liability, automobile, and group health insurance. However, only very large insureds will usually elect these plans.

Underwriting ■

Underwriting is the process of selecting and classifying exposures. It is directly related to the rate-making or pricing function of an insurer, because computed rates contemplate some composition of loss-producing characteristics to which they will be applied. As we noted in Chapter 10, the future experience of the group to

[5]Retrospective rating is discussed in greater detail in Chapter 14.

which the rates are applied will approximate that of the group on which those rates are based only if both have approximately the same loss-producing characteristics. There must be the same proportion of good and bad risks in the group insured as there were in the one from which the basic statistics were taken. The tendency of the poorer-than-average risks to seek insurance to a greater extent than do the average or better-than-average risks must be blocked. The underwriter's main responsibility is to guard against adverse selection. The need for underwriting stems from the fact that the individual or organization to whom an insurance policy is sold is, in a sense, the "product" that the insurer sells. The product is the insurer's promise of indemnity, and the scope of this promise is defined by the combination of hazards and loss-producing characteristics that the individual or organization brings to the insured group. This means that an insurer selling the same policy to different individuals or different firms may be selling dramatically different products.

The goal of underwriting is not the selection of risks that will not have losses. Rather, it is to avoid a disproportionate number of bad risks, thereby equalizing the actual losses with the expected ones. In addition to this goal, there are certain other objectives. While attempting to avoid adverse selection through rejection of undesirable risks, the underwriter must secure an adequate volume of exposures in each class. In addition, he or she must guard against congestion or concentration of exposures that might result in a catastrophe.

The underwriting process often involves more than acceptance or rejection. In some instances, an exposure that is unacceptable at one rate may be written at a different rate. It may be possible to make an otherwise unacceptable applicant acceptable by reducing or removing hazards. Insurer loss-prevention personnel frequently work with applicants who would otherwise be unacceptable to reduce hazards through loss-prevention and control measures. In some cases too, an applicant that is not acceptable under one rating plan might be acceptable under a different rating approach. Under a retrospectively rated program, for example, the insurer has the opportunity to adjust the cost of the insurance after the policy period is over, based on actual losses during the policy period.

UNDERWRITING POLICY

Underwriting begins with the formulation of the company's underwriting policy, which is generally established by the officers in charge of underwriting. The underwriting policy establishes the framework within which underwriting decisions are made. This policy specifies the lines of insurance that will be written as well as prohibited exposures, the amount of coverage to be permitted on various types of exposure, the areas of the country in which each line will be written, and similar restrictions. The desk underwriter, as the individual who applies the underwriting rules and guidelines is called, is usually not involved in forming the company underwriting policy.

THE UNDERWRITING PROCESS

When an insurer considers providing coverage for any applicant, it gathers as much information about the dangers and exposures associated with the applicant as possible within the limitations imposed by time and the cost of obtaining additional data. The desk underwriter must rule on the exposures submitted by the agents, accepting some and rejecting others that do not meet the company's underwriting requirements. When a risk is rejected, it is because the underwriter feels that the hazards connected with it are excessive in relation to the rate. Several sources of information are available to the underwriter regarding the hazards of a commercial applicant for property and liability insurance.

1. Application containing the insured's statements
2. Information from the agent or broker
3. Past loss experience
4. Physical inspections

Application

The basic source of underwriting information is the application, which varies for each line of insurance and for each type of coverage. The broader and more liberal the contract, usually the more detailed the information required in the application. The questions on the application are designed to give the underwriter the information needed to decide whether he or she will accept the exposure, reject it, or seek additional information.

Information from the Agent or Broker

In some lines of insurance, particularly personal lines, the agent may exercise underwriting authority. Even in the commercial lines field, agents are expected to exercise underwriting judgment. Indeed, part of the compensation of property and liability insurance agents is based on the profitability of the business they write. This is accomplished through a device known as a *contingency contract* or *profit-sharing contract*, the terms of which provide the agent with an additional commission at the end of the year if the business he or she has submitted has produced a profit for the company. The intent of these profit-sharing agreements is to encourage the agent to underwrite in his or her office.[6]

Regardless of the agent's underwriting authority, the agent or broker is a prime source of information in the underwriting process. In many cases, the underwriter places much weight on the recommendations of the agent or broker. This varies, of course, with the underwriter's experience with the particular agent in question. In certain cases, the underwriter will agree to accept an exposure that does not meet the underwriting requirement of the company. Such exposures are referred to as *accommodation risks*, because they are accepted to accommodate a valued client or agent.

---

[6]The use of the term *underwriter* in reference to an agent is more common in the field of life insurance than in property and liability, which is surprising in view of the fact that the agent plays a far more important role in the underwriting process in the latter type of insurance.

Information on Past Loss Experience

Based on the premise that the record of past losses is a good indicator of future experience, the underwriter will also want information on an applicant's past loss experience. In the case of workers compensation and other casualty lines, this information is often obtained from a rating bureau that computes the firm's experience modifier. In addition, the applicant will obtain detailed loss information from former insurers and provide it to the prospective insurer.

Physical Examinations or Inspections

In addition, safety and loss-prevention specialists from the insurer will usually inspect the applicant's premises. Although such inspections are not always conducted, the practice is increasing. In some instances, this inspection is performed by the agent, who sends a report to the company with photographs of the property. In other cases, a company representative conducts the inspection. The purpose of the inspection is to confirm the facts indicated in the application or those provided by the agent, and also to detect hazards that are not revealed by these sources of information.

THE UNDERWRITING DECISION

The insurer's investigation determines whether or not the exposure that is offered to the insurer meets the requirements of an insurable risk and whether the hazards the applicant brings to the pool of insureds is commensurate with the premium that can be charged. In some cases, the investigation helps to determine the price at which the coverage will be provided. Although the underwriting begins with a rate based on loss costs and a loading, this rate is sometimes adjusted to meet competition.

Insurers establish underwriting policies to guide desk underwriters in their decisions. The desk underwriters are evaluated based on their compliance with the company's underwriting policy. From a practical point of view, the underwriter has little to gain by *taking a chance* on the applicant that does not fit the insurer's profile of an acceptable risk. Fortunately for buyers, insurers differ in their underwriting philosophy, and an applicant that may be unacceptable to one insurer may be acceptable to a different insurer.

POSTSELECTION UNDERWRITING

In some lines of insurance, the insurer has the opportunity periodically to reevaluate its insured. When the coverage in question is cancelable or optionally renewable,[7] the underwriting process may include *postselection* (or renewal) *underwriting* in which the insurer decides whether the insurance should be continued. When a review of the experience with a particular policy or account indicates that the losses have been

---

[7]Cancellation is the process of terminating coverage prior to the normal expiration date.

excessive, the underwriter may insist on an increased deductible at renewal. In other instances, the underwriter may decide that the coverage should not be continued and will decline to renew it, or even cancel it outright. Insurance companies differ in the extent to which they exercise their renewal underwriting options.

In addition to the fact that postselection underwriting is obviously possible only with policies that may be canceled or in which renewal is optional with the insurer, the ability of insurers to engage in postselection underwriting is considerably less in some lines today than in the past. Because cancellation or the refusal of the insurer to renew some forms of insurance can work an undue hardship on the insured, many states have enacted statutes or have imposed regulations that restrict the insurer's right to exercise these options. Some laws merely require the insurer to give advance notice of its intent to refuse renewal. These laws were designed to prevent an insurer from canceling or from refusing to renew without providing adequate time for the insured to obtain replacement coverage.[8]

Although the restrictions on the right of insurers to cancel or refuse to renew have been beneficial in many areas, they have also made it harder to obtain insurance. When legislative restraints are imposed on the insurers' ability to engage in postselection underwriting, insurers typically become increasingly selective before issuing a policy in the first place.

◢◣ Competition in the Insurance Industry ■■■■■■■■■■

Competition within the insurance industry today is intense, perhaps more so than at any time in history. Briefly, this rivalry takes place in two areas: price and quality.

PRICE COMPETITION

Price competition in the property and liability insurance industry takes place among both companies and agencies. At the company level, price competition takes place between the various types of insurers. Mutual companies compete with stock companies, bureau companies compete with nonbureau companies, and companies operating through the American Agency System compete with direct writers. Although the nature of the price competition at the agency level is less well recognized, it occurs in both personal and commercial lines.

Price Competition Among Companies

Insurers compete on the basis of price by offering a lower priced product than other companies dealing in the same line of insurance. How can insurance com-

---

[8]The most severe restrictions on postselection underwriting apply to personal line insureds (as opposed to commercial or business insureds). In some cases, the laws prohibit midterm cancellation, except for certain specified reasons, once a policy has been in effect for a designated period of time, such as 60 days. In addition, the laws of many states prohibit insurers from canceling or refusing to renew coverage because of an insured's age, sex, occupation, race, or place of residence. In most cases, the laws require the insurer to furnish an explanation of the reason for cancellation or declination.

panies charge significantly different premiums for identical coverage? The price of insurance coverage, like most prices, is a function of the cost of production. The most obvious answer to the question, therefore, is that their costs must also vary significantly. The following costs are common to all insurance companies:

1. Payment of losses
2. Loss-adjustment expense
3. Production cost (sales expense)
4. Administrative expenses
5. Taxes
6. Profits or additions to surplus

If a company succeeds in reducing any of these costs below those of its competitors, it will be able to offer its coverage at a lower premium.

The first of the costs listed can be an area of considerable difference among companies. Some companies, through selective underwriting, have achieved significantly lower loss costs. It should be recognized, however, that lower premiums achieved by selective underwriting reflect a different "product." The unique nature of price competition in insurance rests on the often-neglected fact that the individual to whom an insurance policy is sold is, in a sense, the "product" that the insurer sells. It is the combination of hazards and loss-producing characteristics that the individual brings to the insured group that represents the risk transferred to the insurer. This means that two insurers selling policies to different individuals may be selling dramatically different products. If an insurer succeeds in selecting customers with lower than average probabilities of loss, it sells a product whose cost is lower and for which a lower premium may be charged.[9]

Although the point is seldom recognized, price competition based on selectivity in underwriting has a dual benefit for the competitor. If an insurer is successful in selecting insureds who represent better than average exposures (that is, whose loss experience is better than average), its loss experience will be lower. Moreover, because the better risks are thus removed from the total of exposure units, the average risk in the remaining group will be worse than previously. So when one company or a group of companies succeeds in lowering its loss payments through the selection of better risks, the loss payments of other insurers rise.

The second cost, acquisition expense, can also be altered to reflect substantial premium savings. The major part of the production costs have traditionally been agents' commissions. Some companies, especially the direct writers, have been able to reduce premium costs by reducing or eliminating agents' commissions. Even in life insurance, where the agent's commission is usually a significant cost only in the first years, lower commissions permit lower premiums.

[9]The unique nature of the insurance product, in which the individual insured is, in a sense, the product sold, serves as the foundation for a distinctive form of price competition in insurance markets. The existence of cooperative rate-making, in which competitors charge the same price, is not inconsistent with a competitive market in which insurer's costs differ. In the traditional model of competition suggested by economists, market interaction forces prices downward to the level of costs. In the field of insurance, price competition can also occur in a second way. When prices are fixed and the insurer's costs differ from those on which the bureau rate is predicated, insurers adjust their costs to the market price by altering their underwriting standards.

Administrative expense includes those expenses other than loss costs and acquisition expense that the insurer incurs in providing its product. Administrative costs tend to be relatively fixed, and their influence on the final premium varies with the insurer's efficiency. This efficiency depends on the absolute level of overhead, the quality of the insurer's workforce, and the premium volume over which fixed costs are spread.

Although taxes represent only a small percentage of the total premium, some differences in cost are traceable to the tax element. The state premium tax is levied as a percentage of the total premiums written by an insurer and is added to the individual premiums. It therefore tends to magnify the difference among companies in the other costs.

The final element, the allowance for profit and contingencies, is a residual. In the rate-setting process, it is a hoped-for return on capital. In actual practice, it is a residual that exists only to the extent that projected premiums exceed the aggregate of the projected other expenses.

The differences that can exist in the common costs of insurers help to explain both the differences and the similarities in the premiums charged by insurers. If a company is successful in reducing any of its costs below those of its competitors, it is able to offer coverage at a lower price or derive a higher profit on its operations. Insurers whose costs are excessive find it difficult to maintain an adequate market share.

Price Competition Among Agencies

In the personal lines field, the agent does not (except in extremely isolated cases) participate in setting the price of the product, and the pricing of personal lines products by its companies is a factor outside the agency's control. Price competition in personal lines insurance does, of course, take place, but this price competition is based on the price competition among the companies they represent. There are differences in price among companies and, in the selection of the company that he or she will represent, the agent has some control over the price of the personal lines contracts the agency sells. However, the selection of a company sets the price that the agent must charge at the rate established by the companies the agency represents. Agencies operating through the American Agency System represent companies that are similar in their pricing structure. In many instances, competing agencies represent the same companies, and the contracts they sell are identical in price.

Agents participate more directly in pricing commercial line coverages through a process referred to as *premium modification*. Under this process, the insurer may modify the expense component of the premium to reflect costs. Since the commission payable to the agent is an important component in the final premium, the agent can agree to a modification of the commission, thereby influencing the final premium to be charged. Premium modification dates from the 1960s. Originally, there was little room for adjustment of the filed premium, no matter how large the premium. Some agents argued that because economies of scale are involved in handling larger accounts, rating procedures should make provision for adjusting the premiums on large accounts to reflect these economies. After considerable debate, the industry and regulators agreed on the concept of *premium modification* under which the expense portion of the premium was made subject to adjustment. Originally, only premiums in excess of $10,000 were subject to premium modification. In most jurisdictions, the level at which premium modification is permissible has gradually fallen, so that the agent can negotiate the commission (and therefore participate in price-setting) on most commercial accounts. Generally, the larger the account, the greater the likelihood that a negotiated commission will influence the final premium.

PRODUCT COMPETITION

Product Competition by Insurers

Insurance companies also compete by differentiating their products at both the company and agency level. Companies offer different forms of policies, with broader insuring agreements or additional provisions that are beneficial to the insured. One aspect of this rivalry that has been beneficial to insureds (and, we might add, in some instances detrimental to the companies) has been the continuous broadening of coverage under various policy forms. New policy combinations with wider coverage features are continually introduced as insurers seek to capture additional market share. Most states allow insurers to follow bureau forms or to file their own forms independently. Those companies that make independent filings do so to distinguish their forms from those of the bureau companies, and generally include broader provisions that liberalize the coverage beyond that of the standard bureau forms. Pressure from bureau companies on the bureaus then results in the bureau forms incorporating the provisions of the independently filed forms.

Competition with respect to product also occurs in the area of service. Some insurers excel in providing loss-prevention services to their clients, offering extensive assistance in industrial safety, loss prevention, rehabilitation of injured workers, and similar services. These services are an important part of a bundle of services that represent the total insurance product purchased by corporate insureds.

Product Competition by Agencies

Agencies also compete with one another in the product they offer to their clients. In a real sense, the insurance agent does not sell only insurance; it is possible to purchase insurance without the services of an agent. If the consumer elects to purchase insurance from an agent rather than directly from a company, the cost is likely to be somewhat higher, and the additional premium that the consumer pays is compensation to the agent for the function that he or she performs: that of advising the insured. In this sense, the insurance premium is composed of two parts; one part goes to the insurance company as consideration for the protection granted, and the other part goes to the agent for the service he or she provides. Basically, this service consists of advice in selecting the proper coverage to meet the client's needs, selecting the appropriate insurance, and assisting in claim settlement at the time of a loss.

247

In the area of service, competition depends to a great extent on the technical competence of the personnel employed by the agency or brokerage firm. For this reason, the large national brokers are not considered direct competitors of small local agencies, inasmuch as the small local agency does not have the facilities to provide services required by the large national accounts that represent the target market of the national brokers. On the other hand, many larger local agencies compete effectively with the national brokers.

The insurance marketplace is characterized by numerous competitors offering products with different levels of cost and prices to consumers. Insurers have different levels of selectivity and, consequently, different levels of cost. They also have elected different distribution systems. The differing levels of selectivity in underwriting and the different distribution systems are reflected in the different prices at which insurers offer their products.

Insurance Shortages ■

As in any competitive market, periodic imbalances arise between the demand for insurance and its supply. As a consequence, there are occasional shortages of insurance, which are referred to as *availability* problems. Insurance availability problems arise in part because the absolute supply of insurance is limited by regulatory standards that dictate the relationship between premiums written and insurers' surplus.[10] Insurers, limited in the volume of insurance they can write, must therefore select from among the risks offered to them. An underwriter who must accept some risks and reject others will accept those that have the greatest likelihood of yielding a profit.

Besides of the finite supply of insurance, availability problems arise when the price at which the insurance may be sold is less than the costs that will be incurred by selling it. Even if insurers had unlimited surplus, there would still be some classes of applicants they would reject. Some lines of insurance are demonstrably unprofitable for insurers because the anticipated losses and expenses of providing the insurance exceed the premium the insurer can charge for the coverage. Usually, this occurs in markets where regulatory restrictions on insurer prices are rigid and inflexible, but it can also arise from other causes. One is simply intensive competition. Sometimes, an underwriter will conclude that the price that can be obtained for the coverage is inadequate relative to the loss potential. Given the choice between insuring exposures on which they are almost guaranteed to lose money and those on which they can reasonably expect to earn a profit, insurance companies logically choose the latter.

Finally, the cyclical nature of the insurance industry creates periodic shortages of insurance. The insurance cycle results in changes in insurers' surplus and profit. When surplus falls, the supply of insurance is reduced. The reduction in insurer

[10]This subject is discussed in Chapter 12.

profit that results from the soft phase of the cycle makes insurers more restrictive in their underwriting, further restricting availability.

THE INSURANCE CYCLE

The property and liability industry is highly cyclical, experiencing periods of underwriting profit followed by periods of losses; the insurance market is characterized as "hard" or "soft," depending on the phase of the cycle. During periods when insurers are earning underwriting profits, the market is said to be "soft," as insurers engage in price cutting to increase their market share. The price cutting includes reduction in the absolute level of rates, as well as loosening of underwriting standards. This has the natural result of generating losses, resulting in a "hard" market, during which insurers increase prices and tighten underwriting standards.

Although some observers believe that the underwriting cycle results from mismanagement within the insurance industry, this criticism ignores the fact that in a competitive market competitors do not set the market price. Competitors accept the price that is set by the interaction of market forces. The pricing decisions of insurance companies are a response to the cycle, not a cause. Insurers cut prices not because they want to, but because they are required to by the pressure of market forces. Often, these pressures stem from forces outside the industry itself.

CASH-FLOW UNDERWRITING

It has been said—only half in jest—that property and liability insurers are not so much insurance companies as investment companies that raise the necessary money for their investments by selling insurance. This observation was undoubtedly prompted by the size of the industry's investment portfolio and the importance of investment income in the overall operating profit of property and liability insurers. For the past three decades, property and liability insurers have about broken even or even lost money on underwriting, but investment income has provided an overall operating profit.

The dependence on insurance premiums as funds for investment led to a phenomenon known as *cash-flow underwriting*—the pricing practice aimed at maximizing written premium income rather than underwriting profit. In cash-flow underwriting, insurers price their products below the amount needed to cover losses and expenses to compete for premium dollars that can be invested. The rationale is that during periods of high interest rates, the investment income earned on additional premium volume will more than offset any underwriting loss that may be incurred. Insurers compete for dollars that can be invested at a higher rate than the cost of those funds. An insurer with a combined ratio of, say, 106 percent is, in effect, paying the policyholders 6 percent for the use of their money. If those funds can be invested at some rate greater than 6 percent, the leveraged investment will increase the return to stockholders. As a result, price competition in the industry tends to be driven by the returns available in financial markets where insurers invest their funds.

Access to the Insurance Market ■ ■ ■ ■ ■ ■ ■ ■ ■ ■ ■ ■ ■

The decision to transfer risks to an insurer is implemented by selecting an agent and the insurer or insurers to which the risks will be transferred. Risk managers who decide to transfer part of the organization's risks to a commercial insurer will generally access the insurance market through an insurance agent or broker. There are two reasons, one legal and the other practical. First, most states require that insurance be placed through a licensed agent or broker, and unless the organization owns a captive agency, the risk manager must deal through an intermediary. Even if this requirement did not exist, however, risk managers would still access insurers through agents or brokers for a practical reason: to access the market knowledge of the agency or brokerage firm. Even though the placement of the insurance program occurs with regularity, the risk manager's contact with the insurance market is limited to the placement of the risks of his or her organization. Insurance agencies and brokers, in contrast, deal with many clients and are in constant contact with insurers in placing the business they write.

Placing an insurance program involves significantly more than simply finding an insurer that is willing to write an account. Insurers differ in their attitudes toward different classes of business, and a class that might be unacceptable to one insurer will be appealing to another. Individual insurers have their own strengths and weaknesses. Underwriters, too, have preferences, developed from long years of underwriting. What may be an appealing class of business to one insurer or one underwriter may be distasteful to a different insurer or underwriter. One of the agent's or broker's principal functions is to select from the hundreds of insurers in the market the limited number that are most suitable for the particular combination of risks that is to be transferred.

SELECTING AN AGENT OR BROKER

It is easy to inventory the desirable characteristics of an agent or broker; it is more difficult to guarantee that the agent or broker selected will have these characteristics.

Desirable Characteristics

The most important qualities an agency or brokerage firm can offer a prospective buyer are a competent staff and access to insurance markets. In general, the selection of an agent or broker should focus on whether the firm can provide these qualities.

In many cases, the selection is made on the basis of the agency's reputation. People in the same industry often share information, especially with regard to the services they receive from the agent or broker. Although the agency's general reputation is a starting point, the prudent buyer will investigate the agent's or broker's qualifications before making a commitment. In this connection, one logical step is to ask for references. Once the agency has provided the names of satisfied customers, the buyer can make inquiry of those clients regarding the service they have received from the agency.

The agency or broker's principal service is technical competence and advice on, among other things, the design of the insurance program (coverage), on possible economies that can reduce the cost of insurance (costs), and on insurance markets (companies). Finally, the agency may also provide assistance at the time of a claim (claims). Given the importance of the agent's or broker's technical competence and knowledge to the buyer, many buyers focus on the agency staff's education and training. Advanced education beyond the college level is an indication of continuing professional interest in the subject of risk management. Earning such professional designations as Chartered Property Casualty Underwriter (CPCU), Chartered Life Underwriter (CLU), and Associate in Risk Management (ARM), for example, requires the passing of rigorous examinations in diverse subject matters.

Another indicator of the agency's technical competence is the type of accounts the agency currently handles. Information on the number of accounts of similar size and complexity is important. An agency with a large number of large accounts is more likely to have the technical expertise, market channels, and ancillary services that are required to provide the level of service required.

Still another consideration is the agency staff's familiarity with the buyer's particular industry. Insurance needs differ significantly from industry to industry, and a firm in a particular industry is better served by an agency that has a number of other clients from that same industry. One learns how to program coverage for specialized exposures by programming coverage for specialized exposures. Although some transferability of techniques and solutions takes place from one industry to another, certain exposures are unique to specific industries. An agency whose personnel are experienced in a given industry is likely to provide better service than an agency that is unfamiliar with the industry. In addition, it is more likely to have access to insurers that are interested in and proficient at writing accounts in the industry.

Agency staff may be considered at two levels. The agency contact with the account—usually called an *account executive*—is usually the initial contact; this is the person who solicits the account. In some agencies, this individual is also the principal servicing contact after the account is sold; in other agencies, the account may be serviced by support personnel. For this reason, the size and qualifications of the staff that support the account executives are matters of critical concern. Many agencies operate on a team approach basis, with customer service representatives, account placement specialists (insurance buyers), and claims personnel, who operate together in servicing the account. Virtually all agencies provide some level of claim service, but the level of expertise (and the types of claims the agency is equipped to handle) will differ. In addition, some larger agencies employ their own engineering and loss-prevention personnel.

The Selection Process

Usually, relationships between buyers and agents or brokers develop over a long period of time and continue uninterrupted as long as both parties are satisfied with the arrangement. Occasionally, an agency will become dissatisfied and will then look for another broker. Occasionally, too, a firm will solicit formal bids for its insurance program, inviting a select group of agents and brokers to bid. Although some buyers find this procedure satisfactory, most authorities suggest that the selection of the agent or broker is sufficiently important to warrant separate consideration.

One approach to selecting an agent or broker is a "beauty contest," in which a number of agencies and brokers are invited to make proposals to the organization to handle the insurance program. In some instances, the brokers are asked to submit an insurance program. In other cases, the focus is on selecting the intermediary, and the structure of the program is addressed separately, after the agent or broker has been selected.

The pool of bidders can be selected on the basis of reputation, geographical location, size (income or the number of professional employees), or some other criterion. The selected bidders are asked to present written proposals outlining the services the agency or broker is prepared to offer. After the written proposals are received and reviewed by the risk manager and other top executives of the corporation, the eligible brokerage firms are asked to make an oral presentation. The selection is based on these presentations.

Compensating the Agent or Broker

Traditionally, virtually all compensation to agents and brokers was in the form of the commission payable by the insurer. This was logical, for the agent or broker was viewed primarily as a salesperson for the insurer and like other sales personnel was compensated on the basis of performance. The higher the agent's production, the higher his or her compensation. Because insurance rates were rigidly regulated in most states, there was little room for negotiation and the commission system remained intact.[11]

In the early 1960s, a debate developed over the logic of the commission compensation system. The debate focused primarily on the commercial lines field and the level of commissions on commercial lines policies. Insurance buyers argued that the commission system of compensating the agent or broker was a flawed system for several reasons.

First, under the commission system, the agent's compensation varies with the insured's hazard, not with the amount of work the agency is required to perform. Thus agents were compensated more highly for placing and servicing a frame structure than a fire-resistive one, and the commission on a workers compensation policy for steel workers was higher than the commission on a workers compensation policy for say, clerical operations. In addition, it was argued, a policy with a $100,000

---

[11]The amount of this commission can vary widely, depending on the line of insurance and the size of the premium. In most property and liability lines, it lies between 10 and 15 percent but may be significantly less, depending on the premium. In workers compensation, for example, the commission on very large premiums may be as low as 3 or 4 percent.

premium did not require 10 times as much work by the agency as 10 policies with $10,000 premiums or 100 policies with a premium of $1000 each. Eventually, dissatisfaction with the commission system and changes in the rate regulation system led, first, to a system of negotiated commissions, and then to a fee system for some larger accounts. Today, negotiated commissions on commercial lines accounts are prevalent. Although fixed commissions remain the rule on smaller accounts, for larger accounts fixed commissions are the exception rather than the rule. In the case of very large accounts, the insurer may quote the insurance on a net basis, without making allowance for the agent's commission. The agent then negotiates directly with the client, usually for a fixed annual fee for handling the account.

As might be expected, the subject of fees versus a commission system for compensating the agent or broker is an emotional one. Those who favor the fee system argue that the agent, as a professional, should be compensated as a professional. Others prefer the commission system because this is the traditional system, and some agents are apprehensive about what would happen to their income if the system changed. Although cynics argue that commission income is usually higher than the fees an agent might charge, this is not always the case.

The most logical criticism of the commission system is that it has a perverse effect with respect to those agents who help their clients implement risk management strategies. Under the commission system, an agent who is successful in assisting a client in reducing insurance costs—that is, an agent who does a good job and performs a valuable service for the client—suffers a reduction in income. In fact, under the commission system, the better job the agent does in helping the client reduce insurance costs, the lower will be his or her compensation. For this reason, the use of fees as a method of compensating agents and brokers on larger accounts is expected to increase.

THE NONADMITTED (EXCESS AND SURPLUS LINES) MARKET

Under certain specified conditions defined by state insurance laws, nonadmitted insurers are permitted to write insurance in a state in which they are not licensed. When a buyer is faced with the need for a coverage that is not available from an admitted insurer, such coverage may be placed in the nonadmitted market, also called the *excess and surplus lines market*.[12] The laws vary from state to state, but usually the coverage may be placed only with nonadmitted insurers that have been approved by the state regulatory authority or that have not been "black-listed" by the state insurance department. In addition, all states with surplus lines laws require the payment of a tax that varies from two percent to six percent. The tax is normally the same for an admitted insurer, although in some states it is higher.

[12]While the terms *surplus lines* and *excess lines* are often used interchangeably with the term *nonadmitted market*, these terms have a somewhat narrower meaning. Originally, the term *surplus line* meant part of a line of fire coverage needed by an insured which exceeded the capacity of the admitted market. When those companies that were licensed to do business in the state had written all of the coverage that they were willing to write, the "surplus" was placed in the nonadmitted market, and since it was a surplus, it was referred to as a *surplus line*. The term *excess line* originally meant placement with a nonadmitted insurer of a layer of casualty insurance in excess of that written by an admitted insurer. As these terms are now used, they generally refer to any coverages that admitted insurers are unwilling to write.

State excess and surplus lines (E&S) laws make the agent who places insurance in the nonadmitted market responsible for remitting the premium tax to the state. The premium tax must be collected from the insured and paid to the Insurance Division annually along with an annual report, indicating the total amount of all business written in the nonadmitted market.

Structure of the Nonadmitted Market

The nonadmitted market includes three types of insurers that are not licensed to do business in the state. The first class consists of insurers domiciled outside the United States that operate on a nonadmitted basis in most states. These include Lloyds and other London companies plus insurers domiciled in such jurisdictions as Bermuda, Germany, Ireland, Sweden, and Switzerland. The second class of nonadmitted insurers includes insurers domiciled in the United States but unlicensed in all states where they operate. Some of these were formed specifically for the purpose of writing surplus line business, while others are captives that were organized to write insurance for their parent corporation, but that have expanded to include insuring unaffiliated entities. Finally, there are some domestic insurers that operate on an admitted basis in most states, but that operate on a nonadmitted basis in other states.

Reasons for Use of the Excess & Surplus Lines Market

Originally, the E&S market was developed to accommodate the insurance needs of buyers that exceeded the capacity of admitted insurers. Today, it serves as a source of coverage for all types of insurance that is not available through the admitted market. This naturally raises the question of why nonadmitted insurers are willing to write those coverages that admitted insurers decline. The answer is that non-admitted insurers are not bound by the same regulatory restraints in pricing or form as are admitted insurers.

Business is sometimes placed in the nonadmitted market because of a perceived inadequacy in filed and approved rates. The rates for coverage in the nonadmitted market are usually higher than the rates in the admitted market. Although an approved rate in the admitted market may be lower than the rate charged by a nonadmitted insurer, the difference is meaningless if an admitted insurer will not write the coverage at the approved rate. When insureds cannot obtain needed coverage from admitted insurers at approved rates, they may turn to the nonadmitted market where rates are higher.

Consent-To-Rate Laws

Any discussion of the nonadmitted market would be incomplete without at least a brief mention *consent-to-rate laws.* One of the reasons why nonadmitted insurers are sometimes willing to write insurance that admitted insurers will not write is an imbalance between the hazard for the risk and the rate that the admitted insurer can charge under approved rate filings. In an effort to create equity in the treatment of admitted and nonadmitted insurers, many states have enacted laws that allow an admitted insurer to charge a higher rate than the filed rate at the request of the insured. It would be unfair to deny an admitted insurer the opportunity to write a coverage because the rate is inadequate, and then allow a nonadmitted insurer to write the coverage at an adequate rate. The consent-to-rate provision of the insurance laws addresses this inequity.

Access to the Nonadmitted Market

The nonadmitted market can be approached in several ways. First, an insured can go directly to a London broker or to a nonadmitted insurer and buy coverage. This is possible because the state regulates only insurance sellers, not insurance buyers. An insurance buyer may choose to purchase insurance from any source. However, if the buyer bypasses the state regulatory system, he or she cannot turn to the state for assistance in the event of a dispute with the insurer.

Normally, an insurance buyer accesses the excess and surplus market through an agent that is specifically licensed to place business in the E&S market. If the insured's own agent is not licensed for nonadmitted placement, the agent will place the coverage through a managing general agent (MGA) or an E&S agent who is licensed for the excess and surplus lines market and who is located in the state. Most nonadmitted insurers prefer to deal through MGAs and E&S agents who have the technical expertise to serve as insurance wholesalers. In addition, most agents have found that a knowledgeable broker who is familiar with the surplus lines field can provide valuable assistance in placing the coverage.[13]

SELECTING THE INSURER

The insured may receive assistance from the agent in selecting an insurer if the agent represents several companies. However, in the case of most life insurance agents and certain property and liability agents who represent only one company, the selection of the agent will automatically include the selection of the company. In choosing a company, the major consideration should be its financial stability. In addition, certain aspects of the company's operation, such as its attitude toward claims and cancellation of policyholders' protection, are important. Finally, cost is a consideration.

Financial Strength

Analysis of an insurance company's financial strength follows the same principles used in the financial analysis of any corporation. However, industry accounting practices require certain modifications, making the evaluation of an insurer's financial stability a somewhat more complicated procedure (see Chapter 12). For this reason, the layperson should probably consult an evaluation service rather than attempt the analysis alone. Data on the financial stability of insurance companies are available from several sources that specialize in providing information on the companies' financial strength, the efficiency of their operation, and the caliber of management.

---

[13]The vast majority of MGAs are highly knowledgeable about the excess market and specialty coverages. In some instances, however, these intermediaries have placed business in nonadmitted insurers which subsequently became insolvent. Because the MGA plays a key role in the E&S market, the NAIC has recently focused attention on inadequacies in this area.

For many years, the principal rating agency for both property and liability insurers and life insurers was Alfred M. Best Company. Recently, however, three firms that traditionally specialized in rating debt issues and preferred stocks have entered the insurance rating field. They are Standard and Poor's Corporation, Moody's Investors Service, Inc., and Duff & Phelps/MCM Investment Research Company. Yet another recent entry into the insurer rating field is Weiss Ratings, Inc. Each of the rating services uses a slightly different classification system, and the categories have slightly different designations. All rating services, however, distinguish between insurers whose financial condition is deemed adequate and those insurers classified as vulnerable or weak. The ratings and the descriptions assigned by the rating agency to the various classes are summarized in Table 11.1.

Standard and Poor's, Moody's, and Duff & Phelps rate a far smaller number of companies than does Best's, and it is possible that a particular company in which a prospect is interested will not have been rated by these firms. A. M. Best, in contrast, assigns ratings to the vast majority of insurers and gives a "not rated" classification to those insurers that are not rated.[14]

Best's publishes separate reference guides for insurers in the property and liability and life insurance fields. In the property and liability field, *Best's Insurance Reports: Property-Liability* is a comprehensive analysis of virtually all property and liability insurers.[15] *Best's Key Rating Guide: Property-Liability*, though a smaller and less comprehensive book, offers sufficient information to assist in selecting a company in most cases.[16] Both books include Best's ratings for all companies listed. Two ratings are assigned to each company: a General Policyholders' Rating and a Financial Size Rating; of these, the General Policyholders' Rating is the more important.[17] The General Policyholders' Rating is based on an analysis of (1) underwriting results, (2) economy of management, (3) adequacy of reserves for undischarged liabilities, (4) adequacy of policyholders' surplus to absorb shocks, and (5) soundness of investments. Based on an analysis of these factors, the company is assigned 1 of 15 policyholders' ratings indicated in Table 11.1. The majority of property and liability companies are in the top four classifications.[18]

---

[14]In addition to the standard letter ratings listed in Table 11.1, which apply to approximately 70 percent of the insurers reviewed by Best's, about 30 percent of the companies are not rated, but are assigned to one of nine "Not Assigned" categories: NA-1 (Special Data Filing), NA-2 (Less Than Minimum Size), NA-3 (Insufficient Operating Experience), NA-4 (Rating Procedure Inapplicable), NA-5 (Significant Change), NA-6 (Reinsured by Unrated Reinsurer), NA-8 (Incomplete Financial Information), NA-9 (Company Request), and NA-11 (Rating Suspended).

[15]*Best's Insurance Reports: Property-Liability* (Morristown, NJ: A.M. Best Co., annual).

[16]*Best's Key Rating Guide: Property-Liability* (Morristown, NJ: A.M. Best Co., annual).

[17]The Financial Size Rating indicates Best's estimate of the safety factor of each company and is based solely on the insurer's financial resources as indicated by the sum of net worth, conditional reserves, and the redundancy in liabilities. To avoid confusion with Best's "Policyholders' Ratings," the financial ratings for property and liability insurers are represented by roman numerals, ranging from I for property and liability companies with $1 million or less in adjusted surplus to XV for companies with $2 billion or more in adjusted surplus.

[18]In 1994, 55.7 percent of property and liability companies were assigned to the first four categories (A++ through A–).

TABLE 11.1 Rating Categories Used by Insurer Rating Agencies

A. M. Best		Duff & Phelps		Moody's		Standard & Poor[a]		Weiss	
A++	Superior	AAA	Highest	Aaa	Exceptional	AAA, AAAq	Superior	A+	Excellent
A+	Superior	AA+	Very high	Aa1	Excellent	AA+	Excellent	A	Excellent
A	Excellent	AA	Very high	Aa2	Excellent	AA, AAq	Excellent	A−	Excellent
A−	Excellent	AA−	Very high	Aa3	Excellent	AA−	Excellent	B+	Good
B++	Very good	A+	High	A1	Good	A+	Good	B	Good
B+	Very good	A	High	A2	Good	A, Aq	Good	B−	Good
B	Adequate	A−	High	A3	Good	A−	Good	C+	Fair
B−	Adequate	BBB+	Adequate	Baa1	Adequate	BBB+	Adequate	C	Fair
C++	Fair	BBB	Adequate	Baa2	Adequate	BBB, BBBq	Adequate	C−	Fair
C+	Fair	BBB−	Adequate	Baa3	Adequate	BBB−	Adequate	D+	Weak
C	Marginal	BB+	Uncertain	Ba1	Questionable	BB+	May be adequate	D	Weak
C−	Marginal	BB	Uncertain	Ba2	Questionable	BB, BBq	May be adequate	D−	Weak
D	Very vulnerable	BB−	Uncertain	Ba3	Questionable	BB−	May be adequate	E+	Very weak
E	State supervision	B+	Risk	B1	Poor	B+	Vulnerable	E	Very weak
F	In liquidation	B	Risk	B2	Poor	B, Bq	Vulnerable	E−	Very weak
		B−	Risk	B3	Poor	B−	Vulnerable	F	Failed
		CCC	Substantial risk	Caa	Very poor	CCC, CCCq	Extremely vulnerable	U	Unrated
		DD	In liquidation	Ca	Extremely poor	R	Regulatory action		
				C	Lowest				

[a]Standard and Poor publishes two ratings. The first rating indicated above is the *claims-paying ability rating*, which is computed at the insurer's request and is based on public and nonpublic data provided by the insurer. The second is a *quantitative rating* (indicated by a q in the rating), which is computed solely from public data.

In the field of life insurance, Best's publishes *Best's Life Reports*, which provides detailed financial and historical data on most life insurers.[19] Life insurers are rated on the same basis (i.e., the same 15 classes from A++ to F) as property and liability insurers. Less than a third of the life insurers that are rated are assigned ratings in the four highest categories.[20] The "Not Assigned" ratings for life insurers are the same as for property and liability insurers. As in the case of property and liability insurers, both a Policyholders' Rating and a Financial Size Rating is assigned to life insurers.[21]

When properly used, the ratings assigned by A. M. Best and Company and the other rating services can be effective tools for avoiding delinquent insurance companies. In utilizing the ratings for both property and liability insurers and life insurers, the ratings should be checked for a period of years. If there has been a downward trend in the rating, further investigation into the cause of the change is warranted. For many years, the suggested standard was an A+ rating from A. M. Best and Company for a period of at least six years.[22] A current authority recommends that one should select a life insurance company that has very high ratings from at least two of the four rating firms other than Best. This seems to be a reasonable standard for property and liability insurers as well.[23]

When comparing the ratings assigned by different rating services, the description of the rating assigned by each service should be reviewed. Although all the agencies divide insurers into approximately the same number of rating categories, the financial strength assigned to the categories varies, and insurers ranked in the top six categories by one service may represent a different evaluation than ranking in the top six categories of another service. Table 11.1 indicates the descriptions assigned to the categories by the rating agencies and the dividing line each service uses in distinguishing strong companies from weaker companies.

COMPETITIVE PRICE QUOTATIONS

Usually, the agent or broker who handles an account will shop the market and obtain quotes from insurers the agency represents. Occasionally, however, an insurance buyer wants to seek competitive bids more widely, either for a particular line of insurance or for its entire account.

The issue of requesting bids for insurance is complex. Obtaining bids is a reasonable way of fostering price competition among insurance agencies, but attempting to obtain bids whenever a policy comes up for renewal is impractical. Preparing a quotation for commercial lines insurance can be done superficially, or it can be a time-consuming and complex procedure. Before embarking on a major project to price a commercial account, the insurer wants a reasonable assurance that the work is justified. A company that requests bids annually is likely to find that after the first few years, few insurers are

---

[19] *Best's Life Reports* (Morristown, N.J.: A. M. Best Co., annual).

[20] In 1994, 31.3 percent of the rated life insurers were rated in classes A++ through A-.

[21] For life insurers, Best's Financial Size ratings range from class I for companies with $250,000 in surplus to class XV for companies with $100 million or more in surplus.

[22] See Herbert S. Denenberg, "Is 'A Plus' Really a Passing Grade?" *Journal of Risk and Insurance* 34 (September 1967).

[23] Joseph M. Belth, "Financial Strength Ratings of Life-Health Insurance Companies," *The Insurance Forum*, 21, Nos. 3 and 4 (March/April 1994): p 15.

willing to prepare serious proposals. As a general rule, requests for bids should not be undertaken more often than every three to five years.

There are two basic approaches in a bidding process. In one, selected agencies are asked to propose a program and are given flexibility in the design of coverages they recommend. This has the advantage of tapping the creativity of the bidding agencies. The disadvantage is that it can make the selection decision extremely difficult, for the proposals to be compared will be apples and oranges.

Under the second approach, the agencies are asked to quote a specific package of coverage, in which the coverage specifications are tightly defined. The bidding agencies may be given the option of making an alternative quote, but all bidders are required to present proposals based on the defined coverage specifications.

One problem that can arise in the bidding situation is access to insurance markets. Insurers decided long ago that they did not want to be put in the middle of two of their agents, both of which wanted to bid on a particular account. To eliminate the dilemma they might face in choosing one of their agents over another, insurers devised the *Agent Letter of Record*, a letter from a prospective buyer instructing an insurer to recognize a particular agent as its agent "of record." Once a particular agent has been so designated, the insurer will not entertain applications for the account from other agencies unless and until the insurance buyer has changed the agent of record.

In a bidding process, the organization seeking bids must name each of the bidders through an agent of record letter for the insurers they propose to use. Usually, each agent or broker submits a list of insurers he or she plans to use, listed in order of preference. The risk manager then gives letters of authorization to each broker for those companies he or she appears best able to represent. The usual system for resolving conflicts that arise when a particular company appears on more than one list is that the broker placing the insurer highest on his or her preference list may be authorized to use it.

IMPORTANT CONCEPTS TO REMEMBER

rate	merit rating	managing general agent
premium	credibility factor	(MGA)
gross rate	trend factor	hard market
loading	adjustment bureau	soft market
pure premium	contingency contract	cash-flow underwriting
expected loss ratio	profit-sharing contract	reinsurance
loss ratio	accommodation risk	ceding company
expense ratio	postselection underwriting	cession
permissible loss ratio	staff adjuster	net retention
combined ratio	independent adjuster	facultative reinsurance
class rating	public adjuster	facultative treaty
individual rating	policyholders' rating	automatic treaty
judgment rating	financial rating	quota share reinsurance
schedule rating	nonadmitted market	surplus line reinsurance
experience rating	excess and surplus lines market	excess-loss reinsurance
retrospective rating	consent-to-rate law	

QUESTIONS FOR REVIEW

1. List and briefly explain the steps in the underwriting process.
2. What sources of information are available to the underwriter? Explain the importance of each source. Why are mulitple sources necessary?
3. Sales representatives of property and liability insurance companies sometimes refer to the "sales prevention department." What department of the company are they referring to? Explain.
4. Why is the pricing of the insurance product more difficult than pricing of other products?
5. What is the difference between a premium and a rate?
6. Identify the sources of information on insurer finances that are available to insurance buyers.
7. Briefly explain the nature of retrospective rating plans and why they are used.
8. Distinguish between a *hard market* and a *soft market.*
9. What are the desirable characteristics a buyer should look for in an insurance agent?
10. Explain why "shortages" occur in the insurance market.

QUESTIONS FOR DISCUSSION

1. How do you account for the feeling held by many people that there is something almost "immoral" about an insurance company canceling a policy in the middle of the policy term? Do you agree or disagree with this position?
2. Describe the general nature of the excess and surplus lines market. In what way(s) are the characteristics of the market of significant to the risk manager?
3. The property and liability insurance industry has been castigated for its inability to manage the insurance cycle, which results in wide swings in the price of some forms of insurance. Why do insurers engage in cash flow underwriting? Is this a desirable or undesirable phenomenon from the perspective of insurance buyers?
4. Distinguish between the two approaches that are used to compensate agents and brokers. Which, in your opinion, is the preferred approach?
5. "Pricing is much more difficult in insurance than in other business fields, because the cost of production is not known until after the product has been delivered." To what extent is this statement true and to what extent false?

SUGGESTIONS FOR ADDITIONAL READING

Denenberg, Herbert S. "Is A-Plus Really a Passing Grade?" *Journal of Risk and Insurance,* XXXIV, No. 3 (Sept. 1967).

Donaldson, J.H. *Casualty Claims Practice*, 4th ed. Homewood, IL: Richard D. Irwin, 1984.

Green, Mark R., James S. Trieschmann, and Sandra G. Gustavson. *Risk and Insurance*, 8th ed. Cincinnati: South-Western Publishing, 1992. Chapter 24.

Holtom, Robert B. *Restraints on Underwriting: Risk Selection, Discrimination and the Law*, 2nd ed. Cincinnati: National Underwriter, 1982.

Launie, J.J., J. Finley Lee, and Norman A. Baglini. *Principles of Property and Liability Underwriting*, 3rd Ed. Malvern, PA: Insurance Institute of America, 1986.

Markham, James J. ed. *Property Loss Adjusting*, Vol. I and Vol. II. Malvern, PA: Insurance Institute of America, 1990.

Markham, James J., Kevin M. Quinley, and Layne S. Thompson. *The Claims Environment.* Malvern, PA: Insurance Institute of America, 1993,

Reinarz, Robert C.; Janice O. Schloss, Gary S. Patrik, and Peter R. Kensicki. *Reinsurance Practices*, Vol. I and Vol. II. Malvern, PA: Insurance Institute of America, 1990.

Rosenthal, Norman L. "Insurance Broker as Risk Consultant." *Risk Management* (June 1995), pp. 33–36.

Ralston, August R., ed. *Risk Management Manual*, Santa Monica, CA: (loose-leaf service with monthly supplements), vol. 2, section 1. "Insurance."

West, Kathryn Z. "How Do You Select and Work With an Insurance Broker?" *Risk Management* (February 1966).

Williams, C. Arthur, and Richard M. Heins. *Risk Management and Insurance*. 6th ed. New York: McGraw-Hill, 1989. Chapter 26.

Webb. Bernard L., Howard N. Anderson, John A. Cookman, and Peter R. Kensicki. *Principles of Reinsurance*, Vol. I and Vol. II Malvern, PA: Insurance Institute of America, 1990.

Webb, Bernard L., Connor M. Harrison, and James J. Markham. *Insurance Operations*, 1st ed., Vols I and II. Malvern, PA: American Instutute for Property and Liability Underwriters, 1992.

CHAPTER 12

Regulation of the Insurance Industry

CHAPTER OBJECTIVES

When you have finished this chapter, you should be able to

Identify and explain the reasons why insurance is subject to regulation.

■

Identify the major areas of insurer operations that are regulated.

■

Trace the history of insurance regulation and identify the landmark cases and laws that led to the current regulatory environment.

■

Identify the major aspects of insurance company operations that are subject to regulation.

■

Identify and explain the statutory requirements that exist with respect to insurance rates.

■

Describe the different approaches the states have taken toward regulating insurance rates.

■

Identify the arguments favoring state or federal regulation of insurance.

The Why of Government Regulation of Insurance ■ ■ ■

Many of the original reasons for the regulation of the insurance industry are now being challenged, and new regulatory goals are being proposed. In analyzing the issues discussed in this chapter, the reader should be familiar with the general theory of regulation, which serves as the foundation for the theory of insurance regulation.

THE WHY OF REGULATION GENERALLY

Economists have some important differences of opinion on the subject of government regulation, and much of the controversy concerning insurance regulation stems from these differences. Few disagree in principle on the need for some form of government control of business, but the form this control should take is a matter of some debate.

Some economists believe in the concept of an efficient market and maintain that competition will generally produce the greatest benefits to society. Economists of this school agree that, while some form of government control is necessary, the government's principal role should be that of maintaining competition. Other economists distrust the market, or at least have less confidence in its operation. They believe the lesson of history to be that regulation is often needed to prevent abuse of consumers and that regulations should be imposed wherever there is a likelihood of market failure.

APPROACHES TO GOVERNMENT CONTROL OF BUSINESS

Government control of business takes one of two forms, reflecting the two economic philosophies just described: antitrust and regulation. *Antitrust* concentrates on maintaining competition, whereas *regulation* involves the application of specific performance standards to the firms in an industry. The principal thrust of antitrust is to curtail monopoly power. It focuses on preventing collusion, opposing mergers that lead to excessive concentration, and abating market power. The theory of antitrust is that if the government prevents monopoly and unfair competition, competition will result in the public welfare.

Regulation, in contrast to antitrust, represents a more direct involvement of government in the affairs of business. It usually consists of two types of actions by government: restricting entry into the market (usually because competition is thought to be infeasible, but sometimes on other grounds as well) and controlling prices to guarantee that the firms in an industry do not obtain excessive profits. In a sense, regulation replaces competition in industries that are natural monopolies or in industries that are considered to have special importance because of size or influence.

Natural monopolies, for example, are licensed, and their pricing decisions are controlled to protect the consumer from exploitation. Cartelized industries are regulated for the same reasons. Here regulation is required because of a lack of competition, and it seeks to generate results similar to those that would exist in a competitive industry. In insurance, the problem of monopoly is not significant, but there are still reasons for government restraint.

The rationale for regulation of insurance differs from that of monopolized or cartelized industries because the potential "market failures" are also different. The first of the potential market failures in insurance stems from the fiduciary nature of insurer operations, and the second from the uncertainties inherent in the insurance pricing process.

Vested in the Public Interest Rationale

The first rationale for the regulation of insurance is that it is an industry that is vested in the public interest. The courts have long held that insurance, like banking, is pervasive in its influence, and that failures in this field can affect persons other than those directly involved in the transaction.[1] Individuals purchase insurance to protect themselves against financial loss at a later time, and it is important to the public welfare that the insurer promising to indemnify insureds for future losses fulfill its promises.

Classical economists held that competition serves the consumer by forcing inefficient firms out of the market. Contrary to this classical model, which held that the failure of some firms from time to time was a wholesome phenomenon, the public interest is not served by the failure of insurers, because of the resulting losses to policyholders and claimants. The "vested in the public interest" rationale for regulation of the insurance industry holds that the insurance industry, like any other business holding vast sums of money in trust for the public, should be subject to government regulation because of its fiduciary nature.

Besides the solvency issue, certain other "public interest" reasons have led legislators to regulate the industry. The complex nature of insurance contracts makes them difficult for a consumer to understand, even if he or she should attempt to do so. Regulation is therefore deemed necessary to ensure that the contracts offered by insurance companies are fair and that they are fairly priced.

Although the public interest rationale has a relationship to the area of pricing and competition, its implications are much broader. It implies a need for regulation of insurance in many areas, of which pricing is only one. The fiduciary nature of insurer operations and the extensive influence of insurance on members of society require regulation of entry into the market (i.e., the licensing of companies), the investment practices of insurers, and similar areas related to insurer solvency. In addition, the complexity of the insurance product requires regulatory scrutiny of contracts and the licensing of practitioners to ensure their competence. All of this means that because insurance is "vested in the public interest," the industry would require regulation even if it were not for the second rationale for regulation, destructive competition.

Destructive Competition Rationale

The second rationale for the regulation of insurance—currently being challenged by some parties—is that competition in some fields of insurance, if left unregulated, would become excessive. Although regulation in many other industries aims at enforcing competition and preventing artificially high prices, insurance regulation was designed (at least initially) in the opposite direction: preventing excessive competition. It has long been argued that in the absence of regulation the natural

---

[1]In 1974 the U.S. Supreme Court ruled that insurance was a business "affected with the public interest." See *German Alliance Insurance Company v. Lewis*, 233 U.S. 380 (1914).

tendency in the insurance industry would be to engage in the keenest sort of cut-throat competition. The assumption that the natural tendency in insurance pricing is toward destructive competition rests on two premises:

- The cost of production is not known until the insurance contract has run its full term.

- There are classes of desirable and undesirable insureds. In attempting to compete, insurance companies might assume that their insureds are from the more desirable class and make unwarranted assumptions about their future costs.

As we will see later in the chapter, there is considerable disagreement on this point, and many analysts are now questioning the validity of the argument. Nevertheless, those who argue that insurance regulation must be aimed at preventing too much competition maintain that the basic danger in the insurance industry is the possibility that, in vying for business, companies may underestimate future losses and as a result fail.

GOALS OF INSURANCE REGULATION

Originally, the goals of insurance regulation were clearly understood and generally agreed on by all concerned: to promote the public welfare by ensuring fair contracts at fair prices from financially strong companies. The "market failures" that insurance regulation was intended to correct were insolvencies (no matter what their source) and unfair treatment of insureds by insurers. In short, the dual goals of regulation were solvency and equity.[2]

Although the original goals still dominate the regulatory philosophy, new goals—still emerging—focus on the availability and affordability of insurance. The inability of some consumers to obtain insurance at a price they are willing and able to pay and a growing philosophy of entitlement have created pressure for regulatory measures that will guarantee insurance to all who want it at affordable rates.[3]

A BRIEF HISTORY OF INSURANCE REGULATION

The earliest forms of insurance regulation were related to the premium taxes imposed by the states on out-of-state insurers and grew out of the registration and reporting requirements imposed for the purpose of determining insurers' tax liabilities. By the end of the Civil War, most states had agencies responsible for regulating

---

[2]These goals were articulated by Professor Spencer L. Kimball, who referred to them as the principles of "solidity" and "*aequum et bonum.*" See Spencer L. Kimball, *Essays in Insurance Regulation* (Ann Arbor, Mich.: Spencer Kimball, 1966), pp. 3-10.

[3]The issue of availability and affordability is discussed later in the chapter.

insurers operating within their borders. Perhaps inevitably, a conflict arose over the issue of the right of states to regulate the industry. The 1869 case of *Paul v. Virginia* focused on the preeminence of the right of the states or federal government to regulate insurance. The U.S. Constitution gives the federal government the right to regulate interstate commerce, and the issue in *Paul v. Virginia* was whether insurance is interstate commerce. The case was carried to the U.S. Supreme Court, where it was finally decided in 1869, when the Court ruled that insurance was not interstate commerce and, therefore, was not subject to regulation by the federal government. This decision stood for 75 years.

Seventy-five years later, in the South-Eastern Underwriters Association (SEUA) case, the Supreme Court reversed its decision of *Paul v. Virginia*, stating that insurance is interstate commerce and as such is subject to regulation by the federal government.[4]

In response to the SEUA decision, Congress enacted a law drafted by the National Association of Insurance Commissioners, which provides the insurance industry with a partial exemption from federal regulation. This was *Public Law 15*, or the *McCarran-Ferguson Act*, which become law on March 9, 1945.

In the McCarran-Ferguson Act, Congress reaffirmed the right of the federal government to regulate insurance, but agreed that it would not exercise this right as long as the industry was adequately regulated by the states. In effect, the law explicitly grants to the states the power to regulate the insurance business—a power that the Supreme Court in the SEUA case had concluded was vested in Congress under the Commerce Clause of the Constitution. The exemption from federal law is not complete, however. The act provides that the Sherman Act will continue to apply to boycott, coercion, or intimidation.

■ Regulation Today ■■■■■■■■■■■■■■■■■■■■■■■■

Following enactment of Public Law 15, the states attempted to put their houses in order, passing rating laws, defining fair trade practices, and extending licensing and solvency requirements.

THE CURRENT REGULATORY STRUCTURE

Insurance is presently regulated by the several states through their legislative, judicial, and executive branches of government. The legislative branch enacts laws that govern the conduct of the insurance industry within its boundaries. These laws spell out the requirements that must be met by persons wishing to organize an insurance company in the state and provides for the general regulation of the industry. The judicial branch exercises control over the insurance industry through the courts by rendering decisions on the meaning of policy

---

[4] *United States v. South-Eastern Underwriters Association*, 322 U.S. 533 (1944).

terms and ruling on the constitutionality of the state insurance laws and the actions of those administering the law. The actual regulation of the insurance industry, however, is generally vested in the state's executive branch.

The Commissioner of Insurance

The central figure in the regulation of the insurance industry in each state is the commissioner of insurance.[5] In most states this official is appointed by the governor of the state and is charged with the administration of the insurance laws and the general supervision of the business. Although a part of the executive branch of the state government, the commissioner frequently makes rulings that have the binding force of law and exercises judicial power in interpreting and enforcing the insurance code.

National Association of Insurance Commissioners

The *National Association of Insurance Commissioners* (NAIC) has been an active force in the regulation of insurance since it was founded in 1871. Although it has no legal power over insurance regulation, it is an important influence. Through this body, the 50 state commissioners exchange information and ideas and coordinate regulatory activities. Based on the information exchanged at its two annual meetings, the NAIC makes recommendations for legislation and policy. The individual commissioners are free to accept or reject these recommendations, but in the past most commissioners have seen fit to accept the recommendations appropriate for their particular states.

NAIC State Accreditation Program

In 1989, in an effort to address certain deficiencies in state regulation, the NAIC established minimum standards for financial regulation by the states. The following year, the NAIC created its Financial Regulation Standards Accreditation Program, which is designed to assist state legislatures and insurance departments in developing an effective system of solvency regulation. The program provides for NAIC certification of states that meet the requirements of the accreditation program. The measures that must be adopted by a state to be accredited by the NAIC include 16 model laws and rules affecting regulation of insurance holding companies, managing general agents, reinsurance intermediaries, credit for insurance, examination processes, liquidation proceedings, and risk retention groups. By September 1995, insurance departments in 45 states and the District of Columbia had been awarded formal accreditation certificates by the NAIC. In addition to the original certification, states must submit to an annual evaluation process and must undergo recertification review every five years.

---

[5]Although the title "commissioner of insurance" is the most common, in some states the chief insurance regulator is referred to as the "director of insurance" or the "superintendent of insurance."

Areas Regulated ■■■■■■■■■■■■■■■■■■■■■■■■■■

LICENSING OF INSURERS

The power to license insurance companies (or revoke those licenses) is perhaps the greatest power that the commissioner of insurance possesses. In effect, when a company is licensed, the commissioner certifies the company with regard to its financial stability and soundness of methods of operation. Before licensing a firm to conduct business in the state, the commissioner must be satisfied that the company to be licensed meets the financial requirements specified in the insurance code of the state. To qualify for a license, the insurance company making application must have a certain amount of capital and surplus. The exact amount required varies from state to state, being relatively small in some states and substantial in others.[6] The amount also depends on the type of business the firm will conduct and whether the company is a stock or mutual carrier. These capital and surplus requirements usually apply both to individuals who wish to form an insurer in the state and to foreign companies that request a license to do business in the state.

Besides the capital and surplus requirement, the commissioner also reviews the personal characteristics of the organizers, promoters, and incorporators of the company to determine their competence and experience. The commissioner may deny the application for a license if the company's founders seem unworthy of public trust.

STATUTORY ACCOUNTING REQUIREMENTS

Regulatory requirements for insurance companies extend to the manner in which insurers account for their income and their expenses. The set of accounting procedures embraced by insurance companies is referred to as the *statutory accounting system,* because it is required by the statutes of the various states. Virtually all insurance company accounting is geared to the NAIC *Annual Statement Blank*—a standardized reporting format developed by the NAIC by which each company must file an annual statement with the insurance department of its home state and with every other state in which it is licensed to do business. With minor exceptions, the required information and the manner in which it is to be submitted are the same for all states. There are two versions of the Convention Blank, one for property and liability insurers and one for life insurers. The information required in these documents and the procedures for recording that information (which are also spelled out by the NAIC) set the ground rules for insurance accounting.

Basically, the statutory system is a combination of a cash and an accrual method and differs from generally accepted accounting principles (GAAP) in a number of ways. Because the principal emphasis in statutory accounting is on reflecting the

---

[6]In 1992, the NAIC proposed model legislation for a system of risk-based capital (RBC) requirements for insurers. RBC standards do not replace capital requirements but are designed to assist regulators in accessing solvency. RBC is discussed later in this chapter.

insurer's ability to fulfill its obligations under the contracts it issues, statutory accounting is, in most areas, ultraconservative.

In recent years, the statutory accounting system has come under criticism by independent public accountants, most notably, the American Institute of Certified Public Accountants (AICPA). In 1993, the AICPA notified the NAIC that it would no longer issue unqualified audit opinions on statutory financial statements after 1994. The AICPA argued that statutory accounting principles are not clearly articulated: they are not generally codified in state law, differences exist across states, and the sources of statutory accounting may be found in numerous places (including instructions to the annual statement, NAIC manuals, individual state laws, regulations, and administrative rules). The NAIC has responded to these criticisms of statutory accounting by reaffirming its belief that regulator control over the accounting system is essential for effective solvency regulation and has embarked on a project to more clearly define the principles underlying statutory accounting statements. The NAIC's hope is that the codification of statutory accounting principles project will result in the AICPA recognizing statutory accounting as an *Other Comprehensive Basis of Accounting*, thereby permitting auditors to issue opinions.

Admitted and Nonadmitted Assets

The first difference between GAAP and statutory accounting lies in the criteria for inclusion of assets in the balance sheet. Although most noninsurance companies recognize all assets, insurance companies recognize only those that are readily convertible into cash. These are called *admitted assets*, and only they are included in the balance sheet of an insurance company. Assets such as supplies, furniture and fixtures, office machines and equipment, and premiums past due 90 days or more are *nonadmitted assets* and do not appear on the balance sheet. The elimination of these nonadmitted assets, whose liquidity is questionable, tends to understate the equity section of the balance sheet, which, in statutory accounting terminology, is called *policyholders' surplus*.[7]

Valuation of Assets

A second major difference between the two accounting systems is that investments are carried at cost under GAAP (in some cases the lower of cost or market value), whereas under the statutory system, stocks are carried at market value, as determined by the Security Valuation Committee of the NAIC based on market values

---

[7]The equity section of the balance sheet for any business consists of the excess of asset values over the liabilities of the firm. For an insurance company, it consists of either one or two items. In the case of stock companies, it consists of the capital stock, which represents the value of the original contributions of the stockholders, plus surplus, which represents amounts paid in by the organizers in excess of the par value of the stock and any retained earnings of the company. Because there is no capital stock in mutual insurance companies, the total of the equity section is called surplus. In both stock and mutual companies, this is referred to as *policyholders' surplus*, indicating that this is the amount available, over and above the liabilities, to meet obligations to the company's policyholders.

at the end of the year. Bonds not in default of interest or principal payments are carried at their amortized value.[8] (Bonds in default are carried at market value.) Thus changes in the market value of stocks held by insurers directly influence the equity section of the balance sheet, whereas changes in the market value of bonds do not. Unrealized capital gains or losses on stocks under the statutory system are reported directly as changes in equity. Thus, when the value of an insurer's investment portfolio changes, the equity section of its balance sheet, called *policyholders' surplus*, is altered to reflect the change in the portfolio. Unrealized gains are not recognized under GAAP.

Matching Revenues and Expenses

A final major difference between statutory accounting and GAAP is in the matching of revenues and expenses. Under GAAP, revenues and expenses are matched, with prepaid expenses deferred and charged to operations when the income produced as a result of incurring those expenses is recognized. Under statutory accounting, all expenses of acquiring a premium are charged against revenue when they are incurred, rather than being treated as prepaid expenses that are capitalized and amortized. The related premium income, however, is deferred, and equal portions corresponding to the protection provided over time are recognized only as that time passes. This is done in two ways. First, insurers are permitted to include premiums as income only as the premiums become earned—that is, only as the time for which protection is provided passes. In addition, the insurer is required to establish a deferred income account as a liability, called the *unearned premium reserve*, the primary purpose of which is to place a claim against assets that will presumably be required to pay losses occurring in the future.[9]

Statutory Profit or Loss

The combination of a cash basis of accounting for expenses and an accrual basis for premiums can, as one might suspect, create distortions in the reported underwriting results of an insurer. Because expenses must be paid when the policy is written and before the premium income has been totally earned, and the premiums are included in the computation only as earned, the net effect is to understate profit when premium volume is increasing (whenever premiums written exceed

---

[8]Bonds are evidence of debt and promise to pay their face value at maturity. At maturity, the bond of a solvent corporation will be worth its face value, but the market value of bonds may vary from this face value over time, depending on the bond's interest rate compared with the market rate. When interest rates increase, the market value of bonds falls. Conversely, if the interest rate falls, the market value of the bond will increase above its face value. If a bond is purchased in the market for other than its face amount, the book value will differ from the bond and must gradually be adjusted over time so that it will equal the face of the bond at maturity. The process of gradually writing the value of the bond up or down so that the book value will equal the face at maturity is called amortizing.

[9]In insurance accounting and insurance terminology generally, the term *reserve* is synonymous with *liability*. This usage is probably misleading to the layperson and is contradictory to modern accounting terminology, but unless otherwise specified, when used in insurance accounting, the term *reserve* always refers to a liability.

premiums earned) and to overstate profit when premium volume is declining (when premiums earned exceed premiums written).

A second significant point to be noted is that an increase in premium writings, other things being equal, will result in a reduction in policyholders' surplus. The management of every insurer must constantly watch the growth of its business to make certain that a balance is maintained between its liabilities and its policyholders' surplus. Although no general consensus has been reached on exactly what the ratio should be, agreement is widespread as to some desirable ratio of policyholders' surplus to premiums written or to the unearned premium reserve.[10] The drain on surplus created by the statutory accounting requirements therefore places a limit on an insurer's ability to write new business.

Because statutory accounting provides a distorted picture, instead of depending on the statutory figures, informed observers gauge the profitability of a given company on the basis of its *combined ratio*, which is derived by adding the loss ratio and the expense ratio for the period under consideration. The *loss ratio* is computed by dividing losses incurred during the year by premiums earned. The *expense ratio* is computed by dividing expenses incurred by premiums written. Because the loss ratio is computed on the basis of losses incurred to premiums *earned* and the expense ratio is based on premiums *written*, the combined ratio merges data that are not precisely comparable. Nevertheless, the ratio is widely used as an indication of the "trade" profit of an insurer. If the total of these two ratios is less than 100 percent for the year, underwriting was conducted at a profit, and in the degree indicated.

REGULATION OF RESERVES

Because insurers operate on the unusual plan of collecting in advance for a product to be delivered at some time in the future, insurance laws require specific recognition of the insurer's fiduciary obligations. Life insurers are required to maintain "policy reserves" on outstanding policies, and to reflect these reserves as liabilities in their financial statements. The insurance code of most states specifies the manner in which the reserves must be computed. In addition, the code requires the insurance company to deposit cash or securities with the commissioner of insurance, based on the amount of the reserves. The critical importance of the reserves in the financial stability and solvency of an insurer is apparent when we recognize that the reserves are true liabilities. They are an actuarial measurement of the company's liabilities to its policyholders and claimants that must be offset by assets. If the reserves are understated, the net worth of the company is overstated.

Unearned Premium Reserve

As previously noted, the unearned premium reserve represents the premiums that insureds have paid in advance for the unexpired terms of their outstanding policies.

---

[10]The National Association of Insurance Commissioners' Insurance Regulatory Information System suggests premium writings of three times policyholders' surplus.

Just as the insured carries "prepaid insurance premiums" as an asset on his or her books, so the insurance company enters them as a liability on its books. For each policy, the unearned premium reserve at the inception of the policy period is equal to the entire gross premium that the insured has paid. During the policy period, the unearned premium reserve for the policy declines steadily to zero by a straight mathematical formula.[11]

The unearned premium reserve is sometimes called the *reinsurance reserve* on the premise that it represents the amount that would be required to transfer the insurance in force to another insurer if the primary insurer should retire from the business. The amount that would actually be needed to reinsure existing policies is somewhat less than the full amount of the unearned premium reserve. Even though production and administrative expenses are charged against revenue at the inception of the policy, the insurer is required to establish an unearned premium reserve equal to the entire premium on a policy. This means that there is a redundancy in the unearned premium reserve; because expenses have already been paid, the unearned premium reserve is actually higher than need be. This in turn means that surplus is actually understated to the extent of the excess in the unearned premium reserve.[12]

Loss Reserves

Because there may be delays between the occurrence of a loss and the time when it is actually paid, statutory accounting makes a distinction between incurred losses and paid losses. *Incurred losses* refer to those losses actually taking place during the particular period under consideration, regardless of when they are actually paid. *Paid losses* refer to losses paid during a particular period regardless of the time when the loss occurred. Recognition of the difference between paid and incurred losses is made through liability accounts called loss or claim reserves. The two major classes of loss reserves are a reserve for losses reported but not yet paid, and a reserve for losses that have occurred but have not yet been reported to the insurance company. Reserves for losses reported but not yet paid can be established by examining each claim and making an approximation based on what the loss will ultimately be. Alternatively, averaging formulas can be applied to blocks of outstanding claims. The reserve for losses incurred but not reported (losses the insurer presumes have already taken place but have not been submitted because of a lag in claim reporting) are usually estimated on the basis of the insurer's past experience.

---

[11]The unearned premium reserve is computed by tabulating the premiums on policies in force according to the year (or month) of issue and the term. The most acceptable and most widely used method of calculating unearned premiums is called the monthly pro rata basis. Under this approach, $\frac{1}{24}$ of the premium for an annual policy is considered earned during the month in which the policy is written, $\frac{1}{12}$ is earned each month from month 2 through month 12, and $\frac{1}{24}$ is earned in month 13.

[12]Persons familiar with the property and liability insurance industry are aware of the inaccuracy in the figures presented in the insurer's balance sheets and make allowance for it. There is no universally accepted formula for doing this, but one method is to adjust surplus and the unearned premium reserve by the amount of the redundancy of the unearned premium reserve, usually considered to be about 35 percent.

INVESTMENTS

To the extent that an insurer's promises depend on the value of its investments, those investments must be sound. For this reason, the insurance code of each state spells out the particular investments permitted to each type of insurance company in the state. The investments permitted are usually U.S. government obligations: state, municipal, and territorial bonds; Canadian bonds, mortgage loans, certain high-grade corporate bonds; and, subject to limitations, preferred and common stocks. In general, property and liability insurers are granted greater latitude in their investments than are life insurers. Life insurers are generally allowed to invest only a small percentage of their assets in common stocks.

EXAMINATION OF INSURERS

The insurance code requires every licensed insurance company, foreign and domestic, to submit an annual report to the commissioner of insurance. This report includes information about the assets and liabilities of the company: its investments; its income, loss payments, and expenses; and any other information desired by the commissioner. In addition to the annual report, the commissioner's office makes a periodic inspection of each company conducting business in the state. The insurance commissioner may examine or inquire into the affairs of any company transacting business in the state at any time, but the insurance code normally requires examining domestic companies at least once every three years. The expense of the examination is paid by the insurance company being inspected. It is a detailed procedure, often lasting an extended period, during which the examiners scrutinize every aspect of the firm's operation.

To eliminate duplication of effort, it has become the practice for each state insurance department to examine only those companies that are domiciled in the state. For auditing foreign companies, a *zone examination system* is used, in which each state in a zone (there are four zones) accepts the examination in which a representative from the zone participates. Normally, the zone examination takes place simultaneously with the examination by the insurer's home state, and an examiner from each of the zones participates in the examination. Since January 1994, states accredited by the NAIC may not accept zone examination reports from an unaccredited state unless an examiner from an accredited state participates in the examination.

INSURER INSOLVENCIES

Although the principal thrust of insurance regulation is to avoid insolvencies, on occasion they do occur, and in such instances the commissioner of insurance must institute the necessary proceedings to have the insurer's assets taken over by an official liquidator. Usually, liquidation is a last resort, and the commissioner will often take steps to rehabilitate a company when an examination suggests that it is impaired or in a hazardous condition. In attempting to rehabilitate a company, the commissioner may direct that substantial portions of the firm's business be reinsured with other companies. Sometimes, the shaky firm may be merged with a stronger insurer. Often, the public is unaware that the company was threatened by insolvency.

When these efforts fail or when the company's position is too precarious to attempt rehabilitation, it becomes necessary for the Insurance Department of the state in which the company is domiciled to handle the liquidation. In such circumstances, the commissioner may apply to a district court for permission to take possession of the company to conduct or close its business.

Many states have adopted the *Uniform Insurers Liquidation Act*, developed by the NAIC, which is designed to provide equitable treatment to all parties concerned when the insolvent insurer operates in several states. Under the provisions of this act, creditors in each state are afforded equal treatment, and those located in the state of domicile are treated the same as those from other states.

Insolvency Funds

Insolvency guarantee funds, designed to compensate members of the public who suffer loss because of the failure of property and liability insurers or life and health insurers, exist in all states. Most of the property and liability insolvency guarantee funds date from the early 1970s, when they were established to forestall the formation of a federal agency, which had been proposed to perform the same function.[13] Most operate on a postinsolvency basis, in which insurers operating in the state are assessed their proportionate share of losses after an insolvency occurs. The New York plan for property and liability insurers is based on a preinsolvency assessment. In some states, the assessments are allowed as tax offsets, permitting solvent insurers that have paid assessments to recoup these losses by reducing their premium taxes.

Early Detection of Potential Insolvencies

Although insolvency funds provide some protection to policyholders, it is clear that the real answer to protecting policyholders from insurer insolvencies is in detecting potential failures before they occur. Regulators employ two mechanisms in their efforts to detect financial problems in an insurer: the NAIC *Insurance Regulatory Information System* (IRIS) and *Risk-Based Capital*.

The NAIC Insurance Regulatory Information System   The NAIC *Insurance Regulatory Information System (IRIS)* was adopted in 1974. It is designed to indicate financially troubled insurers by computerized analysis of selected audit ratios. Under the current version of this system, there are 11 ratios for property and liability insurers and 12 for life and health insurers.[14] The eleven ratios for property and liability insurers are as follows:

---

[13]The earliest of the funds were established in New York (1947), New Jersey (1952), and Maryland (1965). However, these early funds did not pay claims on all lines of property and liability insurance, nor did they provide for the return of premiums that policyholders had paid to the insolvent insurer. These laws were revised in the 1970–1971 period when the rest of the plans were established.

[14]*Using the NAIC Insurance Regulatory Information System: Property and Liability Insurers,* 1978 ed. (Milwaukee: National Association of Insurance Commissioners, 1978); and *Using the NAIC Insurance Regulatory Information System: Life and Health and Fraternal Insurers,* 1978 ed. (Milwaukee: National Association of Insurance Commissioners, 1978).

	Ratio		Formula		Acceptable
(1)	Premium to Surplus Ratio	=	$\dfrac{\text{Net Premiums Written}}{\text{Policyholders' Surplus}}$	$\times 100$	$\leq 300\%$
(2)	Change in Premiums Written	=	$\dfrac{\text{Net Premiums Current Year} - \text{Net Premiums Prior Year}}{\text{Premiums Written Prior Year}}$	$\times 100$	$< \pm 33\%$
(3)	Surplace Aid- to Surplus	=	$\dfrac{\text{Surplus Aid}}{\text{Surplus}}$	$\times 100$	$< 25\%$
(4)	Two-Year Overall Operating Ratio	=	$\dfrac{\text{Combined Ratio} - \text{Investment Income}}{}$	$\times 100$	$< 100\%$
(5)	Investment Yield	=	$\dfrac{\text{Net Investment Income}}{\text{Average Invested Assets}}$	$\times 100$	$> 5.0\%$
(6)	Change in Surplus Ratio	=	$\dfrac{\text{Change in Adjusted Surplus}}{\text{Adjusted Surplus Prior Year}}$	$\times 100$	$< 50\%$
(7)	Liabilities to Liquid Assets	=	$\dfrac{\text{Stated Liabilities}}{\text{Liquid Assets}}$	$\times 100$	$< 105\%$
(8)	Agents Balances to Surplus	=	$\dfrac{\text{Agents Balances in Course of Collection}}{\text{Surplus}}$	$\times 100$	$< 40\%$
(9)	One-Year Reserve Development to Surplus	=	$\dfrac{\text{One-Year Reserve Development}}{\text{Prior Year's Surplus}}$	$\times 100$	$< 25\%$
(10)	Two-Year Reserve Development to Surplus	=	$\dfrac{\text{Two-Year Reserve Development}}{\text{Second Year's Surplus}}$	$\times 100$	$< 25\%$
(11)	Estimated Current Reserve Deficiency to Surplus	=	$\dfrac{\text{Estimated Reserve Deficiency}}{\text{Surplus}}$	$\times 100$	$< 25\%$

The eleven ratios may be classified into four groups. The first three ratios are overall operating tests, which measure premiums written to surplus, the change in premiums written, and surplus aid, which is the extent to which surplus has been enhanced through proportional reinsurance. Ratios (4) through (6) test profitability, and ratios (7) and (8) test liquidity. The final three ratios are tests of reserves, and measure the ultimate liability of reserves against the original estimates. Deviations from the expected norms are taken as an indication that closer scrutiny of the insurer is needed. A company that fails four or more of the acceptable levels is targeted for such scrutiny.[15] Although the IRIS has provided useful information for regulators, it has been criticized as an inadequate approach to predicting the financial difficulties of insurers. As a result, regulators have continued their search for a more effective tool for analyzing the financial strength of insurers.

---

[15]A 1990 report issued by the General Accounting Office (GAO) called for the NAIC to expand the IRIS program to incorporate additional information on the conditions of insurers that might make the system more useful. According to the GAO, the IRIS system is often too slow in providing information to regulators.

Risk-Based Capital   In 1992, the NAIC proposed model legislation to the states for risk-based capital (RBC) standards for life insurers. A model Risk-Based Capital law for property and liability insurers was approved by the NAIC in 1993. Under the RBC standards, the amount of capital required for an insurer will vary, based on the specific risks facing the insurer, including risks associated with underwriting, the insurer's investment portfolio, and other risks not reflected by these factors.

Risk-based capital standards do not replace statutory capital and surplus requirements. In fact, RBC ratios cannot be computed until the insurer has developed a book of business. The purpose of the RBC standards is to alert regulators to the need for closer scrutiny of insurers, based on an analysis of the insurer's capital and surplus, relative to the specific risks in its portfolio.

The RBC model requires comparison between the insurer's total adjusted capital and the amount of capital—the risk-based capital—designed to reflect the riskiness of the insurer's activities. This computation yields a ratio, which indicates the action (or inaction) required. For a property and liability insurer, the risks that capital and surplus must protect and absorb are asset risk, underwriting risk, and off-balance sheet risks. Risks that the capital and surplus of a life insurer must protect and absorb are risk of loss due to defaults in assets and variations in the market value of common stock, risk of claims, expenses, and catastrophes, risk of loss due to changes in interest rates, and risks not otherwise reflected.

A deficiency in risk-based capital is indicated by the ratio of the company's actual capital and surplus and the required risk based capital. Depending on the magnitude of the deficiency, the risk-based capital regulations will require specific action, ranging from corrective action by the insurer under a plan approved by the commissioner to seizure of the company by the state insurance department.

REGULATION OF RATES

The original rationale for regulation of insurance rates was that such regulation was needed to achieve the dual goals of regulation (solvency and equity). To the extent that the insurer's promise depends on the price it charges for these promises, it was felt that these rates must be subject to government control. All states (with the exception of Illinois, which does not currently have a rating law) provide for the regulation of insurance rates, requiring that the rates must be adequate, not excessive, and not unfairly discriminatory.

Adequacy is the primary requirement. The rates, with interest income from investments, must be sufficient to pay all losses as they occur and all expenses connected with the production and servicing of the business.

In addition to being adequate, the insurance rates must *not be excessive*. Insurance has become regarded as a product essential to the well-being of society's members, and insurers may not take advantage of this need to realize unreasonable returns.

Finally, insurance rates must *not discriminate unfairly*. The emphasis in this requirement is on *unfairly*, for the very nature of insurance rates requires some degree of discrimination. By not being unfairly discriminatory, we mean that the insurance company may not charge a significantly different rate for two clients with approximately the same degree of risk. Any variation in rates charged must have an actuarial basis.

Although all states have legislation requiring that rates must be reasonable, adequate, and not unfairly discriminatory, the manner in which these requirements are enforced varies with different lines of insurance and, sometimes, also varies from state to state.

Regulation of Life Insurance Rates

Apart from making certain that the companies do not engage in price discrimination, most states do not exercise any form of direct control over the level of life insurance rates. However, life insurance rates are regulated indirectly. Regulation of dividends and mutual insurers' accumulation of surplus represents an indirect control on maximum rates. In addition, legal limits on the expense portion of the premium help to control the cost of life insurance in those states that impose such limits.[16] Finally, state laws prescribe the mortality tables and interest assumptions that must be used in computing policy reserves, which means that the adequacy of life insurance rates is also indirectly regulated. If the insurer's rate structure is too low, premium income will be insufficient to generate the assets required to meet the required reserves.

Regulation of Property and Liability Rates

Although life insurance rates are subject only to indirect forms of regulation, property and liability rates represent a different case. Some states exercise direct control over rates, requiring specific approval of rates before they can be used. Other states follow the life insurance pattern and exercise only indirect forms of regulation. Although there are other systems, regulation of property and liability insurance rates follows one of four approaches: prior approval, open competition or no file, file-and-use, and use-and-file.[17] In addition, we will briefly note the newest system, known as flex rating.[18]

Prior Approval System Most states follow the prior approval approach, patterned after the All Industry Model Rating Law developed by the NAIC in 1946 following the SEUA case. Under this system, the insurance company must obtain approval of

---

[16]New York, for example, limits the amount of commission payable to a soliciting agent in the first year of an ordinary life policy to 55 percent of the premium. Different limitations apply to other types of policies. Companies not licensed to sell in New York sometimes pay commissions as high as 125 percent of the first-year premium.

[17]In addition to these four systems, there have been two other systems, state-made rates and mandatory bureau rates. State-made automobile rates are used in Massachusetts. Mandatory bureau rates are used in the District of Columbia, Louisiana, and Mississippi for fire insurance, and in North Carolina for fire and automobile insurance.

[18]It is difficult to classify states with respect to their system of rate regulation because many states follow more than one system. A given state may use the prior approval system for some lines and file-and-use or use-and-file for others.

its intended rates from the commissioner before they may be used, and the commissioner retains the right to disapprove the rates after they become effective. Statistical data in the form of trended loss experience and projected expenses are filed as supporting data with requests for approval of rates. An insurer may accumulate and file its own loss data, or it may authorize an advisory organization (i.e., *rating bureau*) to file industrywide trended loss data on its behalf. In either case, the insurer must complete the filing data using its own projected expenses. If the commissioner is satisfied that the statistical data support the proposed rate, it is approved. In most states, the law includes a "deemer" provision, which provides that if the rates have not been disapproved within a specified period of time (ranging from 15 to 60 days), they are "deemed" to have been approved.

Open Competition   Although the most common approach to the regulation of property and liability rates remains the *prior approval approach,* pressure mounts from time to time for replacement of this system with so-called open competition laws, which are more accurately described as no-file laws.[19] The no-file approach follows the pattern of a California law, which existed from 1947 until it was repealed by Proposition 103 in 1987.[20] The California law made it clear that competition, not government authority, is the preferred governor of rates and that barring the existence of an anticompetitive situation or practice, the commissioner was not to regulate rates as such. Insurance companies were not required to file their rates for approval, but could use whatever rates their experience or that of a bureau dictates. In effect, the position of property and liability insurers under such a law is much the same as that of life insurers, which, as we have noted, are subject only to indirect control of their rates.

File-and-Use Laws   A third system of rate regulation, *file-and-use laws,* represent something of a compromise between the prior approval system and the no-file or open competition system. Under the file-and-use approach, the insurer must file proposed rate changes but may use the new rates immediately. However, the commissioner may subsequently disapprove of the rates. The chief advantage of the file-and-use system is that there is no delay between the time a rate adjustment is needed and the time it becomes effective.[21]

---

[19]The term *open competition,* which has been used widely to identify this type of law, has proven to be an unfortunate choice, for some have interpreted it to imply an absence of competition in states using the prior approval system. Because prior approval rate regulation is often used in other industries as an alternative to competition, some observers assume that this is also the case with insurance. The truth of the matter is that the industry is highly price competitive, not only in those states with open competition laws but in the prior approval states as well.

[20]Proposition 103 repealed California's 40-year-old open competition law and replaced it with a prior approval system.

[21]The file-and-use system encompasses a wide range of rate regulatory systems, some of which are similar to the prior approval system and others which in effect operate like the open competition system. For example, some states impose a waiting period before the rates may be used, and operate in much the same way as a prior approval law with a deemer period. In other states, rates may be used immediately upon filing but may subsequently be disapproved.

Use-and-File   The fourth system, *use-and-file*, is considered to have virtually the identical effect of the open competition approach. Rates may be used without regulatory approval, but they are filed with the regulator for information purposes.

Flex Rating   The newest approach to rate regulation, known as *flex rating*, combines elements of both the prior approval system and the open competition system. Under the flex rating system, a range is established for insurance rates. Insurers are permitted to change their rates both up and down within the established range in response to market conditions and without prior approval. Increases above or decreases below the established range (e.g., 10 percent) require prior approval.

POLICY FORMS

The insurance product is a contract, and so by its very nature it is technical. In most cases, customers are asked to purchase a product in which they become a party to a contract that they have neither read nor would understand if they had read it. Because insurance contracts are complicated, they must be approved by the regulatory authorities to ensure that the insurance-buying public will not be mistreated as a result of unfair provisions. In addition, the solvency of the insurers must be protected against unreasonable commitments they might make under stress of competition. In some states, new policy forms and endorsements need only be filed with the commissioner's office before they are put into use; if the commissioner does not approve of the form, it is then withdrawn. In most states, however, the law requires that a form be approved before it is adopted.

COMPETENCE OF AGENTS

Because of the technical complications in the insurance product, those selling insurance should understand the contracts they propose to sell. Many states require applicants for a license to demonstrate by examination that they understand the contracts they propose to offer to the public and the laws under which they will operate. The agents must also be respected and responsible residents of their individual communities.

APPROVAL OF NON-ADMITTED INSURERS

States vary in their approach to approving insurers that are permitted to participate in the nonadmitted market under excess and surplus lines laws. In some states, the insurance department issues a *black list*, indicating insurers with which insurance may not be placed. Other states use a *white list* approach, in which the insurance department issues a list of insurers that are eligible to participate in the nonadmitted market. Still other states leave it up to the agent to look into the qualifications of the insurer and make certain that the company is financially solvent and meets the criteria established by the law. This white list is generally based on a quarterly list published by the National Association of Insurance Commissioners. The Non-Admitted Insurers Information Office, which was established by the NAIC to screen insurers for approval, publishes a Non-Admitted Insurers Quarterly listing, indicating insurers who have satisfied the eligibility requirements of one or more states and who have established a trust fund in the United States. The NAIC requires that the trust account be maintained by an alien insurer "at an appropriate level but in no event less than $1,500,000." Over 150 alien insurers maintain such trust funds in the U.S. Although the trust funds serve to safeguard the rights of policyholders, they were originally conceived as a means of providing a cushion against fluctuations in the value of currencies and as a protection against possible impediments to the transfer of funds.

UNFAIR PRACTICES

An insurer might be sound financially and yet indulge in practices that are detrimental to the public, such as unfairly discriminating against an insured or engaging in unethical claim practices. Among the many unfair practices specifically forbidden by many insurance codes are rebating and twisting. *Rebating* consists of directly or indirectly giving or offering to give any portion of the premium or any other consideration to an insurance buyer as an inducement to the purchase of insurance. An example of unlawful rebating would be an offer by an insurance agent to give a part of his or her commission to a prospective insured.

Although antirebating laws have been accepted without much question for about 70 years, they are now being challenged as anticompetitive in effect.[22] Critics of the antirebate laws believe they represent anticompetitive laws, designed to prevent price competition among insurance agents. In fact, the original purpose of the laws was to complement the unfair discrimination provisions in the state rating laws. Legislators understood that it makes little sense to forbid insurers to charge different rates to persons with the same risk, and then permit the companies' agents to adjust the price at the point of sale.[23] Nevertheless, we will undoubtedly see more challenges to the antirebate laws.

Twisting is the practice of inducing a policyholder to lapse or cancel a policy of one insurer in order to replace it with the policy of another insurer in a way that would prejudice the interest of the policyholder. Obviously, there is no crime in a

---

[22]In 1981, the commissioner of insurance in the state of Wisconsin introduced a measure to repeal Wisconsin's antirebate law, but the effort was unsuccessful. In June 1986, the Florida Supreme Court upheld a lower court decision that overturned Florida's antirebate law on the grounds that it was unconstitutional and violated the due process clause of the Florida constitution. In July 1987, a California Superior Court upheld the constitutionality of California's antirebate law. The California law, however, was repealed in the massive overhaul of the California insurance code contained in Proposition 103. A Michigan circuit court upheld that state's antirebate law in 1990.

[23]The original antirebate provisions of the New York Code—Sections 89 and 90—were entitled Discrimination Prohibited and Discrimination Against Colored People. The first antirebate law was designed to protect blacks—the "colored people," in the vernacular of the day—from discriminatory pricing.

complete comparison without misrepresentation that an agent may make between a policy sold by his or her company and one sold by another company. Unfortunately, many agents are reluctant even to talk about replacement of an existing contract with a new contract. It is unfortunate because in a surprising number of cases replacement of a contract would clearly benefit the policyholder.

ACCESS TO INSURANCE

Increasingly, those who cannot obtain insurance at a price they feel they can afford are demanding a subsidy from the rest of society. The traditional approach to this subsidy has been a residual-risk pool.

Distressed and Residual-Risk Pools

Property and liability insurers in all states are required to participate in *shared markets*, a euphemism for the involuntary markets in which insurance is provided to applicants that do not meet normal underwriting standards. In some instances, applicants are shared on some predetermined basis. In others, losses are shared. The following are a few of the more important programs that have been designed to deal with the problem of the high-risk insured.

1. *The automobile shared market*: Some drivers, because of their past records and the likelihood of future losses that those records indicate, are unacceptable to insurers in the normal course of business. However, because it is deemed socially undesirable to permit such drivers on the road without any insurance, the insurance industry has established special mechanisms to provide the necessary coverage. The most widely used approach is the Automobile Insurance Plan (formerly called Assigned Risk Plan), which is currently used in 42 states. This plan functions by sharing applicants, with each automobile insurer operating in a state accepting a share of the undesirable drivers, based on the percentage of the state's total auto insurance that it writes. The remaining 8 states use alternate plans designed to achieve the same purpose.[24]

2. *Workers compensation assigned-risk pools*: Shared-market plans also exist in the field of workers compensation insurance. Here, employers who are not acceptable to insurers in the standard market are assigned to insurers, based on each insurer's percentage of the standard market.

3. *Medical malpractice pools*: In the mid-1970s, because of deteriorating loss experience, many insurers withdrew from the medical malpractice insurance field, creating a "malpractice crisis," in which many physicians found that they were unable to obtain professional liability insurance at any price. The

---

[24]In Maryland, the insurance is available through a state-operated fund. In Massachusetts, New Hampshire, North Carolina, and South Carolina, all auto insurers participate in statewide automobile reinsurance pools, generally called the *facility*. Florida, Hawaii, and Missouri use a *joint underwriting association* for high-risk drivers. The reinsurance facilities and joint underwriting associations operate on the principle of sharing losses rather than sharing applicants.

reaction varied from area to area, but in many states a part of the response was the formation of mandatory participation reinsurance pools, in which all liability insurers in the state share in the premiums and losses associated with medical malpractice insurance.

4. *FAIR plans*: FAIR plans are insurance industry pools designed to provide insurance to property owners in inner-city and other high-risk areas who are unable to obtain insurance through normal market channels because of the location of their property or other factors over which they have no control. If a property owner cannot obtain insurance through normal markets, he or she makes application to the state FAIR plan. After inspecting the property, the FAIR plan assigns the property to a participating insurer or tells the owner which physical hazards must be corrected before the property will be insured.[25]

5. *Beach and windstorm pools*: Special "beach and windstorm plans" exist in seven states.[26] These plans provide property insurance to property owners along the Atlantic and Gulf coasts where vulnerability to hurricanes and other forms of severe windstorm damage is especially high. Like the automobile insurance and FAIR plans, the plans operate by sharing applicants, with each participating insurer accepting a share of the undesirable applicants proportionate to its premiums in the state.

6. *State health insurance plans*: A number of states have addressed the problem of availability of health insurance by creating subsidized state health insurance pools for the uninsurable.[27] Individuals who are not eligible for Medicare or Medicaid and who cannot buy private health insurance obtain coverage from the pools, usually at a subsidized rate. Although the plans differ in detail, the pools provide comprehensive medical coverage that includes in-hospital services, skilled nursing facility care, and prescription drugs. Although the pools are subsidized, even with the subsidy, premiums range from 125 percent to 150 percent of the state's average premiums. Costs in excess of the premiums are covered by a subsidy.[28]

---

[25]The term *FAIR* is an acronym for Fair Access to Insurance Requirements. State FAIR plans currently exist in California, Connecticut, Delaware, Georgia, Illinois, Indiana, Iowa, Kansas, Kentucky, Louisiana, Maryland, Massachusetts, Michigan, Minnesota, Missouri, New Jersey, New Mexico, New York, North Carolina, Ohio, Oregon, Pennsylvania, Rhode Island, Virginia, Washington, and Wisconsin. The FAIR plans were created as an adjunct to a federal riot reinsurance program created by Congress in the aftermath of an epidemic of urban riots that erupted in the summer of 1967. The reinsurance program, which was terminated in 1983, protected the private insurers against catastrophic losses from civil disorders. Participation in the reinsurance program was optional on a state-by-state basis, but if a state chose to participate, all property insurers operating in the state were required to join the state-supervised FAIR plan.

[26]Alabama, Florida, Louisiana, Mississippi, North Carolina, South Carolina, and Texas.

[27]By 1995, the following 23 states had created such pools: California, Colorado, Connecticut, Florida, Georgia, Illinois, Indiana, Iowa, Maine, Minnesota, Montana, Louisiana, Nebraska, New Mexico, North Dakota, Oregon, South Carolina, Tennessee, Texas, Utah, Washington, Wisconsin, and Wyoming.

[28]The source of the subsidy varies by state, and includes state general revenues, a tax on hospital revenues, and assessments on health insurers. Most states fund their plans with an assessment on health insurers.

Virtually without exception, the various assigned risk plans and pools have generated losses far in excess of the premiums collected. These losses must, by definition, be passed on to other insurance buyers in the form of higher premiums or they must be borne by the insurer's stockholders. In either case, they represent a redistribution of wealth through the insurance mechanism.

More recently, the availability/affordability demands have focused on a new issue: the manner in which insurance rates should be determined and the extent to which each insured's costs should be reflected in the hazards he or she brings to the pool of insured persons.[29]

Redlining

Another important controversy in the debate over availability and affordability relates to the alleged practice of *redlining*, which refers to the insurer's policy decision to avoid insuring property located in areas where the expected losses are higher than average. Generally, the areas in which it is alleged that redlining occurs are in urban centers where insurers have experienced excessive losses due to vandalism, arson, and riots. When insurers refuse to sell insurance in such areas, critics argue, insurance is simply not available. Even when they agree to write coverage, it is argued, the coverage is not affordable.[30]

Allegations of redlining and the availability of insurance in urban areas have been issues since the riots that erupted across the country in 1968 in the aftermath of the assassination of Dr. Martin Luther King, Jr. Following these riots, property owners in some urban centers across the country reported difficulty obtaining insurance on their property. The Congress responded by enacting the Federal Riot Reinsurance Program, and the states created FAIR plans, which are designed to provide access to insurance for property owners who have difficulty obtaining insurance because of the location of their property.

The concern about availability and affordability of insurance in urban areas was renewed in the wake of the 1992 riots in Los Angeles. To address the problems related to availability, the NAIC established the Insurance Availability and Affordability Task Force, which reports to the Market Conduct and Consumer Affairs Subcommittee of the NAIC. The task force surveyed the states to determine the

---

[29]The debate over *availability* and *affordability* is reflected in a variety of programs in which insurers are compelled to write insurance for some classes as a loss and then pass these losses on to other consumers. Those who oppose the use of insurance to provide subsidies from one class to another argue that while redistribution of income and wealth may be a legitimate function of government, the use of the insurance mechanism for this purpose will create distortions in the insurance market. Further, it may not achieve a more equitable distribution of income or wealth. See Emmett J. Vaughan and Therese M. Vaughan, *Fundamentals of Risk and Insurance* (New York: John Wiley and Sons, Inc., 1996), pp. 115–122.

[30]The term *redlining* originated in the underwriting departments of insurers and has a historical basis in the "red lines" that were drawn on maps maintained by property insurance underwriting departments of insurers. In an effort to avoid unacceptable concentrations of risk, property insurers maintained maps (published by Sanborne and therefore referred to as "Sanborne" maps) on which underwriting personnel indicated the location of each building insured by the company. When the number of insured buildings in a particular area had reached a saturation point at which additional exposures might create a catastrophe exposure, the insurer declined to accept applicants from the area. In some cases, a red line was drawn around the area to alert underwriting personnel to the concentration of risks.

extent of the information and opinions on urban and rural availability problems. The task force is also charged with responsibility to study and make recommendations with respect to insurer underwriting and marketing practices as they relate to availability and affordability problems and to suggest solutions.

The debate over redlining is based on the premise that redlining is an unfair restriction of insurance availability based on geographic location. All state insurance codes outlaw unfair discrimination in insurance. The issue, of course, is whether an underwriting decision based on the excessive hazard for a particular geographic area constitutes unfair discrimination. When the NAIC addressed the availability problem in mid-1992, several commissioners pointed out that availability and affordability problems also existed in rural areas where individuals and businesses experienced difficulty in obtaining property coverage because of the high incidence of weather-related catastrophes, such as tornadoes and hurricanes. Some industry critics argue that there is a fundamental difference between the refusal to write coverage in a geographic area because of excessive hazard arising from natural perils (such as windstorm and hail) and refusal because of excessive hazard arising from human perils (such as vandalism, arson, and riots). The latter, they argue is a subterfuge for discrimination based on race or color.

In response to recent criticisms about redlining, a number of insurers and insurer groups have actively pursued increased business in inner-city areas. They have added more agents, promoted consumer education, and sponsored programs to upgrade inner-city buildings and reduce loss exposures.

In 23 states, FAIR plans provide access to insurance for property owners who are unable to obtain coverage through normal market channels. To the extent that redlining occurs, the FAIR plan provides access to the insurance market for property owners who are denied access to insurance because of the geographic location of their property. FAIR plans have been criticized for providing more limited coverage than that available in standard markets.

✖ Taxation of Insurance Companies ■ ■ ■ ■ ■ ■ ■ ■ ■ ■ ■ ■

Insurance companies, like all business corporations, are subject to federal, state, and local taxes. At the federal level, insurers are subject to the federal income tax. At the state level, they pay income and property taxes like other businesses and, in addition, are liable for a number of special taxes levied on insurers, the most important of which is the premium tax.

STATE PREMIUM TAX

Taxation of insurance companies by the states grew out of the states' need for revenue and a desire to protect domestic insurers by a tariff on out-of-state companies. As time went by, most states came to levy the *premium tax* on the premium income of both domestic and foreign insurers. Currently, every state imposes a premium tax on insurers operating within its borders. In essence, this tax is a sales tax on the premiums for all policies sold by an insurer in the state. The amount of the tax varies among the states; the maximum in any state is 4 percent, with the most typical amount being 2 percent. The tax paid by the insurer is, of course, added to the cost of the insurance contract and is passed on to the policyholder. Most states tax all companies alike, but some states still apply the tax only to out-of-state companies, or they tax domestic companies at a preferential rate.[31]

FEDERAL INCOME TAXES

For the purpose of taxation under the *Internal Revenue Code*, insurance companies are classified into three categories: life insurance companies, nonlife mutual insurance companies, and insurance companies other than life or mutual. In general, all three classes are subject to the same tax rates as are other corporations. However, they differ from other corporations and from each other in the manner in which taxable income is determined.

Life Insurance Companies

Life insurance companies are taxed at standard corporate rates on their "life insurance company taxable income" (*LICTI*), which is simply life insurance gross income minus deductions. Life insurance gross income includes premiums, decreases in life insurance reserves, and other standard elements of gross income, such as investment income. Deductions include expenses incurred, death benefits, increases in certain reserves, policyholder dividends, and certain miscellaneous deductions.

1. Among the special deductions, the *Internal Revenue Code* (*IRC*) permits a "small company" deduction to life insurers with less than $500 million in assets. The "small company" deduction allows an eligible insurer to deduct 60 percent of its first $3 million in tentative *LICTI*. The deduction is phased out as tentative *LICTI* reaches $15 million.

2. Although life insurers are permitted to deduct an increase in their reserves, the deduction for tax purposes cannot exceed the amount taken into account in computing statutory (annual statement) reserves.

3. The deduction for policyholders' dividends in computing the taxable income of a mutual life insurer is determined under a complex formula, which disallows a part of the dividends as a deduction. The theory is that at least a part of the dividends to policyholders should be viewed at least in part as a return of the mutual life insurance company's profits for the year.

[31]Most states have reciprocal or retaliatory premium tax laws. Under a retaliatory law, the purpose is to impose equally high taxes on the admitted companies of another state as that state imposes on the companies of the initial state doing business in the foreign state. For example, if Iowa taxes all companies doing business within its borders at the rate of 2 percent and Illinois taxes the companies organized in Iowa at the rate of 3 percent, companies from Illinois that are admitted to Iowa would be taxed 3 percent.

4. Finally, life insurers are required to capitalize and amortize policy acquisition expense in computing taxable income. The high first year commissions on life insurance policies produce an underwriting loss which is recouped as future premiums are earned. The amount of premiums capitalized and amortized is based on the percentage of net premiums for the first year of the policy and renewals.

Property and Liability Companies

Property and liability insurers pay the usual corporate income tax on net underwriting profit and investment income. The manner in which taxable income is determined, however, reflects the unique conventions of statutory accounting.

1. The *IRC* provides that only 80 percent of the increase in the unearned premium reserve in a given year is deductible in computing taxes.

2. The *IRC* also requires that property and liability loss reserves be discounted to reflect the time value of money. The annual deduction for incurred losses includes the increase in loss reserves, but the amount deducted is subject to statutory discounting. (A decrease in loss reserves results in income inclusion, also on a discounted basis.) The discount rate to be used is based on the federal mid-term rate.

3. Finally, the *IRC* disallows a portion (15 percent) of property and liability insurer's tax-exempt interest and dividends. This is accomplished by reducing the deduction for incurred losses by 15 percent of tax exempt interest and deductible dividends.[32]

Although the preceding discussion of insurer functions and insurer finance provides only a cursory treatment of these subjects, understanding even these general notions of the ways in which insurers operate will make the material in the following chapters easier to understand.

IMPORTANT CONCEPTS TO REMEMBER

antitrust	National Association of	prior approval law
regulation	Insurance Commissioners	file-and-use law
vested in the public interest	accreditation program	use-and-file law
Paul v. Virginia	zone examination	competitive rating law
SEUA Case	insolvency guarantee funds	no-file approach
Public Law 15	Insurance Regulatory	rebating
McCarran-Ferguson Act	Information System	twisting
domestic insurer	risk-based capital	involuntary markets
foreign insurer	legal requirements of	redlining
alien insurer	insurance rates	availability

[32]Generally, 80 percent of dividends received by corporations are deductible in computing taxable income.

affordability
statutory accounting
admitted assets
nonadmitted assets
policyholders' surplus
written premiums
earned premiums
unearned premium reserve

reinsurance reserve
incurred losses
paid losses
loss reserves
statutory profit or loss
retaliatory premium tax
GAAP
surplus drain

residual risk pool
assigned risk pool
Automobile Insurance Plan
Joint Underwriting
   Association
FAIR Plan
beach and windstorm pool

QUESTIONS FOR REVIEW

1. Explain why the field of insurance has been regarded as a type of business that requires government regulation.

2. Precisely what is meant by the statement that insurance is an industry that is "vested in the public interest."

3. Identify the landmark decisions and statutes that led to the present status of insurance as respects the federal antitrust laws.

4. Describe the four principle approaches to rate regulation in the property and liability field.

5. List and briefly explain the statutory requirements with respect to insurance rates and describe the four principal approaches to rate regulation in the property and liability insurance field.

6. Describe and differentiate between the two analytic tools that are used by regulators in their efforts at early identification of financial difficulties of insurers.

7. Describe the operation of the state insolvency funds. To what types of insurers do they apply?

8. What characteristics of the insurance business make reserves necessary?

9. Define the unearned premium reserve and briefly explain how it is calculated. Why is the unearned premium reserve often referred to as the "reinsurance reserve?"

10. The primary emphasis in statutory accounting is supposedly on financial conservatism. However, some statutory techniques violate this principle. Describe three ways in which statutory accounting is ultraconservative, and two areas where the principle of conservatism is violated.

QUESTIONS FOR DISCUSSION

1. In most states, the office of commissioner of insurance is an appointive office. Do you feel that it would be better if it were elective? Why or why not?

2. While it is generally agreed that unrestricted price competition among insurers could be detrimental to the public, some people argue that antirebating laws

represent an unnecessary restriction on price competition among insurance agents, and that such laws should be repealed. What is your opinion?

3. "Although the state insolvency funds protect consumers against loss resulting from insurer insolvency, it can be argued that these funds require strong companies to subsidize their weaker competitors." Explain why you agree or disagree with this statement.

4. "Competition can be depended upon to keep rates from being excessive, and good management will keep them from being inadequate; regulation of rates is an infringement on the right of management to make business decisions." Do you agree or disagree with this statement? Why?

5. The XYZ Insurance Company had an unearned premium reserve of $20,000,000 at the end of 1994. During 1995 it wrote $25,000,000 in annual premiums. At the end of 1995, its unearned premium reserve was $23,000,000. The company had loss reserves of $7,000,000 at the end of 1994. During 1995, it paid $7,000,000 in losses, and had loss reserves in the amount of $6,000,000 at the end of 1995.
   a. What were earned premiums during 1995?
   b. What were the incurred losses for 1995?

SUGGESTIONS FOR ADDITIONAL READING

Crane, Frederick G. "Insurance Rate Regulation: The Reasons Why." *Journal of Risk and Insurance*, XXXIX, No. 4 (Dec. 1972).

Decaminda, Joseph P. "Insurance Regulation: State or Federal?" *CPCU Journal*, Vol. 41, No. 1 (March 1988).

Gart, Alan, and Nye. David J. *Insurance Company Finance and Investments*, 2nd ed. Malvern, PA: Insurance Institute of America, 1990.

Goodwin, David, "The Case for Abolishing Anti-Rebate Laws." *CPCU Journal*, Vol. XLIII, No. 4 (December 1990).

Hanson, John S., Robert Dineen, and Michael B. Johnson. *Monitoring Competition: A Means of Regulating the Property and Liability Insurance Business.* Milwaukee: National Association of Insurance Commissioners, 1974.

Holtom, Robert B. *Restraints on Underwriting: Risk Selection, Discrimination, and the Law*, 2nd ed. Cincinnati: National Underwriter, 1982.

Insurance Accounting and Systems Association. *Life Insurance Accounting.* 3rd ed. Durham, NC: IASA, 1994.

———. *Property-Liability Insurance Accounting.* 5th ed. Durham, NC: IASA, 1991.

Keeton, Robert E. *Basic Text on Insurance Law.* St. Paul, MN: West Publishing, 1971. Chapter 8.

Kimball, S. L. *Insurance and Public Policy.* Madison, WI: University of Wisconsin Press, 1960.

Macey, Jonathan R. and Geoffrey P. Miller. *Costly Policies: State Regulation and Antitrust Exemption in Insurance Markets.* Washington, DC: The AEI Press, 1993.

Manders, John M. "Proposed Congressional Amendments to the McCarran-Ferguson Act: Their Impact on State Regulation." *Journal of Insurance Regulation*, Volume 9, No. 1 (September 1990).

McNamara, Daniel J. "Discrimination in Property-Liability Insurance Pricing." *Issues in Insurance*, Vol. 1. Malvern, PA: American Institute for Property and Liability Underwriters, 1978.

National Association of Insurance Commissioners. *Issues 1994.* Kansas City, MO: National Association of Insurance Commissioners, 1994.

Tillistrand, John A. "An Analysis of the McCarran-Ferguson Act: Should It be Repealed?" *CPCU Journal*, Vol. XLIII, No. 2 (June 1990).

Troxel, Terrie E.; and Bouchie, George E. *Property-Liability Insurance Accounting and Finance*, 3rd ed. Malvern. PA: American Institute for Property and Liability Underwriters, 1990.

U.S. Department of Justice. *A Report of the Task Force on Antitrust Immunities: The Pricing and Marketing of Insurance.* Washington, DC: U.S. Government Printing Office, 1977.

Using the NAIC Insurance Regulatory Information System: Life and Health and Fraternal Insurance (1978 ed.). Milwaukee: National Association of Insurance Commissioners, 1978.

Using the NAIC Insurance Regulatory Information System: Property and Liability Insurance (1978 ed.). Milwaukee: National Association of Insurance Commissioners, 1978.

Vaughan, Emmett J. "Economic Implications of the Repeal of the McCarran-Ferguson Act." *State Solutions for State Problems.* Tallahassee, FL: The Last Manifesto, 1980.

_____, and Therese M. Vaughan, "Proposition 103: Repealing the Law of Supply. " *CPCU Journal*, Vol. XLIII, No. 1 (March 1990).

_____, "The Case for Retaining Anti-Rebate Laws." *CPCU Journal*, Vol. XLIII, No. 4 (December 1990).

Wenck, Thomas L. "Insurer Insolvency: Causes, Effects and Solutions." *Journal of Insurance Issues and Practices,* Vol. X, No. 2 (June 1987).

Williams, C. A., Jr., and Andrew F. L. Whitman. "Open Competition Rating Laws and Price Competition." *Journal of Risk and Insurance*, XL, No. 4 (Dec. 1973).

CHAPTER 13

Legal Principles Relating to Insurance Buying

CHAPTER OBJECTIVES

When you have finished this chapter, you should be able to

Identify and explain the essential elements of a contract.

Explain how the general law of contracts applies to insurance contracts.

Explain why the principle of indemnity is
important to the operation of the insurance mechanism.

Explain the ways in which the principle of indemnity is enforced in insurance contracts.

Explain what is meant by the statements that insurance contracts
are contracts of adhesion, aleatory contracts, conditional contracts, unilateral contracts,
and contracts of utmost good faith.

Define and explain the nature of waiver and estoppel.

Explain the application of the doctrines of concealment and
misrepresentation in the insurance transaction.

■▪ Introduction ■ ■ ▪ ■ ▪ ■

The transfer of risk from the individual to the insurance company is accomplished through a contractual arrangement under which the insurance company, in consideration of the premium paid by the insured and the insured's agreement to abide by the provisions of the contract, promises to indemnify the insured or pay an agreed amount, in the event of the specified loss. The instrument through which this transfer of risk is accomplished is the insurance contract, which, as a contract, is enforceable by law.

A great deal of the law that has shaped the formal structure of insurance and influenced its content derives from the general law of contracts. But because of the many unique aspects of the insurance transaction, the general law has had to be modified to fit the needs of insurance. Our discussion involves a combination of both general contract law and its modifications relative to insurance, but with particular emphasis on those principles that are peculiar to insurance.

■▪ Insurance and the Law of Contracts ■ ■ ■ ■ ■ ■ ■ ■ ■ ■ ■

We begin our consideration of the legal aspects of insurance with a brief discussion of the general laws of contracts and the manner in which this special branch of law applies to the insurance transaction.

GENERAL REQUIREMENTS OF AN ENFORCEABLE CONTRACT

Insurance law is predominantly derived from the general law of contracts. Insurance policies, as is the case with all contracts, must contain the following elements to be binding legally.

1. Offer and acceptance
2. Consideration
3. Legal object
4. Competent parties
5. Legal form

Offer and Acceptance

To have a legally enforceable contract, a definite, unqualified offer must be made by one party, and this offer must be accepted in its exact terms by the other party. In the case of insurance, the *offer* is normally made by the prospect when applying for insurance. The *acceptance* takes place when the agent binds coverage or when the policy is issued. There is no requirement that the contract be in writing.

Under the Statute of Frauds, some types of contracts must be in writing to be enforceable. The only section of this statute that might be construed to apply to insurance contracts is that which requires written and signed proof of an agreement that by its terms is not to be performed within one year from its effective date. This provision has been interpreted to apply only to agreements that cannot possibly be performed within one year. Because the insurer's promise may be required to be fulfilled within one year, or even within one day, from the issue date of the policy, an insurance contract falls outside the statute. Hence, it may be said that in the absence of specific legislation to the contrary, an insurance contract can be oral in nature.[1] However, most insurance contracts are written, and only rarely is an oral contract used.

An oral contract is just as binding on both parties as is a written one. However, the difficulty of proving the terms of an oral contract, or even its existence, makes it advisable whenever possible to confine contractual agreements to those that are written. In certain instances, however, the situation may arise in which an oral contract of insurance may be necessary. When a prospective insured requests coverage from a property and liability agent, the agent may effect a contract orally, accepting the offer of the prospect. In such instances, coverage begins immediately. If a loss occurs before a written *binder* is issued,[2] or before the policy is issued, the company that the agent bound to the risk will be liable for the loss. However, the courts have ruled that if the agent represents more than one company, he or she must specify the company with which coverage is bound. The life insurance agent cannot bind the insurance company to a risk.

Offer and Acceptance and the Agent's Authority. Before leaving our discussion of offer and acceptance—the actions by which an insurance contract is created—we shall review the role of the insurance agent in creating a contract. In the property and liability field, in particular, the agent often acts for the insurer in accepting the insured's offer, thereby creating a contract. In addition to the power to "bind" the company to a risk by acceptance, the agent often acts on behalf of the insurer in other matters. Basically, the agent's authority to act on behalf of an insurer takes three forms, each derived from a somewhat different source: *express authority, implied authority,* or *apparent authority.*

Express authority, also sometimes called *stipulated authority,* is authority that is specifically granted to the agent. Agents are given express powers by their company in the agency agreement or contract. The agency contract gives the agent express authority to represent the company and generally contains clauses dealing

---

[1]Of course, the states have the power to require that insurance contracts be in writing, and some states have done so. For example, the state of Georgia requires that all contracts of insurance be in writing. Other jurisdictions prohibit oral contracts in the fields of life, health, and, occasionally, property and liability insurance. In the absence of specific legislation specifying that an insurance contract be in writing, such contracts may be oral.

[2]A "binder" is a temporary contract, normally issued for 30 days, that an agent uses as evidence of accepting the offer of the prospect. The binder issued by the company is accepted by the insured with the understanding that it provides the same coverage as the policy form in use by the company.

with such matters as the specific and general powers of the agent, the scale of commissions, and the ownership of the contracts sold, with a provision for cancellation of the contract.

In addition to those expressly granted powers, agents have certain implied powers, sometimes called *incidental authority*. Implied authority is the incidental authority required or reasonably necessary to execute the express authority. Although the agency contract may not specifically authorize the agent to advertise or to collect premiums from insureds, these are acts that are reasonably necessary to the duties expressly authorized.

Finally, under the doctrine of *apparent authority* (also sometimes called *ostensible authority*), the courts have ruled that agents have those powers that the public has come to expect them to have. Because it is accepted by the public that property and liability agents can bind their company to a risk, they have this power, in spite of the fact that the company may not have granted it expressly. Let us say, for example, that the insurance company has told a particular agent not to sell any insurance on match factories, but the agent binds coverage on such an establishment. Even though the company forbids the agent from binding such coverage, it is liable for any loss that occurs. As far as the public is concerned, an act by the agent is an act by the insurance company. He or she acts on behalf of the company in the insurance transaction, and under the laws of agency, these acts are deemed to be those of the company. If the agent binds the company to a risk, it is bound to that risk until such time as it effects cancellation of the contract.

Apparent authority arises only on the condition that the buyer has no way of knowing that the agent has exceeded his or her authority. Furthermore, the agent's authority may be extended by ratification. If the agent exceeds his or her authority and the insurer acquiesces by acting as if the agent actually had authority (e.g., by accepting the premium on coverage the agent bound while exceeding express authority), the agent then does have the authority.

Consideration

The binding force in any contract is the *consideration*, which is the thing of value that each party gives to the other. Like all contractual arrangements, the insurance transaction requires that both parties exchange consideration if the contract is to have proper legal status. The consideration of the insurance company lies in the promises that make up the contract, for example, the promise to pay if a loss should occur. The consideration on the part of the insured is the payment of the premium or the promise to pay it, plus an agreement to abide by the conditions of the contract. The promise to pay the premium is normally sufficient consideration for a legally binding contract in property and liability insurance. However, in life insurance, the first premium must be paid before the contract will take effect. And in a life insurance contract, only the first premium constitutes the consideration. This means that premiums subsequent to the first are not part of the legal consideration, because otherwise the contract could not come into existence until all the premiums were paid. The subsequent premiums, however, are conditions precedent to the continuance of the contract.

293

Legal Object

A contract must be *legal* in its purpose. A contract in which one party agreed to commit murder for a specified amount would be unenforceable in court because its object is not legal. Similarly, an insurance policy that is actually a gambling contract would be unenforceable as contrary to public policy, as would a policy that promised to assume the consequences of the insured's criminal acts. Perhaps the most common example of such a contract is one in which insurable interest does not exist, which the courts have generally refused to enforce. However, lack of insurable interest is not the only possibility. For example, a business interruption policy written on the operations of an illegal whiskey still would not be enforceable. It is even possible that an insurance contract providing physical damage coverage on the contents of an illegal gambling establishment would not be enforceable, but here there is divided legal opinion. Some courts would hold the entire contract unenforceable. Some would hold it unenforceable just with respect to the equipment that can be used only for gambling purposes; other equipment, such as tables, chairs, beds, and the like, if destroyed, would be an enforceable obligation of the insurance company.

Competent Parties

The parties to the agreement must be capable of entering into a contract in the eyes of the law. In most cases, the rules of *competency* are concerned with minors and the mentally incompetent. The basic principle is that some parties are not capable of understanding the contract they would enter into; therefore the courts have ruled that they are not bound by such agreements.

In the absence of a statute to the contrary, a minor is considered to be a person under the age of 21, although the majority of states have passed laws lowering the age to 18 in recent years. In addition, the marriage of a person also creates full contractual competence under the law. The legal rule respecting a contract with a minor is that, except for contracts involving a reasonable value of necessities of life, the contract is voidable at the option of the minor. Because insurance has never been held to be a necessity of life by the courts, a minor could purchase insurance, repudiate the contract later, and receive a refund of all premiums. Several states, however, have enacted statutes conferring on minors of a specified age or over the legal capacity to enter into valid and enforceable life insurance contracts. The age limit varies from 14½ to 18.

Legal Form

We have already noted that there is no requirement that the contract be in writing, but in many instances the form and content of a contract are rather carefully governed by state law. Many states, by law, use a standard fire insurance policy. In life insurance, a standard policy is not required in any state, but most insist on the inclusion of certain standard provisions in all life insurance policies. For example, the policy must provide that it will be incontestable after it has been in force during the lifetime of the insured for two years from the date of issue. Another standard provision also denies the life insurance company the right to void the policy because of a misstatement in age of the insured. In health insurance, the Uniform Law, adopted by practically all the states, demands that all individual and family health insurance contracts include 12 provisions specified and spelled out in the law.

In addition to the use of standard contracts and provisions, states require that all types of policies be filed with, and approved by, the state regulatory authorities before the policy may be sold in the state. This, of course, is to determine if the policy meets the requirements of the law, and to protect the policyholders from an unscrupulous insurance company that otherwise would take advantage of the public.

To be in *legal form*, then, the insurance contract must have the same wording as the legal standard policy, or must contain, in substance, the intent of the standard provisions. It must also follow the proper legal procedure of being filed and accepted by the state regulatory authority.

VOID AND VOIDABLE

The terms *void* and *voidable* are sometimes incorrectly used interchangeably. Actually, to speak of a "void contract" is a contradiction in itself. A contract that is void is not a contract at all but simply an agreement without legal effect. In essence, it lacks one of the requirements specified by law for a valid contract. A void contract cannot be enforced by either party. For example, a contract having an illegal object is void, and neither of the parties to the contract can enforce it. A *voidable contract*, in contrast, is an agreement that, for a reason satisfactory to the court, may be set aside by one of the parties. It is binding unless the party with the right to void it decides to do so. Assume, for example, that the insured fails to comply with a condition of the agreement. The company may elect, if it chooses, to fulfill its part of the contract, or it may elect to avoid it and revoke coverage. A contract may be held to be voidable for any one of a number of legal reasons. If one party was forced into the contract under duress, or if there was an element of fraud involved, the contract may be voidable.

■ Special Legal Characteristics of Insurance Contracts ■ ■ ■ ■ ■ ■ ■ ■ ■ ■ ■ ■ ■ ■ ■ ■ ■

In addition to those principles that apply to all contracts, certain legal characteristics are unique to insurance covenants.

INSURANCE IS A CONTRACT OF INDEMNITY

In many forms of insurance, particularly in property and liability, the contract is one of *indemnity*. This means that the insured is entitled to payment from the insurance company only if he or she has suffered a loss and only to the extent of the financial loss sustained. Put in its simplest terms, the principle of indemnity maintains that an individual should not be permitted to profit from the existence of an insurance contract but should be restored to the same financial condition that existed prior to the occurrence of the loss. Human nature being what it is, the ability to profit from the existence of an insurance policy would lead to the destruction of property as well as to other more serious crimes. The principle of indemnity is enforced through legal doctrines and policy provisions designed to limit the amount the insured can collect to the amount of the loss. The four most important of these principles are the doctrine of insurable interest, the concept of actual cash value, and the "other insurance" and "subrogation" provisions of insurance contracts.

Insurable Interest

The most important legal doctrine giving substance and support to the principle of indemnity is that of *insurable interest.* An insurance contract is legally binding only if the insured has an interest in the subject matter of the insurance and this interest is in fact *insurable.* In most instances, an insurable interest exists only if the insured would suffer a financial loss in the event of damage to, or destruction of, the subject matter of the insurance. To be more specific, an insurable interest involves a relationship between the person applying for the insurance and the subject matter of the insurance, such as a building or a person's life, so that there is a reasonable expectation of benefit or advantage to the applicant from the continuation of the subject matter or an expectation of loss or detriment from its cessation. In property and liability insurance, this relationship requires a pecuniary interest, and insurable interest is limited to the extent of that pecuniary interest. In life insurance, it is broad enough to recognize a sentimental interest or one based on love and affection.

The doctrine of insurable interest was developed as a means of ensuring that the insurance contract would not be used for wagering purposes and also to mitigate the moral hazard. It should be obvious that if Smith can purchase insurance on Brown's house and collect if the house is damaged or destroyed, Smith would be profiting from the insurance. Smith might even be inclined to cause the damage. In the absence of the doctrine of insurable interest, an insurance policy might be used as a gambling contract and could be an inducement to commit arson.

The doctrine is used in life insurance as a means to control wagering with human lives. It is also intended to reduce the threat of murder just as it is used in property insurance to reduce the threat of willful destruction of property. If the class of persons who can legally insure the life of another is restricted to those who are closely related to the insured by blood or marriage, or who possess such a financial relationship to the insured that they stand to gain more by his or her continued life than by death, the temptation to murder the insured will be greatly diminished.[3] A few states even require that the person whose life is to be insured by another must give consent to the transaction.

Insurable interest in property and liability insurance is established by means of a pecuniary relationship between the insured and the subject matter of the insurance.

---

[3]Murder, of course, may still exist. Murder of the insured by the beneficiary will not relieve the insurance company of its obligation to pay the proceeds of the policy. The proceeds will not be paid to the murderer-beneficiary, obviously, but will be paid to a contingent beneficiary or to the estate of the insured.

Perhaps the most obvious of these relationships is *ownership*. For example, if the insured owns an item of property such as a building or an automobile and if the property is destroyed, the insured will suffer a financial loss. Ownership, however, is not the only relationship that gives rise to insurable interest. If one has an interest in property for which title is held by another, then this interest may establish an insurable interest. An example would be property used as collateral for a debt. Thus a mortgagee has an insurable interest in the property mortgaged, and a lienholder has an insurable interest in the property on which the lien is held. In both cases, damage to, or destruction of, the collateral could cause the creditor financial loss.[4] Legal liability for loss of, or damage to, property of others in the care of someone else may also establish an insurable interest. For example, the operators of an automobile storage garage could become legally liable for damage to, or destruction of, customers' cars in their care if the proximate cause of loss was their negligence. The fact that a bailee may become liable for the property of the bailor establishes an insurable interest that is of great importance. There are other relationships that will not be mentioned here. As long as there is a relationship in which a financial loss would arise, it is a proper subject for a legally binding insurance contract.

An important aspect of the application of the doctrine to property and liability insurance involves the time at which the insurable interest must exist. The insurance contract will be valid only if the insurable interest exists at the time of the loss, regardless of whether it was or was not present at the inception date of the contract.

Insurable interest in life insurance requires a somewhat different relationship for its establishment, and it must exist at a different time. Here, a sentimental interest or one based on love and affection is sufficient to satisfy the requirement, even though a financial loss would not necessarily be involved. The family relationship of husband and wife is universally conceded, in and of itself, to satisfy the requirement. A number of courts, although perhaps a minority, have recognized the relationship of parent and child, of brother and sister, of grandparent and grandchild, and the like, as sufficient. In other relationships, particularly those of a business nature, the death of the insured must give rise to the definite and measurable financial loss if insurable interest is to exist. These include the interest of a corporation in the lives of key employees, a theatrical producer in the life of an actor, a professional baseball club in the lives of outstanding players, a partner in the lives of the other partners, and creditors in the lives of debtors.

In contrast to the requirement in property and liability insurance, an insurable interest must exist at the inception of the life insurance contract for the contract to be legal, but it need not be present at the time of the insured's death. For example, if Jones and Smith are partners in a business operation, it is obvious that if Jones should die, the partnership must be dissolved. The heirs of the deceased partner are entitled to his share of the business, even though the sale of the assets will terminate the venture and may involve all concerned in substantial losses. Because of this possibility of financial loss, each partner has an insurable interest in the life of

---

[4]However, the insurable interest of the mortgagee or the lienholder does not extend to the full value of the property used as collateral, but only to the extent of the indebtedness. Obviously, the creditor's financial loss would be limited to the balance of the debt, including unpaid interest.

the other. But what happens to the life insurance policy Jones has purchased on Smith's life if a voluntary dissolution terminates the business? Since the rule in life insurance is that insurable interest is not required at the time of the occurrence of the event insured against, Jones could continue to maintain the policy and collect the proceeds at Smith's death. In the same manner, it is also possible for a creditor to maintain insurance on a debtor's life even though the debt has been paid off.

The extent of the insurable interest depends on a number of factors. First, and perhaps most important, it is assumed that an individual has an unlimited insurable interest in his or her *own* life. This is based on the principle that one should be able to dispose of one's human life value with the same freedom that one can exercise in disposing of other property after death. For example, if a man can find a company that will sell him $1 million worth of life insurance, and if he can pay the premiums on this amount, the contract will be legitimate, even though his death will not cause a financial loss to anyone. His insurable interest in his own life is without limit. The insured has the right to designate anyone he so desires as the beneficiary of his life insurance, and it is not required that the beneficiary have an insurable interest in the life of the insured. The beneficiary has a legal claim to a fixed sum of money on the occurrence of the insured's death and, as a consequence, need not prove that he sustained a financial loss because of the death. A third-party applicant for the insurance, who is to be the beneficiary, however, must possess an insurable interest, and the amount of the insurance must bear a relationship to the extent of the interest. For example, in most jurisdictions, the insurance procured by a creditor on the life of a debtor must not be disproportionate to the amount of the debt as it existed at the time the policy was issued or as it was reasonably expected to be thereafter. The purpose of this requirement is to prevent the use of a debt as a cloak for a wagering transaction.

Actual Cash Value

The second doctrine that is used to enforce the principle of indemnity is the concept of *actual cash value.* No matter how much insurance an individual purchases, the amount one may recover is limited to the amount of his actual loss. If Smith owns a building worth $500,000 and he insures it for $1 million, in the event of a loss, he will be permitted to collect only the actual value of the building. Generally speaking, if persons were permitted to collect the face amount of their insurance contracts, regardless of the extent of the financial loss involved, this again would make the operation of the insurance principle impossible. Overinsurance would be common and would lead to willful destruction of property. As a result, it would upset any possibility of predicting losses with any reasonable degree of accuracy. Both results would be socially and economically undesirable. (The two standard measures of insurable value in property insurance, actual cash value and replacement cost, were discussed in Chapter 7.)

Although actual cash value is the basic measure of the financial loss of the insured in most types of property and liability insurance contracts, it is not the only measure used. In business interruption and in rent insurance, for example, the measure of financial loss is the insured's *loss of income* that arises because of inability to use and occupy the premises owing to physical damage to the property. In extra-expense insurance, the measure is the amount of *abnormal expense* incurred to make possible the continued operation of a business in the event its premises have been damaged or destroyed by certain specified perils. In liability insurance, it would be the amount of damages the insured is obligated to pay a third party in cases in which the proximate cause of the injuries of the third party has been the negligence of the insured. But regardless of the method used in measuring the loss, the principle of indemnity is applicable. The insurance company will pay only if a loss has occurred and only to the extent of the financial loss of the insured, not exceeding the limits of coverage purchased, of course.

Valued Policies and Cash Payment Policies   These are not contracts of indemnity in the strict sense. Under the *valued policy* principle, the insurer agrees on the value of the property at the time the contract begins and in the event of a total loss must pay the face amount of the policy. This type of contract is characteristic of ocean marine insurance and insurance on fine arts. Life insurance contracts, on the other hand, are *cash payment* policies. There is not necessarily an agreement on the value of the life insured, but the company agrees to pay the face value of the policy on the death of the insured.

In ocean marine insurance, the valued policy is more a historical consequence than a modern necessity. Many years ago, if a ship were lost at sea, it could be many months before the loss became known, and in many cases it would be virtually impossible to determine exactly where the loss occurred. As a consequence, the disagreements arising from the attempts to determine the value of the destroyed property at the time and place of the loss were insurmountable. In addition, it is obvious that when a ship is lost at sea, there is no physical evidence that could be used to help establish the value at the time of the loss. The practical alternative to actual cash value was the use of an agreed value for insurance purposes. The principle of insuring on the basis of an agreed value was developed in ocean marine insurance in early times, and it is still used today.

In cases where it would be difficult or impossible to determine the amount of the loss after it has taken place (as in the case of a rare or valuable work of art), the valued policy is used. Under these contracts, the face amount of the policy is paid in the event of a total loss, regardless of the actual amount of financial loss.

Valued Policy Laws   In addition to its use in marine insurance, the valued policy principle has been enacted into law in some form or other in about half of the states.[5] The Nebraska law is an example:

> Whenever any policy of insurance shall be written to insure any real property in this state against loss by fire, tornado, or lightning, and the property insured shall

---

[5]Valued policy laws exist in Arkansas, California, Georgia, Kansas, Minnesota, Mississippi, Missouri, Montana, Nebraska, New Hampshire, North Dakota, Ohio, South Carolina, South Dakota, Texas, and West Virginia.

be wholly destroyed, without criminal fault on the part of the insured or his assignee, the amount of the insurance written in such policy shall be taken conclusively to be the true value of the property insured and the true amount of loss and measure of damages.

This is an ill-conceived law and has little, if any, justification. Fortunately, however, it is limited in its application. The student should note carefully that it is applicable only to *real property*, only to the perils of *fire, lightning*, or *tornado*, and only if the loss to the real property is total.

A valued policy law is perhaps based on the mistaken assumption that if an insured pays for a certain amount of insurance, this is the amount that should be collected if a total loss occurs. If an insured has a dwelling with an actual cash value of $80,000 and purchases $100,000 coverage and the dwelling is totally destroyed by fire, the insurer will be obligated to pay the $100,000, even though this will yield the insured a profit of $20,000 and even though the contract promises to pay only the actual cash value of the destroyed property.[6] To permit the insured to profit through the existence of the insurance contract is in direct contradiction to the principle of indemnity and is contrary to public policy. Nevertheless, most valued policy laws have been in existence for many decades.

Cash Payment Policies   The principle of indemnity is necessary in most forms of property insurance to prevent the insured from profiting on the insurance contract, but in life insurance the principle has limited application. Here, the insurance company contracts to pay a stated sum of money in the event of the insured's death, and this sum is payable without reference to any financial loss resulting from the death. The life insurance contract, therefore, is a cash payment policy. In life insurance, not only is it difficult to place a monetary value on a human life, but to the extent that it can be approximated, most individuals would be substantially underinsured. Overinsurance, with the possibility of profiting through the existence of the insurance contract, is not generally an important problem in life insurance.

The principle of indemnity is applicable only partially in the field of health insurance. Policies providing benefits for loss of income due to disability are cash payment contracts and not contracts of indemnity. The coverage is for a fixed amount, as in life insurance, and this amount will be paid if the insured becomes disabled, even though no financial loss is suffered or the amount of the financial loss is less than the insurance. For example, if X has a disability policy that will pay $2000 per month in the event of total disability arising from sickness or bodily injury by accident, the insurance company must pay the $2000 per month, even though the insured has not had employment for some time and suffers no loss of earnings because of the disability. The basic reasons for the use of the cash payment contracts rather than the indemnity principle are much the same in health as in life insurance. It is so difficult to place an exact monetary value on disability or freedom from it that any attempts to do so after a disability has occurred would be highly impractical.

---

[6]The student is perhaps aware of the fact that, if there is a conflict between the provisions of a contract and a statute, the provisions of the statute will prevail.

Other Insurance

Most insurance contracts, other than life and in most instances health, contain some clause relating to coverage by other insurance; the primary purpose of the restriction is to prevent the insured from collecting for the same loss under two policies, and thereby profiting from the existence of duplicate insurance.

One of the most common of the other insurance clauses is one that is known as a *pro rata clause*. The provision in the basic fire insurance contract may be used as an illustration:

> This Company shall not be liable for a greater proportion of any loss that the amount hereby insured shall bear to the whole insurance covering the property against the peril involved, whether collectible or not.

An example will clarify the meaning. Let us assume that X has a building with an actual cash value of $200,000. She purchases $10,000 fire insurance coverage from Company A and $100,000 from Company B, and then suffers a fire loss of $5000. If X could collect $5000 from each insurance company, which she has every intention of doing, she would obviously profit from the existence of the insurance. But under the provisions of the pro rata clause in each policy, each insurer will be obligated to pay only that proportion of the loss that its insurance bears to the total fire insurance on the property. Each company will pay $2500. This will rather effectively prevent the insured from profiting.

Another common type of other insurance clause is one that makes the insurance excess over other valid and collectible insurance. A partial statement of the other insurance clause in an inland marine personal property floater is as follows:

> If at the time of the loss or damage, there is other valid and collectible insurance which would attach . . . had this policy not been effected, then this insurance shall apply as excess over all such other insurance and in no event as contributing insurance.

This clause is typical of inland marine insurance contracts and is also found to some extent in other property and liability insurance contracts. The excess other insurance clause is a method of distributing the insurance in those instances where more than one policy covers a specific loss, and, similar in purpose with that of the pro rata clause, it prevents the insured from profiting through the existence of the insurance contract.

Another approach to other insurance is a provision in some contracts that makes the insurance inapplicable to property that is covered by other insurance. A common provision of this type states:

> We do not cover articles separately described and specifically insured by other insurance.

Provisions of this type are referred to as *exculpatory clauses*, since they relieve the insurer of liability for loss.

The ocean marine contract provides still another contrast with the pro rata clauses used in property and liability insurance. Under the U.S. rule, if there is double insurance, the ocean marine policy with the earliest effective date is the primary insurance.[7] A policy with a subsequent effective date will be applicable only if the primary insurance is insufficient to provide full coverage for the loss.

Subrogation

Another contractual provision designed to prevent the insured from making a profit is the *subrogation clause.* Here, if the insured collects indemnity under the policy and the loss has been caused by the negligence of some third party, the right to collect damages from the negligent party must be relinquished to the insurance carrier. However, relinquishment is required only to the extent of the amount paid by the insurance company. The right of subrogation is based on the principle that if it did not exist, the insured would be permitted to collect twice for the loss, once from the insurance company and once from the negligent party. This, of course, would be profiting from the existence of the insurance contract.

The doctrine of subrogation is applicable only in property and liability insurance. It is never applied in life insurance and seldom in health insurance. For example, if X has a $100,000 life insurance contract and is killed while crossing the street as the result of the negligence of the operator of a 10-ton truck, the widow-beneficiary can collect the $100,000 from the insurance company and in addition can sue the driver and the trucking firm. The insurance company has no right to reimbursement from the negligent party. The inapplicability of the doctrine is based on the principle that in life insurance the policy is not a contract of indemnity. Support is also provided in the fact that in terms of one's economic value, most individuals will be substantially underinsured. Therefore, the possibility of profiting from the existence of a life insurance contract is relatively slight. The same principles are true in health insurance. For example, if X had a disability income contract that would provide a payment of $500 per week in the event of total disability, and if X is injured seriously as a result of the negligent operation of the 10-ton truck, he or she can collect the $500 per week from the insurance company and can also collect damages from the trucking firm without reference to the insurance coverage. The disability insurance company would have no rights against the negligent third party.

INSURANCE IS A PERSONAL CONTRACT

Although insurance coverage may apply to property, the risk is transferred to the company from an individual. While we speak of "insuring a house" or some other piece of property, the contract is between the company and a specifically named insured. If the insured should sell the property that is "insured," the protection is not binding in favor of the new owner of the property. Since the company has a

---

[7]The English rule involved prorating regardless of the order of the dates on the contracts. Any company providing the insurance may become liable for the full amount of its coverage. However, if the insured collects from one specific insurer, the other companies would then be liable to this insurer for their pro rata share of the loss.

right to decide with whom it will and will not do business, the insured cannot transfer the contract to someone else without the written consent of the insurer. The personal characteristics of the insured and the circumstances surrounding the subject matter of the coverage are important to the insurance company in determining whether it will issue the policy.

One important aspect of the application of the personal contract rule to insurance policies is the right of the insured to assign an insurance policy to another person. Because the general rule states that one cannot be forced to contract against one's will, the right of the insured to assign the policy must require the consent of the insurance company. Otherwise, the company could be legally bound on a contract with an individual to whom it would never have issued a policy originally, and on one in which the nature of the risk is altered substantially. For example, suppose an automobile owner decided to sell his or her car to a 17-year-old boy. If it were possible to assign the insurance policy to the boy without the consent of the insurance company, the company would then be in the position of contracting with a person with whom originally it would not have dealt. The insured has the right to assign his or her policy, but in most contracts the assigned policy will be legally binding only with the written consent of the insurance company.

In some instances, an insured will assign the proceeds of the policy if a loss occurs, for example, to a mortgagee, a lienholder, or another creditor. This type of assignment is valid without the consent of the insurance company. It does not change the contracting parties or the nature of the risk; it merely entitles the recipient to a certain amount of money without making the person a party to the contract.

The requirement of written consent of the insurance company in the event of an assignment of the policy is not applicable to all insurance contracts. Life insurance policies are freely assignable without permission. The applicable rule is that anyone having an interest in a life insurance contract can transfer this interest, even to a person who does not have an insurable interest in his life and under circumstances in which no financial consideration is involved. Although no restrictions are placed on the right of the insured to assign a life insurance policy, the policy provides that the insurance company will not be bound by any assignment until it has received written notice of the assignment. This is simply for the protection of the company. An owner might, for example, assign the policy, and the company, not being aware of the fact, might make payment to someone other than the person to whom the policy was assigned. To avoid litigation and eliminate the possibility of being required to make a double payment, the company requires written notice of any assignment and is not bound by the assignment until the notice is received.

The difference in the application of the rule of assignment in life insurance, as contrasted with its application in the property and liability field, may be explained largely by the fact that an assignment of a life insurance policy does not alter the nature of the risk to the insurance carrier, but merely changes the ownership of the contract. The person whose life is insured is still the person insured, and the assignment should have no appreciable effect on the possibility of the insured's death. In property insurance, however, the assignment could have a substantial effect on the possibility of the occurrence of a loss.

INSURANCE IS A UNILATERAL CONTRACT

Only one party to the contract is legally bound to do anything. The insured makes no promises that can be legally enforced. It is true that an insurance policy is a conditional contract, and if the insured violates certain conditions of the contract he or she may be prevented from collecting in the event of a loss.

INSURANCE IS A CONTRACT OF ADHESION

A *contract of adhesion* is one prepared by one of the parties (the company) and accepted or rejected by the other (the insured). It is not drawn up through negotiation; the insured who does not particularly like the terms of the contract may choose not to purchase it, but if he or she does purchase it, it must be accepted as it is.

Because the insurance company has the right to draw up the contract, the courts have held that any ambiguity in the contract should be interpreted in favor of the insured. It is somewhat like the case of two small children and the device commonly adopted to settle the dispute as to which of the two gets the biggest piece of pie: "One child cuts and the other gets first pick." The company draws up the contract, and the insured gets the benefit of any doubt.

The fact that the insurance policy is a contract of adhesion and the insured must accept or reject the terms as they are written makes the doctrine of "presumption of intent" rather important in the area of insurance. Under this doctrine, the courts have ruled that a person is bound by the terms of a written contract that he or she signs or accepts, whether or not he or she reads the contract. In other words, the court assumes that the insured reads the contract and agrees with the terms thereof.

INSURANCE IS AN ALEATORY CONTRACT

Briefly, the term *aleatory* means that the outcome is affected by chance and that the number of dollars given up by the contracting parties will be unequal. The insured pays the required premium, and if no loss occurs, the insurance company pays nothing. If a loss does occur, the insured's premium is small in relation to the amount the insurer will be required to pay. In the sense that it is aleatory, an insurance contract is like a gambling contract.

INSURANCE IS A CONDITIONAL CONTRACT

Since the promises of the insurance company are conditioned upon the insured paying the initial and subsequent premiums and also his fulfilling any requirements of the contract, insurance is a conditional contract. The insured does not promise to continue paying premiums on the policy, but the promises of the insurer are conditional upon his doing so and upon his fulfilling any policy requirements, such as filing a proof of loss and the like.

INSURANCE IS A CONTRACT OF UTMOST GOOD FAITH

Partly because the contract is aleatory, the insurer and the insured enter into an agreement where mutual faith is of paramount importance. The legal principle of *uberrmae fidei (utmost good faith)* has deep historical roots in its application to insurance. In the early days of marine insurance, an underwriter was often called on to insure a ship that was halfway around the world and had to accept the word of the applicant that the ship was still afloat. The practical effect of the principle of utmost good faith today lies in the requirement that the applicant for insurance must make full and fair disclosure of the risk to the agent and the company. The risk that the company thinks it is assuming must be the same risk that the insured transfers. Any information about the risk that is known to one party should be known to the other. If the insured intentionally fails to inform the insurer of any facts that would influence the issue of the policy or the rate at which it would be issued, the insurer may have grounds for avoiding coverage. The courts have given meaning to the principle of "utmost good faith" through the evolution of the doctrines of misrepresentation, warranty, and concealment.

When disagreement concerning the conditions relating to an insurance contract arises, the insured or the insurer (or both) may turn to the courts for relief. In some cases, the court will be asked to interpret the contract when there is disagreement about its terms. In other cases, the parties may seek rescission or reformation of the contract. Rescission is the annulment or abrogation of the contract. The contract is repudiated and declared null from its beginning. The party seeking rescission of a contract must prove impossibility (usually not the case in insurance) or fraud, misrepresentation of a material fact, or concealment. In insurance, it is usually the insurer that seeks rescission of a contract, usually because of a misrepresentation or concealment of a material fact by the insured.

Reformation is a remedy when a written contract does not reflect the original intent of the parties. It is used to rectify mutual mistakes or unilateral mistakes coupled with fraud by the other party by rewriting the contract to express the original intent of the parties. The purpose of reformation is not to change the terms of the contract. Rather, it is to rectify a misstatement of those terms when they have somehow been incorrectly recorded.

Misrepresentation

A representation is an oral or written statement made by the applicant prior to, or contemporaneously with, the formation of the contract. It constitutes an inducement for the insurer to enter into the contract. Normally, the representations are the answers to certain questions that the applicant gives concerning the subject matter of the insurance. For example, in the negotiation of a life insurance contract, if the prospect states in answer to a question that he or she has never had tuberculosis, this statement is a representation. If the statement is false, a *misrepresentation* exists that may provide grounds for the insurer's avoidance of the contract later on. However, a misrepresentation may give grounds for rescission of a contract only if it involves what is known as a "material fact." A material fact is information that, had it been known, would have caused the insurance company to reject the application or issue the policy on substantially different terms. Facts of minor importance, such as the age at which one's grandparents died, if misrepresented, would have had no influence on the terms of the contract had the truth been known and, therefore, would not provide a basis for rescission of the contract.

The doctrine of misrepresentation is applied with varying degrees of strictness. Since frequently in ocean marine insurance there is little chance for the insurer to inspect the subject matter of the insurance, the company must place greater reliance on the information supplied by the applicant than would be the case in domestic insurance. Therefore, it has always been a rule in ocean marine insurance that a misrepresentation of a material fact, even though there was no bad faith on the part of the insured, is grounds for rescission of the contract. In other words, even though fraud is not involved, the mere fact that certain conditions are misrepresented and exercise an improper influence is sufficient to exonerate the carrier from its contractual obligation.

In most other forms of insurance, the misrepresentation must be made with fraudulent intent before the insurer can use it as grounds for rescission of the contract. This application of the principle is, of course, based somewhat on the assumption that the subject matter of the insurance can be inspected by the insurance company. The company, then, is not obligated to depend so strictly for its knowledge on the information provided by the insured and therefore cannot have grounds for voidance of a contract unless it can prove a willful intent to defraud the company. For example, a provision in the basic fire insurance policy states:

> This entire policy shall be void if, whether before or after a loss, the insured has willfully concealed or misrepresented any material fact or circumstance concerning this insurance or the subject matter thereof.

Thus the fire policy, by its provisions, requires a willful intent on the part of the insured to defraud the company before the policy can be voided.

Many applicants for insurance are inclined to misrepresent important facts. Naturally, the reason for this is to obtain insurance where otherwise no company would issue a policy at all or to obtain the coverage at a lower cost.

Some states have a statutory requirement that the misrepresented or concealed material fact contribute to the loss before it can give grounds for voiding a policy. These are ill-conceived laws and have about as much justification as valued policy legislation. The illogical result of such legislation may be demonstrated rather easily. For example, in a nonmedical life insurance contract, the insured could misrepresent the fact that he has a serious heart impairment. If the insurer had known this fact, it would not have issued the policy. If the insured dies as a result of an automobile accident, and not because of the heart impairment, the company will be obligated to pay the proceeds of the policy because the misrepresented fact did not contribute to the loss. Such legislation seems to put a premium on fraud or at least make contracts based on fraudulent intent much more feasible. The rule followed in most states, that is, the possibility of voidance whether or not the misrepresented or concealed fact contributes to the loss, places the insurance contract on a much more logical and justifiable basis.

In life insurance, a misrepresentation may be used as grounds for voiding a policy only if the false information is part of the written application and only if the application, or a photostatic copy thereof, is attached to the policy. In most other forms of insurance, the application is rarely a physical part of the contract; however, even though the application is not attached to the policy, the doctrine of misrepresentation is still applicable.

Warranties

When a representation is made a part of the insurance contract, usually by physical attachment of the application to the policy, the statements of the insured then become warranties. Warranties, by definition, also include promises of the insured that are set forth in the policy. The promise to maintain certain protective devices, such as burglar alarms, in proper working order at all times would be an example. A *breach of warranty* may give grounds for voiding a policy, and most important, it may do so without reference to the materiality of the statement or promise. Therefore, whether the insurer was prejudiced by the untruth or nonfulfillment of the promise is not a consideration. The mere breach of warranty will provide grounds for voiding the contract. The warranty, therefore, is quite different from a representation in that (1) the warranty need not be material and (2) the warranty must be part of the contractual agreement.

A breach of warranty as a means of avoiding a contract is in general much too harsh a doctrine to be applied to insurance contracts. As a consequence, its unqualified use is found only in ocean marine insurance. Here, for example, if the insured warrants that the ship will be used only in coastwise trade, any use otherwise, even though it would not materially increase the risk, would be a breach of warranty and could void the contract. However, in other forms of insurance, the use of the doctrine has been modified substantially. Courts have tended to look with disfavor on the strict application of the doctrine and, in most instances, have modified it by requiring that the breach of warranty materially increase the risk before it may be used to void an insurance contract. There have also been some statutory modifications of the use of the doctrine. For example, in life insurance, the statements of the insured, regardless of the fact that they are part of the contract, can have the legal effect only of representations. This means that the breach of warranty must involve a material fact. Other statutory modifications provide that the breach of warranty will prevent recovery by the insured only if it increased the risk of loss, or only if it contributed to the loss. The disfavor into which warranties have fallen and the difficulties of enforcing their use is gradually leading to their abandonment except in ocean marine contracts. Instead of a promise in the form of a warranty, such as one requiring the insured to maintain certain protective equipment (e.g., burglar alarms) in proper working order at all times, the policy may provide an exclusion to the effect that the insurance coverage is not applicable while the equipment is in disrepair.

Concealment

The disclosure of proper and accurate information is not all that is required if the knowledge of both parties of the material facts is to be equal. The applicant also has the obligation of voluntarily disclosing material facts concerning the subject matter of the insurance that the company could not be expected to know about. The failure of the insured to disclose such facts constitutes a concealment, and a willful concealment of a material fact will give grounds for voiding the policy.[8]

Since the insurance company cannot be expected to inquire about everything that may be material to the subject matter of the insurance, the insured has an obligation to disclose extraordinary facts within the scope of his or her knowledge. For example, a company normally would not ask the insured in the application whether there is a whiskey still in the basement of his or her home. However, if the insured has such an apparatus, this fact must be revealed to the company. If this is not done, the policyholder may be dismayed to discover that the insurance is without effect. Legislatures have also tampered with this doctrine, and, as is the case with representations, some states require that the fact concealed contribute to the loss before it will give grounds for voiding the policy. So if faulty wiring in the attic, rather than the still, were the cause of the loss, the policy would be valid. There are many other possibilities of concealments, yet this example should be sufficient for the student to recognize that any extraordinary fact related to the subject matter of the insurance, which the insurance company could not be expected to know, requires disclosure of such fact to the insurance company.

Waiver and Estoppel

Directly linked to the doctrines of concealment and misrepresentation are those of waiver and estoppel. These doctrines also relate directly to the law of agency and to the power of the agent.

Waiver is the intentional relinquishment of a known right. If the agent issues a contract, knowing that the conditions are being violated, that agent is deemed to have waived the violation. For example, let us assume that a man takes out an automobile liability policy, and in the application he states that no male drivers under 25 years of age will be operating the car, when the truth of the matter is that his 17-year-old son operates the car almost exclusively (probably in stock car races). Let us assume further that the agent knows full well that this is the case. Since the knowledge of the agent is presumed to be knowledge of the company, the agent is deemed to have waived this violation when issuing the policy.

Estoppel prevents a person from alleging or denying a fact the contrary of which, by his own previous action, he has admitted. The waiving of a violation of the

---

[8]In ocean marine insurance, the concealment does not have to be willful. In other forms of insurance, however, the material fact concealed must be with the intent to defraud.

contract by the agent *estopps* the company from denying liability on the basis of this violation at some time in the future.

The powers of the life insurance agent, as we have said before, are somewhat more limited than are those of the property and liability agent. For the property and liability agent, however, make no mistake: the powers are extremely broad, and the power of waiver on the part of the agent has been extended by court decision. For example, in an attempt to protect themselves from actions on the part of their agents, insurance companies have inserted the following clause in the standard fire policy:

> No permission affecting this insurance shall exist or waiver of any provision be valid, unless granted herein or expressed in writing added hereto.

Does this clause really protect the companies from the waiver powers of agents? Let us suppose that an insurance agent receives a call from a client who says, "I just put a still in my basement and I wondered if this would affect my insurance." (Naturally it would, for this is a provision in the policy suspending coverage at any time the hazard is increased by any means within the control of the insured.) The agent, however, says, "Don't worry about it—it's OK." If a fire occurs, will the insured be able to collect? The company will probably point to the clause stating that no waiver is valid unless expressed in writing, but this may not do much good. Some courts have ruled that the agent can waive the quoted clause along with any other clauses in the contract. In other words, the power of the agent is so strong that he or she can waive the very clause prohibiting waiver of any of the clauses in the contract!

The Parol Evidence Rule

While on the subject of the interpretation of contracts, we should note in passing one of the important principles of law related to the interpretation of written contracts: the *parol evidence rule*. This rule holds that when parties to a contract have committed their agreement to writing, the written contract is presumed to contain the agreement of the parties and that the contract cannot be modified or changed by parol (i.e., oral) evidence. In simple terms, this means that arguments about what the parties "agreed to" cannot be used to contradict what the written contract expresses as the agreement. There are a limited number of exceptions in which the parol evidence rule is not applicable and in which the terms of a written contract can therefore be modified by oral evidence. Parol evidence may be admissible in situations in which the terms of a written contract are incomplete, where the contract is ambiguous, or when there has been a mistake or fraud in the preparation of the written contract.

With respect to insurance contracts, a strict application of the parol evidence rule means that the written contract is the agreement of the parties and that it cannot be modified by the insured's argument that the agent had agreed to provide coverage different from that in the contract.[9]

---

[9]Although the insurer would not be held liable for the agent's agreement to obtain a different form of coverage than that which was written, the agent might be liable to the insured for negligent failure to obtain the appropriate coverage.

THE INSURANCE CONTRACT AS A CONTRACT

When members of society who have entered into a contractual arrangement disagree about the terms of the contract, or one of the parties questions the very existence of the contract, either party has recourse to the courts. The court will decide the issue in question. We have already noted that, with respect to insurance contracts, any ambiguity is interpreted against the insurer. There is a second doctrine of policy interpretation with which the reader should be familiar, the doctrine of reasonable expectation.

Reasonable Expectation

The doctrine of the insured's *reasonable expectations* represents an extension of the general rule that ambiguities are to be interpreted against the insurer. Under this doctrine, the courts interpret an insurance policy to mean what a reasonable buyer would expect it to mean. When it is applied, the "reasonable expectations" of the insured determine the coverage of the policy, even though policy provisions may deny those expectations. An important corollary of this doctrine is that policy language is to be interpreted as a layperson would understand it, and not as it might be interpreted by a lawyer or other person skilled in the law of insurance.[10]

Complexity of Insurance Contracts

The complicated nature of the insurance contract has made it the butt of many jokes. "Why," people often ask, "doesn't the insurance company make the policy language simple enough for the layperson to understand?" "Why not cut out some of the excess wordage?" The answer to both questions is that the companies are in fact attempting to do precisely that. There is a trend within the industry toward simplified policy language, and much progress has been made in this area. However, it is a difficult task. As a contract enforceable by law, the insurance policy must set forth as clearly and as unambiguously as possible every condition and obligation of both parties. In addition, the insurer must attempt to define as precisely as possible the particular event against which protection is provided, while at the same time attempt to protect itself against misinterpretation by the courts. Even though companies are attempting to simplify policy wording, the task is complicated by the stern realities of the law and the possibility that any ambiguity will be interpreted against the insurer.

Insurance and the Courts

The courts play an important role in the operation of private insurance. Court decisions are important in the individual case because they decide the issue. More important from our point of view, they set precedents that are applied in future instances. Court interpretations of insurance policies make policy interpretation difficult in

[10] See Robert E. Keeton, *Basic Text on Insurance Law* (St. Paul, Minn.: West, 1971), p. 357.

one sense, in that there is always the distinct possibility that the court will construe a contract in a way that the insurer had not considered. On the other hand, past decisions are useful in interpreting contracts, for they indicate the court's view of the policy's meaning. Because the insurer has the option of changing future contracts, court decisions often influence the drawing of insurance contracts.

POLICY CONSTRUCTION

In the chapters that follow, we will examine a number of insurance contracts, and although all are different, they are similar in that they are all composed of four basic parts:

1. Declarations
2. Insuring agreements
3. Exclusions
4. Conditions

Declarations

The declarations section contains the statements made by the insured. As we have seen, these are usually considered to be representations by the courts. Also included in this section is information about the location of the property insured, the name of the policyholder, and other matters relating to the identification of the person or property insured.

Insuring Agreements

In this section, the company promises to pay for loss if it should result from the perils covered. Coverage may be provided in one of two principal ways. It is either on a *named-peril* basis, in which case the policy lists the perils insured against, or it is on an *open-peril* basis. Open-peril policies cover loss by any perils except those that are specifically excluded.

Exclusions

In this section, the company states what it will not do. The number of exclusions has a direct relationship to the broadness or narrowness of the insuring agreement. If the policy is written on a named-peril basis, the exclusions may be few. On the other hand, open-peril policies require more exclusions to eliminate coverage for those perils that are uninsurable. The exclusions are a basic part of the contract, and a complete knowledge of them is essential to a thorough understanding of the agreement. Certain perils must be excluded from insurance contracts either because they are not insurable or because the basic premium does not contemplate the exposure and the coverage must be obtained through the payment of an additional premium or under another more specialized contract.

Conditions

This section spells out in detail the duties and rights of both parties. Most of the clauses contained in it are fairly standard; they relate to the duties of the insured in the event of loss, and they protect the insurance company from adverse loss experience through increases in the hazard within the control of the insured.

IMPORTANT CONCEPTS TO REMEMBER

requirements of an enforceable contract	insurable interest	utmost good faith
offer and acceptance	actual cash value	*uberrimae fidei*
consideration	replacement cost	rescission
legal object	valued policies	reformation
legal form	cash payment policies	misrepresentation
competent parties	valued policy law	material fact
binder	pro rata clause	breach of warranty
void	exculpatory clause	concealment
voidable contract	subrogation	waiver
express authority	personal contract	estoppel
implied authority	unilateral contract	parol evidence rule
apparent authority	contract of adhesion	reasonable expectation
contract of indemnity	conditional contract	
	aleatory contract	

QUESTIONS FOR REVIEW

1. The principles of insurable interest, subrogation, actual cash value, and pro rata apportionment all stem from the broader principle of indemnity. Explain what is meant by the principle of indemnity, and indicate specifically in what way each of the four principles mentioned above helps to enforce the principle of indemnity.

2. We have noted several instances in which the principle of indemnity is not enforced in the various fields of insurance. List the exceptions to the principle of indemnity with which you are now familiar and explain why each is permitted.

3. In what ways have the doctrines of warranty and misrepresentation been modified in their application to the field of insurance in the United States?

4. What is the key factor in determining whether a fact is "material" in the application of the doctrines of misrepresentation and concealment?

5. Insurance contracts are said to be aleatory. What important additional feature of insurance contracts follows from this characteristic?

6. In what sense is an insurance contract conditional? In what sense is it unilateral?

7. Strictly speaking, life insurance is not a contract of indemnity. Nevertheless, there are certain applications of the principle of indemnity in this field. To what extent does the principle of indemnity apply to life insurance?

8. Identify and briefly describe the four basic sections of insurance contracts.

9. What is meant by the expression, "The policyholder gets the benefit of the doubt," in connection with any interpretation of the provisions of the life insurance policy?

10. Describe the doctrine of *reasonable expectations*. Does this seem to you to be a reasonable legal doctrine? Why or why not?

QUESTIONS FOR DISCUSSION

1. The insurance buyer for a local retail store calls his insurance agent at 3:00 A.M. and asks the agent to increase the coverage on the firm's inventory from $600,000 to $800,000. The agent binds the coverage. During the night the store burns to the ground and total inventory valued at $1 million is destroyed. The insurer denies liability for the additional $200,000 in coverage. On what ground do you think the denial is based? Should the company be obligated to pay the original $600,000?

2. The subrogation provision enforces the principle of indemnity by preventing the insured from profiting from the existence of the insurance contract. What other beneficial effect might it have?

3. Jones tells the insurance company that his building is equipped with a sprinkler system and that a guard is on duty inside the premises when they are closed. Neither statement is true. The building is destroyed by a windstorm. Do you believe that an intentional misrepresentation by an applicant for insurance should permit the insurer to deny coverage for a loss even if the misrepresented fact had no relationship to the loss? Why?

4. Jones and his partner, Smith, carry insurance on their factory under a Commercial Property Coverage Form. They have both been worried about the recurring operating losses of the firm. Unbeknownst to Jones, Smith torches the building in the hope that the insurance recovery will return at least a part of their investment. The two are equal partners in the enterprise and the building is insured for its full replacement cost value of $2.5 million. There is a $1.5 million mortgage on the building. Shortly after the fire, the state fire marshall apprehends Smith, who confesses to the arson. Discuss the insurer's liability under this contract.

5. In your opinion, is it possible to create insurance contracts that laypeople can understand? Why or why not?

SUGGESTIONS FOR ADDITIONAL READING

Athearn, James L., Travis Pritchett, and Joan T. Schmit. *Risk and Insurance*, 6th ed. St. Paul, MN: West Publishing, 1989. Chapter 4.

Black, Kenneth, Jr., and Harold D. Skipper, Jr. *Life Insurance*, 12th ed. Englewood Cliffs, NJ: Prentice-Hall, 1994. Chapter 8.

Greene, Mark R., James S. Trieschmann, and Sandra G. Gustavson. *Risk and Insurance*, 8th ed. Cincinnati: South-Western Publishing, 1992. Chapters 4–5.

Grieder, J.E., and W.H. Beadles. *Law and the Life Insurance Contract*, 4th ed. Homewood, IL: Richard D. Irwin, 1979.

Horn, R.C. *Subrogation in Insurance Theory and Practice.* Homewood, IL: Richard D. Irwin, 1964.

Keeton, Robert E. *Basic Text on Insurance Law.* St. Paul, MN: West Publishing, 1971.

Lorimer, James J., et. al. *The Legal Environment of Insurance*, 4th ed. Vol. I. Malvern, PA: American Institute for Property and Liability Underwriters, 1993.

McGill, D.M. *Legal Aspects of Life Insurance.* Homewood, IL: Richard D. Irwin, 1959.

Patterson, E.W., and W. F. Young, Jr. *Cases and Materials on the Law of Insurance*, 4th ed. New York: Foundation Press, 1961.

———. *Essentials of Insurance Law*, 2nd ed. New York: McGraw-Hill, 1957.

Vance, W.R., and B.M. Anderson. *Handbook on the Law of Insurance*, 5th ed. St. Paul, MN: West Publishing, 1951.

CHAPTER 14

Risk Financing: Retention

CHAPTER OBJECTIVES

When you have finished this chapter, you should be able to

Describe the distinctions between intentional and unintentional retention, voluntary and involuntary retention, and funded and unfunded retention.

•

Explain the difference between financing losses and financing the cost of risk.

•

Identify the approaches that may be used in selecting appropriate risk retention levels.

•

Describe the current tax treatment with respect to risk retention programs.

•

Explain the advantages and disadvantages of self-insurance.

•

Describe the ways in which retention and transfer may be combined.

•

Explain the rationale for and describe the operation of cash-flow plans.

▧ Introduction ■

Risk retention is one of the two techniques of risk finance, the process whereby the risk manager arranges the availability of funds to replace property, meet obligations, and continue operations in the event of loss. It is an alternative to the other risk-financing technique, insurance.

Risk retention can assume a variety of modes, from an informal arrangement in which losses are simply paid as operating expenses as they occur to a highly structured arrangement in which the entity establishes a captive insurance company. In many instances, risk retention is combined with risk transfer, in arrangements whereby the organization assumes losses up to a specific level and is indemnified for losses above that level. Ideally, risk retention should be supported by risk control measures, since when risk is retained, the organization must bear the financial impact of the losses that occur. To the extent that risk control measures minimize the magnitude of retained losses, risk retention becomes more workable. Although the following discussion is only an introduction to the subject, it should provide an insight into the manner in which risk retention can be used in dealing with the risk management problem.

Risk Retention Techniques Classified ■ ■ ■ ■ ■ ■ ■ ■ ■ ■ ■

As noted above, risk retention may assume a variety of forms and may arise in a variety of circumstances. The following discussion outlines some of the more important distinctions.

INTENTIONAL AND UNINTENTIONAL RETENTION

A little reflection on the matter will indicate that risk retention may be intentional or unintentional. Because risk retention is the "residual" or "default" risk management technique, any exposures that are not avoided, reduced, or transferred are retained. This means that when nothing is done about a particular expo-sure, the risk is retained. Unintentional retention occurs when a risk is not recognized. The firm unwittingly and unintentionally retains the risk of loss arising out of the exposure.

Unintentional retention can occur even when the risk has been recognized, but the measures designed to deal with it are improperly implemented. If, for example, the risk manager recognizes the exposure to loss in connection with a particular exposure and intends to transfer that exposure through insurance, but then acquires an insurance policy that does not fully cover the loss, the risk is retained.

Obviously, unintentional risk retention is always undesirable. Because the risk is not perceived, the risk manager is never afforded the opportunity to make the decision concerning what should be done about it on a rational basis. Also, when the unintentional retention occurs as a result of improper implementation of the technique that was designed to deal with the exposure, the resulting retention is contrary to the intent of the risk manager.

VOLUNTARY–INVOLUNTARY RISK RETENTION

In addition to the distinction between intentional and unintentional risk retention, we can differentiate between those risks that are voluntarily retained and involuntarily retained. Involuntary retention occurs when it is not possible to avoid, reduce, or transfer the exposure to an insurance company. Uninsurable exposures represent a good example of involuntary retention.

Some forms of retention are, in a sense, on the border between voluntary and involuntary retention. In the case of liability insurance, for example, it may be noted that the organization retains the risk of loss in excess of the limits of coverage that it carries. A business that carries a $5 million umbrella, for example, tacitly assumes the risk of all losses in excess of this limit. Although the risk manager may explicitly consider the decision in this context, selecting the $5 million limit is a decision to retain risks in excess of that limit.

FUNDED VERSUS UNFUNDED RETENTION

A final distinction that may be drawn is between funded retention and unfunded retention. In a funded retention program, the firm earmarks assets and holds them in some liquid or semi-liquid form against the possible losses that are retained. The need for segregated assets to fund the retention program will depend on the firm's cash flow and the size of the losses that may result from the retained exposure.

◼️ Financing Losses Versus Financing Risk ◼️◼️◼️◼️◼️◼️◼️◼️◼️

The choice between transfer and retention, or the way in which retention and transfer should be combined, should recognize the distinction between financing losses and financing risk. A brief review of terminology may be helpful. Risk, we have seen, is the possibility of a loss. Not all losses involve risk, which is the possibility of a deviation from what is expected. If "expected" losses are $20,000 a year, but could be as much as $1,000,000, the risk is $980,000 ($1,000,000 minus $20,000).

The $20,000 represents a predictable loss, which may be treated by retention or by transfer to an insurer. The remaining $980,000 represents "risk," which may also be retained or transferred to an insurer. The fact that the funding of losses and financing of risk can use the same techniques often results in both functions being handled in the same way. Under some circumstances, this is perfectly acceptable. The more predictable the normal loss, the less appropriate the transfer for dealing with it. But as the normal loss becomes increasingly variable, it becomes increasingly advantageous to insure the exposure.

THE COST OF FINANCING RISK

The distinction between financing losses and financing risk raises an important principle in the decision to retain or transfer a particular exposure, the *cost of financing risk*. When insurance is purchased, the premium includes provision both for the cost of losses that will be funded by the coverage and for the cost of risk. When a risk is retained, there are also separate costs for funding losses and for financing risk.

For the sake of example, consider a manufacturer that owns buildings worth $1,000,000. Insurance on the buildings will cost $30,000. Assuming a loss ratio of about 65 or 66 percent, the expected loss (that is, the average loss per insured) is roughly $20,000. In fact, let us also assume that the manufacturer's past losses have been about average, at roughly $20,000 per year. If the firm could be certain that losses would not exceed $20,000 a year (actually $30,000 a year), it would save by retaining the entire risk. But losses could conceivably reach $1,000,000.

If the firm decides to retain the entire risk of loss, it will presumably continue to incur $20,000 in losses annually. In addition, to protect against the possibility of a total $1,000,000 loss, it must maintain a liquid reserve of $980,000. The cost of the retention program will be the $20,000 in annual losses that must be paid plus the opportunity cost on the $980,000 reserve. This opportunity cost is measured as the difference that will be earned on the reserve, which must be kept in a semi-liquid form, and the return that could be realized if the $980,000 were applied to the firm's operations. If the average rate of return on funds applied to operations is, say, 15 percent and the interest that can be earned on the invested reserve is 6 percent, the opportunity cost is $88,200 ($147,700 minus $58,800). Thus the cost of insuring is $30,000, while the cost of retention is $108,200 ($20,000 in losses plus the $88,200 opportunity cost).[1] A more complete analysis would consider the effect of taxes on both costs. Assuming a combined state and federal marginal tax rate of 50 percent, the cost of insurance would be $15,000 and the cost of retention would be $54,100.

DETERMINING APPROPRIATE RETENTION LEVELS

Several sophisticated quantitative models have been suggested as an approach to determining retention levels. Generally, however, retention levels are established based on rules of thumb or, in some instances, expected losses. Often, the retention level is determined more by the size of the available premium credits than by the organization's financial ability to withstand potential loss. One of the more or less standard approaches to the determination of the level of risk retention is to measure the potential premium savings for a deductible of a given size against the risk retained. This oversimplified approach generally results in unnecessary costs and inconsistencies in the program. Determination of risk retention levels should be made on the basis of an integrated financial analysis rather than arbitrary guidelines or rules of thumb.

The Normal Loss

The first step in the analysis is the determination of the "normal loss," sometimes called the "expected value of loss." This can be calculated on the basis of past loss experience of the firm, or it may be imputed from the insurance premium. Because a target loss ratio in many property and liability lines is about 65 percent,

---

[1]If the firm decides that it will not maintain a reserve, but will borrow the required $980,000 if a total loss occurs, the net effect is the same, since it will need to maintain $980,000 of its line of credit free for use in the event of a loss. The opportunity cost is the same in either case.

it follows that the average loss per insured—that is, the normal loss—will be roughly 65 percent of the existing premium level.

Loss-Retention Capacity

Once the normal loss has been computed, the second step is to determine the loss-bearing capacity of the firm. This requires measuring the resources that would be available to pay assumed losses in excess of the normal loss (that is, the ability to pay unexpected losses). In calculating the ability to retain losses, it is necessary to look at financial strength indicators.

Working Capital   Perhaps the best measure of the ability to withstand unexpected losses is working capital. Unfortunately, there is no hard and fast rule for the percentage of working capital that should be considered as a maximum level of risk retention. Guidelines used by various firms range from 10 percent to as much as 25 percent. Ten percent might be used when the firm is inventory intensive and cannot liquidate current assets without financial loss. The high range might be used when the firm has a very liquid working capital position.

Total Assets   A second measure of financial strength, although somewhat less useful, is total assets. In a sense, the total assets measure is an indication of the entity's borrowing power and overall financial strength rather than its short-term availability of funds. A range of 1 to 5 percent is sometimes suggested, but since total assets may not reflect liquidity, it is generally considered a poor standard for determining retention levels.

Effect on Earnings   To measure the ability to fund losses through earnings, the retained earnings over an extended period (such as, for example, five years) should be considered. In the case of a nonprofit institution, the excess of revenues over expenses should be considered. Suggested ranges of earnings that may be considered as a possible contribution to earnings are 1 to 3 percent of retained earnings plus 1 to 3 percent of average pretax earnings (five years). The earnings consideration is long range because it depends on the underlying earning power of the firm, as indicated by past history, as the ultimate source of funds to provide for losses in excess of the normal loss.

Earnings Per Share   Although there is considerable room here for flexibility, 10 percent of the earnings per share of a publicly held corporation is a convenient starting point. For a nonprofit organization or a public body, 10 to 50 percent of the excess of revenues over expenses may be used.

Sales Budget   Still another earnings indicator that may be used is the sales budget. A range of 0.5 to 2 percent of annual sales or revenues might be considered.

Cash Flow   A range of 5 to 10 percent of the preceding year's nondedicated cash flow is an appropriate measure of the funds available for allocation to the retention program.

Determining Retention Level an Art, Not Science

There is no hard and fast rule that permits easy computation of a risk retention level. All that can be expected is that you point out the various factors that might be considered, and suggest a range of retention levels with which management might be comfortable. In many instances, each of the factors outlined above will indicate a somewhat different level.

Although the various factors discussed above cannot provide a precise and definite indication of the appropriate retention level, two measures will always be of use. As an initial step in determining the risk retention level for an organization, we can begin with the following measures:

What is the level of uninsured loss that would be beyond the credit capacity of the firm and would result in bankruptcy? $_____

What is the level of uninsured loss that the firm could bear without being forced to borrow? $_____

The answer to the first question provides an absolute maximum retention limit for any exposure. It should be clear that all risks that could result in loss in excess of this limit must be transferred.

ACCOUNTING FOR AND FUNDING RETAINED LOSSES

The formality with which the organization approaches accounting and the funding for retained losses can be very different. First, the organization may simply pay retained losses as they occur, treating them as an operating expense. One problem with this approach is that some losses are not detected at the time they occur. Although a retailer may recognize that shoplifting losses are occurring, the amount that has actually been stolen by customers (and by employees) will not be known until a periodic inventory count has been done. Let's suppose that the firm decides to retain the risk of physical damage to its automobiles. If, on average, a car is demolished once every three years, profitability will be greater in two out of the three years because long-run losses are not recognized.

The second approach to accounting for losses is to explicitly recognize such losses in a loss reserve account (analogous to the reserve for bad debts that was once widely used by businesses). Under this approach, a reserve for retained or uninsured losses is established based on an estimate, and losses are charged against the reserve as they occur. Although losses charged against a loss reserve in this way are not deductible for tax purposes, establishing the reserve and charging losses against the estimate serves as a scorecard and calls attention to the magnitude of losses.

The third approach is to create a fund for retained losses. Here, assets are specifically earmarked to cover retained losses that occur. The purpose of the fund is to guarantee the availability for cash at the time it is needed. Creating a fund recognizes that the reserve for uninsured losses—an accounting convention—does not guarantee the availability of cash at the time it may be needed. Note that a reserve can be established without a fund, and a fund can exist without a reserve.

TAX CONSIDERATIONS AND RISK RETENTION

Federal and state income tax laws play a significant role in determining how a risk retention plan will be structured. For example, premiums for insurance are fully deductible by the insured. In general, *Section 162* of the *Internal Revenue Code* provides a tax deduction for ordinary and necessary business expenses. *Treas. Req. Section 1.162.1(a)* makes it clear that insurance premiums are deductible business expenses. Accordingly, if a risk is covered by insurance, the premium paid is deductible.

Deductibility of Contributions to Self-Insurance Reserves

The subject of deductibility of contributions to self-insurance reserves has been sufficiently addressed by the court to allow the conclusion that contributions made by a corporation to a self-insurance fund are not deductible. Note that the tax law does not eliminate the tax deductibility of self-insurance—it only forces companies to wait until they actually pay a claim before taking the deduction.

Although some earlier case law suggested that deductions to a self-insurance reserve might be allowable in some cases, Congress addressed this issue in the Tax Reform Act of 1984[2] and overturned an earlier decision in which the court had allowed a deduction.[3] The change redefined the *all events test* on which some deductions had been allowed, and provides that the fact of liability is not determined, and thus an expense cannot be accrued, until "economic performance" has occurred. "Economic performance" is defined as the actual payment of a claim. Thus the requirement for economic performance unquestionably denies a tax deduction for liabilities known in the current year but not actually payable until future years. The 1984 legislation provided that the fact of liability is not determined until "economic performance" has occurred, and that economic performance in workers compensation cases occurs only as payments are made. Thus workers compensation liabilities are deductible only on a cash basis.

Net Operating Loss Deduction

Although the taxable organization cannot deduct contributions to a loss reserve, but must deduct losses only in the year in which they are paid, the provisions of the Tax Code regarding net operating loss carryback and carryover provide some relief. Net operating losses may be carried back to each of the preceding three years and carried forward to each of the following 15 years until used up.[4]

---

[2] *Section 91* of the *Act* added *Section 461(h)* to the *Internal Revenue Code of 1954*.

[3] *Kaiser Steel Corporation v. United States.* 717 F.2d 1304 (9th Cir. 1983). In this case, the appeals court ruled that self-insurers could, under certain conditions, take a tax deduction for reserves set up to pay uncontested workers compensation claims. In other words, an employer was entitled to a deduction for the amount of self-funded reserves if all the events governing the employer's liability occurred during the tax year and the amount of liability could be determined with "reasonable accuracy."

[4] Section 172; 1.172-1 to 1.172.8.

FINANCIAL ACCOUNTING STANDARDS BOARD RULE 5

One of the subjects relating to risk retention that has received considerable attention in some quarters is the newly promulgated Financial Accounting Standards Board Rule No. 5 (FASB-5). This ruling announced a change in accounting procedures, which in theory was expected to be of interest only to professional accountants; it has sparked a new interest in accounting for losses under self-insurance and risk retention programs. The critical segment of FASB-5 states:

> An estimated loss from a contingency shall be accrued by a charge to income if both of the following conditions are met:
>
> (a) Information available prior to the issuance of the financial statements indicates that it is probable that an asset has been impaired or a liability has been incurred at the date of the financial statements. It is implicit in this condition that it must be probable that one or more future events will occur confirming the fact of the loss.
>
> (b) The amount of loss can be reasonably estimated.

In simple terms, the ruling says that a firm may not make charges to a current accounting period for any contingency that has not yet occurred. If it has occurred but the cost cannot be determined, charges against the current accounting period still cannot be made. With the adoption of FASB-5, essentially the same rules now apply to financial accounting as previously applied in tax law.

FASB-5 is a rule for public accountants, to be followed if a financial statement issued by a publicly held corporation is certified. It has, by reference, been incorporated into the regulations of the SEC. No annual report or financial statement requiring SEC approval can be issued without complying with FASB-5. FASB-5 does not apply to the financial practices of privately held companies that do not need or are not concerned with certification by a public accountant. In addition, FASB-5 does not apply to nonprofit institutions that do not have shareholders or that do not seek SEC approval.

■ Self-Insurance   ■

In Chapter 10 we noted that although self-insurance is technically a definitional impossibility, the term has found widespread acceptance in the business world. It is widely used (and understood) and there seems little sense in ignoring the widespread use of an established and accepted term.[5] Although there are theoretical defects in the term *self-insurance*, it is a convenient way of distinguishing retention programs that utilize insurance techniques from those that do not. Self-insurance

---

[5]Many state laws, for example, refer to the "self-insurance" of the workers compensation exposure, usually under conditions that do not contemplate any of the requirements specified by textbook writers.

programs are distinguished from other retention programs primarily in the formality of the arrangement. In some instances, this means obtaining approval from a state regulatory agency to retain risks, under specifically defined conditions. In other cases, it means the formal trappings of an insurance program, including funding measures based on actuarial calculations and the contractual definitions of the exposures, are self-insured. When the self-insurance involves third parties (as in the case of employers covered under an employer-sponsored health insurance program), there is a need for the formal trappings of insurance, such as certificates of coverage and premiums. It is in this limited sense that the term *self-insurance* is used in this section.

Over the past three decades, the use of self-insurance by businesses and other organizations in dealing with risk has grown significantly. In some areas, such as employer-sponsored health benefits for employees, it has become a major alternative to commercial insurance. Given the growing importance of this approach to dealing with risks, it seems appropriate that we consider some of the reasons for its growth.

REASONS FOR SELF-INSURANCE

Self-insurance—like any of the other risk management techniques—should be used when it is the most effective technique for dealing with a particular risk. The question is, under what circumstances is self-insurance the most effective technique for dealing with a particular risk? The main reason that firms elect to self-insure certain exposures is that they believe it will be cheaper to do so in the long run. This is particularly true in cases in which there is no need for the financial protection furnished by insurance. When losses are reasonably predictable, with a small likelihood of deviation from year to year, the risk can be retained.

First, as we have noted on several occasions, the cost of insurance must, over the long run, exceed average losses. This is a mathematical truism. In addition to the losses that must be paid, the insurance premium must include a surcharge to cover the cost of operating the insurance company and its distribution system. In addition, commercial insurance is subject to state premium taxes, which represent a cost that must be paid by buyers. Self-insurance avoids certain expenses associated with the traditional commercial insurance market. These include, among other things, insurer overhead and profit, agents' commissions, and the premium taxes paid by insurers. Consider, for example, a typical summary of the expenses used in the loading for a commercial property or liability contract.

Acquisition expense	13.7%
State premium tax	3.6%
General administrative expense	7.5%
Loss adjustment expense	8.6%
Profit and contingency expense	2.5%
	35.9%

Several of these expenses can immediately be eliminated through self-insurance. These are the state premium tax and the allowance for profit and contingencies. In addition, many buyers would also eliminate acquisition expense. Combined, these three elements of the expense loading represent roughly 20 percent of the total premium. The remaining expenses—insurer overhead and loss adjustment expenses—represent an additional potential for saving. This suggests that if the firm can purchase unbundled loss-prevention and adjustment services for less than the expense allowance, it will experience an immediate savings in expenses.

In addition to the potential for expense saving, the organization may believe that its loss experience is significantly better than the average experience on which rates are made, or that the rating system does not accurately reflect the hazards associated with the exposure. This may or may not be true.

One of the major appeals of self-insurance for many organizations is the ability to control the claim process. Many firms insured with commercial insurers for workers compensation or general liability have expressed dissatisfaction over the claim management process, and their lack of control in claims. Too often, they argue, claims are paid that should be contested, and settlements are made that the employer does not believe are justified. This is especially irritating when the business is insured under a loss-sensitive rating program, in which the ultimate premium depends on the amount of losses. By switching to a self-insured program, the business gains control of the claim process and can exercise a greater degree of discretion with respect to the claims that are paid and those that are contested.

Furthermore, in those lines of insurance in which there are long delays between the time that a loss occurs and the time it is paid, insurers hold "reserves," which represent liabilities for unpaid losses. Some insurance buyers believe that the investment income from these reserves is not adequately reflected in rates and that they can reduce the cost of their insurance by capturing these investable funds through self-insurance.

Finally, self-insurers can avoid the social load in insurance rates that results from statutory mandates that insurers cover certain exposures in which premiums are less than the losses for those insured. These underwriting losses are passed on to other insureds in the form of higher premiums than their hazards justify. In the property and liability field, the social load includes the insurer's share of losses under assigned risk plans, FAIR plans, and joint underwriting associations.

DISADVANTAGES OF SELF-INSURANCE

Offsetting the perceived advantages of self-insurance, there are certain disadvantages and *potential* disadvantages.

The greatest disadvantage of self-insurance is that it can leave the organization exposed to catastrophic loss. This disadvantage can be eliminated if the self-insurer purchases reinsurance for potentially catastrophic losses, much in the same way as do insurers.

A second disadvantage of self-insurance is that there may be greater variation of costs from year to year. When the variation in costs from year to year is great, the firm may lose the tax deduction for the losses that occur in years when there are no profits from which to deduct the losses.

In addition, self-insurance of some exposures can create adverse employee and public relations. There may be advantages to the organization in having its employee benefit claims handled by an insurer (as opposed to the staff of the employer organization).

Finally, there is the possible loss of ancillary services. Certain services are provided by insurers which are lost when a company adopts a self-insurance program. Most of these relate to loss prevention and claims handling. These services can be purchased separately from an insurer (under an arrangement called unbundling) or from specialty firms. The cost of obtaining these services must be included in the cost of the self-insurance when a comparison is made with commercial insurance. Usually, a self-insuring organization will hire a *third party administrator* (TPA) to handle the loss-adjusting process, but is able to exercise greater control over the TPA than over a commercial insurer. Although the cost of claims handling is often expressed as a percentage of losses in self-insurance proposals, it is recommended that the TPA not be compensated for loss settlement on a percentage of claims basis. Although the loss-adjustment expense can be expected to range from about 10 to 15 percent of incurred losses, the actual level should be determined by application of a hourly or case rate.

ANALYSIS OF SELF-INSURANCE PROPOSALS

Often, an organization first considers self-insuring a particular exposure when it is approached by an agency or brokerage firm selling self-insurance services. These include third-party administrative services and access to excess stop-loss insurance. The proposing agency may or may not have conducted a feasibility study but will usually propose the self-insurance plan on the premise that it will generate premium savings to the insured.

Many self-insurance proposals focus on the potential savings in administrative expenses. Because administrative expenses are eliminated (or reduced) under a self-insured program, holding other things constant, the reduction in administrative expenses alone should produce a cost advantage in favor of self-insurance. If losses are assumed to be the same under an insured program and the self-insured program, there is a cost advantage in favor of self-insurance. The problem with this analysis is that other things are not equal, and the cost of losses will differ between a commercially insured program and a self-funded one. The difference stems from the distinction between predictable and unpredictable losses.

Every organization can divide its insurance costs, whether fully insured or self-insured, into three broad elements: (1) *administrative costs*, which include those previously discussed expenses other than loss costs; (2) *average predictable losses*, which are those losses that occur regularly and, as a result, are reasonably predictable; and (3) *unpredictable losses*, which are determined by chance and which individually can attain catastrophic proportions.

In a fully insured program, these costs are grouped together in the premium charged by the insurance company. Under a self-insured program, the costs are separated and funded through discrete mechanisms. Proposals for self-insured programs universally address the first two components of cost (administrative costs and average predictable losses). Because catastrophic, unpredictable losses are unpredictable, they are not an appropriate subject for retention. In a properly structured self-insurance program, unpredictable losses are not retained but are insured by some form of excess insurance.

Although protection against catastrophic, unpredictable losses would seem to be essential in any program, the cost of protecting against unpredictable losses is sometimes so high that it eliminates the potential economies in a self-insurance plan. The high cost of protecting against catastrophic or unpredictable losses stems from the law of large numbers. In a fully insured program, the insurer combines a large number of exposures. This reduces the possible variation in loss experience, decreasing the level of unpredictable losses. Because the law of averages operates over a large number of exposures, the variability in an insurer's loss experience is simply less than is the case for a single entity. Even in a fully insured program, however, insurance companies purchase reinsurance to protect against abnormal deviations in actual experience from predicted losses. The insurer's cost for such protection is usually modest, because the likelihood of abnormal deviations is also modest. The greater the number of exposures insured, the better the predictability and the smaller will be the charge for catastrophic, unpredictable losses.

Under a self-insured program, the potential for deviations in actual experience is greater than for an insurer. Because catastrophic losses—the deviations from expected or average losses—are by definition unpredictable, they are not an appropriate subject for retention. A self-insurer, like commercial insurers, must purchase protection against unpredictable and potentially catastrophic losses. Coverage for these losses is available in two separate types of coverage, specific excess insurance and aggregate excess (also called stop-loss) insurance. Because some self-insurance proposals include the cost of specific excess insurance only, it is important that the distinction between specific excess insurance and aggregate excess (stop-loss) coverage be clear. With specific excess insurance, the insured assumes a predetermined amount of the loss arising out of any one occurrence, and the insurance pays losses over this sum up to a specified limit. In workers compensation insurance, for example, specific excess insurance might be written to cover up to $1 million over a $50,000 self-insured retention for any one occurrence. If one accident caused claims totaling $300,000, the insured would pay $50,000 and the specific excess would pay $250,000.

Aggregate excess (stop-loss) coverage provides coverage when the sum of all losses falling within the self-insured retention exceeds a predetermined amount. Normally, the *aggregate stop-loss* amount is a function of the annual manual premium, such as 150 to 200 percent of the manual premium. Under an aggregate excess stop-loss program, a maximum is imposed on the total losses that must be absorbed under the self-insured retention.

Occasionally, we encounter illustrations of the "cost advantages" of self-funded plans that ignore the cost of aggregate stop-loss insurance. A common approach to comparing the cost of a self-funded program with an insured program is to begin with the insurer's retention under the insured program and identify the expenses that would be eliminated or reduced under a self-funded program. Because the insurer's cost of catastrophe protection does not appear as a separate element in the retention, it is sometimes ignored in the analysis. Because an insurer addresses predictability by combining large numbers of insureds, the cost of stop-loss reinsurance is a small part of its overall cost of operation. Conversely, because most organizations cannot spread risk over as large a number of exposures as does an insurer, the cost of catastrophe protection is greater for the self-insurer than for an insurer. Often, it will equal or exceed the reduction in administrative expenses that can be saved in a self-insurance program. Because the cost of adequate catastrophe protection can make a self-funded program appear less attractive, this part of the cost is sometimes ignored by the purveyors of self-funded programs. Obviously, unless adequate stop-loss protection is provided, any comparison of an insured program with a self-insured one is fundamentally invalid.

Combining Retention and Transfer

As we have previously noted, retention is often combined with transfer. Historically, insurers developed the combination programs in order to compete with self-insurance programs. As large insureds began to recognize the advantages of retaining the insurance-related cash flow and the economies in segregating their own experience from that of other insureds, insurance companies responded with programs to facilitate this inclination. The following discussion, though not exhaustive, indicates the major programs currently available that combine retention and transfer.

DEDUCTIBLES

The most familiar technique for combining transfer with retention is through the use of deductibles. Deductible coverage is available in virtually every form of insurance, and a variety of options are often offered. In the property insurance field, for example, coverage is available with a deductible applicable on a per-structure basis, per occurrence, and with an annual aggregate. Deductibles are also available in the general liability and automobile liability fields. In workers compensation, excess workers compensation policies are available, under which the insurer is obligated to pay losses only in excess of a specified amount resulting from a single occurrence. For example, the policy might be written to pay losses in excess of $50,000 or $100,000. In essence, the policy is simply a form of deductible coverage.

RETROSPECTIVELY RATED INSURANCE

A retrospectively rated insurance policy is a self-rated plan under which the actual losses experienced during the policy period determine the final premium for the coverage, subject to a maximum and a minimum. Retrospective rating is most commonly used in the workers compensation field, but sometimes in other lines, such as general liability and automobile liability. The coverage under a retrospectively rated program is precisely the same as if it were rated on a flat basis; the only difference is in the determination of the premium or cost. A retrospective plan is a self-rating plan in which the actual experience under the policy or policies involved determines the final premium.[6]

A deposit premium is charged at the inception of the contract, with an adjustment after the policy has expired to reflect the actual experience during the period of coverage. The final premium is arrived at by adding to the cost of the actual losses a percentage for expenses incurred by the insurer, as well as a charge for shock losses. In a sense, a retrospective program is much like a cost plus contract, the major difference being that the premium is subject to a maximum and a minimum. Viewed from a slightly different point of view, a retrospective program is like a self-insurance program up to the maximum premium. The lower the losses of the insured, the lower will be the final premium. The higher the losses, the higher will be the premium.

The Retrospective Formula

In order to provide a basis for the discussion of the retrospective approach to rating, it may be helpful to briefly explain the formula that is used in determining the final premium under the retrospective plans. In its simplest aspect, the retrospective premium is determined after the rating period is over, based on the following formula[7]:

Retrospective Premium = (Basic Premium + Converted Losses) × Tax Multiplier

Although the formula may appear somewhat complicated, an explanation of each of the factors should help to clarify it.

1. *Basic Premium.* The basic premium is simply a charge for the insurance protection element in the retrospective plan—the fact that there is a maximum to the insured's cost. In a retrospective program that combines several lines of insurance, a basic premium charge is made for each line of insurance: workers compensation, general liability, and auto liability. The basic premium for the general liability and auto liability is a percentage of the premium subject to the retrospective rating. It may be viewed as a flat charge for the administration of the program and for setting a maximum to the program.

2. *Ratable Losses.* Ratable losses are the actual amounts paid out by the insurance company, subject to the excess loss limitation, if any. For example, with a $25,000 loss limitation, in the event of a $100,000 loss, only $25,000 would be included as a "ratable loss."

3. *Loss Conversion Factor.* The loss conversion factor adds a percentage surcharge to every dollar of loss to pay for the cost of claims administration. For exam-

[6]Retrospectively rated plans date from 1943. Originally, there were four *tabular* plans, designated A, B, C, and J. These plans were referred to as tabular because the maximum premium, minimum premium, and basic premium could be taken directly from rating tables. The National Council on Compensation Insurance (NCCI) introduced new plans effective December 31, 1991.

[7]The formula presented above is the simplified version of the retrospective formula. An optional charge called the *excess loss premium* may be added to policies on which the estimated annual standard premium is $100,000 to limit the effect of any one accident to $25,000.

ple, if the loss conversion factor is 1.12, a $10,000 loss would be converted to $11,200 in the formula.

4. *The Tax Multiplier.* The tax multiplier represents the charge required to pay the state premium tax. In general, it is about 1.07, which means that total adjusted losses and the basic premium are increased by 7 percent.

Thus the *basic premium* is the fixed cost element in the plan, which does not vary with the level of losses. *Converted losses* are actual losses sustained, plus a percentage of losses for loss-adjustment expense. The *tax multiplier* is a variable charge, equal to the premium that will be due to the state from the insurer, and is based on the total premium generated by the formula. The final premium for the year is determined by adding the basic premium to actual losses and loss-adjustment expense, and then adding the amount of the premium tax that will be payable by the insurer to the state.

The basic premium, the minimum premium, and the maximum premium are generally expressed as a percentage of the *standard premium*. The standard premium is the manual premium after experience modification, but before any size discounts.[8]

Although the terminology tends to be confusing, we can illustrate the elements in the retrospective rating formula by indicating one set of values for each of the elements in the formula that would apply to a workers compensation policy. Assume an experience-modified annual workers compensation premium for the coming year of, say, $500,000.[9] With the premium discount for size, the premium would be reduced to about $443,375.

	Rating Factor	Dollar Amount
Guaranteed cost premium (Discounted)		$443,375
Standard premium		500,000
Basic premium	.145	72,500
Loss conversion factor	1.120	
Tax multiplier	1.070	
Minimum premium	.60	300,000
Maximum premium	1.30	650,000

The insurer will determine the final premium for the policy after the year is over by adding the *basic premium* indicated above ($72,500) to actual losses incurred plus the cost of adjusting those losses (Table 14.1). The cost of adjusting losses is indicated by the *loss conversion factor* of 1.12 above, which adds a 12-percent surcharge to ratable losses to cover the cost of loss-adjustment expense. After the

---

[8]Because of economies of scale in handling larger policies, workers compensation premiums are subject to a premium discount based on size. The first $5000 in premium is not subject to discount, but the next $95,000 is subject to a discount of 8.4 to 10.9 percent, depending on the state, the next $400,000 is subject to a discount of 10.5 to 16.3 percent, and that part of the premium in excess of $500,000 is subject to a discount of 11 percent to 16.3 percent. The premium discount does not apply to retrospectively rated policies.

[9]The example presented above is from the Appendix of the December 1, 1991 revision of the NCCI *Retrospective Rating Plan Manual.*

charges for losses, loss-adjustment expense, and the basic premium are combined, this total is then increased by the amount of the premium tax that the insurer must pay to the state. In this way, the premium will vary directly with losses, up to the point at which the maximum premium is reached.

The exact "breakeven" point under a retrospectively rated program will depend on the retro plan selected and the maximum, minimum, and basic premiums. For the values indicated in the Table 14.1, the "breakeven" level of losses occurs at about $305,240 in losses, which produces a retrospective rated premium of $443,375, the amount of the guaranteed cost premium computed with the premium discount. Thus, for losses below $305,240, the organization would experience savings, while at losses above the $305,240 level, costs will be greater under the retrospectively rated program than under a guaranteed cost program.

Under a retrospectively rated program, good experience has an immediate impact on insurance costs. More importantly, it reduces the influence of bad past experience on insurance costs, since the annual premium for the coverage is determined primarily by current experience rather than by past experience.

The example clearly illustrates the reason why it is often said that a retrospective program is like a cost plus contract; the final cost of the program varies with the

Table 14.1   Retrospective Rating Illustration

(a) If Losses Are	(b) Converted Losses	(c) Basic Premium	(d) Columns (b) + (c)	(e) With Tax Multiplier	(f) Final Premium	
$0	$0	$72,500	$72,500	$77,575	$300,000	Minimum
40,000	44,800	72,500	117,300	125,511	300,000	Minimum
80,000	89,600	72,500	162,100	173,447	300,000	Minimum
120,000	134,400	72,500	206,900	221,383	300,000	Minimum
160,000	179,200	72,500	251,700	269,319	300,000	Minimum
200,000	224,000	72,500	296,500	317,255	317,255	
240,000	268,800	72,500	341,300	365,191	365,191	
280,000	313,600	72,500	386,100	413,127	413,127	
305,240	341,869	72,500	414,369	443,375	443,375	Breakeven
320,000	358,400	72,500	430,900	461,063	461,063	
360,000	403,200	72,500	475,700	508,999	508,999	
400,000	448,000	72,500	520,500	556,935	556,935	
440,000	492,800	72,500	565,300	604,871	604,871	
480,000	537,600	72,500	610,100	652,807	650,000	Maximum
520,000	582,400	72,500	654,900	700,743	650,000	Maximum
560,000	627,200	72,500	699,700	748,679	650,000	Maximum

costs incurred by the insured, and the "plus" is the charge the insurer makes for limiting the premium to some maximum.

Evaluating Retrospective Plans

The very nature of a retrospectively rated plan makes it difficult to estimate the cost of a policy written on this basis, because the final premium will depend on the actual losses sustained. This is one area in which statistical probability and decision theory techniques are especially useful. In the case of a firm large enough to seriously consider a retrospectively rated workers compensation plan, for example, there is likely to be a record of past losses that will be useful in making projections regarding future losses. These loss projections can aid in the decision as to whether or not a retrospectively rated plan is likely to be advantageous, and if so, the most attractive parameters for a plan.

CASUALTY CASH FLOW PLANS

The traditional approach by casualty insurers has been to invoice premiums on the basis of total incurred claims (paid and reserved) rather than for paid claims, plus a percentage for administration, loss adjustment, profit, contingencies, and state taxes. This practice is due in part to the state insurance laws which require insurance companies to establish reserves on all claims for which they have assumed liability. Because incurred claims are entered on the balance sheet as a liability, they must be secured by a corresponding asset. Normally, the premiums collected from insureds supply this asset. These funds are invested in assets that have yielded a return to the insurers.

Although the premiums charged by insurers implicitly recognize reserves (or their corresponding assets) as a source of investment income, the net effect of the traditional billing procedure represents an added cost of a formal insurance plan. A corporation earning a high rate of return on its investments may find that it can earn a higher return on its reserves than the firm could earn itself. The cash-flow characteristics in prepayment of guaranteed cost programs and retrospectively rated programs brought about the concept of casualty cash-flow plans.

Although retrospective rating plans appeal to the insured who is inclined toward self-insurance because of better than average loss experience, it does not address another attraction of self-insurance, the investment income on policy reserves. To address this feature of self-insurance, insurers developed cash-flow plans. These plans include *compensating balance* plans and *paid-loss retrospective* plans.

Compensating Balance Plan

A compensating balance plan is an insured program in which premiums paid by the insured are deposited in a checking account in the insured's bank and used to meet some of the compensating balance requirements that the bank imposes on the insured. Insured losses and expenses are paid from this account. Compensating

331

balance plans were conceived by insurers to partially offset the cash-flow benefit of self-insurance. Because the deposited funds are available to meet the requirements of the insured's bank, other funds are freed for use in operations.

Paid-Loss Retro Plans

The traditional approach by casualty insurers has been to invoice premiums on the basis of total incurred claims (paid and reserved) rather than for paid claims, plus a percentage for administration, loss adjustment, profit, contingencies, and state taxes. This practice is due in part to the state insurance laws which require insurance companies to establish reserves on all claims for which they have assumed liability. Because incurred claims are entered on the balance sheet as a liability, they must be secured by a corresponding asset. Normally, the premiums collected from insureds supply this asset. Thus, the practice of paying premiums on the basis of reserved as well as paid claims developed. These funds have, of course, generally been invested in liquid assets that have yielded a return to the insurers.

Although the premiums charged by insurers implicitly recognize reserves (or their corresponding assets) to be a source of investment income, the net effect of the traditional billing procedure represents an additional cost of a formal insurance plan. More specifically, a rapidly growing corporation earning a high rate of return on its investments may find the traditional way of insuring disadvantageous, since it represents a diversion from high-yield credits on funds held by the insurer. The undesirable cash-flow characteristics in prepayment of guaranteed cost programs or conventional retrospectively rated programs brought about the concept of casualty cash-flow plans.

The idea of cash flow is, of course, not new. Deferred premium plans, which have some cash-flow advantages, have been in use for many years. In the recent past, however, more and more businesses have recognized the advantages of self-insurance benefits relating to loss reserves. As a result, insurers now offer cash-flow plans based on paid claims rather than incurred claims. Although there is considerable flexibility and these plans may take many forms, most have the following characteristics:

1. The special cash-flow premium payment provisions are simply added to a standard retrospectively rated or guaranteed cost program.

2. Annual premiums are paid at approximately the same rate that claims are actually settled. Premiums are generally based on paid claims plus a servicing cost.

3. The insurance company requires an irrevocable bank letter of credit, based on the amount of reserved claims. This becomes an admitted asset against reserves for state insurance regulatory purposes.

In considering cash-flow plans, it is important to keep one point in mind: any advantages flowing from these plans are basically financial in nature. Instead of paying premiums approximately equal to total incurred claims, the bank's irrevocable letter of credit is posted annually for the outstanding difference between paid losses and incurred losses. The result has a favorable effect on the insured's cash flow. The extent on this cash flow effect will depend on the size of the premium and the rate at which incurred losses convert to paid losses. In workers compensation, for example, only about one-third of incurred losses may be paid out in the year incurred, with another third paid out in the following year. Payment of the final third may require an additional eight years or more.

FINITE RISK INSURANCE

Finite risk insurance (also known as *financial insurance*) has been around in one form or another for several decades. During the 1990s, however, it enjoyed a resurgence in popularity among self-insurers. Finite risk insurance originated from financial reinsurance, which is used by insurance companies to minimize the effects of fluctuations in their loss experience.

Finite risk insurance is a financing tool used in connection with risk retention to smooth the effect of retained loses on the firm's balance sheet. It does this by redistributing large losses over a number of accounting periods so that excessive losses do not become entries into the balance sheet in a single year. Finite risk insurance is based on the premise that the insured will pay its own losses over time, and that fluctuations in loss experience can be smoothed by contractual transfers between the self-insurer and the insurance company. The basic function of finite risk insurance, then, is to reduce the *timing risk* associated with self-insurance and other risk retention programs. It is essentially a *banking* or *funding* concept that provides a means of loss stabilization for balance sheet purposes.

The key element in a finite risk plan is a negotiated premium that varies directly with the losses under the program. Finite risk contracts are usually written for a period of five years or more with premiums based on projected losses but with an agreement by the insured to reimburse the insurer for losses that exceed the premiums paid. This means that finite risk insurance involves very little transfer of underwriting risk; in some instances, there is no risk transfer because of the insured's obligation to reimburse the insurer for all amounts paid under the contract.

To illustrate the operation of finite risk insurance, assume that ABC Manufacturing, Inc. and XYZ Insurance Company enter into a five-year finite risk arrangement. The policy is written to apply to product liability losses in excess of $1 million with a $50 million aggregate limit. The annual premium for this policy is $10 million per year payable by a cash premium of, say, $500,000 per year, plus a note for $9.5 million. The note becomes payable if the insurer requires the funds to pay losses. Over the five-year period, the insured will have paid $50 million in cash and notes. At the end of the five years, the insurer will pay a *commutation profit commission* to the insured based on the losses that have been paid under the policy. If there have been no losses, the insurer will return 99 percent of the premiums paid ($49.5 million) to the insured. If the insurer has sustained losses under the policy, the commutation profit commission will be 99 percent of the cumulative premiums plus interest credited, minus losses paid by the insurer. If the insured incurs $50 million in losses during the policy period, the aggregate limit is exhausted and the insured remains liable for the remaining annual installments of $10 million per year.

Sometimes, the timing risk covered by this arrangement may be combined with underwriting risk. If, for example, the premium terms are as indicated above (i.e., $10 million per year or $50 million over the five years), but the policy aggregate is $75 million, the insurer assumes both timing and underwriting risk.

In some cases, a finite risk plan may provide payment of premiums for a different period than the period for which the protection is provided. Under this arrangement, finite risk coverage might be written for a five-year period with premiums payable over a ten-year period. The premium payable over the ten-year period is determined by the application of a retrospective formula and fully reimburses the insurer for paid losses. The annual premium for the five-year policy period is based on projected losses plus a small loading. The premiums build a fund out of which losses are paid. If losses exceed the amount the insured has paid in, the insurer pays the excess losses up to the policy limit. The insured is then required to reimburse the insurer for the excess losses spread over the next five years, including interest charges and premium taxes.[10]

FRONTING COMPANIES

There are situations in which a risk manager might prefer to self-insure a particular exposure, but state regulations make it impossible. For example, a trucker may be required to file proof of insurance that meets a compulsory auto insurance law with a state agency. In these instances, it is sometimes possible to negotiate with an insurer to act as a *front* in the arrangement. For a fee, the insurance company will issue the required documents while the insured agrees in a letter of indemnity to reimburse the insurer for all losses paid. Although this may be viewed as a violation of the letter or spirit of the law, it is not. The main purpose of statutory insurance requirements is to gain the financial stability of an insurer to back up the insured—a condition that the fronting plan achieves. Although fronting companies are sometimes used in connection with the retention techniques discussed in this chapter, the technique is more commonly used in connection with captive insurers, the subject of the next chapter.

IMPORTANT CONCEPTS TO REMEMBER

intentional retention	self-insurance	loss conversion factor
unintentional retention	loss-sensitive rating program	tax multiplier
involuntary risk retention	third party administrator	converted losses
voluntary retention	administrative costs	standard premium
unfunded retention	average predictable losses	cash flow plans
funded retention	unpredictable losses	compensating balance plan
cost of financing risk	specific excess insurance	paid-loss retro plans
working capital	aggregate excess (stop-loss)	finite risk insurance
self-insurance fund	coverage	funded spread loss plans
all events test	aggregate stop-loss	loss portfolio transfer
FASB-5	retrospective rating	

[10]Some of the anticipated benefits of finite risk insurance were nullified by the Financial Accounting Standards Board's standards FAS No. 113, EITF 93-14, and EITF 93-6. In addition, as one might expect, the IRS refuses to allow a deduction for programs in which there is no transfer of risk.

QUESTIONS FOR REVIEW

1. Identify the ways in which retention can be classified, and describe the distinguishing characteristics of each class.

2. Explain the difference and illustrate by an example the distinction between financing loss and financing the cost of risk.

3. Identify the approaches that may be used in selecting the appropriate retention level for an organization.

4. Explain the requirements of Financial Accounting Standards Board Rule Number 5 (FASB-5).

5. Identify and briefly explain the advantages of self-insurance that may prompt an organization to adopt this approach to dealing with its risks.

6. Identify and briefly explain the possible disadvantages of self-insurance and explain how these disadvantages can be reduced or eliminated.

7. Describe several ways in which retention and transfer may be combined.

8. Explain the rationale for and describe the operation of cash-flow plans. Why do insurers offer such plans?

9. Identify and describe the three components into which an organization can divide its insurance costs. In what way(s) does the distinction among these costs relate to risk retention?

10. How does unintentional risk management occur? Why is it always undesirable?

QUESTIONS FOR DISCUSSION

1. Describe finite risk insurance. In your opinion, why is this designation appropriate or inappropriate for the type of plans it encompasses?

2. Describe the ways in which an organization engaged in an extensive program of risk retention might protect itself from the undesirable consequences of adverse loss experience.

3. What is meant by the statement that "retention is the residual or default risk management technique?"

4. Of the six measures of financial strength discussed in the chapter as possible bases for determining risk retention levels, which do you believe is the most appropriate? Why? Which do you believe is the least appropriate? Why?

5. Describe the current tax treatment of (a) retained losses (b) insurance premiums, and (c) insurance recoveries. In what way(s) does the tax treatment of these expenses or income influence risk management decisions?

SUGGESTIONS FOR ADDITIONAL READING

Banham, Russ. "Shopping the Market for Finite Risk Products." *Risk Management* (September 1994). pages 34–43.

Goshay, R.C. *Corporate Self-Insurance and Risk Retention Plans.* Homewood, IL: Richard D. Irwin, 1964.

Hamer, Michael D., and Thomas R. Dickson. "Finite Risk Contracts: An Enlightened Approach." *Risk Management (August 1995),* pp. 23–28.

Koral, Edward S. "A Tug of War: Accounting Rules and Finite Risk Programs." *Risk Management* (November 1995, pp. 45–57.

MacCorkle, Glenn A. "Accounting for the Cost of the Risk." *Risk Management* (December 1994), pp. 21–28.

Ralston, August R., ed. *Risk Management Manual,* Santa Monica, Ca.: (loose-leaf service with monthly supplements), vol. 2, section 4. "Retention."

Solon, John F. "Risk Retention Demystified." *Best's Review.* Property/Casualty Insurance Edition (March 1988).

Tiller, Margaret Wilkinson, James D. Blinn, and John J. Kelly. George L. Head, ed. *Essentials of Risk Financing.* Malvern. PA: Insurance Institute of America, 1988.

Williams, Numan A., ed. *Risk Retention: Alternate Funding Methods.* Malvern, PA: Society of Chartered Property and Casualty Underwriters, 1983.

CHAPTER 15

Risk Financing: Captive Insurers

CHAPTER OBJECTIVES

When you have finished this chapter, you should be able to

Explain the general nature of a captive insurer and describe the different types of captives.

■

Identify and explain the main reasons for the use of captives.

■

Explain the current tax treatment of captive insurers, and identify the circumstances in which premiums paid to a captive are considered deductible by the Internal Revenue Service.

■

Distinguish between risk retention groups and insurance purchasing groups that are authorized by the Risk Retention Act of 1986.

■■ Types of Captives ■

Captive insurers represent a special case of risk retention, and, in some instances, risk transfer. A captive insurance company is an entity created and controlled by a parent, whose main purpose is to provide insurance to that parent. Within the context of this definition, two types of organizations may be considered.

1. Pure captives
2. Association or group captives

Pure Captives

A pure captive is an insurance company established by a noninsurance organization solely for the purpose of underwriting risks of the parent and its affiliates.

Although the term *captive* has sometimes been applied loosely to include virtually any affiliated insurance company, as used here the term *captive* does not include insurance subsidiaries whose purpose is to write insurance for the general public. J.C. Penney Casualty Insurance, for example, is a subsidiary of J.C. Penney Company, Inc. Under our definition, however, it would not be considered a captive, since it was not organized for the purpose of underwriting the exposures of its parent. Companies such as J.C. Penney Casualty Insurance are more appropriately referred to simply as "insurance subsidiaries." Some pure captives have broadened into writing the business of others and eventually move from captives to ordinary insurance subsidiaries.

Association Captives

An association or group captive is an insurance company established by a group of companies to underwrite their own collective risks. These organizations are also sometimes referred to as trade association insurance companies (TAICs) and also as risk retention groups. The term *risk retention group* was added to the terminology of the captive field by the Risk Retention Acts of 1981 and 1986. As we will see, a risk retention group is simply a group-owned captive organized under the provisions of the Risk Retention Act.

Pools

A risk-sharing pool represents a mechanism that is closely related to and sometimes confused with the association or group captive, but that actually constitutes a separate technique. A group of entities may elect to pool their exposures, sharing the losses that occur, without creating a formal corporate insurance structure. In this case, a separate corporate insurer is not created, but the risks are nevertheless "insured" by the pooling mechanism.

Many authorities believe that pooling is appropriately classified as either transfer or retention, depending on the situation. In one sense, pooling represents a form of transfer, in the sense that the risks of the pooling members are transferred from the individuals to the group. In another sense, however, it is a form of retention in which the organization's risks are retained, along with those of the other pooling members. Viewed from one perspective, pooling represents a form of risk transfer; viewed from another perspective, it is a form of retention. This dual nature of pooling stems from the sometimes-forgotten fact that in a pooling arrangement, the members are both insureds and insurers.

CAPTIVE DOMICILES

Captives have traditionally been classified as onshore or offshore. An onshore captive is incorporated domestically and conducts business in the United States. An offshore captive is incorporated in a foreign jurisdiction and operates from that location, but it may still primarily insure U.S. risks. Usually, foreign captives operate under the surplus line laws of the states.

Historically, most captives have been formed offshore, primarily because the regulatory requirements in foreign jurisdictions were less demanding than those of the individual states and because there were certain tax advantages for offshore captives. Bermuda is the leading offshore site for captives, owing to its attractive legislative and regulatory climate. Other than some nominal levies, no significant tax is imposed on captives.

In 1996, the five domiciles with the largest numbers of captives included Bermuda, with 1,292, followed by the Cayman Islands with 336, the Isle of Guernsey with 300, the state of Vermont with 264, and Luxembourg with 230.[1]

A domestic captive can be organized as an insurance company under the same state laws as other insurance companies. Under this approach, however, the captive is subject to the same capital and surplus requirements and other regulations as any other insurer. More frequently, a domestic captive is formed under the laws of one of several states that are designed to encourage the formation of captives, by granting exemptions from the standard requirements for companies organized as captives. Colorado was the first state to enact legislation (in 1972) specifically designed to encourage the formation of captives, reducing some of the stringent requirements normally applied to insurers in such areas as capitalization, rating, pool participation, and surplus. Since Colorado's legislation authorizing captives, Vermont, Tennessee, Hawaii, and Virginia have passed captive legislation that frees captives from some of the stringent regulations normally applicable to open market insurance companies.

A BRIEF HISTORY OF CAPTIVES

The 35-year period from 1960 to 1995 witnessed a phenomenal growth in the number of captives worldwide. From a hundred or so in the late 1950s, the number of captives licensed worldwide at the end of 1995 grew to 3,199. By 1995, it was estimated that over half of the Fortune 500 companies had established captives.

Although the greatest growth in captives has occurred during the past 35 years, the captive idea is not new. The earliest captives were organized by the railroads in the 1800s. The late 1800s saw a revolt of New England textile manufacturers against the rigid fire insurance rates of the time. They formed a captive that then went into the general insurance business to become the well-known Factory Mutual organization. Many mutual and some stock insurance companies started this way. The Church Insurance Company, possibly the first group captive, was formed by the Episcopal Church in 1929.

The reasons for the phenomenal growth in captives during the past 30 years are complex. Basically, they include a failure of the established insurance market to adjust rapidly enough to the increasingly sophisticated risk-financing needs of insurance users. In addition, as explained later in the chapter, tax considerations also played an important role.

During the 1950s, there was a modest increase in the number of captives, mainly by U.S. companies in the process of transformation to multinational corporations.

[1]"Captive Growth Stable, Outlook Bright," *Business Insurance* (April 22, 1996).

As U.S. firms established plans and acquired subsidiaries in foreign countries, they often found that the insurance available from foreign insurers was more expensive than the prices in the United Sates or more limited in scope. These multinational companies constructed international insurance programs through the use of captives working with foreign insurers. Usually, the parent corporation purchased coverage from local insurers, which then reinsured the coverage with the parent's captive. Although the number of such operations was limited, they demonstrated the potential for the use of captives in structuring international insurance programs.

Another expansion in the number of captives occurred in the 1960s, this time motivated by a shortage of property insurance owing to the insurance cycle. The industry's surplus was limited, restricting its capacity to write coverage. Faced with market restrictions, about 50 large corporations—mainly Fortune 500 companies—created their own insurance market by organizing captives.

A major growth in captives occurred in the 1970s, as a result of restrictions in the market for medical malpractice insurance. Physicians, and then hospitals, organized captive insurance companies to write medical malpractice coverage that was either not available in the standard market or was available only at prices doctors and hospitals judged to be excessive. Interestingly, most of the so-called *bedpan mutuals* were, in fact, organized as mutual insurance companies and were mainly domiciled in the United States.

Encouraged by the apparent success of physicians and hospitals, when manufacturers faced a product liability crisis at the beginning of the 1980s, they followed the same strategy, organizing captive insurers for the purpose of writing product liability insurance. Some of the activity during this phase of captive development was prompted by federal legislation in the form of the Product Liability Risk Retention Act of 1981, special enabling legislation authorizing the formation of risk retention groups to address the product liability exposures of the groups' members. This law was extended in 1986 by the Risk Retention Act of 1986. Whereas the 1981 act had authorized risk retention groups solely for the purpose of writing product liability losses, the 1986 act authorized such groups for all types of general liability insurance.[2]

REASONS FOR GROWTH OF CAPTIVES

The motivation for the expansion of captives during the period of the 1950s through the 1980s was a perceived failure of the traditional insurance market to meet consumers' needs for coverage. Captives were originally conceived primarily because they offered an alternative to the commercial market. A secondary motivation, which later assumed preeminence, was the belief that certain tax benefits were available through captives that could not be attained under a retention program. Although this belief now seems to have been misplaced, many captives that were formed for the expected tax advantages have been continued for other reasons. Although the tax advantages that were anticipated were not, in most cases, realized, the number of captives has continued to grow for other reasons.

[2]The Risk Retention Act and risk retention groups are discussed in greater detail later in the chapter.

It would be an oversimplification to suggest that the growth of captives has been due to the insurance shortages that prompted organization of captives in the fifties, sixties, seventies, and eighties, or that the growth was motivated primarily by the hoped-for tax benefits. In fact, the growth in the number of captives has been due to a variety of reasons. They include:

- Tax considerations
- Inability to obtain needed coverage
- Desire to reduce insurance costs
- Desire to improve cash flow
- Desire to create a profit center
- Need to move capital in international markets

None of these motivations individually could have prompted the spectacular growth in the number of captives worldwide. Collectively, they supported a continuous and increasing rate of growth in captive insurance companies.

Tax Considerations

Premiums paid to commercial insurers qualify as tax deductions because they represent ordinary and necessary business expenses. As noted in the preceding chapter, the Internal Revenue Service (IRS) has persistently refused to recognize contributions to a self-insurance reserve as a deductible expense. An early rationale for captive insurers was the hope that by creating a separate entity to which premiums were paid, the parent company would be permitted to deduct premiums that would not be deductible as contributions to a self-insurance reserve. As we will see, this strategy has generally been rejected by the IRS. Still, the growth of captives continues for other reasons. Although the IRS has generally disallowed a deduction for premiums paid to a captive insurer by its parent, there are exceptions. Premiums paid to a captive may, under very specific and limited circumstances, be deductible by the parent corporation.

Inability to Obtain Coverage

Our review of the growth of captives indicates that the most common reason for the formation of captives in earlier years was the unavailability of a needed coverage from the standard insurance market. The inability to obtain coverage exists at three levels.

1. There are those who cannot get coverage at all; the most difficult lines of coverage have been product liability, professional medical liability, liability for architects and engineers and accountants, pollution liability, and liability insurance for municipalities, petroleum operations, and certain hazardous contractor exposures.
2. Coverage is available but at an enormous price.
3. For some exposures, the traditional market has never provided coverage at all, or any reasonable size market. These include strike insurance, product guarantee insurance, product recall, and other exposures viewed by some to be uninsurable.

The history of the captive movement is replete with examples of individual firms and groups that created captives because of an inability to obtain needed coverage from traditional insurers. A group of paint and varnish manufacturers with high fire risks, for example, could not buy the broad insurance needed and so they formed an association captive (VERLAN) that pooled the lower levels of loss among themselves. Other captives have been formed to write strike insurance and pollution liability insurance, coverage that is not freely available in standard insurance markets.

Reduced Insurance Costs

Although market restrictions and the hope of favorable tax treatment were the early motivations for the formation of captives, most of the captives that have been organized in the past two decades were prompted by the simple desire to reduce insurance costs. As the value of industrial capital has continued to increase and the cost of risk has continued to grow, pressure has grown for measures that will reduce these costs. These pressures and an increased understanding of risk management combined to intensify motivation to use captives as a way to save money on insurance costs.

Lower Expense Ratio

The anticipated savings from the use of captives are the same as those expected from other forms of retention discussed in the preceding chapter. These include the elimination or reduction of the expense component in insurance premiums. Captives have a natural cost advantage compared with conventional insurers. Premium taxes and acquisition cost savings can produce a direct saving of about 5 percent to as much as 15 percent. The saving in expenses, to the extent it is achieved, comes from eliminating these parts of a commercial insurer's overhead. Although the reduction in these expenses is offset by management fees for the captive, these fees are generally lower than the expenses of the insurer.

A major saving can be achieved simply by avoiding the *social load* factor in insurance premiums. The various involuntary markets in which commercial insurers are required to participate, such as automobile and workers compensation assigned risk plans, medical malpractice pools, FAIR plans and beach plans, and state health insurance pools all produce underwriting losses that the insurers must then pass on to other insurance buyers. The only way that insurance buyers can avoid this cost is to avoid being insurance buyers. Some risk managers viewed the captive as a mechanism for avoiding participation in the subsidization of substandard risks.

Still another way in which a captive can reduce the cost of dealing with risk is to reduce the cost of excess insurance by providing direct access to the reinsurance market. Corporations that self-insure their exposures typically deal in the *retail* insurance market in purchasing excess insurance. Corporations are restricted to purchasing excess coverage for self-insured plans from conventional insurance companies and a limited number of reinsurers. When a captive is used, the insurance alternatives become much wider. Many reinsurance companies are unwilling to deal directly with a business corporation that is not an insurer. These same companies, however, have no reservations about dealing with that corporation's captive insurer. Because reinsurers are less rigidly regulated than conventional insurers, they are more flexible and can exercise greater creativity in the design of coverages. As a consequence, gaining direct access to the reinsurance market is beneficial both in terms of cost and coverage design.

Desire to Improve Cash Flow

Insurance buyers had always recognized that insurers enjoyed a cash-flow benefit arising from the timing of the payment of premiums they received and the time at which those premiums were paid out in losses. Only in the last 20 years, however, has the cash-flow benefit that insurers enjoy become sufficiently attractive to insurance buyers to prompt them to do something about it. Although the shift to a risk management philosophy and increasing concerns over the cost of insurance undoubtedly account for part of the shift in buyer attitude, a more important factor is the changing nature of insurance reserves and the shift from property insurance-type reserves to liability-based reserves. Thirty years ago, the bulk of property and liability insurer reserves consisted of unearned premium reserves, the reserves representing the unexpired terms of the policies in force. Over time, the composition of reserves has shifted. With the growth in litigation, loss reserves, especially on casualty lines such as liability and workers compensation, came to dominate insurers' balance sheets. Whereas the turnover in unearned premium reserves was fairly rapid and occurred on schedule, the reserves for unpaid losses are compounded, as each year's unpaid losses are added to the unpaid losses of earlier years. The growth in loss reserves created cash flows of a new magnitude which, combined with record-level interest rates, created a package too appealing to resist.

A majority of corporations that have entered the captive arena during the past two decades have done so primarily to gain the cash-flow benefits that would otherwise have been enjoyed by their insurers. Many of the captives formed during this period were established by companies that had no problems in placing their insurance and whose management no longer believed in the Easter bunny or tax deductions for the parents of captive insurers. The principal motivation was the desire to participate more fully in the investment income potential of their premiums.

A New Profit Center

Hundreds of captives have developed into insurance and reinsurance companies that write the exposures of parties other than their parent. Such captives are generally referred to as *profit center captives* or as *broad captives*. Although it is doubtful that this has served as the prime motivator for the formation of *any* captives, it is an additional benefit that supports other reasons for captive formation. It may be noted parenthetically that, although some captives have actually generated profits for their parents by writing coverage for unaffiliated entities, a number of captives have come to grief through this route. Aspen, the captive insurance subsidiary of Caterpillar equipment dealers, was forced into bankruptcy in 1994, primarily as a result of poor underwriting experience on the outside business it had accepted.

343

Moving Capital in International Markets

Another benefit of a captive, although not necessarily sufficient in itself to justify creating a captive, is the ability to move money in international markets. Exchange controls and restrictions on currency convertibility do sometimes occur, and a captive insurer serves as a means by which these restrictions can be bypassed. A captive provides a means of moving money from one country to another by accepting payments from its parent in the foreign currency. Although this can be a benefit under certain conditions (when currency restrictions exist), it is questionable whether this benefit is sufficient to justify the creation and maintenance of a captive.

Taxation of Captives ■

The taxation of captive insurance companies has been a source of contention between captive owners and the IRS almost from the inception of the captive concept. The disagreement has concerned both the taxation of the captive's income, and the deductibility of the premiums paid by the parent to the captive. There has been a running battle between the owners of captives and the Internal Revenue Service for over 30 years. Initially, offshore captives were a source of concern to the IRS, because of the foreign income aspect, which permitted a captive to retain untaxed income in a foreign jurisdiction. With regard to other captives, the IRS objected to the deduction of what it considered to be essentially loss reserves in a retention (self-insured) program.

DEDUCTIBILITY OF PREMIUMS

Although premiums paid to commercial insurers qualify as tax-deductible expenses, the IRS has consistently refused to recognize contributions to a funded retention plan or self-insurance reserve as a deductible expense. One of the original rationales for captives was the hope that by creating a separate entity to which premiums were paid, the parent company would be permitted to deduct premiums that would not be deductible as contributions to a self-insurance reserve. However, with the exception of group captives, this strategy has been rejected by the IRS.

Early in 1972, IRS agents were given instructions to challenge the deductibility of parent company premium payments to foreign captive insurance companies. Since that time, a number of states have enacted legislation authorizing domestic insurance companies, and the IRS has taken the position (via an interoffice memo) that deductions for premium payments to any captive insurer—foreign or domestic—are not deductible. The IRS position since 1972 has been:

- A captive is an insurance company in form only, not substance. Because no shifting of risk and no loss of control of the premiums take place, the premiums paid to a captive are self-insurance reserves and not deductible.

- The captive has been formed primarily for the purpose of tax avoidance, and therefore premiums to it are not deductible.

The IRS formalized its position in a series of revenue rulings.

Revenue Ruling 77-316

Revenue Ruling 77-316 was issued on August 29, 1977, and formalizes the position taken by the IRS in 1972. It specifically disallows deductibility of insurance premiums paid by a domestic corporation to its insurance subsidiary. The ruling describes three different sets of circumstances:

1. The parent places insurance with the subsidiary, which retains 100 percent of the risk. Here none of the premium is deductible.
2. The parent places insurance with a totally unrelated domestic insurer, which acts as a fronting company, passing 95 percent of the risk to the parent's subsidiary. Here only the premium charged by the fronting company for retaining 5 percent of the risk is deductible.
3. The parent places insurance directly with the captive, which reinsures 90 percent of the risk with an unrelated insurer. Here, the premium paid for the reinsurance is deductible.

Revenue Ruling 78-338, IRB 38,6

In this ruling, the IRS gave approval of the so-called association captives. The insurer in question was owned by 30 shareholders, none of which controlled the company or contributed more than 5 percent of its total premiums. A large number of insureds creates a true element of insurance through the spreading of risk.

Revenue Ruling 78-277, 1978 IRB 29,9

In this ruling, the IRS indicated that a captive's assumption of outside risks is a factor in the taxpayer's favor, permitting deductibility of premiums paid by the parent company. The IRS has not prescribed the percentage of outside risks that must be assumed.

In spite of the IRS's firm stance on the point, many U.S. corporations feel that the IRS position is incorrect. They argue that the IRS is wrong in failing to recognize an offshore captive as a legal entity distinct from its parent, and that a properly structured captive—that is, distinct and separate from its parent and with sufficient assets and capitalization to carry on its business and meet its liabilities—will eventually rebut the IRS position. However, the IRS position on deductibility of premiums to a single-parent captive has been upheld by the courts in *Carnation Company v. Commissioner of Internal Revenue*, 71 T.C., No. 39 (December 26, 1978) and in *Clougherty Packing Company v. Commissioner of Internal Revenue*, U.S.C.A., 9th, No. 85-7707, March 3, 1987.

1991 Victory for Captives

In 1991, the U.S. Tax Court ruled in three separate but related cases that companies may deduct their premiums paid to their wholly owned captive subsidiaries. The three related cases were brought by Harper Group, which owns Rampart Insurance Company, Sears, Roebuck & Company, which owns Allstate Insurance Company, and Amerco Company, which owns Republic Western Insurance Company. The companies argued that taking business deductions for premium payments to their captive subsidiaries was legitimate because the captive insurers were bona fide companies that did business with other unaffiliated companies. The courts previously ruled that the subsidiaries that did most of their business with their parents did not qualify for tax deductions. The Internal Revenue Service argued that a corporate parent and its units constitute a single economic unit and there can be no shifting of risk. The Tax Court rejected the IRS's position by a 12 to 3 majority.

The effect of the court's ruling is that captive owners may deduct premiums from their federal income taxes if the captives write relatively large amounts of business for unrelated or third-party business. The captive must be a separate insurance company, regulated by insurance laws, and have sufficient premium income or retained earnings to pay losses. The Tax Court rejected the contention by the IRS that companies cannot deduct premiums paid to captive subsidiaries because they are part of the same "economic family."

The Sears decision, which the IRS appealed, was upheld by the Seventh Circuit Court of Appeals in 1992. In upholding the Tax Court, the Seventh Circuit adopted a substance-over-form view, holding that the arrangement between Sears and Allstate had economic substance independent of its tax effects and that there was no need to re-characterize the transactions as self-insurance.

The decision in these rulings was not really surprising. What is surprising is that the IRS chose to challenge the deductibility of premiums paid by Sears to Allstate. The IRS challenge appears to directly contradict the Service's own position, as set forth in Revenue Ruling 78-277.

Taxation of Captive Income—TRA-86

Although premiums paid to single-parent captives are nondeductible, the exceptions permitted for group-owned captives created a tax loophole for offshore association captives that was not addressed until the Tax Reform Act of 1986. Prior to TRA-86, the income of an offshore captive derived from premiums on U.S. exposures was taxed under complicated rules applicable to a "controlled foreign corporation" (CFC). Although the law defined a CFC as one in which 25 percent of the shareholders were U.S. residents, only shareholders owning 10 percent or more of the foreign corporation were counted in making the determination. This meant that an offshore captive owned by 20 participants, each with 5 percent of the stock, was not classed as a CFC and escaped taxation of its income, even though the parent recognized a deduction for the premiums paid to the captive. Under TRA-86, each U.S. shareholder who owns stock in a 25 percent or more U.S.-owned foreign corporation is subject to current taxation on a pro rata share of income of the foreign insurer arising from insuring risks of U.S. stockholders and related parties, regardless of the degree of ownership in the company. This means that under prior law, the owners of an offshore captive could defer payment of taxes on the captive's profits until actual receipt, if their ownership in the captive was less than 25 percent. Under the new law, regardless of the percentage of ownership, the profits of the captive are imputed to the shareholders and are currently taxable, whether or not they are paid out. This effectively eliminates the shelter on the earned income of owners of association captives.

State and Foreign Income Taxes

Obviously, a domestic corporation will be subject to any applicable state income taxes. State income taxes normally do not apply to a foreign corporation. A discussion of foreign income taxes is beyond the scope of this chapter except to note that Bermuda has no corporate income tax.

State Premium Taxes

In general, premiums paid to offshore, nonadmitted insurers are not subject to state premium taxes if all negotiations and activities associated with obtaining and signing the policy are conducted offshore. Captives that are actually licensed to do business in a particular state are subject to the premium tax of that state. In those instances in which the captive is not subject to the premium tax because it is not licensed, an excess and surplus line premium tax may apply.

Federal Excise Tax

Section 4371 assesses a 4 percent tax on premiums (except life insurance) written directly to most foreign insurers. There is also a 1 percent tax on premiums ceded (reinsured) with foreign carriers. The excise tax is levied on the insured rather than the carrier, but it is in lieu of the U.S. income taxes the foreign carrier would incur if it operated a business in the United States.

▟ Structuring The Captive ■

There are three choices concerning the corporate structure of a captive insurance company: stock, mutual and reciprocal. We examined the characteristics of each type of insurer in Chapter 11.

CAPTIVE MANAGEMENT COMPANIES

One of the requirements of a captive insurer is management expertise to run the operation. During the past 30 years, a growing number of brokers and consultants have established captive management firms. This relieves the parent of a captive of the need to assemble the technical competence required for managing the captive.

FEASIBILITY STUDIES

A detailed feasibility study is usually made before setting up any captive insurer. Such studies may be made by internal staff, brokers with captive experience, captive management firms, or independent consultants. Recently, a number of public accounting firms have also entered the captive feasibility study field.

Most of the larger brokers and captive company management firms have expertise and knowledge regarding captives. They have two limitations: (1) some have a pro-captive and others an anti-captive bias, and (2) they do not thoroughly explore other techniques, especially self-insurance. Many otherwise sophisticated financial managers will have captive feasibility studies made by brokers who manage captives or captive management firms, an approach akin to asking IBM whether you need a computer.

Captive feasibility studies should not only compare the captive to other risk finance plans, but should also be undertaken only by those who are (1) knowledgeable and (2) unaffected by the outcome of the study.

FRONTING COMPANY ARRANGEMENTS

In some lines of insurance, especially workers compensation and often auto liability, coverage must be written by an insurer licensed in the state where the coverage is provided. Thus an unlicensed captive cannot write these lines directly. Owners of captives can, however, use the captive to reinsure a licensed company. The licensed, or "fronting," company will retain a portion of the risk—either a nominal quota share (10 percent is common) or possibly an upper layer of risk. A fronting company is an insurance company that is unrelated to the captive and that takes all of the risk and reinsures it 100 percent (or substantially, say, 90 percent or 95 percent) according to the requirements of the law in the country or state in which the risk is located.

There is a cost (usually in the range of 10 percent or more of premium) for use of the fronting company designed to cover the fronting company's expenses. The fronting company has to issue the policy. Although the exposure is reinsured with the captive, the fronting company is contractually liable to the insureds, and if the captive cannot meet its obligations, the fronting company must nevertheless pay incurred losses. Fronting companies are also sometimes required to make filings in the local community. They, or an affiliate company, may provide the actual engineering services, loss-prevention services, safety engineering, and claims service.

Not only must the fronting company be financially responsible for the coverage issued, but also it may not be given credit by the state regulatory authorities for reinsurance ceded to the captive. Licensed insurers are limited in the amount of their writings (based on their capital and surplus), which is increased with "authorized" reinsurance. A captive is not usually considered an authorized reinsurer by state regulators. Thus risks reinsured in a captive may adversely affect the fronting company's surplus.

CAPTIVES AS REINSURERS

Captive insurers sometimes function as reinsurers, taking a part of the risk written by other insurance companies. In some cases, the reinsurance arrangement involves the parent company's risk, which is written by a "fronting" company (discussed above) and then reinsured with the captive. In other cases, a captive may reinsure unrelated risks.

Even captive insurance companies have created a captive. Ten companies with active captives formed Corporate Insurance and Reinsurance Company, Ltd. Today, this organization has 14 owners and writes about $50 million in premiums in a pooling operation for its members.

RENT-A-CAPTIVE

The other side of fronting involves the recipient of the program, the rent-a-captive operations, which are usually domiciled in an offshore location such as Bermuda. During the late 1970s and early 1980s, many captive owners found that they were not operating their companies on a cost-efficient basis, because they were not maximizing the use of surplus or spreading administrative costs over a sufficiently large premium base.

One solution, implemented by a number of captive owners, was to increase the volume of business written by their offshore captive by soliciting outside business. An easy way to do this was to offer the captive to other firms that either did not want to make the capital contribution required to form an offshore captive, or who found it difficult to justify creation of their own captive. The result was the "rent-a-captive" concept.

Since that time, rent-a-captive facilities have become popular, and a number of domestic insurance companies and even insurance brokerage houses have become participants in the field. Often, a rented captive is used in conjunction with a fronting company. Fronting companies obviously have a strong interest in the financial soundness of the rented captive, because it is the captive to which the business written by the fronting company is ceded. If the captive is not able to pay the losses generated under the program, the fronting company that has written the coverage remains responsible.

❖ The Risk Retention Act of 1986 ■ ■ ■ ■ ■ ■ ■ ■ ■ ■ ■ ■ ■ ■ ■

A discussion of captives would not be complete without some mention of the Risk Retention Act of 1986, which was signed into law in November 1986 by President Reagan. The Risk Retention Act of 1986, which amended the Product Liability Risk Retention Act of 1981, opened a new era of captives. The original 1981 act, which was passed to provide relief for insurance buyers during the product liability crisis of the late 1970s, limited its application to the *products and completed operations* exposures. The 1986 law expanded the provisions of the law to apply to most liability coverages. (Workers compensation, employers liability, and personal risks are excluded from the new law.) In general, the liability exposures included within the scope of the act include those coverages that would normally be written under the commercial general liability policy, the auto liability form, and the umbrella policy. However, other coverages such as officers and directors liability, errors and omissions liability, and even pollution liability fall within the definition of liability for which the act may provide coverage.

Like its predecessor, the Risk Retention Act of 1986 authorized two mechanisms for group treatment of liability risks:

1. Risk retention groups for self-funding (pooling)
2. Purchasing groups for joint purchase of insurance

The two types of groups are fundamentally different, with resulting differences in their operations and usefulness.

RISK RETENTION GROUPS

A risk retention group is essentially a group-owned insurer whose primary activity consists of assuming and spreading the liability risks of its members. As their name implies, risk retention groups are formed for the purpose of retaining or pooling risk. They are insurance companies, regularly licensed in the state of domicile, and owned by their policyholders who, in effect, double as shareholders. The members are required to have a community of interests (i.e., similar risks), and once organized, they can offer "memberships" to others with similar needs on a nationwide basis.

A risk retention group need be licensed in only one state, but may insure members of the group in any state. The jurisdiction in which it is chartered regulates the formation and operation of the group insurer. This is a major advantage, for it enables the group to operate nationwide, without having to comply with the licensing requirements of the other states in which it does business. Such requirements include capital and surplus requirements, assessments and regulation by insolvency guarantee associations, countersignature requirements, and discriminatory taxes. Once it is chartered in one state, it can operate in any state simply by filing notice of its intent with the respective state insurance department.

Initially, the organizers of a risk retention group submit a business plan or feasibility study to the insurance department of the chartering state. Usually, the feasibility study will include a review of the past premiums and losses of the group, a proposed rating structure, capitalization requirements, projected premiums and losses, and a proposed cost allocation approach. The group may be formed as a captive insurer in one of the states that has enacted legislation to encourage the domicile of captives, or it may be organized as a regular insurance company. In either case, the process of forming the association captive is simplified by an exemption of members from federal security law registration requirements and from state "blue-sky" laws.

Once it is chartered by a state, the risk retention group has the same powers as a regular insurance company. Depending on the state of domicile, the risk retention group can be capitalized at a fraction of the capital and surplus required of a domestic company. It can issue policy contracts, establish rates, retain all or part of the risk, purchase reinsurance, and pay claims—everything a conventional insurer can do.

The principal state regulatory overview is by the chartering state. The group must submit copies of the plan or study to the insurance departments of each other state in which the group will be doing business, but it need not be licensed to operate in other states. However, risk retention groups are subject to the unfair claim settlement practice laws, residual market mechanisms (i.e., assigned risk pools), registration with the state insurance commissioner, filing of data such as losses and expenses, and solvency examinations by insurance commissioners of the states in which they operate. In addition, although the earliest interpretations of the act suggested that rate and policy form regulation did not apply to risk retention groups, this has become an area of some controversy as a number of state commissioners have disagreed.

The group must file with the insurance commissioner, in each state in which it does business, a copy of the annual financial statement it files with the chartering state. The statement must (a) be certified by an independent public accountant and (b) include an opinion of the adequacy of loss reserves by a qualified loss reserve specialist or board-certified actuary.

Although risk retention groups may look like other insurance companies and operate like other insurance companies, they lack one of the principal advantages of an insurer admitted to do business in the state. Risk retention groups are prohibited from joining the state insolvency guaranty fund. In the event of insolvency of a risk retention group, there is no source of recovery other than the assets of the group. Both federal and state law requires that policies issued by risk retention groups include the following notice on the face of the policy:

NOTICE

This policy is issued by your risk retention group. Your risk retention group may not be subject to all of the insurance laws and regulations of your state. State insurance insolvency guaranty funds are not available for your risk retention group.

The exclusion of risk retention groups from the state insolvency funds represents one of the principal dangers to their use.

Requirement for Success

Much of what has been written about the requirements for the successful operation of a risk retention group could have been taken from any well-written principles of insurance textbook. A risk retention group is basically an insurance company, and the elements in its successful operation are basically the same as the requirements for the successful operation of any insurance mechanism.

First, the group must be homogeneous in both interest and in the risks they intend to share. Without homogeneity, the group loses the application of the law of large numbers. In addition, the participants must be willing to share risks with others in the pool. Members of a risk retention group are not only insureds, but also insurers. This means, among other things, that the group must exercise selectivity in the choice of its members. The cost of insurance through a risk retention group will vary directly with the loss experience, and poor experience will generate high costs.

Obviously, the plan must be properly funded. This means, among other things, a rating structure that accurately reflects the likelihood of loss, some provision for fluctuations in experience over time, and adequate protection against catastrophic loss. In this context, the financial stability of the risk retention group's reinsurers is a critical determinant of the plan's ability to indemnify.

In addition, to be successful, the program must be cost effective; it must offer the members a cost advantage as compared with commercial insurance alternatives. This cost advantage may arise in part from lower losses than would be incurred if the risks were commercially insured (e.g., claims handling), from recapture of investment income, and from reduced administrative and marketing expense.

Finally, members must be willing to make a long-term commitment. Although "long-term" cannot be defined precisely in this context, it means at a minimum a three- to five-year commitment by the participants. To encourage the required commitment, some retention groups impose financial penalties for early withdrawal from a risk retention group. (The requirement of the long-term commitment is based on the operation of the law of large numbers; experience may fluctuate in the short run, and continued participation by a large number of the participants is essential to the stability of experience over time.) The problem, of course, is that some members may be tempted to leave the group for the traditional insurance market as market conditions change. Any provision in the plan that penalizes early withdrawal discourages members from taking advantage of a change in the insurance marketplace. With a softening of the market, members would be subject to a penalty for withdrawal. If such a provision is not included, it is reasonable to expect that members would turn to traditional commercial insurance when it offered a lower cost alternative than the risk retention group.

Risk retention groups that have been formed thus far vary widely in their capitalization, reinsurance arrangements, and success in enrolling participants. As yet, there is virtually no way to judge the adequacy of the pricing or capitalization of these new entities.

PURCHASING GROUPS

A "purchasing group" under the Risk Retention Act is a legal entity that purchases insurance for its members. Like participants in risk retention groups, members of purchasing groups must be in similar or related businesses that expose them to similar liability risks. However, unlike a risk retention group, a purchasing group does not retain risk. Rather, it purchases group liability insurance from insurance companies for its members. The coverage is purchased in the conventional insurance market, and state laws that prohibit the group purchase of property and liability insurance are nullified with respect to qualified purchasing groups.

There are no specific requirements regarding the legal structure of a purchasing group. A purchasing group may be formed by an existing organization, or the group may be formed expressly for the purpose of purchasing insurance. Purchasing groups must give advance notice of intention to operate to the insurance departments of those states in which they will be doing business. States cannot, however, interfere with the creation or operation of purchasing groups, provided the group conforms with the provisions of the act.

Obviously, it is easier to form purchasing groups than risk retention groups. Purchasing groups require no capital contribution by the participants, no feasibility study, no business plan, no direct access to the reinsurance market, and no projection of losses and premiums. The absence of these requirements alone makes purchasing groups much simpler to form than risk retention groups, and as a result, they have proliferated at a more rapid rate. In addition, although risk retention groups must have a sufficiently large number of participants to make losses reasonably predictable and must have a minimum annual premium volume, purchasing groups can theoretically be any size, provided the group is acceptable to the insurer.

Purchasing groups have been compared to safety groups, a marketing concept of the late 1960s and early 1970s. The idea for safety groups arose in the workers compensation area where an insurance company insured a group of similar or related risks in a group program. One of the primary requirements for a safety group member was that it adhere to loss control or safety procedures. In return for reduced claims, members were rewarded by a dividend that was then divided pro rata among the group members. Safety groups generally were written only on a statewide basis primarily because of the state regulatory requirements that have been nullified by the Risk Retention Act.

Purchasing group arrangements include both individually issued policies and the use of master policies with individual certificates. Usually, when a master policy approach is used, the policy contains an aggregate limit. This means that in the event that losses of the group exceed the master policy limit, the coverage is exhausted, and there is no coverage left for the losses of other members.

The insurance companies that provide coverage to purchasing groups thus far include a number of the major insurers, such as Aetna, Home Insurance, and Continental. In addition to the traditional insurers who have taken advantage of the new act to sell to purchasing groups, several new insurers have been formed expressly to provide coverage to purchasing groups.

The financial dependability of a purchasing group obviously depends on the solvency of the insurer underwriting the program. In this context, the same standards that apply in the selection of a direct insurer for the city's insurance should also be applied in the case of insurance purchasing groups.

The regulation of purchasing groups by the states in which they operate has become a source of some conflict. For example, an insurance company brought suit against the Superintendent of Insurance in New York State over the issue of whether a state can require a purchasing group insurer to file its rates and forms for prior approval. The judge in the U.S. district court in which the suit was brought ruled in favor of the insurance department, stating that purchasing groups are not exempt from state regulation of forms and rates under the act.

Three additional suits were filed in the state of Iowa over the question of whether or not the insurer for a purchasing group must be licensed in the states in which it insures group members. The federal law requires that the purchasing group obtain insurance from a company that is licensed in the state in which the purchasing group is "located," but does not define what is meant by the term *located*. Under one interpretation, the group is "located" in the state where it is headquartered. Under the interpretation applied by the insurance departments, it is "located" in any state in which it has insured members. In the Iowa cases, the court ruled in favor of the commissioner of insurance, who had argued that the insurer must be licensed in the state in order to sell to members of the group.

In spite of the adverse rulings in the New York and Iowa cases, the growth of purchasing groups has continued at a rapid rate. The premium volume that will ultimately reside in purchasing groups and the success of the groups are yet to be determined. At least some purchasing groups are likely to become a significant factor in the marketplace.

IMPORTANT CONCEPTS TO REMEMBER

pure captives	bed-pan mutuals	controlled foreign
group captives	social load factor	corporations
association captives	profit center captives	fronting company
trade association insurance	broad captives	rent-a-captive
companies (TAICs)	Revenue Ruling 77-316	Risk Retention Act of 1986
risk retention groups	Revenue Ruling 78-338	purchasing group
onshore captive	Revenue Ruling 78-277	safety groups
offshore captive		

QUESTIONS FOR REVIEW

1. Describe the general nature of a captive insurer. What are the corporate objectives of captives?

2. Identify and distinguish among the types of captive insurers. What is the rationale for these different structures?

3. Identify and briefly explain the main motivations for the formation of captive insurers.

4. Briefly summarize the tax treatment of captive insurers, and identify the circumstances in which premiums paid to a captive are and are not considered tax deductible by the Internal Revenue Service.

5. Distinguish between risk retention groups and insurance purchasing groups that are authorized by the Risk Retention Act of 1986.

QUESTIONS FOR DISCUSSION

1. It can be argued that the growth of captives, historically, resulted from dissatisfaction with the traditional insurance market. What were the types of dissatisfaction that it might be argued prompted the growth of captives?

2. What, in your opinion, accounts for the large number of U.S. captive insurers that are domiciled outside the country?

3. Describe what is meant by a *fronting insurer* and explain the benefits to the business firm using a fronting company and the benefits to the fronting company.

4. In what way(s) might a captive insurer protect itself and its parent organization from the adverse consequences of unfavorable loss experience?

5. In your opinion, which of the types of captives discussed in the chapter are likely to experience the greatest growth in the immediate future?

RISK FINANCING: CAPTIVE INSURERS

Barile, Andrew J. *The Captive Insurance Company*. Ada, OK: Intersate Service Corporation, 1987.

Barrese, James, and Jack Nelson. "The Tax Treatment of Captives." *CPCU Journal*, Vol. XLIII, No. 2 (June 1990).

Gillett, Roger C. "Captives Step Up or Move Aside," *Risk Management* (March 1996):

Harkavy, Jon. "The Risk Retention Act of 1986: The Options Increase," *Risk Management*, Vol. 34, No. 3. (March 1987).

Loy, D. and M. Pertl. "Why do Fortune 500 Companies Form Captives?" *Risk Management* (January 1982).

Mulderig, Robert A. "Captives Can Be for Everybody—Rent-A-Captive," *Risk Management* (March 1996).

Wright, P. Bruce. "IRS Fighting Deductibility of Captive Premiums." *Risk Management* (April 1995), pp. 112–114.

CHAPTER 16

Managing Property Risks:
Risk Control

CHAPTER OBJECTIVES

When you have finished this chapter, you should be able to

Describe the elements that are required for a fire and the techniques that may be
used to counteract a fire once it has occurred.

•

Describe the way in which commercial fire rates are determined and explain
how these rates may be useful in fire loss prevention and control.

•

Identify the four factors on which fire insurance rates are based and explain how
each factor influences the rate.

•

Identify and differentiate among the types of sprinkler systems.

•

Describe salvage operations and explain how they serve as a post-event form of loss control.

■■ Introduction ■■■■■■■■■■■■■■■■■■■■■■■■■■■■■■■■■■■■■■■

Loss-prevention and control measures aimed at reducing the frequency and potential severity of losses involving damage to property follow the general principles discussed in Chapter 9. Because property losses can arise from a wide range of perils
and can affect various types of property, it is virtually impossible to inventory the
total range of loss-prevention measures that might be used to prevent or reduce
property losses. The specific measures that will be appropriate for a given exposure

will depend on the exposure itself. We will not attempt to describe loss-prevention and control strategies for all property exposures. Instead, we will concentrate primarily on loss-prevention measures used to prevent and control fire losses. This approach seems justified on two grounds. First, fire is the major threat to property, exceeding damage from most other causes by a significant margin. In addition, by concentrating our discussion on the peril of fire, we can illustrate the application of the general principles discussed in Chapter 9 to the property loss exposure.

Although our major emphasis is on risk control measures directed at the fire peril, we briefly deal with other perils as well. The principal exception is loss by crime, which is addressed in Chapter 19. In addition, we consider only those loss-prevention and control measures that address property at fixed locations. Loss-prevention and control measures directed at property in transit are discussed in Chapter 21.

Avoiding Property Risks ■ ■ ■ ■ ■ ■ ■ ■ ■ ■ ■ ■ ■ ■ ■ ■ ■

Risk Control measures that may be applied in the management of property risks include risk avoidance and risk reduction. The opportunities for avoiding property risks is limited by the organization's need for assets required to achieve its objectives. The organization requires assets to achieve its goals and while the cost of risk associated with these assets can be reduced, it can rarely be avoided. It is sometimes suggested that the risks associated with the ownership of property can be avoided by the simple expedient of leasing rather than owning property. Although this is true in principle, it is an oversimplification. Leasing avoids the risk of property loss, but the costs associated with such risks will not usually be avoided through this strategy. Whether they purchase insurance or self-insure the risk of loss to their property, lessors invariably include in the charge for a lease an element that reflects the long-run expected cost of physical damage to the leased property. This means that the lessee ends up paying the costs associated with possible damage to property even when the ownership of property is avoided.

Noninsurance Transfers ■ ■ ■ ■ ■ ■ ■ ■ ■ ■ ■ ■ ■ ■ ■ ■ ■

Noninsurance transfers—usually under the terms of a lease—represent a common method of managing property risks. For example, a common provision in property leases states that

> At the termination of this lease, lessee shall return the property to the lessor in the same condition as at the commencement of the lease, natural wear and tear only excepted.

By agreeing to return the premises in the same condition as at the commencement of the lease, the lessee has, in effect, taken on the risk of damage from all perils. Note that negligence is not a consideration. If the property is damaged or destroyed by any cause—other than normal wear and tear—the lessee becomes responsible for restoration. Responsibility for insuring the property (or otherwise financing the risk of damage) is shifted from the lessor to the lessee.

⁙ Fire Prevention and Loss Control ■ ■ ■ ■ ■ ■ ■ ■ ■ ■ ■ ■ ■

Because the major hazard affecting buildings is fire, loss prevention in the area of property losses should begin with proper fire protection measures. Although loss-prevention measures aimed at protecting property from other hazards should also be implemented where possible, the following discussion of property loss prevention focuses on fire loss prevention. The discussion illustrates the principles of property loss prevention that may be applied with respect to other perils.

ANALYZING FIRE HAZARDS

The problem in attempting to discuss the area of property loss prevention is not that there is a shortage of material; on the contrary, it is that the information available is overwhelming. The current edition of the National Fire Protection Association (NFPA) *Handbook of Fire Protection*, for example, states that it attempts to include "in compact form only essential information on fire prevention and fire protection that time has crystallized into good practice."

Although we will only note briefly a few of the many considerations in fire prevention, a few specifics should be noted. Perhaps most important, it should be recognized that almost all fires are preventable. Consistent application of time-tried and proven methods of prevention and control would eliminate most fires and would limit the loss from the remainder.

Prevention of the start of fires requires emphasis on the human element in the equation. Most fires are caused by smoking and matches, followed closely by electrical wiring. Once a fire has started, the key to loss control is prompt discovery and extinguishment. With the exception of a few fires initiated by the explosive combustion of dusts, vapors, or other highly inflammable or hazardous substances, most fires start small. Finally, the damage caused by a fire can be limited by controlling the spread of the fire. This can be done by construction design that provides suitable barriers and that holds the volume of structures to a manageable area.

Factors in Fire Losses

A fire is combustion or oxidization proceeding at a rate rapid enough to generate a flame. A fire occurs when the heat applied to a fuel equals or exceeds the ignition point of that fuel. In general, a fire requires a source of heat, oxygen, and fuel. The techniques that may be used to prevent a fire are therefore to prevent the buildup of heat or to separate the heat from combustible fuel. Once a fire has occurred, it is counteracted by

1. Removing the fuel
2. Removing the heat
3. Removing the oxygen
4. Breaking the chain reaction

Most fire-fighting techniques attempt to counteract the interaction of heat, oxygen, and fuel by cooling or by removing the oxygen. Some chemical fire-fighting agents (halogenated hydrocarbons, also known as halogens or "Halon") fight fire by interfering with the chain reaction in oxidization.

FIRE INSURANCE RATING SYSTEMS

One convenient way to examine fire prevention and control efforts is to focus on the fire insurance rating structure, which is designed to reflect the hazards inherent in commercial properties. Because the fire-rating system seeks to measure hazards, it is a convenient guide to analyzing potential sources of loss.

Two basic types of rates are used in the field of fire insurance: class rates and schedule rates.[1] Class rates apply to risks that are so similar in character that it would be an unnecessary expense to differentiate among the various exposure units on the basis of their differing characteristics. Schedule rates are computed individually for each structure, with each building having its own rate, which reflects the hazards of the building.

Prior to 1976, all commercial properties were schedule rated by the local fire-rating bureau, a system that was cumbersome and expensive for many smaller risks. In 1976, the Insurance Services Office (ISO) introduced a new class rating plan for certain commercial classes with similar construction and occupancies. These classes include (1) small mercantile and nonmanufacturing risks (under 15,000 square feet in area) that are not fire resistive, (2) habitational risks of all construction classes regardless of size, and (3) property in the open. Concurrent with the introduction of the Commercial Class Rating Program, ISO withdrew all published rates for buildings eligible for class rating. Commercial risks that are not eligible for the fire class rating plan are specifically rated by ISO, and rates are obtained from ISO Commercial Risk Services, Inc.[2]

Specific loss costs for schedule rated structures are developed through an on-site inspection of the premises by a fire-rating engineer who is an employee of ISO, called a *field-rating representative*. The field-rating representative is trained in fire-rate

---

[1]In most states, ISO no longer publishes commercial fire rates. Instead, it publishes advisory loss costs, which represent the loss component in the final rate. The insurer adds an allowance for expenses and profits to the loss costs. These loss costs, however, serve as the basis for the rates computed by the insurer.

[2]Simultaneous with the introduction of the commercial class rating, ISO also introduced a new *Commercial Fire Rating Schedule* which establishes rates for commercial buildings that do not qualify for the class rating plan. Risks that are schedule rated include hotels, restaurants, manufacturers, processors, and various high-hazard occupancies.

engineering, and computes the loss costs by applying a schedule of debits and credits to a standard benchmark. The specific rates for each building are computed from a schedule of charges and credits after a rating survey of the features of the building. Engineers who have been trained for this specialized field inspect each building and evaluate its hazards, using a standard rate survey form on which the data relating to the specific features of the building are recorded. The report of this rating survey, which is contained in a document known as the *fire-rate makeup*, is the official basis for the specific rate on the building. Since this report enumerates the defects and beneficial features on which the structure's rate is predicated, it may serve as a valuable roadmap for loss prevention and risk improvement.

Although fire insurance schedule rating is a complex subject, an understanding of the fundamentals involved allows one to use the fire-rating schedules as a guide in fire loss prevention. Analysis of the fire-rate makeup can indicate possible loss-prevention measures that will lower the fire rate. With a basic understanding of the approach used in schedule rating, one can readily see what the debits are for, and how much credit can be obtained by remedying certain defects in the property.[3]

Experience has shown that most fire hazards can be grouped under four major building characteristics:

1. Construction

2. Occupancy

3. Protection

4. Exposure

A brief review of the factors related to each of these features that influence the final rate will illustrate the extent to which the fire-rate makeup can provide guidance in loss prevention efforts.

Construction

The loss potential of buildings is measured in terms of their combustibility, as determined by the quantity of burnable material used in their construction. Both the type of materials and the manner in which they are combined are important in measuring the loss potential of a risk. Because the type of construction is an important determinant of hazard, it will be helpful to review the major classes of construction that are used in the commercial fire field.

1. *Class 1: Frame Construction.* Buildings with exterior walls, floors and roof of combustible construction, or buildings with exterior walls of noncombustible or slow-burning construction, with combustible floors and roof. This class

---

[3]Prior to the organization of ISO, state and regional rating bureaus provided rate-making services to insurers. These state and regional rating bureaus used two different rating schedules to establish specific rates for a given risk: The Dean Analytic System, which was used in about half of the states, and the Universal Mercantile Schedule (UMS), which is used in the other half. Although there were differences between the systems, both based the rate for a building on its potential loss-producing characteristics. The schedules have been replaced by a single schedule by the ISO, the new schedule being more closely designed after the Dean Schedule than the UMS.

also includes frame buildings with masonry veneer such as stone or brick, or clad with iron or other metal siding, and also buildings overlaid with stucco or plaster.

2. *Class 2: Joisted Masonry Construction.* Buildings where the exterior walls are constructed of masonry materials such as brick, concrete, hollow concrete block, stone, tile, or similar materials and where the floors and roof are combustible.

3. *Class 3: Noncombustible Construction.* Buildings where the exterior walls and the floors are constructed of and supported by metal, asbestos, gypsum, or other noncombustible materials.

4. *Class 4: Masonry Noncombustible Construction.* Buildings where the exterior walls are constructed of masonry materials as described in Construction Class 2, with the floors and roof of metal or other noncombustible materials.

5. *Class 5: Modified Fire-Resistive Construction.* Although concrete and brick will not burn, the contents in such structures can burn, and the term *fire resistive* refers to the ability of the structure to withstand damage when exposed to the effects of burning contents. A modified fire-resistive structure is one that will "resist" the heat from burning contents for one hour. It is a building in which the exterior walls, floors, and roof are constructed of masonry or other fire-resistive material with a fire-resistance rating of one hour or more, but less than two hours.

6. *Class 6: Fire-Resistive Construction.* These buildings will have the same construction characteristics as Class 5, but with a fire-resistance rating of two hours (as compared with one hour for the modified fire-resistive buildings).

Occasionally, a building of mixed construction is encountered. Mixed construction refers to a structure in which a part of the building meets the standards for one construction class, and a part meets the standards for a different class. In these cases, the rating of the building is determined according to a set of rules that considers the percentage of the structure represented by each class of construction.

Schedule rating begins with a base rate for the particular type of construction under consideration. This base rate is then surcharged to reflect construction deficiencies or negative features of the building. The "standard" for a reinforced concrete wall, for example, is 6 inches. If the wall meets this standard, there is no charge; if the wall is less than 6 inches thick, a surcharge is applied. Structural deficiencies may be concerned with such features as unbroken floor areas, location and characteristics of vertical and horizontal openings, roof features, the structure and arrangement of exterior walls and partition or division walls, skylights, and the amount and location of concealed space.

Large undivided areas are known to contribute to the spread of fire. More important, they make it difficult to extinguish a fire once it has begun. Firemen attempting to extinguish a fire in large open areas cannot reach the center of the fire with water. One way to avoid fire-rate surcharges—and to reduce the hazard associated with such areas—is by creating separate *fire divisions*. A "fire division" is a structure whose characteristics justify its treatment as a separate building for rating purposes. In general, this means a structure physically separated from other buildings by space. When structures are not separated by space, a different definition applies. In this case, a structure is considered a separate fire division if it is separated from other structures by a continuous common wall (also called a "party wall") constructed of masonry at least 8 inches thick or reinforced concrete not less than 6 inches in thickness. If the roof is not masonry, the party wall must pierce the roof and rise above it to form a parapet, with no combustible materials extending across the parapet. Buildings that communicate through openings (doors) protected by an automatic or self-closing fire door labeled "Class A" are considered separate buildings.

Occupancy

Virtually all fire-rating systems recognize that the activities conducted in the premises have an important influence on the fire hazard. Some occupancies are more hazardous than others and have a greater likelihood of causing a fire. In addition, contents differ in their tendency to ignite and to burn once they are ignited, as well as in their susceptibility to damage. Charges for occupancy in commercial fire rates reflect all of these factors. Class rates group risks by occupancy; in the schedule rating system, occupancy is also a major feature in the determination of the rate.

The type of occupancy, however, is not the only factor considered, for hazards may vary considerably from one building to another, even when the occupants are performing the same function. Occupancy charges may reflect variations in hazard based on the way the equipment is installed, its proximity to combustible surfaces, and so on. In general, all of the occupancy factors relate to the ease with which a fire could start, or, if started, the ease with which it could spread.

For many property owners, little can be done about the hazards for which occupancy charges are made. Usually, the conditions for which the charges are made are basic to the type of activity being conducted by the firm. Occasionally, however, there are charges for hazards that are only incidental to the occupancy, such as heating devices, internal combustion engines, and painting operations. The charges for these hazards can sometimes be eliminated through safety measures that do not reduce the efficiency of the operation.

Protection

Fire protection is of two types: *Public*, or *municipal protection*, provided by towns and cities, and *private*, or *internal protection*, provided by the property owner. Private and public protection alike consist of three elements: (1) prevention, (2) detection, and (3) extinguishment.

Public Protection   Public protection refers to the fire-fighting capabilities and certain other factors in the community in which the insured property is located. Communities are divided into 10 categories, based on a Standard Grading Schedule of the Insurance Services Office, and are graded according to the quality of the fire department, water supply, building code, and other factors that bear on the fire hazard. Cities are rated into categories numbered 1 through 10, with 1 designating cities with the lowest exposure and 10 designating "unprotected" exposures. A municipality without rateable protection is classified as Class 10. A municipality with public fire-fighting equipment will be rated from class 1 (the best) to class 9, depending on the characteristics of its fire department, water supply system, and fire alarm system.

Factors considered in evaluating the fire department include (1) number of engine companies, (2) equipment of the engine companies, (3) number of ladder companies, (4) equipment of ladder companies, (5) geographic distribution of engine and ladder companies relative to the builtup areas of the municipality, and (6) personnel training.

Factors considered in rating the water supply are (1) the part of the city protected by fire hydrants, (2) maximum daily water consumption, (3) fire flow and duration, (4) the ability of the water system to deliver the needed fire flow at representative locations in the city, and (5) the condition of the fire hydrants.

The fire alarm rating is based on factors such as adequacy of the telephone system, devices used to record calls to report fires, number of operators on duty to handle fire calls, fire radio communications facilities, and emergency power equipment.

Private Protection Private or internal protection, as distinguished from municipal protection, is the next factor considered. The types of protective features for which rate credits may be allowed include fire protection appliances, such as approved portable extinguishers and stand pipe hose systems, automatic sprinklers, fire doors, alarm systems, outside fire escapes, and heat from outside the building. The most important of these protective devices, and generally the most expensive, is the automatic sprinkler system, discussed later in the chapter.

The effectiveness of portable extinguishers depends on the care and maintenance of the equipment and the familiarity of personnel with its use. For extinguishment purposes, fires are divided into the following classes: Class A is wood, paper, and textiles; Class B is flammable liquids, greases, and waxes; Class C is electrical equipment; and Class D is flammable metals. Most fire extinguishers are classed "ABC," so they are appropriate for several types of fires. The use of a water extinguisher on an electrical fire is dangerous to personnel who should be instructed on the hazards of such extinguishers. Better yet, portable extinguishers should be restricted to the ABC class.

Detection Systems Another protective device for which fire insurance credits may be allowed is a detection or fire alarm system, of which there are several kinds. The major detection systems include (1) private patrol service, (2) guard service with clock, (3) smoke and heat detectors, (4) automatic local alarm, and (5) central station alarm or remote station system.

A local alarm system, triggered by smoke or heat, sounds a bell on the outside of the building and relies on passersby to report the alarm to fire or police officials. A local alarm is not considered effective in reporting fires. A *central station system* is a private service with personnel who monitor the systems of a number of commercial concerns. The service either calls the appropriate authorities or dispatches its own personnel to investigate. A *remote station system* is similar to a central station, except that the mechanical and electrical detection devices are connected directly to the local police and fire stations.

Maximum credit is usually allowed when the building's warning system is connected to a municipal box, so that when the signal is activated in the building an alarm is transmitted through the municipal fire alarm system directly to the fire department. This system may be activated automatically by a detector device for heat, smoke, or fire, or manually by pulling a hook or handle on any fire alarm box in the building. All components of alarm systems, wherever installed, should have the label of approval of Underwriters Laboratories (UL). For an alarm system to be continuously effective, it must be inspected and tested regularly, and maintained as required.

Exposure

The final factor—exposure—reflects the hazards outside the building itself. The "exposure hazard" measures the likelihood that the building may be ignited from outside its own walls. Because the risk to the building (and to its contents) is increased by the possibility of a spread of fire from surrounding buildings (called exposing risks), the rate is modified to reflect the hazards inherent in the neighboring properties, based on the characteristics of the exposing risks and their distance from the exposed risk. The exposure surcharge is based on the rate of the exposing (i.e., the neighboring) building, the size and height of the exposing building, and the distance between the structures. Exposure is explicitly considered in schedule fire rates, but not in class rates.

Faults of Management

"Faults of Management" (also called "after charges") are those penalties assessed for poor housekeeping and temporary deficiencies. Usually, they are hazards in a risk that lend themselves readily to correction, and hence are regarded as temporary. For this reason, rating engineers do not consider them as a proportionate part of the risk, and thus measure them in dollars and cents rather than as percentages of the basis rate. Among the hazards specifically mentioned in the schedule are unsafe, improper handling or storage of flammable oils and gases; hazardous conditions resulting from poor housekeeping practices (such as permitting an accumulation of rubbish or waste on the premises, especially in the basement or attic); unsafe or inadequate electrical wiring, and nonstandard electrical extensions.

FIRE-RATE MAKEUP ANALYSIS

The preceding discussion of the process by which schedule rates are determined illustrates how complex the process is. Fortunately, the process is completed by highly trained engineers from the Insurance Services Office. Why, you may then ask, do we even discuss the subject? The answer is that knowing how schedule rates are determined can serve as a guide to loss control measures.

The document that summarizes and reports the fire-rating engineer's analysis is called a Fire-Rate Survey. It indicates the various factors that were used in calculating the final rate for the particular risk. Because it summarizes the hazards that determine the rate for a particular structure, it can serve as a guide in reducing hazards. Although the construction and occupancy of a particular structure may be beyond the firm's control in the short run, often other improvements in the risk can help to reduce the cost of insurance. Equally important, removal of hazards reduces the likelihood of a loss.

From the risk manager's perspective, the fire-rate makeup is the starting point in fire-rate analysis. The local inspection bureau has on file a copy of the fire-rate makeup for each building rated under its schedule, and copies of the rate makeup are generally available to the property owners and their designated agents. The risk manager should make it a point to obtain a copy of the fire-rate makeup for structures owned by the organization.

Once a copy of the fire-rate makeup has been obtained, it may be examined to determine the nature of the charges and credits. Following this analysis, an inspection of the subject premises will be necessary. During this inspection, the risk manager should focus on five points.

1. Do the conditions for which charges have been made actually exist?
2. Do superior or favorable features for which credits were granted actually exist?
3. Are there new or additional defects for which charges have not been made?
4. Can any of the defects for which charges have been made be removed?
5. Can additional internal protection features be added?

Although the forms initially appear overwhelming, with a little practice and guidance, they can be used effectively as a tool for risk analysis and rate improvement. In addition to the general information that identifies the structure (address and town), the form also includes the date of the inspection and the name of the inspector.

The other information, such as the charges and credits, are entered into the appropriate blocks in the form. In reviewing the fire-rate makeup, it is important to determine whether there have been any changes in the building's conditions since the last inspection which might result in additional charges. This avoids the danger of requesting a re-rate and then finding that there are additional charges which more than offset the credits achieved through the re-rate.

After completion of the analysis, the recommended changes and recommendations that will be made to management should be discussed with an engineer from the ISO or other advisory organization that performed the original survey. This will ensure that loss-prevention measures will actually have a beneficial impact on the fire rate. It is sometimes beneficial to compare the expense of carrying out the recommendations made with the premium savings over some illustrative period of time. When the premium savings over a few years time cover the cost of improvements, management has an obvious financial incentive to implement the recommended changes. Of course, the greater the amounts of insurance carried, the greater will be the premium savings.

It is important to remember, however, that any rate reductions achieved are only a small part of the total benefit picture. In addition to a reduction in insurance costs, the elimination of defects and the addition of protective features make the probability of loss lower than would otherwise be the case.

Preconstruction Analysis

Fire rate analysis is also useful—perhaps even more so—in the case of new buildings. When plans are made to erect new buildings, the plans and blueprints should be checked by the rating bureau prior to the commencement of construction. It is obviously far less expensive to change the plans before the building is completed than to make adjustments after construction. More often than not, the increased cost for more resistive construction is offset by the premium savings over time. In the same way, prior planning can reduce insurance costs relative to additions and remodeling of existing buildings if the revisions are checked out with the rating bureau before the work is begun.

Because of the expense involved, it is generally not practical to remove many of the substandard features for which structural charges have been made, such as walls in an existing building. That should have been done when the plans and specifications were being drawn.

CLASS-RATED SUBSTANDARD CONDITIONS SURCHARGE

Rating data on class-rated properties can also provide guidance on loss-prevention and control measures. When a substandard condition exists in class-rated properties, a charge is added to the loss costs obtained from the manual. Substandard condition charges are expressed in dollars and cents, and are added to the class loss cost as appropriate. (When substandard condition charges apply, the property must be submitted to the insuring company for a review of the charges.) These charges are indicated in Table 16.1.

AUTOMATIC SPRINKLER SYSTEMS

The most effective fire loss control system is an automatic sprinkler system. As its name suggests, the operation of these systems is automatic, for they are activated when a fire occurs. The sprinkler *heads* are opened by a temperature-sensitive fused link that melts at temperatures caused by a fire or electronically by an automatic fire detection system.

Five types of sprinkler systems are in common use today. The selection of a system depends largely on the nature of the area to be protected, its construction, and the hazards involved. However, each system consists of at least a water supply, control valve piping to carry the water throughout the structure, and sprinkler heads to discharge the water. Each system type may have several configurations, depending on the manufacturer and special system requirements.

Wet Pipe Sprinkler Systems

The most common system is a *wet pipe system.* In this system, the automatic sprinklers (sprinkler heads) are attached to the piping system which contains water

Table 16.1   Class Substandard Condition Charges

Substandard Condition	Charge		
	Frame, Non-Combustible or Joisted Masonry Buildings	Masonry, Non-Combustible Buildings	Modified Fire Resistive or Fire Resistive Buildings
Heating and Cooking: Unsafe arrangement of heating including chimneys, stovepipes and gas vents and unsafe arrangement of cooking devices	.50	.25	.12
Wiring: Unsafe or inadequate electric wiring, non-standard extensions, overloading, and overusing	.25	.12	.06
Conversion: Subdivision of conversion of original living spaces into multiple units with overcrowded occupancy	.50	.25	.12
Physical Condition and Housekeeping: Building not in good repair, roof or chimneys deteriorating, wood surfaces unpainted or decaying, garages or porches not well maintained, and yards, basements, hallways or attics not kept clean and free from rubbish and litter	.50	.25	.12
Exposure: For adjoining properties of an exceptionally hazardous nature	.25	.12	.06

under pressure at all times. When a fire occurs, the individual sprinklers are immediately actuated (opened) by the heat and water flows through the open sprinkler heads. The biggest advantage of the wet pipe system is that water is available to start to extinguish the fire immediately. In any other type of a system, some delay is necessary in order to allow time for water to fill the piping prior to being discharged from the sprinkler head.

The riser in the wet pipe system is fitted with an alarm valve. Once a sprinkler head is fused opened, the water is discharged from the sprinkler head and the flow of water activates a water-flow alarm.

As a general rule, wet pipe sprinkler systems are confined to areas where freezing conditions do not occur. Occasionally, it is necessary to extend a wet pipe sprinkler system into an area that is subjected to freezing temperatures during the cold weather. Under these conditions, it may be necessary to deviate from standard practice and turn off this section of the sprinkler piping. The valves that are used to isolate that section of the sprinkler system, so that it can be drained, are commonly referred to as "cold weather valves." For very special applications, the sprinkler piping may be filled with antifreeze solution to eliminate the need to shut off the system and drain it during cold weather. The cost of antifreeze solutions generally prohibits the use of this procedure in large systems.

Dry Pipe Systems

Whenever the sprinkler system is subjected to cold weather conditions and it cannot be properly heated, a dry pipe sprinkler system is generally used. In the *dry pipe system*, the entire sprinkler piping network contains air under pressure until the dry pipe valve is operated. When a fire occurs, a supplementary fire detection system in the protected area detects the presence of a fire and then opens the alarm valve, allowing water to flow into the piping system prior to a sprinkler head opening. Under normal circumstances, the detection system is designed so that it will detect the presence of fire long before a sprinkler head opens.

Because a dry pipe system is filled with air under pressure, the air must be exhausted from the piping before it can fill with water and reach a pressure necessary for proper discharge from the sprinkler heads. Thus there is a time lag between the operation of a sprinkler head and the discharge of water on the fire.

Pre-Action Sprinkler Systems

In buildings where the danger of water damage is a serious problem as a result of damaged sprinklers or broken piping, the pre-action system is generally used. The major difference between the pre-action system and the standard dry pipe system is that the operation of the water supply valve in the pre-action system is *independent* of the operation of any sprinklers. The pre-action type valve is opened manually or by the operation of an independent fire detection system—not by reduction of the air pressure due to the fusing (opening) of a sprinkler head. The pre-action system has several advantages over the standard dry pipe system. Since the valve is opened by the operation of an independent fire detection system, by the time a sprinkler head opens the piping system is already filled with water. In addition, the system used to trip the supply valve generally sounds an alarm and enables the people in the building to hold water damage to an absolute minimum. Because the system is dry, it may be used in areas where freezing conditions occur.

Deluge Systems

A deluge system is similar to a pre-action system except that all or a portion of the sprinkler heads are open at all times. When the fire detection system senses the presence of a fire, the deluge valve (alarm valve) is opened. When the valve opens, water flows into the sprinkler system piping and out the open sprinkler heads deluging the protected area.

In case of fire, the deluge-type sprinkler system wets down the entire area covered by the sprinkler system by admitting water to sprinkler heads that are open at all times. These systems are operated by sensors designed for the detection of extra-hazardous fire conditions. This type of system applies water to the fire more quickly than any other type of system.

It is possible to use open and closed sprinkler heads, in combination, on a system where deluge operation may be needed over only part of the protected area. Because of the use of many open sprinkler (or spray) heads, deluge systems require a larger water supply than any other type of system.

Combined Dry Pipe and Pre-Action Systems

A combined dry pipe and pre-action system uses the actuating features of both the dry pipe and pre-action systems. That is, the loss of air in the system piping or the action of the supplementary detection devices actuate the flow of water into the piping. However, if the detection devices actuate the flow of water, the system will operate in the same manner as a wet pipe system. If the loss of air actuates the flow of water, then the system operates as a dry pipe system. The main purpose of the system is to provide water through two dry pipe valves, connected in parallel, to a sprinkler system of larger size than is permitted for a single dry pipe valve.

OTHER FIRE SUPPRESSION SYSTEMS

The potential for water damage from sprinklers can be averted by installing a system that uses an agent other than water. A carbon dioxide system, for instance, extinguishes fires by reducing the concentration of oxygen. Such a system is not recommended for structures with human occupants, because if actuated, it makes breathing difficult. A Halon 1301 system, on the other hand, interferes with the chemical reaction in a fire. It leaves little residue but dissipates into the atmosphere. If it works correctly, it suppresses a fire immediately and is less toxic to humans than other gases. The premature release of Halon can be prevented by requiring impulses from two systems before release, or by a five-minute delay.

HIGHLY PROTECTED RISKS (HPR)

Our discussion of risk control for property exposures would not be complete without a brief comment on the *Highly Protected Risk (HPR)* market. HPR refers both to a specialized approach in the property insurance field and to the types of property that are eligible for this approach. HPR property is property that, because of its superior construction, fire protection equipment, and management's commitment to loss prevention, is considered to have an extremely low fire hazard. Insurers that specialize in providing coverage on such property are known as *HRP insurers*. Three types of companies dominate this market. They include the companies in the Factory Mutual System, the Industrial Risk Insurers (IRI), and the Kemper Insurance Group. A number of the largest property and liability insurers are members of IRI and participate in the HPR through this organization.

An HPR property is defined by these characteristics: an automatic sprinkler system monitored by a central station supervisory service, superior construction with fire doors and walls to contain fire within a limited area, an adequate water supply, and good local fire protection. Perhaps the most important qualification is a managerial commitment to property loss prevention.

Usually, the values involved in HPR property are substantial. The significant value qualification results from two factors. First, it was the need for capacity to insure large and high-valued complexes that led to the creation of HPR insurers. In addition, the insured entity must generate sufficient premiums to cover the cost of the loss-prevention and control engineering services that are provided as an integral part of the protection package. Because the rates for HPR property are extremely low, the values must be extremely large to cover the insurer's costs.

HPR insurers operate as direct writers and do not pay commissions to agents or brokers. The distinguishing feature of HPR insurers is the broad range of loss prevention and control engineering services they provide to insureds. These include a variety of supporting services, such as consulting on fire protection facilities, loss control training courses, and inspection services. HPR insurers have developed the science of fire protection to a high degree, and the services of HPR insurers account for much of their appeal to insurance buyers with large concentrations of value.

Risk Control Measures for Other Perils ■ ■ ■ ■ ■ ■ ■ ■ ■

Although fire is generally considered the major threat to fixed location property, it is not the only peril that can cause serious loss. Because the cause of a loss is less important than its effect, loss prevention and control measures should be directed at other perils as well as at fire.

WINDSTORM AND HAIL

Windstorms have a greater potential for catastrophic loss than does hail. The major sources of windstorm damage are high winds accompanying cyclonic storms, which often strike in the winter, tornadoes, and hurricanes. Certain areas are especially susceptible to hurricanes or tornadoes. Although windstorm is not susceptible to prevention measures, certain loss control steps can be taken. In addition to the obvious strategy of locating away from areas with frequent severe storms, wind-resistive structures represent the most effective strategy. Buildings with large areas of glass or inadequately anchored roof surfacing are more susceptible to windstorm damage than structures without these vulnerabilities.

Hail consists of ice particles created by freezing atmospheric conditions. Hailstones can cause substantial damage to autos, buildings, and other property in the open. The only strategy effective against hail damage is to protect vehicles and other property that are likely to be damaged by storing them in covered structures.

EXPLOSIONS

Explosions include combustion explosions that result from the ignition of gases, dust, or other explosive materials or from pressure devices, such as steam boilers. For the steam boiler exposure, scheduled inspections are the most effective loss control technique. Other explosions—which are basically rapid combustion—are susceptible to control measures similar to those used for fire. The major difference is the shorter time period available for counteraction. Explosion suppression equipment resembles an automatic fire extinguishing system. It detects a sudden abnormal increase in pressure and automatically floods the incipient explosion with a suppressing agent. Other controls are proper handling, low-oxygen or oxygen-free atmosphere, and venting explosions that do occur.

Separation may also be an effective loss control measure. In the manufacture of volatile substances, for example, multiple small factories make more sense than a large single factory.

WATER DAMAGE

Water damage due to flood, waves, or spray may accompany a windstorm. Water damage can also result from leaking or burst pipes or accidental discharge from a plumbing or heating system. Finally, water damage can result from accidental admission of rain or snow directly into the interior through defective doors, windows, or other openings.

Inspection and maintenance of plumbing systems and roofs, windows, and doors represent obvious control measures. In addition, property that is susceptible to damage by water may be protected by coverings and by skidding. *Skidding* refers to the storage of property on wooden pallets or skids, so that the property does not rest on the floor. This can prevent damage to the property as a result of capillary action, in which water is drawn from the floor up into the property.

SPRINKLER LEAKAGE

If the system is located in an area where no freezing weather is anticipated, then a wet system may be used with water at the sprinkler head. Otherwise, the dry pipe system is employed. An alarm is an important part of the system.

VANDALISM AND MALICIOUS MISCHIEF

Most vandalism is committed by children and young adults. Areas with large populations of children, such as urban areas, are likely to have a higher incidence of vandalism. Other types of vandalism can occur during labor disputes or social protest. Security personnel may be an effective loss control measure, and perimeter security such as a fence may deter vandals. In many instances however, these measures are not feasible. Graffiti-resistant coverages may be applied to exterior walls, but other types of damage can still occur.

EARTHQUAKE

Because it is not possible to control the buildup of energy associated with earthquakes, the loss-prevention and control alternatives are limited. Avoiding earthquake-prone areas is one option, and earthquake-resistant construction is another. The most important loss control strategies, however, are the post-event control measures. When an earthquake occurs, emergency action to prevent fires and explosions (such as shutting off gas lines and electricity) can minimize the damage sustained. Disaster planning can help to guarantee that appropriate measures are taken and can conceivably prevent loss of life.

BOILER EXPLOSION AND MACHINERY HAZARDS

The conventional loss-prevention method for boilers and machinery is inspection and maintenance. At the time they were first introduced, steam boilers were the "nuclear reactors" of their day. Public concern over the dangers associated with steam boilers led to statutory requirements for the inspection of steam boilers by both cities and states. In 1995, 43 states and 28 cities had laws requiring periodic inspection of boilers.[4] The laws vary widely from jurisdiction to jurisdiction, and it is difficult to generalize with respect to the requirements. Some laws apply to steam boilers only, some to both steam and hot water boilers, and others to boilers and certain types of machinery. The greatest degree of uniformity is with respect to high-pressure steam boilers (that is, those operating at over 15 pounds per square inch pressure) for which inspection is uniformly required. In some states, all boilers of the type specified are subject to the law, whereas other states exempt the boilers of public service companies, refineries, and canneries. In some states, the inspection requirement applies only to boilers in places of public assembly.

All state laws accept the inspection service provided by an insurance company as meeting the requirements of the law.[5] As an alternative, state inspectors may perform the inspection for a fee. One of the major reasons for purchase of boiler and machinery insurance is to obtain the inspection services provided the insurer. All boilers, machinery, and other equipment insured under a boiler and machinery policy are routinely inspected by qualified insurance company engineers to determine their operating condition and to be sure that such equipment meets the

---

[4]The states without boiler inspection laws are Alabama, Florida, Georgia, New Mexico, Missouri, South Carolina, and Wyoming.

[5]Boiler and machinery insurance originated in 1966 as a type of guaranteed inspection service when a group of engineers from Hartford, Connecticut, offered a boiler inspection service and promised to indemnify their clients if the boiler exploded while the inspectors were under contract with the boiler owner. This organization, the Hartford Steam Boiler Inspection and Insurance Service, remains the leading writer of boiler and machinery coverage.

engineering requirements of the insurer. Although the policy does not obligate the insurer to provide such inspections, the parties understand that the inspections will be made. The effectiveness of inspection as a means of loss prevention in this instance seems indisputable; the accident rate for insured boilers is about one-twentieth of the rate for uninsured boilers.

Although the field of boiler and machinery insurance began with the inspection and insuring of boilers, it later expanded to include other pressure devices and eventually machinery. Any machine subject to accidental breakdown that could destroy or damage a large part of the machine is eligible. Examples include motors, generators, transformers, switchboards, steam, oil and gas engines, fly-wheels, turbines, hydraulic presses, air compressors, and refrigeration equipment. The growth of automation in industry and the increased sophistication of production facilities have increased the need for loss-prevention efforts for machinery and equipment other than boilers.

Salvage Operations

The term *salvage* refers to the residual value of property that has been damaged. It may be used to mean the property that escaped destruction in a fire or other casualty that caused loss, or the amount of money received from the sale of the undamaged property. Under most forms of property insurance, the insurer reserves the right to pay for the loss in cash, to repair or replace the property. The insurer also usually reserves the right to take salvage.

Salvaging is the cost of saving property from loss, or from further loss, during and after the occurrence of damage. As such, it represents an important post-loss control technique. Salvaging operations may include separating and putting undamaged property in order, inventorying, reconditioning, and, in many cases, selling the salvage. Efforts to protect and preserve any undamaged property at the time of a loss can substantially mitigate the damage that would otherwise be incurred. Salvage efforts include not only those efforts aimed at protecting property from further damage, but also arranging for the sale or other disposition of undamaged property at the highest price. Although most salvaging operations are conducted on behalf of insurers in connection with insured losses, salvage operations are also an important loss control measure for self-insurers.

PROFESSIONAL SALVORS

Except in the case of small losses, insurance company adjusters generally avoid taking over and selling salvage or personally conducting salvage operations. Normally, this function is performed by a professional salvor. The term *salvor* refers to a person or an organization equipped to save, protect, inventory, recondition, and sell damaged property. Reputable and competent salvors perform numerous important services which include inventorying, separating damaged from undamaged stocks, appraising damage, protecting and arranging for reconditioning, and removing and selling stocks. This is their day-to-day business, and their experience in handling salvage makes their services invaluable. Their contacts with salvage buyers in various localities and their knowledge of how best to negotiate with individual buyers help to reduce the amount of loss when salvage is to be sold. Part of the service of qualified salvors is the documentation of their activities, their inventories, sales, and expenses.[6]

RESPONSIBILITY FOR SELECTING SALVOR

In the case of insured losses, the appointment of a salvor is basically the insurer's prerogative. Insurance company adjusters generally know their company's preference regarding the use of salvage companies, or they can quickly find out from the branch or home office. When a salvor is retained, the insurer's claim representative remains responsible for the outcome of the adjustment, and the salvor is under the adjuster's authority.

When a salvor is employed to assist in a loss adjustment, the entire bill is chargeable to the insurer or insurers represented by the company claim representative. Ordinarily, the salvor presents a bill when submitting a report.

SERVICES PERFORMED BY SALVORS

The exact functions the salvor is retained to perform will depend on the circumstances. At some point in the negotiations with the insured, a decision must be reached whether to leave the salvage with the insured at an agreed value or have part or all taken over by the insurer. In some cases, it may not be clear at the outset whether the interests of the parties will be best served by the insurer taking the salvage, or if it will be better to compensate the insured for the damaged property and leave salvage with the insured. This initial decision may dictate the nature and scope of the salvor's duties.

If the decision is made to have the salvor sell the stock, the salvor will be retained to sell the stock as is, where it is, or to remove it from the premises and sell it at some other location. In either event, it is ultimately removed from the insured's place of business by buyers or by the salvor. This is the principal service of salvors for which they are uniquely equipped and qualified. The salvor may, however, provide other services as well.

Protecting and Preserving Property

Cases arise in which the insured is unable to protect the damaged merchandise and put it in order because of lack of the necessary labor, space, and equipment. When the salvor is retained solely for the purpose of assisting in protecting and preserving

---

[6]The Underwriters Salvage Company of Chicago and the Underwriters Salvage Company of New York, both organized and owned by a large group of stock insurers, operated independently until 1975, when they merged under their present name, the Underwriters Salvage Company of Chicago. They are the largest salvors in the country. In addition, there are a number of highly competent independent salvage companies and salvors.

the property or inventorying the property, the salvor will undertake to separate the property and put the property worth saving in order. Because property insurance policies almost universally require the insured to protect and preserve property at and after a loss, judgments must usually be made quickly to avoid unnecessary loss.

If the work of separating the damaged from the undamaged stock has not already been done, the salvor will usually do the separation in connection with the temporary protection. This service is important to keep wet, heavily smoked, or otherwise damaged stocks from contaminating undamaged stocks. Separating and putting stocks in order is also a preliminary to inventorying.

Preparing Inventories

A professional salvor can provide enormous assistance in preparing inventories following a loss. The inventory may involve the entire contents of the premises or only a portion: it may be an inventory of only damaged stock or of both damaged and undamaged. The salvor's inventories may be only for count, but generally they are made for count, value, and damage. When a joint inventory can be made with the property owner and the salvor working together, the loss adjustment will be greatly simplified, for there will be few questions as to quantities.

Verifying Value and Assessing Degree of Damage

Because salvors usually have broad experience regarding replacement values, market values, and depreciation, they are uniquely qualified to assist in verifying values. In this procedure, they often follow the same procedure followed by a loss adjuster in checking invoices and accounting records to verify values. Whether or not a salvaging operation is necessary, the insurer may retain a salvor to verify values and the amount of the loss.

Once an inventory has been prepared and checked and the company adjuster and the insured agree regarding sound insurable value at the time of the loss, the next step is to determine the value of the property immediately after the occurrence of the loss. The difference between the value immediately prior to the loss and the value of the property after the loss is the measure of the damage that has been suffered by the owner. Measuring this difference is one of the principal services offered by the professional salvor. This process will also provide some notion of the amount that may be realized if the damaged property is taken over and sold as salvage.

Removing Part or All of Stock for Sale

In some instances, the parties will agree that the salvage will be sold by the insured and that the insured's net loss will be computed with an allowance for the value of the salvage. This normally occurs when the insured has customers or knows firms in the industry that are likely to be interested in buying damaged material from the insured and who may be willing to pay more for the goods than strangers would be willing to pay. When the insured sells the salvage, ordinarily it is sold on the premises. At times, however, it is advisable to send it away for reconditioning and sell it from the premises where it is reconditioned.

In other situations, the proceeds from salvage will be greater if the merchandise is handled by a competent salvor than if handled by the insured. After review of the facts, it may be agreed that the salvor will sell the salvage. Whenever merchandise is to be put into the hands of a salvor, the transaction is subject to a formal written agreement or a letter confirming the arrangement.

Salvage is sold for account of (1) the insurers, (2) the insured, or (3) whom it may concern, as determined by the insured. Sale for the account of the insurer occurs when the insurer makes full payment to the insured for the loss, takes the salvage, and then has it sold to reduce its loss. Sale for the account of the insured occurs when the insurer pays only for the damaged property or allows the insured to take the salvage, in which case the proceeds of the salvage are payable to the insured. Finally, sale for the account of whom it may concern occurs when it is judged advisable to sell the merchandise before details on the payment of the proceeds can be worked out, or when the insured as well as the insurers will be entitled to part of the proceeds.

Salvage operations represent an important post-loss control measure. Although most such operations are conducted on behalf of insurers, the services of professional salvors can help to minimize losses sustained by self-insurers.

IMPORTANT CONCEPTS TO REMEMBER

class rates	modified fire resistive construction	remote station system
schedule rates		faults of management
fire rate make-up	fire resistive construction	after charges
construction	fire divisions	fire rate survey
occupancy	internal protection	pre-construction analysis
protection	public protection	substandard condition charges
exposure	"unprotected" exposures	
frame construction	private protection	wet pipe system
joisted masonry construction	detection systems	dry pipe system
non-combustible construction	private patrol service	pre-action system
	guard service with clock	deluge system
masonry non-combustible construction	smoke and heat detectors	salvage
	automatic local alarm	salvor
	central station alarm	

QUESTIONS FOR REVIEW

1. Identify the elements that are required for a fire to occur and, by reference to these elements, identify the techniques that may be used to counteract a fire once it has occurred.

2. Describe the two broad classes into which commercial fire rates may be divided. Why are two approaches used rather than a single approach?

3. Identify the four factors upon which commercial fire insurance rates are based and explain the way in which each factor influences the rate.

4. Identify and describe the distinguishing characteristics of the types of building sprinkler systems.

5. Describe what it means by salvage operations and explain how they serve as a post-event form of loss control.

6. Identify the services provided by professional salvors and explain how each of the services may contribute to risk control.

7. Explain the distinction among Class A, B, C, and D portable fire extinguishers.

8. Explain what is meant by a *highly protected risk* and the significance of this classification in property loss prevention and control.

9. Identify the classes of fire detection systems and describe the distinguishing characteristics of the different classes.

10. What loss prevention and control measures can an organization take with respect to perils of nature such as windstorms, earthquake and flood?

QUESTIONS FOR DISCUSSION

1. The primary focus of the discussion in this chapter is on loss-prevention and control measures. To what extent is avoidance an effective approach to managing property loss exposures?

2. To what extent are noninsurance transfers useful in managing the risks of property damage losses?

3. It has been argued that deficiencies in municipal fire protection substitute private expenditures for public expenditures. To what does this argument refer? How might the net system cost be reduced by superior fire protection in a municipality?

4. A risk manager states that "a sprinkler system should be considered when fire insurance premiums saved by the reduction in fire rates will pay for the system over a 20 year period." Evaluate this advice.

5. In some forms of insurance, such as workers conpensation and liability, credits are granted for favorable experience. Why does fire insurance rating not lend itself to experience credits?

SUGGESTIONS FOR ADDITIONAL READING

Head, George L., ed. *Essentials of Risk Control, 2nd ed., vol. I,* Malvern Pa.: Insurance Institute of America, 1989. Chapters 2, 3.

National Board of Fire Underwriters. *Building Codes: Their Scope and Aims.* New York, The Board, 1957.

National Fire Protection Association. *Life Safety Code Handbook.* Boston, MA: The Association, 1991.

National Fire Protection Association. *Fire Protection* Handbook, 18th ed. Boston, MA: The Association, 1996.

CHAPTER 17

Managing Property Risks: Risk Finance

CHAPTER OBJECTIVES

When you have finished this chapter, you should be able to

Identify and distinguish among the four broad classes of commercial property insurance, and explain the distinguishing characteristics of each class.

∎

Describe the general nature of coverage available to business firms with respect to fixed location property.

∎

Describe the types of coverage that are available to business firms with respect to property that is not at a fixed location.

∎

Explain the principal features of boiler and machinery insurance and the feature that distinguishes it from other types of insurance.

▨ Introduction ∎∎∎∎∎∎∎∎∎∎∎∎∎∎∎∎∎∎∎∎∎∎∎∎∎∎∎

In this chapter, we examine the insurance coverage that is available to the risk manager when dealing with property exposures. As the reader will recall, damage to property may produce two types of loss: direct, which consists of the loss of the asset itself; and consequential, or indirect, which results from loss of use of the asset. We examine coverage for direct losses in this chapter.

Commercial property insurance evolved from the separate parallel development of several distinct types of insurance that protect against different types of property losses. This was a natural result of the monoline structure of the industry and the underwriting attitudes of insurers. Commercial fire insurance forms, for example, traditionally provided coverage only at the insured's premises, creating a need for a special class of coverages—the marine forms—to protect property while it is away from the premises. Other forms of property insurance such as crime insurance and boiler and machinery coverage also developed as separate fields of insurance.

Today, these different types of property insurance are often combined into a single package contract, and while the trend toward commercial package policies continues to gain momentum, commercial insurance packages are a case in which the whole is equal to the sum of the parts. Commercial package policies are simply combinations of the individual monoline coverages, which means that one learns about commercial package policies by studying the individual types of insurance that are combined to create the package.

Insurable Interest ■

One of the key elements in determining whether or not a particular piece of property represents an exposure to loss is reflected by the concept of insurable interest. The term is generally understood to mean any lawful economic interest in the safety or preservation of property from loss, destruction, or pecuniary damage. Although insurable interest generally follows title, insurable interest is not limited to owners. The variety of financial interests that can support an insurable interest include

1. The owner.
2. The secured creditor (mortgagor, vendor, etc.).
3. The holder of a mechanic's or contractor's lien.
4. A bailee or other agent or representative of the owner.
5. A lessee or renter of property to the extent of a legal obligation.
6. A tenant who makes improvements on real property owned by another.
7. A party with a contractual or legal expectation of ownership.
8. *Usfruct* interests.[1]

The concept of insurable interest is vital because property may not be insured unless the person insured has an insurable interest. The nature and extent of the insurable interest must be proven at the time of loss.

Commercial Property Direct Loss Coverages ■ ■ ■ ■ ■ ■

Most of the contracts discussed in this chapter are part of the simplified Commercial Property Coverage program that was introduced in 1985 by the Insurance

---

[1] *Usfruct* interest is defined as "the right to utilize and enjoy profits and advantages of something belonging to another so long as the property is not damaged or altered in any way." Examples are easements, permanent use of storage buildings, private roads, and similar interests.

Services Office (ISO).[2] Although these standard contracts are used by many insurers, some insurers have developed their own forms which they file with regulatory authorities independently. In addition, there are some contracts for which ISO has not created standard forms, and these contracts will vary from company to company. Although these forms are not standardized, the forms used by most insurers are similar, and we will describe the provisions included by most companies. In addition to the fact that ISO has not promulgated standard forms for all types of insurance, ISO is an advisory body, and insurers are free to adopt or not adopt the ISO forms. Insurance companies may modify or supplement the ISO forms.

ISO's Commercial Property Coverage program consists of those lines of insurance that were traditionally known as *fire and allied lines*. *Allied lines* referred to coverages such as earthquake and sprinkler leakage that were often allied with fire insurance coverage. Actually, the term *fire insurance* itself was something of a misnomer, because coverage for loss by fire was rarely written alone. Generally, coverage for loss by fire was combined with coverage against other perils; the perils of extended coverage usually represented the minimum coverage package.[3]

COMMERCIAL PROPERTY COVERAGE POLICIES

A Commercial Property Coverage policy is created from modular parts, which include a standard Common Policy Conditions form, a Commercial Property Conditions form, a Commercial Property Coverage Part, and a Causes of Loss form.

Commercial Property Coverage Forms

Different coverage forms are used for different types of property and are designed to provide protection against different types of losses. Twelve property coverage forms are designed for use under the Property Coverage part of the portfolio program.[4] Some of these forms provide coverage for direct loss; others, such as the Business Income and Extra Expense forms, are indirect or consequential loss coverages. The Property Coverage forms must be used with one of several standard Causes of Loss forms that specify the perils for which coverage is provided, along with the relevant exclusions. Because the perils for which protection is provided

---

[2]*Commercial property coverage* is the term used by the ISO to designate those fields that were previously known as "fire and allied lines." Because the term *commercial property insurance* (or *commercial property coverage*) is also used in reference to the range of coverages that provide protection on property of commercial risks (i.e., fire and allied lines, boiler and machinery, plate glass, marine, and crime insurance), this creates a potential for ambiguity. To minimize the confusion, we will follow the ISO's usage of the term *commercial property coverage* to refer to the traditional fields of fire and allied lines, and will use the term *commercial property insurance* when referring to the broad field of property insurance coverage.

[3]"Extended coverage" consisted of a group of perils (windstorm, hail, explosion, riot, civil commotion, aircraft, vehicles, and smoke) that were sold as a package and that came to be considered a more or less standard addition to the fire policy.

[4]The portfolio commercial property forms are the Building and Personal Property Coverage Form, Glass Coverage Form, Condominium Association Coverage Form, Condominium Commercial Unit-Owner's Coverage Form, Builders' Risk Coverage Form, Business Income Coverage (and Extra Expense) Form, Business Income Coverage (Without Extra Expense) Form, Legal Liability Coverage Form, Extra Expense Coverage Form, Leasehold Interest Coverage Form, Mortgage Holder's Errors and Omissions Coverage Form, and Tobacco Sales Warehouses Coverage Form.

are added by another form, the basic coverage is the same regardless of the perils package selected. Although we will not attempt to examine all of these forms, we can provide a general understanding of their nature and give the reader some insights by examining the most commonly used forms.

BUILDING AND PERSONAL PROPERTY COVERAGE FORM

The *Building and Personal Property Coverage Form (BPP)* is the standard form for insuring most types of business property. It may be used to provide direct damage coverage on completed buildings and structures or business personal property, including the personal property of others. Coverage may be written on buildings only, personal property only, or on both in the same contract. In addition, the form can be used to provide coverage on specific classes of property (such as stock, tenants improvements and betterments, or machinery and equipment) by endorsements or by describing the property in the declarations. The coverage is provided under three insuring agreements: Building, Your Personal Property, and Personal Property of Others. Each of the three insuring agreements defines the property that is insured under that item and specifically excludes other property from coverage.

Building

The building coverage defines *building* to include the structure described, completed additions, permanently installed fixtures, machinery and equipment, outdoor fixtures, personal property used to maintain or service the building, and materials and supplies for use in additions, alterations, or repairs of the structure.

Your Personal Property

The definition of *Your Personal Property* includes furniture and fixtures, machinery and equipment, stock, and all other personal property owned by the insured and used in the business. The insured's use interest in tenant's improvements and betterments is also included in the definition of personal property. As in the case of other items of property for which coverage is not desired, improvements and betterments may be excluded by endorsement. Finally, the latest version of the BPP includes coverage for leased personal property, which the insured is contractually obligated to insure, unless such property is insured under the Personal Property of Others insuring agreement.

Personal Property of Others

The *Personal Property of Others* coverage applies to the property of others that is in the insured's care, custody, or control, and that is located in or on the building described in the declarations. Coverage also applies to property in the open, or on a vehicle within 100 feet of the described premises.[5]

[5]Although personal line forms such as the homeowners policies automatically extend coverage to property of others in the insured's custody, commercial line policies generally do not. If coverage is required on the property of others, it must be specifically purchased.

Tenants Improvements and Betterments

The definition of *Your Personal Property* automatically includes the insured's interest in tenants improvements and betterments. In the event of damage or destruction of the tenant's improvements and betterments, payment will depend on whether the damaged property is restored and by whom. The insurance forms generally contemplate three separate possibilities, with different amounts payable in the event of each:

- If the improvements and betterments are repaired or replaced at the expense of the tenant within a reasonable time after the loss, the actual cash value or replacement cost of the improvements and betterments will be paid.

- If the improvements and betterments are repaired or replaced by others for the use of the insured, there is no loss to the insured and therefore nothing is paid.

- If the improvements and betterments are not repaired or replaced, the amount payable is that proportion of the original cost of the damaged or destroyed improvements and betterments that the unexpired term of the lease bears to the period from the date of installation to the expiration of the lease.

The different payment provisions, depending on whether the tenants improvements and betterments are replaced and who replaces them, are a logical extension of the principle of indemnity. They also illustrate the importance of proper planning in arranging the insurance on tenants improvements and betterments.

Additional Coverages

The Building and Personal Property Coverage form includes certain extensions of coverage; some of these are referred to as Additional Coverages, while others are referred to as Coverage Extensions. There are four Additional Coverages.

Debris Removal   The Debris Removal coverage provides payment for the expense of removing the debris of covered property damaged by an insured peril. Coverage for debris removal is limited to 25 percent of the amount paid for direct loss plus the amount of the deductible under the policy. For example, if direct damage to insured property is say, $6000, and the deductible is $250, the insurer will pay $5725 for the direct loss and up to $1500 for debris removal (25 percent of ($5750 + $250)). In the event that the cost of debris removal exceeds this limitation, an additional $10,000 is provided for debris removal under the Limit of Insurance provision. An important exclusion under the Debris Removal coverage eliminates coverage for the cost of removing pollutants. Limited coverage for removal of pollutants is provided under a separate Pollutant Cleanup and Removal additional coverage discussed below.[6]

---

[6]The exclusion of the cost of removing pollutants in the debris removal coverage was introduced in response to court decisions that held insurers liable for extensive pollution cleanup expense under the debris removal provision. Water used to extinguish a fire at a chemical plant, for example, can result in the dispersal of chemicals into the land or water. Under earlier forms, insurers were held liable for such costs up to the face amount of the policy.

Preservation of Property Coverage for removal of covered property is now provided by the Preservation of Property additional coverage. This coverage is on an open-peril basis and runs for 30 days.

Fire Department Service Charges The Fire Department Service Charge coverage is similar to the same coverage in the Homeowners forms. Coverage under the BPP is provided up to a $1000 limit with no deductible.

Pollutant Cleanup and Removal The Pollutant Cleanup and Removal coverage provides limited protection, up to $10,000, for the insured's expense in extracting pollutants from land or water at the described premises when the discharge or release of the pollutants was caused by a covered cause of loss. The $10,000 limit may be increased by endorsement for an additional premium.

Coverage Extensions

Coverage Extensions, like Additional Coverages, provide added coverage for specified exposures. However, unlike the Additional Coverages described earlier, the Coverage Extensions apply only when the policy is written with 80 percent or higher coinsurance.

- When buildings are covered, newly acquired or newly constructed buildings are automatically covered for up to $250,000. The coverage applies for 30 days.
- When personal property is covered, personal property at a newly acquired location is automatically covered, subject to a $100,000 maximum.
- Personal effects and property of others are covered up to a total of $2500.
- The cost of labor and research to reconstruct valuable papers and records for which duplicates do not exist is covered up to $2500 per location when such records are destroyed by an insured peril.
- Coverage applies to personal property while away from the premises, up to $5000.
- Outdoor property such as trees, shrubs, plants, fences, detached signs, and antennas are covered up to $1000 for loss caused by fire, lightning, explosion, riot or civil commotion, or aircraft. A $250 sublimit applies to each tree, shrub, or plant.

Perils Insured

Although the term *fire insurance* is commonly used when referring to property insurance on buildings and contents, coverage is seldom written to cover against loss by fire only. More generally, it is written to include the perils of *Extended Coverage*, vandalism, sprinkler leakage, volcanic eruption, and sinkhole collapse. This coverage is referred to as the *Basic* or *Standard* form, depending on the contract. Coverage may be broadened to include additional named perils, in which case the coverage is referred to as *Broad* form coverage. Finally, coverage may also be written under a *Special* form, which provides coverage on an *open-peril* basis. Thus there are three more or less standard approaches to property insurance, representing three levels of coverage: *Basic, Broad,* and *Special. Basic* and *Broad* form coverage are referred to as *named-peril* coverage, indicating that a loss is covered only if damaged by a named peril. Under *Special* coverage forms, losses are covered unless they are specifically excluded; it is therefore referred to as *open-peril* coverage.[7]

Under the portfolio commercial property program, four Causes of Loss forms are used in connection with the Building and Personal Property Coverage form: Causes of Loss—Basic Form, Causes of Loss—Broad Form, Causes of Loss—Special form and Causes of Loss—Earthquake Form.

The Basic Causes of Loss form covers fire, lightning, explosion, windstorm or hail, smoke, aircraft or vehicles, riot or civil commotion, vandalism, sprinkler leakage, sinkhole collapse, and volcanic action. Windstorm or hail, vandalism, and sprinkler leakage can be excluded. The basic form excludes building ordinance, earth movement, governmental action, nuclear hazard, power failure, war and military action, water (e.g., flood and other types of water losses), electrical apparatus, leakage or discharge of water or steam from appliances other than sprinkler systems, and rupture of water pipes.

The Broad Causes of Loss form includes all Basic form perils plus breakage of glass ($100 per plate and $500 per occurrence), falling objects, weight of snow, ice, or sleet, and water damage. Collapse is included as an additional coverage.

The Special Causes of Loss form provides coverage on an open-peril basis for risks of direct physical loss; it provides additional coverage for collapse and additional coverage extensions for property in transit ($1000 limit for personal property for certain named perils) and water damage (costs to repair damage to buildings to fix system). The Special form excludes pollutants and contaminants and transfer of property due to unauthorized instructions. A theft exclusion endorsement is available.

The Causes of Loss—Earthquake form insures against earthquake and volcanic eruption, explosion, or effusion (from earthquakes or volcanoes that begin during the policy period, even if direct physical loss occurs within 168 hours of the expiration of the policy period).

Need for Open-Peril Coverage

Although the named-peril approach to insuring property is probably the most common practice, it is unsatisfactory from several points of view. It violates the first principle of risk management in that it focuses on the cause of loss rather than on the result. Obviously, the business owner should be concerned about damage to his or her property by *any* cause, not just by fire, tornado, riots, or vandalism. In

---

[7]*Open-peril* coverage was previously referred to as *all-risk* coverage. The insurance industry has discontinued use of the term *all-risk*, which was misleading and which undoubtedly created misconceptions among the insurance-buying public.

the last analysis, it makes little difference what the cause of the loss may be; it is the size of the loss that is important.

Recognition of this principle leads to the conclusion that business property should be insured against as wide a range of perils as possible, rather than against some arbitrary and historical group of perils. The preferred approach is to insure owned buildings and contents on an open-peril basis, where any loss that is not specifically excluded is covered.

Some of the perils excluded under the Standard forms of open-peril coverage represent potentially catastrophic losses. For example, most open-peril forms exclude loss caused by earthquake and flood. Earthquake may be added to the property insurance policy by endorsement, and federally subsidized flood insurance is available through property and liability insurance agents.

Other Provisions

In addition to those provisions outlined above, the coverage part is subject to several other important provisions.

Deductible   The standard deductible under the form is $250, but larger deductions are available and may be scheduled in the declarations. The deductible applies "per occurrence," regardless of the number of buildings affected.

Vacancy Condition   The Vacancy condition provides that 60 days' vacancy bars recovery for loss by vandalism, sprinkler leakage, glass breakage, water damage, theft, and attempted theft. For all other perils, vacancy beyond 60 days results in a 15 percent loss-payment penalty.

Valuation Condition   The Valuation condition provides that covered property will be valued at actual cash value. Building losses of $2500 or less are payable at replacement cost, provided the insured meets the coinsurance requirement. Glass is covered at the cost to replace with safety glazing material if required by law. When duplicates of valuable papers and documents exist, coverage is provided for the cost of transcribing valuable papers and documents. Prepackaged computer software is valued at its actual cash value.

Mortgage Holders Condition   A mortgagee occupies an unusual position in a property insurance contract. Although not involved in the formation of the contract, a mortgagee listed in the policy becomes a party to the contract with rights distinct from those of the insured.[8] The Mortgage Clause grants those rights and imposes

[8]The mortgagee could, if it so desired, take out a separate policy covering its interest in the mortgaged property. However, this would result in a duplication of coverage, since the owner-mortgagor would insure the property to the extent of his or her insurable interest, which includes not only the owner's equity but also the obligation to the mortgagee for the unpaid loan balance. The normal practice is for the owner to purchase a policy naming the mortgagee as an insured under the standard mortgage clause.

certain conditional obligations on the mortgagee. Under the contract, the mortgagee has the right

- To receive any loss or damage payments to the extent of its interest in the property, regardless of any default of the insured with respect to the insurance.
- To receive separate written notice of cancellation.
- To sue under the policy in its own name.

The right of the mortgagee to recover regardless of any default of the insured means that the mortgagee's protection under the policy is unaffected by any violations of the policy provisions or breach of the contract by the insured. The mortgagee's interest would still be covered even if the insured committed arson.

The mortgage clause also provides that policy conditions relating to Appraisal, Suit Against Us, and Loss Payment apply to the mortgagee. As a separate party to the contract, the mortgagee's rights are distinct from those of the insured, and these include the right of a separate legal action against the insurer.

The obligations imposed on the mortgagee are

- To notify the insurer of any change in occupancy, or substantial increase in hazard of which the mortgagee is aware.
- To render proof of loss to the insurer if the owner fails to do so, and thereafter to abide by the policy provisions with respect to appraisal, time of payment, and bringing suit.
- To pay premiums due if the owner fails to do so.
- To surrender to the insurer any claim it has against the mortgagor to the extent that it receives payment in those cases where the company has ruled that no coverage exists for the owner.

Note that these are conditional obligations. They must be met only if the mortgagee wishes to enjoy the coverage of the policy; they are not conditions the mortgagee can be required to keep.

Coinsurance

The Building and Personal Property Coverage Form—like many other commercial property forms—contains a coinsurance clause. Because the coinsurance clause and the principle on which it is based are critical elements in many forms of property insurance, we will stop to examine it more closely. However, before turning our attention to the policy provision itself, it will be helpful to examine the underlying rationale for the coinsurance principle.

Rationale for Coinsurance   To understand the logic of the coinsurance concept, we must begin by recognizing that most fire losses are partial. Insurance Services Office (ISO) loss statistics indicate that about 85 percent of all fire losses are for less than 20 percent of the value of the property, whereas only about 5 percent result in damage over 50 percent of the property's value. Because fire insurance rates are based on the ratio of losses to the total values insured, the rate will be higher if owners insure a lower percentage of their property values than if they insure the property to some high percentage of its value. This relationship can be illustrated by an example.

Assume that an insurance company insures 10,000 buildings worth $10,000 each for 100 percent of their value. On the basis of past experience, the company projects the following losses:

30 partial losses at $1000 each	$30,000
2 total losses at $10,000 each	20,000
	$50,000

Since the company can expect $50,000 in losses on $100,000,000 worth of buildings, it computes the pure rate to be $0.05 per $100:

$$\frac{\$50,000}{\$100,000,000} = 0.0005 \text{ per } \$1, \text{ or } \$0.05 \text{ per } \$100$$

If the insurer assumes that the loss ratio will be 50 percent of gross premiums, it will add a loading, making the gross rate $0.10 per $100.00 of coverage.

If the same buildings are each insured for 50 percent of their value, the rate per $100 will be considerably higher. Assuming the same losses,

30 partial losses at $1000 each	$30,000
2 total losses at $5000 each	10,000
	$40,000

$$\frac{\$40,000}{\$50,000,000} = 0.0008 \text{ per } \$1, \text{ or } \$0.08 \text{ per } \$100$$

Again assuming that the loss ratio will be 50 percent of gross premiums, the gross rate is $0.16 per $100 of coverage.

Because insurance to value has a definite relationship to equity in fire rates, some concession must be made in the rating structure to those who insure their property for a high percentage of its value. The coinsurance clause was invented to support a concession in rates for policyholders who purchase insurance equal to a high percentage of the value of the property. It is designed to enforce the insured's agreement to insure the property for a specified percentage of its value, which is made in return for a lower rate.

Coinsurance Clause   Under the provisions of the coinsurance clause, the insured agrees to maintain insurance equal to some specified percentage of the value of the property (e.g., 80 percent, 90 percent, 100 percent) in return for a reduced rate. In effect, the coinsurance rate is a quantity discount. If the insured fails to maintain insurance to value as agreed, he or she may suffer a penalty at the time of a loss. A simplified language version of the coinsurance clause states that

All property covered by this form must be insured for at least 80 percent of its total value at the time of "loss" or you will incur a penalty. The penalty is that we will pay only the proportion of any "loss" that the Limit of Insurance shown in the Declarations for the property bears to 80 percent of the total value of the property at the premises as of the time of "loss."

More simply, at the time of a loss, the company will make payment on the basis of the following formula:

$$\frac{\text{Amount of Insurance Carried}}{\text{Amount of Insurance Required}} \times \text{Amount of Loss} = \text{Amount Paid}$$

The application of the provision is simple. As long as the insured carries insurance equal to the required percentage, all losses covered by the policy will be paid in full up to the face amount of the policy. If the insured fails to maintain insurance to value as required, only a part of the loss will be collected.

Coinsurance Clause Illustrated   To illustrate, let us assume that the insured has purchased coverage on a $100,000 building, subject to an 80 percent coinsurance clause. In keeping with the requirement of the clause, $80,000 in coverage has been purchased. In the event of a $5000 loss, the company would pay:

$$\frac{\text{Amount of Insurance Carried } (\$80,000)}{\text{Amount of Insurance Required } (\$80,000)} \times \$5000 = \$5000$$

Now let us assume that as time goes by, construction costs go up, increasing the value of the building, but the insured continues to carry $80,000 in coverage. When the next $5000 loss occurs, it is found that the actual cash value of the building is $200,000. To comply with the 80 percent coinsurance clause, the insured should now be carrying $160,000 in coverage. In this case, the insured becomes a coinsurer and suffers a penalty equal to the coinsurance deficiency:

$$\frac{\text{Amount of Insurance Carried } (\$80,000)}{\text{Amount of Insurance Required } (\$160,000)} \times \$5000 = \$2500$$

Two important points are illustrated by the examples. First, the coinsurance requirement applies at the time of the loss, and the amount of coverage required for compliance is based on the value of the property at the time of loss—not the value of the property when the insurance is purchased. Second, the burden of maintaining the proper amount of insurance is on the insured. The insurance company does not check to see if the insured has kept his or her promise until a loss takes place.

Deductibles and Coinsurance   Although the Simplified ISO portfolio property forms stipulate that the deductible is to be applied after the application of the coinsurance penalty, if any, this represents a break with tradition. Prior to the introduction of the portfolio forms, and in many other forms in use today, the deductible is applied to the loss and the coinsurance penalty is applied to the after-deductible portion of the loss. Because contracts differ in this respect, they must be examined individually to determine the manner in which the deductible applies.

Optional Coverages

Three Optional Coverages are available for use with the Building and Personal Property Form: Agreed Value, Inflation Guard, and Replacement Cost. The Inflation

Guard and Replacement Cost coverages are essentially the same as their personal line counterparts examined in connection with the homeowners policies. The Agreed Value Optional Coverage suspends the coinsurance provision for a one-year period, guaranteeing that the insured will not suffer a coinsurance penalty. The insurer will grant agreed value coverage after verifying the values insured.

Specialized Valuation Endorsements

Although the actual cash value and replacement cost valuation provisions are suitable for most property, in some situations it is desirable to modify the basis on which property is insured. Several standard endorsements exist for this purpose.

Ordinance or Law Coverage Endorsement An *Ordinance* or *Law Coverage* endorsement is used to provide three types of coverage related to the enforcement of building codes. Coverage is provided for three types of losses.

First, the endorsement permits a building owner to purchase insurance for an amount required to replace a substandard building with one that will meet code requirements. An increased cost of construction limit is listed in the endorsement. In addition, under the terms of the endorsement, the insurer agrees to pay as a total loss any partial loss in which building code provisions prevent the owner from using the undamaged parts of the building in reconstruction. Finally, coverage may be included for the cost to demolish undamaged parts of a building following damage by an insured peril, when such demolition is required by the building code. Payment for damage to the structure and the cost of demolition cannot, however, exceed the limit of insurance. A limit is indicated in the endorsement for the cost of demolition.

Functional Building Valuation Endorsement Situations sometimes exist in which advances in technology or architecture make it possible to replace an existing structure with one that performs the same function, but at a lower cost than would be required to duplicate the existing building. The Functional Building Valuation endorsement insures buildings for the cost of repairing with less costly materials, but in the architectural style that existed before the loss. For total loss, coverage applies for the cost of replacing the building with a less costly, but functionally equivalent, building. The coinsurance provision does not apply to buildings insured on a functional valuation basis.

Functional Personal Property Valuation (Other Than Stock) Coverage on personal property may also be written on a functional valuation basis. In this case, coverage applies to specifically described property that can be replaced with similar property that performs the same function as the original, when replacement with identical property is impossible or unnecessary. If the property is repaired or replaced, payment is made for replacement with the most closely equivalent property available. If the property is not repaired or replaced, coverage is limited to the lowest of (a) the amount of insurance, (b) the market value of the property, or (c) the actual cash value of the property.

Manufacturer's Selling Price Clause A manufacturer with finished goods on hand faces a loss that is not covered under the standard BPP form, and that is the loss of

389

the expected profits on the goods destroyed. The policy provides coverage on stock for its actual cash value—the replacement cost less depreciation—not the selling price. Coverage for this potential loss can be obtained under the Manufacturer's Selling Price clause endorsement, which provides that the value of finished stock shall be the price at which it would have sold had no loss occurred. The Manufacturer's Selling Price clause is applicable only to the finished stocks of manufacturers and is not available to wholesalers and retailers.[9]

BLANKET INSURANCE

Thus far, we have discussed only one approach to fire insurance, that form known as "specific" insurance, which applies a definite amount of coverage to a stated item. Coverage may also be in the form of *blanket insurance*, under which one amount of insurance covers more than one type of property or property at more than one location. For example, a firm with a number of buildings may purchase specific insurance on each, but it can also insure them on a blanket basis, with a single amount of insurance applicable to all. When coverage is written on a blanket basis, 90 percent coinsurance is usually required.

The blanket approach has significant advantages. The major advantage is that the blanket limit is available to cover loss to any of the individual items insured. For example, suppose that the XYZ Company owns 10 buildings, each worth $100,000. If the properties are insured on a blanket basis, subject to a 90 percent coinsurance clause, XYZ must purchase $900,000 in blanket coverage. In the event of a loss, coverage would apply to any building up to the full $100,000 of its value, provided that XYZ meets the coinsurance requirement at the time of the loss. If the same 10 buildings were insured for $90,000 each on a specific basis, recovery would, of course, be limited to the $90,000 applicable to each. Contents at different locations may also be insured on a blanket basis, or buildings and contents can be insured in this way.

REPORTING FORM COVERAGE

Reporting forms are designed to meet the needs of business firms whose stocks of merchandise fluctuate over time. A reporting form is written with a maximum limit sufficient to cover the highest values expected during the year, and the amount of insurance moves up and down with the values exposed to loss, subject to this maximum. The insured makes periodic reports (monthly or quarterly) of current values on hand and is charged on the basis of these reports, paying only for the values exposed to loss, not the limit of liability. Because the premium cannot be known until the year is over, a provisional premium is paid at the inception of the policy and then adjusted at year's end to reflect the true cost of the protection provided.[10]

---

[9]Retailers and wholesalers do not face the same exposure. They can normally replace their stock within a short time, and the income lost on sales during the period required to replace the stock is covered under the Business Interruption form used for mercantile firms.

[10]When the fluctuation in value is limited to an identifiable period, a Peak Season Endorsement may be used. Here the amount of insurance is increased pro rata for a specified period to cover the increased values, and a pro rata premium charge is made for the added coverage.

The insured must report 100 percent of the values of the property insured. Late reports or underreporting of values, intentional or otherwise, may result in a penalty at the time of a loss. In the event of a late report, the amount of insurance is limited to the values contained in the last previous filing. In addition, the *full value reporting clause* (also called the "honesty clause") provides that if the insured under-reports, the insurer's liability is limited to that percentage of loss that the last stated values bear to the values that should have been reported. Thus, if the insured reports value of $100,000, when the actual value of the property on hand was $200,000, recovery would be limited to 100/200, or 50 percent of the loss sustained. In effect, the full value reporting clause is a 100 percent coinsurance clause.

BUILDERS RISK COVERAGE FORM

When a building under construction is to be insured, it is normally covered under a specialized contract known as the Builders Risk form. There is a single *Builders Risk Form* under the Commercial Property portfolio program, which provides coverage on a "completed value" basis. Under this form, coverage is written for the final full value of the building, and a premium based on 55 percent of the 100 percent coinsurance builders risk rate is charged. Coverage continues during the process of construction but terminates automatically when the structure is completed and occupied. If the insured desires, the coverage can be converted to a reporting basis by endorsement. Builders Risk coverage may be written to cover the interests of the building owner, the general contractor, and subcontractors, all of whom have an insurable interest in the building under construction.

CONDOMINIUM ASSOCIATION COVERAGE FORM

The Condominium Association Coverage form is used in place of the Building and Personal Property Coverage Form when buildings and contents are insured in the name of a condominium association. The form states that certain types of property will be covered or not covered depending on whether the Condominium Association agreement requires the association or the unit owner to insure it. This provision avoids the need to include a specific description of this property in the declarations and permits the form to be used with either a "bare walls" or "all included" type of condominium agreement.

CONDOMINIUM COMMERCIAL UNIT-OWNERS COVERAGE FORM

The Condominium Commercial Unit-Owners Coverage Form dovetails with the Condominium Association Coverage Form. It excludes fixtures, improvements, alterations, and appliances in units unless the Association Agreement places responsibility for insuring them on the unit owner. When Association and Unit-Owners coverage responds to the same loss, the Unit-Owners coverage is excess.

STANDARD PROPERTY POLICY

The Standard Property Policy is a self-contained property damage form that is used to insure buildings and personal property on a somewhat more restrictive basis than the BPP. It is used to insure property assigned to the insurer under FAIR plans or for other properties that do not meet high underwriting standards. The Standard Property Policy is similar to the BPP, but provides coverage only for the perils of the Causes of Loss—Basic form. The provisions regarding cancellation, increase in hazard, and vacancy are more restrictive than those of the BPP.

PLATE GLASS INSURANCE

Although the causes of loss forms applicable to building coverage cover glass constituting a part of the structure, such protection is subject to important exclusions. For example, vandalism and malicious mischief coverage excludes loss to glass, and the Broad Form and Special Form limit coverage for glass breakage to $100 per plate and $500 per occurrence. Because of these limitations, individual business owners may wish to purchase more extensive protection afforded under a Glass Coverage Form, which covers glass on an extremely broad open-peril basis.

The Glass Coverage Form may be combined with other coverage forms in the Commercial Property Coverage part, or it may be written alone. Coverage applies for accidental glass breakage (except by fire) and damage caused by acids or chemicals accidentally or maliciously applied. The only exclusions are fire, war, and nuclear damage. However, only those plate glass panels specifically scheduled are insured, and lettering and ornamentation are not covered unless they, too, have been specifically insured. The policy also covers the cost of repairing or replacing frames or sashes, boarding up or installing temporary plates in broken windows, and removing and replacing fixtures or other obstructions.

✖ Boiler and Machinery Insurance ■ ■ ■ ■ ■ ■ ■ ■ ■ ■ ■ ■ ■ ■

As noted earlier, boiler and machinery insurance originated from the efforts of a group of engineers in Hartford, Connecticut, who offered an inspection service for steam boilers and, for a small additional charge, guaranteed their inspection by providing insurance against loss up to some limit selected by the client. The inspection service that originally served as the basis for this type of insurance remains an important part of the service provided by boiler and machinery insurers today. The boiler and machinery line is a highly specialized field, and insurers who offer this coverage employ trained engineers who seek to discover faulty conditions and mechanical weakness before such defects can cause accidents. The bulk of the boiler and machinery premium goes to pay the cost of inspections.

Although it is common to think of boiler and machinery insurance primarily in terms of steam boilers, the insurance applies to many types of equipment: boilers, pressure containers, refrigerating systems, engines, turbines, generators, and motors. The inspection service that proved so beneficial for steam boilers has established its worth for other types of objects as well. Large and small businesses now rely on a range of equipment that was not imagined when boiler and machinery were invented. These include computers, PBX systems, copier and duplicating machines, and fax machines. Boiler and machinery coverage can be written to cover loss to equipment that is not covered under normal maintenance agreements, including accidental damage and damage by artificial electricity.

Although the inspection service is a critical part of the boiler and machinery product, indemnification for losses that do occur is equally important from the perspective of the insured. Hazards associated with boilers and machinery are usually excluded from other forms of property insurance, so boiler and machinery insurance is needed to fill this gap.

Like other portfolio program coverages, boiler and machinery coverage combines common coverage parts with boiler and machinery forms to create the specialized policies. There are three basic boiler and machinery forms under the portfolio program: the Boiler and Machinery Coverage Form, the Small Business Boiler and Machinery Form, and the Small Business Boiler and Machinery Coverage Broad Form. In addition, Indirect Loss Coverage endorsements are also available.

BOILER AND MACHINERY COVERAGE FORM

The Boiler and Machinery Coverage Form insures against losses resulting from an accident to an insured object. Coverage is provided in a single insuring agreement for both damage to the insured's property and for liability arising out of damage to the property of others in the care, custody, or control of the insured if caused by "a covered cause of loss." A "covered cause of loss" is an "accident" to an insured "object" shown in the declarations. One or more Object Definition forms are used to define the objects to be insured.[11] Indirect loss coverages may be added by endorsement.

An *accident* is defined as "a sudden and accidental breakdown of the 'object' or a part of the object." At the time the breakdown occurs, it must manifest itself by physical damage to the object that necessitates repair or replacement. The definition of *accident* specifically excludes certain specified types of losses, such as depletion, deterioration, corrosion, and erosion; wear and tear; and the functioning of any safety or protective device. In addition to the limitations in the definition of *accident*, the form contains the standard Ordinance or Law, Nuclear, and War or Military Action exclusions. Accidents to objects while being tested are also excluded, as are losses of the type covered under fire insurance policies.

Extensions

There are four extensions in the form: Expediting Expenses, Automatic Coverage, Defense, and Supplementary Payments. The Expediting Expense coverage provides

---

[11]There are six object definition forms: Pressure and Refrigeration Objects, Mechanical Objects, Electrical Objects, Turbine Objects, and two "comprehensive" forms. One comprehensive form covers all objects, and the other covers all objects except those used for manufacturing.

payment for the reasonable extra cost of temporary repairs and expediting permanent repairs. Coverage is limited to $5000, but may be increased. The Automatic Coverage extension provides coverage on newly acquired objects of the type insured for up to 90 days. The Defense and Supplementary Payment extensions are the conventional variety; the insurer agrees to defend the insured in suits seeking damages payable under the policy and to pay reasonable costs incurred by the insured at the company's request. Defense costs are in addition to the policy limit, and the insurer reserves the right to settle any claims it deems expedient.

Loss Payment

The entire amount of insurance is available to pay for loss to property of the insured and property damage liability. Insured property includes not only the boiler itself, but other property such as buildings and contents as well.[12] If the policy limit is not exhausted by loss payment for the insured's property and property damage liability, the policy then pays expediting expenses. Payment for expediting expenses is therefore limited to the insurance remaining after payment for damage to the insured's property and property damage liability, or $5000, whichever is less.

Policy Limits and Deductible

In addition to the limit per accident shown in the declarations, the Boiler and Machinery Coverage form includes four internal limits. Expediting expenses, the cost of cleaning up hazardous substances, damage caused by ammonia contamination, and water damage are each subject to a $5000 limit. These limits are part of and not in addition to the policy limit. All but the hazardous substances limit can be increased for an additional premium. Coverage under the policy is subject to a minimum $250 deductible, and higher deductibles are available.

Suspension

The boiler and machinery policy contains a unique provision permitting the insurance company to suspend coverage on any or all insured objects found to be in a dangerous condition. Suspension may be executed by any insurance company representative by handing notice of suspension to the insured or by mailing the notice to the insured's address stated in the policy or to the location of the object on which coverage is to be suspended. The suspension becomes effective immediately on delivery without prior notice or waiting period. When coverage has been suspended, it may be reinstated only by endorsement to the policy.

---

[12]Since other forms of property insurance generally exclude steam boiler explosion, the limit should be high enough to cover all damage to owned property that may result from an accident. The standard policy covers on a repair or replacement basis (i.e., on a replacement cost basis), but actual cash value coverage is available by endorsement.

SMALL BUSINESS BOILER AND MACHINERY FORMS

Boiler and Machinery Coverage is also available under one of two "small business" boiler and machinery forms—the Small Business Boiler and Machinery Coverage form (SBBM Basic form) and the Small Business Boiler and Machinery Coverage—Broad form (SBBM Broad form). Both forms include the same insuring agreement as the standard boiler and machinery policy and provide coverage for direct loss to insured property resulting from an accident to an insured object. The minimum coverage under either form is $100,000. Coverage is available in $100,000 increments up to $500,000, in $250,000 increments up to $2.5 million, and $500,000 increments up to $5 million. The SBBM Basic form is not available to firms with high-pressure boilers (over 15 pounds of pressure per square inch) or to manufacturing or processing firms. The SBBM Broad form provides coverage on any steam boiler, as long as it is not used in manufacturing or processing.

■ Inland Marine Insurance ■ ■ ■ ■ ■ ■ ■ ■ ■ ■ ■ ■ ■ ■ ■ ■ ■ ■ ■

Inland marine insurance developed as an extension of ocean marine insurance when ocean marine insurers extended their policies to cover property being shipped *from warehouse to warehouse*. Eventually, in 1933, the National Association of Insurance Commissioners (NAIC) defined the scope of inland marine insurance in its *Nationwide Marine Insurance Definition*, specifically limiting the types of insurance marine insurers were permitted to write. Although the original version of the *Definition* defined the types of exposures that could be written as inland marine insurance, the definition was revised in 1953 and again in 1977. The 1977 version assumed the more modest role of defining those types of insurance that are considered marine insurance for rate filings and for the reporting of statistics. The 1977 version of the definition recognizes six broad classes of property that may be insured under marine contracts: (1) imports, (2) exports, (3) domestic shipments, (4) instrumentalities of transportation and communications, (5) personal property floater risks, and (6) commercial property floater risks. The first two classes—imports and exports—are strictly limited to the ocean marine category. Export property is considered to be in the course of transportation and thus eligible for marine coverage as soon as it is designated or prepared for export. Imports are eligible until they reach their intended destination.

For purely *inland* marine risks, the definition recognizes four categories: domestic shipments, means of transportation, personal property floater risks, and commercial property floater risks. Here we are concerned only with the last of these classes, commercial property floater risks.[13] For the purpose of our discussion, it is helpful to divide the NAIC's commercial property floater risks class into four subclasses (business floater policies, dealers' forms, bailee forms, and miscellaneous policies).

[13]We will examine transportation coverages in Chapter 22.

1. *Business floater policies*, which cover personal property (such as construction equipment) that is mobile in nature and, therefore, subject to damage by the perils of transportation.

2. *Dealers forms*, which cover the merchandise of certain types of businesses, such as jewelers, furriers, camera dealers, and musical instrument dealers. These forms cover the merchandise while it is on the insured's premises and also provide incidental off-premises coverage.

3. *Bailee forms*, designed to cover goods that are in the custody of someone other than the owner to whom the goods have been entrusted.[14]

4. *Miscellaneous policies*, which include unrelated and anomalous types of inland marine coverages such as accounts receivables and valuable papers coverages as well as electronic data processing policies.

BUSINESS FLOATER POLICIES

Policies such as the Building and Personal Property Coverage Form discussed early in the chapter provide coverage at fixed locations. Inland marine forms provide coverage that is not location-specific, but instead covers the property wherever it may be, on-premises or off-premises—hence the term *floater* coverage. Commercial inland marine floater policies fall into one of three categories.

1. *Equipment Floaters.* These are designed to cover business property not held for sale or on consignment that is in the hands of the owner for its intended purpose. Examples include the Contractors' Equipment floater, Agricultural Equipment and Livestock floater, and Salesmen's Sample floater.

2. *Processing and Storage Floaters.* These insure property in temporary storage and property undergoing processing outside the owner's premises. A good example is the Garment Contractor's floater, which covers the stock of a manufacturer that has been sent off premises for processing.

3. *Consignment and Sales Floaters.* These policies protect goods being held for sale under consignment, being installed, or being sold under an installment plan. Examples include the Installment Sales floater, which covers goods sold on an installment basis; the Floor Plan Merchandise form, which covers stock pledged as collateral under a "floor plan" arrangement; and the Installation floater, which covers machinery and equipment in transit for installation in a building and while being installed.

The coverage of these forms may be written on both an open-peril or named-peril basis, and the coverage varies under the different forms. In several classes, the insured has a choice between open-peril and named-peril coverage. In addition, the coverage may be written on a schedule or blanket basis.

[14]Bailee forms are treated in greater detail in Chapter 24.

DEALERS FORMS

Dealers forms represent something of an anomaly in inland marine insurance. Although inland marine forms generally cover property that is mobile and that is commonly away from the owner's premises, the dealers forms provide coverage on a dealer's stock of goods. Although coverage applies on and off premises, the major exposure is on premises. Dealers forms are available only for specific classes of dealers. They include jewelers, furriers, musical instrument dealers, camera dealers, equipment dealers, fine arts dealers, and stamp and coin collection dealers. The policies for jewelers and furriers are referred to as the Jeweler's Block policy and the Furrier's Block policy.[15] The other forms are referred to simply as dealer's forms (for example, Musical Instrument Dealer's Form, Camera Dealer's Form, and so on). The Equipment Dealers Coverage Form is typical of these policies. The Equipment Dealers Coverage Form insures the stock in trade of dealers in agricultural equipment and implements and contractors' equipment. Motor vehicles designed for highway use are not eligible for coverage under the form. In addition to the dealer's stock, the form also covers property of others in the custody of the dealers. Such property of others would consist of customers' equipment in the dealer's custody for servicing or repair.

MISCELLANEOUS INLAND MARINE FORMS

The miscellaneous class of inland marine commercial policies includes unrelated and unusual types of inland marine coverages such as Accounts Receivable and Valuable Papers coverages and Electronic Data Processing policies. Accounts Receivable insurance and Valuable Papers insurance are the most common of these coverages.

Accounts Receivable

Accounts receivable insurance protects against the inability to collect amounts owed to the insured because of destruction of records by fire or other insured perils. The coverage is written on an open-peril basis, on either a reporting basis or, subject to an 80 percent coinsurance provision, on a nonreporting basis. The coverage is on an indemnity basis and compensates the insured for any amounts that cannot be collected because of the destruction of the accounting records (with allowance for bad debts). In addition, payment is made for expenses incurred to reconstruct the records, for collection expenses above normal costs, and for the interest charges on loans taken out by the insured to offset the impaired collections.

---

[15]The term *block* as used in connection with the Jeweler's Block and Furrier's Block policies comes from the French phrase *en bloc*, meaning "all together." Thus, block policies are intended to cover all the property of the business in a single contract.

Valuable Papers Insurance

Valuable papers coverage may be written to insure various types of important records, including maps, film, tape, wire or recording media, drawings, abstracts, deeds, mortgages, and manuscripts. Coverage is on an open-peril basis and can be either blanket or scheduled. Items specifically insured are covered for an agreed amount, whereas papers covered on a blanket basis are insured for their actual cash value.

EDP Policy

With the rapid spread of electronic data processing (EDP) equipment and its software, a need quickly developed for insurance coverage to protect against losses arising out of damage to or destruction of this costly equipment. The coverage was originally written by insurers with an extensive background in inland marine insurance, usually on inland marine forms. The coverage is written on an open-peril basis and generally provides coverage under separate insuring agreements for damage to hardware, software, and extra expense or business interruption.

Manufacturers Output Policy

The manufacturers output policy was developed as an inland marine form to cover manufacturers' stocks of merchandise being shipped to dealers. The earliest versions of the policy covered automobiles being shipped from the factory to dealers and covered property only while away from the insured's premises. The standard form excludes property at any manufacturing location owned by the insured, but the policy is usually endorsed to provide open-peril coverage both on- and off-premises.

Difference-in-Conditions Coverage

Difference-in-conditions insurance, generally referred to as DIC coverage, is a special form of open-peril coverage written in conjunction with basic fire coverage and designed to provide protection against losses not reimbursed under the standard fire forms. It is always written as an adjunct to separate policies covering against fire, extended coverage, and vandalism and malicious mischief (plus sprinkler leakage when the exposure exists) and does not provide coverage against losses caused by these perils. It does, however, provide coverage for most other insurable perils, including flood and earthquake. There is neither a coinsurance clause nor a pro rata clause, and the policy may be written for an amount different from the basic policies it complements. The coverage is subject to a deductible, which is usually substantial, ranging upward from $10,000. Protection against earthquake and flood may be subject to limits and deductibles that differ from the remainder of the policy. Each DIC policy is rated individually. The coverage was originally available only to giant firms, but some insurers have recently developed mini-DIC forms for medium to small businesses. In some instances, indirect loss coverage (such as business interruption) and transportation insurance are included.

✖ Flood Insurance ■

Until enactment of the 1968 Housing and Urban Development Act (HUD) which initiated the National Flood Insurance Program, flood insurance on fixed location property was available only on an extremely limited basis. The HUD Act of 1968 created a federally subsidized flood insurance program, under which flood insurance is available to both individuals and businesses.

GENERAL NATURE OF THE PROGRAM

The National Flood Insurance Program (NFIP) is under the jurisdiction of the Federal Insurance Administration in the Federal Emergency Management Agency (FEMA). Flood policies are issued both by the NFIP itself and by private insurers participating in the cooperative program referred to as the Write-Your-Own program. Private insurers issue flood insurance policies on behalf of the NFIP and are reinsured 100 percent against loss. Private insurers participating in the Write-Your-Own program are reimbursed by the NFIP for losses that are not covered by premiums and the investment income on those premiums. Coverage written by both the private insurers and the federal government is sold by private insurance agents who are paid a commission for the coverage sold.

Eligible Communities

The National Flood Insurance Program is open to any community that pledges to adopt and enforce land control measures designed to guide the future development of the community away from flood-prone areas. Cities, counties, or other governmental units seeking approval for the sale of flood insurance must take the initiative and submit an official statement to FEMA indicating a need for the insurance and a desire to participate in the program. To become eligible for the insurance, the community must agree to adopt certain land-use and flood control measures, including zoning ordinances that prohibit new construction in areas where there is more than a 1 percent chance of flooding each year.

Once the community has agreed to adopt the specified controls, it becomes eligible for the Emergency Program. Under this program, coverage is available on eligible properties, up to specified limits, at subsidized rates. Although the program originally provided coverage only for residential property, the eligibility has gradually been expanded. Today, virtually all residential, industrial, commercial, agricultural, and public buildings are eligible for coverage.

Subsidized coverage is available under the emergency program for up to $35,000 on single family dwellings and up to $100,000 on other eligible structures, and up to $10,000 on residential contents and $100,000 on nonresidential contents. The cost of flood insurance under the Emergency Program is identical for all eligible cities and towns, and the rates for the additional coverage under the Regular Program vary with the loss probability of the particular area.

A community enters the Regular Program when the detailed flood risk study has been completed (or waived by FEMA) and the community adopts flood plain management ordinances. Increased amounts of coverage are available once the community enters the Regular Program. Under the Regular Program, available coverage is classed as Basic Insurance Limits and Additional Insurance Limits. Basic Limits are similar to (but not identical with) the limits under the Emergency Program. Rates under the Regular Program are actuarially determined and differ for the Basic Insurance Limit and the Additional Insurance Limit. New limits of coverage were implemented on March 1, 1995. The amounts of coverage under the Emergency Program and the Basic and Additional amounts under the Regular Program are summarized in Table 17.1.

Other Provisions

Federal law now requires the purchase of flood insurance in Special Flood Hazard Areas as a condition for receiving any form of federal financial assistance for acquisition or construction purposes. This means that property owners in those communities where flood insurance is available and whose property is located in a Special Flood Hazard Area, must purchase the flood insurance in order to qualify for federal loans or federally assisted or insured loans (VA, FHA, FDIC, and so on). A Special Flood Hazard Area is specifically designated land within a community in the flood plain which is most likely to be subjected to severe flooding.

Following the floods of 1993, the *National Flood Insurance Reform Act of 1994* significantly strengthened the compliance requirements for lenders. Federally regulated lenders and federal agency lenders must now require flood insurance when making, increasing, extending, or renewing a loan, and the coverage must be maintained for the term of the loan. Lenders are required to notify, in writing, the purchaser or lessor of property that is in a Special Flood Hazard Area of the requirement for flood insurance in advance of the signing of the purchase agreement or lease. If the borrower has not purchased flood insurance within

Table 17.1   Limits on Nonresidential Property Under the Federal Flood Insurance Program

	Emergency Program	*Basic Insurance Limits*	*Additional Insurance Limits*	*Total Insurance Available*
Non-Residential Buildings	$100,000*	$135,000	$365,000	$500,000
Small Business Buildings		135,000	365,000	500,000
Non-Residential Contents	100,000	115,000	365,000	500,000
Small Business Contents		115,000	365,000	500,000

*Non-Residential Buildings in Alaska, Guam, Hawaii and U.S. Virgin Islands are $150,000
Source: *National Flood Insurance Manual*, 1995.

45 days of the notification, the lender must purchase flood insurance on behalf of the borrower.

If the property is not in a Special Flood Hazard Area, the flood insurance is not a prerequisite to obtaining a loan but may, of course, still be insured. The 1973 legislation also eliminates the possibility of receiving federal disaster funds following a flood in any area identified as having a special flood hazard, unless the property owner has purchased flood insurance. The law specifically prohibits any federal agency from approving financial assistance to victims for reconstruction following a flood, if the individual did not purchase flood insurance. This prohibition applies regardless of whether or not the community has become eligible for the flood insurance program.

There is a 30-day waiting period, after application and the payment of the premium, before a flood insurance policy becomes effective. This waiting period is subject to two exceptions. The waiting period does not apply to the initial purchase of flood insurance in connection with making, increasing, extending, or renewing a loan. The waiting period also does not apply to the initial purchase of flood insurance if the purchase occurs during the 13-month period following the revision or update of a Flood Insurance Rate Map.

THE GENERAL PROPERTY FORM
FLOOD INSURANCE POLICY

The Federal Flood Insurance Policy consists of a policy jacket and a form. The flood policy used to insure commercial property is called the General Property form. Protection under this policy is provided under three items, designated Coverages A, B, and C, which insure the building, contents, and debris removal, respectively. Coverage may be purchased on the building, its contents, or on both. The debris removal coverage is included in the limit of liability applicable to the property insured, although it is set forth in a separate insuring agreement.

The coverage for debris removal applies only to removal of debris *of* or *on* the property insured. This is an important limitation. The property owner may incur significant expense in clearing away debris after a flood, but the cost is covered only to the extent of removing the debris of the covered property itself or removing other debris from the covered property. Reimbursement for debris removal is a part of, and not in addition to, the coverage provided on the dwelling or the contents.

Insuring Agreement

The insuring agreement of the Federal Flood Insurance Policy is simple and straightforward. Coverage is provided for "direct physical loss by or from flood" as defined in the contract. Flood is defined in the policy as

A general and temporary condition of partial or complete inundation of normally dry land areas from overflow of inland or tidal waters or from the unusual and rapid accumulation or runoff of surface waters from any source.

Losses caused by flood-related erosion and damage caused by mudslides (that is, mudflows), as specifically defined in the policy, are also covered.

Flood must be a general condition; this is reinforced by specific exclusions of damage by water that stems from sources on the insured's own property or within the insured's control, or from a condition that does not cause general flooding in the area. The policy therefore will not cover as "flood damage" inundations from a broken or stopped-up sewer or a faulty sump pump in the insured's basement. Neither would accumulations of water on the insured property caused by the slope of the lot be covered in the absence of general flooding in the area.

Deductible

The Flood Policy is subject to a deductible that applies separately to the building and to contents. For nonresidential property under the Emergency Program or property that is located in certain zones where the rates used to compute the premium date from before the publication of the Flood Insurance Rate Map, the deductible is $750. In all other cases, it is $500. An additional $250 deductible applies separately to each building and content loss for payments for land subsidence, sewer backup, or seepage of water. Higher optional deductibles have been available, ranging from $1000 up to $5000, in increments of $1000.

Inception of Coverage and Cancellation Provision

During the first 30 days in which flood insurance is available in a community, policies are in force immediately upon issuance. Policies issued after the thirtieth day become effective only after a 30-day waiting period.

The insurer may cancel the policy only for nonpayment of premium, and even in this case 20 days' written notice of cancellation is required. The policy may be dropped by the insured at any time, but if the insured retains title to the property, the premium for the current term is considered fully earned and there is no premium refund. If the insured disposes of the property, the return premium is calculated on a short-rate basis.

 ## Package Policies for Business Firms ■ ■ ■ ■ ■ ■ ■ ■ ■ ■ ■ ■

Although the package policy began with the Homeowners contract, the concept was soon applied to the field of commercial insurance. Eventually, two standard bureau package programs designed for businesses and institutions evolved: the Special Multi-Peril (SMP) Program and the Businessowners Policy (BOP). In addition to these programs, many insurers also developed their own commercial packages, although the independently filed packages usually paralleled the bureau forms. With the introduction of the new portfolio program, the ISO SMP Program was replaced by a new Commercial Package Policy.

There are now two standard package policies for businesses and other organizations—the Commercial Package Policy (CPP) and the Businessowners Policy

(BOP). Both are multiple line policies in the truest sense of the term and provide property and liability insurance in a single contract. The CCP combines the monoline forms discussed in this chapter with liability and automobile insurance forms (discussed in Chapters 24 and 25). The BOP is a package policy approach for business firms similar to the BOP but designed for smaller firms. It is available for small and medium apartments, offices, mercantile, service, and processing firms.[16] Both the CCP and the BOP grant a discount when coverages are combined in a package policy, a convention that was introduced with the Homeowners Policy.

In addition to the standard ISO package policies, many insurers have developed their own unique package policies. Although these independent forms generally parallel the ISO forms, they differ from the ISO forms and from each other in detail.

⚙ Combining Transfer and Retention ■ ■ ■ ■ ■ ■ ■ ■ ■ ■ ■ ■

Commercial property coverages are written with deductibles, allowing the insured to combine transfer and retention. Although the standard deductible on most property forms is $250 to $1000, higher optional deductibles are available. The ISO *Commercial Lines Manual* Insurance indicates rate credits for deductibles up to $75,000. Usually, the deductible applies on a per structure basis but may be written subject to a per occurrence aggregate or an annual aggregate. Higher deductibles are available, but the premium credits are determined by underwriters on a judgment basis.

A second approach to retention in connection with commercial property insurance is to simply not insure some or all property. Some companies, for example, do not insure structures with a value below some specific limit, such as $25,000. Although this can produce economies, the risk manager should consider whether a number of such uninsured structures could be destroyed in a single occurrence (such as a tornado), producing a loss that exceeds the firm's maximum retention.

A final approach to retention of property exposures is underinsuring. As we noted in our discussion of coinsurance, when the amount of insurance carried is less than the amount required by the coinsurance provision, the insured is required to bear a part of the loss. An insured with a $1 million building might purchase $900,000 in coverage with a 100 percent coinsurance requirement, thereby tacitly agreeing to bear 10 percent of every loss. Under this arrangement, the coinsurance provision, in effect, acts as a sliding deductible. In the event of a $100,000 loss, the insured would bear $10,000; in a $200,000 loss, the insured would bear $20,000 of the loss. This arrangement would be advantageous when the premium saved by the purchase of less than full insurance provided a greater premium saving than would a $100,000 deductible.[17]

---

[16]Eligible properties include apartment buildings of six stories or fewer with no more than 60 units and 15,000 square feet or less; office buildings of six stories or fewer and up to 100,000 square feet; and mercantile, processing, and service firms with up to 15,000 square feet.

[17]This could be the case, depending on the credit for the deductible. Purchasing $900,000 in coverage rather than $1 million will save 10 percent. The 100 percent coinsurance agreement will produce an additional 5 percent credit and generate a total premium reduction of 15 percent.

IMPORTANT CONCEPTS TO REMEMBER

portfolio program
Commercial Property
   Coverage
Building and Personal
   Property Coverage form
Condominium Association
   Coverage form
Condominium Commercial
   Unit Owner's Coverage
   form
coinsurance
Causes of Loss—Basic form
Causes of Loss—Broad form

Causes of Loss—Special
   form
Causes of Loss—Earthquake
   form
blanket insurance
reporting forms
full value reporting clause
Agreed Value Coverage
Ordinance or Law Coverage
Businessowners policy
Builders' Risk Coverage form
Demolition Cost Coverage
boiler and machinery
   coverage form

accident
object
consequential damage
equipment floaters
processing and storage
   floaters
consignment and sales
   floaters
dealer's forms
accounts receivable insurance
valuable papers insurance
Commercial Package Policy
difference-in-conditions
   insurance

QUESTIONS FOR REVIEW

1. Explain the general scope of the Building and Personal Property Coverage Form. Your explanation should include (a) the property that may be covered under the form and (b) the perils for which protection may be provided.

2. Distinguish between scheduled coverage and blanket coverage. Which do you believe to be the preferred approach to insuring property? Why?

3. Briefly describe the provisions of a reporting form that apply in the event that the insured (a) is late in filing a report, or (b) underreports the values on hand.

4. Identify and briefly describe the six broad classes into which inland marine coverages may be divided.

5. Briefly describe the coverage of the Boiler and Machinery policy. What property is covered?

6. Why might a business firm that carries property insurance on its buildings and personal property also need to purchase inland marine insurance?

7. Describe the Debris Removal provision of the Building and Personal Property Coverage Form.

8. Identify and briefly explain the general exclusions that are included under the Causes of Loss coverage forms of the simplified portfolio property program. Indicate the reason for each of the exclusions.

9. Briefly describe the provisions of the Flood Insurance policy relating to inception of coverage and cancellation.

10. Briefly describe the purpose of the Standard Property Policy. In what ways is it different from the portfolio Building and Personal Property Coverage Form?

QUESTIONS FOR DISCUSSION

1. The Widget Manufacturing Company insures its plant against loss by fire for $900,000, under a policy with an 80% coinsurance clause. At the time that a $600,000 loss takes place, it is determined that the building is worth $1,250,000. How much will the insurer pay? How much would be paid in the event of a total loss?

2. How are mortgagee rights in property typically provided for in property insurance contracts? How and why did this system probably develop?

3. John Jones carries a Standard Fire Policy on his building, with Easy Money Mortgage Company listed as a mortgagee. Jones tells his agent to cancel the policy because the property has been sold The agent cancels the policy and Jones obtains a return of the premium. About six months later, when the building burns, Easy Money Mortgage Company makes claim for recovery. Investigations reveal that the building was not sold, and that Jones canceled the policy without the knowledge of the mortgage company. Discuss the liability of the insurer and the agent.

4. Do you believe that businesses owning property in the city in which you live should purchase the earthquake insurance? Why or why not?

5. Identify and briefly describe the alternatives to *actual cash value* valuation that are available under commercial property insurance forms.

SUGGESTIONS FOR ADDITIONAL READING

Fire, Casualty and Surety Bulletins. Casualty and Surety Volume. Cincinnati: National Underwriter Company. (Loose-leaf manual service with monthly supplements.) See "Fire," "Miscellaneous Property," "Boiler and Machinery," "Inland Marine," and "Catastrophe" sections.

Hershbarger, Robert A. and Ronald K. Miller, "Differences in Conditions: The Coverage and the Market," *C.P.C.U. Annals,* 29, NO. 1(March 1976).

Huebner, S. S., Kenneth Black, Jr., and Bernard L. Webb. *Property and Liability Insurance,* 4th ed. Englewood Cliffs, NJ: Prentice-Hall, 1996. Chapters 2, 3, 4, 5, 6, 7, 8, 9, 10, 11, 17, and 20.

Malecki, Donald S., Ronald C. Horn, Eric A. Wiening, and James H. Donaldson. *Commercial Liability Risk Management and Insurance,* 2nd ed., Vols. I and II. Malvern, PA: American Institute for Property and Liability Underwriters, 1986.

Policy, Form and Manual Analysis Service. Casualty Coverages Volume. Indianapolis, IN: Rough Notes Company. (Loose-leaf manual service with monthly supplements.) See "Boiler and Machinery" section.

Policy, Form and Manual Analysis Service. Property Coverages Volume. Indianapolis, IN: Rough Notes Company. (Loose-leaf manual service with monthly supplements.) See "Fire and Allied Lines," "Multiple Line" and "Miscellaneous" sections.

Ralston, August R., ed. *Risk Management Manual,* Santa Monica, Ca.: (loose-leaf service with monthly supplements), vol. 2, section 10. "Loss Handling."

Robinson, Linda G. "The 1995 Commercial Property Changes," *The Risk Report.* vol 18, no. 2 (October 1995).

Robinson, Linda G. and Jack P. Gibson. *Commercial Property Insurance* (Dallas, Tx.: International Risk Management Institute, Inc., loose-leaf service with periodic supplements), vol. I, "General Discussion," "Direct Damage," and "Causes of Loss" sections; vol II, "Inland Marine," "Boiler and Machinery," and "Package Policy" sections.

Webb, Bernard L., Stephen Horn II, and Arthur L. Flitner. *Commercial Insurance*, 2nd ed. (Malvern, Pa.: Insurance Institute of America, 1990), Chapters 1, 2, and 5.

Your Guide to the ISO Commercial Line Policies, 3rd ed. Boston, MA: John Liner Organization, 1991.

CHAPTER 18

Managing Consequential Loss Risks: Control and Finance

CHAPTER OBJECTIVES

When you have finished this chapter, you should be able to

Explain what is meant by the term *consequential loss.*

■

Identify the pre-event loss control measures that may be used to address the risk of business interruption and extra expense.

■

Explain how the program evaluation and review technique is useful in dealing with consequential losses.

■

Identify and explain the determinants of loss severity in the event of a business interruption loss.

■

Explain how the amount of insurance should be determined under a business interruption insurance program.

■

Identify the features that distinguish organizations that may require extra expense insurance from those that require business interruption insurance.

❖ Introduction ■■■■■■■■■■■■■■■■■■■■■■■■■■■■

Property losses are of two kinds; direct and indirect, or consequential, losses. Direct losses, which involve the tangible value of the property, were discussed in the preceding chapter. In this chapter we examine the management of consequential loss exposures, which arise from the fact that the damaged property cannot perform its intended function. As the term suggests, *consequential* losses are those that result from direct loss; they are also referred to as *indirect* loss. In those situations in which the amount of the consequential loss is a function of time, some consequential loss exposures are also referred to as *time element* exposures. Although the terms tend to be used interchangeably, not all consequential losses are time element losses. Debris removal losses and losses arising out of the enforcement of building codes, which were examined in the preceding chapter, are examples of consequential loss where the loss is not a function of time.

The simplest example of an indirect time element exposure is business interruption. When a factory burns, the owners lose the value of the factory and its contents. In addition, they also lose the output of the factory for the period of time required for reconstruction. During the period required for the business to get back into operation, the organization suffers a "business interruption."

Another consequential loss exposure is *extra expense*. Sometimes an organization cannot suspend operations in the event of damage to or destruction of facilities, but must continue to provide its services using extraordinary means and at a higher cost. The increased cost of continuing operations when owned property is damaged or destroyed can result in a reduction in profit or, in severe cases, an operating loss.

The importance of consequential loss exposures is frequently underestimated. Although the magnitude of a consequential loss may equal or exceed that of a direct loss, organizations that would not consider going without property insurance ignore the business interruption or extra expense exposure.

In addition to the failure to purchase insurance, the amount of insurance purchased under business interruption and extra expense forms often bears little relationship to the exposure. The inadequacies in the management of the consequential loss exposure is evidenced by the high percentage of business firms that go bankrupt or otherwise cease operations after a major fire. More often than not, insurance to cover the direct loss is adequate enough, but there is no or inadequate business interruption insurance, and the firm never resumes operations.

❖ Controlling Consequential Loss Exposures ■■■■■■■

It should be obvious that since indirect property losses are occasioned by direct property losses, the loss control measures aimed at preventing and reducing direct loss also serve to prevent indirect losses. In addition to measures that are designed to prevent direct loss, a number of loss control measures aim specifically at preventing or controlling indirect loss.

PLANNING FOR INDIRECT LOSSES

The most effective loss control technique for consequential losses is to anticipate such losses and make arrangements prior to a direct loss for continuation of operations. A determination must be made as to whether it will be feasible for the organization to continue operations in the event of damage to or destruction of its property. Often, it is management's intent to attempt to continue operations following a direct loss. But unless specific plans are made as to how and where operations are to be continued, it may be found that it is impossible to obtain access to the facilities required to continue or resume operations. Ideally, a specific continuation plan should be devised, which identifies the requirements that will exist for continuing operations and the manner in which these requirements will be met.

Identifying Bottlenecks

Special attention should be devoted to identifying machines or other elements in the production process that are essential, and the destruction of which would interrupt the entire process. In some situations, a key machine is critical to the entire production process, which means that the loss of the machine could interrupt the entire operation. When such bottlenecks are identified, it may be possible to reduce the interruption period by planning for rapid replacement of the item.

Planning Replacement Facilities

To the extent possible, substitute facilities that could be used in emergency situations should be identified, and if possible, arrangements should be made for their use. In some instances, the organization may be able to enter into a reciprocal arrangement with another firm in the same industry for the use of facilities on a temporary basis. In other cases, the firm may be able to subcontract with another organization during the period required to restore the premises.

Given the increasing dependence of businesses and other organizations on computer systems, many organizations make advance provision for use of an alternate facility in the event the organization's data processing equipment is damaged or destroyed. The usual approach is a *cold site*, an alternate facility that is void of any resources or equipment except air conditioning and a raised floor (to accommodate cables). Equipment and resources must be installed in such a facility to duplicate the critical business functions of the organization, but the advance arrangement of a cold site greatly simplifies the process of reestablishing automated operations. In some cases, the alternate facility will be established as a *hot site*—a facility that has in place the equipment and resources required to recover the business functions affected by a disaster. Hot sites may vary in the type of facilities offered (such as data processing, communication, or any other critical business functions).

When the contingent business income exposure relates to a single source of supply, the firm may consider stockpiling a reserve of the raw materials, thus eliminating the need to suspend operations in the event of the supplier's destruction. In addition, to the extent possible, alternate sources of supply should be identified.

Although the cost of obtaining supplies from the alternate source may be higher, once this has been determined, insurance may be arranged to cover the higher cost.

Redundancy

Another approach to preventing time element losses is to maintain backup facilities that can be used to continue operations in the event of damage to the production facilities. Redundancy in production facilities is similar in effect to stockpiling raw materials; it can permit the firm to continue operations when a direct loss damages property required for the production effort. It can be an effective loss control strategy, but only if the primary and redundant facilities are not subject to loss in the same occurrence.

Post-Loss Control—Resuming Operations

Once a direct loss has occurred, it may be possible to prevent or reduce the amount of the indirect loss by continuing operations at another location or by partial resumption of operations. If the organization can reduce the amount of loss through such efforts, it will obviously seek to do so. As will be noted later in the chapter, when insurance coverage has been purchased to provide indemnity for indirect losses, a condition of the policy requires the insured to use all reasonable means to resume operations as soon as possible. If operations can be continued even on a partial basis, the insured is required to do so. This condition merely requires the insured to use the same loss prevention and control methods when insurance exists as it would use if the risk of loss had been retained.

Even in the absence of the insurance coverage requirement that the insured resume operations as quickly as possible, it is in the insured's interest to do so. The longer a business is interrupted, the greater the likelihood that its customers will turn elsewhere for the goods or services it previously provided. Once an organization's property has been damaged or destroyed, interrupting or reducing business activity, the loss control objective is to resume operations as quickly as possible. Sometimes this can be done by using alternate facilities, but in the long run it will usually require restoration of the premises. The more quickly reconstruction can be completed, the more quickly the firm will be able to resume normal operation. In general, this means expediting the resumption of operations in all ways possible. One technique that is increasingly applied to this problem is Program Evaluation and Review Technique (PERT).

PERT is an analytical technique that is used when a project includes a number of time-critical events whose performance may determine the total time required to complete the project. A PERT chart indicates the various components of a project and defines when each step or project must be completed before subsequent steps or projects can be commenced. The key element in the process is the identification of time-sensitive parts of the project whose completion will determine the total time required for completion of the total project. PERT can be used for managing any project in which some tasks must be completed before others can be begun and in which the timing of certain tasks can have a significant impact on the total time required to complete the project. Applied to a dinner party, PERT means deciding that the pot roast must be purchased before it can be roasted, but the table can be set at any time before, after, or during the shopping and cooking.

The most pervasive use of PERT analysis in risk management is in managing the resumption of operations following damage or destruction of an organization's property. Because the income that will be lost during a period of interruption will vary with the duration of the shutdown, there is an incentive to resume operations as quickly as possible. PERT analysis can help to expedite restoration and resumption of operations. This was dramatically demonstrated in the restoration of the World Trade Center following its bombing by terrorists. An article in the *New York Times* in March of 1993 details the manner in which PERT served the Port Authority of New York and New Jersey in managing the repairs to the World Trade Center, during restoration. Using a desktop personal computer and six laptops, the project manager directed thousands of tasks, from reinforcing girders to installing emergency lighting. Using PERT, Port Authority managers compressed into a few days a system of planning, preliminary design, and detailed design that normally takes months.[1]

Financing Consequential Losses ■ ■ ■ ■ ■ ■ ■ ■ ■ ■ ■ ■ ■ ■

Time element coverages are available to protect against all of the time element exposures discussed in this chapter. The major indirect or consequential loss coverages are business interruption insurance, extra expense insurance, contingent business interruption and contingent extra expense insurance, and leasehold interest coverage.[2]

BUSINESS INTERRUPTION INSURANCE

Business interruption insurance is designed to indemnify business firms for loss of income sustained during the period required to restore property damaged by an insured peril to a useful condition. It pays the expenses that continue and the profits that would have been earned during the period of interruption. Although a valued form of coverage is available, most business interruption is written on an indemnity basis. In determining the amount of loss under the indemnity forms, the insurance company considers the insured's experience before the loss and probable future experience if no loss had occurred.

Perils Insured

As in the case of direct damage property exposures, the greatest errors in arranging business interruption coverage generally relate to the perils insured. Business

---

[1]Matthew L. Wald, "The Twin Towers: How to Fix Them," *New York Times Metro* (Monday, March 8, 1993), B-5.

[2]Prior to the introduction of the portfolio program, another form, Rent Insurance or Rental Value Insurance was written as a separate form in the past. Under the portfolio program, loss of rents or rental value are simply viewed as another form of business interruption and are insured under the standard Business Income form.

interruption insurance may be written to provide coverage against any of the perils available for direct damage coverages, and payment is made only if the interruption results from an insured peril. Just as property should be insured against as wide a range of perils as possible, the business interruption coverage should be arranged to provide protection against any insurable loss that could trigger a suspension of operations. This includes, among other things, not only the broad coverage of an open-peril form, but earthquake and flood as well. Boiler and machinery coverage should be extended to provide coverage for business interruption or extra expense in the same amounts as is insured under the general property insurance part of the program.

Selecting the Form of Coverage

Business interruption coverage may be written in several ways. In most instances, the most appropriate form will be the portfolio Business Income Coverage form. There are two versions of the portfolio business income form, designated *Business Income Coverage (And Extra Expense)* form (CP 00 30) and *Business Income Coverage (Without Extra Expense)* form (CP 00 32). Coverage under either form is written subject to a coinsurance provision, which requires coverage equal to 50 percent, 60 percent, 70 percent, 80 percent, 90 percent, or 100 percent of the firm's annual earnings for the 12-month period of the policy. For those situations in which the business could be shut down for over a year, a 125 percent coinsurance option is available. In addition, however, coverage may also be written on a monthly limitation form, a 120-day indemnity form, or a valued form. The monthly limitation form and the 120-day indemnity form are built into the Business Income form and are triggered by an entry in the policy declarations. The valued form is a nonstandard approach that is available only from certain insurers. Before turning to a more detailed discussion of the coinsurance approach, it may be helpful to describe the alternatives.

Monthly Limit of Indemnity   The first option, the Monthly Limit of Indemnity, is an alternative to the standard coinsurance approach to business interruption insurance, and is the approximate equivalent of the previous Loss of Earnings or No-Coinsurance business interruption form. Under the Monthly Limit of Indemnity option, the insured may collect a specified fraction of the total amount of the insurance during any month for which the business is totally or partially interrupted. Options are available to permit collection of one-third, one-fourth, or one-sixth of the face amount of coverage.

120-Day Indemnity Form   The standard Business Income form can be converted to a 120-day indemnity form by electing the Maximum Period of Indemnity option. Under this provision, the coinsurance clause is replaced with a 120-day limit on the period for which indemnity is payable, with no monthly limit on the amount payable other than the amount of loss.

Valued Business Interruption Insurance   Although most business interruption coverage is written on an actual loss-sustained basis, a valued form of coverage is also available. Under a valued form, the insured purchases coverage with a specified limit of coverage payable per day or week of interruption, and the agreed amount is paid for each day or week of total interruption, regardless of the actual loss sustained. A proportional payment is made for partial interruptions.

The valued form is sometimes used for new businesses where the amount of the business interruption value is uncertain. The valued form of business interruption insurance is most useful when the income is stable and does not fluctuate over time. The greater the fluctuation in values over time, the less appropriate is the valued form.

The cost of a valued form is higher than the actual loss-sustained form. The latter is therefore usually preferred, not only for this reason, but also for the flexibility in loss adjustment. Many risk managers believe the additional administrative cost of proving a loss-sustained claim is outweighed by the more accurate results.[3]

Business Income (Coinsurance) Coverage Forms

The standard forms for insuring the business interruption exposure are the *Business Income Coverage (And Extra Expense)* form and the *Business Income Coverage (Without Extra Expense)* form. As noted above, coverage under either form is subject to a coinsurance provision. Coinsurance options of 50 percent, 60 percent, 70 percent, 80 percent, 90 percent, 100 percent, or 125 percent are available.

Both business income forms require a choice of three options: business income including rental value, business income excluding rental value, and rental value only. Rental Value is the anticipated rental income from tenants at the described premises minus expenses that do not continue or the fair rental value of any part of the premises occupied by the insured. The option selected determines the scope of "income" for which payment is made.

If the business is interrupted, payment is made for the loss of Business Income, defined as the net profit that would have been earned (including or excluding rental income) and the necessary expenses that continue during the "period of restoration." The period of restoration begins 72 hours after the time of the direct physical damage. In determining the amount of loss, the insurer considers the insured's experience before the loss and probable future experience if no loss had occurred. The definition of business income may be modified to delete or limit coverage on ordinary payroll (roughly, the payroll for rank-and-file workers) if the insured does not wish to collect for this expense in the event of interruption.

Loss of income coverage may be written to provide coverage against the same perils as the direct damage coverages, and payment is made only if the interruption results from an insured peril. The damage must occur during the policy period, but the period of indemnity is not limited by the expiration of the policy.

For mercantile and service firms, the net profit that would have been earned and continuing expenses will generally relate to sales. In the case of a manufacturing firm, it may relate to production. It is conceivable that a manufacturer in a

---

[3]At one time, there was a tax advantage to a valued form since recovery was treated as capital gains rather than income; but this situation has been changed by the courts. From a tax standpoint, no difference in treatment now exists between the valued and actual loss-sustained forms.

specialized line might suffer interruption during a period at which it might normally not have sales receipts, but nevertheless suffers loss because production is lost. A firm that manufactures Christmas tree ornaments, for example, whose operations are shut down because of an uninsured loss during the months of March to July, would not feel the impact of the shutdown until November and December. The reduced profit in December which results from the lost production in March to July constitutes an insured loss and would be compensated under the business interruption form. The same is true with respect to the continuing expenses during the period of shutdown that would have been covered out of receipts in November and December. On the other hand, if the firm is able to make up the lost production once the plant is restored, and sales in November and December are unaffected by the shutdown, there is no "loss sustained."

Resumption of Operations   In the event of damage to property that triggers an interruption, the Resumption of Operations provision requires the insured to resume operations as soon as possible, even on a partial basis, using damaged or undamaged property at the described premises or elsewhere. If operations are not resumed when it is possible to do so, the insurer will reduce payment for loss of income by the amount that resumption of operations would have reduced the loss.

Directly related to the provision that requires the insured to resume operations is a provision for payment of the expenses required for such resumption. Two separate provisions relate to the expense to reduce loss. Coverage may be provided either for "expense to reduce loss" or for "extra expenses."

Expense to Reduce Loss/Extra Expense   The principal difference between the two Business Income forms is in the additional coverages. The Without Extra Expense form includes an additional coverage titled Expense to Reduce Loss, which provides payment for expenses incurred by the insured to resume operations or otherwise reduce the amount of the business interruption loss. Expenses incurred to continue operations are payable under the Expense to Reduce Loss additional coverage only to the extent that they actually reduce the business interruption loss. Under the And Extra Expense business income form, the additional coverage is called Extra Expense, and payments are made under this additional coverage for expenses incurred to continue operations whether or not such expenses reduce the business interruption loss. In effect, under the form that includes the Extra Expense additional coverage, the entire amount of insurance is payable for either business interruption or extra expense.

The Extra Expense Additional Coverage of the Business Income form with extra expense is true extra expense coverage, and, in most instances, it pays extra expenses whether or not they actually reduce the amount of the loss. Extra expenses are payable to avoid or minimize the suspension of business and continue operations at the insured premises or substitute premises. In addition, coverage is provided for the cost to repair or replace any property and to research, replace, or restore lost information on damaged valuable papers and records. Payment under this item is limited to the amount by which the expenditures actually reduce the amount of loss that would otherwise be payable. The 72-hour waiting period applicable to the business income coverage does not apply to the Extra Expense Additional Coverage.

Programming Business Interruption Insurance

Measuring the potential magnitude of time element exposures is difficult because estimating the amount of such losses basically requires a prediction. In the case of a direct loss, calculating replacement cost or the actual cash value of property may be difficult, but the object to be valued can be measured and appraised. In the case of business interruption, on the other hand, the risk manager must determine (1) the period of time for which the firm will be interrupted, and (2) the income that will be lost during that period. Since the time at which the interruption will occur is unknown, the earnings that will be lost during the period of interruption is also unknown. Yet, in spite of the difficulties, consequential loss exposures can be measured with greater precision than is generally assumed.

Determining the amount of insurance to be carried under a business interruption form is basically a prediction. More specifically, it is a prediction of the future income and expenses that would be lost in the event of a shutdown. This depends on the time required for restoration, the expenses that would continue, and the seasonality of the firm.

The first step in the process of computing the amount of business interruption to be carried is to estimate the loss that the insured will suffer in the event of a shutdown. This requires determination of the period of restoration and the income that would be lost during that period. It also requires some estimate of the expenses that would continue during the period of shutdown and those that would not. Because expenses that do not necessarily continue are not payable under the business interruption forms, to the extent that such expenses can be identified, they should be deleted from business income in determining the amount of insurance to be carried. Note that in deleting expenses that are not expected to continue in determining the amount of insurance, the insured is not in any sense violating the requirements of the form's coinsurance provision.

Under the latest edition of the business income forms (June 1995), the forms provide that for the purpose of the coinsurance condition, twelve classes of expense are to be deducted from business income. These include Prepaid freight—outgoing; returns and allowances; discounts; bad debts; collection expenses; cost of raw stock and factory supplies consumed (including transportation charges); cost of merchandise sold (including transportation charges); cost of services purchased from outsiders for resale that do not continue under contract; power, heat and refrigeration expenses that do not continue under contract and that have been excluded from coverage; all ordinary payroll expenses that have been excluded from coverage; and special deductions for mining properties.

The insured is not required to purchase coverage for expenses that will not continue. The Business Income Form simply states that the insured may not deduct noncontinuing expenses (other than those specified) in computing business income that serves as the basis for the coinsurance provision.

Once the potential loss has been estimated, the insured should purchase the amount of insurance indicated. Having determined the amount of insurance that is needed and should be carried, the appropriate coinsurance percentage can be selected.

Programming Example   The following schedule of projected earnings, expenses, and profits illustrates the preceding discussion.

Month	Business Income	Noncontinuing Expenses	Continuing Expenses	Profit
January	15,000	5,000	5,000	5,000
February	15,000	5,000	5,000	5,000
March	15,000	5,000	5,000	5,000
April	15,000	5,000	5,000	5,000
May	15,000	5,000	5,000	5,000
June	15,000	5,000	5,000	5,000
July	15,000	5,000	5,000	5,000
August	15,000	5,000	5,000	5,000
September	35,000	5,000	20,000	10,000
October	35,000	5,000	20,000	10,000
November	45,000	5,000	20,000	20,000
December	65,000	5,000	20,000	40,000
	300,000	60,000	120,000	120,000

The insured has a highly seasonal business, with earnings increasing and peaking during the Christmas season. It has been determined that in the event of a loss, the period required to restore the building and the stock would be four months. The problem is to determine the maximum loss that might be incurred by the insured during the four-month period. Given the increase in earnings during the months of September through December, it is obvious that the greatest loss would occur if the interruption took place during this period. Using projected continuing expenses and profit as a measure of loss, we determine the amount of insurance needed for a four-month shutdown to be $160,000. This is the amount of insurance the insured should purchase.

Determining the Coinsurance Percentage

Given a proper determination of the amount of insurance to be carried, the selection of the appropriate coinsurance percentage is relatively simple. Most of the confusion in this area stems from the previously noted misconception that one selects the coinsurance percentage first and that the coinsurance percentage multiplied by Business Income determines the amount of insurance. As we have seen, the proper approach is to determine the amount of insurance that is required to reimburse the insured and purchase this amount. The coinsurance percentage is then determined on the basis of the relationship between the amount of insurance purchased and the annual Business Income.

Once the amount of insurance to be purchased has been determined, it is then appropriate to compute the annual Business Income, using the formula contained in the form (or in the business interruption worksheet). Once the annual Business Income has been determined and the amount of insurance to be carried has been decided, the coinsurance percentage is selected on the basis of the relationship between the annual Business Income and the amount of insurance. In our illustration above, we determined the annual Business Income to be $300,000. We also computed the needed amount of insurance as $160,000. Dividing the insurance to be purchased by the annual Business Income, we find that the insurance to be purchased represents 53 percent of the annual Business Income:

$$\frac{\$160,000}{\$300,000} = .5333$$

Logic dictates that a 50 percent coinsurance clause be selected; if 60 percent were selected, the insured would already have a coinsurance deficiency.

As a further illustration of the principle involved here, let us modify the assumptions in the illustration and assume that the period of restoration is estimated to be six months rather than four. Adding the potential loss for the months of July and August, the amount of insurance needed is $180,000. Under this set of assumptions, the relationship between the amount of insurance and the Business Income is about 60 percent:

$$\frac{\$180,000}{\$300,000} = .60$$

In this case, the insured would select a 60 percent contribution clause. Keep in mind that the insured can always carry more than the amount required by the coinsurance provision. He or she simply cannot carry less without the risk of a coinsurance penalty.

As a final point, note that if the insured anticipates a shutdown for the entire year, the amount of insurance required is the annual profit plus the annual continuing expenses:

$$\frac{\$300,000}{\$240,000} = .80$$

Payroll Endorsements

Because employees will sometimes be laid off during an extended shutdown, business interruption insureds may sometimes elect to cover only the payroll of executive officers or other important employees. When this is done, ordinary payroll may be excluded from coverage under the policy. "Ordinary payroll" is defined as payroll expense for all employees except officers, executives, department managers, employees under contract, and any other employees selected by the insured and designated in the Ordinary Payroll Limitation endorsement.

If the insured wishes to purchase coverage for the payroll of rank and file workers for a short period of time, but exclude it if a shutdown extends beyond a specified period, ordinary payroll may be covered for a specified period, with no coverage after the shutdown extends beyond the selected time. The Ordinary Payroll endorsement may be used to exclude ordinary payroll altogether (by entering "0" under the Limitation Period) or to limit ordinary payroll by entering the appropriate number of days. Coverage on Ordinary Payroll may be limited to 30, 60, 90, 120, 150, or 180 days. The same Ordinary Payroll Endorsement is used with both direct and contingent loss of income coverages. When payroll is excluded or limited, the base Business Income rate is modified as follows:

Number of Days for Which Payroll Coverage Is Provided	Factor
0	1.12
90	1.06
180	1.00

Dealing with the Problem of Underinsurance

One of the most difficult problems in programming business interruption insurance stems from the fact that the loss involved is one that cannot be measured with precision at the time the insurance is purchased. Recognizing the problem facing insurance buyers in attempting to purchase the proper amount of insurance, insurers offer two options whereby an insurance buyer can cope with the problem of inadequate coverage.

Agreed Value Option   The Agreed Value option is the equivalent of the Agreed Amount Endorsement which was previously available as an endorsement to the Gross Earnings form. Like the Agreed Value coverage of the Building and Personal Property Coverage form, the Agreed Value optional coverage of the business interruption form suspends the coinsurance provision and guarantees that the insured will not suffer a coinsurance penalty on a partial loss. The Agreed Value option of the business interruption form suspends the coinsurance provision for a period of one year. It protects against a coinsurance penalty that might result from an inadvertent insurance deficiency if the insured's earnings increase more than anticipated. When the Agreed Value option is added to the policy, the base Business Income rate is modified by a factor of 1.10.

Premium Adjustment Endorsement   The Premium Adjustment Endorsement, like the Agreed Value coverage, is designed to protect against an inadvertent deficiency in the amount of business interruption insurance. However, the approach used in the Premium Adjustment Endorsement is fundamentally different; in a sense, the Premium Adjustment Endorsement is a type of reporting form, with a single report at the end of the year to determine both the amount of insurance that was in force during the year and the premium for the coverage. The insured selects a provisional amount of insurance that is higher than the anticipated level of protection that will be required. In addition, a coinsurance percentage is selected. After the period of coverage is over (under most circumstances a policy year), the amount of insurance actually in force during the coverage period is determined by multiplying the coinsurance percentage selected by the actual business income of the firm. In other words, the amount of insurance in force is the amount that permits the insured to comply precisely with the coinsurance percentage selected.

Assume that the Widget Corporation's annual business income has grown at an annual average rate of say, 10 percent. Its present level of business income is $1 million. It is estimated that 50 percent of expenses would continue during a period of interruption and that profit equal to 10 percent of sales would be lost. The firm's loss in the event of an interruption would be 60 percent of its income. Anticipating a 10 percent increase in the coming year, the Widget Corporation might purchase $660,000 in business income coverage, perhaps with the Agreed Amount provision applicable. As an alternative, Widget might purchase coverage under the Business Income form with a Premium Adjustment Endorsement. In this case, the provisional amount of insurance might be set at $800,000 rather than the $660,000. The amount of insurance in force during the year will equal the amount required to comply with the 60 percent coinsurance requirement. If earnings increase to $1.1 million, Widget will have $660,000 in business income coverage. If earnings increase to $1.2 million, the amount of coverage will be $720,000. And if earnings remain at $1 million, the coverage will be $600,000. A provisional premium is paid at the inception of the policy, based on the provisional amount of insurance, and is adjusted after expiration based on the reported actual income.

Unlike the Agreed Amount option, there is no surcharge to the rate when coverage is written with the Premium Adjustment Endorsement. The cost is the interest foregone on the overpaid premium:

Premium for $6 million coverage	$6300
With Agreed Amount endorsement	$6930
$8 million with Premium Adjustment	$8400
Refund	$2100
Net Premium + Opportunity cost at 10%	$6510

Special Exposures to Consider

When programming business income insurance or evaluating an existing business interruption program, attention should be given to the existence of any special exposures that may require modification of the standard business interruption forms. These may include difficulties that might be encountered in resuming operations, a lag in the resumption of income after restoration, or special types of property, such as computers, that may require special treatment.

Alterations and New Buildings Specific consideration should be given to the need for business interruption coverage on new facilities. Although a limited amount of coverage is provided in the standard business interruption forms for new facilities at the insured location, the coverage is extremely limited. The Alterations and New Buildings Additional Coverage extends coverage to buildings under construction at the described premises. In addition, if the policy is written with a 50 percent or higher coinsurance provision, the Newly Acquired Location Extension provides $100,000 additional coverage at any newly acquired location. Specific business interruption coverage should be arranged for new facilities, including the period during which the facility is being constructed.

Lag in Earnings After Restoration   Sometimes a firm's income can be anticipated to remain depressed following restoration of the premises. Old customers may have turned to new sources during the period of interruption, and the process of rebuilding a clientele may require time beyond the period of restoration. In the absence of a provision to the contrary, payments under the business income form would cease once the premises were restored. The latest versions of the business interruption forms provide coverage for a period of 30 days beyond the date of restoration, under a provision entitled "Extended Business Income."[4] For those situations in which the potential lag in income following restoration may exceed this 30-day period, the Extended Period of Indemnity optional coverage permits the insured to extend this 30-day extension. Extended Period of Indemnity optional coverage is available in 30-day increments up to six months, with 90-day increments thereafter up to 365 days.

Building Code Requirements   One of the special conditions that is sometimes overlooked is the increase in time required to replace a building that does not conform to the local building code. The standard business interruption forms cover for the time necessary to rebuild, repair, or replace damaged property with "due diligence and dispatch." It does not pay for the additional time needed due to ordinances that require demolition or change of undamaged property. Therefore, it may well be worthwhile to investigate the need for an *Ordinance or Law-Increased Period of Restoration endorsement.* The name of the form may vary by rating bureau jurisdiction; the important point is that two forms are needed to cover the exposure: (1) statutory demolition requirements and (2) increased cost to rebuild (because of building codes being more restrictive than when the structure was first built).

Electronic Media and Records   As in the earlier business interruption forms, there is a limitation on the payment of business interruption income when the interruption is caused by damage to electronic data processing records or data. Payment is limited to 60 days, or the period required to repair or rebuild other damaged property. Under earlier forms, coverage for loss resulting from damage to electronic media and records was limited to 30 days.

EDP Consequential Exposures   Firms with computerized production equipment or that depend on computerized information to support production and firms that process data for others may need business interruption insurance under an EDP

---

[4]Under earlier forms, this coverage was available only by endorsement and required an additional premium. The 30-day limit may be extended for an added charge.

form to cover breakdown and unusual perils. Such an exposure exists, for example, when a key piece of machinery is computer-controlled. The boiler policy covers breakdown of machinery but not of computerized equipment. An EDP policy will cover breakdown of the computer but not of production equipment. This means that either the boiler policy or the EDP policy must be modified to provide coverage.

EXTRA EXPENSE INSURANCE

Under some circumstances, it may be necessary for a business to continue operations after its facilities have been destroyed. For example, a bank's earnings, which are derived from loans and investments, would not be affected by destruction of the bank's premises, but the bank would need other facilities to continue to service its accounts. Extra expense insurance is an alternative to business interruption insurance for those enterprises that can continue operations with other facilities. It provides payment for expenses above normal costs when such expenses are incurred to continue operations after damage to the premises by an insured peril.

The Extra Expense Coverage form contains a schedule of cumulative monthly limits, expressed as a percentage of the face amount of the policy, and the insured's recovery is limited to these percentages. The most commonly used schedule permits the policyowner to collect up to 40 percent of the face of the policy during the first month following damage, up to 80 percent during the first two months, and up to 100 percent for three months or more. An insured anticipating a more extended period requiring extra expenses can select a smaller monthly limitation (for example, 10 percent during the first month, 20 percent in the first two months, and so on). The rate for the coverage decreases as the percentage of the face amount collectible in the first and succeeding months decreases.

INDIRECT BOILER AND MACHINERY COVERAGES

As in the case of the portfolio Property Coverage form, indirect loss coverages may be added to the Boiler and Machinery portfolio form by endorsement. There are three boiler and machinery consequential loss coverages.[5]

Business Interruption

Boiler and machinery business interruption (formerly called Use and Occupancy coverage) provides coverage for loss due to a total or partial interruption of business as a result of an accident to an insured object. Coverage also applies for the

---

[5]The third boiler and machinery indirect loss coverage, Consequential Damage coverage, provides indemnity for the actual loss of insured property due to spoilage resulting from lack of power, light, heat, or refrigeration at described premises caused by an accident to an insured object. A freezing plant or meat locker might purchase consequential damage coverage for indirect loss resulting from the breakdown of its freezing equipment.

expenses incurred to reduce loss resulting from such interruption. The coverage is written on both an indemnity basis and a valued basis.

Extra Expense

The extra expense coverage available under the boiler and machinery policy performs essentially the same function as the extra expense coverage sold under fire policies.

CONTINGENT BUSINESS INTERRUPTION AND EXTRA EXPENSE

Contingent business interruption insurance is a means of protecting a firm against interruption losses resulting from damage caused by an insured peril to property that it does not own, operate, or control. This coverage is used in three situations:[6]

1. When the insured depends on one or a few manufacturers or suppliers for most of its materials. The firm on which the insured depends is called the contributing property.
2. When the insured relies on one or a few businesses to purchase the bulk of its products. The firm to which most of the insured's production flows is called the recipient property.
3. When the insured counts on a neighboring business to help attract customers. A common way of referring to the neighboring firm is the leader property.

The contributing or recipient property need not be shut down in order for the insured's contingent interruption loss to be payable. For example, a supply of finished goods intended for the insured may be destroyed at a contributing plant, with only the insured's operations affected. The key element is an interruption of the insured's business caused by damage to nonowned property.

Contingent Business Income Endorsements

The contingent business income endorsements revise the Business Income coverage to apply to contingent loss of income due to direct physical loss at another location that is not owned and operated by the insured. There are two versions of the Contingent Business Income Endorsement: a Broad form and a Limited form.

The Broad Form Contingent Business Income Endorsement provides coverage in addition to the direct Business Income coverage and for the same limit. The Limited Form Contingent Business Income Endorsement provides coverage when

---

[6]Some sources refer to four situations in which the coverage is needed: Contributing properties (suppliers of materials); Recipient properties (purchasers of products); Manufacturing properties (suppliers of products to sales customers); and Leader properties (businesses that attract customers to the insured's location).

written without direct Business Income coverage or when the limit for contingent business interruption coverage differs from the direct Business Income limit.

Contingent Extra Expense

Contingent extra expense insurance operates in much the same way as contingent business interruption, but is designed for the firm that would incur increased costs as a result of damage to a contributing or recipient firm's property.

Interruption of Utilities

Another subject that has created some confusion is the interruption of businesses that occurs as a result of the suspension of utilities. The usual trigger for business interruption losses is damage by an insured peril at the insured location. If coverage for interruption caused by damage at some other location is desired, it must be purchased in the form of contingent business interruption.

A very specialized form of contingent business interruption is coverage for interruption of business due to the suspension of utility service caused by damage to the utility (or transmission media) away from the premises by the Utility Services—Time Element Endorsement. The particular type of utility service for which coverage is desired must be indicated. There are five options:

- Water supply
- Communication, not including transmission lines
- Communication, including transmission lines
- Power supply, not including transmission lines
- Power supply, including transmission lines

Coverage for interruption due to the interruption of Off-Premises Services applies when the insured's business is interrupted because of damage by an insured peril.

The interruption of power and other utility services away from the premises is an often misunderstood exposure, and the insurance designed to protect against this exposure can be confusing. The problem stems from the fact that the loss of off-premises power or other utility services can be a source of both direct loss and indirect loss. Separate endorsements are designed to cover each exposure.[7]

With respect to the time element exposure, the Utility Service Interruption endorsement provides coverage for lost income or extra expenses owing to failure of communications services, water supply services, or power services. The endorsement is subject to a 12-hour waiting period deductible, which applies to all perils.

---

[7]Coverage for direct damage losses arising out of the interruption of power, water, or communication services is provided under two separate endorsements. The Utility Services—Direct Damage endorsement (CP 04 17) provides coverage for damage to insured property arising out of the interruption of insured services, resulting from damage to the facilities supplying the services. The insured may elect coverage for any (or all) of "water supply services, communication supply services, or power supply services." The insured may include or reject coverage for overhead transmission lines.

BUSINESS INTERRUPTION FOR INDIVIDUALS

Although business interruption is usually regarded as a loss exposure of a firm, in some situations an individual's income may be insured. A store manager whose income is tied to sales or receipts would suffer a considerable financial loss if the store were shut down. Such persons can purchase coverage under a form that provides for payment of personal income lost because of damage to the property of a named business. Similarly, commission salespeople whose line of goods consists primarily of the output of a single manufacturer may obtain coverage for the loss they would suffer if the manufacturer's operations were suspended because of an insured peril. For individuals in these situations, such coverages are an important form of protection.

Although no business interruption forms available are designed specifically for the individual exposure, the exposure is basically a contingent business interruption one and can be written under the contingent business interruption form, provided the insurer is willing to provide the coverage.

LEASEHOLD INTEREST INSURANCE

Leasehold interest coverage protects against loss due to the termination of a favorable lease caused by fire or other insured peril. Consider, for example, a property leased for $1000 a month, subject to a lease that may be canceled in the event of fire or other damage to the premises. When prevailing conditions make it impossible to secure similar quarters at less than, say, $2500 a month, the existing contract will create a leasehold interest loss of $1500 a month for the remaining period of the lease.

Under earlier versions of the leasehold interest form, coverage applied only if the termination of the lease was triggered by a provision in the lease, and a copy of the lease provision was inserted in the policy as part of the insuring agreement. Under the portfolio version, reference to the fire clause is deleted, so coverage applies whenever a peril insured against results in the cancellation of a lease. The Building Ordinance exclusion does not apply to this coverage.

The amount of coverage under leasehold interest coverage decreases month by month, with the amount of insurance always about equal to the insured's interest in the lease. In the event of a loss that terminates the rental agreement, the insured is paid a lump sum equal to the discounted value of the leasehold interest for the remaining months of the lease.

Simplified coverage for Leasehold Interest permits selection of interest rates between 5 and 15 percent. Separate Leasehold Interest Factor forms are provided in the forms portfolio (but are not available through ISO distribution). A copy of one of these forms must be attached to the policy when Leasehold Interest is written. The form to choose is based on the interest rate selected.

This form may be used to cover leasehold interest exposure, but it may also be used to provide coverage for bonus payments, improvements and betterments, and prepaid rent.

RAIN INSURANCE

Before leaving the subject of business interruption, we should briefly note another specialized indirect loss coverage, rain insurance. Rain insurance is a consequential loss coverage. It protects not against damage to property, but against loss of income or the incurring of extra expenses due to rain, snow, sleet, or hail. It is usually sold to cover outdoor events scheduled for a certain day dependent on favorable weather for success. The coverage may be written on an indemnity basis to cover the loss of income suffered or additional expenses incurred, or it may be written on a valued basis. Some contracts specify the amount of rain that must fall before payment will be made, whereas in other contracts any amount of rain will require payment by the insurer. The policy must usually be taken out at least seven days before the event and is not subject to cancellation by either party. Although rain insurance is a specialty coverage and many companies design their own forms, the Crop-Hail Insurance Actuarial Association has developed a standardized form for its member companies.

BUYING CONSEQUENTIAL LOSS COVERAGE

In general, it is recommended that consequential loss coverage be purchased from the same insurer as provides the direct loss coverage. Direct loss settlement and reconstruction are expedited and loss adjustments are made more quickly because the insurer is anxious to minimize time element losses.

IMPORTANT CONCEPTS TO REMEMBER

consequential loss
time element exposures
bottlenecks
substitute facilities
reciprocal arrangement
cold site
hot site
redundancy
Program Evaluation and
    Review Technique
    (PERT)
business interruption
    insurance
extra expense insurance
contingent basis interruption
contingent extra expense
    insurance
leasehold interest coverage
monthly limit of indemnity
120-day indemnity form
maximum period of
    indemnity option

valued business interruption
    insurance
rental value
resumption of operations
    provision
expense to reduce loss
    additional coverage
extra expense additional
    coverage
ordinary payroll
ordinary payroll limitation
    endorsement
agreed value option
premium adjustment
    endorsement
extended business
    income
"consequential damage"
    coverage
broad form contingent
    income endorsement

limited form contingent
    business income
    endorsement
business interruption
    insurance
business income
Business Income Coverage
    (And Extra Espense) form
Business Income Coverage
    (Without Extra Expense)
    form
Resumption of Operations
    provision
contingent business
    interruption
contributing property
manufacturing property
recipient property
leader property
Extra Expense Coverage form
Leasehold Interest Coverage

QUESTIONS FOR REVIEW

1. Explain what is meant by the term *consequential loss*. What are the subclasses of consequential loss?

2. Identify the pre-event loss control measures that may be used to address the risk of business interruption and extra expense.

3. Explain how the program evaluation and review technique can be useful in dealing with consequential loss.

4. Identify and explain the determinants of loss severity in the event of a business interruption loss.

5. Identify the features that distinguish organizations that face an extra expense exposure from those that face a business interruption exposure.

6. Describe the differences between the two standard Business Income Coverage Forms. Of what significance to the insured are these differences at the time of a loss?

7. Describe the contingent business interruption exposure. How are contingent business interruption exposures generally classified?

8. Under what circumstances would you recommend that coverage for ordinary payroll be included in a business interruption insurance policy?

9. Under what circumstances is the monthly-limitation approach to business interruption insurance appropriate? Why is it not appropriate for other business interruption situations?

10. Give two specific examples in which Contingent Business Interruption insurance would be needed.

QUESTIONS FOR DISCUSSION

1. Describe the two broad approaches available to insurance buyers that may be helpful in avoiding underinsurance in business interruption coverage. Which of the two approaches do you believe is preferable?

2. XYZ carries a Business Income Coverage form for $200,000, written under the Maximum Period of Indemnity option. XYZ suffers a windstorm loss, which causes damage to the roof of the factory. The time required to repair the roof and replace the damaged contents forces XYZ to suspend operations for six months. During the period of suspension, XYZ incurs $20,000 per month in continuing expenses and $20,000 per month in lost profits. How much will be payable under the Business Income Coverage form?

3. Explain how the coverage under the Business Income Form is modified by each of the following optional coverages:
   (1) Agreed Value Coverage
   (2) Maximum Period of Indemnity
   (3) Monthly Limit of Indemnity
   (4) Extended Period of Indemnity

4. ABC purchases business interruption coverage in the amount of $250,000, subject to a 50% coinsurance clause. It suffers a business interruption loss in which it is forced to totally suspend operations for a period of four months. During the previous year, its operations produced the following results:

Sales   1,200,000

Cost of goods sold   600,000

Income and expenses are relatively constant throughout the year and do not fluctuate significantly from month to month. It is agreed that the continuing expenses and lost profit during the period of shutdown would have been consistent with income and expenses in the past. How much will be payable under ABC's business interruption policy?

5. Jacobs invested $80,000 in improvements and betterments that became a permanent part of the premises when he leased a building under a ten-year lease. Jacob insured the improvements and betterments under a Commercial Property Coverage Form. A fire occurred when the lease had seven years left to run, and the fire caused $35,000 in damage to the improvements and betterments. Describe the various bases upon which the loss might be settled, and indicate the amount payable under each.

SUGGESTIONS FOR ADDITIONAL READING

Head, George L., ed. *Essentials of Risk Control*, 2nd ed., vol. I, Malvern, Pa.: Insurance Institute of America, 1989. Chapter 8.

Huebner, S.S., Kenneth Black, Jr., and Bernard L. Webb. *Property and Liability Insurance,* 4th ed. Englewood Cliffs, NJ: Prentice-Hall, 1996. Chapters 18 and 19.

Jorgensen, James R. *Business Income Insurance—How It Works,* 3rd ed. Boston, MA: The John Liner Organization, 1991.

Morrison, Robert M., Alan G. Miller and Stephen J. Paris. *Business Interruption Insurance: Its Theory and Practice.* Cincinnati, OH: National Underwriter Company, 1986.

Robinson, Linda G. and Jack P. Gibson. *Commercial Property Insurance* (Dallas, Tx.: International Risk Management Institute, Inc., loose-leaf service with periodic supplements), vol. I, "Time Element" section.

Webb, Bernard L., Stephen Horn II, and Arthur L. Flitner. *Commercial Insurance* 2nd ed. (Malvern, Pa.: Insurance Institute of America, 1990), Chapter 3.

CHAPTER 19

Managing Crime Risks: Risk Control

CHAPTER OBJECTIVES

When you have finished this chapter, you should be able to

Identify the two broad classes of criminal loss to which business and organizations are exposed.

■

Explain the principal loss prevention and control measures that are appropriate for addressing employee crime.

■

Identify the specific types of criminal acts that are directed at the organization by nonemployees.

■

Explain why nonemployee criminal losses are particularly susceptible to loss-prevention and control measures.

■

Identify the major approaches that are used to prevent and control losses by burglary, robbery, and shoplifting.

■

Identify and distinguish among the major types of burglar alarm systems, both with respect to the activation mechanism and to the location at which the alarm is sounded.

⚏ Introduction ■

No one knows for sure how much business this country loses to crime each year, despite the many surveys, estimates, and opinions on how large this loss is. It is safe to say, however, that the loss is in the billions of dollars, and a conservative estimate places the crime loss at between 2 and 5 percent of the gross revenues of business. This loss can be equal to the profit margin in many types of business and can make the difference between success and failure, profit or loss.

The actual loss may be even higher because of undiscovered crime. A business owner may know that he or she is not making a profit, but is not sure why not. This uncertainty may be partly because the organization does not have a good record and inventory system and management does not realize how much merchandise is unaccounted for. Part of it may be missing because of customer thefts, employee thefts, and fraud or embezzlement, for much crime is undiscovered and often overlooked.

The fact that many criminal losses are not detected obviously makes insurance an inappropriate approach to dealing with such losses. Insurance policies that cover against dishonesty generally specify the criminal peril or perils for which coverage is provided. Without exception, these contracts exclude losses whose existence is provable only by an inventory or a profit and loss computation. Thus a criminal loss is collectible under an insurance contract only when it is detected and when the specific cause of the loss is known.

CRIMES AGAINST BUSINESS

Broadly speaking, crimes against businesses are classified according to the perpetrator as employee crime and nonemployee crime. Nonemployee crime is further divided according to the type of crimes: burglary, robbery, shoplifting, forgery, and bad checks. In addition, there are a variety of other related crimes: usually related to one of these categories but distinguishable by their unique character. Computer crimes, which may be committed by employees or nonemployees, is an example. Before turning to a discussion of the loss-prevention and control measures that may be used to address criminal losses, it may be helpful to define the crimes with which we will be concerned in this chapter.

Robbery

The term *robbery* refers to taking property (1) by inflicting violence on the custodian of the property or by putting the custodian in fear of violence, and (2) by any other obviously unlawful act witnessed by the person from whom the property is taken. The infliction of violence or putting the victim in fear of violence includes killing or rendering the victim unconscious, as well as armed holdups. The second type of robbery (taking property by an obviously unlawful act) is robbery, even in

429

the absence of violence or threat of violence. If an employee sees a thief grab an item and run out of the store, the loss is considered robbery because the robber committed an obviously unlawful act witnessed by the employee. For the same reason, loss resulting from smashing a show window while the premises are open for business is considered robbery.

Burglary

Burglary consists of stealing property when the premises are not open for business by a person or persons making forcible entry into the premises. Insurance policies covering loss by burglary typically require visible evidence of forcible entry into the premises or forcible exit.

Theft

Theft is much broader in meaning than either burglary or robbery; it includes any illegal taking of property, thus embracing both burglary and robbery. It encompasses shoplifting losses, but may also include taking property through fraud. A "customer" who takes a test drive in the auto dealer's car and simply does not return commits theft, even though the dealer gave him the keys and invited him to take the car for a drive. Similarly, the customer who trades in a car he or she does not own commits theft.

Forgery

Forgery is the crime committed when someone falsifies an authorized signature on a check or other financial instrument or modifies a check or order to pay by increasing the amount payable. It also includes altering the payee. Forgery crimes may be committed by employees or by nonemployees.

Bad Checks

Crimes involving bad checks are distinguishable from forgery losses. Whereas forgery usually involves outgoing instruments, the bad check exposure relates to incoming checks. Bad check losses may involve insufficient fund checks or nonexistent account checks issued in payment for merchandise. Passing bad checks is the most frequent crime in America. Usually, the amount per loss is modest, but with a high frequency, the aggregate annual loss can be significant.

CRIME AND TYPE OF BUSINESS

The type of loss to crime varies with the business. Some retailers, for example, have virtually no shoplifting problem; no one shoplifts a car from an auto dealer. Other types of business, such as supermarkets or discount stores, have a heavy loss to shoplifters as do most self-service stores. The loss varies with type of location and type of customer. Bad-check writers target all types of business. Burglars and robbers may hit any place, but isolated businesses or those in certain neighborhoods are usually most likely victims of burglars whereas robbers like places that stay open late at night with few employees on duty.

Employee thefts can occur in any business unless the owner is the only employee. Even employing only relatives does not assure that there will be no employee thefts. Thefts by employees can range from pilferage of small items such as office supplies up to hundreds of dollars a week, with the total loss in the hundreds of thousands. The potential severity of employee theft is much greater than that for nonemployee thefts. The burglar or the holdup man victimizes any one business only once in a while. Shoplifters are limited to what they can conceal and carry out. Bad-check writers have trouble with large checks because everyone is more careful then. But employees are on the job daily, and their thefts are often limited only by their needs.

❖ Loss Control and Crime Generally ■ ■ ■ ■ ■ ■ ■ ■ ■ ■ ■ ■ ■

Of the various exposures facing the organization, loss by crime is probably the most susceptible to control measures. Because criminal acts are acts of people, techniques aimed at preventing criminal loss are effective in two respects. First, they make criminal acts more difficult for those who are inclined to commit such acts. In addition, by making the acts more difficult, loss-prevention and control measures discourage attempts by criminals. Most crime exposures are characterized by a high-frequency low-severity type of losses that risk management theory suggests are most susceptible to loss control measures. The principal exception is the case of employee dishonesty, where a high frequency of thefts by an employee over an extended period of time can produce a high severity loss.

As in the case of other loss-prevention and control measures, those directed at the crime exposure may be classified according to the time of application (pre-event, at the time of the event, and post-event) and according to whether the measure is aimed at persons, mechanical devices, or the environment. As we discuss specific loss-prevention and control measures, attempt to classify them according to the matrix we discussed in Chapter 9.

THE DETERRENCE FACTOR

Because crime losses are a result of human acts, loss-prevention measures can have a dual effect on the likelihood of losses. Like a fire alarm, a burglary alarm alerts friendly forces that a loss is occurring, thereby permitting a timely response. In addition, the burglar alarm acts as a deterrent. In fact, the deterrent effect may be the most significant benefit of crime loss control measures.

■ Employee Dishonesty Loss Control   ■ ■ ■ ■ ■ ■ ■ ■ ■ ■ ■

As in the case of criminal acts by nonemployees, the type of employee thefts varies with the type of business. In some organizations, the major exposure is theft of materials and supplies; in other firms, it is manipulation of records and embezzlement of funds. This makes it difficult to develop an employee-crime deterrent program that is applicable to all types of businesses. Each type of business must be studied and security methods developed for the specific problems.

Although cash and negotiable instruments are always attractive, the dishonest individual is also tempted by merchandise that can be turned into cash or put to personal use. Some objects may be carried out, but entire truckloads of material can be diverted by the thief who takes the time to organize and plan. Although employee pilferage may seem insignificant in the grand scheme of the organization's risks, it can be a major drain on the organization's resources.

SELECTION OF EMPLOYEES

At one time, a standard loss-prevention measure with respect to employee crime was a job application and background check of individual applicants. Based on the assumption that a person who has stolen once is likely to steal again, a criminal record was taken as a good reason not to hire the individual. Although there is still more or less general agreement that employee thefts can be reduced by carefully investigating the background of all employee applicants, state and federal legislation has made this increasingly difficult. Information about the history and activities of employees and job applicants is now far less available to employers than was formerly the case. In fact, state and federal legislation often denies a prospective employer information on the criminal record of job applicants. The trend has been to deny such information to private employers except where it is specifically authorized to them by the provisions of federal or state statute, executive order, or regulation. At the state level, the approaches to disclosure of criminal record information vary. A few states do not address the issue of nonconviction information to private employers, but most states do. Some states permit disclosure of criminal records to prospective employers,[1] but other states strictly prohibit the release of such information.[2] The most general pattern is to permit access only to criminal *conviction* information (as opposed to information on *arrests*) and to allow such information only to employers authorized by statute or regulation.

Even when information on an individual's arrest and conviction record is available, a number of cases in various jurisdictions hold that such information cannot be used as the sole reason for rejecting a candidate for employment. The rule is

---

[1]Florida, Illinois, Kentucky, Minnesota, Montana, Nebraska, Nevada, Pennsylvania, and West Virginia. In Montana, Nebraska, Nevada, and West Virginia, the subject's written consent is required.

[2]Alabama, Arizona, California, Delaware, Iowa, New York, North Carolina, Oregon, Rhode Island, Virginia, Wyoming, and the District of Columbia.

that a criminal conviction record is one factor among all factors to be considered in assessing an applicant's suitability. Major crimes, especially those which if committed in the workplace would pose a serious threat to coworkers, have generally been regarded as seriously disqualifying. In other words, rejection must relate to a crime that is somehow linked to the workplace or to job performance. The courts do not generally support terminating employees for off-the-job criminal conduct that does not pose a threat on the job.

Other techniques that were previously used in evaluating prospective employees are also barred because of privacy considerations. The Federal Employee Polygraph Protection Act of 1988[3] has made preemployment tests of this type unavailable in preemployment selection for most U.S. employers. Prior to the act, some states had banned the use of polygraph examinations, and other states have added state laws to the federal statute.

INTERNAL CONTROLS

The term *internal control* refers to the elements that are incorporated into the organization's accounting system designed to prevent employees from stealing and concealing theft from the organization. There are four basic elements of an effective control system. The first is a clear assignment of responsibility, in which identifiable persons are accountable for defined functions. Second, duties must be divided among employees in a way that separates the performance of a function from the recording of that function in the books of account. Third, there must be an adequate paper trail to assure continuous control. Finally, the proper operation of the plan must be verified on a regular basis by someone who has no accountability for the assets controlled.

When employee theft or embezzlement occurs in a corporate or business operation, investigation invariably shows that it stemmed primarily from weaknesses in four areas of the company's policies and procedures, namely, cash controls, disbursements, accounts receivable, and purchasing and receiving. Consequently, a well-designed system of internal controls will establish appropriate controls in each of these areas.

Cash Control Procedures

Internal controls begin with proper cash control procedures. Basically, this involves dividing the receipt and disbursement of funds to be received among individuals. Accounting for receipts and accounting for disbursements should generally be performed by different persons. In addition, the individual or individuals responsible for recording the transactions in the organization's books of account—the bookkeeper in a small firm or the accounting department in a larger organization—should not be permitted to perform either of these functions. As a basic principle, control of records and recording of transactions should be separated from the functions of receiving and disbursing cash.

---

[3] *29 U.S.C* 2001.

Separation of responsibilities with respect to cash receipts should also be incorporated into the organization's banking practices. The individual who prepares bank deposits, for example, should be different from the person who actually takes the deposits to the bank. In this respect, it is also recommended that responsibility for actually making deposits be separated. Bank deposits should not always be made by the same person; the task can be divided among a number of employees, with the duty scheduled among these people on an irregular and random basis. This can reduce the potential for embezzlement that involves collusion between the persons who prepare the deposit and the messenger who will be responsible for actually taking the deposit to the bank.

All cash receipts should be properly recorded and documented. The documentation should indicate the source of the funds, which will allow auditors to verify receipts against deposits. This is accomplished through a monthly reconciliation of the bank statements. Obviously, the reconciliation should be performed by employees who have no role in either the receipt or deposit of funds. Because the bank statement is one record that is not subject to falsification by persons within the organization, it is a critical tool in the internal control system. Where necessary, measures should be implemented to guarantee that the bank statement is delivered to the appropriate person and cannot be intercepted by employees.

Disbursement Procedures

Proper disbursement procedures begin with payment of all bills and accounts by check, regardless of the amount. Payment by check requires that funds be channeled through the organization's bank, which is essential to achieve the reconciliation discussed earlier. All checks should be prenumbered, and the disposition of all checks should be accounted for in periodic inventories. Checks marked "spoiled" should not be discarded; they should be maintained in the record system along with canceled checks that have been processed through the bank. There should be no gaps in the numerical sequence of "used" checks, whether they have been processed through the bank or voided because of errors.

Checks should be prepared in a way that guards against alteration. In general, this means printing or typing that resists erasure. The preferred approach is a check-writing machine that punches through the paper on which the check is made. When check-writing equipment incorporates a signature device, the mechanism should be treated in the same way as cash. The signature equipment should be in the custody of staff who are not responsible for the preparation of checks.

Once a check has been prepared, it should be compared against the authorization for payment before it is signed or sent to the party responsible for signing. After verification, the authorization should be canceled or marked in some way to indicate that the check has been prepared. This prevents the preparation of duplicate checks based on the same authorization.

Accounts Receivable and Sales Procedures

Many embezzlements occur in the manipulation of accounts receivables or in connection with sales in which an employee receives funds directly from a customer for sales. The first step in guarding against loss in this area is to set up procedures that require full documentation of the details of every sale, no matter how large or small. A second step is to ensure that correspondence and other communications regarding sales or billings with customers are not handled by the same person who prepared the monthly statements of accounts receivable.

Contrary to the common practice in many organizations, neither the bookkeeping nor the accounting department should be responsible for collecting overdue accounts receivable. Embezzlements can occur when accounting or bookkeeping personnel collect accounts that have been characterized as "bad debts" and write the accounts off as uncollectible. Final approval to write off an account receivable as a bad debt should be reserved to an executive of the organization outside the sales, bookkeeping, or accounting department. The individual authorized to approve writeoffs should have no direct relationship to any of the operations or responsibilities associated with the accounts.

Accounts receivable invoices should be treated in much the same manner as checks. As with checks, accounts receivable invoices should be numbered sequentially, and procedures should be established that require accounting for all numbered invoices and bills. Voided or spoiled invoices or bills should be retained and accounted for in the same way as checks.

Procedures for Purchasing, Receiving, and Accounts Payable

Purchase orders should be handled in essentially the same manner as blank checks and billing invoices. They should be numbered sequentially, and procedures should be established to ensure accounting for every number. Purchase orders should always be prepared in multiple copies, with copies distributed to the party to receive the goods or services and to the accounting department. The multiple copies can help prevent the use of purchase orders for dishonest ends by making it difficult for an individual to create fictitious purchase orders.

All purchases should be made on the basis of formal purchase orders. The only exceptions are in the case of inconsequential amounts that may be purchased out of petty cash. The formal purchase orders should require approval by a specified individual other than the person making the purchase. This can eliminate the opportunity for individuals to purchase goods and services for their personal use and charge the purchase to the organization.

Responsibility for determining what has been received should be assigned to personnel other than those from the purchasing department. This can help to prevent actions on the part of dishonest employees to hide their actions.

AUDITS

Given satisfactory control procedures in the financial area, an effective audit program helps to ensure that control requirements are being followed. An audit program is an important function, even though a company may have an outstanding control system. Companies have been defrauded over a period of time because their system of internal control, which they consider adequate, in actuality breaks down without anyone knowing it. This makes it imperative to check the systems periodically to ensure that they actually work.

An audit program should provide for a complete review of all procedures and control systems at least once a year. In addition, the annual financial review by a certified public accountant, conducted by most companies, should review the internal controls as a matter of routine. A review by such an outsider often results in suggestions for improving internal controls.

In addition, the audit and security organizations should undertake periodic joint reviews of financial controls. Although the audit is an important factor in discouraging dishonesty, it cannot uncover all irregularities. Even the most meticulous audit review will not detect some manipulations. The clever thief manipulates books and records, supply invoices, and cash receipts and, where necessary, forges signatures.

PROSECUTION OF DISHONEST EMPLOYEES

As stated earlier, one of the most effective crime barriers to employee crime is the deterrent effect of loss-prevention and control measures. The employee who is genuinely afraid of getting caught is less likely to steal than the employee who has little fear, either because controls are lax or because the employee is confident that the employer will not prosecute if he or she is caught. Many employees are reluctant to bring criminal charges against the employee who is caught stealing. In many instances, the thief is not even discharged. There are countless examples in which a dishonest employee is caught, begs forgiveness, promises not to do it again, and is given a second chance. Not surprisingly, many use the second chance to steal again. The employer who gives the dishonest employee a second chance takes a risk in two ways. The first is that the employee will steal again. The second relates to insurance coverage. As will be explained in the next chapter, standard forms of employee dishonesty insurance specifically exclude theft by any employee after the employer becomes aware of a previous dishonest act. If the employee is given a second chance, it is the employer that takes the risk, not the insurer.

✕ Nonemployee Crime Loss ■ ■ ■ ■ ■ ■ ■ ■ ■ ■ ■ ■ ■ ■ ■ ■ ■ ■

Much nonemployee crime is "crime of opportunity." A potential thief, often a juvenile, sees a lock on the back door of the neighborhood store that he can open with his pocketknife. He gets to talking to his friends about it, and on the spur of the moment, they decide to break in. If the lock had been just a little bit better, there might have been no burglary and no juveniles in trouble. Of course, a good burglar, given enough time, can break in almost any place, but increased security will deter many potential thieves and delay the others as well as cause them to make more noise and so increase their chances of capture.

Loss-prevention measures designed to deter nonemployee crime are difficult to classify because of the variety of forms that crimes may take. For the major crimes of burglary and robbery, the standard loss control measures are barriers, alarms, and guards. We will address these measures first, and then cover some of the specialized loss control measures applicable to other forms of crime.

BARRIERS

Barriers are the perimeter protection that is designed to deny unauthorized persons entry to the premises when they are not open for business. They consist of the structure and the devices that cover holes in the structure. It is an axiom of security management that a security system is only as strong as its weakest link; the integrity of a building is only as secure as its weakest link.

Doors are a critical point in security. You normally go into a building through a door, and so it is only logical for a burglar to do the same. As with all security, the door is only as strong as its weakest point. Doors designed to serve as barriers should be strong enough to do so. This means not only the door itself, but also the hinges and locks that are used to secure the door. If there is a glass panel in the door, it should be covered with a grill or be made of an unbreakable material such as Lexan. Even if the glass area is too small for entrance, it may allow the thief to reach through and open the door.

A firm policy should be established for keys and then carefully followed. Only the smallest possible number of keys should be issued, and these keys should be kept on the person to whom they are issued at all times. It only takes a little while to duplicate a key, so if one can be taken for only a short time, key control has broken down. For the same reason, employees should not be allowed to lend their key to another employee who is not authorized to have one.

Some types of occupancy require panic locks on certain exits—that is, a lock, usually a bar extending across the door, that can be opened from the inside in case of an emergency. When the place is closed for the night, these locks should be deadlocked for two reasons. First, the panic lock alone is usually not secure enough to prevent entry from the outside. Second, if someone hides in the premises, escape through the panic lock is simple.

The lock is the most often attacked point of entry. This is understandable for many locks in use in business places are inadequate. The most effective form of lock is a dead bolt or dead lock. This means that the locking bolt is so designed that it can't be pushed back by slipping a credit card, knife blade, or similar tool through the crack at the lock. An adequate lock will have a minimum "throw" of one inch. High-quality locks are designed with security in mind, and will resist the standard attacks of burglars such as saw blades, cylinder pullers, and pipe wrenches that are used to turn the cylinder out.

Windows are second only to doors as a favorite point of entry for burglars. The fact that in most cases they contain easily broken glass has done much for their popularity as a point of entrance. The most effective barriers for windows are steel bars, a metal grill, or an unbreakable material. Most industrial-type steel windows have small panes, and a lock on the window will go a long way toward preventing entry.

In many areas of the country, display windows are the prime target. This is a smash and grab operation so that the thief is there for only a matter of seconds, too short a time for an alarm to be effective. Usually, they confine their thefts to small, high-value items, such as jewelry, but not necessarily; other targets are color TV sets, hi-fi equipment, cameras, or records. There are three basic methods of protection. One is to take the high-value items out of the windows when the store is closed, or at least when foot traffic decreases. This is always time consuming, so not too many business places want to do it; moreover, with large items, such as TV sets, it is not practical. A second way is to protect with grill-type shutters or sliding grills. The objection here, besides the cost, is that it reduces the effectiveness of the window display. A third method is of recent origin. This is the use of clear plastics that are highly resistant to force. The basic problem is the cost, and the plastic does tend to scratch easier than glass.

Walls are seldom considered a vulnerable point for burglaries. However, going through a wall may be faster than breaking in a door or a window, depending on the material and thickness of the walls. Although little can be done to alter the structure, recognizing the deficiencies of a barrier permits it to be addressed in other ways (with an alarm, for example).

Finally, a fence can be an effective barrier and deterrent to crime. A fence keeps people out in two ways. First, it establishes a boundary, and anyone within that boundary is immediately suspect. Second, it physically keeps people out. How well it does this job depends on how it is made and designed. It will completely turn back some intruders, but to others it is not a real barrier. A fence also keeps people in. A burglar knows he can climb the fence in just 15 to 20 seconds. This is not a problem when he is going in, but he can't afford the loss of 15 or 20 seconds in an escape as the police approach. As a result, burglars don't like fences.

BURGLAR ALARM SYSTEMS

The first line of defense against burglary and the best single method of protection is an alarm system. Locks, safes, bars, and similar devices will slow the criminal down, but an alarm system will notify the police so that there will be a capture in most cases or will at least severely limit the time the thief can work. A security alarm installation provides prompt warning signals of any abnormal situation in the area or building that requires protection. Intruder detection systems vary from the simple electronic switch on a door to solid state audio microphone analog accumulators that detect extraneous noises and eliminate the effect of random noises.

Types of Alarm Systems

The three major types of alarm systems are: perimeter systems, area or space systems, and point or spot systems.

A *perimeter system* is triggered by penetration of a structure. Perimeter systems may be classified as *partial perimeter systems*, which protect exterior doors, windows, and other openings, and *complete perimeter systems*, which protect not only doors, windows and openings, but walls, ceilings, and floors as well. The most popular type of system in use today for mercantile premises consists of a partial perimeter system, with contact devices, switches, and metallic foil tape on all doors and windows. These form a continuous closed-circuit loop connected to alarm relays. If an attempt is made to enter through one of the protected points, the circuit will be broken and will set off the alarm. A complete perimeter system requires the addition of wired panels applied to the walls, ceilings, and floors or vibration detectors on walls, ceilings, and floors. A complete perimeter system is more expensive than a partial system, but the cost is justified when criminals might bypass openings and punch a hole in a wall or roof.

Perimeter systems may also be used to surround the entire premises and may be combined with a fence. Outdoor perimeter alarm systems are usually expensive and have the potential to generate nuisance alarms. Still, in the appropriate situation, an outdoor system can provide a part of an effective defense-in-depth strategy.

An *area* or *space system* is triggered by penetration of a portion of, or the total interior of, a room or building. One of the most popular area systems is the *ultrasonic system*, which generates a train of high-frequency sound waves which saturate an enclosed area with a pattern of standing waves. A sensitive receiver connected to an electronic amplifier picks up the waves. Motion within the protected area distorts the standing wave pattern and sends back a reflected wave of a different frequency. This change is detected and amplified in the control unit to trigger the alarm. *Microwave* systems operate on a similar basis. In a microwave system, a train of waves is produced which are partially reflected back to an antenna. If all objects within the range of the waves remain stationary, the reflected waves return in the same frequency. If they strike a moving object, they return at a different frequency, thus triggering the alarm. Finally, radar systems operate in much the same way as microwave systems. However, radio waves are highly penetrating and are not easily confined within a closed area such as a room or building, which may result in accidental alarms by persons or vehicles moving outside the building. Other types of interior intrusion systems that are classed as area or space systems include photoelectric beams, pressure-sensitive mats, and trip wires.

A *point* or *spot system* is an alarm system that is designed for the protection of safes, files, or small areas within a room or building. It is triggered when the specific point or spot is attacked. The best example of a point system is an alarm connected to a safe. These include *thermo acoustic alarms* and *capacity alarms*. A thermo acoustic alarm is installed inside the safe or other container. It is designed to detect heat, vibration, or sounds caused by a physical attack on the protected object. The alarm will also detect unauthorized opening of the safe by use of the combination lock. A *capacity alarm* operates on a somewhat different principle. The protected object acts as part of the capacitance (storage mechanism for an electric charge) of a tuned circuit. If a change occurs in the region of the protected object—such as the approach by an individual—there will be a change in capacitance of sufficient magnitude to upset the balance of the system and sound the alarm. In effect, the system sets up a protective field around the object which, if penetrated, will sound the alarm.

The most effective alarm system is a defense in depth, which combines the three types of alarm systems. The criminal's difficulty in overcoming one system, only to be faced with another, perhaps even more effective system, is a major psychological deterrent as well as a physical deterrent.

Alarm System Transmission Lines

A second distinction among alarm systems involves transmission of the alarm signal. Alarm systems may be classified as (1) local station alarms, (2) central station systems, (3) remote station alarms, and (4) proprietary alarm systems.

A *local station alarm* simply sounds a bell, siren, horn, or a similar device at the premises in the event of a burglary. There is an ongoing argument about local alarms. Some people like them on the theory that they will scare a burglar off before he steals anything. This is only partly true. If the location is such that no one is likely to hear it, and the burglar knows it, he can work on undisturbed. He may also realize that he has at least the minute or two that it takes someone to realize that an alarm is sounding and then phone the police. In that time he can steal a lot. A local alarm can also be defeated in many cases; that is, the horn, siren, or bell wires may be cut or the system silenced in some other way before the break-in starts.

The police don't particularly like local alarms because they would prefer to catch a thief rather than scare him away. If a burglar runs into a local alarm, all he has to do is hunt around and find another place to hit. He can't do this if he is caught. Local alarms have the advantage of being low cost, for there are no telephone line charges to pay. This often is the deciding factor, especially if the location is at a distance so that the charges would be unusually high or if the location is very far from a law enforcement agency so that response time would be slow.

A *central alarm system* is owned and operated by a private security firm (such as, for example, American District Telegraph or ADT) for the protection of its customers. Most large cities have an alarm central station, maintained by a commercial alarm company that has a location into which all of their alarms are wired. When an alarm is received, they notify the police and in most cases send one of their own men to the location. In addition to burglar, holdup, and fire alarms, central stations often monitor such things as temperatures, water levels, and a variety of industrial processes. Well-operated central stations are very efficient, but of course they vary in quality.

A *remote station alarm* is directly wired to the off-premises office of a fire department or police station or the owner of the protected property. Normally, a remote station alarm is wired directly to the police or fire department station.[4] There are many arguments pro and con as to where the alarm signal should be received, but the police do have the advantage of rapid response time if they receive the alarm signal directly. Numerous studies have shown that rapid response time is essential if captures are to be made. The additional time needed for a central station to interpret their alarm signal and then relay the message to the police often is the difference between an arrest or a miss.

A *proprietary alarm system* is similar to a central station alarm, but in this system the alarm sounds at a central office in the protected premises. It is generally used when the organization has its own security personnel, and it may be combined with a video camera premises surveillance system. Some proprietary systems are wired to the owner's home or the home of an employee, particularly when the owner lives nearby

---

[4]A variation of the remote station alarm system is called an *auxiliary alarm system*, in which the alarm triggers a fire alarm box of a public fire department.

so that wires can be run directly without the cost of leasing phone lines. Relatively few alarm systems use this method, and they are generally located in small towns or rural areas where it would take considerable time for a law enforcement agency to arrive.

Nighttime Security

In addition to barriers and alarms, a variety of other loss-prevention measures can help to reduce or control burglary losses. Some techniques may seem excessive, but the ingenuity of burglars requires that all reasonable measures be taken to bar penetration. One measure is to check restrooms and other enclosures when the premises are being closed. People can be accidentally locked in a business place, and this is only an inconvenience. On the other hand, some burglars hide so that they will be locked in, knowing it is always easier to break out than it is to break in. Unless there is an alarm system with interior protection, the thief is then free to move around and steal all he wishes. Even if there is an alarm on doors and windows, it is common practice for the burglar to gather all of his loot at a specific door and then at a predetermined time an accomplice will drive up, the thief will break out, setting off the alarm, but they will be loaded up and gone in a matter of seconds. Another variation, employed when the burglars are skilled, is to disable the alarm system; again this is not too difficult when the burglar is on the inside.

HOLDUP ALARM SYSTEMS

Holdup alarm systems are widely used by banks, financial institutions, jewelers, and other organizations using central station, police, or other response termination alarm systems. Convenient and unobtrusive switches are installed on desks, counters, stairwells, and in vaults. A variety of activating switches are available for such systems. These include double-pinch, which help to reduce accidental activation since finger-and-thumb squeeze action is required, and silent tumbler switches and push buttons, which automatically restore themselves after activation so that the robber cannot identify the originator of the alarm. Money clip switches installed in cash drawers are activated by removal of currency, which activates an electronic contact, triggering the alarm. No unusual movements on the part of the attendant are required.

The installation of a holdup system is relatively low in cost, particularly when it is incorporated into an existing burglar alarm system. Supervised wiring circuits are being widely used for 24-hour monitoring of the holdup switches and circuits to prevent tampering with the system. Other refinements include separate monitoring panels to alert guards or police to the exact whereabouts of the attempted holdup.

CASH HANDLING

Still another area in which standard security policies can be helpful in reducing and controlling criminal loss relates to the handling of cash. In evaluating the organization's cash-handling policies, the following should be considered.

First, the amount of cash on hand should be limited to the amount needed to meet actual requirements. Too many businesses allow cash to accumulate until it becomes convenient to go to the bank. As a result, if they have a loss, it is likely to be larger than necessary. It is not difficult to determine the maximum amount of cash on hand needed and then to bank it so that this level is not exceeded. Excess cash should be removed from the registers regularly.

Reasonable security measures should also be implemented for cash off-premises, such as when cash is being conveyed to the bank by a messenger. The messenger should avoid going to the bank at the same time and by the same route every day.

All checks should be stamped for deposit as soon as they are received. This will prevent a thief stealing one or anyone finding a lost check from cashing it. This policy should apply especially to payroll checks, government checks, and other checks where your business is not the payee.

SAFE SECURITY

Some people regard any metal box with a combination lock as a safe. Basically, there are two types—one for record storage and designed to protect against fire and one designed to protect against attack by burglars. Safes of fairly recent manufacture will usually carry an Underwriters Laboratory label. This label will tell how the safe is intended to protect plus a rating as to how well it will do its job. However, many safes are so old that they do not have this label, and although they look strong and fireproof, they may not be. Most businessmen pay little attention to the safe as long as the lock works, or they do not have a fire or burglary. In some types of business, a good safe will pay for itself in a few years through the reduction in insurance premiums. If the business holds considerable cash or valuables in the safe, it is in the owner's interest to see how well the reduction in insurance premiums would offset the cost of a suitable safe.

Unless there is an Underwriters Laboratory label, it is not always easy to determine a safe's burglar resistance. Some old safes are quite tough, whereas others that look equally strong can be opened with simple tools in 30 seconds. Safes with an Underwriters Laboratory label will indicate the safe's burglary-resistant rating, which is usually expressed as a delay time—the minimum period that it will require a burglar to penetrate the protection.

The safe, if there is one, should be fastened in place. One of the most common methods of safe burglary is to take the safe to a location where it can be worked on without interruption, and then even an unskilled thief can usually get it open, one way or another. The Underwriters require that a safe weigh at least 750 pounds for one classification or 1000 for another or that it be anchored down. It is a good practice to anchor even heavier safes if large amounts of money are kept. In one case a safe weighing 1500 pounds was moved several hundred feet on a hand truck especially designed by the burglars for the job.

In addition to being fastened in place, the safe should be placed where it is visible from the exterior. The safe can be put in the front window where the patrol car can see it every time it goes by. With some types of business, this is not practical, but if at all possible, it should be located so that it can be seen. If this cannot be done, the safe should carry a high rating, and an alarm system should be used if security is expected.

Some organizations—banks, for example—have a vault instead of a safe. Although vaults usually provide better protection against burglary, they may create additional risks. Ideally, the vault should have ventilation in case of lock-in. It is convenient for holdup men to lock employees and customers in the vault. If the door is tight, oxygen may be depleted before their plight is noted. In addition, it is good practice to have an alarm button inside the vault. This does not, however, serve as a substitute for a ventilation system, for there may be a delay in opening the vault.

The first rule in safe management is that the combination should be changed whenever there is a turnover in personnel and a person who leaves knows the combination. It is a simple matter to change a combination. The owner can change many modern safe combinations in just a few minutes using a special key. Other safes require a locksmith. But even if the owner can change the combination, it is a good idea to have a locksmith clean and check the combination every few years, for they do wear and get dirty. If this is not done, at some inopportune time the combination may fail to work and getting the safe open then can be expensive.

The number of persons who have access to the combination should be limited to those for whom the knowledge is absolutely necessary. Not every employee needs to know the combination, but unless it is treated as a carefully guarded secret, soon many people will know it. Equally important, it should not be written in a convenient place, such as the pull-out board on a desk.

Responsibility for locking the safe at night should be assigned as a specific duty to an individual or individuals. It seems logical that the safe would always be locked at night, but this does not always happen as police cases will attest. A closely related duty is to see that everything that should be in the safe is in it when it is locked. Some crime reports that show money missing out of a locked safe without a mark on it have turned out to be cases where the money was never placed in the safe.

In some instances, the safe should be locked not only at night, but in the daytime whenever access to the contents is not required. This is a sound practice for a number of reasons. The contents of many unlocked safes are often stolen during open hours, especially when the safe is in an office, a back room, or some other point where it is not readily seen. Employees, salesmen, deliverymen, or customers may take advantage of an unlocked safe. Even in the case of a robbery, opening the safe will delay the holdup, and some robbers may be in such a hurry that they will not even require it to be opened.

MERCHANDISE SECURITY (SHOPLIFTING)

Merchandise security relates to the shoplifting exposure. Shoplifting losses are second only to employee-dishonesty losses in magnitude. Standard merchandise security measures include the following.

Serial numbers on high-ticket items should be recorded. All television sets, cameras, watches, and other merchandise of the same model look exactly alike. The only difference is the serial number. If the serial numbers of merchandise are not recorded, the chances of recovering it if stolen are greatly reduced. It is very frustrating to the police to catch a known thief with a great deal of merchandise that they are sure is stolen, and then be unable to prove it was stolen because none of the serial numbers were recorded. On the other hand, through the use of serial numbers and computer systems, merchandise stolen months before and many states away has been recovered. Businesspeople should keep the serial numbers of items in stock, and as they are sold, drop those numbers from their inventory. In addition, they should keep the serial numbers of their office and other equipment, for they, too, can be stolen.

A standard loss control measure for high-value items on hangers is to alternate the direction in which the hangers are hung so that an armload can't be lifted off at one time. Most burglars and many shoplifters like to be able to grab an armload of merchandise at one time. If the hangers are alternated, they can't do this, and so maybe won't be able to steal as much. It's a simple thing to do, but helpful.

Shoplifting losses can also be controlled by limiting the access of customers, delivery persons, and others to stockrooms. In many business places, the stockroom is a regular shortcut for many people. It may even be an unofficial lounge. This is a bad practice, for all of that merchandise lying around is a temptation to some people. The fact that it can be easily stolen is compounded because it is often some time before an item is missed from the stockroom. You think you still have one more, and then miss a sale because you don't.

Little-used doors through which a thief might enter or leave undetected should be eliminated. Although it should be convenient to get in and out of a business place, this convenience should be balanced against the possible loss by theft. Sometimes back or side doors that are not used more than once or twice a day by customers should remain unlocked.

This inventory of loss control measures merely scratches the surface, but all the same it indicates the range of measures that are possible. The specific loss control measures that are required in a given situation depend on the value of the property to be protected and the frequency and severity of loss in the absence of protective measures.

Types of Shoplifters

Fortunately for their potential victims, the majority of shoplifters are amateurs rather than professionals. Juvenile offenders make up about 50 percent of all shoplifters, and there are indications that this type of offender is increasing. Juveniles steal "for kicks" or because they have been "dared" to do so. Other amateur shoplifters include adults who steal because of a momentary impulse, kleptomaniacs (who do not need the items they pick up), and narcotic addicts or vagrants.

The professional shoplifters are the most difficult type to detect and apprehend, mainly because they are clever at their craft. When they enter the store, professional shoplifters often pretend that they are shopping for a gift. The professional shoplifter is in business for money, not for the items that may be stolen. They usually steal to resell the loot to established fences. Often, the professional shoplifter has been caught before and will have a police record. Because they are experienced, professional shoplifters will be discouraged if they detect that anti-shoplifting measures are in effect.

Notifying Police

Regardless of the type of shoplifter, the common answer that most shoplifters give when caught is: "I have never done this before." Failure to prosecute "first offenders" encourages shoplifting. It is best to operate on the premise that he who steals will also lie, and the standard operating procedure should be to call the police. When a merchant (or all merchants) follow the policy of prosecuting shoplifters, word gets around. Hardened professionals are deterred, and amateurs will think twice before yielding to the temptation to pocket a choice item.

Protective Personnel and Devices

In reducing shoplifting losses, the deterrent factor is all important. Protective devices help to discourage borderline shoplifters—those who don't steal unless the coast is clear—and to trap bold ones. Among these devices are two-way mirrors, peepholes, closed-circuit television, radio communication, and detectives posing as customers. Some large stores use uniformed guards and plain-clothes personnel who serve as a reminder to patrons that only legally purchased merchandise may be removed from the premises. One way to identify such merchandise is to use stapled packages with receipts attached outside.

The most effective deterrents to shoplifting are the electronic devices now available which expose the shoplifter by sounding an alarm when goods are stolen. The earliest versions of these devices were electronic pellets or wafers attached to garments so that they could not be removed without tearing the merchandise. If a shopper tried to remove the garment from the store, the pellet or wafer sent out signals. The cashier removed the pellet with special shears when the customer purchased the garment. Newer versions of these electronic devices can be attached to virtually any type of property and desensitized only at checkout counters.

OTHER PHYSICAL SECURITY MEASURES

Guards

For some installations, security personnel represent an important element in the security control program. Security personnel may range from watchmen to a uniformed security force to plain-clothes security personnel. Guards have been generally recognized throughout the private sector and the government as an essential element in the protection of assets and personnel.

If the organization has a security force, it should, of course, be properly trained, and corporate policies relating to the responsibilities and conduct of the guards should be well defined. An improperly trained security force and the absence of policies relating to security activities can involve the organization in litigation for violation of the rights of individuals. Thirty-eight states and the District of Columbia and Puerto Rico now have laws regulating private security operations. These laws regulate such things as formal training of security personnel and the use of lethal and nonlethal weapons.

Use of Dogs for Asset Protection

A dog utilized for protection purposes represents a great psychological deterrent to potential violators, and the mere fact that an animal is present in an area will serve as an effective preventive measure. Obviously, guard dogs must be properly trained, and their use should be appropriate to the organization's overall security needs. There are some exposures—such as guarding warehouses or other facilities—for which guard dogs are ideally suited. In some instances, the dogs are used with handlers, whereas in other situations they may be used without handlers. One area in which guard dogs are extremely effective is in helping to locate and then hold violators after an area has been penetrated.

As valuable as dogs are for protection purposes, it should be kept in mind, as with all other protection techniques, that their use may create other hazards. Because dogs do not distinguish between criminal and noncriminal intruders, their use should be announced by appropriate signs indicating that guard dogs are in use in the premises. Signs of this type serve two functions. First, they serve as a deterrent to criminals and, second, they serve as a warning to innocent persons.

Although some organizations maintain their own guard dogs, many organizations contract with an outside vendor to provide guard dog service. In many major cities, firms lease trained dogs for security purposes. In these areas, trucks and vans can be seen daily delivering guard dogs to car lots, warehouses, construction sites, and a variety of other facilities where they are released without handlers to protect property during nonworking hours.

Closed-Circuit Television

Television equipment may be used in conjunction with an alarm system or independently. In many cases the principal use is as a deterrent to crime. The equipment may be used to produce a photographic record, or it may be part of a closed-circuit television system that permits remote viewing of a situation, condition, or activity. The viewing might be in real time, as when a security console operator observes the condition simultaneously with its occurrence; or it might be delayed, as when a videotape is made for later viewing; or it might be both immediate and delayed. This third case is becoming the typical security model. A scene is viewed in real time by an operator and a videotape is also made for later review by others.

Financial institutions universally employ video recording systems, and an increasing number of retailers have adopted video recorders to deter robbery. Another application of photographic records is to deter bad check writers. A popular model camera automatically takes a picture of the check, the identification presented, and the individual cashing the check. The principal effect of these techniques is to serve as deterrents.

❖ Computer Security ■

Criminal acts directed at a firm's computers or computer system represent a type of loss that cannot be classified neatly into the *employee crime* and *nonemployee crime* dichotomy.

Computer security originally focused on protecting computer mainframe installations against damage by sabotage, industrial espionage and the loss of corporate secrets, and unauthorized access that could be used for embezzlement. The standard techniques were to treat the centralized computer facility as a restricted area to which access was limited. State of the art fire detection and suppression systems were an integral feature of every installation, and security of data media was achieved through the use of fire and heat resistive vaults and off-premises storage of duplicate copies of the media. While these techniques remain an important part of computer security, they are now only one element in a total computer security system. What has changed is the nature of computer systems and the growth of distributed data processing. With the proliferation of personal computers and the growth of networks—including external networks—access to computer facilities that was previously denied by physical barriers is now achieved electronically. Consequently, the nature of computer security has changed. Today, computer crime is a major threat to all organizations that depend on computers. The threat to organizations from this source has initiated a competition between computer security specialists and those who would use computers for personal gain at the expense of others.

Today, the computer security measures required depend on the organization and its computer operations. Different measures are required for the protection of mainframe computers, minicomputers, personal computers, and local area networks. For each type of operations, the threat and the response will differ. In general, however, the threats related to computers can be classified into four general classes:

- loss of or damage to the computer system itself.
- system outages.
- theft of money or property after penetrating the system.
- theft of proprietary information or corporate secrets.

Although our primary concern here is with respect to the threats arising out of criminal acts, we include loss or damage to the system and system outages that result from criminal acts. Criminal acts, in this context, include the unique form of electronic vandalism in which the objective is to sabotage the system. The damage may be caused by a disgruntled employee, or it may be a stranger whose gain is the satisfaction in penetrating the system. In either case, the result can be a serious disruption of operations and financial loss to the organization. Computer viruses are a variation of the vandalism threat.

Theft of money, property, and information requires access to a computer. In some cases the access is granted because the individual is an employee. An employee who is computer-knowledgeable may be able to manipulate the system in a way that not only permits theft from the employer, but conceals the theft. In addition to theft and fraud by employees, outsiders who penetrate the system can transfer assets to their accounts and electronically "wipe out" their footprints.

Because computer security is highly specialized field that depends heavily on expertise, the computer security system should logically be designed by specialists. The level of expertise required will depend on the complexity of the system and the potential loss if it is successfully penetrated. The specialists who are charged with the design of the computer security system may be staff employees or it may be necessary to retain a consultant. In either case, the success of the system will depend on the extent to which employees incorporate the security standards into their daily operations. An additional measure is to ensure that the external accounting auditors who have been trained as programmers are experts in checking all phases of a computerized system to detect fraud. Computerized embezzling is more difficult to detect than the traditional version of embezzlement. An audit program can be conducted by persons who are knowledgeable in the computer area.

Terrorism and Bomb Threats ■ ■ ■ ■ ■ ■ ■ ■ ■ ■ ■ ■ ■ ■ ■

It is difficult to decide exactly where the subject of bomb threats and terrorism should be discussed. Because many of the control measures designed to thwart terrorists are similar to those aimed at crime, it seems logical to discuss the topic here, as a part of the general discussion on crime loss control measures.[5]

Although the threat of terrorist bombs was once considered a threat primarily in connection with foreign operations, the bombing of the World Trade Center in New York City on February 26, 1993, raised the specter of terrorism in America. The subsequent explosion of a 4,800-pound fertilizer bomb at the Alfred P. Murrah Federal Building in Oklahoma City on April 19, 1995, killed 168 people and wounded many others, forever shattering the assumption that "it can't happen here."

The threat of terrorism, which can include bomb threats, product tampering, and kidnapping, have become a part of the portfolio of pure risks with which the risk manager must be concerned. Because bombs are the terrorist's weapon of preference, many of the techniques that are used to protect sensitive facilities are also useful as anti-terrorist measures. However, anti-terrorism is a highly specialized field, and we will not even attempt to list the complex and extensive features of an anti-terrorist program. For the organization that is a potential target for such attacks, the recommended approach is to retain the services of a professional security consulting firm. There are a number of specialist security companies that can provide practical guidance in connection with virtually any aspect of terrorism. Even those organizations with an in-house security system will benefit from the advice and counsel of specialists in this area.

[5]A related risk that poses the same problem with respect to where it should be discussed is kidnapping. The kidnapping risk is discussed in Chapter 28.

Although the design of anti-terrorist efforts are the domain of the specialist, a properly designed disaster plan will provide for an appropriate response to a range of disasters, including a terrorist threat or actual bombing. Even when the disaster plan is not conceived with terrorism in mind, the planning and emergency organization will help to minimize the after effects of the disaster.

Outside Crime Control Services ■ ■ ■ ■ ■ ■ ■ ■ ■ ■ ■ ■ ■ ■

Outside security professionals are a valuable source of assistance in designing anti-crime loss-prevention and control measures. In addition to the specialists in computer security and anti-terrorist measures we have noted, professional advice on internal controls is advisable. Advice on internal controls is provided by certified public accountants.

The three largest security firms are Pinkerton, Burns, and Wackenhut, with offices across the nation and abroad. They provide every kind of security service, including electronic surveillance, guard service, pre-employment investigation, hand writing experts, workers compensation and insurance claims investigation, as well as security consultation. In addition to these firms, many local firms can also provide security assistance. Moreover, outside auditors can be very useful in pinpointing weaknesses in internal controls. Yet, organizations that supply security services *and* counsel may not provide objective counsel because of their conflict of interest. If counsel is needed, an attempt should be made to obtain such advice from a source that cannot profit from the recommendations.

Last but not least, an important source of assistance for small businesses is a crime prevention program conducted by local police. Crime prevention programs in police departments are relatively new, but many police departments offer advice to business on methods of crime prevention.

SECURITY STANDARDS

One of the most widely circulated sources of security standards is the *Industrial Security Manual* (ISM) of the Department of Defense. This document is intended for use by firms that have contracts with any of the military departments and that must have access to classified defense information for that purpose. Although the ISM is mandatory only for those suppliers, it contains a great wealth of security information that may be useful to business organizations. The ISM is supplied directly to the regulated contractors, but is available to anyone else through the U.S. Government Printing Office.

Although the ISM is intended to assure protection of classified defense information, it is an excellent model for the development of programs to protect any proprietary information. It is not suggested that nondefense firms adopt it in its procedural entirety. Indeed, over the years, there has been much criticism that the ISM is burdensome in many areas, chiefly because of its procedural requirements. However, the general scheme of protection it describes is valid and sound, and could save an inexperienced manager many hours. Its sections dealing with the handling of information, control of areas, visitor control procedures, and graphic arts are of special value.

In addition to the Department of Defense ISM, statutory loss-prevention standards apply to certain banks and financial institutions. The Bank Protection Act of 1968 gave four federal agencies (the Federal Reserve System, the Federal Home Loan Bank Board, the Federal Deposit Insurance Corporation, and the Controller of the Currency) authority to make regulations concerning the security practices of the banking and financial institutions that they regulate. These agencies have published regulations relating to intrusion and robbery alarm systems, lighting, locks, surveillance, and vault and safe requirements. Although these regulations are binding only on the regulated banks and institutions, they represent useful guidance for all institutions concerned with the protection of cash and negotiable instruments.[6]

IMPORTANT CONCEPTS TO REMEMBER

robbery	perimeter alarm system	microwave alarm system
burglary	partial perimeter alarm system	point or spot alarm system
theft		
forgery	complete perimeter alarm system	local station alarm
bad check losses		central alarm system
deterrence	area or space alarm system	remote station alarm
internal control		proprietary alarm system
barriers	ultrasonic system	virus

QUESTIONS FOR REVIEW

1. Identify the two broad categories into which crime exposures are traditionally classified.

2. Identify and briefly distinguish among the common crime perils that are directed against businesses.

3. Of the various crime perils facing the organization, which has the greatest potential severity? Why?

4. Describe the two ways in which risk control measures directed at preventing crime can be effective in reducing criminal losses. Which of the effects is probably the most significant?

5. What are the four basic elements of an effective internal control system identified in the text? Identify the areas of a firm's internal control system for which specific control measures are recommended and cite a method of loss control that can reduce or deter loss for each of the four areas.

---

[6]Another excellent reference for banking security standards and bank security in general is *Bank Security Desk Reference*, 2nd ed., with supplement by Richard F. Cross, CPP, published by Warren, Gorham and Lamont, Inc., Boston, Mass.

6. Identify and distinguish among the types of alarm systems discussed in the chapter and the alarm transmission systems. What are the advantages and disadvantages of each type?

7. Explain what is meant by the term internal control and identify the four elements of an effective internal control system.

8. Identify the four types of loss related to computer systems and describe the loss control measures that may be employed to reduce the frequency or severity of such loss.

9. Identify two areas in which it may be desirable for an organization to seek assistance from an outside security specialist.

10. Which of the risk control measures discussed in connection with the non-employee crime exposure are likely to be effective in an antiterrorist program?

QUESTIONS FOR DISCUSSION

1. What elements of the employee dishonesty exposure make it difficult to estimate the size of the loss that can occur? In what way does the fidelity exposure differ from other property exposures?

2. Why is the crime exposure considered to be particularly susceptible to treatment by risk control measures?

3. Cite two risk control measures discussed in the chapter that may be classified as pre-event, event, or post event measures.

4. The text describes four types of loss that may arise in connection with an organization's computer system. Describe the computer security measures used by the college or university in which are you enrolled and identify the type of loss against which these measures are directed. What computer security measures do you personally use and which of the four types of loss are these measures designed to prevent?

5. Which of the crime exposures discussed in the chapter are most susceptible to retention? Which of the exposures are the most likely candidates for transfer?

SUGGESTIONS FOR ADDITIONAL READING

Bradford, Michael, Douglas McLeod, and Mark H. Hoffman, "Shock Waves From Bombing Losses." *Business Insurance*, (April 24, 1995).

Dobbs, Peter. "Postwar Terrorism Triggers Insurance Dilemma," *Risk Management* (June 1991).

Krauss, Leonard I., and MacGahan, Aileen, *Computer Fraud and Countermeasures*. (Englewood Cliffs, N.J.: Prentice-Hall, 1979).

Moeller Robert. *Computer Audit, Control, and Security*, (Boca Raton, Fl.: CRC Press, 1989).

Ralston, August R., ed. *Risk Management Manual*, Santa Monica, Ca.: (loose-leaf service with monthly supplements), vol. 1, section 3. "Computer Center Risk Control," "The White Collar Crime Problem and Business," "Embezzler and Bankruptcy Fraud," and "Crime by Computer."

Walsh, Timothy J., *Protection of Assets* Santa Monica, Ca.: The Merritt Company (loose leaf service with monthly supplements).

CHAPTER 20

Managing Crime Risks: Risk Finance

CHAPTER OBJECTIVES

When you have finished this chapter, you should be able to

Differentiate between the two broad classes of crime insurance and explain
the general nature of each.

■

Explain the difference among the crime perils of robbery, burglary, and theft.

■

Interpret major features of the fidelity bonds, including the provisions
relating to thefts that occur prior to the inception of the bond.

■

Be able to determine the minimum level of fidelity coverage that is appropriate for a
business or other organization based on the financial characteristics of the organization.

■

Differentiate among the standard forms of nonemployee crime coverage and be able
to select the appropriate form for a particular exposure.

■ Introduction ■

The broad field of crime insurance includes all cases in which the cause of the loss
is the wrongful taking of property belonging to the insured. Historical development led to the development of two distinct classes of dishonesty coverages:

1. Fidelity bonds, which are designed to cover theft or dishonesty on the part of
   employees of the insured.

2. Nonemployee crime coverages, which are designed to cover dishonest acts of persons who are not employees of the insured.

Each of these classes provides incomplete protection against the peril of dishonesty. In order to provide more complete protection, they must be combined, so it is appropriate to discuss them together. The artificial distinction between "employee" and "nonemployee" dishonesty insurance is gradually disappearing; with the advent of package policies, both types of criminal losses are frequently insured in the same contract.

With the development of multiple line underwriting, the coverage of open-peril fire insurance forms has been expanded to include loss by theft. This has resulted in a decrease in the level of monoline nonemployee crime insurance. Increasingly, the exposures of burglary, robbery, and theft of merchandise and equipment are insured under fire policies. Virtually all property forms, however, exclude losses due to employee dishonesty. In addition, fire policies (and now the Portfolio property forms) exclude money and securities. The need to cover loss of property from employee dishonesty, and the need for open-peril coverage on money and securities, still require separate contracts, generally classified as crime insurance. In addition, other crime forms exist to cover the traditional crime perils of burglary, robbery, and theft, even though these perils are often covered under open-peril property policies.

The Portfolio Crime Coverage Forms ▪ ▪ ▪ ▪ ▪ ▪ ▪ ▪ ▪ ▪ ▪

As a part of its revision and simplification of the commercial lines forms, ISO introduced a new set of commercial crime forms in 1986. Like other commercial portfolio forms, the Portfolio Commercial Crime monoline policy is composed of modular parts.

The Crime Coverage forms describe the subject of insurance, designating whether the coverage applies to money and securities, to all property, or to property other than money and securities. In addition, they describe the perils for which the insured property is covered. The coverage forms also describe any Coverage Extensions, and indicate the Limit of Insurance and Deductible provisions. Finally, the coverage forms contain additional exclusions, conditions, and definitions that are not contained in the Common Conditions or the Crime General Provision forms.

There are seventeen Crime Coverage forms (actually eighteen, since Coverage Form A, which covers employee dishonesty has two versions—one that provides blanket coverage and another schedule coverage). Fourteen forms were included in the original simplified portfolio crime program that was introduced in 1986. Three additional forms were added in 1990.

In general, the new coverage forms parallel the crime policies that existed at the time the portfolio program was introduced, although there have been some important modifications in the coverage. The new crime forms are presented in Table 20.1.

Table 20.1   Portfolio Crime Coverage Forms

Coverage Form A	Employee Dishonesty
Coverage Form B	Forgery or Alteration
Coverage Form C	Theft, Disappearance, and Destruction
Coverage Form D	Robbery and Safe Burglary
Coverage Form E	Premises Burglary
Coverage Form F	Computer Fraud
Coverage Form G	Extortion
Coverage Form H	Premises Theft and Robbery Outside the Premises
Coverage Form I	Lessees of Safe Deposit Boxes
Coverage Form J	Securities Deposited with Others Form
Coverage Form K	Liability for Guests' Property-Safe Deposit Box
Coverage Form L	Liability for Guests' Property-Premises
Coverage Form M	Safe Depository Liability
Coverage Form N	Safe Depository Direct Loss
Coverage Form O	Public Employee Dishonesty Per Loss
Coverage Form P	Public Employee Dishonesty Per Employee
Coverage Form Q	Robbery and Safe Burglary—Money and Securities

CRIME COVERAGE GENERAL PROVISIONS FORM

The Crime General Provisions Form (CR 10 00) contains General Exclusions, General Conditions, and General Definitions that apply to all Crime Coverage forms except certain Innkeepers Liability and Safe Depository forms (which have their own general provisions). Before turning to our examination of the individual coverage forms, we will briefly examine the Crime General Provisions form, which is used with both employee and nonemployee crime coverages. The Crime General Provisions form contains six general exclusions, 18 general conditions, and four exclusions. These exclusions, conditions, and definitions were historically included in the individual crime coverage parts. Under the simplified program, they are included only once, in the Crime General Provisions form.

General Exclusions

Six general exclusions are contained in the Crime Policy General Provisions form, most of which were used in the previous crime coverage forms.

1. Loss resulting from dishonesty or criminal acts by the insured or any partner while acting alone or in collusion with others.

2. Loss resulting from seizure or destruction of property by order of government authority.

3. Indirect or consequential loss resulting from any covered event, such as the cost of audits to establish the amount of the loss or loss of income that would have been earned except for the loss.

4. Expenses related to any legal action.

5. Loss resulting from nuclear reaction, radiation, or radioactive contamination.

6. Loss resulting from war, whether or not declared, warlike action, insurrection, rebellion, or revolution.

In addition to these general exclusions, the individual coverage forms include additional exclusions that are pertinent to the particular coverage being provided by the individual form.

General Conditions

The Crime General Conditions form lists 18 conditions. Most of these conditions deal with general agreements, such as the insured's duties in the event of loss, coverage in the event of merger (additional employees of the merged firm are automatically covered for 30 days), and the policy territory (United States, Canada, the Virgin Islands, Puerto Rico, and the Canal Zone). The following provisions are noteworthy.

Discovery Period for Loss   The insurer is liable only for losses discovered within one year of the end of the policy period.

Loss Sustained During Prior Insurance   The Loss Sustained During Prior Insurance clause provides a form of "discovery" coverage when the bond in force replaces a prior bond without a break in coverage. Prior to the portfolio program, bonds were written on a continuous basis and ran until canceled. Because the crime must, in general, occur and be discovered during the term of the bond for coverage to apply, the continuous bond made sense. Under the portfolio program, however, bonds, like other coverages, are written for a specified term. To provide continuity of coverage, the Loss Sustained During Prior Insurance provision stipulates that coverage is provided for loss that occurred during a prior bond but that is not covered because the period during which the loss must have been discovered has expired. This provision applies only if there has been absolutely no gap in coverage between the termination of the prior bond and the inception of the existing bond.

Note that the continuity of coverage is maintained even if the bond in force has replaced a bond of another insurer. This assumption of coverage by a subsequent insurer was originally called the Superseded Suretyship provision. It provides continuity of coverage when the insured changes insurers. Subject to certain restrictions, this clause provides that if a bond is replaced by another with a different company, the succeeding insurer becomes liable for losses that occurred during the term of the first bond. This provision applies only when there is absolutely no lapse in coverage from the old bond to the new and the loss is discovered after the end of the discovery period of the old bond. If the amounts of the bonds differ, the lower penalty will apply. Insurers are willing to pick up coverage for losses under prior bonds because in the absence of such a provision, it would be difficult if not impossible for bonding companies to compete for new business. In the absence of such a provision, an insured would be penalized by changing insurers, since he or she would forfeit coverage for any losses that had occurred but had not yet been discovered. The Loss Under Prior Bond provision guarantees the insured against a break in coverage when changing bonding companies.

Noncumulation of Limit of Insurance   The limit of insurance is not cumulative from year to year. This is an important limitation, because employee infidelity can take place over an extended period of time, and all thefts by a given employee are considered a single loss.

Recoveries   This is the "salvage" provision of the policy. It states that if the insured sustains a loss exceeding the amount of coverage under the bond, he or she will be entitled to any recoveries from the embezzler in excess of the limit of insurance and amount of the deductible. Recoveries in excess of this amount go to the insurer, until the insurer is fully reimbursed. Finally, recoveries in excess of the insurer's reimbursement go to the insured, up to the amount of the deductible.

Transfer of the Insured's Rights of Recovery Against Others   This is the standard subrogation clause and requires the insured to transfer to the insurer all rights of recovery against others to the extent that the insurer has made payment. The insured must do everything necessary to secure right of recovery against others and shall do nothing after a loss to impair that right.

Valuation   Different valuation provisions apply to different classes of property. Money is valued at more than its face value. Foreign money is valued at either its face value or its value in U. S. dollars at the rate of exchange for the day the loss is discovered. Securities are valued at not more than their worth at the close of the day on which the loss is discovered. The insurer reserves the right to pay for the loss of the securities or replace them. Property other than money and securities is valued, at the option of the insurer, at its actual cash value or the cost of repairing or replacing the property.

▰ Employee Crime Coverages ■ ■ ■ ■ ■ ■ ■ ■ ■ ■ ■ ■ ■ ■ ■ ■

Each year, thefts by employees amount to several times the amount lost by burglary, robbery, and other forms of larceny. Less than 10 percent of these losses are insured. Coverage for loss by employee dishonesty is covered under contracts called *fidelity bonds,* which cover loss or damage to money, securities, or other property, resulting from the dishonest acts of the person bonded, up to the face amount of the bond, which is called the "Penalty."

The penalty under a bond is never cumulative from year to year. The dishonesty must occur after the inception of the bond and must be discovered while the bond is in force or within a designated "discovery period" following termination of the bond. However, there are exceptions to this general principle, as explained later in the text.

Coverage can exist for losses that occurred prior to inception and that would have been covered under a prior bond which the existing bond replaced. In addition, a bond may be written on a "discovery" basis, in which case losses that occurred prior to inception are covered if they are discovered during the coverage period of the bond. A bond written on a "discovery basis" will cover a loss that occurred prior to the inception of the bond, if the loss is discovered during the bond or during the discovery period.

Coverage under a fidelity bond may apply to specifically designated individuals, to persons occupying specified positions, or to all employees. The mode of coverage depends on whether the bond is written on a name schedule basis, a position basis, or a blanket basis.

Form A: Employee Dishonesty

Coverage Form A, Employee Dishonesty, provides fidelity bond coverage to protect against loss resulting from employees' dishonesty, and covers loss of money, securities, or other property resulting from acts (fraud, forgery, embezzlement, theft) by persons bonded, up to the face amount of the bond, which is called the penalty. The dishonesty must occur while the bond is in force, although a provision called the "discovery period" stipulates that losses detected within a stated period after the bond terminates (usually one year) will be covered if the loss took place during the bond period. Coverage is written on both a blanket and a scheduled basis.

Employee Dishonesty Blanket Coverage   Coverage Form A Blanket basis (CR 00 01) is the most attractive approach to fidelity coverage for the organization. Under this approach, coverage is designed to cover all employees, regardless of position, with new employees covered automatically. Coverage applies to dishonest acts of employees, whether or not the employee is identified. In contrast, as noted below, the scheduled form requires that the dishonest employee be identified. The coverage is subject to a one-year discovery period.

Definition of Employee   One of the important determinants of coverage under the employee crime forms is, of course, the definition of employee. The term is defined as follows:

The term employee is defined to include:

A. Any natural person
   1. while in your service (and for 30 days after termination of service);
   2. whom you compensate directly by salary, wages, or commissions; and

3. whom you have the right to direct and control while performing services for you.

B. Any natural person employed by an employment contractor while that person is subject to your direction and control and performing services for you, excluding, however,
any such person while having care and custody of property outside the "premises."
But employee does not mean any:

1. Agent, broker, factor, commission merchant, consignee, independent contractor or
representation of the same general contractor; or

2. Director or trustee except while performing acts coming within the scope of the
usual duties of an employee.

Although the definition might appear to be quite comprehensive, there are significant omissions. First, manufacturers representatives are not considered employees. In addition, directors and trustees of the insured are not "employees" of the
insured unless they are compensated by the insured, and then only while there are
performing acts that are the normal duties of an employee. Standard endorsements are available to add these persons to the definition of "employee."

Coverage may also be extended to cover the trustee of the insured's qualified
pension plan. The Employee Retirement Income Security Act (ERISA) requires
that persons handling funds for pension and welfare plans be bonded. Although
such persons would not fit the above definition (unless they were also employees
of the insured), a standard endorsement is available to broaden the definition of
"employee" to include persons handling welfare or pension funds.

Application of Penalty   The "penalty" (or limit of coverage) under the Blanket
Employee Dishonesty Coverage form applies on a "per loss" basis rather than "per
employee." This means that if several employees are involved in a collusive loss, the
maximum payable for that loss is the limit specified.[1]

Employee Dishonesty Schedule Coverage   The second approach to fidelity coverage
is provided under Coverage Form A Schedule (CR 00 02), which may be written on
either a name schedule basis or a position schedule basis. When fidelity coverage is
written on an individual name basis, the person to be bonded is specifically named.
When several persons are listed in a single bond, it is known as a Name Schedule
Bond. Under a Position Schedule Bond, positions to be covered are listed rather
than the individuals. If a person leaves the firm or moves to another position, his
or her successor is covered in the scheduled position. When more individuals
occupy a scheduled position than the number originally specified, all are covered

[1]Prior to the introduction of the new portfolio crime forms, there were two forms of blanket bond,
the Commercial Blanket Bond and the Blanket Position Bond. The principal difference between the
two was the manner in which the penalty applied to loss. Under the Commercial Blanket Bond, the face
amount of the bond applied on a "per loss" basis, whereas the Blanket Position Bond applied on a "per
employee" basis. The new portfolio Employee Dishonesty Blanket Coverage form follows the format of
the Commercial Blanket Bond.

but on a decreased basis. For example, if the bond provides for two cashiers with a $10,000 penalty on each, and there are actually four cashiers, loss by any of the four would be covered but only up to $5,000 each. For coverage to exist under the scheduled form of coverage, the dishonest act must have been committed by an identified employee.

Exclusions   In addition to the exclusions in the Crime General form already noted, Coverage Form A contains two additional exclusions.

1. There is no coverage for loss caused by an employee for whom coverage has been canceled under the policy or a similar policy and not reinstated. An important provision in this respect is the condition relating to cancellation of an employee's coverage. The policy states that coverage is canceled on any employee upon discovery by the insured or a partner, officer, or director not in collusion with the employee, of any dishonest act committed by the employee before or after becoming an employee of the insured.

2. There is no coverage for any loss or part of a loss, the existence of which can be proved only by a profit and loss computation or an inventory.

Determining Fidelity Limits

The fact that all thefts by an individual are considered to be a single loss, regardless of the period of time over which the loss occurs, combined with the fact that the penalty under a fidelity bond is noncumulative from year to year, makes it difficult to select a fidelity limit that will protect against the worst possible loss. Some years ago, the American Institute of Certified Public Accountants and the Surety Association of America developed a Dishonesty Exposure Index, to be used in determining the level of fidelity coverage that should be purchased by corporations. Actually, there are three separate indexes, one for manufacturers and retailers, one for commercial banks, and one for public bodies. Based on selected variables from the organization's financial statement, an index is calculated which, through reference to a table, indicates the minimum level of fidelity coverage that should be purchased. The Dishonesty Exposure Indexes for manufacturers and retailers, commercial banks, and public entities are reproduced in the three accompanying tables.

Table 20.2 indicates the minimum limits of fidelity coverage for manufacturing and mercantile establishments for various levels of the Dishonesty Exposure Index. The Index for these classes is based on the value of goods on hand, current assets other than goods on hand, and gross annual sales. The Dishonest Exposure Index for commercial banks is in Table 20.3. For commercial banks, the Index is based on the bank's deposits. Finally, the Dishonesty Exposure Index for public bodies (such as municipalities, school districts, and other political subdivisions) is presented in Table 20.4. For public bodies, the Dishonesty Exposure Index is based on total annual receipts from all sources and the market value of all negotiable securities held by the public body.

Table 20.2   Determining Fidelity Bond Limits: Mercantile and Manufacturing Firms

5% of the value of goods on hand: $ _____

20% of current assets other than goods on hand: $ _____

10% of annual gross sales: $ _____

    Dishonesty Exposure Index: $ _____

    Minimum fidelity coverage limit: $ _____

Exposure Index			Bracket	Minimum Fidelity Coverage		
Less than		$25,000	1	$15,000	to	$25,000
$25,000	to	125,000	2	25,000	to	50,000
125,000	to	250,000	3	50,000	to	75,000
250,000	to	500,000	4	75,000	to	100,000
500,000	to	750,000	5	100,000	to	125,000
750,000	to	1,000,000	6	125,000	to	150,000
1,000,000	to	1,375,000	7	150,000	to	175,000
1,375,000	to	1,750,000	8	175,000	to	200,000
1,750,000	to	2,125,000	9	200,000	to	225,000
2,125,000	to	2,500,000	10	225,000	to	250,000
2,500,000	to	3,325,000	11	250,000	to	300,000
3,325,000	to	4,175,000	12	300,000	to	350,000
4,175,000	to	5,000,000	13	350,000	to	400,000
5,000,000	to	6,075,000	14	400,000	to	450,000
6,075,000	to	7,150,000	15	450,000	to	500,000
7,150,000	to	9,275,000	16	500,000	to	600,000
9,275,000	to	11,125,000	17	600,000	to	700,000
11,125,000	to	15,000,000	18	700,000	to	800,000
15,000,000	to	20,000,000	19	800,000	to	900,000
20,000,000	to	25,000,000	20	900,000	to	1,000,000
25,000,000	to	50,000,000	21	1,000,000	to	1,250,000
50,000,000	to	87,500,000	22	1,250,000	to	1,500,000
87,500,000	to	125,000,000	23	1,500,000	to	1,750,000
125,000,000	to	187,500,000	24	1,750,000	to	2,000,000
187,500,000	to	250,000,000	25	2,000,000	to	2,250,000
250,000,000	to	333,325,000	26	2,250,000	to	2,500,000
333,325,000	to	500,000,000	27	2,500,000	to	3,000,000
500,000,000	to	750,000,000	28	3,000,000	to	3,500,000
750,000,000	to	1,000,000,000	29	3,500,000	to	4,000,000
1,000,000,000	to	1,250,000,000	30	4,000,000	to	4,500,000
1,250,000,000	to	1,500,000,000	31	4,500,000	to	5,000,000

Table 20.3   Determining Fidelity Bond Limits: Banks

Total Deposits	$
Dishonesty Exposure Index	$
Minimum fidelity coverage limit	$

Bank's Deposits			Bracket	Minimum Fidelity Coverage		
Less than		$750,000	1	$25,000	to	$50,000
$750,000	to	1,500,000	2	50,000	to	75,000
1,500,000	to	2,000,000	3	75,000	to	90,000
2,000,000	to	3,000,000	4	90,000	to	120,000
3,000,000	to	5,000,000	5	120,000	to	150,000
5,000,000	to	7,500,000	6	150,000	to	175,000
7,500,000	to	10,000,000	7	175,000	to	200,000
10,000,000	to	15,000,000	8	200,000	to	250,000
15,000,000	to	20,000,000	9	250,000	to	300,000
20,000,000	to	25,000,000	10	300,000	to	350,000
25,000,000	to	35,000,000	11	350,000	to	450,000
35,000,000	to	50,000,000	12	450,000	to	550,000
50,000,000	to	75,000,000	13	550,000	to	700,000
75,000,000	to	100,000,000	14	700,000	to	850,000
100,000,000	to	150,000,000	15	850,000	to	1,200,000
150,000,000	to	250,000,000	16	1,200,000	to	1,700,000
250,000,000	to	500,000,000	17	1,700,000	to	2,500,000
500,000,000	to	1,000,000,000	18	2,500,000	to	4,000,000
1,000,000,000	to	2,000,000,000	19	4,000,000	to	6,000,000
Over $2,000,000,000			20	$6,000,000 and up		

Table 20.4   Determining Fidelity Bond Limits: Public Bodies

10% of total annual receipts $ _____
20% of market value of all negotiable
      securities held $ _____
      Dishonesty Exposure Index $ _____
      Minimum fidelity coverage limit $ _____

Exposure Index			Bracket	Minimum Fidelity Coverage		
Up to		$25,000	1	$15,000	to	$25,000
$25,000	to	125,000	2	25,000	to	50,000
125,000	to	250,000	3	50,000	to	75,000
250,000	to	500,000	4	75,000	to	100,000
500,000	to	750,000	5	100,000	to	125,000
750,000	to	1,000,000	6	125,000	to	150,000
1,000,000	to	1,375,000	7	150,000	to	175,000
1,375,000	to	1,750,000	8	175,000	to	200,000
1,750,000	to	2,125,000	9	200,000	to	225,000
2,125,000	to	2,500,000	10	225,000	to	250,000
2,500,000	to	3,325,000	11	250,000	to	300,000
3,325,000	to	4,175,000	12	300,000	to	350,000
4,175,000	to	5,000,000	13	350,000	to	400,000
5,000,000	to	6,075,000	14	400,000	to	450,000
6,075,000	to	7,150,000	15	450,000	to	500,000
7,150,000	to	9,275,000	16	500,000	to	600,000
9,275,000	to	11,125,000	17	600,000	to	700,000
11,125,000	to	15,000,000	18	700,000	to	800,000
15,000,000	to	20,000,000	19	800,000	to	900,000
20,000,000	to	25,000,000	20	900,000	to	1,000,000
25,000,000	to	50,000,000	21	1,000,000	to	1,250,000
50,000,000	to	87,500,000	22	1,250,000	to	1,500,000
87,500,000	to	125,000,000	23	1,500,000	to	1,750,000
125,000,000	to	187,500,000	24	1,750,000	to	2,000,000
187,500,000	to	250,000,000	25	2,000,000	to	2,250,000
250,000,000	to	333,325,000	26	2,250,000	to	2,500,000
333,325,000	to	500,000,000	27	2,500,000	to	3,000,000

⊞ Nonemployee Crime Coverages ■ ■ ■ ■ ■ ■ ■ ■ ■ ■ ■ ■ ■ ■

Policies designed to cover against loss of money or other property through dishonest acts of persons other than employees are classified according to peril. Some policies protect against burglary, robbery, theft, forgery, and so on. Only the specified type of criminal activity indicated is covered, and coverage exists only when the loss occurs under conditions that meet the policy definition of the crime. For example, burglary consists of stealing property when the premises are not open for business and requires forcible entry into the premises. Insurance policies covering loss by burglary typically require visible evidence of forcible entry into the premises or forcible exit. Robbery, on the other hand, consists of taking property by violence or threat of violence. Theft, which is much broader in meaning than either burglary or robbery, includes any illegal taking of property, thus embracing both burglary and robbery.

Form B: Forgery or Alteration Coverage

Forgery or Alteration coverage promises to pay for loss sustained by the insured resulting from forgery or alteration "of, on, or in any covered instrument." The coverage does not distinguish between handwritten signatures and mechanically reproduced (machine) signatures; forgery of either is covered. A "covered instrument" is a check, draft, promissory note, or similar written promise or an order or direction to pay money that is drawn on or by the insured, the insured's agent, or by anyone else against the insured's account. Note that "alteration" is covered in addition to forgery. This means that if the signature on an instrument is genuine, but the amount has been altered, coverage will apply.

The Crime General Conditions form exclusions apply to the Forgery or Alteration coverage, but there is only one additional exclusion: loss caused by dishonest or criminal acts of the insured's employees, directors, or trustees. This exclusion cannot be removed.

Form C: Theft Disappearance and Destruction Form

The Theft, Dishonesty and Destruction form is the approximate equivalent of an older form called the Money and Securities Broad form. It covers money and securities for loss by theft, but it goes further and also provides coverage against loss by "disappearance and destruction." In effect, it provides open-peril coverage on money and securities. Like the other crime coverages discussed in this section, employee infidelity is excluded. Coverage is available under two separate agreements applying to losses on premises and losses off premises. Each section is independent of the other, and the insured may select either or both. Separate limits apply to each coverage.

Section 1 covers money and securities inside the insured's premises (or inside banking premises) against theft, disappearance, or destruction. The term *theft* includes both robbery and burglary.

Section 2 covers money and securities outside the premises while in the care and custody of a "messenger." A "messenger" is defined as the named insured, any partner of the named insured, or any employee while having custody of covered property outside the premises.

The off-premises coverage applies within the United States, the District of Columbia, the Virgin Islands, Puerto Rico, the Canal Zone, and Canada. There is no coverage for losses occurring outside these limits. Coverage applies to money and securities in the custody of a messenger, and while being conveyed by an armored car company.

Exclusions   In addition to the general crime exclusions previously discussed, the Theft, Disappearance and Destruction form contains eight exclusions, many of which are found in other crime forms.

Accounting or Arithmetical Errors or Omissions. This excludes losses that result from both accounting mistakes and simple losses that might result, for example, from giving a customer too much change.

Acts of Employees, Directors, Trustees or Representatives. This is the fidelity exclusion, which is common to all portfolio crime forms except Form A.

Exchanges or Purchases. Any loss resulting from giving or surrendering property in any exchange or purchase is excluded. This excludes losses in which the firm suffers a loss of property in a fraudulent transaction (e.g., the "return" of an item by a customer that was not purchased and paid for).

Fire. There is no coverage for fire damage to the premises, no matter how it is caused. Burglary is sometimes accompanied by fire damage, from fires set by the burglars to conceal evidence. Fire damage will be covered under the Portfolio property forms.

Money-Operated Devices. There is no coverage for theft or "burglary" from a coin-operated device, unless the amount of money deposited in the device is recorded by a continuous recording instrument in the device.

Transfer or Surrender of Property. This provision excludes loss by transfer or surrender of property to a person or place outside the premises or banking premises, as a result of (a) unauthorized instructions, or (b) a threat to do bodily harm to a person or damage to property. Coverage for loss resulting from transfer of property as a result of unauthorized instructions can be covered, in part, under the Computer Fraud coverage. Coverage for loss resulting from threat to do bodily harm to a person may be covered under the Extortion coverage.

Vandalism and Malicious Mischief. There is no coverage for damage to the premises, its interior, or containers of covered property by vandalism and malicious mischief.

Voluntary Parting of Title to or Possession of Property.   This provision excludes loss resulting from the insured or anyone acting on the insured's authority being tricked into voluntarily parting with title to or possession of covered property.

Protective Devices or Services Provision   When the insured claims credit for the existence of protective devices (such as burglar alarms) or protective services (such as guards), and receives credit in the policy premium for such protection, the Protective

Devices or Services Provision endorsement (CR 15 09) is attached to the policy. Under the terms of this endorsement, the insured promises that the devices or services will be maintained at all times during the policy. (This same endorsement is also used with Forms D, E, and H.)

If, for reasons within the control of the insured, the protective devices or services claimed in the policy are not maintained, the insurance ceases for any period of nonmaintenance, but only for the premises or messengers affected. If the failure to maintain the protective devices or services is for reasons beyond the insured's control, different provisions apply. If, for reasons beyond the insured's control, an alarm system for which the insured has received credit is inoperative, but as long as the insured provides at least one additional "watchperson" (in addition to any for which credit has been received), the coverage is continued. If, for reasons beyond the insured's control any device *other than an alarm system* or protective service is not maintained, the limit of insurance is reduced to the amount that the premium paid would have purchased without credit for the device or service.

Form D: Robbery and Safe Burglary Coverage Form

The Robbery and Safe Burglary Policy covers property other than money and securities and may be written to cover three exposures: on-premises robbery; off-premises robbery; and safe burglary. The policy covers property other than money and securities inside or outside the premises (or both) against actual or attempted robbery. The Robbery and Safe Burglary Coverage Form was developed to separate an insured's property other than money and securities exposure from the money and securities exposure, and thus to help the insurer charge a proper premium for both. The insured may select any or all of the coverages, and separate amounts of insurance may be written for each coverage.

Robbery Coverage   The robbery coverage is written in two separate, independent sections; robbery within the premises and robbery outside the premises. The insured may select either or both, and separate amounts of insurance are purchased for each.

Coverage either on or off premises applies for the peril of robbery, as defined at the beginning of this section. The term is defined in the policy to include the taking of property:

1. By violence inflicted on a custodian or putting the custodian in fear of violence.

2. By any other obviously unlawful act witnessed by the person from whom the property is taken.

Note that the definition of "robbery" includes the taking of property even where no violence is inflicted or threatened. If an employee sees a thief grab an item and run out of the store, the loss will be considered robbery since the robber committed an obviously unlawful act witnessed by the employee. For the same reason, loss resulting from smashing a show window while the premises are open for business is considered robbery.

With respect to on-premises robbery, the form refers to the taking of property from a "custodian" of the property. "Custodian" is defined to include the named insured, any of the named insured's partners, or any "employee" as defined in the General Conditions while having care and custody of covered property. However, the definition excludes any "watchperson" or janitor.

For off-premises robbery coverage, the coverage applies to the robbery of a "messenger," who is defined to include the named insured, any partner of the named insured, or any employee while having care and custody of covered property outside the premises.

Under an extension of coverage, the Outside the Premises Robbery coverage is extended to cover loss of property while in the care and custody of an armored motor vehicle company. However, coverage under this extension is excess over any recovery from the armored motor vehicle company or under any insurance carried by the armored motor vehicle company.

Safe Burglary Coverage Safe Burglary coverage is designed to protect against direct loss of any property, including money and securities, when such property is lost as a result of forcible entry into a safe or vault. Again, the loss must be the result of forcible entry; if the burglar opens the safe by manipulation of the dial, there is no coverage. Removal of the entire safe from the premises is construed as safe burglary and is covered.

The policy also covers damage to the safe or vault, furniture or fixtures, equipment, or other property owned by the insured which are damaged by safe burglary or attempted safe burglary. As long as an attempt at safe burglary is made, any other property damage is also covered. In this connection, it is important to note that forcible entry into the premises does not constitute safe burglary unless there is also forcible entry (or attempt) into the safe. There is no requirement that the premises be entered forcibly.

In addition to the general theft exclusions, there are four exclusions in this form, all of which have previously been discussed and apply in addition to the general theft exclusions: the fidelity exclusion, the fire exclusion, transfer or surrender of property, and the vandalism exclusion. In addition to these four exclusions, for some reason the form also excludes loss of motor vehicles. Although loss of motor vehicles by robbery or safe burglary might seem to be a remote exposure, strange things can happen.

In addition to paying for loss of insured property by robbery and safe burglary, the form agrees to pay for damage to the premises or its exterior resulting directly from safe burglary if the insured is the owner of the property or is liable for the loss.

Form E: Premises Burglary Coverage

The Premises Burglary Coverage (formerly called Mercantile Open Stock Burglary) covers loss of merchandise, furniture, fixtures, and equipment as a result of burglary. It does not cover money or securities. Visible evidence of forcible entry or forcible exit is required, and the policy covers damage caused by burglars. In addition, the policy is extended to cover loss by robbery or attempted robbery of a watchperson employed exclusively by the insured while on duty within the premises.

"Watchperson" is defined as any person employed by the named insured "specifically to have care and custody of property inside the premises and who has no other duties." This definition would not, for example, include a janitor, although the definition can be modified by endorsement to include a janitor.

Exclusions   In addition to the exclusions in the Crime General Conditions form, the Premises Burglary form includes a number of exclusions or other limitations defining the coverage.

First, the loss must be the result of burglary (or robbery of a watchperson). Unless there are marks of forcible entry into or out of the premises, coverage does not apply. In addition to the standard fidelity and vandalism exclusions, the form has two additional noteworthy exclusions: an exclusion of a loss during a change in the conditions of the premises that is within the insured's control and that increases the probability of loss; and a two-part fire exclusion. The first part excludes damage caused by fire, except to a safe or vault. The second part excludes loss occurring during a fire in the premises. This means there is no coverage for burglary if the burglary occurs during a fire.

Although the provision is not listed in the exclusions section of the form, the policy provides (under the Limit of Insurance provision) that in the event of loss, coverage is suspended until the premises are restored to the same condition as existed prior to the loss. The suspension may be avoided if, until the premises are restored, the insured adds a watchperson within the premises when the business is closed.

Form F: Computer Fraud Coverage

The Computer Fraud Coverage form provides protection for loss of money, securities, and property other than money and securities by computer fraud.

> Computer Fraud means theft of property following and directly related to the use of any computer to fraudulently cause a transfer of that property from inside the "premises" or "banking premises" to a person (other than a "messenger") outside those premises or to a place outside those premises.

This form contemplates losses in which a person outside the firm uses a computer to break into the computer system of the insured and instruct the insured's computer to transfer funds to a fictitious payee at a particular location.

Exclusions   There are only two exclusions under this form (other than the general crime exclusions): the employee dishonesty exclusion and an exclusion of inventory shortages. There is no coverage for any loss, the existence or amount of which can be proved only by an inventory or profit and loss computation.

Form G: Extortion Coverage Form

The off-premises crime coverages we have examined (Forms C, D, and H) all exclude the transfer or surrender of property resulting from a threat to do bodily harm to any person or damage to any property. Coverage for this exposure is called Extortion Coverage, and is covered under Form G, the Extortion Coverage form, which covers money, securities, and other property against such loss.

The term *extortion*, as used in the form, has a specialized meaning in Coverage G, which is somewhat narrower than the extortion excluded in the other forms. *Extortion* means the surrender of property away from the "premises" as a result of a threat communicated to (the named insured) to do bodily harm to (the named insured) or a relative or invitee of either, who is, or allegedly is, being held captive.

Note that the definition refers to the surrender of property only as a result of a threat to do bodily injury to a person who is being held (or is allegedly being held) by the extortionist. The policy does not cover extortion involving the threat to do damage to property.

Exclusions   There are two exclusions under the Extortion Coverage: (1) the standard Employee, Directors, Trustees or Representatives fidelity exclusion; and (2) the Non-Notification of Authorities exclusion, which excludes coverage for loss of property surrendered before a reasonable effort has been made to report the extortionist's demands to all of the following: an associate; the Federal Bureau of Investigation; and local law enforcement authorities. Quite obviously, what constitutes a "reasonable" effort will depend on the facts of the particular situation.

The special nature of the extortion coverage requires modification in certain of the standard conditions. First, the Policy Period condition is modified to provide that loss is covered only if the threat to do bodily harm is first communicated to the insured during the policy period.

In addition, the policy territory is amended to cover loss only if the captivity (or alleged captivity) takes place within the United Sates of America, U.S. Virgin Islands, Puerto Rico, the Canal Zone, or Canada.

The policy makes provision for participation (or nonparticipation) in the loss. If the insured elects "participation," the policy will pay no more than the specified percentage of the loss indicated or the applicable limit of the policy.

Form H: Premises Theft and Robbery Outside Premises

The Premises Theft and Robbery Outside Coverage form offers those insureds who desire it broader coverage than that available under Forms D and E. The Premises Theft coverage is a modification of the Premises Burglary coverage form and is the equivalent of the older Mercantile Open Stock Theft form. It covers property other than money and securities inside or outside the premises (or both) against actual or attempted theft inside the premises. The Robbery Outside the Premises provides essentially the same coverage as the outside robbery coverage of Form D: loss of property other than money and securities by actual or attempted robbery outside the premises.

Exclusions   In addition to the general theft exclusions, Form H contains seven exclusions that have already been discussed: infidelity, change in condition of the premises, exchanges or purchases, fire, inventory shortages, transfer or surrender of property, and vandalism and voluntary parting with title or possession of property.

As in the case of the Premises Burglary coverage, the Limit of Insurance Provision states that coverage is suspended until the premises are restored to the same condition as prior to the loss. However, the suspension does not apply if the insured maintains at least one watchperson while the premises are closed for business.

Summary of Forms

There are a confusing number of differences among the various crime coverage forms, and it is sometimes difficult to keep the features of the various forms straight. The accompanying table, which summarizes the significant features of the major crime coverage forms, may be helpful in this respect.

Coverage Form	Causes of Loss	Property Covered	Where Applicable	Culprit
A	Employee Dishonesty	All property including Money and Securities	US & Canada plus 90-day travel extension	Any employee
B	Forgery— Alteration	Checks and drafts issued by the Insured, Credit Cards by endorsement	Insured's Bank Account	Anyone *except* an employee
C	Theft, Disappearance, and Destruction	Money and Securities only	Inside and Outside the Premises	Anyone *except* an employee
D	Robbery and Safe Burglary	Property other than Money and Securities	Inside and Outside the Premises	Anyone *except* an employee
E	Burglary and Robbery of a Watchman	Property other than Money and Securities	Inside the Premises only	Anyone *except* an employee
F	Computer Fraud	All property including Money and Securities	U.S. and Canada	Anyone *except* an employee
G	Extortion	Property Other than Money and Securities	U.S. and Canada	Anyone *except* an employee
H	Theft	Property other than Money and Securities	Inside the Premises	Anyone *except* an employee
	Robbery of a Messenger		Outside the Premises	Anyone an employee

Other Portfolio Crime Forms

The remaining crime forms are specialized policies designed to insure the unique needs of depository organizations or bailees.

Form I: The Lessee of Safe Deposit Boxes Coverage Form   This form is written for firms that rent safe deposit boxes to the public. It covers securities inside a safe deposit box or depository premises against theft, disappearance, or destruction. Coverage may also be provided on property other than money and securities, but only against actual or attempted burglary or robbery and vandalism. Thus, while securities are covered on an open-peril basis, other property, such as jewelry or other valuables inside the safe deposit box or depository premises, is covered against loss by burglary or robbery. Separate limits apply to Section 1 and Section 2.

Form J: Securities Deposited With Others Coverage Form   Coverage under this form applies while securities are inside the custodian's premises, while they are being conveyed outside the custodian's premises by the custodian or an employee of the custodian, and while the custodian has the securities in a depository for safekeeping. The custodian with whom securities are deposited must be named in the form. If the custodian places the securities in a depository, that depository must also be named.

Form K and L: Coverage for Guest's Property   *Innkeepers Laws* of most states require hotels, motels, and other organizations that provide lodging to the public to provide a place of safekeeping for the valuables of their tenants. Form K, the Liability for Guest's Property—Safe Deposit Coverage form, covers property of a guest in a safe deposit box on the premises, and pays damages for which the insured is legally liable because of loss, destruction, or damage of such property. Coverage is also provided to defend the insured in suits seeking damages payable under the form.

A companion coverage, Form L (Liability for Guest's Property—Premises Coverage Form) covers guests' property (other than vehicles, samples, or articles for sale) that is not deposited with the innkeeper for safekeeping. It provides coverage to pay damages for which the insured is legally liable because of loss, destruction, or damage of such property and also provides defense for the insured in suits seeking damages payable under the form. State innkeepers laws generally limit an innkeepers liability for loss to property of guests that is not given to the innkeeper for safekeeping to a dollar amount, such as $500 or $1000 per guest. It is this liability that is covered under Form L.

Forms M and N: Safe Depository Liability and Direct Loss   Forms M and N are designed for organizations—other than banks—that provide safe depository facilities to the public. These forms cover customer's property on an insured's premises inside the customers' safe deposit boxes in vaults, stored in vaults, or while in the course of deposit or removal from boxes or vaults. Form M pays for damages for which the insured is legally liable because of loss, destruction, or damage to property in the depository facility. The form also covers defense for suits seeking damages payable under the form. Form N provides coverage for losses sustained by safe-depository customers for which the insured is not legally liable.

■ Package Crime Policies ■ ■ ■ ■ ■ ■ ■ ■ ■ ■ ■ ■ ■ ■ ■ ■ ■ ■

Package crime policies, which combine several dishonesty coverages into a single contract, have existed for many years. The ISO Portfolio program contemplates continuation of the packaging of crime coverages, under a series of Coverage Plans. There are nine coverage plans in all, most of which involve the combination of individual forms of crime coverage into packages that more or less parallel the package crime policies that existed when the portfolio program was introduced. Three of the plans (designated Plans 3 through 5) are the Storekeepers Broad Form, the Storekeepers Burglary and Robbery Package, and the Office and Burglary Package. These packages are designed for small businesses and provide limited amounts of coverage. Of the remaining plans, the most widely used, and by far the most important of the crime packages, is Plan 1, Combined Crime—Separate Limits form.[2]

PLAN 1: COMBINATION CRIME—SEPARATE LIMITS

Portfolio Crime Plan 1 is designated the Combination Crime—Separate Limits Option. It is an excellent example of the package approach to crime coverage, including both fidelity and nonemployee crime coverages in a single contract. The insured may select any combination of coverage Forms A through J, and none of the coverages are mandatory. In addition, there is no required relationship among the limits of the various coverages. The plan may be written for any insured except certain organizations that are eligible for a financial institutions bond (discussed next). Although none of the coverages are mandatory in this package and there are no insurance-to-value requirements, there is no discount for the packaging.

FINANCIAL INSTITUTIONS BONDS

Financial institution bonds represent a specialized class of coverages designed for a specialized clientele. Although the contracts are referred to as bonds, they actually represent a package approach to crime coverage, including not only fidelity coverage but nonemployee crime coverages as well. Although a variety of financial institution bonds are designed to provide coverage to organizations with slightly different needs, the most commonly used form is the Financial Institutions Bond (Form 24) which was formerly known as the Bankers Blanket Bond.

The Financial Institutions Bond contains six insuring agreements, which more or less parallel the crime coverages already discussed. The Financial Institutions Bond coverages are

---

[2]Originally, there were 10 plans. The rules for Plan 2 were eliminated in 1988. Crime coverage plans 6 through 10 are specialized forms of protection, providing coverage primarily for exposures related to the custodial or fiduciary exposure. They are designed for hotels, innkeepers, banks, and depository institutions that are exposed to loss in connection with property of others placed in their custody.

Fidelity

On-premises coverage

In-transit coverage

Forgery or alteration

Securities coverage

Counterfeit currency

Coverage for Fidelity, On-Premises, and In-Transit is mandatory with a single limit of coverage and a single deductible. If the optional coverages Forgery, Securities, or Counterfeit, are elected, they are subject to their own internal limits and to the policy aggregate limit.

The property insured includes an extensive list of negotiable and nonnegotiable financial instruments owned by the insured or in the insured's care. Coverage on the property of others applies regardless of the insured's liability or lack of liability for the loss. The On-Premises coverage provides coverage for loss of insured property by robbery, burglary, misplacement, mysterious, unexplainable disappearance, damage, or destruction.

The Forgery or Alteration coverage of the Financial Institutions Bond protects the insured financial institution against loss resulting from giving anything in value on the faith of instruments that turn out to have been forged or altered.

Unlike the other forms of crime insurance that have been examined, there is no discovery period following termination of the bond. However, at any time prior to termination, the insured can elect to purchase a "tail" coverage, providing a discovery period of 12 months in which to discover losses that may have occurred prior to termination.

Financial Institution Combination Safe Depository Form

The Financial Institution Bond excludes property of customers in safe deposit boxes, unless the loss results from employee infidelity and then only if the bank is legally liable for the loss. The Financial Institution Combination Safe Depository form is designed to protect against loss to customers' property in the safe deposit boxes of the institution. The form provides essentially the same type of coverage as was examined in connection with the depository coverages designed for organizations other than financial institutions (Portfolio form M and N).

Retention of Crime Exposures ■ ■ ■ ■ ■ ■ ■ ■ ■ ■ ■ ■ ■ ■ ■

Although employee crime represents an exposure of catastrophic proportions and is therefore rarely an appropriate subject for retention, there are many non-employee crime exposures for which retention, combined with loss control, is the most appropriate approach to dealing with risk. Many, but not all, nonemployee crime exposures represent high-frequency, low-severity exposures. Shoplifting, for example, is rarely insurable. Retention through noninsurance may be appropriate for some crime exposures. Unless the property consists of extremely high valued items, such as jewelry, the amount of property that burglars or robbers are likely to get away with will generally be limited. When insurance is purchased, both employee and nonemployee crime coverages may be written with deductibles.

IMPORTANT CONCEPTS TO REMEMBER

portfolio crime coverage forms
Crime Policy General Provision Form
Loss Sustained During Prior Insurance
discovery coverage
superseded suretyship provision
fidelity bond
penalty
discovery period
employee dishonesty blanket coverage
employee dishonesty schedule coverage
dishonesty exposure index

Forgery or Alteration Coverage Form
Theft, Disappearance and Destruction Form
Robbery and Safe Burglary Coverage Form
custodian
messenger
Safe Burglary Coverage Form
Premises Burglary Coverage
Computer Fraud Coverage Form
Extortion Coverage Form
Premises Theft and Outside Robbery Coverage Form

Lessee of Safe Deposit Boxes Coverage Form
Securities Deposited With Others Coverage Form
Liability for Guests' Property –Safe Deposit Form
Liability for Guests' Property –Premises Form
Safe Depository Liability
Combination Crime– Separate Limits package
Financial Institutions Bond
Financial Institutions Combination Safe Depository Form

QUESTIONS FOR REVIEW

1. To what extent is protection for loss of insured property covered for loss by crime under commercial property forms such as the Building and Personal Property Coverage form? To what extent is property not covered for loss by crime under such policies?

2. Briefly describe the coverage provided by the portfolio Computer Fraud coverage.

3. Identify the six general exclusions contained in the Crime Policy General Provisions form.

4. Explain the "Loss Sustained During Prior Insurance" provision. Why is such a provision required in fidelity bonds? Does it make any difference whether the prior insurance was written by the same insurer or a different insurer?

5. XYZ carries a blanket fidelity bond with a $25,000 penalty. The company's treasurer absconded with $85,000. He was apprehended, but not before his had lost $40,000 of the money at a casino. Describe the way in which $45,000 funds he has not spent will be apportioned between the insured and the insurer.

6. Explain the significance of the *discovery* period in a fidelity bond.

7. Describe the distinction between blanket fidelity coverage and scheduled coverage. In what circumstances would the difference be significant at the time of a loss?

8. Who is covered as an employee under the employee dishonesty blanket coverage? Are there any additional parties that should be added to the policy?

9. Describe the provision of the Employee Dishonesty form that deals with knowledge on the part of the insured concerning dishonesty on the part of employees.

10. What type of property is covered under the *Theft, Disappearance and Destruction* form and for what perils is coverage provided?

QUESTIONS FOR DISCUSSION

1. The Loss Sustained During Prior Insurance provision seems reasonable when the insurer at the time of loss has collected premiums from the insured for many years before a loss is discovered. Is it equally reasonable for a new insurer to cover a loss that occurred before its policy was written? Why are insurers writing crime insurance so generous?

2. Describe what you would imagine to be the underwriting process for a discovery basis bond.

3. Describe the provisions of the portfolio crime forms dealing with failure of the insured to maintain protective devices for which credit has been granted in the rating for the coverage. In your opinion, are these reasonable?

4. The Widget Manufacturing Company purchased an Employee Dishonesty Coverage form (Portfolio Crime Form A) with a $10,000 penalty on June 1, 1990, and canceled the bond on June 1, 1992. Which of the following losses would be covered and to what extent?
   a. Employee A embezzled $5000 in 1989 and $5000 in 1991 the total $10,000 loss being discovered in January 1992.
   b. Employee B embezzled $15,000 in 1984, but the loss was not discovered until January 1993.
   c. Employees C and D embezzled $7500 each in a collusive loss during 1992, but the loss was not discovered until May 1993.

5. The *Computer Fraud Coverage* form insures against loss of money, securities, and property other than money and securities resulting from the use of a computer to fraudulently transfer the property from the premises or from banking premises to a person or place outside the premises. What types of computer-related crime losses can you identify that go beyond the scope of this coverage?

SUGGESTIONS FOR ADDITIONAL READING

Fire, Casualty and Surety Bulletins. Casualty and Surety Volume. Cincinnati: National Underwriter Company. (Loose-leaf manual service with monthly supplements.) See "Crime," "Burglary," and "Miscellaneous Casualty" sections.

Huebner, S.S., Kenneth Black, Jr., and Bernard L. Webb. *Property and Liability Insurance*, 4th ed. Englewood Cliffs, NJ: Prentice-Hall, 1996. Chapter 22.

Robinson, Linda G. and Jack P. Gibson. *Commercial Property Insurance* (Dallas, Tx.: International Risk Management Institute, Inc., loose leaf service with periodic supplements), vol. II, "Crime" section.

Webb, Bernard L., Stephen Horn II, and Arthur L. Flitner. *Commercial Insurance* 2nd ed. (Malvern, Pa.: Insurance Institute of America, 1990), Chapter 5.

CHAPTER 21

Managing Transit Risks: Risk Control

CHAPTER OBJECTIVES

When you have finished this chapter, you should be able to

Identify the parties exposed to loss as a result of the inland transportation of goods.

Distinguish among the classes of carriers that may be used to transport goods and explain the liability of each class for goods in its custody.

Distinguish among classes of bills of lading and explain the importance of the distinction from a risk management perspective.

Explain what determines the risk of loss to goods in transit and the manner in which terms of sale can influence this determination.

Identify the principal loss prevention and control measures that may be used in dealing with the transit exposure.

Introduction

It has been said that American business moves on wheels. The vast landmass of the continental United States created an early demand for efficient and economical means of transportation. Most businesses send or receive raw materials and finished products, and the shipment of these goods creates a potential for financial loss. Goods in transit may be damaged in a collision, they may be stolen, or they may be damaged by fire, windstorm, or flood. Determining how severe such losses are likely to be is an important step in the process of deciding how the risks should be addressed.

Commercial goods may be shipped by parcel post, rail, truck, and air. When the goods are shipped by rail or air, the transportation company is probably a common carrier. When goods are shipped by truck, the transportation company may be a common carrier or a contract carrier. In this chapter, we examine the risks associated with the transportation of property and describe the loss-prevention measures.

Identifying and Measuring Transportation Risks ▪ ▪ ▪ ▪

The risk associated with the shipment or transportation of goods depends on several factors. These include the issue of title or ownership and the responsibility of the carrier for damage to goods in its custody.

PARTIES EXPOSED TO LOSS

Damage to property in the course of transportation may cause financial loss to two interests: (1) owner of the goods, and (2) the person or organization to whom the goods have been entrusted for transportation. In some situations, damage to goods in transit can be a source of loss to a creditor who has a security interest in such goods.

Title to Goods in Transit

The first issue to be addressed is the question of who is the owner of the goods in transit. Goods in the course of transportation are generally goods in the course of commerce—that is, goods that have been bought and sold by the parties. The question of ownership depends on the terms of the sale, which determine the point at which title to the goods passes from the seller to the buyer. When the sale of goods involves some element of transportation, the terms of the sale will specify whether the goods must be transported to the buyer by the seller, or if the seller's obligation is satisfied once the goods are delivered to the buyer. This determines the point at which title passes, and the risk of loss to goods being shipped may rest with the buyer or the seller, depending on the terms of the sale.

The terms of sale define the point at which the seller is obligated to deliver the goods *free-on-board* or *F.O.B.* When goods are shipped *F.O.B. Point of Origin,* title passes to the buyer when the goods are loaded on the conveyance. Goods shipped *F.O.B. Destination,* in contrast, remain the property of the seller until they arrive at their destination. This means that the point at which title passes (and the risk of loss to goods) is subject to agreement by the parties.

Sellers that ship goods F.O.B. Point of Origin (where the title to the goods passes when the goods have been loaded on the transporting conveyance) often arrange coverage to protect the interest of the buyer, thereby making certain that the goods are insured and that their interest in the goods is protected. When the seller prefers to arrange for insurance on the goods being shipped to the buyer, the goods may be sold F.O.B. Destination, *c.i.f.* The term *c.i.f.* indicates that the price quoted to the buyer includes the *cost* of the goods, plus *insurance* and *freight.*

477

Under these terms, the seller is obligated to place the goods in the possession of the carrier, pay the transportation charges, and arrange for insurance. The seller may prefer to arrange insurance on the goods, even when title to the goods passes to the buyer at the point of origin when the seller has not yet paid for the goods. If the goods are damaged or destroyed in transit, there is nothing for the seller to attach or repossess in the event of a payment default by the buyer.

The Liability of Common Carriers

One of the most important principles related to the risk of loss to goods in the course of transportation is the legal liability of a carrier for goods which it transports. A carrier is one who undertakes to transport goods, regardless of the methods of transportation. There are three types of carriers: *common carriers*, which hold themselves out to transport goods for all members of the public for a fee; *contract carriers*, which transport goods for specific firms under individual contracts; and *private carriers*, which transport their own goods.

Common carriers are subject to strict regulation, both at the state and federal level. Until 1996, interstate common carriers were regulated by the Interstate Commerce Commission (ICC). In December of 1995, President Clinton signed legislation abolishing the ICC and transferring its functions to a new federal agency, the Surface Transportational Board, within the Department of Transportation. Personnel of the ICC were transferred to the new STB and, for the present, little has changed except the name. The regulations previously enforced by the ICC are now enforced by the DOT. Intrastate common carriers are regulated by the states, which usually impose regulations on intrastate truckers similar to the federal regulations.

The legal liability of a common carrier for goods entrusted into its care for transportation is quite strict. Only a few causes of loss are considered to be beyond the control of the common carrier, and with the exception of these exclusions, the common carrier is legally liable for any loss of or damage to goods which it transports. Losses resulting from the following causes are excepted and relieve the common carrier from liability.

1. Acts of God.

2. Acts of the public enemy (a foreign power).

3. Exercise of public authority.

4. Fault or neglect of the shipper.

5. Inherent vice, which is defined as a quality in a good that causes the good to destroy itself (e.g., butter will spoil).

Even loses caused by one of the five causes listed above may result in the carrier being held liable, if the carrier's negligence contributed to the loss. For example, although wind and hail are acts of God, if the trailer failed to exercise proper care in protecting the property from such perils, it could be held liable for damage.

Released Bills of Lading

With the broad liability imposed on common carriers by the common law, it should not be surprising that common carriers have sought ways of avoiding a part of this liability. However, the only way that a common carrier can limit its liability to the owner of property to less than the full value of that property is to enter into a contract to this effect.

The contract between a carrier and a shipper for transportation of the goods is called a *bill of lading*. The terms and conditions of the bill of lading of carriers operating in interstate commerce are tightly controlled by the Bill of Lading Act, an amendment to the Interstate Commerce Act. Most states have similar laws relating to bills of lading used in intrastate transportation.

A bill of lading may be a *straight bill of lading* or a *released bill of lading*. Under the terms of a *released bill of lading*, the common carrier limits its liability for damage to goods in its custody to a specific dollar amount. The shipper under a released bill of lading pays a freight rate based on what is known as a *released value*, i.e. a value which may be substantially below the value of the commodities being transported. The liability of the common carrier is then limited to this released value. A common value under a released bill of lading is $.50 per pound. The shipper may declare a greater value than the released value but subject to payment of excess valuation charges. Usually, the excess valuation charges are higher than the premiums insurers charge a shipper for insurance equal to the full value of the goods. Shippers generally find it cheaper to accept the limitation of liability and finance losses in excess of the carrier's liability through retention or insurance.

Measuring Frequency and Severity

If a shipper sends a large number of shipments on a regular basis, it may generate sufficient experience to establish a frequency rate for lost or damaged shipments. Depending on the amount of experience on which this frequency rate is based, it may be possible for the shipper to make reasonably accurate estimates of future losses.

The potential loss severity associated with the transit exposure varies with the value of the largest shipment made. In measuring potential loss, the maximum dollar value for shipments by any one truck, train, or aircraft should be determined. Except in unusual circumstances, the value of any single shipment is likely to be within the organization's retention level.

⠿ Loss Prevention and Control for Transit Risks ▪ ▪ ▪ ▪ ▪ ▪

Transit losses are highly susceptible to loss control measures. The extent of the organization's loss control efforts will depend on the exposure. A firm that makes frequent shipments needs to consider control measures to control loss frequency. A firm that makes only occasional shipments, on the other hand, will probably judge the transit exposure to be insignificant. As in the case of other risks, there are standard approaches and methods to transit loss control. The following discussion summarizes the most common control measures.

DEPARTMENT OF TRANSPORTATION STANDARDS

Among the responsibilities of the secretary of transportation is the regulation of carriers involved in interstate commerce. As part of this responsibility, the Department of Transportation (DOT) has issued advisory standards for transportation operations. Although these standards are not mandatory, they represent valuable guidance for shippers and consignees. The DOT's Cargo Security Advisory Standards deal with seal accountability, high-value commodity storage, and internal accountability procedures. Before releasing these advisory standards, DOT solicited and received the comments of many large air and surface carriers in the United States. Hence they reflect widely held professional views and should be consulted in any protection program involving transport and related storage of material.

TITLE DURING TRANSIT

From our discussion concerning the relationship between the terms of sale and the risk of loss to goods in transit, it is clear that the risk of loss to goods in transit can be transferred to the other party in the transaction through the terms of the sale. A seller will prefer terms of sale that transfer title to the buyer at the point of origin (F.O.B. point of origin), and the buyer will prefer terms that transfer title at the end of the transportation (F.O.B. destination). Other factors, such as industry convention, however, may outweigh the preferences of the parties.

PACKAGING

The standard loss control method for transportation losses is the packaging of the goods to be shipped. Usually, the buyer or consignee has little control over how the goods are packaged. For this reason, the terms of sale become particularly relevant if shipments are damaged because of poor packaging. Packaging is a science, and packaging engineer specialists can design packaging that can withstand possible rough handling.

A second feature of packaging is labeling. Except where necessary for other reasons, packages should not be labeled in a way that reveals that the contents are worth stealing. Many view labeling high-valued items as an invitation to steal.

SELECTION OF THE CARRIER

The second loss control measure with respect to the transportation exposure is the selection of the carrier. Despite the liability of common carriers, some organizations find that they can control transit losses better by operating their own delivery fleet. The organization that delivers or picks up goods on its own trucks often does so in order to achieve increased security and control losses.

When goods are to be shipped by common carrier or contract carrier, the selection of the particular carrier that will be used is a loss control factor. A carrier with a good safety record and experience in transporting the type of goods involved should be selected. In addition, the particular type of carrier to be used should be considered. In addition to truckers, which are the most common type of carrier, other carriers include railroads, air carriers, and U.S. parcel post.

Railroads

As common carriers, railroads also limit their liability through their bills of lading. A straight bill of lading makes the railroad liable for the full value of the property being transported. A released bill of lading limits the railroad's liability to a specified value, based on the carrier's *tariff* or charges, which vary with the type of goods being transported. Railroads may also include a theft deductible in their bill of lading, which states that the railroad is not liable for theft or pilferage losses up to the specified deductible limit.[1]

Air Freight

Air carriers are subject to essentially the same liability for goods being transported as outlined above, subject to the same common law exceptions. Like truckers and railroads, air carriers limit their liability through their bills of lading. The normal limit of liability for air freight carriers is a specified dollar amount per pound or per 100 pounds.

Air carriers may use independent truckers to make deliveries as well as to transfer goods between terminals. These may or may not be agents of the airlines. Quite often they may be local truckers that are exempt from regulations of the Interstate Commerce Commission (ICC). Therefore, liability for goods while in their care may not fall to the airline but to the trucker. Airlines are regulated by the Civil Aeronautics Board, which allows each carrier to file his own tariff, whereas truckers are regulated by the ICC, which publishes uniform tariffs and rates.

U.S. Parcel Post

The federal government is not a common carrier and does not incur any liability for damage to or loss of property transported unless the parcel is insured by the Post Office. U.S. Postal Service offers insurance up to $200 per parcel for third and fourth class and priority mail. Registered mail can be insured up to $10,000 per parcel. Because of the cost, the use of U.S. Postal Service as a carrier is an option only for small shipments.

SEPARATION OF VALUES

A standard loss control method for transit exposures is the separation of values technique, originally noted in Chapter 9. Where possible, the concentration of values on a single conveyance should be limited to reduce the severity of any loss

[1]Congress authorized the theft deductible in the Staggers Act of 1980.

that does occur. When goods are shipped by common carrier, shipments should be scheduled to avoid higher concentrations of values at any one terminal.

COLLECTING FROM THE COMMON CARRIER

Collecting for lost or damaged shipments from the common carrier is a post-event loss control measure. It is usually easier and quicker to collect a claim from an insurance company than from a common carrier. Regardless of whether reimbursement is sought from the common carrier who transported the goods or from the insurer, the following factors should be kept in mind.

Inspection for Concealed Damage

Merchandise received by common carrier should be inspected immediately upon receipt by specifically designated employees of the consignee. When the property is shipped by sealed container, the seal should be inspected to verify that it remains intact and that the seal numbers agree with those recorded by the shipper on the bill of lading. If there is any suspicion that the seal has been subject to tampering, the container should not be accepted. Failure to detect a broken or altered seal will usually make it impossible for the consignee to collect from the carrier for lost, stolen, or damaged property. Once accepted, the container should be unloaded as soon as possible, since it usually offers little protection against intruders. The goods should be checked for concealed damage as soon as possible, since bills of lading usually require that the carrier be notified of concealed damage within 15 days. If the shipment is damaged, the carrier should be notified immediately so a representative can be assigned to inspect the damage.

Filing Shipping Claims

When freight is received in damaged condition, the extent of the damage should be determined. Goods that have been received damaged or opened, or in any other way not acceptable, should be marked as such, and the actual count verified, signed, and dated. A claim should be filed with the appropriate source of indemnification immediately by someone within the organization who is familiar with the proper procedure. The undesirable practice of allowing damaged merchandise to accumulate and submit a consolidated claim for multiple shipments should be avoided.

Time Limit For Notice

Timing is a vital element in getting reimbursement for transit losses. The time limit for notice of loss required by common carriers is usually shorter than that required by insurance companies and is stipulated either in the bill of lading or in the carrier's tariffs. Shippers usually prefer to seek reimbursement from the common carrier first before charging a loss against their own insurance carrier because most transit policies are experience rated; the fewer the losses, the lower the premium. Usually common carriers rigidly enforce the time limits for making claims.

Air carriers require prompt notification in case of loss. Concealed damage may have to be reported within 15 days. The courts have upheld denial of coverage for late notice, even though reporting requirements are not spelled out in the air bill. Most domestic airlines allow nine months for filing claims and two years for filing suit if the claim is denied. However, air freight forwarders have not generally adopted these provisions and may allow considerably less time.

Ocean Marine Transportation Risks

MARINE RISKS RELATED TO COMMERCE

Marine risks, as risks of transportation, are principally the risks of commerce and trade. Many years ago, when land transportation was slow and hazardous, oceans and waterways were the avenues of commerce. Dependence on water transportation was so great in the early days of the United States that a number of canals were built to provide waterways where nature had neglected to supply a sea or river route. Cities were dependent on commerce for growth, and most major cities were located on waterways or harbor sites.

Transportation by water remains the most inexpensive mode of transportation and is still used extensively where speed of delivery is not essential or when bulk makes other media inappropriate. Much international trade between continents is by water, and inland waterways also provide a common method of transporting goods within many countries. Water transportation is slower than other modes, but it is the most economical for movement of staple goods that do not justify high shipping costs.

HAZARDS OF OCEAN SHIPPING

Although transportation by water is an inexpensive means of transporting commodities, it exposes property to a variety of hazards and perils that almost defy the imagination. Even though modern safety devices and precautions are used in maritime transportation, the perils of the sea can strike at any time, sometimes with unbelievable force. Waves several stories high can engulf a ship and drop tons of water on the deck with crushing force. The pressure of the wind against the surface of the ship which rides above the water line is tremendous. Errors in navigation, fog, hidden objects, and frequent fires make this form of transportation extremely hazardous.

INSURANCE AS A GUARANTEE FOR LOANS OR CREDIT

Most of today's ocean commerce, like that on land, depends on borrowed money or credit. Because ships may be on the open sea for weeks or even months, the merchant who has sold goods to a foreign purchaser does not want to wait for delivery of the goods to receive his money. He may sell the documents representing his shipment to a bill broker who then receives payment through commercial banking channels upon delivery of the goods. All of the mortgages on ships, loans, and other commercial transactions are guaranteed financially by the insurance written to protect the interest of the owner, be it owner of the ship or owner of the cargo.

Commercial transactions are simply a matter of buying and selling at an agreed price if delivery is immediate and payment is by cash or a direct credit agreement between buyer and seller. However, frequently in domestic and foreign commerce this type of sale is impossible. The seller may wish cash on delivery, or the buyer may not have the money to pay for the goods until he gets delivery. A document known as an order bill of lading is used to handle such situations and will be discussed later in this chapter under inland marine insurance. The time goods may be in transit, as well as the remote location of the purchaser, makes it even more important for the foreign trader to receive payment when goods are shipped. Thus a system of bills of lading and commercial drafts has been developed under which the seller receives cash or credit through his or her own bank or through other commercial channels. Upon receipt of the goods, the buyer makes payment through a bank in his or her own country. There is no direct exchange of currency between buyer and seller.

PARTIES EXPOSED TO LOSS OF OCEAN CARGO

One of the most complicated aspects of ocean marine transportation is in determining which interest is at risk when goods are shipped from a seller to a buyer and when the risk of loss passes from the seller to the buyer. Although the general principles are the same as those discussed for domestic shipments, their application can be more complicated.

There are six basic terms of sale: *Ex Point of Origin*, in which the buyer takes title to the goods at the warehouse or factory and is responsible for all charges from that point; *Free Along Side (F.A.S.)*; *Free On Board (F.O.B.)*, and *Ex Ship's Tackle*, which require the seller to be responsible for the goods until they are placed alongside the ship, on board the ship at some designated point, or delivered on the dock at the port of destination; *Cost and Freight (c.f.)*, in which the seller is responsible for transportation charges to the final destination, but the buyer is responsible for loss or damage; and *Cost Insurance and Freight (c.i.f.)*, in which the seller is responsible for transportation charges as well as insurance coverage up until the final point of destination.

OCEAN MARINE BILLS OF LADING AND DRAFTS

The objective of the seller of goods in international commerce is to get the sold merchandise delivered to the foreign buyer and to get his or her payment in the most expeditious manner. Ordinarily, the contract to carry the goods, arrangements for transfer of money or credit, and insurance on the investment are intermingled.

The Ocean Marine Bill of Lading

The basic shipping document is the bill of lading, which has two basic purposes: to serve as a receipt from the carrier of the goods and to serve as a contract for transportation of the goods. The simplest form of bill of lading is used for financial arrangements directly between shipper and consignee. In such case, the bill of lading is a contract for delivery of the goods to the consignee at the place named in the bill of lading. The carrier accepts the goods, transports same, delivers, and secures a receipt. The carrier is not concerned with payment for the goods.

Order Bill of Lading   An order bill of lading is, in a sense, a "claim check" for goods that have been shipped. It entitles the holder to receive the goods from the ocean carrier at the shipping destination. It is used in conjunction with drafts or bills of exchange through banking channels and is a closely guarded document because it is endorsed to the agent who is to receive the goods. It is employed in cases where there is no direct financial arrangement between seller and buyer (consignee). Because direct financial arrangements between buyers and sellers in widely separated countries are difficult to establish, this document is commonly employed.

The order bill of lading is (1) a receipt for the goods, (2) a contract for transportation of the goods, and (3) an order for delivery. Normally, it provides that goods will be delivered to the shipper or to whoever's favor the shipper endorses the document. The shipper then endorses the bill of lading in blank and delivers it to her bank for forwarding to the country where the goods are destined. An order bill of lading thus endorsed in blank is equivalent to title to the goods and is handled with as much care as a signed blank check. It passes through international banking channels and eventually arrives in the country to which the goods are shipped. The consignee (buyer) arranges for payment or credit through his bank, and the foreign bank at the destination then fills in the name of the consignee in the blank space on the endorsement. The buyer now has title to the goods. He takes the order bill of lading to the carrier and is given the goods.

Provision for Damage

The bill of lading, as a receipt for merchandise, indicates that goods were received in good condition as far as can be determined by external examination. In case goods are received in a damaged condition, a notation to that effect is entered on the bill of lading. A "bad order" notation may interfere with acceptance of the goods and payment therefor. Carriers are reluctant to accept goods for overseas shipment if there is a possibility of the consignee's refusal.

Other Accompanying Documents

Other documents are sent with the order bill of lading to enable the shipper to collect his money from the consignee. An invoice shows the amount due, including the freight charges if they are shown separately and are to be paid by the consignee. A draft or bill of exchange is written by the shipper ordering the consignee to pay the amount due. This bill of exchange becomes an obligation of the consignee if he accepts it and agrees to pay the amount. Should the sale be on a cost-plus-insurance-plus-freight basis (*c.i.f.*), an ocean marine insurance policy also accompanies the other documents.

Ocean marine policies covering cargo are generally assignable. This is different from assignment of policies in other forms of insurance and does not apply to insurance on hulls. The order bill of lading and the insurance policy are either endorsed to the consignee or are endorsed in blank so that the consignee's name may be filled in by his bank upon acceptance of the bill of exchange and arrangements for payment for the goods.

A typical package of documents that passes through banks or other financial channels includes (1) an *invoice* showing the sales contract and the amount due the shipper/seller; (2) an *order bill of lading*, which is the receipt of the carrier for the goods and the contract of transportation; (3) a *bill of exchange*, which the consignee accepts and agrees to pay; and (4) an *ocean marine insurance policy*, obligating the underwriters to pay for any loss caused by perils insured against.

The seller/shipper is customarily credited with the amount of money due her when she presents the above set of documents to her bank, and she has nothing more to do with the transaction. The seller may, if she chooses, sell the package of documents to a dealer in commercial paper rather than handle the transaction through a bank. Some merchants import goods regularly from a country, and they find it advantageous to maintain a bank account in the country from which they are receiving goods. In all of these varying transactions, the insurance is essential to assure reimbursement to the party holding title to the goods in case there is a loss.

MARITIME LAW AND OCEAN MARINE INSURANCE

Because England was for many years the most significant maritime nation and because of the United States' ties with that nation down through the years, present practices in international ocean marine insurance were developed by that great nation. England has no formal constitution, and its body of law springs from common law and acts of Parliament. English maritime laws and practices have had a strong effect on American law and practices.

Liability of Carriers by Sea   There is a substantial difference between the liability of a carrier on land and the liability of a carrier on the sea. As explained earlier, land carriers in the United States are responsible for the safe delivery of goods in their custody, except for the few uncommon perils over which they have no control. If the carrier does not deliver the property in good condition, it is liable and must normally compensate the shipper, regardless of negligence.

The liability of a carrier by sea is not nearly as extensive as the liability of a carrier by land. As a result of custom developed over many years, the carrier by sea is liable only for loss caused by negligence. The provisions of maritime law in this area are quite complicated, but in effect ocean carriers are legally liable only for losses caused by negligence.

MARITIME LAW AND AVERAGE LOSSES

The term *average* may be the most important single word in the terminology of ocean marine insurance. It is synonymous with *loss*. *Average* or *loss* under an ocean marine policy may be a *Particular Average* or *General Average.* A Particular Average is defined as a partial loss to the property of a particular interest only. It is borne entirely by the owner of the property involved in the loss. A Particular Average is contrasted with a General Average loss, which is a loss that is borne by all parties to the venture.

General Average Losses

A *General Average loss* is a form of liability that admiralty courts impose on the participants in a maritime venture (voyage). The *participants* include all parties with property exposed to loss in the venture. It is a doctrine based on the principle of equity and imposed liability on all persons who have goods or property at risk in a maritime venture, when part of the goods are sacrificed for the benefit of the entire venture. It is based on ancient maritime law and requires that all persons involved in a venture share in the loss of the goods of one individual that are sacrificed to save the entire venture.

The simplest example of a General Average loss involves the jettisoning of part of the cargo to lighten the ship in time of stress. If goods are intentionally jettisoned in an attempt to save the ship, and the attempt is successful, the ship owner and the other cargo owners will share in the loss of the jettisoned cargo with its owner, based on the proportion of the total value of the venture that each owned. To illustrate, assume that a ship, valued at $5 million, is carrying cargo belonging to five different parties, each valued at $1 million. In the middle of the voyage, the ship runs into bad weather and is in danger of sinking. In order to lighten the ship, the goods belonging to "X" are thrown overboard. The jettison is successful, and the ship reaches port safely. The entire burden of the loss will not fall on "X" or on the insurer. "X" will be forced to bear 10 percent of the loss because this was the proportion of the total value of the venture that was owned. If the cargo was insured, the insurer will indemnify "X" for this 10 percent. The owner of the ship will bear 50 percent of the value of the cargo jettisoned, and each of the remaining cargo owners will bear 10 percent. The other parties become liable to "X" for their share of the General Average loss.[2]

The following elements must be present for payment of a General Average loss:

- The existence or imminence of some risk that appears to threaten all interests—that is, both ship and cargo (heavy seas, for example).

- A voluntary sacrifice, or some extraordinary expense, with the purpose of avoiding loss or reducing it for the common interest of all owners.

- Some practical effect of the effort, with at least some part of the total values in the venture saved.

- A freedom from any fault on the part of the interests claiming contribution from the rest of the venture. For example, if the owners of a ship are claiming General Average contribution, they must show that they were not at fault in connection with the risk that threatened the ship and cargo.

[2]As explained in the next chapter, ocean marine policies include coverage for general average charges levied against the insured.

Salvage

In marine commerce, the term *marine salvage* is intended to mean the rescue of ships and cargoes at sea. A person or organization engaging in salvage operations is known as a salvor. The obligation to save life at sea is imposed on all mariners. The saving of life without the saving of property does not entitle the mariner to a salvage award. The person who does save property of another from a maritime peril is entitled to an award for his effort. Maritime law imposes a liability on the thing saved. This is a salvage award and is compensation for the services of the person who aided the distressed property. Most insurance policies pay salvage charges for rescue of a ship which is covered by the policy.

IMPORTANT CONCEPTS TO REMEMBER

free-on-board	common carrier	Ex Ship's Tackle
F.O.B. destination	contract carrier	cost and freight (*c.f.*)
F.O.B. point or origin	private carrier	order bill of lading
cost, insurance and freight	bill of lading	average
(*c.i.f.*)	straight bill of lading	particular average
Interstate Commerce	released bill of lading	general average
Commission (ICC)	Ex Point of Origin	salvage
Surface Transportation	Free Along Side (F.A.S.)	
Board (STB)		

QUESTIONS FOR REVIEW

1. Risk follows ownership. What determines ownership with respect to goods that are sold and for which there is an element of transportation? Explain.

2. Identify the three classes into which carriers can be divided and explain the important of the distinction from the perspective of risk management.

3. Describe the liability of a common carrier operating in the U.S. for damage to or loss of goods it undertakes to transport.

4. Explain how the bill of lading affects a common carrier's liability for damage to goods it has undertaken to transport.

5. Why is the transit exposure considered to be particularly susceptible to treatment by risk retention?

6. Why might a firm that ships its products FOB buyer's premises elect to insure outgoing shipments?

7. In what way is the liability of an ocean common carrier different from the liability of an inland common carrier? To what do you attribute the difference?

8. Describe the nature of an *order bill of lading* used in international transactions. What function does this document serve other than as a contract for the transportation of goods?

9. Explain the nature of *general average* liability. In what sense is it appropriate to refer to this concept as a type of liability loss?

10. What is the nature of the Department of Transportation's Cargo Security Advisory Standards. To whom do the standards apply and what is their source? Of what assistance are these standards to the risk manager?

QUESTIONS FOR DISCUSSION

1. In addition to the fact that it reduces the potential severity from any single loss, assuming that the cost of transportation is the same, are there any other advantages to a firm that makes a large number of small shipments rather than fewer large shipments?

2. A vessel and its cargo are valued as follows:

Vessel	$6,000,000
Abel's Cargo	$ 500,000
Baker's Cargo	$1,000,000
Cole's Shipment	$2,500,000

If Abel's shipment is jettisoned to save the vessel from sinking, how will the loss be distributed?

3. From a risk management perspective, what considerations might lead a firm to operate its own fleet of trucks for transporting its products, rather than using a common carrier?

4. Identify and briefly explain the post-event risk control measures that can be applied in the management of transportation exposures.

5. ABC, Inc. manufacturers has experienced a high incidence of theft losses in connection with shipments of goods shipped by common carrier. What caveats should the firm consider with respect to packaging of its products?

SUGGESTIONS FOR ADDITIONAL READING

Gilmore, Grant, and Charles L. Black, Jr. *The Law of Admiralty.* Mineola, NY: The Foundation Press, Inc., 1957.

Parks, Alex L., *The Law and Practice of Marine Insurance and Average.* Centerville, MD: Cornell Maritime Press, 1987.

Winter, William D., *Marine Insurance: Ocean and Inland,* 3rd ed. New York, McGraw-Hill Book Company, 1952.

CHAPTER 22

Managing Transit Risks: Risk Finance

CHAPTER OBJECTIVES

When you have finished this chapter, you should be able to

Describe the form of inland marine insurance designed for common carriers and other carriers for hire.

•

Explain what the owner of goods shipped by common carrier may elect to insure such shipments.

•

Identify and differentiate among the standard inland marine forms that are used to insure an owner's goods.

•

Identify and explain the coverage of the four types of insurance that may be written under an ocean marine policy.

•

Explain the admiralty law principle of general average.

Introduction ■

Transportation exposures often represent ideal risks for retention. More often than not, transit losses represent a relatively small risk. When the firm makes a large number of shipments, each of which can produce only a modest loss, the firm will generally find retention to be cheaper than the purchase of insurance. Shipments with high concentrations of value, where the loss of a single shipment would represent a significant dollar loss, represent an obvious exception.

The answer to the question of how the economically-irreducible risk should be financed—whether transportation insurance should be purchased—depends on the situation, the types of property shipped, the value of the shipments, the frequency of shipments, and whether the shipments are made by common carrier, by contract carrier, or on the organization's own trucks. We turn now to a discussion of the options available for those who must insure goods in the course of transportation. This includes carriers for hire who are required to carry insurance on the goods they carry for the benefit of the public.

Inland Marine Insurance ■

Although the term *inland marine* is something of a contradiction in terms, it represents a well-established part of insurance terminology. It designates the forms of coverage designed to protect property that is mobile in nature, primarily while that property is away from the premises of the owner. It has been suggested that the term *transportation insurance* better describes the nature of the coverage. This may be true in the sense that some element of transportation is usually involved, but in some instances the transportation exposure is slight.

The need for a special form of coverage to protect property while away from the owner's premises arose because fire insurance contracts have traditionally covered insured property only while at fixed locations. Although some fire contracts provide a limited amount of protection on property while away from the premises, these are the exception rather than the rule, and fire insurance underwriters have generally based their rates on the exposures at a specific location. Because the hazards that threaten property while off premises differ from those on the premises, a separate form of coverage is needed to cover property while off premises.

Coverage for property while away from the owner's premises is usually written under an *inland marine* form. The particular class of inland marine forms with which we are concerned here are the transportation forms. These forms are designed to cover shipments of goods by common carriers such as railroads, trucking firms, air carriers or by postal service, or by the owner of the goods. Some forms are available to cover the interest or legal liability of common carriers and contract carriers, and other forms protect the owner of the goods against loss resulting from damage to the goods.

COVERAGE OF INLAND MARINE POLICIES

Inland marine insurance grew out of ocean marine insurance. Because ocean marine insurers were accustomed to providing coverage on a broad basis, the earliest forms of inland marine insurance were also written to cover a wide variety of loss. In fact, inland marine insurers innovated the concept of "all-risk" coverage, which was later adopted by fire insurers and is now referred to as "open-peril" coverage.

Because many inland marine contracts are written on an open-peril basis, there is sometimes a tendency to equate the term *inland marine* with *all-risk*. However, many inland marine contracts are written on a named-peril basis. For some exposures, there is both a named-peril and an open-peril form. When coverage is written on an open-peril basis, it is obviously subject to exclusions, and many of the exclusions are fairly standardized. All inland marine policies contain a war exclusion and a nuclear exclusion. In addition, virtually all policies exclude wear and tear, gradual deterioration, inherent vice, and similar inevitable losses. Loss due to carelessness of an insured, such as marring and scratching, may also be excluded, along with damage caused by dampness, freezing, or other loss due to a change in temperature. Other specialized exclusions will be added, depending on the nature of the property and the exposure to which it is subject.

When coverage is written on a named-peril basis, it usually provides protection against perils of fire, lightning, wind, hail, earthquake, flood, and the *perils of transportation*. *Perils of transportation* may or may not be defined in the policy. In most policies, specific perils are listed, including collision or overturn of vehicles, and damage by stranding, sinking, burning, or collision while being transported on ferries. Theft may or may not be included. When theft is included, it is often subject to special restrictions and limitations. For both named-peril and open-peril forms, both the actual insuring agreement and the exclusions must be examined to determine the scope of the coverage.

Controlled and Uncontrolled Forms

One often encounters the terms *controlled* and *uncontrolled* in connection with inland marine forms. The distinction refers to the degree of standardization and to whether an advisory organization or rating bureau maintains trended loss data for the particular form. "Controlled" forms are inland marine forms that have become standardized and that are filed with the insurance department by an advisory organization such as the ISO (Insurance Services Office) or the AAIS (American Association of Insurance Services). The terms of uncontrolled forms can differ from insurer to insurer, depending on underwriting philosophy. The importance of the distinction between controlled and uncontrolled forms lies in the standardization of controlled forms and the differences that can exist in uncontrolled forms. Because advisory organizations do not develop or file uncontrolled forms, the form used by individual insurers for a particular coverage may differ significantly. Most of the forms discussed in this chapter are uncontrolled forms. It should be evident that it is virtually impossible to describe the scope of coverage under the uncontrolled forms, and the provisions of an uncontrolled form from a particular company may vary from the terms discussed in this chapter.

■ Transportation Coverages ■ ■ ■ ■ ■ ■ ■ ■ ■ ■ ■ ■ ■ ■ ■ ■ ■ ■

Measured in terms of premium volume, transportation forms constitute the largest single segment of the inland marine field. In general, the transportation forms are designed to protect the insured against loss or damage to goods in transit, usually by express, railroad freight, public trucking, owners' trucks, coastwise steamers, inland steamers, air, or any combination of these. Some forms are designed to cover the legal liability of carriers who transport goods for others, as well as contracts to cover the interest of the owner of goods in transit. There are also forms designed to cover property while it is being shipped by mail.

MOTOR TRUCK CARGO POLICY—TRUCKER'S FORM (U)

The Motor Truck Cargo Policy Trucker's form is designed to insure public truckers against their legal liability for loss or damage to merchandise in their possession. The coverage is a specialized form of liability coverage and indemnifies the trucker for legal liability arising out of damage to property in the trucker's custody. There is no coverage under the form unless the carrier is legally liable for the loss.

The Trucker's form is not a standardized contract, and in many cases it is tailor-made to the insured's needs. However, the policies of most companies tend to be quite similar, and a discussion of the general nature of the contract is possible. The specific policy used by each company should be examined to determine the scope of the coverage; policies will differ somewhat from one insurer to another.

Method of Coverage

Coverage is generally written under one of two approaches. Under the first, vehicles are specifically scheduled, and coverage applies only to property on scheduled vehicles or on a temporary substitute. When coverage is written on scheduled trucks, a limit is designated for each truck. Coverage is subject to a 100 percent coinsurance provision, which requires full insurance to value for property on each truck.

Coverage is also written on a gross receipts basis, under which blanket coverage applies to property on all vehicles owned, leased, or operated by the insured, and without the requirement that the vehicles be listed. Coverage is subject to a per truck limit and a limit for any one casualty. The initial premium for the gross receipts policy is based on the estimated premium for several months. The insured makes monthly reports of earnings, and additional premiums are paid when the earned premium exceeds the initial deposit premium. Failure to make premium payments when due automatically terminates the coverage.

Perils Insured

The insuring agreement covers the insured's legal liability for damage to the specified types of property while on trucks and in transit when damage is caused by an insured peril. Although coverage is available on an open-peril basis, most coverage is written on the named-perils form. Although there is some variation from company to company, the perils normally included in the named-peril form are:

1. Fire.
2. Cyclone, windstorm, tornado.[1]

---

[1]Although these are acts of God, the carrier could be held liable for loss resulting from one of them, if the loss was in part due to the negligence of the carrier or its employees.

493

3. Perils of the sea, lakes, rivers, and inland water while on a ferry.

4. Collision.

5. Upset and overturn of the motor truck.

6. Collapse of bridges.

7. Flood.

8. Theft is sometimes added by endorsement, often with a sizable deductible and a provision that only theft of an entire shipping package is covered, thus excluding loss by pilferage.

Exclusions

The exclusions applicable to the Trucker's form of the Motor Truck Cargo Policy may vary somewhat from form to form, but most forms tend to be similar. It is common to exclude loss of high-value property, such as bills, currency, evidences of debt, securities, money, notes, jewelry, or similar valuables. Most forms also exclude loss to livestock except death caused by a specifically insured peril. When the peril of theft is added to the policy, theft by employees of the insured, acting alone or in collusion with others, is excluded. Other exclusions may be added in special situations involving particularly hazardous exposures.

Terminal Coverage

An important limiting feature of the cargo policy is that coverage is provided only for loss or damage to the goods while on an insured vehicle. This limitation may pose problems in those instances in which goods are unloaded from a truck at a terminal, sorted out by routes, and transshipped. The common carrier's liability is applicable to the goods in its care in the terminal just as it would be while the goods are on the truck. As a consequence, it is now customary to extend the coverage of the policy to include coverage on the goods while in terminals, but only within specified limits. The usual extension limits terminal coverage to 24, 48, or 72 hours.

Interstate Commerce Commission Endorsement

During the early 1930s, it became increasingly evident that interstate motor truck carrier operations should be regulated. In 1935, Congress passed the Motor Carrier Act as an amendment to the Interstate Commerce Act, providing for the regulation of motor common carriers. One of the most important provisions of the Motor Carrier Act dealt with insurance and provided that the commissions may require insurance policies or other evidence of security to make certain that the truckers will meet their obligations to the public. Under the authority of this provision, the commission requires that the trucker provide insurance of $5000 for loss or damage to the contents of each vehicle, and $10,000 in coverage for aggregate losses or damages at any one time and place.

Insurance policies issued to interstate motor common carriers must contain an endorsement prescribed by the ICC. This endorsement makes the insurance company responsible for any claim for which the policyholder is liable, regardless of cause, up to the limits of $5000 per truck and $10,000 per accident. This responsibility is not limited to the coverage written into the policy, but covers the full common carrier liability.

The policy includes a reimbursement clause which provides that the insured will reimburse the insurer for any loss paid by the insurance company for which the insurance company is not liable under the terms of the basic policy. Thus, if a loss occurs as a result of a peril not covered under the basic policy (which is usually written to cover the perils of fire, windstorm, perils of the sea while on a ferry, collision, upset, collapse of bridges, and flood), the insurance company is required under the terms of the ICC endorsement to make payment to the owner of the goods, but may then seek reimbursement from the insured for the amount paid. In actual practice, truckers report losses to the insurer only when the loss is covered by the basic policy. The truckers pay their customers directly for other losses. It is uncommon that the insurance company pays losses under the ICC endorsement and then seeks recovery from the insured. The risk that the insurer assumes under the ICC endorsement is that the trucker may be unable to reimburse the insurer for losses it has paid under the ICC endorsement, which occurs in the case of the trucker's bankruptcy.

INSURANCE NEEDS OF SHIPPERS AND OWNERS

As noted in the preceding chapter, although the legal liability of a common carrier is extremely broad, the owner of goods being shipped by common carrier may still need insurance on his or her goods. We noted that common carriers are exempt from liability for losses arising out of certain causes and that they further limit their liability through a release bill of lading. In addition to these factors which leave the owner of goods in transit exposed to the risk of loss, there is another reason why those who ship by common carrier may elect to insure their shipments, and that is to expedite the recovery process. It may be cost effective for a shipper to insure commercially, collect from the insurer, and leave the task of collecting from the shipper to the insurer. In these cases, the objective is not really protection from financial loss. Rather, it is to transfer to an insurance company the burden of collecting for the loss from a common carrier that may be responsible for the loss or damage.[2]

In addition, the owner of goods being shipped by means other than common carrier may also need some form of transportation insurance. The contract carrier's liability is more limited than that of a common carrier, which means there is a lower chance of collecting from the carrier. When goods are shipped on the owner's own conveyances, there is no third party from whom the owner can

---

[2]As a historical footnote, inland transit coverage became popular during World War I, when the federal government took over and operated railroads in the United States. Rather than deal with the federal bureaucracy, shippers elected to insure with private insurers and to assign their rights to recover from the government to the insurer. After the railroads were returned to private control, many organizations elected to continue the arrangement with insurers.

recover in the event of loss. In these cases, the owner must decide on the most appropriate financing technique—retention or transfer.

APPROACHES TO INSURANCE FOR SHIPPERS AND OWNERS

The owner of goods in transit may insure these goods in one of several ways, depending on the method of shipment. When goods are shipped by truck, coverage may be obtained under a Motor Truck Cargo Policy similar to the one discussed in connection with the carrier's liability, but with a form tailored to the insured's exposure. There are two forms available for insuring the owner of goods being shipped by truck: the Owner's form and a Shipper's form. The Owner's form is used to cover owner's goods on owner's trucks, whereas the Shipper's form covers goods being shipped by common carrier or contract carrier.

A second approach, which is fundamentally different from the Motor Truck Cargo Policy, is the Transportation Policy. This policy may be written to cover goods in transit by a variety of modes. Although the Motor Truck Cargo Policy covers goods in transit by truck, a Transportation Policy can be used to cover goods shipped by rail, contract, or common carrier truckers, or even on the insured's own trucks. The policy is written as a Trip Transit form to cover a single shipment, or as an Annual Transit form to cover all shipments during the course of a year. Coverage under the Trip Transit and Annual Transit policies is essentially the same, except for the duration of the contract.

Motor Truck Cargo Policy—Shipper's Form (U)

The Shipper's form of the Motor Truck Cargo Policy is similar in format to the Trucker's form in that it uses the same basic policy, but the form attached to the policy is fundamentally different. Whereas the Trucker's form is a liability contract, the Shipper's form is a property coverage protecting the owner of goods that have been shipped by a trucker operating as a common or contract carrier for loss to those goods.

Property Insured   The specific type of property to be insured is designated in the form. Coverage is usually written to cover the interest of the owner only, covering property in the course of transit until it is delivered at its destination or until the insured's interest ceases. Coverage may be provided on incoming shipments, outgoing shipments, or both. The same classes of property excluded under the Trucker's form are also usually excluded under the Shipper's form. In addition, the form generally excludes insured goods while on the insured's premises.

Perils Insured   The Shipper's form may be written on an open-peril or named-peril basis. Coverage under either approach is approximately the same as under the equivalent Trucker's form; the named-peril form covers the same perils as the Trucker's named-peril form, and the open-peril form excludes the same losses as the Trucker's open-peril form.

Premium Basis Coverage can be written on a monthly reporting basis, an annual adjustment basis, or for a flat premium. Under the monthly reporting form, the insured pays a provisional premium at the inception of the policy and makes monthly reports of shipments. The monthly earned premium is applied to the deposit premium until it has been exhausted, after which the premium is payable monthly. The flat annual premium is used only for small shippers with a limited but predictable volume of shipments.

Valuation The Trucker's form, being a liability coverage, does not include a valuation clause. The Shipper's form includes a provision that specifies the value of insured property in the event of loss as "the amount of invoice, if any; otherwise, the cash market value on the date and place of shipment."

Motor Truck Cargo Policy—Owner's Form (U)

The Owner's form of the Motor Truck Cargo Policy is designed to provide transportation coverage for the business firm that owns trucks on which it transports its own goods. The owned trucks are usually scheduled in the form, and coverage applies to goods while loaded for shipment and in the course of transportation. A limit is specified for each truck, and the coverage is subject to a 100 percent coinsurance provision. Like the Trucker's form and the Shipper's form discussed earlier, the Owner's form is an uncontrolled form.

Property Insured The definition of insured property can be tailored to meet the need of the insured and can be arranged to cover not only property owned by the insured, but also property sold by the insured or property sold by the insured and on which the insured has agreed to provide coverage. The specific type of property being transported is usually specified in the form, and the radius of operation for the owned trucks is also indicated.

Perils Insured Again, coverage is available on both a named-peril basis and an open-peril form. The perils covered under the named-peril form, the exclusions of the open-peril form, and the specific types of property that are excluded are essentially the same as in the Trucker's form.

Transportation Policy—Annual Transit Form (U)

The Annual Transit Policy is designed for business firms that want to protect property of all kinds from being shipped to others or being received from other shippers. Coverage may be written to cover outgoing shipments, incoming shipments, or both. Coverage applies to insured property while in the course of transportation from the time it leaves the initial point of shipment until delivered at its destination, and applies not only while the goods are loaded on conveyances, but also while on docks, wharves, piers, in depots, stations, and on platforms while in the custody of a common carrier. In addition to shipments by land transportation companies such as rail carriers and truckers, coverage can also be written on shipments by scheduled airlines and coastal steamers.

Policy Limits   In most instances, there are two limits of liability. The first is a limit on the amount the insured can collect for loss or damage in any one place, and the second limit applies to all losses in any one disaster.

Perils Insured   The perils insured against may vary from a few specified perils to an open-peril insuring agreement. When coverage is written on a named-peril basis, the usual perils are:

1. Fire and lightning.
2. Windstorm.
3. Flood.
4. Earthquake.
5. Landslide.
6. Theft.
7. Collision, derailment, or overturn of transportation vehicles.
8. Stranding, sinking, burning, or collision while on ferries.

Open-Peril Exclusions   Exclusions under the open-peril form vary from insurer to insurer, but most open-peril Annual Transit policies exclude loss caused by

1. Improper packing, rough handling, or unexplained shortages.
2. Insects, vermin, or inherent vice.
3. Leakage, evaporation, shrinkage, breakage, heat or cold, mold, rust, wet or dry rot, bending, chipping, marring or scratching unless caused by fire, lightning, windstorm, flood, explosion, collision derailment or overturn, or by stranding, sinking, or burning of a ferry.
4. Delay or loss of market value.
5. Strikes, riots, or civil commotion.
6. War.
7. Nuclear damage.

Other exclusions may be added, depending on the nature of the property being shipped, the method and distance of shipment, and other factors bearing on the exposure to loss.

Limitations on Insured Property   Both the named-peril form and the open-peril form often contain limitations or restrictions on the types of property insured. First, shipments by mail are excluded. In some contracts, damage to paintings, statuary, or other works of art is excluded; in other contracts, it is limited to specifically named perils and to a dollar amount.

Impairment of Recovery Rights   One of the most important provisions in the Transportation Policy is a provision that voids the policy if the insured enters into any agreement that releases any carrier or bailee from liability or impairs the right of recovery. The provision may be modified to permit the insured to accept a standard Released Bill of Lading. Some contracts automatically permit such releases, whereas the permission must be added by endorsement in other policies.

Valuation Valuation of insured property is usually set at actual invoice cost, including prepaid or advance freight. If there is no invoice, the value is the actual cash value of the property insured at the point of destination on the date of loss.

Trip Transit Policy (U)

This form fills the same function as the Annual Transit Policy, except that it covers a specified lot of goods for a specified trip. Coverage may be written in a specific policy, or it may be written under a master policy with certificates of insurance for each trip. Rates vary with type of carrier (common, contract, or the insured's own trucks), length of trip, and type of goods.

Parcel Post Policy (U)

This form is designed for the firm that makes many parcel post shipments and wishes to avoid the inconvenience caused by waiting in line at a post office to obtain government insurance. Claim settlements are usually made much sooner under the Parcel Post Policy purchased from a private insurer than is the case with government insurance. The contract provides open-peril coverage on goods shipped by parcel post, registered, or unregistered mail. The policy does not cover money and securities. Money and securities must be covered under a Mail Coverage form described below.

The coverage applies only within the continental United States, Canada, and Alaska. The coverage is written on an "open" form with no expiration date. An initial premium is paid at inception, with additional premiums due and payable as shipments are made. The insured registers each shipment on the day that it is made in a register. Only those shipments the insured wants to insure are recorded, and premiums are charged on the basis of those recorded.

Mail Coverage Form (C)

The Mail Coverage form is written for banks, trust companies, insurance companies, and similar firms that have occasion to mail money or other items of high value. It covers first-class mail, certified mail, U.S. Postal Service express mail, and registered mail. The form must be written on a reporting basis, with reports and premiums sent to the insurer on a regular schedule. Coverage applies to different classes of property depending on the type of mail used. Separate limits are specified for any one shipping package and to any one addressee per day, for each of the following classes of property sent by the specified types of mail:

First class and certified mail

United States Postal Service express mail

Registered mail

Coverage applies to the property while sent between the insured's offices or between the insured's office and banks, trust companies, insurance companies, security brokers, investment firms or corporations, stock-clearing corporations, and corporations that act as transfer agents or registrars for their own clients.

Insured Property   Bonds, stock certificates, certificates of deposit, other securities, coupons if detached from bonds, money orders (postal, express, or other), postal and revenue stamps, checks, drafts, warehouse receipts, other commercial papers, and other documents and papers of value are covered when sent by first-class mail, certified mail, United States Postal Service express mail, or registered mail. Separate limits are specified for various types of property, such as nonnegotiable securities, detached coupons, and all other covered property. Bullion, platinum, other precious metals, currency, unsold travelers checks, jewelry, watches, precious and semiprecious stones, and similar valuable property are insured only when sent by registered mail.

⚎ Ocean Marine Insurance ■ ■ ■ ■ ■ ■ ■ ■ ■ ■ ■ ■ ■ ■ ■ ■ ■ ■

Ocean marine insurance is considered to be the oldest form of the modern insurance coverages; in fact, it was probably the first form of insurance written. Early traders recognized that perils were involved in the use of the waters of the world as a means of transportation, and the logical result was the institution of some type of share-loss and risk transfer arrangements. In spite of the technological advances in marine transportation, ocean disasters remain an ever present hazard for those engaged in foreign trade.

TYPES OF LOSS AND OCEAN MARINE COVERAGES

Ocean marine insurance consists of four distinct types of coverage, which are written to cover the four corresponding types of losses that may be involved in ocean forms of transportation. The four classes into which the ocean marine coverages are divided are:

1. *Hull Insurance.* Hull insurance is designed to protect the owner of a vessel against loss to the ship itself. The hull insurance coverage is generally written on a modified open-peril basis.

2. *Cargo Insurance.* Cargo insurance, which is written separately from the insurance on the ship, protects the owner of the cargo from financial loss that would result if the cargo were lost or destroyed.

3. *Freight Insurance.* Freight insurance is written to protect the owner of the vessel from the loss of the charges made for carrying the goods. If the ship is lost, the income that would have been earned upon the completion of the voyage is also lost. Under the freight insurance coverage, the owner of the ship is reimbursed for the loss of these charges.

4. *Protection and Indemnity.* Protection and indemnity coverage under ocean marine contracts is essentially liability insurance that protects the owner of the ship from the consequences of his negligent acts or the negligent acts of his agents. If the owner were held legally liable for damages to a third party, the protection and indemnity coverage would provide protection against financial losses by paying those sums that the insured became legally liable to pay.

Because hull, freight, and protection and indemnity coverages are coverages designed for shipowners, they represent a highly specialized area. We will concentrate on ocean marine cargo insurance, which has wider application in business firms generally.

OCEAN MARINE CARGO INSURANCE

The most frequently used policy in ocean marine is ocean cargo. Therefore, most of our discussion of ocean marine insurance will involve this contract. Because the basic parts of the policies used for the insurance of hulls, cargo, and freight are essentially the same, the discussion of the cargo policy will provide some understanding of the hull and freight coverages as well.

The Open Policy and the Special Marine Policy

At one time, the practice was to arrange specific marine insurance policies only when they were needed; this method is still used by those who make shipments only infrequently. It is now more common to insure cargo under contracts that are known as "open policies," which insure every shipment reported to the insurance company and which remain in force until canceled. Two methods are used to report shipments to the insurer. In those cases in which the individual insured under the open policy is insuring the goods for his own interest, a short form of notice suffices. This notice indicates the name of the vessel, sailing date, point of shipment and destination, the nature of the commodity, the amount of insurance desired, and the number of the open policy under which the insurance is being provided. In those cases in which the insured is required to furnish evidence of insurance to the other party in the import-export transaction, a "special marine policy" or "certificate" is issued. This certificate indicates that the shipment has been insured. It makes no reference to the open policy and is independent of the open policy. It may be used to insure the interest of either party in the transaction and is negotiable. When a special marine policy or certificate is issued under an open policy, it is as if the insurer had issued a separate policy insuring the single shipment involved.

Perils Insured Against Because ocean marine insurance is internationally competitive, there is no standard policy. One of the interesting aspects of ocean marine policies is their wording in language and terms of an age long past. A typical perils clause in a modern American policy reads as follows:

> While the goods are waterborne, the perils hereby insured against are of the seas, fires, jettisons, assailing thieves, barratry of the Master and Mariners, and all other like

perils losses and misfortunes that have or shall come to hurt, detriment or damage of said goods and merchandise, or any part thereof except as may be otherwise provided for herein or endorsed hereon.

The insuring agreement is open-peril but with qualification. Damage arising from perils "of the seas" is covered, and here the clause is definitely open-peril. Damage could be caused by waves, the ship stranding on reefs or rocks, lightning, collisions, or the ship could sink from any number of causes due to perils of the sea. The list of such perils is almost endless. The clause also provides for coverage for "*perils on the seas*" specifically listed, including fires, jettisons,[3] assailing thieves, barratry,[4] and all other like perils. The coverage for perils on the seas does not provide coverage for anything that could happen on the seas but only loss or damage arising from perils of the same nature as those specifically listed. The perils must be similar in nature to the perils that are listed.

In addition to the specified perils, marine policies are frequently expanded to include other specified perils. A good example is the "Inchmaree clause," which covers the bursting of boilers and latent defects in machinery or errors in navigation or management of the vessel by the master or crew.[5]

Certain perils that would otherwise be included in the broad insuring agreement are specifically excluded. The two most important exclusions are the *Free of Capture and Seizure clause* (F.C.&S.) and the *Strike, Riot, and Civil Commotion clause* (S.R.&C.C.).

The F.C.&S. Clause   The basic insuring agreement covers war perils; however, it is customary to incorporate into all marine policies a war exclusion known as the Free of Capture and Seizure clause. This provision excludes virtually everything that could be considered war in any of its aspects, including collision with a mine or torpedo where there was no hostile act. The policy could be made to include the war peril simply by deleting the FC&S clause, but the common practice is to issue a separate war risk policy to provide coverage for the perils of war.

The S.R.&C.C. Clause   The basic policy also excludes, by means of the Strikes, Riot, and Civil Commotion clause, loss or damage caused by the acts of strikers, rioters, or persons engaged in civil commotion. This exclusion may be deleted if the underwriter is willing to assume the risk.

Average Conditions

Average conditions in an ocean marine policy include the *General Average* provision and clauses relating to *Particular Average*.

---

[3]Jettison is the voluntary act of destruction in which cargo is cast overboard in order to save the ship.

[4]Barratry involves a situation in which the master or mariners steal the ship and its cargo, willfully sink or desert the ship, or put the ship in peril by disobeying instructions.

[5]This clause is named after the ship *Inchmaree*, which suffered loss as a result of breakage of a pump resulting from negligence in maintenance by the crew. The British House of Lords decided that the loss was not covered since it was not of the same nature as a "peril of the sea." To counteract this decision, the *Inchmaree* clause was added to hull policies.

General Average Losses   The ocean marine cargo policy, like the hull policy, includes coverage for general average losses. As a participant in the ocean venture, the party shipping cargo may be held liable for General Average charges as discussed in the preceding chapter. Under the terms of the General Average condition of the ocean marine cargo policy, the insurance company providing the cargo insurance will pay the insured's share of any general average loss[6] in addition to amounts payable for loss of the insured property. Coverage is also provided under the policy for the insured's share of salvage charges.

Particular Average

A Particular Average is a partial loss to the property of a particular interest. It is borne entirely by the property owner and is distinguished from a General Average loss, which is borne by all interests in the venture. Ocean marine policies frequently contain clauses pertaining to particular average, such as a clause limiting the amount of loss to a certain percentage or a clause removing particular average completely except for a specified peril. A Particular Average loss generally is adjusted by determining the proportion by which the value of the property has been lessened.

Free of Particular Average Clause   The *Free of Particular Average* or F.P.A. clause of the ocean marine policy is essentially an exclusion of all partial losses except those caused by a few specified perils. The Free of Particular Average clause provides that in addition to total losses, partial losses resulting from perils of the sea are recoverable, but only if the vessel has been stranded, sunk, on fire, or in a collision. Partial losses resulting from other causes are excluded.[7]

With Average Clause   As an alternative to the Free of Particular Average arrangement, coverage may be provided *With Average.* Under the "With Average" provision, partial losses (other than those caused by stranding, sinking, burning, or collision) are excluded only if they are less than a specified percentage of the value (e.g., 3 percent). Partial losses involving stranding, sinking, burning, or collision are covered regardless of the amount. Thus, under the With Average clause, the provision states that the policy is "Warranted Free of Particular Average If Less Than 3 Percent." If the loss is less than this amount, there is no recovery. If the loss exceeds the percentage specified, it is paid in full.

Total Loss of Part of a Shipment   When a shipment consists of several parts or separate units, policies usually provide that a total loss of one or more units is not considered

---

[6]Salvage charges are expenses payable to third parties known as salvors for assistance rendered in saving property exposed to loss. Such charges may be incurred under contract or they may be incurred independently of a contractual obligation. The shipowner and cargo owners may be assessed salvage damages if the ship is in danger of sinking and accepts help from another vessel in order to reach port.

[7]There are actually two forms of the F.P.A. clause: Free of Particular Average English Conditions and Free of Particular Average American Conditions. The English conditions merely require that one of the enumerated perils has taken place, without requiring that the damage result from the peril. The American conditions require that the damage must be caused by stranding, sinking, burning, or collision.

a particular average. The amount of insurance on the unit loss can be determined from the insurance policy, and this amount is paid to the insured as the loss.

Total Losses

Ocean marine insurance recognizes two types of total loss; *actual total loss* and *constructive total loss*. An *actual total loss* is a loss in which there is no value left in the property. This is a simple kind of loss to adjust because most policies are on a *valued* basis; in other words, the amount of insurance carried is the amount of loss. The fact that a loss has occurred must be verified, and the ownership and interest must be checked to determine whether they are in order for payment of the loss. With cargo losses, it is necessary to secure the invoices to prove invoice value and to make whatever additions of freight or percentages may be called for by the valuation clause of the policy.

A *constructive total loss* is considered to have occurred when the cost of salvaging the damaged cargo or ship, or of making repairs, would be more than the actual value of the property when it is salvaged or repaired. The insurer has the right to any salvage value it may recover on making payment for a constructive total loss.

Abandonment   Unlike the case with most insurance contracts in which abandonment to the insurer is prohibited, abandonment is simply a step in submitting a claim to the insurer. The owner abandons the remaining property to the insurer in the event of constructive total loss. If the insurer refuses to accept abandonment, the insured is still obligated to use all reasonable means to recover the property until he can demonstrate conclusively that a constructive total loss has occurred. Abandonment is optional with the insured and cannot be forced by the insurer. The insured must tender abandonment promptly if he sees that his situation is such that abandonment is desirable.

Other Important Features

Many of the practices and policy provisions in the field of ocean marine are unique and should be noted for a fuller understanding of the field.

Valuation Clause   One of the most important clauses in the policy is the Valuation clause. Before proceeding with a specific analysis of the valuation principles, it is important to point out that almost all ocean marine policies are valued contracts.[8] In addition, most ocean marine policies are interpreted as if they contained a 100 percent coinsurance clause.[9] A typical Valuation clause reads as follows:

---

[8] You will recall that in a valued policy, the face amount of insurance is payable in the event of a total loss.

[9] The policy does not specifically contain a 100 percent coinsurance clause, but the legal custom of 100 percent insurance to value has been in existence for so long that legally it is considered to be a condition of the contract.

The value of the shipments insured under this policy shall be the amount of the invoice, including all charges therein plus any prepaid and/or advanced and/or guaranteed freight not included in the invoice, plus . . .

A percentage (e.g., 10 percent) is designated to provide for the additional value of the cargo to the insured at the point of destination. This amount is the insured value and will be paid in the event of a total loss, even though the market value of the goods at the port of destination may be substantially greater or less than this amount.

Implied Warranties In the field of ocean marine, there are, in addition to the express warranties which may be included in the contract, four warranties that are not stated but, rather, are implied. Here, in making the contract, the parties agree by implication that certain conditions exist and that certain rules will be followed in the conduct of the voyage. The first warranty involves legal conduct, and it is warranted that the venture is not illegal. The second implied warranty is that the vessel is seaworthy.[10] The third involves prompt attachment of the risk. Because weather conditions may affect the risk involved, the underwriter has a right to assume that insurance purchased on a shipment of goods in May will not be providing protection against loss on a voyage in the middle of January. The final warranty is that of no deviation. It is warranted that the vessel will proceed without deviation by the most direct or customary route. There are excusable deviations, such as deviation arising from stress of weather or an errand of mercy to save life, but inexcusable deviations will void the policy.

The Warehouse-to-Warehouse Clause Unless the policy designates to the contrary, coverage is provided only from the time the goods are actually loaded on the transporting vessel. However, since a shipment may originate at a point far from the place of ocean shipment, policies may be endorsed to cover the goods during transportation to the vessel. In these cases it is customary for the ocean marine insurer to endorse the policy in order to provide coverage for the entire exposure from the time the goods leave the premises of the shipper until they arrive at the premises of the consignee under the "Warehouse-to-Warehouse" clause.

Other Insurance Once in a great while a cargo owner may inadvertently have double insurance on his property—that is insurance in two different companies on the same property. The American rule is that the policy dated first must pay as the primary insurance, and that dated later will be relieved of all liability except insofar as the prior policy is deficient in amount. The company with the later dated policy then returns the premium on that amount that constitutes overinsurance. If the two policies are identical in date, each company will pay its pro rata share of the loss and will retain only its pro rata share of the premium. Under English law, each company is liable for the full amount of its policy, regardless of the inception dates. However, since the insured cannot collect for more than the amount of the

---

[10]The owner of cargo shipped on someone else's vessel probably has little opportunity to verify the seaworthiness of the vessel. Therefore the cargo policy typically contains a provision in which the seaworthiness of the vessel is admitted.

loss, the insured collects from any one of the insurers, and this insurer then has a valid claim on the other insurers for a ratable contribution to the loss.

The Sue and Labor Clause   The Sue and Labor clause requires the insured to use all reasonable means to protect the property from further damage after a loss has occurred and to prevent or reduce the amount of the loss. The provision also requires the insured to enforce legal rights against any third party who may be responsible for the loss. The policy authorizes the insured to incur expenses for these purposes and will reimburse the insured for any expense so incurred. The insurer may be required to pay more than the amount of the insurance. If after incurring expenses to save the cargo or a vessel a total loss still occurs, the insured must be indemnified for the total loss, plus the expenses incurred under the Sue and Labor clause.

Extended Cover or Marine Extension Clauses

The cargo insurance covers during deviation, delay, forced discharge, or reshipment because the voyage is terminated. It does not cover a loss *from* deviation or delay, but merely continues coverage during the extra time or other method of shipment to the destination. The intention is to protect the insured when the extension is beyond his control, and there may or may not be an additional premium charge.

On-Deck Cargo

Cargo transported on the open deck is much more subject to damage. A customary clause in cargo policies provides that particular average will not be paid on cargo above deck unless loss is caused by stranding, sinking, burning, collision, or jettison or washing overboard.

OCEAN MARINE INSURANCE PREMIUM RATES

Ocean marine insurance rates are handled quite differently from conventional "land" insurance rates. Rates are calculated by underwriters (insurers) for each policy or risk. There is virtually no governmental control over them because of the nature of this kind of insurance. It is worldwide; therefore, foreign underwriting would not be subject to U. S. control.

Freedom from filing and control is justified, not only because of the international nature of the insurance but also because of the continuous variations in ships, voyages, and cargoes. Weather conditions vary from season to season, and the route of the ship has a large bearing on rates. Competition is the best method of control over these rates, if indeed controls are necessary.

Factors considered by an underwriter in making a rate are the ship's ability to withstand perils of the sea, the route over which operations will occur, the safety or dangers of the harbors involved, the type of cargo and its inherent hazards, the coverages applicable to the individual risk, the experience of the shipowner, and the world competitive situation.

THE OCEAN MARINE INSURANCE MARKET

Ocean marine insurance in the United States is placed largely in American insurance companies or in American branches of foreign insurance companies. A big share of the English market is written by Lloyds of London, and Lloyds also participates heavily in the American market.

Insurance on large ships or fleets may exhaust almost the entire world insurance market, and in some cases, such as for war risks, interested governments need to participate in order to obtain sufficient coverage.

Groups or syndicates of insurance companies have banded together in order to provide sufficient coverage and some uniformity of underwriting. Some groups have developed uniform policy forms and clauses.

The broker plays a major role in the ocean marine market. The brokers are highly specialized and have intimate knowledge of the field, including the needs of the shipowners and markets available. The broker also performs many of the functions of the insurer, such as participation in details concerning the application of general average and in collection of losses.

IMPORTANT CONCEPTS TO REMEMBER

inland marine insurance
perils of transportation
controlled form
uncontrolled form
Motor Truck Cargo Policy—
　Trucker's Form
terminal coverage
Interstate Commerce
　Commission (ICC)
　Endorsement
Motor Truck Cargo Policy—
　Shipper's Form
Motor Truck Cargo Policy—
　Owner's Form

Transportation Policy—
　Annual Transit Form
Transportation Policy—
　Trip Transit Policy
Parcel Post Policy
Mail Coverage Form
hull insurance
cargo insurance
freight insurance
protection and indemnity
open policy
special marine policy
Free of Capture and
　Seizure (F.C.&C.) Clause

Strike, Riot and Civil
　Commotion (S.R. & C.C.)
　Clause
general average loss
free of particular average
actual total loss
constructive total loss
abandonment
implied warranties
warehouse-to-warehouse
　clause
sue and labor clause

QUESTIONS FOR REVIEW

1. Identify the two broad classes of insureds whose interest may be covered under inland marine transportation forms, and briefly describe the general nature of the coverage available for each class.
2. Briefly describe the nature of the Motor Truck Cargo Trucker's Form, and the purpose of the Interstate Commerce Commission endorsement to the Motor Truck Cargo Trucker's Form.
3. Explain the distinction between *controlled* and *uncontrolled* inland marine forms.

4. What is the purpose of the Interstate Commerce Commission Endorsement to the Trucker's Coverage form?

5. List and briefly distinguish among the four coverages that are written as a part of an ocean marine policy.

6. Distinguish between a general average loss and a particular average loss in ocean marine insurance. What is a "free of particular average" clause?

7. To what extent do you agree that transportation exposures often represent ideal risks for retention? What characteristics of the transportation exposure make these risks suited to retention?

8. Explain specifically how the ICC endorsement affects the liability of (a) the insurance company and (b) the insured trucking company under the Motor Truck Cargo Policy.

9. Briefly explain the meaning of the term "free of particular average" as it is used in the field of ocean marine insurance.

10. Name and describe three implied warranties in ocean marine insurance policies. What is the rationale for these warranties?

QUESTIONS FOR DISCUSSION

1. In view of the broad liability of a common carrier, why might a business firm choose to carry insurance on shipments that are made by common carrier?

2. Which of the forms of transportation coverage discussed in the text would a manufacturer that ships its products by rail use to insure those shipments?

3. The limits of the ICC endorsement that is required on a trucker's Motor Truck Cargo Policy seem ridiculously low. Does the requirement that a truck obtain this endorsement really provide much protection to the public?

4. What is the justification for allowing common carriers to limit their liability in a bill of lading?

5. Which of the transit exposures discussed in the chapter are most susceptible to retention? Which of the exposures are the most likely candidates for transfer?

SUGGESTIONS FOR ADDITIONAL READING

Brunck, Arthur E.; Victor P. Simone; and C. Arthur, Williams Jr. *Ocean Marine Insurance*, Vol. I and II. Malvern, PA: Insurance Institute of America, 1988.

Fire, Casualty and Surety Bulletins. Casualty and Surety Volume. Cincinnati: National Underwriter Company. (Loose-leaf manual service with monthly supplements.) See "Inland Marine" section.

Huebner, S.S., Kenneth Black, Jr., and Bernard L. Webb. *Property and Liability Insurance*, 4th ed. Englewood Cliffs, NJ: Prentice-Hall, 1996. Chapters 12, 13, 14, 16.

McNamara, Roderick; Robert A. Laurence; and Glenn L. Wood, *Inland Marine Insurance*, Vol. I and II. Malvern, Pa: Insurance Institute of America, 1987.

Policy, Form and Manual Analysis Service. Property Coverages Volume. Indianapolis, In: Rough Notes Company. (Loose-leaf manual service with monthly supplements.) See "Inland Marine," "Ocean Marine."

Robinson, Linda G. and Jack P. Gibson. *Commercial Property Insurance* (Dallas, Tx.: International Risk Management Institute, Inc., loose leaf service with periodic supplements), vol. II, "Inland Marine" section.

Rodda, William H.; James S. Trieschmann; Eric A. Wiening; and Bob A. Hedges, *Commercial Property Risk Management and Insurance*, 3rd ed. Vol. I and Vol. II. Malvern, PA: American Institute for Property and Liability Underwriters, 1988.

Webb, Bernard L., Stephen Horn II, and Arthur L. Flitner. *Commercial Insurance* 2nd ed. (Malvern, Pa.: Insurance Institute of America, 1990), Chapter 4.

Winter, W.D. *Marine Insurance,* 3rd ed. New York: McGraw-Hill, 1952.

Youd, James D. *A Practical Approach to Inland Marine Insurance.* Boston: Standard Publishing Company, 1979.

CHAPTER 23

━━━━━━━━━━

Managing Liability Risks:
Risk Control

CHAPTER OBJECTIVES

When you have finished this chapter, you should be able to

Distinguish between criminal acts and torts and define negligence, giving
the requirements to support a claim of negligence.

■

Explain what is meant by vicarious liability.

■

Explain the obligations of property owners to those on their property.

■

Identify and describe the types of damages that may be awarded to an injured party
and explain how each is determined.

■

Explain the defenses to negligence.

■

Apply the law of negligence to specific fact situations.

■

Explain the problems in the tort system and identify the proposals for change.

■

Identify and describe pre-event and post-event liability loss control measures.

⊞ Introduction ■

A risk confronting every business or organization is that of legal liability for injury or damage to other people or their property. It is a risk that can, and in many instances has, attained catastrophic proportions, and one that can materialize at any time. There is no way of estimating the amount of legal liability in advance. It may be a mere thousand dollars, or it may be a half-million. It is a risk that has no maximum predictable limit.[1] Before we study the role of insurance in protecting the individual from the legal liability hazard, we will examine the hazards that can give rise to legal liability. Basically, liability can arise from two sources: torts and contracts, which represent the two broad branches of civil law.

Simply by being in business, an organization is exposed to the threat of legal liability. It is an exposure that cannot be avoided and for which loss prevention is an inadequate response. In the last analysis, the only practical solution is transfer through insurance. Before we examine the role of insurance in protecting businesses and organizations from the legal liability hazard, we will examine the principles of negligence and legal liability.

⊞ The Law of Torts ■

Legal liability stems from the law of torts, which is that branch of the law that deals with the violation of a person's rights by another. Basically, a person can commit two classes of wrongs: public and private. A public wrong is a violation of one of the laws that govern the relationships of the individual with the rest of society; it is called a crime and is the subject of criminal law. Crimes include a wide range of acts: treason, murder, rape, arson, larceny, trespass, disorderly conduct, assault, vagrancy, and so on. Most crimes are defined by statute. Criminal acts are prosecuted by the state as the moving party (plaintiff) against any citizen for violation of a duty prescribed by law, and they are punishable by fine, imprisonment, or death.

A private wrong, on the other hand, is an infringement of the rights of another individual. A private wrong is called a *tort*, and the person who commits such a wrong is called a *tort feasor*. Commission of a tort may give the person whose rights were violated a right of action for damages against the tort feasor.[2] Such an action is

---

[1]For many risks, the maximum predictable loss can be calculated precisely. For example, owning a car entails the possibility of the loss of the value of the auto itself, a loss with a maximum limit equal to the value of the car. But with respect to the legal liability arising from driving it, the loss will depend upon the severity of the accident and the amount the jury is willing to award the injured parties.

[2]The concept of tort liability grew out of the ancient and deep-rooted *lex talionis*—the law of retaliation. Originally, absolute liability was the rule, and it was harshly applied. If a stone fell from a building and killed an occupant, the builder was put to death. Later, it seemed to make more sense to make the builder support the dead man's widow instead of killing him, and the idea of compensation developed. Gradually, the courts shifted away from the concept of absolute liability, under which liability was imposed regardless of fault, to the doctrine of negligence, under which a person cannot be held responsible unless proven negligent or at fault.

called a civil action. Torts may be subdivided into intentional and unintentional. *Intentional torts* include infringements on the rights of others such as assault and battery, libel, slander, false arrest or imprisonment, trespass, or invasion of privacy. Persons who suffer injury as a result of these intentional torts have the right to sue for damages. *Unintentional torts* are those that result from negligence or carelessness; in these cases, the injured party may also be entitled to damages in a civil action, even though the tort feasor had no malicious intent, as in an intentional tort.[3]

Liability insurance is rarely concerned with the legal penalties resulting from criminal behavior. Although insurance is available to protect against loss resulting from some intentional torts, most liability policies exclude injury or damage caused deliberately or at the direction of the insured. In liability insurance, we are concerned primarily with unintentional torts or losses arising from negligence.

NEGLIGENCE AND LEGAL LIABILITY

The most important cause of legal liability is negligence. Although many of the doctrines relating to the law of negligence are found in statutes, its primary development has been through common law. The basic principle of common law is that most people have an obligation to behave as a reasonable and prudent individual would. Failure to behave in this manner constitutes negligence, and if this negligence leads to an injury to another, or to damage of another's property, the negligent party may be held liable for the damage. Legal liability is imposed by the courts when it has been established that all the following occurred:

1. There was negligence.
2. There was actual damage or loss.
3. The negligence was cause of the damage.
4. The person injured was free from fault.

Because the application of these four requirements becomes complex when applied in real-world situations, a brief examination of each will be helpful.

THERE MUST BE NEGLIGENCE

The basic concept of our law holds that unless a party is at fault—unless he or she has unreasonably and unlawfully invaded the rights of another—that party is not liable. The basic question in all cases concerning legal liability must be, "Has there been negligence?" Negligence is defined as the failure of a person to exercise the proper degree of care required by the circumstances.

---

[3]An act can be both a crime and a tort. If Smith assaults Jones, he commits a crime and he may go to jail, but in addition he has committed a tort and he may be liable for civil damages if Jones decides to sue.

What Constitutes Negligence?

As we noted previously, negligence is defined as the failure of a person to exercise the proper degree of care required by the circumstances. As a rule, the duty to exercise care is owed to anyone who might suffer injuries as a result of a person's breach of duty, even if the negligent party could not have foreseen a risk of harm to someone because of the behavior.

One of the major problems is to determine what constitutes correct action in any given situation. To make this determination, the courts apply what is known as the "prudent man rule," which seeks to ascertain what would have been a reasonable course of action under the circumstances. The mere fact that some other course of action might have avoided the accident does not make the individual liable. The negligent person is entitled to have his or her actions judged by this "prudent man standard" rather than hindsight. The judge and jury are not permitted to look back at the situation in light of what happened and to judge liability on the basis of whether some other course of action would have prevented the accident. The action must be judged by what a reasonable and prudent person, confronted with the same situation, might normally and properly have done.

Because the standard is rather vague and the variety of circumstances and conditions precludes hard and fast rules, in the final analysis whether the duty has been breached will be for a court of law to decide.[4] Normally, the burden of proof of negligence is on the injured party. However, certain doctrines impose liability by statute or shift the burden of proof from the injured party to the defendant.

Negligence Per Se In many circumstances, what constitutes the standard of care to be met by an individual is set arbitrarily by statute. For example, speed limits in most states set the rate of speed for driving an automobile. These speed limits amount to the establishment of a rule that no reasonable person should violate. If the law is violated, it is referred to as *negligence per se* (negligence of itself), and the injured party is relieved of the obligation to prove that the speed was unreasonable.

Absolute Liability Under certain circumstances, liability may be imposed simply because "accidents happen," and it is imposed regardless of whether anyone was at fault. In such cases we have the application of the rule of strict or *absolute liability*. The injured party will be awarded damages even though there was nothing legally wrong in what the other person was doing or the manner in which it was done.

One of the most important examples of absolute liability is employment-connected injuries. All the states have enacted workers compensation laws, which impose absolute liability on employers for injuries to employees who are covered under the laws. In this sense, there is a departure from the basic laws of negligence

[4]Not all situations arising from negligence, particularly those in which insurance is involved, become subjects of court litigation. Adjusters can determine the existence or nonexistence of legal liability in the vast majority of cases without court action. Only those in which the facts or issues are debatable reach court, and these constitute a relatively small percentage of the total.

in the case of an injured worker, for the worker does not have to prove negligence on the part of the employer. Workers compensation laws, then, represent an exception to the rule that there can be no liability without fault, and the injured worker is entitled to indemnity regardless of the employer's negligence or lack of it.

The second application of the rule of strict liability is with respect to extra hazardous activities. The principle is that one who maintains a dangerous condition on his or her premises, or who engages in an activity that involves a high risk to the person or property of others in spite of all reasonable care, will be strictly liable for the harm it causes. Customary examples are keeping wild animals, blasting, explosives manufacture, oil well drilling, crop spraying by airplane, and containment of water.

Res Ipsa Loquitur   A significant doctrine in the operation of the law of negligence is that of *res ipsa loquitur,* a phrase meaning "the thing speaks for itself." This doctrine is concerned with circumstances and types of accidents that afford reasonable evidence, in the absence of some specific explanation, that negligence existed. The accident is of a type that normally does not occur without someone's negligence, and the doctrine recognizes the persuasive force of a particular kind of circumstantial evidence. The characteristics of the event constitute an inference, or *prima facie* evidence, of negligence. In the operation of the doctrine, the law reverses the burden of proof. When the instrumentality causing the damage was under the exclusive control of the defendant, and the accident is the type that would not usually happen in the absence of negligence, the law holds that the very fact that the accident happened is proof that the defendant was negligent. For example, if Mr. Brown walks down the sidewalk and a 2000-pound safe being lowered by a rope falls on him, he is not required to prove that the person or persons lowering the safe failed to exercise due care. The fact that the safe fell on him (or that he is 18 inches shorter) is evidence of this negligence. The burden of proof is shifted, and the defendants must prove that care *was* exercised.

For the doctrine to be applicable, certain conditions are generally required. First, the event must be of a type that normally does not occur in the absence of negligence. Second, the instrumentality causing the injuries must be shown to have been under the defendant's exclusive control. Finally, the injured party must in no manner have contributed to his or her own injuries. The injured party must be completely free from fault.

THERE MUST BE ACTUAL DAMAGE OR LOSS

The mere fact that carelessness existed is not sufficient cause for legal liability. Actual injury or damage must have been suffered by the party seeking recovery. In most cases it is not difficult to prove that injury or damage has occurred, but establishing the amount of damages is often extremely difficult.

A tort may result in several types of injuries to another. The most common types of injuries are bodily injury and property damage. In additional to these, the courts recognize other types of injuries, usually referred to as *personal injury.* Some personal injuries result from intentional torts, such as libel, slander, defamation of character, or invasion of privacy. Newer types of injuries that have been recognized by the courts include intangible losses, such as those that might result from discrimination in employment, sexual harassment, or the loss that results from the failure of a fiduciary to meet an obligation. The common feature of all of these injuries is the attempt legally to measure them in financial terms.

In the case of property damage, the extent of the loss is relatively simple to determine. Generally, it is measured by the actual monetary loss to the injured party. If, for example, another driver negligently collides with your auto and "totals" it, it is relatively simple to place a value on the car. Market or depreciated value is the normal measure. An additional loss could involve the loss of use of your car. If you needed an auto in your business and had to rent one, the rental expenses would be included in the damages. The loss of use of property could amount to a large sum if, for example, a large building were destroyed. In some cases, punitive damages (discussed shortly) may also be awarded for property damage.

In the case of bodily injury, fixing damages can be considerably more complicated. Bodily injuries may lead to claims for medical expenses, lost income (present and future), disfigurement, pain and suffering, mental anguish, and loss of consortium.[5] Three classes of damages may be awarded:

Special Damages *Special damages* are designed to compensate for measurable losses, such as medical expenses and loss of income caused by the injury.

General Damages *General damages* compensate the injured party for intangible losses, such as pain and suffering, disfigurement, mental anguish, and loss of consortium. Determination of the amount that should be awarded for these damages is clearly subjective.

Punitive Damages *Punitive damages* are amounts assessed against the negligent party as a form of punishment when the injury resulted from gross negligence or willful intent. They are intended not only as punishment, but also as a means of deterring others from similar behavior in the future.[6]

The great difficulty in determining the award for each of these types of losses should be fairly obvious. First, although the medical and hospital expenses incurred by an injured party are subject to fairly accurate measurement, an injury that will require expenditures for many years into the future can pose valuation problems at the time damages are determined. The same is true with respect to loss

---

[5]*Loss of consortium* originally referred to the loss of a wife's companionship. Under a common law rule still retained in most states, a husband has the right to the services and consortium of his wife. A husband has an ancillary cause of action against a negligent party who is responsible for the loss of his wife's services and consortium, as well as for reasonable expenses incurred for her recovery. Originally, loss of consortium applied only to the husband's right to sue for loss of the wife's services, and a wife had no corresponding right vis-à-vis her husband's services, but most jurisdictions now permit damages for loss of consortium by either husband or wife.

[6]The subject of punitive damages has been subject to considerable debate. Although some states do not allow punitive damages, in 1991, the U.S. Supreme Court upheld punitive damages. (*Pacific Mutual Life Insurance Company v. Cleopatra Haslip, Cynthia Craig, Alma M. Calhoun and Eddie Halgrove*, U.S. Supreme Court, No. 89-1279).

of future earnings. If the injury will prevent the victim from ever working again, the problem becomes one of determining the present value of his or her probable future earnings.

In determining the amounts that should be awarded as general damages, we enter the world of fantasy. What, for example, is the "price" for the pain and suffering and mental anguish over the loss of an arm or leg? The best answer is, "The amount that an attorney can convince a jury it is worth."

Finally, with respect to punitive damages, there is no necessary relationship between the extent of the injured party's loss and the amount awarded. Punitive damages tend to vary with the conduct of the negligent party rather than with the extent of the injured party's loss and, in a sense, represent a windfall to the injured party.

Collateral Source Rule

Damages for bodily injury can be assessed against the negligent party even when the injured person recovers the amount of his or her loss from other sources. A basic principle of common law, the *collateral source rule*, holds that the damages assessed against a tort feasor should not be reduced by the existence of other sources of recovery available to the injured party, such as insurance or a salary continuation plan provided by an employer. If X is injured by Y and X has full insurance to compensate for the injury, he or she can still sue Y for the amount of medical expenses and lost income he or she would have incurred had there been no insurance.

NEGLIGENCE MUST BE THE PROXIMATE CAUSE OF THE DAMAGE

The negligence must have been the proximate cause of the damage if the injured party is to collect for the damage. This means that there must have been an unbroken chain of events beginning with the negligence and leading to the injury or damage. The negligence must have been the cause without which the accident would not have happened.

The negligent person is usually held to be responsible not only for the direct consequences of his or her action, but also for the consequences that follow naturally and directly from the negligent conduct. Even if an intervening force arises, the negligent party may still be held responsible for the damage if the intervening force was foreseeable. For example, suppose that Brown decides to burn his leaves but takes no precautions to confine the fire. The wind begins to blow (an intervening cause), and the flying embers set Brown's neighbor's house on fire. The negligence began the direct chain of events, and in spite of the intervening cause, Brown could be held liable. The wind is an intervening cause, but one that Brown should have foreseen and for which he should have provided.[7]

---

[7]In addition to an intervening cause, the chain of casualty can be interrupted by a "superseding" cause. A superseding cause is one that is more immediate to the event and "replaces" a prior event as the proximate cause. The doctrine of last clear chance discussed later in the chapter is an example of a superseding cause.

Vicarious Liability

Under some circumstances one person may become legally liable for the negligent behavior of another person. This type of liability is known as "imputed" or *vicarious liability* and is based on the common law principle of *respondeat superior*, "let the master answer." For example, principals are liable for the negligent acts of their agents. Employers are liable for the negligence of their employees when they are acting within their capacity as employees. In some instances, vicarious liability is imposed by statute. For example, in many states a car's owner is held liable for the negligent acts of anyone driving it with his or her permission. Note that this is not liability without negligence; there is negligence, but the negligence of one person makes another person liable.

To illustrate the principle of vicarious liability, let us assume that an employee owns his or her own automobile, has no automobile liability insurance, and is using the car in the business of her employer. Through his or her negligent driving, a pedestrian is injured seriously. The injured party has a right of action against both the employee and the employer, and any judgment would be binding on both.[8] If the employee is financially irresponsible, the vicarious liability rule will obligate the employer to pay the damages.

Joint-and-Several Liability

Instances sometimes occur in which the negligence of two or more parties contributes to the injury or damage. In such cases, the question of who is to be held liable is of critical importance. An important doctrine in this area is the concept of *joint-and-several liability*. A liability is said to be joint and several when the plaintiff obtains a judgment that may be enforced against multiple tort feasors collectively or individually. In effect, this doctrine permits an injured party to recover the entire amount of compensation due for injuries from any tort feasor who is able to pay, regardless of the degree of that party's negligence. If A and B are both negligent and C is injured, the doctrine of joint-and-several liability permits C to collect the entire amount of damages from either A or B, even if A were 98 percent at fault and B were 2 percent at fault. The doctrine has been attacked by critics who argue that it is merely a manifestation of the "deep pocket" theory of recovery. A number of states passed laws in 1986 and 1987 to abolish or modify the doctrine of joint-and-several liability,[9] replacing it with several liability or a system for apportionment of damages based on the degree of fault.

---

[8]The injured pedestrian will probably sue both or, in legal parlance, "everybody in sight." The purpose of the doctrine of *respondeat superior* is to permit the inclusion of other parties who probably will be better able to pay for the injury. Note that vicarious liability does not relieve the agent of liability. It merely makes it possible to impute his or her negligence to additional persons.

[9]Alaska, Arizona, California, Colorado, Connecticut, Florida, Georgia, Hawaii, Idaho, Illinois, Iowa, Louisiana, Michigan, Missouri, Montana, New Hampshire, New York, Nevada, New Mexico, North Dakota, Oregon, South Dakota, Texas, Utah, and Washington.

LIABILITY EXPOSURES CLASSIFIED

Broadly speaking, liability exposures may be divided into three broad categories, corresponding to the types of insurance that have evolved to insure them. They are:

1. Employers' Liability (and workers compensation)
2. Liability arising out of automobiles
3. General liability

Each type of liability is insured under a separate type of contract and covers only that specific exposure. Liability to employees is the subject of employers' liability and workers compensation laws, which differ from the general law of torts. It is insured under the Workers Compensation and Employers' Liability Policy. Automobile liability is part of the general law of torts but is insured under automobile coverage forms which cover liability arising out of automobiles, but excluding injury to employees. The third category—general liability—is the residual class. It refers to liability to persons other than employees of the insured that arises out of sources other than automobiles.

This classification stems from the types of insurance contracts that provide protection for liability losses. Each type of liability is insured under a separate type of contract that covers only that specific exposure.

General Liability Exposures of Businesses and Organizations

Because business firms vary greatly in their activities, their liability exposures also vary. The same is true with respect to not-for-profit organizations and governmental units. Every organization, however, is subject to one or more of the following liability exposures.

Premises Liability   The basic exposure of the individual in owning property also threatens the business firm. The owner or tenant of a building may be held liable for damages if a member of the public is injured, or if the property of others is damaged as a result of a condition in or arising out of the premises. The owner of business premises usually has a greater exposure with respect to premises than does the individual property owner. In most jurisdictions, the courts distinguish among several classes of persons who enter onto premises, with differing obligations on the part of the property owner toward each. The obligation of a business to people who come onto the premises will usually be greater than that of the individual property owner. The classes of persons who enter premises and the degree of care that must be shown to each are as follows:

1. *Trespasser.* This is a person who comes onto the property without right and without consent. The property owner is obliged only to abstain from doing intentional harm.
2. *Licensee.* This is a person who comes onto the property with the knowledge or the toleration of the owner, but for no purpose of or benefit to the owner. In

addition to the duty to avoid intentional harm, the owner must warn the licensee of any hidden dangers.

3. *Social Guest.* Several states distinguish between the social guest and the invitee. The majority of the courts hold that a social guest is the same as a licensee. Other courts hold that a social guest is the same as an invitee.

4. *Invitee.* The invitee is a person who has been invited in or onto the property for some purpose of the owner. The best example of an invitee is a customer in a store. In addition to the obligation to refrain from intentional harm and warning of any hidden dangers, the owner must keep the premises safe so that no harm will come to the invitee.

The distinction among these four classes is not always clear-cut, and it is often difficult to determine whether a person is an invitee or a licensee, or whether a person is a trespasser or a licensee. Business customers and those who enter the premises of organizations open to the public, however, will generally be considered invitees and will be entitled to the highest degree of care.[10]

Children   The law imposes a greater responsibility with regard to the degree of care that must be exercised with regard to children. It is an accepted fact that children do not always act prudently; this being the case, the law requires property owners to protect the children from themselves. The doctrine of "*the attractive nuisance hazard*" holds the property owner liable for injury to any child by an attractive hazard. An attractive hazard is anything that would attract and injure a child of tender years. Examples are piles of lumber, animals, or even trees. The doctrine is applied in the case of construction equipment more frequently than any other item.

Conduct of Business Operations Liability   In addition to the liability exposure from premises occupied, the firm may be liable if a member of the public or property of others is injured on or away from the premises by an activity of the owner or an employee. For example, employees of a contractor may injure someone at some place other than the firm's premises.

Products Liability   The legal liability exposure of a manufacturer or seller does not end when the product is sold and delivered to the customer. The manufacturer or distributor of a faulty product that injures someone or damages property may be held legally liable, and such liability may be established on one of three bases: negligence, breach of warranty, and strict liability.

If a product is negligently made or improperly designed, or if proper warning is not given to the consumer about its dangerous qualities, the manufacturer may be found negligent and can be held responsible for the resulting injury or damage. Liability can also arise under the doctrine of breach of warranty. When a product is

---

[10]The once firmly established distinction among trespassers, licensees, and invitees has been modified by the courts in some jurisdictions. For example, courts in California and Hawaii have abolished the distinction. See William L. Prosser, *Handbook of the Law of Torts* (St. Paul, Minn.: West, 1971), p. 398 f.

sold, there is an implied warranty that it is fit for the purpose intended. If it should prove defective and injurious in use or consumption, the warranty is breached and liability can result. Breach of warranty is a type of contractual liability.[11] Finally, in the case of some products, product liability can also arise under the doctrine of strict liability. Under this doctrine, a seller engaged in the business of selling a product that is inherently dangerous may be held liable.[12]

Product liability losses mushroomed during the 1970s, as both the number of losses and the size of the awards mounted. In many cases, manufacturers were held liable for injuries caused by machines manufactured 10, 20, or 30 years prior to the time of the injury. Faced with an increasing number of losses and escalating judgments, insurers reacted by increasing their premiums. For most buyers, the cost of product liability insurance skyrocketed, and in some instances the protection was difficult or impossible to obtain.

In the wake of this product liability crisis, many proposals were made during the 1970s for changes in the tort system as it relates to product liability. These proposals suggested modification of statutes of limitations, adoption of the rule that manufacturers be held responsible only to the extent of the "state of the art" at the time the product was originally produced, and even a no-fault approach to products liability. By 1990, two-thirds of the states had actually enacted legislation that in one way or another limited the injured party's right to sue or provided a defense for the manufacturer.[13] Although the exact nature of the laws differs, most include a "period of repose" doctrine, which requires that the suit must be brought within a certain time from the manufacture or sale of the product, a statute of limitations ranging from 2 years to 11 years, consideration of the state of the art when the product was manufactured, and mitigation of damages in cases involving misuse or alteration of the product. In spite of the changes, the product liability exposure remains a severe one.

Liability for defective products can give rise to three types of losses. First, and most obvious, is the cost of defending and paying any claims that may be brought by injured users of these products. The second cost is the cost of recalling any batches of products that are suspected of being defective before these products cause additional injuries. The final possible cost of defective products consists of fines that may be imposed for violation of state or federal laws pertaining to product quality, such as the federal Consumer Product Safety Act.

---

[11]Under common law, the seller or distributor of a product could be liable for breach of warranty only to those with whom he or she was in privity of contract (i.e., with whom the seller had a direct contractual relationship). However, most courts have abandoned the requirement of privity of contract and permit suits based on breach of warranty to be brought against the manufacturer as well as the retailer. Most courts also permit persons other than the direct purchaser to bring action based on the breach of warranty doctrine.

[12]Restatement, Second, Torts. Section 401-A.

[13]Alabama, Arizona, Arkansas, California, Colorado, Connecticut, Florida, Georgia, Idaho, Illinois, Indiana, Iowa, Kansas, Kentucky, Louisiana, Maine, Michigan, Minnesota, Missouri, Montana, Nebraska, New Hampshire, New Jersey, North Carolina, North Dakota, Oregon, Rhode Island, South Carolina, South Dakota, Tennessee, Texas, Utah, and Washington. The Alabama law was held to be unconstitutional.

Completed Operations Liability   The completed operations exposure is quite similar to the products exposure, and consists in the possibility of liability arising out of work that has been performed. Such work is, in a sense, the product of the firm, and any damage arising out of it may result in liability if it is defective. If the work causes injury or damage at any time after it is completed, the contractor or mechanic who performed the work may be held liable for the resulting loss.

Contingent Liability   It is possible for an individual or a business to be held liable because of work performed by independent contractors. As a general rule, the principal does not control the actions of an independent contractor, and is therefore generally not liable for the negligence of such contractor. But there are important exceptions. In instances where the work being performed by the independent contractor is unlawful in itself, or the work is inherently dangerous, or where the principal exercises any supervision, the principal may be held liable. In addition, the principal may also be held liable because there are certain duties and obligations that cannot be delegated. Thus, in spite of the general rule, in many cases the negligence of an independent contractor may be imputed to the owner of property who has engaged that contractor. Every firm that may have occasion to hire contractors, or a contractor who hires subcontractors, has a contingent liability exposure.

Errors and Omissions Liability   The term errors and omissions encompasses a wide range of wrongful acts that can occasion loss or damage. With respect to organizations, errors and omissions may include breaches in the organization's responsibility to its employees (called employment-practices liability) or breaches in the responsibility of the organization's officers and directors to stockholders or to the public (called directors and officers, or D&O liability).

Miscellaneous Liability Exposures   In addition to these major exposures, there may be additional exposures that result from specialized activities of the organization. For example, some states impose strict liability on sellers of alcoholic beverages. Organizations that take custody of property of others for storage or to perform work on that property are subject to bailee liability. Other even more specialized exposures may exist for individual firms.

Legal Liability of Organizations

As a final point on the subject of legal liability, we should briefly examine the effect of legal forms of ownership on the liability exposure.

The Corporate Form of Ownership   One of the frequently cited distinctions between corporations, proprietorships, and partnerships is the limited liability associated with the corporate form. Although there is some limitation in liability associated with the corporate form of ownership, this limitation is frequently misunderstood and has received far more attention than it deserves. For some reason, the notion persists that the corporate form of ownership is a means of protecting oneself from the legal liability exposure.

In general, stockholders are not personally liable for corporate obligations; consequently, each shareholder risks only the amount of capital that he or she has invested in the enterprise. In the case of a proprietorship, the individual becomes personally and fully responsible for the obligations of the business. Similarly, the individual partners are fully responsible for the obligations of the partnership. Thus, although it is true that corporate stockholders enjoy a limitation on their liability that does not exist for the other forms of ownership, it does not represent the extensive "limited liability" shield that is sometimes suggested.

One of the features of the corporate form of ownership is the limited liability of stockholders. Nevertheless, it should be stressed that this limitation on liability applies to stockholders only in their role as stockholders. Individuals employed by the corporation—including its stockholders—are personally liable for their own torts, the same as any other individual. This seriously reduces the "limited liability" shield for those stockholders who are active in the operations of the organization. To restate the limited liability principle as it applies to the corporate form of ownership, it can be said that the corporate form of ownership protects shareholders from the vicarious liability arising out of the acts of employees of the organization other than themselves. Obviously, the corporation should not under any circumstances be considered a shield against tort liability suits, for an injured party may bring suit against both the corporation and the individual whose negligence caused the loss or damage.

DEFENSES TO NEGLIGENCE

Thus far in our discussion of negligence, we have been concerned with the existence of a duty owed to others and a breach of that duty. But an individual's negligent behavior does not necessarily mean that a person has a legal liability. For many torts predicated on negligence alone, the presumed negligent parties may have certain defenses that could free them from legal liability in spite of the negligent behavior.

Assumption of Risk

An excellent defense to tort actions is that of *assumption of risk* by the injured party. If one recognizes and understands the danger involved in an activity and voluntarily chooses to encounter it, this assumption of the risk will bar any recovery for injury caused by negligence. Perhaps the most common application of this doctrine is attendance at certain types of sporting events such as baseball and hockey. Courts have held that in seeking admission, a spectator must be taken to have chosen to undergo the well-known risk of having his or her face smashed by a baseball or a hockey puck. Another common example is the guest passenger in an automobile. If the car is driven in a grossly negligent manner and the guest fails to protest the dangerous driving, he or she may be considered to have assumed the risk of injury.

Negligence on the Part of the Injured Party

Negligence on the part of the injured party may also serve as a bar to recovery or, in some jurisdictions, reduce the amount to which the injured party is entitled as damages. Two doctrines have developed in this connection: contributory negligence and comparative negligence.

Contributory Negligence   As an outgrowth of the idea that every person has an obligation to look out for his or her own safety and cannot blame someone else for damage where personal negligence is to blame, the common law principle of *contributory negligence* developed.[14] To collect, the injured party must come into court with clean hands. Under the doctrine of contributory negligence, any negligence on the part of the injured party, even though slight, will normally defeat the claim. Note that the degree of contributory negligence is of no consequence. Its existence on the part of the injured party, even though slight, will defeat the claim.

Contributory negligence is an important and effective defense, but it is an extremely harsh doctrine to apply in modern society. It seems unfortunate that some courts continue to follow the common law maxim of refusal to apportion blame. For example, one could seriously question the virtue of a legal doctrine under which a person who is 90 percent to blame for an accident should be free of liability just because the injured party was 10 percent responsible.[15]

The number of instances in which contributory negligence has qualified as a defense is practically infinite. One of the most common examples in automobile liability is jaywalking. Failure to signal a turn could be contributory negligence on your part, even though your car was rear-ended by an oncoming automobile. Being drunk, running down poorly lighted stairs, teasing an animal, and engaging in horseplay have all qualified at one time or another, to name just a few examples of contributory negligence.

Comparative Negligence   Because of the harshness of the contributory negligence doctrine, the majority of the states have adopted a somewhat more lenient doctrine, that of *comparative negligence.* Here contributory negligence on the part of the injured party will not necessarily defeat the claim, but will be used in some manner to mitigate the damages payable by the other party. Comparative negligence rules divide into two broad types. One is the so-called pure rule, sometimes called the Mississippi rule because it was first adopted by that state in 1910. Under this rule, any defendant who is only partly at fault must still pay in proportion to his or her blame.[16] Most other states follow the Wisconsin rule, first asserted in 1933, under

---

[14]Contributory negligence is a defense only to tort actions based on negligence. It is not a defense to intentional torts such as assault and battery or to any tort predicated on strict liability.

[15]Because of the obvious and unjust harshness of the doctrine, some courts by judicial interpretation use the rule of comparative negligence discussed next. In practice, many courts are inclined perhaps to ignore slight degrees of contributory negligence.

[16]States following the "pure" comparative negligence rule are Alaska, California, Florida, Illinois, Louisiana, Michigan, Mississippi, Missouri, New Mexico, New York, Rhode Island, and Washington.

which the defendant who was least at fault is not required to pay at all.[17] By 1995, all but seven states had adopted one or the other of these rules.

To illustrate the difference between the two approaches, and to provide a contrast with the common law principle of contributory negligence, assume that Brown and White are injured in an accident, each suffering losses in the amount of $10,000. Assume also that Brown is 40 percent and White 60 percent at fault. Recovery under each of the systems would be as indicated by the accompanying table.

The comparative negligence principle has much to commend it. It helps temper the harshness of the contributory negligence doctrine, particularly in situations in which only a slight degree of contributory negligence will defeat an injured party's claim. It seems unfair to disallow a claim in cases in which the negligence of the injured party is slight, but it also seems illogical to allow a person to recover complete damages in such instances. If the jury can separate degrees of negligence, the comparative negligence principle will produce logical and fair results.

	Recovery Under Common Law (18 states)	Recovery Under Wisconsin Law (6 states)	Recovery Under Mississippi Rule (26 states)
Brown, 40% at fault, $10,000 loss	0	$6,000	$6,000
White, 60% at fault, $10,000 loss	0	0	4,000

Last Clear Chance   The doctrine of last clear chance is an additional modification of the doctrine of contributory negligence. Under this tenet, as utilized in practically all legal jurisdictions, it is recognized that the contributory negligence of an injured party will not bar his or her recovery if the other party immediately prior to the accident had a "last clear chance" to prevent it but failed to seize that chance. Its logic is obvious. If a person can avoid an accident and does nothing to prevent its occurrence, that person should be legally liable for damages, regardless of the contributory negligence of the injured party.

To illustrate the doctrine, let us assume that X drives onto a highway after stopping at a stop sign. He gets partially onto the highway, when his automobile stalls. He tries frantically to get the car started but to no avail. A car driven by Ms. Y is speeding down the highway. Although Y notices X's car well in advance of the accident, she slows down very little and makes no attempt to drive to the other side of the road. From the resulting collision, X may be entitled to collect a considerable amount in damages, even though he had no right to be on the highway and even though he knew that his car was in the habit of stalling. Here, Y was negligent because of her failure to use reasonable care in driving her car. She saw X's predicament and could have avoided the accident by slowing down, or, if necessary, by

[17]States that follow the Wisconsin rule may be divided into two classes: those that permit recovery when the injured party's negligence is "less than that of the other person" (the 49 percent rule) and those that permit recovery when the injured party's negligence is "not greater than the other person" (the 50 percent rule). States that follow the "less than" rule are Arkansas, Colorado, Georgia, Idaho, Kansas, Maine, North Dakota, Utah, West Virginia, and Wyoming. In addition, Arizona, Nebraska, South Dakota, and Tennessee have a special version of the "less than" rule and use the terms "slight" and "gross" negligence. States following the "not greater than" rule are Connecticut, Hawaii, Indiana, Iowa, Massachusetts, Minnesota, Montana, Nevada, New Hampshire, New Jersey, Ohio, Oklahoma, Oregon, Pennsylvania, Texas, Vermont, and Wisconsin.

coming to a halt. She could also have driven to the other side of the road if it had been clear of oncoming traffic. One of the most difficult lessons for a driver to learn is that having the right-of-way does not mean that this right can be used without reasonable regard for the safety of others, even though the others have placed themselves negligently in situations that may imperil their persons or property.

Immunity

Another defense, which has gradually eroded, is immunity from tort liability, which previously existed for government bodies and for charitable institutions.

Government Bodies   At common law, sovereign powers can be sued only with their permission. Any government unit that shares in the sovereignty is immune from liability unless it is engaging in proprietary functions. When performing strictly government functions, it is said to have *sovereign immunity*. This government immunity is based on the old common law maxim that "the king can do no wrong." The doctrine has been modified significantly—both by statute and by court decision. One of the most important qualifications is the Federal Tort Claims Act,[18] which provides that the United States shall be liable for money damages to the same extent as a private individual. Government immunity also has been modified at the state level in many jurisdictions by similar statutes. Finally, in a growing number of instances, the courts have attempted to find exceptions to the doctrine of government immunity, and some have rejected it entirely.[19]

Even in those areas where the doctrine has not been abrogated, the immunity does not extend to the employees of the government unit who are acting in their capacity as employees. If Mr. Brown is struck by a city vehicle and the damage is the result of the negligence of the vehicle's driver, the city itself may not be held liable, but the driver does not enjoy the same immunity.

Charitable Institutions   Formerly there was a distinct difference between the respective liability exposures of a charitable and a profit-making institution, but this distinction has gradually disappeared. At one time, the courts were reluctant (and some still are) to hold charitable institutions liable, but the recent trend has been to treat them in the same manner as profit-making institutions.

Survival of Tort Actions

Under common law, tort actions do not survive the death of the person committing the injury or the person injured. This obviously prevents any recovery by the deceased individual's estate or personal representative. The responsible person

---

[18]Title 28, Sections 1346(b), 2401, and 2671–2680.

[19]States in which government immunity has been substantially affected by statute include Alaska, Hawaii, Illinois, Iowa, Kansas, New York, Oregon, Rhode Island, Utah, Vermont, and Washington. The doctrine has been judicially invalidated in the states of Arizona, California, Colorado, Idaho, Indiana, New Jersey, New Mexico, Pennsylvania, and Wisconsin. In some states, the immunity is waived if insurance is in effect; these include Georgia, Maine, Mississippi, Missouri, Montana, North Carolina, North Dakota, Ohio, and Tennessee.

could be held criminally but not civilly responsible. It is clear, therefore, that this rule had the unusual characteristic of making it more profitable to kill than to maim a person. In almost every jurisdiction, this rule has been changed to some extent. Some statutes declare merely that cause of action for damage to property survives the death of either the plaintiff or the defendant. But most go further and allow the survival of causes of action for personal injuries as well.

Every jurisdiction now has some sort of statute of wrongful death. The most common creates a new cause of action for the benefit of particular surviving relatives—usually the spouse, children, or parents—which permits the recovery of the damage sustained by such persons. The new cause of action, however, does not eliminate any defenses available to the responsible party. Thus the decedent's contributory negligence, assumption of risk, or release executed by him or her before death for the full recovery of a judgment by the deceased are all held to bar wrongful death actions in most states.

Legal Liability and Bankruptcy

Bankruptcy is a process recognized by our legal system by which a debtor can, in effect, pay into court what he has, be relieved of existing debts, and start with a clean slate. The question naturally arises whether bankruptcy is an approach that will address debts arising out of tort actions.

A number of major firms have sought protection under Chapter 11 bankruptcies, usually when faced with massive legal liability claims. In 1988, for example, the Manville Corporation sought protection from thousands of claims arising out of the disease asbestosis, which resulted from the firm's products. Under the terms of the bankruptcy, Manville was reorganized and the *Manville Personal Injury Settlement Trust* was established to pay claimants. Over 198,000 persons have filed claims against the firm. Settlement of the first 25,000 of these claims totaled nearly $2 billion.[20]

Another example of resort to bankruptcy for protection from claimants was the A. H. Robins Company bankruptcy in 1989. A. H. Robins, which manufactured the Dalkon Shield, an intrauterine birth control device, faced thousands of suits, despite the fact that the product had been taken off the market in 1974. Under the terms of its bankruptcy, Robins established the *Dalkon Shield Claimants Trust* to pay women with claims against the company. By 1996, 186,000 claimants had been paid $2.3 billion from the fund, with about 38,000 cases yet to be settled.[21]

In a more recent case, Dow Corning filed for Chapter 11 federal bankruptcy law protection in 1995, in the face of thousands of suits over alleged injuries arising out of the breast implants manufactured by the company. In the Dow Corning case, a $4.25 billion trust fund was established for the payment of claims.[22]

[20]See "Manville Trust Seeks Single Settlement," *Best's Insurance News* (September 20, 1990).

[21]Despite the 1989 settlement with claimants, in 1996, the U.S. Supreme Court refused to overturn an appellate court ruling that allowed a woman to pursue a lawsuit over a 20-year old injury, in the face of hundreds of suits against its manufacturer, A. H. Robins Company. See Wojcik, Joanne. "Court Lets Dalkon Ruling Stand," *Business Insurance* (March 25, 1996).

[22]"Breast Implant Settlement Seriously Underfunded," *Best's Insurance News* (June 21, 1995); Sclafane, Susanne. "Dow Corning Wins Implant Coverage," *National Underwriter* (February 19, 1996).

POSSIBLE CHANGES IN THE TORT SYSTEM

In the 1980s, a debate over the tort system, which had begun with dissatisfaction over the "automobile problem," moved from the auto field into the field of general liability. Initially, agitation for reform came from the medical profession, whose members complained that the costs of insuring against tort losses had become an unbearable burden. Later, manufacturers complained that liability suits involving defective products had also reached an unbearable level. Eventually, the high cost of insuring against liability losses produced what many called a liability insurance crisis, affecting classes as diverse as day care centers, recreational facilities, medical practitioners, architects, product manufacturers, governmental bodies, and the officers of major corporations. Dissatisfaction with the system reached a peak in the period from 1985 to 1987, when many buyers faced astronomical increases for liability insurance, which the insurance industry blamed on a tort system out of control. Pressure for reform came from a coalition of insurance buyers and the insurance industry. Opposition to reform has come principally from the American Trial Lawyers Association and other groups representing the plaintiff's bar.

The changes in the tort system that are collectively considered to be tort *reform* include

1. Alternative dispute resolution mechanisms, such as binding arbitration for small claims to reduce the cost of litigation.
2. Elimination of the doctrine of joint-and-several liability.
3. Establishment of a sliding fee schedule for plaintiffs' attorneys in place of the contingency fee system.
4. Limitations or "caps" on awards for noneconomic damages (pain and suffering).
5. Elimination of the collateral source rule (subtracting from the award for economic damages any reimbursement from other sources, such as personal health insurance).
6. Periodic payment of awards (also called structured settlements) in place of lump-sum awards.
7. Elimination of punitive damages or making punitive damages payable to the state rather than to the injured party.

In response to the pressure, most states have enacted some elements of tort reform. In general, however, the impact of reform on liability insurance costs has been modest. The failure of the reform measures that have been adopted thus far to reduce insurance costs is blamed on two factors.

First, the reforms were virtually all at the state level, which means that their impact would be localized. Those who advocate serious tort reform have always been skeptical that state-by-state reform would solve the problem. In the case of products liability, for example, they point out that we are a national market and that only a national system of product liability tort reform will eliminate the problems that underlie the crisis.

Second, because insurers had not maintained loss data in a form that indicates the proportion of liability losses attributable to pain and suffering, punitive damages, or contingency fees, they have had difficulty in judging the amount by which the reforms were likely to reduce future losses. As a result, many states enacted legislation requiring insurers to accumulate loss data according to categories that will permit measurement of such factors in the future.

Although the impact of tort reform on insurance prices has not met consumer expectations, there is evidence that even the regional changes in the tort system had a positive effect on insurer losses and on premiums. The limitations on joint-and-several liability, pain and suffering, and punitive damages significantly reduced insurers' losses, and the reductions were passed on to buyers in the form of premiums that were lower than otherwise would have been the case.[23]

LIABILITY ARISING OUT OF CONTRACT

In addition to liability arising out of torts, an organization may incur liability by virtue of a contractual assumption. In Chapter 9 we noted that hold-harmless agreements, exculpatory agreements, and indemnity agreements may be used as a method of transferring risk to another party. Here, we are concerned with the result of such transfers, the contractual assumption of liability by the transferee.

Contractual liability coverage becomes a factor when one party, the indemnitor, agrees to indemnify another party, the indemnitee, for liability to a third party. For example, a contractor might agree to defend and indemnify the owner of a project for liability to injured third parties arising from the owner's and contractor's negligence. If a member of the public is subsequently injured and brings suit against both the contractor and owner, the owner will be protected by the hold-harmless agreement. This protection is, of course, defined and limited by the indemnitor's ability to make good on the promise to indemnify. The contractual transfer does not affect the indemnitee's obligation to an injured third party. If Smith is injured as a result of negligence by Jones, and Johnson has agreed to hold Jones harmless, nothing prevents Smith from suing Jones. If Jones is held liable, Johnson must pay the judgment. If Johnson cannot pay the judgment, Jones remains liable for Smith.

Uses of Hold-Harmless Agreements

Contractual assumptions of liability, hold-harmless agreements, and exculpatory clauses arise in connection with a variety of contractual relationships. They are often included in leases, construction agreements, purchase orders, maintenance and service agreements, and easement agreements.

It is difficult to generalize as to who will be the indemnitor and who will be the indemnitee in a particular type of contract. In the case of leases, for example,

---

[23]See Glenn Blackmon and Richard Zeckhauser, "State Tort Reform Legislation: Assessing Our Control of Risks," *Tort Law and the Public Interest* (New York: The American Assembly, W. W. Norton, 1991).

sometimes the property owner is the indemnitee, and sometimes the tenant is the indemnitee. The role of the parties in the agreement will depend on their relative bargaining power, and the roles may be completely reversed from one contract to another. The same is true with respect to contractors and subcontractors and buyers and sellers.

Classes of Contractual Liability

Historically, contractual assumptions of liability have been classified into three broad categories designated limited, intermediate, and broad. (Actually, the number and types of hold-harmless agreements are limited only by the ingenuity of the drafters.)

In a limited agreement, the indemnitor reaffirms responsibility for *his own negligent acts*. The indemnitee is thus protected in cases where he is held vicariously responsible. He has acquired a *contractual* right to indemnity where the basic tort law of the jurisdiction may or may not entitle him to it.

Under an intermediate agreement, the indemnitor assumes responsibility for *all liability* except that arising out of the *sole negligence* of the indemnitee. Here, the indemnitor assumes all responsibility for joint negligence regardless of the degree of fault.

Finally, under a broad contractual agreement, the indemnitor assumes responsibility for *all liability without regard to fault*. Here, the indemnitor assumes not only the responsibility for the sole negligence of the indemnitee, but also the negligence of third parties over whom he has no control.

Public Policy Issues

In general, a contract which protects the indemnitee against the consequences of an act that is not a crime or a civil wrong or contrary to public policy is not illegal. Although these agreements conflict with the common law concept that a person is responsible for his or her own wrongs, they have generally been held to be enforceable. The enforceability of hold-harmless agreements depends both on state laws and on the interpretation of the courts.

Some states have enacted statutes prohibiting the enforcement of some contractual indemnity clauses. These states declare indemnity provisions that attempt to transfer an indemnitee's sole negligence to the indemnitor void and unenforceable as against public policy. In most cases, these statutes apply only to construction contracts or to other specialized activities, such as, for example, oil drilling.

■ Liability Loss Prevention and Control ■ ■ ■ ■ ■ ■ ■ ■ ■

Given the peril that gives rise to legal liability—negligent acts—the simplistic response to the question of how to reduce the frequency of liability losses is to reduce the number of negligent acts. Although this response seems simplistic, it is only through the reduction in negligent acts that liability claims are reduced.

PRE-EVENT LOSS CONTROL

Pre-event loss control measures aimed at reducing the likelihood of liability include all efforts to reduce hazards that might result in injury to the public. Some of these measures are discussed below. In addition to efforts to reduce hazards, a second pre-event loss control measure is to prepare a defense against suits before a loss has occurred. This consists of building documentation that demonstrates that the organization took reasonable means to safeguard the public from injury.

Premises Hazards

Several areas may be addressed here. The first is the removal of hazards on the premises that could injure those who enter. This requires inspections by qualified safety personnel as well as conscientious housekeeping and employee training. Also, because the responsibility differs with the status of the person who enters the premises, measures aimed at drawing a clear distinction between trespassers and invitees are beneficial. The use of signs stating *Not Open to Public* or *Employees Only* are intended to accomplish precisely this end. By restricting public access to defined parts of the premises, the organization's responsibility and liability may be reduced if a member of the public is injured outside those defined parts.

Product Liability

Product liability loss control begins with product design. Engineers and designers must assure the safety and strength of the product at its theoretical level. The design should be judged against the standards of the Consumer Product Safety Commission.

Next, high standards of quality control in the production process are required to guarantee that the finished product meets the engineers' design specifications. The design and production quality control measures should be documented, for use as evidence in the event of a claim. Punitive damage awards in connection with production liability suits are invariably based on the accusation that the manufacturer showed a wanton disregard for the safety of the consumers. Documentation of the firm's efforts to produce a safe product can serve as a defense against such accusations.

Packaging and labeling should be reviewed by the firm's legal counsel. Instructions for use of the product and warnings about hazards or side effects represent attempts by the manufacturer to meet the prudent man rule.

Contracts with suppliers should be reviewed and revised when necessary to make certain that suppliers of components for the firm's product assume liability for failure of their component-product.

The final element in a product liability loss control program is a contingency plan to be activated in the event of a product safety crisis. The purpose of the contingency plan is to allow the company to recall defective products or locate consumers and repair faults in the field.

Contractual Liability

Contractual transfers and assumptions of liability are pervasive in the business world. They represent a hazard of enormous magnitude that firms often enter into without realizing they are doing so. The obvious control measure is to have all contracts the firm enters into reviewed by legal counsel. Although the bargaining power of the parties in the contract may be such that the firm must accept the contractual assumptions of liability in the contract if it wants the relationship, an informed judgment cannot be made without a full appreciation of the extent of the contractual assumption.

Environmental Impairment Liability

Although environmental impairment liability is actually a part of the premises and operations exposure, it deserves separate comment because of its significance and its unique basis, which is the statutory imposition of retroactive liability, with and without fault. More than a half-dozen federal statutes establish regulations relating to the environment and pollution,[24] and many states have added their own laws in this area. The Environmental Protection Agency (EPA) has identified 40,000 hazardous waste sites in need of cleanup or containment and estimates that at least 25 percent of the nation's 2.3 million underground gasoline storage tanks may be leaking into the soil and groundwaters. These and other inactive and abandoned hazardous waste disposal sites are the subject of the Comprehensive Environmental Response, Compensation, and Liability Act (CERCLA, also known as Superfund), which was passed in 1980 and renewed in 1986 and 1991. The original act established a $1.6 billion fund, principally from taxes on the chemical industry, to be used to clean up old waste dumps, and the 1986 act increased the fund to $8.5 billion. In those instances in which responsible parties cannot be identified, the cleanup costs are covered by the Superfund. Where responsible parties (an owner and operator, the transporter who selected the site, or the generator of the waste) can be identified, such party is responsible for the cleanup cost. If the parties responsible for a particular site fail to respond, the government can fund the cleanup from the $8.5 billion fund and then sue for reimbursement plus punitive damages equal to three times the cleanup costs. The 1991 renewal extended Superfund until 1995. Although Congress did not extend Superfund before it adjourned in 1995, Congress was considering renewal in mid-1996, and there seemed little question that pollution liability would remain an important hazard for business and industry.

For environmental claims arising out of the discharge or release of pollutants at some time in the distant past, the only risk control measure is an effective defense. This, however, is expensive and may not be successful. The prospects for success in controlling future pollution-related losses, on the other hand, are good

---

[24]These include, for example, the Resource Conservation and Recovery Act, the Clean Water Act, the Clean Air Act, the Safe Drinking Water Act, the Toxic Substances Control Act, and the Comprehensive Environmental Response, Compensation, and Liability Act (Superfund).

for the organization that is willing to address the hazard. A number of consulting firms specialize in environmental compliance engineering. The first step in an effective pollution liability loss control program is a survey by qualified engineers to detect potential emission hazards. The second step is a program to remove those hazards.

Employment-Related Practices Liability

The 1990s witnessed an exponential rise in the incidence of tort actions alleging wrongful employment practices. Suits alleging discrimination in the workplace, wrongful termination, and sexual harassment have grown at an exponential rate for a variety of reasons. One reason has been the growth in federal legislation that specifically outlaws various types of discrimination in the workplace.[25] Another reason is a heightened sensitivity on the part of those who are wrongly treated in connection with employment. Regardless of the reasons, suits by employees who suffer discrimination or harassment have become a major exposure for employers.

Employment-related practices loss is preventable, but it requires a commitment from management in the form of corporate policies that address discrimination, sexual harassment, and other employment-related practice torts and a willingness to aggressively enforce the policy. Again, this is an area in which professional legal help is a requisite. Corporate policies should be reviewed by attorneys who are knowledgeable in the area of employment law.

POST-EVENT LOSS CONTROL

In the post-loss phase of liability loss control, the organization can attempt to reduce the amount of loss in two ways. The first is to attempt to negotiate a settlement with the claimant or the claimant's attorneys that is less than the amount of the judgment that is likely to be rendered. In negotiating a settlement, the defendant will save defense and other costs that would be incurred in addition to the amount of the judgment.

Negotiation and Settlement

Both sides to a claim are pressured to negotiate by the possibility of a worse outcome at trial. Even claimants who face little chance of losing at trial overwhelmingly prefer to settle than to litigate. In the settlement of the typical claim, negotiations begin with a demand by the claimant's attorney for a specific sum of

---

[25]Title VII of the Civil Rights Law of 1964, The Equal Pay Act, The Age Discrimination in Employment Act of 1967, The Rehabilitation Act of 1973, The Pregnancy Discrimination Act of 1978, The Americans with Disabilities Act of 1990, The Older Workers Benefit Protection Act of 1990, The Civil Rights Act of 1991, and The Family and Medical Leave Act of 1993.

money. The opening demand is usually a very high evaluation of the case. Usually, the adjuster responds to the attorney's demand with a settlement offer that is a lower evaluation of the case. The attorney and the adjuster discuss the merits of their case and the weaknesses of the other side's case and exchange further counter-demands and counter-offers. If they believe they can settle, they continue to negotiate until they agree on a specific settlement amount.

Alternative Dispute Resolution

Even if a settlement is not reached, negotiation may produce a limit on the amount of loss. First, the claimant may be persuaded to agree to an alternative form of dispute resolution, such as arbitration. If this is done, the legal costs associated with a court trial can be avoided, and the amount of the settlement is likely to be more reasonable than the amount that might be awarded in a jury trial.

High/Low Agreement

Alternately, the parties may enter into a *High/Low Agreement* in which the parties to the settlement agree to guaranteed minimum and maximum settlement amounts of claims in litigation. A verdict below the minimum will result in the minimum limit being paid, whereas a verdict above the maximum will be capped at the maximum. This type of agreement is appropriate when the plaintiff's case is doubtful but because of the seriousness of the injuries could result in a significant judgment. The defendant is able to limit its liability to the specified maximum, which might be exceeded by a jury judgment.

Structured Settlements

In cases that involve a serious disabling injury, the plaintiff's major concern is in obtaining some form of support for the remainder of his or her life. As part of the negotiation process, the plaintiff may be offered an income payable for life, rather than a lump sum. If the plaintiff accepts the offer, an annuity is generally purchased from a life insurer to provide the promised benefits. These arrangements are called *structured settlements.*

Although structured settlements were used as early as the 1950s, they did not become a serious factor in liability negotiations until the 1970s. Their status was significantly elevated in 1982, when Congress passed the Periodic Payments Act of 1982.[26] This law codified the tax-free status of periodic payments in personal injury settlements. It also established guidelines that allow a property and liability insurer to transfer its obligation to the plaintiff to a third party (the life insurer issuing the annuity). Structured settlements have proven to be an effective post-event loss control measure and will probably be pursued aggressively in the future.

[26]Public Law 97-473.

Aggressive Defense

The second post-loss control measure is to resist the claims and attempt to build a strong defense that may defeat the claim or minimize the damages that are awarded. This is in direct opposition to the philosophy that it will be cheaper in the long run to offer settlement, even when it is perhaps not warranted, to avoid litigation and the possibility of a large jury award. Some organizations believe that settling claims leads to more claims and that an aggressive defense will deter nuisance claims.

Although we have surveyed only the more fundamental aspects of legal liability, the tremendous exposure facing businesses and other organizations in this area should be evident. The complexities of tort law, as illustrated by the preceding discussion, indicate how impossible it is for businesses and organizations of all types to avoid this exposure or to reduce it to a manageable level. Although loss-prevention and control measures can reduce the frequency and sometimes the severity of loss, the exposure cannot be eliminated. The catastrophic proportions that the liability loss can assume dictate that the risk management device used to deal with it be risk transfer. This is accomplished for the most part by transfer of the risk to an insurance company through the purchase of liability insurance, the subject of the next chapter.

IMPORTANT CONCEPTS TO REMEMBER

law of torts	proximate cause	contingent liability
tort feasor	vicarious liability	assumption of risk
intentional tort	*respondeat superior*	contributory negligence
unintentional torts	joint-and-several liability	comparative negligence
negligence	trespasser	last clear chance
prudent man rule	licensee	sovereign immunity
negligence *per se*	social guest	alternative dispute resolution
absolute liability	invitee	contingency fee system
res ipsa loquitur	attractive nuisance hazard	structured settlements
special damages	product liability	exculpatory agreement
general damages	breach of warranty	hold-harmless agreement
punitive damages	strict liability	environmental liability
loss of consortium	period of repose doctrine	employment related practices
collateral source of rule	completed operations liability	high/low agreement

QUESTIONS FOR REVIEW

1. What conditions must exist before a person or organization may be held legally liable in a tort action?

2. Distinguish among invitee, licensee, and trespasser, and describe a property owner's responsibilities to each.

3. Give an example of the legal doctrines of *res ipsa loquitur* and negligence *per se.*

4. Explain fully what is meant by the term vicarious liability, giving examples of several situations in which vicarious liability is likely to exist.

5. Identify and briefly explain the defenses that may be used against a tort action.

6. Identify and briefly explain the basis upon which liability for products may be established.

7. What factors are considered in determining the amount of damages to which a person who suffers bodily injury is entitled in a tort action?

8. Distinguish between the concepts of contributory negligence and comparative negligence. Which doctrine is used in your state? Which do you feel is the more reasonable, and why?

9. On what grounds are hold-harmless agreements and other types of contractual transfers allowed by the state laws? On what grounds have such contracts been prohibited?

10. Identify and briefly explain the post-event risk control measures that can be applied in the management of general liability risks.

QUESTIONS FOR DISCUSSION

1. The question of whether punitive damages should be covered under liability policies remains an issue of contention. What are the arguments for and against including coverage for punitive damages in liability policies?

2. Describe the types of torts that are included in the areas of employment-related practices liability. What are the public policy arguments for and against allowing organizations to purchase insurance for losses of this type?

3. Explain the provisions of the Superfund law and explain how it is a source of legal liability for business and industry. What, in your opinion, is the underlying philosophy on which this legislation is based?

4. Liability suits for injuries caused by products have increased considerably over the last ten years. In many cases, manufacturers are held liable for injuries arising out of products that were considered to meet the state of the art at the time they were manufactured, but do not include safety features that were introduced later. What is your opinion concerning the standard to which manufacturers should be held?

5. Hold-harmless and indemnity agreements are widely used in the business world and some authorities have argued that they should be outlawed. What, in your opinion, are the features of hold-harmless agreements that justifies their existence and what are the arguments in favor of their elimination?

SUGGESTIONS FOR ADDITIONAL READING

Anderson, R. A. *The Insurer's Tort Law.* Ocean City, NJ: Insurance Press, 1964.

Blackmon, Glenn and Richard Zeckhausser. "State Tort Reform Legislation: Assessing Our Control of Risk." *Tort Law and the Public Interest.* (New York, The American Assembly, W. W. Norton & Co., 1991.

Grimaldi, John V., and Rollin H. Simonds. *Safety Management, 3rd ed.* (Homewood, Illinois, 1975), Chapters 24 and 25.

Harris, John, and Jane Tarver. "Structured Settlements." *The Risk Report,* vol. VI, no. 4, (December 1983).

Head, George L., ed. *Essentials of Risk Control,* 2nd ed., vol. I, Malvern, Pa.: Insurance Institute of America, 1989. Chapter 6. liability losses

Huebner, S. S., Kenneth Black, Jr., and Robert S. Cline. *Property and Liability Insurance, 3rd ed.* Englewood Cliffs, NJ: Prentice-Hall, 1982. Chapter 29.

Keeton, Robert E. *Basic Text on Insurance Law.* St. Paul, Mn: West Publishing, 1971.

Parkerson, G. Bruce. "The Enforceability Of Broad Form Hold Harmless Clauses". *The Risk Report,* vol. XVI, no. 7, (March 1994).

Prosser, William L., et al. *Handbook on the Law of Torts,* 5th ed. St. Paul, Mn: West Publishing, 1984.

Ralston, August R., ed. *Risk Management Manual,* Santa Monica, Ca.: (loose-leaf service with monthly supplements), vol. 1, section 3. "Risk Control and Product Liability," and "Product Liability and Product Recall."

Riswadkar, A. V. "Contingency Plans Needed for Product-Recall Crises," *National Underwriter: Property Casualty/Risk & Benefits Management Edition* (April 15, 1996).

Schroeder, Beth, and Andrew Kaplan. "Policy Manuals Help Shield Employers From Liability," *The Risk Management Letter.* Vol. 16. (Issue 1, 1995).

Sclafane, Susanne. "Dow Corning Wins Implant Coverage," *National Underwriter,* no. 8, (February 19, 1996).

CHAPTER 24

Managing Liability Risks: Risk Finance

CHAPTER OBJECTIVES

When you have finished this chapter, you should be able to

Identify and differentiate among the three broad categories into which liability insurance for business firms may be divided.

■

Identify and explain the general liability exposures facing a business.

■

Identify the major coverages of a Commercial General Liability policy.

■

Explain the purpose and intent of each exclusion in a Commercial General Liability policy.

■

Explain the difference between an occurrence general liability policy and a claims-made liability form.

■

Identify and differentiate among the types of bailment and explain the liability associated with each class.

■

Explain how bailee liability coverages differ from other forms of liability insurance.

■

Describe the characteristics of commercial excess liability policies and commercial umbrella liability policies.

Introduction ■

The liability exposures arising from business operations are both numerous and varied, and for the business firm as for the individual, there is virtually no calculable limit to the losses that can arise from legal liability. The sources from which liability can result multiply with the complexity of the business, and as a result, the field of commercial liability insurance has become increasingly more complicated over time.

As noted earlier, liability coverages can be conveniently divided into three classes: employers' liability and workers compensation, automobile liability, and general liability. In addition to these three standard classes of liability insurance, we will also discuss bailee liability coverages in this chapter.[1]

Legal Liability and Liability Insurance ■ ■ ■ ■ ■ ■ ■ ■ ■ ■

Liability insurance is designed to provide protection for the individual or business firm against the financial loss that might result from legal liability. In its simplest form, the liability insurance policy undertakes to pay all sums that the insured becomes legally obligated to pay, up to the limit of the policy. It is commonly referred to as third-party coverage, because it undertakes to compensate someone who is not a party to the contract, the injured party to whom the insured is liable. It is important to recognize that this "third party" is not an insured and has no direct claim against the insurance company. The insurer is bound to pay only when the insured has become legally obligated for damages, which occurs when a judgment has been granted in court.

In addition to the promise to pay all sums which the insured becomes legally obligated to pay, most liability policies include a promise to defend the insured in any lawsuit involving the type of liability insured under the contract. Thus automobile liability insurance will pay for defense in connection with lawsuits involving the ownership, operation, or maintenance of an automobile; a premises liability policy will pay defense costs connected with suits alleging liability in connection with the premises. The insurance company is obligated to pay the defense costs even if the grounds of the suit are false or fraudulent. The basic principle is that the company must pay defense costs if it would be obligated to pay the damages should the insured be found liable.

As a practical matter, very few liability claims ever reach trial. The insurance companies realize that the interests of all concerned will best be served if a settlement can be reached without litigation, and the company normally attempts to reach an out-of-court settlement with the injured party. Most liability policies reserve this right to the insurer. Even though the insurance company often deals directly with the injured party, it should be remembered that the injured party's claim is against

---

[1]Bailee liability coverage is classed as inland marine insurance and is traditionally treated with the floater policies discussed in Chapter 17. I believe that they are more appropriately treated in this chapter with other liability coverages.

the negligent insured and not the company. Technically, the company is not bound to make payment until actual liability has been determined in a court of law.

One of the areas frequently misunderstood by the public is the distinction between the liability of the insured and coverage under the liability policy. When presented with a claim, an insurer may attempt to negotiate a settlement, or it may refuse to consider payment. The insurer's denial of payment may be based on two different reasons. One is that the loss is not covered under the policy. Here, the insured must assume his or her own defense and, if held liable, must pay the claim. An entirely different situation exists when the company denies payment because it does not feel that the insured is liable for the damage or injury. In this case, the insurer is obligated to defend the insured, and if the insured is eventually found liable, the insurer will pay for the loss up to the policy limits.

❖ General Liability Insurance ■ ■ ■ ■ ■ ■ ■ ■ ■ ■ ■ ■ ■ ■ ■ ■ ■

COMMERCIAL GENERAL LIABILITY COVERAGE

General liability coverage for organizations is provided under the Commercial General Liability (CGL) Policy, which was introduced by the Insurance Services Office in January 1986 as part of the commercial lines simplification program, also known as the portfolio program. The Commercial General Liability forms replaced the Comprehensive General Liability Policy (which was also known as the CGL).

The new CGL—like the old CGL—is designed to insure those general liability exposures that are common to most organizations: premises and operations, products and completed operations, liability arising out of independent contractors, and contractual assumptions of liability. However, the new CGL form offers two approaches to the provision of this coverage: an "occurrence form" and a "claims-made form." Under the older program, most general liability policies were written on an "occurrence basis," which means that they covered injuries and damage that occurred during the policy period, regardless of when a claim was made or suit was brought. Under a claims-made form, coverage applies to injury or damage for which claim is made during the policy period.

Occurrence-form liability policies, which cover losses arising out of *occurrences* during the policy period, have served the marketplace well, virtually from the inception of liability insurance. When the injury is of an obvious nature and is recognized when it occurs, there is no problem. Unfortunately, however, some types of injuries that are not discovered until long after they occur. These are referred to as *latent injuries*. Latent injuries have required insurers to pay losses under occurrence policies long expired, because the injury or damage was not discovered until long after it had occurred.

The phenomenon of latent injury is best illustrated by asbestosis, an occupational lung disease incurred by workers in a variety of industries. Persons who suffer asbestosis may not discover the injury until long after it occurs. Employees who began working with asbestos in the 1950s did not discover they had contracted the disease until the 1970s or 1980s. The insurers who provided the products liability coverage for asbestos manufacturers in the 1950s on an "occurrence" basis found themselves paying for losses in the 1980s on policies that had long since expired. The problem was compounded by conflicting court decisions as to precisely when the "occurrence" covered under the policy occurs.[2]

ISO and its member companies believed that a new approach to liability insurance was needed to counter the legal theories adopted by the courts in long-term exposure cases. The solution was the introduction of a new claims-made form for the general liability field, under which coverage applies, not based on the time at which the injury or damage occurs, but on the time that the claim is filed with the insurer. Although some insurers argued for a complete shift to claims-made coverage, ISO developed two new forms, one written on the claims-made basis and the other on the traditional occurrence basis. At the time it was introduced, there was concern that the claims-made form would be widely used and that it might even replace the occurrence form. In fact, its use has been limited. Despite the lower cost of the claims-made form, few insureds have chosen to purchase it. In addition, insurers have insisted on using the claims-made form only in those situations in which the latent injury exposure is significant.

Because the occurrence form remains the most common approach to general liability insurance, we will concentrate on its provisions. We can then examine the specific differences between the two forms.

Coverage A: Bodily Injury and Property Damage

Both versions of the CGL policy provide coverage against two major exposures: premises and operations, and products and completed operations. The insuring agreement for these coverages is designated Coverage A, Bodily Injury and Property Damage Liability. In addition, coverage is provided for Personal and Advertising Injury Liability as Coverage B and for Medical Payments as Coverage C.

Like its predecessor, the Comprehensive General Liability Policy, the Commercial General Liability Policy automatically covers new exposures. The premium for the CGL begins with an advance payment determined at inception. After the policy period, an audit is performed to determine what, if any, additional exposures have developed, and an additional charge is made for these.

Insuring Agreements   The Coverage A insuring agreement contains the different terminology to provide coverage on an occurrence basis or a claims-made basis. The occurrence insuring agreement states that

[2]In what has been called the triple trigger, courts ruled that the occurrence that "triggers" the insurer's liability was the initial inhalation of asbestos fibers, the continued exposure to the hazard, or the diagnosis of the disease. This decision said that all insurers that had provided coverage from the time of inhalation through manifestation of an asbestos-related disease are liable for defense and indemnification costs. In some cases, the firms had been uninsured for extended periods, and the courts sought an interpretation that would find coverage under any (or all) of their expired contracts. *Insurance Company of North America v. Forty-Eight Insulations, Inc.*, 633 F.2d 1212 (6th Cir., 1980), cert. denied 102 S. Ct. 686 (1981); *Eagle-Picher Industries, Inc. v. Liberty Mutual Insurance Co.*, 523 F. Supp. 110 (D. Mass., 1981); *Keene Corporation v. Insurance Company of North America.*, 667 F.2d 1034 (D.C. Cir., 1981).

We will pay those sums that the insured becomes legally obligated to pay as damages because of "bodily injury" or "property damage" to which this insurance applies. The "bodily injury" or "property damage" must be caused by an "occurrence." The "occurrence" must take place in the "coverage territory." We will have the right and duty to defend any "suit" seeking those damages.

The claims-made form adds the statement

This insurance applies to "bodily injury" or "property damage" only if a claim for damages because of "bodily injury" or "property damage" is first made against any insured during the policy period.

These broad insuring agreements, which provide coverage for liability "to which this insurance applies," are modified by the exclusions in the contract.

Exclusions There are 15 exclusions in the CGL, designated a. through o. Coverage for some of the excluded exposures is available under other forms of coverage, such as the auto policy or workers compensation policy. Other exclusions eliminate coverage for exposures that require an additional premium, and provision is made for a "buy-back" of the coverage. Finally, some of the excluded exposures are simply considered uninsurable by insurers. The following are the exclusions of the CGL form.

a. *Expected or intended injury.* The policy excludes bodily injury or property damage that is either expected or intended by the insured. An exception to the exclusion states that it does not apply to the use of reasonable force to protect persons or property.

b. *Contractual assumptions.* Liability assumed under contracts is excluded, but there are several important exceptions. Coverage applies to "insured contracts" (leases, sidetrack agreements, easement agreements, and agreements and contracts pertaining to the insured's business under which the insured assumes the tort liability of another). In addition, the exclusion does not apply to liability that the insured would have in the absence of the contract or agreement.

c. *Liquor liability.* The policy excludes liability imposed under a liquor liability statute or at common law for causing or contributing to the intoxication of any person, or furnishing alcoholic beverages to a person under legal drinking age or who is intoxicated. The exclusion applies only to organizations in the business of manufacturing, selling, or distributing alcoholic beverages, and the courts have interpreted it narrowly. The courts have refused to apply the exclusion, for example, to injuries arising out of the selling or serving of alcoholic beverages by churches or other nonprofit organizations at social functions or fund-raising activities, on the grounds that these organizations are not in the business of serving or selling alcoholic beverages. In response to these decisions, the ISO developed an optional endorsement that insurers can add to the policy when they anticipate a liquor liability exposure. The Amendment of Liquor Liability Exclusion endorsement (CG 21 50) expands the exclusion to eliminate coverage for anyone who serves alcoholic beverages for a charge, whether or not the activity is for the purpose of financial gain. This includes a variety of fund-raising and social activities sponsored by nonprofit organizations. If the insurer is willing, the exposure can be covered by scheduling the specific functions at which the liquor will be sold using the Amendment of Liquor Liability Exclusion—Exception for Scheduled Activities endorsement (CG 21 51).

d. *Workers compensation.* There is an exclusion of benefits payable under any workers compensation, disability benefits, or unemployment compensation law.

e. *Employers' liability.* The policy excludes bodily injury to employees of the insured arising out of and in the course of employment. As in the workers compensation exposure, losses of this type are intended to be covered under the Workers Compensation and Employers' Liability Policy.

f. *Pollution exclusion.* The pollution exclusion has two parts. In addition to an exclusion of bodily injury and property damage arising out of the discharge, release or escape of pollutants, the policy separately excludes liability for cleanup costs. Unlike earlier policies, in which the exclusion did not apply if the emission was sudden and accidental, the new form excludes all forms of pollution. The only exception is with respect to the Products/Completed Operations hazard. Even here, however, the exclusion of cleanup costs applies. As discussed later in the chapter, the policy may be endorsed to provide pollution coverage and two Pollution Liability Coverage forms are available.

g. *Aircraft, autos, and watercraft.* This exclusion eliminates liability arising out of the ownership, maintenance, use, or entrustment to others of aircraft, motor vehicles, and watercraft that are owned or operated by or rented or loaned to any insured. Nonowned watercraft of less than 26 feet in length are covered by an exception to the exclusion. The definition of motor vehicle does not include "*mobile equipment*" (bulldozers, farm machinery, forklifts, and other vehicles designed for use principally off public roads), which means that coverage is provided for vehicles of this type.

h. *Mobile equipment* is excluded while being transported by an auto, or while being used in any racing, speed, or demolition contest, or while practicing for such activities.

i. *War exclusion.* Liability arising out of war is excluded, if such liability is assumed in a contract. (No one knows why, so don't ask your instructor.)

j. *Care, custody, and control.* This exclusion excludes property damage to property owned by, rented to, or in the care, custody, and control of the insured. It also excludes damage to premises sold, given away, or abandoned unless such premises are the insured's work (formerly called the alienated premises). The exclusion of property in the insured's care, custody, and control applies only to personal property. Finally, property damage is excluded for the particular part of real property on which the insured or any subcontractor is working or the particular part of any property that must be restored, repaired, or replaced because work was incorrectly performed on it.[3]

[3]The care, custody, and control exclusion of the CGL form is both long and complex. It incorporates a number of provisions that were previously available only by endorsement and generally broadens the coverage in this area from that of earlier forms.

k. *Damage to the insured's product.* The policy excludes property damage to the insured's product arising out of the product. Many people find this exclusion confusing, but the concept is simple enough. If a service station sells a defective tire to a customer and it blows out, there is no coverage for the loss of the tire. If, on the other hand, the blowout causes the customer to lose control of the car and demolish it or other property, everything except the tire would be covered. The basic point is that the products coverage is designed to cover damage caused *by* the product and not damage to the product.

l. *Damage to the insured's work.* The exclusion of damage to the insured's work is similar in intent to the exclusion of damage to the insured's product. Although the situation is somewhat more complicated, the principle remains the same. The exclusion of damage to the insured's work applies only under the Products and Completed Operations coverage, which means that it applies only after the work is completed. In addition, an exception to the exclusion makes it inapplicable if the damaged work or the work out of which the damage arises was performed on the named insured's behalf by a subcontractor.

m. *Property damage to impaired property.* The policy excludes loss arising out of "impaired property" (property not actually injured or damaged) arising out of a defect, deficiency, or condition in the insured's work or product or delay or failure by the insured to perform a contract or an agreement in accordance with its terms. The term *impaired property* distinguishes property that is diminished in value or usefulness from property that has actually been damaged. It is property that cannot be used or is less useful because of a defect in the insured's product or work, but the situation is correctable. If, for example, the insured manufactures aviation navigation equipment, defects in such equipment might result in grounding of aircraft in which it has been installed. The aircraft are not damaged; they are "impaired property." The distinction between "impaired" property and "damaged" property is whether the property can be restored by removal or replacement of the insured's product, or by the insured fulfilling the terms of the contract or agreement.

n. *Product recall.* The policy excludes liability for damage or claims arising out of the withdrawal or repair of products that are, or are believed to be, defective. The cost of recalling defective products can be considerable, and coverage for this exposure is available from specialty insurers on a limited basis.

o. *Employment-related practices.* The policy may be modified by endorsement to exclude coverage for bodily injury arising out of employment practices. Suits by employees alleging wrongful termination, sexual harassment, and discrimination proliferated during the 1980s and 1990s. Although such offenses do not meet the policy definition of bodily injury, some plaintiffs argued successfully that the employment practices caused bodily injuries such as emotional distress, trauma, and anxiety. Efforts to deny such claims based on the employee injury exclusion also failed as courts ruled that the employment-related activities fell outside "the course of employment." Responding to these decisions, ISO developed the *Employment-Related Practices Exclusion Endorsement* (CG 21 47) that may be added to the policy. The endorsement excludes bodily injury arising out of any refusal to employ, termination, coercion, demotion, evaluation, reassignment, discipline, defamation, harassment, humiliation, discrimination, or other employment-related practices, policies, acts, or omissions. Although the endorsement is designated as an optional modification, it is almost universally included in CGL policies.

Coverage B: Personal and Advertising Injury Liability

Personal injury and advertising injury liability were originally available as optional coverages under the CGL form. They are now included as standard components of the coverage. Personal Injury is defined to include

1. False arrest, detention, or imprisonment.
2. Malicious prosecution.
3. Wrongful entry into or eviction of a person from a room, dwelling, or premise that the person occupies.
4. Oral or written publication of material that slanders or libels a person or organization or disparages a person's or organization's goods, products, or services.
5. Oral or written publication of material that violates a person's right of privacy.

Advertising injury means injury arising out of oral or written publication of materials that slanders or libels a person or an organization, that disparages a person's or organization's goods, products, or services, or that violates a person's right of privacy. It also includes misappropriation of advertising ideas or style of doing business or infringement of copyright, title, or slogan. The trigger of coverage for Personal and Advertising Injury Liability is on an occurrence basis in the occurrence form and on a claims-made basis in the claims-made form.

There are relatively few exclusions. Liability assumed under contract is excluded, as is personal or advertising injury arising out of the willful violation of a penal statute. Libel, slander, or defamation committed by the insured before the inception of the policy or done by or at the direction of the insured with knowledge that the statements were false is also excluded. As in the case of the Bodily Injury coverage, Personal Injury coverage may be endorsed to exclude personal injury arising out of employment practices.

Coverage C: Medical Payments Coverage

The Medical Payments coverage is similar in nature and intent to the Medical Payments coverage examined in the homeowners forms. It pays reasonable medical expenses incurred within three years of an accident to persons injured on the premises, regardless of liability. The Medical Payments coverage excludes injury to all insureds (instead of just the named insured). In addition, for tenants in residence, coverage applies only with respect to nonoccupied areas.

Other Coverages

Several coverages that were previously available only by endorsement are now incorporated into the basic policy by virtue of the absence of exclusions. Two of these are fire legal liability and contractual liability insurance.

Fire Legal Liability   A special problem created by the "care, custody, and control" exclusion is the lack of coverage for damage to property rented or leased to the insured. If a tenant (or an employee of the tenant) negligently sets fire to a leased or rented structure, the owner (or the owner's insurer) may seek to recover the amount of the loss from the tenant. Fire Legal Liability coverage is covered by virtue of an exception to the care, custody, and control exclusion. The coverage applies only to real property and is subject to a separate limit of liability stated in the declarations. Exclusions c. through o. do not apply to damage by a fire to premises rented to the insured.[4]

Contractual Liability Coverage   Under earlier versions of the general liability forms, a separate contractual liability coverage part was used to provide protection for liability arising out of contractual assumptions. The exceptions to the contractual exclusion we noted earlier automatically provide coverage for contractual liability without a separate form or insuring agreement. The coverage for liability assumed under contract is subject to the other exclusions of the form. This means, for example, that contractual assumptions of liability involving motor vehicles are excluded and must be covered elsewhere. (The Business Auto Coverage form includes coverage for contractual liability related to motor vehicles.)

In the early 1990s, a debate evolved over the scope of the contractual liability coverage—more specifically over whether the obligation to defend the insured against claims that are covered under the policy extends to a third party indemnitee. In 1996, ISO introduced a revision in the CGL to clarify this feature of coverage. The 1996 edition the CGL incorporates two extensions of coverage to insured indemnitors and their indemnitees who have been promised a defense in a hold-harmless agreement. Under the first extension, contractually assumed defense costs are considered *damages* when they are part of the liability assumed by the CGL insured. As damages, such costs are subject to the policy limits. Under the second extension, the policy covers contractually assumed defense costs under the supplementary payments when the indemnitees is joined in a suit against the named insured. Under this provision, the defense costs are payable in addition to the policy limit.

Policy Limits

The application of the policy limits differs from previous forms in several ways. A combined single limit applies to bodily injury and property damage on a "per occurrence" basis. In addition, an aggregate limit applies to the products/completed operations hazard, with a separate aggregate limit applicable to all other coverages combined. Finally, separate sublimits apply on a "per person" basis to personal and advertising injury liability, "per person" to medical payments, and "per fire" to fire damage legal liability.

[4]Fire Legal Liability coverage may also be purchased separately under the Commercial Property Coverage portion of the portfolio program. The separate coverage may be purchased by attaching a legal liability form to a portfolio property insurance policy. The coverage may be limited to real property, or it may include personal property as well. Although the standard liability form applies to fire only, the fire policy version may be written to include additional perils such as internal explosion and, in some areas, extended coverage.

Occurrence Form Compared with Claims-Made Version

The major difference between the occurrence and claims-made versions of the CGL is, of course, the difference in the trigger of coverage, but this difference dictates other differences as well. The claims-made trigger is the date when a claim is "reported and recorded" by the insured or the company, for injury or damage that occurred after the policy's *retroactive date.*

A *retroactive date* in a claims-made liability policy is a coverage restriction. It limits coverage to claims arising out of events that occur after the specified retroactive date.[5] Initially, the retroactive date will be the date on which a claims-made form first replaces an occurrence form. Thus, if an occurrence policy is replaced by a claims-made policy on June 1, 1995, the retroactive date of the claims-made form will be June 1, 1995. This is a natural approach to eliminating duplication of coverage between a claims-made form and an occurrence form. The retroactive date eliminates coverage for claims arising out of occurrences before inception, because such losses will presumably be covered under the expired occurrence policy that was replaced. Ideally, renewals of claims-made policies should have the same retroactive date as the policy being renewed, which would be the same as the first claims-made policy (and the expiration of the last occurrence policy).

If all claims-made policies subsequent to the first are issued with the same retroactive date as the initial claims-made policy, coverage will be provided on an uninterrupted basis from the last occurrence form up to the latest claims-made form. Losses that occurred prior to the retroactive date (that is, before inception of the first claims-made form) will be covered under the occurrence forms that preceded the change to a claims-made basis. Coverage for losses that occurred after the retroactive date will be provided by the claims-made form that is in effect at the time the claim is made.

As long as the retroactive date in claims-made forms remains the same as the date the last occurrence policy expired, there is no gap in coverage. If the retroactive date in any renewal of a claims-made policy is advanced, however, a gap in coverage is created.[6] The expired claims-made policy will not cover claims that are filed after its expiration, and the new claims-made policy will not cover claims arising out of occurrences prior to its retroactive date (inception). Thus a claim made during the renewal policy arising out of an occurrence during the expired policy would not be covered.

The traditional solution to this gap in claims-made policies has been for the insured to purchase an extended reporting date endorsement (commonly called "tail" coverage) for the expiring policy. An "extended reporting period" provision

---

[5]Although it is possible to write a claims-made form without a retroactive date, most claims-made policies will be written with a retroactive date. The insurer may eliminate the retroactive date feature of the coverage by entering "none" in the policy declarations entry entitled "retroactive date."

[6]The claims-made form allows the insurer to advance the retroactive date in a renewal under specified conditions: (1) when there is a substantial change in the insured's operations that increases the hazard; (2) when the insured fails to provide the insurer with information known or that should have been known to the insured about the nature of the risk; (3) with the agreement of the insured; and (4) when there is a change in insurer.

stipulates that any claim reported within the designated extended reporting period will be deemed to have been reported during the policy and will be covered.

Extended Reporting Period Provisions The revised version of the claims-made form includes three extended reporting provisions. Two are built into the basic policy and together are called Basic Extended Reporting Period Coverage. The third provision is provided by endorsement for an additional premium and is referred to as the Supplemental Extended Reporting Period Coverage.

The *basic extended reporting period* begins when the policy period ends and is activated when there is an interruption in claims-made coverage—that is, when the policy is canceled or nonrenewed, renewed with an advanced retroactive date, or is replaced with an occurrence policy. The basic extended reporting period has two elements. First, claims arising out of occurrences after the retroactive date but before the policy expiration are covered if reported during the 60-day period following expiration. In addition, the policy covers claims reported within five years of the expiration of the policy, which arise out of occurrences reported to the insured or the insurer during the policy period or within 60 days following expiration.[7]

Claims covered under the basic extended reporting period provisions are subject to the policy limits, and the limits are not increased or reinstated with respect to claims under these provisions. In addition, the coverage applies only in the absence of future insurance that applies to the claims or that would apply except for the exhaustion of limits.

The insured may elect, within 60 days of the expiration of the policy, to purchase a *Supplemental Extended Reporting Period Endorsement* for an additional premium. The endorsement extends the reporting period indefinitely. Unlike the provisions of the basic extended reporting period, the coverage of the Supplemental Extended Reporting Period Endorsement applies even if the loss is covered by other insurance. Also, when the Supplemental Extended Reporting Period Endorsement is purchased, the original policy limits are reinstated.[8]

OTHER PORTFOLIO LIABILITY COVERAGES

In addition to the two CGL forms, there are a number of other specialized forms of liability coverage under the new program. Although products and completed operations coverage is included in the CGL, instances arise in which the coverage

---

[7]The five-year extended reporting period seems peculiar without an explanation of its rationale. In the first version of the claims-made form, an actual claim for damages had to be received during the policy period to trigger coverage. Insurance buyers argued that an insurer, learning of an occurrence that had not yet generated an actual claim, might advance the retroactive date or decline to renew, forcing the insured to purchase the optional extended reporting period coverage for an additional premium. Responding to the criticism, ISO added the five-year tail for claims arising out of occurrences reported during the policy period or within 60 days of the end of the policy.

[8]The premium for the extended reporting period is limited to 200 percent of the final annual premium of the terminated policy. Factors considered in determining the premium for the endorsement include the exposures insured, the previous types and amounts of insurance, the limits purchased, and "other related factors."

must be written separately, and separate occurrence and claims-made forms of the coverage are available. *Owners and Contractors Protective Liability Coverage* is also available under a separate coverage part to insure liability arising out of independent contractors.[9] *Railroad Protective Liability Coverage* is a special form of contractual liability required for those who perform construction or demolition work on or near railroad property.

OTHER GENERAL LIABILITY COVERAGES

In addition to the CGL and those liability coverages that have been noted, there are a number of specialized liability coverages designed to meet specific exposures. Some of the more interesting of these coverages are discussed in the paragraphs that follow.

Liquor Liability Coverage

Another exclusion of the CGL creating a need for a specialized coverage is that of liability arising out of the business of manufacturing, selling, or serving of alcoholic beverages. Many states have special statutes, called "dram shop" laws, that provide a right of action against the seller in the event that the purchaser injures a third party. The laws vary greatly in their detail. Some apply only when the injury results from sale to a minor or intoxicated person, whereas others have no such qualification. Some laws provide for liability only to those injured by the intoxicated person, whereas others permit liability for loss of support by dependents of the intoxicated party or even injuries sustained by the intoxicated person. Even in those states where such laws do not exist, similar liability may be imposed under common law.[10] When the expanded liquor liability exclusion endorsement is attached to the policy, coverage is excluded not only for insureds in the liquor business, but also for anyone who serves alcoholic beverages for a charge, whether or not the activity is for the purpose of financial gain. This would include a variety of fund-raising and social activities sponsored by nonprofit organizations. These activities may be covered by endorsement to the CGL, or they may be covered under a Dram Shop or Liquor Liability Policy in the same manner as firms in the business of manufacturing, selling, or distributing alcoholic beverages. Occurrence and claims-made Liquor Liability Coverage forms were introduced as a part of the portfolio general liability program. Both cover liability arising out of the selling, serving, or furnishing of alcoholic beverages but differ in the coverage trigger. Coverage provisions of the claims-made version generally parallel those of the claims-made CGL already discussed.

[9]Liability arising out of independent contractors is covered under the CGL, but the exposure is sometimes insured under a separate contract in order to isolate the cost of the insurance and shift it to the independent contractor.

[10]Dram shop liability laws exist in Alabama, Alaska, California, Colorado, Florida, Georgia, Illinois, Iowa, Maine, Michigan, Minnesota, New Mexico, New York, North Carolina, North Dakota, Ohio, Oregon, Pennsylvania, Rhode Island, Utah, Vermont, and Wyoming. Liability has been imposed on sellers of alcoholic beverages under common law in Arizona, Colorado, Hawaii, Idaho, Indiana, Kentucky, Louisiana, Massachusetts, Mississippi, Missouri, New Jersey, New Mexico, North Carolina, South Dakota, Washington, Wisconsin, and Wyoming.

Pollution Liability Insurance Coverage

As we noted in our discussion of the CGL, the latest version of the CGL excludes all liability arising out of pollution. An endorsement is available under which an insurer can add pollution coverage to the CGL, but most insurers have been unwilling to extend the policy.

In addition to the pollution liability endorsement, ISO introduced two simplified pollution liability forms as part of the portfolio revision. The two new pollution liability forms are designated Pollution Liability Coverage form—Designated Sites and Pollution Liability Limited Coverage Form—Designated Sites. The principal difference between the two forms is that the limited form does not provide coverage for "mandated off-site cleanup costs," whereas coverage for such costs is specifically insured in the standard form.

Federal law requires owners and operators of certain hazardous properties, such as landfills, land treatment facilities, and similar surface impoundments, to carry environmental liability coverage for nonsudden occurrences of at least $3 million per occurrence and $6 million aggregate. These limits are in addition to a requirement of $1 million per occurrence and $2 million annual aggregate limits of coverage for sudden and accidental occurrences. The coverage is available only from a limited number of insurers.[11]

Pension Fiduciary Liability

The Pension Reform Act of 1974 (ERISA) imposed new responsibilities on employers and fiduciaries supervising pension plans and group life and health insurance programs, holding them liable to beneficiaries for violation of the prudent man rule in the supervision of such a plan. Pension fiduciary liability insurance protects against this exposure. The coverage is sometimes written to include employee benefit errors and omissions coverage, which protects against liability arising from errors in advising employees and from other types of mistakes related to a fringe benefit program.

Directors and Officers Errors and Omissions Insurance

A special form of coverage known as Directors and Officers Errors and Omissions insurance is available to protect corporate officers and directors from suits alleging mismanagement. Such suits may be brought by stockholders or by persons outside the firm. The coverage is subject to a deductible, and the insured is usually required to bear 5 percent of any loss in excess of the deductible. The coverage excludes losses based on alleged personal gain by the insured and losses resulting from failure to purchase proper insurance coverage.

Variations of this coverage are available to protect elected and appointed public officials. These include a Board of Education Liability Policy and a Public Official Liability Policy. Like the Officers and Directors coverage, above, there is no standard form for these coverages, and they are usually sold by specialty insurers.

[11]ISO introduced a pollution liability policy in 1982. In 1984, a Pollution Liability Insurance Association (PLIA) was formed for the purpose of handling the pollution liability insurance written by its 49 member companies. The PLIA was dissolved in 1989 after the number of participating members had fallen to 14.

Employment Related Practices

The rapid growth in employment practices liability discussed in the preceding chapter led to a demand for insurance to cover such losses. Although it was sometimes possible to find coverage for employment-related practices under other forms of liability insurance in the past, the vestiges of coverage were unintended and have been removed. General liability insurers, workers compensation insurers, and umbrella liability insurers have all added the Employment-Related Practices Liability Exclusion Endorsement to their policies.

A limited number of insurers offer employment practices liability policies, which cover discrimination, sexual harassment and wrongful termination. Fines and criminal penalties are universally excluded.[12] Some insurers include coverage for punitive damages, and some do not. In most cases, defense costs are included in the policy limit, rather than "outside" the policy limit as in the case of the CGL and most other liability contracts. Coverage is written on a claims-made basis with a retroactive date and a limited discovery period. Extended reporting coverage is available for an additional premium if coverage is canceled or nonrenewed by the insurer. Deductibles range upward from a low of $1000 to $25,000. In addition to the deductible, policies also include a coinsurance provision that functions as a copayment provision. The insured must usually share a percentage of defense and settlement costs, normally ranging from 5 to 25 percent, with most being either 5 or 10 percent.

❖ Insurance for Bailees ■

A bailment consists of the delivery of property of one person, the "bailor," to another, the "bailee," for some specific purpose. The property may be in the care of the bailee to be worked on, as in the case of an automobile being repaired, or in storage, or for some other purpose. If property in the hands of a bailee is damaged or destroyed, the bailee may be liable to the owner.

BAILEE LIABILITY

In general, there are three types of bailment, and the degree of care that the bailee must exercise in protecting the property depends on the nature of the bailment. The first is gratuitous bailment for the benefit of the bailor. For example, you may ask your neighbor to take care of your cat while you are on vacation. In this situation,

---

[12]Initially, there was a serious debate over whether insurance for employment-related practices—which are illegal—violates public policy. The Civil Rights Act of 1964 recognizes two distinct types of discrimination: that of "disparate treatment" and that of "disparate impact." Disparate treatment is where you treat people differently and it is an intentional act. Disparate impact is where treatment is actually the same but results in *de facto* discrimination. This may not be an intentional act. In addition, coverage is deemed permissible for the vicarious liability of an employer even when the act committed by an employee is criminal.

perhaps *slight care* is all that is necessary, since the bailment is gratuitous and for the benefit of the bailor. The second type of bailment is also gratuitous, but here it benefits the bailee. For example, if you borrow your neighbor's lawn mower, you must exercise extraordinary care to protect it from loss. The third type of bailment is bailment for mutual benefit. Here the bailment may be gratuitous, or in the case of most business firms, it involves bailment for hire. For example, if you store your auto in an overnight parking garage, the situation is a bailment for mutual benefit, but it is also bailment for hire. In general, bailees in mutual benefit bailments must use reasonable care—that is, the same degree of care they would exercise with respect to their own property. However, the degree of care that must be used is greater in bailment for hire than for gratuitous bailment.

A bailee may extend or limit its liability for the bailed property by contract or advertisement. The bailee may assume complete responsibility for damage to property of customers, regardless of negligence. A bailee may also, by contract, limit its liability. For example, the bailee may specify that its total liability for a single fur coat in storage will be $200. Normally, it is legal for the bailee to limit its liability. However, the courts frown on a bailee's attempts to relieve itself of liability completely. The decided trend of modern decisions is against the validity of exculpatory clauses or provisions of parking lots, garages, checkrooms, and warehouses, where business firms undertake to protect themselves against liability by posting signs or printing limitations on the receipts delivered to the bailor-owner at the time of bailment.

BAILEE LIABILITY COVERAGES

The need for specialized coverages to protect against liability as a bailee arises because of the care, custody, and control exclusion of the general liability policies. If it were not for this exclusion, the bailee's liability because of damage to customers' goods would be covered under the general liability policies. Bailed property has traditionally been insured under property insurance forms, most frequently under inland marine contracts.[13]

Bailee liability coverages sometimes depart from the other liability coverages we have noted in a very fundamental respect. Under some bailee forms, payment is made by the insurer regardless of the liability of the bailee, as long as the cause of the loss is a peril under the policy. This approach is the result of the demand of customers that their property be returned to them in good condition, regardless of the liability of the bailee. A merchant who refused to reimburse a customer for the loss of property because of not being liable under the specific set of circumstances might soon find him- or herself without customers. Although some bailee coverages provide for payment only when the insured is legally liable, these are the exceptions rather than the rule.

[13]The bailor may, of course, insure his or her property under all conditions, including the period while it is in the custody of the bailee, but the general principle is that coverage purchased by the bailor shall not benefit the bailee. If the bailor collects from his or her insurance company, the insurer may then subrogate against the bailee.

BAILEE'S CUSTOMER POLICY

The Bailee's Customer Policy is the basic policy for bailees' customer insurance. It is completed by the attachment of a special form designed for the particular class of business. Coverage may be provided under these forms for such businesses as laundries, dyers and dry cleaners, processors, and service-type firms. There are special forms for appliance repair stores, radio and television repair stores, and other similar establishments.

In general, the Bailee's Customer Policy covers all kinds of lawful goods and articles that are the property of customers in the custody of the insured. Coverage applies regardless of the bailee's liability. The normal perils insured against include fire, lightning, windstorm, riot, earthquake, sprinkler leakage, burglary, robbery, and confusion of goods caused by any of the perils insured against.[14] In addition, the usual perils of transportation are covered and coverage applies to the property while in transit or at the insured's premises. The normal exclusions are loss while the goods are in the custody of other processors, unless specifically endorsed onto the policy; loss due to shortage (unless caused by burglary or holdup); loss resulting from delay, misdelivery, or mysterious disappearance; and losses from infidelity, nuclear energy, and war.

OTHER BAILEE FORMS

In addition to the Bailee's Customer policy, there are more specialized bailee forms for certain business classes. There is a Furrier's Customer policy, which covers customers' coats in storage; a Cold Storage Locker Bailee floater, which covers customers' property in public freezers; and a special form for hotels and motels, the Innkeepers Liability policy. In some instances, the coverage applies regardless of the bailee's liability. In others, it applies only when the insured is actually liable. In some cases, such as the Garagekeeper's coverage, the insured may elect coverage on either basis. Each of these forms has special provisions necessary to tailor the protection to the unique exposures of the business involved.

■ Excess Liability and Umbrella Liability Coverage ■ ■ ■ ■ ■ ■ ■ ■ ■ ■ ■ ■ ■ ■ ■

The average size of liability claims has increased steadily over time and will undoubtedly continue in this direction in the future. The occasional gigantic liability claims that appear in the newspapers are stark reminders of the catastrophic proportions the liability risk may assume. To provide protection against the devastating losses that businesses may suffer in this area, excess liability policies and the blanket catastrophe excess liability policy (frequently called the "umbrella") were developed.

[14]Confusion of goods refers to the inability to identify the ownership of the goods even though they are not destroyed, but the confusion must result from an insured peril.

EXCESS LIABILITY DISTINGUISHED FROM UMBRELLA LIABILITY CONTRACTS

The term *umbrella liability policy* was originally intended to describe a blanket excess liability policy, which provides broadened excess coverage over a schedule of underlying contracts. Unfortunately, there is no official definition of an "umbrella," and the term is also used loosely to describe not only contracts with the original characteristics but narrower excess contracts as well.

There is no "standard" umbrella or excess liability policy. Each insurer draws up its own contract, and although most of the contracts are similar, there may be substantial differences. Because insurers use the term *umbrella* to designate contracts with different characteristics, the true nature of a particular contract can be determined only by a detailed analysis of the specific contract being considered. In general, umbrella and following-form excess policies fall into one of three broad classes:

1. *Following-Form Excess Liability Policies.* The first of the three types of policies, the "following-form" excess liability policy, is subject to all the terms and conditions of the scheduled underlying policies. It provides coverage identical to that of the underlying contracts, although sometimes this type of policy includes a few terms and conditions of its own that may further restrict the coverage.

2. *Excess Umbrella Liability Policy.* This is the contract that most agents have in mind when referring to an "umbrella." The distinguishing feature of this type is a self-insured retention (SIR) in areas of no underlying insurance, which indicates that the policy is broader, at least in some areas, than the underlying coverage.

3. *Combination Umbrella and Following-Form Excess.* This is sometimes called the "two-step" umbrella. It combines the two above types, with the umbrella provisions applying to some aspects of the program, and other areas of the insurance subject to following-form coverage only. Not only does it provide a combination of agreements, but it also may be a combination of occurrence and claims-made forms, depending on the coverages for which it is used as excess.[15]

UMBRELLA LIABILITY POLICIES

The umbrella policy is a form of excess liability insurance and differs from primary liability insurance in that the insurer promises to indemnify insureds for their ultimate net loss in excess of some retained limit. The policy limits are quite high, ranging upward from $1 million. When purchased in conjunction with the liability policies normally purchased by the business firm, the umbrella serves three functions:

1. *Excess coverage.* The umbrella policy applies as excess coverage over the other liability coverage purchased by the insured. It takes over when the limits of the basic policies are inadequate to pay any judgment against the insured.

---

[15]In addition to excess liability policies and umbrella liability, there is a third form, known as a "bumbershoot," which covers marine liability as well as nonmarine liability.

2. *More comprehensive coverage than is afforded under the underlying policies.* Certain losses that are not covered by the underlying insurance may be included within the broad scope of the umbrella liability policy. In these instances, the umbrella provides protection subject to a deductible called a self-insured retention, or SIR, usually ranging from $10,000 upward. The deductible or SIR applies only in cases where the loss is not covered by the underlying coverage. In other words, there is no deductible on those losses that are covered by underlying coverage.

3. *Drop-down coverage.* If the underlying coverage is exhausted, the umbrella becomes the underlying coverage, subject to the terms and conditions of the underlying contracts.

Underlying Insurance Requirements

In general, the umbrella liability policy is written only for insureds that have a broad and substantial program of underlying coverage. Normally, the insurer requires comprehensive general liability coverage with bodily injury limits of $250,000/$500,000, property damage limits of $100,000, and automobile liability coverage with the same limits. Employers' liability coverage is required, usually in the amount of $100,000 (although some insurers have begun to require a $500,000 limit). In addition, when the exposure exists, bailee liability and aviation liability coverage may also be required. The policy conditions call for the maintenance of the underlying coverage, and the liability of the umbrella insurer is determined as if the underlying coverage were in force, whether or not it is.

Defense Coverage

In some contracts, the policy limit includes defense and investigation costs. In other policies, the defense coverage is in addition to the policy limit. Other policies may not include defense coverage at all. Individual policies must be examined to determine the manner in which defense coverage is treated. Practically all umbrella liability contracts have a provision that in effect provides that the insurer may take over or participate in the defense of a claim in which it may be involved.

Coverage Under the Umbrella Liability Policy

There is no "standard" form of commercial umbrella liability insurance. Each insurer draws up its own contract, and although most contracts are similar, there are substantial differences. These differences can be identified only through a detailed analysis of the specific contract being considered. In general, the insuring agreements are broad and comprehensive. It is common to provide coverage under three sections:

1. Personal injury liability
2. Property damage liability
3. Advertising liability

Although some umbrella policies separate coverage for "bodily injury" and "personal injury," the most common approach is to include bodily injury in the Personal Injury insuring agreement. In the broadest contracts, Personal Injury is defined to include bodily injury, mental injury or mental anguish, sickness, disease, disability, false arrest or imprisonment, wrongful eviction, detention, malicious prosecution, and humiliation, as well as libel, slander, defamation of character, and invasion of rights of privacy that are not the result of advertising activity. One type of action that is usually excluded is discrimination.

Exclusions

Although the coverage under the Umbrella Liability Policy is far broader than that of standard general liability and automobile liability contracts, it is not all-risk. There are exclusions, and many of the exclusions are quite important. Some of the more common exclusions contained in the current umbrella liability contracts are the following:

1. The policies exclude any liability arising out of any workers compensation, unemployment compensation, or disability benefits law. As in the case of the underlying contracts, this exclusion does not apply to liability of others assumed by the insured under contract. Employers' liability, however, is covered.

2. The policies exclude liability arising out of claims against the insured for repairing or replacing any defective products manufactured, sold, or distributed by the insured, or for the cost of repairing or replacing defective work performed by the insured.

3. Most policies exclude liability arising out of the ownership, maintenance, use, loading, or unloading of any aircraft owned by or chartered without a pilot by the insured. Some policies totally exclude liability arising out of aircraft, including both owned and nonowned.

4. There is an exclusion of liability of any employee with respect to liability for injury to or death of a fellow employee.

5. Most umbrella policies also exclude any error or omission, malpractice, or mistake of a professional nature committed by or alleged to have been committed by or on behalf of the insured.

6. All umbrella policies exclude liability for damage to property owned by the insured.

7. Most policies include some variation of the "care, custody, and control exclusion." Usually, only property with respect to which the insured is obligated to provide property insurance is excluded. Some policies also exclude damage to aircraft, watercraft, or automobiles in the insured's care, custody, and control.

8. Increasingly, umbrella liability policies include a sweeping pollution liability exclusion, generally patterned after the pollution exclusion of the 1986 version of the CGL form.

9. Finally, some umbrella insurers include an exclusion of punitive damages.

The recent trend has been toward higher and higher liability suits, particularly in the case of the individual versus the corporation. The liability contracts discussed in this chapter represent the major forms of coverage that are available to businesses to protect against this exposure. The umbrella liability policy is part of the total framework of liability protection and constitutes a critical part of the overall protection of the business firm.

Combining Retention with Transfer ■ ■ ■ ■ ■ ■ ■ ■ ■ ■ ■

Although few organizations are sufficiently large to fully retain the legal liability exposure, transfer can be combined with retention in several ways. The first is through the use of deductibles. Although most people think of deductibles in connection with property insurance, general liability coverage may also be written with a deductible. Deductibles are available in amounts ranging upward from $250. Premium credits are displayed in the ISO Commercial Lines Manual for deductibles from $250 up to $25,000. The credits for higher deductibles must be obtained from the insurer. When coverage is written on a deductible basis, the insurer provides investigation and defense coverage and the deductible is applied only to the amount of damages. The insurer reserves the right to settle with a claimant. The insured reimburses the insurer for the payment within the deductible.

In addition to the use of deductibles, part of the liability risk can be retained under a retrospectively rated program. Although retrospective rating is most frequently used in the field of workers compensation, it may also be used for general liability and automobile programs. In fact, large firms sometimes combine workers compensation, automobile coverage, and general liability coverage into a single retrospectively rated program. In such cases, the entire workers compensation premium is usually included in the computation. With respect to auto and general liability coverage, however, it is common to include only part of the total coverage in the retrospective plan. For example, an automobile policy with a $1 million limit of liability might include only the first $10,000 or $25,000 of the total coverage limit in the retrospective plan. In this case, only the premium for the limit of liability selected to be subject to retrospective rating is included in the retrospective computation. The premium for the limits of liability in excess of the selected limit is treated as a flat charge. In a sense, it is as if the insured had purchased two separate liability insurance programs: one subject to the retrospective rating program and the other written on a flat basis. Obviously, the higher the limits of coverage on the part of the program included under the retrospective rating program, the higher will be the premium for that portion, and conversely, the lower will be the premium for the excess limits.

A combination retrospectively rated program might provide for the following limits of coverage to be retrospectively rated:

$25,000 per occurrence auto

$25,000 per occurrence CGL

$25,000 general aggregate CGL

$25,000 products aggregate CGL

Premiums for coverage and losses up to the specified limits would be included in the computation of the retrospectively rated plan. Premiums for coverage in excess of these limits are rated on a flat basis, and losses in excess of the limits are not included in the retrospective premium computation.

IMPORTANT CONCEPTS TO REMEMBER

occurrence form	malicious prosecution	pollution liability insurance
latent injury	wrongful entry	pension fiduciary liability
triple trigger	eviction	directors and officers errors
claims-made form	fire legal liability	and omissions insurance
personal injury	contractual liability	bailee
advertising injury	coverage	bailor
medical payments	retroactive date	bailee liability coverage
coverage	basic extended reporting	Bailee's Customer Policy
liquor liability	period	umbrella liability policy
mobile equipment	Supplemental Extended	following-form excess
impaired property	Reporting Period	liability policy
product recall	Endorsement	excess umbrella liability
false arrest	dram shop law	policy

QUESTIONS FOR REVIEW

1. For what types of liability exposures is coverage included in the Commercial General Liability policy?

2. Distinguish between premises and operations coverage and products and completed operations coverage. What is the line of demarcation between the two?

3. Describe the application of the limits of liability under the Commercial General Liability Coverage form.

4. What is meant by the term "impaired property?" Why is the term important?

5. Identify the five torts for which coverage is provided under the Personal Injury coverage of the CGL.

6. Describe the nature of the exposure directors and officers liability insurance is intended to cover. Identify and describe the two insuring agreements usually found in directors and officers liability policies.

7. Without going into great detail, what is the distinction between a motor vehicle and mobile equipment under the CGL policy? What is the significance of the distinction?

8. Distinguish between a "claims made" malpractice policy and an "occurrence" policy. What conditions led to the introduction of the claims-made form?

9. Briefly describe the coverage provided by the Commercial General Liability Coverage form for liability assumed under contract.

10. Briefly describe the general nature of an umbrella policy. In your definition identify the features of an umbrella that distinguish it from other excess liability contracts in the market.

QUESTIONS FOR DISCUSSION

1. Joe Smith has been in the plumbing business as a sole proprietor for the past 35 years and is now planning to retire. His insurance agent has told him that he should continue to carry products and completed operations liability coverage. Do you agree with the agent's recommendation? Why or why not?

2. In view of the fact that many insurers have adopted trade names for their umbrella policies that may or may not be descriptive, how can one tell whether a particular contract is a true umbrella or a following-form excess liability policy?

3. There was a time when it was argued that liability insurance would undermine the tort system, which, among other things is designed to punish and to deter negligence. Do you think that the existence of liability insurance causes one to be less careful than he or she might otherwise be?

4. Identify and briefly explain the post-event risk control measures that can be applied in the management of general liability risks.

5. Bailee liability policies may be written to cover not only the legal liability of the insured bailee, but the interest of the owner of the bailed property. What is the rationale for this arrangement?

SUGGESTIONS FOR ADDITIONAL READING

Bergman, Robert A. "Employment Practices Liability Insurance," *The Risk Report,* vol. 17, no. 4 (December 1994).

Griffin, Gary W. "Employment Practices Liability Insurance: Practical Tips for Comparing Coverage-Part 1," *The Risk Management Letter,* vol. 16, (Issue 4).

Griffin, Gary. "Employment Practices Liability Insurance, Part Two: What Is A Claim," *The Risk Management Letter.* vol. 16 (Issue 6, 1995).

Harrington, Scott E. "Liability Insurance: Volatility in Prices and in the Availability of Coverage," *Tort Law and the Public Interest.* New York, The American Assembly, W. W. Norton & Co., 1991.

Harrington, E. Scott. "A Retrospective on the Liability Insurance Crisis," *CPCU Annals,* vol. XLIII, No. 1 (March 1990).

Huber, Peter. "The Environmental Liability Dilemma," *CPCU Journal,* vol. 40, No. 4 (December 1987).

Webb, Bernard L., Stephen Horn II, and Arthur L. Flitner. *Commercial Insurance* 2nd ed. (Malvern, Pa.: Insurance Institute of America, 1990), Chapters 6, 7, and 11.

Woodward, W. Jeffrey. "The 1996 ISO CGL Program," *The Risk Report.* vol. 18, no. 5 (January 1996).

CHAPTER 25

Managing Auto Risks: Control and Finance

CHAPTER OBJECTIVES

When you have finished this chapter, you should be able to

Explain the special provisions of tort law applicable to automobiles.

Explain the principles of vicarious liability and the special provisions applicable to guests.

Explain the legal requirements imposed by the states regarding automobile liability insurance.

Explain the no-fault concept and the basic philosophy on which this concept is based.

Be able to explain the distinction between hired automobiles and nonowned automobiles.

Identify the four standard commercial automobile forms and explain the difference in eligibility for these forms.

Explain the scope of coverage under the Business Auto Coverage form and be able to apply the provisions of the form to specific loss situations.

Explain the unique pollution liability cleanup provision of the Business Auto Coverage form.

Explain the structure of the trucking industry in the United States, and explain how that structure created the need for a specialized policy for truckers.

Explain the insurance requirements for truckers and be able to explain the manner in which the special features of the Truckers Coverage form meet these needs.

■ Introduction ■

Organizations, like individuals, are exposed to a range of losses in connection with the use of automobiles. The major exposure is, of course, liability arising out of the use of automobiles. In addition, the firm faces the possibility of damage or loss to the vehicles it owns or for which it may be liable. Finally, the operation of vehicles also includes the possibility of employee injuries. In this chapter, we focus on the first two exposures, liability (to persons other than employees) and loss or damage to vehicles.

Before turning to the legal environment, it may be helpful to review briefly the automobile coverage available to protect against loss arising out of automobile use.

■ An Overview of Automobile Coverages ■ ■ ■ ■ ■ ■ ■ ■ ■ ■

For the purpose of our discussion, it will be helpful if the reader will keep in mind the distinctions among the following four automobile insurance coverages: Automobile Liability Insurance, Medical Payments coverage, Physical Damage coverage, and Uninsured Motorists coverage.

AUTOMOBILE LIABILITY INSURANCE

Automobile Liability Insurance protects the insured against loss arising from legal liability when his or her automobile injures someone or damages another's property. Usually, a single limit of liability pays for bodily injury or property damage arising out of the use of an insured automobile.

MEDICAL PAYMENTS COVERAGE

Automobile *Medical Payments coverage* reimburses the insured and members of the insured's family for medical expenses that result from automobile accidents. The protection also applies to other occupants of the insured's automobile. Automobile Medical Payments coverage is distinct from the liability coverage; it applies as a special form of accident insurance to cover medical expenses of occupants of an insured auto. It is written with a maximum limit per person per accident, which usually ranges from $500 to $5000.

PHYSICAL DAMAGE COVERAGE

Automobile *Physical Damage coverage* insures against loss of the policyholder's own automobile. The coverage is written under two insuring agreements: Other Than Collision (formerly called Comprehensive) and Collision. Collision, as the name implies, indemnifies for collision losses; Other Than Collision is a form of open-peril coverage that provides protection against most other insurable perils. Physical Damage coverage applies to the insured auto regardless of fault.

UNINSURED MOTORISTS COVERAGE

Uninsured Motorists coverage is an imaginative form of auto insurance under which the insurer agrees to pay the insured, up to specified limits, the amount the insured could have collected from a negligent driver who caused injury, when that driver is uninsured or is guilty of hit and run. Uninsured Motorists Coverage usually has the same limits as the bodily injury coverage in the liability section of the policy. A related coverage, *Underinsured Motorists Coverage*, applies when the other driver has insurance but limits are less than the limits of the Underinsured Motorists Coverage.

❖ The Legal Environment of the Automobile ▪ ▪ ▪ ▪ ▪ ▪ ▪

The liability of the owner or operator of an automobile is largely governed by the principles of negligence discussed in Chapter 23. However, special laws affecting automobile liability have been enacted to modify some of the basic principles of negligence. Several of these statutes relate to the responsibility of others when the driver is negligent.

VICARIOUS LIABILITY AND THE AUTOMOBILE

As you will recall from Chapter 23, vicarious liability describes a situation in which one party becomes liable for the negligence of another. When one thinks of being held liable for the operation of a motor vehicle, one normally has in mind a situation in which he or she is the driver. However, because of vicarious liability laws and doctrines, an individual can be held liable in situations where someone else is the operator. For the business firm or other organization, the significant doctrine is *respondent superior,* which holds a principal responsible for the acts of an agent. An organization is vicariously responsible for injuries or damage caused by employees or other agents, both when they are operating the organization's vehicles and when they drive their own cars on company business. In addition to this imputed liability, an organization may also be vicariously liable as the owner of a vehicle that is not being operated on behalf of the organization. Some states have enacted *permissive use statutes,* which impose liability on the owner of an auto for liability arising out of someone operating it with the owner's permission.[1] A corporation that

---

[1]California, Connecticut, Florida, Idaho, Iowa, Massachusetts, Michigan, Minnesota, New York, North Carolina, Rhode Island, Tennessee, and the District of Columbia.

gives employees permission for personal use of company cars is exposed to vicarious liability as owners in these states.[2]

AUTOMOBILE LIABILITY INSURANCE AND THE LAW

As late as 1971, only Massachusetts, North Carolina, and New York had *compulsory automobile liability insurance laws*. However, with the enactment of the no-fault laws discussed later in this chapter, many legislatures also made automobile liability insurance compulsory. By 1995, 40 states and the District of Columbia had laws requiring the owners of automobiles registered in the state to have liability insurance or, sometimes, an approved substitute form of security.[3]

Before the widespread enactment of compulsory auto insurance laws, most states attempted to solve the problem of the financial responsibility of drivers through what are known as financial responsibility laws. These laws require a driver to show proof of insurance (or some other approved form of security) when he or she is involved in an accident. Because they require proof of "financial responsibility" only after an accident, these laws are sometimes called "free-bite laws." Most states that have enacted compulsory auto insurance laws retained their financial responsibility law, and drivers are subject to the requirements of both.[4]

In most states, the financial responsibility laws take the form of a "security-type" law. It provides that any driver involved in an auto accident that causes bodily injury or damage to the property of others (the property damage must exceed a specified minimum, usually $100 or $200) must demonstrate the ability to pay any judgment resulting from the accident or lose his or her license. If a driver's license is suspended, then security for future accidents must be posted before it will be restored. The financial responsibility laws apply to all parties in an accident, even those who do not appear to have been at fault.

The requirements of the law are met if an insurer files a certificate (called an SR-21) indicating that, at the time of the accident, the driver had liability insurance with limits that meet the state's requirements (typically $50,000). If the driver cannot provide evidence of insurance, the requirements of the law can be met by depositing security (money) with the specified authority in an amount determined by the authority. A person who does not have liability insurance and cannot make any other arrangements for settlement of the loss will lose his or her driving

---

[2]In addition to the vicarious liability of organizations, state laws impose vicarious liability on the head of a family for the operation of a family automobile by a family member. Other states impose liability on the parents of a minor or anyone who furnishes an automobile to a minor or, in some states, any person who signs a minor's application for a driver's license for the negligent acts of such minor in the operation of the automobile. See Vaughan, Emmet J, and Therese M. Vaughan, *Fundamentals of Risk and Insurance*, 7th ed. (New York: John Wiley and Sons, Inc., 1996), p. 511.

[3]The states without compulsory auto insurance laws are Alabama, Iowa, Mississippi, New Hampshire, Rhode Island, Tennessee, Vermont, Virginia, Washington, and Wisconsin.

[4]All states except Kansas, Maryland, Massachusetts, and Minnesota have some form of financial responsibility law (and these four states have compulsory insurance laws).

privileges.[5] Driving privileges remain suspended until any judgment arising out of the accident is satisfied and until proof of financial responsibility for future accidents is demonstrated. Judgments are deemed satisfied, regardless of the amounts awarded, when the payment equals the required liability limits. The requirement that any judgment be satisfied may also be met by filing with the authority (1) signed forms releasing the driver from all liability for claims resulting from the accident, (2) a certified copy of a final judgment of nonliability, or (3) a written agreement with all claimants providing for payment in installments of an agreed amount for claims resulting from the accident. Financial responsibility for future accidents normally is proven by the purchase of automobile liability insurance in the limits prescribed by the state. The insurance company then submits a certificate, an SR-22, showing that the insurance is in force. Financial responsibility may also be demonstrated by posting a surety bond or, as a final resort, by the deposit of a stipulated amount of cash or securities (for instance, $25,000 or $50,000) with the proper authorities. The length of time for which proof is required varies from state to state, but the usual time is three years.

In many states, a person's license to drive may also be revoked or suspended if that person is convicted of certain traffic violations. After the period of suspension, the restoration of the license requires proof of financial responsibility. This can be accomplished as was just discussed. Offenses leading to suspension vary among the states. Practically all states suspend licenses for driving while intoxicated, reckless driving, being convicted of a felony in which a motor vehicle was used, operating a car without the owner's permission, or for a series of lesser offenses.

NO-FAULT LAWS

The easiest way to understand the no-fault idea is to contrast it with the traditional tort system. Under the tort system, if you are involved in an accident and the accident is your fault, you may be held liable for injury to others or damage to their property. If you are found liable, you will be required to compensate the injured party through payment of damages. If you have liability insurance, your insurance company will pay for the other party's injuries. If the other party is found to have been negligent, his or her company will pay for your damages. If you are injured through your own negligence, you must bear the loss yourself, either out of existing resources or under some form of first-party insurance where the insurance company makes direct payment to you.

Under a *no-fault system*, no attempt is made to fix blame or to place the burden of the loss on the party causing it; each party collects for any injuries sustained from his or her own insurance company. Under a pure no-fault system, the right to sue the driver who caused an accident would be entirely abolished, and both the innocent victim and the driver at fault would recover their losses directly from their own insurance. Compulsory first-party coverage would compensate all accident victims regardless of

[5]The financial responsibility law of a particular state applies to nonresidents who have accidents in the state. The suspension of the license and registration of a nonresident normally affect driving privileges only in that state. But some states have reciprocal provisions, and if the nonresident's home state has reciprocity, his or her license and registration will be suspended in the home state as well.

fault. Although some no-fault proposals have included abolition of tort actions for damage to automobiles, the principal focus has been on bodily injuries.

Although the basic no-fault concept is simple enough, several modifications of the idea have developed, and there are significant differences among the various proposals. We can distinguish among three different approaches.

1. *Pure No-Fault Proposals:* Under a pure no-fault plan, the tort system would be abolished for bodily injuries arising from auto accidents. (Some proposals would also abolish tort actions for damage to automobiles.) Anyone suffering loss would seek recovery for medical expenses, loss of income, or other expenses from his or her own insurer. Recovery for general damages (pain and suffering) would be eliminated.

2. *Modified No-Fault Proposals:* Modified no-fault proposals would provide limited immunity from tort action to the extent that the injured party was indemnified under a first-party coverage. Tort action would be retained for losses above the amount recovered under first-party coverage. In some modified no-fault plans, payment for pain and suffering would be limited or eliminated. In 1995, 14 states had laws that provided compulsory first-party benefits with some restriction on lawsuits.[6]

3. *Expanded First-Party Coverage:* Here there is no exemption from tort liability. Instead, the injured party collects benefits under a first-party coverage, retaining the right to sue for losses more than the amount paid by the first-party coverage. Most important, the responsibility of the negligent driver is retained by permitting subrogation by the insurer paying the first-party benefits. In 1995, 11 states had laws that provided first-party benefits on a compulsory or optional basis, but with no restriction on lawsuits.[7]

DEPARTMENT OF TRANSPORTATION INSURANCE REQUIREMENTS

The term *business automobile* may include private passenger vehicles, buses, and trucks. When the vehicles to be insured are trucks, special federal insurance requirements may apply. Broadly speaking, trucks may be classified into two categories: private carriers, whereby owners transport their own goods on their own trucks; and carriers for hire, whereby owners transport goods belonging to others. Historically, carriers for hire have been highly regulated, with restrictions on entry into this field imposed by the Interstate Commerce Commission (ICC) at the interstate level, and by state agencies with respect to intrastate trucking. In addition to regulating entry into the field, the ICC and state agencies have also regulated the financial responsibility of carriers for hire by specifying the limits of automobile liability insurance such firms were required to carry.

---

[6]Colorado, Hawaii, Kansas, Kentucky, Massachusetts, Michigan, Minnesota, New Jersey, New York, North Dakota, Pennsylvania, and Utah.

[7]Arkansas, Delaware, New Hampshire, Maryland, Oregon, South Carolina, South Dakota, Texas, Virginia, Washington, and Wisconsin.

During the 1970s, growing dissatisfaction with government controls in general brought about a general movement toward deregulation in many areas. The trucking industry (that is, carriers for hire) was partially deregulated by the Motor Carrier Act of 1980, which eliminated some of the barriers to entry. The act was passed in the hope that the removal of barriers to entry would promote more competitive and efficient transportation services. However, Congress feared that the ease of entry into the trucking field would bring in new, untried firms and increase the likelihood of severe accidents, especially for trucks hauling hazardous commodities. In order to create incentives to motor carriers to maintain and operate their vehicles in a safe manner and to assure that motor carriers maintain an appropriate level of financial responsibility, the act authorized the Department of Transportation to set insurance requirements for persons and organizations engaged in trucking. In June of 1981, the Department of Transportation, as required by the act, issued final regulations setting financial responsibility for motor carriers. These regulations became effective on December 1, 1981. The ICC modified its insurance requirements to conform with those of the DOT and relinquished responsibility for enforcement of insurance requirements to the DOT.

Although the DOT financial responsibility requirements originated in the deregulation of the trucking industry, it is important to note that the requirements adopted apply not only to carriers for hire, but to some private carriers as well. Under the regulations, trucks with a gross vehicle weight rating of 10,000 pounds or more were separated into three categories for different levels of financial responsibilities which must be met with insurance policies or surety bonds.

- Type 1 vehicles are trucks that are operated for hire and engage in interstate commerce but that do not carry hazardous cargo, as defined in the law. Type 1 vehicles have been subject to a single-limit insurance requirement of $750,000.

- Type 2 vehicles include both for-hire and private trucks engaged in interstate or intrastate commerce and carrying defined hazardous substances. Type 2 vehicles are subject to a single-limit requirement of $5 million.

- Type 3 vehicles include for-hire and private trucks engaged in interstate commerce and carrying specified substances other than "defined" hazardous substances. Type 3 vehicles are subject to a $500,000 single-limit requirement.

The insurance requirements have been effective since July 1, 1983. The financial responsibility requirements may be met either through an automobile liability policy or by posting a surety bond. (When the surety bond approach is used, the surety guarantees the financial responsibility of the trucker, but may seek reimbursement from the trucker in the event of a loss.) The most common approach to compliance is through insurance.

Motor Carrier Act Endorsement

Policies issued to comply with these insurance regulations must include an endorsement (Form MCS-90, Endorsement for Motor Carrier Policies of Insurance for Public Liability Under Sections 29 and 30 of the Motor Carrier Act of

1980) to the policy providing the insurance. The endorsement provides that "no condition, provision, stipulation, or limitation contained in the policy . . . shall relieve the company from liability." This means that the insurer's liability with regard to claimants under the endorsement is absolute, subject only to the limit for which the coverage is written. If the insurer is required to pay a loss excluded by the policy or for which it would not be responsible except for the provisions of the mandatory endorsement, it may seek reimbursement from the insured. The endorsement is, in effect, a surety bond guaranteeing payment of certain types of losses by the insured. The endorsement stipulates that coverage will remain in effect continuously until terminated. Cancellation by the insurer requires 35 days' written notice.

Anyone who knowingly violates the rules pertaining to the financial responsibility requirements is subject to a fine of up to $10,000 for each violation.

Fleet Safety ■

Like the other business exposures we have discussed, the risks related to the ownership and operation of vehicles in a business should be addressed by loss-prevention and control measures. Highway safety is an area in which safety programs can produce positive results, reducing the cost of automobile insurance and of retained losses.

Automobiles may be a source of potential loss to the business or organization in three ways. First, there is the potential for legal liability. As noted earlier, the employer may be held liable for the employee's negligence whether the employee is operating a corporate or his or her own vehicle.

In addition to the possibility of liability to persons involved in accidents with the firm's employees, there is the possibility of injury to the employees. According to the Occupational Safety and Health Administration (OSHA), about 38 percent of all job-related fatalities involve a motor vehicle. Although the cost associated with injury to employees is properly considered part of the workers compensation exposure, it is an auto exposure as well.

Finally, there is the risk of loss to the organization's vehicles, which may be demolished in a collision, stolen, burned, or otherwise damaged. Although this exposure is modest compared with the risks of liability losses and employee injuries, frequent vehicle collisions can be costly to the organization over time.

ELEMENTS OF A FLEET SAFETY PROGRAM

The loss prevention and control measures addressed as the automobile risk may be classified according to the general framework discussed in Chapter 9, whether they are directed at personnel, equipment, or the environment, and according to the timing (pre-event, at the time of the event, post-event). Fleet safety measures will include both the engineering approach and the human behavior approach.

Vehicle Maintenance

Fleet safety begins with well-maintained vehicles. A principal factor in the safe operation of vehicles is the proper running condition of the vehicle, which means that vehicle maintenance is an essential part of the fleet safety program. Inspections by the vehicle drivers should be a standard operating procedure and should be conducted in the same way as a pre-flight check used by pilots. A defect record should be filled out by the driver in reporting the defects in his or her vehicle. This should be completed at the end of each trip. This continuous driver-inspection program should then be supported with scheduled inspections and maintenance by qualified mechanics. The inspection program should verify not only that the vehicles are in good working condition mechanically, but that they are equipped with the appropriate vehicle safety kits, containing items such as first aid kits, safety vests, and fire extinguishers.

Selection of Drivers

Individuals selected as drivers for an organization's vehicles may vary widely in their physical and mental abilities. Testing and selecting drivers therefore deserves careful attention. Driver qualifications may be determined through written and road or driving tests. These tests are useful in the selection of new drivers and can also be used in determining faults of existing drivers.

Supervision

One of the challenges in safety management as it relates to automobiles is the supervision of drivers away from the firm's premises. Drivers are entrusted with expensive equipment and valuable cargo, and are often their own supervisors for extended periods of time. Some firms use mobile observers who monitor drivers to detect traffic violations, unsafe practices, and instances of discourtesy. In operations that involve long distances from a main terminal, some firms post signs on their vehicles, asking members of the public to report unsafe driving.

Accident Database

Driver performance should be continually monitored. A database of vehicle accidents, by driver, should be maintained and analyzed on a regular basis to identify drivers with a high accident frequency. A properly designed database can also indicate accident patterns that may be useful in designing loss control measures. The time of day, weather conditions at the time of the accident, and even the day of the week may provide an indication of why accidents are occurring.

Driver Training and Safety Education

Because driver error is responsible for the vast majority of accidents, driver training and safety education programs are also key elements in a fleet safety program. The drivers' training program focuses on driving skills. It may include seminars and workshops, videotaped instruction, instruction in dual-control vehicles, and simulator training. An increasing number of employers have all employees take a defensive driving course.

Safety education aims at creating safety awareness on the part of the employee. Whereas the vehicle maintenance program emphasizes the engineering approach, safety education represents the human behavior school. Because many of the elements in the safety education program for vehicles follow the same principles as safety training generally, we will defer our discussion of this subject until Chapter 26, which deals with risk control for employee injuries.

Loading and Unloading Vehicles

Proper loading of the vehicle is necessary to ensure against damage to freight and to facilitate safe operation of the vehicle en route. When drivers do not supervise the loading, they should be advised of any unusual or hazardous cargo. Special attention should be given to shipments involving flammables, explosives, or corrosive substances. Before the vehicle leaves, load coverings, tarpaulins, and vehicle bodies should be checked for leaks that might cause damage to freight in stormy weather.

Fire Prevention and Fire Fighting

Fire losses to cargo, vehicles, and garages amount to millions of dollars annually. Proper precautions should be taken to prevent fires, but personnel should also be taught how to act quickly in case of a fire in a garage, warehouse, or on the road.

DRUG AND ALCOHOL TESTING PROGRAM

Risk managers have long considered alcohol and drug testing programs to be a valuable feature of a fleet safety program. One deterrent to such programs has been the argument that requiring such tests constitutes a search that may violate the individual's constitutional rights.[8] The risk manager's dilemma with respect to testing appears to have been resolved by federal legislation that mandates such tests. The Omnibus Transportation Employee Testing Act of 1991 required the U.S. Department of Transportation (DOT) to develop and promulgate rules for testing persons who hold a commercial driver's license for drug and alcohol use.[9] The rules became effective for organizations with 50 employees or more in 1994 and to other employers on January 1, 1996. The thrust of the rules is to prohibit commercial vehicle drivers from certain types of conduct and to require tests designed to detect such conduct.

Under federal regulations, an employer must now adopt, issue, and enforce a policy forbidding illegal drug use at all times by employees who hold a commercial driver's license and who perform *safety sensitive activities. Safety sensitive functions*

---

[8]See *Skinner v. Railway Labor Executives Association*, 489 U.S. 602, 109 S. Ct. 1402 (1989).

[9]Different rules apply to the operators of commercial motor vehicles, employees subject to Federal Transit Administration, and employees subject to the Federal Aviation Administration.

include driving, waiting to be dispatched, inspecting, servicing or conditioning any commercial motor vehicle. It also includes all time spent in the motor vehicle, other than time in a sleeper berth, loading or unloading a vehicle, or assisting in loading or unloading the vehicle. In addition to the prohibition of illegal drug use at all times, a driver may not report for duty, remain on duty, or perform safety-sensitive functions while using any controlled substance. The sole exception is when a physician has advised the driver that the substance will not impair his or her ability to safely operate a vehicle.

With respect to alcohol, drivers may not report for duty or remain on duty that requires performance of a safety-sensitive function with an alcohol concentration of 0.04 or greater. Furthermore drivers may not possess alcohol while on duty unless the alcohol is part of a manifest load being transported. "Alcohol" includes medications containing alcohol and "non-alcoholic" beer. Drivers are also prohibited from using alcohol while performing safety-sensitive functions and may not perform safety-sensitive functions within four hours of using alcohol.

Testing Requirements

Employers must give pre-employment controlled substance and alcohol tests to prospective employees. Tests are also required at the time of an accident. In addition, employers must, on an annual basis, randomly test 50 percent of their drivers for drugs and 25 percent of the drivers for alcohol. Finally, the employer must test any employee if a trained supervisor or official observes the employee exhibiting behavior or appearance characteristic of drug or alcohol misuse.

A driver who is found to have engaged in prohibited activity must immediately be removed from duty. The organization must have a substance abuse professional evaluate the employee and must inform the employee of resources available to resolve problems associated with substance abuse. These services must be provided to the employee even if he or she is terminated for the violation.

All drivers subject to the regulations must be provided with a copy of the policy statement and other information related to the law's requirements. These materials include a clear description of the drivers who are subject to the rules and the period of the workday during which they are required to comply with the rules, the circumstances under which testing will occur, and a description of the penalties for violation.

Penalties for violation of the rules are defined by federal statute and include disqualification and other penalties for conviction.[10] Employers and drivers who violate the rules are subject to civil penalties up to $10,000.

❖ Commercial Automobile Insurance　■ ■ ■ ■ ■ ■ ■ ■ ■ ■ ■

In those cases in which a business is organized as a proprietorship, a "business" automobile may be insured under a Personal Auto Policy, the contract designed for insuring individuals and families. However, if the firm is a partnership or cor-

[10]49 UCS §521(b).

poration, or if the automobile itself is not eligible for a Personal Auto form, coverage must be provided under a commercial auto form. There are four commercial automobile forms designed to cover different types of commercial automobile exposures, notably the Business Auto Coverage Form, the Garage Coverage Form, the Trucker's Coverage Form, and the Motor Carriers Coverage Form. These forms may be used to create a monoline auto policy, or they may be included with other coverage forms in a package policy. Although we make some general observations on each, our discussion will concentrate on the Business Auto Coverage Form, since it is the most widely used of the three contracts.[11]

BUSINESS AUTO COVERAGE FORM

The standard form for insuring commercial automobiles, the Business Auto Coverage Form, may be used to provide Liability Medical Payments, Physical Damage, and Uninsured Motorist coverages. It can also be endorsed to provide no-fault benefits in states where such coverage is required.

Liability Coverage

The Business Auto Coverage (BAC) Form liability insuring agreement is similar in most respects to the liability insuring agreements that have been examined thus far. It begins with the traditional wording in which the insurer states:

> We will pay all sums an "insured" legally must pay as damages because of "bodily injury" or "property damage" to which this insurance applies, caused by an "accident" and resulting from the ownership, maintenance or use of a covered "auto."

The form then goes on to add a unique insuring agreement, under which the insurer agrees to pay for certain pollution costs:

> We will also pay all sums an "insured" legally must pay as a "covered pollution cost or expense" to which this insurance applies, caused by an "accident" and resulting from the ownership, maintenance or use of covered "autos." However, we will only pay for the "covered pollution cost or expense" if there is either "bodily injury" or "property damage" to which this insurance applies that is caused by the same "accident."

"Covered pollution cost or expense" is defined in the policy to mean the cost or expense arising out of any request, demand, order, or claim or suit by or on behalf of the government demanding that the insured clean up the pollutants. The coverage for "covered pollution cost or expense" means that under the defined conditions (i.e., when there is a covered bodily injury or property damage loss), the BAC will cover not only damage caused by pollutants, but also the cost of cleaning up such pollutants when such cleanup is mandated by government order.

[11]In those instances in which a smaller business is organized as a proprietorship, a "business" automobile may be insured under one of the personal auto forms, such as the Family Auto Policy or the Personal Auto Policy, provided the automobile itself is otherwise eligible. However, if the firm is a partnership or a corporation, or if the automobile itself is not eligible for one of the personal automobile forms, coverage must be provided under a different form.

Covered Auto In describing those autos that are covered for each of the coverages the insured selects, the Business Auto Coverage Form uses the term *Covered Auto*. A series of numerical designations, each representing a class of autos, is entered in the declarations opposite the various coverages, indicating the types of autos covered under the policy. Nine numerical symbols are used to designate the autos for which the policy provides coverage:

1. Any Auto
2. Owned Autos Only
3. Owned Private Passenger Autos Only
4. Owned Autos Other than Private Passenger Autos Only
5. Owned Autos Subject to No-Fault
6. Owned Autos Subject to Compulsory Uninsured Motorists Law
7. Specifically Described Autos
8. Hired Autos Only
9. Nonowned Autos Only

Historically, auto liability insurance for commercial insureds has recognized three classes of autos: owned autos, hired autos, and nonowned autos. The classes hired autos and nonowned autos are mutually exclusive. *Hired autos* are those autos that are leased, hired, rented, or borrowed, excluding autos that are owned by employees. Autos leased, hired, rented, or borrowed from employees are considered *nonowned autos*. Thus, the distinction between a "hired" and "nonowned automobile" does not depend on whether payment is made for the use of the auto, but rather on whether it is owned by an employee. This somewhat artificial distinction exists primarily for the purpose of rating and premium determination.

The preferred approach is symbol 1, Any Auto (also referred to as comprehensive auto liability coverage). When comprehensive auto liability coverage is written, coverage is provided for liability arising out of the ownership, maintenance, or use of all owned, nonowned, and hired autos, including replacements and additionally acquired autos. All owned and hired autos are scheduled at the inception of the policy, and additional exposures are automatically covered. After the policy, an audit of the exposure that developed is made, and any additional premium due to the company is charged.

In some situations, the insurer is unwilling to provide coverage on a comprehensive basis, in which case the insured must accept coverage on Specifically Described Autos (symbol 7). When Specifically Described Auto coverage is selected, newly acquired autos are covered only if the company insures all autos owned by the insured or if the newly acquired auto replaces a described auto. Notice to the company is required within 30 days. Also, when owned autos are insured on a specifically described basis, hired autos and nonowned autos should be covered by entering symbols 8 and 9 in the declarations of the policy.

Persons Insured The Business Auto Coverage Form includes coverage for the named insured, permissive users, and persons or organizations vicariously liable for acts or omissions of the named insured or permissive users. As in the case of the Personal Auto Policy, coverage for those held vicariously liable does not apply to the owner of a nonowned vehicle.

Exclusions   Twelve exclusions apply to the liability coverage of the Business Auto Coverage form: (1) expected or intended injury, (2) contractual, (3) workers compensation, (4) employers' liability, (5) fellow employee, (6) care, custody, and control, (7) handling of property, (8) movement of property by mechanical device, (9) operation of mobile equipment, (10) completed operations, (11) pollution, and (12) war. Most of the exclusions are similar to their counterparts in the Commercial General Liability form (CGL). Several, however, deserve special comment.

The handling of property, movement of property by mechanical device, and operation of mobile equipment exclusions eliminate duplication with the CGL, which is designed to cover these exposures.

The pollution exclusion contains an exception that adds back coverage for pollution resulting from the discharge or leakage of fuels, lubricants, exhaust gases, or similar pollutants from the vehicle itself. The principal thrust of the remainder of the pollution exclusion is to exclude only pollution arising out of property being transported (i.e., cargo). This means that neither liability for bodily injury and property damage nor "covered pollution cost or expense" is provided with respect to pollutants that are being transported by the insured. Coverage for this exposure may be added by endorsement.

Physical Damage Coverage

Physical damage coverage for owned and nonowned automobiles is available under the Business Auto Coverage form, which provides essentially the same forms of protection that are available for personal autos. The insured may select from among three options with respect to the perils insured against, and different classes of vehicles may be insured for different perils. The available coverages include Comprehensive Coverage, Specified Perils Coverage, and Collision Coverage. The Specified Perils Coverage is an alternative to the Comprehensive Coverage and provides protection against the perils of fire or explosion, theft, windstorm, hail, earthquake, flood, vandalism and malicious mischief, and the perils of transportation (sinking, burning, collision, or derailment of any conveyance transporting the covered auto). Numerals corresponding to the class of autos for which each coverage is desired are entered in the appropriate sections of the policy declarations.

GARAGE COVERAGE FORM

The Garage Coverage form is designed to provide comprehensive liability coverage for businesses commonly known as garages and other automotive firms such as automobile sales agencies, repair shops, service stations, storage garages, and public parking places. Like the Business Auto Coverage form, the Garage Coverage form is a self-contained document that provides both liability and physical damage coverages.

The Garage Coverage form provides for legal liability arising out of three classes of hazards: premises and operations, products and completed operations, and automobile liability. In addition, the contract may be used to provide physical damage coverage on owned and hired automobiles, including the stocks of automobiles held for sale by automobile dealers.

The premises and operations as well as the products and completed operations coverage of the Garage Coverage form are essentially the same as the separate coverage parts providing these forms of protections and with the same exclusions. The "care, custody, and control" exclusion causes an inordinate number of problems in this class of business, because it excludes damage to automobiles of customers that are in the care of the insured.

Garagekeeper's Insurance

Because most garages take custody of customers' cars, there is a need for a special form of bailee liability insurance. The Garage Coverage form includes a coverage known as Garagekeeper's insurance, which provides coverage on customers' autos while in the care of the garage. The insured may choose from among Collision, Comprehensive, or Specified Perils coverage. (Specified Perils include fire, explosion, theft and vandalism, and malicious mischief.) Loss to the customer's automobile must fall within the definition of the coverage or coverages selected.

Besides selecting the perils to be covered, the insured may also select the basis on which the coverage will apply. Three options are offered: legal liability basis, direct coverage—primary basis, and direct coverage—excess basis. Under the first of these three options, coverage applies only if the garage is legally liable for damage. Under the second option, the Garagekeeper's coverage becomes primary with respect to the customer's automobile and regardless of the liability of the garage. Under the third option, the Garagekeeper's coverage responds regardless of liability, but only if the customer has no physical damage coverage.

TRUCKERS COVERAGE FORM

The Truckers Coverage form is a modified version of the Business Auto Coverage form, designed to meet the special needs of truckers. ISO rules define a "trucker" as "a person, firm, or corporation in the business of transporting goods, materials, or commodities for another."

The form adapts the provisions of the Business Auto Coverage form to deal with the special practices of the trucking industry and the insurance requirements imposed by those practices. Because entry into the trucking business is controlled, those firms that hold licenses or certificates authorizing them to operate in a particular area often permit unlicensed independent "owner-operators" (who own a tractor or trailer but who do not have a license) to use the licensed carrier's permit by leasing the independent operator's equipment. Because both state and federal regulatory authorities require the licensed trucker to provide insurance for all vehicles being used under their permits, the insurance coverage of the licensed trucker must be written to cover the equipment of the owner-operators that the licensed carriers lease. This means that unlike most forms of auto liability insurance, the Truckers form provides coverage on hired autos, not only for the named insured, but for the owner of the hired vehicle as well.

Coverage for Owner-Operators

An owner-operator who leases vehicles to a licensed trucking firm is covered under the lessee's policy while the equipment is being operated over routes the licensee is authorized to serve. However, owner-operators must obtain insurance to cover liability when they are not operating under the certificate of a licensed carrier. Nontrucking use of a tractor without a trailer is called "bobtailing," and operating a tractor with an empty trailer is known as "deadheading." Coverage for bobtailing and deadheading is provided for owner-operators under a special endorsement to the Business Auto Coverage Form, Truckers Insurance for Non-trucking Use. This form provides coverage only when the vehicle is not being used to carry goods.

Trailer Interchange Coverage

The loan of trailers between truckers is usually accomplished under a "trailer interchange agreement" that requires the borrower to assume responsibility for damage to the trailer. The Truckers Coverage form includes a special type of contractual liability coverage, Trailer Interchange coverage, which provides protection for losses involving damage to leased or rented trailers for which liability is assumed under contract.

THE MOTOR CARRIER COVERAGE FORM

The Motor Carrier Coverage form was introduced in response to the changing regulatory environment in the trucking industry which was introduced by the Motor Carrier Act of 1980. This legislation significantly changed the manner in which the motor carrier industry is regulated and consequently in the way it operates.

The major effect of the Motor Carrier Act of 1980 was to reduce the ICC's regulatory authority over some of the operations of the truckers it regulates. With this deregulation, the Interstate Commerce Act now allows the mixing of exempt and regulated commodities as long as the motor carrier also has ICC authority to haul the regulated commodities. Truckers may now enter into operations that would not have been possible prior to deregulation.

The Motor Carrier Coverage Form was developed to respond to the needs of both regulated and unregulated motor carriers. The Truckers Coverage form is structured as if all motor carrier operations were subject to exactly the same regulations and all operations were conducted in accordance with operating rights granted by a public authority. It automatically presumes that in all but specifically excepted cases, the liability insurance of the motor carrier under whose authority the transportation is being conducted will be primarily for the benefit of owners of leased commercial vehicles, for example, owner-operator units. The Motor Carrier Coverage Form, on the other hand, makes no reference to such regulations. It addresses the needs of both ICC-regulated motor carriers and private motor carriers.

▞ Buying Commercial Auto Insurance ■■■■■■■■■■

The principles of risk management and insurance buying discussed earlier in the text also apply to commercial auto or fleet insurance.

Uninsured Motorist Coverage

One area in the commercial auto area in which there is disagreement is the uninsured motorists coverage and underinsured motorists coverage. The disagreement arises from the nature of the coverage. Uninsured or Underinsured Motorists coverage does not provide protection for the firm; it is designed to cover loss sustained by employees or other occupants of insured vehicles when they are injured by another driver who is uninsured or whose limits of coverage are inadequate to cover the injured employee's loss, a hit and run driver, or a driver who is insured by an insolvent insurance company. In the event of injury during the course of employment, an injured worker would be entitled to workers compensation benefits, which would cover the full cost of medical expenses plus a portion of lost wages. Still, an injured worker might be entitled to collect under the uninsured motorist coverage for disfigurement, mental anguish, pain and suffering, and similar losses. Although the coverage is designed to protect passengers in vehicles and not the business, some authorities argue that uninsured motorist coverage should be included in an employer's automobile policy. Given the litigious nature of our society, it is conceivable that an injured employee might file suit against the employer for failure to provide the coverage. The decision to include or not include Uninsured Motorists Coverage and Underinsured Motorists coverage in the corporate auto policy is a judgment call, and there are persuasive arguments on both sides.

Automobile Physical Damage Coverage

Automobile physical damage insurance is an area in which there is widespread violation of the principles of risk management. Many firms purchase comprehensive and collision coverage on their fleet, often with modest deductibles. Collision losses tend to be isolated events, and it is unlikely that a large enough number of vehicles would be demolished in a given period to create a financial catastrophe. Even if physical damage coverage is purchased, the highest deductible possible should be considered.

▞ Aviation Insurance ■■■■■■■■■■■■■■■■■■■■■■

Aviation insurance is a general term embracing the risks encountered in or associated with the ownership, maintenance, or use of aircraft. The aviation insurance coverages with which the agent will normally be concerned are in the field of "general aviation," which refers to all flying except by military and commercial airline aircraft. The most common aviation coverages are:

575

- Aircraft Liability Insurance
- Hull Insurance
- Airport Liability Insurance
- Hangarkeepers Legal Liability Insurance

The first two coverages are written together in an Aviation Policy and provide coverage analogous to that given under an automobile policy. Because aircraft range from privately owned single-engine planes to commercial jets, the coverage must be tailored to the specific exposure to be insured. Airport Liability Insurance and Hangarkeepers Legal Liability Insurance are analogous to the Garage Policy and Garagekeepers Insurance studied in the Commercial Auto section.

INSURANCE ON AIRCRAFT

The Aviation Policy may be written to cover Aircraft Liability, Hull Insurance, or both. Because aircraft differ significantly in design, capability, and use, the classification of the aircraft is an important element in the underwriting process.

Aviation Underwriting and Rating Classes

Six general classes are used in underwriting and rating general aviation aircraft.

1. *Business and Pleasure Use*—usually applies to individuals who operate an aircraft for their own pleasure and family use. The classification permits the individual to use the aircraft for business purposes, but it is not intended to include corporate-owned aircraft, aircraft used for instructional purposes, or aircraft used to carry passengers for hire.

2. *Industrial Aid*—designed for corporate aircraft used to transport executives, employees, guests, or customers in the usual course of business. It is not intended for instructional purposes or carrying passengers for hire.

3. *Limited Commercial*—designed for aircraft that are used for instructional and rental purposes. The classification does not permit the aircraft to carry passengers for hire.

4. *Commercial Excluding Instruction*—designed to cover aircraft that transport passengers or cargo for hire. It is not intended for aircraft used for instructional purposes or those rented to others. Again, this classification permits the other uses described under the Business and Pleasure Use and Industrial Aid classifications above.

5. *Commercial*—designed for aircraft rented to others and those used to transport passengers for hire. In effect, it incorporates all of the uses permitted in both the limited commercial and commercial excluding instruction classes, as well as the uses permitted by the business and pleasure and industrial aid classes.

6. *Special Uses*—a catch-all classification used for aircraft that do not fall into any of the previously listed classes. It could include, for example, aircraft used in testing or racing.

The majority of the aviation insurance written in the United States is written by two multicompany pools, the United States Aircraft Insurance Group (USAIG) and the Associated Aviation Underwriters (AAU).

AVIATION LIABILITY INSURANCE

Aircraft liability coverages are quite similar to automobile liability coverages with one major difference—Bodily Injury Liability is divided into two coverages:

1. Passenger Liability
2. Bodily Injury Excluding Passengers

Although the basic limits of aircraft liability insurance are patterned after those of auto liability, we must remember that most insureds desire much higher limits of liability to adequately cover the catastrophe exposure involved. It is possible to cover Bodily Injury Excluding Passengers, Passenger Bodily Injury, and Property Damage Liability with a single limit to cover all three exposures.

The aviation liability coverage may be written to include Medical Payments coverage. The Medical Payments coverage is similar to that of the auto policy except that the injury must be sustained while in, entering, or alighting from the insured aircraft. Medical Payments coverage is included only when the policy contains Passenger Bodily Injury Liability.

Admitted Liability

Admitted Liability coverage, also known as Voluntary Settlement coverage, is available only in conjunction with Passenger Legal Liability. It is written on a per seat limit basis, and it promises to pay a certain sum for loss of life, limb, or sight by a passenger. When voluntary settlement is offered, a release of liability against the insured is obtained from the passenger to whom the settlement is paid. Although payment is made regardless of liability, if the injured party refuses to sign a release, the offer of payment is withdrawn. The injured party must then bring suit against the insured, who is then protected by the Passenger Bodily Injury coverage.

Aviation Policy Exclusions   Most of the policy provisions are quite similar to those of the auto policy. There are, however, certain unique exclusions that are applicable only in the field of aviation coverages:

1. The policy excludes loss involving any aircraft not registered under a "Standard" Category Airworthiness Certificate issued by the Federal Aviation Agency.
2. The policy excludes loss when the aircraft is operated, while in flight, by other than the pilot or pilots stated in the declarations.

3. The policy excludes loss when the aircraft is operated in violation of the Civil Air Regulations.

Aviation Policy Warranties

Aircraft policies, like ocean marine contracts, contain specific warranties, the truth of which is a factor in the validity of coverage. The two most important warranties in the aircraft policy deal with the fitness and qualification of the aircraft and the qualifications of the operator or operators.

The aircraft must have a current certificate of airworthiness issued by the Federal Aviation Administration in order to comply with the policy warranty. The certificate is usually updated annually or every 100 hours of operation. The updating is done by a certified mechanic who determines whether the aircraft meets the minimum mechanical qualifications required to call the aircraft "airworthy." In the event the aircraft fails to maintain its airworthiness, the insured is deemed to have breached the warranty and the coverage is void.

The pilot or operator warranty is based on the minimum qualifications an underwriter will accept with respect to the number of hours the pilot has operated the described aircraft, the type of license held by the pilot, his or her rating, and proof that the license is not under revocation or suspension.

Usually, the pilot warranty shows the names of the individual pilots who are qualified in the underwriter's opinion. Underwriters use the named pilot technique because it gives them the opportunity to review the pilot's qualifications before coverage becomes effective.

The policy may also contain an "open pilot warranty" that authorizes other pilots to fly the aircraft provided they meet the minimum qualifications indicated in the warranty. The open pilot warranty does not name individuals but grants authority to unnamed pilots to operate the aircraft, provided they meet the standards indicated in the open pilot warranty. These standards usually relate to the type of license held by the pilot and the number of hours he or she has flown in the make and model of the particular aircraft insured.

Nonowned Aircraft Liability Insurance

Basic Aircraft liability policies provide coverage only for the aircraft designated in the declarations or a temporary substitute. A temporary substitute is an aircraft that is used as a substitute for the listed aircraft, when it is withdrawn from use because it is being serviced or repaired, or because it has been damaged. Usually, the policy covers only a temporary substitute that is the same type of aircraft and sometimes even the same seating capacity.

This means that the standard Aircraft Policy does not cover liability arising out of airplanes that are chartered or rented by the insured. In addition, they do not provide coverage on aircraft owned, rented, or borrowed by employees. In other words, Aircraft policies do not provide the equivalent of "hired" or "nonowned" auto coverage. If nonowned aircraft coverage is required, it must be obtained by endorsement to the Aircraft Policy.

Nonownership protection is provided by endorsement to the Aircraft Policy. The standard version of the endorsement covers the named insured and corporate officers and directors. Some companies provide coverage for employees for planes not owned by them or by members of their household.

Nonowned aircraft coverage usually applies to nonowned aircraft in the FAA's "standard category" certification requirements and used in the insured's business. Properly worded, the endorsement will provide coverage for virtually all nonowned exposures: planes owned or rented by employees, planes rented or chartered in the name of the insured, and nonowned aircraft operated by qualified officers or employees.

Aircraft liability coverage may also be written to cover the nonowned exposure only. In this case, coverage is provided under an Aircraft Policy with the ordinary Nonowned Aircraft Endorsement attached. Some companies use a separate Nonowned Aircraft Policy, but the terms and conditions are essentially the same under both approaches.

AVIATION HULL COVERAGE

Hull insurance provides physical damage coverage on the aircraft itself, and is the equivalent of comprehensive and collision coverage of the automobile insurance policy. There are two basic forms of Hull coverage. The first is the equivalent of comprehensive and collision under the automobile policy, and is referred to as *All-risk on Ground and in Flight*. The second variation, called *All-risk on Ground, Limited Coverage in Flight*, provides more limited coverage.

All-Risk on Ground and in Flight

This is the broadest form of Hull coverage and provides open-peril coverage on the aircraft both while it is on the ground and while it is in flight. Deductibles may be purchased applying to the aircraft while on the ground or while in flight or taxiing.

All-Risk on the Ground—Limited in Flight

Under this form of Hull coverage, open-peril coverage is provided on the aircraft while on the ground. The coverage while the aircraft is in flight is limited to the perils of fire, lightning, and explosion, but not fire or explosion following a crash or collision. The major perils not covered in flight are, therefore, crash or collision. The coverage is usually written with a deductible which applies to all losses except fire, lightning, explosion, vandalism and malicious mischief, transportation, or theft. The deductible may be written so that it applies while the aircraft is not in motion or when the aircraft is taxing.

IMPORTANT CONCEPTS TO REMEMBER

Uninsured Motorists
    Coverage
Underinsured Motorists
    Coverage
financial responsibility law
no-fault law
pure no-fault
modified no-fault
expanded first party
    coverage
Motor Carrier Act of 1980
Form MCS-90
Omnibus Transportation
    Employee Testing Act of
    1991

Business Auto Coverage
    Form
covered pollution cost or
    expense
"Covered Auto"
owned auto
hired auto
nonowned auto
mobile equipment
Garage Coverage Form
Garagekeepers Insurance
Truckers Coverage Form
owner-operator
bobtailing

deadheading
trailer interchange coverage
Motor Carrier Coverage
    Form
aviation insurance
hull insurance
hangarkeepers legal liability
    insurance
passenger liability
admitted liability coverage
voluntary settlement
    coverage
nonowned aircraft liability
    insurance

QUESTIONS FOR REVIEW

1. Identify and briefly explain the distinction among the three broad classes of automobiles for which coverage may be provided under the Business Auto Coverage Form.

2. Briefly describe the distinction between scheduled automobile coverage (provided by symbol 7) and comprehensive automobile coverage (symbol 1). How does the coverage on newly acquired automobiles differ under the two approaches?

3. Who is included in the definition of *Insured* with respect to the owned, hired, and nonowned automobiles under the Business Auto Coverage form? Are there any significant parties that are omitted or excluded from coverage?

4. To what extend does the contractual liability exposure arise in connection with automobiles? How is this exposure insured?

5. Describe the coverage for pollution liability contained in the Business Automobile Coverage form.

6. Why is it advisable for an employer to purchase employers' nonownership automobile liability coverage, even though the firm's employees may carry their own insurance?

7. Describe the two auto physical damage coverages.

8. Describe the types of organization for which the Garage Coverage Form was developed. Why was it considered necessary to create a separate policy form for this type of business?

9. What practices of the trucking industry create the need for a special policy for truckers? In what way is the coverage modified to meet the need?

10. What three basic types of liability insurance are provided under the Garage Coverage form?

QUESTIONS FOR REVIEW

1. Identify the major elements of a fleet safety program.
2. In your opinion, should a business firm purchase uninsured motorists coverage on company vehicles driven by employees? Why or why not?
3. Which of the automobile exposures discussed in the chapter are most susceptible to retention? Which of the exposures are the most likely candidates for transfer?
4. Describe the provisions of the Omnibus Transportation Employee Testing Act of 1991. In your opinion, does legislation such as the Omnibus Transportation Employee Testing Act make the risk manager's job easier or harder?
5. Do you believe employers should be able to require drug tests of their employees? In your opinion, does the type of work in which the employees are involved make any difference?

SUGGESTIONS FOR ADDITIONAL READING

Fire, Casualty and Surety Bulletins. Casualty and Surety Volume. Cincinnati: National Underwriter Company. (Loose-leaf manual service with monthly supplements.) See "Auto" section.

Grimaldi, John V., and Rollin H. Simonds. *Safety Management*, 3rd ed. Homewood, Illinois, 1975, Chapter 23.

Huebner, S.S., Kenneth Black, Jr., and Bernard L. Webb. *Property and Liability Insurance*, 4th ed. Englewood Cliffs, NJ: Prentice-Hall, 1996. Chapter 33.

Levick, Dwight E. *Risk Management and Insurance Audit Techniques.* Boston: Standard Publishing Company, 1995.

Levick, Dwight E., and Barbara Grzincic. *Commercial Auto Insurance Guide.* Boston: Standard Publishing Company, 1995.

McLendon, Maureen C. "A Review Of The Commercial Auto Coverage Form Revisions," *The Risk Report*, vol. XVI, no. 10, (June 1994).

McLendon, Maureen C. "Rental Car Risk Management," *The Risk Report*, vol. 17, no. 10 (June 1995).

McLendon, Maureen C. "The New Motor Carrier Coverage Form," *The Risk Report*, vol. XVI, no. 6, (February 1994).

Parker, David. "Commercial Motor Vehicles: Navigating Federal Testing Rules," *Public Risk* (March 1995).

Toms, Gary L., and Robert Kreamer. "Ensuring a Safe Fleet," *Risk Management* (February 1993).

Vendetti, James G. "Getting a Handle on Commercial Automobile Costs," *Risk Management* (March 1995).

Webb, Bernard L., Stephen Horn, II, and Arthur L. Flitner. *Commercial Insurance*, 2nd ed. Malvern, Pa.: Insurance Institute of America, 1990, Chapter 8.

CHAPTER 26

Managing Employee Injury Risks: Risk Control

CHAPTER OBJECTIVES

When you have finished this chapter, you should be able to

Describe the general features of the Occupational Safety and Health Act.

■

Identify and briefly describe the importance of the seven elements in an effective safety program.

■

Describe the three major approaches to identifying job-safety hazards.

■

Describe the process of job-safety analysis.

■

Compute and interpret the standard ratios that are used to measure performance in job safety.

■

Identify the measures that may be used to address the problem of fraud in workers compensation.

■

Describe what is meant by rehabilitation and explain why it is important in managing the risk of employee injuries.

✖ Introduction ■

For many businesses, the largest single element in the cost of dealing with pure risk is the cost associated with employee injuries and occupational disease. Under our current system of law, an employer is held absolutely liable for injuries to employees that arise out of and in the course of employment. Compensation to injured workers is made under a statutory schedule of benefits that is payable in addition to the total cost of medical expenses associated with the injury.

In this chapter, we begin our discussion of the ways in which businesses can deal with the risk of injury to employees and occupational diseases. First, we discuss the workers compensation system, followed by a brief summary of the provisions of the Occupational Safety and Health Act, the federal law that mandates work conditions related to safety in the workplace. Next we turn to the subject of loss-prevention and control measures designed for the employee injury exposure.

✖ The Workers Compensation System ■ ■ ■ ■ ■ ■ ■ ■ ■ ■

In general, without negligence there can be no liability for injury to another. Workers compensation laws represent a modification of this basic principle, since such laws impose liability on the employer for injuries suffered by an employee without regard to the question of fault.

Under English common law, which developed in a society dominated by handicraft industries, certain legal principles evolved as a branch of law known as *employers' liability*. The general thrust of these principles was to make it difficult, if not impossible, for an injured worker to collect indemnity for an industrial injury. The heart of the employers' liability law was a set of obligations known as the employers' *common law obligations*. Failure of the employer to meet these obligations gave the employee who suffered an injury a right of legal action. The employer had five common law obligations:

1. To provide a reasonably safe place to work.
2. To provide reasonably safe tools.
3. To provide reasonably sane and sober fellow employees.
4. To set up safety rules and enforce them.
5. To warn the worker of any dangers inherent in the work that the worker could not be expected to know about.

Failure by the employer to meet these obligations constituted negligence and gave an injured worker the right to sue the employer in a tort action. If the employee sued, the employer could interpose one of three common law defenses; contributory negligence, the fellow servant rule, or assumption of risk. The doctrine of contributory negligence denied the worker recovery if his or her own negligence was partly responsible for the injury. The fellow servant rule was an exception to the general principle of *respondeat superior,* and held that an employer was not vicariously liable for injuries caused to an employee by a fellow worker. Finally, the assumption of risk doctrine was used to argue that the worker was compensated for taking the risks inherent in the job and that by accepting employment the employee assumed the risk of injury.

To collect under employers' liability law, litigation was necessary. Even if the worker won the suit, a substantial portion of the judgment went to the attorney who had accepted the case on a contingency basis. Finally, in some cases in which workers were injured there was no employer negligence.

It became apparent that some modification of the principles of legal liability and negligence was necessary to protect the workers and their families from the tragic economic aftermath of industrial accidents. The unsatisfactory status of the worker under common law, and the social and economic consequences of industrial injuries, finally led to a new way of distributing the financial costs of industrial accidents, workers compensation.

The workers compensation principle is based on the notion that industrial accidents are inevitable in an industrialized society. Because the entire society gains from industrialization, it should bear the burden of these costs. Workers compensation laws are designed to make the cost of industrial accidents a part of the cost of production by imposing absolute liability on the employer for employee injuries regardless of negligence. The costs are thus built into the cost of the product and are passed on to the consumer. The purpose of the laws is to avoid litigation, lessen the expense to the claimant, and provide a speedy and efficient means of compensating injured workers.

In the United States the first law to survive a constitutional challenge was the Wisconsin law, which became effective in 1909. Workers compensation laws now exist in all 50 states.[1]

PRINCIPLES OF WORKERS COMPENSATION

Although the laws of the various states differ somewhat in detail, the basic principles they embody are more or less uniform. There are five general principles, as follows.

Negligence Is No Longer a Factor in Determining Liability

The workers compensation laws impose absolute liability on the employer for injury suffered by the employee that arises *out of and in the course of employment.* If the worker is injured, the employer is obligated to pay benefits according to a schedule in the law regardless of whose negligence caused the injury. The employer is considered liable without any necessary fault on his or her part and will be assessed the compensable costs of the job-connected injury, not because he or she was responsible for it, caused it, or was negligent, but simply because of social policy.[2]

---

[1]There are also workers compensation laws in Puerto Rico and Guam in addition to three federal laws (applicable to civilian workers of the federal government, longshoremen and harbor workers, and nongovernment workers of the District of Columbia) making a total of 55 laws.

[2]The passage of workers compensation laws did not eliminate the employers' liability laws. These still apply to employment that is not covered under workers' compensation. For example, in most states

Indemnity Is Partial But Final

The second principle of workers compensation involves the amount of the benefit. In general, no attempt is made to provide an injured worker with complete damages. The worker gives up the right to sue the employer in return for a schedule of benefits set forth in the law. The amount of these benefits is based on the severity of the injury, the employee's wage, and, in some states, the number of dependents. Usually, the total benefits payable are less than the employee could receive if he or she were permitted to sue and establish a case of negligence on the part of the employer. However, the worker is entitled to the benefits as a matter of right, without having to go through the courts.

Payments Are Made Periodically

Usually, the indemnity is paid periodically instead of in a lump sum, although the periodic payments may sometimes be commuted to a lump sum. The requirement of periodic rather than lump-sum settlement is designed to protect the recipient against financial ineptness and the possibility of squandering a lump sum.

Cost of the Program Is Made a Cost of Production

The employer must pay the premium for the insurance coverage, or pay the benefits required by law, without any contribution by workers. The employer can predict the cost of accidents under a workers compensation program and build this into the price of the product, thereby passing the cost of industrial accidents on to the consumer.

Insurance Is Required

As a general rule, the employer must purchase and maintain workers compensation insurance in order to protect against the losses covered under the law. Most states will permit the employer to self-insure the workers compensation exposure, if the firm has a sufficiently large number of employees and some protection against catastrophic loss through the physical dispersion of workers. In 6 states the insurance must be purchased from a monopolistic state insurance fund. In 13 states the private insurance industry operates side by side with the state workers comp insurance funds.[3]

---

an injured farm worker or domestic servant has a remedy against the employer only under employers' liability laws. Thus, the negligence of the employer must be the cause of the injury, and the employer would usually have the right to interpose the common law defense.

[3] The 6 states that maintain monopolistic workers compensation programs are Nevada, North Dakota, Ohio, Washington, West Virginia, and Wyoming. The 13 states in which the workers compensation fund operated by the state competes with private insurers are Arizona, California, Colorado, Idaho, Maryland, Michigan, Minnesota, Montana, New York, Oklahoma, Oregon, Pennsylvania, and Utah.

PROVISIONS OF WORKERS COMPENSATION LAWS

Although the details of the state laws and the benefit levels differ, the laws are similar in intent and operation. The following are some of the similarities and differences.

Persons Covered Under State Laws

None of the state workers compensation laws covers all employees in the state. Although at one time many laws listed only the occupations that were covered, the standard approach today is to exclude some occupations and cover all others. Those most frequently exempted are agricultural and domestic employees.[4] The laws usually allow the employer of persons omitted from the law to bring these workers under the law voluntarily.

Elective and Compulsory Laws

At one time, about half the states had elective laws, under which either the employer or the employee could choose to be exempt from the law.[5] Today, all but three states are compulsory.[6] The compulsory laws require every employer defined therein to accept the act and to pay the compensation specified.

Injuries Covered

The workers compensation laws stipulate that employee injuries are compensable only when connected with employment, requiring that the injury arise out of and in the course of employment. In addition to the traumatic type of injury, all laws provide compensation for occupational disease. All states provide coverage for all occupational diseases, either under a separate occupational disease law or by defining injury broadly enough under the workers compensation law to include disease.

Workers Compensation Benefits

Generally, seven classes of benefits are payable to the injured worker or his or her dependents under the workers compensation laws:

1. Medical expenses
2. Total temporary disability
3. Partial temporary disability

[4]Two other major groups outside the coverage of workers compensation laws are railroad employees engaged in interstate commerce and sailors in the U.S. merchant marine. These workers are covered by federal statutes that give the employee the right to sue the employer in the event of injury.

[5]The elective laws were patterned after the earliest laws, which were made elective so that they would not be declared unconstitutional on the grounds that they deprived the employer of property without due process. The constitutionality of compulsory workers compensation laws was settled by the U.S. Supreme Court in 1917 in *The New York Central Railroad v. White* (243 U.S. 188). The Court upheld the state's right to pass a compulsory law under its police power. In spite of this decision, many states enacted laws with elective provision.

[6]Coverage is compulsory for most private employment covered except in New Jersey, South Carolina, and Texas. In these states the coverage is elective.

4. Total permanent disability

5. Partial permanent disability

6. Survivors' death benefits

7. Rehabilitation benefits

Medical expense benefits account for about one-third of total benefit payments under workers compensation. In most states, medical expenses incurred through employment-connected injuries are covered without limit. Four states impose a dollar limit on medical expenses, but even these laws, upon authorization of the administrative body, may permit exceeding the limitation.

The disability benefits and the death benefits under workers compensation laws are designed to replace an injured or killed workers income. The amount of the benefit generally depends on the workers' pre-injury wage. Compensation for permanent partial disability (the loss of a member, sight, or percentage disability of the body) is often commuted into a lump sum (e.g., an amount equal to 250 times the weekly disability benefit).

Slightly over three-fifths of the state laws contain specific *rehabilitation benefit provisions*, but even where state law does not enumerate such benefits, they are provided. Injured workers may be entitled to additional compensation during a period of vocational training, transportation, and other necessary expenses, artificial limbs and mechanical appliances, and other benefits. Funds for rehabilitation benefits may come from the employer or its insurance company. In some cases, state funds are used. Finally, the Federal Vocational Rehabilitation Act provides for federal funds to aid states in this program.

⬛ The Occupational Safety and Health Act (OSHA) ■ ■ ■ ■ ■ ■ ■ ■ ■ ■ ■ ■ ■ ■ ■ ■ ■

Any discussion of workplace safety in the United States should begin with a description of the federal standards that serve as a backdrop for virtually all efforts by employers to address the issue of safety. The Williams-Steiger Occupational Safety and Health Act (OSHA) was signed into law on December 20, 1970, and became effective on April 28, 1971. As declared by the Congress, this landmark legislation is designed to "assure so far as possible every working man and woman in the Nation safe and healthful working conditions and to preserve our human resources."

The provisions of the law apply to every employer engaged in a business affecting commerce who has employees. The law applies in all 50 states, the District of Columbia, and U.S. territories and possessions. Federal, state, and local government employees are specifically excluded from coverage, but they may be covered by equally effective requirements. In addition, the act specifically provides that its terms shall not apply to working conditions protected under the federal occupational safety and health laws (such as those under the Federal Coal Mine Health and Safety Act and under the Atomic Energy Act of 1954 as amended, including state agreements under that act).

587

STATE PARTICIPATION

The act encourages the states to assume responsibility for the administration and enforcement of their own occupational safety and health laws, which a state may do by submitting a plan for a state program to the U.S. secretary of labor for approval. Federal funds are provided for the support of state OSHA agencies. State plans approved by the secretary of labor must include standards and enforcement procedures at least as demanding as those of the federal law. If the secretary of labor refuses to approve a state plan, he or she must provide the state submitting the plan due notice and opportunity for hearing before so doing. Once a state plan is approved, the secretary is required to evaluate it on a continuing basis and to withdraw approval if there is a failure to comply substantially with the federal standards. The subsequent withdrawal of an approved state plan or the rejection of a state's plan is subject to review by the U.S. Court of Appeals. In 1996, twenty-three states plus Puerto Rico and the Virgin Islands had OSHA-approved plans.[7]

DUTIES OF EMPLOYERS AND EMPLOYEES UNDER OSHA

Each employer under the act has the general duty to furnish each of his employees employment and places of employment that are free from recognized hazards causing or likely to cause death or serious physical harm. The employer has the specific duty of complying with the safety and health standards set forth under the act. Each employee has the duty to comply with these standards and all pursuant rules, regulations, and orders that are applicable to his own actions and conduct. This responsibility extends to standards and guidelines.

Notices

Employers are required to post in prominent places (such as bulletin boards, cafeteria, and locker rooms) notices to keep employees informed of their protection and obligations under the act. Appropriate posters are available from area offices of the Occupational Safety and Health Administration.

STANDARDS

In general, job-safety and health standards consist of rules for avoiding hazards that research and experience have proven to be harmful to personal safety and health. They constitute an extensive compilation of wisdom which sometimes applies to all employees. An example would be fire protection standards. A great many standards, however, apply only to workers who are engaged in specific types of work, such as handling compressed gases. All employers and employees are required to familiarize themselves with those standards that apply to them and to

---

[7]Alaska, Arizona, California, Connecticut, Hawaii, Indiana, Iowa, Kentucky, Maryland, Michigan, Minnesota, Nevada, New Mexico, New York, North Carolina, Oregon, South Carolina, Tennessee, Utah, Vermont, Virgin Islands, Virginia, Washington, and Wyoming.

observe them at all times. The standards applicable to general industry are known as 29 CFR Part 1910.

INSPECTION

The act gives the Department of Labor broad powers of entry and inspection of any place of business. The OSHA compliance officers are authorized to inspect and investigate all pertinent conditions, structures, machines, apparatus, devices, equipment, and materials in the place of business. They can do so during regular working hours and at other reasonable times, and within reasonable limits, and in a reasonable manner. Interpretation of "reasonable times, limits, and manner" is within the discretion of the secretary.

The act provides that an employer representative and an authorized employee representative be afforded the opportunity to accompany the compliance officer during the physical inspection of the workplace. If there is no authorized employee representative, then the compliance officer will consult with a reasonable number of employees about safety and health in the workplace.

IMMINENT DANGER

One of the most important provisions of the act is that covering imminent danger. It permits the secretary to apply to a U.S. District Court for a temporary restraining order requiring the shutdown of any business operation when he believes that a danger reasonably could be expected to cause death or serious physical harm immediately or before it can be eliminated through the normal enforcement procedures of the act.

COMPLAINTS

Any employee (or representative thereof) who believes that a violation of a job-safety or health standard exists which threatens physical harm, or that an imminent danger exists, may request an inspection by sending a signed written notice to the Department of Labor. Such a notice must set forth with reasonable particularity the grounds for the notice, and a copy is provided the employer or his agent. The names of the complainants need not, however, be furnished to the employer.

If the secretary finds no reasonable grounds for the complaint and a citation is not issued, the secretary is required to notify the complainants in writing of his determinations of final disposition of the matter. The secretary is also required to set up procedures for informal inquiry in a case where a citation is not issued.

VIOLATIONS

Upon determination that an alleged violation of a standard, rule, order, or regulation exists, the area director of the OSHA Administration may issue to the employer either a citation for the alleged violation or a notice of *de minimis* violation. *De minimis* violations are those that have no direct or immediate relationship to safety and health. All citations describe the standard allegedly violated and the conditions that violated the standard and specify a time for abatement. All citations must be posted by the employer at or near the place(s) of violation to which they refer. The citation must remain posted until the violation(s) cited are abated, or for three working days, whichever period is longer. The employer will also receive a notice of proposed penalty, if any, for each citation.

CIVIL ENFORCEMENT PROCEDURES

Jurisdiction for settling contested cases rests with the Occupational Safety and Health Review Commission, which is an independent establishment of the executive branch of the U.S. government. The Commission is the final administrative authority to rule on a particular case, but its findings and orders can be subject to further review by the courts. The secretary of labor or any person adversely affected by orders of the Review Commission may appeal them to a U.S. Court of Appeals within 60 days. Failing there, they may take the appeal to the U.S. Supreme Court.

Penalties

The law makes provision for both civil and criminal penalties. Civil penalties are determined largely by the seriousness of the offense. The maximum civil penalty is $70,000 for each willful or repeated violation. For other violations, a fine up to $7,000 may be imposed, plus $7,000 for each day beyond a stated abatement date for failure to correct a violation. For serious violations, a minimum penalty of $5,000 applies. The application of the civil penalties on an *each-violation* basis has resulted in numerous multi-million dollar fines against corporations. Penalties may, however, be reduced for small employers. For employers with one to 25 workers, the penalty is reduced 60 percent; with 26 to 100 workers, the reduction is 40 percent; 101 to 250 workers, the reduction is 20 percent. An additional 25 percent reduction may be granted for evidence that the employer is making a good faith effort to provide a safe workplace. Finally, there is a 10 percent reduction if the employer has not been cited by OSHA for any serious, willful or repeat violations in the past three years.

The act also includes criminal penalties for making false official statements and for giving unauthorized advance notice of any inspections to be conducted under the act. Criminal penalties that may be imposed when death results form willful violation of a standard, rule, or order include a fine up to $10,000 and/or imprisonment for up to six months for the first offense. A second conviction for a willful violation resulting in death carries a $20,000 fine and/or imprisonment for up to one year. The maximum penalty under the act is life imprisonment for killing an OSHA inspector.

Notification of Proposed Penalty

Within a reasonable time after a citation is issued for a job-safety or health violation, the Labor Department must notify the employer by certified mail of the penalty, if any, which is proposed to be assessed. The employer then has 15 working days within which to notify the department that he wishes to contest the citation or proposed assessment of penalty. If the employer does contest the penalty within the specified time, a hearing is held by the Occupational Safety and Health Review Commission. Upon completion of the hearing, the Commission will issue orders affirming, modifying, or vacating the citation or proposed penalty. The Commission's orders are final 30 days after issuance. Review of Commission orders may be obtained in the U.S. Court of Appeals.

Time for Abatement of Hazards

A citation issued by the department shall prescribe a reasonable time for elimination or abatement of the hazard. This time limit may also be contested if notification of such is filed with the department within 15 days. The time set by the department for correcting a violation shall not begin to run until there is a final order of the Review Commission, if the employer initiates the review in good faith and not solely for delay or avoidance of penalties. Employees (or their representatives) also have the right to object to the period of time fixed in the citation for the abandonment of a violation. If, within 15 days after a citation is issued, an employee files a notice with the department alleging that an unreasonable time was allowed for abatement, review procedures similar to those specified above apply.

Failure to Correct Violation in Allowed Time

Where time for correction of a violation is allowed, but the employer fails to abate within such time, the secretary of labor shall notify the employer by certified mail of such failure and of the proposed penalty. Such notice and assessment shall be final unless the employer contests the same by notice to the secretary within 15 days.

Upon the employer's showing of a good-faith effort to comply with the abatement requirements of a citation, but that abatement has not been completed because of factors beyond his reasonable control, an opportunity for a hearing is provided, after which an order affirming or modifying the abatement requirement will be issued.

RECORDKEEPING

Most employers of 11 or more employees are required to maintain records of occupational injuries and illnesses as they occur. Employers with ten or fewer workers and employers regardless of size in certain industries are exempt from the record-keeping requirements unless they are selected by the Bureau of Labor Statistics (BLS) to participate in its Annual Survey of occupational injuries and illnesses. Recordkeeping is not required for employers in retail trade, finance, insurance, real estate and service industries (except building materials and garden supplies, general merchandise and food stores, hotels and other lodging places, repair services, amusement and recreation services, and providers of health services).

Failure to maintain the required records is punishable by a fine of up to $7000. The records that must be maintained include:

1. A log (OSHA Form Number 100) of injuries and illnesses, or any private equivalent.

2. A supplementary record (OSHA Form No. 101) of recordable occupational injuries and illnesses or an acceptable alternative, such as a workers compensation report containing all the information required in the supplementary record.

3. An annual summary (OSHA Form No. 102) of occupational injuries and illnesses, based on the information contained in the log.

Both the log and the supplementary record entries must be made within six working days after information is received that a recordable case has occurred. However, if the log is maintained in a computer or at a location other than the local establishment, an updated copy of the log, no more than 45 days old, must be kept at the local establishment.

The annual summary must be completed within one month of the close of each calendar year. A copy of it must be posted for 30 days in a prominent place in each of the employer's establishments.

OSHA APPRAISED

Although OSHA has not been in effect for more than 20 years, many businesspeople continue to question its effectiveness. OSHA critics argue that employers were concerned about safety for economic reasons long before the federal law was enacted and that they remain committed, sometimes in spite of OSHA rather than because of it.

Many people believe that a nonprofit, nonpolitical organization known as the National Safety Council has had a far greater influence on safety in the workplace than OSHA. The National Safety Council serves as a clearinghouse for all accident prevention information and coordinates the activities of all other organizations working in the field of employment safety. It publishes technical, statistical, and educational materials on workplace safety and serves as the leading authority on job-safety issues. Its *Accident Prevention Manual for Industrial Operations* and *Supervisors Safety Manual* are considered the most complete references in the field. In addition, the Council publishes a monthly magazine devoted to industrial safety, the *National Safety News.*

◼️ Design of Effective Safety Programs ◼️◼️◼️◼️◼️◼️◼️◼️◼️◼️◼️

The National Safety Council has suggested that an industrial safety program should involve

1. Commitment of management

2. Assignment responsibility for safety

3. Hazard identification

4. Job safety

5. Employee education

6. Accident record system

7. Interest in safety

These elements provide a convenient framework for our discussion, which, because of the complexity of the subject, must address a diverse range of topics.

COMMITMENT OF MANAGEMENT

Management must recognize its responsibility for making both the workplace and the employee as safe as humanly possible. Safety efforts will succeed only if management really wants to reduce accidents. The management commitment must begin at the top of the organization and extend down to the supervisor level. Supervisors must accept accident prevention as a normal part of their job.

Management's commitment to safety should be formalized in a written safety policy that affirms this commitment. The safety policy should be typed on the organization's stationery and posted so that all employees are aware of the administration's attitude toward safety. The following wording is typical.

XYZ CORPORATION POLICY ON SAFETY

The directors and managers of the XYZ Corporation consider accident prevention to be of utmost importance. Accident control involves the safety and well-being of our employees and the public, in addition to affecting costs and services.

The firm is committed to providing a safe working environment for its employees. To accomplish this, management believes that nothing is more important than making certain that

1. You are provided all reasonable safeguards to ensure safe working conditions.

2. You are provided with neat, clean, attractive, and healthful working conditions.

3. We maintain all equipment, tools, and machines in good repair.

4. We study and develop safe work methods, and train employees in these methods.

5. We comply with federal, state, and local laws regarding accident prevention and working conditions.

Management recognizes that more than personnel safety is involved, because the existence of accident hazards is proof of a wasteful, inefficient operation. Accidents lead to interference with work plans, complaints, dissatisfaction, and loss of good will.

The success of our Accident Prevention Program depends on the sincere, constant, and cooperative effort of all employees and their active participation and support. If you see a hazard, report it immediately.

A copy of the policy should be posted in a conspicuous place in all facilities along with the required OSHA notices and copies of general safety rules.

Once safety has been established as a corporate objective, the responsibility for achieving it rests with the organization's chief operating officer. This is not to suggest that he or she will be directly involved in the execution of safety plans. It merely recognizes the fact that the CEO is ultimately accountable for good or bad performance in this area.

Management commitment to safety must, of course, be real. When the CEO is personally interested in safety, the entire organization is aware of it, and this can influence performance. The CEO can indicate his or her interest in safety in a variety of ways, including the maintenance of a noticeable safety profile by complying with all safety rules and insisting that others do so as well.

ASSIGNMENT OF RESPONSIBILITY FOR SAFETY

Responsibility for safety may be assigned to the risk management department, or there may be a separate industrial safety department (usually located in the production division). When safety is assigned as a risk management responsibility, there may be a separate safety director, or the duties of safety director may be performed by the risk manager, depending on the size of the firm and the risk management division. Regardless of the location, responsibility for safety should be specifically assigned to an executive who is sufficiently high in the organization to be effective.

Safety Director

The manager of the safety effort, whom we will refer to as the safety director, should be given overall responsibility for personnel safety, developing and implementing the complete safety program. Specifically, the safety director is expected to

1. Coordinate safety activities through the organization.
2. Plan and direct safety inspections and initiate correction of safety hazards.
3. Establish and review the organization's safety regulations.
4. Check for compliance with federal, state, and city safety rules and regulation.
5. Maintain and analyze all accident reports.
6. Review accident, injury, and illness reporting procedures for compliance with OSHA requirements.
7. Conduct educational activities for supervisors and employees.
8. Design and conduct activities to maintain the interest of employees using safety bulletins, posters, and the like.
9. Investigate accidents and near accidents.
10. Serve as a member of the safety committee.

Safety Committee

Safety committees are a vital asset in the risk control function. They encourage employee participation in the safety program and provide a channel for actions on suggestions and ideas submitted by employees. The basic purpose of the safety committee is to serve as a vehicle for management in communicating to its employees and to create and maintain active employee interest in safety. To accomplish these objectives, the safety director should form a committee to assist him or her in formulating policy, performing inspections, assuring that necessary corrections are made, and conducting safety training of all employees. Many employers find safety committees to be useful tools in finding and reporting unsafe conditions, in helping to develop safety regulations, and in identifying the causes of accidents. In addition, safety committees can help get safety ideas across to all employees by developing their interest through gaining their participation.

HAZARD IDENTIFICATION

Until they are recognized, hazards cannot be eliminated. The first step in creating a safe work environment, then, is hazard identification. Although identifying unsafe work conditions is a specialized function, it generally follows the format discussed in our earlier chapter on risk identification. There are three basic approaches to the identification of hazards in the workplace: safety inspections, accident investigations, and the systems safety procedures we discussed in Chapter 9. Here we will focus on the first two of these, safety inspections and accident investigations.

Safety Inspections

An important element in any safety program is to conduct regular, thorough general inspections of the entire facility. A thorough safety inspection should detect and identify physical conditions and unsafe employee acts that may cause accidents. A *Safety Inspection Checklist* can be useful in indicating to inspectors what to look for, and will also provide a formal record of the inspections. Inspection forms should be designed to check a department's specific hazards.

Before beginning the inspection, the inspector should review previous inspection reports to help familiarize him or her with all related problems in the plant. A good inspector will look for off-the-floor and out-of-the-way items as well as those that are in the areas of the plant or facility that are most frequently used. Notes should be methodical and thorough and should clearly describe specific hazards and their exact location. An attempt should be made to classify each hazard by its *potential loss severity*. This will aid management in its remedial decisions. Those hazards with imminent chance for loss of life or body part should be considered critical hazards and marked for immediate correction.

The follow-up phase of the inspection process is to correct the defects that have been identified. Properly conducted safety inspections should produce a steady flow of recommendations for correcting unsafe working conditions and practices. Unless some action is taken on these recommendations, however, the inspections will have been a waste of time.

Accident Investigations

The purpose of accident investigation is to obtain information through which recommendations for corrective action can be developed for the prevention of similar accidents throughout the firm. First, the cause of accidents is determined by seeking out the elements and sources from which the accident developed, and then corrective measures are determined by analyzing the causal factors and making recommendations for their elimination. Accident investigations should include inquiry not only into injury accidents, but also noninjury accidents and "near misses."

Accident investigations should be made as soon as possible after the accident. Delay can permit information or items of importance to be removed, destroyed, or forgotten. The time for accident investigation is always as soon as possible. The less time between the accident and the investigation, the better and more accurate the data that can be obtained.

Accident investigation begins with the *accident report*, which is basically the supervisor's analysis and account of an accident, based on factual information gathered by a thorough and conscientious examination of all factors involved. Accident investigation report forms may differ from company to company, but the information they seek is fairly standard. It should include the name of the injured worker, the department or division, the date and time of the injury, the nature of the injury, and the cause of the injury.

Once the accident report has been reviewed, the investigator should examine the scene of the accident. Like the scene of a crime, the scene of an accident should be kept as undisturbed as possible. Whenever possible, the initial phase should be conducted at the scene of the accident and as promptly as possible following its occurrence. When appropriate, the investigator should take photographs and make drawings or measurements. All witnesses should be interviewed, one at a time and separately, as soon as practical. No attempt should be made to fix blame or to find fault during the investigation. The purpose is simply to get the facts and to record them as accurately as possible.

JOB SAFETY

Once hazards have been identified, the logical next step is to eliminate as many unsafe conditions as possible. Making the job safe is primarily a safety-engineering problem. It involves the analysis and redesign of layout, workflow, lighting, ventilation, and other physical aspects of the work environment to eliminate hazards, not only with respect to the characteristics of the facilities, equipment and materials, but with respect to the possible actions of workers. The objective is to make working conditions as foolproof as possible, in order to reduce the effect of the human element. Making the job safe includes the installation of guards, providing safety devices, and reducing or eliminating work hazards. It is the science of ergonomics—the designing of the workplace and work methods to fit the worker. Key elements in the process include job-safety analysis, engineering controls, and personal protective equipment.

Job-Safety Analysis

Job analysis is standard methodology for examining the steps involved in a particular task for the purpose of defining the most efficient method of performing the task. The term *job-safety analysis* (JSA) defines the process of analyzing a task to determine the hazards associated with the job so that they can be eliminated or the consequences of accidents can be reduced.

The earliest application of job-safety analysis seems to have been the military close-order drill and manual of arms during the early era of gunpowder. It grew out of the natural concern that musketeers might wound each other while using their weapons. Musketeers ranked in close order, especially in the early days of gunpowder when scattered loose powder near slow-burning matches threatened to set off a chain of accidental discharges, required that all men performed the many steps in loading, aiming, and firing in exact unison. The musketry drill books were the equivalent of industrial safety manual task descriptions, dividing the sequence into numerous precise actions.[8]

Modern job analysis developed as an approach to work simplification, the traditional arena of the time and motion expert. The original purpose of job analysis was to identify the most efficient approach to performing each task. Job-safety analysis simply changes the emphasis in the process from operational efficiency to safety. The basic methodology of job-safety analysis is much the same as the methodology used to construct the musketry books centuries ago. The specific steps in the sequence are identified and then analyzed. The prescribed steps are then defined, based on an analysis of safety hazards in each step. Once completed, a good job analysis provides the blueprint to teach any worker how to do a critical job the safe, productive way. The actual preparation of a job analysis provides another enormous opportunity to detect actual or potential sources of occupational injury or health problems at the precontact stage of accident control.

JSA incorporates information from workers and first-line supervisors who are familiar with the process being studied. Their familiarity with the process can provide information that a safety analyst might not detect.

Methodology Jobs that are determined to be serious risks to safety, quality, or production become the "critical few" first targets for analysis. Selection may be based on the frequency or severity of past loss history or the potential for loss. A job analysis is best prepared by actual observations of a worker or workers doing the job. When infrequent tasks prevent the observation method of conducting a job analysis, the technique of group discussion can be employed as an alternative.

The four basic steps in conducting a job analysis are (1) selecting the job to be analyzed, (2) breaking the job down into a sequence of steps, (3) determining key factors related to each job step, and (4) performing an "efficiency check." The final step involves determining that each step of the job is done in the best and most efficient way. This final step frequently involves a job procedure or methods change, a job environment change, or a technique to reduce the number of times the job must be done. The savings alone that result from accomplishing this step have consistently proven to be justification for introducing the program.

Materials Handling and Storage The handling of materials is one area in which job-safety analysis can provide significant benefits. About one-fourth of all compensable work injuries are traceable to manual handling of materials. The primary

[8]John Keegan, *A History of Warfare* (New York: Vantage Books: 1994), p. 342.

cause of injuries arising from this source is unsafe working habits: improper lifting, carrying a load that is too heavy, and failure to wear personal protective equipment. Of the materials-handling accidents, about one-half result from improper lifting—simply picking something up and setting it down. If improperly handled, objects weighing no more than a few pounds can cause injuries that are just as serious as those caused by heavy objects. There are two solutions to the hazards associated with lifting; training in proper lifting techniques, and use of personal protective equipment such as safety shoes.

Repetitive Motion Injuries   One of the fastest growing costs in workers compensation is that related to repetitive motion injuries, such as *carpal tunnel syndrome* and *tendinitis*. The most effective loss-prevention and control measures for the hazards associated with these injuries is the ergonomic analysis of work stations. Job safety analysis can sometimes reduce repetitive motions and alleviate awkward postures in the work process to eliminate reaching and twisting motions. Also, workers should be educated to recognize early symptoms of repetitive motion injuries so early treatment can be applied.

Engineering Controls

Most hazardous conditions can be predicted or anticipated at the design, purchase, maintenance, or work-standard development stages of plant operation. Unsafe conditions, such as inadequate guards and devices, inadequate warning systems, fire and explosion hazards, projection hazards, congestion and close clearances, hazardous atmospheric conditions, and inadequate illumination or noise, are good examples of the more common causes of accidents that can be prevented by effective engineering at the precontact stage of accident control.

Machine Guarding   An unguarded machine is almost always a serious work hazard, whether or not it is used constantly. Machine guards prevent direct contact by the worker with an injury-producing part of the machine, such as the point of operation of circular saws and punch presses or parts of the transmission apparatus, such as drive belts and gears. Machine guards also protect the worker from the material being processed, such as kickbacks of stock during sawing operations or chips from machining or grinding operations. Finally, guards are designed to protect against human failure resulting from fatigue, distraction, deliberate chance-taking, or other physical causes.

Occupational Health Hazards   A second area in which engineering controls can reduce hazards is with respect to *occupational health hazards*—those conditions that cause illness or impair the health of workers. These conditions may involve chemical, biological, or ergonomic hazards.

Most occupational diseases arise from inhaling chemical agents in the form of vapors, gases, dusts, or fumes. General methods for controlling harmful environmental factors include the substitution of less harmful materials for those that are dangerous to health, isolating or enclosing the work operation to reduce the number of persons exposed to the hazard, and installation of exhaust systems. Also included may be personal protective equipment with specialized respiratory mechanisms.

Industrial hygiene specialists periodically examine those employees who are working with or who are exposed to hazardous materials. When periodic examinations indicate that it is warranted, employees are restricted from further exposure to the harmful conditions.

Personal Protective Equipment

The preferred way to deal with an industrial hazard is to eliminate it by *engineering out* the hazard through redesign, automation, or, if necessary, machine-guarding the exposed area that can cause injury. Sometimes, however, neither elimination of the hazard nor control is practical. In these cases, the best way to protect workers from the hazard is to package the people in personal protective equipment.

Personal protective equipment ranges from common equipment such as safety shoes, hard hats, and safety glasses to specialized equipment such as welding helmets and respirators. In all instances, the purpose of the equipment is to protect the individual from injury when an accident occurs. Traditionally, the blue-collar, heavy-industry segments of the workplace have had the greatest need for personal protective equipment.

OSHA standards relating to personal protective equipment are included in Subpart I of the OSHA standards. Separate sections set forth the requirements for Eye & Face Protection, Respiratory Protection, Occupational Head Protection, Occupational Foot Protection, and Electrical Protective Devices. As a general rule, suitable protective equipment is required "where there is a reasonable probability of injury that can be prevented by such equipment." In such cases, employers must make conveniently available a type of protector suitable for the work to be performed, and employees must use the protectors.

The Post-Contact Stage of Accident Control

Once an accident has occurred and an injury results, measures may be taken to reduce the amount of the loss. Two approaches that have become increasingly beneficial in reducing the cost of injuries to employees are prompt medical treatment and rehabilitation.

Emergency Medical Treatment   The logic of utilizing prompt emergency care as an effective countermeasure to reduce death and disability in industry is supported by many occupational medicine specialists. There is no way of knowing how many lives might have been saved over the years had this care been more readily available. When expert consultants returned from Vietnam, for example, they publicly asserted that, if seriously injured, their chances of survival would be better in the combat zone than in most American cities. Prompt emergency care proved to be the major factor in the phenomenal decrease of death rates from battle casualties among those who reached medical facilities, from 4.5 percent in World War II to less than 2 percent in Vietnam. This experience suggests that emergency care in the industrial workplace can provide substantial benefits in the important post-accident phase of loss control.

An emergency care program includes minimum facilities and resources, including first, a properly equipped first-aid area for treatment of all general injuries and certified first-aid attendants or medical professionals on all shifts. Many firms have established in-plant training programs. In addition, a plan should be implemented for handling serious injury cases, including provision for emergency transportation to a properly equipped medical facility. In larger organizations, this may include a trained rescue team or an ambulance team on each shift.

Rehabilitation   The goal of rehabilitation is to restore injured or disabled persons to the highest possible level of functionality through medical rehabilitative and vocational training techniques. Rehabilitation is an effective post-loss-reduction technique that can reduce the cost of bodily injuries. Although rehabilitation is generally considered a technique for handling bodily injury to employees, it can also reduce the cost of bodily injuries to others in cases where the organization might be legally liable at tort.

Rehabilitation of a disabled worker may require physical, vocational, and psychological rehabilitation. The major emphasis in physical rehabilitation is on restoring motor skills that may have been damaged or impaired by the occupational injury. Vocational rehabilitation, which may be accomplished through state rehabilitation agencies or through private facilities supported by insurers, concentrates on restoring job skills or, when necessary, creating new ones.

Although rehabilitation is often thought of only in terms of physical therapy and vocational rehabilitation, it also has psychological aspects. Psychological rehabilitation seeks to restore the healthy mental condition the disabled worker enjoyed before becoming disabled. Disabilities can create fears about the ability to cope with life, and professional help may be required to establish confidence in a person's ability to resume life.

Rehabilitation of an injured worker is generally considered a team effort, involving physicians, rehabilitation specialists, and the employer. The employer's role is to encourage the employee to return to work as quickly as possible and to arrange accommodations in job duties that facilitate the return.

Some employers have had considerable success with *light duty* programs, under which employees who have been injured and who cannot return to their regular duties are assigned to work within their physical capacity. When it is known that the employee will eventually return to his or her regular job, light duty assignments may speed the return. Some workers would prefer to sit around the house and watch television during their recuperative period; light duty programs deny them this option. Thus, since injured workers have to go to work anyway, a light duty program may motivate them to return to the regular job more quickly.

Americans with Disabilities Act   The subject of rehabilitation naturally raises the matter of the Americans with Disabilities Act (ADA), which was enacted in 1990 and took effect on July 26, 1992. The basic philosophy of this law is that most people with disabilities can and should work and that discrimination against qualified disabled candidates should be outlawed. The ADA applies to all organizations in interstate commerce that employ 15 or more persons.

The ADA prohibits employers, state and local governments, employment agencies, and labor unions from discriminating against qualified individuals with disabilities.[9] The prohibitions of discrimination against any qualified individual with a disability apply to all aspects of the employment relationship. Prohibited acts include (1) using standards, criteria, or methods of administration that have the effect of discriminating on the basis of disability, (2) excluding or otherwise denying equal jobs or benefits to a qualified person because of the known disability of an individual with whom the qualified person is known to have a relationship or association, and (3) using qualification standards, employment tests, or other selection criteria that screen out or tend to screen out an individual with a disability. The act requires that employers base employment decisions on the individual's ability to perform the job rather than on presumptions or generalizations about what "people with disabilities" can or cannot do.

The new act goes beyond merely prohibiting discrimination. It requires that employers "reasonably accommodate" individuals with disabilities, if necessary. A "reasonable accommodation" is defined to include (1) making existing facilities used by employees readily accessible to and usable by individuals with disabilities; and (2) job restructuring including hours, vacant positions, equipment (necessary as aid), and policies and procedures that are reasonable and achievable. An employer does not have to provide an accommodation if it would result in "undue hardship." In general, "undue hardship" would occur if the particular accommodation imposes significant difficulty or expense to the employer. When the accommodation would impose an undue hardship on the employer, the employer must provide the disabled applicant with an opportunity to pay for the accommodation him- or herself before rejecting the applicant from the job.

EMPLOYEE EDUCATION

The employee education function as it relates to job safety involves the training of new employees and an ongoing safety education program designed for existing employees. These are part of the human behavior approach to loss control.

The importance of entry training cannot be overemphasized. When a new employee comes to work, he or she immediately begins to learn and form new attitudes. The wise employer takes advantage of this situation and makes sure that the new employee learns correctly those things that will make the employee a safe and efficient worker. It is always easier to train employees to form new and safe habits while they are learning their jobs than it is to correct established unsafe habits later.

THE ACCIDENT RECORD SYSTEM

Information is the raw material from which decisions are made, and the accumulated data on the organization's past losses can provide input for better decisions

---

[9]In addition to the employment-related provisions, the law addresses several other areas. The scope of the law's coverage is indicated by the five titles into which it is divided: (1) Employment, (2) Public Service and Public Accommodations, (3) Services Operated by Private Entities, (4) Telecommunications, and (5) Miscellaneous Provisions.

related to loss prevention and control. Accumulating and analyzing information on the organization's losses helps measure performance. Accurate information on the trend in losses and comparison of the organization's experience against standards can indicate whether performance is satisfactory or requires attention. Accumulating and analyzing information on past losses is also useful in identifying the causes of losses, thereby allowing management to address those causes and hopefully prevent future losses. Records that classify injuries by type and by cause are particularly useful in hazard identification. A high incidence of minor eye injuries, for example, indicates that either the source of flying particles should be eliminated or protective glasses should be worn.

Illness and Injury Statistics

The information on past losses contained in the database can provide valuable information that will aid in planning loss-prevention measures. But while the loss records have a story to tell, they can't talk. Someone must interpret them.

An absolute statement, such as "The XYZ Corporation suffered 112 work-related injuries in 1995," is, in itself, not very useful. A record of 112 injuries might be good for a firm with a large workforce engaged in hazardous operations, but poor for a firm with a smaller workforce in which the work is not particularly hazardous. It is only when the 112 injuries are compared with something else that the analysis becomes meaningful. For this reason, the most popular approach to the analysis of financial statements is the use of ratios.

A ratio is simply one number expressed in terms of another; it is computed by dividing one number, the base, into another. For example, the ratio of work-related injuries might be expressed as a ratio to hours worked by dividing the number of injuries by the number of hours worked.

$$\frac{\text{Total injuries}}{\text{Number of hours worked}}$$

It is conventional in computing ratios related to work injuries to express the ratios in terms of 200,000 worker hours, regardless of the number of hours actually worked. This reflects 100 employee-years, computed on the basis of a 40-hour workweek for 50 weeks a year. Thus, regardless of the size of the organization or its number of employees, the injury rates are expressed for every 200,000 worker hours.

The three standard ratios used to measure performance in the area of employee safety are

1. The total recordable case incidence rate.
2. The lost-workday case incidence rate.
3. The lost-workday incident rate.

The first ratio measures frequency by expressing the number of recordable disabling injuries per 100 employees per year. The other two ratios represent slightly different measures of severity, measured in terms of the number of injuries that involved lost time and the number of days lost because of workplace injuries or illnesses. Because these ratios are the basis for the reports that employers are required to file with OSHA and because the Bureau of Labor Statistics publishes national ratios computed on the same basis, they represent a logical way for the organization to keep score.[10]

The numerator of the three ratios differs to reflect different measures of work injury. The numerator for the recordable case rate is the number of recordable disabilities suffered by employees during the year. The numerator for the *lost-workday case rate* is the number of cases during the year in which an employee was injured or became occupationally ill on the job and did not return to work on the day of the disability or the day after. Finally, the numerator of the *lost-workday rate* is the number of days (excluding the day of injury or illness at work) lost by all employees during the year.

To illustrate the manner in which the rates are computed, consider an employer with 120 full-time employees who receive two weeks' annual vacation. The annual employee hours would be $120 \times 40 \times 50$ or 240,000 hours. Dividing 240,000 hours by 200,000, we derive a ratio of 1.20. If the employees of this organization suffered 32 recordable cases of workplace injury or illness (for which the employee left work for at least some part of the day), and if, of these 32 cases, 12 also required the employee to miss at least the next workday, accounting for a total of 150 employee workdays lost during the year, then the recordable case, lost-workday case, and lost-workday rates would be computed as follows:

$$\text{Recordable Case Rate} = \frac{\text{Recordable Disabling Cases per Year}}{\text{Annual Employee Hours}/200,000}$$

$$\frac{32}{(120 \times 40 \times 50)/200,000} = 26.66 \text{ cases per 100 employees per year}$$

$$\text{Lost-Workday Case Rate} = \frac{\text{Cases Involving Lost Days per Year}}{\text{Annual Employee Hours}/200,000}$$

$$\frac{29}{(120 \times 40 \times 50)/200,000} = 24.16 \text{ cases per 100 employees per year}$$

$$\text{Lost-Workday Rate} = \frac{\text{Lost Workdays per Year}}{\text{Annual Employee Hours}/200,000}$$

$$\frac{150}{(120 \times 40 \times 50)/200,000} = 125 \text{ lost workdays per 100 employees per year}$$

---

[10]These ratios have replaced the ratios developed by the American National Standards Institute (ANSI), which computed work injuries in terms of one million man-hours worked. With the exception of the base used in the computation, the ANSI standards were computed in the same way as the OSHA standards.

Comparison With Standards

Once the ratios have been computed, they are compared with some standard. Virtually all standards fall into one of three broad categories:

1. A historical standard
2. An industry standard
3. A preconceived or "judgment" standard.

Historical Standards   The most common approach to evaluation of ratios—but not necessarily the best approach—is to compare the firm's performance over time. Comparing the current year's performance with the previous year's is a quick and simple way of measuring progress or lack of it. Unfortunately, a comparison between current figures and historical figures can only show if the current period is "better" or "worse" than the past. In many instances, this does not provide a sound basis for evaluation, for the historical figures may not have represented an acceptable starting point.

Industry Standards   In addition to comparisons of the organization's own performance over time, it is also useful to compare its performance with that of other organizations within the same industry to see how safety performance stacks up against other agencies. This task is facilitated by the availability of safety ratios on an industry-by-industry basis. The United States Bureau of Labor Statistics publishes these ratios annually for every Standard Industrial Classification (SIC) code.

Significant differences between the firm's ratios and those published by OSHA may indicate areas that should be examined more closely. The word *indicate* is a key one here. Standard ratios are a useful means of comparison, but they should not be considered operating rules of thumb to be followed slavishly. Organizations differ considerably from each other, even within the same industry, and these differences can produce marked differences in ratios. This doesn't mean that comparison of the organization's ratios with industry averages isn't valuable. It is—and, when it is used over a period of years, it can be valuable in detecting trends. But the variations among firms must always be kept in mind when ratio comparisons are made.

Preconceived Standard   Still another standard against which performance can be measured is a "judgement" standard, based on a predetermined goal. Most safety directors set goals that indicate the levels of performance that they hope to achieve. If actual performance corresponds with the goal, it seems reasonable to conclude that performance was good. However, if the goal was not established carefully, the comparison of performance with the goals will be as meaningless as the goals themselves. Moreover, goals are established on the basis of certain assumptions regarding conditions that were expected during the period. If these circumstances change, the goal figures are incorrect measures of the results that should have been expected under the prevailing circumstances.

Which Standard to Use?   Although each of these three standards has advantages and disadvantages, all can be useful. When the information is available for comparison, there does not seem to be any good reason not to compare performance against all three of the standards. Significant trends in the organization's ratios over time, a wide difference between the organization's ratios and the industry ratios published by the Department of Labor, or failure to achieve the ratio objectives may all indicate the need for more detailed analysis of the differences. The most meaningful information is derived by analysis of the trends in ratios over a longer period of time, such as five years. Time series analysis can help to identify points in time at which significant changes in safety performance have occurred.

ACCIDENT COSTS

Another part of the accident record system that is useful in measuring performance is the information on the cost of losses. Usually, the information available will indicate only the direct costs resulting from an accident. These consist, in the main, of workers compensation costs: the medical expenses associated with the injury, workers compensation disability benefits paid to the injured worker, and rehabilitation costs. Some authorities have recommended that in addition to these direct costs, indirect costs for injuries should also be estimated and recorded. Indirect costs are the costs other than workers compensation costs that rise from a work-related injury. These include the time spent by supervisors and other personnel in completing accident reports, the general reduction in productivity that results from the distraction of other workers from their duties, the lower productivity of a replacement worker, and other miscellaneous costs.

Various attempts have been made over the years to estimate the level of indirect costs as a function of direct costs. Heinrich suggested a ratio of $4 in indirect costs for every $1 in direct costs. Most authorities reject this approach, arguing that the indirect costs associated with employee injuries probably vary with the type of injury, being greater for some losses than for others. Simonds and Grimaldi suggest that indirect costs be computed by determining an indirect cost factor for lost time cases, doctor's cases, first aid cases, and no-injury accidents. The total amount of indirect costs are then computed by multiplying the dollar indirect cost determined for each type of loss by the number of such losses.[11]

The original interest in indirect costs associated with work-related injuries is understandable. Safety personnel often met resistance from management in their efforts to implement safety equipment and procedures. Often, the impediment was cost. Management sometimes balked at safety expenditures because the costs proposed for the prevention of losses were often higher than the historical costs for the losses the measures were designed to prevent. Safety personnel argued that this was so because only direct costs were recorded. They noted that if management would consider total costs—direct and indirect—the expenditures would be justified.

INTEREST IN SAFETY

Given a commitment of management to job safety, there remains the job of obtaining the commitment of employees. Although one might presume that workers will be interested in safety for personal reasons, experience proves otherwise. Whether

---

[11]John V. Grimaldi and Rollin H. Simonds, *Safety Management* (Homewood, Il.: Richard D. Irwin, 1975), p. 411.

or not one accepts Heinrich's estimate that 88 percent of all industrial injuries are the result of unsafe acts, it is indisputable that most worker injuries are due to carelessness on the part of the injured worker or coworkers. Workers need to be educated regarding the need for and benefits of safety, and must be motivated to follow safe working practices.

Not all workers will be interested in accident prevention for the same reasons. Whereas one worker might take an active part in accident prevention efforts because of his concern for his personal welfare and the security of his family, another may be motivated by her pride in doing her work well or by her fear of personal injury. To interest all workers in safety, various means have been used: award systems, suggestion systems, slogan contests, and unit pride. A wealth of material is available from the National Safety Council and from other sources. Safety education and promotion materials include leaflets, booklets, films, posters, and technical materials. Although such materials are not, in themselves, a solution to the job-safety problem, they provide an effective part of an overall system.

ADDITIONAL CHALLENGES IN MANAGED JOB SAFETY

In addition to those hazards already discussed, three additional hazards challenge risk managers in their efforts to control the cost of workplace injuries, violence in the workplace, alcoholism and substance abuse, and fraudulent claims.

Workplace Violence

Workplace violence has emerged as a critical safety and health hazard. According to Bureau of Labor statistics, homicide is the second leading cause of death to American workers (behind vehicle-related fatalities), claiming the lives of 1,071 workers in 1994 and accounting for 16 percent of the 6,588 fatal work injuries in the United States. Workplace homicides are only part of the problem. According to BLS statistics, about 21,300 workers were injured in nonfatal assaults in the workplace in 1993. Women were victims in 56 percent of these assaults.

As in the case of other hazards, loss prevention and control measures can reduce the risks of workplace violence to workers. Although not every incident can be prevented, many can, and the severity of injuries sustained by employees reduced. Some employees are more exposed to violence than others. Of the 1,071 deaths due to workplace violence in 1994, as in prior years, half occurred during robberies of small retail establishments, including grocery or convenience stores, restaurants and bars, liquor stores, fast-food restaurants, and gas stations. Shootings accounted for four-fifths of fatal workplace assaults, with robbery being the motive in 75 percent of the homicides. Statistics indicate that robberies are not randomly distributed, but that robbers are selective in their targets. Stores most likely to be robbed are those that have large amounts of cash on hand, an obstructed view of counters with inattentive clerks, poor outdoor lighting, and easy escape routes. This suggests logical prevention measures, making the target less attractive by reducing the amount of cash on hand, maximizing the "take-to-risk" ratio for perpetrators, and training employees not to resist. Standard anti-crime security measures discussed in Chapter 19 are also effective measures for protecting employees from workplace violence.

Workplace violence can also arise *among* employees. The recurring episodes of workers gone berserk, spraying a workplace with gunfire, are stark reminders of this workplace hazard. Although mental health researchers generally agree that it is very difficult to predict violent behavior, most acts of employee violence follow recognized threats. A history of violent behavior and open threats are indisputable warning signals and the employer should consider training front-line supervisors how to recognize warning signs and diffuse anger. If extreme behavior occurs, it should be addressed immediately. Other pre-event measures include communicating a zero-tolerance for violence to employees and a good reporting system. To the extent allowable, hiring practices should avoid those likely to be violent.

The employer must be cautious to avoid legal repercussions when taking action against an employee whose behavior makes him or her suspect. Under the ADA, an employer may require that employees not pose a direct threat to the health and safety of themselves or others. This means that the employer can, if proper procedures are followed, terminate an employee who poses a threat to others, if the threat cannot be eliminated through a reasonable accommodation. The employer cannot discharge an employee merely on the basis of suspicion. The risk must be substantial. When an emotional or mental disability is involved, the employer must identify the specific behavior on the part of the worker that poses a direct threat to other workers.

Substance Abuse and Addiction

It is estimated that more than 10 million employees in the workforce are alcoholics, that 20 million of the nation's workers smoke marijuana and 5 million habitually use cocaine. Although it is difficult to measure the effect of substance abuse in terms of increased employer costs for work related injuries, it is indisputable that a link exists. In addition to the costs for work related injuries, substance addiction exacerbates the cost of medical care generally, both for employers and for society. The high incidence of drug and alcohol abuse and its effect on workers compensation and health care costs has led to the search for ways to address this problem.

Drug Testing and Screening The U.S. Supreme Court has ruled that the federal government can require drug-testing of both private and government employees whose work involves public safety or law enforcement, but the question of the constitutionality of random testing is still fiercely debated. Fourteen states have enacted drug screening statutes that allow the use of substance screening tests and personnel action against employees on the basis of such tests.[12] All state laws permit testing on the basis of a reasonable suspicion of illegal use and some allow random testing as well. As discussed in Chapter 25, federal law *requires* testing for commercial vehicle operators.

[12]Connecticut, Iowa, Kansas, Louisiana, Maine, Maryland, Montana, Nebraska, Rhode Island, South Dakota, Tennessee, Utah, and Vermont.

Employee Assistance Programs An *employee assistance program* (EAP) is an employer-sponsored benefit aimed at helping employees overcome personal problems, including dependency on alcohol and drugs. Usually, the EAP program provides assistance to employees for a variety of personal problems, including not only alcoholism and substance abuse, but emotional and personal problems as well.

Employee assistance programs may be internal or external. In the external model, workers are referred to an outside agency. Internal EAPs provide in-house diagnosis and counseling. The purpose of an EAP is to make treatment readily available to employees and, in some cases, to their dependents. The EAP program is coordinated with the organization's health insurance program, which is structured to provide inpatient and outpatient treatment options. An essential element in both internal and external programs includes training for supervisory personnel in the early identification of employees who have addiction or other problems.

Addiction and the ADA Clinical alcoholism may be classified as a disability, and the ADA protects alcohol dependent workers who are participating in a recovery program and are able to perform the duties of their job. The ADA permits an employer to forbid drinking alcohol on the job or working under the effects of alcohol, and workers suffering from alcoholism may also be required to meet the same standards of performance as other workers. If alcohol affects performance, the employee may be disciplined or terminated as long as the same penalties are applied to nonalcoholic employees who commit the same infractions.[13] The ADA requirement that the employer make "reasonable accommodations" might mean a leave of absence for treatment.

Fraudulent Claims

Fraud is a pervasive problem in the field of workers compensation. Although most of this fraud is perpetrated by employees, some physicians and attorneys are accomplices. The National Insurance Crime Bureau has estimated that as much as 20 percent of all claim payouts in some states may involve some type of fraud.

In some ways, it is easy to understand this fraud. Consider the plight of the assembly-line worker who has just been told that he will be on the company's next list of layoffs. The likelihood of finding another job is poor. He has a mortgage payment and three mouths to feed, and the state maximum benefit for unemployment is $155 a week. The present workers compensation benefit in the same state is $545 a week. Without condoning the action, many people would not be surprised if this employee chose to make a fraudulent workers compensation claim. Similarly, an employee who has no health insurance and sustains a serious knee injury playing touch football on the weekend may consider claiming that the injury was work related to cover medical bills.

In other instances, fraudulent workers compensation claims indicate an animosity toward the employer (or toward society generally). In other cases, they repre-

---

[13]*Americans With Disabilities Act of 1990*, Section 104(b), also 26 C.F.R. 36.209.

sent the employee's perverted notion of redress for what he or she may consider unfair treatment. A recent study from the Boeing Company, for example, documented that the best predictor of a costly back injury was totally unrelated to physical factors. The most significant predictor was a supervisor's negative report on an employee's work performance during the previous six months.[14]

The first line of defense in dealing with fraudulent claims is careful investigation of work-related injuries of a questionable nature. Some of the major signs that a claim may be fraudulent include a delay in reporting the incident, the absence of witnesses to the injury, the injury occurred early Monday morning, or a history of prior claims of injuries. Sometimes, circulating rumors about injuries are based on direct knowledge of fellow workers. Such rumors should always be investigated.

Some authorities argue that another defense against employee fraud is a properly structured employee benefit package, which includes adequate health insurance for employees. Employees who know that another source of recovery will be available to cover their medical expenses are less likely to file fraudulent claims.[15]

IMPORTANT CONCEPTS TO REMEMBER

employers liability	survivors' death benefit	occupational health hazards
employers common law obligations	rehabilitation benefits	total recordable case incident rte
common law defenses	Federal Vocational Rehabilitation Act	lost-workday case incident rate
out of and in the course of employment	Occupational Safety and Health Act (OSHA)	lost workday incident rate
total temporary disability	*de minimis* violations	rehabilitation
partial temporary disability	accident report	Americans With Disabilities Act
total permanent disability	job safety analysis	reasonable accommodation
partial permanent disability	engineering controls	

QUESTIONS FOR REVIEW

1. Identify and explain the five common law obligations of an employer with respect to employees and the three common law defenses to employers' liability suits.

---

[14]Bigos, Battie, Spengler, *et.al.*, A Prospective Study of Work Perceptions and Psychosocial Factors Affecting the Report of Back Injury," *Spine*, Vol. 16, No. 1, 1991, pp 1–6.

[15]A local school district in the midwest that did not provide health insurance on part-time employees used part-time drivers for its school bus system. Analysis of the district's workers compensation loss experience revealed that the injury frequency rate for part-time employees was four times as high as for full-time employees. After the group health insurance program was extended to cover part-time employees, the injury frequency rate for these employees fell to approximately the same rate as for full-time employees.

2. Identify and explain the six principles of workers' compensation and the manner in which these principles modified the common law principles of employers' liability.

3. Explain the distinction between an employee and an independent contractor for worker's compensation purposes.

4. Briefly describe the purpose of the Occupational Safety and Health Act and indicate the manner in which the Occupational Safety and Health Administration seeks to achieve this purpose.

5. Describe the general types of injuries that are covered under workers' compensation laws.

6. Describe the job safety analysis process and explain how it contributes to accident control.

7. John is injured in the course of his employment in State X. John's employer is located in State Y, where John is normally employed. What are John's rights? Explain.

8. Identify the three standard ratios that are used to measure performance in the area of employee safety. How is each computed and what do they measure?

9. H. W. Heinrich's writings emphasized efforts aimed at reducing the number of unsafe acts as the best approach to loss control. What was the premise for this emphasis?

10. In what way is the accident investigation system a useful tool for hazard identification? What questions can the accident investigation system help answer?

QUESTIONS FOR DISCUSSION

1. The management of ABC Trucking has become increasingly concerned about suspected use of alcohol and drugs by its drivers. You are retained as a consultant. What approach would you recommend to the firm as the most effective approach to addressing this problem?

2. Many employers have found the requirements of the Occupational Safety and Health Act to be burdensome. In your opinion, is regulation of this type an appropriate realm of government activity?

3. In what way does the successful contribution of personal protective equipment depend on both the engineering approach and the human behavior approach to risk control in the area of employee injuries?

4. Of the seven elements that the National Safety Council has suggested are important to an effective industrial safety program, which do you believe is the most important? Why?

5. Discuss the significance of the Americans With Disabilities Act for job safety.

SUGGESTIONS FOR ADDITIONAL READING

Fletcher, Meg. "Encouraging Safety Not Always Easy." *Business Insurance*, October 9, 1995, p. 3.

Grimaldi, John V., and Rollin H. Simonds. *Safety Management*, 3rd ed. (Homewood, Illinois, 1975).

Hammer, Willie. *Occupational Safety Management and Engineering*. Englewood Cliffs, NJ: Prentice Hall, Inc. 1976.

Hampson, David G. "New And Emerging Exposures in Workers Compensation," *The Risk Report*, vol. VI, no. 4, (December 1983).

Head, George L., ed. *Essentials of Risk Control*, 2nd ed., vol I Malvern, Pa.: Insurance Institute of America, 1989. Chapters 4, 5.

Heinrich, H.W., Dan Petersen, and Nester Roos. *Industrial Accident Prevention: Safety Management Approach*, 5th ed. New York: McGraw-Hill Book Company, 1980.

Mitchell, William J. "Workers Compensation Cost Management," *The Risk Report*, vol. XVIII, no. 4, (December 1995).

Shafer, Rebecca A., and Graham, Elizabeth S. "Simplifying the Return-to-Work Maze." *Risk Management* (February 1995), pages 45-47.

CHAPTER 27

Managing Employee Injury Risks: Risk Finance

CHAPTER OBJECTIVES

When you have finished this chapter, you should be able to

Explain the insurance coverage provided by the insuring agreements of the standard Workers Compensation and Employers Liability Policy.

■

Understand the purpose of the common endorsements used to modify the Workers Compensation and Employers Liability Policy.

■

Be able to identify and explain the factors that determine the workers compensation premium and the rating approaches that influence that premium.

Introduction ■

The workers compensation system can be viewed from two perspectives. The first is its role as a social insurance mechanism designed to provide income to wage earners in the event of occupational disability. In this chapter we are concerned with the second perspective: the obligations that these laws impose on the employer. All states require the employer to insure the workers compensation exposure or to qualify as a self-insurer. Usually, only the largest firms self-insure, and even in these instances, some form of catastrophe coverage is normally purchased.

In addition to the liability imposed on the employer under the workers compensation laws, injury to employees may be a source of liability in still another way—a suit at common law. Although the workers compensation system was intended as an exclusive remedy for injured workers, in some situations an employer may be sued for injury to an employee. Thus some form of coverage is needed to defend the employer in the event of such suits, as well as to pay any resulting judgments. Protection for Employers Liability is provided as part of the standard Workers Compensation Policy.

Workers compensation benefits may be paid directly out of the firm's own income or assets (we will call this self-insurance) or through insurance. Self-insurance is permitted in all states except North Dakota, Texas (except for public bodies), Wyoming, Guam, Puerto Rico and the Virgin Islands. In Indiana, only private firms may self-insure; state and political subdivisions may not.

Workers Compensation Insurance ■ ■ ■ ■ ■ ■ ■ ■ ■ ■ ■ ■ ■

Workers compensation insurance—like general liability and auto liability insurance—undertakes to pay those sums for which the insured is legally liable, those that fall within the insuring agreements of the contract. In the case of workers compensation insurance, the liability covered is the insured's liability under the workers compensation law of one or more states. Coverage is standardized by law, and all insurers use essentially identical contracts.

THE WORKERS COMPENSATION AND EMPLOYERS LIABILITY POLICY

Workers compensation insurance is currently provided under the 1992 edition of the Workers' Compensation and Employers Liability Insurance Policy (WCELIP), which was developed by the National Council on Compensation Insurance (NCCI). The policy is written in simplified language and contains two standard coverages, Workers Compensation and Employers Liability. An optional coverage, Other States Insurance, is printed in the policy and is activated by an entry in the declarations. Other coverages are available by endorsement.

Part One: Workers Compensation Insurance

The workers compensation insuring agreement obligates the insurer to pay sums that the insured is legally obligated to pay under the workers compensation law of the state or states listed in the declarations. This is an extremely broad commitment. There are no exclusions under the workers compensation coverage, and there is no maximum limit on the amount payable.

In a legal sense, the workers compensation portion of the policy is not simply an agreement to pay benefits on behalf of the insured; it goes beyond indemnifying the insured, and it makes the insurer directly and primarily liable to employees who are entitled to benefits, even though such employees are not named in the policy. A Statutory Provision in the policy in effect incorporates the provisions of the workers compensation law of the designated state into the contract, just as if it had been fully written into the policy. The insurer's obligation to employees is affected neither by any default of the insured under the policy, nor by the failure

of the insured to comply with the policy provisions. As respects the insurer's obligation under the compensation law or laws listed in the policy, it is never a defense
to a compensation claim that the policy is not written broadly enough to cover the
loss or that the insured violated a policy provision. The only matter to be determined is whether or not the employer is liable under the law. If the employer is
liable, the insurer is liable.

Although the insurer's liability to the employee is governed by the workers compensation law, the insurer's liability to the employer is governed by the policy terms.
The insurer may recover from the employer amounts that would not have been paid
except for the employer's unique position as a direct beneficiary under the policy.
These amounts include any benefits paid because of the insured's serious and willful
misconduct, because of knowingly employing a person in violation of the law, because
of failure to comply with health or safety regulations, or because of discrimination
against any employee in violation of the workers compensation law.

Part Two: Employers Liability Insurance

The Employers Liability Insurance provides protection for common law suits by
employees who suffer bodily injury. The coverage is subject to a per accident limit
and a separate limit per employee occupational disease limit. In addition, there is a
policy aggregate for occupational disease. The standard limits for Employers Liability coverage, which may be increased for an additional premium, are $100,000
per accident, $100,000 per employee for occupational disease, and $500,000 aggregate for occupational disease.

Originally, Employers Liability coverage was included in the WCELIP primarily
as a defense coverage. As we saw in the preceding chapter, one of the principles of
workers compensation laws is that the compensation to the injured employee represents a "partial but final indemnity." This meant that in return for the schedule
of benefits for which the employer became absolutely liable, the employer was
granted immunity from tort action. Because workers compensation was intended
as an exclusive remedy, suits by employees were once considered unlikely. Moreover, if an injured employee brought suit, the legal principles generally favored the
employer. Nevertheless, it was argued, the cost of defending the suits could be
expensive, and the Employers Liability coverage provided such defense. In effect,
Employers Liability coverage was purchased primarily as a defense coverage.

Recently, the exclusive remedy theory of workers compensation has become
subject to attack and is gradually being eroded. As a result, Employers Liability coverage can no longer be considered merely a defense coverage. It is an increasingly
important component of the liability insurance program.

Attacks on the exclusive remedy theory of employer protection have come in several forms. Some states permit the spouse of an injured worker to bring action against
the employer for the spouse's loss (as opposed to the loss suffered by the insured
worker). Another approach is the so-called *third party over suit*, in which the
employer is sued by a third party who, having been found liable to the injured
employee, seeks to pass part of the responsibility on to the employer. Third party
over suits arise when an employee is injured in the course of employment and the

injury is caused by a negligent third party. The employee collects workers compensation from this employer, but also brings a tort action against the third party. The third party, having been found liable, then seeks to pass part of the liability on to the employer, usually arguing that the employer's negligence was partly responsible for the injury.[1]

Still another doctrine under which employees have been permitted to recover from the employer in a common law suit is *dual capacity*. This doctrine permits the employee to bring action against the employer if the employer was acting in a different capacity at the time of the injury. A classic illustration of this doctrine arose in connection with a hospital employer providing medical treatment to an injured employee. The court held that the employee had two relationships with the hospital; that of employee and that of patient. Although the employee was barred from bringing suit as an employee, he could sue as a patient.[2] The doctrine has also been applied to incidents in which the worker was injured by a product manufactured by the employer, even when the injury occurred in the course of employment.[3]

The insuring agreement of the Employers Liability section of the policy makes specific references to such suits, indicating that coverage is provided for damages under the doctrine of dual capacity, claims in third party over suits, and damages for loss of care and consequential bodily injury to relatives of an injured employee.

Employers Liability Exclusions

The Employers Liability coverage is subject to several exclusions:

1. Liability assumed under contract. Contractual liability coverage in the general liability field covers liability for injuries to employees assumed under contract.

2. Punitive or exemplary damages because of injury to an employee employed in violation of the law.

3. Bodily injury to an employee while employed in violation of the law with the insured's knowledge or with the knowledge of any of the insured's executive officers.

4. Obligations under a workers compensation, occupational disease, unemployment compensation, or disability benefits law, or any similar law. This exclusion makes it clear that Workers Compensation and Employers Liability coverages are separate and distinct.

5. Bodily injury caused or aggravated intentionally by the insured.

6. Bodily injury outside the United States, its territories or possessions, or Canada. An exception to this exclusion makes it inapplicable to a citizen

---

[1]The landmark case in this area is *Doe v. Dow Chemical Company*, 331 N.Y. Supp. 2d 382 288 (1972). Here the court ruled that the employer was liable to a manufacturer.

[2]*Tatrai v. Presbyterian University Hospital*, 439 A.2d 1162(1982).

[3]In an Ohio case, a truck driver was injured when his tire blew out, and he brought a tort action against the employer who was the manufacturer of the tire. See *Mercer v. Uniroyal*, 49 Ohio 279 (1977). In a well-known 1977 California case, an employee who was injured on a scaffold manufactured by his employer successfully brought suit against his employer in its capacity as the scaffold manufacturer. *Douglas v. E. and J. Gallo Winery*, 69 Cal. App. 3d 103 (1977). See also *Bell v. Industrial Van Gas*, 110 Cal. App. 3d 463 (1980).

or resident of the United States or Canada who is injured while temporarily outside the specified areas.

7. Damages arising out of discharge of, coercion of, or discrimination against an employee in violation of the law.

8. Bodily injury to persons in work subject to the Longshore and Harborworkers Compensation Act (or amendments to the act) or any other federal workers compensation law.

9. Bodily injury to persons in work subject to the Federal Employers Liability Act or any other federal law obligating an employer to pay damages because of bodily injury to an employee.

10. Bodily injury to a master or member of the crew of any vessel.

11. Fines or penalties imposed for violation of federal or state laws.

12. Damages payable under the Migrant and Seasonal Agricultural Protection Act and under any other federal law awarding damages for violation of those laws or regulations issued thereunder.

Several of these exclusions were omitted in the 1984 edition of the WCELIP but were added by endorsement. The 1992 edition of the policy incorporates the exclusions into the policy itself.

Part Three: Other States Insurance

Other States Insurance provides essentially the same coverage that was previously available by an endorsement called the Broad Form All States Endorsement. The coverage is designed to protect against liability under the workers compensation laws of states in which the employer does not expect to have employees, but in which a workers compensation obligation could conceivably be incurred.

Most workers compensation laws are "extraterritorial"—that is, the provisions of the law apply to injuries employees suffer while in the state and also while traveling outside its boundaries. Some laws have further extraterritorial effect in that they impose liability on an employer who is located in another state if an employee is injured in a state where he or she is working. For example, the employee of a Nebraska firm who is injured while working in Iowa may bring action for workers compensation benefits under the Nebraska law. In addition, however, the injured worker may decide to bring action under the law of the state where he or she was injured, particularly if the benefits of that state are higher. The worker in our example may elect benefits under either the Nebraska law or the Iowa law, and the employer will be obligated to make payment in either case. However, if Nebraska is the only state listed in the declarations, the policy will not pay the employer's obligation under the Iowa law.

Initially, the employer should list all states in which the firm has employees. The Other States Insurance may then be used to further broaden the policy. The Other States Insurance extends the policy to provide workers compensation benefits in any state listed in the declarations for Other States coverage if the employer becomes liable under the law of such state. Rather than listing other states individually, it is common to use a blanket designation, stipulating that coverage applies to "*all states except. . . .*"

The states excepted are those with monopolistic state funds (Nevada, North Dakota, Ohio, Washington, West Virginia, and Wyoming), and the state or states designated for Section One coverage. Some insurers also exclude states in which they are not licensed to write insurance.

WORKERS COMPENSATION ENDORSEMENTS

The WCELIP is sometimes modified by endorsement to provide coverage for workers compensation benefits and for employers liability exposures that are not covered under the basic policy itself. Various federal acts apply to railroads, work on the continental shelf, maritime activities, and members of the merchant marine. Where operations are such that exposures to these laws exist, special endorsements may be needed. Among the endorsements used to modify the policy, the following are among the more common.

Voluntary Compensation Insurance

Voluntary Compensation Insurance is an optional coverage that may be added to the policy by endorsement, using the Standard Voluntary Compensation and Employers Liability Coverage Endorsement (WC 00 03 11). This endorsement is used when an employer wishes to provide workers compensation benefits to employees even though the law does not require payment of benefits to such employees. The insured selects a state law (usually the state of employment), and, in the event of injury to a member of the class of employees for whom voluntary compensation is provided, the policy will provide benefits as if the employee were subject to the law.

Employers Liability (Stop Gap) Endorsement

The Employers Liability Endorsement (WC 00 03 03) is an advisory endorsement that may be used to provide Employers Liability coverage in a state or states—including the monopolistic-fund states—in which the policy does not provide workers compensation coverage. The state funds in monopolistic states write only workers compensation, not employers' liability. An employer who has operations in those states with monopolistic workers compensation state funds can insure the employers' liability exposure in connection with such operations through the Employers Liability Coverage Endorsement, also referred to as Stop Gap coverage. If the employer has a WCELIP covering operations in other states, the Stop Gap coverage may be added to the WCELIP written to cover operations in those states. Employers whose operations are confined to the monopolistic-fund states use a different Stop Gap endorsement, which is added to the general liability policy.

Monopolistic-Fund State Coverage

Nevada, North Dakota, Ohio, Washington, West Virginia, and Wyoming (as well as all provinces of Canada) have monopolistic-state funds and do not allow private insurance. However, Nevada, Ohio, Washington, and West Virginia do allow self-insurance. Some insurers will endorse the WCELIP to provide indemnification for any loss inadvertently incurred in such states prior to the insured's knowledge of any such exposure or requirement to insure in the fund.

Federal Coal Mine Act Endorsement

The Federal Coal Mine Health and Safety Act established a schedule of compensation benefits for persons who had contracted "black lung" disease. Coverage for this act must be added to the policy by the Federal Coal Mine Health and Safety Act Endorsement (WC 00 01 02).

Federal Employers Liability Act

Special note should be made of the Federal Employers Liability Act and the status of coverage for this law under the WCELIP. The Federal Employers Liability Act is an employers liability law rather than a workers compensation law. It predated workers compensation laws and makes an interstate railroad liable for bodily injuries sustained by employees.[4] Coverage for liability under the Federal Employers Liability Act is excluded from the Employers Liability section of the WCELIP and must be added by endorsement.

Federal Longshore and Harbor Workers Compensation Act Endorsement

Persons (other than seamen) who are engaged in maritime employment are covered under a federal workers compensation statute, the U.S. Longshore and Harbor Workers Compensation Act (LHWCA). Although this is a complex area of law, in general a worker is covered under the LHWCA only if he or she meets a *situs* and a *status* test. The injury must occur on the navigable waters or on an adjoining wharf, pier, dock, or similar facility used in loading, unloading and building or repairing vessels. In addition, the individual must have been engaged in maritime employment when injured. Public bodies do not have this exposure because the act excludes "an officer or employee of the United States or any agency thereof or any state or foreign governments or of any political subdivision thereof." Because the LHWCA is a federal statute, it does not fall within the scope of the workers compensation insuring agreement. When coverage is required for the LHWCA, it may be added to the policy by the Longshore and Harbor Workers Compensation Act Endorsement.

The federal LHWCA has been amended several times to cover special groups of workers. These include persons employed on the continental shelf, employees of contractors employed by the federal government outside the United States, and civilian

[4]Federal Employers' Liability Act (45 U.S. Code 51-60).

employees of certain Department of Defense nonappropriated fund installations (PXs and base exchanges).[5] The LHWCA Endorsement does not cover liability under these acts; they are insured under separate endorsements discussed below.

Defense Base Act Coverage Endorsement

The Defense Base Act, an amendment to LHWCA, applies to contractors performing work at overseas military bases.[6] Coverage for such contractors who perform work at specifically designated overseas sites is added to the WCELIP by the Defense Base Act Coverage Endorsement (WC 00 01 01).

Nonappropriated Fund Instrumentalities Act Endorsement

The Nonappropriated Fund Instrumentalities Act, which is an amendment to the LHWCA, applies to civilian employees of PXs, base exchanges, and other instrumentalities of the United States government under the jurisdiction of the armed forces.[7] The Nonappropriated Fund Instrumentalities Act Endorsement (WC 00 01 08) extends the Workers Compensation and Employers Liability Policy to cover such operations.

Outer Continental Shelf Lands Act Endorsement

The Outer Continental Shelf Lands Act, which is an amendment to the LHWCA,[8] applies to work involving the development of resources of the "outer continental shelf." In general, this consists of offshore drilling rigs on the continental shelf. Coverage for employment subject to this act is added to the WCELIP by the Outer Continental Shelf Lands Act Endorsement (WC 00 01 09). The state whose boundaries, if extended to the continental shelf, would include the worksite are scheduled in the endorsement.

Maritime Employment Endorsement

Liability to masters of vessels and members of the crew of a ship is exempt from workers compensation laws, and is covered under admiralty law and under an amendment to the Federal Employers Liability Act, the so-called Jones Act. This act applies to members of the U.S. merchant marine and gives members of the merchant marine a right to bring suit in a federal court.[9] Prior to enactment of the Jones Act, a sailor's only recourse to recovery for injury was through the admiralty courts.[10] The act gives the injured worker a choice between admiralty law and a suit in a federal court.

[5]Longshoremen's and Harbor Workers' Compensation Act (33 U.S Code 901-952).
[6]Defense Base Act (42 U.S. Code 1651-1654); Compensation Act for Employees of Contractors with the United States Outside the United States (42 U.S. Code 1701-1717)
[7]5 U.S. Code 2105, 8171-8173.
[8]Outer Continental Shelf Lands Act (43 U.S Code 1331-1343, Section 1331 and 1333).
[9]Jones Act (Injury or death of seamen), (46 U.S Code 688).
[10]High Seas Death Act (46 U.S Code 761-768); Convention No. 55, "'Shipowners' Liability (sick and injured seamen) Convention, 1936" (54 U.S. Statute 1693).

Liability to the master or member of the crew of a vessel is specifically excluded under the Employers Liability coverage of the WCELIP. When a maritime exposure exists, it must be covered by endorsement. The Maritime Coverage Endorsement (WC 00 02 01A) modifies the Employers Liability coverage of the WCELIP to include coverage with respect to bodily injury to the master or a member of the crew of a vessel. Coverage applies only within the continental United States, Alaska, Hawaii, and Canada, and while sailing directly between the ports of these territories. (Maritime coverage for other territories is written as a part of the Protection and Indemnity coverage of the ocean marine policy.)

■ Workers Compensation Rating Plans ■ ■ ■ ■ ■ ■ ■ ■ ■ ■

In the area of workers compensation, state laws require that all workers compensation insurers adhere to a uniform classification system and uniform experience rating system filed with the commissioner by an advisory organization designated by the commissioner. The standard rating bureau for workers compensation insurance is the National Council on Compensation Insurance. The *Basic Manual for Workers Compensation and Employers Liability Insurance* is the NCCI's compilation of rules, classifications, and basic rates for workers compensation insurance approved and issued by the director of insurance. It establishes the rates, by type of employment, for workers compensation insurance coverage written in each state. Minimum premium rates for workers compensation insurance are approved by the insurance commissioner, and no insurer may charge less than the published minimum rates.

Understanding the options available to the firm in connection with its workers compensation exposure requires at least a familiarity with the rating structure for workers compensation insurance.

STANDARD PREMIUM AND GUARANTEED COST PLANS

The standard approach to workers compensation rating is the guaranteed cost plan. This is the premium generated by the insured's payroll and rates, modified to reflect experience for those risks subject to experience rating. Manual rates are published by the NCCI. Rates are published per $100 of payroll for hundreds of different occupational categories. These rates multiplied by the insured's projected payroll figures develop the standard premium. Because the exposure is measured by the insured's estimated payroll for the year, the premium is subject to adjustment at the end of the policy period, when the actual payroll is multiplied by the rates in force to determine the final premium. In addition, the premium may also change as a result of changes in rates during the policy period. Workers compensation rates are unique, in the sense that changes in rates during the policy period that result from changes in benefit levels apply to policies already in force. This stems from the fact that changes in workers compensation benefits enacted by the Assembly apply to policies already in force. A "guaranteed cost" premium is "guaranteed" in the sense that it is subject to change only if rates change or if the actual payroll differs from the estimated payroll.

EXPERIENCE RATING

The insured's manual premium may be modified by an experience rating factor to reflect the firm's past experience. Experience rating is a mandatory feature that applies to all employers who generate a specified premium (generally $2500). Losses incurred during the period of experience (usually three years) are compared with average losses for the classifications of the insured involved. The resulting "experience modification" is a ratio applied to manual rates. The modification, however, is prospective; that is, it applies to the following year's premium rather than to the years for which it was calculated.

Experience rating is not intended to punish employers with poor experience (although it does tend to punish); rather, it is based on the assumption that past experience is a good indicator of future experience. The fundamental operation of experience rating measures past actual incurred losses for a particular insured and then relates them to the losses that the insured was expected to incur based on the average indications of the classifications under which the firm was rated. Experience rating determines whether an individual risk is better or worse than the average and also how much the premium should be modified to reflect this variation. When the actual losses incurred are less than those expected from an average risk of the same size and type, a credit is produced and the premium is reduced. When the actual losses incurred are more than those expected from an average risk of the same size and type, a debit is produced and the manual premium is increased.

Experience rating was devised to encourage loss-prevention activities and to discriminate fairly among insureds so that each insured pays its fair share of the cost of insurance. The experience rating plan has proven useful for measuring differences in hazard between two risks in the same classification.

As noted earlier, a three year experience period is used for the rating. The three-year period begins four years prior to the date for which the rating will be applied, and it terminates one year in advance of the rating becoming effective. The data for the most recent year are considered too new and unreliable to be included in the computation. As an example, for a policy period beginning January 1, 1996, the experience period would include the following:

1–1–1992 to 1–1–1993	Included
1–1–1993 to 1–1–1994	Included
1–1–1994 to 1–1–1995	Included
1–1–1995 to 1–1–1996	Not Used

The theory of experience rating is to allow an insured's past experience to influence the premium for future coverage, on the premise that past experience is a good predictor of future experience. The plan compares the actual experience of each organization to the industry average. Based on this comparison,

NCCI computes an experience modifier, expressed as a percentage of the manual premium. If the policyholder's experience modification is 0.90, the premium charged will be 10 percent lower than indicated in the manual. If the experience modification is 1.25, a surcharge (debit) over the manual premium will be imposed.

PARTICIPATING OR DIVIDEND PLANS

A *participating* or *dividend plan* is similar to a guaranteed cost plan, except that a dividend may be returned as a result of good loss experience. No penalty is levied if loss experience is poor. Generally, the dividend is based on the experience of the insurer for all workers compensation insureds in the state. By law, dividends cannot be guaranteed, and it is a violation of the law to promise the payment of a dividend. Participating or dividend plans are generally independent filings.

RETENTION PROGRAMS

Basically, a retention program is a dividend plan. The insurer determines a charge or "retention" for its services expressed as a percentage of the standard premium (say, 20 to 30 percent). This retention includes commissions, other expenses, and the insurer's profit. Losses, multiplied by a "loss conversion factor" (to cover adjusting costs), are added to the retention to get the final premium. If there are no claims, the retention is the total premium. The final premium is reached when the insurer calculates what the retention plus converted losses should be and then subtracts this amount from the deposit premium. As in the case of dividend and participating plans, retention plans are generally independent filings.

RETROSPECTIVE RATING PLANS

A retrospective rating plan is much like a retention plan, the difference being that under a retrospectively rated plan, the insured will be penalized for poor experience. Retrospective rating is similar to a cost-plus contract and bases the insured's premium for the current period on actual losses in the current period. With good experience, the insured pays less than normal; with poor experience, he pays more. Although insureds use them for potential cost savings, they may also be employed to persuade an insurer to accept an otherwise unacceptable account. The Retrospective Rating section of the NCCI manual includes several retrospective rating plans approved by the department of insurance.

WORKERS COMP ASSIGNED RISK PLANS

Workers Compensation assigned risk plans provide those employers who are unable to secure coverage in the voluntary market with a means of obtaining insurance. Insurance through these plans is available only to employers who have been turned down for coverage within the 60 days preceding application by two nonaffiliated insurers that are licensed to write workers compensation in the state. Like automobile assigned risk plans after which they are patterned, the workers compensation plans operate on a risk sharing basis, under which applicants are assigned to insurers based on the proportion of the total workers compensation premium that each insurer writes in the state. The insured is required to submit the premium with the application and must pay the premium for renewal policies in advance. The employer who is able to obtain insurance in the voluntary market after obtaining coverage from the plan may withdraw from the plan at any time, without a premium penalty. The insurer can discontinue coverage only in the case of nonpayment of premium.

EMPLOYEE LEASING AND WORKERS COMPENSATION

Employee leasing arrangements were conceived as a means by which an employer could avoid the administrative details associated with the employment of a workforce. Through these arrangements, the firm's employees are transferred to a *labor contractor*, who in theory becomes their employer. The employees are then leased back to the labor contractor's client, the previous employer of the leased employees.

Labor contractors provide personnel administration services to client companies. Usually, the labor contractor assumes responsibility for computing and distributing payroll, maintaining payroll records, and preparing all employee-related reports and audits. Most labor contractors also act as an employee benefits department for the client, procuring health and pension benefits and workers compensation coverage for the client companies. The client companies thus remain the actual source of the funds used to meet payroll, pay taxes, and obtain insurance coverage. In effect, the client companies are simply channeling their payroll functions through the labor contractor, which charges a fee for handling these matters.[11]

The growth of the employee leasing industry has been attributed to the 1982 Tax Equity Fiscal Responsibility Act (TEFRA), which gave employers who leased employees certain advantages under the IRS pension laws. In addition, employee leasing was, and still is by some, promoted as a way to avoid unionization. It is also a way for small and midsize employers to cooperatively purchase certain benefit programs that they would be unable to afford individually. Employee leasing has also been promoted as a way for employers to avoid the costs of workers compensation insurance premiums.

[11]Labor contractors should be distinguished from temporary labor companies (such as Manpower and Kelley). The temporary labor business consists largely of furnishing employees to others, frequently to solve short-term staffing problems. In the labor contracting business, the workers for a particular client company were usually hired initially by the client company. The workers usually work for the same client company at the same location throughout the duration of their employment.

The Legal Status of Leased Employees

The legal question naturally arises as to who is the employer of leased employees for the purpose of workers compensation: the labor contractor who issues the paychecks or the client company which is paying the labor contractor to issue the paychecks? The answer, which begs the question, is whichever party is the *employer* of the employee.

The answer to the question of *who is the employer* is a legal one that is decided by the courts. In general, the courts have followed one of two doctrines in deciding who the employer is: the *right to control* doctrine and the *economic reality* doctrine. The majority of jurisdictions have adopted the right to control test, which holds that the employer is the party that exercises control over the employee. If the party has the right to direct the person performing services and to control the time, place, degree and amount of such services, the person performing the services is held to be an employee.[12]

Under the economic reality test, courts often focus on the nature of the claimant's work in relation to the regular business of the employer and whether the work being done by the injured worker was an integral part of the employer's regular business.[13]

Under typical employee leasing contracts, the employee is controlled and directed by the client company (not the labor contractor), and the employee does work that is an integral pert of the client company's business (and not the labor contractor's). Thus, under both the majority and minority approaches to the definition of employer-employee, the client company would be considered the employer, despite the employee leasing arrangement.

Under a traditional common law analysis, leased workers are the employees of the client company, under both the majority and minority approaches. Absent statutory or regulatory action to the contrary, however, common law controls, and only the entity that directs and controls the employee or for whose primary economic benefit the employee works will be considered the employer.

National Council on Compensation 1991 Rule

Faced with the complexity of employee leasing arrangements and some uncertainty regarding the status of leased employees for the purpose of workers compensation, in 1991 the NCCI added a new rule to its manual addressing the subject of employee

[12]*Ford v. Mitcham.* 298 So. 2d 34 (Ala. Civ.. App. 1974); *City of Los Angeles v. Vaughn.* 358 P.2d 913,914 (Ca. 1951); *Clark v. Lynch.* 294 S.W. 2d 294 (Tex. Civ. App. 1940); *Vorston v. Pennell,* 153 A.2d 255, (Penn. Sup. Ct. 1959); *Barton-Mansfield Co. v. Bogey.* 147 S.W. 2d 977,980 (Ark. 1941);*Vacek v. State* 142 A. 491,493 (Md. App. 1928).

[13]*United States v. Silk,* 331 U.S. 704,67 S.Ct. 1463,91 LEd. 1757 (1947); *Hyslop v. Klein,* 85 Mich. App. 149,270 N.W. 2d 540(1978); *White v. Central Transport. Inc.,* 150 Mich. App. 128,388 N.W. 2d 274(1986); *Bowser v. State Industrial Accident Commission,* 182 Ore. 42' 185 P.2d 891 (1947): *Powell v. Employment Security Commission,* 345 Mich. 455, 75 N.W. 2d 874 (1956); *Oilfield Safety & Machines Specialities. Inc. v. Harman Unlimited. Inc.,* 625 F.2d 1248(5th Cir. 1980); and *Haynie v. Tideland Welding Service,* 631 F.2d 1242(5th Cir. 1980).

leasing arrangements. Under the terms of this rule, NCCI proposes that whoever is the *employer* should retain workers compensation coverage for the leased employees. Although under a traditional common law analysis, the client would generally be considered the employer of its leased workers, a labor contractor may obtain coverage for its leased workers if it can clearly demonstrate that it is the employer.

Two endorsements support the new rule: the Employee Leasing Client Endorsement—00 03 19, and the Labor Contractor Endorsement—WC 00 03 20. The Employee Leasing Client Endorsement may be attached to a policy issued to a labor contractor. This endorsement requires that the labor contractor provide its workers compensation insurance carrier with specific information relative to its clients, including proof that the client has secured its workers compensation obligations for the leased workers. It further specifies that the labor contractor's failure to secure such proof of coverage will result in the labor contractor being charged for the premium for the leased employees and may result in cancellation of the labor contractors policy.

The Labor Contractor Endorsement may be attached to a policy issued to a client when the client is determined to be the employer of its leased workers. This endorsement provides insurance to the labor contractor specified in the schedule relative to claims for bodily injury to covered leased employees. The Alternate Employer Endorsement—WC 00 03 01A, which has been in existence for some time, may be attached to a policy issued to a labor contractor when it is desired to extend coverage to its client with respect to leased workers.

Assigned Risk Exception to General Rule

By far the most significant problem associated with the emergence of the employee leasing industry has been the undermining of the experience rating system. This problem has occurred because many labor contractors have marketed their services by representing to client/employers that the employers may escape their experience modification factors through the device of employee leasing. Essentially, a labor contractor with a relatively low modification factor (mod), or with a 1.0 *unity* modifier, will represent to an insurer that the workers of its client company (which has a relatively high experience modifier) are the employees of the labor contractor.

In response to the insurer's difficulties in obtaining the proper premium in the case of employee leasing operations, NCCI added an exception to the rule for leased workers under the Workers Compensation Assigned Risk Plans over which it exercises jurisdiction. This rule provides that workers compensation coverage for leased employees shall be provided under the workers compensation insurance plan by a policy issued in the name of the *client company*. The rule also provides that the client be recognized as the party primarily responsible for providing workers compensation coverage for leased workers. This is designed to prevent the use of leaseback arrangements to avoid unfavorable loss experience of some risks. Application is made in the name of the client company, and a separate policy is issued for each client company. The premium for the client company continues to be calculated using the experience modification factor of the client company. Essentially, the employee leasing arrangement is not taken into consideration in the premium calculation.

✖ Self-Insurance and Workers Compensation ■ ■ ■ ■ ■ ■ ■

Workers compensation is more frequently self-insured than many other corporate exposures. Self-insurance has become a popular method of dealing with the workers compensation exposure because it is characterized by a high frequency of loss, because the benefits are defined by statute and thus limited, and because it generates more premiums than most other lines of casualty insurance.

Private employers are permitted to self-insure the workers compensation exposure in all states except North Dakota, Wyoming, and Texas. Although self-insurance in some lines of insurance can be implemented informally, self-insuring workers compensation usually requires filing an application and obtaining approval from the state to act as a self-insurers. Depending on the size of the organization, the self-insurer will usually be required to provide some form of security—in most instances a workers compensation bond. Most insurers also arrange some form of excess workers compensation coverage to protect against catastrophic loss. The usual excess workers compensation coverage is written with a $250,000 self-insured retention and a maximum limit ranging from $1 million to $5 million. This is in contrast with the WCELIP, under which there is no limit on the amount payable by the insurer for workers compensation benefits.

✖ The Workers Compensation Crisis ■ ■ ■ ■ ■ ■ ■ ■ ■ ■ ■

In the 1980s, the workers compensation system created new challenges for employers, their workers, and the insurance industry. Almost everyone associated with the system voices dissatisfaction with the way the system has developed, and the term *crisis* is increasingly used in discussions of workers compensation.

Employers complain about the soaring cost of workers compensation insurance or, in the case of self-insured firms, the cost of benefits. Insurance companies complain that the workers compensation line has been consistently unprofitable, and an increasing number of insurers have restricted their writings. Organized labor complains that workers have become the target of those concerned with runaway costs. Instead of focusing corrective action on creating safer work sites, efforts are being made to lower workers compensation benefits or to change the definition of injury or illness.

Three factors combined to create the almost universal dissatisfaction with the current status of the workers compensation system. The first is the soaring level of benefits, both for disabilities and for medical expenses. The changes enacted by most states during the 1970s (in response to the recommendations of the *National*

Commission on State Workmen's Compensation Laws) tied benefit levels in most states to the state average weekly wage. This resulted in an automatic escalation in benefits over time. In addition to the increasing level of benefits, new occupational injuries and diseases have appeared. The courts have expanded the concept of occupational disease, providing coverage for aggravation of nonoccupational injuries and disabilities, cumulative trauma, and psychiatric and mental stress claims.[14] The doctrine of cumulative trauma makes the employer liable for the total effects of an injury worsened by employment, even though the injury was initiated by causes unrelated to employment. Back injuries are a good example. Employees who suffer lower-back pain often seek and are awarded workers compensation benefits. Although the injury results from the totality of the person's lifestyle, the award of benefits is justified on the grounds that the condition was aggravated by repetitive acts associated with their work. Not surprisingly, the incidence of cumulative trauma increases for workers approaching retirement.

The greatest increases in workers compensation costs have been in the area of medical expenses, which account for 40 percent of workers compensation costs. Although the escalation in medical expenses is a universal problem nationally, the cost of medical expenses in workers compensation has increased even faster than other medical costs. While U.S. expenditures on health care increased 100 percent between 1980 and 1987, the cost of medical treatment under workers compensation laws increased 150 percent. The abnormal escalation in medical costs occurred because workers compensation laws pay the entire cost of treatment for covered injuries and occupational disease, without a copayment by the patient who, in most jurisdictions, is allowed to choose the physician. Unlike Medicare and Medicaid, the system sets no limits on providers' fees, and workers have resisted the cost containment efforts that characterize other fields of health care.

The second factor in the developing crisis has been a significant increase in litigation of workers compensation claims. One of the basic principles on which the workers compensation concept was based was the elimination of litigation, but over during the 1980s, litigation, with its attendant delay and expense, has become the norm when it should be the exception. In some states, lawyers are involved in half of all workers compensation claims. Although fault is not an issue, litigation over causation and the degree of disability are chronic issues. A significant percentage of the litigation involves back injuries, cumulative trauma, and psychiatric and mental stress claims.

In response to these cost-drivers, a number of states enacted workers compensation reforms in the late 1980s and early 1990s. Many states enacted measures aimed at containing medical costs, including restricting the employee's choice of healthcare provider, instituting provider feel schedules and encouraging managed care. Insurers and regulators also focused on ways to reduce fraud. These reforms, coupled with increased loss control efforts by both employers and insurers, and regulatory approval

[14]The Bureau of Labor Statistics Annual Survey for 1988 indicated a 58 percent increase in the number of reported cumulative trauma disorders, such as carpal tunnel syndrome. This category now accounts for nearly half of all occupational disease cases.

of requested rate increases have had a dramatic effect on insurer results. In 1990, the countrywide combined ratio for workers compensation was 122.6 percent. By 1995, it had fallen to 103 percent. Many states were experiencing rate decreases in 1995 and 1996. Despite the improvement, there are some who believe that the relief is only temporary and that a major change in the system is required.

WORKERS COMPENSATION AND 24-HOUR COVERAGE

Nearly a decade ago, one authority recommended that the reliance on workers compensation as the primary payer of benefits for work-related injuries be reduced,[15] and suggested that other available mechanisms could fill this role. Instead of a specialized program dealing with occupational injuries, it was suggested that the coverage under public and private benefit plans be expanded to pay for occupational and nonoccupational disabilities alike.

The original proposals for combining the state workers compensation programs with programs for nonoccupational disabilities focused on the disability benefit part of workers compensation. They were based on the notion that the need for income is the same whether one is disabled on or off the job. In addition to the disability coverage under the social security system, six states have established some form of compulsory nonoccupational disability coverage program.

With the growing crisis in workers compensation and the focus on controlling health care costs generally, the focus changed from the disability portion of the workers compensation programs to the medical expense portion, and the notion of 24-hour health care coverage has been discussed with increased frequency. Some insurers, with regulatory approval, are experimenting with this coverage.

WORKERS COMPENSATION AND ERISA

ERISA Section 514(a) provides that ERISA will supersede any state law that "relates to" an employee benefit plan. This preemption of state laws by ERISA has been the subject of an increasing amount of litigation, and the rulings in preemption cases have varied from court to court.

The U.S. Supreme Court ruled that a workers compensation program that combines nonworkers compensation benefits with workers compensation benefits is preempted under the ERISA statute.[16] Litigation on this point continues, and the states have generally taken the position that workers compensation remains subject to state regulation. Following the ruling by the Supreme Court, several state insurance departments warned insurers, agents, and brokers that they may face disciplinary action if they make any stated or implied representation that an ERISA plan meets state workers compensation requirements.

---

[15]See Michael L. Murray, "Workers Compensation—A Benefit Out of Time," *Benefits Quarterly*, 1 No. 2 (Second Quarter 1985).

[16]*The Greater Washington Board of Trade v. District of Columbia*, 948 F.2d 1317, 14 EBC 1791 (D.C. Cir. 1991), cert. granted, 112 S.Ct. 1584 (1992).

IMPORTANT CONCEPTS TO REMEMBER

Workers Compensation and
  Employers Liability
  Insurance Policy
employers liability insurance
third party over suit
dual capacity doctrine
extraterritorial
voluntary compensation
  insurance
Employers Liability (Stop
  Gap) Endorsement
Federal Coal Mine Act
  Endorsement

black lung disease
Federal Longshore and
  Harbor Workers
  Compensation Act
  Endorsement
Defense Base Act
  Endorsement
Nonappropriated Fund
  Instrumentalities Act
  Endorsement
Outer Continental Shelf
  Lands Act Endorsement

Maritime Employment
  Endorsement
guaranteed cost plan
experience rating
experience modification
participating plan
dividend plan
retention program
loss conversion factor
retrospective rating plan
assigned risk plan
24-hour coverage

QUESTIONS FOR REVIEW

1. Why does the Workers' Compensation and Employers' Liability policy not contain a specific statement of the benefits which it provides?

2. What is the purpose of the Other States Coverage option that is available under the Workers Compensation and Employers Liability policy? Why is it needed? When added, does it leave any unprotected gaps?

3. Describe the purpose of the Voluntary Compensation Endorsement to the Workers' Compensation policy. When is the endorsement used? Would you classify it as an essential, important, or optional insurance coverage?

4. In what ways do the factors that determine the workers compensation premium for a particular organization encourage loss prevention and control?

5. Describe the objective of workers compensation assigned risk plans and explain the manner in which they achieve this objective.

6. What characteristics of the workers compensation exposure make it suited to retention? What characteristics of the exposure make it unsuited to retention?

7. You have been retained as a consultant by a manufacturer to review the firm's industrial safety program. What features of the program would you stress in your review?

8. A risk manager, reporting to the president of the firm on the large number of cumulative trauma workers compensation claims stated that "the problem with carpal tunnel syndrome is that it is contagious." To what did she probably have reference?

9. What choices does a risk manager have concerning the degree of retention and transfer with respect to workers compensation claims?

10. Explain the effect of the Statutory Provision included in the Workers Compensation and Employers Liability Insurance Policy.

QUESTIONS FOR DISCUSSION

1. Retrospective rating is more widely used in the workers compensation field than in any other filed. What prompted insurers to create retrospectively rated workers compensation programs?

2. Workers compensation was originally designed as an exclusive remedy. In what ways has the system departed from this original concept?

3. A multi-employer welfare association (MEWA) offers to provide workers compensation to employers that join the program at premiums computed without experience modification. What is the inevitable result of a plan of this nature?

4. A Minnesota manufacturer maintains a branch office in North Dakota, a state that requires that workers compensation insurance be purchased from its monopolistic state fund. Are there any features of this arrangement about which the risk manager should be concerned? If so, is there any solution to the problem?

5. What is your personal opinion of the proposal for 24-hour coverage? Do you see any philosophical issues that need to be considered in connection with this idea?

SUGGESTIONS FOR ADDITIONAL READING

Chamber of Commerce of the United States. *Analysis of Workers Compensation Laws.* Washington, DC: U.S. Chamber of Commerce, annual.

Fire, Casualty and Surety Bulletins. Casualty and Surety Volume. Cincinnati: National Underwriter Company. (Loose-leaf manual service with monthly supplements.) See "Workers Compensation" section.

Gentile, Williard J. *The Workers Compensation and Employers Liability Policy,* 7th ed. New York: Insurance Advocate, 1974.

Huebner, S.S., Kenneth Black, Jr., and Bernard L. Webb. *Property and Liability Insurance,* 4th ed. Englewood Cliffs, NJ: Prentice-Hall, 1996. Chapters 28 and 29.

Lewis, John H. "24 Hour Coverage: Less Than Meets The Eye," *The Risk Management Letter.* vol. 16, (Issue 3, 1995).

Mitchell, William J. "Workers Compensation Cost Management," *The Risk Report.* vol. 18, no. 4 (December 1995).

Murray, Michael L. "Workers Compensation—A Benefit Out of Time." *Benefits Quarterly,* Vol. I, No. 2 (Second Quarter 1985).

Policy, Form and Manual Analysis Service. "Casualty Coverages Volume." Indianapolis: Rough Notes Company. (Loose-leaf manual service with monthly supplements.) "Workers Compensation" sections.

Report of the National Commission on State Workmen's Compensation Laws. Washington, DC: U.S. Government Printing Office, 1972.

State Workers Compensation Laws. Washington, DC: U.S. Department of Labor, revised annually.

Webb, Bernard L., Stephen Horn II, and Arthur L. Flitner. *Commercial Insurance,* 2nd ed. (Malvern, Pa.: Insurance Institute of America, 1990), Chapter 10.

Whiteaker, Raymond E. "Exclusive Remedy Doctrine under Siege," *For The Defense,* Vol. 1984, No. 3. Milwaukee, WI: Defense Research Institute, 1984.

Workmen's Compensation Law Reporter. New York: Commerce Clearing House, Biweekly.

CHAPTER 28

Managing International Risks

CHAPTER OBJECTIVES

When you have finished this chapter, you should be able to

Describe what is meant by a multinational corporation and explain why companies become multinational corporations.

∎

Identify the two major policy issues that arise in connection with management of international risks.

∎

Distinguish between admitted and nonadmitted insurance and explain why the distinction is an important issue of risk managers.

∎

Identify and evaluate the markets from which the multinational corporation may purchase insurance and the advantages of each segment.

∎

Describe what is meant by political risk and explain the methods that may be used to address it.

▟ Introduction ∎

Although the United States has traditionally dominated the world insurance market, its domination has declined over the past two decades, as insurers outside the United States have increased their share of the world premium volume. In 1970, the United States controlled 70 percent of the world premium volume; by 1990, its share had fallen to 38 percent. The three largest insurance companies in the world today are Japanese.

Part of the growing percentage of world premiums written by foreign insurers simply reflects the growth in the gross national product of foreign countries relative to the United States. As economic activity increases in a nation, the premiums written to protect assets against loss also increase. Thus, part of the United States' decreased share of world premiums results not from a decrease in U.S. premiums, but from an increase in premiums in other nations. Individuals and businesses in a particular country tend to purchase their insurance from domestic insurers, and the growth of other economies has brought a corresponding growth in the insurance premiums in other countries.

A point that is sometimes ignored in the discussion of changing shares in the world insurance market is the role that the growth of U.S. corporations abroad has had on the distribution of insurance expenditures. The growth in the investment of U.S. corporations in international operations has created a corresponding growth in the international risk management responsibilities of U.S. risk managers. Many a risk manager has suddenly found him- or herself responsible for arranging foreign insurance coverage, dealing with foreign employee benefit requirements, and monitoring international exchange rates. Increasingly, corporate managers are recognizing the importance of risk management in international operations. Because U.S. corporations cannot ignore the opportunities abroad, they are dependent on the risk manager to ensure that the same protection against loss from pure risks exists for foreign operations as for domestic activities.

How does risk management in a multinational enterprise differ from that in a domestic firm? In principle, the concepts of protecting the organization against unbearable loss are the same for both types of companies, but the environment in which these decisions are made is different. This chapter considers the institutional factors that make the risk management of a multinational company somewhat different from that of a domestic company. In this regard, we examine the statutory requirements with respect to purchase of insurance from admitted insurers, the tax environment, and political risks. Our purpose is to provide not an in-depth understanding but rather an exposure to those factors that influence a firm's basic risk management decisions in an international setting.

Multinational Corporations ■ ■ ■ ■ ■ ■ ■ ■ ■ ■ ■ ■ ■ ■ ■ ■ ■ ı

International business enterprises may be classified as either *limited international corporations* or *multinational corporations*.[1] A limited international corporation is a business with limited commitment to the international market. Its major activity in the world economy is exporting its product to other nations, or, in some cases, importing the products of foreign producers. In contrast, a multinational corporation (MNC) is one that not only sells, but also produces in foreign markets. Consider, for example, McDonald's, our international conduit of American culture. McDonald's does not

---

[1]Norman A. Baglini, *Global Risk Management* (Risk Management Society Publishing, 1983), p. 2.

ship its Big Macs around the world from grills in the United States. It produces them in hundreds of outlets located all over the world. Nor does Pepsi ship its products around the world. People in foreign countries that purchase Big Macs and Pepsi are buying American products that were produced in their own country. Obviously, McDonald's and PepsiCo are only two of the literally thousands of U.S.-based multinational corporations. Other U.S. multinationals include the names of numerous leading corporations in the United States—Ford, General Motors, IBM, and many others.

What persuades a firm to produce in factories in foreign countries rather than just sell its product overseas? The answer is clear enough in the case of McDonald's, but perhaps less so in the case of IBM. The answer, as you might suspect, is profit. A business usually begins the journey toward multinationalism as an exporter. As the foreign market grows, it eventually becomes more profitable for the firm to organize an overseas production operation. This permits savings in transportation and sometimes in tariffs. It is also likely to reduce labor costs. Most importantly from our perspective, MNCs represent a flow of investment capital internationally. It is this flow of capital that creates the need for international risk management.

U.S. corporations that operate overseas customarily do so through subsidiaries, often incorporated in the various countries where they carry on business. Throughout this discussion, therefore, although reference may loosely be made to American or U.S. corporations, it is important to remember that, in fact, the corporation owning the foreign property is likely to be a foreign corporation, though one owned wholly or in part by a U.S. parent. From our generalized equation on the existence of risk, the ownership of assets that are subject to damage or destruction creates financial risk. This risk is the focus of international risk management.

THE GROWTH OF MULTINATIONAL OPERATIONS

Economists point out that not only is the absolute level of international trade increasing, the relative importance of that trade is also increasing, both for individual countries and for all nations as a group. More important for our purposes, U.S. investment abroad continues to increase, as U.S. corporations acquire assets or subsidiaries in foreign nations. The breakup of the Soviet Union and privatization of eastern European nations witnessed the opening of an enormous consumer market, a market in which U.S. corporations are intensely interested. Privatization is creating new opportunities for investment. Simultaneously, it is requiring new investment in national infrastructures, including telecommunications and transportation systems and power production facilities. All of these provide a backdrop for a variety of new trade pacts—such as the North American Free Trade Agreement (NAFTA)—as nations jockey to exploit the consumer demand in new markets. Countries such as China and India—the world's most populated nations—represent markets of enormous potential.

At one time, U.S. multinational corporations dominated the international scene. Today, they struggle to hold their own in a fiercely competitive world economy. Multinational corporations from other nations—both European and Asian—now challenge U.S. multinationals both domestically and in foreign markets.[2] Large corporations in general and multinational corporations in particular will continue to play an expanding role in the world economy as international trade barriers continue to fall.

Although the principal focus in international risk management is on the large multinational corporation, small businesses in the United States have sought and found opportunities abroad. Although the foreign link for small businesses is generally trade, rather than investment, they face many of the same problems in managing the risks associated with their international activities as do larger corporations.

▓ Complications in International Risk Management ■■■■■■■■■■■■■■■■■■■■■

One would suspect that the international distribution of assets across national borders would complicate the process of risk management. According to Dr. Norman Baglini, the factors that tend to complicate international insurance management are:

- The wide range of insurance regulations from country to country (including compulsory insurance).

- The prohibition against insurance policies purchased out of the country where the risk is located (including severe penalties for violations).

- The many alternative types and combinations of insurance coverages from which to choose (U.S. insurance contracts, foreign language contracts, and combinations).

- The pros and cons of using various brokers, consultants, insurers, and combinations thereof (U.S. international brokers with correspondents or local brokers, for example).

- The potential violation (due to currency devaluations) of policy clauses requiring insurance to value.

- The peculiar income tax problems concerning the nondeductibility of some insurance premiums and the absorption of loss payments.

- The attitude and sometimes conflict of interest of the affiliate manager with respect to insurance purchasing.

- The many languages involved and legal interpretations of the various insurance policies.

- The absence of customary insurer services.

- The foreign exchange regulations and the need to be kept up to date.[3]

---

[2]In 1980, of the 25 largest industrial corporations in the world, 18 were headquartered in the U.S. By 1990, the number had dropped to 12.

[3]Baglini, *Global Risk Management*, p. 16.

Dr. Baglini's inventory of issues provides a convenient outline through which we can explore the problems and opportunities of international risk management.

CENTRALIZATION VERSUS DECENTRALIZATION

An initial risk management policy issue for the MNC is that of centralization versus decentralization of the risk management function—the extent to which decision making with respect to pure risks should be delegated to the management of foreign subsidiaries or affiliates. Although there is room for debate, Dr. Baglini provides the following argument for centralization:

> Since the decision to commit assets to foreign operations is made by the parent corporation, the parent corporation should likewise make the decision regarding the methods best suited for the protection of those assets and the flow of earnings emanating therefrom. Depending upon the structure of the organization, that decision may be implemented locally with a certain amount of flexibility, but the basic policy should be determined by the parent corporation and local management held accountable to top management for compliance with its policy.

The disagreement that is sometimes expressed over the question of centralization or decentralization of the risk management function is actually a debate on a different issue—whether insurance should be purchased centrally or at the local level of the foreign affiliate. This issue is sometimes equated with the question of centralization or decentralization, but they are actually two separate issues.

A centralized risk management program is not inconsistent with the purchase of local insurance. The purchase of insurance might be delegated to the foreign affiliate, but with guidelines and strict performance standards on how it is to be done. Such guidelines could include minimum standards with respect to insure perils, methods of asset valuation, limits of liability, financial stability of the insurer, and qualifications and duties of the broker. There may be valid reasons for decentralizing the insurance-buying function, but the decision to decentralize the insurance-buying function does not automatically imply decentralization of the risk management function. On the issue of centralization or decentralization of the risk management function, Dr. Baglini's observation seems persuasive. Because it is the assets of the parent corporation that have been committed and are exposed to risk, the parent corporation should also make the decisions regarding the measures to protect those assets.

CENTRALIZED VERSUS LOCAL INSURANCE BUYING

MNCs consist of those groups that regard insurance as a matter for local procurement and those that regard it as a matter for centralized buying. The issue of centralized versus decentralized insurance buying arises for several reasons. The most important is legal.

Reasons for Purchase of Foreign/Admitted Insurance

Nonadmitted insurance is prohibited in a majority of countries in the world because of the legal requirement that insurance covering persons or companies located in the country be provided by insurers "admitted" to do business in that country.[4] It is sometimes argued that the prohibitions against nonadmitted insurance represent a form of protectionism, designed to protect a domestic insurance industry from foreign competition. Although some foreign countries have adopted protectionist policies with respect to their domestic insurance industry, requirements that insurance be placed in admitted insurers should not be regarded as an effort to keep foreign competition out. After all, the identical pattern exists in the system of state regulation in the United States. U.S.-based MNCs are familiar with the concept of admitted and nonadmitted insurers because it is a pervasive feature of the U.S. insurance market. Just as individual states in the United States require that insurers be licensed before operating within the state, most foreign nations require that insurance written in the country be written by an admitted insurer. In some instances, the choice is limited when it comes to admitted companies. Still, the system is not particularly foreign, but reflects the structure of the U.S. market.

Dealing with a foreign/admitted insurer presents certain advantages, mostly financial and based on a differential tax treatment of premiums paid for admitted and nonadmitted insurance. In many countries, only premiums paid to admitted insurers are allowable as tax-deductible expenditures. Adding insult to injury, when a foreign affiliate receives a loss payment from a nonadmitted insurer, it may be treated as taxable income. The same payment received from a foreign-admitted insurer would be treated as a nontaxable reimbursement for the restoration of the damaged property.

A second advantage of insurance purchased through a foreign/admitted insurer is that premiums will be paid in the foreign currency and loss payments will be received in the foreign currency. This provides some protection against fluctuations in exchange rates as well as against currency inconvertibility. Because many foreign countries have exchange controls, it is desirable to expend local currency that might not otherwise be remissible.

Still another advantage of purchasing insurance locally is what might be termed *reciprocity*. Often, a foreign affiliate will prefer to deal with a foreign insurer. In some instances, where the foreign affiliate was acquired by the MNC, the insurance relationship may be a long and cordial one. In the case of a newly acquired overseas affiliate, the MNC may chose not to disturb the relationships upon which the affiliate relies. Sometimes reciprocal business advantages are to be gained from local purchase of insurance—for example, when a firm sells business machines to local insurance companies. Similarly, in the case of a partially owned subsidiary, there may be an understanding that insurance is one of the matters to be handled by the local shareholders. Finally, sometimes loans may have been advanced to the

---

[4]The creation of the European Union and the end of the Cold War in the early 1990s eliminated many of the restrictions on *across-border* insurance in Europe. By 1995, the first full year of Europe's single insurance market, most of the 15 member countries in the European Union had implemented the directives that enable an insurer in one country to establish an insurance subsidiary in another member country, subject only to the "home" state's insurance regulations.

subsidiary by a group of insurance companies on the understanding that part of the consideration is the placement of the insurance with the lenders.

Reasons Against Purchase of Foreign/Admitted Insurance

The purchase of insurance locally is a piecemeal approach to the purchase of insurance that may result not only in inadequate insurance but also in the purchase of coverage that the parent would not consider essential to its program. No doubt, local management will be more familiar with local conditions, but this does not necessarily qualify them as knowledgeable purchasers of insurance. Nor does it mean that the insurance forms customary in the local market entirely meet the corporation's actual needs. One major reason why U.S.-based MNCs prefer to purchase nonadmitted insurance rather than foreign-admitted coverage is the difference in the ancillary services available from U.S. insurers compared with foreign insurers.

A piecemeal approach to insurance buying is also likely to be more costly in the aggregate than a centralized program. This simply reflects of the fact that, when many exposures are brought together in a single plan, it is usually possible to insure them more cheaply than if each exposure is insured individually with many different underwriters.

A major danger of unsupervised local purchase of insurance is the possibility of placement with insurers whose financial resources are not commensurate with the risks they assume. Fortunately, the overwhelming majority of insurance companies overseas, as in the United States, are eminently sound and failures are relatively few. Failures do occur, however. In the United States, there are laws governing the size of a policy that a company may issue in relation to its capital and surplus, but, generally speaking, no such laws exist overseas. It is not unusual for a small company to assume quite large commitments, relying on reinsurance for as much as 99 percent. Thus, a perfectly solvent company might be put into difficulties when one of its reinsurers fail to respond in case of a dispute, for instance. Not only may the regulatory requirements differ, but also there is likely to be little in the way of assistance in evaluating the foreign insurer.

Finally, the purported reciprocal business advantages derived from local procurement of insurance may be exaggerated. Sometimes these advantages are nothing more than local management's vague feeling that local placement generates goodwill, which in turn results in more business. However, carried to its logical conclusion, this would be tantamount to procuring all goods and services locally and abandoning centralized purchasing altogether with its consequent effect on costs.

COVERAGE UNDER FOREIGN/ADMITTED INSURANCE

The coverage offered by foreign insurers tends to be narrower in scope than that to which most U.S. insurance buyers are accustomed. Named-peril coverage is the rule, and replacement cost coverage is far from standard in many foreign countries. Not only does the coverage of foreign insurers differ from that of U.S. insurers, but it also differs from country to country. For the MNC that operates in multiple countries and purchases admitted insurance in each area, the differences in coverage from country to country will result in significant inconsistencies in the overall program. The perils, deductibles, coinsurance requirements, and valuation provisions may all vary from one country to another.

Some of the coverage differences are not particularly troublesome. Most foreign insurers, for example, usually require 100 percent coinsurance, as compared with the 80 percent or 90 percent that is typical in the United States. Although this could conceivably cause a coinsurance problem, a coinsurance deficiency is much more likely to result from runaway inflation in the foreign country or from currency exchange rate fluctuations. In fact, currency fluctuations can be a major problem. An MNC that secures adequate insurance to value could end up being penalized because of a change in the U.S.-foreign currency exchange rate.

Fortunately, there is a solution to the problem of coverage differences. The MNC with an international program composed of multiple insurance purchases in different jurisdictions can purchase a *difference-in-conditions* (DIC) policy that serves as a wraparound and brings the overall level of protection up to a specified level. The DIC policy, which is usually purchased from a U.S. insurer, provides coverage excess over the coverage from the various foreign/admitted insurers. The coverage may be written to include not only property exposures, but casualty coverages as well, including general liability coverage and auto liability.

A DIC property policy typically affords all risk protection that covers losses not covered by foreign/admitted named-peril policies. DIC policies do more than cover additional perils; they fill other gaps as well. They can provide more favorable valuation provisions than are usually encountered with admitted policies. Under a DIC, coverage can be written to cover on a replacement cost or functional replacement cost basis.

With the exception of the issue of economies that can be achieved by centralized buying, the other objections to foreign/admitted placement of insurance seem manageable, especially if the risk management function remains centralized. Obviously, the first concern should be the financial strength of the local insurers, but if this concern can be resolved the question then becomes one of price. The question will be whether the financial penalties from taxation are greater or less than the economies that are achievable using a nonadmitted insurer.

In countries where a competitive insurance market does not operate, the MNC may be faced with excessive prices. In this situation, most risk managers attempt to purchase the minimum permissible amount of insurance in the foreign country and cover the bulk of the exposures under the DIC policy. If the foreign market is competitive and the rates are reasonable, there is no reason not to purchase coverage locally. In fact, there may be definite advantages. The greater the level of coverage purchased in the foreign country, the less the need to depend on the coverage in the DIC policy.

THE GLOBAL INSURANCE PROGRAM

A global insurance program is one in which insurance is purchased centrally, with a master program that covers all of the organization's risks. Such programs combine coverage on the MNC's exposures in the United States with exposures abroad. This approach provides potential economy in centralized buying. A potential disadvantage is finding an insurer with a global network of engineers, adjusters, and other service personnel who can support the program.

Some observers question the value of global programs. For one thing, they argue that an MNC can easily segment its overseas and domestic exposures, making it relatively easy to set up an international insurance program that is separate and distinct from its domestic program. In practice, some U.S. MNCs do actually maintain two separate insurance programs—one for U.S. operations and a separate program for foreign operations. Furthermore, some observers point out that relatively few insurers can handle a global program, while there are many more domestic insurers.

INTERNATIONAL CAPTIVES

Some MNCs have found that they can exercise greater control over the insurance facet of their international risk management program through the use of a captive. One approach is to use a foreign admitted insurer as a fronting company that issues admitted coverage and then reinsures the risks with the MNC's captive. This allows the MNC to comply with the foreign insurance regulations and at the same time self-fund the exposures. In some cases, captives may reinsure only those risks that a country requires be insured through an admitted insurer. The captive will then write the remaining coverage on a direct basis.

U.S. INSURERS ABROAD

Although less than 5 percent of the U.S. insurance industry's premium writings is generated in foreign countries, 60 to 70 U.S. insurers have established a significant presence abroad. At the top of this list is the American International Group (AIG). AIG is the largest commercial and industrial insurer in the United States, and over one-half its total operating income comes from foreign sources. AIG is the largest non-Japanese life insurance operation in Japan, as well as the largest non-Japanese property and liability insurance operation. Some foreign insurers have acquired U.S. subsidiaries and provide a global network of related companies. The classic example is Allianz, AG, the giant German insurer, which purchased Fireman's Fund in 1971 for an adjusted price of about $3.1 billion. With other subsidiaries throughout the world, Allianz offers international buyers access to a range of companies that are licensed in most jurisdictions. Other leading U.S. insurers with a significant presence in the overseas and international market include CIGNA, Chubb, and Reliance National Insurance Company. Several U.S. insurers that have not maintained a presence in foreign markets have moved to establish such a presence. Late in 1990, for example, the St. Paul Fire and Marine Insurance Company became the first American-owned insurer to take advantage of the new European regulations, permitting cross-frontier underwriting of large risks.

PLACING THE INSURANCE

Having secured all necessary information and formulated an insurance program, the risk manager must decide how it is to be placed. The manager has three basic choices.

First, he or she may decide to place the insurance in the various local markets where the corporation's exposures are located, perhaps using for this purpose the services of one of the American brokerage firms with offices or correspondents in the various countries concerned.

The second possibility is to offer the business to the London market. Although local markets have grown and in many instances thrown off their former almost total dependence on London, London remains the foremost world market. The major British companies have an overseas branch office and agency network, but Lloyd's is primarily a nonadmitted market.

Finally, U.S. insurers, with their extensive system of overseas branch offices, offer excellent facilities and the great advantage of being able to deal with a problem on the spot whenever it arises, which is usually easier than if there must be resort to correspondence.

AGENTS AND BROKERS IN THE INTERNATIONAL MARKET

Many of the problems in dealing with the foreign admitted insurance market are addressed through domestic brokers that have established an international network. Major U.S. brokerage firms have established a presence in many foreign counties and have contracts with foreign insurers. In fact, with a few exceptions, such as AIG, U.S. brokers have become international at a faster rate than have U.S. insurers. Even brokers that do not have offices in foreign countries have established working relationships with affiliate agencies abroad, giving them access to foreign markets and providing a network through which they can serve the foreign insurance needs of their U.S. clients.

FOREIGN EXCHANGE RISKS

Several of the risks facing an MNC relate to foreign exchange rates, and it is therefore appropriate that we briefly consider exchange rates. An exchange rate represents the number of units of currency of one country that can be exchanged for another. The currencies of the major countries are traded in an active market where rates are determined by supply and demand.

Foreign exchange risk is the risk that the currency of a country in which a U.S. country does business is devalued relative to the dollar, that the market price of the currency declines relative to the dollar in the absence of an official devaluation or that its convertibility is restricted.

When a currency declines in value relative to the dollar, the U.S. company suffers a loss on the currency and on the assets payable in currency it holds. Thus a significant devaluation or drop in price of a currency can be very costly to the multinational company. The impact of fluctuations in exchange rates was dramatically illustrated by the devaluation of the Mexican peso by more than 35 percent late in 1994. This devaluation had the potential to create insurance problems for U.S. companies doing business in Mexico, depending on whether their insurance was written in dollars or in pesos. For those firms whose insurance was written in dollars, the devaluation did not pose problems. However, for those firms whose property insurance was written in pesos, the limits of insurance were made inadequate because of the devaluation. An MNC with a factory valued at $100 million in U.S. dollars would have been adequately insured with 350 million pesos in coverage prior to the devaluation. Without a revision in coverage, however, the loss payment of 350 million pesos for a destroyed factory after devaluation would convert to roughly $63 million in dollars. If the facility included a substantial amount of imported equipment, the impact was even more dramatic.

In addition to its effect on the value of tangible assets in the foreign country, the exchange rate risk arises from the holdings of foreign exchange by MNCs. The MNC with a Mexican subsidiary might have had bank deposits of $35 million pesos. At the 1993 exchange rate, this represented about $10 million in U.S. dollars. When the peso was devalued by 35 percent in 1994, the MNC's peso holdings became worth $6.5 million in U.S. currency.

One approach to managing the foreign exchange exposure is to minimize the amount of foreign currency held. Because there are practical limitations on this approach, most companies use some other approach. Retention is, of course a possibility. Another strategy is to hedge in the futures market for foreign currencies. Under a futures contract, the seller (our MNC) agrees to deliver the specified currency to a buyer at some specified time in the future at a price agreed on when the futures contract is executed. If the value of the currency falls before the due date of the futures contract, the seller can purchase the currency required to meet the contract obligation at a reduced price. The profit made on the transaction will offset the loss the MNC suffers on the decline in the value of its holdings in the foreign currency. The principal drawback to the use of futures contracts is that these contracts involve a cost. Generally, the weaker the currency, the greater will be the cost.

■ Managing Political Risks   ■ ■ ■ ■ ■ ■ ■ ■ ■ ■ ■ ■ ■ ■ ■ ■ ■ ■ ■

Political risks are those risks sometimes encountered in international operations that stem from the actions of government or other political organizations or from the political acts by business or terrorists. Political risks include confiscation of assets of the foreign subsidiary without compensation, damage to property or personnel by antigovernment activity, and kidnapping and murder of the firm's employees. The ultimate political risk is expropriation or confiscation, in which the government nationalizes foreign companies without compensating the owners. In addition to these major causes of loss, the political risks facing an MNC include mild interferences with business transactions of a lesser severity. These interferences may include such things as laws that may require that the MNC employ some minimum percentage of nationals or that it invest in local social and economic projects. Political risk may also involve restrictions on the convertibility of currency. In between the extremes of mild interference and outright expropriation of assets are a range of actions that can cause financial loss to the MNC operating in foreign nations. Discriminatory practices such as higher taxes, higher utility charges, and the requirements to pay higher wages than a national company are examples. In effect, they place the foreign operation of the U.S. company at a competitive disadvantage.

U.S. corporations operating in foreign countries are also protected by a number of enactments and international agreements. Although the sanctions for which these agreements provide are rarely imposed, they serve as a threat that can reduce losses from political risks. The Hickenlooper Amendment requires the president of the United States to suspend foreign aid to any country that has expropriated property of a U.S. company without providing proper compensation. In addition, included in the agreement of the *Generalized System of Preferences* (which provides lower tariffs for developing countries' products) is a section providing protection for multinationals. The agreement states that any country that nationalizes U.S. property without offering settlement will forfeit favorable tariff status.

Despite these protections, political risks remain an important consideration in international risk management. The techniques available to address political risk are the same as those we have discussed throughout the text: risk control and risk financing, which together encompass avoidance, reduction, retention, and transfer.

POLITICAL RISK LOSS CONTROL

Risk control as regards political risk should begin with the analysis of foreign investments before they are made. The initial risk control measure should be a thoughtful and thorough consideration of the political risk potential in the project. Essentially, this is a job of forecasting political instability. Important considerations include the stability of the government, the existence of resistance or opposition to the government, and an estimate of any new government's view of foreign investments. Other important considerations include the rate of inflation and the existence, if any, of economic instability. The decision to enter a foreign country as an investor should be made only after a review of the political risk involved in the investment.

Avoidance

In some instances, the review of the political environment of the foreign country in which operations are contemplated will indicate that the most prudent approach is risk avoidance. Regrettably, the risk manager may not be involved in this stage of the decision-making process. Although measures can be taken to protect an investment once it is made, in many instances, once a political change has occurred, little can be done. The time to look hardest at political risk is before the investment is made.

Reduction

Once a company decides to invest in a foreign company or in foreign assets, it should take steps to protect itself. One of the most common approaches is to enter into a joint venture with local investors to establish local support for the firm and to provide better information on the country's political and economic conditions.[5] Shared ownership reduces both the likelihood and the potential severity of loss.

A second approach is to limit the amount of capital invested in the foreign venture (and thereby the amount that could be lost through political risks). Borrowing funds locally will lessen the investment exposure should nationalization occur. In the same way, keeping fixed investments and assets to a minimum by leasing whenever possible and by keeping research and development activities in the United States reduces the exposure. The exposure can also be reduced by making all payments in a convertible currency to guarantee that money can be removed from the country.

POLITICAL RISK INSURANCE

Political risk insurance provides protection against seizure of assets, currency inconvertibility, and interference with contractual performance. The sources of political risk insurance are extremely limited. Political risk insurance is available from three types of insurers: U.S. government agencies, a limited number of U.S. insurers, and Lloyds of London.

The Foreign Credit Insurance Association

The Foreign Credit Insurance Association (FCIA) is an association of roughly 50 U.S. insurance companies which was organized in 1961 to assist U.S. exporters in international trade by writing export credit insurance. The Export-Import Bank of the United States, a U.S. government agency, reinsures virtually all of the political risk insurance written by the FCIA.

The FCIA offers two versions of coverage. Comprehensive coverage includes all risks including insolvency of the debtor. Political risk coverage protects against war, revolution, insurrection, confiscation, and currency inconvertibility. Comprehensive coverage insures 90 percent of the loss, while political risk coverage can be written to cover 100 percent of the loss. Although a blanket form of coverage is available (under what is called a *discretionary credit limit* coverage), coverage is usually subject to prior approval by the FCIA before a shipment is made.

---

[5]In some nations, the laws require some minimum level of ownership by the country's nationals as a condition to operation within the country. Kuwait, for example, requires that all commercial enterprises conducting business in the country be 51 percent owned by Kuwait partners.

The Export-Import Bank

The Export-Import Bank (EXIM) of the United States which reinsures the credit insurance contracts issued by the FCIA, has provided credit insurance and reinsurance to U.S. exporters and financial institutions since 1961. Congress authorized EXIM to provide such insurance to encourage the development of U.S. export trade. It was initiated to match foreign officially supported competition. The credit insurance sold by EXIM guarantees a seller or a bank financing the seller against default on the credit obligation by a foreign buyer. EXIM provides two types of coverage: commercial risk of default, which covers the buyer's inability to pay the receivable due to financial difficulties, and political risk of default, which covers defaults beyond the control of the buyer, such as those resulting from government intervention, cancellation of an export or import license, political violence, or currency inconvertibility. Although currency inconvertibility is covered, currency devaluation is not. However, if the devaluation causes the purchaser to default, the loss is covered as a commercial risk default.

Exporters and banks purchase export credit insurance for several reasons. First, foreign buyers often demand credit, or credit terms are necessary if the U.S. firm is to be able to sell to the foreign buyer. When U.S. goods are sold on credit, there is obviously an increased risk to the U.S. seller. When the receivable from a foreign buyer has been insured, the exporter can assign the receivable, borrowing against it or selling it.

Overseas Private Investment Corporation

The FICA and EXIM provide political risk insurance only in connection with the extension of credit to foreign buyers; they do not provide coverage to protect the assets located in a foreign country. In some cases, coverage for this exposure may be available from another U.S. government agency, the Overseas Private Investment Corporation (OPIC). OPIC was created in 1969 to stimulate investment by U.S. corporations in less developed nations. OPIC provides loans and guarantees financial assistance to banks for proposed overseas projects. It also provides insurance for private investments abroad.

Coverage is available only in specified developing countries that have diplomatic relations with the United States, whose governments have signed an agreement with the United States and recognize the subrogation rights of the U.S. government when payment is made under a policy. Currently, about 140 countries worldwide are on the eligibility list. Coverage is written for periods up to 20 years and low rates. Because OPIC was created to encourage investment in less developed nations, it does not insure existing installations. OPIC includes coverage for expropriation, nationalization, or confiscation of the foreign investment, war, revolution, insurrection, and inconvertibility of currency. It also insures against normal business losses. The insured is required to self-insure at least 10 percent of any loss.

Because OPIC was formed to encourage investment in less developed countries, only new investments in eligible countries are eligible for coverage. New investment is defined to include expansion or modernization of existing projects. Approval of the investment by the host country's government is a prerequisite for coverage.[6]

Lloyds

In addition to the FCIA and OPIC, a limited number of U.S. insurers also offer political risk insurance, as does Lloyd's of London. Coverage is written to protect against expropriation, nationalization, and deprivation and, in some cases, terrorism and war risk coverages may be written. Limits of up to $40 million for any one loss can be considered.

Coverage Under Political Risk Insurance

The definition of political risk should be carefully examined to ensure that all pertinent exposures are included. The degree of risk retention required may be a percentage of the limit of liability or loss sustained or a flat dollar amount, and is negotiable with insurers. The length of the waiting period varies from insurer to insurer and is sometimes a negotiable coverage point.

Exclusions typically found in political risk policies include currency fluctuation or devaluation, losses due to fraudulent, criminal, or dishonest acts by the insured, losses caused by failure to comply with local laws, labor disputes, losses caused by investors' or their foreign operations' financial insolvency, and physical damage losses arising from hostile or warlike actions. (OPIC is currently the only domestic market for this coverage.)

KIDNAPPING AND RANSOM LOSSES

Kidnapping threats to the organization's employees can be divided into criminal acts, in which the objective is to obtain ransom for the release of the victim; and political acts, in which the objective is not financial but ideological. At the risk of oversimplification, political kidnapping tends to be a greater exposure outside the country, whereas criminal kidnapping can occur both at home and abroad. Sometimes criminal and political kidnapping merge when a political group seizes on kidnapping as a means of obtaining funds. For this type of kidnapping, the hazard to business executives is probably greater than the threat of kidnapping to diplomatic personnel. This is because, as a rule, governments refuse to pay ransom to kidnappers, but corporations may be willing to do so.

Criminal Kidnapping

In the United States, kidnapping losses typically involve executives of financial institutions who are kidnapped and forced to have money withdrawn from the bank. Wealthy individuals and their families are also subject to the kidnapping peril.

---

[6]A draft U.S. Senate Budget Committee Report early in 1995 called for cutbacks in the funding for OPIC. The proposed cutbacks were part of the Republican majority's efforts to cut back on spending for international aid.

For those cases in which the kidnappers' demands are financial, kidnap/ransom insurance is available. The Surety Association of America, which is the major rating bureau for dishonesty insurance, excludes kidnap/ransom losses from the basic forms of blanket bond coverage, but provides an endorsement that extends the bond to cover such losses for an additional premium. In addition, specialty underwriters in the United States and the Lloyd's market have developed forms to cover potential situations where business corporations might suffer kidnap ransom losses. Companies that send executives or key employees overseas are especially prone to this exposure. As a result, the market for kidnap/ransom insurance is very tight and the cost for international risks is high.

A standard feature of kidnap/ransom insurance is the requirement imposed on the insured that the existence of the insurance not be revealed. This requirement is based on the assumption that if criminals know that kidnap/ransom insurance exists, they may be encouraged to kidnap the individual whose kidnapping will trigger the coverage. It has been argued that the purchase of kidnap/ransom insurance may create an exposure to kidnapping that would not otherwise exist. As a consequence of this belief, and because of the high cost of the coverage, many firms assume the risk of financial loss associated with the kidnapping of personnel.

Kidnapping and Terrorism Abroad

Although kidnapping losses occur in the United States as well as abroad, the exposure is generally thought to be more prevalent in foreign countries than in the United States. For the multinational corporation, the risk of loss relating to personnel includes loss not only from the death or disability of the individual, but also financial losses arising out of kidnapping, terrorism, and acts of rebels or forces hostile to the government of the host country.

In some cases, when the exposure is severe, the risk should be avoided through the simple expedient of not assigning personnel to especially hazardous areas. When avoidance is not possible, the major emphasis should be on loss-prevention measures. Although the security measures that will be appropriate will depend on the situation, security specialists are often retained to educate and train personnel assigned responsibilities in foreign nations and to act as bodyguards for the personnel while they are in the hazardous area.

When kidnapping occurs abroad, it is often the act of a group whose goals are political rather than financial. In these cases, the demands are not for ransom but for the release of political prisoners or some similar demand. Typically, the security forces of the foreign country, sometimes in cooperation with the U.S. government, attempt to obtain the release of the victim. When the demands are political, the decision as to whether or not they will be met does not rest with the corporation, but with the host government (or other government on which the demands are made).

For kidnapping losses, the first recommended procedure is to verify that the individual has actually been kidnapped. Many abductions are actually hoaxes in which—after ransom has been paid—the supposed victim is found not to have been in the custody of the kidnappers at all. Kidnappers will often instruct that law enforcement agencies not be notified, but the conventional wisdom is that the next step should be to notify appropriate law enforcement officials.

Once the abduction has been verified, the response will depend on the demands. In the case of political demands, the decision will usually rest with the host country (or the other organization on which the demands are made). In criminal kidnapping cases, where the demands are financial, a decision must be made as to whether or not to pay the ransom. This is a policy decision of monumental proportions, and there are persuasive arguments on both sides.

IMPORTANT CONCEPTS TO REMEMBER

limited international corporation
multinational corporation
reciprocity
difference-in-conditions policy

international captive
foreign exchange risk
political risk
expropriation
confiscation

Foreign Credit Insurance Association (FCIA)
Export-Import Bank
Overseas Private Investment Corporation

QUESTIONS FOR REVIEW

1. Describe what is meant by a multinational corporation and explain why companies become multinational corporations.

2. Identify the two major policy issues that arise in connection with management of international risks.

3. Why may the distinction between admitted and nonadmitted insurance be a more important consideration in a foreign jurisdiction than it is in the U.S.?

4. Identify and evaluate the markets from which the multinational corporation may purchase insurance and the advantages of each segment.

5. Identify the risks facing a multinational corporation in overseas operations that are different from those encountered within the United States.

6. What are some of the problems encountered in administering a risk management program for firms operating abroad?

7. In your opinion, in what ways are the risks of multinational enterprise greater than domestic risks?

8. In your opinion, in what ways are domestic risk greater than the risks of multinational enterprise?

9. Why is the insurance on investments abroad that is available from OPIC limited to new investments only?

10. In what way(s) is the *difference-in-conditions* (DIC) insurance suggested for use by multinational companies (a) the same as the DIC policies used domestically (that were discussed in Chapter 17), and (b) different from the DIC policies used in the domestic market?

QUESTIONS FOR DISCUSSION

1. In what way is a captive insurer useful to the risk manager of a multinational corporation?

2. Explain how the risk of currency fluctuation can complicate the design of the multinational corporation's insurance program in foreign jurisdictions.

3. What are the sources from which political risk insurance can be obtained by a multinational corporation? Under what circumstances is the coverage available from each source?

4. To what extent do U.S. brokers and insurance companies maintain a presence abroad? Is this presence increasing or decreasing? What do you believe is the target market for these brokers and insurers?

5. Most standard forms of property insurance written in the U.S. exclude damage caused by war. Does damage caused by terrorists fall within the scope of this exclusion? To what extent is loss caused by war insurable?

SUGGESTIONS FOR ADDITIONAL READING

Carris, Richard. "Global Flow of Insurance Premium," *Risk Management* (October 1995).

Baglini, Norman A. *Global Risk Management.* New York: Rims, 1983.

Baglini, Norman A. *Risk Management in International Corporations.* New York, Risk Studies Foundation, 1976.

Balbinot, Sergio. "Emergency Assistance for International Risks," *Risk Management* (June 1993).

Hutchin, James W. "Managing Risks in a Global Environment," *The John Liner Letter* (Fall 1995).

O'Hare, Dean. "The Rise of Kidnap & Ransom Risk," *Risk Management* (June 1994).

Pahl, Teresa L. "New Challenges in Overseas Exposures." *Risk Management* (December 1994), pages 15–17.

Skipper, Harold D. "Captive Use in Developing Countries—Boon or Bust?," *Risk Management* (February 1988).

Slattery, Thomas J. "Globalization a Necessity for Insurers." *National Underwriter Property and Casualty Edition* (June 24, 1991).

CHAPTER 29

Managing Organization Risks from Death and Disability

CHAPTER OBJECTIVES

When you have finished this chapter, you should be able to

Define personal risks and identify the personal risks that can exist in an organization.

▪

Identify the major uses of life insurance and disability in protecting the organization.

▪

Describe the general nature of a deferred compensation plan and explain the advantages and disadvantages of such plans.

▪

Explain the relationship of business perpetuation planning to the risk management function of the organization.

▪

Identify and differentiate between the two types of arrangements that may be used in business buyout agreements.

▪

Explain the essential elements of an effective buyout arrangement.

▰ Introduction ▪▪▪▪▪▪▪▪▪▪▪▪▪▪▪▪▪▪▪▪▪▪

Life and health insurance find applications in the business world in three areas. The first is as a part of a business organization's own risk management program. In some instances, individuals represent key assets in an organization; when the loss of such persons by death or disability would cause the organization financial loss, the exposure must be "managed" in the same manner as other potentially catastrophic exposures. In addition to the possible loss of key employees as a result of death and disability, key employees can also be lost to other organizations that are willing to pay more for their services. Life insurance is sometime used as part of an incentive package designed to retain valuable employees—often referred to as *golden handcuffs*.

Life and health insurance may also find application in protecting business owners against the financial loss that might arise from the death or disability of other owners. The exposure here is "business continuation" or "business perpetuation." The business continuation exposure is not a risk for the organization in the same sense as the loss of a key employee. Although the business continuation exposure sometimes seems to be a risk that threatens the business, this is because the business owner is also a key employee. Unless the owner is also a key employee, the business continuation problem is a risk for the owners—not for the business itself. After all, when the owner of a business dies, the business automatically gets a new owner. The problem arises when the surviving owners prefer not to share ownership with the beneficiary of the deceased owner. The standard solution to this exposure has been a buy-sell agreement among owners. Such agreements may or may not be funded by insurance.

Finally, life and health insurance is widely used in business as part of the compensation package to workers. Often, the risk manager will be responsible for managing the organization's employee benefit program.

In this chapter, we examine the first of these three applications of life and health insurance: protecting the organization and the organization's owners against financial loss arising out of death or disability. We discuss employee benefits in the next four chapters. Before turning to our discussion of the business uses of life insurance, we will briefly discuss the types of life insurance available.

⬛ Types of Life Insurance Contracts ■ ■ ■ ■ ■ ■ ■ ■ ■ ■ ■ ■

The six distinct types of life insurance contracts are term insurance, whole life, endowment, universal life, adjustable life, and variable life policies. Term insurance, whole life, and endowment contracts are the traditional forms of life insurance and have existed for many years. Universal life, variable life, and adjustable life are relatively recent innovations, dating only from the 1970s. Ignoring the subtle differences among some of these types of policies for the moment, we can divide life insurance products into two classes: those that provide pure life insurance protection, called *term insurance*, and those that include a savings or investment element, which we will call *cash value policies*.

Term Insurance *(Pure Insurance Protection)*	*Cash Value Insurance* *(Protection and Savings)*
Term Insurance	Whole Life Insurance
	Endowment Insurance
	Universal Life Insurance
	Adjustable Life Insurance
	Variable Life Insurance

Although important differences exist among the policies classified together as cash value policies, they are more similar than they are different. The basic distinction in life insurance is between term insurance and those policies that combine protection with savings.

The simplest form of life insurance is yearly renewable term. This type provides protection for one year only, but it permits the insured to renew the policy for successive periods of one year, at a higher premium rate each year, without having to furnish evidence of insurability at the time of each renewal. This is life insurance protection in its purest form.

The easiest way to understand the operation of any mechanism is to try it. In life insurance, as in other forms of insurance, the fortunate many who do not suffer loss share the financial burden of the few who do. In life insurance, each member of the group pays a premium that represents the member's portion of the benefit to be paid to the beneficiaries of those who die. Mortality data tell us that at age 21, 1.07 out of every 1000 females will die. To simplify the mathematics, let us assume that there are 100,000 females in the group. On the basis of past experience, we may expect 107 of them to die, and if we wish to pay a death benefit of $1000 to the beneficiary of each woman who dies, we will need $107,000. Ignoring, for the present, the cost of operating the program and any interest that we might earn on the premiums we collect, and assuming that the mortality table is an accurate statement of the number who will die, it will be necessary to collect $1.07 from each individual in the group to provide the needed $107,000.[1] During the year, 107 members of the group will die, and $107,000 will be paid to their beneficiaries.

The next year we would find that the chance of loss has increased, for all the members of the group are now older, and past experience indicates that a greater number will die per 1000. At age 25, it will be necessary to collect $1.16 from each member. At age 30, the cost will be $1.35. At age 40, the cost per member will have almost doubled from the cost at age 21, and it will be necessary to collect $2.42. By the time the members of the group reach age 50, we will have to collect $4.96 from each. At age 60, we will need $9.47, and at age 70, we will need $22.11 from each member. It does not take a great deal of insight to recognize that before long the plan is going to bog down, if it has not already done so before the members reach age 70. At age 70, when the probability of death is greater than ever before, the members of the group may find that they cannot afford the premium that has become necessary. At age 80, we will need $65.99 from each member, and at age 90, $190.75.

The increasing mortality as a group of insureds grows older makes yearly renewable term (and other forms of term) impractical as a means of providing insurance protection at advanced ages. Yet many insurance buyers want coverage that continues throughout their lifetimes. Insurers have found a practical solution in the con-

---

[1]The $1.07 indicated in our simplified calculation reflects mortality only. In actual practice, life insurance rates include two additional factors: interest and loading. Life insurers specifically recognize the investment income that will be earned on premiums by assuming that premiums will be paid at the beginning of the year and that deaths will occur at the end of the year. The discounted value of future mortality costs is called the *net premium*. A loading for expenses is added to the net premium to derive the gross premium, which is the amount the buyer pays.

cept of *permanent* life insurance, covering an individual for his or her entire lifetime, but with a level premium. This level premium is set higher than necessary to fund the cost of death claims during the early years of the policy, and the excess premiums are used to meet the increasing death claims as the insured group grows older.

The level premium for an ordinary life policy of $1000 purchased by a female at age 21 and the one for yearly renewable term insurance beginning at age 21 are illustrated in Figure 29.1. The line that constitutes the level premium is the exact mathematical equivalent of the yearly renewable term premium curve. This means that the insurance company will obtain the same amount of premium income and interest from a large group of insureds under either plan, assuming that neither group discontinues its payments.

The level premium plan introduces features that have no counterpart in term insurance. Figure 29.1 shows that under the level premium plan, the insured pays more than the cost of pure life insurance protection during the early years the policy is in force. This overpayment is indicated by the difference between the term and the level premium lines up to the point at which the lines cross. The overpayment is necessary so that the excess portion, when accumulated at compound interest, will be sufficient to offset the deficiency in the later years of the contract. The excess payments during the early years of the contract create a fund that the insurance company holds for the benefit and credit of the policyholders. The fund is invested, usually in long-term investments, and the earnings are added to the accumulating fund to help meet the future obligations to the policyholders. The insurer establishes a reserve or liability on its financial statement to reflect these future obligations.

From Figure 29.1 it appears that the reserve should increase for a time and then diminish. It also appears that the area of redundant premiums in the early years of the contract will never be sufficient to equal the inadequacy in the later years. In the case of a single individual, this would be true, but many insureds are involved, and the law of averages permits a continuously increasing reserve for each policy in force. Some insureds will die during the early years of the contracts, and the excess premiums that they have paid are forfeited to the group. The excess premiums forfeited by those who die, together with the excess premiums paid by the survivors, will not only offset the deficiency in later years but, with the aid of compound interest, will also continue to build the reserves on the survivors' policies until they equal the face of the contract at age 100. Death is bound to occur at some time, and in a whole life policy, the insurance company knows that a death claim must ultimately be paid.[2] Although aggregate reserves for the entire group of insureds increase and then decrease, individual policy reserves continue to climb, mainly because the aggregate reserves are divided among a smaller number of survivors each year. Figure 29.2 shows the growth in the reserve on an ordinary life policy purchased at age 20.

The level premium plan introduces the features of the redundant premium during the early years of the contract and the creation of the reserve fund. The

---

[2]The mortality table indicates that all policyholders will have died by age 100. If the insured has not died by this time, the insurance company will declare him dead and pay the face of the policy.

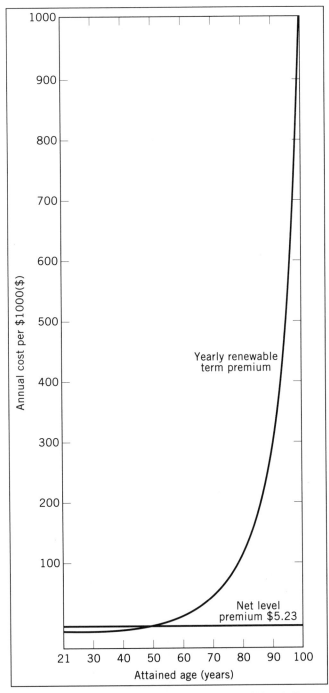

Figure 29.1 Comparison of Net Premiums per $1,000 of Yearly Renewable Term and Whole Life (*Source:* 1980 Commissioners' Standard Ordinary Mortality Table, 4.5% interest assumption.)

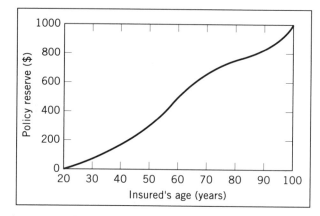

Figure 29.2   Increase in Reserve on Whole Life Policy. (*Source:* 1980 Commissioners' Standard Ordinary Mortality Table, 4.5% interest assumption.)

insured has a contractual right to receive a part of this reserve in the event the policy is terminated, under a policy provision designated the *nonforfeiture value.* The contractual right to receive part of the excess premiums that are paid under the level premium plan, therefore, represents an investment element in the contract for the insured. When a policyholder dies, the death benefit could be viewed as being composed of two parts—the portion of the reserve to which the insured would have been eligible and an amount of pure insurance. Under this view, the face amount of the policy is seen as a combination of a decreasing amount of insurance (the net amount at risk) and the increasing investment element (the growing reserve). The decreasing insurance and the increasing investment element always equal the face of the policy.

The policy reserve is not solely the property of the insured. It is the insured's only if and when the policy is surrendered. If this occurs, the contract no longer exists, and the insurance company is relieved of all obligations on the policy. As long as the contract is in full force, the reserve belongs to the insurance company and must be used to help pay the death claim if the insured should die. As mentioned, the reserve must be accumulated by the company to take care of the deficiency in the level premium during the later years of the contract.

Tax Treatment of Life Insurance

The accumulating fund that arises from the overpayment of premiums and the insured's right to withdraw the cash values based on these overpayments adds an investment element to the protection function of life insurance. Life insurance proceeds and this investment element in the life insurance contract are both granted favorable tax treatment under the *Internal Revenue Code.* First, amounts payable to a beneficiary at the death of an insured are generally not included in taxable income.[3] In addition, income earned on the cash surrender value of life insurance policies is not taxed currently to the policyholder. The investment gain on a life insurance policy is taxed at the termination of the contract prior to death only to the extent that the cash value exceeds the policyholder's investment in the contract (i.e., the sum of all premiums paid on the contract). Because the total amount of premiums paid includes the cost of life insurance protection, this represents an understatement of the taxable gain. Both features of this tax treatment are obviously beneficial to the insured or beneficiaries.[4]

Other Life Insurance Contracts

In addition to term life insurance and whole life, several other forms of life insurance are sufficiently unique to justify comment.

Universal Life   Universal life was introduced in 1979 by Hutton Life, a subsidiary of the stock brokerage firm, E. F. Hutton. The essential feature of universal life, which distinguishes it from traditional whole life, is that, subject to specified limitations, the premiums, cash values, and level of protection can be adjusted up or down during the term of the contract to meet the owner's needs. A second distinguishing feature is the fact that the interest credited to the policy's cash value is geared to current interest rates but is subject to a minimum such as 4 percent.

In effect, the premiums under a universal life policy are credited to a fund (which, following traditional insurance terminology, is called the cash value), and this fund is credited with the policy's share of investment earnings, after a deduction for expenses. This fund provides the source of funds to pay for the cost of pure protection under the policy (term insurance), which may be increased or decreased, subject to the insurer's underwriting standards. Universal policyholders receive annual statements indicating the level of life insurance protection under their policy, the cash value, the current interest being earned, and a statement of the amount of the premium paid that has been used for protection, investment, and expenses.

---

[3]An exception exists in the case of "transfer for value." An example of a policy transferred for value would be if A purchases from B an existing policy for $10,000 on B's life, paying B $3000 for the policy. If B dies, A will be taxed on the $7000 gain. The taxation of policies transferred for value does not apply if the transferee is the person insured, a partner of the insured, or a corporation of which the insured is a director or stockholder.

[4]In the Tax Reform Act of 1984, Congress enacted a new definition of life insurance designed to limit favorable tax treatment to contracts in which a substantial element of protection exists. It did this by establishing two tests which, in effect, limit the permissible savings element in the contract. Contracts that fail these tests at any time lose the tax-deferred status on their investment element. In addition, all income previously deferred will be included in the insured's income in the year the contract fails to qualify as a life insurance contract. The new definition of life insurance generally applies to policies issued after 1984. The two tests for determining whether a contract qualifies as life insurance are the *cash value accumulation test* and a combined *guideline premium test* and *cash value corridor* test. Both tests require that the cash value of the contract not exceed specified actuarial levels.

Variable Life Insurance   Variable life insurance is a whole life contract in which the insured has the right to direct how the policy's cash value will be invested and the insured bears the investment risk in the form of fluctuations in the cash value and in the death benefit. Variable life insurance is designed as a solution to the problem of the decline in the purchasing power of the dollar that accompanies inflation. Under the plans that have been offered in the United States, the amount of the premium is fixed, but the face amount of the policy varies up and down, subject to a minimum, which is the original amount of insurance. The cash value of the policy is not guaranteed and fluctuates with the performance of the portfolio in which the premiums have been invested by the insurer. This fluctuating cash value provides the funds to pay for the varying amount of death protection. Some insurers offer policyholders a choice of investments, with the underlying fund invested in stock funds, bond funds, or money market funds.

Variable Universal Life   The latest innovation, variable universal life insurance, was introduced in 1985. It combines the flexible premium features of universal life with the investment component of variable life. The policyholder decides how the fund will be invested, and the fund's performance is directly related to the performance of the underlying investments.

Adjustable Life   The adjustable life policy was introduced in 1971[5] and was proposed as a solution to the dilemma posed by an individual's changing need for and ability to pay for life insurance. The *adjustable life policy* allows the buyer to adjust various facets of the policy over time as the need for protection and the ability to pay premiums change. Within certain limits, the insured may raise or lower the face amount of the policy and increase or decrease the premium over the life of the policy. Increases in the amount of protection can be offset by increased premiums, and reductions in coverage will permit reduced premiums, but other options are also possible. When the premiums paid exceed the cost of protection, the policy cash value increases; when the cost of protection exceeds the premiums paid, the cash value diminishes.

▚ Key Employee Insurance ■

One of the most valuable assets of any business is the skill of its employees. Since every employee contributes to the success of a business, the death of any employee is a source of loss to the firm. The extent of this loss varies with the individual's contribution to the success of the firm. The risk of loss of employees who make a critical contribution to this success—the so-called key employees—may be suffi-

---

[5]Adjustable life was introduced by Minnesota Mutual in 1971 and was also offered shortly thereafter by Bankers Life of Des Moines, Iowa, which had independently developed the same concept. See Charles L. Trowbridge, "Adjustable Life—A New Solution to an Old Problem," *CLU Journal* (October 1977).

cient to warrant risk management efforts. The key person may be a crucial factor in sales, production, finance, management, or some combination of these functions. The distinguishing characteristic is that the success or failure of the firm depends to a great degree on his or her continued efforts. In many cases, when the loss of an individual connected with the business may cause a financial loss through imperiled credit, loss of leadership, reduced profits, or reduced ability to secure new business, the firm has an insurable interest in that individual.

KEY PERSON LIFE INSURANCE

Many businesses purchase insurance to compensate the business for its loss should the key person die or become disabled. Proceeds from the key person life insurance can be used to replace the lost revenue that results from loss of the person's services. Alternatively, the insurance proceeds can be used to fund a search for someone to replace the key person or the cost of training someone to serve as a replacement for the individual whose services were lost.

Determining the value of a key employee is often the most difficult phase in managing the risk of loss associated with such employees. This value may be unrelated to his or her compensation. A key employee earning, say $100,000 a year might be responsible for essentially the entire profit of the organization, which could greatly exceed the compensation. Rather than focusing on the compensation paid to the key employee, valuation must look to the loss that would be suffered by the employer corporation. The valuation may be based on an estimate of the probable loss of income that might result from his or her loss, based on estimates of the decline in sales or general slowdown of operations. In addition, it may be based on an estimate of the *additional* expense that would be involved in obtaining a replacement, including the cost of finding, hiring, and training a comparable individual. Because the organization will have available the funds that were previously paid to the key employee for payment to a replacement, it is the additional expense that is relevant. In the last analysis, determining the value of the key person will be an educated guess based on a combination of the above factors.

The type of insurance used to insure the life of the key person will vary. Sometimes permanent life insurance is purchased to serve a dual role of protecting the corporation against the loss of the key employee, while at the same time accumulating funds that may be paid to the employee at retirement (see the discussion of nonqualified deferred compensation later in this chapter). Technically, because the value of the key employee decreases as he or she approaches retirement (since the number of years the business can expect to have his or her services decreases), decreasing term life insurance might be the most appropriate choice.

When a corporation purchases life insurance on a key employee, the premium paid is not deductible as a business expense. This is in contrast to the deductibility of premiums paid to insure other assets. Offsetting the nondeductibility of the premium, the death benefits received by the corporation are not taxable to the corporation.[6] Because the key person has no rights in the policy, there are obviously no tax consequences for him or her.

KEY PERSON DISABILITY INSURANCE

When a key employee does exist, the organization needs protection against the loss of his or her services from any cause, not just death. For this reason, key disability insurance is growing in popularity. Here, the employer corporation purchases a disability income policy that pays benefits to the corporation when the key employee is unable to perform the usual duties of his or her job due to injury or sickness. Although some disability income policies provide coverage only when the insured person is unable to engage in *any* occupation, the key person disability exposure requires the more limited coverage definition, which is the inability of the individual to engage in the duties of his or her *own* occupation.[7]

The amount of disability income coverage that will be required to compensate the organization for loss resulting from disability of a key employee will depend on the circumstances. As in the case of the death of a key person, the salary previously paid should be available. This assumes that the employer is not required to continue compensating the disabled employee out of corporate funds, as will be the case if disability income benefits are payable to the disabled person as an employee benefit. Because disability income benefits are *usually* payable on a periodic (that is, monthly) basis, the amount of coverage to be purchased will generally be a specified amount per month, payable for a specified period of time. Presumably, the need for income to support replacement of the key employee or to compensate for the loss suffered will be a short-term income need, payable for a period of perhaps one or even two years. Insurance companies generally place a key person's value at twice his or her salary level (including the value of benefits paid to the disabled key person). This means that the corporation can insure up to 100 percent of the individual's salary, usually up to a specified maximum, such as $10,000 per month. Disability income insurance is usually written with a *waiting period*, which serves as a deductible. Waiting periods typically range from 30 to 180 days.

Personal Replacement Expense Disability Coverage

As an alternative to the traditional form of disability income insurance, a limited number of insurers write a personal replacement expense coverage that is designed

---

[6]*IRC* Sections 264(a)(1) and 101(a)(1). Although the policy proceeds are not taxable as income, they may increase the corporation's tax by increasing the alternative minimum taxable income. Under the complex rules of the *IRC* related to the corporate alternative minimum tax, the excess of the death benefit over premiums paid is a tax preference item that *may* increase the alternative minimum tax.

[7]A policy that covers the insured's inability to engage in any occupation provides broader coverage than one that covers only the insured's inability to engage in his or her own occupation. A salesperson might conceivably be able to perform certain clerical duties and would not therefore qualify for benefits under a contract that pays benefits only when the insured is unable to engage in any occupation.

to reimburse the employer for specific costs incurred in securing a replacement for a key employee. This coverage is on an indemnity basis, and it compensates the employer only for expenses actually incurred and submitted to the insurer for reimbursement. Coverage may be written for a lump sum, usually up to a maximum of $50,000, to cover all expenses actually incurred by the firm in securing a replacement. The expenses that are generally covered include the salary of the replacement for a limited period of time (e.g., three months), moving expenses paid to the new employee, and the cost of searching for a replacement (such as advertising and fees paid to employment agencies or executive search firms).

When a corporation purchases a disability income policy on a key employee under which the benefits are payable to the corporation, the premium paid for the policy, like the premium for a key person life insurance policy, is not deductible. Benefits payable under the policy, however, are received by the corporation income-tax free.[8]

Nonqualified Deferred Compensation Plans

In addition to its use in qualified employee benefit plans, life insurance is sometimes used as a nonqualified employee benefit, especially in the case of highly paid executives. Sometimes, an employer will design a benefit package for a valued employee that defers a part of the employee's compensation, but with conditions under which the compensation may be forfeited if the employee leaves the firm.

Technically, any arrangement under which a portion of an individual's current earnings are made payable at some time in the future is a "deferred compensation plan." Such plans fall into two categories: qualified plans and nonqualified plans. Qualified plans include pension and profit sharing plans that meet the requirements of Section 401 of the *IRC*, thereby qualifying for special tax treatment.[9] The major tax benefits that are granted to qualified plans are deferral of taxation on the benefits until they are actually received by the employees, with a current tax deduction to the employer for contributions made to fund the benefits. In addition, earnings on the employer's contributions accumulate on a tax-free basis until they are paid out, and the benefits payable to the employees or their survivors are subject to favorable income and estate tax treatment. Although nonqualified plans do not qualify for the same tax treatment as qualified plans, they may still have tax advantages.

The basic idea of a nonqualified deferred compensation plan is a simple one: instead of being paid in full for services as they are currently provided, an employee is paid in part in the current year, with the rest of his or her compensation deferred until a later time. In this sense, nonqualified deferred compensation plans are similar to qualified plans. The principal difference is in the tax treatment of the deferred amounts and the employer's contribution to fund the benefits. Although

[8]*IRC* Sections 104, 105, 106, 213, and 265.
[9]Qualified plans are discussed in Chapter 34.

the requirements for qualified plans are rigid and demanding, there is much greater flexibility and employer discretion if the plan meets the *IRC* definition of an unfunded nonqualified plan. Under federal rules an "unfunded plan established for a select group of management or highly-paid employees" is exempt from the nondiscrimination, vesting, and funding requirements of ERISA. A deferred compensation plan that meets this definition does not require any IRS approval and may cover employees on a discriminatory basis.

The basic theory of a nonqualified deferred compensation plan is that the employer promises to pay part of the income currently due to an employee at some later time, usually after retirement. The plan is usually established so that the deferred income is payable for a specified period of years following retirement or termination of employment, but it may also provide for payment to the survivors of the worker in the event of his or her death. If desired, the plan can also provide disability benefits as well.

The most limited plans provide annual payments for a specified period of years. Usually, provision is made for payments to a beneficiary if the employee dies before the number of years specified has elapsed. A deferred compensation plan might provide, for example, payments of $25,000 a year for a period of 10 years, with payment to a beneficiary if the employee dies after retirement, but before the 10 years are completed. A deferred compensation plan may also provide for payment of a death benefit if the employee dies before reaching retirement. In this case, some form of life insurance, payable to the employer, is generally used to fund the plan. Finally, the plan may provide benefits if the employee becomes disabled. When benefits are payable in the event of disability, they are also usually funded by insurance.

Tax Treatment of Nonqualified Deferred Compensation Plans   Under Revenue Ruling 60-31, a participant in an unfunded, nonqualified plan will not be currently taxed on the compensation deferred under such a plan as long as the employer's obligation is merely a contractual obligation and is not represented by any evidence of indebtedness or other security.

The essential requirement in obtaining deferral of taxes on the deferred compensation is to avoid "constructive receipt" of the benefits to the employee. Under the doctrine of constructive receipt, income is taxable when it is credited to an employee without substantial restrictions or limitations on the power to withdraw. In other words, if the employee has the right to withdraw the funds at will, he or she has constructive receipt of the income regardless of whether or not it is actually paid. On the other hand, where limitations or conditions are attached to the right to withdraw or receive the compensation, there is no constructive receipt until the conditions are met. Thus to successfully defer income tax on the deferred compensation, it is important to establish conditions that could deny the employee the right to the income. This is generally done by establishing a contingency in the agreement that may cause the employee to forfeit his or her right to the payment. Such a condition might, for example, provide that the deferred compensation be payable only if the individual continues in the employ of the firm until retirement, disability, or death. As long as the possibility of forfeiture exists, there should be no constructive receipt.[10]

In addition to the provisions designed to deny the employee constructive receipt, the agreement must be entered into before the employee earns the compensation in question, and the employer's promise should not be secured in the sense of a formal liability. The employer's obligation should therefore not be recognized in any way in the firm's balance sheet.

Funding The requirement that the nonqualified deferred compensation plan for a select group of management employees not be funded does not mean that the corporation cannot accumulate funds to meet its obligation under the agreement. The "unfunded" requirement refers to the type of funding contemplated by qualified retirement programs such as pensions or qualified deferred profit-sharing plans. The requirement that the plan be "unfunded" does not prevent the employer from accumulating the required cash to meet its obligation in the form of life insurance, mutual funds, or other investments. What is important is that any funds designated for payment of the deferred compensation obligation must remain solely the property of the corporation and must always be available to satisfy corporate creditors. The employee must rely only on the employer's unsecured promise to pay the promised benefits if the employee is to avoid current taxability.[11]

Historically, nonqualified deferred compensation plans for employees of closely held corporations have been funded largely with cash value life insurance. Because earnings on funds accumulated for deferred payment do not accumulate tax-free as do funds accumulated for qualified plans, the tax-free accumulation of life insurance cash values nullifies the taxability of investment earnings on the accumulating funds. With the general increase in interest rates during the past two decades, there has been a shift to other funding instruments, including universal life and interest sensitive life insurance products.

Regardless of the funding method selected, the corporation must retain absolute ownership of the fund. Where life insurance is used, the corporation will be the applicant, policyowner, premium payer, and beneficiary. As owner of other assets, the corporation will incur taxes on any realized gains, interest, or dividend income. However, the increase in life insurance cash values and the possible growth in value of a variable or fixed dollar annuity are not subject to current taxability.

The Split-Dollar Plan

Split-dollar insurance is the name given to an arrangement whereby an employer and an employee share the premium cost of an insurance policy on the life of the employee. The employer and employee usually enter into an agreement whereby the employer will contribute a portion of each annual premium equal to the

---

[10]Regs. 1.451-1, 1.451-2.
[11]Rev. Rul. 60-31, 1960-1 C.B. 174.

increase in the tabular cash value which will result from such premium payment. The employer will collect the balance of such premium from the employee. The employer, as owner of the policy, is responsible for paying the full premium to the life insurance company.

The employer is usually the owner of the policy. The employer is also the beneficiary of the policy to the extent of an amount equal to the cash value as of the date to which premiums have been paid at the time of the employee's death less any indebtedness. The employee's spouse or other personal beneficiary is designated as beneficiary to the extent of any balance of the death proceeds. Under the basic split-dollar plan, the employer may not change the portion of the beneficiary designation dealing with the insured's personal beneficiary without the consent of the insured. To exclude the proceeds of the policy from the insured's gross estate for federal estate tax purposes, the insured designates an irrevocable beneficiary.

Many concrete benefits accrue to an employee under a split-dollar plan. First, the employee is afforded the opportunity of obtaining additional life insurance with a minimum outlay of his own funds. In addition, split-dollar insurance has the additional advantage of being permanent insurance—not term insurance—and can be continued beyond retirement age. Finally, split-dollar insurance provides an incentive and an inducement for the employee to remain with the firm.

A drawback to the split-dollar plan is that the amount payable to the insured's personal beneficiary decreases year by year as the cash value of the policy increases.

The Business Continuation Exposure ■ ■ ■ ■ ■ ■ ■ ■ ■ ■

The death or disability of the owner of a business, the member of a partnership, or a stockholder of a close corporation may create serious problems for that business. If the business is a sole proprietorship, it may be necessary to liquidate and sell the specific assets, rather than the going business. Any value based on goodwill or earnings may be wiped out. In the case of a partnership, the disabled partner or the executor of the estate of a deceased partner may find it necessary to sell the interest in the business at the best offer that can be obtained from the other partners. Finally, in the case of the corporation, the corporation will continue, but either the dependents or the heirs of a disabled or deceased stockholder may not desire to continue their ownership, or the remaining stockholders may not wish to share ownership and control of the corporation with the heirs.

The ideal solution to these problems is to make prior arrangements for the sale of the individual's interest prior to the death or disability through a buy and sell agreement. Under the terms of this agreement, each owner agrees that his share of the business is to be sold to the remaining owners in the event of death or permanent disability, and each owner agrees to buy the share of the deceased or disabled owner. In the case of a proprietorship, the parties to the purchase agreement may be the owner and an employee or the owner and a competitor. The agreement may contain a formula to be used in setting the value of the business at the time of sale, thus eliminating difficulty at the time of the sale.

ORGANIZATIONAL FORMS AND THE PERPETUATION PROBLEM

The perpetuation problem exists for every business, regardless of the business's form of organization. The need for continuation planning is as great in the case of a corporation as it is in the case of a partnership or a proprietorship—although at times the perpetual existence of a corporation tends to obscure the fact. That the business is organized as a corporation is of little consequence if there is no one to take over the operation of the business. What is important is that there is someone who is willing and able to buy the business owner's interest in the business. For this reason, the problem is most acute in the case of the single-owner business, because a successor who can continue the business may not be readily available. However, even when there are other owners, the need exists for some type of agreement under which the surviving owners agree to purchase the interest of the deceased, and the heirs of the deceased are obligated to sell that interest.

Sole Proprietorships

Clearly, the sole proprietorship is the most vulnerable, although there are several possible solutions for this form. If the surviving members of the family can take over and operate the business, it may be passed through the will. When there are no relatives or survivors who are capable of, or interested in, operating the business upon the death of the owner, arrangements might be made with a competitor or with the employees of the business to purchase the business upon the death of the owner. If none of these alternatives can be developed, the best approach is to take someone into the business who is interested in eventually acquiring ownership.

The Partnership

A partnership is usually dissolved immediately at the death of a partner—or at best within a few months. Thus, the death of a partner involves a serious hazard to the continuity of the business that operates under a partnership arrangement. Under common law and the Uniform Partnership Act, a partnership is automatically dissolved at the death of one of the partners, unless an express agreement to the contrary has been made. The surviving partners become obligated to liquidate the business. They are considered trustees for the deceased partner's interest and, as such, are responsible to the probate court. Surviving partners may not conduct business, except such as is incidental to the liquidation. If this rule is violated, they must account to the deceased partner's estate for any profit made and must bear any losses alone.

As in the case of a proprietorship, several alternatives are available. An attempt might be made to continue the business with the deceased partner's surviving spouse or estate as the owner of the deceased partner's interest. Here, however, there is likely to be a problem with respect to the sharing of income, particularly when the previous division was based on the active service of the deceased. Theoretically, the surviving partners could sell the entire business, but this would rarely be desirable. The surviving partners might also induce some new individual to join the firm, purchasing the interest of the decedent, but such a person would have to be acceptable to all of the partners. The preferred solution, of course, is to make arrangements during the lifetime of all partners for the survivors to purchase the interest of the one who dies. This precludes the entry of strangers or relatives of the decedent into the firm and is also probably in the best interest of the survivors of the deceased partner.

Corporate Form No Solution

Although perpetual existence is a basic feature of the corporation, the corporate form of ownership does not solve the perpetuation problem. Although the corporate existence as such does not terminate upon the death of a stockholder, the impact of such a death can be as severe as in the case of a partnership. Upon death, the shares become part of the deceased stockholder's estate. The estate will require cash for death taxes and other costs. If the shares of stock represent the bulk of the estate, and no advance arrangements have been made, there may be no alternative but to convert them into cash. If the shares do not involve control, it may be difficult to find a buyer. If the heirs choose to retain the stock because it does represent control—but are unable to contribute to the operation of the business—the remaining shareholders who are active in the business's operation may become disgruntled. Dissension may result, and the business will suffer. When the corporation is a one-person enterprise, most of the problems of the sole proprietorship will be present.

THE BUY-SELL AGREEMENT AS A SOLUTION

The ideal solution to the perpetuation problem, and the technique that should be used for transferring an owner's interest in his or her business to another person is, of course, the purchase and sale agreement, more commonly known as a buy-and-sell agreement. A buy-and-sell agreement provides that one party promises to sell his or her business interest at a specified time to another person, and concurrently, that another party promises to purchase that interest under specified terms. The time specified is usually the death of the person owning the business interest, but a specified date of retirement may also be used. Where death is used as the date at which transfer is to be made, the agreement must be binding on the decedent's estate. The buy-and-sell agreement should also stipulate a price at which the interest is to be sold, or contain a formula for setting the price at the time of sale, thus eliminating difficulties on this point at a later time.

Basic Approaches

Although the basic intent is the same under all buy-and-sell agreements—to provide for the mandatory sale and purchase of a business interest at some designated time—the operational details of buy-and-sell agreements can differ considerably. In general, there are two basic approaches. Under the first, the owners of the partnership or corporation enter into an agreement under the terms of which the estate of a survivor is obligated to sell the deceased's interest, and the survivors are obligated to purchase that interest. Under the second approach, the partnership or corporation itself agrees to purchase the interest of the deceased owner, thereby proportionately increasing the interest of the remaining owners.

In the case of a partnership, for example, a cross-purchase plan involves an agreement under which each partner agrees to purchase a proportionate share of the deceased member's interest. If Abner, Baker, and Cole each own one-third of a business valued at $900,000 and Abner dies, Baker and Cole would each purchase one-half of Abner's interest for $150,000. As an alternative, the partnership agreement might provide that the partnership will purchase the interest of a deceased partner, an approach called the *entity plan*. In this case, if Abner dies, the partnership would purchase his interest in the partnership from the heirs, thereby increasing Baker's and Cole's interest.

In the case of a corporation, the two approaches are referred to as a stockholder's buy-and-sell agreement and a stock redemption agreement. Under a stockholder's buy-and-sell agreement, the surviving shareholders agree to buy the stock of a deceased shareholder. A stock retirement agreement is an agreement between the corporation and the shareholders whereby the corporation agrees to purchase the stock in the corporation owned by the shareholder upon the shareholder's death. The corporation may then hold or cancel the stock. Although there are certain tax differences (discussed later), buy-sell agreements for Subchapter S corporations operate in essentially the same way as for regular (C) corporations.

The choice of an entity or cross-purchase plan or a stockholder's buy-sell agreement or stock redemption agreement will depend on the circumstances, but will generally be determined by the tax treatment of each approach and the tax situations of the participants. Under a cross-purchase plan, the surviving stockholders get a stepped-up basis for their shares purchased from a deceased stockholder's estate. Subsequent sale of the stock will be made with an allowance for the cost of the stock in computing the capital gain. Under a stock retirement agreement, the proportionate interests of the surviving owners are increased, but there is no stepped-up basis. In addition, when the agreement is funded with life insurance, the insurance policies owned by the individual shareholders on the lives of other shareholders are not subject to the claims of the corporation's creditors. The principal disadvantage of a cross-purchase plan arises when there is a vast difference in the ages of the stockholders and their respective shareholdings, and insurance is to be used as a funding vehicle. Younger shareholders with small interests may be unable (or unwilling) to pay the larger premiums required under the cross-purchase arrangement. When the cross-purchase plan is used, the individual shareholders must come up with personal funds to purchase the stock or to pay the premiums on the life insurance used to fund the arrangement.

The "Wait and See" Arrangement

Because there are sometimes uncertainties as to whether a stock redemption agreement or a cross-purchase buy-sell agreement will be advantageous, perpetuation planners developed the concept of an optional buy and sell agreement (sometimes known as a "wait and see" arrangement). The wait and see arrangement provides increased flexibility in deciding who will purchase the stock of a deceased shareholder. This flexibility is created by granting the first option to purchase any or all of the stock of a deceased shareholder to the corporation. If the corporation declines to exercise the option, the surviving shareholders are also granted an option to purchase the stock. If the shareholders decline to exercise their option and purchase the stock, the agreement will require the corporation to purchase the decedent's stock.[12]

FINANCING THE PURCHASE

Merely providing for the mandatory purchase and sale of the business interest is not a complete solution. Consideration must also be given to financing the transaction. In many instances, this financing becomes one of the most difficult details to arrange. The purchaser may pay for the business out of savings, borrowings, earnings of the business after transfer, or life insurance proceeds. Sometimes a combination of these funds must be used. When arrangements for the purchase of the interest of a deceased proprietor, partner, or shareholder are made, they must necessarily include provisions for ready access to sufficient cash to accomplish the transfer. The surviving owners may not have sufficient money available to complete the agreed-upon transaction, and there may be legal restrictions on the use of partnership or corporate assets for this purpose.

Payment Out of Earnings After Transfer

The purchase price of the business can often be paid in installments, out of the earnings of the business. This arrangement can be used under either the cross-purchase plan or the entity plan. However, if the deceased owner was active in the business, a replacement will probably have to be hired, thereby reducing the funds available to pay for the business.

When the decision is made to fund the transfer from future income, the sellers' interest will generally be purchased with an interest-bearing note. The note must bear interest at a minimum rate specified by the IRS. When the deceased owner's interest is purchased on an installment basis, the deductibility of interest will be a consideration in choosing between a stockholder's buy-sell agreement and a stock redemption plan.

Accumulated Earnings

As an alternative to purchase out of future earnings, the owners in a corporate business may elect to accumulate funds to meet the corporation's obligation under

---

[12]When life insurance is used to fund a wait and see arrangement, the policies should be purchased on a cross-purchase basis. Upon the death of a stockholder, the survivors will receive the insurance proceeds (tax free) and will then decide whether to purchase the stock after the corporation's option has expired. If the surviving stockholders decide not to purchase the stock, they can contribute the insurance proceeds to the corporation as a contribution to capital, thereby increasing their cost basis in the shares they hold.

the agreement. The accumulation of cash or near cash for the purpose of stock redemption is facilitated by the corporate tax structure, under which the tax rate on the first $50,000 of corporate profits is only 15 percent and the rate on the next $50,000 is only 25 percent. Because personal tax rates are somewhat higher, there is an advantage to retention of earnings within the corporation.

Accumulating corporate earnings to fund a future stock redemption agreement could conceivably lead to an accumulated earnings tax problem under Section 531 of the *Internal Revenue Code.* Section 531 imposes an additional tax on a corporation which accumulates earnings for the purpose of avoiding a tax on its shareholders. The rate of this additional tax is 27.5 percent of the first $100,000 accumulated taxable income and 38.5 percent of the accumulated taxable income in excess of $100,000. A credit is granted (the "accumulated earnings credit"), which provides that the IRS cannot assess the accumulated earnings tax where the sum of accumulated and current earnings and profits does not exceed $150,000. Even where earnings and profits exceed $150,000, there is no tax if the funds are being accumulated for the reasonable needs of the business. Many authorities feel that a strong argument can be made that a corporation which accumulates funds to redeem the stock of a deceased stockholder in accordance with the terms of a stock retirement agreement is accumulating such funds for the reasonable needs of the business.

Life Insurance

When the prospective seller is insurable, a business life insurance policy is an attractive approach to obtaining the funds needed to effect the transfer. Many business owners take advantage of life insurance as a means of economically and efficiently providing ready cash with which to purchase the interest of a deceased owner. As in the case of the purchase agreements themselves, the operational details of the life insurance purchases will vary. Under the cross-purchase plan of a partnership or the stockholder's buy-and-sell agreement, each of the owners carries enough insurance on the lives of the others to permit the purchase of a proportionate share of the deceased member's interest. In our earlier example in which Abner, Baker, and Cole each owned one-third of a $900,000 business, Abner would buy $150,000 in life insurance on Baker and Cole, Baker would buy $150,000 on Abner and Cole, and Cole would buy $150,000 on Abner and Baker. If one partner dies, the remaining two will receive sufficient proceeds for their policies to permit them to purchase the decedent's interest.

As an alternative, the policy on each owner could be purchased by the firm itself. Under this arrangement, the firm owns the policies and is the beneficiary. The policy proceeds payable upon the death of one of the owners is used by the partnership or corporation to purchase the interest of the deceased owner, and the interest of the survivors is proportionately increased. Generally, premiums on business life insurance are not deductible for federal income tax purposes.[13] On the other hand, the proceeds of the policy paid at the death of the insured are not generally taxable as income to the recipient.[14]

[13] *IRC,* Section 264(a)(1).
[14] *IRC,* Section 101 (a)(l).

Much of the literature that discusses the subject of business purchase agreements assumes that individual policies will be purchased on each of the owners. An alternative approach that may be more cost-effective is to use a joint life policy, insuring two or more lives, which pays upon the death of the first. However, there may be other reasons for the purchase of individual policies. When cash value policies are used, the policies may be used for funding the purchase of stock at retirement, as well as upon the death of the individual insured.

Life insurance proceeds on the lives of the partners or stockholders owned by and payable to other owners or the corporation should not be included in the gross estates of the respective insureds. Under Section 2042 of the *IRC*, the proceeds of life insurance payable to beneficiaries other than the estate of the insured will be included in the insured's gross estate for federal estate taxes only if the insured possessed any "incidents of ownership" in the policy, exerciseable alone or in conjunction with others. Incidents of ownership include the right to change beneficiaries, to surrender the policy, or to assign the policy or borrow against it.[15]

BUY-SELL AGREEMENTS AND THE ESTATE TAX

The IRS will normally recognize the value established in the buy-sell agreement as determinative in setting the value of the business interest of a decedent for estate tax purposes. In the absence of a buy-and-sell agreement, the IRS may place a value on the business interest that will result in a greater tax burden on the survivors. The negotiated value established in a buy-and-sell agreement will prevail if (1) the agreement requires the estate to sell, (2) the survivors have a legally binding contract or an option to purchase, (3) the agreement prohibits the shareholder from disposing of the stock during his or her lifetime without first offering the stock to the corporation or other shareholders at the agreed purchase price, and (4) the purchase price was reached through an arm's length negotiation and the price agreed upon is the result of bargaining by the parties who are concerned with securing a fair price.[16]

DISABILITY OF AN OWNER

Many business owners have taken steps to avoid some of the problems that might otherwise arise at their deaths by entering into a business-purchase agreement with fellow shareholders or partners. Many others, however, have made no arrangements to meet the problem associated with total and permanent disability.

When a disabled individual is an owner of the business, his or her contribution to the success of the business ceases. This has serious implications for the other

---

[15]However, federal estate tax regulations provide that the term *incidents of ownership* include the power to change a beneficiary reserved to the corporation in which the insured is the sole stockholder.

[16]*Roth v. United States*, 511 F. Supp. 653 (E.D. Mo. 1981).

owners, as well as for the disabled person. In the absence of disability income insurance which provides income to the disabled owner, it is likely that both the disabled person and the other owners will suffer. Often, out of a sense of moral obligation, the nondisabled owners will continue a salary to the disabled party for as long as possible, but there is a point at which a small business cannot afford to pay a salary to a person who is not earning one. At this point, the nondisabled partners are torn between their sense of moral obligation and the practical realities of income and outgo.

A proper view of the disability exposure facing business owners recognizes that there are two separate problems when an owner is disabled. First, there is the problem of a continuing income to the disabled owner. The solution to this problem is the same as the disability problem facing every individual: disability income insurance provided by the employer or purchased individually.

The second problem is the transfer of the disabled owner's interest in the business to the nondisabled owners. The solution to this problem is essentially the same as the solution to the problem associated with the death of an owner: a buy-sell agreement designed to become effective upon the occurrence of a designated event—in this case, the total and permanent disability of the owner.

The shareholders of a business can develop a plan of action to meet the disability of an owner that does not require the sale of the disabled person's interest in the business. For example, a recapitalization or adjustment of the profit formula might be an acceptable solution under certain circumstances. In general, however, all parties will probably desire to arrange for the transfer of the disabled individual's interest to the nondisabled owners. One approach to this solution is a disability buyout agreement, setting forth the conditions under which such a sale is to be made. Disability income policies designed to fund buy-sell agreements generally provide lump-sum benefits rather than periodic income. This permits the nondisabled owners to make a lump-sum payment for the interest being acquired.

As in the case of life insurance, premiums paid by a corporation or partnership on shareholders or partners are not deductible as an expense. However, as long as the benefits under the policy are paid directly to the partner who is disabled, they are excluded from the recipient's income under Section 104(a)(3) of the *IRC*.

Disability Overhead Insurance

In addition to policies that cover the living expenses needed by their families in the event of disability, some self-employed persons carry disability "overhead" insurance, which is designed to pay business expenses, such as rent and clerical costs, while the individual is disabled. Disability overhead insurance is needed by individuals whose services represent the principal source of income to the business and whose disability would halt that income. Even a short period of disability can pose a problem to a personal service business. Disability income insurance can be arranged to replace the income lost and thereby provide for continued payment of the firm's fixed expenses.

IMPORTANT CONCEPTS TO REMEMBER

business continuation
business perpetuation
term insurance
cash value insurance
permanent life
   insurance
whole life
universal life
adjustable life
variable life

cash value accumulation
   test
guideline premium test
cash value corridor test
key person life insurance
key person disability
   insurance
nonqualified deferred
   compensation plan
constructive receipt

split dollar plan
cross-purchase plan
entity plan
stockholders buy-and-sell
   agreement
stock redemption
   agreement
disability overhead
   insurance

QUESTIONS FOR REVIEW

1. Distinguish between term insurance policies and cash value policies. Explain what is meant by the statement that term insurance is "pure protection."

2. Under a whole life policy, the overpayment by the insured during the early years of the contract offsets underpayments in later years. This being the case, the reserve should reach a peak and then gradually decline. How do you explain the fact that it does not?

3. Under a whole life policy, the amount payable in the event of the insured's death can be viewed as consisting of two parts. Explain this concept.

4. Describe the ways in which life insurance policies receive favorable tax treatment.

5. Distinguish between individual and group life insurance arrangements and identify the sources of the cost advantage for group life insurance.

6. In what sense is key-employee insurance analogous to property insurance on a valuable piece of equipment?

7. What are the reasons a business firm might want to purchase key-employee insurance? What are the income tax consequences for the employer? For the employee?

8. Briefly outline the provisions of the tax code relating to deductibility of premiums and taxation of policy proceeds in key person life insurance.

9. For what reasons might an organization decide to establish a nonqualified deferred compensation program? Has the number of nonqualified programs increased or decreased since enactment of ERISA? Why?

10. In funding business continuation agreements with life insurance for partnerships or close corporations the arrangement made may be known as a *cross-purchase* plan or an *entity* plan. What are the differences between these two approaches to funding?

QUESTIONS FOR DISCUSSION

1. The alumni at the state university are considering a nonqualified deferred compensation arrangement with the school's football coach and have asked you to explain the benefits of the plan to the coach. You have agreed to do so, but have told the alumni you feel compelled to make full disclosure, and present both the advantages and disadvantages. What do you plan to tell the coach about the proposed plan?

2. When you meet with the coach, he says that he finds the proposal appealing, but that the alumni from another school that is attempting to hire him have offered to fund a split-dollar life insurance plan. He asks your opinion regarding which "is the better deal." Assuming the contributions the alumni are proposing to make at the two schools are approximately equal, what do you tell him?

3. Three stockholders in a highly successful insurance agency are preparing to enter into a buy-sell agreement and cannot decide whether to use a stockholders buy-sell arrangement or a stock redemption plan. What are the advantages and disadvantages of each approach? What factors will influence the decision?

4. To what do you attribute the significant increase in the number of nonqualified deferred compensation plans over the past two decades?

5. One of the difficulties that sometimes arises in deferred compensation arrangements is that the Internal Revenue Service will regard the deferred payments as having been constructively received by the employee and tax them accordingly. Discuss the concept of constructive receipt as it relates to deferred compensation and give an example of a situation where difficulty might arise.

SUGGESTIONS FOR ADDITIONAL READING

Doyle, Robert J., Jr., et. al., *The Financial Services Professional's Guide to the Tax Reform Act of 1986*. Bryn Mawr, PA: American College, 1986.

Graves, Edward., (ed.). *McGill's Life Insurance*. Bryn Mawr, PA: The American College, 1994. Chapters 2, 3, 4, 33.

Hallman, G. Victor and Karen L. Hamilton, *Personal Insurance: Life, Health, and Retirement*. Malvern, Penn.: American Institute for CPCU, 1994, Chapters 7, 8.

Leimberg, Stephan R., et. al., *The Financial Services Professional's Guide to the State of the Art*, 2nd ed. Bryn Mawr, PA: American College, 1991.

Williams, C. Arthur and Richard M. Heins. *Risk Management and Insurance*, 6th ed. New York: McGraw-Hill, 1989. Chapters 21, 22, 25.

Wood, Glenn L.; Lilly, Claude C., III; Malecki, Donald S.; Graves, Edward E.; and Rosenbloom, Jerry S., *Personal Risk Management and Insurance*, 4th ed., vol. II. Malvern, PA: American Institute for Property and Liability, 1989. Chapters 12, 13, 14.

CHAPTER 30

Employee Benefits

CHAPTER OBJECTIVES

When you have finished this chapter, you should be able to

Identify the major classes of employee benefits that are provided by employers to their employees, and describe the tax treatment of these benefits.

∎

Identify the different possibilities regarding responsibility within a corporation for employee benefits.

∎

Explain how the administration of employee benefit plans is different and similar to a risk manager's other responsibilities.

∎

Explain the statutory requirements that apply to qualified employee benefits plans generally.

∎

Identify and explain the characteristics of the funding alternatives available to employers with respect to qualified retirement plans.

∎

Explain the role of a third-party administrator in the management of employee benefit programs.

▚ Introduction ∎∎∎∎∎∎∎∎∎∎∎∎∎∎∎∎∎∎∎∎∎∎∎∎∎∎

In addition to the uses in protecting the organization and its owners, life and health insurance are also used extensively as an employment benefit. It is common for an employer to offer an employee some life insurance, health insurance, or retirement benefits in the employment setting. In many cases, the employer pays a part of the cost. This may be viewed as another form of compensation, since it benefits the employee. These arrangements fall under the broad classification of *employee benefits*. In this chapter, we begin our discussion of employee benefits with an overview of the nature and tax treatment of employee benefits generally. In the next three chapters, we examine specific employee benefit programs.

Responsibility for Employee Benefits ■ ■ ■ ■ ■ ■ ■ ■ ■ ■

In many organizations, the risk manager does not have direct responsibility for employee benefits. In fact, surveys of risk managers generally indicate that something less than half of the responding risk managers have responsibility for employee benefits. Many firms assign administration of employee benefits to a department other than risk management because both the employer and employees consider employee benefits to be part of the compensation package, payable in lieu of wages. For this reason, the administration of employee benefits is often viewed as a natural extension of the personnel or human resource division's responsibility for payroll.

Other organizations recognize that the design of an employee benefit plan and many of the decisions related to such plans involve essentially the same types of decisions that are involved in managing the organization's own risks. Many plans are insured with commercial insurers, and the risk manager's familiarity with insurance buying generally gives him or her a natural advantage in this area. Furthermore, when the plans are self-insured, the considerations are similar to those that are addressed in the retention of the organization's own risks. Although employee benefits are a part of the employee-compensation function and are therefore within the realm of the human resource managers of the organization, the risk manager's expertise in insurance buying has direct relevance to the design and funding of employee benefit plans. Consequently, many risk management departments have responsibilities related to employee benefits. Even when the risk manager is not responsible for the employee benefits function, he or she serves as an important source of expertise for those who have this responsibility.

Employee Benefits Defined ■ ■ ■ ■ ■ ■ ■ ■ ■ ■ ■ ■ ■ ■ ■ ■

Broadly speaking, any nonmonetary compensation provided by an employer to its employees can be termed an "employee benefit." Unfortunately, this definition is too broad to be of much use in analyzing and evaluating employee benefit programs. If one wishes to compare the cost of benefit programs among organizations, for example, some standard classification of benefits whose cost is to be compared is needed. For this reason, it seems important to at least agree at the outset on the package of benefits we will consider to be "employee benefits."

NARROW DEFINITION

In its annual review of employee benefits plans, the *Social Security Bulletin* uses a fairly narrow definition of employee benefit plans. The benefit plans for which the Social Security Administration publishes data are based on the following definition of employee benefits:

> Any type of plan sponsored or initiated unilaterally or jointly by employers or employees and providing benefits that stem from the employment relationship and that are not underwritten or paid directly by government. . . In general, the intent is to include plans that provide in an orderly predetermined fashion for:
>
> 1. income maintenance during periods when regular earnings are cut off because of death, accident, sickness, retirement, or unemployment; and
> 2. benefits to meet medical expenses associated with illness or injury.

Although this limited definition includes death benefits, sickness and disability benefits, retirement income, and medical expense insurance or reimbursement, it does not include such benefits as paid vacations, holidays, rest periods, child care benefits, or certain other employee benefits for which the *Internal Revenue Code* provides a tax exemption. Interestingly, it also does not include any of the legally required benefits, such as social security, workers compensation, or unemployment compensation.

BROAD DEFINITION

The broader view of employee benefits takes the position that virtually any benefit provided to employees by an employer other than wages and salary for work performed is to be considered an employee benefit. This definition coincides with the one suggested by the United States Chamber of Commerce, which classifies employee benefits into five categories:

1. Legally required payments for employee security, such as, for example, workers compensation, unemployment compensation, and social security.
2. Pensions and other negotiated or agreed-upon benefit programs, including group life, group accident and health, travel accident, sick leave, allowances paid at termination of employment, purchasing discounts, free meals, tuition refunds, and stock purchase plans.
3. Payment for nonproductive time while on the job, including rest periods, lunch periods, wash-up time, travel time, or time for changing clothes.
4. Payments for time when the employee is not at work. In this category are such things as vacations for which pay is provided, paid holidays, paid sick leave, jury duty, or death in the family.
5. Other payments not categorized above, such as profit-sharing plans, Christmas bonuses, medical examinations, recreation facilities, group property and liability insurance, and group prepaid legal benefits.

This broader view of "employee benefits" includes all nonpaycheck benefits provided to employees, and covers the range reaching from social security benefits to such fringe benefits as payment for vacation and other time not worked. The fifth category, "other payments not categorized above," extends the definition to include other "perks" associated with employment.

The broad Chamber of Commerce definition is probably the most useful one for analyzing employee benefit plans. It is this measure, for example, for which cost estimates are most frequently given; current estimates place the cost of employee benefits broadly defined in the range of 38 to 40 percent of payroll. In contrast, the cost of employee benefits included under the narrower social security definition probably ranges roughly 12 to 13 percent of payroll.

■ Employee Benefits Generally ■ ■ ■ ■ ■ ■ ■ ■ ■ ■ ■ ■ ■ ■ ■ ■ ■

Regardless of the definition, employee benefits clearly represent a significant part of the compensation of many employees. Medical expense coverage for most employees and their dependents is obtained through an employer-sponsored health insurance plan. Over half of all employees are covered by employer-sponsored retirement plans. Over two-thirds of all employees are covered by life insurance offered by their employer. Although private disability insurance is less likely to be offered by an employer, it is estimated that about one of every four employees is covered by employer-sponsored long-term disability plans.

There are several reasons for the prevalence of employer-sponsored insurance benefits. First, employees may find it advantageous to accept insurance as part of their compensation, primarily because of the favorable tax treatment of employee benefits. In addition, most life and health insurance provided by employers is part of a group insurance contract which, as we have seen, tends to be less expensive than individual insurance. There are several reasons for this, including lower underwriting expenses and administrative costs, as well as reduced costs from adverse selection. In addition to the fact that employees may find insurance benefits to be an attractive form of compensation, employers may have other objectives for offering employee benefits. Some plans are established in the hope that they will improve employee morale and motivation. Plans may be designed to address certain specific goals, such as reducing employee turnover or encouraging early retirement.

Levels of benefits vary by industry and employee size. Employee benefits are more likely to be offered by large employers than by smaller employers. In addition, employers typically differentiate between full-time and part-time employees in the design of their plans. Often, full-time employees are eligible for a variety of benefits for which part-time employees are not eligible. Waiting periods for participation may be imposed, so that seasonal and short-term employees are eliminated from the various plans.

The design of an employer's plan must carefully consider the employer's objectives and employee's needs, the various options available, and their cost. Typically, the employer will want to consider how its employee benefit plan compares to other firms that it competes with for employees. In addition, the employer must decide how the plan will be financed (whether through insurance or some other mechanism) and who will administer the plan. Finally, the employer must effectively communicate the plan to employees if it is to have the intended impact. Frequently, the employer will retain a consultant to assist in this process.

HISTORY OF EMPLOYEE BENEFITS

Employee benefit programs are of relatively recent origin. Prior to the twentieth century, the risks of premature death, superannuation, disability, and medical expenses were considered the responsibility of the individual. Although some cooperative efforts were made to address these risks, these efforts were usually cooperative associations among workers rather than programs that involved the employer. Most of these were voluntary cooperative associations in which members of a particular group, such as a guild or union combined to share risks. These voluntary associations began with the Greek and Roman benevolent societies, were later followed by the guilds, and still later by mutual benefit societies and so-called "friendly societies" in England in the 1600s. The general pattern in all of these organizations was the payment of a weekly or monthly benefit to members who suffered sickness or injury. Eventually—shortly after the Civil War in the United States—mutual benefit associations came to be associated with employment. Mutual benefit associations, called *establishment funds*, usually organized by employees, were sometimes funded by the employer. The first formal employee benefit plan in the United States was probably the pension plan started in 1875 by the American Express Company for its employees. In 1910, Montgomery Ward and Company, which had funded an employee establishment fund for its employees, replaced the fund with what is generally regarded to be the first group health insurance contract. The program provided weekly benefits for nonoccupational disability. Group life insurance originated in 1911.

Other employers followed, but the spread of employee benefit plans was slow. In the Great Depression of the 1930s, employee benefit plans suffered a serious setback, and many of the plans that had been established collapsed. The collapse of pension plans, in particular, was one of the reasons for the creation of the social security system. At the beginning of the 1940s, the employee benefit arena was in complete disarray.

World War II

During World War II, the federal government imposed price and wage controls throughout the economy in an attempt to control inflation. Interestingly, despite the freeze on wages and salaries, the Wage Stabilization Board did not freeze employee benefit plans. Because labor was in short supply, employers used employee benefits to enhance the compensation package for workers. Employee benefit plans increased dramatically and by the end of the war had become a standard part of the employee compensation package.

Organized Labor

Following World War II, organized labor adopted employee benefits as an integral part of its negotiation efforts. The economy was expanding and the demand for labor was high. More importantly, federal legislation, in the form of the National Labor Relations Act of 1935 (better known as the Wagner Act) gave workers the specific right to bargain over wages, hours, and conditions of employment.[1] Organized labor's interest in employee benefits was based on the favorable tax treatment afforded such benefits under the *Internal Revenue Code*.

TAX TREATMENT OF QUALIFIED EMPLOYEE BENEFITS

Some employee benefits are popular because such programs receive favorable treatment under the tax laws. Most of the employee benefits discussed in the following chapters have been granted special tax-exempt status under the *Internal Revenue Code* and are called qualified employee benefits. As the term is generally used, the *qualified* employee benefit plan refers to a benefit that meets specific requirements of the *Internal Revenue Code* and for which favorable tax treatment is provided. Basically, this favorable tax treatment consists of the fact that contributions made by the employer for a qualified employee benefit are deductible by the employer but are not taxable to the employee as income. Some benefits, such as pension plans and qualified deferred profit-sharing plans, are granted a tax deferral. The employer's contribution is deductible by the employer at the time that it is made, but is not taxable to the employee until a later date when the accumulated benefits are eventually paid. In addition, during the period of accumulation, investment income is not taxed, but, like the contributions to the plan, will be taxed at a later time when paid out. Although some employee benefits are taxable, most are not. The preferential tax treatment of qualified employee benefits provides a net system saving to the employees, since the cost of the employee benefits is significantly less than if they were purchased with after-tax dollars.

Requirements for qualification vary. Usually, the benefit must be provided to all eligible employees on a nondiscriminatory basis. In a limited number of cases, the benefits may be granted selectively.

The Tax Reform Act of 1984 Act (TRA-84) added a new section to the *Internal Revenue Code* (Section 132) that specifically excludes certain fringe benefits from taxable income, and provides for taxation of some fringe benefits if they are not provided on a nondiscriminatory basis. If a fringe benefit is not specifically excluded under the new provisions or under earlier exemptions, the fair market value of the benefit is taxable as income to the recipient. The *Internal Revenue Code* now denominates certain types of benefits for which employer contributions are tax exempt to the employees, and also designates specific employee benefits that are exempt. The employee benefits exempted from taxation by the changes introduced by the new

---

[1]The U.S. Supreme Court ruled in 1949 that the term *wages* must be construed to include "emoluments of value, like pensions and insurance benefits." See *Inland Steel Company v. National Labor Relations Board*, U.S. Supreme Court (cert. denied, 336 U.S. 960, 1949).

Section 132 added by the TRA–84 include a variety of benefits such as (1) no-additional-cost services (services offered by the employer to employees in the ordinary course of business and for which the employer incurs no substantial additional cost in providing the benefit), (2) qualified employee discounts, (3) employee parking, (4) working condition fringes (such as subscriptions to business publications and professional organization memberships, (5) *de minimis* fringes (fringes whose value is so small that accounting for them would be administratively impractical, (6) certain subsidized eating facilities provided on a nondiscriminatory basis, (7) athletic facilities, and (8) a tuition-reduction plan for employees of educational institutions.

Fringe benefits that were statutorily exempt before 1984 were unaffected by the provisions of the 1984 law. Section 132 did not affect the other statutorily conferred tax-exempt status for benefits such as meals and lodging furnished for the convenience of the employer (Section 119), employer-provided van pooling (Section 124), and employer-provided dependent care assistance programs (Section 129).

Although some attempts have been made to unify the tax treatment of different types of employee benefits, currently the tax treatment of employee benefits differs for different types of benefits. The nondiscrimination rules of some employee benefits prohibit discrimination in favor of "key employees," whereas other rules prohibit discrimination in favor of "highly compensated employees," and the definitions of these terms differ. Different employee benefits also have different standards regarding eligibility and benefit levels.[2]

With the addition of Section 132 to the *Internal Revenue Code* by the TRA–84, it is now possible to define the classes of "qualified" fringe benefits and the requirements that must be met for qualification. Table 30.1 summarizes the taxation of employee benefits.

For the "qualified" employee benefits, the favorable tax treatment means that the cost of a benefit to the employee in terms of wages that must be given up is less than the dollars that would have to be spent personally by the employee to acquire the benefit. All in all, the inclusion of group insurance as part of the compensation package of employees has permitted a significant expansion of private insurance coverage. In many instances, it is the only form of protection available to the individual covered. For others, it represents an important "sandwich" layer of protection between social security and individually purchased coverages.

Cafeteria Employee Benefit Plans

A *cafeteria plan* is an employee benefit plan that meets the design conditions outlined in Section 125 of the *IRC*, and in which employees have the right to choose from among a range of benefits. The normal approach to a cafeteria plan is a program that grants employees credits that may be used to "buy" benefits. Credits can be based on salary, years of service, or a combination of factors, but cannot discriminate in favor of key employees. The employee then selects benefits most appropriate to his or her

---

[2]The Tax Reform Act of 1986 introduced a new set of antidiscrimination rules known as Section 89, which established a complex series of tests designed to measure discrimination in employee benefit plans. Section 89 was repealed in November 1989, reinstating the rules that existed prior to the Tax Reform Act of 1986.

Table 30.1   Tax Status of Employee Benefits (Narrow Definition)

Free Only Under a Nondiscriminatory Plan

Contributions to qualified retirement plans	Section 401
Qualified Pension Plan	
Qualified Deferred Profit Sharing Plan	
Simplified Employee Pension	
Keogh Plan	
Section 401 (k) Cash or Deferred Plan	
Employee Stock Ownership Plan	
Life insurance coverage up to $50,000	Section 79
Medical expense benefits or insurance	Section 105, 106
Insured medical reimbursement plans	Section 106
Uninsured medical expense reimbursement plan	Section 105
Cafeteria plan benefits	Section 125
Dependent care assistance programs	Section 129

Always Tax-Free to Employees

Disability benefits or insurance	Section 105, 106
$5,000 death benefit to surviving spouse or family member	Section 101(b)
Physical examinations, diagnostic tests	Section 105
Bargain element of excess term life insurance	Section 79

need from the range of choices offered, which can include any nontaxable benefits, such as group term life insurance, health insurance, dependent care, or participation in a group legal service plan. The employer may also permit the employee to take some or all of the credit in the form of additional cash compensation (but not as taxable benefits).[3] Section 401(k) cash or deferred profit sharing or stock bonus plans can be included in the list of choices. Other deferred compensation plans, such as pensions, must be provided separately from the flexible program.

In some cases, flexible benefits are funded directly through salary reduction; employees can reduce their salaries by a certain amount and use the money tax-free to pay for certain benefits. Such arrangements, though technically cafeteria plans, are called *flexible spending accounts*.

As in the case of other qualified employee benefits, a cafeteria plan may not discriminate in favor of highly compensated participants as to benefits or contributions. Under a restriction added by the Tax Reform Act of 1984, key employees will be taxed on otherwise nontaxable benefits in any year for which the qualified benefits for key employees exceed 25 percent of such benefits for all employees under the plan.[4]

---

[3]Originally, participants under cafeteria plans were offered a choice from a wide range of nontaxable benefits, taxable benefits, and cash. Since 1988, cafeteria plans may include only cash or nontaxable benefits, such as coverage under group health insurance, group term life insurance, or other qualified benefits.

[4]*IRC*, Section 125(b)(2).

■■ ERISA   ■■■■■■■■■■■■■■■■■■■■■■■■■■■■■■■

The Employee Retirement Income Security Act of 1974 (ERISA) is the principal federal law regulating employee benefits. Although the law was enacted to address flaws in the pension system of the country, it addresses other employee benefit programs as well. The tax aspects of ERISA are administered by the IRS. Otherwise, the law is administered by the Department of Labor.

ERISA formalized two definitions relating to the employee benefit field: the *employee pension plan* and the *employee welfare-benefit plan*. The welfare-benefit plan, which refers to employee benefits other than pensions to which ERISA applies, is defined as

> any plan, fund or program which was heretofore or is hereafter established or maintained by an employer or by an employee organization or by both, to the extent that such plan, fund, or program was established or is maintained for the purpose of providing participants or their beneficiaries through the purchase of insurance or otherwise, (A) medical, surgical, or hospital care or benefits, or benefits in the event of sickness, accident, disability, death or unemployment, or vacation benefits, apprenticeship or other training programs, or day care centers, scholarship funds, or prepaid legal services or (B) any benefit described in Section 186(c) of this title (other than pensions on retirement or death, and insurance to provide such pensions).[5]

This definition is somewhat narrower than that proposed by the Chamber of Commerce, but it is broader than the Social Security Administration definition.

General Requirements of ERISA

ERISA addressed three general responsibilities of the sponsors of employee benefit plans: disclosure and reporting, fiduciary responsibility, and claim procedures. Although some of the specific requirements will be discussed in later chapters in connection with individual types of employee benefits, we may at this point note the general disclosure and reporting requirements imposed by ERISA.

Summary Plan Description

For employee benefit plans that cover 100 or more lives, ERISA requires the plan administrator to file a description of the plan with the U.S Department of Labor. The plan administrator (usually the group policyholder or plan sponsor) must file a Summary Plan Description (SPD) with the Department of Labor within 120 days after the plan is initiated. All plan participants must be provided a written copy of the SPD within 90 days of becoming a participant. The SPD includes the name of the plan, the name and address of the policyholder, the type of benefit plan, and the name, address, and telephone number of the plan administrator. In addition, the SPD must include all of the following information:

[5]29 USC, Section 1002(1).

- Plan requirements concerning eligibility for participation and benefits.
- A list of the circumstances that may result in disqualification or denial of benefits.
- The source of a method of determining the amount of contribution to the plan.
- Procedures for presenting claims for benefits.
- Remedies available for redress of claim benefits that have been denied.
- The date ending the plan fiscal year.

Once a plan is established, if it is changed a summary description of material changes must be filed with the Department of Labor no later than 210 days after the close of the plan year in which the modification occurred. These filings are available to plan participants and beneficiaries from the plan administrator upon request.

Reporting Requirements

In addition to the initial filing of the SPD plan, sponsors must file an annual report (Form 5500) summarizing the financial aspects of the plan's operation. Separate information is required for pension plans and for welfare plans. The information on welfare plans (which includes life, health, and disability programs) includes information on the name of the insurance company providing the coverage, the number of persons covered during the year, and the total amount of fees and commissions paid to agents or brokers. Information is also required on premium rates and subscription charges, contributions to the plans, and benefit payments.

ERISA Preemption

One of the more controversial features of ERISA is a provision in the law preempting state laws covering employee benefits plans. This preemption has been the subject of numerous legal challenges. Although the courts have generally supported the federal preemption, there are exceptions. The major exception is that, although the states may not regulate employee benefit plans, the employers who maintain them, or trust funds established in connection with such plans, the states may regulate insurers and insurance policies that are used to provide coverage under such plans.

◼ Group Insurance Funding Issues ◼ ◼ ◼ ◼ ◼ ◼ ◼ ◼ ◼ ◼ ◼ ◼ ◼

The alternatives available to an employer for financing its life and health benefits for employees range from a fully insured plan to a fully self-funded plan, with many variations in between. Throughout this text, we have examined the proper role of insurance in the risk management plan of an individual. Recall that four alternatives are available for dealing with a pure risk faced by an individual or firm: transfer, retention, avoidance, and loss control. The factors that influence the choice of each alternative were discussed in Chapter 3. There we noted that insurance tends to be an expensive mechanism for treating risk, since it involves expenses beyond the payment for losses (insurer marketing expenses, premium taxes, insurer profit, etc.). Where the risk is characterized by a high frequency and low severity, and, therefore, relatively predictable expenses, insurance is not likely to be cost-effective. Retention, on the other hand, is likely to be appropriate where expenses are highly predictable.

These same considerations will affect an employer's choice of a funding mechanism for its employee benefit plans. Where losses tend to be unpredictable and there is a potential for large severe losses that would adversely affect the firm, self-funding is unlikely to be an attractive option. On the other hand, where losses are stable and relatively predictable, self-funding may be attractive. In addition to these general considerations, specific tax and other legal considerations may affect the choice of funding vehicle. Finally, if an employer decides to self-fund, it must also decide whether to administer the plan itself or to retain an outside administrator to make benefit determinations.

Consider, for example, the case of health insurance. The level of technology used in the delivery of medical care has increased dramatically in recent decades. Along with this increase has come an increase in the potential severity of medical claims. The cost of caring for a single infant born prematurely, organ transplants, and heart surgery, for example, can run in the hundreds of thousands of dollars.

Because of the potential severity of loss, historically only very large employers self-insured their medical expense plans. Those employers whose size was insufficient to justify self-funding may have been subject to experience rating, retrospective rating, or some other loss-sensitive program. In recent years, however, it has become increasingly common for even smaller employers to engage in some degree of self-funding, while capping their exposure through the use of stop-loss insurance.

STOP-LOSS INSURANCE

Stop-loss insurance limits the amount of loss that the employer is required to fund. The most common form of stop-loss insurance is *aggregate stop-loss*. With aggregate stop-loss insurance, the employer agrees to pay all claims up to an agreed-upon limit for the year, and the insurer pays for all claims beyond the limit. In a sense, the stop-loss limit acts as an annual deductible, and the policy caps the employer's loss exposure for the year. The employer self-funds losses within the limit but is protected if losses exceed the limit. Frequently, the stop-loss limit is set at 120 to 140 percent of the employer's expected losses. Stop-loss policies are increasingly made available to small employers and have fueled a dramatic growth in self-funding among this employer group. An alternative form of stop-loss insurance, specific stop-loss, caps the amount of claims for one individual. When the claims of one employee or dependent exceed the stop-loss limit, any excess is covered by the insurer. The use of stop-loss insurance by small employers has grown significantly in recent years in response to the increased interest of small employers in self-funding their medical expense benefits.

The reasons for the greater interest in self-funding in recent years are numerous. Some observers point out that self-funded plans are not subject to state insurance laws, thanks to a preemption in the Employee Retirement Income Security Act (ERISA). They see the increasing growth of self-funded plans as driven by a desire to escape state regulation. Most states have mandated benefits laws requiring certain benefits to be provided in insured plans. Self-insured plans are not subject to these mandates. In addition, most states have passed small-group reform laws that impose rate limitations, require guaranteed issue of small-employer policies, and limit preexisting conditions exclusions. Although these reforms make insurance more available and less expensive for those firms where employees have health problems, they also tend to increase the cost modestly for other firms. These other firms might find it more attractive to escape the insured market and thereby avoid the mandated subsidy of the poorer risks under small-group reform.

Although some groups have attempted to modify the ERISA preemption, these efforts have been opposed by large employer groups. Many employers argue that ERISA preemption is necessary because of the burden that would exist if employers operating in multiple states were forced to comply with the wide variety of health insurance laws in the states. At the moment, the states are attempting to stem the flow of small employers to the self-funded market by limiting the use of stop-loss insurance. Current proposals would prohibit stop-loss insurance with a loss limit of less than $20,000. Many small employers would be unable to self-fund at that level.

THIRD-PARTY ADMINISTRATORS

With the exception of very large employers, most employers that decide to self-fund their medical expense benefits will seek the assistance of an outside administrator. Administering a medical expense plan requires significant expertise, and the employer is often not interested in developing and maintaining that expertise internally. In addition, some employers are concerned that internal administration creates the possibility for conflict between the employer and employee over benefit decisions.

Third-party administrators (TPAs) are business firms that contract to provide administrative services in connection with employee benefit plans, especially for employers that elect to self-insure their programs.[6] Many TPAs are owned or managed by insurance agencies or brokerage firms. They assist the employer in the design of the employee benefit plan and sometimes in the purchase of insurance. Their primary function, however, is the administration of the plan once it is established. The TPA processes applications for coverage under the plan, issues certificates or booklets to participants, maintains all records associated with the plan, and processes and pays claims. ERISA places responsibility on third-party administrators by requiring that they be bonded and that they submit an annual report covering all financial aspects of each plan they administer.

The outside administrator may be a TPA or an insurance company. Where the employer has arranged stop-loss insurance, it is common for the insurer to be the administrator. Where the plan is fully self-funded, the contract between the administrator and employer is often called an administrative services only (ASO) agree-

---

[6]Although TPAs normally contract with an employer, an insurance company will often hire a TPA to provide services in an area in which it does not maintain an office or staff.

ment, in recognition of the fact that no insurance is being provided. Under an ASO arrangement, some insurance companies act as TPAs for self-insuring employers. In an ASO arrangement, the insurance company acts only as an administrator and does not bear the risk of insurance. This is borne by the employer. Most ASO contracts involve medical and dental coverages only, although a few insurers also offer ASO arrangements in connection with disability coverage.

FUNDING THROUGH A 501(C)(9) TRUST

An employer who self-funds certain employee benefits may establish a 501(c)(9) trust vehicle. Section 501(c)(9) of the *Internal Revenue Code* allows employers to establish a voluntary employees' beneficiary association (VEBA) and to use the trust to fund certain benefits for members. Benefits that may be funded through a 501(c)(9) trust include those payable because of death, medical expenses, disability, legal expenses, and unemployment. Retirement and deferred compensation benefits may not be funded through this vehicle. These funds may be used to pre-fund retiree life insurance or medical benefits, subject to special rules.

Certain additional requirements apply. Membership in the trust is limited to employees, former employees who are retired, disabled, or laid off, and their dependents. Benefits must not discriminate in favor of highly compensated individuals (although benefits may be based on a uniform percentage of compensation). If the plan requires contributions, membership in the trust must be voluntary on the part of employees.

In any year, contributions to the trust are limited to the sum of (1) direct benefit costs for that year, (2) additional amounts necessary to fund benefits that were incurred but have not yet been paid, and (3) administrative costs. The employer may not deduct excess contributions, which may result in adverse tax consequences.

◼ A Profile of Employee Benefit Programs ◼ ◼ ◼ ◼ ◼ ◼ ◼ ◼

In 1991, the U.S. Department of Labor's Bureau of Labor Statistics released the findings of its first survey of employee benefits in small private-industry establishments. The 1990 survey covered establishments with fewer than 100 employees and provided a useful benchmark for evaluating the employee benefits of an organization. The establishments surveyed had less extensive employee benefits coverage than the medium and large establishments (those with 100 workers or more) that the Bureau had surveyed in 1989.

The small establishment survey of 1990 provides information on the incidence and characteristics of benefit plans for an estimated 40.8 million employees (nearly two-fifths of the nation's civilian employed persons) in establishments with fewer than 100 employees. An estimated 32.6 million full-time and 8.2 million part-time employees were covered by the survey, which included all private industries, except farms and households. The survey included small establishments that were part of larger enterprises, such as a local service unit of a large manufacturing company, and small independent businesses, such as an independent agency. Three-fourths of the covered employees were in independent small businesses, and the remainder were in small units of larger companies.

The findings from the survey are presented in Table 30.2, together with data from the Bureau's medium and large private establishment survey, which provides a perspective for the data on small businesses.

Table 30.2 Percentage of Employees Covered for Particular Employee Benefits Small Businesses and Medium and Large Firms—1990

| Employee Benefit Program | Small Private Business | | Employees of Medium and Large Private Business |
	Full-Time Employees	Part-Time Employees	
Insurance			
Sickness and accident Insurance	28%	10%	43%
Long-term disability Insurance	19%	6%	45%
Medical care	69%	6%	92%
Dental care	30%	3%	66%
Life insurance	64%	6%	94%
Paid Time Off			
Holidays	83%	28%	97%
Vacations	88%	29%	97%
Personal leave	11%	4%	22%
Rest period	48%	27%	71%
Funeral leave	47%	11%	84%
Jury duty leave	54%	13%	90%
Military leave	21%	3%	53%
Sick leave	48%	11%	68%
Maternity leave	2%	1%	3%
Paternity leave	—	—	1%
Unpaid Time Off			
Maternity leave	17%	4%	37%
Paternity leave	8%	2%	18%
Retirement Benefits	42%	10%	81%
Defined benefit pension	20%	4%	83%
Defined contribution	31%	7%	48%
Other Benefits			
Flexible benefits	2%		9%
Reimbursement accounts	8%		23%
Child care	1%		5%

BENEFITS FOR FULL-TIME WORKERS
Insurance and Disability Benefits

Medical care and life insurance protection (covering about two-thirds of full-time employees) were the most prevalent insurance benefits found in the 1990 survey of small establishments. This compares with over 90 percent coverage for such benefits in medium and large establishments. Among part-time workers in small establishments in 1990, less than one-tenth had medical care benefits. (The survey of medium and large establishments covered only full-time employees.)

Coverage for other types of protection was less extensive. Three-tenths of full-time employees received dental care benefits; one-fourth had income replacement for short-term disabilities through sickness and accident insurance; and one-fifth had income replacement through long-term disability insurance.

Three-fourths of the full-time workers with medical care benefits were covered by a traditional fee-for-service plan. Under such plans, payments are made to the care provider or to the patient after care has been received. Another one-eighth of the full-time participants were covered by fee-for-service plans with a preferred provider option. Participants choosing the option received care at lower costs if treatment was provided by designated hospitals, physicians, or dentists. Health maintenance organizations, which provide a predetermined set of benefits for a fixed cost, typically from a predetermined group of providers, covered the remaining one-eighth of full-time plan participants.

About two-fifths of full-time employees with medical care benefits were required to contribute to the cost of individual coverage; two-thirds contributed for family coverage. When employee contributions were required, they averaged about $25 per month for individual coverage and $110 per month for family coverage.

Life insurance protection, typically paid for entirely by employers, was provided to two-thirds of full-time workers in small establishments. About three out of five life insurance plan participants had benefits specified as flat amounts, averaging slightly more than $15,000. Most of the remaining participants were provided life insurance benefits based on salary, typically one or two times annual pay.

Additional life insurance protection could be obtained by about one-fourth of those employees covered by a basic life insurance plan. In nearly all cases, this supplemental coverage, though available at group insurance rates, was paid for entirely by the employee. One-fifth of life insurance participants were in plans that continued benefits after retirement. In nearly all cases, these benefits were reduced at retirement, but remained in effect for life.

Sickness and accident insurance plans, which provide either a percentage of a worker's pay or a flat amount per week during a period of disability, were available to one-fourth of full-time workers in the 1990 small-establishment survey. A typical sickness and accident insurance plan imposes a seven-day waiting period before benefits (often half or two-thirds of regular pay) begin, with payments continuing for 26 weeks.

When an employee is disabled for a longer period of time, or indefinitely, income replacement benefits may be available through a long-term disability insurance plan. About one-fifth of full-time employees in the 1990 small-establishment survey participated in a long-term disability insurance plan; three out of four of these workers had coverage fully paid by their employer. Typical long-term disability insurance plans provided payments equal to 60 percent of pre-disability pay.

Paid and Unpaid Leave

Time off with pay is available to employees in a variety of forms—from a few minutes for a daily rest break to several weeks of annual vacation. Paid military leave was available to one-fifth of full-time employees in small establishments in 1990. Such plans were typically designed for short-term reserve duty; the average maximum amount of paid military leave available for full-time workers was 11 workdays per year.

Paid holidays and vacations were available to over four-fifths of the full-time workers in small establishments. Workers receiving such leave averaged 9.5 paid holidays a year and annual paid vacation of 11.5 days after five years of service. Sick leave plans, providing full pay for some or all of a period of short-term disability, were available to half of the full-time workers in small establishments.

The needs of households where parents are employed were addressed by a number of employee benefits in the 1990 survey. Unpaid maternity leave was available to about one-sixth of full-time workers in small establishments; unpaid paternity leave was available to nearly one-tenth of full-time workers. Parental leave plans provide time off for mothers and fathers to care for newborn or newly adopted children. These plans, as defined by the survey, are separate from other leave benefits, such as sick leave and paid vacations, which at times also may be used for parenting purposes. *Paid* parental leave was rare.

One percent of full-time employees were eligible for child care benefits subsidized by their employer. These benefits include both on-site and near-site child care facilities and full or partial payment of child care expenses. Another method of assisting employees with child care expenses was through reimbursement accounts. Such accounts, typically financed with employee pretax dollars, may be used to pay for expenses that are not covered by other benefit plans, such as dependent care expenses and out-of-pocket medical care expenses. Fewer than one-tenth of full-time employees in small establishments were eligible for such accounts in 1990.

Retirement Programs

Defined-benefit pension plans, which specify a formula for determining an employee's annuity, covered one-fifth of full-time workers in small establishments in 1990—approximately 6.5 million workers. Defined-contribution plans, which usually specify the employer's contribution but do not indicate the actual amount of employee benefit, were available to three-tenths of full-time workers (approximately 10 million workers). (Because some employees were covered under both defined-benefit and defined-contribution plans, the number of persons covered under both types of plans combined exceeds the number of employees covered for all pension plans.)

In 1990, a large majority of participants with defined-contribution plans had limited access to funds prior to retirement age. About two-fifths of full-time employees in small establishments were covered by some type of retirement plan—either a defined-benefit plan or a defined-contribution plan that restricted access to benefits, or both.

The most prevalent type of defined-benefit pension plan found among participants in small establishments was the terminal earnings plan, which bases pension payments on an employee's average earnings in the last few years prior to retirement.

Several types of defined-contribution plans were provided to employees in small establishments. Deferred profit sharing plans, which set aside funds for employees based on company profits, were provided to one in seven full-time workers in small establishments; savings and thrift plans, which specify an employee contribution that is typically matched, in whole or in part, by the employer, were provided to one in ten workers; money purchase plans, which receive a fixed periodic contribution from the employer, were provided to one in seventeen workers; and Simplified Employee Pension plans (SEPs), which are specifically designed for small establishments to create retirement accounts for employees, were rarely provided.

One-sixth of the full-time workers covered by the survey participated in 401(k) plans (also known as cash or deferred arrangements), which permit pretax employee contributions to a retirement account. Most of these plans were salary reduction plans, allowing employees to reduce their current taxable income by making voluntary contributions that are not taxed until withdrawn from the plan. For example, savings and thrift plans commonly allow participants to make some or all of their contributions in pretax dollars.

BENEFITS FOR PART-TIME WORKERS

For the first time, the Bureau's data on the incidence and details of employee benefits include information on part-time workers. As might be expected, the pattern of benefits for full-time employees was higher than the pattern of benefits for part-time employees. Paid vacations and holidays were the most prevalent benefits available to part-time workers, whereas insurance and retirement protection was rare. Because of the limited incidence of benefits among part-time workers, plan provisions could not be examined to the same extent as for full-time workers.

Just fewer than three in ten part-time employees in small establishments in 1990 received paid vacations and paid holidays. When these benefits were provided, they were typically similar to those of full-time workers but prorated based on the work schedule of the part-time employee. Insurance and retirement benefits were generally available to fewer than one-tenth of part-time employees in small establishments.

IMPORTANT CONCEPTS TO REMEMBER

employee benefits
broad definition of
   employee benefits
narrow definition of
   employee benefits
qualified employee benefit
cafeteria plan

flexible spending account
Employee Retirement
   Income Security Act
   (ERISA)
Summary Plan Description
Form 5500
stop-loss insurance

aggregate stop-loss
third-party administrator
administrative services only
   (ASO)
voluntary employee's beneficiary association (VEBA)
Section 501(c)(9) trust

QUESTIONS FOR REVIEW

1. (a) Distinguish between the broad definition of employee benefits and the narrow definition. (b) To what do you attribute the fact that two definitions have developed? (c) Which of the definitions of employee benefits comes the closest to the class of benefits for which risk managers are responsible?

2. Using the narrow definition of employee benefits, identify the major classes of employee benefits that are provided by employers to their employees, and describe the tax treatment of these benefits.

3. Identify the different possibilities regarding responsibility within a corporation for employee benefits. To what extent are risk managers generally assigned responsibility for employee benefit programs?

4. What factors are responsible for the popularity of employee benefits?

5. What is the cost of employee benefits to employers based on each definition?

6. Approximately what portion of the workforce is covered for the various types of employee benefits included in the narrow definition of employee benefits?

7. Explain the role of a third-party administrator in the management of employee benefit programs.

8. What is meant by the term cafeteria employee benefit plan? To what do such plans owe their increased popularity?

9. Describe the three general responsibilities of the employee benefit plan sponsor addressed by ERISA.

10. In what way does the favorable tax treatment of group life and group health insurance differ from the tax treatment of qualified retirement plans?

QUESTIONS FOR DISCUSSION

1. Describe the ERISA preemption of state laws with respect to employee benefit plans. Why has this preemption been the subject of litigation and controversy?

2. What is meant by the term "key employee" and why are key employees important with respect to employee benefit plans?

3. What factors are generally considered by an employer in the design of an employee benefits package?

4. What are some of the reasons for the increased interest in self-funding health insurance benefits in recent years? How extensive is self-funding of employer sponsored group health insurance?

5. The conventional wisdom suggests that the expansion of employee benefits has been due both to collective bargaining and to the favorable tax treatment of such benefits under the *Internal Revenue Code*. Which of these factors, in your opinion, has had the greatest influence on the growth of employee benefits?

SUGGESTIONS FOR ADDITIONAL READING

Allen, Everett T., Joseph J. Melone, Jerry S. Rosenbloom, and Jack L. VanDerhei. *Pension Planning*, 7th ed. Homewood, IL: Richard D. Irwin, Inc., 1992.

American Council of Life Insurance. *Pension Facts*. Washington, DC: American Council of Life Insurance, published annually.

Beam, Burton T., Jr. *Group Benefits: Basic Concepts and Alternatives*, 4th ed. Bryn Mawr, Pa: The American College, 1991.

Beam, Burton T., Jr. and John J. McFadden. *Employee Benefits*, 3rd ed. Brookfield, WI: Dearborn Financial Publishing, Inc., 1994.

Black, Kenneth, Jr., and Harold D. Skipper, Jr. *Life Insurance*, 12th ed. Englewood Cliffs, NJ: Prentice-Hall, 1994. Chapter 7, 14, 28.

Brahs, Stuart J. "Tax Reform in 1986: What It Means for Employee Benefits." *Benefits Quarterly*. vol. III, no. 1 (First Quarter 1987).

Fundamentals of Employee Benefit Programs, 4th ed. Washington, DC: Employee Benefit Research Institute, 1990.

Leimberg, Stephan R., et al., *The Financial Services Professional's Guide to the State of the Art*, 2nd ed. Bryn Mawr: Pa: American College, 1991.

McNamara, Michael J. "Managing the Risk of Employee Benefits Exposures," *CPCU Journal*, vol. 44, no. 1 (March 1991).

Ralston, August R., ed. *Risk Management Manual*, Santa Monica, Ca.: (loose-leaf service with monthly supplements), vol. 3, section 13, "Employee Benefits."

Rosenbloom, Jerry S., ed. *The Handbook of Employee Benefits: Design, Funding and Administration*. Homewood, Il: Richard D. Irwin, 1984.

CHAPTER 31

Social Insurance Programs

CHAPTER OBJECTIVES

When you have finished this chapter, you should be able to

Identify and describe the major classes of benefits in the Old-Age, Survivors, Disability, and Health Insurance program (OASDHI).

■

Identify the persons who are eligible for benefits under the OASDI program and how eligibility for benefits is derived.

■

Explain how benefits under the OASDI program are financed.

■

Explain how the amount of benefits received under OASDI is determined and the circumstances that can lead to a loss of benefits.

■

Evaluate the financial soundness of the Social Security system and identify the proposals that have been suggested to improve that soundness.

■

Describe the features of state unemployment compensation laws and explain how one becomes eligible for benefits.

■

Describe state temporary disability laws and explain how one becomes eligible for benefits.

Introduction ■■■■■■■■■■■■■■■■■■■■■■■■■■■■■■

Before turning to the specific employee benefits for which the risk management department may have responsibility, it will be helpful if we briefly examine the social insurance program with which the employee benefit programs must be coordinated. We have already noted one of the nation's three major social insurance programs, workers compensation. In this chapter, we briefly review the social security system, unemployment compensation, and the nonocccupational disability programs.

The Old-Age, Survivors, and Disability Insurance Programs ■■■■■■■■■■■■■■■■■■■■■

The Old-Age, Survivors, Disability, and Health Insurance (OASDHI) program (Commonly known as Social Security) protects eligible workers and their dependents against the financial losses associated with death, disability, superannuation, and sickness in old age. The benefits available under the program to the dependents of a deceased worker or to the worker and dependents when the worker is disabled are an important part of an individual's income-protection program. The retirement benefits are also a fundamental element in the individual's retirement program. The employee benefit program builds on this floor of protection. There are four classes of benefits under OASDHI.

Old-Age Benefits—The old-age part of OASDHI provides a lifetime pension beginning at age 65 (or a reduced benefit as early as age 62) to each eligible worker and certain eligible dependents. The amount of this pension is based on the worker's average earnings during some period in the working years and is subject to automatic adjustments for increases in the cost of living. Benefits for all recipients are increased automatically each January if the consumer price index (CPI) shows an increase in the cost of living during the preceding year. Congress retains the right to legislate increases in benefits, but there is no automatic increase in any year for which Congress has not legislated one.

Survivors' Benefits—Originally, the Social Security Act provided only retirement benefits. Complaints that the system was unfair to workers who died before retirement (or after retirement) persuaded Congress to expand the program, extending benefits to the dependents of a deceased worker or retiree. The survivors' portion of the program provides covered workers with a form of life insurance, the proceeds of which are payable to their dependent children and, under some conditions, surviving spouses.

Disability Benefits—Disability benefits were added to the program in 1956, when benefits were extended to insured workers who became disabled between the ages of 50 and 64. In 1960, this coverage was broadened to all workers who meet certain eligibility requirements.[1] A qualified worker who becomes totally and permanently disabled is treated as if he or she had reached retirement age, and the worker and dependents become eligible for the benefits that would otherwise be payable at age 65.

Medicare Benefits—The Medicare portion of the system was added in 1965. It offers people over 65 and certain disabled persons protection against the high cost of hospitalization, skilled nursing, hospice care, home health services, and other kinds of medical care. In addition, it provides an option by which those eligible for the basic benefits under the medical program may purchase subsidized medical insurance to help pay for doctors' services and other expenses not covered by the basic plan.[2]

ELIGIBILITY AND QUALIFICATION REQUIREMENTS

Initially, only about 60 percent of the civilian workforce was covered under the act. The major classes not included were the self-employed, agricultural workers, government employees, and employees of nonprofit organizations. Coverage has gradually been expanded until virtually all private employment and self-employment are covered by OASDHI. Over 95 percent of the labor force is covered, most of them on a compulsory basis. Those not covered under the act are excluded because they are state, local, or federal employees.[3]

Qualification for Benefits

To qualify for benefits, an individual must have credit for a certain amount of work under Social Security. When a worker is covered by the law, a tax is paid on a portion of his or her wages, and insured status is determined by the earnings that have been credited. Insured status is measured by "quarters of coverage." Some benefits are payable only if the worker has enough quarters of coverage to be considered "fully insured," whereas other benefits are payable if the worker is merely "currently insured."

Quarter of Coverage   For most employment before 1978, *one quarter of coverage* was earned for each calendar quarter in which the Federal Insurance Contribution Act (FICA) tax was paid on $50 or more in wages. (A "calendar quarter" is any three-month period beginning January 1, April 1, July 1, or October 1.) The level of

---

[1]Discussed later in the chapter.

[2]The Medicare program is discussed in Chapter 33.

[3]Employees who are covered under a state or local government retirement system may elect to be included under OASDHI by referendum; the employing government enters into a contract with the federal government to cover the employees. About 75 percent of state and local government employees are so covered. The 1983 amendments eliminated an option under which state and local governments could terminate coverage on their employees. Federal employees hired after December 31, 1993 are included in the OASDHI program.

earnings on which FICA taxes must be paid for a quarter of coverage is adjusted annually for inflation, based on increases in average total wages for all workers. By 1996, one quarter of coverage was granted for each $640 of earnings, up to a maximum of four quarters a year. Further increases will take place as average total wages for all workers increases.

Fully Insured Status   *Fully insured status* is required for retirement benefits. To be fully insured the worker must have one quarter of coverage for each year after the year in which he or she reaches age 22, up to, but not including, the year in which the worker reaches age 62, becomes disabled, or dies. For most people, this means 40 quarters of coverage. No worker can achieve fully insured status with fewer than 6 quarters of covered employment, and no worker needs more than 40 quarters. Once a worker has 40 quarters of coverage, he or she is fully insured permanently.

Currently Insured Status   To be currently insured, a worker needs six quarters of coverage during the 13-quarter period ending with the quarter of death, entitlement to retirement benefits, or disability. Basically, currently insured status entitles children of a deceased worker (and the children's mother or father) to survivor benefits and provides a lump-sum benefit in the event of the worker's death.

FINANCING

The OASDHI program is financed through a system of payroll and self-employment income taxes levied on all persons in the program. For wage earners, a tax is paid on wages up to a specified maximum by both employers and the employee. In the original act of 1935, a tax rate of 1 percent applied to the first $3000 of an employee's wages, and the employer and employee were each liable for the tax up to a $30 annual maximum. When the Medicare program was added in 1965, a separate *Hospital Insurance tax* was added, which is combined with the *Old-Age, Survivors and Disability tax* to comprise the total FICA tax. Both the tax rate and taxable wage base to which it applies have increased over time as the program has expanded. The most recent change in the tax rate occurred in 1990, when the Old-Age, Survivors and Disability tax was increased to 6.2 percent and the Medicare tax was increased to 1.45 percent, making a combined rate of 7.65 percent, payable by the employee and matched by the employer.

The Old-Age, Survivors, and Disability tax applies to a taxable wage base that automatically increases in the year following an automatic benefit increase. Like the automatic increases in benefit levels, congressional changes in the taxable wage base override the automatic adjustment provisions. Automatic increases in the earnings base are geared to the increase in average wages for all workers. With the legislated changes and automatic adjustments, the taxable wage base had increased to $62,700 by 1996. This taxable wage base will continue to increase in the future. Historically, the Medicare tax applied only up to the maximum taxable wage base. The 1993 Tax Reform Act eliminated the maximum wage base for the Medicare tax, and the tax now applies to total earned income without limit.

Self-employed persons pay a tax rate that is equal to the combined employer-employee contribution (i.e., 15.30 percent in 1996). Self-employed persons are allowed a deduction against income taxes equal to half the self-employment taxes paid for the year.

AMOUNT OF BENEFITS

All OASDI income benefits are based on a benefit called the *Primary Insurance Amount* (PIA). The PIA is the amount of the retirement benefit payable to a worker who retires at age 65. It is computed from the individual's *Average Indexed Monthly Earnings* (AIME), which is the worker's average monthly wages or other earnings during his or her computation years, indexed to current wage levels. All monthly income benefits under OASDHI to the worker and his or her eligible dependents are based on the PIA.

Computing the Primary Insurance Amount The first step in computing the primary insurance amount (PIA) is to determine the computation period, based on the number of "elapsed years." For workers born in 1930 or after, elapsed years are the years beginning with the year in which the worker reached age 22 and ending with the year before the one in which the worker becomes 62, dies, or is disabled. Five years with the lowest earnings are then eliminated from total elapsed years to determine the computation years. The remaining years are the computation years and are the basis for computing the average earnings on which benefits are based. Because a maximum of five years may be eliminated, some years in which there was no income may have to be included. At least two years must be used for the computation.

Indexing the Earnings The worker's covered earnings are indexed to the average earnings in his or her "indexing year," which is the second year before the year of eligibility, using the average annual wages since 1950 published by the Social Security Administration. The actual earnings of the worker (up to the maximum taxed) in each year are indexed by multiplying the earnings by the fraction:

$$\frac{\text{Average Earnings in the Indexing Year}}{\text{Average Earnings in the Year Being Indexed}}$$

If the year being indexed is say, 1970, when average earnings were $6186.24, and the indexing year is 1990, when average earnings were $21,027.98, the worker's wages for 1970 would be inflated by a 3.399 multiplier ($21,027.98/$6186.24). The purpose of the indexing is to adjust the worker's past income to current levels.

All elapsed years are indexed, and the total indexed earnings in the computation years are divided by the number of months in those years to determine the worker's average indexed monthly earnings (AIME). The AIME serves as the basis for determining the worker's PIA. Once the AIME has been determined, it is converted to a *primary insurance amount* (PIA), using a formula prescribed by law. The formula used in converting AIME to PIA provides for a higher percentage of the average indexed earnings at lower income levels than at higher income levels.[4]

The computation of AIME and PIA is obviously complex. Fortunately, the Social Security Administration will provide a history of any worker's earnings and an estimate of his or her monthly benefits upon request. A *Personal Earnings and Benefit Statement* can be obtained through any Social Security Office by completing Form SSA-7004.[5] The statement provides an estimate of the benefits for retirement at age 62, 65, and 70, as well as the estimated benefits payable to a spouse and children upon the worker's retirement, disability, or death.

Retirement Benefits

Workers reaching age 65 who are fully insured are entitled to receive a monthly pension for the rest of their lives.[6] A fully insured worker who retires at age 65 receives a benefit equal to 100 percent of his or her PIA. Workers who elect to receive benefits before reaching age 65 may do so as early as age 62, but the benefit that would be payable at age 65 is reduced five-ninths of 1 percent for each month prior to age 65 that benefits commence (a 20 percent reduction at age 62). Workers who delay retirement receive an increase of 1/4 percent in their PIA for each month between the ages of 65 and 72 that they delay retirement.

Benefit for the Spouse of a Retired Worker   The spouse of a retired worker (or a spouse divorced after 10 years of marriage) is entitled to a retirement benefit at age 65 equal to 50 percent of the retired worker's benefit. Like the retired worker, the spouse may choose a permanently reduced benefit.[7] The worker must have been fully insured.

Children's Benefit   The benefit for children of a retired worker is payable to three classes of dependent children of a retired worker who is fully insured: (1) unmarried children under age 18, (2) unmarried children age 18 or over who are disabled, provided that they were disabled before reaching age 22, and (3) unmarried children under age 19 who are full-time students in an elementary or secondary school. The benefit to each eligible child of a retired worker is 50 percent of the worker's PIA, subject to a family maximum (discussed below).

---

[4]For workers reaching age 62 in 1994, PIA was computed on the basis of the following formula: 90 percent of the first $422 of AIME, plus 32 percent of AIME from $422 to $2545, plus 15 percent of AIME above $2545. The dollar amounts in the formula, known as "bend points," are subject to adjustment based on changes in the national average monthly wages.

[5]Persons who do not have access to a Social Security office can obtain the earnings and benefit statement from the Consumer Information Center, Dept. 55, Social Security Administration, Pueblo, Colorado 81000. Persons age 60 and older can obtain an estimate of future retirement benefits by telephone, using a toll-free number (1-800-772-1213).

[6]The age at which full retirement benefits are payable—now age 65—is scheduled to be increased to age 67 in very gradual steps, beginning in the year 2000. When this change is fully phased in, a worker will still be able to receive benefits at age 62 as now, but the benefit rate will be lower than the rate at age 62 under present law.

[7]Since 1985, a divorced spouse is entitled to receive a retirement benefit even if the worker on whose account the benefit is based continues working. This provision applies if both parties are at least age 62, were married 10 years, and have been divorced at least 2 years.

Mother's or Father's Benefit   A retired worker's spouse who has not yet reached age 62 may still be entitled to a benefit, if he or she has care of a child who is receiving a benefit. A *mother's benefit* or a *father's benefit* is payable to the spouse of a retired worker if that spouse has care of a child under 16 or a disabled child who is receiving a benefit.[8] The mother's or father's benefit is 50 percent of the worker's PIA, subject to the family maximum. The worker must have been fully insured.

Family Maximum   All benefits payable to a worker and his or her dependents are subject to a family maximum. The family maximum is based on a formula applied to the PIA.[9]

Survivors' Benefits

Benefits are payable to certain dependents of a deceased worker, provided that the worker had the required insured status, which varies for the different classes of survivor's benefits. The benefits payable under this part of the program include the following.

Lump-Sum Death Benefit—When a fully or currently insured worker dies, a $255 lump-sum death benefit is payable to the surviving spouse or children of the deceased worker.

Children's Benefit—The children's benefit is payable to dependent children of a deceased worker in any of the three classes noted earlier if the deceased worker was either fully or currently insured. The benefit to each eligible child of a deceased worker is 75 percent of the worker's PIA, subject to the family maximum.

Mother's or Father's Benefit—A mother's or father's benefit is payable to the widow or widower of a deceased worker who has care of a child under 16 (or a disabled child over 16) who is receiving benefits. The worker may have been either fully or currently insured. The benefit to a surviving spouse who has care of a child under 16 or a disabled child who is entitled to a benefit is 75 percent of the worker's PIA, subject to the family maximum.

Widow's or Widower's Benefit—The widow or widower of a deceased worker who was fully insured is entitled to a retirement benefit at age 65, equal to 100 percent of the worker's PIA. A divorced wife who was married to a fully insured deceased worker for at least 10 years is entitled to the same benefit. The widow or widower may elect to receive a permanently scaled-down benefit as early as age 60. The *widow's or widower's benefit* is also payable to the spouse of a deceased worker who becomes disabled after age 50 if the disability commences within seven years of the worker's death or the end of the beneficiary's

[8]Prior to 1975, the law provided only for a "mother's" benefit (i.e., a benefit to the female spouse of a retired or deceased worker with a child in her care). The U.S. Supreme Court ruled that the provision of such a benefit to females only was unconstitutional and that it deprived working women of a form of protection afforded to working men.

[9]This formula, like the PIA formula, includes dollar "bend points" that are subject to adjustment based on increases in the average total wages of all workers.

entitlement to a mother's or father's benefit. A disabled widow or widower age 50 to 59 who is entitled to a benefit receives 71.5 percent of the PIA.

Parents' Benefit—The *parents' benefit* is payable to a deceased worker's parents who are over age 62, if they were dependent on the worker for support at the time of death. The dependent parents of a deceased worker are entitled to a retirement benefit at age 62 equal to 82.5 percent of the worker's PIA. The maximum benefit for two dependent parents is 150 percent of the worker's PIA (75 percent each). The son or daughter must have been fully insured.

Disability Benefits

Disability benefits are payable to a worker and eligible dependents when a worker who meets special eligibility requirements is disabled as defined by the law. Disability is defined as a "mental or physical impairment that prevents the worker from engaging in any substantial gainful employment." The disability must have lasted for six months and must be expected to last for at least 12 months or be expected to result in the prior death of the worker. Persons who apply for social security benefits are referred to the state agencies called Disability Determination Services (DDS) to evaluate the disability. If the state agency is satisfied that the worker is disabled as defined by the Social Security Act, the individual is certified as such and benefits are paid. However, benefits do not start until the worker has been disabled for five full calendar months.

Qualification requirements for disability benefits depends on the worker's age. Workers who become disabled before reaching age 24 qualify if they have 6 quarters out of the 12 quarters ending when the disability began. Workers who become disabled between ages 24 and 31 must have 1 quarter of coverage for each 2 quarters beginning at age 21 and ending with the onset of disability. Workers over age 31 must be fully insured and must have 20 out of the last 40 quarters in covered employment.

In general, disability benefits are payable to the same categories of persons and in the same amounts as retirement benefits, but are subject to a special family maximum. Total monthly benefits for a disabled worker with one or more dependents are limited to the lower of 85 percent of the worker's AIME or 150 percent of the worker's disability benefit.[10]

A second limit on disability benefits deals with the manner in which AIME and PIA are determined for younger workers. Workers under age 27 may not eliminate any years with low earnings in the computation. Workers age 27 through 31 may eliminate one year, those 32 through 36 may eliminate two, those 37 through 41 three, and workers 42 through 47 may eliminate four years. A worker age 47 or older may eliminate the full five years.[11]

---

[10]Disability benefits under OASDHI may be reduced if the individual also receives workers compensation benefits. The law limits combined benefits to 80 percent of the disabled worker's recent earnings. Some states have reverse offset plans, under which workers compensation benefits are reduced if the worker is entitled to social security benefits.

[11]A worker under age 37 may drop an additional year for each year in which he or she had no earnings and had a child under age 3 in the household. In no case, however, can the total number of dropout years exceed 3.

The disability insurance program has a number of provisions designed to encourage beneficiaries to return to gainful employment. Beneficiaries may be referred to state vocational rehabilitation agencies for assistance. They are also permitted to return to employment for a "trial work period" without adversely affecting their benefits. After this nine-month period of employment, benefits will continue if average monthly earnings have not exceeded $500.[12] If average earnings are greater than $500, benefits continue for a three-month grace period, then cease.

Summary of Qualification Requirements

Although the preceding discussion may seem complicated, the nature of the qualification requirements can be summarized concisely, and while all qualifications are important, some seem more so than others. The survivors' benefits payable to children and mother's or father's benefits require only that the worker must have been fully or currently insured. To be eligible for any retirement benefits, the worker must have been fully insured. Table 31.1 summarizes the qualification requirements for the various categories of benefits under OASDHI.

Table 31.1   Insured Status Required for OASDHI Benefits

Benefit	Insured Status Required of Workers
Survivor benefits	
Children's benefits	Fully or currently insured
Mother's or father's benefit	Fully or currently insured
Dependent parent's benefit	Fully insured
Widow or widower age 60 or over	Fully insured
Lump-sum death benefit	Fully or currently insured
Retirement benefits	
Retired worker	Fully insured
Spouse of retired worker	Fully insured
Child of retired worker	Fully insured
Mother's or father's benefit	Fully insured
Disability benefits	
Disabled worker	20 or last 40 quarters fully insured or
Dependent of disabled worker	6 of last 12 quarters if under are 24 or
	1 of every 2 quarters since age 21 if between 23 and 31
Hospital benefits	Entitlement to cash benefits under social security or railroad retirement or have reached age 65 before 1968, or meet special eligibility requirement.

[12]The nine months need not be consecutive.

Loss of Benefits—OASDHI Program

A person receiving benefits may lose eligibility for benefits in several ways. The most common causes of disqualification under the law are the following:[13]

1. *Divorce from a person receiving benefits.* For example, a retired worker's wife or husband who is receiving a benefit based on the qualification of that worker loses the right to the benefit upon divorce, unless he or she was married to the worker for 10 years or longer.

2. *Attainment of age 18 by a child receiving benefits.* The benefit payable to the child of a deceased, retired, or disabled worker stops automatically when the child reaches age 18, unless the child is still in high school, in which case the benefit is payable until age 19. When the child reaches age 16, the mother's or father's benefit stops even though the child continues to receive a benefit. The child-raising widow or widower of a deceased worker, therefore, faces a period during which no benefits are payable. Between the time the youngest child turns 16 and the time the widow or widower reaches age 60, no benefits are payable. This period is commonly referred to as the "blackout period."

3. *Marriage.* The rules governing the loss of benefits through marriage or remarriage are rather complicated. As a rule, if a person receiving a monthly benefit as a dependent or survivor marries someone who is not also a beneficiary, his or her payment stops. Thus the payments to a dependent child would halt if the child married. On the other hand, a widow who marries a man receiving a benefit as a widower, parent, or disabled child over age 18 would not have her benefits affected. A widow or widower receiving a benefit who marries someone not drawing one, or someone who is getting a retirement benefit, does not lose the widow's or widower's benefit. If the benefit due the widow or widower as the spouse of a retired worker (on the new husband or wife's account) is larger than that received as a widow or widower, he or she will receive the larger of the two benefits.[14]

4. *Adoption.* If a child receiving a benefit is adopted by anyone except a step-parent, grandparent, aunt, or uncle, the payment to the child stops.

5. *Disqualifying income.* Sometimes, persons receiving social security benefits continue to work. Some work full time, others only part time. The same is true with respect to dependents receiving benefits. The social security laws provide that if a person receiving benefits earns additional income, he or she may lose a part or all of his or her benefits, depending on the amount earned. Exempt amounts of earnings are permitted, and earnings in excess of these amounts reduce the social security benefit.

---

[13]In addition to the causes of disqualification listed above, benefits may also be lost because of conviction of treason, sabotage, or subversive activity, deportation, work in foreign countries unless that work is also covered under OASDHI, and the refusal of rehabilitation by a disabled beneficiary.

[14]In a change added by the 1983 amendments, benefits payable to a divorced surviving spouse age 60 or over are no longer terminated if he or she remarries after age 60.

Disqualifying Income The disqualifying income provisions of the law are not intended as a needs test, but rather as a retirement test. The purpose is to determine whether the person has retired or is still working. In general, the idea is that a person should be able to have modest annual earnings without losing retirement status, so the law permits a small amount of earnings without loss of benefits. Different amounts of exempt earnings are established for beneficiaries under age 65, over 65 but under 70, and age 70 and older. The annual exempt amount of earnings is determined by the escalator provisions of the law, based on increases in national earnings. For 1996, the exempt amount of earnings for persons under age 65 was $8280. For persons over age 65 it was $12,500. These amounts will increase in the future with increases in the national wage. After age 70, the individual may earn any amount and no benefits will be withheld.

Even if the earnings exceed the exempt amounts, the individual may be entitled to a part of the benefit. The law provides that for beneficiaries under age 65, $1 in benefits will be withheld for each $2 in earnings in excess of the exempt amount. For persons age 65 and over, $1 in benefits is withheld for each $3 in earnings above the annual limit. Earnings by the retired worker offset not only the retiree's benefits, but those of other family members as well. However, if a family member works, the family member's earnings affect only his or her benefits, not the family benefit.

Because Social Security benefits can be diminished by earnings, it is important to distinguish those types of income that do not bar one from receiving benefits. Among the items that do not count as disqualifying income are (1) pensions and retirement pay, (2) insurance annuities, (3) dividends from stock (unless the person is a dealer in stock), (4) interest on savings, (5) gifts or inheritances of money or property, (6) gain from the sale of capital assets, and (7) rental income (unless the person is a real estate dealer or participating farm landlord).

Taxation of Benefits

Although Social Security benefits were originally exempt from taxes, since 1984 Social Security beneficiaries who have significant income in addition to the Social Security benefits have been taxed on a portion of those benefits. If combined income for a single person is between $25,000 and $34,000, up to 50 percent of benefits may be taxed. For combined income above $34,000, up to 85 percent of benefits may be taxed. For those filing joint returns, the respective break points are $32,000 and $44,000. The Treasury collects taxes paid on Social Security benefits as a part of the income tax and credits them to the Social Security trust funds.

SOUNDNESS OF THE OASDHI PROGRAM

One of the central issues in the debate over passage of the Social Security Act was the system's financing. Many authorities proposed that the federal government support the program out of general revenues; others maintained that it should be financed completely by the contributions of the workers and their employers. The decision was eventually reached that only revenues provided by social security taxes would be used to pay benefits. The intent at that time (and the principle that has, for the most part, been carried down to the present) was that the system should be self-supporting from contributions of covered workers and their employers. The bases for this decision were complex, but one of the primary reasons was to give the participants a legal and moral right to the benefits.[15]

Once the issue of a self-supporting program had been settled, the disagreement centered on whether the program was to be funded with a reserve similar to that used in private insurance or whether it was to be operated on a "pay-as-you-go" basis. The proponents of a "pay-as-you-go" approach eventually prevailed, creating the system currently in use.

Pay-As-You-Go System

Under the *pay-as-you-go system*, those who are eligible receive benefits out of social security taxes paid by those who are working. In turn, today's workers will receive benefits upon retirement from funds that are paid by the labor force at that time. The monies collected are allocated to trust funds, from which the benefits are paid. There are separate trust funds for the Old-Age and Survivors' program, the Disability program, the Hospital Insurance program of Medicare, and the Supplementary Medical Insurance program. The trust funds were conceived as a contingency reserve to cover periodic fluctuations in income, not to fund liabilities to future recipients.

The rationale for the pay-as-you go system seems logical. Given a stable system with a high number of taxpayers to beneficiaries, modest tax rates can support relatively generous benefits. When current workers retire, their retirement benefits will be funded by a new generation of taxpayers (and a presumably larger one, if there is population growth). Moreover, those taxpayers will make contributions based on higher earnings as a result of improved national productivity. In theory, this results in an ever-increasing level of benefits.

Difficulties arise, however, when the relationship between the number of beneficiaries and the number of taxpayers changes adversely. If there are fewer taxpayers to support the benefits, tax rates must rise. That is, in fact, what has happened.

The combined Social Security contributions for employers and employees climbed from a modest $348 in 1965 to $9593 for workers earning $62,700 in 1996, with further increases likely in the future. For the average wage earner, the greatest increase in the cost of living over the past 30 years has been the hike in social security taxes.

The increasing tax for workers covered under the program and the financial difficulties that are predicted stem from two causes: the increasing number of beneficiaries under the program and the increasing level of benefits. In 1947, when only retired persons and survivors were eligible for benefits, about 1 out of every 70 Americans received Social Security checks. With the expansion of the program to include disabled workers and their dependents, by 1996 the fraction of the population

[15]As Franklin D. Roosevelt aptly put it, "Those taxes were never a problem of economics. They are politics all the way through. We put those payroll contributions there so as to give the contributors a legal, moral, and political right to collect their pensions and their unemployment benefits. With those taxes in there, no damn politician can ever scrap my social security program." Quoted in Arthur M. Schlesinger. Jr., *The Coming of the New Deal* (Boston: Houghton Mifflin, 1959), pp. 308f.

receiving benefits had increased to 1 out of 6. More importantly, by 1996 the ratio of taxpayers to beneficiaries had increased to about 1 out of 3. Over the next 35 years, as the large post-World War II baby boom reaches age 65, this ratio will become even worse. In 2029, it is projected that there will be fewer than two taxpayers for each beneficiary.

At the same time that the proportion of the population entitled to benefits has grown, the level of those benefits has also increased. For most periods since the introduction of the automatic adjustment in benefits, average benefits paid to retired workers have increased at a faster rate than the CPI or the increase in wages. As benefits have increased, the percentage of pre-retirement income replaced by Social Security has also risen, from a replacement rate of about 31 percent in 1970 to over 40 percent by 1996.

With the growth in the number of recipients and the increasing level of benefits, the system reached a critical point in the late 1970s. In December 1977, Congress enacted a social security "bailout plan" to save the system from impending bankruptcy. It included the largest peacetime tax increase in the history of the United States up to that time. In signing the 1977 amendments, President Carter stated, "Now this legislation will guarantee that from 1980 to the year 2030, the Social Security funds will be sound." Unfortunately, the measures designed to save the system did not contain a sufficient margin of safety. As a result, the salvation was short-lived and another financing crisis occurred in 1981–1983. By 1981, the system's Board of Trustees warned in its annual report to Congress that, even under the most optimistic assumptions, the OASDHI Trust Fund would be bankrupt by the end of 1982. In mid-1983 Congress enacted legislation, including massive tax increases in 1988 and 1990, an increase in the retirement age beginning in the year 2000, and taxation of Social Security benefits for persons with incomes above a certain level.

In an effort to avoid repetition of what occurred as a result of faulty assumptions in the 1977 legislation, the changes enacted in 1983 were made on the basis of ultra-conservative estimates. Because the economy performed better than had been anticipated, revenues have exceeded disbursements by a significant margin, and the social security trust funds increased from modest contingency funds totaling about $39 billion in 1982 to over $479 billion by 1992. The trust funds are expected to peak in 2013. After 2020-2029, large annual deficits will occur, depleting the fund in 2030.[16]

The dramatic growth in the trust funds that will occur over the next 45 years has led to a new concern over how those funds are invested. By law, the trust funds are invested in U.S. government bonds. In effect, the federal government is borrowing money from the trust funds to cover current operations and is issuing IOUs to the funds. Of course, in the next century, these bonds will have to be redeemed as the trust fund balances are depleted. This leaves the question: Where will the money come from to redeem the bonds? Presumably it will come from taxpayers at that time. In that case, the Social Security funding problem hasn't been resolved. Rather, it has been replaced by a massive new tax problem. This has led some critics

[16] *1995 Annual Report of the Board of Trustees of the Old-Age and Survivors Insurance (OASI) and Disability (DI) Trust Funds.*

to suggest abandoning the current attempt to accumulate large trust funds with high taxes and instead to move closer to a system in which today's taxes are just enough to fund today's benefits. While that will lead to a day of reckoning, they argue, that day will come anyway given how the funds are currently invested. Moreover, they argue, reduced payroll taxes could lead to greater economic growth.

Thus the long-run soundness of the program continues to be a concern. Although the 1983 amendments appear to have solved the system's financial problems for the immediate future, some people believe that the means by which the solution was achieved—increasing the Social Security tax for workers—is a cure worse than the disease. Furthermore, the fundamental imbalance between the workers and recipients will continue to grow, increasing the difficulty of funding benefits to future recipients. At the same time, the automatic cost-of-living adjustments will continue to push the amounts paid out to beneficiaries to higher and higher levels. With the growing imbalance between the number of workers and benefit recipients and the automatic cost-of-living benefit and wage base adjustments, the cost of the program for workers cannot help but escalate even more. Meeting the obligations for benefits promised to workers entering the workforce today will require higher payroll tax rates, including both the employer and the employee share, of up to 40 percent, compared to the current 15 percent.

PROPOSALS FOR CHANGE

In the face of these prospective difficulties, a number of proposals have been made for changes in the system. Some suggest a revision in the financing of the system; others call for a reevaluation of benefit levels.[17]

Proposals For Changes in Financing

The proposals for changes in financing the system have been many and varied. One approach suggests that the increased costs of the system be financed through higher taxes rather than through raising the earnings base. Proponents of this position argue that benefit increases should not be financed by the "painless" process of simply increasing the tax base. Higher tax rates would require all covered workers to share in the increased cost, thereby making the desirability of the increased benefits an issue to be considered by all.

Other proposals for changes in the system's funding take a directly opposite position, maintaining that the system is already highly regressive (most burdensome on low-income groups) and that the tax base should be eliminated completely, with Social Security taxes applying to all income earned. Others of this school have suggested that the system should be financed out of general revenues rather than through a separate tax.

[17]For a summary of the many proposals for change, see Dorcas R. Hardy and C. Colburn Hardy, *Social Insecurity: The Crisis in America's Social Security System and How to Plan Now for Your Own Financial Survival* (New York: Villard Books, 1991).

Proposals for Change in Benefit Levels

The Social Security system was originally developed on the principle that the amount of social insurance benefit should be sufficient to provide a *floor of protection*, meaning an amount sufficient to maintain a minimum standard of living. This floor of protection was then to be supplemented by the individual through private insurance or other devices. Some critics believe that the system currently provides benefits to recipients far in excess of this "floor of protection" level. They have suggested that the level of benefits be limited.

A second proposal for changing the benefits structure focuses on the age for receiving full retirement benefits. When the Social Security Act was passed in 1935, the normal retirement age for benefits was 65. The 1983 Amendments have instituted a gradual increase in this age, to 67 in the year 2022. Some critics argue that this compromise did not go far enough, and that there should be a significant and faster increase in the normal retirement age. They base this argument on the dramatic improvements in life expectancy since 1935, resulting in a much longer period of retirement for current retirees.[18]

Still another proposal argues that the solution to the problem is to permit workers to avail themselves of private alternatives to the Social Security system, through a system of credits for contributions to private retirement programs, such as individual retirement accounts (IRAs), and that the level of contribution to these programs should be increased. In the official report of the U.S. Advisory Council on Social Security which was released in 1996, a minority of the council members recommended that the U.S. Social Security System be *privatized*. Under this proposal, tax funds collected by the Social Security Administration would be invested not in U.S. treasury instruments, as is now the case, but in private stocks and bonds. Whether privatization is the solution to the OASDI funding problems depends on one's point of view, but there is a strong case for the proposal.

According to Professor Martin Feldstein (former chairman of the President's Council of Economic Advisers and professor of economics at Harvard University), the fundamental problem with the Social Security system is the pay-as-you-go financing system. With benefits financed by current tax revenues, the 600 percent increase in the tax rate and the growth in the labor force since the Social Security Act was adopted, has permitted the system to pay retirees significantly more in benefits than those retirees had paid in taxes during their working years. The problem is that the demographics have changed and increasing tax rates as a means of paying out more to beneficiaries than they paid in isn't going to work in the future.

For current workers, and for those who will be entering the labor force, Social Security tax rates will have to increase to balance the aging of the population and the increasing number of retirees relative to those who are working. This means that the rate of return that future workers will receive on their contributions is limited to the rate at which S. S. tax revenues will increase. This, it appears, will be limited to the increases that results from higher incomes and any growth in population. According to Feld-

[18]According to Hardy and Hardy, *Social Insecurity*, in 1935, the remaining life expectancy for a man retiring at age 65 was 11.9 years and for a woman it was 13.2 years. Today, the life expectancy of a 65-year-old male is 16 years and that of a woman of the same age is 19.2 years.

stein, the implicit rate of return that is achievable from these sources is a modest 2.5 percent. Professor Feldstein estimates that if contributions were invested in a funded account earning a real return of 9 percent—roughly the rate that has been earned on funds invested in stocks and bonds in the private sector—the cost of financing Social Security benefits would be cut by about 80 percent. For a person earning $40,000 in 1996, the cost of providing his or her retirement benefit would be cut from $4,960 to about $1,066. The difference—80 percent of the current contribution—would be retained by the individual. This, according to Feldstein, would reduce the national marginal tax rate from about 25 percent to roughly 15 percent.

The difficulty, of course, is that a privatized system could not be achieved immediately. There would be a transition period during which the Social Security Administration would have to continue to pay benefits to existing retirees while new funds are accumulated and invested through the individual accounts. There are several ways in which this could be done.

Many other nations around the world have already done precisely what the minority members of the U.S. Advisory Council on Social Security members recommended, shifting from unfunded pay-as-you-go systems to funded privatized systems. Although the approach adopted by other countries differs in detail, the common thread is requiring that employer and employee contributions be invested in mutual funds or similar private assets.[19]

The extent to which any of the proposals for change will be implemented and whether they will solve the financial problems of the social security system remains to be seen. The financial difficulties in financing the system will remain a haunting problem for our society.

Workers Compensation ■■■■■■■■■■■■■■■■■■■

The workers compensation laws and the insurance these laws require represent another major social insurance program. In Chapter 26, we viewed workers compensation as a part of the organization's liability exposure. From the worker's perspective, however, it is a social insurance program that provides an important element of protection for workers and their dependents. As such, it also represents a part of the social insurance floor of protection on which employee benefit programs build.

Unemployment Insurance ■■■■■■■■■■■■■■■■■■■

In addition to the perils of death and disability, the individual faces loss of income from another source: unemployment. This has been one of the major problems in our economy in the recent past; it promises to become even more critical in the future. Commercial insurance companies cannot deal with the peril of unemploy-

[19]Martin Feldstein, "Time to Privatize Social Security," *The Wall Street Journal,* March 8, 1996.

ment; the government has therefore undertaken a system of *unemployment compensation* to protect members of the society against loss from this ever-present threat.[20]

The unemployment insurance program of the United States is subject to control by both the federal and state governments. This division of control resulted from the reluctance of the states to enact unemployment insurance programs and the manner in which states were encouraged to establish unemployment insurance programs by the federal government. Although reformers had long argued for a system of unemployment insurance, by the middle of the 1930s, only two states (Wisconsin and New York) had established such programs. Most states were reluctant to enact such programs because they feared that their industries would suffer a competitive disadvantage with other states whose firms were not burdened by the cost of such programs. Eventually, the federal government used its power to tax to force states to establish unemployment insurance programs.

The Social Security Act of 1935 imposed a payroll tax of 1 percent on the total wages of all employers who had eight or more employees in each of 20 weeks during the year and who were not exempted because of occupational classification.[21] After imposing the tax, the law went on to provide that employers would be permitted to offset 90 percent of the tax through credit for taxes paid to a state unemployment insurance program meeting standards specified in the law. In effect, this meant that any state that did not enact a qualified unemployment insurance law would experience a financial drain that could be avoided by instituting an unemployment compensation system. It is not surprising that all the states elected to enact programs meeting the conditions required by the federal law and so qualified for the tax offset.

Over time, participation has been extended to include employers of one or more employees in 20 separate weeks or firms that have a quarterly payroll of $1500 or more. In addition, coverage has been extended to nonprofit institutions, state hospitals and educational institutions, municipalities and school districts. In January 1978, coverage was also extended to agricultural workers whose employer's payroll is $20,000 or more per year and to domestic workers of employers with a quarterly payroll of at least $1000.

The tax rate has been increased several times and was 6.2 percent in 1996. The wage base has been reduced from total wages and applied to the first $7000 of each worker's wages in 1996.[22]

---

[20]A few private insurers offer private unemployment insurance in connection with consumer installment debt. The insurance covers the payments on an installment debt when the insured debtor becomes involuntarily unemployed. The amounts of insurance are small, and the coverage is generally overpriced.

[21]The occupations exempted from the act included agricultural employees, domestic employees, crews of vessels on navigable waters of the United States, immediate members of the employer's family, federal government or federal agency employees, state and local government or agency employees, and employees of nonprofit organizations of a religious, charitable, scientific, literary, or educational nature.

[22]The actual tax is 6 percent and the federal retention is 10 percent of the tax, or 0.6 percent. There is also 0.2 percent temporary tax that will be levied by the federal government until all outstanding advances to the Federal Extended Unemployment Compensation Account are repaid, making the federal retention 0.8 percent. The total tax and the federal retention will drop from 6.2 percent and 0.8 percent to 6.0 percent and 0.6 percent respectively, when the Federal Extended Unemployment Compensation Account advances are repaid.

Because each state has enacted separate legislation and operates a separate program, the programs differ considerably in almost every respect. However, it will be useful to discuss their general nature.[23]

ELIGIBILITY FOR BENEFITS

The eligibility requirements vary from state to state, but all call for previous employment in a covered occupation and continued attachment to the labor force as a prerequisite for benefits. A few states cover occupational classifications excluded under the federal standards, but in general the occupations omitted under the federal law are also left out under the state laws.

In addition to the requirement of covered employment (which means that a tax must have been paid on behalf of the worker), other qualifications are also mandated. In most states, the worker must also have earned a certain minimum income during the preceding year, referred to as the *base period*. Some states require that the worker must have been paid a stated dollar minimum during the base period, and a few demand a specified number of weeks of employment with a minimum amount of earnings each week. Most states require the employee to have earned some multiple of the weekly benefit amount that he or she will receive (e.g., 30 times).

Continued attachment to the labor force is also required. The basic philosophy of the unemployment compensation program is that only those workers who are legitimate members of the labor force are eligible for benefits. Therefore, unemployment must be involuntary before the worker can collect benefits, which means that the worker must be willing and able to work. This is the principal reason why benefits are payable through the state employment offices. The worker desiring to draw benefits must present himself or herself at the employment office to collect the money and must be willing to accept suitable work if it is offered.[24] The question of what constitutes suitable employment can be thorny, but normally the administrative staff of the state employment office decides whether the work is appropriate. The worker who feels that he or she has been unfairly treated is entitled to a hearing. Following the philosophy that only those who are involuntarily unemployed are entitled to benefits, most state laws deny or limit benefits to workers who quit without sufficient reason or who are discharged for misconduct.[25]

---

[23]As in the case of the workers compensation laws discussed earlier in the chapter, the student will no doubt want to look at the unemployment compensation act of his or her own state. One of the most up-to-date compilations of the laws of all the states is *The Unemployment Insurance Reporter*, a loose-leaf reporting service published weekly by the Commerce Clearing House in New York.

[24]For example, students not available for work while attending school and women who quit their jobs because of pregnancy or to get married are not eligible for benefits. However, starting in 1978, states are prohibited from automatically disqualifying women from unemployment benefits solely on the basis of pregnancy.

[25]In such circumstances benefits may be completely or only partially forfeited. For example, under the Iowa law a worker discharged for misconduct forfeits four to nine weeks of benefits. A worker who voluntarily quits a job forfeits all benefits for which he or she had accumulated credit in that particular job, but the benefits given up are those accumulated only during the job the worker quit.

AMOUNT AND DURATION OF BENEFITS

The worker who meets the requirements of previous employment and involuntary unemployment is entitled to certain benefits as a matter of right, without the necessity of meeting a needs test. There is no uniformity among the states in the amount of benefits to which the qualified worker is entitled, and the benefits payable in some states are far higher than those in others. Some states have accumulated substantial reserves, whereas others with more generous benefits constantly face depleted accounts.

In all states the amount of the benefits to which the worker is entitled is related to previous earnings. In most states the method of determining benefits is to take some percentage or fraction of the worker's wages during the quarter of highest earnings in his or her base year. One of the most commonly used fractions is 1/26. If the worker was fully employed during the quarter, the 1/26 benefit provides a weekly benefit equal to approximately 50 percent of his or her normal full-time earnings. The amount of the benefit is subject to a state weekly maximum and minimum. Most states now provide for an automatic adjustment of the benefit maximum to coincide with changes in the state's average weekly wage of those in covered employment. A few provide for a sliding maximum based on the number of dependents the unemployed worker has. The maxima in effect under the various state laws in 1995 varied from $133 to $487 a week. Actual payments to recipients on a state-by-state basis in 1995 averaged $173 countrywide. Most states provide for a one-week waiting period before benefits begin, but some states use a shorter waiting period, and in 10 states there is no waiting period.

In addition to imposing limits on the amount, all states stipulate a maximum period for which benefits are payable. In 44 states, this is 26 weeks, whereas in 6 states and the District of Columbia it is longer. The maximum in any state is 39 weeks.[26]

In all states, benefits may be extended during periods of high unemployment by 50 percent for up to 13 weeks under the federal-state *extended unemployment compensation program.* Extended benefits are triggered when the unemployment rate in a state averages 5 percent or more over a 13-week period and is at least 20 percent higher than the rate for the same period in the two preceding years.

FINANCING

The federal law permits the states to impose tax rates higher than the 6.2 percent specified by the federal statute, and also to increase the tax base. A number of states (35 in 1994) have increased the tax base above the federal $7000, and 34 have also elected to levy taxes at a higher rate.

In addition, all states except Alaska have enacted "experience-rating" provisions in their laws that relate the taxes paid by an employer to the benefits that have

[26]In Alaska, California, Connecticut, Hawaii, and Oklahoma, benefits are extended under exclusively state funded programs when unemployment in the state reaches a specified level. In all states benefits may be extended during periods of high unemployment by 50 percent for up to 13 weeks under federal-state extended unemployment compensation program.

been paid out to its former workers who were involuntarily terminated. The basic intent of the experience-rating plans is to promote employment stability by rewarding those employers exhibiting a low turnover rate with a lower premium requirement. The rate paid by the employer under an experience-rated plan is based on the ratio of past premiums paid to past benefits paid. The lower the benefits in relation to tax deposits made by the employer, the lower its current tax rate.[27]

UNEMPLOYMENT COMPENSATION LAWS APPRAISED

From our short discussion, it is apparent that the unemployment insurance programs of the individual states are essentially short term. They are designed to provide additional income to the worker who is temporarily idle—the "between-jobs" worker. In addition, the programs may serve to provide income to jobless workers during periods of cyclical unemployment. The underlying assumption is that the premium tax will be more than sufficient to provide benefits during peak employment periods, with the excess used to meet the additional benefits payable during periods of mass short-run employment. Although the program was devised during a period of mass unemployment, it is not designed to cope with large-scale unemployment over an extended period. Structural and technological unemployment must be met through other income redistribution techniques and retraining of workers.

State unemployment insurance programs serve a variety of functions. Although they provide only a modest level of benefits for a limited period of time, they represent an important part of the individual's floor of protection against fundamental risks. In addition, unemployment insurance exerts a countercyclical influence on the economy. During periods of high employment, payroll taxes drain purchasing power from the economy, dampening inflationary pressures. During periods of high unemployment, benefit payments return purchasing power to consumers and can have a stimulating effect. Finally, state experience-rating programs may have an effect on employment stability, although this influence is probably modest.

✛ Compulsory Temporary Disability Insurance Laws ■

Workers who are incapacitated because of an injury resulting from an industrial accident are entitled to disability income benefits under the workers' compensation laws. In addition, persons in covered employment who are able to work, and are available, and who are involuntarily unemployed, are entitled to unemployment compensation benefits. The OASDHI program, as we have seen, provides disability income benefits for covered employees who become totally and permanently disabled. In spite of the broad coverage of these three programs, there exists an

---

[27]Only the state portion of the tax is subject to experience rating. The federal 0.8 percent remains unchanged.

income risk that is not generally protected under the social insurance programs: loss of income from temporary nonoccupational disability. Although many private employers have established plans covering their employees against loss of income due to nonoccupational injuries, only six jurisdictions require such coverage by law: California, Hawaii, New Jersey, New York, Rhode Island, and Puerto Rico. The basic emphasis of these laws differs from both workers compensation and unemployment insurance. Workers compensation provides protection against job-connected disabilities; unemployment compensation pays benefits to the healthy person who is out of work. The temporary disability laws of these six jurisdictions provide benefits for loss of income from nonoccupational disabilities.

IMPORTANT CONCEPTS TO REMEMBER

social security	currently insured	widow's (widower's) benefit
OASDHI	primary insurance amount	disqualifying income
old-age benefit	(PIA)	trial work period
survivors' benefit	average indexed monthly	pay-as-you-go system
disability benefit	earnings (AIME)	floor of protection
Medicare	children's benefit	unemployment insurance
quarter of coverage	mother's (father's) benefit	base period
FICA tax	lump sum death benefit	compulsory temporary
fully insured	parents' benefit	disability insurance

QUESTIONS FOR REVIEW

1. Identify and briefly describe the four classes of benefits available to those covered under OASDHI.

2. Explain how benefit levels are automatically adjusted under OASDHI. How are the increases in benefits financed?

3. Outline the requirements for "fully insured" status under OASDHI.

4. What benefits does a "fully insured" worker have that a "currently insured" worker does not?

5. What benefits does a worker who is only currently insured have?

6. Under what circumstances can a person who is entitled to social security benefits become ineligible for benefits?

7. Under what conditions is a "children's" benefit payable under social security? How is "child" defined for benefit purposes?

8. Individual states were initially reluctant to enact unemployment insurance laws, fearing that such laws would place their states at a competitive disadvantage. Describe the strategy the federal government used to induce the individual states to enact unemployment insurance laws.

9. Unemployment comes in many forms and is caused by many factors. With what particular forms of unemployment are the state unemployment compensation programs designed to deal?

10. John Jones, Jr. recently dropped out of high school and has been looking for work. Unfortunately, he cannot find employment, primarily because of a lack of work experience and education. He would like to apply for unemployment compensation. Advise him.

QUESTIONS FOR DISCUSSION

1. Many observers have voiced concern about the soundness of the social security system, pointing to the growing number of recipients and the increasing benefit levels. To what extent do you believe that the OASDHI system is still in trouble? What would you recommend in the way of corrective action?

2. The Old Age, Survivors', Disability and Health Insurance program has been called "the greatest chain letter in history." To what aspect of the social security system does this probably refer? Do you agree or disagree with the observation and why?

3. The social security trust funds are invested in U.S. Treasury securities. Although there is little question regarding the safety of these instruments, many observers have expressed alarm over this arrangement. Do you believe that the current arrangement, in which the trust funds are invested in Treasury bonds is a good thing, a bad thing, or a matter of no consequence? Why?

4. For what reasons do you believe that supplemental unemployment benefits have not been more widely adopted as a part of employee benefit programs?

5. Unemployment results in a loss of income regardless of the cause. We should, therefore, eliminate the distinction in social insurance programs between unemployment resulting from occupational or nonoccupational disability and unemployment not connected with disability. Do you agree or disagree?

SUGGESTIONS FOR ADDITIONAL READINGS

Black, Kenneth, Jr. and Harold D. Skipper, Jr. *Life Insurance,* 12th ed. Englewood Cliffs, NJ: Prentice-Hall, 1994. Chapter 25.

Hardy, Dorcas R. and C. Colburn Hardy. *Social Insecurity: The Crisis in America's Social Security System and How to Plan Now for Your Own Survival.* New York, NY: Villard Books, 1991.

Matthews, Joseph L. *Social Security, Medicare and Pensions.* Berkeley, CA: Nolo Press, 1991.

Mehr, Robert I. and Sandra G. Gustavson. *Life Insurance: Theory and Practice.* 4th ed. Plano, Tx.: Business Publications, 1987. Chapter 18.

Myers, Robert J. *Social Security,* 3rd ed. Homewood IL: Richard D. Irwin, 1985.

_____. "A Reappraisal of the Basic Purposes of Social Security." *Journal of the American Society of Chartered Life Underwriters,* vol. XXXI, no. 1 (Jan. 1977).

_____. Will Social Security Have Another Financing Crisis Soon?" *Benefits Quarterly,* Vol. I, No. 1 (First Quarter 1985).

_____. "Social Security's Health Is Really Robust." *Benefits Quarterly,* Vol. V, No. 4, 1989.

Poortvliet, William G. and Thomas P. Laine. "A Global Trend: Privatization and Reform of Social Security Pension Plans," *Benefits Quarterly,* Vol. 11, No. 3 (Third Quarter 1995).

Rejda, G.E. *Social Insurance and Economic Security*, 5th ed. Old Tappan, NJ: Prentice-Hall, 1994.

_____. "Social Security and the Paradox of the Welfare State." *Journal of Risk and Insurance*, Vol. XXXVII, No. 1 (March 1970).

Robertson, A. Haeworth. "Is the Current Social Security Program Financially Feasible in the Long Run?" *Benefits Quarterly*. Vol. I, No. 3 (Third Quarter 1985).

_____. *Social Security: What Every Taxpayer Should Know*. Washington, DC: Retirement Policy Institute, 1992.

Schlesinger, A.M., Jr. *The Coming of the New Deal*. Boston: Houghton-Mifflin. 1959.

Social Security Manual. Cincinnati, OH: National Underwriter Company, 1995.

Thomas, William W., III, ed. *Social Security Manual*. Cincinnati, Oh.: The National Underwriter Co., 1995.

Unemployment Insurance Reporter. A loose-leaf reporting service. New York: Commerce Clearing House.

CHAPTER 32

▓▓▓▓▓▓

Managing Employee Benefits: Life and Disability

CHAPTER OBJECTIVES

When you have finished this chapter, you should be able to

Explain the provisions of the *Internal Revenue Code* relating to the provision of life insurance as an employee benefit.

■

Identify and briefly explain the life insurance products that may be used to provide permanent life insurance protection to employees.

■

Differentiate between *short-term disability* insurance and *long-term disability* insurance.

■

Identify and contrast the alternative definitions of total disability.

■

Identify ways in which benefits are provided for partial disabilities.

■

Explain how the maximum benefit period and the waiting period affect the cost of a disability income insurance policy.

■

Explain how disability income insurance can be integrated with social security and workers compensation benefits.

⬚ Life Insurance as an Employee Benefit ■ ■ ■ ■ ■ ■ ■ ■ ■ ■ ■

Both group life insurance and group health insurance are widely used as part of the compensation package for workers. In part, the growth of group life and health insurance has been encouraged by collective bargaining and the demands of the workforce. A more important impetus has probably been the favorable tax treatment of contributions made by employers for such coverage. Before turning to our discussion of life insurance as an employee benefit, we should first distinguish among the broad classifications of life insurance.

GENERAL CLASSIFICATIONS OF LIFE INSURANCE

In addition to the distinctions among the various types of life insurance contracts, life insurance may also be divided according to the way in which it is marketed. The two major marketing approaches are *ordinary life* insurance, which is sold to individuals, and *group life* insurance, which is marketed through employers or other sponsors and which covers more than one life.[1]

Ordinary Life Insurance

Ordinary life insurance constitutes the oldest and largest of the classes. In ordinary life, individual policies are marketed with a face amount of $1000 or more. Their premiums are paid annually, semiannually, quarterly, or monthly. The main characteristics of ordinary life are purchases on an individual basis and policy amounts of $1000 or more. It currently accounts for about 58 percent of all life insurance in force in the United States.

Group Life Insurance

Group life insurance is a plan whereby coverage can be provided for a number of persons under one contract, called a master policy, usually without evidence of individual insurability. It is generally issued to an employer for the benefit of employees but may also be used for other closely knit groups. The individual members of the group receive certificates as evidence of their insurance, but the contract is between the employer and the insurance company. Group life insurance programs sponsored by an employer may be contributory or noncontributory. Under a contributory plan, which is the more common approach, employer and employees share the cost of the insurance. Under a noncontributory plan, the employer pays the entire cost.

---

[1] In addition to ordinary life and group life, there are two other marketing classes—credit life and industrial life insurance. Credit life is sold in connection with the extension of credit by banks and other lenders and covers the unpaid balance of a loan. Industrial life insurance is marketed to individuals in amounts of $1000 or lower face amount, with the premium paid weekly. Credit life insurance and industrial life insurance account for less than 2 percent of total life insurance in force.

In most states, the groups to which group life insurance may be issued are defined by laws patterned after an NAIC Model Group Life Insurance Law. The NAIC Model Group Life Insurance Law definition includes

1. Current and retired employees of one employer.

2. Multiple employer groups.

3. Members of a labor union.

4. Debtors of a common creditor.

5. Members of associations formed for purposes other than to obtain insurance, provided the association has at least 100 members and has been in existence for at least two years.

6. Members of credit unions.

In addition to these standard groups defined in the NAIC model law, some state laws authorize "any other group approved by the commissioner," generally referred to as "discretionary groups." The requirements for the first six groups are defined in the law, and no specific permission is required for the purchase of insurance by such groups. Discretionary groups require specific approval by the insurance commissioner, which will be granted only if the proposed coverage meets a balancing test set forth in the law. Generally, the laws state that the commissioner will approve such groups if the plan meets three conditions. First, the issuance of the group policy must be judged to be not contrary to the best interest of the public. Second, the insurance of the group policy will result in economies of acquisition or administration costs. Finally, the benefits under the group policy must be reasonable in relation to the premium charged.

The basic feature of group life insurance is the substitution of group underwriting for individual underwriting. This means that no physical examination or other individual underwriting methods are applicable to individual employees. The insurance company's major problem is, therefore, that of holding adverse selection to a minimum, and many of the features of group life insurance derive from this requirement. For example, when the premium is paid entirely by the employer, 100 percent of the eligible employees must be included. When the plan is contributory, with the premium paid jointly by the employer and the employees, not less than 75 percent of the eligible employees must participate. Furthermore, the amount of insurance on each participant must be determined by some plan that will preclude individual selection. In most instances, either the amount of insurance is a flat amount for all employees, or it is determined as a percentage or multiple of the individual's salary. It should be obvious that if group life insurance were provided without any required minimum number or percentage of employees, and if the employees could choose to enter the plan or stay out, a disproportionate number of impaired individuals would subscribe to the insurance. If the employee could choose the amount of insurance, the impaired lives would tend to take large amounts, whereas those in good health would opt for only small amounts. For group insurance to be practical, safeguards must be provided to prevent and minimize the element of adverse selection.

Although the original group idea of substituting group underwriting and group marketing for individual underwriting and marketing, group underwriting has changed somewhat since the beginning of group life insurance. Under the first group life insurance laws, the definition of "groups" for insurance purposes were restrictive, requiring a minimum number of members, usually 50 or 100 lives.[2] Over time, statutory requirements concerning the minimum number of individuals in a "group" have shrunk, and with the decrease in the number, the nature of group underwriting has changed. As the minimum number of members required for group coverage fell, insurers introduced elements of individual underwriting for smaller groups. Although group underwriting is still used for large groups, state laws often allow insurers the right to require evidence of individual insurability on groups. Whether an insurer will require evidence of individual insurability for group coverage depends on the size and nature of the group.

Group life insurance has become an important branch of life insurance today, accounting for about 40 percent of total life insurance in force. For many persons who would not be insurable under ordinary life insurance, it provides the only means for obtaining coverage. For others, the low-cost group life insurance is an excellent supplement to the individual life insurance program.

GROUP TERM LIFE INSURANCE

The *Internal Revenue Code*, Section 79, exempts from taxable income of employees amounts paid by their employer on the first $50,000 of group term life insurance. Although the premium on such coverage is not taxable to the employee, it is nevertheless deductible by the employer as a business expense.

Prior to 1964, the premiums paid by employers for group term life insurance on employees were totally exempt from the employee's income. Some companies took undue advantage of the exclusion by providing large amounts of group term life insurance on executives. The IRS was particularly dissatisfied with the arrangement, and persuaded Congress to enact Section 79 of the IRC, which sanctions an exclusion only for the premiums paid on the first $50,000 of group-term life insurance. For each $1000 of coverage in excess of $50,000, the employee must include as income an amount that represents the taxable value of the premium paid by the employer. The taxable value of group term life insurance in excess of $50,000 is not the amount actually paid by the employer, but rather an imputed cost contained in the regulations.[3] Section 79 provides that the cost shall be determined on the basis of uniform premiums computed on the basis of five-year age brackets. Table 32.1 indicates the rates that are used in imputing income to employees for group term life insurance in excess of $50,000.

A group term life insurance plan will be considered nondiscriminatory if it does not discriminate in favor of key employees as to eligibility and amount of benefits. A plan is nondiscriminatory if it benefits 70 percent or more of all employees; at

[2]The first NAIC model group law, adopted in 1917, set the minimum for groups at 50. Many states reduced this to 25, and the number has gradually dropped to 10.
[3]See *IRS Regulations*, Section 1.79-3(d)(2).

Table 32.1   Uniform Premiums for $1000 Group Term Life Insurance

5-year Age Bracket	Cost per month
Under 30	$.08
30 to 34	.09
35 to 39	.11
40 to 44	.17
45 to 49	.29
50 to 54	.48
55 to 59	.75
60 to 64	1.17

least 85 percent of all employees who are plan participants are not key employees; and the plan benefits employees who qualify under a classification established by the employer and found by the IRS not to discriminate in favor of key employees.[4]

The requirement that the group term insurance benefits not discriminate can be satisfied if the amount of insurance bears a uniform relationship to total compensation of the persons covered. This means that a formula that provides life insurance equal to, say, two times the individual's annual salary is nondiscriminatory, even though it produces a higher amount of life insurance for more highly compensated individuals.

Contributory-Noncontributory Plans

Group life insurance programs sponsored by an employer may be contributory or noncontributory. Under a contributory plan, the employer and employee share the cost of the insurance, and at least 75 percent of the eligible employees must participate. Under a noncontributory plan, whereby the employer pays the entire premium, all employees (or all employees in a particular class) must be covered. Contributory plans are the most common arrangement. Under a contributory plan, the employee pays, normally through payroll deduction, a flat rate regardless of age, and employer pays the balance. Usually, the cost is not shared equally between the employee and the employer, and the employer pays a larger share of the cost than does the employee. The customary flat charge paid by the employees is 60 cents per month per $1000 of insurance, although this may be higher or lower in some states. The employer's contribution will be quite substantial for

---

[4]If a group term insurance plan discriminates in favor of key employees, the key employees are taxed on the value of the benefits, but the benefits remain tax exempt to other workers. Under a technical correction in the Tax Reform Act of 1986, the taxable value of coverage provided to key employees under a discriminatory plan is the greater of (1) the actual cost or (2) the cost indicated in the Section 79 cost table.

older employees, yet the employer's contribution for all employees remains relatively constant. As older employees retire, die, or leave the firm, their places are taken by younger workers, and as a consequence the age composition of the group remains quite stable. Under a noncontributory plan, the employer pays the entire cost of the program.

Another important distinction between a contributory plan and a noncontributory plan is that a noncontributory plan has only a probationary period, whereas a contributory plan has both a probationary period and an eligibility period. Under a noncontributory plan, the probationary period is usually a period of one to six months, during which the employee is not covered but after which coverage is automatic. Under a contributory plan, the probationary period is followed by an eligibility period (usually 31 days) during which the new employee can apply for group coverage without evidence of insurability. After the end of the eligibility period, the insurer may require evidence of insurability if the employee requests coverage.

Cost

The cost of group life insurance is comparatively low. The reasons are quite simple. First, the basic plan under which most group life insurance is provided is yearly renewable term insurance, which provides the lowest cost form of protection per premium dollar. For employer-sponsored plans, the flow of insureds through the group maintains a stable average age as older employees retire, die, or leave the firm and their places are taken by younger workers. Second, the expenses of medical examinations and other methods of determining insurability are largely dispensed. Third, group life involves mass selling and mass administration with the result that expenses per life insured will be less under group policies than under the marketing of individual policies. In addition, when group life insurance is offered as an employee benefit, the tax advantage noted above reduces the cost of insurance to employees, who would have to receive something more in salary than the amount paid by the employer to purchase an equivalent amount of life insurance individually.[5]

Most group insurance is experience-rated; that is, the group's past experience affects the premium. If the group's experience was good (i.e., better than average), then both participating and nonparticipating companies allow a credit to the policyowner. This credit, usually referred to as a dividend, actually takes the form of a reduction in the next year's premium. Of course, experience rating can also reflect bad experience. When this is the case, the premium for the next year is increased.

Coverage Terms

The coverage of most group life insurance contracts is extremely liberal; there are no exclusions, and the insurance proceeds are paid for death from any cause, including suicide, without restrictions as to time. In addition, most policies include a conversion provision, under which the insured employee may, within 31 days after termination of

---

[5]For example, an employee in a 28 percent tax bracket would have to receive $277 in before-tax income to pay the equivalent of $200 in premiums contributed by the employer for group life insurance.

employment, convert all or a portion of the insurance to any form of individual policy currently offered by the insurance company, with the exception of term insurance. Conversion is at the attained age of the employee, and the insurance company cannot refuse conversion because of the worker's uninsurability.

GROUP PERMANENT LIFE INSURANCE

Group permanent life insurance plans are those in which a permanent benefit accrues to the plan participant. This permanent benefit may be used to provide retirement benefits to the employee or to create group paid-up insurance. Group permanent insurance differs from group term insurance in that a benefit accumulates to which the employee will be entitled upon leaving the group.

Under group permanent life insurance, the premium paid by the employer is divided into two parts. One part is used to fund the cash value of the contract and thus does not qualify for the tax exemption under Section 79. The other part goes to pay the term insurance portion of the plan. The employee pays the permanent premium or is taxed on the premium paid by the employer. IRS regulations determine the minimum value of the permanent insurance benefit, which may be greater than the premium allocated by the life insurance company.

Group Paid-Up Life Insurance

Group paid-up life is designed to provide a limited amount of permanent insurance to employees at retirement. This is usually achieved through the purchase of paid-up units of single-premium whole life insurance during the employee's working years in combination with decreasing term insurance. The whole life units are purchased by the employee's contribution. As the amount of paid-up whole life increases, the employee's contribution is usually reduced. At retirement, the employee may withdraw the cash value or leave the policy in force for the remainder of his or her life.

Group Universal Life

Group Universal Life is similar in most respects to individual universal life and differs primarily in the same ways that other forms of group life differ from individual contracts. Usually coverage is written without evidence of insurability and is subject to lower administrative costs than individually written universal life. There is no tax advantage in employer funding, and premiums are generally paid by employees.

Retired Lives Reserve

Usually, the employer's deductible contribution for group term insurance for employees terminates when the employee retires. Retired lives reserve is a mechanism for funding the continuation of yearly renewable term after the employee's retirement. The employer makes contributions to a trust fund during the employee's working years in an amount sufficient to fund the cost of term insurance after the worker retires.

Survivor Income Benefit Insurance

Survivor income benefit insurance (SIBI) is life insurance payable to dependents as a monthly benefit rather than in a lump sum. The coverage is unique because payment on the benefit depends on the beneficiary's status. For example, the monthly benefit to a surviving spouse terminates if the spouse remarries. Otherwise, benefit payments continue until the spouse reaches a specified age (usually 65) or until he or she dies. SIBI benefits are payable to children until they reach a specified age, usually age 19 or until age 23 if attending school on a full-time basis. The child's benefit also terminates if the child dies or remarries. SIBI may be written as a rider to another form of group life insurance, or it may be written as a separate contract.

EMPLOYEE DEATH BENEFIT

Under the provisions of the IRC, an employer can make payments to a deceased employee's widow, children, or other beneficiaries, even if there is no legal or moral obligation to do so. Thus the question arises as to whether the employer's payments will be treated as a gift to the recipient. Generally, the position of the IRS is that such payments are compensation for prior services rendered by the deceased employee rather than a gift.

Section 101(b) of the IRC attempts to eliminate or reduce the controversy in this area by providing an automatic exclusion of the first $5000 paid by an employer to the employee's beneficiaries. When the employer's payments exceed $5000, the beneficiaries may still be able to exclude the entire amount received as a gift, if they are able to show gratuitous intent on the part of the employer.

❖ Disability Income Benefits ■ ■ ■ ■ ■ ■ ■ ■ ■ ■ ■ ■ ■ ■ ■ ■ ■

Two separate types of insurance are included in the generic term "health insurance": *disability income insurance*, which provides periodic payments when the insured is unable to work because of sickness or injury, and *medical expense insurance*, which pays the costs of medical care that result from sickness or injury. In this chapter, we deal with the first type, disability income. Coverage for the expenses relating to health care is discussed in the next chapter.

NEED FOR DISABILITY INCOME PROTECTION

Because disability can be both total and permanent, the exposure ranks in severity with the death of the wage earner. In fact, some authorities argue that loss-of-income protection should come even before life insurance. When a wage earner is disabled, his or her earnings stop just as surely as if death had occurred. This "living death" of disability can be economically more severe than actual death. If the breadwinner of the family dies, the family's income stops; if he or she is disabled, not only does the income stop but expenses remain the same and usually increase. Because a disabled person—by definition—is one whose ability to work is impaired, he or she must depend on sources other than employment for income. When persons other than the disabled individual were also supported by the lost income, the problem is compounded. The disability income protection provided by employers as an employee benefit addresses this important exposure.

Protection Available from Other Sources

Employees who suffer a disabling injury that occurs in the course of their employment are entitled to the workers compensation benefits discussed in Chapter 26. In addition, workers in California, Hawaii, New Jersey, New York, Rhode Island, and Puerto Rico are covered for nonoccupational disabilities by compulsory programs, under which the benefits are also prescribed by law. Finally, workers who are totally and permanently disabled and who meet special eligibility requirements for disability under the federal Old-Age, Survivors, and Disability Insurance program qualify for benefits under that program.

Besides these government-sponsored or -supervised programs, the most common source of recovery is employee benefit programs. Many employers provide paid sick leave, usually up to some maximum, such as 30 days. This modest form of protection may be supplemented by disability income benefits. When disability income protection is provided as an employee benefit, coverage is often purchased from a commercial insurer. Although some larger employers partially or totally self-insure the exposure, even in these cases the scope of the protection usually follows the format developed by commercial insurers.

Extent of Coverage for Disability

Because of some overlap, it is difficult to measure precisely the extent of disability income coverage applicable to the labor force. Excluding the coverage under workers compensation laws and the OASDI program, approximately two-thirds of the U.S. labor force had some sort of disability income coverage by 1995. About 57 percent of nongovernment workers and self-employed persons were covered under short-term disability plans, including sick leave programs.[6] Of this total, about two-thirds were insured with commercial insurers.[7] At the same time, slightly less than 30 percent of the nongovernment labor force had long-term disability protection, all of which was provided through commercial insurers. Because some workers participate in both short- and long-term programs, total coverage is less than would be suggested by combining these two categories.

---

[6]When persons covered under the state compulsory temporary disability plans and railroad workers are excluded, the total covered for short-term disability is less than 50 percent of the nongovernment labor force.

[7]Health Insurance Institute, *Source Book of Health Insurance Data* (New York: Health Insurance Institute, 1995).

GENERAL NATURE OF DISABILITY INCOME INSURANCE

Disability income insurance provides periodic payments to the person insured when he or she is unable to work because of injury or illness. Coverage may be provided for disabilities resulting from accidents only or for disabilities resulting from accidents or sickness. Coverage for disability resulting from sickness only is rarely written. Benefit eligibility presumes a loss of income, but in practice this is usually defined as the inability to pursue an occupation.

Methods of Marketing

Disability income insurance is marketed through groups and to individuals. Approximately four-fifths of the disability income insurance in the United States is sold on a group basis. Group underwriting in the disability income field employs much the same principle as does group life insurance. A minimum-sized group is required, and its nature must be such that insurance is incidental to its existence. In other words, the group cannot be organized primarily for the purpose of purchasing the group insurance. Most group disability income coverage is written under employer-sponsored employee benefit plans, but some is also written under association group plans.

As in the case of group life insurance, the group approach to disability income insurance provides some economies. The insurer enjoys some freedom from adverse selection, and the employer usually performs certain administrative functions. Finally, the agent usually receives a lower commission rate.

SHORT-TERM VERSUS LONG-TERM DISABILITY COVERAGE

In addition to the distinction between group and individual marketing, a distinction among disability income coverage is drawn on the basis of the periods for which coverage is provided. *Short-term disability* insurance provides coverage for disabilities up to two years, whereas *long-term disability* protects the individual for a longer time, often until age 65 for illness and for life in the case of accident. Short-term disability policies are written with benefit periods of 13, 26, 52, or 104 weeks. Long-term disability policies, also called LTD policies, provide benefits for 5 years, 10 years, until age 65, or even for the lifetime of the insured.

The distinction between short-term disability and long-term disability is not merely in the length of time for which benefits are payable. The short-term/long-term distinction also reflects a difference in pricing, in underwriting, and in the breadth of coverage. The earliest forms of disability income coverage provided indemnity for 13 weeks. Gradually, the period was extended, first to 26 weeks and eventually to one year and finally to two years. The disinclination of insurers to provide coverage for longer periods reflects the caution insurers felt was required in a field in which the potential for both morale and moral hazard exists. When long-term disability contracts were eventually placed on the market, insurers did so with some apprehension. In time, it became clear that the long-term disability exposure was an insurable one and that the underwriting considerations that had deterred insurers from offering the coverage could be addressed. Because most disabilities are short term, the insurer's risk decreases as the contract lengthens. A 26-week plan does not cost twice as much as one for 13 weeks. Most disabilities will not exceed 13 weeks, so the insurer does not have to pay out twice as much in benefits under a 26-week plan. The longer the contract, other things being equal, the lower the cost of the additional protection. Approximately 82 percent of the short-term disability coverage and 78 percent of the long-term disability coverage are sold through groups.

DISABILITY INCOME UNDERWRITING AND PRICING

Disability income insurance is a field in which moral hazard and morale hazard are high. These hazards are reflected in insurers' underwriting and marketing practices and explain some of the unusual features in the disability income field. Insurers are cautious about the amount of coverage they are willing to allow on a given individual and exhibit a concern about adverse selection that to the detached observer seems to border on obsession.

Occupational Classes and Underwriting

Nearly 150 years ago, one of the earliest insurers to offer insurance coverage with benefits to bodily injury that did not cause death, the Accidental Death Association, recognized the necessity for differences in rates for different occupations. Interestingly, its classification system divided risks into four classes: (1) professional, (2) master tradesmen doing no manual labor, (3) mechanics or operative classes, and (4) all others, who were considered the most hazardous.[8] After a century of experimentation with more sophisticated classification systems, modern insurers generally classify insureds into categories that are surprisingly similar. Although the defining characteristics may vary, the most common rating classes today divide risks into professional, white collar, and blue collar, in descending order of underwriting desirability. Not only do these occupational classes affect rates, but they affect the breadth of the coverage that will be offered as well. Coverage for blue-collar workers may have more restrictive definitions of disability, and may provide coverage for a shorter period and for lesser amounts.

Group Versus Individual Coverage

In the field of life insurance and group medical expense insurance, group policies tend to be more liberal in their provisions than individual policies, with fewer restrictions and a generally more liberal underwriting attitude. In the disability income field, group policies are often more restrictive in their coverage features than individual policies. Although group policies tend to be cheaper than individual policies, they are also likely to include restrictive provisions that are not imposed in individual policies.

---

[8]Edwin J. Faulkner, *Health Insurance* (New York: McGraw-Hill, 1960), pp. 513-514.

Actually, the demarcation in liberality of policy provisions in disability income insurance is not the group-individual dichotomy, but rather between short-term and long-term coverage. Although the insurer's potential liability may be greater under a long-term disability policy than under a short-term policy, the different classes insured under short-term and long-term coverage and the difference in coverage features permit somewhat more liberal features in LTD policies. Short-term disability insurance tends to cover blue-collar workers, whereas long-term disability is more often sold to cover white-collar and professional employees.

DISABILITY INCOME CONTRACTS

Because there is no such thing as a standard disability income policy, the discussion of this kind of coverage must focus on the differences in the provisions likely to be included in such contracts. The following features, which reflect differences among the contracts offered by commercial insurers, are also incorporated into the provisions of self-funded disability income programs.

Perils Covered

The disability income policy may provide coverage for loss of income caused by accident, or it may cover loss of income that results from either accident or sickness. Few companies are willing to sell disability income protection covering the peril of sickness only. The reason, of course, is the moral hazard involved. It is relatively easy to feign sickness, but it is more difficult to feign accidental injury. For the same reason, insurance companies will not sell disability income protection to homemakers; it is difficult to determine when a homemaker is disabled.

When a disability income policy is written to cover both sickness and accidents, the intervals for which benefits are payable may be different, depending on the cause of the disability. Thus one policy will pay benefits for two years if the disability is brought on by illness and for five years if it results from accident. Long-term contracts often pay to age 65 for sickness and for life if the disability results from accident.

Occupational-Nonoccupational Disability

Another important distinction in the disability insurance field is between policies that cover both occupational and nonoccupational disabilities and those that cover nonoccupational disabilities only. Some disability income policies exclude losses arising out of the occupation of the insured for which the insured is entitled to receive workers compensation benefits. These contracts are called *nonoccupational disability insurance.* Most short-term disability income coverage is written on a nonoccupational basis, but some policies provide workers compensation "wrap around" coverage, which supplements workers compensation benefits. In the event of occupational injury, the benefit is equal to the difference between the workers compensation payment and the payment under the policy for nonoccupational disabilities. This then provides the same income replacement for the individual whether the injury is occupational or nonoccupational.

Long-term disability may be written on a nonoccupational basis or may provide coverage for both occupational and nonoccupational disabilities ("24-hour coverage"). When coverage is written on an occupational basis, some insurers provide for a reduction in benefits equal to the amount received under workers compensation, whereas still others pay the full policy benefit regardless of the occupational or nonoccupational character of the injury.

Waiting Periods

The *waiting period* in disability income policies acts like a deductible, forcing the insured to bear a part of the loss. The purpose of the waiting period is to eliminate coverage for short-term disabilities of the "sniffle" type and to help to control the morale hazard. Waiting periods of 3, 7, 15, 30, 60, 90, 180, and 365 days are available. As might be expected, short-term disability coverage generally has shorter waiting periods than long-term coverage. Although coverage for losses resulting from accident may be written without a waiting period, a three-day waiting period is about as short a time as it is possible to purchase under sickness coverage. In addition, the waiting period in a given contract may differ for accident and sickness losses. One widely used plan in the short-term disability income field is the "1-8-26" formula. This coverage provides benefits from the first day if the disability results from an accident and from the eighth day if it is caused by illness. The "26" indicates the number of weeks for which benefits are payable. Waiting periods for long-term disability coverage range upward from 30 days, and most coverage is written with longer waiting periods.

Limitations on Amount of Coverage

Ideally, the disability income policy should restore the income of the incapacitated worker as closely as possible to what was earned before the disability. However, insurance companies typically limit the amount of coverage under short-term policies to a percentage of gross weekly income, usually from 50 to 70 percent, with 66 2/3 percent being the most common. Coverage may also be set at a flat amount (e.g., $500 per week), or it may be based on a schedule, with a weekly benefit specified for different salary ranges. Under long-term contracts, coverage is sometimes written for as much as 70 percent of the worker's monthly wage, but most insurers impose a dollar limit (such as $3000 or $4000) on the maximum monthly benefit that will be provided. Such limits are considered necessary to prevent moral hazard. If a policy could be purchased that would pay as much as or more than the worker's regular income, there would be an incentive to feign illness and contrive accidents. In addition, the worker collecting benefits would have little reason to return to the job as quickly as possible.

Because of the potential for morale hazard, LTD policies sometimes include a provision relating to income the insured may have from other sources. Other income might include, for example, Social Security benefits or disability benefits under a corporate pension plan. In some cases, income from such sources serves as an offset against the policy's benefits, and the amount of the income is subtracted from the benefits payable. In other instances, the policy may provide for a cap on benefits if income from all sources exceeds a percentage of the insured's pre-disability income (e.g., 70 percent). When an LTD policy includes an income offset or cap on total income received, there may be an exception for social security benefits, called a *Social Security Freeze*. The Social Security Freeze provision provides a modest element of protection against inflation; it provides that increases in social security benefits after LTD payments have commenced will not reduce the LTD benefits.

Definitions of Disability Income Policies

The definitions are of utmost importance in disability income policies, for the broadness of the coverage is based on the definitions of "disability," "injury," and "sickness."

Definition of Disability Disability may be defined in various ways, but most definitions fall into one of three categories:

- The inability of the insured to engage in his or her own occupation.
- The inability of the insured to engage in any reasonable occupation for which he or she is or might easily become qualified.
- The inability of the insured to engage in any occupation.

The most liberal, of course, is the one that defines disability as the inability of the insured to engage in his or her own occupation, and the narrowest, as the inability to engage in any occupation. Short-term disability coverage almost universally uses the *any* occupation definition.

Most long-term policies use one or a combination of the first two definitions. Many policies use a split definition that defines disability as the inability of the insured to engage in his or her occupation for some initial period (e.g., two years) and the inability to engage in any occupation for which he or she is suited or might become qualified after that period. This time period, which was originally two years, has gradually increased as a result of competition among insurers. For example, if a dentist should lose his or her right arm in an accident, he or she will be totally disabled in the occupation of dentistry, and the benefits will be paid. However, if a college professor teaching economics should lose his or her right arm, the loss presumably will have little effect on his or her ability to engage in that occupation. But after a period of two years, if the dentist is able to pursue some occupation for which he or she is reasonably fitted by education, training, or experience, or for which he or she becomes reasonably suited, the benefits will then cease. Therefore, if the dentist becomes a faculty member in a dental college or a sales representative for a dental supply firm, it will be a job for which education, training, or experience have prepared him or her. Of course, if the policyholder is hospitalized, or if a sickness or an accident keeps the individual confined to bed, disability will exist under any of these definitions.

Definition of Injury The most common definition of injury today is "accidental bodily injury," which requires that the result (bodily injury) be accidental or unintended. Older policies sometimes used the definition of "bodily injury by accidental means," which required not only that the result must have been accidental, but also that the cause of the injury must have been accidental.

Definition of Sickness   The definition of sickness is often used to exclude preexisting conditions in disability contracts.[9] For example, the definition of sickness in one contract specifies that "The company will pay the total disability benefit for total disability resulting from sickness first manifesting itself while the policy is in force."

Thus coverage would be provided for a preexisting condition that did not manifest itself until after the inception of the policy. Group disability income plans tend to have either no exclusions or limited exclusions for preexisting conditions. A typical exclusion might eliminate coverage for a disability starting within one year of inception if the sickness was diagnosed or treated in the year prior to being covered.

Exclusions in Disability Income Contracts

Although the coverage of the policy is generally defined and limited by the insuring agreement and the policy definitions, group disability income coverage provided as an employee benefit has relatively few exclusions. Nonoccupational contracts may bar work-connected injuries by an exclusion or in the insuring agreement. Pregnancy is generally not excluded in group plans. Federal and state laws require that disability plans offered by most employers treat disability from pregnancy or childbirth the same as any other disability.[10]

Payments for Other than Total Disability

Although disability coverage is usually payable only when the insured is totally disabled, some contracts provide for payment of a reduced benefit when the insured resumes work on a partial basis after a period of total disability. The two approaches to the payment of such benefits are a *partial disability benefit* and a *residual disability benefit.*

Partial Disability Benefit   Partial disability is usually defined as the inability to perform some specified percentage of the duties of the insured's usual occupation. A common definition of partial disability is "the inability of the insured to perform some, but not all of the important duties of his or her occupation," or "the inability to engage in his or her regular occupation for longer than one-half the time normally spent in performing the usual duties of the regular occupation." If the individual cannot perform the duties of the job, it is presumed that his or her income will decrease, but partial disability does not base its benefits on the reduction in income. It is based on the inability to perform the specified percentage of the functions that constitute the person's normal job. The customary payment under a partial disability benefit is a monthly indemnity equal to one-half the monthly benefit for total disability. Usually, the partial disability benefit is payable for the period of partial disability, but not exceeding a specified term, such as five or six months. The provision usually states that it will be payable only for a partial disability that immediately follows a period of total disability for which benefits were payable. In fact, one of the motivations for

---

[9]Preexisting conditions are not normally excluded under group contracts.

[10]In some individual policies, preexisting conditions are eliminated by an exclusion rather than by the definition of sickness. Some individual disability policies exclude normal pregnancy (depending on the state), but disability from complications of pregnancy would generally be covered.

offering partial disability coverage was as an encouragement for the insured to resume employment as quickly as possible, even on a part-time basis.

Residual Disability Benefit   Increasingly, a somewhat different provision is used to provide benefits for partial disabilities. As in the case of the partial disability benefit discussed earlier, a *residual disability benefits* provision provides coverage for partial disabilities but focuses on the amount of income lost rather than on the physical inability to work. Residual disability coverage is particularly appropriate for self-employed persons, who may suffer a loss of income after returning to work, even though they are now capable of performing all of the functions of their occupation (owing to a loss of clients, for example).

The amount of the benefit is tied to the amount of lost income. For example, an insured suffering a 40 percent loss of income would be paid 40 percent of the benefit that would be payable for total disability. Insureds must usually have a 20 percent income loss to be eligible for the residual disability benefit. Although some policies require a prior total disability, it is increasingly common for residual disability benefits to cover lost income because of accident or sickness even in the absence of a prior total disability.

Although there is a similarity between the partial disability benefit and the residual disability benefit, there are important differences. A partial disability benefit is payable in an amount equal to one-half the total disability benefit, regardless of the reduction in earnings. In contrast, the residual disability benefit is payable in proportion to the individual's reduced earnings. In addition, coverage under a partial disability benefit is limited to a specified period such as five or six months. Residual disability benefits are usually not limited in duration, other than the maximum benefit period provided under the basic plan.

Rehabilitation Provision   In addition to the partial disability and residual disability benefits, some long-term disability contracts include a *rehabilitation provision*, which provides for continuation of disability benefits or other financial assistance while a totally disabled person is retraining or attempting to acquire skills to return to work.

Presumptive Disability   Some contracts include a provision entitled *presumptive disability*, which provides that loss of the use of two bodily members or the loss of sight will be considered as total disability, regardless of whether the insured can do any work for remuneration. This means that an insured who suffers a stroke, for example, and loses the use of an arm and leg, would be entitled to full benefits under the policy, even though the crippling of these members did not affect the person's income-earning ability.

Cost-of-Living Adjustment Benefit   The *cost-of-living adjustment benefit* is designed to offset the decline in purchasing power of disability benefits that result from inflation. Under this provision, disability benefits are increased by the lesser of the increase in the consumer price index or a percentage specified in the policy. The percentage specified is usually 5 to 10 percent, and the increase applies after disability benefits have been paid for a year.

Accidental Death and Dismemberment   Some disability income policies provide a death benefit, expressed as some multiple of the weekly benefit specified in the policy (e.g., 200 weeks) to be paid to a beneficiary if the insured dies as a result of accidental bodily injury. The policy usually provides that death must occur within 90 days from the date of the accident claimed to be the cause of death. In addition to the principal amount payable in the event of death, there is usually a scaled-down benefit payable for loss of sight or loss of a body member. For example, a policy might provide payment of a sum equal to 200-weeks indemnity in the event of the death, and a schedule such as the following for dismemberment:

Payable in the event of death by accidental bodily injury	200 weeks
Loss of 2 hands, feet, or sight of both eyes	200 weeks
Loss of one hand and one foot	200 weeks
Loss of one hand	100 weeks
Loss of one foot	100 weeks
Loss of sight of one eye	65 weeks
Loss of thumb and index finger	50 weeks

In addition to its inclusion in some disability income policies, this accidental death and dismemberment coverage may be written as a separate contract. In such cases, the face amount is expressed as a dollar limit rather than a number of weeks. The indemnity for loss of members or loss of sight is expressed as a percentage of the principal amount:

Payable in the event of death by accidental bodily injury	Principal sum
Loss of 2 hands, feet, or sight of 2 eyes	Principal sum
Loss of one hand and one foot	Principal sum
Loss of one hand	Principal sum
Loss of one foot	1/2 principal sum
Loss of sight of one eye	1/3 principal sum
Loss of thumb and index finger	1/4 principal sum

As in the case of the double indemnity provision of the life insurance policy, there is no logic whatsoever to this form of coverage. If an individual dies, his or her family's need is the same regardless of whether the death is caused by accident or otherwise.

DESIGN OF A DISABILITY INCOME BENEFIT PROGRAM

From the variety of provisions discussed, it is clear that the cost of disability income benefit program can be controlled by the design of the program. A major goal in this respect is to coordinate the benefits of the disability income coverage with protection from other sources, most notably OASDI and workers compensation insurance. In addition, when the firm also offers paid sick leave, the waiting period under the program should be coordinated with the paid sick leave program.

As in the case of workers compensation claims, a major cost-control measure for a disability income program is rehabilitation. It is generally agreed that it is beneficial to the employer and to the disabled person to encourage the employee to return to work as soon as possible. For this reason, the design of a disability income program should include some consideration for the return of disabled workers to gainful employment. For temporary disabilities, this may involve a return to *light duty* or a gradual return to the individual's previous position. For permanent disabilities, it may include vocational evaluation and retraining for a different occupational specialty. Under the provisions of the Americans With Disabilities Act, the employer will be required to make reasonable accommodations to facilitate the disabled worker's employment.

TAXATION OF DISABILITY INCOME BENEFITS

The tax treatment of disability income benefits has an important effect on the amount of income that needs to be replaced. Sick pay and other disability income payments that have been paid for by the employer are treated essentially the same as wages and are taxable to the employee. If the employee was required to contribute to the disability income plan as a condition for being covered, the portion of the benefits paid for by the employee is received tax free.[11]

IMPORTANT CONCEPTS TO REMEMBER

ordinary life insurance
group life insurance
group term life insurance
I.R.C. Section 79
contributory plan
noncontributory plan
group permanent life
   insurance
group paid-up life insurance
group universal life
   insurance

retired lives reserve
survivor income benefit
   insurance
employee death benefit
short-term disability
   coverage
long-term disability
   coverage
occupational disability
nonoccupational disability
accidental bodily injury

bodily injury by accidental
   means
disability
partial disability
sickness
social security substitute
presumptive disability
preexisting condition
waiting period
residual disability benefit
rehabilitation provision

QUESTIONS FOR REVIEW

1. Distinguish between individual and group life insurance arrangements and identify the sources of the cost advantage for group life insurance.

2. Explain the provisions of the *Internal Revenue Code* relating to the provision of group term life insurance as an employee benefit.

3. Identify and briefly explain the life insurance products that may be used to provide permanent life insurance protection to employees.

[11]Disability income benefits received from individually owned disability income policies are not subject to the federal income tax. Premiums paid by individuals for disability income insurance is not deductible for federal income tax purposes.

4. In what way(s) does the substitution of group underwriting for individual underwriting produce economies?

5. Describe the benefit to employees when the employer offers the option of obtaining group term life insurance in excess of the $50,000 limit permitted by the *Internal Revenue Code.*

6. Describe the tax treatment of permanent life insurance that is provided as a part of an employee benefit package.

7. What sources of protection other than disability income insurance may the individual have to protect against loss of earnings? Why is disability income insurance a necessary supplement to these forms of protection?

8. In your own words, explain the basic difference between the two common definitions of sickness contained in disability income policies. Explain which would be preferable from the insured's point of view and why.

9. Briefly distinguish between long-term and short-term disability income contacts. Of what significance is the distinction other than with respect to the time for which coverage is provided?

10. Identify and briefly describe three optional benefits that may be included in disability income policies.

QUESTIONS FOR DISCUSSION

1. What characteristics of the disability income exposure make this employee benefit susceptible to retention by the organization? Why is disability income often insured rather than self-insured?

2. Describe the ways in which disability income coverage provided as an employee benefit can be integrated with other forms of protection against disability that may be available to the individual.

3. Which type of hazard (physical, moral, or morale) do you believe would pose the greatest problem for an insurer writing disability income insurance?

4. You have been retained by an insurer to design a disability income policy covering both accident and sickness, but with appropriate provisions to protect against the special hazards associated with writing sickness coverage. What provisions or conditions would you incorporate into the policy?

5. One of the major problems facing a person who is permanently disabled is the possibility of erosion of purchasing power when price level changes occur during the period of disability. To what extent could the concept of variable annuity or variable life insurance be used in the field of disability income?

SUGGESTIONS FOR ADDITIONAL READINGS

Beam, Burton T., Jr. and John J. McFadden. *Employee Benefits,* 3rd ed. Brookfield, WI: Dearborn Financial Publishing, Inc., 1994.

Black, Kenneth, Jr. and Harold D. Skipper, Jr. *Life Insurance,* 12th ed. Englewood Cliffs, NJ: Prentice-Hall, 1994. Chapters 26, 27.

Crawford, Muriel L. *Life and Health Insurance Law,* 7th ed. Homewood, IL: Richard D. Irwin, 1994.

Graves, Edward E., (ed.). *McGill's Life Insurance.* Bryn Mawr, PA: The American College, 1994. Chapters 2, 3, 4, 7, 33.

Hallman, G. Victor and Karen L. Hamilton. *Personal Insurance: Life, Health & Retirement.* Malvern, PA: American Institute for CPCU, 1994. Chapter 4.

Mehr, Robert I., and Sandra G. Gustavson. *Life Insurance: Theory and Practice.* 4th ed. Plano, TX: Business Publications, 1987. Chapters 14, 15.

Price, Daniel N. "Cash Benefits for Short-Term Sickness." *Social Security Bulletin,* vol. 47, no. 8 (Aug. 1984).

Rosenbloom, Jerry S., ed. *The Handbook of Employee Benefits: Design, Funding and Administration,* 3rd ed. Homewood, IL: Richard D. Irwin, 1991.

CHAPTER 33

▨▨▨▨▨

Managing Employee Benefits: Health Expense Coverage

CHAPTER OBJECTIVES

When you have finished this chapter, you should be able to

Identify and describe the traditional forms of medical expense insurance, distinguishing between basic policies and major medical insurance.

▪

Distinguish among traditional fee-for-service policies, health maintenance organizations, preferred provider organizations, and point-of-service plans.

▪

Identify common cost-containment activities that have been adopted by health insurers.

▪

Identify and explain the important considerations in buying health insurance.

▪

Identify and describe the major problems associated with the current health care system and the proposed solutions.

▨ Health Care as an Employee Benefit ▪▪▪▪▪▪▪▪▪▪▪▪

Health care benefits represent the most popular insurance benefit offered by employers. Over 90 percent of the employees of medium and large corporations are covered by health care benefits, while about 70 percent of the employees of smaller firms are insured. The importance of health care as an employee benefit is evidenced by the fact that slightly fewer than 10 million persons, less than 5 percent of the total population, obtain their health insurance coverage under individually-purchased health insurance policies. The overwhelming majority of persons covered by private health insurance obtain their coverage under group plans, usually sponsored by an employer. These plans cover the worker and his or her dependents. Most persons under age 65—approximately 85 percent—are covered by private health insurance, usually under an employer-sponsored plan.[1]

There are two reasons for the overwhelming dominance of employee benefits as a source of financing for health care benefits. The first reason why medical expense financing is typically provided through an employment relationship has to do with taxes. An employer's contributions made as payment for employee's health insurance premiums or as direct payments for medical expenses of employees are deductible as a business expense for the employer, but the amount of premiums is not taxable as income to the employee. Further, the employee is not taxed on benefits received under such a program if they are reimbursement of medical expenses actually incurred.[2]

The second reason for the popularity of employer sponsored plans is the economy of the group insurance approach, which makes group coverage cheaper than individually written coverage. The potential for cost savings inherent in the operation of the group mechanism was discussed in Chapter 29. Group insurance provides opportunities for cost savings because of lower underwriting expenses, reduced agents' commissions, and reduced potential for adverse selection. Where the individual is insured as a member of a group, the premium tends to be lower than if the individual had purchased the insurance on his or her own.

Group health insurance plans, like group life insurance, were originally distinguished from individual health insurance in the fact that group underwriting and group rating were substituted for individual underwriting and individual rating. As in the case of group life insurance, the nature of group health insurance has changed since its inception. As a result of health insurance reform, the regulations for group health insurance have changed dramatically. By 1995, 44 states had adopted some form of small group health insurance reform. In most states, this reform imposed standards designed to improve the availability and portability of insurance for employees. Most laws followed an NAIC Small Group Law, which defined a small group as 2 to 50 lives.[3]

---

[1]Although employee benefits represent an important source of financing for health care expenditures, most expenses are covered from other sources. An astounding 47 percent of health care expenses in the United States are covered by state and federal reimbursement under Medicare and Medicaid. Out of pocket expenditures from private resources cover about 23 percent of total expenditures for health care. Finally, private insurance, including self-insurance, provides financing for the remaining 30 percent of health care expenditures. Health Care Financing Administration, *HCFA Financial Report Fiscal Year 1993*, April 1994, p. 8. In addition to these sources, workers compensation pays for most medical expenses arising out of work-related injuries.

[2]In those instances in which the employer pays the entire cost of the plan, benefit payments in excess of the actual expenses incurred are taxable to the employee. If the employee paid the premium on the policy, the excess is not taxed. When the cost of the insurance is shared by the employer and the employee, the employee is taxed on that part of the excess reimbursement attributable to the employer's contribution.

[3]In March 1995 the NAIC adopted a controversial new Small Group Model Act, which includes "groups" of one life (sole proprietorship) in the mandated reforms. It remains to be seen whether the individual states will accept this new approach.

CONTRIBUTORY-NONCONTRIBUTORY PLANS

Health care programs are often written on a contributory basis, meaning that the employer and employee share the cost of the program. Often, the employer pays the premium for the employee's coverage, and the employee is responsible for the cost of coverage for dependents, but other cost-sharing arrangements exist. The ultimate *contributory plan* is one in which the employee pays the entire cost of the coverage. Fortunately, employees can make their contributions on a tax-sheltered basis using flexible spending accounts.

Premium Only Plan

The efficiency the group approach to health insurance and the benefits of the favorable tax treatment is indicated by the willingness of employees to pre-fund their own health care expenses through a group program sponsored by their employer. One approach to employee funding is known as the *premium only plan.* Under a *premium only plan*, the employee accepts a reduction in salary and allows the employer to use the reduction to pay insurance premiums on a before-tax basis. The employee saves the income and FICA taxes that would otherwise be payable on the amount by which salary is reduced. (These plans also reduce the employer's FICA tax, which allows the employer to fund a part of the premium without any out-of-pocket cost). The potential drawback is that any funds that are set aside but not used for health insurance premiums or health care costs are forfeited by the employee. This so-called *use it or lose it* is not a problem when the premiums that will be payable are known to the employee and the salary reduction reflects the amount of anticipated premiums.

Medical Savings Accounts

Medical savings accounts (MSAs) are a version of the flexible spending account idea that many employees have used with positive results. The employee requests a reduction in salary, with the amount by which the salary is reduced set aside for out-of-pocket medical expenses in an MSA. The salary reduction reduces the state and federal income taxes and FICA tax. The employee then draws money from the MSA to pay medical expenses as they arise. The principal drawback to MSAs is the IRS use it or lose it rule, under which amounts that are not spent during the year are forfeited. Although this deters some employees from designating a part of their salary for an MSA, an individual should be able to make a reasonable estimate of the amount of out-of-pocket medical expenses that the family is likely to incur.

In its 1995 Balanced Budget Act, Congress proposed a new type of MSA for Medicare and for health care financing generally that would be subject to different tax rules.[4] Under the Medicare MSA option in the *Balanced Budget Act of 1995* (that

---

[4]The idea of Medical Savings Accounts has been around at least since 1965. See Thomas L. Wenck, "Financing Senior Citizen Health Care: An Alternative Approach," *Journal of Risk and Insurance*, vol. XXXII, no. 2, pp. 165-175. Prior to the Congressional debate in 1995, 13 states had enacted MSA legislation and more than 40 states had considered such legislation.

President Clinton vetoed), Medicare beneficiaries would have the option of electing an MSA instead of Medicare benefits. The beneficiaries would receive cash vouchers to be used to purchase high-deductible health care coverage and would deposit a part of the payment in an MSA, which would be used to pay out-of-pocket medical costs, with unexpended contributions carried forward from year to year. Accumulations in excess of a specified level could be withdrawn by the individual as taxable income and could be used for other purposes. It was hoped that MSAs would serve as an incentive to consumers to control medical care expenses. Critics of MSAs argue that they may discourage people from seeking needed health care. They also argue that individuals with poor health are more likely to elect lower deductibles, while the healthier insured population will elect the MSA approach. In that case, premiums for low deductible plans will increase and may become unaffordable for some insureds.

❖ Approaches to Financing Health Care Benefits ■ ■ ■ ■

Health care employee benefits may be self-insured or they may be fully insured. As expected, larger employers tend to self-insure, while smaller firms transfer the risk of loss to an insurer. In between, there are a variety of arrangements with different degrees of retention.

INSURED PLANS

The private health insurance industry is composed of three broad types of organizations: commercial insurance companies, Blue Cross and Blue Shield organizations, and capitated health care providers.

Commercial Insurance Companies

Private commercial insurance companies selling medical expense protection include property and liability insurers, life insurers, and monoline health insurers. There are about 1200 insurance companies that sell health insurance, providing about 75.1 million persons with hospital and surgical expense benefits. This includes 36.2 million persons covered under fully insured group plans and 9.5 million persons covered under individual policies. The remaining 29.4 million persons consist of those who are covered under programs that are fully or partially self-insured by employers and administered by insurance companies.

Blue Cross and Blue Shield Plans

The Blue Cross and Blue Shield plans (the "blues") are nonprofit associations usually organized under special state-enabling legislation to provide for prepayment of hospital and surgical expenses. The Blue Cross plans were originally organized by individual hospitals to permit and encourage prepayment of hospital expenses. Blue Shield plans occupy approximately the same position in the surgical expense field as Blue Cross plans occupy in the hospitalization field. Both Blue Cross and Blue Shield market "service" contracts under which service benefits, rather than a dollar indemnity, are provided to insured members. Thus, although a commercial insurer's contract might, for example, provide for payment up to a specified dollar maximum per day while the insured is confined to a hospital, a Blue Cross contract would provide a semiprivate room in a member hospital. Although Blue Cross and Blue Shield organizations were originally organized as nonprofit and tax-exempt organizations, in recent years a number of these organizations have converted to mutual life/health insurers or mutual property/liability insurers. In 1995, Blue Cross and Blue Shield organizations insured an estimated 68.1 million persons, a part of whom represent participants in employer self-funded plans that are administered by the Blue Cross and Blue Shield organizations.

Capitating Health Care Providers

Capitating health care providers include Health Maintenance Organizations (HMOs) and Physician-Hospital Organizations (PHOs), also sometimes called Organized Delivery Systems (ODSs). HMOs and PHOs differ from commercial insurers in that they are also health care providers. The insurance element in the operation of HMOs and PHOs derives from the manner in which they charge for their services, which is called capitation. Under the capitation approach, individual subscribers pay an annual fee and in return receive a wide range of health care services. HMOs insure an estimated 22.2 million persons and provide administrative services for an additional 14.4 million. Because PHOs are relatively new, they presently insure a small number of persons. That number, however, is growing. (The operation of HMOs and PHOs is discussed later in the chapter.)

SELF INSURED PLANS

In addition to the coverage underwritten by commercial insurers, the "blues," and health expense associations, a growing number of organizations self-insure their group health benefit programs. Many large employers have opted to self-fund their employee health insurance programs as a way to reduce costs. The cost advantages of self-insurance stem from two major sources. First, by eliminating the premium, the employer eliminates the premium taxes assessed by state governments. Second, most states require that group insurance policies include certain "mandated benefits." These may include, for example, coverage for chiropractors and podiatrists, mammographies, and mental illness. Self-insured plans are exempt from these mandated benefits requirements. Employers who self-insure may use a third-party administrator or an insurance company to administer their benefit program. It is estimated that in 1996, over two-thirds of large employers were self-insured, with programs covering approximately 54.8 million persons.

There are two basic approaches to self-funding health care benefits. The simpler of the two is the *disbursed self-funded* technique. Under this method, employees' claims are paid directly out of the firm's cash flow, as part of the expense of doing business. Claims are tax deductible when they are paid. The second approach to self-funding is a tax-exempt trust. Contributions are paid into the trust, from which claims and expenses are paid. Contributions are deductible when made, and excess funds are invested as reserves. In a tax-qualified trust, the trust's investment income is exempt from taxation. Self-insured plans also include multiple employer plans, such as multiple employer trusts and Multiple Employer Welfare Arrangements (MEWAs).

Multiple Employer Trusts

As their name states, Multiple Employer Trusts (METs) are in the legal form of trusts, usually with a corporate fiduciary (such as a bank) serving as trustee. They are formed to provide health (and life) insurance to employer-employee groups too small for economic purchase of group insurance individually. METs are sponsored by insurance companies and by other organizations formed for this purpose. METs differ widely in their operation. Some operate on a self-funded basis, using the premiums collected from trust members to fund the health care costs of the group. Other METs operate on a fully insured basis, purchasing group health insurance coverage from commercial insurers for their members.

Multiple Employer Welfare Arrangements

MEWAs are multiple employer trusts that provide health and welfare benefits under the provisions of ERISA. When Congress enacted ERISA in 1974, it included a broad preemption of state regulation for employee benefit plans, specifically providing that states may not treat certain self-funded employee benefit arrangements as insurance. The decision to exempt these plans from state regulation proved ill-advised. After a number of financial failures owing to the absence of regulatory oversight, the 1982 amendments to ERISA authorized states to apply state insurance laws to self-funded MEWAs. Unfortunately, because of ERISA's complex and confusing provisions, some ambiguity remains concerning regulatory responsibility for MEWAs. Persons covered by MEWAs are included in the number of persons covered by self-insured plans.

⚙ Health Insurance Coverage Options ■ ■ ■ ■ ■ ■ ■ ■ ■ ■

The number of options available to employees has increased dramatically in the last two decades. Twenty years ago, the two major providers of group health insurance were Blue Cross/Blue Shield plans and commercial insurers. Both groups provided a type of benefit known as "fee-for-service" benefits. The insured who became ill or was injured would seek service from a medical care provider (e.g., a physician or hospital), and the policy would pay. The policy would pay the provider directly, or it would reimburse the insured for amounts the insured paid. In either case, there was little interference with the way in which care was provided. The provider and insured agreed on the level of care, and the insurer paid the bill.

As medical expenses began to rise dramatically following the enactment of Medicare in 1965, employers and others became concerned. More attention was given to the problems inherent in the fee-for-service system. Many experts argued that this system provided an incentive to overutilize health care, since the decision makers (the insured and provider) had nothing to lose as more health care was provided. When the insurer paid the costs, insureds and providers had no incentive to reduce costs. Moreover, it was argued, the provider stood to gain when more services were provided, because the amount he or she was paid would increase. Insurers, employers, and public policymakers began to look for ways to alter the relationship between the way the care was financed and provided in order to give providers an incentive to reduce medical expenses.

The trend in recent years has been away from traditional indemnity "fee-for-service" plans and toward several types of plans that involve a more direct relationship between provider and insurer or, in the case of self-insured plans, employer. These plans include health maintenance organizations, preferred provider organizations, and point-of-service plans. Because of the stronger relationship with providers, these programs are often referred to as managed care. Before turning to a discussion of these alternative programs, we will review the traditional indemnity or fee-for-service plans offered by insurers and "the blues."

TRADITIONAL FEE-FOR-SERVICE HEALTH INSURANCE PLANS

Medical expense insurance provides for the payment of medical care costs that result from sickness and injury. Its benefits help to meet the expenses of physicians, hospital, nursing, and related services, as well as medications and supplies. Benefits may be in the form of reimbursement of actual expenses (up to a limit), cash payments, or the direct provision of services. Because employees are sensitive to the nature of their health care coverage, self-insured plans generally follow the format and use provisions that were developed by the sellers of health insurance.

Broadly speaking, traditional forms of health insurance are divided into four broad classes of coverage: hospital insurance, surgical expense, physician's expense coverage, and major medical coverage.

Hospital Expense Insurance

Hospital expense (or hospitalization) insurance provides specific benefits for daily room and board, plus ancillary hospital-provided services. Most hospitalization insurance is sold under two types of contracts: service contracts, originally developed by Blue Cross, and expense reimbursement contracts, marketed by insurance companies. Either plan may be written to cover the individual or an entire family. When coverage is written to include dependents, "dependents" usually include the spouse and unmarried children under age 19. Some policies provide coverage for children over 19 years of age if they are unmarried and full-time students, up to a maximum age of 23 to 26.

Hospital Service Contracts   A hospital service plan provides actual services of the hospital to the insured person for a stated number of days, rather than a cash benefit. Blue Cross organizations maintain contracts with hospitals in the state or region where they operate. These member hospitals agree to accept scheduled fees from Blue Cross in full payment for the services rendered to the patient. The number of days varies widely in different Blue Cross organizations, but generally ranges from 70- to 365-day plans. If the subscriber desires a private room, he or she may reimburse the hospital for the difference between the cost of the private room and the charges paid by Blue Cross. Like disability insurance, the cost of protection does not increase proportionately with an increase in the number of days covered. A policy with a 365-day limit will be only slightly more expensive than one providing 120-day coverage.

Not all hospitals are members of Blue Cross, and service benefits are usually available only in those that are. When a subscriber is admitted to a nonmember hospital, benefits are on a cash payment basis. The insured is reimbursed on a cash basis for the Blue Cross organization's cost of a semiprivate room in a member hospital.

Hospital Reimbursement Contracts   Hospital expense policies offered by commercial insurers are designed to pay all or some of the cost of room and board when the insured is confined to a hospital. The cost of hospital room and board is usually written for a flat daily amount for a specified number of days such as 31, 70, 120, or 365. Early contracts provided that costs up to the maximum benefit per day (e.g., $100, $200, or $300) would be paid while the insured or an eligible dependent was in the hospital, up to the number of days specified. Room and board expenses in excess of the amount provided in the policy must be paid by the insured.

From the insured's point of view, policies offering reimbursement benefits were inferior to those offering service benefits because they failed to provide protection against rising costs. For example, the insured with a hospitalization policy providing a daily benefit of $100 would be responsible for the increase if hospital room costs in the area rose above this amount. Persons covered under a service benefit contract, on the other hand, would still be protected in full. In response to that concern, many policies today have dropped the dollar limit and instead pay benefits based on "reasonable and customary" charges. Under this arrangement, the policy pays a benefit based on the prevailing charges for hospitals in the region. As hospital room costs increase, the insurer's reimbursement automatically increases, providing built-in protection against inflation. These plans operate very much like service benefit policies.

In addition to the semiprivate room or reimbursement, hospitalization policies usually provide coverage for *hospital miscellaneous expenses* or *incidental hospital expenses* covered under reimbursement contracts written by commercial insurers. These expenses include incidental hospital expenses such as the use of the operating room, Xrays, drugs, anesthesia, and laboratory charges.

741

Surgical Expense and Physicians' Expense Insurance

Two types of basic coverages pay for physicians' fees. Surgical expense insurance provides coverage for surgeons' fees, and physicians' expense insurance covers nonsurgical physicians' fees. Like hospitalization coverage, these coverages were originally written on a reimbursement basis by insurance companies and on a service basis by Blue Shield organizations.

Blue Shield organizations agree to pay the physician's usual, customary, and reasonable (UCR) charges. *UCR* means the usual fee charged by the provider for the particular service, the *customary* or prevailing fee in that geographic area, and a *reasonable* amount based on the circumstances. The usual, customary and reasonable standard is a statistically determined value, based on surveys of what doctors and hospitals charge. Based on the survey, the UCR level is set at a percentile of what providers charge. For example, if the UCR is set at the 85th percentile and the UCR for a particular operation is $1500, this means that 85 percent of doctors charge $1500 or less for the procedure. If the patient patronizes one of the 15 percent of doctors who charge more than $1500 for the procedure, the patient must absorb the difference.

Although conventional insurers originally sold surgical expense coverage on a reimbursement basis, they have gradually transitioned to the *UCR* approach pioneered by Blue Shield. Some insurers, however, still offer reimbursement contracts, which reimburse the insured according to a schedule that assigns a dollar value to different types of operations. Surgical procedures are assigned relative values, depending on the difficulty of the operation. A typical schedule might provide the following benefits:

Procedure	Surgery Value
Appendectomy	$ 40
Aortic valvuloplasty, open repair	200
Gall bladder removal	60
Gastrectomy, complete	50
Stomach, total resection of	100

The amount payable for a particular procedure is determined by multiplying the surgery value shown in the schedule by the dollar unit value indicated in the policy. If the dollar value for the indicated schedule is $20, the contract will pay $800 for an appendectomy and $4000 for open-heart-surgery. The actual schedule in the policy would be far more complete. In addition, benefits are payable for operations that are not listed in the policy based on the difficulty involved. If the physician charges more than the schedule's maximum for a procedure, the patient is responsible for the excess charges.

Physician's Expense Reimbursement Insurance

Physician's expense insurance (formerly called regular medical expense insurance) provides benefits to cover a physician's fees for nonsurgical care in a hospital, home, or doctor's office. The coverage is seldom written alone, but must be included with one of the other medical expense coverages (hospital or surgical expense). Physician's expense insurance pays for visits to a doctor's office or for a doctor's house calls or hospital visits, usually with a limit per visit (e.g., $25 to $50) and a maximum number of calls per sickness or injury.

Major Medical Insurance

The major medical policy is the contract that is most appropriate for the large medical expenses that would be financially disastrous for the individual. It is designed to provide protection against catastrophic losses and at the same time eliminate the dollar trading inherent in the insurance contracts that are written on a first-dollar basis.

One of the distinguishing characteristics of the major medical policy is the high limit per loss and the relative absence of exclusions. Major medical policies are commonly written with a limit as high as $500,000 or $1 million. The policy maximum may apply to each accident or illness, or it may apply as a lifetime maximum. Some policies, especially group contracts, are written without a maximum limit. Originally, there were no restrictions on how much of this amount could be spent for doctor bills, private nursing, medicines, or other expenses as long as the expenses were reasonable and necessary. The more recent major medical policies include internal limitations, restricting the amount payable for specific types of expense (for example, mental illness). In general, major medical policies still go far beyond the usual health insurance contracts, providing payment for blood transfusions, prescriptions and drugs, casts, splints, braces and crutches, artificial limbs or eyes, and even the rental of wheelchairs.

A second characteristic of the major medical policy is its deductible, which may be $100, $200, $250, $300, $500, or even higher. The application of the deductible differs from contract to contract. Most policies make the deductible applicable to a time period, such as a calendar year. Under this form, the deductible applies only once per member of the family during the stated period. Other policies apply the deductible on a disability basis, requiring that the deductible be paid only once for any disability. Many policies have both individual and maximum family deductibles. For example, a policy may have a $200 individual deductible and a $400 family deductible. The first $200 of expenses for each individual are not reimbursed, but after the family has had a total of $400 in nonreimbursed expenses, the individual deductibles no longer apply. In some instances, the individual deductible applies on a family basis if two or more members of the family are injured in the same accident. By eliminating small claims through a deductible, the insurer can offer a high limit at a premium that is moderate in comparison with plans on a first-dollar basis.

In addition to the deductible, the major medical policy also requires the insured to share part of the loss in excess of the deductible. For example, the insurance company may pay 80 percent of the loss in excess of the deductible, with the insured paying the other 20 percent. The insurer may pay a lower percentage for certain classes of expenses (e.g., mental illness). In the newest forms of major medical plans, there is usually a cap on the out-of-pocket costs borne by the insured—commonly $2000 or $3000—beyond which the insurance pays 100 percent of covered expenses up to the policy limit.

This share-loss or coinsurance requirement is necessary because of the breadth of the contract. Once the insured has met the deductible, most other medical expenses are covered, and insurers feel that the coinsurance provision is necessary to control utilization. Without the coinsurance clause, neither the insured nor the doctor would have an incentive to keep expenses within reasonable limits.

The broad class of major medical contracts includes supplemental major medical and comprehensive major medical policies.

Supplemental Major Medical   The first major medical policies were written to supplement a first-dollar coverage plan, which is called the base plan in such cases. Normally, when the major medical policy is written with a base plan, a corridor deductible is used. The corridor represents a specified amount of expense that the insured must incur personally before the major medical plan becomes applicable. The deductible amounts to whatever the base plan pays plus the corridor of $50, $100, or $200. Whenever medical bills not covered by the base plan exceed the corridor deductible, the major medical policy becomes operative. Because many items are payable under the major medical policy that are not covered under the base plan, benefits may actually be payable before the limits of the base plan have been exhausted.

Figure 33.1 illustrates a major medical policy written with a base hospital and surgical expense plan. Expenses covered under the base plan are payable up to the scheduled limits without a deductible or participation. Expenses that are not covered under the base plan are covered by the major medical policy, once the insured has satisfied the $100 corridor deductible. The next layer of coverage is

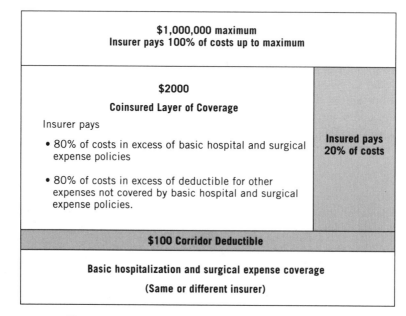

Figure 33.1   Supplementary Major Medical Policy

subject to a 20 percent coinsurance provision, and expenses in excess of this layer are covered in full. The insured's maximum out-of-pocket cost under this plan would be $500 (the $100 corridor deductible plus 20 percent of $2000).

Comprehensive Major Medical   The most recent version of major medical coverage, the comprehensive major medical, combines the best features of a base plan and the major medical contract into a single policy. There are many variations in comprehensive major medical plans, and many are individually tailored to the needs of the group.

Under the earliest comprehensive major medical plans, coverage was written to pay hospital charges, surgical expenses, and other medical costs through a single contract, subject to a small deductible, with a coinsurance provision applicable to all expenses above the deductible. Later variations of the plan eliminated the deductible for hospital charges and sometimes for surgical charges as well. They provided for payment of these expenses without a coinsurance provision up to some specified maximum, with coinsurance applicable above this limit. A sample comprehensive major medical plan is depicted in Figure 33.2.

As an illustration of how this policy operates, let us assume that a person insured under a contract with the features indicated in Figure 33.2 suffers a $20,000 loss in connection with hospital and doctor bills. Payment would be made on the following basis:

Amount of loss	$20,000
Less: Deductible	250
	19,750
Insured pays 20% of expense over deductible up to $10,000	2,000
Insurer pays balance	$17,750

The insured pays a total of $2250, and the insurer pays $17,750.

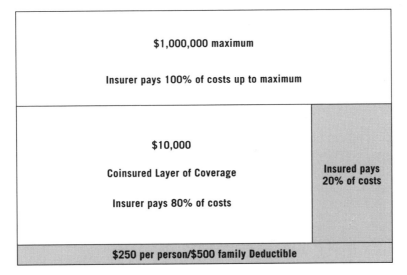

Figure 33.2   Comprehensive Major Medical Plan

The cost of a comprehensive major medical policy varies with the maximum limit, the deductible, and the coinsurance percentage. The insured's age, the number of dependents, and the area where the insured resides also affect the premium. One company offers a stand-alone major medical with the following coverage: $1 million per person maximum limit, 90 percent coinsurance on the first $2500 of covered expenses per person, full coverage after $2500, with a $250 individual deductible per calendar year (subject to a $500 annual family maximum).

Exclusions Under Major Medical Policies   Like all insurance policies, major medical contracts are subject to exclusions. Exclusions in individual policies tend to be more extensive than those in group policies, and some group contracts contain more exclusions than others. Most employer sponsored health plans exclude expenses payable under workers compensation or any occupational disease law, elective cosmetic surgery, dental work, and experimental procedures. Expenses arising out of mental or nervous disorders may be excluded or subject to a lower maximum or only a percentage of the costs may be covered. Maternity benefits may or may not be included in individual contracts. If they are included, they usually have a specified maximum payment. It is also customary to include maternity benefits in individual contracts only after the dependent has been covered under the policy for 9 or 10 months. Maternity benefits are usually covered under group contracts on the same basis as any other condition.[5]

Most policies contain limitations on coverage for preexisting conditions. These tend to be less restrictive in group policies. Group policies frequently impose a waiting period (e.g., six months or one year) before a preexisting condition will be covered.[6] Other policies may provide some coverage immediately, but subject to a low dollar limit for a period.

ALTERNATE APPROACHES TO HEALTH CARE FINANCING

As health insurance costs have increased in the last 30 years, dramatic changes have taken place in the health insurance marketplace. Traditional plans are no longer the predominant form of insurance for most employees. Many employers offer health maintenance organizations (HMOs), physician hospital organizations (PHOs), and preferred provider organizations (PPOs), and many employees have elected to enroll in one or the other. More recently, employers have

---

[5]The Pregnancy Discrimination Act of 1975 amended the Civil Rights Act of 1964 to prohibit employment discrimination with respect to pregnancy, childbirth, or related medical conditions. Besides prohibiting discriminatory employment practices, the law prohibits such discrimination in company-funded employee benefit programs. Prior to the passage of the act, many firms did not include coverage for pregnancy-related conditions in health insurance and disability plans. If maternity benefits were included, coverage was often subject to benefit limits different from those for other illness. Since passage of the act, all employer-sponsored health and disability insurance plans must provide equal benefits for pregnancy-related conditions and other medical conditions.

[6]The waiting period may be shorter if it is a condition for which the insured is not receiving ongoing treatment.

begun to offer point-of-service (POS) plans. Even where indemnity plans are offered, they now contain cost-containment features that encourage efficient provision of care.

The dramatic growth in popularity of HMOs, PHOs, PPOs, and POS plans can be seen by examining the enrollment trends in recent years. Twenty years ago, approximately 90 percent of insured employees were covered under traditional plans offered by commercial insurers and Blue Cross and Blue Shield plans. By 1993, that figure had fallen to 46 percent. Approximately 22 percent of employees are enrolled in PPOs, 25 percent are enrolled in HMOs, and about 7 percent in POS plans.

Health Maintenance Organizations

Health maintenance organizations were first seen as a solution to the problem of overutilization of medical care. A health maintenance organization provides a wide range of comprehensive health care services to a group of subscribers in return for a fixed periodic payment. The distinguishing characteristic is that the HMO not only provides for the financing of health care—as do commercial insurers and the "blues"—it also delivers that care. In some sense, the provider and financing mechanisms are merged. An HMO, then, is an alternative not only to other forms of insurance but to other health delivery systems as well. The HMO may be sponsored by a group of physicians, hospital or medical school, an employer, labor union, consumer group, an insurance company, or Blue Cross and Blue Shield plans.

Although these organizations have been around for at least as long as the Blue Cross and Blue Shield plans, public and government attention did not focus on them until the late 1960s, bringing them their current popularity.[7] Their increasing popularity dates from 1973, when Congress enacted the Health Maintenance Organization Act of 1973.[8] This law encouraged HMOs by providing funding for the development of new HMOs and the expansion of existing ones. Perhaps most important, the law required employers with 25 or more workers who are subject to the Fair Labor Standards Act to offer, as part of its health benefit program, the option of membership in a federally qualified HMO if one is available.

During the period since the enactment of this legislation, HMOs have proliferated at what can only be described as a phenomenal rate. From about 25 in the early 1970s the number of operational HMOs had increased to over 700 by 1995. Although the original organizations were independent plans, both commercial insurers and the Blue Cross and Blue Shield organizations have embraced the idea. By 1995, insurance companies were administering over 200 HMO projects.

---

[7]Although the roots of the HMO idea can be traced back to the 1800s, their modern history dates from 1938, when industrialist Henry Kaiser adopted the idea of prepaid group medical practice and capitation for his employees working on the Grand Coulee Dam. The idea spread to Kaiser shipyards and other Kaiser industries during World War II, and the result was the Kaiser Permanente Medical Care Program, the largest HMO in the country. Prior to the 1970s, the HMO idea spread slowly, but several plans were established, including the New York Health Insurance Plan (HIP), the United Mine Workers' Plans, the Ross-Loos Medical Group in Los Angeles, the Metro Health Plan of Detroit, and the San Joaquin Plan.

[8]P.L. 93-222.

Blue Cross and Blue Shield organizations have been equally active, with more than 90 HMOs in operation by 1995.

Operation of HMOs   The HMO functions as a provider of health care services, but it does so on a considerably different basis from the traditional fee-for-service methods for delivering health care. Under the HMO idea, comprehensive health care is provided in return for a prenegotiated lump sum or periodic payment. HMOs often operate their own hospitals. HMOs include a variety of arrangements but consist mainly of four types:

- *Staff model.* Under the staff model HMO, physician services are provided through a group of multispecialty physicians who are salaried employees of the HMO.

- *Group model.* Under the group model, physicians' services are provided by a multispecialty group of physicians who are independent of the HMO, but who contract with the HMO to provide service. The physicians primarily serve members of the HMO but may serve other patients as well. The physicians' group is compensated in the form of a capitation payment, that is, on a per capita basis.

- *Individual practice associations.* The individual practice association (IPA) type of HMO involves physicians who practice in their own offices but agree to provide medical services to the HMO. IPA physicians are typically reimbursed on a fee-for-service basis within agreed-upon ranges. They bill the association rather than the patient, and the association agrees to provide comprehensive health care to its enrolled population for a per capita payment. The IPA physicians are subject to the risk that their normal fees may be reduced if the HMO revenue is insufficient for full payment.

- *Network model.* The network model is similar to the group practice model, except that the HMO enters into contracts with several mutispecialty groups of physicians. The groups are compensated by a fixed monthly fee per enrollee. The group decides how the fees will be distributed to individual physicians.

The newest type of HMO, the open-ended HMO, was created by the Health Maintenance Organization Act of 1988. Prior to this act, services could be provided only by physicians employed by or under contract with the HMO. Under the new laws, up to 10 percent of an HMO's services may be provided by physicians who are not affiliated with the HMO.[9]

Whatever the arrangement with the physicians, from the subscriber's point of view, the fee-for-service system is replaced by a system of capitation, under which the membership fee paid by the individual subscribers pays for all or almost all services

---

[9]The Health Maintenance Organization Act of 1988 (P.L. 100-517). This law also changed several other requirements for federally qualified HMOs. Prior to this law, the HMO Act required HMOs to develop their rates on a community basis. The law also permits experience rating of individual groups of 100 or more persons. In addition, the 1988 law changed the rules for employer contributions to HMOs. Prior to the 1988 act, the employer was required to contribute the same dollar amount toward the cost of an HMO as would have been made to an insured plan. Under the new rules, the employer is required to contribute only the same percentage of cost as it contributes toward an insured plan.

received. In return for a fixed monthly fee, the individual receives virtually all the medical care required during the year. There may be a nominal charge, on the order of $5, paid by the participant when visiting the physician, but this charge is the same regardless of the service rendered. Care is managed by a primary care physician, also known as the "gatekeeper," who is responsible for determining what care is received and when the individual is referred to specialists.

Premiums for HMO contracts may be higher or lower than those charged by private insurance companies or the Blue Cross and Blue Shield organizations for traditional indemnity insurance. However, even where higher, the difference in cost may be justified by the all-inclusive nature of the HMO's benefit package. Initial studies suggest that HMOs not only reduce the family's total health bill but can also provide better health care at the same time.

One factor that helps to control costs in the long run is that subscribers are generally encouraged to have regular medical checkups and see their physician as often as necessary. In addition, care is more likely to be provided in an outpatient setting. Because inpatient care tends to be expensive and HMO subscribers tend to be hospitalized less, this reduces the net system cost.

A major disadvantage of HMOs, from the perspective of many employees, is that the subscriber is not covered when he or she uses a provider other than the HMO, unless it's for an emergency. In some cases, subscribers may want to seek treatment from specialists outside the HMO. Unless the HMO refers them and agrees to pay the costs, there is no coverage.

Physician Hospital Organizations

Physician Hospital Organizations (PHOs), also sometimes called Organized Delivery Systems (ODSs), are relatively recent entrants into the insurance marketplace and are a key feature in many of the national health care reform proposals. Like HMOs, they combine the delivery and financing of health care. Physician Hospital Plans are a type of joint venture in which hospitals and physicians combine to provide a full range of health care services to subscribers. PHOs are paid a capitated fee for the services they provide. The fee is divided among the providers based on a prenegotiated arrangement. Because PHOs are a relatively new player in the health insurance market, they cover a relatively small, but growing, segment of the health care market.

Preferred Provider Organizations

Although health maintenance organizations have enjoyed greater popularity in the last 20 years, many individuals objected to the limitations placed on their ability to select the physicians and hospitals that would provide their care. As a result, early enrollment in HMOs was disappointing. Insurers and employers began to consider other ways they could reduce costs by contracting with providers, while still allowing insureds the option to choose their provider. This led to the development of preferred provider organizations.

A preferred provider organization is a network of health care providers (doctors and hospitals) with whom an employer or insurance company contracts to provide medical services. The provider typically offers to discount those services and to set up special utilization review programs to control medical expenses. In return, the employer or insurer promises to increase patient volume by encouraging insureds to seek care from preferred providers. The insurer does this by issuing contracts that provide higher rates of reimbursement when the care is received from the network. The insured is still permitted to seek care from other providers, but will suffer a penalty in the form of increased deductibles and coinsurance. Unlike HMOs and PHOs, PPOs are reimbursed on a fee-for-service basis, so they bear no risk.

This arrangement preserves the employee's option to choose a provider outside the network, should he or she desire. Where the insured stays in the network, the discounted fees to providers should provide some cost savings, although the potential for savings is lower than with an HMO. In 1995, there were over 1000 preferred provider organizations operating countrywide.

Point-Of-Service Plans

The newest development in the health insurance field has been the creation of point-of-service (POS) plans. In one respect, a POS plan operates like a PPO, for employees retain the right to use any provider but have to pay a higher proportion of the costs when they use a provider outside the network. On the other hand, a POS plan is like an HMO, inasmuch as care received through the network is managed by a primary care physician, or "gatekeeper." In fact, the first POS plans were created when HMOs allowed their subscribers to use nonnetwork providers. The penalties for using a nonnetwork provider are typically greater than the penalties under a PPO. It is hoped that the use of the "gatekeeper" approach in POS plans will provide greater cost control than that provided by a PPO arrangement.

HEALTH CARE BENEFITS FOR OLDER WORKERS AND RETIREES

Because the federal Medicare program covers a large part of the medical expenses of persons over age 65, there is sometimes a tendency to dismiss the role of employee benefits in financing the health care costs of older workers and retired workers. The Age Discrimination in Employment Act (ADEA), which requires equal treatment of older workers, makes the health care needs of older and retired workers relevant for the organization's employee benefit program. The special requirements in this area relate to the three types of insurance designed to cover health care costs of the elderly: Medicare, Medicare supplement insurance, and long-term care insurance.[10]

---

[10]In addition to Medicare, Medicare Supplement policies, and long-term care insurance, some elderly obtain assistance with the medical expenses under the Medicaid program, a federal-state program that provides financial assistance for medical expenses to the indigent. The Medicaid program was established in 1965 as Title XIX of the Social Security Act, entitled "Grants to States for Medical Assistance Programs."

The Medicare Program

There are two separate programs under Medicare: Part A-Hospital Insurance, which provides coverage for the cost of hospital care, nursing home care, hospice care, and home visits, and Part B-Supplementary Medical Insurance, an optional coverage for which the insured must pay a monthly premium and which covers doctors' fees and certain other costs.

Medicare Part A–Hospital Insurance   Almost all persons age 65 or over are eligible for Part A–Hospital Insurance, which is financed by part of the Social Security payroll tax that is paid by workers and their employer, and by self-employed persons.[11] Medicare Part A helps pay for medically necessary inpatient care in a general hospital, skilled nursing facility, psychiatric hospital or hospice care. When the beneficiary is hospitalized, Medicare will pay for all covered hospital services during the first 60 days of a benefit period, except for the deductible. The Part A deductible in 1996 was $736 per benefit period. A benefit period begins the day the beneficiary is hospitalized. It ends after the beneficiary has been out of the hospital or other facility that primarily provides skilled nursing or rehabilitation services for 60 days in a row. If the beneficiary is hospitalized after 60 days, a new benefit period begins. With each new benefit period, Part A hospital and skilled nursing facility benefits are renewed except for any lifetime reserve days or psychiatric hospital benefits used. There is no limit to the number of benefit periods a beneficiary can have for hospital or skilled nursing facility care.

In addition to the initial benefit period deductible, if the beneficiary is hospitalized for more than 60 days in a benefit period, he or she is responsible for a share of the daily costs for the 61st through the 90th day. In 1996, this copayment was $184 a day. After the 90th day, a beneficiary may draw on a *lifetime reserve* of 60 days for inpatient hospital care. These lifetime reserve days may be used whenever the individual is in the hospital for more than 90 days in a benefit period. Once used, the reserve days are not renewed. When a reserve day is used, Part A pays for all covered services except for coinsurance of $368 a day in 1996.

Medicare Part A also pays part of the cost in a skilled nursing facility for up to 100 days, subject to a coinsurance provision ($92 per day in 1996). Coverage also applies to benefits for home health care and for hospice care for terminally ill beneficiaries who choose to receive hospice care rather than regular Medicare benefits for management of their illness.

Medicare Part B –Supplemental Medical Insurance   Persons who are eligible for Part A of Medicare have the option of purchasing Part B–Supplemental Medical Insurance (SMI). SMI is a voluntary coverage financed jointly by monthly premiums

---

[11]Persons who are entitled to benefits under Social Security or Railroad Retirement systems or who worked long enough in federal, state or local government employment to be insured, do pay any premium for Part A. In addition, all persons who have received OASDI disability benefits for at least 2 years are also entitled to Medicare benefits. Finally, chronic kidney patients requiring dialysis or renal transplant, who are fully and currently insured or who are dependents of a fully and currently insured worker, are also eligible for Medicare Part A coverage.

paid by persons who elect the coverage and a contribution for each participant by the federal government. For the 12-month period beginning January 1, 1996, the monthly Medicare Part B premium was $42.50.

The coverage under Supplementary Medical Insurance is much like a major medical contract. Benefits begin after a deductible ($100 in 1996), and nothing is paid until this initial expense has been met by the insured. Medical insurance pays 80 percent of the covered expenses in excess of the deductible, provided that the charges are "reasonable" (based on customary and prevailing charges). Covered expenses include charges for physicians' and surgeons' services, no matter where rendered, home health services (even if the insured has not been in the hospital), surgical dressings, splints, and rental or purchase of medical equipment, and all outpatient services of a participating hospital, including diagnostic tests and treatments. In addition, since 1991, Medicare Part B has provided coverage for screening mammography—the radiological procedure used for the early detection of breast cancer in women. Coverage depends on the beneficiary's age, but for women over age 64, payment is made for screening mammography biennially.

Employer Group Medicare Coverage   Under certain circumstances, persons who are eligible for Medicare but who are still employed must be given the option of enrolling (with their spouses) in their employer's health insurance plan. Federal Law requires that employers with 20 or more employees must also offer the same health benefits, under the same conditions, to employees age 65 or over and to their spouses who are 65 or over, that they offer to younger employees and spouses. Employers must also offer health care coverage to employees' spouses who are between 65 and 69 even if the employee is under age 65. The employee may accept or reject coverage under the employer group health plan. If the individual accepts the employer plan, it will be the primary payer and Medicare becomes excess. If the individual rejects the plan, Medicare will be the primary payer for Medicare-covered health services that he or she receives. If the employee rejects the employer plan, an employer cannot provide a plan that pays supplemental benefits for Medicare-covered services or subsidize such coverage. An employer may, however, offer a plan that pays for health care services not covered by Medicare, such as hearing aids, routine dental care, and physical checkups.[12]

Medicare Supplement Coverage

When employees who are eligible for Medicare or retired employees are included in an employee benefit health care program, the coverage is integrated with Medicare, under an arrangement called a *carve-out plan*, which is the employee-benefit approach to Medicare supplement coverage. Under a carve-out plan, the participant

[12]The Tax Equity and Fiscal Responsibility Act of 1982 required employers with more than 20 employees to offer workers between ages 65 and 69 the choice of enrolling in the corporate plan or sticking with the federal Medicare program for their health care coverage. If these older workers had spouses who also were between 65 and 69, employers had to offer the corporate health care plan to the spouses. The Deficit Reduction Act of 1984 further requires employers to offer health care coverage to employee's spouses who are between 65 and 69 even if the employee is under age 65.

receives the amount payable under the plan, minus the amount paid by Medicare. The effect is to produce the same payment by the participant as for other workers who are under age 65. To illustrate, assume that an employee incurs $12,000 in medical expenses, of which the group employee benefit plan, in the absence of Medicare, would pay $11,000. If Medicare pays $7,000 of the total expenses, the employee benefit plan will pay $4,000, leaving the insured with the same $1000 in uninsured expense he or she would incur without Medicare coverage.[13]

Accounting for Retirees' Health Care Coverage Surveys indicate that three-fourths of large employers provide retiree health benefits.[14] Many employers introduced retiree medical benefits at about the time Medicare was introduced, assuming that this extension of coverage would be a low-cost addition to the employee benefit package. Experience with retiree health coverage has given employers cause to question their assumptions. In addition, retirees' health care coverage has become a concern for employers for yet another reason, the manner in which the employer must account for such benefits.

In 1990, the Financial Accounting Standards Board (FASB) adopted a new standard that significantly changes the methods by which most companies account for health care provided to retirees.[15] In the past, employers that provide health insurance to retired employees have funded the cost of such programs on a pay-as-you-go basis. The FASB believes that retiree health care should be accrued while an employee is still working for the company. Starting in 1997, a company's balance sheet must reflect a liability equal to the unfunded obligations to retirees. Benefit analysts estimate the unfunded liability for post-retirement health care benefits at over $400 billion.[16]

Long-Term Care Policies

With the increase in life expectancy and improved medical care, people are living longer and an increasing number of our aged are spending their final days in nursing homes and extended care facilities with annual costs that range from $25,000 to $50,000.[17] Although Medicare provides coverage for the normal health care needs of older persons, it does not meet the long-term care need, such as the cost of custodial care in a nursing home. Nor do Medicare supplement policies provide coverage for extended care. The need therefore exists for a form of insurance that

[13]Employees over age 65 whose employer does not provide Medicare carve-out coverage and retired persons who are no longer covered under an employee benefit program may purchase individual Medicare Supplement policies, also called *Medigap* policies.

[14]Donald G. Lightfoot, "Retiree Health Care Costs: A Workable Plan," *Benefits Quarterly*, vol. 7, no. 1 (First Quarter 1991), p. 17.

[15]Financial Accounting Standards Board, "Employers Accounting for Post-Retirement Benefits Other Than Pensions," February 4, 1989.

[16]Lee Berton, "FASB Rule of Retirees to Cause Furor," *The Wall Street Journal*, February 9, 1989, p. A2.

[17]A study published in the *Journal of the American Medical Association* in February 1991 indicates that 43 percent of persons who reach age 65 will enter a long-term care facility before they die. For 24 percent of the elderly, the stay will be at least a year. For 9 percent, it will be five years or more.

will assist in meeting the costs of long-term care for the aged. Long-term care coverage was developed by insurers to meet this need.

The typical long-term care policy provides coverage for care in a skilled, intermediate, or custodial nursing home, often with a different limit of indemnity for each. The policies are designed to pay a specific dollar amount per day for an extended period of time, with benefit periods ranging from two years up to a lifetime benefit. Daily benefits range from about $30 a day for home health care to a maximum of $150 a day for nursing home care. There is usually a waiting period, eliminating coverage for a period of confinement before benefits are payable. Waiting periods range from 20 to 100 days, and maximum benefit periods range from two years up to a lifetime benefit.

Unlike most other types of health insurance discussed in this chapter, long-term care has rarely been included in employee benefit plans. This has been due in part because the coverage is new, but also because of the uncertainty about the eventual cost of such plans and the tax treatment of long-term care insurance. The *Internal Revenue Code* does not include long-term care insurance under the definition of health insurance for which employer-paid premiums are deductible. The 1996 Congressional health care reform package addressed the issue of tax treatment by granting the same favorable tax treatment to long-term care insurance as exists for other types of health insurance.

COST CONTAINMENT PROVISIONS

In addition to the rapid growth of managed care arrangements such as HMOs, PPOs, and POS plans, most traditional indemnity plans have adopted provisions designed to control the employer's costs. In fact, employee benefit managers have been a major force in the nation's search for a solution to the rapidly increasing cost of health care.

Increased Employee Cost Sharing

The trend in recent years has been to increase the portion of medical expenses funded by the employee. Employee contributions to purchase coverage have generally increased, as have deductibles, the employee's share of covered expenses, and out-of-pocket maximums.

Coordination of Benefits

Most plans today have a provision that reduces benefits if the expenses are also covered by a spouse's plan. With the dramatic increase in the two-income family, situations often arise in which a married couple will both be covered under medical expense policies provided by their employers. When an employer-provided policy includes coverage on dependents, one or both partners may be covered under two policies: the policy provided by their own employer and the policy provided by their spouse's employer.

Insurers developed the coordination of benefits provision to eliminate double payment when two policies exist and to establish a priority of coverage for payment of losses. Under a standard coordination of benefits provision, if a wife is covered by her employer and as a dependent under her husband's policy, her policy applies before the husband's policy. The husband's policy pays nothing if the wife's policy covers the total cost of the expenses.[18]

Covering Alternative Sites of Care

Originally, hospital insurance policies covered only care administered in a hospital. Today, most policies recognize that there may be less costly alternative, but still appropriate, sites for delivering care. Policies are likely to cover outpatient surgery and ambulatory care. Birthing facilities are often covered as a less expensive alternative to in-hospital maternity care. Policies are also likely to cover care delivered in skilled nursing facilities, home health care, and hospice care.

Addressing Utilization

A number of policy provisions are designed to encourage the cost-effective delivery of care. *Second surgical opinion* programs will pay for the cost of a second opinion prior to surgery, with the belief that this might reduce the incidence of unnecessary surgeries. *Preadmission certification* programs require the insured to receive the insurer's approval prior to being admitted to the hospital for certain conditions. The object is to prevent unnecessary admissions for ailments that can be treated on an outpatient basis. Under a *concurrent review* program, the insurer reviews the care while the insured is in the hospital to determine whether continued hospitalization is necessary. It authorizes an appropriate length of confinement and may authorize more inpatient days if the patient's condition requires it. Many companies have case management programs under which cases that have very high medical expenses are reviewed individually, with an attempt to design a plan of care that will reduce overall costs. This plan may result in the insurer covering expenses that are otherwise excluded but that will result in eliminating other unnecessary costs.

MANDATED ACCESS TO INSURANCE

Although the debate over the nation's health care delivery and financing system has addressed a variety of issues, two problems have taken center stage: the lack of coverage for some segments of society and the escalating costs from year to year. A number of measures have already been tried in attempts to correct the flaws in the system. Legislated mandates dictating access to health insurance are of particular relevance to the subject of employee benefits.

---

[18]Children are covered under the policy of the parent whose birthday falls earlier in the year.

Cobra

The Consolidated Omnibus Budget Reconciliation Act of 1986 (COBRA) requires that employees and certain beneficiaries be allowed to continue their group health insurance coverage following a qualifying loss of coverage. The law applies to the employers with group plans covering 20 or more persons and permits continuation when coverage would otherwise be ended as a result of termination of employment, divorce, legal separation, eligibility for Medicare, or the cessation of dependent-child status. The employer must provide the coverage for up to 18 months for terminated employees and up to 36 months for spouses of deceased, divorced, or legally separated employees and for dependent children whose eligibility ceases. Generally, the COBRA participant pays a premium based on the existing group rate.[19]

Small Group Reform

At the state level, many states have passed small-group reform, intended to improve the availability of health insurance coverage to small businesses and their employees. Typically, these laws require insurers to offer plans to small groups on a guaranteed issue basis. The insurer may not exclude individual employees and may exclude preexisting conditions only for a limited period. Having met the preexisting conditions requirement in one plan, coverage must be "portable." That is, a new insurer may not impose a new preexisting conditions requirement. Rating rules limit the rate the insurer may charge and the annual rate increases allowed. Insurers are allowed to nonrenew only for certain specified reasons. These plans may also be exempt from mandated benefits laws, allowing the insurer to offer less comprehensive, but less expensive, coverage.

■ Dental Expense Insurance   ■ ■ ■ ■ ■ ■ ■ ■ ■ ■ ■ ■ ■ ■ ■ ■

Dental expense insurance is a specialized form of health expense coverage designed to pay for normal dental care as well as damage caused by accidents. Most of the coverage is written on a group basis. It is offered by insurance companies, the Blue Cross and Blue Shield organizations, and dental service corporations similar to the "blues." The "blues" and dental service corporations provide benefits on a service basis. The coverage may be integrated with other medical expense coverage (integrated plans), or it may be written separately from other health care coverages (nonintegrated plans).

Dental expense coverage is written on a scheduled or nonscheduled basis. Scheduled plans provide a listing of various dental services, with a specific amount available for each. Unscheduled plans generally pay on a "reasonable and customary" basis, subject to deductibles and coinsurance.

---

[19]Several features of COBRA have been liberalized since its enactment. The 18-month extension for terminated employees can be extended up to 29 months if the individual met the OASDI definition of total disability at the time of the termination. *I.R.C.* Section 4980B.

Usually, dental expense insurance distinguishes among several classes of dental expenses and provides somewhat different treatment for each. The coverage is usually subject to a calendar-year deductible of $50 or $100 and a coinsurance rate that varies with the type of service provided. In addition, usually a dollar maximum per insured person is applicable on a calendar-year basis, except for orthodontia services, which may be subject to a lifetime maximum. A typical dental insurance plan might provide the following benefits, with the indicated limits and coinsurance provisions.

Category	Limit	Deductible	Coinsurance
Preventive and diagnostic services	$1000 annual	None	90%/10%
Basic services	Included in annual	$100	80%/20%
Major services	Included in annual	$100	60%/40%
Orthodontia	$1000 Lifetime	$250	50%/50%

Routine care and preventive maintenance are often covered without a deductible and with a modest coinsurance requirement, such as 90 percent. This part of the coverage includes payment for routine examinations and teeth cleaning once a year, full-mouth Xrays once every three years, and topical fluoride treatments as prescribed. The absence of a deductible and low coinsurance provision is intended to encourage preventive maintenance. Basic services include endodontics, periodontics, and oral surgery, including anesthesia. These services are subject to a slightly higher coinsurance provision and to the annual maximum. Major services include restorative services, such as crowns, bridges, and dentures. These services are subject to a still higher coinsurance requirements, usually in the range of 60 percent/40 percent. Orthodontic care is subject to a separate maximum and a separate deductible, which may differ from the deductible for restorative care. It is also subject to the highest coinsurance provision, under which the insured is required to pay 50 percent of the cost of treatment.

Because the maximum annual benefit under most dental plans is in the range of from $1000 to $2000, maximum losses are reasonably predictable and these programs lend themselves to self-insurance.

⠿ Funding Arrangements ■ ■ ■ ■ ■ ■ ■ ■ ■ ■ ■ ■ ■ ■ ■ ■ ■ ■ ■

Over the past two decades, a revolution has occurred in the funding of employer-provided health care benefits. Like other changes in insurance financing, the revolution was motivated by an increased understanding of risk management, by pressure on corporate managers to control costs, and by high interest rates. Increasingly, employers have turned to self-funding approaches for their health care benefit package. In many ways, the changes in financing health care benefits parallel the shift to self-funding in the field of workers compensation. This is not particularly surprising, inasmuch as the shift in the two fields was driven by the same factors. Employers who have turned to self-funding health care benefits have been motivated by the desire to

- Participate in the cash flow that insurers enjoyed under traditional insurance programs.
- Avoid the social load imposed by mandated health insurance benefits in many states.
- Reduce the expense component of the premium allocated to agents' commissions, insurer overhead, and premium taxes.
- Avoid pooling the group's experience with the experience of other buyers, usually under the assumption that the group's experience is more favorable than average.

As in the case of workers compensation insurance, as insurance buyers turned to self-funding approaches, insurers designed products designed to compete with self-insurance. Some insurers also offer their services as third-party administrators (TPAs).

STOP LOSS INSURANCE

As in the case of workers compensation insurance, firms that elect to self-fund their health care benefits may purchase *stop loss* insurance to protect against the risk of abnormally large losses or severe loss experience. Aggregate stop loss and specific stop loss contracts are available for this purpose.

Specific stop lost insurance protects against large claims incurred by a single insured. This would include, for example, major operations such as bypass surgery or other expensive procedures. The specific stop loss is expressed as a dollar amount, such as $25,000, $50,000, or $100,000. Although some insurers have offered specific stop loss limits as low as $10,000, state insurance regulators are attempting to stem the flow of small employers to the self-funded market by limiting the use of stop-loss insurance. Current proposals would prohibit stop-loss insurance with a loss limit of less than $20,000. Many small employers would be unable to self fund at that level.

Aggregate stop loss insurance is written to trigger payment by the insurer when claims exceed a specified limit during a specific period, such as a policy year. The limit is usually determined as a percentage of the expected claims, usually in the range from 120 percent to 140 percent.

Although there are many who argue that self-insurance of health care benefits is unwise for the smaller organization, a properly structured retention corridor can reduce costs for smaller firms in the same way that more complete self-insurance works for larger firms. When the health benefits are written with a participant-payable deductible, the employer can retain a layer of risk by opting for a self-insured retention of deductible that applies once the participant deductible has been met. In this case, the employer's total retained risk is the amount of this corridor deductible multiplied by the total number of participants. One estimate suggests that the actual payout by the employer will be in the range of 20 percent to 30 percent of this retained risk.[20]

[20]Charles R. Sundermeyer, "Employee Benefit Planning for Small Businesses," *Benefits Quarterly*, vol. 9, no. 4 (Fourth Quarter 1993).

RETROSPECTIVELY RATED PREMIUM ARRANGEMENTS

The retrospective rating approach has found wide application in financing employer-provided health care programs. Under these programs, the policyholder's premium fluctuates directly with loss experience, subject to a maximum. A typical maximum premium under a health insurance retrospectively rated program might be 115 percent of the conventional premium. This means that the insurer assumes the risk that claims will exceed the sum of expected claims and the retrospective rating basic premium.

EXTENDED GRACE PERIOD ARRANGEMENTS

Under the terms of a conventional group health insurance arrangement, the policyholder is allowed a grace period of 31 days from the due date within which to pay the premium. In response to buyers' desire to participate in the cash-flow benefits associated with insurance premiums, some insurers offered plans extending the grace period to 60 or 90 days. This allows the employer to retain the premiums for a longer period of time and thereby enjoy the investment income on such premiums.

MINIMUM PREMIUM ARRANGEMENTS

A minimum premium arrangement is a partially self-funded plan. Plan participants receive certificates of coverage from the insurer, the same as under a conventionally insured program, subject to a notice that the employer has assumed responsibility for plan benefits. The employer pays benefits under the plan up to a predetermined limit, which is based on projected claims. If claims exceed the projected level, the insurer then assumes responsibility for claims. The plan sponsor pays the insurer a premium that reflects the insurer's risk: the possibility that actual claims will exceed expected claims.

In a sense, the minimum premium arrangement is much like a self-insured plan with stop-loss insurance set at the level of projected claims. The economies under a minimum premium plan stem from the fact that the premium payable to the insurer for the risk it assumes is a fraction of the conventional premium. In addition, state premium taxes are usually payable only on the premium paid to the insurer, not on the amount of benefits paid to plan participants.

ADMINISTRATIVE SERVICES ONLY ARRANGEMENTS

Under an Administrative Services Only (ASO) arrangement, buyers self-insure the benefits under the plan and the insurer has no risk. The insurer's function is limited to the provision of administrative services such as the payment of claims and administration of the programs. The range of services provided under an ASO contract can vary significantly, ranging from claims-paying services only to a full range of services virtually identical to the services provided to the insurer's conventionally insured buyers.

IMPORTANT CONCEPTS TO REMEMBER

"fee-for-service"
service benefit contract
reimbursement contract
"usual, customary, and
    reasonable" contract
surgical expense insurance
physician's expense
    insurance
major medical policy
coinsurance
corridor deductible
comprehensive major
    medical
health maintenance
    organization (HMO)

capitation
primary care physician
    ("gatekeeper")
preferred provider
    organization
cost containment
coordination of benefits
    provision
third-party administrator
    (TPA)
flexible spending accounts
Medicare
Medicare supplement
    policies

long-term care insurance
insurance-encouraged
    utilization
cost-shifting
mandated benefits
COBRA
small group reform
individual mandates
physician hospital
    organization
point of service plan (POS)
UCR
"usual, customary, and
    reasonable" contract
dental expense insurance

QUESTIONS FOR REVIEW

1. List the four classes into which medical expense insurance may be divided, and briefly describe the coverage afforded by each.

2. Compare and contrast the typical provisions and benefits of a commercial hospitalization policy with a Blue Cross contract, and a commercial surgical expense contract with a Blue Shield contract.

3. Suppose you decide to buy a basic hospitalization and surgical expense policy. What points of coverage would you check if you were presented with two apparently similar contracts, but with substantially different premiums?

4. Briefly describe the distinguishing characteristics of (a) a major medical policy written with a base plan, and (b) a comprehensive major medical policy.

5. Give reasons for the coinsurance feature and the deductible in the major medical policy. Are both really necessary?

6. Briefly describe the distinguishing characteristics of a health maintenance organization. How does it differ from the other insurers operating in the health insurance field?

7. Distinguish among the health insurance organizations that are characterized by their emphasis on managed care.

8. Identify and briefly describe four techniques that have been adopted as cost-containment strategies.

9. Describe the arrangement(s) that may be used to provide a tax shelter to employees who pay for the cost of their own health care coverage. What are the advantages of these arrangements? What are the disadvantages?

10. Identify and describe the provisions of the legislative efforts that have been enacted to facilitate access to health insurance.

QUESTIONS FOR DISCUSSION

1. A noted insurance authority has said "Because the financing of long term care is inconsistent with insurance principles, it is a problem that does not lend itself to solution through insurance." In what ways is the financing of long term care inconsistent with insurance principles? What, in your opinion, is the solution to the problem of financing long term care?

2. Briefly explain the basic features of each of the three approaches that have been suggested for a national health insurance plan. Which do you prefer and why?

3. An insurance company executive recently observed that "insuring a person who has contracted AIDS is like insuring a burning building." Do you believe that insurers should be compelled to insure individuals who have contracted AIDS? Should insurers be permitted to refuse to insure individuals who have not contracted the virus but whose lifestyle makes them statistically at high risk?

4. It has been suggested that hospital confinement rates are lower among HMO-insured persons than for persons insured by traditional insurers. What are the reasons for the lower hospitalization of HMO subscribers compared with persons covered under insurance company plans or Blue Cross and Blue Shield plans?

5. "Much of the increase in the cost of medical care can be attributed to unnecessary and undesirable overutilization of health services, often prompted by the existence of insurance." To what extent do you believe that the insurance industry is to blame for the health care crisis in this country?

SUGGESTIONS FOR ADDITIONAL READING

Ahmad, Khurshid, et. al. "Long Term Care: An Insurance Industry Perspective," *Journal of the American Society of CLU/ChFC*, 62 (March 1992).

Beam, Burton T., Jr. and John J. McFadden. *Employee Benefits*, 3rd ed. Brookfield, WI: Dearborn Financial Publishing, Inc., 1994.

Black, Kenneth, Jr. and Harold D. Skipper, Jr., *Life Insurance*, 12th ed., Englewood Cliffs, NJ: Prentice Hall, 1994, Chapters 26, 27.

Bowen, Howard R. and James R. Jeffers. *The Economics of Health Services*. New York: General Learning Press, 1971.

Berton, Lee. "FASB Rule of Retirees to Cause Furor," *Wall Street Journal*, February 9, 1989, p. A2.

Crowell, Michael J. and Walter H. Hoskins. *AIDS, HIV Mortality and Life Insurance*. Itasca, IL: Society of Actuaries, 1987.

Davis, Karen, et. al. *Health Care Cost Containment*. Baltimore, MD: Johns Hopkins University Press, 1990.

Eilers, R. D. *Regulation of Blue Cross and Blue Shield Plans*. Homewood, IL: Richard D. Irwin, 1963. Chapters 1–5, 8–11.

Enthoven, Alain C. "Consumer Centered vs. Job Centered Health Insurance. *Harvard Business Review* (Jan.–Feb. 1979).

Fernstrom, Stephen C. and Ning Y. Chen. "Accounting for Post-retirement Benefits Other Than Pensions," *Benefits Quarterly*, vol. 7, no. 2 (Second Quarter 1991).

Fields, Joseph A., Frances S. Lilly, and Nancy Sutton-Bell. "Health Care Challenges and Opportunities in the 1990s," *Benefits Quarterly*, Vol. 7, No. 4 (Fourth Quarter 1991).

Financial Accounting Standards Board, "Employers Accounting for Post-Retirement Benefits Other Than Pensions," February 4, 1989.

Finkel, Madelon Lubin. *Health Care Cost Management: A Basic Guide*, 2nd ed. Brookfield, WI: International Foundation of Employee Benefit Plans, 1991.

Health Care Financing Administration, Office of the Actuary: Data from the Office of National Cost Estimates. *Medical Benefits*, July 15, 1990.

Health Insurance Association of America. *Group Life and Health Insurance: Part A* (5th ed.) (Washington, DC: Health Insurance Association of America, 1994).

_____. *Group Life and Health Insurance: Part B* (5th ed.) (Washington, DC: Health Insurance Association of America, 1994).

_____. *Group Life and Health Insurance: Part C* (4th ed.) (Washington, DC: Health Insurance Association of America, 1994).

_____. *Long-Term Care: Needs, Costs, and Financing* (Washington, DC: Health Insurance Association of America, 1992).

_____. *Managed Care: Integrating the Delivery and Financing of Health Care: Part A* (Washington, DC: Health Insurance Association of America, 1995).

Letsch, Suzanne W., Helen C. Lazenby, Katharine R. Levit, and Cathy A. Cowan. *Health Care Financing Review* (Washington, DC: Health Care Financing Administration (Winter 1992).

Lightfoot, Donald G. "Retiree Health Care Costs: A Workable Plan," *Benefits Quarterly*, Vol. 7, No. 1 (First Quarter 1991), p. 17.

Mehr, Robert I. and Sandra G. Gustavson. *Life Insurance: Theory and Practice*. 4th ed. Plano, TX: Business Publications, 1987. Chapters 14, 15.

Myers, Robert J. "The Future Financing of Medicare," *Benefits Quarterly*, Vol. 10, No. 3 (Third Quarter 1994), page 23.

Rosenbloom, Jerry S., ed. *The Handbook of Employee Benefits: Design, Funding and Administration*, 3rd ed. Homewood, IL: Richard D. Irwin, 1991.

U.S. Bipartisan Commission on Comprehensive Health Care, *Access to Health Care and Long-Term Care for All Americans*, Recommendations to the Congress, 101st Congress, 2nd Session, Washington, D.C.: U.S. Government Printing Office, 1990.

Yamamoto, Dale H. "Retiree Medical—Round 2," *Benefits Quarterly*, Vol. 10, No. 3 (Third Quarter 1994).

CHAPTER 34

Managing Employee Benefits: Qualified Retirement Plans

CHAPTER OBJECTIVES

When you have finished this chapter, you should be able to

Explain the way in which employer contributions to a qualified pension plan
are treated under federal tax laws and the way in which this treatment
benefits workers covered under such plans.

Identify and explain the difference between the defined contribution
and defined benefit approaches in qualified retirement plans.

Describe the basic features of qualified retirement plans,
including benefits and vesting.

Explain the provisions of the Tax Code relating to Individual Retirement Accounts
(IRAs) and explain the benefits that arise from both deductible
and nondeductible contributions to IRAs.

Pensions

A pension is a payment, other than wages, that is made to a person (or to his or her
family) who has fulfilled certain conditions of service or who has reached a certain
age. The idea of pensions appears to have originated in ancient Rome and was initially provided to soldiers who had completed their terms of enlistment. The pensions were administered by societies known as *Collegia* and were funded by the
donativa or spoils of war that the government periodically awarded to the military.

Eventually, pensions spread to the business world, where they were viewed as a reward for long and faithful service. Although private pension plans in the United States have been in existence since the late 1800s, their greatest growth has taken place since World War II. In 1940, about 4 million people—less than 20 percent of all employees in government and industry—were covered by private pensions. By 1995, over 100 million persons, including about one-half of all workers in private business and three-fourths of all government workers, were enrolled in retirement programs other than Social Security. Sixty million of these were covered by plans insured or administered by insurance companies.

Before turning to our examination of qualified retirement plans, we will first examine the concept of an *annuity*, which is a fundamental element in many pension plans.

THE ANNUITY PRINCIPLE

Before turning to an examination of pension design, it will be helpful to pause and briefly discuss the annuity principle, which is fundamental to the operation of pension plans. Annuities have been called "upside-down life insurance," and in a sense they are a reverse application of the law of large numbers as it is used in life insurance. An *annuity* is a contract that provides periodic payments for a specified period of time, such as a number of years or for life. The payments may begin at a stated or contingent date and may be payable for a specified number of years or for the duration of a person's life or the lives of more than one person. The person whose life governs the duration of the payments is called the *annuitant*. If the payments are to be continued for a specified period but only for as long as the annuitant lives, the contract is known as a temporary life annuity. Because the temporary life annuity is used only infrequently, our discussion of annuities will concentrate on life annuities.

The basic function of a life annuity is to liquidate a principal sum, regardless of how it was accumulated, and it is intended to provide protection against the risk of outliving one's income. It may involve the liquidation of a sum derived from a person's savings (including the annuity itself or the cash value of life insurance policies) or the liquidation of life insurance death benefits in the form of a life income to the beneficiary of the policy.

Under the annuity principle, the law of averages operates to permit a lifetime guaranteed income to each annuitant. Some people who reach age 65 will die before they reach 66. Others will live to be 100. Those who live longer than average will offset those who live for a shorter period than average, and those who die early will forfeit money to those who die later. Every payment the annuitant receives is part interest and part principal. In addition, each payment is part survivorship benefit, in that it is composed in part of the funds of group members who have died.

Classification of Annuities

Annuities may be classified in six different ways: (1) they may be classed as *individual* or *group*, depending on the way in which they are marketed; (2) they are classified according to the manner in which the premium is paid, which may be in *install-ments* or as a *single premium*; (3) they are further divided according to the time at which the annuity benefits will commence, which may be on an *immediate* or *deferred* basis; (4) they may be classified according to the number of lives over which bene-fits will be paid, referred to as *single life* or *joint life*; (5) they may be classified as *fixed dollar* or *variable*, indicating whether the accumulation is on a fixed (guaran-teed) rate or varies with the performance of an underlying portfolio, generally con-sisting of common stocks; and, finally (6) annuities may be classified according to the insurer's obligation, as a *pure life annuity* or a *period certain annuity*. Under a pure life annuity, payments are made only for the balance of the annuitant's life-time, regardless of how long or short this period might be. Under an annuity cer-tain, payment is made for the lifetime of the annuitant, but at least for a specified number of years.

As will be clear from the discussion that follows, most annuities used in quali-fied pension plans are group-deferred-installment annuities, which means that periodic contributions are made toward an accumulation that will not be distrib-uted until sometime in the future, presumably at retirement. They may be fixed dollar annuities or variable annuities, single or joint life, straight life or period certain annuities.

▓ Qualified Retirement Plans ■ ■ ■ ■ ■ ■ ■ ■ ■ ■ ■ ■ ■ ■ ■ ■ ■

Retirement plans are established by employers and sometimes jointly by unions and employers in order to provide workers with a retirement income that will sup-plement Social Security retirement benefits. The plan may be set up for the employees of a particular firm, or it may be a "multiemployer" plan, serving work-ers from a number of unrelated firms.

A "qualified" retirement plan is one that conforms to the requirements of the federal tax laws and for which the IRS recognizes contributions to the plan as a tax-deductible expense for the employer. When a plan is qualified under the IRC, it receives favorable tax treatment. Employer contributions are a tax-deductible expense at the time they are made, and the employee is not taxed on the employer's contributions until benefits are actually received (usually at retirement). In addi-tion, during the accumulation period, investment income on accumulating funds is not subject to taxation and will be taxed only when paid out to the employee. This means that funds in a retirement plan will accumulate to a larger amount on an after-tax basis than funds held in other (nontax-deferred) forms.

LEGISLATION AFFECTING PENSION PLANS

Two major pieces of legislation stand out in the history of pensions in the United States: the Employee Retirement Income Security Act of 1974 (ERISA) and the Tax Equity and Fiscal Responsibility Act of 1982 (TEFRA). In addition, several other acts establish conditions that must be observed by employers in establishing retirement plans for their employees.[1]

Employee Retirement Income Security Act of 1974

Any discussion of private pension plans in the United States today must begin with the Employee Retirement Income Security Act (ERISA) of 1974,[2] which embodied the most sweeping overhaul of private pensions in the history of the country. The act was passed in response to a growing concern over the soundness and equity of the pension system. Although few pension plans had actually failed, in many instances workers lost the benefits they had been counting on for retirement.[3] The funding provisions of many plans were unsound, and the vesting requirements, under which an employee's right to the pension was established, were often severe. To correct these and other deficiencies in the existing pension system, Congress passed ERISA to establish standards for pension programs that would provide a better guarantee to the workers they covered.

The goal of ERISA was to increase the rate of national participation in pension plans, prevent loss of benefits by persons who terminate employment before retirement, establish minimum standards for funding and vesting, and provide for the overall control of new and existing pension plans. Although the law does not require an employer to establish or maintain a pension plan, if such a plan exists, it must conform to the provisions of the law. ERISA prescribes which employees must be included in a plan, establishes minimum vesting requirements, specifies the amounts that must be contributed, and sets forth minimum funding requirements. The act also requires extensive reporting and disclosure information about pension and welfare programs, their operations, and their financial conditions to the secretary of labor, to the Internal Revenue Service, and to those covered by the plan and their beneficiaries.

Tax Equity and Fiscal Responsibility Act of 1982

The second major law affecting pension plans was the Tax Equity and Fiscal Responsibility Act of 1982 (TEFRA).[4] With respect to qualified retirement programs, TEFRA had two basic objectives: to require more equal treatment of highly compensated employees and rank-and-file workers, and to make noncorporate retirement plans and corporate plans more similar. To achieve these two goals, Congress modified the rules for both corporate pension plans and Keogh plans. The maximum limits for contributions to corporate plans were reduced, and the limits for individual plans were increased. In addition, both corporate and individual plans were made subject to new rules with respect to "top-heavy" plans, that is, plans that discriminate in favor of stockholders, key employees, or highly paid executives.

---

[1]Other recent legislation includes the Deficit Reduction Act and the Retirement Equity Act of 1984, as well as the Tax Reform Act of 1986, all of which modified the rules related to qualified plans.

[2]P.L. 93–406.

[3]A well-publicized example of this occurred when the Studebaker auto factory closed in 1963. Although pensions for workers age 60 and over were paid, the pension rights of workers under age 60 (some of which were vested) were lost.

[4]P.L. 97–248.

Title VII of Civil Rights Act of 1964

In addition to the requirements of the IRC, pension plans are also subject to laws relating to employment practices, and the U.S. Supreme Court has ruled that the design of a pension plan may violate the equal employment provisions of the Civil Rights Act of 1964. In a 1978 case, the Court ruled that when benefits to men and women under a pension plan are equal, it is illegal for an employer to require higher contributions to the plan by women than by men.[5] In another case, the Court ruled that when men and women make equal contributions to a pension plan (or when equal contributions are made by the employer on their behalf), women cannot receive a smaller monthly benefit than men, either directly from the plan or under an annuity purchased by an insurer selected by the employer.[6] The net effect of the Court's decisions is that a retirement plan cannot pay women lower retirement benefits and cannot require women to make higher contributions because of their generally longer life expectancy.

QUALIFICATION REQUIREMENTS

For a plan to be qualified by the IRS, it must conform to certain standards specified in the tax code. In general, to be qualified, the plan must meet the following standards:

1. The plan must be designed for the exclusive benefit of employees and their beneficiaries. Officers and stockholders who are *bona fide* employees may participate in the plan.

2. Contributions and benefit formulas cannot be designed to discriminate in favor of officers, stockholders, or highly compensated employees.

3. The plan must be in writing, and a written description of the plan must set forth all the provisions necessary for qualification.

4. The plan must be communicated to the employees. Plan administrators must furnish participants with a written description summarizing the major provisions and clearly describing their rights and obligations.

5. The plan must specifically provide for nondiversion of contributions, making it impossible for the employer to divert or recapture contributions made until all liabilities under the plan have been satisfied.

6. The plan must provide either for definite contributions by the employer or a definite benefit to the worker at the time of retirement.[7]

---

[5] *City of Los Angeles Department of Water and Power v. Manhart* (435 U.S. 702).

[6] *Norris v. Arizona Governing Committee for Tax Deferred Annuity and Deferred Compensation Plans.* This 1983 ruling on defined benefit plans was limited to future retirees, to avoid the risk of bankrupting pension plans nationwide if retroactivity were invoked.

[7] Employers who do not want to commit to a defined contribution rate or a defined benefit at retirement may establish a qualified profit-sharing plan under which the contributions may (but need not) vary with the profits of the firm.

7. The plan must be permanent, and although modifications in the plan over time are permitted, the employer cannot terminate the plan except for "business necessity."

8. Vesting must be provided. (See discussion of vesting later in this chapter.)

9. Life insurance benefits may be included in the plan only on an incidental basis.[8]

Participation Requirements

Prior to ERISA, many plans provided that employees were not eligible to participate in the pension plan until they had been employed by the firm for long periods of time. The obvious intent was to reduce the employer's cost by eliminating benefits for persons involved in the firm's labor turnover. ERISA set standards for participation in qualified pension plans, requiring that all employees with one year of service who had reached age 25 be included in the plan and that years of service after age 22 be counted for vesting purposes. The Retirement Equity Act of 1984 reduced the age at which employees must be allowed to participate to 21, and the Tax Reform Act of 1984 required that years of service after age 18 be considered for vesting purposes.[9]

Vesting Requirements

The tern *vesting* refers to the right of a covered employee to retain a claim to the benefits accrued, even though his or her employment terminates before retirement. Under current law, qualified retirement plans are generally subject to the following vesting requirements.

1. No vesting for five years, with 100 percent vesting after five years (called "cliff vesting").

2. Twenty percent vesting after three years of service, with 20 percent per year thereafter, so that 100 percent vesting exists after seven years of service.

The vesting schedules are minimum requirements, and an employer may provide vesting at a more rapid rate.

Top-Heavy Plans

The most far-reaching feature of TEFRA in the area of retirement programs was a new set of rules applicable to so-called top-heavy plans—those plans that do not provide what Congress considered a sufficient portion of their benefits to rank-

---

[8]Life Insurance is considered incidental if the cost of the life insurance is less than 25 percent of the cost of providing all benefits under the plan. Under a *defined benefit plan*, the requirement is that life insurance benefits not exceed 100 times the expected monthly retirement benefit. Under a defined contribution plan, less than 50 percent of the total contributions may go toward the purchase of ordinary life insurance. See *Rev. Rul.* 68–453, 1968-2 CB 163.

[9]Part-time employees who work less than 1000 hours a year need not be included in the plan. Plans with immediate vesting may require three years of employment as a prerequisite to participation.

and-file workers. If a plan is top heavy, it must satisfy several special requirements designed to ensure that it provides a floor of benefits to nonkey employees. In particular, top-heavy plans are subject to special minimum vesting provisions and minimum benefits or contributions for nonkey employees.

In general, a top-heavy plan is one that provides a disproportionate share of its benefits to "key employees" (owners and certain other highly compensated employees). More specifically, a pension plan is top heavy if over 60 percent of the accumulated account balances or 60 percent of the present value of all accrued benefits are for key employees.

For top-heavy plans, the vesting requirements of ERISA are superseded by the special "top-heavy" vesting requirements. A top-heavy plan must provide either 100 percent vesting for participants after three years of service or graded vesting at the rate of 20 percent after two years and an additional 20 percent each year thereafter, so that a participant will be fully vested after six years of service. The vesting schedules are minimum requirements, and an employer may provide vesting at a more rapid rate.

Top-heavy plans are required to provide minimum contributions for nonkey employees. For *defined contribution plans*, the minimum annual contribution is 3 percent of the employee's compensation. In defined benefit plans, it is the contribution necessary to provide a life annuity at the plan's normal retirement age, equal to 2 percent of the employee's average annual compensation during the five highest paid years of employment, multiplied by the number of years employed by the firm. However, the minimum benefit need not exceed 20 percent of such average annual compensation.

TYPES OF QUALIFIED PLANS

The *Internal Revenue Code* recognizes several distinctly different qualified plans that employers may offer to their employees. Most of these plans are for corporate employers, but there are separate plans for self-employed persons and their employees and for the employees of nonprofit organizations. The qualified plans include the following:

1. *Defined Benefit Pension Plan* A defined benefit pension plan is a retirement plan in which the employer promises to pay the employee a specific income at retirement. The benefit the employee will receive at retirement is specified in a benefit formula, and the employer's contribution is the amount that will be required, together with the investment earnings on the contributions, to provide the specified benefit and pay the expenses of the plan.

2. *Defined Contribution Pension Plan* Under defined contribution plans (also called money purchase plans), the employer's contribution is specified. For example, the employer may promise to make contributions equal to 10 percent of the employee's salary each year. The retirement benefit to which the employee is entitled is simply the amount that the accumulated contributions and investment earnings on those contributions will provide at retirement age.

3. *A Qualified Profit-Sharing Plan*   A qualified profit sharing plan is a form of defined contribution plan, since ultimate benefits depend on the amount contributed by the employer. *Qualified* profit sharing plans are distinguished from other profit sharing arrangements in which part of the firm's profits are distributed to employees. When the distribution is on a cash basis, it is deductible as a business expense to the firm, but it is also taxable as income to the recipients. The *Internal Revenue Code* grants qualified status to profit sharing plans only when distribution is on a deferred basis. A major distinction between a qualified profit sharing plan and a defined contribution pension is that the contribution under a profit sharing plan need not be fixed; employers may vary the contribution from year to year.[10]

4. *Employee Stock Ownership Plan*   An employee stock ownership plan (ESOP) is a qualified stock bonus plan closely related to the qualified profit sharing plan. The principal difference is that under an ESOP, instead of giving the employees a part of the profits of the firm, the employer gives them part of the firm itself in the form of stock in the corporation. Although contributions to an ESOP may be made in cash rather than in stock, the accumulation in the employees' portfolio is nevertheless based on the value of the employer's stock.

5. *Keogh Plans*   Keogh plans allow self-employed persons to make tax-deductible contributions to a retirement plan, provided the plan includes coverage for all other eligible employees on a nondiscriminatory basis. A Keogh plan may be established as a pension or profit sharing plan. Keogh plans are subject to essentially the same limitations, deductions, and benefits as are applicable to corporate pension or profit sharing plans.

6. *Simplified Employee Pension Plans*   Individual retirement accounts (IRAs) may be used by employers to establish simplified employee pensions (SEPs). An SEP permits employers to provide retirement benefits under a less complex arrangement than a qualified pension plan by making a contribution to an employee's individual retirement accounts. Employer contributions to a SEP are included in the employee's income, and the employer may claim a deduction for the distribution to the SEP. The employee then claims a deduction on his or her own Form 1040 for the amount of the contribution made by the employer, subject to specified limits. SEPs are essentially a type of defined contribution plan.

7. *Section 401(k) Plan*   Section 401(k) plans, also referred to as cash or deferred plans, derive their name from the section of the IRC that outlines the rules for these plans. A 401(k) plan is a special type of profit sharing or stock bonus plan that permits an employee to make contributions to the plan on a pretax basis. These plans provide a mechanism for accomplishing two apparently

---

[10]Although a profit sharing plan need not contain a formula for determining the annual contributions, it must provide a formula for allocating the contributions that are made among employees on a nondiscriminatory basis. The most common approach is to allocate contributions according to the ratio of each employee's earnings to the earnings of the group.

conflicting goals: increasing the retirement income of some employees, while increasing the current compensation of others. This is accomplished through a profit sharing plan under which employees *individually* elect whether to receive their contributions currently or have them deferred. In practice, the employees elect to contribute a portion of their income to a profit sharing plan and instruct their employer to make contributions on their behalf. The IRC provides that amounts that an employee elects to defer under Section 401(k) are treated as contributions by the employer rather than by the employee. This makes all monies set aside in the plan deductible by the employer, and the contribution and its earnings are tax free to the employee until withdrawal. The effect is that the plan is a tax-deductible savings account for employees. Section 401(k) plans must provide 100 percent immediate vesting.[11]

8. *Section 403(b) Plans for Employees of Nonprofit Organizations* The employees of certain nonprofit organizations (referred to in the IRC as Section 501(c)(3) organizations) are permitted to establish individual retirement programs (called 403(b) plans), under which the tax on contributions to a tax-sheltered annuity is deferred. Usually, the employee makes an agreement with the employer to reduce his or her salary by an amount equal to the contribution to the retirement plan. In effect, these plans work in essentially the same way as 401(k) plans.

Although each of these programs is similar to the others in its use as a tax-sheltered retirement program, there are fundamental differences among them. Each is subject to different provisions of the IRC, and each may be used for a slightly different purpose. In addition to these qualified plans, which are provided by employers for their employees, individuals may make contributions to a type of qualified plan called an Individual Retirement Account or IRA.

FACTORS INFLUENCING BENEFIT LEVELS

The amount of benefits the employee receives at retirement is based on a formula applicable to all employees. Although the various plans noted above differ in their design, all fall into one of the two basic benefit formula categories: the defined contribution approach and the defined benefit approach. The IRC imposes a maximum permissible contribution for each type of plan.[12]

---

[11]Because the cash or deferred plan is based on a voluntary contribution by the employee of a part of his or her income, Section 401(k) plans have also been referred to as salary reduction plans. For obvious reasons, at least from the employer's perspective, the term *cash or deferred* is a more appealing designation. Employees are likely to misconstrue the nature of the plans and perhaps may be turned off by the designation "salary reduction plan."

[12]If an employee is covered under a defined contribution and a defined benefit plan with the same employer, benefits or contributions may exceed the separate limits for separate plans. Such plans are subject to a complicated "joint limitation rule" under Section 415 of the IRC.

Employee Contributions

Plans may be noncontributory, in which case the entire cost of the pensions is borne by the employer, or they may be contributory, with employees making contributions in addition to those made by the employer. Employee contributions may be voluntary, or they may be required for participation. Other things being equal, retirement benefits will generally be higher in a contributory plan, which acts as a form of forced savings by the employee. Employees have a nonforfeitable right to their contributions. Because it is an oxymoron to speak of employee contributions to a "profit sharing plan," when employees contribute their own funds into a plan, the plan is usually called a "thrift" or "savings" plan. Although employee contributions are not usually deductible by the employees, the investment income on such contributions is exempt from federal taxes until distributed, which makes savings plans a form of tax-favored deferred compensation.[13]

The Amount of Benefits or Contributions

Because a defined contribution plan works exactly as its name implies, the employer's contribution to a defined contribution plan is set by the employment agreement. Usually, it is set as a percentage of compensation, such as, for example, 5 percent or 10 percent of the employee's wages.

In a *defined benefit plan*, the amount of benefits the employee will receive is specified in the benefit formula, and the employer's contribution is the amount that is required, together with the investment earnings on those contributions, to provide the benefit specified and to pay the expenses of the plan.[14] Under most benefit formulas in use today, the employee's retirement benefit payable at normal retirement age is a function of the employee's salary, the benefit accrual rate, and the employee's years of service. Most plans are *final average salary plans*, and the benefit depends on the salary earned in the later years of employment. For example, a plan may promise a monthly benefit equal to 1 percent of the average monthly salary in the last three years of employment. An employee with 35 years of service would receive a benefit equal to 35 percent of the final three-year average salary. Other plans are *career average salary plans*, and the benefit is a function of the salary earned in all years of employment. Obviously, because the salary earned in the early years is lower than that earned in the later years (because of inflation, promotions, etc.), a career average plan must have a higher accrual rate to generate retirement benefits comparable to a final salary plan.

---

[13]Section 401(k) "cash or deferred plans" and Section 403(b) plans are exceptions to the rule that employee contributions are not deductible.

[14]Some plans use a "target benefit plan," which is a cross between a defined benefit and a defined contribution plan. The annual contribution is the amount needed each year to accumulate (at an assumed rate of interest) a fund sufficient to pay a defined retirement benefit (the "target benefit") at retirement age. Once made, contributions are allocated to separate accounts for each participant. If earnings on each fund are different from those assumed, the benefits payable to the participant at retirement are increased or decreased (similar to a defined contribution plan).

Maximum Contributions Under the *Internal Revenue Code*

The *Internal Revenue Code* limits the amount of benefits or contributions that a qualified retirement plan may provide to employees.

Defined Contribution Plans   The employer's maximum annual contribution on behalf of any employee is limited to 25 percent of the individual's earnings for the year, subject to a dollar maximum. This dollar maximum was $30,000 in 1995. Under new rules enacted in 1994, the 1995 dollar limit will be indexed for inflation in increments of $5000; that is, the limit will not be increased until the adjustments reach $35,000.[15]

The compensation to which the contribution percentage applies under a defined contribution plan is subject to a dollar maximum which, like the dollar maximum on the amount of the contribution, is indexed for inflation. In 1995 the dollar limit on income to which the contribution percentage could be applied was $150,000. This means, for example, that a plan that provides an employer contribution equal to 10 percent of compensation would provide a $10,000 contribution for a person earning $100,000, but only $15,000 for a person earning $200,000. Under 1994 changes in the law, the amount of compensation a plan may take into consideration ($150,000 in 1996) will be indexed in increments of $10,000.

The maximum allowable *addition* to an employee's account in a profit sharing plan is the same as the defined contribution pension plan limit (i.e., $30,000 adjusted for inflation). This limit applies to employer contributions, forfeitures credited to the employee, and the employee's voluntary contributions. The limit on the employer *tax deductions* for contributions to a qualified profit sharing plan is 15 percent of the annual compensation of covered employees.

Because an ESOP is basically a type of profit sharing plan, it is subject to the same limits as those outlined above for profit sharing plans: up to 15 percent of covered compensation. However, a money purchase ESOP (in which annual contributions are in cash and are made according to a predetermined formula) of up to 10 percent of payroll can be combined with a stock bonus plan, for a maximum annual contribution of 25 percent of qualified annual payroll.

Defined Benefit Plans   The maximum deductible contribution to a defined benefit plan is expressed in terms of the maximum benefit that the contribution may provide. The maximum retirement benefit that may be provided by a defined benefit plan is 100 percent of the employee's earnings in his three consecutive years of highest earnings. As with defined contribution plans, there is also a dollar limit that is adjusted automatically for cost-of-living increases. In 1996, the dollar limit maximum for defined benefits had reached $120,000. Like the dollar maximum

---

[15]The method by which limits on contributions and benefits are indexed for inflation was changed by provisions included in the General Agreement on Tariffs and Trade (GATT) enacted in 1994. What do pension benefits have to do with the GATT Treaty? Nothing really. The pension provisions were attached to the legislation on trade because the GATT approval was on a "fast-track" and could not be amended. Sponsors of the pension reforms did not believe the legislation would pass if considered separately.

on defined contributions, the indexing of the dollar maximum for defined benefits is adjusted in $5000 increments. This maximum benefit is the amount that may
be paid at the social security retirement age (currently 65). If benefits are paid earlier, the maximum is reduced.[16]

Minimum Contribution or Benefit for Top Heavy Plans   Top heavy plans are required
to provide a minimum contribution on behalf of nonkey employees. For defined contribution plans, the minimum annual contribution is 3 percent of the employee's
compensation. In defined benefit plans, it is the amount required to provide a single life annuity beginning at the plan's normal retirement age, equal to 2 percent
of the employee's average annual compensation during the five highest paid years
with the employer, multiplied by the employee's years of service with the employer.
However, the minimum benefit need not exceed 20 percent of such average
annual compensation.

Contribution for Keogh Plans   Although the same contribution limits apply to a
Keogh plan as to corporate plans discussed above, a special definition of "earned
income" is used to make contributions by a self-employed person correspond to
those for a common law employee, and the percentage limitations apply after the
contribution to the plan has been made. For instance, if a partnership established
a 25 percent money purchase Keogh plan, and a partner earned $100,000, the
deductible contribution on his or her behalf would be $20,000 (25 percent of
earned income of $80,000), not $25,000. With this adjustment, earned income for
a self-employed person corresponds to a common law employee's compensation.[17]

Integrated Benefit Formulas   Although the rules of the tax code require that contribution rates be nondiscriminatory, employers may recognize the FICA payments
made on behalf of employees and consider benefits under social security in establishing contribution levels. This process is referred to as "integration." Both
defined benefit plans and defined contribution plans may be "integrated" with
social security.

In a defined contribution plan, the employer reduces the contribution to the pension plan on part of the wages subject to the FICA tax (the integration level). The
integration level can be any amount up to the social security taxable wage base for
the year. The amount contributed to the plan in excess of the integration level (the
excess level contribution) cannot exceed the base contribution level by more than
(1) the base contribution level itself or (2) the non-Medicare social security tax rate

---

[16]The full $120,000 benefit is permitted at the social security retirement age (age 65 for persons
born in 1938 or before, age 67 for persons born after 1938). For retirement before the social security
retirement age, the $120,000 is reduced in the same manner that social security benefits are adjusted
for early retirement.

[17]For a common law employee, the employer's contribution to a qualified retirement plan is added
to earned income, creating a maximum for taxable income and nontaxable deferred income equal to
125 percent of earned income. This means that 80 percent of the total compensation is taxable and 20
percent is a nontaxable deferral. A self-employed person qualifies for the $30,000 maximum contribu-
tion if he or she has $150,000 in earned income [25 percent of ($150,000 − $30,000)].

(6.2 percent in 1995). Thus a plan with a base contribution level of 2 percent can have an excess contribution level of 4 percent, or a plan with a base contribution level of 5 percent can have an excess contribution level of not more than 10 percent. However, if the base contribution rate is 7 percent, the excess contribution rate cannot be more than 13.2 percent (i.e., the base contribution rate plus 6.2 percent).

In a defined benefit plan, integration is accomplished through a formula that replaces a higher percentage of earnings in excess of some level than is provided for earnings below that level. One of two approaches is used:

1. An excess plan, which provides greater benefits on compensation that exceeds the integration level than on benefits below that level. The excess benefit percentage cannot exceed the base benefit percentage by more than three-fourths of 1 percent for any year of service, or in total, three-fourths of 1 percent times the employee's number of years of service.

2. An offset plan, which provides benefits on the employee's full compensation but then reduces the benefits by a percentage of the benefits received under social security. An offset provision cannot reduce the benefit by more than 50 percent of the benefit computed without the offset.

The offset method may not result in a reduction in private benefits to persons receiving a pension or disability benefit or to vested persons when social security benefits are increased in the future.

Although the provisions for integration initially appear to discriminate against lower-paid workers, they are designed to compensate for the fact that social security benefits provide for replacement of a higher percentage of a lower-paid worker's pre-retirement income than they do for the higher-paid employees. Integration formulas are designed to provide approximately the same percentage of income replacement after retirement for all workers.

Maximum Contribution to Section 401(k) Plans and 403(b) Plans   The limit on an employee's voluntary contribution to a 401(k) plan is the lesser of 25 percent of compensation or a dollar maximum, indexed for inflation. In 1996, the dollar maximum was $9500.[18] This limit applies only to the employee's elective deferrals, not to the employer's matching funds. The combined employer and employee contribution may total the lesser of the qualified pension defined-contribution maximum, or 25 percent of earnings.

The maximum permissible contribution under a 403(b) plan for the employees of nonprofit organizations is 20 percent of the employee's salary, multiplied by the number of years of service, less contributions made in previous years to either the 403(b) plan or a qualified plan. If the plan allows elective deferrals, the maximum deduction allowed for such deferrals is $9500 per year. Employee deferrals plus employer's contributions cannot exceed the 20 percent limitation.[19]

---

[18]Beginning in 1996, the limit on elective deferrals under 401(k) plans will be indexed for inflation in increments of $500.

[19]The $9500 limit will be indexed for changes in the cost of living at the same rate as 401(k) plans.

Significance of the Nature of the Employer's Promise

Defined contribution plans and defined benefit plans differ in the manner in which the employer's contribution is determined, but this difference creates other differences from the employee's perspective.

Investment Risk   Under a defined contribution plan (which includes defined contribution pension plans, profit sharing plans, ESOPs, Section 401(k) plans, and SEPs), the employer promises to make contributions to an account that earns investment income. The employer does not make any guarantee concerning the amount of the retirement benefit. The accumulated contributions will ultimately be available to provide a benefit to the employee. The amount of the benefit will depend on both the level of contributions and the amount of investment income. If investment income is less than anticipated, the accumulation will be less than expected, and the retirement benefit will be lower. Similarly, a higher investment income will increase the retirement income available to the employee. Because the employer promises only to make contributions to the plan, but does not guarantee any level of benefits, the employee bears the investment risk in a defined contribution plan.

Because the employee bears the investment risk in a defined contribution plan, he or she is likely to have a say in how the funds are invested. Employees in 401(k) plans, for example, are often offered a choice concerning how their accumulating funds will be invested. A typical arrangement might offer the participant a choice among a money market fund, an equity fund, and a guaranteed-investment-contract (GIC) option. Although the employer selects the options from which the employee can choose, the employee has greater discretion than in the case of traditional pension plans. In an employee stock option plan, the employer is only required to allow the employee to direct the investment of a portion of his or her account balance (25 percent or 50 percent, depending on the situation). The remainder is typically invested in employer securities.

In a defined benefit plan, the employer's promise is to provide a certain level of retirement benefits to the employee, starting at normal retirement age. The employer determines the required contributions to the pension fund by making assumptions about the number of employees that will reach retirement age, the time for which benefits will be paid, and the rate of investment income earned on the pension fund. The higher the assumed investment income, the lower the employer's required contribution. If, however, investment income goes down and is therefore inadequate to fund the benefits, the employer must increase the contributions because the employer's obligation is to provide the promised benefits.

Advantages to Younger and Older Employees   In addition to the difference between who bears the investment risk, defined benefit and defined contribution plans differ in their relative advantages to young and older employees. In general, a higher proportion of the ultimate retirement benefits are earned in the early years of participation in a defined contribution plan. This is because the contribution in early years will accumulate with investment income for a longer period than the contribution in later years. Hence, the accumulation at retirement will be larger, and the benefits it can purchase will be greater. On the other hand, the present value of the benefits promised to a young worker under a defined benefit plan tends to be small compared to the present value of the benefits promised when the worker is closer to retirement.

Forfeitures Finally, defined contribution and defined benefit plans may differ in how they deal with amounts forfeited by employees who terminate before being fully vested. In a defined contribution plan, amounts that are forfeited by employees who leave before being fully vested may be used to reduce future employer contributions, or they may be reallocated among remaining participants on a nondiscriminatory basis. In a defined benefit plan, gains from employee termination may be used only to reduce future employer contributions.

Employer contributions to defined contribution plans that are forfeited by employees who leave before being fully vested may be used to reduce future employer contributions, or they may be reallocated among remaining participants on a nondiscriminatory basis. Forfeited contributions to defined benefit plans may be used only to reduce future employer contributions.

Protection for Inflation Given the long period between the time an employee begins to work for an employer and the time retirement benefits are paid, the employee would be wise to consider how the plan protects against the risk of inflation during the working years. Similarly, the individual may be retired for many years, and the effect of inflation during retirement on the purchasing power of the benefits should be considered.

Defined benefit final average salary plans provide the greatest protection against inflation during the employee's working years, because the retirement benefits are based on the employee's earnings during the period immediately preceding retirement. Career average salary plans, on the other hand, base the benefits on the employee's salary throughout his or her career. Inflationary periods will reduce the value of the salary paid in early years, and hence the benefits based on those early salaries. Defined contribution plans have, to some extent, a built-in protection against the risk of inflation, for the investment earnings on the funds are likely to be higher in inflationary periods.

Defined contribution plans based on variable annuities also provide protection against inflation; in fact, the variable annuity was conceived as a response to the impact of inflation on retirement incomes. It attempts to counter the effect of inflation by linking the accumulation of retirement funds to the performance of common stocks. The annuitant's premiums are used to purchase units in a fund of securities, much like an open-end investment company. These units are accumulated until retirement, and a retirement income is then paid to the annuitant based on the value of the units accumulated. The concept is based on the assumption that the value of a diversified portfolio of common stocks will change in the same direction as the price level.

Some private plans provide cost-of-living adjustments during retirement years to protect against decreases in the purchasing power of benefits after retirement. This tends to be uncommon, however, and even where offered, the adjustment is subject to an annual cap.

OTHER BENEFITS

Although the basic purpose of a pension plan is to provide retirement benefits, some plans include other features such as death benefits and disability benefits.

Pre-Retirement Death Benefits

A death benefit prior to retirement of the employee is an optional feature in pensions, except in the case of a contributory plan, where the employee's contribution is payable as a death benefit. Some employers also provide for a death benefit before retirement based on the employer's contributions. Federal regulations require that a qualified plan must provide that if a vested participant dies before the annuity starting date leaving a surviving spouse, benefits will be paid in the form of a "qualified pre-retirement survivor annuity." In addition, some plans include pre-retirement death benefits via life insurance. As a rule, a defined contribution plan (i.e., a money purchase pension or a profit sharing plan) can provide (1) term insurance, as long as the premiums are less than 25 percent of the allocation to the employees account, or (2) permanent insurance, as long as premiums are less than 50 percent of the allocation.[20]

Post-retirement Death Benefits

Post-retirement death benefits may be provided by annuities with joint and survivor options or by annuities with period-certain payments.

Required Joint and Survivor Option   ERISA required any participant who has been married for at least one year specifically to decline or else default to accepting a joint and survivor option of at least 50 percent of the participant's retirement benefit. The Retirement Equity Act of 1984 extended this requirement, mandating that qualified retirement plans provide automatic survivor benefits to the surviving spouse of a retiree or to the surviving spouse of a vested participant who dies before retirement. Spousal consent is required for a participant to elect out of joint and survivor annuity or pre-retirement survivor annuity coverage.

Period-Certain Payments   It is possible to arrange the benefits under a pension plan so that a benefit is payable for a minimum period of time, regardless of the death of the beneficiary. So-called period-certain arrangements require that the plan pay for the lifetime of the beneficiary or for a specified period of time (such as 5 or 10 years), whichever is longer. Election of the period-certain option reduces the amount payable to the beneficiary on a lifetime basis.

---

[20]The cost of permanent life insurance protection is treated as a distribution from the plan and is taxable income to the employee for the year in which the premium is paid. The cost taxable to the participant is determined using one-year term insurance rates ("P.S. 58 Table Rates") published by the IRS at the employee's age equal to the "pure insurance" amount in the contract (the excess of the face amount of the policy over its cash surrender value at the end of the year).

Disability Benefits

Some pension plans also make provision against the contingency of the employee's total and permanent disability. A plan may provide for the payment of disability benefits, as long as the costs of such benefits, when added to any life insurance protection provided by the plan, are subordinate (less than 50 percent of cost) to the retirement benefits. Under some plans, disability is simply treated as a form of early retirement, with a reduced retirement benefit payable. A more favorable approach provides for continued contributions to the plan on behalf of the disabled employee. The contributions are based on the compensation the employee would have received if he or she was paid the compensation earned immediately before becoming totally and permanently disabled.[21]

DISTRIBUTION REQUIREMENTS

The provisions that limit contributions and the accrual of benefits are supported by requirements regarding the time at which benefits may commence, the time at which they must commence, and also by a tax on excess contributions.

Commencement of Benefits

All qualified plans have a uniform required beginning date, at which the participant must commence receiving benefits. Plan participants must begin to draw benefits from the plan no later than April 1 following the year in which they reach age 70 1/2. This requirement applies whether or not the participant has actually retired. The distribution must be made over one of the following periods:

- The life of the participant or the lives of the participant and a designated beneficiary.
- A period not extending beyond the life expectancy of the participant and his or her beneficiary.

Under the first option, the accumulation is annuitized, and the plan administrator makes payments for the entire lifetime of the participant (and beneficiary if the joint life option is selected). The annuity may be based on one or two lives, and the annuitant may elect a minimum guaranteed number of payments. The key feature is that benefits are payable based on a life contingency.

Under the second option, distributions are *based* on the life expectancy of the individual (or the individual and his or her spouse) but cease when the funds are exhausted. If the entire accumulation is not paid out before the individual dies, the balance is paid to the designated beneficiary or to the decedent's estate. The key feature in this arrangement is that the accumulation is distributed based on a life expectancy but is not guaranteed for life.

---

[21]The election to continue deductible contributions on behalf of a disabled employee cannot be made for a disabled employee who is an officer, owner, or highly compensated employee.

Premature Withdrawals   A 10 percent penalty applies to premature withdrawals, which are withdrawals made before the individual reaches age 59 1/2. The penalty does not apply to withdrawals that are rolled over into another qualified plan or an IRA. The penalty also does not apply if (1) the distribution is made on account of the employee's death or disability; (2) the distribution is used to pay deductible medical expenses; (3) the distribution is received as an annuity over the lifetime of the employee or under a joint life annuity including a beneficiary; or (4) the individual is at least age 55 and meets the requirements of a plan that permits retirement at his or her age.

An important difference between qualified profit sharing plans and qualified pension plans concerns withdrawals. Although distributions from pension plans are permitted only at retirement, termination of employment, death, or disability, distributions from a qualified profit sharing plan may also be permitted "after a fixed number of years."[22] Distributions prior to age 59 1/2 at any time other than one of the specified events will be subject to the 10 percent penalty on premature withdrawals.

Tax on Excess Distributions   A 15 percent excise tax applies to "excess distributions" from qualified plans, tax-sheltered annuities, and IRAs. The tax applies to the amount by which annual annuity payments exceed $150,000 and lump-sum distributions exceed $750,000.[23]

TAXATION OF DISTRIBUTIONS

Distributions from a qualified pension are taxable to the recipient when received, under special rules. In addition, if the participant dies, a distribution to his or her dependents is taxable as income and, in some cases, is also subject to estate taxes.

Income Taxes

Most retirement plans provide for optional methods of receiving distributions. For example, a participant may receive plan benefits in a lump sum or in installments over his or her lifetime. The method of distribution determines the taxation.

Installment Distributions   Retirement benefits have traditionally been paid to participants as lifetime annuities. Amounts distributed in installments will generally be taxable to the distributee under special annuity rules of IRC Section 72. Installment distributions are taxable only to the extent that they exceed the employee's investment in the contract. Every payment, beginning with the first, is considered part taxable income and part nontaxable. The nontaxable part consists of the portion of the

---

[22]Reg. 1.40-1(b)(1)(ii). The Internal Revenue Service decided long ago that the phrase "*after a fixed number of years*," as used in the regulations, means after at least two years.

[23]An inflation-adjusted amount will be substituted for the $150,000 and $750,000 limits in the future. The inflation-adjusted limit on annual withdrawals is 125 percent of the defined benefit limit under the law. This limit had reached $136,204 by 1991. It will apply once it exceeds the $150,000 limit.

payment that represents the employee's nondeductible contribution and is referred to as the "exclusion ratio."[24] The exclusion ratio apportions distributions between recovery of previously taxed contributions and taxable income. It excludes from taxable income the portion of each payment that the after-tax contributions have to the expected return under the program. The expected return is the annual amount to be paid to the retiree multiplied by the number of years of life expectancy using annuity tables prescribed by the IRS. The exclusion ratio formula is

$$\text{Payment} \times \frac{\text{Previously Taxed Contributions}}{\text{Expected Return}} = \frac{\text{Nontaxable}}{\text{Return of Capital}}$$

To illustrate the operation of the formula, assume that Brown has a taxable basis of $60,000 in her retirement plan and will receive $500 per month for life. She is 65 years old and has a life expectancy of 15 years, which means that she "expects" to receive $90,000 ($6000 per year for 15 years). Applying the exclusion ratio formula to the $6000 benefit Brown receives in the first year:

$$\$6000 \times \frac{\$60,000}{(\$500 \times 12 \times 15 \text{ years})} = \$4000$$

The $4000 is a nontaxable return of capital, and $2000 is taxable income. Once the annuitant has recovered the full amount of his or her investment in the contract, the exclusion ratio no longer applies and subsequent payments are fully taxable. If the annuitant dies before his or her basis is fully recovered, the unrecovered basis may be deducted from the decedent's final tax return. (In the case of contracts annuitized before January 1, 1987, the exclusion ratio applies to all payments, including those made after the annuitant's basis has been recovered.)

For variable annuities, the amount excluded from taxable income each year is also the total investment divided by the number of years the annuitant is expected to live. However, if losses on the underlying portfolio result in payments that are less than the excludable amount for that payment, the investment in the contract for future payments is recalculated. The amount of nontaxable return of principal that was not deductible is factored into the computation of taxable gain for future installments. Suppose, for example, that Brown is receiving a distribution under a variable annuity in which his basis is $300,000. He is 65 years old, and his life expectancy is 15 years. Brown may exclude $20,000 of the variable payment he receives each year. After receiving benefits for four years, the variable benefit in the fifth year drops to $15,000, which is less than the excludable $20,000. The $5000 exclusion is not lost. At this point, Brown is 74 years old and has a life expectancy of 10.1 years. The $5000 exclusion that was not taken may be added to the initial $20,000 exclusion over the 10.1 years, (495.05 per year), making the new excludable amount $20,495.05.

Lump-Sum Distributions An employee who receives a lump-sum distribution can choose from among several alternatives. He or she can roll the distribution over

---

[24]Annuity payments beyond the individual's life expectancy will be fully taxable. Should the retired person die before reaching full life expectancy, his or her heirs may take a deduction on the deceased's final return for the amount of any unrecovered contributions.

into an IRA or another qualified retirement plan, in which case there is no tax on the distribution until it is eventually received from the IRA or other plan. As an alternative, within 60 days of receiving a lump-sum distribution, an employee may use the distribution to purchase a single-premium nontransferable annuity, in which case the distribution will be taxed under the annuity rules.

If the lump-sum distribution is not rolled over and is not used to purchase an annuity within 60 days, it is subject to five-year averaging if the recipient so elects. The actual approach used in averaging is rather complex, but in effect it spreads the taxable gain to the recipient over a five-year period, thereby taxing it at a lower marginal rate. (Prior to TRA-86 the lump sum was subject to a 10-year averaging.) In addition, the portion of a lump-sum distribution attributable to pre-1974 plan years was eligible for capital gain treatment.

Death Benefits   If all or part of a plan's death benefits are payable from the proceeds of a life insurance policy, the excess of the face amount of the policy over its cash surrender value is excludable from income of the beneficiary (as life insurance proceeds). In addition, the beneficiary may exclude an additional amount up to $5000 as a death benefit paid by the employer under code Section 101(b). The remainder of the distribution resulting from the death of a covered employee is usually taxed to the beneficiary in the same manner as it would have been to the deceased worker.

A surviving spouse can roll over to an IRA all or part of a lump-sum death benefit distribution received on account of the deceased employee's death. The amount rolled over is not includable in the surviving spouse's taxable income but will be taxed as ordinary income when it is subsequently distributed and will not be eligible for five-year averaging, even if paid in a lump sum.

If an employee dies before his or her entire interest is paid and a joint and survivor option is not in effect, or if payments are being made to a surviving spouse who dies before the entire interest is received, the balance will generally have to be distributed to beneficiaries within five years.

Estate Taxes

Distributions from qualified plans are not subject to the estate tax if the benefits are paid to a surviving spouse. Other distributions are includable in the estate and are subject to the estate tax.

Limitations on Loan Transactions

The substantial accumulation of funds in qualified pension plans has been an appealing source of loans to the plan participants. Such loans, however, are subject to restrictions imposed by the *IRC*. A loan from a qualified plan to an employee is treated as a distribution (and is therefore taxable) to the extent that it exceeds prescribed limits. Furthermore, a loan to a participant may not exceed the lesser of $50,000 or one-half of the participant's vested accrued benefit (but not less than $10,000). The loan must be repaid within five years, and the repayment must be on an amortized basis. An exception to the five-year payback rules applies to a loan used to acquire the principal residence of the participant.[25]

◼ Funding ◼◼◼◼◼◼◼◼◼◼◼◼◼◼◼◼◼◼◼◼◼◼◼◼◼◼◼◼◼◼◼◼

The term *funding* refers to the preparation the employer makes for provision of the benefits under the plan. In a funded plan, monies are set aside in advance of the date that they are payable, normally as the liability for the benefits accrues. ERISA now requires full funding for currently incurred liabilities. Liability for past service (i.e., for benefits due to workers for service before the adoption of the plan or the establishment of the fund) must be amortized over a period of not more than 30 or 40 years. An employer failing to meet the funding requirement is subject to an excise tax equal to 5 percent of the unfunded liability. If the deficiency is not corrected within a period allowed after notice by the IRS, a 100 percent tax is imposed on it.

Two principal types of funding agencies are used for pension plans: trustees and insurance companies. In either case, the employer's contributions are paid to the funding agency, where they accumulate with investment earnings until they are paid to the pension plan participants. The use of two or more agencies for the funding of a single pension plan is called *split funding*. Usually, split funding takes the form of a partial funding through insurance, with another part of the employer's contribution paid to a trustee for investment in equities.

TRUST FUND PLANS

Under a *trust fund plan*, the employer usually retains a consulting actuary to determine the contributions necessary to fund the benefits specified in the plan. Contributions by the employer (and by employees in a contributory plan) are paid to a trustee, usually a bank or trust company, that holds and invests the contributions and pays benefits according to the terms of the trust agreement and the pension plan provisions. The funds are invested in a variety of instruments, including some issued by insurance companies. Since the 1970s, many trust fund plans have invested in instruments called *guaranteed investment contracts* (GICs) issued by insurance companies. GICs are similar to the CDs issued by commercial banks; they are generally issued for a fixed and fairly short period, such as two to five years, and bear a guaranteed rate of interest. Unlike bonds, the value of GICs does not fluctuate with the interest rate; their value does, however, depend on the financial strength of the issuer. A number of trust fund plans suffered losses on their GIC portfolios when insurers encountered financial difficulties in the early 1990s.

Although a trustee holds the assets, trust fund plans are self-insured by the employer, who is ultimately responsible for the payment of benefits under the plan.

---

[25]Self-employed (owner-employees) are prohibited from borrowing from their Keogh plan.

The trustee makes no guarantee as to the adequacy of the employer's contributions to meet the obligations under the plan.

INSURED PLANS

For *insured plans*, the funding agency is an insurance company. Although funding through insurers once provided little flexibility, insurers now offer a variety of approaches for funding pension plans.

Individual Policies

Individual cash value life insurance and annuity policies are sometimes used by smaller employers as funding devices. When individual contracts fund a pension plan, the employer's (and employee's) contributions are paid to an "individual policy pension trust," a trustee who arranges for the purchase of the individual policies, serves as a custodian, and pays the premiums. The cash values that accumulate provide the retirement benefits under the policy settlement options.

Group Permanent Plans

Group permanent life insurance, which consists of cash value life insurance written on a group basis, may also be used as a funding vehicle for a pension plan. When group permanent life insurance funds a pension plan, the amount of life insurance is usually set at $1000 per $10 of annuity benefits.

Group-Deferred Annuities

When a *group-deferred annuity* is the plan chosen, the annual contributions are used to purchase a deferred annuity for each employee each year. Under both the defined benefit and defined contribution plans, a paid-up unit of benefit is purchased with each year's contribution. Thus, under the defined contribution plan, the annual contribution is used to purchase a single-premium deferred annuity, payable to the employee at retirement. The deferred annuity may be of the fixed-dollar or variable type. A defined benefit plan might purchase an annuity equal to 2 percent of the employee's current income; over a period of, say, 30 years, the cumulative value of such annuities would equal 60 percent of the employee's average earnings.

Deposit Administration Plans

Under a *deposit administration plan*, the insurer establishes a single fund for all personnel under the plan. Contributions are not allocated to specific workers until retirement, when a withdrawal is made from the fund to purchase a single-premium immediate annuity sufficient to provide the retirement benefits due the employee. Under the deposit administration plan, the insurer guarantees the interest rate that will be credited to the account for the first five years and also guarantees the annuity rates for five years, but both are changeable annually thereafter. The insurer does not guarantee the adequacy of the unallocated account to meet the accrued liabilities under the plan. It does, however, guarantee the benefits payable to retired employees for whom annuities have been purchased.

Immediate Participation Guarantee Plans

Immediate participation guarantee plans (IPG plans) are a variation of the deposit administration plan in which the gains or losses from mortality or investment of the account are segregated from the rest of the insurer's operations, giving the employer an "immediate participation" in the favorable (or unfavorable) experience of the plan. There is no guaranteed rate of interest credited to the fund; instead, the fund receives its share of the actual investment earnings of the company. In addition, annuities are not purchased for retiring workers as under the basic deposit administration plan; instead, annuity payments are made directly out of the IPG fund. As in deposit administration plans, the insurer makes no guarantee regarding the adequacy of the fund to meet the plan's obligations. If at any time the amount of the fund falls to a level required to purchase annuities for already retired workers, annuities are actually purchased for such workers.

Separate Accounts

A *separate account* is a fund held by an insurance company apart from its general assets, to be used for investment of pension assets in equities. These accounts are "separate" in the sense that the funds are not commingled with the insurer's other funds, but contributions from a particular pension plan are usually commingled with those of other plans. Separate accounts were designed by insurers to compete with trusted plans, which had always had the advantage of investing in equities. They are permitted under special legislation enacted by the states in the 1960s.

Individual policy pension trust programs, group permanent life insurance, and group-deferred annuities are collectively referred to as *allocated funding instruments* because the employer's contributions are specifically allocated to the individual participants. Deposit administration plans, immediate participation guarantee plans, and separate account plans are *unallocated funding instruments.*

ERISA Pension Plan Termination Insurance ■ ■ ■ ■ ■ ■

In addition to the other provisions designed to increase the security of benefits under pension plans, ERISA also established the Pension Benefit Guarantee Corporation (PBGC) within the Department of Labor. All employers with defined benefit plans are required to insure the benefits of their plan with the PBGC, paying a premium that varies with the nature of the plan. In 1995 the rate for multi-employer plans was $2.60 per participant. For single-employer plans, a variable rate applies. In 1995 the premium was $19 per plan participant, with an additional charge of $9 per participant for each $1000 of underfunding. Prior to 1995, the premium was limited to a maximum of $72. As a result of legislation enacted in 1994, this cap will be phased out gradually and eliminated completely in 1997.

The benefits of a covered pension are guaranteed up to 100 percent of the average wages of the worker during his or her five highest earning years, subject to a dollar maximum. The dollar maximum was originally set at $750 per month, but varies with the social security taxable wage base.[26] By 1995, the maximum coverage per employee had increased to $2250 per month.

Although the original provisions of ERISA which established the PBGC permitted voluntary termination of any single-employer pension plan on the grounds of "business necessity," the provisions regarding terminations were significantly strengthened by the Single Employer Pension Plan Amendments Act of 1986 (SEP-PAA). Under the provisions of SEPPAA, terminations in which the plan assets are insufficient to pay accumulated nonforfeitable benefits ("distress terminations") are permitted only if the sponsor can prove financial distress. "Standard" terminations, in which the plan assets are sufficient to pay benefits due may still be terminated for "business necessity." If a plan is terminated with insufficient assets, the employer must reimburse the PBGC for the deficiency. This "contingent employer liability" is limited to 30 percent of the net worth of the employer plus 75 percent of the remaining liability. The PBGC must permit the employer to pay the additional 75 percent under commercial reasonable terms. The SEPPAA makes provision for the PBGC to appoint a trustee to collect additional payments from the employer over future years. The payments collected are paid to the plan beneficiaries along with the assets from the plan.

In 1994, motivated by increasing concern about the financial condition of the PBGC, Congress enacted a pension reform package that significantly strengthened the funding requirements for private pension plans. Over the years, the PBGC has accumulated a deficit of $2.9 billion from pension plans that terminated with insufficient funding. Features of the 1994 law, which was enacted as part of the General Agreement on Tariffs and Trade, would reduce underfunding by requiring companies to use more conservative mortality and interest assumptions when valuing plan liabilities and to accelerate contributions to underfunded plans.[27] In addition, the elimination of the $72 cap on plan termination insurance premiums noted above will increase PBGC premium revenue by $2 billion over the next five years. PBGC officials have projected that the reforms could wipe out the agency's current deficit within 10 years.

---

[26]The original $750 limit is increased by the same percentage as the social security taxable wage base increases over the 1974 wage base of $13,200.

[27]Employers will be required to use the 1983 Group Annuity Mortality table (GAM 83) to calculate life expectancies of plan participants, and the Treasury Department will develop a new mortality table to be used beginning in 2000. With respect to the interest rate assumptions, employers were previously required to use an interest rate between 90 percent and 110 percent of the four-year weighted average rate for 30-year Treasury bonds. The top of that range will gradually fall to 105 percent by 1999.

IMPORTANT CONCEPTS TO REMEMBER

annuity
fixed-dollar annuity
variable annuity
immediate annuity
deferred annuity
joint life annuity
qualified retirement plans
ERISA
vesting
top-heavy plan
defined benefit plan
defined contribution plan
profit-sharing plan
employee stock ownership
   plan

Keogh plan
simplified employee pension
   plan
section 401(k) plan
final average salary plan
career average salary plan
maximum benefit
   limitations
social security integration
thrift plan
forfeitures
joint and survivor option
premature withdrawal
exclusion ratio
funding

trust fund plan
insured plan
split funding
group deferred annuity
guaranteed investment
   contract (GIC)
deposit administration plan
immediate participation
   guarantee plan
separate account
PBGC
allocated funding
   instrument
unallocated funding
   instrument

QUESTIONS FOR REVIEW

1. It has been stated that an annuity is "upside down" life insurance. Explain what is meant by this notion.

2. Identify the various ways in which annuities may be classified and list the different types of annuities in each classification.

3. Briefly distinguish between a defined benefit pension plan and a defined contribution plan. Which of these would a variable annuity be?

4. What is the purpose of a Keogh plan? What is the maximum deductible contribution that may be made on behalf of a self-employed person under a Keogh plan?

5. Describe the various provisions that may be included in a pension plan with respect to death or disability of a plan participant.

6. The obvious difference between defined contribution plans and defined benefit plans is in the formula by which the contribution is determined. Identify and explain the significance of the other differences between defined benefit and defined contribution plans.

7. Identify and briefly explain the requirements for a pension plan to be "qualified" under ERISA. What are the advantages of qualification?

8. What is the basic difference between "allocated funding instruments" and "unallocated funding instruments?" Identify the funding instruments that fall into each category.

9. In what way does the employer assume a greater element of risk under an immediate participation guarantee pension plan than under a group deferred annuity?

10. Briefly describe the special requirements that apply to a top-heavy plan. Why were these requirements enacted?

QUESTIONS FOR DISCUSSION

1. Many of the decisions relating to pension plans were formerly regarded to be management prerogatives, but are now dictated by federal regulations. To what extent does the Pension Reform Act of 1974 violate the freedom of choice of business managers with respect to pension plans? Is this violation justified?

2. A self-employed chiropractor has three full-time employees and is considering establishing a qualified retirement plan. What are the options with respect to the type of plan that she should establish and the features that will be included in the plan?

3. You are considering employment with two corporations and, among other things, you would like to compare their pension plans. What features of the two plans would you be most interested in?

4. Over the past 40 years, Carl's employer-funded defined contribution retirement program has been invested in a variable annuity. Now that he has reached retirement age, he is elated by the fact that the value of the accumulation exceeds $1 million dollars. He anticipates that the investment income on the accumulation will be between seven and eight percent annually. Because this amount is sufficient for his and his wife's needs, he looks forward to leaving his two children approximately a half million dollars each. Advise him.

5. The PBGC guarantees insured plan participants against loss of benefits that can result from funding deficiencies. How can funding deficiencies arise? In what way(s) does the Pension Benefit Guarantee Corporation protect (a) employees and (b) employers?

SUGGESTIONS FOR ADDITIONAL READINGS

Allen, Everett T., Joseph J. Melone, Jerry S. Rosenbloom, and Jack L. VanDerhei. *Pension Planning*, 7th ed. Homewood, IL: Richard D. Irwin, Inc., 1992.

American Council of Life Insurance. *Pension Facts*. Washington, DC: American Council of Life Insurance, published annually.

Beam, Burton T., Jr. *Group Benefits: Basic Concepts and Alternatives*, 4th ed. Bryn Mawr, PA: The American College, 1991.

———— and John J. McFadden. *Employee Benefits*, 3rd ed. Brookfield, WI: Dearborn Financial Publishing, Inc., 1994.

Black, Kenneth, Jr., and Harold D. Skipper, Jr. *Life Insurance*, 12th ed. Englewood Cliffs, NJ: Prentice-Hall, 1994. Chapters 7, 14, 28.

Brahs, Stuart J. "Tax Reform in 1986: What It Means for Employee Benefits." *Benefits Quarterly*. Vol. III, No. 1 (First Quarter 1987).

Doyle, Robert J., Jr., et al. *The Financial Services Professional's Guide to the Tax Reform Act of 1986*. Bryn Mawr, Pa: American College, 1986.

Fundamentals of Employee Benefit Programs, 4th ed. Washington, DC: Employee Benefit Research Institute, 1990.

Leimberg, Stephan R., et al. *The Financial Services Professional's Guide to the State of the Art*, 2nd ed. Bryn Mawr, Pa: American College, 1991.

Liscio, John. "Safe GICs: Everyone Wants Them But Do They Exist?" *Barons* (July 29, 1991).

Mark L. Cross, Steven M. Flory and Thomas J. Phillips Jr. "Implications of the FASB Proposal for Accruing Postretirement Health Care Benefits," *Benefits Quarterly*, Vol. V, No. 3, 1989.

Mehr, Robert I., and Sandra G. Gustavson. *Life Insurance: Theory and Practice.* 4th ed. Plano, TX: Business Publications, 1987, Chapters 16, 17.

Rosenbloom, Jerry S., ed. *The Handbook of Employee Benefits: Design, Funding and Administration.* Homewood, IL: Richard D. Irwin, 1984.

Shilling, Dana. *Financial Planning for the Older Client,* 2nd ed. Cincinnati, Ohio: The National Underwriter Co., 1994.

Williams, C. Arthur, and Richard M. Heins. *Risk Management and Insurance*, 6th ed. New York: McGraw-Hill, 1989. Chapters 21, 22, 25.

Wood, Glenn L. Lilly, Claude C., III; Malecki, Donald S., Graves, Edward E., and Rosenbloom, Jerry S., *Personal Risk Management and Insurance,* 4th ed., vol II. Malvern, PA: American Institute for Property and Liability, 1989. Chapters 12, 13, 14.

Author Index

Subject Index